k_{sL} Cost of equity of a levered firm
k_{sU} Cost of equity of an unlevered firm
M/B Market to book ratio
MCC Marginal cost of capital
MIRR Modified internal rate of return
N Calculator key denoting number of periods
n (1) Life of a project (periods or years)
   (2) Number of shares outstanding
MVA Market value added
NAL Net advantage to leasing
NPV Net present value
NWC Net working capital
P (1) Price of a share of stock
   (2) Price per unit of output
   (3) Probability of occurrence

P/E Price/earnings ratio
PI Profitability index
PMT (1) Annuity payment
   (2) Payment key on calculators
PV Present value
Q Unit sales
r Correlation coefficient
ROA Return on assets
ROE Return on equity
RP Risk premium
   RP_M Market risk premium
S (1) Dollar sales
   (2) Total market value of equity
SML Security Market Line
Σ Summation sign (capital sigma)
σ Standard deviation (lowercase sigma)
T Tax rate
t Time
TIE Times-interest-earned ratio
V (1) Value
   (2) Variable cost per unit
V_L Total market value of a levered firm
V_U Total market value of an unlevered firm
w Proportion or weight
   w_d Weight of debt
   w_{ps} Weight of preferred stock
   w_{ce} Weight of common equity
WACC Weighted average cost of capital
YTC Yield to call
YTM Yield to maturity

FINANCIAL MANAGEMENT

Theory and Practice

Eighth Edition

Eugene F. Brigham
UNIVERSITY OF FLORIDA

Louis C. Gapenski
UNIVERSITY OF FLORIDA

THE DRYDEN PRESS
HARCOURT BRACE COLLEGE PUBLISHERS

FORT WORTH   PHILADELPHIA   SAN DIEGO   NEW YORK   AUSTIN   ORLANDO   SAN ANTONIO
TORONTO   MONTREAL   LONDON   SYDNEY   TOKYO

PUBLISHER	Christopher P. Klein
ACQUISITIONS EDITOR	Mike Reynolds
DEVELOPMENTAL EDITOR	Shana Lum
PROJECT MANAGEMENT	Elm Street Publishing Services, Inc.
COMPOSITOR	The Clarinda Company
TEXT TYPE	10/12 ITC Garamond Book
TEXT DESIGNER	Linda Harper
COVER DESIGNER	Linda Wooton

Address for Editorial Correspondence
The Dryden Press, 301 Commerce Street, Suite 3700, Fort Worth, TX 76102

Address for Orders
The Dryden Press, 6277 Sea Harbor Drive, Orlando, FL 32887
1-800-782-4479, or 1-800-433-0001 (in Florida)

ISBN: 0-03-017789-8

Library of Congress Catalog Card Number: 96-85290

Printed in the United States of America

7 8 9 0 1 2 3 4 5   039   9 8 7 6 5 4 3 2

The Dryden Press
Harcourt Brace College Publishers

THE DRYDEN PRESS SERIES IN FINANCE

Gitman and Joehnk
Personal Financial Planning
Seventh Edition

Greenbaum and Thakor
Contemporary Financial Intermediation

Harrington and Eades
Case Studies in Financial Decision Making
Third Edition

Hayes and Meerschwam
Financial Institutions: Contemporary Cases in the Financial Services Industry

Hearth and Zaima
Contemporary Investments: Security and Portfolio Analysis

Johnson
Issues and Readings in Managerial Finance
Fourth Edition

Kidwell, Peterson, and Blackwell
Financial Institutions, Markets, and Money
Sixth Edition

Koch
Bank Management
Third Edition

Leahigh
Pocket Guide to Finance

Maisel
Real Estate Finance
Second Edition

Martin, Cox, and MacMinn
The Theory of Finance: Evidence and Applications

Mayes and Shank
Advanced Financial Analysis with Microsoft Excel

Mayes and Shank
Financial Analysis with Lotus for Windows

Mayes and Shank
Financial Analysis with Microsoft Excel

Mayo
Financial Institutions, Investments, and Management: An Introduction
Fifth Edition

Mayo
Investments: An Introduction
Fifth Edition

Pettijohn
PROFIT+

Reilly and Brown
Investment Analysis and Portfolio Management
Fifth Edition

Reilly and Norton
Investments
Fourth Edition

Sears and Trennepohl
Investment Management

Seitz and Ellison
Capital Budgeting and Long-Term Financing Decisions
Second Edition

Siegel and Siegel
Futures Markets

Smith and Spudeck
Interest Rates: Principles and Applications

Stickney
Financial Reporting and Statement Analysis: A Strategic Perspective
Third Edition

Weston, Besley, and Brigham
Essentials of Managerial Finance
Eleventh Edition

The HB College Outline Series

Baker
Financial Management

PREFACE

Our goal in writing *Financial Management: Theory and Practice* was to create a text (1) that is sufficiently current and complete to give students an operational knowledge of finance, (2) that combines theory and applications, and (3) that is sufficiently self-contained for use in an introductory finance course, in follow-on case courses, and, upon graduation, in practice. Further, we wanted a text that students find "user friendly" in the sense that they can learn from it on their own.

The book begins with some basic concepts, including the economic and financial environment, financial statement analysis, risk analysis, and the valuation process. Then it goes on to show how specific techniques and decision rules can be used to help maximize the firm's value. This structure has four important advantages:

1. The early discussion of financial statements provides a bridge from accounting to finance, thus easing students into finance from familiar ground. Also, covering financial statements early provides a vehicle for showing students how financial decisions affect the firm's future profitability and risk. This helps students recognize how the various types of decisions discussed in the course are interrelated, and how they can be integrated into a firm's plans for the future. Finally, if instructors plan to emphasize spreadsheets in the course, financial statements provide an excellent starting point for illustrating the usefulness of spreadsheets.

2. Explaining early in the book how financial markets operate, and how security prices are determined within these markets, lays the groundwork for explaining how financial management can affect the value of the firm. Also, this organization exposes students early to methods of risk analysis, to discounted cash flow techniques, and to valuation concepts, which, in turn, permits us to use and reinforce these key concepts throughout the book.

3. Structuring the book around markets and valuation provides a unifying theme. Some texts develop a series of topics in modular form and then attempt to

integrate them in later chapters. The organization of *Financial Management* gives students a better and more comprehensive understanding of how the topics interact with one another.

4. Students — even those who do not plan to major in finance — generally find stock and bond valuation models, rates of return, and the like, inherently interesting. Since a student's ability to learn a subject is a function of his or her interest and motivation, and since *Financial Management* begins with a discussion of security markets and prices, the book's organization is sound from a pedagogic standpoint.

INTENDED MARKET AND USE

Financial Management is designed primarily for use as an introductory MBA text; however, it can also serve as a reference work for later use. Typically, selected "core" chapters are covered in the introductory course, and then the other chapters are covered in advanced courses (along with readings and/or cases) or used for reference purposes if and when they are needed. Also, the book can be used as an undergraduate introductory text either with exceptionally good students or in schools in which the introductory course is taught over two terms.

We have made a special effort to make the text useful both in the introductory finance class and as a reference book for case courses and for on-the-job applications after graduation. However, to create a useful reference book, we had to include more material than can be covered thoroughly in one term. Still, most students, and especially MBA students, can read on their own and understand reasonably well all but the most technical sections, so classroom coverage of all topics is not necessary. Furthermore, as we discuss later in this preface, we have made a special effort to organize the material in a manner which facilitates coverage of the essential topics in one term.

MAJOR CHANGES IN THE EIGHTH EDITION

The financial environment has changed significantly since 1993, when we last updated the book. Academic researchers have been busy developing new theory, business practitioners have made increasing use of financial theory, and feedback from the real world has led to modifications and improvements in existing theory. We have incorporated these changes into the eighth edition. Additionally, we received many comments from users who liked the book but felt that it was getting too long to handle easily in one term. After careful consideration, we implemented the following changes in the eighth edition:

1. **General update.** The entire book has been reviewed for completeness, ease of exposition, and currency. Hundreds of small changes have been made to keep the text up-to-date. Particular emphasis has been placed on updating the real-world examples and including the latest changes in the financial environment and in financial theory.

2. **Concentration of key topics.** One primary focus in the revision was to make the text easier to use in a one-semester course, but without jeopardizing its usefulness as a reference book. This led us to reorganize the coverage of investment risk, capital structure, and working capital management.

   In the seventh edition, our discussions of investment risk and capital structure were each spread over two chapters, which made it necessary to cover all four chapters to get a coherent picture of these topics. In the revision, each topic still has two chapters, but the first covers essential material and the second adds depth that is useful but not essential for an overview of financial management. This gives instructors greater flexibility in choosing how much time to devote to these topics. Instructors who want to cover more topics can elect not to cover the "extension" chapters, while those who want more depth can include them.

   Similarly, the working capital material has been reorganized so that the essential concepts of working capital management are contained in two chapters. A third chapter provides extension material.

   With the revised organization, all the core material is contained in 19 chapters, which is manageable in one semester with good students. Instructors who want to cover fewer topics but in more depth, or to cover some of the special topics, will find sufficient material in the text to do so.

3. **Chapter organization.** The organization of the text has been changed somewhat to provide a smoother flow. Note, though, that the chapters are generally self-contained and modular, so the topic ordering can be altered to fit different instructors' situations.
   a. The chapter on long-term financial planning (forecasting) has been moved up to precede capital structure and dividend policy. This makes it easier to discuss the use of planning models when making capital structure and dividend policy decisions.
   b. The section on long-term financing has been moved ahead of that on working capital. Although we were reluctant to push working capital farther back in the text, the new organization places the discussion of long-term capital sources immediately behind strategic financing decisions, which results in a more natural progression. Further, our streamlining of the subject makes it easier to actually cover working capital in the course.

4. **New chapters.** The changing financial environment motivated us to add the following two chapters:
   a. A chapter on derivatives and risk management was added to the special topics section. Derivatives and risk management have become so important in financial management that additional coverage was warranted.
   b. We also added a chapter on pension plan management. This topic is important to students not only because corporate managers are responsible for establishing and managing a firm's pension plan but also because students must know enough about pension plans to make intelligent choices in plotting their own personal retirement strategies.

5. **Spreadsheet analysis.** Since spreadsheet analysis is now an integral part of financial management, we added Spreadsheet Applications sections to the end-

of-chapter materials for 21 chapters. These sections contain Spreadsheet Problems, Spreadsheet Exercises, or both, and these models, along with the models that accompany the *Dryden Request* cases, permit instructors to incorporate spreadsheets into the course at three levels: (1) The Spreadsheet Problem models which accompany selected end-of-chapter problems introduce students to the power of spreadsheets without requiring them to construct models. (2) The Spreadsheet Exercises help students learn basic spreadsheet skills. (3) The cases require students to do varying amounts of actual spreadsheet modeling to deal with real-world decisions.

The Spreadsheet Exercises are relatively short and focused, and they allow students to develop, review, and extend their spreadsheet skills. These 19 exercises, along with the accompanying models, examine numerous aspects of spreadsheets such as formulas, linear regression, @functions, data tables, and macros. By working through these exercises, students can increase their spreadsheet competency and confidence. As students see what spreadsheets can do, they become better able to use them to work cases and to help solve real-world finance problems.

The models that accompany the Spreadsheet Problems and Spreadsheet Exercises are contained on a diskette that is packaged with the text.

LECTURE SUPPORT MATERIALS

The eighth edition of *Financial Management* contains a complete "classroom package" that instructors can use to increase the efficiency and effectiveness of their lectures.

The information used in the classroom package is contained in each chapter's Mini Case. The Mini Cases are, in essence, integrated problems that cover all the key material presented in the chapter. The solutions to the Mini Cases, which are contained in the *Instructor's Manual,* have been set up as lectures. Thus, when an instructor discusses the solution to the Mini Case, he or she is actually giving a lecture on the most important elements of the chapter.

The Mini Case format has several advantages over conventional lectures. First, by presenting material in a case setting, students can see more easily the relevance of the concepts, which motivates them to learn the material. Second, since the basis for the lecture — the Mini Case — is in the textbook, students can prepare for the lecture by reading the Mini Case. Although reading the Mini Case is not a substitute for reading the chapter, this is better than no preparation at all. Finally, if the lecture— the Mini Case solution — is not completed in the allotted time, students know precisely what has not been covered, and instructors can, if they choose, pass out full or partial solutions or place them on reserve.

For the seventh edition of *Financial Management,* we developed a set of Lecture Presentation Software (LPS), or "slide show," materials. Since then, we have worked extensively to improve this product, and the new eighth edition version is, according to reviewers, really quite good. This software, available in *Microsoft PowerPoint* for both IBM-compatible and Macintosh systems, consists of computerized slides created with *PowerPoint* that contain solutions to the Mini Cases. Each chapter's slide show has about 40 to 50 slides that contain the lists, graphs, tables, and calculations that an instructor might put on a blackboard, but they are much easier to read and are color-coded so that key elements of a topic tie together.

Initially, we were concerned that the slide show would severely restrict flexibility — an instructor cannot easily change the slides in the classroom. However, an instructor who uses *PowerPoint* can customize the slides to meet individual needs. Also, we have found that it is easy to add variety and spontaneity by alternating between the slide show and the blackboard. This approach permits us to add new material or to deal with student questions as necessary right in the classroom.

If instructors cannot use the slide show, an alternative is to use our Transparency set, which consists of both transparencies and hard-copy masters. We created the masters by first reviewing the slides and then distilling the 1,000+ individual slides into approximately 200 masters. Transparencies were then created from the masters. Instructors who want to use transparencies in the classroom can modify the masters as desired, as well as create new masters of their own, and then use the modified and new masters to make additional transparencies. In effect, instructors will be using a somewhat abbreviated version of the slide show, but with transparencies rather than a computer as the medium. The slide show is superior because it is in color and contains many more individual slides. However, the transparencies are a reasonable substitute when conditions do not permit the use of the slide show.

Directly related to the slide show and transparency masters, we also developed a significantly modified version of an old ancillary called *Blueprints,* which was designed to help students follow the lecture and take notes. The new *Blueprints* is basically a hard copy of the slides/transparencies. We learned long ago that students want and need hard copies of transparencies or other materials to reduce pointless copying and to free them to listen and comprehend. *Blueprints* contains statements of the Mini Cases plus three-to-a-page copies of the slides/transparencies. There is plenty of white space for notes directly adjacent to the images. *Blueprints* comes in a form that instructors can have copied and made available to students, or it can be ordered so as to come shrink-wrapped with the text.

Finally, the classroom package includes a comprehensive set of Cases available for purchase that were specifically designed to accompany *Financial Management.* The cases can be obtained in two versions: a "directed" version with end-of-case questions and a "nondirected" version that provides less structured guidance. The best choice depends on the structure of the course and the familiarity of students with case work. Although most introductory MBA finance courses consist primarily of lectures, the cases make it easy to demonstrate that financial decisions often have important qualitative elements along with the more obvious quantitative elements. Further, if the book is used over two terms, the cases give instructors the opportunity to introduce a wide variety of real-world situations into the classroom.

Taken together, the classroom package for *Financial Management* provides a proven, comprehensive system which facilitates student learning. All instructors, regardless of experience or teaching style, should consider using all or parts of the classroom package.

For our own classes, we develop a Course Pack, which contains (1) our syllabus, (2) instructions for use of a selected financial calculator (taken from the

Technology Supplement discussed below), (3) some of our old exams to give the students a good idea of how we plan to test them, (4) the appropriate *Blueprints* chapters as taken directly from the *Blueprints* supplement, and (5) several "exam-type" questions and problems for each chapter, which we place directly after each *Blueprints* chapter. Since we use the Mini Cases as the basis for our lectures, we ask students to read the chapter and scan the Mini Case. Then we lecture on the chapter by going through the case. We use the slide show or transparencies to save time (writing on the blackboard can be very time consuming), and the use of *Blueprints* enables our students to listen to the lecture and still have coherent notes. We encourage questions and discussions, and the Mini Case format stimulates both. Generally, it takes about two hours to lecture on each Mini Case, so we allocate that much time to them. If we have extra time, we go into the exam-type problems at the end of the *Blueprints* chapter. (We try to schedule pre-exam reviews, and if we do, we use these or similar questions for the review.) In the past, we copied the Mini Case solution from the *Instructor's Manual* and placed it in the library, but with the new *Blueprints* format, students find this unnecessary.

ANCILLARY MATERIALS

The following materials are available to adopters free of charge:

1. **Instructor's Manual.** This comprehensive manual contains (1) a suggested course outline, (2) expanded solutions to the Mini Cases, (3) answers to all end-of-chapter questions and problems, and (4) an instructor's diskette with all the spreadsheet applications for professors and the entire manual in *Word-Perfect* for easy modification and use.

2. **Lecture Presentation Software.** A *PowerPoint* slide show with more than 1,000 computer graphics slides (40 to 50 per chapter). The slide shows are keyed to the end-of-chapter Mini Cases, and hard copies of the slides are contained in the *Blueprints* ancillary.

3. **Transparencies and Masters.** A set of more than 200 transparency acetates with masters, designed to accompany the Mini Cases for use as lecture illustrations, is available from The Dryden Press. Note that the transparency masters can be modified, and new transparencies can be created, so instructors can tailor lectures to meet their unique requirements.

4. **Technology Supplement.** The *Technology Supplement,* coauthored by Stan Eakins of East Carolina University, contains tutorials for the most commonly used financial calculators and the most popular spreadsheet program, *Microsoft Excel* (with additional instructions for users of *Lotus for Windows*). In addition, we have included a new tutorial on *Microsoft PowerPoint* to help instructors using the Lecture Presentation Software and students preparing presentations for class assignments and projects. This supplement can be copied and made available to students as well. We generally include calculator information in our Course Pack.

5. **Blueprints.** *Blueprints* provides students with an efficient system for note taking when the Mini Cases are used as the basis for class lectures. Like the *Technology Supplement, Blueprints* can be ordered with the text or copied and made available for purchase by students.

6. **Test Bank.** A *Test Bank* with more than 1,000 class-tested multiple-choice questions and problems is available both in book form and on diskettes. The diskettes may be obtained in either a computerized test bank format or in *WordPerfect*. The questions are arranged within each chapter by type (true/false, multiple-choice questions, and multiple-choice problems), by topic, and by degree of difficulty. Some of these problems can be extracted and included in a Course Pack, as discussed previously.

7. **Supplemental Problems.** In addition to the end-of-chapter problems, the Mini Cases, and the *Test Bank* problems, a set of supplemental problems, organized by topic and level of difficulty, is also available.

Several additional items are available for purchase by students through bookstores:

1. **Study Guide.** This supplement outlines the key sections of each chapter and provides students with a set of questions and solutions similar to those in the text and in the *Test Bank.* Instructors seldom use the *Study Guide,* but students find it extremely useful, so we recommend that instructors ask their bookstores to have copies available. Our bookstore generally has to reorder the *Study Guide. Study Guides* (and/or *Blueprints*) can be ordered to come shrink-wrapped with the text at a relatively low cost.

2. **Casebooks.** *Cases in Financial Management — Dryden Request* by Eugene F. Brigham, Louis C. Gapenski, and Linda S. Klein, contains cases which illustrate applications of the concepts and methodologies developed in *Financial Management.* The directed versions contain end-of-case questions which help students toward a reasonable resolution to the case. The nondirected versions contain a guidance paragraph in place of the questions. Thus, the nondirected version requires students to develop their own solution strategy for each case. Most of the cases (both directed and nondirected) have accompanying spreadsheet models. Spreadsheets are not absolutely essential for working most cases, but they do reduce number crunching and thus leave more time for students to consider conceptual issues. Also, some type of sensitivity analysis, which is really feasible only with a spreadsheet, is becoming essential for most types of financial analysis.

   Dryden Request is a custom casebook database containing more than 75 cases, with 10 or 20 new or substantially modified cases being added each year. The database system is used to generate customized casebooks, which give instructors the flexibility to mix and match cases to best meet the needs of each particular class and section. We usually assign a few directed cases in the introductory MBA finance course, but we have students retain *Financial Management* for use in the second corporate finance course, where we use about 12 nondirected cases. The steady stream of new and modified cases — similar enough to the old ones to make it easy for users to prepare for class —

makes it simple to avoid the problem of students having access to previous students' work.

It is worth noting that we have our second-course students make presentations, using *PowerPoint* software, on the cases. The presenters represent a team of consultants, and the rest of the class represents the firm's board of directors. This works out extremely well.

3. Readings Books. A readings book, *Issues in Managerial Finance* (Dryden Press, 1995) edited by Ramon E. Johnson, provides an excellent mix of theoretical and practical articles which can be used to supplement the text. Another supplemental reader is *Advances in Business Financial Management: A Collection of Readings* (Dryden Press, 1996), edited by Philip L. Cooley, which provides a broader selection of articles from which to choose.

4. Microcomputer Books. Two new microcomputer books are now available from The Dryden Press: *Financial Analysis with Microsoft Excel* and *Financial Analysis with Lotus for Windows*, both by Timothy Mayes and Todd Shank. These books are not just software tutorials — rather, they present an integrated approach to finance concepts and spreadsheet analysis.

The Dryden Press will provide complimentary supplements or supplement packages to those adopters qualified under our adoption policy. Please contact your sales representative to learn how you may qualify. If as an adopter or potential user you receive supplements you do not need, please return them to your sales representative or send them to:

Attn: Returns Department
Troy Warehouse
465 South Lincoln Drive
Troy, MO 63379

This will help hold down the publisher's cost, hence the price of books.

ACKNOWLEDGMENTS

This book reflects the efforts of a great many people over a number of years. First, we would like to thank Mike Ehrhardt of the University of Tennessee, who reviewed this edition in detail and provided many useful comments and suggestions.

Second, we sincerely appreciate the efforts of the following people, who gave their time and insights during the development of the eighth edition:

Martha Schary Amram, Analysis Group Economics, Inc.

Nasser Arshadi, University of Missouri

Abdul Aziz, Humboldt State University

Gordon R. Bonner, University of Delaware

E. Bruce Frederickson, Syracuse University

Hal Heaton, Brigham Young University

John Helmuth, Rochester Institute of Technology

Hugh Hunter, Eastern Washington University

James F. Jackson, Oklahoma State University

Vahan Janjigian, Northeastern University

Keith H. Johnson, University of Kentucky

Richard LeCompte, Wichita State University

Ilene Levin, University of Minnesota–Duluth

James T. Lindley, University of South Mississippi

R. Daniel Pace, Valparaiso University

Ralph A. Pope, California State University–Sacramento

Allen Rappaport, University of Northern Iowa

Fiona Robertson, Seattle University

G. Bennett Stewart, Stern, Stewart, and Company

Eugene Swinnerton, University of Detroit-Mercy

Robert A. Taggart, Boston College

Sheridan Titman, Boston College

David Vang, University of St. Thomas

Gary R. Wells, Idaho State University

Earlier versions of individual chapters or entire sections were sent to professors and professionals doing research on specific topics. We are grateful for the insights provided by:

- Edward I. Altman of New York University on "Bankruptcy, Reorganization, and Liquidation."
- William Beranek of the University of Georgia on "Working Capital Management and Financing."
- Ben S. Branch of the Bank of New England and the University of Massachusetts on "Bankruptcy, Reorganization, and Liquidation."
- David T. Brown of the University of Florida on "Bankruptcy, Reorganization, and Liquidation."
- Myron Gordon of the University of Toronto on "Capital Structure Decisions and Dividend Policy."
- Robert Kieschnick of George Mason University on "Mergers, LBOs, Divestitures, and Holding Companies."
- James Schallheim of the University of Utah on "Lease Financing."
- Robert Strong of the University of Maine at Orono on "Valuation Models."
- Robert Taggart of Boston College on "The Cost of Capital," "The Basics of Capital Budgeting," and "Project Cash Flow Analysis."
- Jonathan Tiemann of Wells Fargo Nikko Investment Advisors on "Common Stock and the Investment Banking Process."

- Sheridan Titman of the University of California, Los Angeles, on "Risk and Return."
- Alan L. Tucker of Temple University on "Multinational Financial Management."
- David Ziebart of the University of Illinois at Urbana on "Analysis of Financial Statements."

In addition, we would like to thank the following people, whose reviews and comments on prior editions and companion books have contributed to this edition: Mike Adler, Syed Ahmad, Ed Altman, Bruce Anderson, Ron Anderson, Bob Angell, Vince Apilado, Henry Arnold, Bob Aubey, Gil Babcock, Peter Bacon, Kent Baker, Tom Bankston, Les Barenbaum, Charles Barngrover, Bill Beedles, Moshe Ben-Horim, Bill Beranek, Tom Berry, Bill Bertin, Roger Bey, Dalton Bigbee, John Bildersee, Russ Boisjoly, Keith Boles, Geof Booth, Kenneth Boudreaux, Helen Bowers, Oswald Bowlin, Don Boyd, G. Michael Boyd, Pat Boyer, Joe Brandt, Elizabeth Brannigan, Greg Brauer, Mary Broske, Dave Brown, Kate Brown, Bill Brueggeman, Kirt Butler, Robert Button, Bill Campsey, Bob Carleson, Severin Carlson, David Cary, Steve Celec, Don Chance, Antony Chang, Susan Chaplinsky, Jay Choi, S. K. Choudhury, Lal Chugh, Maclyn Clouse, Margaret Considine, Phil Cooley, Joe Copeland, David Cordell, John Cotner, Charles Cox, David Crary, John Crockett, Roy Crum, Brent Dalrymple, Bill Damon, Joel Dauten, Steve Dawson, Sankar De, Miles Delano, Fred Dellva, Anand Desai, Bernard Dill, Greg Dimkoff, Les Dlabay, Mark Dorfman, Gene Drycimski, Dean Dudley, David Durst, Ed Dyl, Dick Edelman, Charles Edwards, John Ellis, Dave Ewert, John Ezzell, Richard Fendler, Michael Ferri, Jim Filkins, John Finnerty, Susan Fischer, Steven Flint, Russ Fogler, Dan French, Michael Garlington, Jim Garvin, Adam Gehr, Jim Gentry, Philip Glasgo, Rudyard Goode, Walt Goulet, Bernie Grablowsky, Theoharry Grammatikos, Ed Grossnickle, John Groth, Alan Grunewald, Manak Gupta, Sam Hadaway, Don Hakala, Sally Hamilton, Gerald Hamsmith, William Hardin, John Harris, Paul Hastings, Bob Haugen, Steve Hawke, Del Hawley, Robert Hehre, George Hettenhouse, Hans Heymann, Kendall Hill, Roger Hill, Tom Hindelang, Linda Hittle, Ralph Hocking, J. Ronald Hoffmeister, Jim Horrigan, John Houston, John Howe, Keith Howe, Steve Isberg, Jim Jackson, Kose John, Craig Johnson, Keith Johnson, Ramon Johnson, Ray Jones, Manuel Jose, Gus Kalogeras, Mike Keenan, Bill Kennedy, Joe Kiernan, Rick Kish, Linda Klein, Don Knight, Dorothy Koehl, Jaroslaw Komarynsky, Duncan Kretovich, Harold Krogh, Charles Kroncke, Joan Lamm, P. Lange, Howard Lanser, Martin Laurence, Ed Lawrence, Wayne Lee, Jim LePage, Jules Levine, John Lewis, Chuck Linke, Bill Lloyd, Susan Long, Judy Maese, Bob Malko, Ileen Malitz, Phil Malone, Terry Maness, Chris Manning, Terry Martell, D. J. Masson, John Mathys, John McAlhany, Andy McCollough, Bill McDaniel, Robin McLaughlin, Tom McCue, Jamshid Mehran, Larry Merville, Rick Meyer, Jim Millar, Ed Miller, John Mitchell, Carol Moerdyk, Bob Moore, Barry Morris, Gene Morris, Fred Morrissey, Chris Muscarella, David Nachman, Tim Nantell, Don Nast, Bill Nelson, Bob Nelson, Bob Niendorf, Tom O'Brien, Dennis O'Connor, John O'Donnell, Jim Olsen, Robert Olsen, Coleen Pantalone, Jim Pappas, Stephen Parrish, Glenn Petry, Jim Pettijohn, Rich Pettit, Dick Pettway, Hugo Phillips, John Pinkerton, Gerald Pogue, R. Potter, Franklin Potts, R. Powell, Chris Prestopino, Jerry Prock, Howard Puckett, Herbert Quigley, George Racette, Bob Radcliffe, Bill Rentz, Ken Riener, Charles Rini, John Ritchie, Pietra Rivoli, Antonio Rodriguez, E. M. Roussakis, Dexter Rowell, Jim Sachlis, Abdul Sadik, Thomas Scampini, Kevin Scanlon, Frederick Schadler, Mary Jane Scheuer, Carl Schweser, John

Settle, Alan Severn, Sol Shalit, Frederic Shipley, Dilip Shome, Ron Shrieves, Neil Sicherman, J. B. Silvers, Clay Singleton, Joe Sinkey, Stacy Sirmans, Jaye Smith, Steve Smith, Don Sorenson, David Speairs, Ken Stanly, Ed Stendardi, Alan Stephens, Don Stevens, Jerry Stevens, Glen Strasburg, Philip Swensen, Ernie Swift, Paul Swink, Gary Tallman, Dennis Tanner, Russ Taussig, Richard Teweles, Ted Teweles, Andrew Thompson, George Trivoli, George Tsetsekos, Mel Tysseland, David Upton, Howard Van Auken, Pretorious Van den Dool, Pieter Vanderburg, Paul Vanderheiden, Jim Verbrugge, Patrick Vincent, Steve Vinson, Susan Visscher, John Wachowicz, Mike Walker, Sam Weaver, Kuo Chiang Wei, Bill Welch, Fred Weston, Norm Williams, Tony Wingler, Ed Wolfe, Don Woods, Michael Yonan, Dennis Zocco, and Kent Zumwalt.

Special thanks are due to Fred Weston, Myron Gordon, Merton Miller, and Franco Modigliani, who have done much to help develop the field of financial management and who provided us with instruction and inspiration; to Roy Crum, who coauthored the multinational finance chapter; to Jim Bicksler, who coauthored the pension plan management chapter; to Larry Wolken, who offered his hard work and advice for the development of the *Lecture Presentation Software;* to Dana Aberwald Clark, Susan Ball, Mary Alice Hanebury, and Kay Mangan, who helped us develop the spreadsheet models; to Dana Aberwald Clark and Dan Gregory, who helped on the ancillaries; and to Carol Stanton and Susan Purcell, who provided both word processing and editorial support.

Both our colleagues and our students at the University of Florida gave us many useful suggestions, and the Dryden Press and Elm Street Publishing Services staffs — especially Shana Lum and Sue Nodine — helped greatly with all phases of text development, production, and marketing.

ERRORS IN THE TEXT

At this point, authors generally say something like this: "We appreciate all the help we received from the people listed above, but any remaining errors are, of course, our own responsibility." And in many books, there are plenty of remaining errors. Having experienced difficulties with errors ourselves, both as students and as instructors, we resolved to avoid this problem in *Financial Management.* As a result of our error-detection procedures, we are convinced that the book is relatively free of mistakes.

Partly because of our confidence that few such errors remain, but primarily because we want very much to detect any errors that may have slipped by so we can correct them in subsequent printings, we decided to offer a reward of $10 per error to the first person who reports it to us. For purposes of this reward, errors are defined as spelling errors, errors in finance content, or other errors that inhibit comprehension. Typesetting problems, such as spacing, or differences in opinion regarding grammatical or punctuation convention do not qualify for the reward. Finally, any qualifying error that has follow-through effects is counted as two errors only. Errors should be reported to Eugene F. Brigham at the address given on the following page.

CONCLUSION

Finance is, in a real sense, the cornerstone of the free enterprise system. Good financial management is therefore vitally important to the economic health of business firms, hence to the nation and the world. Because of its importance, financial management should be thoroughly understood, but this is easier said than done. The field is relatively complex, and it is undergoing constant change in response to technological developments and shifts in economic conditions. All of this makes finance stimulating and exciting, but also challenging and sometimes perplexing. We sincerely hope that the eighth edition of *Financial Management* will help you understand the financial problems faced by businesses today, as well as the best ways to solve those problems.

Eugene F. Brigham
Louis C. Gapenski

College of Business Administration
University of Florida
Gainesville, Florida 32611

September 1996

Brief Contents

Contents

APPENDIXES

CHAPTER 1

AN OVERVIEW OF FINANCIAL MANAGEMENT

It took General Dynamics, a major defense contractor, 43 years to get the value of its stock to $2.7 million. Netscape Communications accomplished the same feat in about one minute in August 1995, when technology-crazed investors had their first chance to buy Netscape's stock on the open market. Never mind that Netscape had never earned a profit or that it had been giving away its primary product free on the Internet.

Netscape produces Netscape Navigator, a "web browser" program that enables users to view information on the World Wide Web, the graphical interface portion of the Internet. The company was founded in April 1994 by James Clark, a noted Silicon Valley pioneer, and Marc Andreesen, a 24-year-old techie from the University of Illinois. The IPO (initial public offering) created a nest egg of $565 million for Mr. Clark, who owned 9.7 million shares of Netscape's stock. Mr. Andreesen's gain of $58 million, while not on par with Mr. Clark's, was not bad for 16 months' work.

How did this all happen? Until August, Netscape had been a privately owned company, with most of the stock owned by four investors: Clark, Andreesen, James Barksdale, who was brought in from McCaw Cellular to be Netscape's president and chief executive officer, and John Doerr, a Silicon Valley venture capitalist. (A venture capitalist is an investor who makes equity investments in startup firms.) To support development of its Netscape Navigator and related software, the company needed additional capital, and its best means of raising new funds was to sell common stock to the public. So, on August 8, 1995, the company sold 5 million shares of common stock at a price of $28 per share. Original plans called for issuing 3.5 million shares at $14 per share, but demand was so great during the weeks prior to the sale that both the amount and price were increased. Still, investor demand for the stock was so great that the company could have sold 100 *million shares. This pent-up demand caused a near panic on August 9, the first day the shares were publicly traded. Lucky investors who got stock for $28 saw it open at $71 per share on the over-the-counter market, be bid up to $75, and then drop back to end the day at $58.*

Once the hype of the initial public offering dies down, it will be up to Barksdale to convert Clark's entrepreneurial vision and Andreesen's technological genius into a viable, well-run business. To do that, he and Netscape's other managers will have to make a whole range of financial decisions. The first decision, the form of business organization, was decided some time ago, but now the firm must decide on such things as the type and amount of debt financing it should use, which projects it should undertake in the future, and how to manage its current assets. If things go well in the future, then at some point more earnings will be generated than are needed for reinvestment in the company, and then the firm must decide how much of its earnings to pay out as dividends. Above all, Netscape's managers must be aware of the goals of the company and how alternative actions impact these goals, including the effect on the firm's stock price. When you have finished your study of this book, you will have a good understanding of the types of financial decisions facing Netscape, and, more importantly, you will be armed with the tools to help make such decisions in your own company.

The purpose of this chapter is to give you an overview of financial management. After you finish the chapter, you should have a reasonably good idea of what finance majors might do after graduation. You should also have a better understanding of (1) some of the forces that will affect financial management in the future; (2) the way businesses are organized; (3) the place finance has in a firm's organization; (4) the relationships between financial managers and their counterparts in accounting, marketing, production, and personnel departments; (5) the goals of a firm; and (6) the way financial managers can contribute to the attainment of these goals.

CAREER OPPORTUNITIES IN FINANCE

Finance consists of three interrelated areas: (1) *money and capital markets,* which deals with securities markets and financial institutions; (2) *investments,* which focuses on the decisions of both individual and institutional investors as they choose securities for their investment portfolios; and (3) *financial management,* or "business finance," which involves the actual management of firms. The career opportunities within each field are many and varied, but financial managers must have a knowledge of all three areas if they are to do their jobs well.

MONEY AND CAPITAL MARKETS

Many finance majors go to work for financial institutions, including banks, insurance companies, mutual funds, and investment banking firms. For success here, one needs a knowledge of valuation techniques, the factors that cause interest rates to rise and fall, the regulations to which financial institutions are subject, and the various types of financial instruments (mortgages, auto loans, certificates of deposit, and so on). One also needs a general knowledge of all aspects of business administration, because the management of a financial institution involves accounting, marketing, personnel, and computer systems, as well as financial management. An ability to communicate, both orally and in writing, is important, and "people skills," or the ability to get others to do their jobs well, are critical.

One common entry-level job in this area is a bank officer trainee, where you go into bank operations and learn about the business, from tellers' work, to cash management, to making loans. You could expect to spend a year or so being rotated among these different areas, after which you would settle into a department, often as an assistant manager in a branch. Alternatively, you might become a specialist in some area such as real estate, and be authorized to make loans going into millions of dollars, or in the management of trusts, estates, and pension funds. Similar career paths are available with insurance companies, investment companies, credit unions, and consumer loan companies.

INVESTMENTS

Finance graduates who go into investments often work for a brokerage house such as Merrill Lynch, either in sales or as a security analyst. Others work for banks, mutual funds, or insurance companies in the management of their investment portfolios; for financial consulting firms which advise individual investors or pension funds on how to invest their funds; or for an investment banker whose primary function is to help businesses raise new capital. The three main functions in the investments area are (1) sales, (2) the analysis of individual securities, and (3) determining the optimal mix of securities for a given investor.

FINANCIAL MANAGEMENT

Financial management is the broadest of the three areas, and the one with the greatest number of job opportunities. Financial management is important in all types of businesses, including banks and other financial institutions, as well as industrial and retail firms. Financial management is also important in governmental operations, from schools to hospitals to highway departments. The job opportunities in financial management range from making decisions regarding plant expansions to choosing what types of securities to issue to finance expansion. Financial managers also have the responsibility for deciding the credit terms under which customers may buy, how much inventory the firm should carry, how much cash to keep on hand, whether to acquire other firms (merger analysis), and how much of the firm's earnings to plow back into the business versus pay out as dividends.

Regardless of which area a finance major goes into, he or she will need a knowledge of all three areas. For example, a banker lending to businesses cannot do his or her job well without a good understanding of financial management, because he or she must be able to judge how well businesses are operated. The same thing holds true for one of Merrill Lynch's security analysts, and even stockbrokers must have an understanding of general financial principles if they are to give intelligent advice to their customers. At the same time, corporate financial managers need to know what their bankers are thinking about, and how investors are likely to judge their corporations' performances and thus determine their stock prices. So, if you decide to make finance your career, you will need to know something about all three areas.

Suppose you do not plan to major in finance. Is the subject still important to you? Absolutely, for two reasons: (1) You need a knowledge of finance to make many personal decisions, ranging from investing for your retirement to deciding whether to lease versus buy a car. (2) Virtually all important business decisions have financial implications, as well as implications for all parts of the firm, so important decisions are generally made by teams from the accounting, finance, legal, marketing, personnel, and production departments. Therefore, if you want to succeed in the business arena, you must be highly competent in your own area, say marketing, and also have a familiarity with the other business disciplines, including finance.

SELF-TEST QUESTIONS

What are the three main areas of finance?

If you have definite plans to go into one area, why is it necessary that you know something about the other areas?

Why is it necessary for business students who do not major in finance to know the basics of finance?

FINANCIAL MANAGEMENT IN THE 1990s

When financial management emerged as a separate field of study in the early 1900s, the emphasis was on the legal aspects of mergers, the formation of new firms, and the various types of securities that firms could issue to raise capital. During the Depression of the 1930s, the emphasis shifted to bankruptcy and reorganization, to corporate liquidity, and to the regulation of security markets. During the 1940s and early 1950s, finance continued to be taught as a descriptive, institutional subject, viewed more from the standpoint of an outsider rather than from that of management. However, a movement toward theoretical analysis began during the late 1950s, and the focus shifted to managerial decisions regarding the choice of assets and liabilities so as to maximize the value of the firm. The focus on valuation has continued on into the 1990s, but the analysis has been expanded to include (1) *inflation* and its effects on business decisions; (2) *deregulation* of financial institutions and the resulting trend toward large, broadly diversified financial services companies; (3) the dramatic increase in both the use of *computers* for analysis and the electronic transfer of information; and (4) the increased importance of *global markets and business operations*. The two most important future trends are likely to be the continued globalization of business and the increased use of information technology.

GLOBALIZATION OF BUSINESS

Four factors have led to the increased globalization of businesses: (1) Improvements in transportation and communications, which lowered shipping costs and made international trade more feasible. (2) The political clout of consumers, who desire low-cost, high-quality products, has helped lower trade barriers designed to protect inefficient, high-cost domestic manufacturers. (3) As technology has become more advanced, the cost of developing new products has increased. This has led to joint ventures between such companies as General Motors and Toyota, and global operations for many firms in an effort to expand markets and thus spread development costs over higher unit sales. (4) In a world populated with multinational firms able to shift production to wherever costs are lowest, a firm whose manufacturing operations are restricted to one country cannot compete unless costs in its home country happen to be low, a condition that does not necessarily exist for many U.S. corporations. As a result of these four factors, survival requires that most manufacturers produce and sell globally.

Service companies, including banks, advertising agencies, and accounting firms, are also being forced to "go global," because such firms can better serve their multinational clients if they have worldwide operations. There will, of course, always be some purely domestic companies, but you should keep in mind that the most dynamic growth, and the best employment opportunities, are often with companies that operate worldwide.

Even businesses that operate exclusively in domestic U.S. markets are not immune to the effects of globalization. For example, the costs to a homebuilder in rural Nebraska will be affected by interest rates and lumber prices — both of which are determined by worldwide supply and demand conditions. Furthermore, demand for the homebuilder's houses will be influenced by interest rates and by conditions in the local farm economy, which depend to a large extent on foreign demand for wheat. To operate efficiently, the builder must be able to forecast the demand for houses. So, at least some knowledge of global economic conditions is important to virtually everyone, not just to those involved with businesses that operate internationally.

Information Technology

The remainder of the 1990s will see continued advances in computer and communications technology, and this will revolutionize the way financial decisions are made. Companies will have networks of personal computers linked to one another, to the firms' own mainframe computers, to the Internet and the World Wide Web, and to their customers' and suppliers' computers. Thus, financial managers will be able to share information and to have "face-to-face" meetings with distant colleagues through video teleconferencing. The ability to access and analyze data on a real-time basis will also mean that quantitative analyses will become more important, and "gut feel" less important, in business decisions. As a result, the next generation of financial managers will need stronger computer and quantitative skills than were required in the past.

How has financial management changed from the early 1900s to the 1990s? **Self-Test**
How might a person become better prepared for a career in financial management? **Questions**

Increasing Importance of Financial Management

The historical trends discussed in the previous section have greatly increased the importance of financial management. In earlier times, the marketing manager would project sales, the engineering and production staffs would determine the assets necessary to meet those demands, and the financial manager's job was simply to raise the money needed to purchase the required plant, equipment, and inventories. That situation no longer exists — decisions are now made in a much more coordinated manner, and financial managers generally have direct responsibility for the control process.

Eastern and Delta airlines can be used to illustrate both the importance of financial management and the effects of financial decisions. In the 1960s, Eastern's stock sold for more than $60 per share while Delta's sold for $10. By the mid 1990s, Delta had become one of the world's strongest airlines, and its stock was selling for more than $80 per share. Eastern, on the other hand, had gone bankrupt and was no longer in existence. Although many factors combined to produce these divergent results, financial decisions exerted a major influence. Because Eastern had traditionally used a great deal of debt while Delta had not, Eastern's costs increased significantly, and its profits were lowered, when interest rates rose during the 1980s. Rising rates had only a minor effect on Delta. Further, when fuel price increases made it imperative for the airlines to buy new, fuel-efficient planes, Delta was able to do so, but Eastern was not. Finally, when the airlines were deregulated, Delta was strong enough to expand into developing markets, to buy assets from failing airlines, and to cut prices as necessary to attract business, but Eastern was not.

The Delta-Eastern story, and others like it, are now well known. As a result, all companies today are greatly concerned with financial planning, and this has increased the importance of corporate financial staffs. Indeed, the value of financial management is reflected in the fact that more chief executive officers (CEOs) of the top 1,000 U.S. companies started their careers in finance than in any other functional area.

It is also becoming increasingly important for people in marketing, accounting, production, personnel, and other areas to understand finance in order to do a good job in their own fields. Marketing people, for instance, must understand how marketing decisions affect and are affected by funds availability, by inventory levels, by excess plant capacity, and so on. Similarly, accountants must understand how accounting data are used in corporate planning and are viewed by investors.

Thus, there are financial implications in virtually all business decisions, and nonfinancial executives simply must know enough finance to work these implications into their own specialized analyses.[1] Because of this, every student of business, regardless of his or her major, should be concerned with financial management.

SELF-TEST QUESTIONS   Explain why financial planning is important to today's chief executives.
Why do marketing people need to know something about financial management?

THE FINANCIAL MANAGER'S RESPONSIBILITIES

The financial manager's task is to acquire and use funds so as to maximize the value of the firm. Here are some specific activities:

---

[1] It is an interesting fact that the course "Financial Management for Nonfinancial Executives" has the highest enrollment in most executive development programs.

1. **Forecasting and planning.** The financial manager must interact with other executives as they look ahead and lay the plans which will shape the firm's future.

2. **Major investment and financing decisions.** A successful firm usually has rapid growth in sales, which requires investments in plant, equipment, and inventory. The financial manager must help determine the optimal sales growth rate, and he or she must help decide what specific assets to acquire and the best way to finance those assets. For example, should the firm finance with debt, equity, or some combination of the two, and, if debt is used, how much should be long term and how much should be short term?

3. **Coordination and control.** The financial manager must interact with other executives to ensure that the firm is operated as efficiently as possible. All business decisions have financial implications, and all managers — financial and otherwise — need to take this into account. For example, marketing decisions affect sales growth, which, in turn, influences investment requirements. Thus, marketing decision makers must take account of how their actions affect (and are affected by) such factors as the availability of funds, inventory policies, and plant capacity utilization.

4. **Dealing with the financial markets.** The financial manager must deal with the money and capital markets. As we shall see in Chapter 3, each firm affects and is affected by the general financial markets where funds are raised, where the firm's securities are traded, and where its investors either make or lose money.

5. **Risk management.** All businesses face risks, including natural disasters such as fires and floods, uncertainties in commodity and security prices, volatile interest rates, and fluctuating foreign exchange rates. However, many of these risks can be reduced by purchasing insurance or by hedging in the derivatives markets. The financial manager is usually responsible for the firm's overall risk management program, including identifying the risks that should be hedged and then hedging them in the most efficient mannner.

In summary, financial managers make decisions regarding which assets their firms should acquire, how those assets should be financed, and how the firm should manage its existing resources. If these responsibilities are performed optimally, financial managers will help to maximize the values of their firms, and this will also maximize the long-run welfare of consumers and employees.

What are five specific activities with which financial managers are involved?

SELF-TEST QUESTION

ALTERNATIVE FORMS OF BUSINESS ORGANIZATION

The three main forms of business organization are (1) sole proprietorships, (2) partnerships, and (3) corporations. In addition, there are several hybrid forms, which are discussed at the end of this section. In terms of numbers, about 80 percent of businesses are operated as sole proprietorships, while the remainder are divided equally between partnerships and corporations. Based on dollar value of sales, however, about 80 percent of all business is conducted by corporations, about 13 percent by sole proprietorships, and about 7 percent by partnerships. Because most business is conducted by corporations, we will concentrate on them in this book. However, it is important to understand the differences among the various forms.

Sole Proprietorship

A *sole proprietorship* is an unincorporated business owned by one individual. Going into business as a sole proprietor is easy — one merely begins business operations. However, even the smallest businesses normally must be licensed by a governmental unit.

The proprietorship has three important advantages: (1) It is easily and inexpensively formed, (2) it is subject to few government regulations, and (3) the business pays no corporate income taxes.

The proprietorship also has three important limitations: (1) It is difficult for a proprietorship to obtain large sums of capital; (2) the proprietor has unlimited personal liability for the business' debts, which can result in losses that exceed the money he or she invested in the company; and (3) the life of a business organized as a proprietorship is limited to the life of the individual who created it. For these three reasons, sole proprietorships are used primarily for small-business operations. However, businesses are frequently started as proprietorships and then converted to corporations when their growth causes the disadvantages of being a proprietorship to outweigh the advantages.

Partnership

A *partnership* exists whenever two or more persons associate to conduct a noncorporate business. Partnerships may operate under different degrees of formality, ranging from informal, oral understandings to formal agreements filed with the secretary of the state in which the partnership was formed. The major advantage of a partnership is its low cost and ease of formation. The disadvantages are similar to those associated with proprietorships: (1) unlimited liability, (2) limited life of the organization, (3) difficulty of transferring ownership, and (4) difficulty of raising large amounts of capital. The tax treatment of a partnership is similar to that for proprietorships, which is often an advantage, as we demonstrate in Chapter 3.

Regarding liability, the partners can potentially lose all of their personal assets, even those assets not invested in the business, because, under partnership law, each partner is liable for the business's debts. Therefore, if any partner is unable to meet his or her pro rata claim in the event the partnership goes bankrupt, the remaining partners must make good on the unsatisfied claims, drawing on their personal assets if necessary. The partners of the national accounting firm Laventhol and Horwath, a huge partnership which recently went bankrupt as a result of suits filed by investors who relied on faulty audit statements, learned all about the perils of doing business as a partnership. Thus, a Texas partner who audits a business which goes under can bring ruin to his New York partners who never went near the business.

The first three disadvantages — unlimited liability, impermanence of the organization, and difficulty of transferring ownership — lead to the fourth, the difficulty partnerships have in attracting substantial amounts of capital. This is no particular problem for a slow-growing business, but if a business's products or services really catch on, and if it needs to raise large amounts of capital in order to capitalize on its opportunities, the difficulty in attracting capital becomes a real drawback. Thus, growth companies such as Hewlett-Packard and Microsoft generally begin life as a proprietorship or partnership, but at some point they find it necessary to convert to a corporation.

CORPORATION

A *corporation* is a legal entity created by a state. It is separate and distinct from its owners and managers. This separateness gives the corporation three major advantages: (1) *Unlimited life*. A corporation can continue after its original owners and managers are deceased. (2) *Easy transferability of ownership interest*. Ownership interests can be divided into shares of stock, which in turn can be transferred far more easily than can proprietorship or partnership interests. (3) *Limited liability*. To illustrate the concept of limited liability, suppose you invested $10,000 in a partnership which then went bankrupt owing $1 million. Because the owners are liable for the debts of a partnership, you could be assessed for a share of the company's debt, and you could be held liable for the entire $1 million if your partners could not pay their shares. Thus, an investor in a partnership is exposed to unlimited liability. On the other hand, if you invested $10,000 in the stock of a corporation which then went bankrupt, your potential loss on the investment would be limited to your $10,000 investment.[2] These three factors — unlimited life, easy transferability of ownership interest, and limited liability — make it much easier for corporations than for proprietorships or partnerships to raise money in the general capital markets.

The corporate form offers significant advantages over proprietorships and partnerships, but it also has two disadvantages: (1) Corporate earnings may be subject to double taxation — the earnings of the corporation are taxed at the corporate level, and then any earnings paid out as dividends are taxed again as income to the stockholders. (2) Setting up a corporation, and filing the many required state and federal reports, is more complex and time-consuming than for a proprietorship or a partnership.

A proprietorship or a partnership can commence operations without much paperwork, but setting up a corporation requires that the incorporators prepare a charter and a set of bylaws. Although personal computer software that creates charters and bylaws is now available, a lawyer is required if the fledgling corporation has any nonstandard features. The *charter* includes the following information: (1) name of the proposed corporation, (2) types of activities it will pursue, (3) amount of capital stock, (4) number of directors, and (5) names and addresses of directors. The

---

[2]In the case of small corporations, the limited liability feature is often a fiction, because bankers and other lenders frequently require personal guarantees from the stockholders of small, weak businesses.

charter is filed with the secretary of the state in which the firm will be incorporated, and, when it is approved, the corporation is officially in existence.[3] Then, after the corporation is in operation, quarterly and annual employment, financial, and tax reports must be filed with state and federal authorities.

The *bylaws* are a set of rules drawn up by the founders of the corporation to aid in governing the internal management of the company. Included are such points as (1) how directors are to be elected (all elected each year, or perhaps one-third each year for three-year terms); (2) whether the existing stockholders will have the first right to buy any new shares the firm issues; and (3) procedures for changing the bylaws themselves, should conditions require it.

The value of any business other than a very small one will probably be maximized if it is organized as a corporation for the following three reasons:

1. Limited liability reduces the risks borne by investors, and, other things held constant, *the lower the firm's risk, the higher its value.*

2. A firm's value is dependent on its *growth opportunities,* which, in turn, are dependent on the firm's ability to attract capital. Since corporations can attract capital more easily than can unincorporated businesses, they are better able to take advantage of growth opportunities.

3. The value of an asset also depends on its *liquidity,* which means the ease of selling the asset and converting it to cash at a "fair market value." Since an investment in the stock of a corporation is much more liquid than a similar investment in a proprietorship or partnership, this too means that the corporate form of organization can enhance the value of a business.

As we will see later in the chapter, most firms are managed with value maximization in mind, and this, in turn, has caused most large businesses to be organized as corporations.

Hybrid Forms of Organization

Although the three basic types of organization — proprietorships, partnerships, and corporations — dominate the business scene, several hybrid forms are gaining popularity. For example, there are some specialized types of partnerships that have somewhat different characteristics than the "plain vanilla" kind. First, it is possible to limit the liabilities of some of the partners by establishing a *limited partnership,* wherein certain partners are designated *general partners* and others *limited partners.* In a limited partnership, the limited partners are liable only for the amount of their investment in the partnership, while the general partners have unlimited liability. However, the limited partners typically have no control, which rests solely with the general partners, and their returns are likewise limited. Limited partnerships are common in real estate, oil, and equipment leasing ventures, but they are not widely used in general business situations because no one partner is usually willing to be

---

[3]Note that more than 60 percent of major U.S. corporations are chartered in Delaware, which has, over the years, provided a favorable legal environment for corporations. It is not necessary for a firm to be headquartered, or even to conduct operations, in its state of incorporation.

the general partner and thus accept the majority of the business's risk, while would-be limited partners are unwilling to give up all control.

The *limited liability partnership (LLP)*, sometimes called a *limited liability company (LLC)*, is a relatively new type of partnership that is now permitted in many states. In both regular and limited partnerships, at least one partner is liable for the debts of the partnership. However, in an LLP, all partners enjoy limited liability with regard to the business's liabilities, and, in that regard, they are similar to shareholders in a corporation. In effect, the LLP form of organization combines the limited liability advantage of a corporation with the tax advantages of a partnership. Of course, those who do business with an LLP as opposed to a regular partnership are aware of the situation, which increases the risk faced by lenders, customers, and others who deal with the LLP.

There are also several different types of corporations. One type that is common among professionals such as doctors, lawyers, and accountants is the *professional corporation (PC)*, or in some states, the *professional association (PA)*. All 50 states have statutes that prescribe the requirements for such corporations, which provide most of the benefits of incorporation but do not relieve the participants of professional (malpractice) liability. Indeed, the primary motivation behind the professional corporation was to provide a way for groups of professionals to incorporate and thus avoid certain types of unlimited liability, yet still be held responsible for professional liability.

Finally, note that if certain requirements are met, particularly with regard to size and number of stockholders, one (or more) individuals can establish a corporation but elect to be taxed as if the business were a proprietorship or partnership. Such firms, which differ not in organizational form but only in how their owners are taxed, are called *S corporations*. Although S corporations are similar in many ways to limited liability partnerships, LLPs frequently offer more flexibility and benefits to their owners — so many that large numbers of S corporation businesses are converting to this relatively new organizational form.

What are the key differences between sole proprietorships, partnerships, and corporations?

Explain why the value of any business other than a very small one will probably be maximized if it is organized as a corporation.

SELF-TEST QUESTIONS

FINANCE IN THE ORGANIZATIONAL STRUCTURE OF THE FIRM

Organizational structures vary from firm to firm, but Figure 1-1 presents a fairly typical picture of the role of finance within a corporation. The chief financial officer — or CFO, who often has the title of vice-president: finance — reports to the president. The financial vice-president's key subordinates are the treasurer and the controller. In most firms the treasurer has direct responsibility for managing the firm's cash and marketable securities, for planning its capital structure, for selling stocks and bonds to raise capital, for overseeing the corporate pension plan, and for managing risk. The treasurer also supervises the credit manager, the inventory manager, and the director of capital budgeting (who analyzes decisions related to investments in fixed

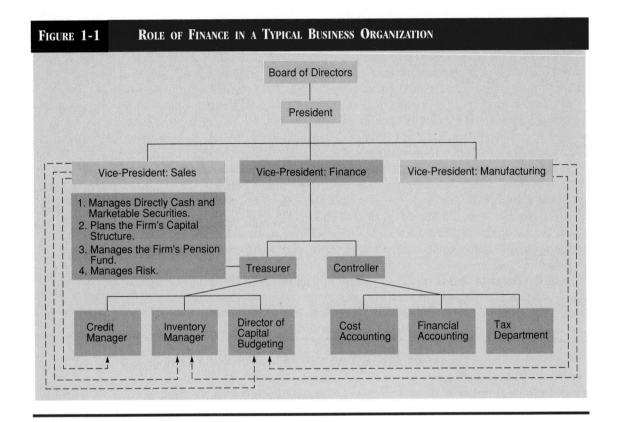

FIGURE 1-1   ROLE OF FINANCE IN A TYPICAL BUSINESS ORGANIZATION

assets). The controller is typically responsible for the activities of the accounting and tax departments.

SELF-TEST QUESTION   Identify the two primary subordinates who report to the firm's chief financial officer, and indicate the primary responsibilities of each.

THE GOALS OF THE CORPORATION

Business decisions are not made in a vacuum — decision makers have some objectives in mind. Throughout this book we operate on the assumption that management's primary goal is *stockholder wealth maximization,* which, as we shall see, translates into *maximizing the price of the firm's common stock.* Firms do, of course, have other objectives — in particular, the managers who make the actual decisions are interested in their own personal satisfaction, in their employees' welfare, and in the good of the community and of society at large. Still, for the reasons set forth in the following sections, *stock price maximization is the most important goal in most corporations.*

MANAGERIAL INCENTIVES TO MAXIMIZE SHAREHOLDER WEALTH

Stockholders own the firm and elect the board of directors, which then elects the management team. Management, in turn, is supposed to operate in the best interests of the stockholders. We know, however, that because the stock of most large firms is widely held, the managers of large corporations have a great deal of autonomy. This being the case, might not managers pursue goals other than stock price maximization? For example, some have argued that the managers of a large, well-entrenched corporation could work just hard enough to keep stockholder returns at a "reasonable" level and then devote the remainder of their efforts and resources to public service activities, to employee benefits, to higher executive salaries, or to golf.

It is almost impossible to determine whether a particular management team is trying to maximize shareholder wealth or is merely attempting to keep stockholders satisfied while pursuing other goals. For example, how can we tell whether employee or community benefit programs are in the long-run best interests of the stockholders? Similarly, are huge executive salaries really necessary to attract and retain excellent managers, or are they just another example of managers' taking advantage of stockholders?

It is impossible to give definitive answers to these questions. However, we do know that the managers of a firm operating in a competitive market will be forced to undertake actions that are reasonably consistent with shareholder wealth maximization. If they depart from this goal, they run the risk of being removed from their jobs, either by the firm's board of directors or by outside forces. We will have much more to say about this in a later section.

SOCIAL RESPONSIBILITY

Another issue that deserves consideration is *social responsibility.* Should businesses operate strictly in their stockholders' best interests, or are firms also responsible for the welfare of their employees, customers, and the communities in which they operate? Certainly firms have an ethical responsibility to provide a safe working environment, to avoid polluting the air or water, and to produce safe products. However, socially responsible actions have costs, and it is questionable whether many businesses would voluntarily incur all such costs. If some firms do act in a socially responsible manner while others do not, then the socially responsible firms will be at a disadvantage in attracting capital. To illustrate, suppose the firms in a given industry have profits and rates of return on investment that are close to "normal," that is, close to the average for all firms and just sufficient to attract capital. If one company attempts to exercise social responsibility, it will have to raise prices to cover the added costs. If the other businesses in its industry do not follow suit, their costs and prices will be lower. The socially responsible firm will not be able to compete, and it will be forced to abandon its efforts. Thus, any voluntary socially responsible acts that raise costs will be difficult, if not impossible, in industries that are subject to keen competition.

What about oligopolistic firms with profits above normal levels — cannot such firms devote resources to social projects? Undoubtedly they can, and many large, successful firms do engage in community projects, employee benefit programs, and the like to a greater degree than would appear to be called for by pure profit or wealth maximization goals.[4] Furthermore, many such firms contribute large sums to charities. Still, publicly owned firms are constrained in such actions by capital market forces. To illustrate, suppose a saver who has funds to invest is considering two alternative firms. One firm devotes a substantial part of its resources to social actions, while the other concentrates on profits and stock prices. Most investors are likely to shun the socially oriented firm, thus putting it at a disadvantage in the capital market. After all, why should the stockholders of one corporation subsidize society to a greater extent than those of other businesses? For this reason, even highly profitable firms (unless they are closely held rather than publicly owned) are generally constrained against taking unilateral cost-increasing social actions.

Does all this mean that firms should not exercise social responsibility? Not at all, but it does mean that most significant cost-increasing actions will have to be put on a *mandatory* rather than a voluntary basis to ensure that the burden falls uniformly on all businesses. Thus, such social benefit programs as fair hiring practices, minority training, product safety, pollution abatement, and antitrust actions are most likely to be effective if realistic rules are established initially and then enforced by government agencies. Of course, it is critical that industry and government cooperate in establishing the rules of corporate behavior, that the costs as well as the benefits of such actions be estimated accurately and then taken into account, and that firms follow the spirit as well as the letter of the law in their actions.

In spite of the fact that many socially responsible actions must be mandated by government, in recent years numerous firms have been voluntarily taking actions, especially in the area of environmental protection, because these actions help sales. For example, many detergent manufacturers now use recycled paper for their containers, and food companies are packaging more and more products in materials that consumers can recycle or that are biodegradable. To illustrate, McDonald's replaced its styrofoam boxes, which take years to break down in landfills, with paper wrappers that are less bulky and decompose more rapidly. Some companies, such as the Body Shop and Ben & Jerry's Ice Cream, go to great lengths to be socially responsible. According to the president of the Body Shop, the role of business is to promote the public good, not just the good of the firm's shareholders. Furthermore, she argues that it is impossible to separate business from social responsibility. For some firms, socially responsible actions may not even be very costly, because the companies often heavily advertise such actions, and many consumers prefer to buy from socially responsible companies rather than from companies that shun social responsibility.

STOCK PRICE MAXIMIZATION AND SOCIAL WELFARE

If a firm attempts to maximize its stock price, is this good or bad for society? In general, it is good. Aside from such illegal actions as attempting to form monopolies, violating safety codes, and failing to meet pollution control requirements, *the same actions that maximize stock prices also benefit society.* First, note that stock price

---

[4]Even firms like these often find it necessary to justify such projects at stockholder meetings by stating that these programs will contribute to long-run profit maximization.

maximization requires efficient, low-cost operations that produce high-quality goods and services at the lowest possible cost. Second, stock price maximization requires the development of products and services that consumers want and need, so the profit motive leads to new technology, to new products, and to new jobs. Finally, stock price maximization necessitates efficient and courteous service, adequate stocks of merchandise, and well-located business establishments — factors that are all necessary to make sales, which are necessary for profits. Therefore, most actions which help a firm increase the price of its stock also benefit society at large. This is why profit-motivated, free-enterprise economies have been so much more successful than socialistic and communistic economic systems. Since financial management plays a crucial role in the operations of successful firms, and since successful firms are absolutely necessary for a healthy, productive economy, it is easy to see why finance is important from a social standpoint.[5]

**SELF-TEST
QUESTIONS**

What is management's primary goal?

What actions could be taken to remove management if it departs from the goal of maximizing shareholder wealth?

What would happen if one firm attempted to exercise costly social responsibility, while its competitors did *not* exercise social responsibility?

How does the goal of stock price maximization benefit society at large?

BUSINESS ETHICS

The word *ethics* is defined in Webster's dictionary as "standards of conduct or moral behavior." Business ethics can be thought of as a company's attitude and conduct toward its employees, customers, community, and stockholders. High standards of ethical behavior demand that a firm treat each party that it deals with in a fair and honest manner. A firm's commitment to business ethics can be measured by the tendency of the firm and its employees to adhere to laws and regulations relating to such factors as product safety and quality, fair employment practices, fair marketing and selling practices, the use of confidential information for personal gain, community involvement, bribery, and illegal payments to foreign governments to obtain business.

There are many instances of firms engaging in unethical behavior. For example, in recent years the employees of several prominent Wall Street investment banking houses have been sentenced to prison for illegally using insider information on proposed mergers for their own personal gain, and E. F. Hutton, a large brokerage firm,

---

[5]People sometimes argue that firms, in their efforts to raise profits and stock prices, increase product prices and gouge the public. In a reasonably competitive economy, which we have, prices are constrained by competition and consumer resistance. If a firm raises its prices beyond reasonable levels, it will simply lose its market share. Even giant firms like General Motors lose business to the Japanese and Germans, as well as to Ford and Chrysler, if they set prices above levels necessary to cover production costs plus a "normal" profit. Of course, firms *want* to earn more, and they constantly try to cut costs, to develop new products, and so on, and thereby to earn above-normal profits. Note, though, that if they are indeed successful and do earn above-normal profits, those very profits will attract competition which will eventually drive prices down, so again the main long-term beneficiary is the consumer.

lost its independence through a forced merger after it was convicted of cheating its banks out of millions of dollars in a check kiting scheme. Drexel Burnham Lambert, one of the largest investment banking firms, went bankrupt, and its "junk bond king," Michael Milken, who had earned $550 million in just one year, was sentenced to 10 years in prison plus charged a huge fine for securities-law violations. Recently, Salomon Brothers was implicated in a Treasury-auction bidding scandal which resulted in the removal of key officers and a significant reorganization of the firm.

In spite of all this, the results of a recent study indicate that the executives of most major firms in the United States believe that firms do try to maintain high ethical standards in all of their business dealings. Furthermore, most executives believe that there is a positive correlation between ethics and long-run profitability. For example, Chemical Bank suggested that ethical behavior has increased its profitability because such behavior (1) avoids fines and legal expenses, (2) builds public trust, (3) attracts business from customers who appreciate and support its policies, (4) attracts and keeps employees of the highest caliber, and (5) supports the economic viability of the communities in which it operates.

Most firms today have in place strong codes of ethical behavior, and about half of all large firms conduct training programs designed to ensure that all employees understand the correct behavior in different business situations. However, it is imperative that top management — the chairman, president, and vice-presidents — be openly committed to ethical behavior, and that they communicate this commitment through their own personal actions as well as through company policies, directives, and punishment/reward systems.

Conflicts often arise between profits and ethics. Sometimes ethical considerations are so strong that they clearly dominate, but in many cases the choice between ethics and profits is not clear cut. For example, if Norfolk Southern's managers know that its coal trains are polluting the air along its routes, but the amount of pollution is within legal limits and preventive actions would be costly, are the managers ethically bound to reduce pollution? Similarly, if a medical products company's own research indicates that one of its new products may cause problems, but the evidence is relatively weak while evidence of benefits to patients is strong, and independent government tests show no adverse effects, should the company make the potential problem known to the public? If it does release the negative (but questionable) information, this will hurt sales and profits, and possibly keep some patients who would benefit from the new product from using it. There are no obvious answers to questions such as these, but companies must deal with them on a regular basis, and a failure to handle the situation properly can lead to huge product liability suits and even to bankruptcy, as Dow-Corning recently learned.

Self-Test Questions   How would you define "business ethics"?

Is "being ethical" good for profits in the long run? In the short run?

AGENCY RELATIONSHIPS

It has long been recognized that firms' managers may have personal goals that compete with shareholder wealth maximization. The fact that managers are empowered by the owners of the firm — the shareholders — to make decisions creates a potential conflict of interest that falls under the general concept of *agency theory.*

An *agency relationship* arises whenever one or more individuals, called *principals,* hire another individual, called an *agent,* to perform some service and then delegate decision-making authority to that agent. Within the financial management context, the primary agency relationships are those (1) between stockholders and managers and (2) between debtholders and stockholders.[6]

AGENCY CONFLICTS

A potential problem arises whenever the manager of a firm owns less than 100 percent of the firm's common stock. If a firm is a proprietorship managed by the owner, the owner-manager will take actions to maximize his or her own welfare or, in economic terms, utility. The owner-manager will probably measure utility primarily by personal wealth, but other factors, such as leisure time and perquisites, will be traded off against personal wealth in the utility maximizing process.[7] Thus, not only will the owner-manager derive all of the benefits from actions that maximize the business's value, but he or she will also bear all of the costs of leisure time and perquisite consumption. However, if the owner-manager relinquishes a portion of his or her ownership by selling some of the firm's stock to outside investors, a potential conflict of interest, called an *agency conflict,* arises. For example, the owner-manager may now decide to lead a more relaxed lifestyle and not work as strenuously to maximize shareholder wealth, because less of this wealth will now accrue to the owner-manager. Also, the owner-manager may decide to consume more perquisites, because some of their costs will now be borne by the outside shareholders. In essence, the fact that the owner-manager will neither gain all the benefits of the wealth created by his or her efforts nor bear all of the costs of perquisite consumption will increase the incentive to take actions that are not in the best interests of the nonmanager shareholders.

In most large corporations, potential agency conflicts are quite important, because large firms' managers generally own only a small percentage of the stock. In this situation, shareholder wealth maximization could take a back seat to any number of possible managerial goals. For example, many people have argued that agent/managers' primary goal is to maximize the size of the firm.[8] By creating a large, rapidly growing firm, managers (1) increase their job security because a hostile takeover is less likely; (2) increase their own power, status, and salaries; and (3) create more opportunities for their lower- and middle-level managers. Furthermore, since the managers of most large firms own only a small percentage of the stock, it has been argued that they have a voracious appetite for salaries and perquisites and that they generously contribute corporate dollars to their favorite charities because they get the glory but outside stockholders bear the cost.

---

[6]The classic work on the application of agency theory to financial management is Michael C. Jensen and William H. Meckling, "Theory of the Firm, Managerial Behavior, Agency Costs, and Ownership Structure," *Journal of Financial Economics,* October 1976, 305–360.

[7]*Perquisites* are executive fringe benefits such as luxurious offices, executive assistants, expense accounts, limousines, corporate jets, generous retirement plans, and the like.

[8]See J. R. Wildsmith, *Managerial Theories of the Firm* (New York: Dunellen, 1974).

AGENCY COSTS

Obviously, managers can be encouraged to act in the stockholders' best interests through a set of incentives, constraints, and punishments. But these tools are effective only if shareholders can observe all of the actions taken by managers. A potential *moral hazard* problem, wherein agents take unobserved actions in their own behalf, arises, because it is virtually impossible for shareholders to monitor all managerial actions. In general, to reduce both agency conflicts and the moral hazard problem, stockholders must incur *agency costs,* which include all costs borne by shareholders to encourage managers to maximize the firm's stock price rather than act in their own self-interests. There are three major categories of agency costs: (1) expenditures to monitor managerial actions, such as audit costs; (2) expenditures to structure the organization in a way that will limit undesirable managerial behavior, such as appointing outside investors to the board of directors; and (3) opportunity costs which are incurred when shareholder-imposed restrictions, such as requirements for stockholder votes on certain issues, limit the ability of managers to take timely actions that would enhance shareholder wealth.

In the absence of any type of shareholder effort to affect managerial behavior, and hence with zero agency costs, there will almost certainly be some loss of shareholder wealth due to improper managerial actions. Conversely, agency costs would be very high if shareholders attempted to ensure that every managerial action coincided exactly with shareholder interests. Thus, the optimal amount of agency costs to be borne by shareholders should be viewed like any other investment decision — agency costs should be incurred as long as each dollar spent returns more than a dollar in shareholder wealth.

MANAGERIAL INCENTIVES

There are two extreme positions regarding how to deal with shareholder–manager agency conflicts. At one extreme, if a firm's managers were compensated solely on the basis of stock price changes, agency costs would be low because managers would have a great deal of incentive to maximize shareholder wealth. However, it would be difficult if not impossible to hire competent managers under these terms, because the firm's earnings stream would be affected by economic events that were not under managerial control. At the other extreme, stockholders could monitor every managerial action, but this would be costly and inefficient. The optimal solution lies somewhere between the extremes, where executive compensation is tied to performance, but some monitoring is also done. Some specific mechanisms which encourage managers to act in shareholders' interests include (1) performance-based incentive plans, (2) direct intervention by shareholders, (3) the threat of firing, and (4) the threat of takeover.

PERFORMANCE-BASED INCENTIVE PLANS   Firms are increasingly tying managers' compensation to the company's performance by instituting performance-based incentive plans. In the 1950s and 1960s, most of these plans involved *executive stock options,* which allow managers to purchase stock at some time in the future at a given price. Here the options have value only if the market price of the stock rises above the exercise price of the option. These plans relied on the assumption that allowing managers to purchase stock at a fixed price would provide an incentive for them to take actions that would increase the stock's price. This type of plan lost favor in the 1970s, however, because the options generally did not pay off; the stock market declined during the 1970s because of rising interest rates, so stock prices did not necessarily reflect managerial performance. Further, it was recognized that if interest rates fall in the economy, stock prices will tend to rise, even for poorly managed firms. This situation existed during the 1980s. Since incentive plans should be based on factors over which managers have control, and since managers cannot control broad market movements, stock option plans proved to be poor incentive devices.

Because of concerns over stock option plans, there has been a trend away from the exclusive use of such plans as managerial incentives. Rather, many firms are now using some form of performance shares. *Performance shares* are shares of stock given to executives on the basis of performance as defined by objective measures such as earnings per share, return on assets, return on equity, and so forth. For example, Honeywell uses growth in earnings per share as its primary performance measure. The firm has two overlapping four-year periods, beginning two years apart. At the start of each period, participating executives are allocated a certain number of performance shares, say, 10,000 shares for the president down to 1,000 shares for a lower-level manager. If the company achieves, say, a targeted 13 percent average annual growth in earnings per share, the managers will earn 100 percent of their shares. If corporate performance is above the target, Honeywell's managers can earn even more shares, up to a maximum of 130 percent, which requires a 16 percent growth rate. However, if growth is below 13 percent, they get less than 100 percent of the shares, and below a 9 percent growth rate they get none. Executives must remain with the firm through the entire performance period (four years) to qualify for the performance shares.

Performance shares will have value even when the company's stock price remains flat or decreases because of poor stock market conditions, whereas stock options have no value under similar conditions, even if managers have been successful in boosting per-share earnings. Of course, the value of the performance shares received depends on market performance, because 1,000 shares of Honeywell stock are a lot more valuable if the stock sells for $60 than if it sells for only $40.

A relatively new measure of managerial performance, *economic value added (EVA)*, is being used by more and more firms to tie executive compensation to stockholder wealth maximization. EVA is a way to measure a firm's true profitability. The cost of debt capital (interest expense) is deducted when accountants calculate net income, but no cost is deducted to account for the cost of common equity. Therefore, in an economic sense, net income overstates "true" income. EVA overcomes this flaw in conventional accounting.

EVA is found by taking the after-tax operating profit and subtracting the annual cost of *all* the capital a firm uses. If EVA is positive, then management is creating value for the stockholders, but if EVA is negative, management is destroying value. Obviously, the higher its EVA, the more wealth the firm is creating for its shareholders. There is a better link between EVA and stock prices than between accounting measures such as earnings per share and stock prices, so compensation based on

EVA provides managers with stronger incentives to maximize shareholder wealth. EVA, and its companion measure, market value added (MVA), will be discussed in more depth in Chapter 2.

All incentive-based compensation plans — executive stock options, performance shares, profit-based bonuses, and so forth — are supposed to accomplish two goals. First, they provide executives with an incentive to take actions that will contribute to shareholder wealth maximization. Second, incentive compensation plans help companies attract and retain managers who have enough confidence to stake their financial future on their own abilities and efforts, and such individuals make the best top-level executives. Well-designed plans can accomplish both goals.

DIRECT INTERVENTION BY SHAREHOLDERS   Although a great deal of stock is owned by individuals, an increasing percentage is owned by institutional investors such as insurance companies, pension funds, and mutual funds. Indeed, in 1996 more than half of all stock was owned by institutions. Therefore, the institutional money managers have the clout, if they choose to use it, to exercise considerable influence over most firms' operations. First, they can talk with a firm's management and make suggestions regarding how the business should be run. In effect, institutional investors can act as lobbyists for the body of stockholders. Second, any shareholder who owns at least $1,000 of a company's stock for one year can sponsor a proposal which must be voted on at the annual stockholders' meeting, even if the proposal is opposed by management. Although shareholder-sponsored proposals are nonbinding and are limited to issues outside day-to-day operations, the results of such votes are clearly heard by top management.

Why are institutions suddenly taking such an interest in the management of companies they own? The primary reason is that they no longer have an easy exit from the market. Their portfolios are so big that if they decided to dump a stock in a hurry, the stock's price would take a free-fall. Rather than throwing up their hands and selling the stock, many institutional investors have decided to stay and work with management. Also, there has been considerable pressure on pension fund managers from the Department of Labor, which supervises pension fund investment practices under the Employee Retirement Income Security Act (ERISA). Under ERISA, pension fund managers are required to vote in the best interests of the funds' beneficiaries, which often means voting against corporate management. Finally, the Securities and Exchange Commission (SEC) has been expanding the number of issues that shareholders can address in shareholder-sponsored proposals. In its latest move, the SEC ruled that executive compensation is a legal topic for proposals. In the past, executive compensation was classified as a matter of "ordinary business" and hence not addressable in shareholder proposals. Similarly, the SEC recently forced several companies to allow shareholders to vote on "golden parachute" executive retirement packages.[9]

The most fundamental change that institutional investors are lobbying for is a more independent board of directors — institutional investors see a management-

---

[9]A *golden parachute* is a contract provision that gives a corporate executive a large severance payment if the company is taken over by another company and the executive loses his or her job.

controlled board as the weak link in the chain of managerial accountability to share-holders.[10] Too often, according to most experts on corporate control, the directors are in management's hip pocket, which is why institutional investors are pressing for truly independent boards. In fact, many institutional investors would like to see an outside director installed as chairman of the board, as was done recently by GM, because they do not trust an inside chairman to serve the shareholders first and his or her management's interests second.

THE THREAT OF FIRING Until recently, the probability of a large firm's management being ousted by its stockholders was so remote that it posed little threat. This situation existed because the ownership of most firms was so widely distributed, and management's control over the voting mechanism so strong, that it was almost impossible for dissident stockholders to get the votes needed to overthrow the managers. However, as noted previously, that situation is changing.

Consider the case of Baltimore Bancorp. Recently, its chairman, Harry L. Robinson, spurned a friendly $17-per-share takeover offer from rival First Maryland Bancorp. Dismayed stockholders saw the stock price drop to $5 a share, and, led by a Baltimore businessman, they revolted. A slate of dissident directors was nominated, and they lined up the support of T. Rowe Price, a Baltimore mutual fund management company which held about 9 percent of the bank's stock. At Baltimore Bancorp's next annual meeting, shareholders elected the dissident directors, who won all six of the board seats that were up for election. Subsequently, the board ousted Robinson, and a new management team was put in place.

For every obvious case of shareholders' exercising their ownership rights and ousting current management, such as at Baltimore Bancorp, there have been many more less obvious occurrences. In recent years, the CEOs or other top executives at American Express, Goodyear, General Motors, and IBM have all resigned amid speculation that their departures were connected to their companies' poor performance. More and more, the reasons for executive departures are shifting from "poor health" and "personal reasons" to "at the request of the board."

TAKEOVERS *Hostile takeovers* (when management does not want the firm to be taken over) are most likely to occur when a firm's stock is undervalued relative to its potential because of poor management. In a hostile takeover, the managers of the acquired firm are generally fired, and any who are able to stay on lose the autonomy they had prior to the acquisition. Thus, managers have a strong incentive to take actions which maximize stock prices. In the words of one company president, "If you want to keep your job, don't let your company's stock sell at a bargain price."

---

[10]To this end, confidential proxy voting is important because corporate executives have been known to threaten to move pension fund assets from fund managers who vote against management. Because the executives of one company often serve on other companies' boards, a "club" attitude prevails, and the CEO of Company A might take action against his or her pension fund manager if that manager voted against the management of Company B. Company B's management, of course, would be expected to protect Company A's management in return. Because of this situation, public pension fund managers, such as the managers of the California Public Employees' Retirement System (CALPERS), have thus far taken the lead in exercising their voting power.

ANOTHER AGENCY CONFLICT: STOCKHOLDERS VERSUS CREDITORS

In addition to the agency conflict between stockholders and managers, there is also an agency conflict between creditors and stockholders. Creditors have a claim on part of the firm's earnings stream (the interest and principal payments on the debt) as well as on the firm's assets in the event of bankruptcy. However, stockholders have control (through the firm's managers) of the decisions that affect the profitability and risk of the firm. Creditors lend funds to a firm at rates that are based on (1) the riskiness of the firm's existing assets, (2) expectations concerning the riskiness of future asset additions, (3) the firm's existing capital structure (that is, the amount of debt financing used), and (4) expectations concerning future capital structure decisions. These are the primary determinants of the riskiness of a firm's cash flows, hence the safety of its debt issues.

Now suppose its stockholders, acting through management, cause a firm to take on a large new project that has more risk than was anticipated by the creditors. This increased risk will cause the required rate of return on the firm's debt to increase, which, in turn, will cause the value of the outstanding debt to fall. If the risky project is successful, all of the benefits go to the stockholders, because creditors' returns are fixed at the old, low-risk rate. However, if the project is unsuccessful, the bondholders may have to share in the losses. From the stockholders' point of view, this amounts to a game of "heads I win, tails you lose," which is obviously not a good game for the creditors. Similarly, suppose its managers borrow additional funds and use the proceeds to repurchase some of the firm's outstanding stock in an effort to leverage up stockholders' return on equity. If the old debt does not have seniority over the new debt, its value will decrease, because more debt will have a claim against the firm's cash flows and assets. In both the riskier asset and the increased leverage situations, stockholders gain at the expense of creditors.

Can and should stockholders, through their managers/agents, try to expropriate wealth from creditors? In general, the answer is no. First, such behavior is unethical, and there is no room for unethical behavior in the business world. Second, if such attempts are made, creditors will protect themselves against stockholders by placing restrictive covenants in future debt agreements. Finally, if creditors perceive that a firm's managers are trying to take advantage of them, they will either refuse to deal further with the firm or else will charge a higher than normal interest rate to compensate for the risk of possible exploitation. Thus, firms which deal unfairly with creditors either lose access to the debt markets or are saddled with high interest rates and restrictive covenants, all of which are detrimental to shareholders.

In view of these constraints, it follows that to best serve their shareholders, managers must play fairly with creditors, which means abiding by both the letter and the spirit of credit agreements. Managers, as agents of both shareholders and creditors, must act in a manner that is fairly balanced between the interests of the two classes of security holders. Similarly, because of other constraints and sanctions, management actions which would expropriate wealth from any of the firm's other *stakeholders,* including its employees, customers, suppliers, and community, will ultimately be to the detriment of its shareholders. We conclude that in our society, stock price maximization requires the fair treatment of all parties whose economic position is affected by managerial decisions.

What are agency conflicts? Within corporate finance, what are the two major agency conflicts?

What are agency costs, and who bears them?

What are some mechanisms that encourage managers to act in the best interests of stockholders? To not take advantage of bondholders?

Why should managers not take actions that are clearly unfair to any of the firm's stakeholders?

MANAGERIAL ACTIONS TO MAXIMIZE SHAREHOLDER WEALTH

To maximize the price of a firm's stock, what types of actions should its management take? First, consider the question of stock prices versus profits: Will *profit maximization* also result in stock price maximization? In answering this question, we must consider the matter of total corporate profits versus *earnings per share (EPS)*.

For example, suppose Xerox had 100 million shares outstanding and earned $400 million, or $4 per share. If you owned 100 shares of the stock, your share of the total profits would be $400. Now suppose Xerox sold another 100 million shares and invested the funds received in assets which produced $100 million of income. Total income would rise to $500 million, but earnings per share would decline from $4 to $500/200 = $2.50. Now your share of the firm's earnings would be only $250, down from $400. You (and other current stockholders) would have suffered an earnings dilution, even though total corporate profits had risen. Therefore, other things held constant, *if management is interested in the well-being of its current stockholders, it should concentrate on earnings per share rather than on total corporate profits.*

Will maximization of expected earnings per share always maximize stockholder welfare, or should other factors be considered? Think about the *timing of the earnings.* Suppose Xerox had one project that would cause earnings per share to rise by $0.20 per year for 5 years, or $1 in total, while another project would have no effect on earnings for 4 years but would increase earnings by $1.50 in the fifth year. Which project is better? In other words, is $0.20 per year for 5 years better or worse than $1.50 in Year 5? The answer depends on which project adds the most to the value of the stock, which, in turn, depends on the time value of money to investors. Thus, timing is an important reason to concentrate on wealth as measured by the price of the stock rather than on earnings alone.

Another issue relates to *risk.* Suppose one project is expected to increase earnings per share by $1, while another is expected to raise earnings by $1.20 per share. The first project is not very risky; if it is undertaken, earnings will almost certainly rise by about $1 per share. However, the second project is quite risky, so, although our best guess is that earnings will rise by $1.20 per share, we must recognize the possibility that there may be no increase whatsoever, or even a loss. Depending on how averse stockholders are to risk, the first project might be preferable to the second.

The riskiness inherent in projected earnings per share (EPS) also depends on *how the firm is financed.* As we shall see, many firms go bankrupt every year, and the greater the use of debt, the greater the threat of bankruptcy. *Consequently, while the use of debt financing may increase projected EPS, debt also increases the risk-iness of projected future earnings.*

Another issue is the matter of paying dividends to stockholders versus retaining earnings and reinvesting them in the firm, thereby causing the earnings stream to grow over time. Stockholders like cash dividends, but they also like the growth in EPS that results from plowing earnings back into the business. The financial manager must recommend exactly how much of the current earnings to pay out as dividends rather than to retain and reinvest — this is called the *dividend policy decision.* The optimal dividend policy is the one that maximizes the firm's stock price.

We see, then, that the firm's stock price is dependent on the following factors:

1. Projected earnings per share

2. Timing of the earnings stream

3. Riskiness of the projected earnings

4. Use of debt

5. Dividend policy

Every significant corporate decision should be analyzed in terms of its effect on these factors and, hence, on the price of the firm's stock. For example, suppose Kerr-McGee's coal division is considering opening a new mine. If this is done, can it be expected to increase EPS? Is there a chance that costs will exceed estimates, that prices and output will fall below projections, and that EPS will be reduced because the new mine was opened? How long will it take for the new mine to show a profit? How should the capital required to open the mine be raised? If debt is used, by how much will this increase Kerr-McGee's riskiness? Should Kerr-McGee reduce its current dividends and use the cash thus saved to finance the project, or should it maintain its dividends and finance the mine with external capital? Financial management is designed to help answer questions like these, plus many more.

SELF-TEST QUESTIONS   Will profit maximization always result in stock price maximization?

Identify five factors which affect the firm's stock price, and explain the effects of each of them.

THE EXTERNAL ENVIRONMENT

Although managerial actions affect the value of a firm's stock, stock prices are also affected by external factors, including legal constraints, the general level of economic activity, tax laws, and conditions in the stock market. Figure 1-2 diagrams these general relationships. Working within the set of external constraints shown in the box at the extreme left, management makes a set of long-run strategic policy decisions which chart a future course for the firm. These policy decisions, along with the general level of economic activity and the level of corporate income taxes, influence the firm's expected profitability, the timing of its cash flows, their eventual transfer to stockholders in the form of dividends, and the degree of risk inherent in projected earnings and dividends. Profitability, timing, and risk all affect the price of

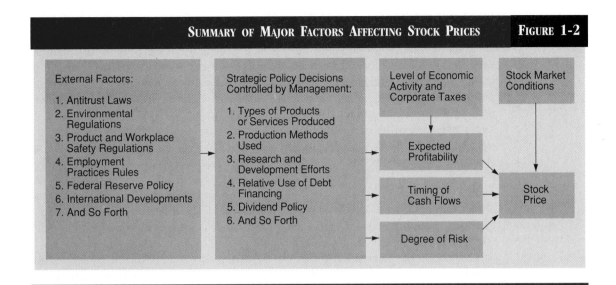

SUMMARY OF MAJOR FACTORS AFFECTING STOCK PRICES — **FIGURE 1-2**

the firm's stock, but so does another factor, conditions in the stock market as a whole.

Identify some factors beyond a firm's control which influence its stock price.   **SELF-TEST QUESTION**

ORGANIZATION OF THE BOOK

The primary goal of management is to help maximize the value of the firm. To achieve this goal, managers must have a general understanding of how businesses are organized, how financial markets operate, how interest rates are determined, how the tax system operates, and how accounting data are used to evaluate a business's performance. In addition, managers must have a good understanding of some fundamental concepts, including discounted cash flow analysis, risk analysis, asset valuation, and evaluation of investment opportunities. This background information is essential for anyone involved with making the kinds of decisions that affect the value of a firm's securities.

The organization of this book reflects these considerations, so we begin, in Part I, with some background information on financial markets, institutions, taxes, and interest rates, plus a discussion of how accounting data are used to evaluate the firm's past performance, present condition, and forecasted future condition.

Part II covers the fundamental concepts upon which financial management is built — risk analysis, the relationship between risk and return, discounted cash flow analysis, and the formal models used to evaluate securities and other assets. The concepts discussed in Parts I and II are used throughout the remainder of the book.

Part III covers *capital budgeting,* a key financial management decision area which involves investments in fixed assets. In a sense, firms make two types of decisions: *strategic decisions* and *operating decisions.* Every successful firm of any size has a business plan, which is a guide to future operations, and specific decisions are made within the framework of the plan. For example, if General Motors plans to revamp its North American operations to reduce costs, it will have to invest in equipment to automate some of its plants. Specific investment decisions will be made within the framework of the corporate plan, using the capital budgeting analysis techniques discussed in Part III.

If GM or any other company is to acquire new assets, it will have to obtain capital, and Part IV deals with long-term financial planning and alternative financing strategies. Most well-run businesses use computer models as an integral part of their planning process, because such models are ideally suited for showing what can be expected under different financial policies and under different economic conditions. For example, General Motors has a long-term model that forecasts the company's financial requirements, its key financial ratios, and its earnings per share under different financial plans.

The primary financing decision relates to the use of debt versus equity, or the *capital structure decision.* There are advantages and disadvantages to using debt, and capital structure decisions can have a profound effect on a firm's risk, profitability, and stock price. A related decision, the *dividend policy decision,* involves how much of its earnings the firm should retain to support growth versus paying dividends to the stockholders. Stockholders like the growth that reinvested earnings provides, but they also like cash dividends, and deciding how to allocate earnings between retentions and dividends involves some complex issues.

Part V focuses on the institutional details of long-term financing. Here we discuss the key features of stocks and bonds, the characteristics of warrants, convertibles, and lease financing, and procedures for issuing securities.

Part VI deals with current assets and current liabilities, or *working capital management.* Companies make policy decisions regarding the optimal amounts of inventory, accounts receivable, and cash to hold, and about the optimal types and amounts of short-term credit to use. These policy decisions always recognize that the optimal levels of current assets and types of short-term credit are directly related to the level of sales, that sales levels can change quickly, and, hence, that working capital decisions must be made continuously and in "real time." Some people regard short-term decisions as being "less glamorous" than long-term decisions, but (1) most corporate failures result from a failure at the operating level, not at the strategic level, (2) most business students will spend most of their time dealing with current assets and liabilities, and (3) success in short-term operations is a requirement for promotion to the strategic arena, where long-term decisions are made.

Finally, in Part VII, we take up several special topics, including derivatives and risk management, bankruptcy, mergers, multinational financial management, and pension plan management, all of which can best be handled after you have covered the basics presented in the earlier chapters.

It is worth noting that there is no perfect organization for a book such as this. Therefore, some instructors may choose to cover the chapters in a sequence different from the order in the book. Accordingly, we wrote the chapters in a modular, self-contained format, which will make reordering relatively easy.

SUMMARY

This chapter provides an overview of financial management. The key concepts covered are listed below.

- Finance consists of three interrelated areas: (1) *money and capital markets*, (2) *investments*, and (3) *financial management*.

- Financial management has undergone significant changes over time, but four issues have received the most emphasis in recent years: (1) *inflation* and its effects on interest rates, (2) *deregulation of financial institutions*, (3) a dramatic increase in the use of *telecommunications* for transmitting information and *computers* for analyzing the effects of alternative financial decisions, and (4) the increased importance of *global financial markets and business operations*.

- *Financial managers* are responsible for *obtaining and using funds* in a way that will *maximize the value of their firms*.

- The three main forms of business organization are the *sole proprietorship,* the *partnership,* and the *corporation.*

- Although each form of organization offers some advantages and disadvantages, *most business is conducted by corporations because this organizational form maximizes most larger firms' values.*

- The primary goal of management should be to *maximize stockholders' wealth,* and this means *maximizing the price of the firm's stock.* Furthermore, actions which maximize stock prices also increase social welfare.

- An *agency relationship* arises whenever one or more individuals (principals) hire another individual (their agent) to perform some service and then delegate decision-making authority to the agent. The primary agency relationships encountered in financial management are those between stockholders and managers and those between debtholders and stockholders.

- A *moral hazard* problem, wherein agents take unobserved actions that are in their own best interests, can arise, because it is virtually impossible for shareholders to monitor all managerial actions.

- To reduce potential agency conflicts and moral hazard problems, stockholders must incur *agency costs,* which come in three major categories: (1) expenditures to monitor managerial actions, (2) expenditures to structure the organization in a way that will limit undesirable managerial behavior, and (3) opportunity costs which are incurred when shareholder-imposed restrictions limit managers' ability to take actions that contribute to shareholder wealth.

- In addition to monitoring, there are a number of ways to encourage managers to act in the best interests of stockholders, including (1) *performance-based incentive plans,* (2) *direct intervention by shareholders,* (3) *the threat of firing,* and (4) *the threat of takeover.*

■ The *price of the firm's stock* depends on the firm's *projected earnings per share*, the *timing of its earnings*, the *riskiness of the projected earnings*, its *use of debt*, and its *dividend policy.*

QUESTIONS

1-1   Define each of the following terms:

    a. Proprietorship; partnership; corporation

    b. Stockholder wealth maximization

    c. Social responsibility; business ethics

    d. Normal profits; normal rate of return

    e. Agency relationships; agency costs

    f. Leveraged buyout (LBO)

    g. Economic value added (EVA)

    h. Performance shares; executive stock options

    i. Profit maximization

    j. Earnings per share

    k. Dividend policy

1-2   What are the three principal forms of business organization? What are the advantages and disadvantages of each?

1-3   Would the "normal" rate of return on investment be the same in all industries? Would "normal" rates of return change over time? Explain.

1-4   Would the role of the financial manager be likely to increase or decrease in importance relative to other executives if the rate of inflation increased? Explain.

1-5   Should stockholder wealth maximization be thought of as a long-term or a short-term goal — for example, if one action would probably increase the firm's stock price from a current level of $40 to $50 in 6 months and then to $60 in 5 years, but another action would probably keep the stock at $40 for several years but then increase it to $80 in 5 years, which action would be better? Can you think of some specific corporate actions which might have these general tendencies?

1-6   Drawing on your background in accounting, can you think of any accounting procedure differences that might make it difficult to compare the relative performance of different firms?

1-7   Would the management of a firm in an oligopolistic or in a competitive industry be more likely to engage in what might be called "socially conscious" practices? Explain your reasoning.

1-8   What is the difference between stock price maximization and profit maximization? Under what conditions might profit maximization not lead to stock price maximization?

1-9   If you were the president of a large, publicly owned corporation, would you make decisions to maximize stockholders' welfare or your own personal interests? What are some actions stockholders could take to ensure that management's interests and those of stockholders coincided? What are some other factors that might influence management's actions?

1-10 The president of International Microchips Inc. (IMI) made this statement in the company's annual report: "IMI's primary goal is to increase the value of the common stockholders' equity over time." Later on in the report, the following announcements were made:

   a. The company contributed $2 million to the symphony orchestra in Seattle, its headquarters city.

   b. The company is spending $600 million to open a new plant in Venezuela. No revenues will be produced by the plant for 4 years, so earnings will be depressed during this period versus what they would have been had the decision not been made to open the new plant.

   c. The company is increasing its relative use of debt. Whereas assets were formerly financed with 30 percent debt and 70 percent equity, henceforth the financing mix will be 45/55.

   d. The company uses a great deal of electricity in its manufacturing operations, and it generates most of this power itself. Plans are to utilize nuclear fuel rather than coal to produce electricity in the future.

   e. The company has been paying out half of its earnings as dividends and retaining the other half. Henceforth, it will pay out only 40 percent as dividends.

Discuss how each of these actions would be reacted to by IMI's stockholders, customers, and labor force, and then how each action might affect IMI's stock price.

MINI CASE

Suppose you went home for a quick visit early in the term, and, over the course of the weekend, your brother, who received his MBA three years ago, asked you to tell him about the courses you are taking. After you told him that financial management was one of the courses, he asked you the following questions:

   a. What kinds of career opportunities are open to finance majors?

   b. What are the most important financial management issues of the 1990s?

   c. What are the primary responsibilities of a corporate financial staff?

   d. (1) What are the alternative forms of business organization?

   (2) What are their advantages and disadvantages?

   e. What is the primary goal of the corporation?

   (1) Do firms have any responsibilities to society at large?

   (2) Is stock price maximization good or bad for society?

   (3) Should firms behave ethically?

   f. What is an agency relationship?

   (1) What agency relationships exist within a corporation?

   (2) What mechanisms exist to influence managers to act in shareholders' best interests?

   (3) Should shareholders (through managers) take actions that are detrimental to bondholders?

   g. What factors can managers influence that affect stock price?

SELECTED ADDITIONAL REFERENCES

For alternative views on firms' goals and objectives, see the following articles:

Cornell, Bradford, and Alan C. Shapiro, "Corporate Stakeholders and Corporate Finance," *Financial Management,* Spring 1987, 5–14.

Donaldson, Gordon, "Financial Goals: Management versus Stockholders," *Harvard Business Review,* May-June 1963, 116–129.

Meckling, William H., and Michael C. Jensen, "Reflections on the Corporation as a Social Invention," *Midland Corporate Finance Journal,* Fall 1983, 6–15.

Seitz, Neil, "Shareholder Goals, Firm Goals and Firm Financing Decisions," *Financial Management,* Autumn 1982, 20–26.

The following articles extend our discussion of agency relationships:

Barnea, Amir, Robert A. Haugen, and Lemma W. Senbet, "Market Imperfections, Agency Problems, and Capital Structure: A Review," *Financial Management,* Summer 1981, 7–22.

Hand, John H., William P. Lloyd, and Robert B. Rogow, "Agency Relationships in the Close Corporation," *Financial Management,* Spring 1982, 25–30.

For a general review of academic finance, together with an extensive bibliography of key research articles, see

Brennan, Michael J., "Corporate Finance Over the Past 25 Years," *Financial Management,* Summer 1995, 9–22.

Cooley, Philip L., and J. Louis Heck, "Significant Contributions to Finance Literature," *Financial Management,* Tenth Anniversary Issue 1981, 23–33.

For more information on managerial compensation, see

Cooley, Philip L., and Charles E. Edwards, "Ownership Effects on Managerial Salaries in Small Business," *Financial Management,* Winter 1982, 5–9.

Hudson, Carl D., John S. Jahera, Jr., and William P. Lloyd, "Further Evidence on the Relationship between Ownership and Performance," *Financial Review,* May 1992, 227–239.

Lambert, Richard A., and David F. Larker, "Executive Compensation, Corporate Decision-Making and Shareholder Wealth: A Review of the Evidence," *Midland Corporate Finance Journal,* Winter 1985, 6–22. The Winter 1985 issue of the *Midland Corporate Finance Journal* contains several other articles pertaining to executive compensation.

Long, Michael S., "The Incentives Behind the Adoption of Executive Stock Option Plans in U.S. Corporations," *Financial Management,* Autumn 1992, 12–21.

Sridharan, Uma V., "CEO Influence and Executive Compensation," *Financial Review,* February 1996, 51–66.

"Stern Stewart Roundtable on Management Incentive Compensation and Shareholder Value," *Journal of Applied Corporate Finance,* Summer 1992, 110–130.

Stern, Joel M., G. Bennett Stewart, III, and Donald H. Chew, "The EVA® Financial Management System," *Journal of Applied Corporate Finance,* Summer 1995, 32–46.

For more information on the role of corporate directors, see

"Corporate Governance: The Role of Boards of Directors in Takeover Bids and Defenses," *Journal of Applied Corporate Finance,* Summer 1989, 6–35.

CHAPTER 2

ANALYSIS OF FINANCIAL STATEMENTS

*O*f all the documents that large companies publish, none is prepared as carefully as the annual report to shareholders. At some companies, top executives begin work on the report as much as six months before its publication, and most hire professional designers and writers to ensure that the final product looks sharp and reads well.

Obviously, so much fuss would hardly be necessary if the only goal of an annual report were to inform shareholders about financial results. But, in fact, most big companies have turned their annual reports into flashy management showcases. In slick magazine format, using four-color photos, feature stories, and elaborate graphics, each firm tells the story its chairman would like to see told. Indeed, to get the desired results, most annual reports are now produced by the director of public relations instead of the chief financial officer.

Because of their puffery, annual reports have lost credibility with serious seekers of financial information. Instead, Wall Street analysts and other sophisticated investors prefer more straightforward financial disclosure documents, such as 10-Ks, which contain more detailed and unadorned information and which must by law be filed with the Securities and Exchange Commission.

Of course, a company's philosophy and personality do count, and few other documents can offer better insights into these intangibles than an annual report. Most financial analysts believe, however, that companies owe it to their investors to distinguish between fanfare and facts. They want to see annual reports that realistically examine the firm's business affairs and that factually discuss likely events which will affect corporate performance. Indeed, they would like to see annual reports become the equivalent of management report cards, detailing strengths and weaknesses and plans for improvement. Given *such information, shareholders would be better equipped to make intelligent investment decisions.*

One chief executive who agrees with the financial analysts is Warren Buffett, legendary chairman of Berkshire Hathaway and former chairman of Salomon Brothers Inc. Describing his attitude toward his readers, Buffett says, "I assume I have a very intelligent partner who has been away for a year and needs to be filled in on all that's happened." Consequently, in his chairman's letter, which begins the annual report, Buffett often admits mistakes and emphasizes the negative. For example, in one recent report he wrote, "We continue to look for ways to expand our insurance operation, but your reaction to this intent should not be unrestrained joy. Some of our expansion efforts — largely initiated by your chairman — have been lackluster, while others have been expensive failures."

Buffett also uses his letters to educate his shareholders and to help them interpret the data presented in the rest of the report. In one letter he lamented the complexities of accounting and observed, "The Yānomamö Indians employ only three numbers: one, two, and more than two. Maybe their time will come."

Buffett's letters, although probably a bit too subjective for financial reporting purists, represent a giant step in the desired direction. In fact, Berkshire Hathaway's annual reports contain no photographs, colored ink, bar charts, or graphs, freeing readers to focus on the company's financial statements and Buffett's interpretation of them. Some CEOs might contend that such a barebones approach is too dull for the average stockholder and, further, that some readers may actually be intimidated by the information overload. But Buffett would no doubt counter that, whatever its shortcomings, his approach shows much greater respect for shareholders' intelligence and capacity to understand than does the average annual report.

As you read this chapter, think about the kinds of information that corporations provide their stockholders. Do the basic financial statements provide adequate data for investment decisions? What other information might be helpful? Also, consider the pros and cons of Chairman Buffett's decision to include long, frank, and frequently self-critical letters in his company's annual reports. Would you suggest that other companies follow suit?

If management is to maximize shareholder value, it must take advantage of the firm's strengths and correct its weaknesses. Financial statements are like report cards on companies' financial health, and financial statement analysis involves a comparison of a firm's performance with that of other firms in the same industry. This helps management identify deficiencies and then take actions to improve performance. In this chapter, we discuss how managers (and investors) evaluate the firm's current position. Then, in later chapters, we will examine the types of actions that a manager can take to improve his or her company's position in the future, thus increasing the price of its stock.

The chapter should, for the most part, be a review of concepts you learned in accounting. However, accounting focuses on how financial statements are *made*, whereas our focus is on how they are *used* by management to improve the firm's performance and by investors to set a value on the firm's stock.

FINANCIAL STATEMENTS AND REPORTS

Of the various reports corporations issue to their stockholders, the *annual report* is probably the most important. Two types of information are given in this report. First, there is a verbal section, often presented as a letter from the chairman, that describes the firm's operating results during the past year and then discusses new developments that will affect future operations. Second, the annual report presents four basic financial statements — the *income statement*, the *balance sheet*, the *statement of retained earnings*, and the *statement of cash flows*. Taken together, these statements give an accounting picture of the firm's operations and financial position. Detailed data are provided for the two or three most recent years, along with historical summaries of key operating statistics for the past five or ten years.[1]

The quantitative and verbal information are equally important. The financial statements report *what has actually happened* to assets, earnings, and dividends over the past few years, whereas the verbal statements attempt to explain why things turned out the way they did. For example, the earnings of MicroDrive Inc., a producer of disk drives for microcomputers, dropped in 1996, to $113.5 million versus $118 million in 1995. Management reported that the decline resulted from a 3-month strike that kept the firm from fully utilizing a new plant that had been financed mostly with debt. However, management then went on to paint a more optimistic picture for the future, stating that full operations had been resumed, that several new products had been introduced, and that 1997 profits were expected to rise sharply. Of course, an increase in profitability may not occur, and analysts should compare management's past statements with subsequent results. In any event, *the information contained in an annual report is used by investors to help form expectations about future earnings and dividends*.

For illustrative purposes, we shall use data taken from MicroDrive's financial statements throughout this chapter. Formed in 1982, MicroDrive has grown steadily and has earned a reputation for being one of the best firms in the microcomputer components industry. .

THE INCOME STATEMENT

Table 2-1 gives the 1996 and 1995 *income statements* for MicroDrive. Net sales are shown at the top of each statement, after which various costs, including income

---

[1]Firms also provide quarterly reports, but these are much less comprehensive. In addition, larger firms file even more detailed statements, giving breakdowns for each major division or subsidiary, with the Securities and Exchange Commission (SEC). These reports, called *10-K reports*, are made available to stockholders upon request to a company's corporate secretary. Finally, many larger firms also publish *statistical supplements*, which give financial statement data and key ratios going back 10 to 20 years.

TABLE 2-1	MICRODRIVE INC.: INCOME STATEMENTS FOR YEARS ENDING DECEMBER 31 (MILLIONS OF DOLLARS, EXCEPT FOR PER-SHARE DATA)		
		1996	**1995**
Net sales		$3,000.0	$2,850
Costs excluding depreciation		$2,616.2	$2,497
Depreciation		100.0	90
Total operating costs		$2,716.2	$2,587
Earnings before interest and taxes (EBIT)		$ 283.8	$ 263
Less interest		88.0	60
Earnings before taxes (EBT)		$ 195.8	$ 203
Taxes (40%)		78.3	81
Net income before preferred dividends		$ 117.5	$ 122
Preferred dividends		4.0	4
Net income available to common stockholders		$ 113.5	$ 118
Common dividends		$ 57.5	$ 53
Addition to retained earnings		$ 56.0	$ 65
Per-share data:			
Common stock price		$23.00	$24.00
Earnings per share (EPS)[a]		$ 2.27	$ 2.36
Dividends per share (DPS)[a]		$ 1.15	$ 1.06

[a]There are 50,000,000 shares of common stock outstanding. Note that EPS is based on earnings after preferred dividends—that is, on net income available to common stockholders. Calculations of EPS and DPS for 1996 are as follows:

$$\text{EPS} = \frac{\text{Net income}}{\text{Common shares outstanding}} = \frac{\$113,500,000}{50,000,000} = \$2.27.$$

$$\text{DPS} = \frac{\text{Dividends paid to common stockholders}}{\text{Common shares outstanding}} = \frac{\$57,500,000}{50,000,000} = \$1.15.$$

taxes, are subtracted to obtain net income available to common stockholders. Per-share data are given at the bottom of the statement. In financial management, earnings per share (EPS) is called "the bottom line," denoting that of all the items on the income statement, EPS is the most important. MicroDrive earned $2.27 per share in 1996, down from $2.36 in 1995, but it still raised the dividend from $1.06 to $1.15.

THE BALANCE SHEET

The left-hand side of MicroDrive's year-end 1996 and 1995 *balance sheets*, which are given in Table 2-2, shows the firm's assets, while the right-hand side shows the liabilities and equity, or the claims against these assets. The assets are listed in order of

ASSETS	1996	1995	LIABILITIES AND EQUITY	1996	1995
Cash	$ 10	$ 15	Accounts payable	$ 60	$ 30
Marketable securities	0	65	Notes payable	110	60
Accounts receivable	375	315	Accruals	140	130
Inventories	615	415	Total current liabilities	$ 310	$ 220
Total current assets	$1,000	$ 810	Long-term bonds	754	580
Net plant and equipment	1,000	870	Total debt	$1,064	$ 800
			Preferred stock (400,000 shares)	$ 40	$ 40
			Common stock (50,000,000 shares)	$ 50	$ 50
			Paid-in capital *(surplus)*	80	80
			Retained earnings	766	710
			Common equity	$ 896	$ 840
Total assets	$2,000	$1,680	Total liabilities and equity	$2,000	$1,680

MicroDrive Inc.: December 31 Balance Sheets (Millions of Dollars)   TABLE 2-2

NOTE: The bonds have a sinking fund requirement of $20 million a year. Sinking funds are discussed in Chapter 17, but in brief, a sinking fund simply involves the periodic repayment of long-term debt. Thus, MicroDrive was required to pay off $20 million of its mortgage bonds during 1995 and 1996. The current portion of the long-term debt is included in notes payable here, although in a more detailed balance sheet it would be shown as a separate item under current liabilities.

their "liquidity," or the length of time it typically takes to convert them to cash. The claims are listed in the order in which they must be paid: Accounts payable must generally be paid within 30 days, notes are payable within 90 days, and so on, down to the stockholders' equity accounts, which represent ownership and need never be "paid off."

Some additional points about the balance sheet are worth noting:

1. **Cash versus other assets.** Although the assets are all stated in terms of dollars, only cash represents actual money. Marketable securities are highly liquid investments which can be converted to cash quickly; receivables are bills others owe MicroDrive; inventories show the dollars the company has invested in raw materials, work-in-process, and finished goods available for sale; and net plant and equipment reflect the amount of money MicroDrive paid for its fixed assets when it acquired those assets at some time in the past, less accumulated depreciation. MicroDrive can write checks at present for a total of $10 million (versus current liabilities of $310 million due within a year). The noncash assets should produce cash over time, but they do not represent cash in hand, and the amount of cash they would bring if they were sold today could be higher or lower than the values at which they are carried on the books.

2. **Liabilities versus stockholders' equity.** The claims against assets are of two types — liabilities (or money the company owes) and the stockholders' owner-

ship position.[2] The *common equity*, or *net worth*, is a residual. For example, at the end of 1996,

$$\text{Assets} \quad - \quad \text{Liabilities} \quad - \quad \text{Preferred stock} = \text{Common equity.}$$
$$\$2,000,000,000 \quad - \quad \$1,064,000,000 \quad - \quad \$40,000,000 \quad = \quad \$896,000,000.$$

Suppose assets decline in value — for example, suppose some of the accounts receivable are written off as bad debts. Liabilities and preferred stock remain constant, so the value of the common equity must decline. Therefore, the risk of asset value fluctuations is borne by the common stockholders. Note, however, that if asset values rise (perhaps because of inflation), these benefits will accrue exclusively to the common stockholders.

3. **Preferred versus common stock.** As we will see in Chapter 19, preferred stock is a hybrid, or a cross between common stock and debt. In the event of bankruptcy, preferred stock ranks below debt but above common stock. Also, the preferred dividend is fixed, so preferred stockholders do not benefit if the company's earnings grow. Finally, many firms do not use any preferred stock, and those that do generally do not use very much of it. Therefore, when the term "equity" is used in finance, we generally mean "common equity" unless the word "total" is included.

4. **Breakdown of the common equity account.** A detailed discussion of the common equity accounts is given in Chapter 16, but a brief preview of that discussion is useful here. First, note that the common equity section is divided into three accounts — common stock, paid-in capital, and retained earnings. The *retained earnings* account is built up over time as the firm "saves" a part of its earnings rather than paying all earnings out as dividends. The other two common equity accounts arise from the issuance of stock to raise capital. In the remainder of this chapter, we generally aggregate the three common equity accounts and call this sum *common equity* or *net worth*.

5. **Depreciation methods.** Companies often use the most accelerated method permissible to calculate depreciation for tax purposes but use straight line, which results in a lower depreciation charge, for stockholder reporting. However, MicroDrive has elected to use rapid depreciation for both stockholder reporting and tax purposes. Had MicroDrive used straight line depreciation for stockholder reporting, its 1996 depreciation expense would have been almost $25 million less, so its net income would have been higher, as would its EPS. The $1 billion shown for "net plant" on its balance sheet, and its retained earnings, would also have been approximately $25 million higher.

---

[2]One could divide liabilities into (1) debts owed to someone and (2) other items, such as deferred taxes, reserves, and so on. Because we do not make this distinction, the terms *debt* and *liabilities* are used synonymously. It should be noted that firms occasionally set up reserves for certain contingencies, such as the potential costs involved in a lawsuit currently in the courts. These reserves represent an accounting transfer from retained earnings to the reserve account. If the company wins the suit, retained earnings will be credited, and the reserve will be eliminated. If it loses, a loss will be recorded, cash will be reduced, and the reserve will be eliminated.

MICRODRIVE INC.: STATEMENT OF RETAINED EARNINGS FOR YEAR ENDING DECEMBER 31, 1996 (MILLIONS OF DOLLARS)	TABLE 2-3

Balance of retained earnings, December 31, 1995	$710.0
Net income, 1996	113.5
Dividends to common stockholders	(57.5)[a]
Balance of retained earnings, December 31, 1996	$766.0

[a]Here, and throughout the book, parentheses are used to denote negative numbers.

6. **The time dimension.** The balance sheet is a snapshot of the firm's position *at a point in time* — for example, on December 31, 1995. Thus, on December 31, 1995, MicroDrive had $65 million of marketable securities, but this account had been reduced to zero by the end of 1996. The income statement, on the other hand, reports on operations *over a period of time.* For example, during 1996 MicroDrive had sales of $3 billion, and its net income available to common stockholders was $113.5 million. The balance sheet changes every day as inventories are increased or decreased, as fixed assets are added or retired, as bank loans are increased or decreased, and so on. Companies whose businesses are seasonal have especially large changes in their balance sheets from month to month during the year.

STATEMENT OF RETAINED EARNINGS

Changes in common equity between balance sheet dates are summarized in the *statement of retained earnings*. Table 2-3 shows that MicroDrive earned $113.5 million during 1996, paid out $57.5 million in common dividends, and plowed $56 million back into the business. Thus, the balance sheet item "retained earnings" increased from $710 million at the end of 1995 to $766 million at the end of 1996.

Note that the balance sheet account "retained earnings" represents a *claim against assets*, not assets per se. Further, firms retain earnings primarily to expand the business, and this means investing in plant and equipment, in inventories, and so on, *not* in cash. *Thus, retained earnings as reported on the balance sheet do not represent cash and are not "available" for the payment of dividends or anything else.*[3]

---

[3]The amount reported in the retained earnings account is *not* an indication of the amount of cash the firm has. Cash (as of the balance sheet date) is found in the cash account—an asset account. A positive number in the retained earnings account indicates only that in the past, according to generally accepted accounting principles, the firm has earned an income, but its dividends have been less than its reported income. Even though a company reports record earnings and shows an increase in the retained earnings account, it still may be short of cash.

The same situation holds for individuals. You might own a new BMW (no loan), lots of clothes, and an expensive stereo, hence have a high net worth, but if you had only 23 cents in your pocket plus $5 in your checking account, you would still be short of cash.

ACCOUNTING INCOME VERSUS CASH FLOW

When you studied income statements in accounting, the emphasis was probably on determining the net income of the firm. In finance, however, we focus on *cash flows*. The value of an asset (or a whole firm) is determined by the cash flows it generates. The firm's net income is important, but cash flows are even more important, because dividends must be paid in cash and because cash is necessary to purchase the assets required to sustain operations.

As we discussed in Chapter 1, the primary goal of the firm is to maximize the price of its stock. Since the value of any financial asset, including a share of stock, depends on the cash flows produced by the asset, managers should strive to maximize cash flows available to investors over the long run. A business's cash flows are generally equal to cash from sales, minus cash operating costs, minus interest charges, and minus taxes. Before we go any further, though, we need to examine depreciation, which is classified by accountants as an operating cost.

Depreciation is an annual charge against income to reflect the estimated dollar cost of the capital equipment used up in the production process. For example, suppose a machine with a life of 5 years which has a zero expected salvage value was purchased in 1995 for $100,000 and placed into service in 1996. This $100,000 cost is not expensed in the purchase year; rather, it is charged against production over the machine's 5-year depreciable life. If the depreciation expense were not taken, profits would be overstated, and taxes would be too high. The annual depreciation charge is deducted from sales revenues, along with such other costs as labor and raw materials, to determine income. However, because the $100,000 was expended back in 1995, the depreciation charged against income in 1996 through 2000 is not a cash outlay. *Since depreciation is a noncash charge, it must be added back to net income to obtain an estimate of the cash flow from operations.*

To see how depreciation affects cash flows, consider the following simplified income statement (Column 1) and cash flow statement (Column 2). Here we assume that all sales revenues were received in cash during the year and that all costs except depreciation were paid in cash. Cash flow is equal to net income plus depreciation:

	INCOME STATEMENT (1)	CASH FLOW STATEMENT (2)	
Sales revenues	$1,500	$1,500	
Costs except depreciation	1,050	1,050	
Depreciation (DEP)	150	—	
Total costs	$1,200	$1,050	(Cash costs)
Earnings before taxes	$ 300	$ 450	(Pre-tax cash flow)
Taxes (40%)	120	120	(From Column 1)
Net income (NI)	$ 180		
Add back depreciation	150		
Net cash flow = NI + DEP	$ 330	$ 330	

As we shall see in Chapter 7, a stock's value is based on the *present value of the cash flows* which investors expect it to provide in the future. Although any individual investor could sell the stock and receive cash for it, the *cash flow* provided by the stock itself is typically the expected future dividend stream, and expected dividends provide the fundamental basis for the stock's value.

Because dividends are paid in cash, a company's ability to pay dividends depends on its cash flows. Although companies with relatively high accounting profits generally have relatively high cash flows, the relationship is not precise. Therefore, investors are concerned about cash flow projections as well as profit projections.

STATEMENT OF CASH FLOWS

The firm's cash flows, as opposed to accounting profits, are reported in the annual report as the *statement of cash flows*. This statement is designed to show how operations have affected the cash position and to help answer questions such as these: Is the firm generating the cash needed to purchase additional fixed assets for growth? Is growth so rapid that external financing is required both to maintain operations and for investment in new fixed assets? Is the firm generating excess cash flows that can be used to repay debt or to invest in new products? This information is useful for both managers and investors, so the statement of cash flows is an important part of the annual report. Table 2-4 is MicroDrive's statement of cash flows as it would appear in the company's annual report.

The top part of the table shows cash flows generated by and used in operations — operations provided net cash flows of *minus* $2.5 million. The operating cash flow is generated principally from the day-to-day operations, and it is found by adjusting the net income figure to account for other cash flows related to operations plus non-cash items. The day-to-day operations in 1996 provided $257.5 million of funds; however, increases in receivables and inventories during the year more than offset these inflows.

The second section shows long-term fixed asset investment activities. MicroDrive acquired fixed assets totaling $230 million; this was its only long-term investment activity during 1996.

MicroDrive's financing activities, shown in section III, included borrowing from banks (notes payable), selling new bonds, and paying dividends on its common and preferred stock. MicroDrive raised $224 million by borrowing, but it paid $61.5 million in preferred and common dividends, so its net inflow of funds from financing activities during 1996 was $162.5 million.

The summary section shows that when all sources and uses of cash are totaled, MicroDrive had a $70 million cash shortfall during 1996. It met that shortfall by drawing down its cash and marketable securities holdings by $70 million.

MicroDrive's statement of cash flows should concern its managers and outside analysts. The company had a $2.5 million cash shortfall from operations, it spent an additional $230 million on new fixed assets, and it paid out another $61.5 million in dividends. It covered these cash outlays by borrowing heavily, by selling off marketable securities, and by drawing down its cash account. Obviously, this situation cannot continue year after year, so something will have to be done. We will consider some of the actions the financial manager might recommend to improve the situation, but first we must examine the financial statements in more depth.

TABLE 2-4	MICRODRIVE INC.: STATEMENT OF CASH FLOWS FOR 1996 (MILLIONS OF DOLLARS)

I. OPERATING ACTIVITIES

Net income	$ 117.5
Additions (sources of cash)	
Depreciation[a]	100.0
Increase in accounts payable	30.0
Increase in accruals	10.0
Subtractions (uses of cash)	
Increase in accounts receivable	(60.0)
Increase in inventories	(200.0)
Net cash flow from operations	($ 2.5)

II. LONG-TERM INVESTING ACTIVITIES

Acquisition of fixed assets[b]	($230.00)

III. FINANCING ACTIVITIES

Increase in notes payable	$ 50.0
Increase in bonds	174.0
Payment of common and preferred dividends	(61.5)
Net cash flow from financing	$ 162.5

IV. SUMMARY

Net reduction in cash and marketable securities	($ 70.0)
Cash and securities at beginning of year	80.0
Cash and securities at end of year	$ 10.0

[a]Depreciation is a noncash expense that was deducted when calculating net income. It must be added back to show the correct cash flow from operations.
[b]The net increase in fixed assets was $130 million; however, this net amount included a deduction for the year's depreciation expense. Depreciation expense was added back to show the increase in gross fixed assets. From the company's income statement, we see that 1996 depreciation expense was $100 million; thus, the acquisition of fixed assets equaled $230 million.

SELF-TEST QUESTIONS

Identify the two types of information given in the annual report.

Describe these four basic financial statements: (1) the income statement, (2) the balance sheet, (3) the statement of retained earnings, and (4) the statement of cash flows.

Explain the following statement: "Retained earnings as reported on the balance sheet do not represent cash and are not 'available' for the payment of dividends or anything else."

In accounting, the emphasis is on the determination of net income. What is emphasized in finance, and why is that emphasis important?

Assuming that depreciation is the only noncash cost, how can someone calculate a business's cash flow?

RATIO ANALYSIS

Financial statements report both on a firm's position at a point in time and on its operations over some past period. However, the real value of financial statements lies in the fact that they can be used to help predict future earnings and dividends. From an investor's standpoint, *predicting the future is what financial statement analysis is all about*, while from management's standpoint, *financial statement analysis is useful both as a way to anticipate future conditions and, more important, as a starting point for planning actions that will influence the future course of events*.

An analysis of a set of ratios designed to show relationships between financial statement accounts is the first step in a financial analysis. For example, Firm A might have debt of $5,248,760 and interest charges of $419,900, while Firm B might have debt of $52,647,980 and interest charges of $3,948,600. Which company is stronger? The true burden of these debts, and the companies' ability to repay them, can be ascertained (1) by comparing each firm's debt to its assets and (2) by comparing the interest it must pay with the income it has available for payment of interest. Such comparisons involve *ratio analysis*.

In this section, we calculate MicroDrive's key financial ratios and then compare them with industry averages. In a later section, we discuss where industry averages can be found. Note that all dollar amounts in the calculations are in millions.

LIQUIDITY RATIOS

A *liquid asset* is one that can be easily converted to cash at a "fair market value," and a firm's "liquidity position" deals with this question: Will the firm be able to meet its current obligations? MicroDrive has debts totaling $310 million that must be paid off within the coming year. Will it have trouble satisfying those obligations? A full liquidity analysis requires the use of cash budgets (described in Chapter 20), but by relating the amount of cash and other current assets to the firm's current obligations, ratio analysis provides a quick, easy-to-use measure of liquidity. Two commonly used *liquidity ratios* are discussed in this section.

CURRENT RATIO The *current ratio* is calculated by dividing current assets by current liabilities:

Liquidity Ratio

$$\text{Current ratio} = \frac{\text{Current assets}}{\text{Current liabilities}}$$

$$= \frac{\$1,000}{\$310} = 3.2 \text{ times.}$$

Industry average = 4.2 times.

Lower than industry of 4.2 therefore it is weak.

Current assets normally include cash, marketable securities, accounts receivable, and inventories. Current liabilities consist of accounts payable, short-term notes payable, current maturities of long-term debt, accrued income taxes, and other accrued expenses (principally wages and taxes).

If a company starts getting into financial difficulty, it will begin paying its bills (accounts payable) more slowly, borrowing from its bank, and so on. Current liabilities then rise faster than current assets, the current ratio begins to fall, and this spells trouble. Because the current ratio provides an indicator of the extent to which the claims of short-term creditors are covered by assets that will soon be converted to cash, it is a commonly used measure of liquidity.

MicroDrive's 3.2 current ratio is well below the 4.2 average for its industry, so its liquidity position is relatively weak. Still, since current assets should be converted to cash in the near future, it is highly probable that they could be liquidated at close to their stated value. With a current ratio of 3.2, MicroDrive could liquidate current assets at only 31 percent of book value and still pay off current creditors in full.[4]

We should note that an industry average is not a magic number that all firms should strive to maintain—in fact, some very well-managed firms will be above the average while other good firms will be below it. However, if a firm's ratios are far removed from the average for its industry, an analyst should be concerned about why this variance occurs. Thus, a deviation from the industry average should signal the analyst (or management) to check further.

QUICK, OR ACID TEST, RATIO   The *quick*, or *acid test*, *ratio* is calculated by deducting inventories from current assets and then dividing the remainder by current liabilities:

$$\text{Quick, or acid test, ratio} = \frac{\text{Current assets} - \text{Inventories}}{\text{Current liabilities}}$$

$$= \frac{\$385}{\$310} = 1.2 \text{ times.}$$

Industry average = 2.1 times.

Inventories are typically the least liquid of a firm's current assets, so they are the assets on which losses are most likely to occur in the event of liquidation. Therefore, a measure of the firm's ability to pay off short-term obligations without having to liquidate inventories is important.

The industry average quick ratio is 2.1, so MicroDrive's 1.2 ratio is low. Still, if the accounts receivable can be collected, the company can pay off its current liabilities even without having to liquidate its inventory.

ASSET MANAGEMENT RATIOS

Asset management ratios measure how effectively the firm is managing its assets. These ratios are designed to answer this question: Does the amount of each type

---

[4]$1/3.2 = 0.31$, or 31 percent. Note that $0.31(\$1,000) = \$310$, the amount of current liabilities.

of asset seem reasonable, too high, or too low in view of current and projected sales levels? MicroDrive and other companies generally borrow when they acquire assets. If they have too many assets, their interest expenses will be too high, hence profits will be depressed. On the other hand, if assets are too low, profitable sales may be lost.

INVENTORY TURNOVER   The *inventory turnover ratio* is defined as sales divided by inventories:

$$\text{Inventory turnover ratio} = \frac{\text{Sales}}{\text{Inventories}}$$

$$= \frac{\$3,000}{\$615} = 4.9 \text{ times.}$$

Industry average = 9.0 times.

As a rough approximation, each dollar of MicroDrive's inventory is sold out and restocked, or "turned over," 4.9 times per year.[5]

MicroDrive's turnover of 4.9 times is much lower than the industry average of 9 times. This suggests that MicroDrive is holding too much inventory. This is, of course, unproductive because excess inventory represents an investment with a low or zero rate of return. MicroDrive's low inventory turnover ratio also makes us question the current ratio. With such a low turnover, one wonders whether the firm is holding damaged or obsolete goods not actually worth their stated value.[6]

---

[5]"Turnover" is a term that originated many years ago with the old Yankee peddler, who would load up his wagon with goods, then go off on his route to peddle his wares. The inventory was his "working capital," because it was what he actually sold, or "turned over," to produce profits, whereas his "turnover" was the number of trips he took each year. Annual sales divided by inventory equaled turnover, or trips per year. If he made 10 trips per year, carried 100 pans, and made a gross profit of $5 per pan, his annual gross profit would be (100)($5)(10) = $5,000. If he went faster and made 20 trips per year, his gross profit would double, other things held constant.

[6]Two problems arise in calculating and analyzing the inventory turnover ratio. First, sales are stated at market prices, so if inventories are carried at cost, as they generally are, the calculated turnover overstates the true turnover ratio. Therefore, it would be more appropriate to use cost of goods sold in place of sales in the numerator of the formula. However, established compilers of financial ratio statistics, such as Dun & Bradstreet, use the ratio of sales to inventories carried at cost. To develop a figure that can be compared with those published by Dun & Bradstreet and similar organizations, it is necessary to measure inventory turnover with sales in the numerator, as we do here.

The second problem lies in the fact that sales occur over the entire year, whereas the inventory figure is for one point in time. For this reason, it is better to use an average inventory measure. Preferably, the average inventory value should be calculated by summing the monthly figures during the year and dividing by 12. If monthly data are not available, one can add the beginning and ending figures and divide by 2; this will adjust for growth but not for seasonal effects. If the firm's business is highly seasonal, or if there has been a strong upward or downward sales trend during the year, it is essential to make some such adjustment. To maintain comparability with industry averages, however, we did not use the average inventory figure.

DAYS SALES OUTSTANDING   *Days sales outstanding (DSO)*, also called the *average collection period (ACP)*, is used to appraise accounts receivable, and it is calculated by dividing average daily sales into accounts receivable to find the number of days' sales that are tied up in receivables. Thus, the DSO represents the average length of time that the firm must wait after making a sale before receiving cash. MicroDrive has 45 days' sales outstanding, well above the 36-day industry average.[7]

$$\text{DSO} = \begin{matrix}\text{Days} \\ \text{sales} \\ \text{outstanding}\end{matrix} = \frac{\text{Receivables}}{\text{Average sales per day}} = \frac{\text{Receivables}}{\text{Annual sales}/360}$$

$$= \frac{\$375}{\$3,000/360} = \frac{\$375}{\$8.333} = 45 \text{ days.}$$

Industry average = 36 days.

The DSO can also be evaluated by comparison with the terms on which the firm sells its goods. For example, MicroDrive's sales terms call for payment within 30 days, so the fact that 45 days' sales, not 30 days', are outstanding indicates that customers, on the average, are not paying their bills on time. If the trend in DSO over the past few years has been rising, but the credit policy has not been changed, this would be even stronger evidence that steps should be taken to expedite the collection of accounts receivable.

Note that an alternative measure of inventory management is *days inventory on hand*, which is defined as inventories divided by average sales per day. For example, the auto companies often report that they have 45 (or some other number) of days sales in stock. With inventories of $615 and average sales per day of $8.333, Micro-Drive's days inventory on hand is $615/$8.333 = 74 days. Thus, MicroDrive's current inventory level would support 74 days of sales without restocking.

FIXED ASSETS TURNOVER   The *fixed assets turnover ratio* measures how effectively the firm uses its plant and equipment. It is the ratio of sales to net fixed assets, or the amount of sales generated by each dollar of fixed assets:

---

[7]Because information on credit sales is generally unavailable, total sales must be used. Since all firms do not have the same percentage of credit sales, there is a chance that the days sales outstanding will be somewhat in error. Also, note that by convention the financial community often uses 360 rather than 365 as the number of days in the year for purposes such as this. Finally, it would be better to use *average* receivables, either an average of the monthly figures or (Beginning receivables + Ending receivables)/2 = ($315 + $375)/2 = $345 in the formula. Had the annual average receivables been used, MicroDrive's DSO would have been $345.00/$8.333 = 41 days. The 41-day figure is the more accurate one, but because the industry average was based on year-end receivables, we used 45 days for our comparison. The DSO is discussed further in Chapter 20.

$$\text{Fixed assets turnover ratio} = \frac{\text{Sales}}{\text{Net fixed assets}}$$

$$= \$3,000/\$1,000 = 3.0 \text{ times.}$$

Industry average $= 3.0$ times.

MicroDrive's ratio of 3.0 times equals the industry average, indicating that the firm is using its fixed assets about as intensively as are the other firms in the industry. It has neither too much nor too few fixed assets in relation to other firms.

A major potential problem can exist when the fixed assets turnover ratio is used to compare different firms. Recall from accounting that most balance sheet values reflect historical costs. Inflation has caused the values of many assets that were purchased in the past to be seriously understated. Furthermore, older assets have been depreciated by a greater amount, regardless of the actual impact of age on value. Therefore, if we were comparing an old firm which had acquired many of its fixed assets years ago at low prices with a new company which had acquired its fixed assets only recently, we probably would find that the old firm had a higher fixed assets turnover ratio. However, this would be more reflective of the inability of accountants to deal with fixed asset values than of any inefficiency on the part of the new firm. The accounting profession is trying to devise ways of making financial statements reflect current values rather than historical values. If balance sheets were actually stated on a current value basis, this would eliminate the problem of comparisons, but at the moment, the problem still exists. Since financial analysts typically do not have the data necessary to make adjustments, they must simply recognize that a problem may exist and deal with it judgmentally. In MicroDrive's case, the issue is not a serious one because all firms in the industry have been expanding at about the same rate, so the balance sheets of the comparison firms are indeed comparable.[8]

TOTAL ASSETS TURNOVER The final asset management ratio, the *total assets turnover ratio*, measures the turnover of all of the firm's assets, and it is calculated by dividing sales by total assets:

$$\text{Total assets turnover ratio} = \frac{\text{Sales}}{\text{Total assets}}$$

$$= \frac{\$3,000}{\$2,000} = 1.5 \text{ times.}$$

Industry average $= 1.8$ times.

---

[8]See FASB Statement 33, *Financial Reporting and Changing Prices*, September 1979, for a discussion of the effects of inflation on financial statements and what the accounting profession is trying to do to provide better and more useful balance sheets and income statements.

MicroDrive's ratio is somewhat below the industry average, indicating that the company is not generating a sufficient volume of business given its total asset investment. Sales should be increased, some assets should be disposed of, or a combination of these steps should be taken.

Recall that MicroDrive's 1996 fixed assets turnover is in line with the industry average, but its total assets turnover is weak. This indicates that the problem lies with MicroDrive's current assets. Examination of the firm's current assets turnover ratio confirms this observation.

DEBT MANAGEMENT RATIOS

The extent to which a firm uses debt financing, or *financial leverage*, has three important implications: (1) By raising funds through debt, stockholders can control a firm with a limited investment. (2) Creditors look to the equity, or owner-supplied funds, to provide a margin of safety, so if the stockholders have provided only a small proportion of the total financing, the risks of the enterprise are borne mainly by its creditors. (3) If the firm earns more on investments financed with borrowed funds than it pays in interest, the rate of return on the owners' capital is magnified, or "leveraged."

To see how the use of debt, or financial leverage, affects risk and return, consider Table 2-5. Here we are analyzing two companies that are identical except for the way they are financed. Firm U (for "unleveraged") has no debt, whereas Firm L (for "leveraged") is financed half with equity and half with debt that costs 15 percent. Both companies have $100 of assets and $100 of sales. Their expected ratio of operating income (also called earnings before interest and taxes, or EBIT) to assets, or the *basic earning power (BEP) ratio*, is EBIT/Total assets = $30/$100 = 0.30 = 30%. Thus, both firms expect to earn 30 percent, before interest and taxes, on their assets. Of course, things could turn out badly, in which case the basic earning power ratio would be lower; in the table, we show the earning power ratio declining from 30 percent to 2.5 percent under poor conditions.

Even though both companies' assets have the same 30 percent expected pre-tax earning power under normal conditions, Firm L should provide its stockholders with an after-tax return on equity of 27 percent versus only 18 percent for Firm U. However, financial leverage can cut both ways. As we show in Column 2 of the income statements, if sales are lower and costs are higher than were expected, the return on assets will be lower than was expected. Under these conditions, the leveraged firm's return on equity falls especially sharply, and losses occur. For example, under the "bad conditions" in Table 2-5, the unleveraged firm still shows a profit, but the firm which uses debt shows a loss, and a negative return on equity. This occurs because Firm L needs cash to service its debt, while Firm U does not. Firm U, because of its strong balance sheet, could ride out the recession and be ready for the next boom. Firm L, on the other hand, must pay interest of $7.50 regardless of its level of sales. Consequently, when day-to-day operations do not generate sufficient operating income to provide cash to meet the interest payments, cash would be depleted and the firm probably would need to raise additional funds. This situation is evident for Firm L when poor economic conditions exist, because only $2.50 in operating income is generated, but the interest payment for debt is three times this amount.

EFFECTS OF FINANCIAL LEVERAGE ON STOCKHOLDERS' RETURNS TABLE 2-5

FIRM U (UNLEVERAGED)

Current assets	$ 50	Debt	$ 0
Fixed assets	50	Common equity	100
Total assets	$100	Total liabilities and equity	$100

	EXPECTED CONDITIONS (1)	BAD CONDITIONS (2)
Sales	$100.00	$82.50
Operating costs	70.00	80.00
Operating income (EBIT)	$ 30.00	$ 2.50
Interest	0.00	0.00
Earnings before taxes (EBT)	$ 30.00	$ 2.50
Taxes (40%)	12.00	1.00
Net income (NI)	$ 18.00	$ 1.50
$ROE_U = NI/Common\ equity = NI/\$100 =$	18.00%	1.50%

FIRM L (LEVERAGED)

Current assets	$ 50	Debt (interest = 15%)	$ 50
Fixed assets	50	Common equity	50
Total assets	$100	Total liabilities and equity	$100

	EXPECTED CONDITIONS (1)	BAD CONDITIONS (2)
Sales	$100.00	$82.50
Operating costs	70.00	80.00
Operating income (EBIT)	$ 30.00	$ 2.50
Interest	7.50	7.50
Earnings before taxes (EBT)	$ 22.50	($ 5.00)
Taxes (40%)	9.00	(2.00)
Net income (NI)	$ 13.50	($ 3.00)
$ROE_L = NI/Common\ equity = NI/\$50 =$	27.00%	(6.00%)

Because it would be running a loss, Firm L would have a hard time selling stock to raise capital, and the losses would cause lenders to raise the interest rate or maybe not even extend the existing loans, increasing L's problems still further. As a final result, Firm L just might not survive to enjoy the next boom.

We see, then, that firms with relatively high debt ratios have higher expected returns when the economy is normal, but they are exposed to risk of loss when the economy goes into a recession. Firms with low debt ratios are less risky, but they also forego the opportunity to leverage up their return on equity. The prospects of high returns are desirable, but investors are averse to risk. Therefore, decisions about the use of debt require firms to balance higher expected returns against increased risk. Determining the optimal amount of debt for a given firm is a complicated process, and we defer a discussion of this topic until Chapters 13 and 14. However, analysts use two key ratios when they analyze financial statements: (1) They determine the extent to which borrowed funds have been used to finance assets *(the debt ratio),* and (2) they determine the number of times fixed charges are covered by operating profits *(the times interest earned ratio* and the *fixed charge coverage ratio).* These two sets of ratios are complementary, so analysts use both types.

Total Debt to Total Assets The ratio of total debt to total assets, generally called the *debt ratio,* measures the percentage of funds provided by creditors:

$$\text{Debt ratio} = \frac{\text{Total debt}}{\text{Total assets}}$$

$$= \frac{\$310 + \$754}{\$2,000} = \frac{\$1,064}{\$2,000} = 53.2\%.$$

$$\text{Industry average} = 40.0\%.$$

Total debt includes both current liabilities and long-term debt. Creditors prefer low debt ratios, because the lower the ratio, the greater the cushion against creditors' losses in the event of liquidation. Stockholders, on the other hand, can benefit from leverage because it magnifies earnings.

MicroDrive's debt ratio is 53.2 percent, which means that creditors have supplied more than half the firm's total financing. Since the average debt ratio for this industry — and for manufacturers generally — is about 40 percent, MicroDrive would find it difficult to borrow additional funds without first raising more equity capital. Creditors would be reluctant to lend the firm more money, and management would probably be subjecting the firm to the risk of bankruptcy if it sought to increase the debt ratio any further by borrowing additional funds.[9]

---

[9]The ratio of debt to equity is also used in financial analysis. The debt-to-assets (D/A) and debt-to-equity (D/E) ratios are simply transformations of each other:

$$D/E = \frac{D/A}{1 - D/A}, \text{ and } D/A = \frac{D/E}{1 + D/E}.$$

MicroDrive's debt-to-equity ratio is

$$\frac{0.532}{1 - 0.532} = \frac{0.532}{0.468} \approx 1.14.$$

Thus, for each dollar of capital supplied by stockholders (including preferred), creditors have supplied $1.14.

TIMES INTEREST EARNED The *times-interest-earned (TIE) ratio* is determined by dividing earnings before interest and taxes (EBIT in Table 2-1) by the interest charges:

$$\text{Times-interest-earned (TIE) ratio} = \frac{\text{EBIT}}{\text{Interest charges}}$$

$$= \frac{\$283.8}{\$88} = 3.2 \text{ times.}$$

Industry average = 6.0 times.

The TIE ratio measures the extent to which operating income can decline before the firm is unable to meet its annual interest costs. Failure to meet this obligation can bring legal action by the firm's creditors, possibly resulting in bankruptcy. Note that earnings before interest and taxes (EBIT) rather than net income is used in the numerator. Interest is paid with pre-tax dollars, so the firm's ability to pay current interest is not affected by taxes.

MicroDrive's interest is covered 3.2 times. Thus, the firm generates $3.20 in operating income for every dollar of interest expense. Since the industry average is 6 times, MicroDrive is covering its interest charges by a relatively low margin of safety. Therefore, the TIE ratio reinforces our conclusion based on the debt ratio that Micro-Drive would face difficulties if it attempted to borrow additional funds.

FIXED CHARGE COVERAGE The *fixed charge coverage ratio* is similar to the times-interest-earned ratio, but it is more inclusive because it recognizes that many firms use long-term leases and also must make sinking fund payments.[10] Leasing has become widespread in certain industries in recent years, making the fixed charge coverage ratio preferable to the times interest earned ratio for many purposes. MicroDrive's annual long-term lease payments are $28 million, and it must make an annual $20 million sinking fund payment to help retire its debt. Because sinking fund payments must be paid with after-tax dollars, whereas interest and lease payments are paid with pre-tax dollars, the sinking fund payment must be divided by (1 − Tax rate) to find the before-tax income required to pay taxes and still have enough left to make the sinking fund payment.

---

[10]Generally, a long-term lease is defined as one that extends for more than 1 year. Thus, rent incurred under a 6-month lease would not be included in the fixed charge coverage ratio, but rental payments under a 1-year or longer lease would be defined as a fixed charge and would be included. A sinking fund is a required periodic payment designed to reduce the balance of a debt or preferred stock issue. Sinking funds are discussed in Chapter 17.

Fixed charges include interest, annual long-term lease obligations, and sinking fund payments, and the fixed charge coverage ratio is defined as follows:[11]

$$\text{Fixed charge coverage ratio} = \frac{\text{EBIT} + \text{Lease payments}}{\text{Interest charge} + \text{Lease payments} + \dfrac{\text{Sinking fund payments}}{(1 - \text{Tax rate})}}$$

$$= \frac{\$283.8 + \$28}{\$88 + \$28 + \dfrac{\$20}{0.6}} = 2.1 \text{ times.}$$

Industry average = 5.5 times.

MicroDrive's fixed charges are covered only 2.1 times, versus an industry average of 5.5 times. Again, this indicates that the firm is weaker than average and that it would probably encounter difficulties if it attempted to increase its debt.[12]

PROFITABILITY RATIOS

Profitability is the net result of a number of policies and decisions. The ratios examined thus far provide some information about the way the firm is operating, but the *profitability ratios* show the combined effects of liquidity, asset management, and debt management on operating results.

PROFIT MARGIN ON SALES   The *profit margin on sales*, often just called the *profit margin*, is calculated by dividing net income by sales, and it gives the profit per dollar of sales:

$$\text{Profit margin on sales} = \frac{\text{Net income available to common stockholders}}{\text{Sales}}$$

---

[11]Note that $20/0.6 = $33.33. Therefore, if the company had pre-tax income of $33.33, it could pay taxes at a 40 percent rate and have exactly $20 left with which to make the sinking fund payment. Thus, a $20 sinking fund payment requires $20/0.6 = $33.33 of pre-tax income. Dividing by $(1 - T)$ is called "grossing up" an after-tax value to find the corresponding pre-tax value. Also note that the fixed charge coverage ratio can be defined in several different ways, depending on what management regards as "fixed" charges. For example, the grossed up preferred stock dividend could be added to the denominator if management was totally committed to maintaining the preferred dividend.

[12]Note that depreciation cash flow can be used to pay fixed charges, so the TIE and fixed charge coverage ratios understate a firm's ability to cover its fixed charge obligations, at least in the short run. The ratios could be modified to recognize the availability of depreciation cash flow by adding depreciation expense to the numerator of each equation.

$$= \frac{\$113.5}{\$3,000} = 3.8\%.$$

Industry average = 5.0%.

MicroDrive's profit margin is below the industry average of 5 percent, indicating that its sales are too low, its costs are too high, or both.

BASIC EARNING POWER (BEP) The *basic earning power (BEP) ratio*, which we discussed earlier, is calculated by dividing earnings before interest and taxes (EBIT) by total assets:

$$\text{Basic earning power ratio} = \text{BEP} = \frac{\text{EBIT}}{\text{Total assets}}$$

$$= \frac{\$283.8}{\$2,000} = 14.2\%.$$

Industry average = 17.2%.

This ratio shows the raw earning power of the firm's assets, before the influence of taxes and leverage, and it is useful for comparing firms with different tax situations and different degrees of financial leverage. Because of its low turnover ratios and low profit margin on sales, MicroDrive is not getting as high a return on its assets as is the average computer component company.[13]

RETURN ON TOTAL ASSETS The ratio of net income to total assets measures the *return on total assets (ROA)* after interest and taxes:

$$\frac{\text{Return on total assets (ROA)}}{} = \frac{\text{Net income available to common stockholders}}{\text{Total assets}}$$

$$= \frac{\$113.5}{\$2,000} = 5.7\%.$$

Industry average = 9.0%.

MicroDrive's 5.7 percent return is well below the 9 percent average for the industry. This low return results from the company's low basic earning power plus its

---

[13]Notice that EBIT is earned throughout the year, whereas the total assets figure is an end-of-the-year number. Therefore, for a rapidly growing company it would be better to calculate this ratio as EBIT/Average assets = EBIT/[(Beginning assets + Ending assets)/2]. We have not made this adjustment because the published ratios used for comparative purposes do not include it, but when we construct our own comparative ratios, we do make the adjustment. Incidentally, the same adjustment would also be appropriate for the next two ratios, ROA and ROE.

above-average use of debt, both of which cause its net income to be relatively low. Note that this ratio is often just called the *return on assets*.

RETURN ON COMMON EQUITY   The ratio of net income to common equity measures the *return on common equity (ROE)*, or the rate of return on stockholders' investment:

$$\text{Return on common equity (ROE)} = \frac{\text{Net income available to common stockholders}}{\text{Common equity}}$$

$$= \frac{\$113.5}{\$896} = 12.7\%.$$

Industry average = 15.0%.

MicroDrive's 12.7 percent return is below the 15 percent industry average, but it is not as bad in a relative sense as the return on total assets. This somewhat better result is due to the company's greater use of debt, a point that is analyzed in detail later in the chapter. For companies that do not have preferred stock, this ratio is just called the *return on equity*.[14]

MARKET VALUE RATIOS

A final group of ratios, the *market value ratios,* relates the firm's stock price to its earnings and book value per share. These ratios give management an indication of what equity investors think of the company's past performance and future prospects. If the firm's liquidity, asset management, debt management, and profitability ratios are all good, then its market value ratios will be high, and its stock price will probably be as high as can be expected.

PRICE/EARNINGS RATIO   The *price/earnings (P/E) ratio* shows how much investors are willing to pay per dollar of reported profits. MicroDrive's stock sells for $23, so with an EPS of $2.27, its P/E ratio is 10.1:

---

[14]Another ratio that is frequently used to measure rate of return is the following:

$$\text{Rate of return on investors' capital} = \frac{\text{Net income + Interest}}{\text{Debt + Equity}}.$$

The numerator shows the dollar return to investors, the denominator shows the total amount of money investors have put up, and the ratio itself shows the rate of return on all investors' capital. This ratio is especially important in the public utility industries, where regulators are concerned about the companies' using their monopoly positions to earn excessive returns on investors' capital. In fact, regulators try to set utility prices (service rates) at levels that will force the return on investors' capital to equal a company's cost of capital as defined in Chapter 8.

$$\text{Price/earnings (P/E) ratio} = \frac{\text{Price per share}}{\text{Earnings per share}}$$

$$= \frac{\$23.00}{\$2.27} = 10.1 \text{ times.}$$

Industry average = 12.5 times.

P/E ratios are higher for firms with higher growth prospects, other things held constant, but they are lower for riskier firms. Since MicroDrive's P/E ratio is below the average of other computer components companies, this suggests that the company is regarded as being somewhat riskier than most, as having poorer growth prospects, or both.

MARKET/BOOK RATIO The ratio of a stock's market price to its book value gives another indication of how equity investors regard the company. Companies with relatively high rates of return on equity generally sell at higher multiples of book value than those with low returns. First, we find MicroDrive's book value per share:

$$\text{Book value per share} = \frac{\text{Common equity}}{\text{Shares outstanding}}$$

$$= \frac{\$896}{50} = \$17.92.$$

Now we divide the market price per share by the book value to get a *market/book (M/B) ratio* of 1.3 times:

$$\text{Market/book ratio} = \frac{\text{Market price per share}}{\text{Book value per share}}$$

$$= \frac{\$23.00}{\$17.92} = 1.3 \text{ times.}$$

Industry average = 1.7 times.

Investors are willing to pay less for a dollar of MicroDrive's book value than for other computer components companies.

The typical railroad, which has a very low rate of return on assets, has a market/book value ratio of less than 0.5. On the other hand, very successful firms such as Microsoft (which makes the operating system for virtually all PCs) achieve high rates of return on their assets, and their market values are well in excess of their book values. At the beginning of 1996, Microsoft's book value per share was $12.50 versus a market price of $103, so its market/book ratio was $103/$12.50 = 8.2 times.

COMPARATIVE AND TREND ANALYSES

In our discussion of MicroDrive's ratios, we focused on *comparative analysis;* that is, we compared MicroDrive's ratios with the average ratios for its industry. Another useful ratio analysis tool is *trend analysis,* where we analyze the trend of a single ratio over time. Trend analysis gives clues as to whether a firm's financial situation is improving, holding constant, or deteriorating. Table 2-6 summarizes MicroDrive's comparative and trend analyses for the past two years.

It is easy to combine comparative and trend analyses in a single graph such as the one shown in Figure 2-1. Here we plotted MicroDrive's ROE and the industry average ROE over the past five years. The graph shows that MicroDrive's ROE has been declining since 1993 even though the industry average has been relatively stable. Other ratios could be analyzed similarly.

DU PONT ANALYSIS

At this point, you may be thinking, "There are too many ratios. I understood each one as I read about it, but I'm confused about how to remember and use them." Years ago, Donaldson Brown, Du Pont's chief financial officer, faced the same problem, and to solve it, he developed the famous *Du Pont equation.*

Brown recognized that a company's stock price depends on many things, including its rate of return on equity:

| FIGURE 2-1 | RATE OF RETURN ON COMMON EQUITY, 1992–1996 |

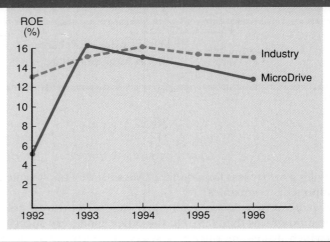

MICRODRIVE INC.: SUMMARY OF FINANCIAL RATIOS — TABLE 2-6

RATIO	FORMULA FOR CALCULATION	1995	1996	1996 INDUSTRY AVERAGE	COMMENT
LIQUIDITY					
Current	$\dfrac{\text{Current assets}}{\text{Current liabilities}}$	3.7×	3.2×	4.2×	Poor
Quick, or acid, test	$\dfrac{\text{Current assets} - \text{Inventories}}{\text{Current liabilities}}$	1.8×	1.2×	2.1×	Poor
ASSET MANAGEMENT					
Inventory turnover	$\dfrac{\text{Sales}}{\text{Inventories}}$	6.9×	4.9×	9.0×	Poor
Days sales outstanding (DSO)	$\dfrac{\text{Receivables}}{\text{Annual sales}/360}$	40 days	45 days	36 days	Poor
Fixed assets turnover	$\dfrac{\text{Sales}}{\text{Net fixed assets}}$	3.3×	3.0×	3.0×	OK
Total assets turnover	$\dfrac{\text{Sales}}{\text{Total assets}}$	1.7×	1.5×	1.8×	Somewhat low
DEBT MANAGEMENT					
Total debt to total assets	$\dfrac{\text{Total debt}}{\text{Total assets}}$	47.6%	53.2%	40.0%	High (risky)
Times-interest-earned (TIE)	$\dfrac{\text{Earnings before interest and taxes (EBIT)}}{\text{Interest charges}}$	4.4×	3.2×	6.0×	Low (risky)
Fixed charge coverage	$\dfrac{\text{Earnings before interest and taxes} + \text{Lease payments}}{\text{Interest charges} + \text{Lease payments} + \dfrac{\text{SF payment}}{(1 - T)}}$	2.4×	2.1×	5.5×	Low (risky)
PROFITABILITY					
Profit margin on sales	$\dfrac{\text{Net income available to common stockholders}}{\text{Sales}}$	4.1%	3.8%	5.0%	Poor
Basic earning power	$\dfrac{\text{Earnings before interest and taxes (EBIT)}}{\text{Total assets}}$	15.7%	14.2%	17.2%	Poor
Return on total assets (ROA)	$\dfrac{\text{Net income available to common stockholders}}{\text{Total assets}}$	7.0%	5.7%	9.0%	Poor
Return on common equity (ROE)	$\dfrac{\text{Net income available to common stockholders}}{\text{Common equity}}$	14.0%	12.7%	15.0%	Poor
MARKET VALUE					
Price/earnings (P/E)	$\dfrac{\text{Price per share}}{\text{Earnings per share}}$	10.2×	10.1×	12.5×	Low
Market/book	$\dfrac{\text{Market price per share}}{\text{Book value per share}}$	1.4×	1.3×	1.7×	Low

> ROE → Stock price.

It is intuitively obvious that the higher a firm's ROE, other things held constant, the higher its stock price. Moreover, management can influence (though not completely control) its ROE, hence its stock price.

Brown began by looking at the ROEs of Du Pont's competitors, of Du Pont as a whole, and of its different business units. He wanted Du Pont's ROE to exceed that of its competitors, and he knew that the corporate ROE depended on the ROEs of its business units. Brown also noted that ROE depends on three factors: (1) the profit margin on sales, (2) the total assets turnover ratio, and (3) the use of debt. He combined these factors to form the Du Pont equation:[15]

$$
\begin{aligned}
\text{ROE} &= (\text{Profit margin})(\text{Total assets turnover})(\text{Equity multiplier}) \\
&= \frac{\text{Net income}}{\text{Sales}} \times \frac{\text{Sales}}{\text{Total assets}} \times \frac{\text{Total assets}}{\text{Common equity}}.
\end{aligned}
$$

2-1

We can obtain MicroDrive's profit margin, turnover, and equity multiplier from Table 2-6 and insert them into Equation 2-1:

$$
\begin{aligned}
\text{ROE} &= (3.8\%)(1.5)(2.23) \\
&= 12.7\%.
\end{aligned}
$$

The 12.7 percent rate of return could, of course, be calculated directly: Net income/Common equity = \$113.5/\$896 = 12.7%. However, the Du Pont equation shows how the profit margin, the total assets turnover ratio, and the use of debt interact to determine the return on equity.[16]

MicroDrive's financial analysts can use the Du Pont equation to analyze ways of improving the firm's performance. The profit margin focuses on sales and expenses, so MicroDrive's analysts can study the effects of raising sales prices (or lowering them to increase volume), of moving into new products or markets with higher margins, and of cutting costs. Total asset turnover measures asset utilization, and Micro-Drive's analysts, working with production and marketing people, can investigate

---

[15]Equation 2-1 is slightly different from the original Du Pont equation, which did not include the leverage variable.

[16]Note that in our Du Pont analysis we have treated preferred stock as debt. Thus, the relevant net income is that available to common stockholders, and the relevant equity multiplier, is Total assets/Common equity. The resulting ROE is, therefore, a measure of return to common stockholders. This treatment is consistent with the facts that the common stockholders have voting control of the firm and that preferred stock, with its fixed dividend payments, is closer to debt than to common stock for purposes of financial analysis. For a specification of the Du Pont equation that treats debt and preferred stock separately, see G. Michael Boyd, "Some Suggestions for a 'New and Improved' Du Pont Model," *Journal of Financial Education,* Fall 1989, 29-32.

ways of minimizing the investment in various types of assets. At the same time, the treasury staff can analyze the effects of alternative financing strategies on the equity multiplier, seeking to hold down interest expense and the risks brought on by using debt while still using leverage to increase the rate of return on equity.

The Du Pont equation provides a useful comparison between a firm's performance as measured by ROE and the performance of an average firm in the industry:

$$\text{MicroDrive: ROE} = (3.8\%)(1.5)(2.23) \approx 12.7\%.$$

$$\text{Industry: ROE} = (5.0\%)(1.8)(1.67) \approx 15.0\%.$$

We see that the average computer components company has (1) a significantly higher profit margin, and thus better control over expenses; (2) a higher total asset turnover, and thus is using its assets more productively; but (3) that MicroDrive has offset some of these advantages with its higher financial leverage, although this increased use of leverage increases its risk.

The Du Pont equation provides a good starting point for analyzing a firm's financial condition because it highlights three important factors: (1) expense control, (2) asset utilization, and (3) debt utilization. Thus, analysts often use it to get a "quick and dirty" feel for a firm's financial condition, after which they can focus on those aspects of the firm's operations that appear to be sub par.

SELF-TEST QUESTIONS

Identify two ratios that measure firm's liquidity position, and write out their equations.

Identify four ratios that measure how effectively a firm is managing its assets, and write out their equations.

Identify three ratios that measure the extent to which a firm uses debt financing, and write out their equations.

Identify four ratios that show the combined effects of liquidity, asset management, and debt management on profitability, and write out their equations.

Identify two ratios that relate a firm's stock price to its earnings and book value per share, and write out their equations.

Explain how the Du Pont equation combines three ratios to reveal the basic determinants of ROE.

How can comparative and trend analyses be used to help interpret ratio results?

COMMON SIZE ANALYSIS

In a *common size analysis,* all income statement items are divided by sales, and all balance sheet items are divided by total assets. Thus, a common size income statement shows each item as a percentage of sales, and a common size balance sheet shows each item as a percentage of total assets. The advantage of common size analysis is that it facilitates comparisons of balance sheets and income statements over time and across companies.

Table 2-7 contains MicroDrive's 1995 and 1996 common size income statements, along with the composite statement for the industry. (Note: Rounding may cause

TABLE 2-7	MICRODRIVE INC.: COMMON SIZE INCOME STATEMENTS		
	1995	**1996**	**1996 INDUSTRY AVERAGE**
Net sales	100.0%	100.0%	100.0%
Costs excluding depreciation	87.6	87.2	86.7
Depreciation	3.2	3.3	2.8
Total operating costs	90.8%	90.5%	89.5%
Earnings before interest and taxes (EBIT)	9.2%	9.5%	10.5%
Less interest	2.1	2.9	1.7
Earnings before taxes (EBT)	7.1%	6.5%	8.8%
Taxes (40%)	2.8	2.6	3.8
Net income before preferred dividends	4.3%	3.9%	5.0%
Preferred dividends	0.1	0.1	0.0
Net income available to common stockholders (profit margin)	4.1%	3.8%	5.0%

TABLE 2-8	MICRODRIVE INC.: COMMON SIZE BALANCE SHEETS		
	1995	**1996**	**1996 INDUSTRY AVERAGE**
ASSETS			
Cash and marketable securities	4.8%	0.5%	3.2%
Accounts receivable	18.8	18.8	15.3
Inventories	24.7	30.8	22.7
Total current assets	48.2%	50.0%	41.2%
Net plant and equipment	51.8	50.0	58.8
Total assets	100.0%	100.0%	100.0%
LIABILITIES AND EQUITY			
Accounts payable	1.8%	3.0%	2.6%
Notes payable	3.6	5.5	3.2
Accruals	7.7	7.0	7.3
Total current liabilities	13.1%	15.5%	13.1%
Long-term bonds	34.5	37.7	26.9
Total debt	47.6%	53.2%	40.0%
Preferred equity	2.4	2.0	0.0
Common equity	50.0	44.8	60.0
Total liabilities and equity	100.0%	100.0%	100.0%

addition/subtraction differences in Tables 2-7 and 2-8.) MicroDrive's operating costs are somewhat above average, as are its interest expenses, but its taxes are relatively low because of its low EBIT. The net effect of all these forces is a relatively low profit margin.

Table 2-8 shows MicroDrive's common size balance sheets, along with the industry average. Its accounts receivable are significantly higher than the industry average, its inventories are significantly higher, and it uses far more fixed charge capital (debt and preferred) than the average firm.

How are common size statements created?
What advantage do common size statements have over regular statements?

SELF-TEST QUESTIONS

PERCENTAGE CHANGE ANALYSIS

A final technique used to help analyze a firm's financial statements is *percentage change analysis.* In this type of analysis, growth rates are calculated for all income statement items and balance sheet accounts. To illustrate, Table 2-9 contains Micro-Drive's income statement percentage change analysis for 1996. Sales increased at a

MICRODRIVE INC.: INCOME STATEMENT PERCENTAGE CHANGE ANALYSIS (MILLIONS OF DOLLARS, EXCEPT FOR PER-SHARE DATA)			TABLE 2-9
	1995	**1996**	**PERCENT CHANGE**
Net sales	$2,850	$3,000.0	5.3%
Costs excluding depreciation	$2,497	$2,616.2	4.8%
Depreciation	90	100.0	11.1
Total operating costs	$2,587	$2,716.2	5.0%
Earnings before interest and taxes (EBIT)	$ 263	$ 283.8	7.9%
Less interest	60	88.0	46.7
Earnings before taxes (EBT)	$ 203	$ 195.8	(3.5%)
Taxes (40%)	81	78.3	(3.3)
Net income before preferred dividends	$ 122	$ 117.5	(3.7%)
Preferred dividends	4	4.0	0
Net income available to common stockholders	$ 118	$ 113.5	(3.8%)
Common dividends	$53	$57.5	8.5%
Addition to retained earnings	$65	$56.0	(13.8%)
Per-share data:			
Common stock price	$24.00	$ 23.00	(4.2%)
Earnings per share (EPS)	$ 2.36	$ 2.27	(3.8%)
Dividends per share (DPS)	$ 1.06	$ 1.15	8.5%

5.3 percent rate during 1996, while total operating costs increased at a slower 5.0 percent rate, leading to 7.9 percent growth in EBIT. The fact that sales increased faster than operating costs is positive, but this "good news" was offset by a 46.7 percent increase in interest expense. The significant growth in interest expense caused growth in both earnings before taxes and net income to be negative. Thus, the percentage change analysis points out that the decrease in reported income in 1996 resulted almost exclusively from an increase in interest expense. This conclusion could be reached by analyzing dollar amounts, but percentage change analysis simplifies the task. The same type of analysis applied to the balance sheets would show that assets grew at a 19.0 percent rate, largely because inventories grew at a whopping 48.2 percent rate. With only a 5.3 percent growth in sales, the extreme growth in inventories should be of great concern to MicroDrive's managers.

The conclusions reached in common size and percentage change analyses generally parallel those derived from ratio analysis. However, occasionally a serious deficiency is highlighted by only one of the three analytical techniques. Also, it is often useful to have all three analyses to drive home to management, in slightly different ways, the need to take corrective actions. Thus, a thorough financial statement analysis will include ratio, percentage change, and common size analyses, as well as a Du Pont analysis.

SELF-TEST
QUESTIONS

What is percentage change analysis, and how is it used in financial statement analysis?

Why is it useful to include in a financial statement analysis ratio, percentage change, and common size analyses?

MVA AND EVA[17]

Thus far in this chapter, we have focused on accounting data and its use in assessing firms' financial conditions. However, accounting data have some severe limitations, so in this section we discuss two new measures of profitability and managerial performance, *Market Value Added (MVA)* and *Economic Value Added (EVA)*.

MARKET VALUE ADDED (MVA)

The primary goal of most firms is to maximize shareholder wealth. This goal obviously benefits shareholders, and it also ensures that scarce resources are allocated efficiently. Shareholder wealth is maximized by maximizing the *difference* between

---

[17]The rationale underlying MVA and EVA have been around for many years, but the concepts as used in industry today were developed and popularized by Joel Stern and Bennett Stewart, and their consulting firm, Stern Stewart & Company. Stern Stewart has a copyright on the term EVA. For more information on MVA and EVA, including the details of how they are calculated, see G. Bennett Stewart III, *The Quest for Value* (New York: HarperBusiness, 1991).

the market value of equity and the amount of equity capital that investors have supplied to the firm. This difference is called *Market Value Added (MVA)*:[18]

$$\text{MVA} = \text{Market value of equity} - \text{Equity capital supplied.}$$

To illustrate, consider Coca-Cola. In 1995, its total equity value was $69 billion, while its stockholders had put up only $8 billion. Thus, Coca-Cola's MVA was $69 − $8 = $61 billion. This $61 billion represents the difference between the money that Coca-Cola's equity investors have put into the corporation since its founding — including retained earnings — and the cash they could get if they sold the business. By maximizing this spread, management maximizes the wealth of its shareholders.

While the managers of Coca-Cola have done a spectacular job of maximizing shareholder wealth, General Motors' managers have done poorly. In 1995, GM's total market value was $69 billion, which, on the surface, makes it look as if its managers have done as good a job as those of Coca-Cola. However, investors have supplied GM with $87 billion of capital, so GM's MVA was a *negative* $18 billion. In effect, GM has only $0.79 of wealth remaining for every dollar investors put up, whereas Coca-Cola has turned $1 of investment into $8.63. Put another way, Coca-Cola's managers have created $61 billion of wealth for its stockholders, while GM's managers have destroyed $18 billion.

ECONOMIC VALUE ADDED (EVA)

Whereas MVA measures the effects of managerial actions since the inception of the company, *Economic Value Added (EVA)* focuses on managerial effectiveness in a given year. The basic formula for EVA is this:

$$\text{EVA} = \text{Operating profit after taxes} - \text{Cost of all capital}$$

$$= \left(\begin{matrix} \text{Sales} \\ \text{revenues} \end{matrix} - \begin{matrix} \text{Operating} \\ \text{costs} \end{matrix} - \text{Taxes} \right) - \left(\begin{matrix} \text{Total} \\ \text{capital} \\ \text{supplied} \end{matrix} \times \begin{matrix} \text{Cost} \\ \text{of} \\ \text{capital} \end{matrix} \right).$$

Here operating profit is defined as sales revenues minus operating costs and taxes, while the cost of the capital used is total capital times the weighted average cost of that capital. To illustrate, suppose a firm in 1996 had $100 million of sales, $80 million of operating costs, and $10 million of taxes, so its operating profits were $10 million. Suppose further that the firm had $50 million of investor-supplied debt and equity capital, and the weighted average cost of that capital was 10 percent. The firm's 1996 EVA would thus be $5 million:

$$\text{EVA} = \$10 - \$50(0.10) = \$10 - \$5 = \$5 \text{ million.}$$

EVA is an estimate of a business's true economic profit for the year, and it differs substantially from accounting profit. EVA represents the residual income that remains

---

[18]MVA can also be defined in terms of total capital supplied, including both debt and equity. However, the definition presented here, which focuses solely on equity capital, is easier to use and is generally consistent with the broader definition.

after the opportunity cost of all capital has been deducted, whereas accounting profit is figured without imposing a charge for equity capital.

EVA depends on both operating efficiency and balance sheet management: without operating efficiency, operating profits will be low, and without efficient balance sheet management, there will be too many assets, hence too much capital, which results in higher-than-necessary capital costs.

Note that EVA (but not MVA) can be applied to divisions as well as to entire companies, and the charge for capital should reflect the risk of the business unit, be it the whole company or an operating division. Note also that the specific calculation of EVA for a company is much more complex than presented here because many accounting issues, such as inventory valuation, depreciation, amortization of research and development costs, lease financing, and the like must be handled properly when estimating a firm's operating profit.

USING EVA AS A MANAGERIAL INCENTIVE

In the past few years, many highly successful firms including Coca-Cola, Quaker Oats, Briggs & Stratton, and CSX have adopted incentive compensation systems based on EVA. Tying executive compensation to EVA gives managers strong incentives to take the set of actions that contributes the most to shareholders' wealth. The advantages of using EVA as the centerpiece of a completely integrated framework for financial management and incentive compensation were stated this way by George McFadden, chief financial officer of Palwaukee Industries:

> We have not had a single capital budgeting project turned down since we adopted EVA. With EVA as the basis for our capital budgeting decisions, performance evaluations, and bonus determinations, our managers spend money like it's their own, and that's paying big dividends for them and for our shareholders.

A firm's MVA is equal to the PVs of its expected future EVAs:

$$MVA = \text{Sum of PVs of expected future EVAs.}$$

If investors expect a zero EVA in each future year, then they expect no value to be created or lost, hence the stock should sell at its book value. It should sell above book if investors expect positive EVAs, but below book if they expect negative EVAs. Note also that operating profit is dependent on (1) past investments and (2) management's operating efficiency. If past managers have identified and invested in good projects, then current managers should be able to generate high operating profits and report high EVAs, provided they operate efficiently.

This means that financial management involves two somewhat different types of decisions: (1) decisions related to the acquisition of new assets, or capital budgeting, and (2) decisions related to the efficient utilization of existing assets. Both are important, and both affect EVA and MVA. When managerial performance is evaluated by the MVA/EVA system, managers have strong incentives to make correct capital budgeting decisions, to use existing assets in an optimal manner, and to finance the firm's operations in an optimal manner. This is, of course, exactly what stockholders want managers to do.

SELF-TEST
QUESTIONS

What is market value added (MVA), and how it is measured?
What is economic value added (EVA), and how is it measured?
Why is EVA a better measure of managerial performance than accounting measures
such as return on equity?

SOURCES OF INDUSTRY DATA

The preceding analysis pointed out the need to compare the company in question
with other firms in its industry. We now describe some of the sources of industry
data.

EXTERNAL SOURCES

One useful set of comparative data is Dun & Bradstreet (D&B), which in its *Key
Business Ratios* provides 14 ratios for a number of industries. Useful ratios can also
be found in the *Annual Statement Studies* published by Robert Morris Associates,
which is the national association of bank loan officers. The Federal Trade Commission's *Quarterly Financial Report* gives a set of ratios for manufacturing firms by
industry group and size of firm. Trade associations also compile industry average
financial ratios.

Each of the listed organizations uses a somewhat different set of ratios, designed
for its own purposes. For example, D&B deals mainly with small firms, many of
which are proprietorships, and it is concerned largely with the creditors' viewpoint.
Accordingly, D&B's ratios emphasize current assets and liabilities, and it provides no
market value ratios whatever. Therefore, when you select a comparative data source,
be sure that your emphasis is similar to that of the organization whose data you use,
or else recognize the limitations of its ratios for your purposes. Additionally, there
are often definitional differences in the ratios presented by different sources — for
example, one may report ROE as net income divided by year-end common equity
(Value Line does this), while another may divide by average common equity
(Salomon Brothers does this). Therefore, before mixing ratios from different sources,
be sure to verify the exact definitions of the ratios used.

INTERNAL SOURCES

Larger firms often create their own comparative data using a computerized database
supplied by a financial services firm. For example, Standard and Poor's Compustat
Services markets CDs which cover several thousand industrial and nonindustrial
companies. The data are broken down by industry and are available for the past 20
years. *Compustat* updates on a weekly basis to reflect new data as companies report
them. Firms can use *Compustat* data to create up-to-date, tailor-made statistics that
best serve their individual needs.

What are some external sources of comparative industry data?
Explain how a firm could create its own comparative industry financial database.

SELF-TEST
QUESTIONS

PROBLEMS IN FINANCIAL STATEMENT ANALYSIS

In our earlier discussion of the ratios, we mentioned some of the problems one encounters in financial statement analysis. In this section, we extend the discussion of problems and limitations.

DEVELOPING AND USING COMPARATIVE DATA: BENCHMARKING

Many large firms operate a number of different divisions in quite different industries, and in such cases it is difficult to develop meaningful industry averages. This tends to make financial statement analysis more useful for small, single-product firms than for large, multiproduct companies.

Additionally, most firms want to be better than average (although half will be above and half below the median). Therefore, merely attaining average performance is not particularly good. Compilers of ratios such as D&B and Robert Morris Associates generally report industry ratios in quartiles. For example, D&B might report that 25 percent of the firms in the aluminum industry have a current ratio above 4.8, that the median is 2.5, and that 25 percent are below 1.6. This gives the analyst an idea of the distribution of ratios within an industry, and he or she can make better judgments about how his or her firm compares with the top firms in its industry.

In addition to comparisons with industry averages, firms today often use *benchmarking* comparisons, which means comparing their ratios with those of specific firms in their industry. For example, MicroDrive benchmarks against Apex Systems, Cablenet, Carter Controls, BMR Corporation, Magnetic Sciences, and Luxor Corporation. MicroDrive's management considers these companies the best-managed set of companies with operations similar to its own. Here is the comparison of Micro-Drive's ROE versus those of the benchmark firms:

	ROE
Cablenet	28%
Carter	26
BMR	22
Magnetic Sciences	19
Luxor	16
MicroDrive	**13**
Apex	9

Similar comparisons are made for the other key ratios, and this procedure allows management to see, on a company-by-company basis, how it stacks up against its major competitors.

DISTORTION OF COMPARATIVE DATA

Inflation has badly distorted firms' balance sheets. Further, reported profits are affected because past inflation affects both depreciation charges and the cost of inventory included in the cost of goods sold. Thus, a financial statement analysis for one firm over time, or a comparative analysis of firms of different ages or which use different accounting methods, must be interpreted with caution and judgment. Inflation's effects are discussed in detail in a later section.

Seasonal factors can also distort ratio analysis. For example, the inventory turnover ratio for a food canning company will be radically different if the balance sheet figure used for inventory is the one just before versus just after the close of the canning season. Receivables, and also current liabilities, are often similarly affected. These problems can be minimized by using 12-month average figures for balance sheet items.

NOTES TO FINANCIAL STATEMENTS

Information which can significantly affect a firm's financial condition is often contained in the notes to its financial statements. Included is information on the pension plan, noncapitalized lease agreements, recent acquisitions and divestitures, accounting policies, and so forth. For example, the notes to MicroDrive's financial statements contain the following information:

1. Inventories are valued at the lower of cost or market, with costs determined by the last-in, first-out (LIFO) method.

2. Receivables were reduced by $51.3 million in 1996 and by $42.7 million in 1995 to allow for doubtful accounts.

3. Noncancellable operating lease commitments are $26.8 million for 1997, $23.3 million for 1998, and $21.1 million for 1999.

4. As of December 31, 1996, the firm had a $968.2 million actuarial present value of vested pension benefits versus $881.6 million in pension fund assets, so its unfunded pension liability was $86.6 million.

This information has a bearing on MicroDrive's financial position, and it should be considered, either directly or indirectly, by financial analysts. The decreasing lease commitment means that, other factors held constant, MicroDrive's fixed charge coverage ratio will improve in the future unless it signs new lease contracts. The unfunded pension liability means that the book value of the equity is in a sense overstated. Other potential problems might be revealed in a more detailed analysis. Indeed, some professional analysts use the footnote information to recast different companies' financial statements on a common basis before they even begin to develop and compare ratios.

INTERPRETATION OF RESULTS

It is difficult to generalize about whether certain ratios are "good" or "bad." For example, a high quick ratio may show a strong liquidity position, which is good, but it could also mean that the firm is holding an excessive amount of cash, which is bad because cash is a nonearning asset. Similarly, a high total assets turnover ratio could denote either a firm that uses its assets efficiently or one that is undercapitalized and simply cannot afford to buy enough assets. Also, firms often have some ratios which look "good" and others which look "bad," making it difficult to tell whether the firm is, on balance, in a strong or a weak position. For this reason, ratio analysis is normally used as an input to judgmental decisions.[19]

DIFFERENCES IN ACCOUNTING TREATMENT

Different accounting practices can distort ratio comparisons. For example, there are four commonly used inventory valuation methods: (1) specific identification, (2) first-in, first-out (FIFO), (3) last-in, first-out (LIFO), and (4) weighted average. During inflationary periods, LIFO produces a higher cost of goods sold and a lower end-of-period inventory valuation than do the other methods. So, the ratios of a company that uses FIFO are not directly comparable to those of one that uses LIFO.

Other accounting practices can also create distortions. For example, if one firm uses short-term, noncapitalized leases to obtain a substantial amount of its productive equipment, then its reported assets may be low relative to its sales, hence improving its turnover ratio. At the same time, if the lease liability is not shown as a debt, then leasing will artificially improve the debt ratio. This problem has been reduced but not eliminated by the accountants' requirement that firms capitalize most large nonoperating leases.

Of course, few problems would occur if firms being compared used the same accounting policies. Fortunately, most firms in a given industry normally do use similar procedures.

WINDOW DRESSING

Firms sometimes employ *window dressing* to make their financial statements look better to analysts. To illustrate, a Chicago builder borrowed on a 2-year note on December 29, 1996, held the proceeds of the loan as cash for a few days, and then paid off the loan ahead of time on January 4, 1997. This improved his current and quick ratios, and made his year-end 1996 balance sheet look good. However, the improvement was strictly temporary; a week later, the balance sheet was back at the old level.

On an even larger scale, E. F. Hutton and several other brokerage houses followed the practice of recording checks they had written, but which had not yet been cleared through the banking system, as current liabilities rather than simply deducting them from reported cash balances. Hutton had been systematically overdrawing its bank accounts, and the question was raised, during investigations into this practice, why its negative cash balances did not alert its bankers that something was amiss. It turned out that to avoid having to report negative cash, Hutton recorded checks received as cash but recorded checks written as current liabilities rather than as deductions from cash. Hutton is no longer in business.

EFFECTS OF INFLATION

The high inflation rates of the late 1970s and early 1980s drew increased attention to the need to assess both the impact of inflation on businesses and the success of

---

[19]There are several quantitative approaches to summarizing the information obtained from a ratio analysis. For one example, see Chapter 24, where we discuss multiple discriminant analysis, a procedure which uses a set of ratios to estimate a firm's probability of going bankrupt.

managements in coping with it. Numerous reporting methods have been proposed to adjust accounting statements for inflation, but no consensus has been reached either on how to do this or even on the practical usefulness of the resulting data. Nevertheless, the Financial Accounting Standards Board issued Statements 33, 82, and 89, which encourage but do not require businesses to disclose supplementary data to reflect the effects of general inflation.

FINANCIAL STATEMENT EFFECTS Traditionally, financial statements have been prepared on the basis of historical costs, that is, the actual dollars paid for each asset purchased. However, inflation has caused the purchasing power of dollars to change over time, and as a result, financial statements can be badly distorted. To illustrate, a $100,000 expenditure on industrial land in 1996 would, in general, purchase far less acreage than a $100,000 expenditure in 1956, so adding 1996 dollars and 1956 dollars is much like adding apples and oranges. Nevertheless, this is done when the typical balance sheet is constructed. To help reduce this disparity, the assets acquired in different years may be restated in *constant* dollars, each of which has equal purchasing power.

To reflect the effects of inflation, and thus to express operating results in dollars of comparable purchasing power, the Financial Accounting Standards Board (FASB) encourages companies to show in annual reports what it characterizes as "income from continuing operations" calculated as if all of its depreciable assets had been purchased with current-year dollars, and consequently its depreciation charges were based on higher-valued assets. Such an adjustment comes closer to showing what profits might be in the long run, when the old, undervalued assets have been replaced with new, inflated-value assets, and depreciation is correspondingly higher.

FASB also encourages firms to present a supplementary 5-year comparison of selected financial data stated in current dollars. Operating revenues, net income, and cash dividends per common share are the items most often restated in constant dollars. This allows investors to see what portion of growth stems from inflation as opposed to true economic growth.

EFFECTS OF INFLATION ON RATIO ANALYSIS If ratio analysis is based on "regular" financial statements, unadjusted for inflation, then distortions can creep in. Obviously, there will be a tendency for the value of the fixed assets to be understated, and inventories will also be understated if the firm uses LIFO accounting. At the same time, an increasing rate of inflation will lead to increases in interest rates, which, in turn, will cause the value of any outstanding long-term debt to decline. Further, profits will vary from year to year as the inflation rate changes, and these variations will be especially severe if the cost of goods sold is based on the FIFO method.

These factors tend to make ratio comparisons less reliable than would be the case in the absence of inflation. This is especially true if a company changes its accounting procedures (say, from straight line to accelerated depreciation, or from FIFO to LIFO), or if various companies in a given industry use different accounting methods. Analysts can attempt to restate financial statements to put everything on a common basis, but, at best, this can only reduce the problem, not eliminate it. As a result, financial analysts generally base their analyses on reported accounting data, but then apply judgment when interpreting the findings.

Financial statement analysis is useful, but analysts should be aware of the problems discussed in this section. An analysis conducted in a mechanical, unthinking manner is dangerous, but when used intelligently and with good judgment, it can provide useful insights into a firm's operations and prospects.

SELF-TEST QUESTIONS

Explain how each of the following factors could present problems to an analyst conducting a financial statement analysis:

(1) Seasonal/cyclical data distortions
(2) Differences in accounting treatments
(3) Window dressing
(4) Inflation

Should analysts consider the information contained in the notes to the financial statements when analyzing a firm's financial condition? Explain.

SUMMARY

The primary purposes of this chapter were (1) to describe the basic financial statements and (2) to discuss how investors and managers analyze the statements. The key concepts covered are listed below.

■ The four basic statements contained in the annual report are the *balance sheet*, the *income statement*, the *statement of retained earnings*, and the *statement of cash flows*. Investors use the information provided in these statements to form expectations about the future levels of earnings and dividends, and about the firm's riskiness.

■ *Operating cash flows* differ from reported *accounting income*. Investors should be more interested in a firm's projected cash flows than in reported earnings, because it is cash, not paper profits, that is paid out as dividends and plowed back into the business to produce growth.

■ *Financial statement analysis* generally begins with a set of *financial ratios* designed to reveal the relative strengths and weaknesses of a company as compared with other companies in the same industry, and to show whether the firm's position has been improving or deteriorating over time.

■ *Liquidity ratios* show the relationship of a firm's current assets to its current liabilities, and thus indicate the firm's ability to meet its maturing debts.

■ *Asset management ratios* measure how effectively a firm is managing its assets.

■ *Debt management ratios* reveal (1) the extent to which the firm is financed with debt and (2) its likelihood of defaulting on its debt obligations.

■ *Profitability ratios* show the combined effects of liquidity, asset management, and debt management policies on operating results.

■ *Market value ratios* relate the firm's stock price to its earnings and book value per share.

■ *Trend analysis* reveals whether the firm's ratios are improving or deteriorating over time, while *comparative analysis* indicates how the firm compares with other firms or with industry averages.

■ *Du Pont analysis* is designed to show which of the basic determinants of ROE — the profit margin on sales, the total assets turnover ratio, and the use of debt — are most in need of improvement.

■ In a *common size analysis*, a firm's income statement and balance sheet are expressed in percentages. This facilitates comparisons among firms of different sizes and for a single firm over time.

■ *Percentage change analysis* focuses on the growth rate of income statement items and balance sheet accounts.

■ Financial statement analysis has some inherent problems, including (1) development of comparative data, (2) distortion of comparative data, (3) interpretation of results, (4) window dressing, and (5) effects of inflation.

■ In addition to comparisons with industry average ratios, firms' managements often *benchmark*, which involves designating a set of leading companies in their industry as "benchmark companies" and then comparing their ratios with those of the selected companies.

■ Two new performance measures have been developed that focus directly on management's success or failure in increasing shareholder wealth. *Market value added (MVA)* is the difference between the firm's market value of equity and the amount of equity capital that investors have supplied. *Economic value added (EVA)* measures income after all costs, including the opportunity cost of capital, have been deducted. MVA reflects the sum of the EVAs throughout the company's history, and both are used as the basis for incentive compensation plans.

Financial statement analysis has limitations, but used with care and judgment, it can be very helpful.

QUESTIONS

2-1 Define each of the following terms:

a. Annual report; income statement; balance sheet
b. Equity, or net worth; paid-in capital; retained earnings
c. Statement of retained earnings; statement of cash flows
d. Depreciation; inventory valuation methods
e. Liquidity ratios: current ratio; quick, or acid test, ratio

   f. Asset management ratios: inventory turnover ratio; days sales outstanding (DSO); fixed assets turnover ratio; total assets turnover ratio

   g. Financial leverage: debt ratio; times-interest-earned (TIE) ratio; fixed charge coverage ratio

   h. Profitability ratios: profit margin on sales; basic earning power (BEP) ratio; return on total assets (ROA); return on common equity (ROE)

   i. Market value ratios: price/earnings (P/E) ratio; market/book (M/B) ratio

   j. Trend analysis; comparative analysis

   k. Du Pont equation

   l. "Window dressing"; seasonal effects on ratios

   m. Common size statements

   n. Percentage change analysis

   o. MVA; EVA

2-2   What four statements are contained in most annual reports?

2-3   If a "typical" firm reports $10 million of retained earnings on its balance sheet, could its directors declare a $10 million cash dividend without any qualms whatsoever?

2-4   Financial ratio analysis is conducted by four groups of analysts: managers, equity investors, long-term creditors, and short-term creditors. What is the primary emphasis of each of these groups in evaluating ratios?

2-5   Why would the inventory turnover ratio be more important when analyzing a grocery chain than an insurance company?

2-6   Profit margins and turnover ratios vary from one industry to another. What differences would you expect to find between a grocery chain and a steel company? Think particularly about the turnover ratios and the profit margin, and think about the Du Pont equation.

2-7   How does inflation distort ratio analysis comparisons, both for one company over time (trend analysis) and when different companies are compared? Are only balance sheet items or both balance sheet and income statement items affected?

2-8   If a firm's ROE is low and management wants to improve it, explain how using more debt might help.

2-9   How might (a) seasonal factors and (b) different growth rates distort a comparative ratio analysis? Give some examples. How might these problems be alleviated?

2-10   Indicate the effects of the transactions listed in the following table on total current assets, current ratio, and net income. Use (+) to indicate an increase, (−) to indicate a decrease, and (0) to indicate either no effect or an indeterminate effect. Be prepared to state any necessary assumptions, and assume an initial current ratio of more than 1.0. (Note: A good accounting background is necessary to answer some of these questions; if yours is not strong, just answer the questions you can handle.)

	TOTAL CURRENT ASSETS	CURRENT RATIO	EFFECT ON NET INCOME
a. Cash is acquired through issuance of additional common stock.	_____	_____	_____
b. Merchandise is sold for cash.	_____	_____	_____
c. Federal income tax due for the previous year is paid.	_____	_____	_____
d. A fixed asset is sold for less than book value.	_____	_____	_____
e. A fixed asset is sold for more than book value.	_____	_____	_____
f. Merchandise is sold on credit.	_____	_____	_____
g. Payment is made to trade creditors for previous purchases.	_____	_____	_____

	TOTAL CURRENT ASSETS	CURRENT RATIO	EFFECT ON NET INCOME
h. A cash dividend is declared and paid.	_____	_____	_____
i. Cash is obtained through short-term bank loans.	_____	_____	_____
j. Short-term notes receivable are sold at a discount.	_____	_____	_____
k. Marketable securities are sold below cost.	_____	_____	_____
l. Advances are made to employees.	_____	_____	_____
m. Current operating expenses are paid.	_____	_____	_____
n. Short-term promissory notes are issued to trade creditors in exchange for past due accounts payable.	_____	_____	_____
o. Ten-year notes are issued to pay off accounts payable.	_____	_____	_____
p. A fully depreciated asset is retired.	_____	_____	_____
q. Accounts receivable are collected.	_____	_____	_____
r. Equipment is purchased with short-term notes.	_____	_____	_____
s. Merchandise is purchased on credit.	_____	_____	_____
t. The estimated taxes payable are increased.	_____	_____	_____

SELF-TEST PROBLEMS

(SOLUTIONS APPEAR IN APPENDIX C)

ST-1 **DEBT RATIO** K. Billingsworth & Co. had earnings per share of $4 last year, and it paid a $2 dividend. Total retained earnings increased by $12 million during the year, while book value per share at year end was $40. Billingsworth has no preferred stock, and no new common stock was issued during the year. If Billingsworth's year-end debt (which equals its total liabilities) was $120 million, what was the company's year-end debt/assets ratio?

ST-2 **RATIO ANALYSIS** The following data apply to A.L. Kaiser & Company (millions of dollars):

Cash and marketable securities	$100.00
Fixed assets	$283.50
Sales	$1,000.00
Net income	$50.00
Quick ratio	2.0×
Current ratio	3.0×
DSO	40 days
ROE	12%

Kaiser has no preferred stock — only common equity, current liabilities, and long-term debt.

a. Find Kaiser's (1) accounts receivable, (2) current liabilities, (3) current assets, (4) total assets, (5) ROA, (6) common equity, and (7) long-term debt.

b. In Part a, you should have found Kaiser's accounts receivable = $111.1 million. If Kaiser could reduce its DSO from 40 days to 30 days while holding other things constant, how much cash would it generate? If this cash were used to buy back common stock (at book value) and thus reduced the amount of common equity, how would this affect (1) the ROE, (2) the ROA, and (3) the total debt/total assets ratio?

PROBLEMS

2-1   **RATIO ANALYSIS** Data for Bowlin Beverages Company and its industry averages follow.

a. Calculate the indicated ratios for Bowlin.

b. Construct the Du Pont equation for both Bowlin and the industry.

c. Outline Bowlin's strengths and weaknesses as revealed by your analysis.

d. Suppose Bowlin had doubled its sales as well as its inventories, accounts receivable, and common equity during 1996. How would that information affect the validity of your ratio analysis? (Hint: Think about averages and the effects of rapid growth on ratios if averages are not used. No calculations are needed.)

BOWLIN BEVERAGES COMPANY: BALANCE SHEET AS OF DECEMBER 31, 1996

Cash	$ 77,500	Accounts payable	$ 129,000
Receivables	336,000	Notes payable	84,000
Inventories	241,500	Other current liabilities	117,000
Total current assets	$ 655,000	Total current liabilities	$ 330,000
Net fixed assets	292,500	Long-term debt	256,500
		Common equity	361,000
Total assets	$ 947,500	Total liabilities and equity	$ 947,500

BOWLIN BEVERAGES COMPANY: INCOME STATEMENT FOR YEAR ENDED DECEMBER 31, 1996

Sales		$ 1,607,500
Cost of goods sold:		
Materials	$717,000	
Labor	453,000	
Heat, light, and power	68,000	
Indirect labor	113,000	
Depreciation	41,500	1,392,500
Gross profit		$ 215,000
Selling expenses		115,000
General and administrative expenses		30,000
Earnings before interest and taxes (EBIT)		$ 70,000
Interest expense		24,500
Earnings before taxes (EBT)		$ 45,500
Federal and state income taxes (40%)		18,200
Net income		$ 27,300

RATIO	BOWLIN	INDUSTRY AVERAGE
Current assets/current liabilities	_____	2.0×
Days sales outstanding	_____	35 days
Sales/inventories	_____	6.7×
Sales/total assets	_____	3.0×
Net income/sales	_____	1.2%
Net income/total assets	_____	3.6%
Net income/equity	_____	9.0%
Total debt/total assets	_____	60.0%

2-2   **BALANCE SHEET ANALYSIS** Complete the balance sheet and sales information in the table that follows for Visscher Industries using the following financial data:

Debt ratio: 50%

Quick ratio: 0.80×

Total assets turnover: 1.5×

Days sales outstanding: 36 days

Gross profit margin on sales: (Sales − Cost of goods sold)/Sales = 25%

Inventory turnover ratio: 5×

BALANCE SHEET

Cash	_____	Accounts payable	_____
Accounts receivable	_____	Long-term debt	60,000
Inventories	_____	Common stock	_____
Fixed assets	_____	Retained earnings	97,500
Total assets	$300,000	Total liabilities and equity	_____
Sales	_____	Cost of goods sold	_____

2-3   **DU PONT ANALYSIS** The Lanser Lighting Company, a manufacturer and wholesaler of high-quality light fixtures, has been experiencing low profitability in recent years. As a result, the board of directors has replaced the president of the firm with a new president, Joan Lamm, who has asked you to make an analysis of the firm's financial position using the Du Pont equation. The most recent industry average ratios and Lanser's financial statements are as follows:

INDUSTRY AVERAGE RATIOS

Current ratio	2×	Sales/fixed assets	6×
Debt/total assets	30%	Sales/total assets	3×
Times-interest-earned	7×	Profit margin on sales	3%
Sales/inventory	10×	Return on total assets	9%
Days sales outstanding	24 days	Return on common equity	12.9%

LANSER LIGHTING COMPANY: BALANCE SHEET AS OF DECEMBER 31, 1996 (MILLIONS OF DOLLARS)

Cash	$ 45	Accounts payable	$ 45
Marketable securities	33	Notes payable	45
Net receivables	66	Other current liabilities	21
Inventories	159	Total current liabilities	$111
Total current assets	$303	Long-term debt	24
Gross fixed assets	$225	Total liabilities	$135
Less depreciation	78	Common stock	$114
Net fixed assets	$147	Retained earnings	201
		Total stockholders' equity	$315
Total assets	$450	Total liabilities and equity	$450

LANSER LIGHTING COMPANY: INCOME STATEMENT
FOR YEAR ENDED DECEMBER 31, 1996 (MILLIONS OF DOLLARS)

Net sales	$795.0
Cost of goods sold	660.0
Gross profit	$135.0
Selling expenses	73.5
Depreciation expense	12.0
Earnings before interest and taxes	$ 49.5
Interest expense	4.5
Earnings before taxes (EBT)	$ 45.0
Taxes (40%)	18.0
Net income	$ 27.0

a. Calculate those ratios that you think would be useful in this analysis.
b. Construct the Du Pont equation for Lanser, and compare the company's ratios to the industry average ratios.
c. Do the balance sheet accounts or the income statement figures seem to be primarily responsible for the low profits?
d. Which specific accounts seem to be most out of line in relation to other firms in the industry?
e. If Lanser had a pronounced seasonal sales pattern, or if it grew rapidly during the year, how might that affect the validity of your ratio analysis? How might you correct for such potential problems?

2-4   RATIO CALCULATION Assume you are given the following relationships for Delano Designs Inc:

Sales/total assets	1.5×
Return on assets (ROA)	3%
Return on equity (ROE)	5%

Calculate Delano's profit margin and debt ratio.

2-5   LIQUIDITY RATIOS The Ezzell's Apparel Company has $1,312,500 in current assets and $525,000 in current liabilities. Its initial inventory level is $375,000, and it will raise funds as additional notes payable and use them to increase inventory. How much can Ezzell's short-term debt (notes payable) increase without pushing its current ratio below 2.0? What will be the firm's quick ratio after Ezzell has raised the maximum amount of short-term funds?

2-6 RATIO CALCULATIONS The Ferri Furniture Company had a quick ratio of 1.4, a current ratio of 3.0, an inventory turnover of 6 times, total current assets of $810,000, and cash and marketable securities of $120,000 in 1996. What were Ferri's annual sales and its DSO for that year?

2-7 TIMES-INTEREST-EARNED RATIO Swensen Associates has $500,000 of debt outstanding, and its pays an interest rate of 10 percent annually. Swensen's annual sales are $2 million; its average tax rate is 20 percent; and its net profit margin on sales is 5 percent. If the company does not maintain a TIE ratio of at least 5 times, its bank will refuse to renew the loan, and bankruptcy will result. What is Swensen's TIE ratio?

2-8 RETURN ON EQUITY Powell Manufacturing's ROE last year was only 3 percent, but its management has developed a new operating plan designed to improve things. The new plan calls for a total debt ratio of 60 percent, which will result in interest charges of $300 per year. Management projects an EBIT of $1,000 on sales of $10,000, and it expects to have a total assets turnover ratio of 2.0. Under these conditions, the average tax rate will be 30 percent. If the changes are made, what return on equity will Powell earn?

2-9 RETURN ON EQUITY The Martell Auto Parts Company, which is just being formed, needs $1 million of assets, and it expects to have a basic earning power ratio of 20 percent. Martell will own no securities, so all of its income will be operating income. If it chooses to, Martell can finance up to 50 percent of its assets with debt, which will have an 8 percent interest rate. Assuming a 40 percent tax rate on all taxable income, what is the *difference* between its expected ROE if Martell finances with 50 percent debt versus its expected ROE if it finances entirely with common stock?

2-10 CONCEPTUAL: RETURN ON EQUITY Which of the following statements is most correct? (Hint: Work Problem 2-9 before answering 2-10, and consider the solution setup for Problem 2-9 as you think about Problem 2-10.)

a. If a firm's expected basic earning power (BEP) is constant for all of its assets and exceeds the interest rate on its debt, then adding assets and financing them with debt will raise the firm's expected rate of return on common equity (ROE).

b. The higher its tax rate, the lower a firm's BEP ratio will be, other things held constant.

c. The higher the interest rate on its debt, the lower a firm's BEP ratio will be, other things held constant.

d. The higher its debt ratio, the lower a firm's BEP ratio will be, other things held constant.

e. Statement a is false, but b, c, and d are all true.

2-11 RETURN ON EQUITY The Quigley Company has sales of $200,000, net income of $15,000, and the following balance sheet:

Cash	$ 10,000	Accounts payable	$ 30,000
Receivables	50,000	Other current liabilities	20,000
Inventories	150,000	Long-term debt	50,000
Net fixed assets	90,000	Common equity	200,000
Total assets	$300,000	Total liabilities and equity	$300,000

a. The company's new owner thinks that inventories are excessive and can be lowered to the point where the current ratio is equal to the industry average, 2.5×, without affecting either sales or net income. If inventories are sold off and not replaced so as to reduce the current ratio to 2.5×, if the funds generated are used to reduce common equity (stock can be repurchased at book value), and if no other changes occur, by how much will the ROE change?

b. Now suppose we wanted to take this problem and modify it for use on an exam, that is, to create a new problem which you have not seen to test your knowledge of this type of problem. How would your answer change if (1) We doubled all the dollar amounts? (2) We stated that the target current ratio was 3.0×? (3) We stated that the target was to achieve an inventory turnover ratio of 2× rather than a current ratio of 2.5×? (Hint: Compare the ROE obtained with an inventory turnover ratio of 2× to the original ROE obtained before any changes are considered.) (4) We said that the company had 10,000 shares of stock outstanding, and we asked how much the change in Part a would increase EPS? (5) What would your answer to (4) be if we changed the original problem to state that the stock was selling for twice book value, so common equity would not be reduced on a dollar-for-dollar basis?

c. Now explain how we could have set the problem up to have you focus on changing accounts receivable, or fixed assets, or using the funds generated to retire debt (we would give you the interest rate on outstanding debt), or how the original problem could have stated that the company needed *more* inventories and it would finance them with new common equity or with new debt.

SPREADSHEET APPLICATIONS

SPREADSHEET PROBLEM

Horrigan's Accessories Inc. forecasted 1997 financial statements follow, along with some industry average ratios.

a. Calculate Horrigan's 1997 forecasted ratios, compare them with the industry average data, and comment briefly on Horrigan's projected strengths and weaknesses.

b. What do you think would happen to Horrigan's ratios if the company initiated cost-cutting measures that allowed it to hold lower levels of inventory and substantially decreased the cost of goods sold? No calculations are necessary. Think about which ratios would be affected by changes in these two accounts.

HORRIGAN'S ACCESSORIES INC.: FORECASTED BALANCE SHEET AS OF DECEMBER 31, 1997

Cash	$ 72,000	Accounts and notes payable	$ 432,000
Accounts receivable	439,000	Accruals	170,000
Inventories	894,000		
Total current assets	$ 1,405,000	Total current liabilities	$ 602,000
Land and building	238,000	Long-term debt	404,290
Machinery	132,000	Common stock	575,000
Other fixed assets	61,000	Retained earnings	254,710
Total assets	$ 1,836,000	Total liabilities and equity	$ 1,836,000

HORRIGAN'S ACCESSORIES INC.: FORECASTED INCOME STATEMENT FOR 1997

Sales	$ 4,290,000
Cost of goods sold	3,580,000
Gross operating profit	$ 710,000
General administrative and selling expenses	236,320
Depreciation	159,000
Miscellaneous	134,000
Earnings before taxes (EBT)	$ 180,680
Taxes (40%)	72,272
Net income	$ 108,408
Number of shares outstanding	23,000

PER-SHARE DATA

EPS	$4.71
Cash dividends	$0.95
P/E ratio	5×
Market price (average)	$23.57

INDUSTRY FINANCIAL RATIOS (1997)[a]

Quick ratio	1.0×
Current ratio	2.7×
Inventory turnover[b]	7.0×
Days sales outstanding	32 days
Fixed assets turnover[b]	13.0×
Total assets turnover[b]	2.6×
Return on assets	9.1%
Return on equity	18.2%
Debt ratio	50.0%
Profit margin on sales	3.5%
P/E ratio	6.0×

[a]Industry average ratios have been constant for the past four years.
[b]Based on year-end balance sheet figures.

c. Suppose Horrigan's Accessories Inc. is considering installing a new computer system which would provide tighter control of inventories, accounts receivable, and accounts payable. If the new system is installed, the following data are projected (rather than the data given earlier) for the indicated balance sheet and income statement accounts:

Accounts receivable	$ 395,000
Inventories	700,000
Other fixed assets	150,000
Accounts and notes payable	275,000
Accruals	120,000
Cost of goods sold	3,450,000
Administrative and selling expenses	248,775
P/E ratio	6×

How do these changes affect the projected ratios and the comparison with the industry averages? (Note that any changes to the income statement will change the amount of retained earnings; therefore, the model is set up to calculate 1997 retained earnings as 1996 retained earnings plus net income minus dividends paid. The model also adjusts the cash balance so that the balance sheet balances.)

d. If the new computer were even more efficient than Horrigan's management had estimated, and thus caused the cost of goods sold to decrease by $125,000 from the projections in Part c, what effect would that have on the company's financial position?

e. If the new computer were less efficient than Horrigan's management had estimated, and caused the cost of goods sold to increase by $125,000 from the projections in Part c, what effect would that have on the company's financial position?

f. Change, one by one, the other items in Part c to see how each change affects the ratio analysis. Then think about, and write a paragraph describing, how computer models like this one can be used to help make better decisions about the purchase of such things as a new computer system.

MINI CASE

Donna Jamison was recently hired as a financial analyst by Computron Industries, a manufacturer of electronic calculators. Her first task was to conduct a financial analysis of the firm covering the last two years. To begin, she gathered the following financial statements and other data.

BALANCE SHEETS	1996	1995
ASSETS		
Cash	$ 52,000	$ 57,600
Accounts receivable	402,000	351,200
Inventories	836,000	715,200
Total current assets	$1,290,000	$1,124,000
Gross fixed assets	$ 527,000	$ 491,000
Less accumulated depreciation	166,200	146,200
Net fixed assets	$ 360,800	$ 344,800
Total assets	$1,650,800	$1,468,800

(continued)

LIABILITIES AND EQUITY	1996	1995
Accounts payable	$ 175,200	$ 145,600
Notes payable	225,000	200,000
Accruals	140,000	136,000
Total current liabilities	$ 540,200	$ 481,600
Long-term debt	$ 424,612	$ 323,432
Common stock (100,000 shares)	$ 460,000	$ 460,000
Retained earnings	225,988	203,768
Total equity	$ 685,988	$ 663,768
Total liabilities and equity	$1,650,800	$1,468,800

INCOME STATEMENTS

	1996	1995
Sales	$3,850,000	$3,432,000
Cost of goods sold	$3,250,000	$2,864,000
Other expenses	430,300	340,000
Depreciation	20,000	18,900
Total operating costs	$3,700,300	$3,222,900
EBIT	$ 149,700	$ 209,100
Interest expense	76,000	62,500
EBT	$ 73,700	$ 146,600
Taxes (40%)	29,480	58,640
Net income	$ 44,220	$ 87,960
EPS	$0.442	$0.880

OTHER DATA

	1996	1995
December 31 stock price	$ 6.00	$ 8.50
Number of shares	100,000	100,000
Dividends per share	$ 0.22	$ 0.22
Lease payments	$ 40,000	$ 40,000

STATEMENT OF CASH FLOWS FOR 1996

OPERATING ACTIVITIES

Net income	$ 44,220	
Additions (sources of cash):		
Depreciation	20,000	
Increase in accounts payable	29,600	
Increase in accruals	4,000	
Subtractions (uses of cash):		
Increase in accounts receivable	(50,800)	
Increase in inventories	(120,800)	
Net cash flow from operations		($ 73,780)

(continued)

LONG-TERM INVESTING ACTIVITIES

Investment in fixed assets	($ 36,000)

FINANCING ACTIVITIES

Increase in notes payable	$ 25,000	
Increase in long-term debt	101,180	
Payment of cash dividends	(22,000)	
Net cash flow from financing		$ 104,180
Net increase (decrease) in cash		($ 5,600)
Cash at beginning of year		57,600
Cash at end of year		$ 52,000

INDUSTRY AVERAGE DATA FOR 1996

RATIO	INDUSTRY AVERAGE
Current	2.7×
Quick	1.0×
Inventory turnover	7.0×
Days sales outstanding (DSO)	32.0 days
Fixed assets turnover	10.7×
Total assets turnover	2.6×
Debt ratio	50.0%
TIE	2.5×
Fixed charge coverage	2.1×
Profit margin	3.5%
Basic earning power	19.1%
ROA	9.1%
ROE	18.2%
Price/earnings	14.2×
Market/book	1.4×

Assume that you are Donna Jamison's assistant, and that she has asked you to help her prepare a report which evaluates the company's financial condition. Then answer the following questions.

a. What can you conclude about the company's financial condition from its statement of cash flows?

b. What is the purpose of financial ratio analysis, and what are the five major categories of ratios?

c. What are Computron's current and quick ratios? What do they tell you about the company's liquidity position?

d. What are Computron's inventory turnover, days sales outstanding, fixed assets turnover, and total assets turnover ratios? How does the firm's utilization of assets stack up against that of the industry?

e. What are the firm's debt, times-interest-earned, and fixed charge coverage ratios? How does Computron compare to the industry with respect to financial leverage? What conclusions can you draw from these ratios?

f. Calculate and discuss the firm's profitability ratios — that is, its profit margin, basic earning power (BEP), return on assets (ROA), and return on equity (ROE).

g. Calculate Computron's market value ratios — that is, its price/earnings ratio and its market/book ratio. What do these ratios tell you about investors' opinions of the company?

h. Use the Du Pont equation to provide a summary and overview of Computron's financial condition. What are the firm's major strengths and weaknesses?

i. Use the following simplified 1996 balance sheet to show, in general terms, how an improvement in one of the ratios, say the DSO, would affect the stock price. For example, if the company could improve its collection procedures and thereby lower the DSO from 37.6 days to 27.6 days, how would that change "ripple through" the financial statements (shown in thousands below) and influence the stock price?

Accounts receivable	$ 402	Debt	$ 965
Other current assets	888	Equity	686
Net fixed assets	361		
Total assets	$ 1,651	Total liabilities and equity	$ 1,651

j. What are MVA and EVA? How can they be used to judge managerial performance?

k. Although financial statement analysis can provide useful information about a company's operations and its financial condition, this type of analysis does have some potential problems and limitations, and it must be used with care and judgment. What are some problems and limitations?

SELECTED ADDITIONAL REFERENCES AND CASES

The effects of alternative accounting policies on both financial statements and ratios based on these statements are discussed in the investment textbooks referenced in Chapter 4, and also in the many excellent texts on financial statement analysis. For example, see

Fraser, Lyn M., *Understanding Financial Statements* (Englewood Cliffs, N.J.: Prentice-Hall, 1992).

Gibson, Charles H., and Patricia A. Frishkoff, *Financial Statement Analysis* (Boston: Kent, 1986).

Hawkins, David F., *Corporate Financial Reporting and Analysis* (Homewood, Ill.: Irwin, 1986).

For further information on the relative usefulness of various financial ratios, see

Chen, Kung H., and Thomas A. Shimerda, "An Empirical Analysis of Useful Financial Ratios," *Financial Management*, Spring 1981, 51–60.

Considerable work has been done to establish the relationship between bond ratings and financial ratios. For one example, see

Belkaoui, Ahmed, *Industrial Bonds and the Rating Process* (London: Quorum Books, 1983).

For sources of ratios and common size statements, see the following:

Dun & Bradstreet, *Key Business Ratios* (New York: Updated annually).

Financial Research Associates, *Financial Studies of the Small Business* (Arlington, Va.: Updated annually).

Robert Morris Associates, *Annual Statement Studies* (Philadelphia: Updated annually).

The following cases from the Cases in Financial Management: Dryden Request *series focus on financial analysis*:

Case 35, "Mark X Company (A)," which illustrates the use of ratio analysis in the evaluation of a firm's existing and potential financial positions.

Case 36, "Garden State Container Corporation," which is similar in content to Case 35.

Case 36A, "Safe Packaging Corporation," which updates Case 36.

THE FINANCIAL ENVIRONMENT:
MARKETS, INSTITUTIONS,
INTEREST RATES, AND TAXES

recent newsletter sent to investors by the Variable Annuity Life Insurance Company (VALIC) contained an article entitled "Interest Rates: The Long and Short of Them." Here are some of the key ideas contained in the article:

Monetary policy and the actions of the Federal Reserve (the Fed) are not necessarily your standard watercooler conversation fare, unless, of course, your office happens to be on Wall Street. However, ripples from Fed decisions eventually wash up on nearly every American's shore.

Interest rates — the cost of money — play a crucial role in how your investments perform, whether you invest in stocks, bonds, mutual funds, variable annuities, T-bills, or money market accounts. Interest rates also impact the cost of mortgage, credit card, and auto loans. Scan almost any newspaper's business section and you will find a story titled something like this: "Analysts pore over economic data . . . nervously awaiting Fed action." As the nation's money supply regulator, the Fed has a significant impact on all interest rates. When the demand for money exceeds the supply, interest rates rise, and when supply exceeds demand, interest rates decline.

Trying to keep the economy growing, but controllably, the Fed must perform a tightrope walk to keep inflation at bay while holding interest rates to relatively low levels. Following the 1974 recession, the Fed reduced the rate that it charges on loans to member banks (the discount rate) six times over a two-year period. As a result, the prime rate — the rate that banks charge their most creditworthy customers — dropped from 10.25 percent to 6.5 percent. Conversely, after a boom in early 1980, the Fed increased the discount rate a full percentage point four times in under a year. This action, in turn, drove the prime rate to record levels, rising to 20.5 percent in 1981.

The direction that interest rates are moving, and expectations about future rate movements, play a major part in stock price performance. For example, a story in the February 7, 1994, Wall Street Journal *contained this statement: "The interest rate bogeyman finally struck last week and knocked the stock market for a loop. Stock prices plunged Friday on news that the Federal Reserve boosted the fed funds rate [the rate that member banks must charge one another for loans] from 3 percent to 3.25 percent. The Dow tumbled 96.24 points, or by 2.4 percent." In another story, this time in the July 7, 1995, edition of* USA Today, *the writer stated that "News that the fed funds rate was cut from 6 percent to 5.75 percent sent the Dow soaring 48.77 points to a record 4664."*

Financial managers must understand the markets where capital is raised, securities are traded, and stock prices are established, as well as the institutions which operate in these markets. They should also understand how money costs are determined and the principal factors that determine the level of interest rates in the economy. In addition, since taxes are critically important in financial decisions, they should also understand the basic features of U.S. tax laws.

THE FINANCIAL MARKETS

AN OVERVIEW

Business firms, individuals, and government units often need to raise capital. For example, suppose Carolina Power & Light (CP&L) forecasts an increase in the demand for electricity in North Carolina, and the company decides to build a new power plant. Because CP&L almost certainly will not have the $2 billion or so necessary to pay for the plant, the company will have to raise this capital in the financial markets. Or suppose Mr. Fong, the proprietor of a San Francisco hardware store, decides to expand into appliances. Where will he get the money to buy the initial inventory of TV sets, washers, and freezers? Similarly, if the Johnson family wants to buy a home that costs $100,000, but they have only $20,000 in savings, how can they raise the additional $80,000? Finally, if the city of New York wants to borrow $200 million to finance a new water treatment plant, or if the federal government needs more than $200 billion to cover its projected 1997 deficit, they too need access to the capital markets.

On the other hand, the incomes of some individuals and firms are greater than their current expenditures, so they have funds available to invest. For example, Kathy Hanks has an income of $36,000, but her expenses are only $30,000, while Ford Motor Company recently accumulated more than $19 billion of excess cash, which it plans to invest.

People and organizations needing money are brought together with those having surplus funds in the *financial markets*. Note that "markets" is plural — there are a great many different financial markets, each one consisting of many institutions, in a developed economy such as ours. Each market deals with a somewhat different type of instrument in terms of the instrument's maturity and the assets backing it. Also, different markets serve different types of customers or operate in different parts of the country. Here are some of the major types of markets:

1. *Physical asset markets* (also called "tangible" or "real" asset markets) are those for such products as wheat, autos, real estate, computers, and machinery. *Financial asset markets* deal with stocks, bonds, notes, mortgages, and other *claims on real assets,* as well as options and other *derivative* securities whose values are *derived* from changes in the prices of other financial assets.

2. *Spot markets* and *futures markets* are terms that refer to whether the assets are being bought or sold for "on the spot" delivery (literally, within a few days) or for delivery at some future date, such as six months or a year into the future. The futures markets are growing in importance, but we shall not discuss them until Chapter 23.

3. *Money markets* are the markets for short-term, highly liquid debt securities. The New York and London money markets have long been the world's largest, but Tokyo's is rising rapidly. *Capital markets* are the markets for long-term debt and corporate stocks. The New York Stock Exchange, where the stocks and bonds of the largest U.S. corporations are traded, is a prime example of a capital market. There is no hard and fast rule on this, but when describing debt markets "short-term" generally means one year or less, "intermediate term" means one to ten years, and "long term" means more than ten years.

4. *Mortgage markets* deal with loans on residential, commercial, and industrial real estate, and on farmland, while *consumer credit markets* involve loans on autos and appliances, as well as loans for education, vacations, and so on.

5. *World, national, regional,* and *local markets* also exist. Thus, depending on an organization's size and scope of operations, it may be able to borrow all around the world, or it may be confined to a strictly local, even neighborhood, market.

6. *Primary markets* are the markets in which corporations raise new capital. If GE were to sell a new issue of common stock to raise capital, this would be a primary market transaction. The corporation selling the newly created stock receives the proceeds from the sale in a primary market transaction. *Secondary markets* are markets in which existing, already outstanding, securities are traded among investors. Thus, if Margaret White decided to buy 1,000 shares of IBM stock, the purchase would occur in the secondary market. The New York Stock Exchange is a secondary market, since it deals in outstanding as opposed to newly issued stocks and bonds. Secondary markets also exist for mortgages, various other types of loans, and other financial assets. The corporation whose securities are being traded is not involved in a secondary market transaction and, thus, does not receive any funds from such a sale.

7. *Private markets,* where transactions are worked out between two parties, are differentiated from *exchange markets,* where standardized contracts are traded. This distinction is especially important in the case of derivative securities such as options and futures. Note also that in our economy there is a tendency for a newly developed security to first trade in the private market,

then for standardized contracts suitable for trading on an exchange to be developed. Standardization and exchange trading lowers transactions costs, increases market efficiency, and facilitates funds flows, which improves the general economy.

Other classifications could be made, but this breakdown is sufficient to show that there are many types of financial markets.

A healthy economy is dependent on efficient transfers of funds from people who are net savers to firms and individuals who need capital. Without efficient transfers, the economy simply could not function: Carolina Power & Light could not raise capital, so Raleigh's citizens would have no electricity; the Johnson family would not have adequate housing; and Kathy Hanks would have no place to invest her savings. Obviously, the level of employment and productivity, hence our standard of living, would be much lower. Therefore, it is absolutely essential that our financial markets function efficiently — not only quickly, but also at a low cost.[1]

Table 3-1 gives a listing of the most important instruments traded in the various financial markets. The instruments are arranged from top to bottom in ascending order of typical length of maturity. As we go through the book, we will look in much more detail at many of these instruments. For example, we will see that there are actually many varieties of corporate bonds, ranging from "plain vanilla flavored" bonds, to bonds that are convertible into common stocks, and to bonds whose interest payments vary depending on the rate of inflation. Still, the table gives an idea of the characteristics and costs of the instruments traded in the major financial markets.

Most financial investments are in *direct claim securities* such as those listed in Table 3-1. However, money can also be invested in options and financial futures, which, as noted earlier, are called *derivatives* and whose values are derived from changes in the prices of underlying securities. Derivatives are complex, generally highly leveraged instruments whose primary purpose is to hedge against the risks inherent in commodities or direct claim securities. However, in recent years derivatives have increasingly been used to speculate in the markets. Because they are leveraged, a relatively small change in the value of the underlying asset will result in a large change in the value of the derivative, which is appealing to speculators. Since one cannot understand derivatives without an understanding of their related direct claim instruments, we defer a detailed discussion of derivatives until Chapter 23.

RECENT TRENDS

The financial services industry from 1980 to 1995 can be divided into two distinct periods. First, from 1980 to 1987 we saw unprecedented growth, innovation, and, in many cases, speculative excess. This period witnessed reduced regulation in most markets, a stock market boom, a surge in financially driven mergers, the develop-

---

[1]As the Commonwealth of Independent States (the former Soviet Union) and the Eastern European nations move toward capitalism, just as much attention must be paid to the establishment of cost-efficient financial markets as to electrical power, transportation, communications, and other infrastructure systems. Economic efficiency is simply impossible without a good system for allocating capital within the economy.

SUMMARY OF DIRECT CLAIM SECURITIES, MARKET PARTICIPANTS, AND SECURITY CHARACTERISTICS	TABLE 3-1

			SECURITY CHARACTERISTICS		
SECURITY	**MARKET**	**MAJOR PARTICIPANTS**	**RISKINESS**	**ORIGINAL MATURITY**	**INTEREST RATE ON 4/10/96[a]**
U.S. Treasury bills	Money	Sold by U.S. Treasury to finance federal expenditures	Default-free	91 days to 1 year	5.2%
Banker's acceptances	Money	Firm's promise to pay, guaranteed by bank	Low degree of risk if guaranteed by a strong bank	Up to 180 days	5.4%
Commercial paper	Money	Issued by financially secure firms to large investors	Low default risk	Up to 270 days	5.4%
Negotiable certificates of deposit (CDs)	Money	Issued by major money-center commercial banks to large investors	Riskier than Treasury bills	Up to 1 year	5.3%
Money market mutual funds	Money	Invest in Treasury bills, CDs, and commercial paper; held by individuals and businesses	Low degree of risk	No specific maturity (instant liquidity)	5.0%
Eurodollar market time deposits	Money	Issued by banks outside U.S.	Default risk is a function of issuing bank	Up to 1 year	5.6%
Consumer credit loans	Money	Issued by banks/ credit unions/ finance companies to individuals	Risk is variable	Variable	Variable
U.S. Treasury notes and bonds	Capital	Issued by U.S. government	No default risk, but price can decline if interest rates rise	2 to 30 years	6.9%
Mortgages	Capital	Borrowings from commercial banks and S&Ls by individuals and businesses	Risk is variable	Up to 30 years	7.2%

[a]Interest rates are for longest maturity securities of the type and for the strongest securities of a given type. Thus, the 6.0% interest rate shown for state and local government bonds reflects the rate on 30-year, Aaa bonds. Lower-rated bonds had higher interest rates.

continued

TABLE 3-1	CONTINUED				

| | | | SECURITY CHARACTERISTICS | | |
SECURITY	MARKET	MAJOR PARTICIPANTS	RISKINESS	ORIGINAL MATURITY	INTEREST RATE ON 4/10/96[a]
State and local government bonds	Capital	Issued by state and local governments to individuals and institutional investors	Riskier than U.S. government securities, but exempt from most taxes	Up to 30 years	6.0%
Corporate bonds	Capital	Issued by corporations to individuals and institutional investors	Riskier than U.S. government securities, but less risky than preferred and common stocks; varying degree of risk within bonds depending on strength of issuer	Up to 40 years[b]	7.8%
Leases	Capital	Similar to debt in that firms can lease assets rather than borrow and then buy the assets	Risk similar to corporate bonds	Generally 3 to 20 years	Similar to bond yields
Preferred stocks	Capital	Issued by corporations to individuals and institutional investors	Riskier than corporate bonds, but less risky than common stock	Unlimited	6 to 8%
Common stocks	Capital	Issued by corporations to individuals and institutional investors	Risky	Unlimited	10 to 15%[c]

[b]In recent years several companies have issued 100-year bonds. However, most corporate bonds have maturities of 40 years or less.

[c]Common stocks are expected to provide a "return" in the form of dividends and capital gains rather than interest. Of course, if you buy a stock, while you may *expect* to earn 10 percent on your money, the stock's price may decline and cause you to experience a 100 percent loss. Also, tax considerations tend to lower the interest (dividends) paid on preferred stock.

ment of the junk bond market, and a sharp rise in business and consumer debt. The financial services industry grew at an unsustainably high rate, but that growth was halted, at least for a while, by the crash of October 1987, when the stock market fell by 25 percent in just one day.

The period from 1987 to 1995 was characterized by adjustment. Growth slowed, and the financial services industry turned more to consumer services rather than corporate services to stabilize earnings. Mergers among banks, investment banking houses, insurance companies, and mutual fund organizations occurred in an effort to gain economies of scale and thus to cut costs and become more competitive.

The period from 1996 to 2000 is shaping up to be a time of resurgence. Capital market activities, corporate lending, and investing are all rebounding. However, many of the growth opportunities will come from international rather than domestic markets. Technology, globalization, competition, and deregulation have all combined to revolutionize worldwide financial markets, and the result is an efficient, internationally linked market.

Throughout the period, investment bankers have been developing new financial products. Much of the innovation has involved derivatives which, as we noted earlier, can be used either to reduce risk or to speculate. To illustrate their use to reduce risk, a company that exports to Japan will see its net income fall if the value of the dollar rises relative to the yen, because the yen it receives from its Japanese customers can be exchanged for fewer dollars. The company could reduce its exposure to exchange rate fluctuations by purchasing derivatives that increase in value whenever the dollar rises against the yen. This use of derivatives is called *hedging*, and its purpose is to reduce the company's risk exposure to changing exchange rates. Speculation, on the other hand, is done in the hopes of gaining high returns on a limited investment. For example, Procter & Gamble recently disclosed that it lost $150 million on derivatives, and Orange County (California) went bankrupt after losing about $2 billion on an "investment" in derivatives.

How does the introduction of derivatives influence the financial markets? The size and complexity of derivatives transactions have concerned regulators, academics, and politicians. Federal Reserve Board Chairman Alan Greenspan noted that, in theory, derivatives should allow firms to manage risk better, but he also stated that it is not clear whether derivatives actually increase or decrease the inherent stability of the financial system.

<table>
<tr><td>Distinguish between physical asset markets and financial asset markets.
What is the difference between spot and futures markets?
Distinguish between money and capital markets.
What is the difference between primary and secondary markets?
Why are financial markets essential for a healthy economy?
What are derivatives, and how are they used?</td><td>**SELF-TEST
QUESTIONS**</td></tr>
</table>

FINANCIAL INSTITUTIONS

Transfers of capital between savers and those who need capital take place in the three different ways diagrammed in Figure 3-1:

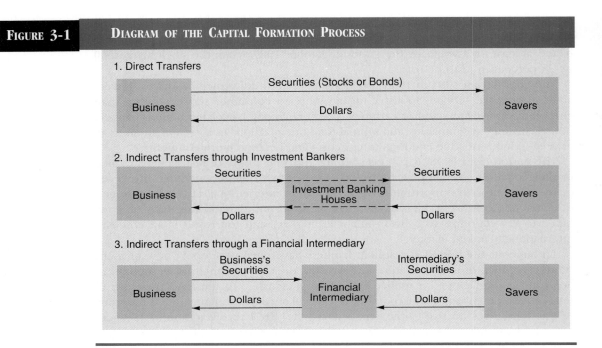

FIGURE 3-1   DIAGRAM OF THE CAPITAL FORMATION PROCESS

1. **Direct transfers** of money and securities, as shown in the top section, occur when a business sells its stocks or bonds directly to savers, without going through any type of financial institution. The business delivers its securities to savers, who in turn give the firm the money it needs.

2. As shown in the middle section, transfers may also go through an *investment banking house* such as Morgan Stanley, which serves as a middleman and facilitates the issuance of securities. The company sells its stocks or bonds to the investment bank, which in turn sells these same securities to savers. The businesses' securities and the savers' money merely "pass through" the investment banking house. However, the investment bank does buy and hold the securities for a period of time, so it is taking a chance — it may not be able to resell the securities to savers for as much as it paid. Because new securities are involved and the corporation receives money from the sale, this is a primary market transaction.

3. Transfers can also be made through a *financial intermediary* such as a bank or mutual fund. Here the intermediary obtains funds from savers, issuing its own securities in exchange, and it then uses the money to purchase and then hold a business's securities. For example, a saver might give dollars to a bank, receiving from it a certificate of deposit, and then the bank might lend the money to a small business in the form of a mortgage loan. Thus, intermediaries literally create new forms of capital — in this case, certificates of deposit, which are both safer and more liquid than mortgages and thus are better secu-

rities for most savers to hold. The existence of intermediaries greatly increases the efficiency of money and capital markets.

For simplicity, we assumed that the entity which needs capital is a business, specifically a corporation, but it is easy to visualize the demander of capital as a home purchaser, a government unit, and so on.

Direct transfers of funds from savers to businesses are possible and do occur on occasion, but it is generally more efficient for a business to enlist the services of an *investment banking house*. Merrill Lynch, Salomon Brothers, Smith Barney, and Goldman Sachs are examples of financial service corporations which offer investment banking services. Such organizations (1) help corporations design securities with features that are currently attractive to investors, (2) buy these securities from the corporation, and (3) then resell them to savers. Although the securities are sold twice, this process is really one primary market transaction, with the investment banker acting as a middleman to facilitate the transfer of capital from savers to businesses.

The *financial intermediaries* shown in the third section of Figure 3-1 do more than simply transfer money and securities between firms and savers — they literally create new financial products. Since the intermediaries are generally large, they gain economies of scale in analyzing the creditworthiness of potential borrowers, in processing and collecting loans, and in pooling risks and thus helping individual savers diversify, hence "not put all their financial eggs in one basket." Further, a system of specialized intermediaries can enable savings to do more than just draw interest. For example, individuals can put money into banks and get both interest income and a convenient way of making payments (checking), or put money into life insurance companies and get both interest income and protection for their beneficiaries.

In the United States and other developed nations, a large set of specialized, highly efficient financial intermediaries has been developed. The situation is constantly evolving, however, and different types of institutions are performing services that were formerly reserved for others, causing institutional distinctions to become blurred. Still, there is a degree of institutional identity, and here are the major classes of intermediaries:

1. *Commercial banks,* which are the traditional "department stores of finance," serve a wide variety of savers and those with needs for funds. Historically, the commercial banks were the major institutions which handled checking accounts and through which the Federal Reserve System expanded or contracted the money supply. Today, however, several other institutions also provide checking services and significantly influence the effective money supply. Conversely, commercial banks are providing an ever-widening range of services, including stock brokerage services and insurance.

   Note that commercial banks are quite different from investment banks. Commercial banks lend money, whereas investment banks help companies raise capital from other parties. Prior to 1933, commercial banks offered investment banking services, but the Glass-Steagall Act, which was passed in 1933, prohibited commercial banks from engaging in investment banking. Thus, the Morgan Bank was broken up into two separate organizations, one of which is now the Morgan Guaranty Trust Company, a commercial bank, while the other is Morgan Stanley, a major investment banking house. Note also that Japanese and European banks can offer both commercial and investment banking services. This hinders U.S. banks in global competition, so efforts are being made by many commercial bankers to get Glass-Steagall repealed.

2. *Savings and loan associations (S&Ls),* which have traditionally served individual savers and residential and commercial mortgage borrowers, take the funds of many small savers and then lend this money to home buyers and other types of borrowers. Because the savers obtain a degree of liquidity that would be absent if they bought the mortgages or other securities directly, perhaps the most significant economic function of the S&Ls is to "create liquidity" which would otherwise be lacking. Also, the S&Ls have more expertise in analyzing credit, setting up loans, and making collections than individual savers, so they reduce the cost and increase the availability of real estate loans. Finally, the S&Ls hold large, diversified portfolios of loans and other assets and thus spread risks in a manner that would be impossible if small savers were making direct mortgage loans. Because of these factors, savers benefit by being able to invest their savings in more liquid, better managed, and less risky accounts, whereas borrowers benefit by being able to obtain more capital, and at lower costs, than would otherwise be possible. In the 1980s, the S&L industry experienced severe problems when (1) short-term interest rates the S&Ls paid savers rose well above the returns they were earning on mortgages and (2) commercial real estate suffered a severe slump resulting in high mortgage default rates. Together, these events forced many S&Ls to either merge with stronger institutions or close their doors.

3. *Mutual savings banks,* which are similar to S&Ls, operate primarily in the northeastern states, accept savings primarily from individuals and lend mainly on a long-term basis to home buyers and consumers.

4. *Credit unions* are cooperative associations whose members have a common bond, such as being employees of the same firm. Members' savings are loaned only to other members, generally for auto purchases, home improvements, and home mortgages. Credit unions often are the cheapest source of funds available to individual borrowers.

5. *Life insurance companies* take savings in the form of annual premiums, then invest these funds in stocks, bonds, real estate, and mortgages, and finally make payments to the beneficiaries of the insured parties. In recent years, life insurance companies have also offered a variety of tax-deferred savings plans designed to provide benefits to the participants when they retire.

6. *Mutual funds* are corporations which accept money from savers and then use these funds to buy stocks, long-term bonds, or short-term debt instruments issued by businesses or government units. These organizations pool funds and thus reduce risks by diversification. They also achieve economies of scale, which lower the costs of analyzing securities, managing portfolios, and buying and selling securities. Different funds are designed to meet the objectives of different types of savers. Hence, there are bond funds for those who desire safety, stock funds for savers who are willing to accept significant risks in the hope of higher returns, and still other funds that are used as interest-bearing

checking accounts (the *money market funds*). There are literally thousands of different mutual funds with dozens of different goals and purposes.

We cannot in this book discuss the pros and cons of the literally thousands of different mutual funds, but virtually all libraries subscribe to services such as Weisenberger and Value Line which provide information on each fund's objectives, past performance, fees, and so on.

7. *Pension funds* are retirement plans funded by corporations or government agencies for their workers and administered generally by the trust departments of commercial banks or by life insurance companies. Pension funds invest primarily in bonds, stocks, mortgages, and real estate.

Changes in the structure of pension plans over the last decade have had a profound impact on both individuals and financial markets. Historically, most large corporations and governmental units used *defined benefit* plans to provide for their employees' retirement. In a defined benefit plan, the employer specifies, or guarantees, the level of benefits the employee will receive when he or she retires, and it is the employer's responsibility to invest funds to ensure that it can meet its obligations when its employees retire. Under defined benefit plans, employees have little or no say about how the money in the pension plan is invested — this decision is made by the corporate employer. Note that employers, not employees, bear the risk that investments held by the plan will not perform well.

In recent years many companies (and virtually all new companies, including those in the rapidly growing high-tech sector) have begun to use *defined contribution* plans, under which employers make specified, or defined, payments into the plan. Then, when the employee retires, his or her pension benefits are determined by the amount of assets in the plan. Therefore, in a defined contribution plan the employee bears the risk inherent in investments, and the employee has the responsibility for making investment decisions.

The most common type of defined contribution plan is the *401(k)* plan, named after the section in the federal act which established the legal basis for the plan. Governmental units, including universities, can use *403(b)* plans, which operate essentially like 401(k) plans. In all of these plans, employees must choose from among a set of investment alternatives. Typically, the employer agrees to make some "defined contribution" to the plan, and the employee can also make a payment. Then, the employer contracts with an insurance company plus one or more mutual fund companies, and then employees must choose among investments ranging from "guaranteed investment contracts" to government bond funds to domestic corporate bond and stock funds to international stock and bond funds. Under most plans, the employees can, within certain limits, shift their investments from category to category. Thus, if someone thinks the stock market is currently overvalued, he or she can tell the mutual fund to move the money from a stock fund to a money market fund. Similarly, employees can gradually shift from 100 percent stock to a mix of stocks and bonds as they grow older.

This change in the structure of pension plans has had two extremely important effects. First, individuals must now make the primary investment decisions for their pension plans. Since such decisions can mean the difference between a comfortable retirement and barely getting by, it is important that those covered by defined contribution plans understand the fundamentals of investing. Second, whereas defined benefit plan managers typically invest in individual stocks and bonds, most individuals invest 401(k) money through mutual funds. Since 401(k) defined contribution plans are growing rapidly, the result is rapid growth in the mutual fund industry. This, in turn, has implications for the security markets, and for businesses that need to attract capital.

Financial institutions have historically been heavily regulated, with the primary purpose of this regulation being to ensure the safety of the institutions and thus to protect depositors. However, these regulations — which have taken the form of prohibitions on nationwide branch banking, restrictions on the types of assets the institutions can buy, ceilings on the interest rates they can pay, and limitations on the types of services they can provide — have tended to impede the free flow of capital from surplus to deficit areas, and thus have hurt the efficiency of our capital markets. Recognizing this fact, Congress has authorized some major changes, and more will be forthcoming.

The result of the ongoing regulatory changes has been a blurring of the distinctions among the different types of institutions. Indeed, the trend in the United States today is toward huge *financial service corporations,* which own banks, S&Ls, investment banking houses, insurance companies, pension plan operations, and mutual funds, and which have branches across the country and even around the world. Examples of financial service corporations, most of which started in one area and have now diversified to cover most of the financial spectrum, include Transamerica, Merrill Lynch, American Express, Citicorp, Fidelity, and Prudential.

SELF-TEST QUESTIONS

Identify the three primary ways capital is transferred between savers and borrowers.

What is the difference between a commercial bank and an investment bank?

List the similarities and differences between investment banking houses and financial intermediaries.

List the major types of intermediaries, and briefly describe each's function.

THE STOCK MARKET

As noted earlier, secondary markets are those in which outstanding, previously issued securities are traded. By far the most active secondary market, and the most important one to financial managers, is the *stock market,* where the prices of firms' stocks are established. Since the primary goal of financial management is to maximize the firm's stock price, a knowledge of the stock market is essential for anyone involved in managing a business.

THE STOCK EXCHANGES

There are two basic types of stock markets: (1) *organized exchanges,* which include the New York Stock Exchange (NYSE), the American Stock Exchange (AMEX), and several regional exchanges and (2) the less formal *over-the-counter market.* Since the organized exchanges have actual physical market locations and are easier to describe and understand, we shall consider them first.

The *organized security exchanges* are tangible physical entities. Each of the larger ones occupies its own building, has specifically designated members, and has an elected governing body — its board of governors. Members are said to have "seats" on the exchange, although everybody stands up. These seats, which are bought and sold, give the holder the right to trade on the exchange. There are more than 1,300 seats on the New York Stock Exchange, and they recently were selling for about $1.3 million.

Most of the larger investment banking houses operate *brokerage departments,* which own seats on the exchanges and designate one or more of their employees as members. The exchanges are open on all normal working days, with the members meeting in a large room equipped with telephones and other electronic equipment that enable each member to communicate with his or her firm's offices throughout the country.

Like other markets, security exchanges facilitate communication between buyers and sellers. For example, Merrill Lynch (the largest brokerage firm) might receive an order in its Atlanta office from a customer who wants to buy 100 shares of IBM stock. Simultaneously, Dean Witter's Denver office might receive an order from a customer wishing to sell 100 shares of IBM. Each broker communicates by wire with the firm's representative on the NYSE. Other brokers throughout the country are also communicating with their own exchange members. The exchange members with *sell orders* offer the shares for sale, and they are bid for by the members with *buy orders.* Thus, the exchanges operate as *auction markets.*[2]

THE OVER-THE-COUNTER MARKET

In contrast to the organized security exchanges, the *over-the-counter market* is a nebulous, intangible organization. An explanation of the term "over-the-counter" will

---

[2]The NYSE is actually a modified auction market, wherein people (through their brokers) bid for stocks. Originally — about 200 years ago — brokers would literally shout, "I have 100 shares of Apex for sale; how much am I offered?" and then sell to the highest bidder. If a broker had a buy order, he or she would shout, "I want to buy 100 shares of Apex; who'll sell at the best price?" The same general situation still exists, although the exchanges now have members known as *specialists* who facilitate the trading process by keeping an inventory of shares of the stocks in which they specialize. If a buy order comes in at a time when no sell order arrives, the specialist will sell off some inventory. Similarly, if a sell order comes in, the specialist will buy and add to inventory. The specialist sets a *bid price* (the price the specialist will pay for the stock) and an *asked price* (the price at which shares will be sold out of inventory). The bid and asked prices are set at levels designed to keep the inventory in balance. If many buy orders start coming in because of favorable developments or sell orders come in because of unfavorable events, the specialist will raise or lower prices to keep supply and demand in balance. Bid prices are somewhat lower than asked prices, with the difference, or *spread,* representing the specialist's profit margin.

Special facilities are available to help institutional investors such as mutual funds or pension funds sell large blocks of stock without depressing their prices. In essence, brokerage houses which cater to institutional clients will purchase blocks (defined as 10,000 or more shares) and then resell the stock to other institutions or individuals. Also, when a firm has a major announcement which is likely to cause its stock price to change sharply, it will ask the exchanges to halt trading in its stock until the announcement has been made and digested by investors. Thus, when Texaco announced that it planned to acquire Getty Oil, trading was halted for one day in both Texaco and Getty stocks.

help clarify exactly what this market is. The exchanges operate as auction markets—buy and sell orders come in more or less simultaneously, and exchange members match these orders. If a stock is traded less frequently, perhaps because it is the stock of a new or a small firm, few buy and sell orders come in, and matching them within a reasonable length of time would be difficult. To avoid this problem, some brokerage firms maintain an inventory of such stocks—they buy when individual investors want to sell and sell when investors want to buy. At one time the inventory of securities was kept in a safe, and the stocks, when bought and sold, were literally passed over the counter.

Today, the over-the-counter market is defined to include all facilities that are needed to conduct security transactions not conducted on the organized exchanges. These facilities consist of (1) the relatively few *dealers* who hold inventories of over-the-counter securities and who are said to "make a market" in these securities, (2) the thousands of brokers who act as *agents* in bringing these dealers together with investors, and (3) the computers, terminals, and electronic networks that provide a communications link between dealers and brokers. The dealers who make a market in a particular stock continuously quote a price at which they are willing to buy the stock (the *bid price*) and a price at which they will sell shares (the *asked price*). Each dealer's prices, which are adjusted as supply and demand conditions change, can be read off computer screens all across the country. The spread between bid and asked prices represents the dealer's markup, or profit.

Brokers and dealers who make up the over-the-counter market are members of a self-regulating body known as the *National Association of Securities Dealers (NASD)*, which licenses brokers and oversees trading practices. The computerized trading network used by NASD is known as the NASD Automated Quotation System (NASDAQ), and *The Wall Street Journal* and other newspapers provide information on NASDAQ transactions.

In terms of numbers of issues, the majority of stocks are traded over-the-counter, and trading volume is greater on NASDAQ stocks than on the NYSE. However, because the stocks of most large companies are listed on the exchanges, about half of the dollar volume of stock trading takes place on the exchanges. In recent years, many large companies, including Microsoft, Intel, MCI, and Apple, have elected to remain NASDAQ stocks, so the over-the-counter market is growing faster than the exchanges.

SOME TRENDS IN SECURITY TRADING PROCEDURES

From the NYSE's inception in 1792 until the 1970s, the vast majority of all stock trading occurred on the Exchange and was conducted by member firms. The NYSE established a set of minimum brokerage commission rates, and no member firm could charge a commission lower than the set rate. This was a monopoly, pure and simple. However, on May 1, 1975, the Securities and Exchange Commission (SEC), with strong prodding from the Antitrust Division of the Justice Department, forced the NYSE to abandon its fixed commissions. Commission rates declined dramatically, falling in some cases as much as 90 percent from former levels.

These changes were a boon to the investing public, but not to the brokerage industry. Several of "full-service" brokerage houses went bankrupt, and others were forced to merge with stronger firms. The number of brokerage houses has declined from literally thousands in the 1960s to a much smaller number of large, strong, nationwide companies, many of which are units of diversified financial service corporations. Deregulation has also spawned a number of "discount brokers," some of which are affiliated with commercial banks or mutual fund investment companies.[3]

There has also been a rise in the so-called "third market," where large financial institutions use computers to trade both listed and unlisted stocks among themselves on a 24-hour basis. Buyers and sellers in this market are located all around the globe — in New York, San Francisco, Tokyo, Singapore, Zurich, and London — and this makes 24-hour trading a necessity. The exchanges have resisted extending their trading hours because it would inconvenience members, but competition will eventually force all major exchanges to operate around the clock. Today, institutional investors, and even some individuals, can trade by computer at any time, day or night.

What are the two basic types of stock markets, and how do they differ?
How has deregulation changed security trading procedures?

SELF-TEST QUESTIONS

THE COST OF MONEY

Capital in a free economy is allocated through the price system. *The interest rate is the price paid to borrow debt capital. In the case of equity capital, investors expect to receive dividends and capital gains, and these are the components which determine the cost of equity money.* The factors which affect the supply of and the demand for investment capital, hence the cost of money, are discussed in this section.

The four most fundamental factors affecting the cost of money are (1) *production opportunities,* (2) *time preferences for consumption,* (3) *risk,* and (4) *inflation.* To see how these factors operate, visualize an isolated island community where the people live on fish. They have a stock of fishing gear which permits them to survive reasonably well, but they would like to have more fish. Now suppose Mr. Crusoe had a bright idea for a new type of fishnet that would enable him to double his daily catch. However, it would take him a year to perfect his design, to build his net, and to learn how to use it efficiently, and Mr. Crusoe would probably starve before he could put his new net into operation. Therefore, he might suggest to Ms. Robinson, Mr. Friday, and several others that if they would give him one fish each day for a year, he would return two fish a day during all of the next year. If someone accepted the offer, then the fish which Ms. Robinson or one of the others gave to Mr. Crusoe would constitute *savings;* these savings would be *invested* in the fishnet; and the extra fish the net produced would constitute a *return on the investment.*

---

[3]"Full-service brokers" give investors information on different stocks and make recommendations as to which stocks to buy. "Discount brokers" generally do not give advice—they merely execute orders, although there has been a growing trend toward providing limited investment advice in recent years. Some brokerage houses (institutional houses) cater primarily to institutional investors such as pension funds and insurance companies, while others cater to individual investors and are called "retail houses." Large firms such as Merrill Lynch generally have both retail and institutional brokerage operations.

Obviously, the more productive Mr. Crusoe thought the new fishnet would be, the higher he would expect the return on his investment to be, and the more he could afford to offer potential investors for their savings. In this example we assume that Mr. Crusoe thought he would be able to pay, and thus he offered, a 100 percent rate of return—he offered to give back two fish for every one he received. He might have tried to attract savings for less—for example, he might have offered only 1.5 fish next year for every one he received this year, which would represent a 50 percent rate of return to Ms. Robinson and the other potential savers.

How attractive Mr. Crusoe's offer appeared to a potential saver would depend in large part on the saver's *time preference for consumption.* For example, Ms. Robinson might be thinking of retirement, and she might be willing to trade fish today for fish in the future on a one-for-one basis. On the other hand, Mr. Friday might have a wife and several young children and need his current fish, so he might be unwilling to "lend" a fish today for anything less than three fish next year. Mr. Friday would be said to have a high time preference for consumption and Ms. Robinson a low time preference. Note also that if the entire population were living right at the subsistence level, time preferences for current consumption would necessarily be high, aggregate savings would be low, interest rates would be high, and capital formation would be difficult.

The *risk* inherent in the fishnet project, and thus in Mr. Crusoe's ability to repay the loan, would also affect the return investors would require: The higher the perceived risk, the higher the required rate of return. Also, in a more complex society there are many businesses like Mr. Crusoe's, many goods other than fish, and many savers like Ms. Robinson and Mr. Friday. Further, people use money as a medium of exchange rather than barter with fish. When money is used, its value in the future, which is affected by *inflation*, comes into play: The higher the expected rate of inflation, the larger the required return.

Thus, we see that the interest rate paid to savers depends in a basic way (1) on the rate of return producers expect to earn on invested capital, (2) on savers' time preferences for current versus future consumption, (3) on the riskiness of the loan, and (4) on the expected future rate of inflation. The rate of return producers expect on their business investments sets an upper limit on how much they can pay for savings, while consumers' time preferences for consumption establish how much consumption they are willing to defer, hence how much they will save at different levels of interest offered by producers.[4] Higher risk and higher inflation also lead to higher interest rates.

What is the price paid to borrow money called?
What do investors expect to get when they supply equity capital?
What four fundamental factors affect the cost of money?

---

[4]The term "producers" is really too narrow. A better word might be "borrowers," which would include corporations, home purchasers, people borrowing to go to college, or even people borrowing to buy autos or to pay for vacations. Also, the wealth of a society and its demographics, influence its people's ability to save and thus their time preferences for current versus future consumption.

INTEREST RATE LEVELS

Capital is allocated among borrowers by interest rates: Firms with the most profitable investment opportunities are willing and able to pay the most for capital, so they tend to attract it away from inefficient firms or from those whose products are not in demand. Of course, our economy is not completely free in the sense of being influenced only by market forces. Thus, the federal government has agencies which help designated individuals or groups obtain credit on favorable terms. Among those eligible for this kind of assistance are small businesses, certain minorities, and firms willing to build plants in areas with high unemployment. Still, most capital in the U.S. economy is allocated through the price system.

Figure 3-2 shows how supply and demand interact to determine interest rates in two capital markets. Markets A and B represent two of the many capital markets in existence. The going interest rate, which can be designated as either k or i, but for purposes of the discussion here is designated as k, is initially 10 percent for the low-risk securities in Market A.[5] Borrowers whose credit is strong enough to qualify for this market can obtain funds at a cost of 10 percent, and investors who want to put their money to work without much risk can obtain a 10 percent return. Riskier borrowers must obtain higher-cost funds in Market B. Investors who are more willing to take risks invest in Market B expecting to earn a 12 percent return but also realizing that they might actually receive much less.

INTEREST RATES AS A FUNCTION OF SUPPLY AND DEMAND FOR FUNDS	FIGURE 3-2

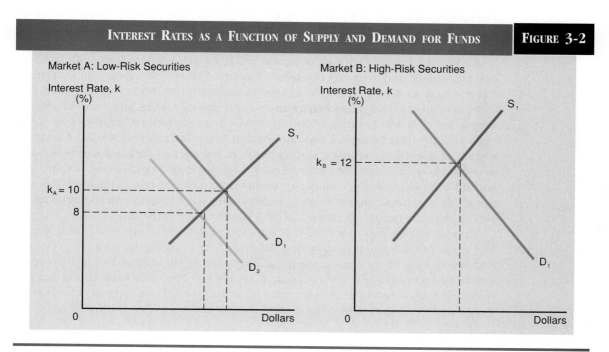

If the demand for funds declines, as it typically does during business recessions, the demand curve will shift to the left, as shown in Curve D_2 in Market A. The market-clearing, or equilibrium, interest rate in this example declines to 8 percent. Similarly, you should be able to visualize what would happen if the Federal Reserve tightened credit: The supply curve, S_1, would shift up, or to the left, and this would raise interest rates and lower the level of borrowing in the economy.

Capital markets are interdependent. For example, if Markets A and B were in equilibrium before the demand shift to D_2 in Market A, this means that investors were willing to accept the higher risk in Market B in exchange for a *risk premium* of $12\% - 10\% = 2\%$. After the shift to D_2, the risk premium would initially increase to $12\% - 8\% = 4\%$. In all likelihood, this much larger premium would induce some of the lenders in Market A to shift to Market B; this, in turn, would cause the supply curve in Market A to shift to the left (or up) and that in Market B to shift to the right. The transfer of capital between markets would raise the interest rate in Market A and lower it in Market B, thus bringing the risk premium back closer to the original level, 2 percent.

There are many capital markets in the United States. U.S. firms also invest and raise capital throughout the world, and foreigners both borrow and lend capital in the United States. There are markets in the United States for home loans; farm loans; business loans; federal, state, and local government loans; and consumer loans. Within each category, there are regional markets as well as different types of submarkets. For example, in real estate there are separate markets for first and second mortgages and for loans on single-family homes, apartments, office buildings, shopping centers, vacant land, and so on. Within the business sector, there are dozens of types of debt and also several different markets for common stocks.

There is a price for each type of capital, and these prices change over time as shifts occur in supply and demand conditions. Figure 3-3 shows how long- and short-term interest rates to business borrowers have varied since the 1950s. Notice that short-term interest rates are especially prone to rise during booms and then fall during recessions. (The shaded areas of the chart indicate recessions.) When the economy is expanding, firms need capital, and this demand for capital pushes rates up. Also, inflationary pressures are strongest during business booms, and that also exerts upward pressure on rates. Conditions are reversed during recessions such as the one in 1991 and 1992. Slack business reduces the demand for credit, the rate of inflation falls, and the result is a drop in interest rates. Furthermore, the Federal Reserve often lowers short-term rates during recessions to help stimulate the economy.

These tendencies do not hold exactly — the period after 1984 is a case in point. The price of oil fell dramatically in 1985 and 1986, reducing inflationary pressures and easing fears of serious long-term inflation. Earlier, these fears had pushed interest rates to record levels. The economy from 1984 to 1987 was fairly strong, but the declining fears about inflation more than offset the normal tendency of interest rates to rise during good economic times, and the net result was lower interest rates.[6]

---

[6]Short-term rates are responsive to current economic conditions, whereas long-term rates primarily reflect long-run expectations for inflation. As a result, short-term rates are sometimes above and sometimes below long-term rates. The relationship between long-term and short-term rates is called the *term structure of interest rates*. This topic is discussed later in the chapter.

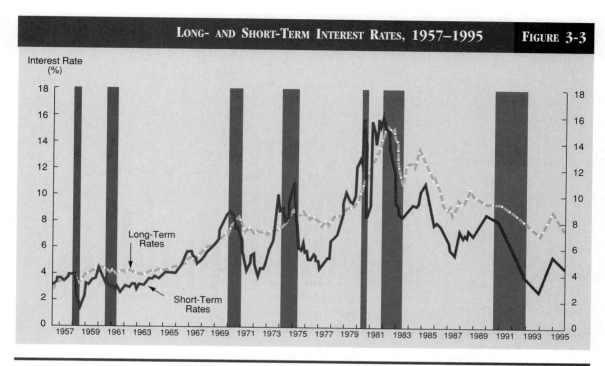

LONG- AND SHORT-TERM INTEREST RATES, 1957–1995   **FIGURE 3-3**

The shaded areas designate business recessions.
Short-term rates are measured by four- to six-month loans to very large, strong corporations, and long-term rates are measured by AAA corporate bonds.
SOURCE: *Federal Reserve Bulletin.*

The relationship between inflation and long-term interest rates is highlighted in Figure 3-4, which plots rates of inflation along with long-term interest rates. Prior to 1965, when the average rate of inflation was about 1 percent, interest rates on AAA-rated bonds generally ranged from 4 to 5 percent. As the war in Vietnam accelerated in the late 1960s, the rate of inflation increased, and interest rates began to rise. The rate of inflation dropped after 1970, and so did long-term interest rates. However, the 1973 Arab oil embargo was followed by a quadrupling of oil prices in 1974, which caused a spurt in inflation which in turn drove interest rates to new highs in 1974 and 1975.

In 1980, inflation rates hit the highest level on record, and fears of continued double-digit inflation pushed interest rates up to historic highs. From 1981 through 1986, the inflation rate dropped sharply, and in 1986 inflation was only 1.1 percent, the lowest level in 25 years.

In recent years, inflation has been running at less than 3 percent a year. However, long-term interest rates have been volatile, because investors are not sure if inflation is truly under control or will jump back to the higher levels of the 1980s. In the years ahead, the level of interest rates will vary with changes in the current rate of inflation and with expectations about future inflation.

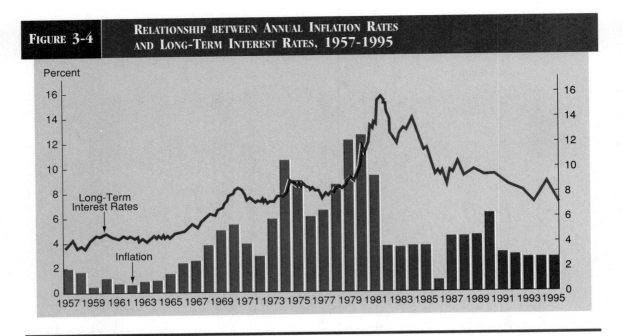

FIGURE 3-4   RELATIONSHIP BETWEEN ANNUAL INFLATION RATES AND LONG-TERM INTEREST RATES, 1957-1995

NOTES:
a. Interest rates are those on AAA long-term corporate bonds.
b. Inflation is measured as the annual rate of change in the Consumer Price Index (CPI).
SOURCE: *Federal Reserve Bulletin.*

SELF-TEST
QUESTIONS

How are interest rates used to allocate capital among firms?

What happens to market-clearing, or equilibrium, interest rates in a capital market when the demand for funds declines? What happens when inflation increases or decreases?

Why does the price of capital change during booms and recessions?

How does risk affect interest rates?

THE DETERMINANTS OF MARKET INTEREST RATES

In general, the quoted (or nominal) interest rate on a debt security, k, is composed of a real risk-free rate of interest, k*, plus several premiums that reflect inflation, the riskiness of the security, and the security's marketability (or liquidity). This relationship can be expressed as follows:

$$\text{Quoted interest rate} = k = k^* + IP + DRP + LP + MRP.$$

3-1

Here

k = the quoted, or nominal, or market, rate of interest on a given security.[7] There are many different securities, hence many different quoted interest rates, that is, different k's.

k^* = the real risk-free rate of interest; k^* is pronounced "k-star," and it is the rate that would exist on a riskless security in a zero inflation world.

IP = inflation premium. IP is equal to the average expected inflation rate over the life of the security.

DRP = default risk premium. This premium reflects the possibility that the issuer will not pay the promised interest or principal on a security. DRP is generally thought to be zero for U.S. Treasury securities, but it rises as the riskiness of issuers increases.

LP = liquidity, or marketability, premium. This is a premium charged by lenders on securities that cannot be converted to cash on short notice at a "reasonable" price. LP is very low for Treasury securities, but it is relatively high on securities issued by very small firms.

MRP = maturity risk premium. As we will explain later, longer-term bonds are exposed to a significant risk of price declines, and a maturity risk premium is charged by lenders to reflect this risk.

If we combine $k^* + IP$ and let this sum equal k_{RF}, then we have this expression:

$$k = k_{RF} + DRP + LP + MRP. \qquad \text{3-2}$$

Here,

k_{RF} = the quoted, or market, rate of interest on riskless securities in a world where inflation exists. This is the quoted interest rate on a security such as a U.S. Treasury bill, which is very liquid and free of most risks. Note that k_{RF} does include a premium for expected inflation, because $k_{RF} = k^* + IP$.

We discuss the components whose sum makes up the quoted, or nominal, rate on a given security in the following sections.

---

[7]The term *nominal* as it is used here means the *stated* rate as opposed to the *real* rate, which is adjusted to remove the effects of inflation. If you bought a 10-year Treasury bond in April 1996, the quoted, or nominal, rate would be about 6.5 percent, but if inflation averages 4 percent over the next 10 years, the real rate would be about $6.5\% - 4\% = 2.5\%$. In Chapter 6 we will use the term nominal in yet another way: to distinguish between quoted rates and effective annual rates when compounding occurs more frequently than once a year.

THE REAL RISK-FREE RATE OF INTEREST, k*

The *real risk-free rate of interest, k**, is defined as the interest rate that would exist on a riskless security in an inflation-free world. The real risk-free rate is not static — it changes over time depending on economic conditions, especially (1) on the rate of return corporations and other borrowers can expect to earn on productive assets and (2) on people's time preferences for current versus future consumption. Borrowers' expected returns on real assets set an upper limit on how much they can afford to pay for borrowed funds, while savers' time preferences for consumption establish how much consumption they are willing to defer, hence the amount of funds they will lend at different levels of interest. It is difficult to measure the real risk-free rate precisely, but most experts think that in the United States k* has fluctuated in the range of 1 to 4 percent in recent years.

THE NOMINAL, OR QUOTED, RISK-FREE RATE OF INTEREST, k_RF

The *nominal*, or *quoted, risk–free rate, k_RF*, is the real risk-free rate plus a premium for expected inflation: $k_{RF} = k^* + IP$. To be strictly correct, the risk-free rate should mean the interest rate on a totally risk-free security — one that has no risk of default, no maturity risk, no liquidity risk, and no risk of loss if inflation increases. There is no such security, hence there is no observable truly risk-free rate. However, there is one security that is free of most risks — a U.S. Treasury bill (T-bill), which is a short-term security issued by the U.S. government. Treasury bonds (T-bonds), which are longer-term government securities, are free of default and liquidity risks, but T-bonds are exposed to some risk due to changes in the general level of interest rates.

If the term "risk-free rate" is used without either the modifier "real" or the modifier "nominal," people generally mean the quoted (nominal) rate, and we will follow that convention in this book. Therefore, when we use the term "risk-free rate" or the symbol "k_RF," we mean the nominal risk-free rate, which includes an inflation premium equal to the average expected inflation rate over the life of the security. In general, we use the T-bill rate to approximate the short-term risk-free rate, and the T-bond rate to approximate the long-term risk-free rate. So, whenever you see the term "risk-free rate," assume that we are referring either to the quoted U.S. T-bill rate or to the quoted T-bond rate.

INFLATION PREMIUM (IP)

Inflation has a major impact on interest rates because it erodes the purchasing power of the dollar and lowers the real rate of return on investments. To illustrate, suppose you invested $1,000 in a Treasury bill that matures in 1 year and will pay 5 percent interest. At the end of the year you will receive $1,050 — your original $1,000 plus $50 of interest. Now suppose the inflation rate during the year is 10 percent, and it affects all items equally. If beer was $1 per bottle at the beginning of the year, it would cost $1.10 at the end of the year. Therefore, your $1,000 would have bought $1,000/$1 = 1,000 bottles at the beginning of the year but only $1,050/$1.10 = 955 bottles at the end. Thus, in *real terms*, you would be worse off — you would receive $50 of interest, but it would not be sufficient to offset inflation. You would thus be better off buying 1,000 bottles of beer (or some other storable asset such as land, timber, apartment buildings, wheat, or gold) than buying the Treasury bill.

Investors are well aware of all this, so when they lend money, they build in an *inflation premium (IP)* equal to the expected inflation rate over the life of the security. As discussed previously, for a short-term, default-free U.S. Treasury bill, the actual interest rate charged, k_{T-bill}, would be the real risk-free rate, k^*, plus the inflation premium (IP):

$$k_{T-bill} = k_{RF} = k^* + IP.$$

Therefore, if the real risk-free rate of interest were $k^* = 3\%$, and if inflation were expected to be 4 percent (hence $IP = 4\%$) during the next year, then the quoted rate of interest on 1-year T-bills would be 7 percent. In April 1996, the expected 1-year inflation rate was about 3 percent, and the yield on 1-year T-bills was about 5.5 percent. This implies that the real risk-free rate on short-term securities at that time was about 2.5 percent.

The rate of inflation built into interest rates is the *rate of inflation expected in the future*, not the rate experienced in the past. Thus, the latest reported figures might show an annual inflation rate of 3 percent, but that is for a past period. If people on average expect a 6 percent inflation rate in the future, then 6 percent would be built into the current rate of interest. Note also that the inflation rate reflected in the quoted interest rate on any security is the *average rate of inflation expected over the security's life*. Thus, the inflation rate built into a 1-year bond is the expected inflation rate for the next year, but the inflation rate built into a 30-year bond is the average rate of inflation expected over the next 30 years.[8]

Expectations for future inflation are closely, but not perfectly, correlated with rates experienced in the recent past. Therefore, if the inflation rate reported for last month increased, people would tend to raise their expectations for future inflation, and this change in expectations would cause an increase in interest rates.

DEFAULT RISK PREMIUM (DRP)

The risk that a borrower will *default* on a loan, which means to not pay the promised interest or principal, also affects the market interest rate on a security: The greater the default risk, the higher the interest rate lenders charge. Treasury securities have no default risk; thus, they carry the lowest interest rates on taxable securities in the United States. For corporate bonds, the higher the bond's rating, the

---

[8]To be theoretically precise, we should use a *geometric average*. Also, because millions of investors are active in the market, it is impossible to determine exactly the consensus expected inflation rate. Survey data are available, however, which give us a reasonably good idea of what investors expect over the next few years. For example, in 1980 the University of Michigan's Survey Research Center reported that people expected inflation during the next year to be 11.9 percent and that the average rate of inflation expected over the next 5 to 10 years was 10.5 percent. Those expectations led to record-high interest rates. However, the economy cooled in 1981 and 1982, and, as Figure 3-4 showed, actual inflation dropped sharply after 1980. This led to gradual reductions in the *expected future* inflation rate. In 1996, as we write this, the expected future inflation rate is about 3 percent. As inflationary expectations dropped, so did quoted market rates of interest.

lower its default risk, and, consequently, the lower its interest rate.[9] Here are some representative interest rates on long-term bonds during April 1996:

	RATE	DRP
U.S. Treasury	6.9%	—
AAA	7.6	0.7%
AA	7.9	1.0
A	8.2	1.3

The difference between the quoted interest rate on a T-bond and that on a corporate bond with similar maturity, liquidity, and other features is the *default risk premium (DRP)*. Therefore, if the bonds listed above were otherwise similar, the default risk premium would be DRP = 7.6% − 6.9% = 0.7 percentage points for AAA corporate bonds, 7.9% − 6.9% = 1.0 percentage point for AA, and 8.2% − 6.9% = 1.3 percentage points for A corporate bonds. Default risk premiums vary somewhat over time, but the April 1996 figures are representative of levels in recent years.

LIQUIDITY PREMIUM (LP)

Liquidity is defined as the ability to convert an asset to cash quickly at a "fair market value." Thus, a liquid security is highly marketable, and a large dollar amount of the security can be offered for sale without depressing its price. Assets have varying degrees of liquidity, depending on the characteristics of the market in which they are traded. For instance, there exist very active and easily accessible secondary markets for financial assets such as government notes and bonds, and for the stocks and bonds of large corporations, but the markets for real estate are illiquid because it takes time to ascertain the value of a piece of property and to locate a suitable buyer. Therefore, most financial assets are considered more liquid than real assets. Of course, the most liquid asset of all is cash, and the more easily an asset can be converted to cash at a "fair market value," the more liquid it is. Because liquidity is important, investors evaluate liquidity and include *liquidity premiums (LPs)* when market rates of securities are established.

Although it is very difficult to accurately measure liquidity premiums, a differential of at least two and probably four or five percentage points exists between the least liquid and the most liquid financial assets with similar default risk and maturity.

MATURITY RISK PREMIUM (MRP)

U.S. Treasury securities are free of default risk in the sense that one can be virtually certain that the federal government will pay interest on its bonds and will also pay them off when they mature. Therefore, the default risk premium on Treasury securities is essentially zero. Further, active markets exist for Treasury securities, so their

---

[9]Bond ratings, and bonds' riskiness in general, will be discussed in detail in Chapter 17. For now, merely note that bonds rated AAA are judged to have less default risk than bonds rated AA, AA bonds are less risky than A bonds, and so on. Ratings are designated AAA or Aaa, AA or Aa, and so forth, depending on the rating agency. In this book, the designations are used interchangeably.

Note also that in 1996 an argument between the Republican Congress and the Democratic White House threatened to cause a default. That intragovernment fight led to a small, hopefully temporary, default premium on Treasury bonds.

liquidity premiums are also close to zero. Thus, as a first approximation, the rate of interest on a Treasury bond should be the risk-free rate, k_{RF}, which is equal to the real risk-free rate, k^*, plus an inflation premium, IP. However, an adjustment is needed for long-term Treasury bonds. The prices of long-term bonds decline sharply whenever interest rates rise, and since interest rates can and do rise, all long-term bonds, even Treasury bonds, have an element of risk called *interest rate risk*. As a general rule, the bonds of any organization, from the U.S. government to Continental Airlines, have more interest rate risk the longer the maturity of the bond.[10] Therefore, a *maturity risk premium (MRP)*, which is higher the longer the years to maturity, must be included in the required interest rate.

The effect of maturity risk premiums is to raise interest rates on long-term bonds relative to those on short-term bonds. This premium, like the others, is extremely difficult to measure, but (1) it seems to vary over time, rising when interest rates are more volatile and uncertain, then falling when interest rates are more stable, and (2) in recent years, the maturity risk premium on 30-year T-bonds appears to have generally been in the range of one or two percentage points.[11]

We should mention that although long-term bonds are heavily exposed to interest rate risk, short-term bills are heavily exposed to *reinvestment rate risk*. When short-term bills mature and the funds are reinvested, or "rolled over," a decline in interest rates would necessitate reinvestment at a lower rate, hence would lead to a decline in interest income. To illustrate, suppose you had $100,000 invested in 1-year T-bills, and you lived on the income. In 1981, short-term rates were about 15 percent, so your income would have been about $15,000. However, your income would have declined to about $5,200 by 1996. Had you invested your money in long-term T-bonds, your income (but not the value of the principal) would have been stable.[12] Thus, although "investing short" preserves one's principal, the interest income provided by short-term T-bills varies from year to year, depending on reinvestment rates.

Write out an equation for the nominal interest rate on any debt security. Distinguish between the *real* risk-free rate of interest, k^*, and the *nominal*, or *quoted*, or *market*, risk-free rate of interest, k_{RF}.

SELF-TEST QUESTIONS

---

[10]For example, if someone had bought a 30-year Treasury bond for $1,000 in 1972, when the long-term interest rate was 7 percent, and held it until 1981, when long-term T-bond rates were about 14.5 percent, the value of the bond would have declined to about $514. That would represent a loss of almost half the investment, and it demonstrates that long-term bonds, even U.S. Treasury bonds, are not riskless. However, had the investor purchased short-term T-bills in 1972 and subsequently reinvested the principal each time the bills matured, he or she would still have had $1,000 in 1981, in spite of the rise in interest rates. This point will be discussed in detail in Chapter 7.

[11]The MRP has averaged 1.4 percentage points over the last 70 years. See *Stocks, Bonds, Bills, and Inflation: 1996 Yearbook* (Chicago: Ibbotson Associates, 1996).

[12]Long-term bonds also have some reinvestment rate risk. To actually earn the quoted rate on a long-term bond, the interest payments must be reinvested at the quoted rate. However, if interest rates fall, the interest payments must be reinvested at a lower rate; thus, the realized return would be less than the quoted rate. Note, though, that the reinvestment rate risk is lower on a long-term bond than on a short-term bill because only the interest payments (rather than interest plus principal) on the long-term bond are exposed to reinvestment rate risk. Only zero coupon bonds, discussed in Chapters 7 and 17, are completely free of reinvestment rate risk.

How is inflation taken into account when interest rates are determined by investors in the financial markets?

Does the interest rate on a T-bond include a default risk premium? Explain.

Distinguish between liquid and illiquid assets, and identify some assets that are liquid and some that are illiquid.

Briefly explain the following statement: "Although long-term bonds are heavily exposed to interest rate risk, short-term bills are heavily exposed to reinvestment rate risk."

THE TERM STRUCTURE OF INTEREST RATES

A study of Figure 3-3 reveals that at certain times such as 1996, short-term interest rates were lower than long-term rates, whereas at other times such as 1980, short-term rates were higher than long-term rates. The relationship between long- and short-term rates, which is known as the *term structure of interest rates*, is important to corporate treasurers, who must decide whether to borrow by issuing long- or short-term debt, and to investors, who must decide whether to buy long- or short-term bonds. Thus, it is important to understand (1) how long- and short-term rates are related to each other and (2) what causes shifts in their relative positions.

To begin, we can find in a source such as *The Wall Street Journal* or the *Federal Reserve Bulletin* the interest rates on Treasury bonds of various maturities at a given point in time. For example, the tabular section of Figure 3-5 presents interest rates for different maturities on two dates. The set of data for a given date, when plotted on a graph such as that in Figure 3-5, is called the *yield curve* for that date. The yield curve changes both in position and in slope over time. In March 1980, all rates were relatively high, and short-term rates were higher than long-term rates, so the yield curve on that date was *downward sloping*. However, in April 1996, all rates had fallen, and short-term rates were lower than long-term rates, so the yield curve in 1996 was *upward sloping*. Had we drawn the yield curve during January 1982, it would have been essentially horizontal, because long-term and short-term bonds on that date had about the same rate of interest. (See Figure 3-3.)

Figure 3-5 shows yield curves for U.S. Treasury securities, but we could have constructed them for corporate bonds; for example, we could have developed yield curves for Exxon, General Motors, Continental Airlines, or any other company that borrows money over a range of maturities. Had we constructed such curves and plotted them on Figure 3-5, the corporate yield curves would have been above those for Treasury securities on the same date because the corporate yields would include default risk premiums, but they would have had the same general shape as the Treasury curves. Also, the riskier the corporation, the higher its yield curve; thus Continental, which is in a relatively weak financial position, would have had a yield curve substantially higher than that of Exxon, which is rated AAA.

Historically, in most years long-term rates have been above short-term rates, so usually the yield curve is upward sloping. For this reason, people often call an upward-sloping yield curve a *"normal"* *yield curve* and a yield curve which slopes downward an *inverted*, or *"abnormal,"* *yield curve*. Thus, in Figure 3-5 the yield curve for March 1980 was inverted, but the one for April 1996 was normal. We

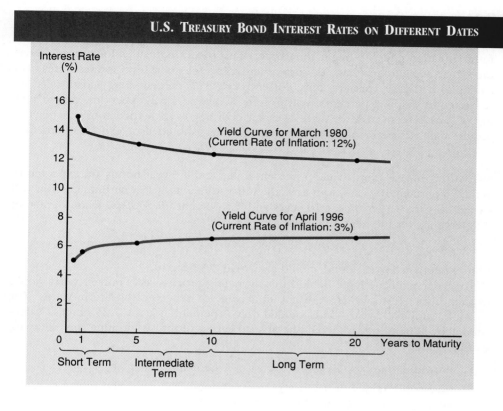

U.S. TREASURY BOND INTEREST RATES ON DIFFERENT DATES   FIGURE 3-5

| TERM TO MATURITY | INTEREST RATE | |
	MARCH 1980	APRIL 1996
6 months	15.0%	5.2%
1 year	14.0	5.6
5 years	13.5	6.3
10 years	12.8	6.6
20 years	12.5	6.8

explain in the next section why an upward slope is the normal situation, but briefly, the reason is that short-term securities have less interest rate risk than longer-term securities, hence short-term rates are normally lower than long-term rates.

TERM STRUCTURE THEORIES

Several theories have been proposed to explain the shape of the yield curve. The three major ones are (1) the expectations theory, (2) the liquidity preference theory, and (3) the market segmentation theory.

EXPECTATIONS THEORY

The *expectations theory* states that the yield curve depends on expectations about future inflation rates. To begin, the expectations theory notes that long-term interest rates are a weighted average of current and expected short-term interest rates. For example, if 1-year Treasury bills currently yield 7 percent and 1-year bills are expected to yield 7.5 percent a year from now, investors will expect to earn an average of 7.25 percent over the next 2 years. According to the expectations theory, this implies that a 2-year Treasury note purchased today should also yield 7.25 percent:[13]

$$(7\% + 7.5\%)/2 = 7.25\%.$$

Similarly, if 10-year bonds yield 9 percent today, and if 5-year bonds are expected to yield 7.5 percent 10 years from now, then investors with a 15-year time horizon will expect to earn 9 percent for 10 years and 7.5 percent for 5 years, or an average of 8.5 percent over the next 15 years:

$$[(10)(9\%) + (5)(7.5\%)]/15 = 8.5\%.$$

Consequently, a 15-year bond should also yield 8.5 percent.

To understand the logic behind this averaging process, ask yourself what would happen if long-term yields were not an average of expected short-term yields. For example, suppose 2-year bonds yielded only 7 percent, not the 7.25 percent calculated above. Bond traders would be able to earn a profit by adopting the following trading strategy:

1. Borrow money for 2 years at a cost of 7 percent.

2. Invest the money in a series of 1-year bonds. The expected return over the 2-year period would be $(7.0 + 7.5)/2 = 7.25\%$.

In this case, bond traders would rush to borrow money (demand funds) in the 2-year market and invest (or supply funds) in the 1-year market. Recall from Figure 3-2 that an increase in the demand for funds raises interest rates, whereas an increase in the supply of funds reduces interest rates. Therefore, bond traders' actions would push up the 2-year yield but reduce the yield on 1-year bonds. The net effect

---

[13]Technically, we should be using geometric averages rather than arithmetic averages, but the differences are not material in this example. To illustrate, if the 1-year T-bill rate is 7 percent in 1997 and 7.5 percent in 1998, the geometric average 2-year Treasury note rate is

$$[(1.07)(1.075)]^{1/2} - 1.0 = 0.0725 = 7.25\%,$$

which in this example equals the 7.25 percent arithmetic average. Note, however, that the differences between arithmetic and geometric averages are significant when interest rates run in double digits.

In general, the geometric average inflation rate is found as

$$[(1 + I_1)(1 + I_2) \ldots (1 + I_t) \ldots (1 + I_n)]^{1/n} - 1.0,$$

where I_t is the expected inflation rate in Year t and n is the number of years in the geometric average. For a discussion of this point, see Robert C. Radcliffe, *Investment: Concepts, Analysis, and Strategy*, 4th ed. (Glenview, Ill.: Scott, Foresman, 1993), Chapter 6.

would be to bring about a market equilibrium in which the 2-year rate was a weighted average of expected 1-year rates.

The pure expectations theory assumes that investors establish bond prices and interest rates strictly on the basis of expectations for inflation. This means that they are indifferent with respect to maturity in the sense that they do not view long-term bonds as being riskier than short-term bonds. Therefore, according to the pure expectations theory, the maturity risk premium (MRP) is equal to zero.

Expressed as an equation, according to the pure expectations theory, k_t, the nominal interest rate on a U.S. Treasury bond that matures in t years, would be found as follows:

$$k_t = k^* + IP_t.$$

Here k^* is the real risk-free rate and IP_t is an inflation premium found as the average inflation rate over t years until the bond matures. The real risk-free rate tends to be fairly constant over time; therefore, changes in Treasury interest rates are driven largely by changes in expected inflation. As noted above, under the pure expectations theory, the MRP is assumed to be zero, and for Treasury securities, the default risk premium (DRP) and liquidity premium (LP) are also zero.

To illustrate the pure expectations theory, suppose that in late December 1996 the real risk-free rate of interest was $k^* = 3\%$ and expected inflation rates for the next 3 years were as follows:

	EXPECTED ANNUAL (1-YEAR) INFLATION RATE	EXPECTED AVERAGE INFLATION RATE FROM 1996 TO INDICATED YEAR
1997	3%	3%/1 = 3.0%
1998	5%	(3% + 5%)/2 = 4.0%
1999	7%	(3% + 5% + 7%)/3 = 5.0%

Given these expectations, the following pattern of interest rates should exist:

	REAL RISK-FREE RATE (k*)		INFLATION PREMIUM, WHICH IS EQUAL TO THE AVERAGE EXPECTED INFLATION RATE (IP_t)		NOMINAL TREASURY BOND RATE FOR EACH MATURITY (k_T-BOND)
1-year bond	3%	+	3.0%	=	6.0%
2-year bond	3%	+	4.0%	=	7.0%
3-year bond	3%	+	5.0%	=	8.0%

Had the pattern of expected inflation rates been reversed, with inflation expected to fall from 7 percent to 5 percent and then to 3 percent, the following situation would have existed:

	REAL RISK-FREE RATE		AVERAGE EXPECTED INFLATION RATE		TREASURY BOND RATE FOR EACH MATURITY
1-year bond	3%	+	7.0%	=	10.0%
2-year bond	3%	+	6.0%	=	9.0%
3-year bond	3%	+	5.0%	=	8.0%

These hypothetical data are plotted in Figure 3-6.

FIGURE 3-6	HYPOTHETICAL EXAMPLE OF THE TERM STRUCTURE OF INTEREST RATES

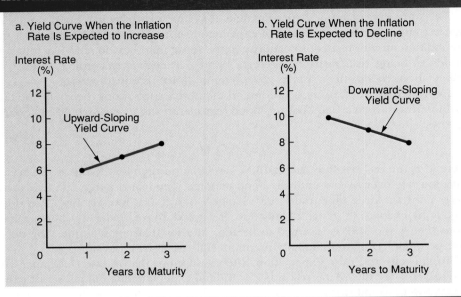

According to the pure expectations theory, an upward-sloping yield curve implies that interest rates are expected to increase in the future. This increase could be due to an increase in expected inflation (as is the case in the example above) or to an increase in the expected real risk-free rate. By contrast, a downward-sloping yield curve would suggest that interest rates are expected to decline.

In practice, we can never actually observe the marginal investor's expected inflation rate or real risk-free rate. However, if the pure expectations theory were correct, we could "back out" of yield curve data the bond market's best guess about future interest rates. If, for example, you observe that Treasury securities with 1- and 2-year maturities yield 7 percent and 8 percent, respectively, this information can be used to back out the market's forecast of what 1-year rates will yield one year from now. If the pure expectations theory is correct, the rate on 2-year bonds is the average of the current 1-year rate and the 1-year rate expected one year from now. Since the current 1-year rate is 7 percent, this implies that the 1-year rate one year from now is expected to be 9 percent:

$$\text{2-year yield} = 8\% = \frac{7\% + X\%}{2}$$

$$X = 9\% = \text{1-year yield expected next year.}$$

LIQUIDITY PREFERENCE THEORY

The pure expectations theory assumes that the maturity risk premium (MRP) is zero. However, convincing evidence suggests that there is a positive maturity risk premium; that is, investors require higher rates of return on longer-term bonds, other things held constant.

This has given rise to the *liquidity preference theory*, which states that long-term bonds normally yield more than short-term bonds for two reasons: (1) Investors generally prefer to hold short-term securities because such securities are more liquid in the sense that they can be converted to cash with little danger of loss of principal. Investors will, therefore, generally accept lower yields on short-term securities, and this leads to relatively low short-term rates. (2) Borrowers, on the other hand, generally prefer long-term debt because short-term debt exposes them to the risk of having to repay the debt under adverse conditions. Accordingly, borrowers are willing to pay a higher rate, other things held constant, for long-term funds than for short-term funds, and this also leads to relatively low short-term rates. Thus, lender and borrower preferences both operate to cause short-term rates to be lower than long-term rates. Taken together, these two sets of preferences imply that under normal conditions, a positive maturity risk premium (MRP) exists, and the MRP increases with years to maturity, causing the yield curve to be upward sloping.

MARKET SEGMENTATION THEORY

The expectation theory is based on the assumption that investors have no maturity preferences. However, empirical studies suggest that different lenders and borrowers have different preferred maturities. For example, a person borrowing to buy a long-term asset such as a house, or an electric utility borrowing to build a power plant, would want a long-term loan. However, a retailer borrowing in September to build inventories for Christmas would prefer a short-term loan. Similar differences exist among savers — for example, a person saving for a vacation next summer would want to lend in the short-term market, but someone saving for retirement 30 years hence might prefer long-term securities.

This thinking led to the *market segmentation theory*, which states that the slope of the yield curve depends on supply/demand conditions in the long-term and short-term markets. Thus, according to this theory, the yield curve could at any given time be either flat, upward sloping, or downward sloping. An upward-sloping yield curve would occur if there were a large supply of short-term funds relative to demand, but a shortage of long-term funds. Similarly, a downward-sloping curve would indicate relatively strong demand by borrowers in the short-term market compared with that in the long-term market. A flat curve would indicate balance between the two markets.

Various tests of the term structure theories have been conducted. While these tests indicate that all three theories have some validity, they also indicate that in recent years inflation, hence the expectations theory, has had the strongest influence. Thus, while the shape of the yield curve at any given time is affected (1) by supply/demand conditions in long- and short-term markets, (2) by liquidity preferences, and (3) by expectations about future inflation, the last factor generally dominates.

Self-Test
Questions
What is a yield curve, and what information would you need to draw this curve?

Discuss each of the following theories: (1) expectations theory, (2) liquidity preference theory, and (3) market segmentation theory.

Distinguish between the shapes of a "normal" yield curve and an "abnormal" yield curve, and explain when each might exist.

Factors That Influence Supply/Demand Conditions

As stated earlier, supply/demand conditions are a primary determinant of the yield curve. The four most important factors that influence the supply and demand for money are (1) Federal Reserve policy, (2) the level of the federal budget deficit, (3) the foreign trade balance, and (4) the level of business activity.

Federal Reserve Policy

As you probably learned in your economics courses, (1) the money supply has a major effect on both the level of economic activity and the rate of inflation, and (2) in the United States, the Federal Reserve Board controls the money supply. If the Fed wants to stimulate the economy, as it did in 1995, it increases growth in the money supply. The initial effect of such an action is to cause interest rates to decline. However, a larger money supply may also lead to an increase in the expected rate of inflation, which, in turn, could push interest rates up. The reverse holds if the Fed tightens the money supply.

To illustrate, in 1981 inflation was quite high, so the Fed tightened up the money supply. The Fed deals primarily in the short-term end of the market, so this tightening had the direct effect of pushing short-term interest rates up sharply. At the same time, the very fact that the Fed was taking strong action to reduce inflation led to a decline in expectations for long-run inflation, which led to a drop in long-term bond yields. That situation produced a downward sloping yield curve.

In 1991, the situation was just the reverse. To combat the recession, the Fed took steps to reduce interest rates. Short-term rates first fell, and later long-term rates also dropped, but not as sharply. These lower rates benefitted heavily indebted businesses and individual borrowers, and home mortgage refinancings put additional billions of dollars into consumers' pockets. Savers, of course, lost out, but the net effect was a benefit to the economy. Lower rates also encouraged businesses to borrow for investment, gave new life to the housing market, and brought down the value of the dollar relative to other currencies, which helped U.S. exporters and lowered the trade deficit.

Federal Deficits

If the federal government spends more than it takes in from tax revenues, it runs a deficit, and that deficit must be covered either by borrowing or by printing money (increasing the money supply). If the government borrows, this added demand for funds pushes up interest rates. If it prints money, this increases expectations for future inflation, which also drives up interest rates. Thus, the larger the federal deficit, other things held constant, the higher the level of interest rates. Whether long- or short-term rates are more affected depends on how the deficit is financed, so we cannot state, in general, how deficits will affect the slope of the yield curve.

FOREIGN TRADE BALANCE

Businesses and individuals in the United States buy from and sell to people and firms in other countries. If we buy more than we sell (that is, if we import more than we export), we are said to be running a *foreign trade deficit*. When trade deficits occur, they must be financed, and the main source of financing is debt. In other words, if we import $200 billion of goods but export only $100 billion, we run a trade deficit of $100 billion, and we must borrow the $100 billion.[14] Therefore, the larger our trade deficit, the more we must borrow, and as we increase our borrowing, this drives up interest rates. Also, foreigners are willing to hold U.S. debt if and only if the interest rate on this debt is competitive with interest rates in other countries. Therefore, if the Federal Reserve attempts to lower interest rates in the United States, causing our rates to fall below rates abroad, then foreigners will sell U.S. bonds, those sales will depress bond prices, and the result will be higher U.S. rates. Thus, the existence of a deficit trade balance hinders the Fed's ability to combat a recession by lowering interest rates.

The United States has been running annual trade deficits since the mid-1970s, and the cumulative effect of these deficits is that the United States is by far the largest debtor nation of all time. As a result, our interest rates are very much influenced by interest rate trends in other countries around the world (higher rates abroad lead to higher U.S. rates). Because of all this, U.S. corporate treasurers — and anyone else who is affected by interest rates — must keep up with developments in the world economy.

BUSINESS ACTIVITY

Figure 3-3, presented earlier, can be examined to see how business conditions influence interest rates. Here are the key points revealed by the graph:

1. Because inflation increased from 1955 to 1981, the general tendency during that period was toward higher interest rates. However, since the 1981 peak, the trend has generally been downward.

2. Until 1966, short-term rates were almost always below long-term rates. Thus, in those years the yield curve was almost always "normal" in the sense that it was upward sloping.

3. The shaded areas in the graph represent recessions, during which both the demand for money and the rate of inflation tend to fall, and, at the same time, the Federal Reserve tends to increase the money supply in an effort to stimulate the economy. As a result, there is a tendency for interest rates to decline during recessions. Currently, in April 1996, we are in a period of relatively stable, but slow, growth. The Fed is reluctant to lower interest rates because it is

---

[14]The deficit could also be financed by selling assets, including gold, corporate stocks, entire companies, and real estate. The United States has financed its massive trade deficits by all of these means in recent years, but the primary method has been by borrowing.

afraid that action would speed up the economy too much and lead to higher inflation. At the same time, the Fed does not want to raise rates, because that might drive the economy into a recession. Therefore, interest rates are currently relatively stable.

4. During recessions, short-term rates decline more sharply than long-term rates. This occurs because (1) the Fed operates mainly in the short-term sector, so its intervention has the strongest effect there, and (2) long-term rates reflect the average expected inflation rate over the next 20 to 30 years, and this expectation generally does not change much, even when the current rate of inflation is low because of a recession. So, short-term rates are more volatile than long-term rates.

SELF-TEST
QUESTIONS

Name four factors which influence supply/demand conditions, hence interest rates, and explain their effects.

How does the Fed stimulate the economy? How does the Fed affect interest rates?

INTEREST RATE LEVELS AND STOCK PRICES

Interest rates have two effects on corporate profits: (1) First, because interest is a cost, the higher the rate of interest, the lower are firms' profits, other things held constant. (2) Second, interest rates affect the level of economic activity, and economic activity affects corporate profits. Interest rates obviously affect stock prices because of their effects on profits, but perhaps even more important, they have an effect due to competition in the marketplace between stocks and bonds. If interest rates rise sharply, investors can get higher returns in the bond market, which induces them to sell stocks and to transfer funds from the stock market to the bond market, which obviously depresses stock prices. Of course, the reverse occurs if interest rates decline. Indeed, the bull market of December 1991, when the Dow Jones Industrial Index rose 10 percent in less than a month, was caused almost entirely by a sharp drop in long-term interest rates.

The experience of Kansas City Power, the electric utility serving western Missouri and eastern Kansas, can be used to illustrate the effects of interest rates on stock prices. In 1983 the firm's stock sold for $9.50 per share, and, since the firm paid a $1.17 dividend, the dividend yield was $1.17/$9.50 = 12.3%. Kansas City Power's bonds at the time yielded about the same amount. Thus, if someone had saved $100,000 and invested it in either the stock or the bonds, his or her annual income would have been about $12,300. (The investor might also have expected the stock price to grow over time, providing some capital gains, but that point is not relevant to this example.)

By 1996, interest rates were lower, and Kansas City Power's bonds were yielding only 8 percent. If the stock still yielded 12.3 percent, investors would be much more inclined to invest in the stock than in the bonds. Thus, investment money would flow into the stock rather than the bonds, and the stock price would be bid up. Indeed, this is exactly what happened, and Kansas City Power's stock sold for $25 in early 1996. In all, the stock price rose 163 percent over the period, while the firm's dividend increased from $1.17 to $1.56, or by 33 percent. Thus, the major factor in the stock price rise was not the growth in dividends but rather the fact that interest rates had fallen. The $25 stock price produced a dividend yield of $1.56/$25 = 6.2%, which was in line with the firm's current bond yield and, hence, with interest rates in general.

In what two ways do changes in interest rates affect stock prices?

SELF-TEST QUESTION

INTEREST RATES AND BUSINESS DECISIONS

The yield curve for April 1996, shown earlier in Figure 3-5, indicates how much the U.S. government had to pay in 1996 to borrow money for 1 year, 5 years, 10 years, and so on. A business borrower would have had to pay somewhat more, but assume for the moment that we are back in April 1996 and that the yield curve for that year also applies to your company. Now suppose your company has decided (1) to build a new plant with a 20-year life which will cost $1 million and (2) to raise the $1 million by selling an issue of debt (or borrowing) rather than by selling stock. If you borrowed in 1996 on a short-term basis — say, for one year — your interest cost for that year would be only 5.6 percent, or $56,000, whereas if you used long-term (20-year) financing, your cost would be 6.8 percent, or $68,000. Therefore, at first glance, it would seem that you should use short-term debt.

However, this could prove to be a horrible mistake. If you use short-term debt, you will have to renew your loan every year, and the rate charged on each new loan will reflect the then current short-term rate. Interest rates could return to their March 1980 levels, in which case you would be paying 14 percent, or $140,000, per year. These high interest payments would cut into, and perhaps eliminate, your profits. Your reduced profitability could easily increase your firm's risk to the point where its bond rating would be lowered, causing lenders to increase the risk premium built into the interest rates they charge. That would force you to pay even higher rates, which would further reduce your profitability, worrying lenders even more, and making them reluctant to renew your loan. If your lenders refused to renew the loan and demanded payment, as they have every right to do, you might have to sell assets at a loss, which could lead to bankruptcy.

On the other hand, if you used long-term financing in 1996, your interest costs would remain constant at $68,000 per year, so an increase in interest rates in the economy would not hurt you. You might even be able to buy up some of your bankrupt competitors at bargain prices — bankruptcies increase dramatically when interest rates rise, primarily because many firms do use short-term debt.

Does all this suggest that firms should always avoid short-term debt? Not necessarily. If inflation falls in the next few years, so will interest rates. If you had borrowed on a long-term basis for 6.8 percent in April 1996, your company would be at a major disadvantage if it locked in a 6.8 percent cost while its competitors (who used short-term debt in 1996 and thus rode interest rates down in subsequent years) had a borrowing cost of only 3 or 4 percent.

Financing decisions would be easy if we could develop accurate forecasts of future interest rates. Unfortunately, predicting future interest rates with consistent accuracy is somewhere between difficult and impossible — people who make a living by selling interest rate forecasts say it is difficult, but many others say it is impossible.

Even if it is difficult to predict future interest rate *levels*, it is easy to predict that interest rates will *fluctuate*—they always have, and they always will. This being the case, sound financial policy calls for using a mix of long- and short-term debt, as well as equity, to position the firm so that it can survive in any interest rate environment. Further, the optimal financial policy depends in an important way on the nature of the firm's assets—the easier it is to sell off assets and thus to pay off debts, the more feasible it is to use large amounts of short-term debt. This makes it more feasible to finance current assets than fixed assets with short-term debt. We will return to this issue later in the book, when we discuss working capital policy.

Changes in interest rates have implications for savers as well as borrowers. For example, if you had a 401(k) plan—and someday you will—you would probably want to invest some of your money in a bond mutual fund. You could choose a fund that had an average maturity of 25 years, 20 years, and so on, down to only a few months (a money market fund). How would your choice affect your investment results, hence your retirement income? First, the annual interest income earned by the plan would be affected. For example, if the yield curve were upward sloping, as it normally is, you would earn more interest if you chose a fund that held long-term bonds. Note, though, that if you chose a long-term fund and interest rates then rose, the market value of the bonds in the fund would decline. For example, as we will see in Chapter 7, if you had $100,000 in a fund whose average bond had a maturity of 25 years and a coupon rate of 6 percent, and if interest rates then rose from 6 percent to 10 percent, the market value of your fund would decline from $100,000 to about $64,000. Of course, if rates declined, your fund would increase in the value. In any event, your choice of maturity would have a material effect on your investment performance, hence your future income.

SELF-TEST QUESTIONS

If short-term interest rates are lower than long-term rates, why might a firm still choose to finance with long-term debt?

Explain the following statement: "The optimal financial policy depends in an important way on the nature of the firm's assets."

THE FEDERAL INCOME TAX SYSTEM

The value of any financial asset, including stocks, bonds, and mortgages, as well as most real assets such as plants or even entire firms, depends on the stream of cash flows produced by the asset. Cash flows from an asset consist of *usable* income plus depreciation, and usable income means income *after taxes*.

Our tax laws can be changed by Congress, and in recent years changes have occurred almost every year. Indeed, a major change has occurred, on average, every three to four years since 1913, when our federal income tax system began. Further, certain parts of our tax system are tied to the rate of inflation, so changes occur automatically each year, depending on the rate of inflation during the previous year. Therefore, although this section will give you a good background on the basic nature of our tax system, you should consult current rate schedules and other data published by the Internal Revenue Service (available in U.S. post offices) before you file your personal or business tax return.

Currently (1996), federal income tax rates for individuals go up to 39.6 percent, and, when Social Security, Medicare, and state and city income taxes are included, the marginal tax rate on an individual's income can easily exceed 50 percent. Business income is also taxed heavily. The income from partnerships and proprietorships is reported by the individual owners as personal income and, consequently, is taxed at federal-plus-state rates going up to 50 percent or more. Corporate profits are subject to federal income tax rates of up to 39 percent, in addition to state income taxes. Furthermore, corporations pay taxes and then distribute after-tax income to their stockholders as dividends, which are also taxed. So, corporate income is really subject to double taxation. Because of the magnitude of the tax bite, taxes play a critical role in many financial decisions.

As this text is being written, a Republican Congress and a Democratic administration are debating the merits of different changes in the tax laws. To stimulate investment, depreciation schedules may be liberalized, and capital gains may be taxed at a lower rate. Even in the unlikely event that no explicit changes are made in the tax laws, changes will still occur because certain aspects of the tax calculation are tied to the inflation rate. Thus, by the time you read this chapter, tax rates and other factors will almost certainly be different from those we provide. Still, if you understand this section, you will understand the basics of our tax system, and you will know how to operate under the revised tax code.

Taxes are so complicated that university law schools offer master's degrees in taxation to lawyers, many of whom are also CPAs. In a field complicated enough to warrant such detailed study, only the highlights can be covered in a book such as this. This is really enough, though, because business managers and investors should and do rely on tax specialists rather than trusting their own limited knowledge. Still, it is important to know the basic elements of the tax system as a starting point for discussions with tax experts.

INDIVIDUAL INCOME TAXES

Individuals pay taxes on wages and salaries, on investment income (dividends, interest, and profits from the sale of securities), and on the profits of proprietorships and partnerships. Our tax rates are *progressive* — that is, the higher one's income, the larger the percentage paid in taxes. Table 3-2 gives the tax rates for single individuals and married couples filing joint returns under the rate schedules that were in effect in April 1996.

1. *Taxable income* is defined as gross income less a set of exemptions and deductions which are spelled out in the instructions to the tax forms individuals must file. When filing a tax return in 1996 for the tax year 1995, each taxpayer received an exemption of $2,500 for each dependent, including the taxpayer, which reduces taxable income. However, this exemption is indexed to rise with inflation, and the exemption is phased out (taken away) for high-income taxpayers. Also, certain expenses including mortgage interest paid, state and local income taxes paid, and charitable contributions, can be deducted and thus be used to reduce taxable income, but again, high-income taxpayers lose some of these deductions.

TABLE 3-2   INDIVIDUAL TAX RATES IN APRIL 1996

SINGLE INDIVIDUALS

IF YOUR TAXABLE INCOME IS	YOU PAY THIS AMOUNT ON THE BASE OF THE BRACKET	PLUS THIS PERCENTAGE ON THE EXCESS OVER THE BASE	AVERAGE TAX RATE AT TOP OF BRACKET
Up to $23,350	$ 0	15.0%	15.0%
$23,350–$56,550	3,502.50	28.0	22.6
$56,550–$117,950	12,798.50	31.0	27.0
$117,950–$256,500	31,832.50	36.0	31.9
Over $256,500	81,710.50	39.6	39.6

MARRIED COUPLES FILING JOINT RETURNS

IF YOUR TAXABLE INCOME IS	YOU PAY THIS AMOUNT ON THE BASE OF THE BRACKET	PLUS THIS PERCENTAGE ON THE EXCESS OVER THE BASE	AVERAGE TAX RATE AT TOP OF BRACKET
Up to $39,000	$ 0	15.0%	15.0%
$39,000–$94,250	5,850.00	28.0	22.6
$94,250–$143,600	21,320.00	31.0	25.5
$143,600–$256,500	36,618.50	36.0	30.1
Over $256,500	77,262.50	39.6	39.6

NOTES:

a. These are the tax rates in April 1996. The income ranges at which each tax rate takes effect, as well as the ranges for the additional taxes discussed below, are indexed with inflation each year, so they will change from those shown in the table.

b. The average tax rate approaches 39.6 percent as taxable income rises without limit. At $1 million of taxable income, the average tax rates for single individuals and married couples filing joint returns are 37.6 percent and 37.2 percent, respectively, while at $10 million it is 39.4 percent.

c. In 1995, a *personal exemption* of $2,500 per person or dependent could be deducted from gross income to determine taxable income. Thus, a husband and wife with two children would have a 1995 exemption of 4 × $2,500 = $10,000. The amount of the exemption is scheduled to increase with inflation. However, if the gross income exceeds certain limits ($172,050 for joint returns and $114,700 for single individuals in 1995), the exemption is phased out, and this has the effect of raising the effective tax rate on incomes over the specified limit by about 0.5 percent per family member, or 2.0 percent for a family of four. In addition, taxpayers can claim *itemized deductions* for charitable contributions and certain other items, but these deductions are reduced if the gross income exceeds $114,700 (for both single individuals and joint returns), and this raises the effective tax rate for high-income taxpayers by another 1 percent or so. The combined effect of the loss of exemptions and the reduction of itemized deductions is about 3 percent, so the marginal federal tax rate for high-income individuals goes up to about 42.6 percent.

In addition, there is the Social Security tax, which amounts to 6.2 percent (12.4 percent for a self-employed person) on up to $60,600 of earned income, plus a 1.45 percent Medicare payroll tax (2.9 percent for self-employed individuals) on *all* earned income. Finally, older high-income taxpayers who receive Social Security payments must pay taxes on 85 percent of their Social Security receipts, up from 50 percent in 1994. All of this pushes the effective tax rate up even further.

2. *The marginal tax rate* is defined as the tax rate on the last unit of income. Marginal rates begin at 15 percent and rise to 39.6 percent. Note, though, that when consideration is given to the phase-out of exemptions and deductions, to Social Security and Medicare taxes, and to state taxes, the marginal tax rate can actually exceed 50 percent.

3. One can calculate *average tax rates* from the data in Table 3-2. For example, if Jill Smith, a single individual, had taxable income of $35,000, her tax bill

would be $3,502.50 + ($35,000 − $23,350)(0.28) = $3,502.50 + $3,262 = $6,764.50. Her *average tax rate* would be $6,764.50/$35,000 = 19.3% versus a *marginal rate* of 28 percent. If Jill received a raise of $1,000, bringing her income to $36,000, she would have to pay $280 of it as taxes, so her after-tax raise would be $720. In addition, her Social Security and Medicare taxes would increase by $76.50, which would cut her net raise to $643.50.

4. As indicated in the notes to the table, the tax code indexes tax brackets to inflation to avoid the *bracket creep* that occurred during the 1970s and that in reality raised tax rates substantially.[15]

TAXES ON DIVIDEND AND INTEREST INCOME   Dividend and interest income received by individuals from corporate securities is added to other income and thus is taxed at rates going up to about 50 percent.[16] Since corporations pay dividends out of earnings that have already been taxed, there is *double taxation* of corporate income—income is first taxed at the corporate rate, and when what is left is paid out as dividends, it is taxed again at the personal rate.

It should be noted that under U.S. tax laws, interest on most state and local government bonds, called *municipals* or "*munis*," is not subject to federal income taxes. Thus, investors get to keep all of the interest received from most municipal bonds but only a fraction of the interest received from bonds issued by corporations or by the U.S. government. This means that a lower-yielding muni can provide the same after-tax return as a higher-yielding corporate bond. For example, a taxpayer in the 39.6 percent marginal tax bracket who could buy a muni that yielded 5.5 percent would have to receive a before-tax yield of 9.11 percent on a corporate or U.S. Treasury bond to have the same after-tax income:

$$\text{Equivalent pretax yield on taxable bond} = \frac{\text{Yield on muni}}{1 - \text{Marginal tax rate}}$$

$$= \frac{5.5\%}{1 - 0.396} = 9.11\%.$$

---

[15]For example, if you were single and had a taxable income of $23,350, your tax bill would be $3,502.50. Now suppose inflation caused prices to double and your income, being tied to a cost-of-living index, rose to $46,700. Because our tax rates are progressive, if tax brackets were not indexed, your taxes would jump to $9,760.50. Your after-tax income would thus increase from $19,847.50 to $36,939.50, but, because prices have doubled, your real income would *decline* from $19,847.50 to $18,469.75 (calculated as one-half of $36,939.50). You would be in a higher tax bracket, so you would be paying a higher percentage of your real income in taxes. If this happened to everyone, and if Congress failed to change tax rates sufficiently, real disposable incomes would decline because the federal government would be taking a larger share of the national product. This is called the federal government's "inflation dividend." However, since tax brackets are now indexed, if your income doubled due to inflation, your tax bill would double, but your after-tax real income would remain constant at $19,847.50. Bracket creep was a real problem during the 1970s and early 1980s, but indexing—if it stays in the law—put an end to it.

[16]You do not pay Social Security and Medicare taxes on interest, dividends, and capital gains, only on earned income, but state taxes are generally imposed on dividends, interest, and capital gains.

If we know the yield on the taxable bond, we can use the following equation to find the equivalent yield on a muni:

$$\text{Equivalent yield on muni} = \left(\begin{array}{c} \text{Pretax yield} \\ \text{on taxable} \\ \text{bond} \end{array} \right)(1 - \text{Marginal tax rate})$$

$$= 9.11\% \, (1 - 0.396) = 9.11\%(0.604) = 5.5\%.$$

The exemption from federal taxes stems from the separation of federal and state powers, and its primary effect is to help state and local governments borrow at lower rates than would otherwise be available to them.

Munis always yield less than corporate bonds with the same risk, maturity, and liquidity. Because of this, it would make no sense for someone in a very low tax bracket to buy munis. Therefore, most munis are owned by high-bracket investors.

CAPITAL GAINS VERSUS ORDINARY INCOME   Assets such as stocks, bonds, and real estate are defined as *capital assets*. If you buy a capital asset and later sell it for more than your purchase price, the profit is called a *capital gain*; if you suffer a loss, it is called a *capital loss*. An asset sold within one year of the time it was purchased produces a *short-term gain or loss*, whereas one held for more than one year produces a *long-term gain or loss*. Thus, if you buy 100 shares of Disney stock for $42 per share and sell it for $52 per share, you make a capital gain of $100 \times \$10$, or $1,000. However, if you sell the stock for $32 per share, you will have a $1,000 capital loss. If you hold the stock for more than one year, the gain or loss is long-term; otherwise, it is short-term. If you sell the stock for exactly $42 per share, you make neither a gain nor a loss; you simply get your $4,200 back, and no tax is due.

Short-term capital gains are added to such ordinary income as wages, dividends, and interest and then are taxed at the same rate as ordinary income. However, long-term capital gains are taxed differently in that the rate on long-term capital gains is capped at 28 percent. Thus, if in 1995 you were in a tax bracket of 28 percent or less, any capital gains you earned would be taxed just like ordinary income, but if you were in the 31, 36, or 39.6 percent bracket, your long-term capital gains would only be taxed at a 28 percent rate. Thus, long-term capital gains are better than ordinary income for many people because more of it is left after taxes.

Capital gains tax rates have varied over time, but they have generally been lower than rates on ordinary income. The reason is simple — Congress wants the economy to grow. For that to happen we need investment in productive assets, and low capital gains tax rates encourage investment. To see why, suppose you owned a company that earned $1 million after corporate taxes. Because it is your company, you could have it pay out the entire profit as dividends, or you could have it retain and reinvest all or part of the income to expand the business. If it pays dividends, they will be taxable to you at a rate of 39.6 percent. However, if the company reinvests its income, that reinvestment should cause the company's earnings and stock price to increase. Now, if you wait for a year, then sell some of your stock at a now-higher price, you will have earned capital gains, which will be taxed at only 28 percent. Further, you can postpone the capital gains tax by simply not selling the stock.

It should be clear that a lower tax rate on capital gains will encourage investment. The owners of small businesses will want to reinvest income to get capital gains, as will stockholders in large corporations. Individuals with money to invest will understand the tax advantages associated with investing in newly formed companies versus buying bonds, so new ventures will have an easier time attracting equity capital. All in all, lower capital gains tax rates stimulate capital formation and investment.[17]

CORPORATE INCOME TAXES

The corporate tax structure, shown in Table 3-3, is relatively simple. To illustrate, if a firm had $75,000 of taxable income, its tax bill would be

$$\text{Taxes} = \$7,500 + 0.25(\$25,000)$$
$$= \$7,500 + \$6,250 = \$13,750,$$

and its average tax rate would be $13,750/$75,000 = 18.3%. Note that corporate income above $18,333,333 has an average and marginal tax rate of 35 percent.[18]

INTEREST AND DIVIDEND INCOME RECEIVED BY A CORPORATION Interest income received by a corporation is taxed as ordinary income at regular corporate tax rates. *However, 70 percent of the dividends received by one corporation from another is excluded from taxable income, while the remaining 30 percent is taxed at the*

---

[17]Capital gains on the newly issued stock of certain small companies are taxed at one-half the regular capital gains tax rate if the stock is held for five years or longer. Thus, if one bought newly issued stock from a qualifying small company and held it for at least five years, any capital gains would be taxed at a maximum rate of 14 percent. This provision is designed to help small businesses obtain equity capital.

[18]Prior to 1987, many large, profitable corporations such as General Electric and Boeing paid no income taxes. The reasons for this were as follows: (1) expenses, especially depreciation, were defined differently for calculating taxable income than for reporting earnings to stockholders, so some companies reported positive profits to stockholders but losses — hence no taxes — to the Internal Revenue Service; and (2) some companies which did have tax liabilities used various tax credits to offset taxes that would otherwise have been payable. This situation was effectively eliminated in 1987.

The principal method used to eliminate this situation is the Alternative Minimum Tax (AMT). Under the AMT, both corporate and individual taxpayers must figure their taxes in two ways, the "regular" way and the AMT way, and then pay the higher of the two. The AMT is calculated as follows: (1) Figure your regular taxes. (2) Take your taxable income under the regular method and then add back certain items, especially income on certain municipal bonds, depreciation in excess of straight line depreciation, certain research and drilling costs, itemized or standard deductions (for individuals), and a number of other items. (3) The income determined in (2) is defined as AMT income, and it must then be multiplied by the AMT tax rate to determine the tax due under the AMT system. An individual or corporation must then pay the higher of the regular tax or the AMT tax. In 1996, there were two AMT tax rates for individuals (26 percent and 28 percent, depending on the level of AMT income and filing status); the corporate AMT remained unchanged at 20 percent.

TABLE 3-3	CORPORATE TAX RATES		
IF A CORPORATION'S TAXABLE INCOME IS	IT PAYS THIS AMOUNT ON THE BASE OF THE BRACKET	PLUS THIS PERCENTAGE ON THE EXCESS OVER THE BASE	AVERAGE TAX RATE AT TOP OF BRACKET
Up to $50,000	$ 0	15%	15.0%
$50,000–$75,000	7,500	25	18.3
$75,000–$100,000	13,750	34	22.3
$100,000–$335,000	22,250	39	34.0
$335,000–$10,000,000	113,900	34	34.0
$10,000,000–$15,000,000	3,400,000	35	34.3
$15,000,000–$18,333,333	5,150,000	38	35.0
Over $18,333,333	6,416,667	35	35.0

ordinary tax rate.[19] Thus, a corporation earning more than $18,333,333 and paying a 35 percent marginal tax rate would pay only (0.30)(0.35) = 0.105 = 10.5% of its dividend income as taxes, so its effective tax rate on dividends received would be 10.5 percent. If this firm had $10,000 in pretax dividend income, its after-tax dividend income would be $8,950:

$$\text{After-tax income} = \text{Before-tax income} - \text{Taxes}$$
$$= \text{Before-tax income} - (\text{Before-tax income})(\text{Effective tax rate})$$
$$= \text{Before-tax income}(1 - \text{Effective tax rate})$$
$$= \$10,000 [1 - (0.30)(0.35)]$$
$$= \$10,000(1 - 0.105) = \$10,000(0.895) = \$8,950.$$

If the corporation pays its own after-tax income out to its stockholders as dividends, the income is ultimately subjected to *triple taxation*: (1) the original corporation is first taxed, (2) the second corporation is then taxed on the dividends it received, and (3) the individuals who receive the final dividends are taxed again. This is the reason for the 70 percent exclusion on intercorporate dividends.

If a corporation has surplus funds that can be invested in marketable securities, the tax factor favors investment in stocks, which pay dividends, rather than in bonds, which pay interest. For example, suppose GE had $100,000 to invest, and it could buy either bonds that paid interest of $8,000 per year or preferred stock that paid dividends of $7,000. GE is in the 35 percent tax bracket; therefore, its tax on the interest, if it bought bonds, would be 0.35 ($8,000) = $2,800, and its after-tax income would be $5,200. If it bought preferred (or common) stock, its tax would be 0.35[(0.30)($7,000)] = $735, and its after-tax income would be $6,265. Other fac-

---

[19]The size of the dividend exclusion actually depends on the degree of ownership. Corporations that own less than 20 percent of the stock of the dividend-paying company can exclude 70 percent of the dividends received; firms that own more than 20 percent but less than 80 percent can exclude 80 percent of the dividends; and firms that own more than 80 percent can exclude the entire dividend payment. We will, in general, assume a 70 percent dividend exclusion.

	USE BONDS (1)	USE STOCK (2)
CASH FLOWS TO INVESTORS UNDER BOND AND STOCK FINANCING		**TABLE 3-4**
Sales	$5,000,000	$5,000,000
Operating costs	3,500,000	3,500,000
Earnings before interest and taxes (EBIT)	$1,500,000	$1,500,000
Interest	1,500,000	0
Taxable income	$ 0	$1,500,000
Federal-plus-state taxes (40%)	0	600,000
After-tax income	$ 0	$ 900,000
Income to investors	$1,500,000	$ 900,000
Rate of return on $10 million of assets	15.0%	9.0%

tors might lead GE to invest in bonds, but the tax factor certainly favors stock investments when the investor is a corporation.[20]

INTEREST AND DIVIDENDS PAID BY A CORPORATION A firm's operations can be financed with either debt or equity capital. If it uses debt, it must pay interest on this debt, whereas if it uses equity, it will pay dividends to the equity investors (stockholders). The interest *paid* by a corporation is deducted from its operating income to obtain its taxable income, but dividends paid are not deductible . Therefore, a firm needs $1 of pretax income to pay $1 of interest, but if it is in the 40 percent federal-plus-state tax bracket, it needs $1.67 of pretax income to pay $1 of dividends:

$$\frac{\text{Pretax income needed}}{\text{to pay \$1 of dividends}} = \frac{\$1}{1 - \text{Tax rate}} = \frac{\$1}{0.60} = \$1.67.$$

Proof: After-tax income = $1.67 − Tax = $1.67 − $1.67(0.4) = $1.67(1 − 0.4) = $1.00.

Table 3-4 shows the situation for a firm with $10 million of assets, sales of $5 million, and $1.5 million of earnings before interest and taxes (EBIT). As shown in Column 1, if the firm were financed entirely by bonds, and if it made interest payments of $1.5 million, its taxable income would be zero, taxes would be zero, and its investors would receive the entire $1.5 million. (The term *investors* includes both stockholders and bondholders.) However, as shown in Column 2, if the firm had no debt and was therefore financed only by stock, all of the $1.5 million of EBIT would

---

[20]This illustration demonstrates why corporations favor investing in lower-yielding preferred stocks over higher-yielding bonds. When tax consequences are considered, the yield on the preferred stock, [1 − 0.35(0.30)](7.0%) = 6.265%, is higher than the yield on the bond, (1 − 0.35)(8.0%) = 5.200%. Also, note that corporations are restricted in their use of borrowed funds to purchase other firms' preferred or common stocks. Without such restrictions, firms could engage in *tax arbitrage*, whereby the interest on borrowed funds reduces taxable income on a dollar-for-dollar basis, but taxable income is increased by only $0.30 per dollar of dividend income. Thus, current tax laws reduce the 70 percent dividend exclusion in proportion to the amount of borrowed funds used to purchase the stock.

be taxable income to the corporation, the tax would be $1,500,000(0.40) = $600,000, and investors would receive only $0.9 million versus $1.5 million under debt financing. The rate of return to investors on their $10 million investment is also much higher if debt is used.

Of course, it is generally not possible to finance exclusively with debt capital, and the risk of doing so would offset the benefits of the higher expected income. *Still, the fact that interest is a deductible expense has a profound effect on the way businesses are financed — our corporate tax system favors debt financing over equity financing.* This point is discussed in more detail in Chapters 13 and 14.

CORPORATE CAPITAL GAINS   Before 1987, corporate long-term capital gains were taxed at lower rates than ordinary income, as is true for individuals. Under current law, however, corporations' capital gains are taxed at the same rates as their operating income.

CORPORATE LOSS CARRY-BACK AND CARRY-FORWARD   Ordinary corporate operating losses can be carried back (*carry-back*) to each of the preceding 3 years and forward (*carry-forward*) for the next 15 years to offset taxable income in those years. For example, an operating loss in 1997 could be carried back and used to reduce taxable income in 1994, 1995, and 1996, and forward, if necessary, and used in 1998, 1999, and so on, to the year 2012. The loss is typically applied first to the earliest year, then to the next earliest year, and so on, until losses have been used up or the 15-year carry-forward limit has been reached.

To illustrate, suppose Apex Corporation had $2 million of *pre-tax* profits (taxable income) in 1994, 1995, and 1996, and then, in 1997, Apex lost $12 million. Also, assume that Apex's federal-plus-state tax rate is 40 percent. As shown in Table 3-5, the company would use the carry-back feature to recompute its taxes for 1994, using $2 million of the 1997 operating losses to reduce the 1994 pretax profit to zero. This

TABLE 3-5	APEX CORPORATION: CALCULATION OF LOSS CARRY-BACK AND CARRY-FORWARD FOR 1994–1996 USING A $12 MILLION 1997 LOSS		
	1994	**1995**	**1996**
Original taxable income	$ 2,000,000	$ 2,000,000	$ 2,000,000
Carry-back credit	− 2,000,000	− 2,000,000	− 2,000,000
Adjusted profit	$ 0	$ 0	$ 0
Taxes previously paid (40%)	800,000	800,000	800,000
Difference = Tax refund	$ 800,000	$ 800,000	$ 800,000

Total refund check received in 1998: $800,000 + $800,000 + $800,000 = $2,400,000.

Amount of loss carry-forward available for use in 1998–2012:

1997 loss	$12,000,000
Carry-back losses used	$ 6,000,000
Carry-forward losses still available	$ 6,000,000

would permit it to recover the amount of taxes paid in 1994. Therefore, in 1998 Apex would receive a refund of its 1994 taxes because of the loss experienced in 1997. Because $10 million of the unrecovered losses would still be available, Apex would repeat this procedure for 1995 and 1996. Thus, in 1998 the company would pay zero taxes for 1997 and also would receive a refund for taxes paid from 1994 through 1996. Apex would still have $6 million of unrecovered losses to carry forward, subject to the 15-year limit, until the entire $12 million loss had been used to offset taxable income. The purpose of permitting this loss treatment is, of course, to avoid penalizing corporations whose incomes fluctuate substantially from year to year.

IMPROPER ACCUMULATION TO AVOID PAYMENT OF DIVIDENDS   Corporations could refrain from paying dividends to permit their stockholders to avoid personal income taxes on dividends. To prevent this, the Tax Code contains an *improper accumulation* provision which states that earnings accumulated by a corporation are subject to penalty rates *if the purpose of the accumulation is to enable stockholders to avoid personal income taxes*. A cumulative total of $250,000 (the balance sheet item "retained earnings") is by law exempted from the improper accumulation tax for most corporations. This is a benefit primarily to small corporations.

The improper accumulation penalty applies only if the retained earnings in excess of $250,000 are *shown to be unnecessary to meet the reasonable needs of the business*. A great many companies do indeed have legitimate reasons for retaining more than $250,000 of earnings. For example, earnings may be retained and used to pay off debt, to finance growth, or to provide the corporation with a cushion against possible cash drains caused by losses. How much a firm should properly accumulate for uncertain contingencies is a matter of judgment. We shall consider this matter again in Chapter 15, which deals with corporate dividend policy.

CONSOLIDATED CORPORATE TAX RETURNS   If a corporation owns 80 percent or more of another corporation's stock, it can aggregate income and file one consolidated tax return; thus, the losses of one company can be used to offset the profits of another. (Similarly, one division's losses can be used to offset another division's profits.) No business ever wants to incur losses (you can go broke losing $1 to save 35¢ in taxes), but tax offsets do help make it feasible for large, multidivisional corporations to undertake risky new ventures or ventures that will suffer losses during a developmental period.

TAXATION OF SMALL BUSINESSES: S CORPORATIONS

The tax code provides that small businesses which meet certain restrictions as spelled out in the code may be set up as corporations and thus receive the benefits of the corporate form of organization — especially limited liability — yet still be taxed as proprietorships or partnerships rather than as corporations. These corporations are called *S corporations*. ("Regular" corporations are called C corporations.) If a corporation elects S corporation status for tax purposes, all of the business's income is reported as personal income by its stockholders and thus is taxed at the rates that apply to individuals. This would be preferred by owners of small corporations in which all or most of the income earned each year will be distributed as dividends, because then the income would be taxed only once, at the individual level.

SELF-TEST
QUESTIONS

Explain what is meant by the statement: "Our tax rates are progressive."

Are tax rates progressive for all income ranges?

Explain the difference between marginal tax rates and average tax rates.

What are capital gains and losses, and how are they differentiated from ordinary income?

How does the federal income tax system treat corporate dividends received by a corporation versus those received by an individual? Why is this distinction made?

What is the difference in the tax treatment of interest and dividends paid by a corporation? Do tax laws favor debt or equity financing?

DEPRECIATION

Depreciation plays an important role in income tax calculations — the higher the depreciation, the lower the taxable income and thus the lower the tax bill. Congress specifies, in the tax code, the life over which assets can be depreciated for tax purposes and the methods of depreciation which can be used. We will discuss in detail how depreciation is calculated, and how it affects income and cash flows, when we take up project cash flow analysis in Chapter 10.

SUMMARY

In this chapter we discussed the nature of financial markets, the types of institutions that operate in these markets, how interest rates are determined, some of the ways in which interest rates affect business decisions, and the Federal income tax system. The key concepts covered are listed below.

- There are many different types of *financial markets*. Each market serves a different region or deals with a different type of security.

- Transfers of capital between borrowers and savers take place (1) by *direct transfers* of money and securities; (2) by transfers through *investment banking houses*, which act as middlemen; and (3) by transfers through *financial intermediaries*, which create new securities.

- The *stock market* is an especially important market because this is where stock prices (which are used to "grade" managers' performances) are established.

- There are two basic types of stock markets — the *organized exchanges* and the *over-the-counter market*.

- Capital is allocated through the price system — a price must be paid to "rent" money. Lenders charge *interest* on funds they lend, while equity investors receive dividends and capital gains in return for letting firms use their money.

- Four fundamental factors affect the cost of money: (1) *production opportunities*, (2) *time preferences for consumption*, (3) *risk*, and (4) *inflation*.

■ The *risk-free rate of interest*, k_{RF}, is defined as the real risk-free rate, k^*, plus an inflation premium (IP): $k_{RF} = k^* + IP$.

■ The *nominal* (or *quoted*) *interest rate* on a debt security, k, is composed of the real risk-free rate, k^*, plus premiums that reflect inflation (IP), default risk (DRP), liquidity (LP), and maturity risk (MRP):

$$k = k^* + IP + DRP + LP + MRP.$$

■ If the *real risk-free rate of interest and the various premiums were constant over time*, interest rates in the economy would be stable. However, both the real rate and the premiums — especially the premium for expected inflation — *do change over time, causing market interest rates to change*. Also, Federal Reserve intervention to increase or decrease the money supply, as well as international currency flows, lead to fluctuations in interest rates.

■ The relationship between the yields on securities and the securities' maturities is known as the *term structure of interest rates*, and the *yield curve* is a graph of this relationship.

■ The yield curve is normally *upward sloping* — this is called a *normal yield curve* — but the curve can slope downward (an *inverted yield curve*) if the demand for short-term funds is relatively strong or if the rate of inflation is expected to decline.

■ *Interest rate levels have a profound effect on stock prices*. Higher interest rates (1) slow down the economy, (2) increase interest expenses and thus lower corporate profits, and (3) cause investors to sell stocks and transfer funds to the bond market. Each of these factors tends to depress stock prices.

■ Interest rate levels have a significant influence on *corporate financial policy*. Because interest rate levels are difficult if not impossible to predict, sound financial policy calls for using a mix of short- and long-term debt, and also for positioning the firm to survive in any future interest rate environment.

■ The value of any asset depends on the stream of *after-tax cash flows* it produces. Tax rates and other aspects of our tax system are changed by Congress every year or so.

■ In the United States, income tax rates are *progressive* — the higher one's income, the larger the percentage paid in taxes, up to a point.

■ Assets such as stocks, bonds, and real estate are defined as *capital assets*. If a capital asset is sold for more than the purchase price, the profit is called a *capital gain.* If the capital asset is sold for a loss, it is called a *capital loss*.

■ Operating income paid out as dividends is subject to *double taxation*: the income is first taxed at the corporate level, and then shareholders must pay personal taxes on their dividends.

■ *Interest income* received by a corporation is taxed as *ordinary income*; however, 70 percent of the dividends received by one corporation from another are excluded from *taxable income*. The reason for this exclusion is that corporate dividend income is ultimately subjected to *triple taxation*.

■ Because interest paid by a corporation is a *deductible* expense while dividends are not, our tax system favors debt financing over equity financing.

■ Ordinary corporate operating losses can be *carried back* to each of the preceding 3 years and *carried forward* for the next 15 years to offset taxable income in those years.

■ *S corporations* are small businesses which have the limited-liability benefits of the corporate form of organization yet are taxed as a partnership or a proprietorship.

QUESTIONS

3-1 Define each of the following terms:
  a. Money market; capital market
  b. Primary market; secondary market
  c. Investment banker; financial service corporation
  d. Financial intermediary
  e. Mutual fund; money market fund
  f. Organized security exchanges; over-the-counter market
  g. Production opportunities; time preferences for consumption
  h. Real risk-free rate of interest, k^*; nominal risk-free rate of interest, k_{RF}
   i. Inflation premium (IP)
  j. Default risk premium (DRP)
  k. Liquidity; liquidity premium (LP)
   l. Interest rate risk; maturity risk premium (MRP)
  m. Reinvestment rate risk
  n. Term structure of interest rates; yield curve
  o. "Normal" yield curve; inverted ("abnormal") yield curve
  p. Market segmentation theory; liquidity preference theory
  q. Expectations theory
  r. Progressive tax
  s. Marginal and average tax rates
  t. Bracket creep
  u. Capital gain or loss
  v. Tax loss carry-back and carry-forward
  w. Improper accumulation
  x. S corporation

3-2 What are financial intermediaries, and what economic functions do they perform?

3-3 Suppose interest rates on residential mortgages of equal risk were 7 percent in California and 9 percent in New York. Could this differential persist? What forces might tend to equalize rates? Would differentials in borrowing costs for businesses of equal risk located in California and New York be more or less likely to exist than differentials in residential mortgage rates? Would differentials in the cost of money for New York and California firms be more likely to exist if the firms being compared were very large or if they were very small? What are the implications of all this for the pressure now being put on Congress to permit banks to engage in nationwide branching?

3-4   What would happen to the standard of living in the United States if people lost faith in the safety of our financial institutions? Why?

3-5   How does a cost-efficient capital market help to reduce the prices of goods and services?

3-6   Which fluctuate more, long-term or short-term interest rates? Why?

3-7   Suppose you believe that the economy is just entering a recession. Your firm must raise capital immediately, and debt will be used. Should you borrow on a long-term or a short-term basis? Why?

3-8   Suppose the population of Area Y is relatively young while that of Area O is relatively old, but everything else about the two areas is equal.
   a. Would interest rates likely be the same or different in the two areas? Explain.
   b. Would a trend toward nationwide branching by banks and savings and loans, and the development of nationwide diversified financial corporations, affect your answer to Part a?

3-9   Suppose a new process was developed which could be used to make oil out of seawater. The equipment required is quite expensive but it would, in time, lead to very low prices for gasoline, electricity, and other types of energy. What effect would this have on interest rates?

3-10 Suppose a new and much more liberal Congress and administration were elected, and their first order of business was to take away the independence of the Federal Reserve System and to force the Fed to greatly expand the money supply. What effect would this have
   a. On the level and slope of the yield curve immediately after the announcement?
   b. On the level and slope of the yield curve that would exist two or three years in the future?

3-11 It is a fact that the federal government (1) encouraged the development of the savings and loan industry; (2) virtually forced the industry to make long-term, fixed-interest-rate mortgages; and (3) forced the savings and loans to obtain most of their capital as deposits that were withdrawable on demand.
   a. Would the savings and loans be better off in a world with a normal or an inverted yield curve?
   b. Would the savings and loan industry be better off if the individual institutions sold their mortgages to federal agencies and then collected servicing fees or if the institutions held the mortgages that they originated?

3-12 Suppose interest rates on Treasury bonds rose from 7 to 14 percent as a result of increased government borrowing. What effect would this have on the price of an average company's common stock?

3-13 Suppose you owned 100 shares of Ford Motor stock, and the company earned $3 per share during the last reporting period. Suppose further that Ford could either pay all its earnings out as dividends (in which case you would receive $300) or retain the earnings in the business, buy more assets, and cause the price of the stock to go up by $3 per share (in which case the value of your stock would rise by $300).
   a. How would the tax laws influence what you, as a typical stockholder, would want the company to do?
   b. Would your choice be influenced by how much other income you had? Why might the desires of a 45-year-old doctor differ with respect to corporate dividend policy from those of a pension fund manager or a retiree living on a small income?
   c. How might the corporation's decision with regard to dividend policy influence the price of its stock?

3-14 What does *double taxation of corporate income* mean?

3-15   If you were starting a business, what tax considerations might cause you to prefer to set it up as a proprietorship or a partnership rather than as a corporation?

3-16   Explain how the federal income tax structure affects the choice of financing (use of debt versus equity) of U.S. business firms.

3-17   For someone planning to start a new business, is the average or the marginal tax rate more relevant?

SELF-TEST PROBLEMS

(SOLUTIONS APPEAR IN APPENDIX C)

ST-1   **INFLATION RATES** Assume that it is now January 1, 1997, and the rate of inflation is expected to be 6 percent throughout 1997. However, increased government deficits and renewed vigor in the economy are then expected to push inflation rates higher. Investors expect the inflation rate to be 7 percent in 1998, 8 percent in 1999, and 9 percent in 2000. The real risk-free rate, k*, is currently 3 percent. Assume that no maturity risk premiums are required on bonds with 5 years or less to maturity. The current interest rate on 5-year T-bonds is 11 percent.

   a. What is the average expected inflation rate over the next 4 years?

   b. What should be the prevailing interest rate on 4-year T-bonds?

   c. What is the implied expected inflation rate in 2001, or Year 5, given that bonds which mature in that year yield 11 percent?

ST-2   **EFFECT OF FORM OF ORGANIZATION ON TAXES** John Thompson is planning to start a new business, JT Enterprises, and he must decide whether to incorporate or to do business as a sole proprietorship. Under either form, Thompson will initially own 100 percent of the firm, and tax considerations are important to him. He plans to finance the firm's expected growth by drawing a salary just sufficient for his family living expenses, which he estimates will be about $40,000, and by retaining all other income in the business. Assume that as a married man with one child, Thompson has income tax exemptions of 3 × $2,500 = $7,500, and he estimates that his itemized deductions for each of the three years will be $8,750. He expects JT Enterprises to grow and to earn income of $60,000 in 1997, $90,000 in 1998, and $110,000 in 1999. Which form of business organization will allow Thompson to pay the lowest taxes (and retain the most income) during the period from 1997 to 1999? Assume that the tax rates given in the chapter are applicable for all future years. (Social Security taxes would also have to be paid, but ignore them.)

PROBLEMS

(Note: By the time this book is published, Congress may have changed rates and/or other provisions of current tax law — as noted in the chapter, such changes occur fairly often. Work all problems on the assumption that the tax tables in the chapter are still current.)

3-1 **YIELD CURVES** Suppose you and most other investors expect the rate of inflation to be 7 percent next year, to fall to 5 percent during the following year, and then to remain at a rate of 3 percent thereafter. Assume that the real risk-free rate, k^*, is 2 percent and that maturity risk premiums on Treasury securities rise from zero on very short-term bonds (those that mature in a few days) by 0.2 percentage points for each year to maturity, up to a limit of 1.0 percentage point on 5-year or longer-term T-bonds.

a. Calculate the interest rate on 1-, 2-, 3-, 4-, 5-, 10-, and 20-year Treasury securities, and plot the yield curve.

b. Now suppose Exxon, an AAA-rated company, had bonds with the same maturities as the Treasury bonds. As an approximation, plot an Exxon yield curve on the same graph with the Treasury bond yield curve. (Hint: Think about the default risk premium on Exxon's long-term versus its short-term bonds.)

c. Now plot the approximate yield curve of Long Island Lighting Company, a risky nuclear utility.

3-2 **YIELD CURVES** The following yields on U.S. Treasury securities were taken from a recent issue of *The Wall Street Journal*:

TERM	RATE
6 months	5.7%
1 year	5.9
2 years	6.1
3 years	6.2
4 years	6.3
5 years	6.4
10 years	6.7
20 years	6.8
30 years	6.9

Plot a yield curve based on these data. (Note: If you looked the data up in the *Journal*, you would find that one of the bonds — the 3.5 percent issue which matures in November 1998 — will show very low yields. These are "flower bonds," which are generally owned by older people and are associated with funerals because they can be turned in and used at par value to pay estate taxes. Thus, flower bonds always sell at close to par and have a yield which is close to the coupon yield, irrespective of the "going rate of interest." "Flower" bonds no longer are issued; the November 1998 bond, which was issued in 1971, is the last one outstanding. Also, the yields quoted in the *Journal* are not for the same point in time for all bonds, so random variations will appear. An interest rate series that is purged of flower bonds and random variations, and hence provides a better picture of the true yield curve, is known as the "constant maturity series"; this series can be obtained from the *Federal Reserve Bulletin*.)

3-3 **INFLATION AND INTEREST RATES** In late 1980 the U.S. Commerce Department released new figures which showed that inflation was running at an annual rate of close to 15 percent. However, many investors expected the new Reagan administration to be more effective in controlling inflation than the Carter administration had been. At the time, the prime rate of interest was 21 percent, a record high. However, many observers believed that the extremely high interest rates and generally tight credit, which resulted from the Federal Reserve System's attempts to curb the inflation rate, would shortly bring about a recession, which in turn would lead to a decline in the inflation rate and also in the rate of interest. Assume that at the beginning of 1981 the expected rate of inflation for 1981 was 13 percent; for 1982, 9 percent; for 1983, 7 percent; and for 1984 and thereafter, 6 percent.

a. What was the average expected inflation rate over the 5-year period 1981–1985? (Use the arithmetic average.)

b. What average *nominal* interest rate would, over the 5-year period, be expected to produce a 2 percent real risk-free rate of return on 5-year Treasury securities?

c. Assuming a real risk-free rate of 2 percent and a maturity risk premium which starts at 0.1 percent and increases by 0.1 percent each year, estimate the interest rate in January 1981 on bonds that mature in 1, 2, 5, 10, and 20 years, and draw a yield curve based on these data.

d. Describe the general economic conditions that could be expected to produce an upward-sloping yield curve.

e. If the consensus among investors in early 1981 had been that the expected rate of inflation for every future year was 10 percent (that is, $I_t = I_{t+1} = 10\%$ for $t = 1$ to ∞), what do you think the yield curve would have looked like? Consider all the factors that are likely to affect the curve. Does your answer here make you question the yield curve you drew in Part c?

3-4 **LOSS CARRY-BACK, CARRY-FORWARD** The Keenan Company has made $150,000 before taxes during each of the last 15 years, and it expects to make $150,000 a year before taxes in the future. However, in 1996 the firm incurred a loss of $650,000. The firm will claim a tax credit at the time it files its 1996 income tax return, and it will receive a check from the U.S. Treasury. Show how it calculates this credit, and then indicate the firm's tax liability for each of the next 5 years. Assume a 30 percent tax rate on *all* income to ease the calculations.

3-5 **LOSS CARRY-BACK, CARRY-FORWARD** The projected taxable income of the Kalogeras Corporation, formed in 1996, is indicated in the table below. (Losses are shown in parentheses.) What is the corporate tax liability for each year? Use tax rates as shown in the text.

YEAR	TAXABLE INCOME
1996	($95,000)
1997	70,000
1998	55,000
1999	80,000
2000	(150,000)

3-6 **PERSONAL TAXES** Mary Jane Scheuer has this situation for the year 1996: salary of $60,000; dividend income of $10,000; interest on McDonnell Douglas bonds of $5,000; interest on state of Florida municipal bonds of $10,000; proceeds of $22,000 from the sale of Microsoft stock purchased in 1984 at a cost of $9,000; and proceeds of $22,000 from the November 1996 sale of Microsoft stock purchased in October 1996 at a cost of $21,000. Mary Jane gets one exemption ($2,500), and she has allowable itemized deductions of $5,000; these amounts will be deducted from her gross income to determine her taxable income.

a. What is Mary Jane's federal tax liability for 1996?

b. What are her marginal and average tax rates?

c. If she had some money to invest and was offered a choice of either state of Florida bonds with a yield of 9 percent or more McDonnell Douglas bonds with a yield of 11 percent, which should she choose, and why?

d. At what marginal tax rate would Mary Jane be indifferent in her choice between the Florida and McDonnell Douglas bonds?

3-7 **EXPECTED RATE OF INTEREST** Suppose the annual yield on a 2-year Treasury bond is 11.5 percent, while that on a 1-year bond is 10 percent. k^* is 3 percent, and the maturity risk premium is zero.

a. Using the expectations theory, forecast the interest rate on a 1-year bond during the second year. (Hint: Under the expectations theory, the yield on a 2-year bond is equal to the average yield on 1-year bonds in Years 1 and 2.)

b. What is the expected inflation rate in Year 1? Year 2?

3-8   EXPECTED RATE OF INTEREST Assume that the real risk-free rate is 4 percent and that the maturity risk premium is zero. If the nominal rate of interest on 1-year bonds is 11 percent and that on comparable-risk 2-year bonds is 13 percent, what is the 1-year interest rate that is expected for Year 2? What inflation rate is expected during Year 2? Comment on why the average interest rate during the 2-year period differs from the 1-year interest rate expected for Year 2.

3-9   CORPORATE TAX LIABILITY The Tanner Corporation had a 1996 taxable income of $365,000 from operations after all operating costs but before (1) interest charges of $50,000, (2) dividends received of $15,000, (3) dividends paid of $25,000, and (4) income taxes. What is the firm's income tax liability and its after-tax income? What are the company's marginal and average tax rates on taxable income?

-10   CORPORATE TAX LIABILITY The Apilado Corporation had $200,000 of taxable income from operations in 1996.
   a. What is the company's federal income tax bill for the year?
   b. Assume the firm receives an additional $40,000 of interest income from some bonds it owns. What is the tax on this interest income?
   c. Now assume that Apilado does not receive the interest income but does receive an additional $40,000 as dividends on some stock it owns. What is the tax on this dividend income?

-11   MATURITY RISK PREMIUM Assume that the real risk-free rate, k^*, is 3 percent and that inflation is expected to be 8 percent in Year 1, 5 percent in Year 2, and 4 percent thereafter. Assume also that all Treasury bonds are highly liquid and free of default risk. If 2-year and 5-year Treasury bonds both yield 10 percent, what is the difference in the maturity risk premiums (MRPs) on the two bonds, that is, what is MRP_5 minus MRP_2?

-12   AFTER-TAX YIELD The Cotner Corporation has $10,000 which it plans to invest in marketable securities. It is choosing between AT&T bonds, which yield 11 percent, state of Florida muni bonds, which yield 8 percent, and AT&T preferred stock, with a dividend yield of 9 percent. Cotner's corporate tax rate is 20 percent, and 70 percent of the dividends received are tax exempt. Assuming that the investments are equally risky and that Cotner chooses strictly on the basis of after-tax returns, which security should be selected? What is the after-tax rate of return on the highest-yielding security?

13   INTEREST RATES Due to the recession, the rate of inflation expected for the coming year is only 3 percent. However, the rate of inflation in Year 2 and thereafter is expected to be constant at some level above 3 percent. Assume that the real risk-free rate, k^*, is 2 percent for all maturities and that the expectations theory fully explains the yield curve, so there are no maturity premiums. If 3-year Treasury bonds yield 2 percentage points more than 1-year bonds, what rate of inflation is expected after Year 1?

SPREADSHEET APPLICATIONS

SPREADSHEET PROBLEM

Carol Moerdyk has operated her small repair shop as a sole proprietorship for several years, but projected changes in her business's income have led her to consider incorporating.

Moerdyk is married and has two children. Her family's only income, an annual salary of $45,000, is from operating the business. (The business actually earns more than $45,000, but Carol reinvests the additional earnings in the business.) She itemizes deductions, and she is able to deduct $6,000. These deductions, combined with her four personal exemptions for $4 \times \$2,500 = \$10,000$, give her a taxable income of $\$45,000 - \$6,000 - \$10,000$. (Assume the personal exemption remains at $2,500.) Of course, her actual taxable income, if she does not incorporate, would be higher by the amount of reinvested income. Moerdyk estimates that her business earnings before salary and taxes for the period 1996 to 1998 will be:

YEAR	EARNINGS BEFORE SALARY AND TAXES
1996	$65,000
1997	85,000
1998	95,000

a. What would her total taxes (corporate plus personal, assuming joint filing) be in each year under
   (1) A non-S corporate form of organization?
   (2) A proprietorship?
b. Should Moerdyk incorporate? Discuss.
c. Suppose Moerdyk decides to pay out (1) 50 percent or (2) 100 percent of the after-salary corporate income in each year as dividends. Would such dividend policy changes affect her decision about whether or not to incorporate?
d. Suppose business improves, and actual earnings before salary and taxes in each year are twice the original estimate. Assume that if Moerdyk chooses to incorporate she will continue to receive a salary of $45,000 and to reinvest additional earnings in the business. (No dividends would be paid.) What would be the effect of this increase in business income on Moerdyk's decision to incorporate or not incorporate?

MINI CASE

Assume that you recently graduated with a degree in finance and have just reported to work as an investment advisor at the firm of Balik and Kiefer Inc. Your first assignment is to explain the nature of the U.S. financial markets and institutions to Michelle DelaTorre, a professional tennis player who has just come to the United States from Chile. DelaTorre is a highly ranked tennis player who expects to invest substantial amounts of money through Balik and Kiefer. She is also very bright, and, therefore, she would like to understand in general terms what will happen to her money. Your boss has developed the following set of questions, which you must ask and answer to explain the U.S. financial system to DelaTorre.

a. What is a financial market? How are financial markets differentiated from markets for physical assets?
b. Differentiate between money markets and capital markets.

c. Differentiate between a primary market and a secondary market. If Apple Computer decided to issue additional common stock, and DelaTorre purchased 100 shares of this stock from Merrill Lynch, the underwriter, would this transaction be a primary market transaction or a secondary market transaction? Would it make a difference if DelaTorre purchased previously outstanding Apple stock in the over-the-counter market?

d. Describe the three primary ways in which capital is transferred between savers and borrowers.

e. Securities can be traded on organized exchanges or in the over-the-counter market. Define each of these markets, and describe how stocks are traded in each of them.

f. What do we call the price that a borrower must pay for debt capital? What is the price of equity capital? What are the four most fundamental factors that affect the cost of money, or the general level of interest rates, in the economy?

g. What is the real risk-free rate of interest (k^*) and the nominal risk-free rate (k_{RF})? How are these two rates measured?

h. Define the terms inflation premium (IP), default risk premium (DRP), liquidity premium (LP), and maturity risk premium (MRP). Which of these premiums is included when determining the interest rate on (1) short-term U.S. Treasury securities, (2) long-term U.S. Treasury securities, (3) short-term corporate securities, and (4) long-term corporate securities? Explain how the premiums would vary over time and among the different securities listed above.

i. What is the term structure of interest rates? What is a yield curve? At any given time, how would the yield curve facing a given company such as AT&T or Revlon (Revlon's bonds are classified as "junk bonds") compare with the yield curve for U.S. Treasury securities? Draw a graph to illustrate your answer.

j. Several theories have been advanced to explain the shape of the yield curve. The three major ones are (1) the market segmentation theory, (2) the liquidity preference theory, and (3) the expectations theory. Briefly describe each of these theories. Do economists regard one as being "true"?

k. Suppose most investors expect the rate of inflation to be 5 percent next year, 6 percent the following year, and 8 percent thereafter. The real risk-free rate is 3 percent. The maturity risk premium is zero for bonds that mature in 1 year or less, 0.1 percent for 2-year bonds, and the MRP increases by 0.1 percent per year thereafter for 20 years, after which it is stable. What is the interest rate on 1-year, 10-year, and 20-year Treasury bonds? Draw a yield curve with these data. Is your yield curve consistent with the three term structure theories?

l. Working with DelaTorre has required you to put in a lot of overtime, so you have had very little time to spend on your private finances. It's now April 1, and you have only two weeks left to file your income tax return. You have managed to get all the information together that you will need to complete your return. Balik and Kiefer Inc. paid you a salary of $45,000, and you received $3,000 in dividends from common stock that you own. You are single, your personal exemption is $2,500, and your itemized deductions are $4,650.

   (1) On the basis of the information above and the 1995 individual tax rate schedule, what is your tax liability?

   (2) What are your marginal and average tax rates?

m. Assume that a corporation has $100,000 of taxable income from operations, $5,000 of interest income, and $10,000 of dividend income. What is the company's tax liability?

n. Assume that after paying your personal income tax, as calculated in Part 1, you have $5,000 to invest. You have narrowed your investment choice down to California bonds with a yield of 7 percent or IBM bonds with a yield of 10 percent. Which one should you choose, and why? At what marginal tax rate would you be indifferent to the choice between California and IBM bonds, assuming equal risk?

SELECTED ADDITIONAL REFERENCES AND CASES

Textbooks which focus on interest rates and financial markets include

Fabozzi, Frank J., *Bond Markets: Analysis and Strategies* (Englewood Cliffs, N.J.: Prentice-Hall, 1992).

Johnson, Hazel J., *Financial Institutions and Markets: A Global Perspective* (New York: McGraw-Hill, 1993).

Kidwell, David S., Richard Peterson, and David Blackwell, *Financial Institutions, Markets, and Money* (Fort Worth, Tex.: Dryden Press, 1993).

Kohn, Mier, *Money, Banking, and Financial Markets* (Fort Worth, Tex.: Dryden Press, 1993).

Livingston, Miles, *Money and Capital Markets* (Cambridge, Mass.: Blackwell, 1996).

Smith, Stephen D., and Raymond E. Spudeck, *Interest Rates: Theory and Application* (Fort Worth, Tex.: Dryden Press, 1993).

For current empirical data and a forecast of monetary conditions, see the most recent edition of this annual publication:

Salomon Brothers, *Supply and Demand for Credit* (New York).

The classic works on term structure theories include the following:

Culbertson, John M., "The Term Structure of Interest Rates," *Quarterly Journal of Economics,* November 1957, 489–504.

Fisher, Irving, "Appreciation and Interest," *Publications of the American Economic Association,* August 1986, 23–29 and 91–92.

Hicks, J. R., *Value and Capital* (London: Oxford University Press, 1946).

Lutz, F. A., "The Structure of Interest Rates," *Quarterly Journal of Economics,* November 1940, 36–63.

Modigliani, Franco, and Richard Sutch, "Innovations in Interest Rate Policy," *American Economic Review,* May 1966, 178–197.

For additional information on financial institutions, see

Greenbaum, Stuart I., and Anjan V. Thakor, *Contemporary Financial Intermediation* (Fort Worth: Dryden, 1995).

Kaufman, George G., *The U.S. Financial System* (Englewood Cliffs, N.J.: Prentice-Hall, 1995).

The following articles provide additional information on the effect of corporate taxes on business behavior:

Angell, Robert J., and Tony Wingler, "A Note on Expensing versus Depreciating under the Accelerated Cost Recovery System," *Financial Management,* Winter 1982, 34–35.

Comiskey, Eugene E., and James R. Hasselback, "Analyzing the Profit and Tax Relationship," *Financial Management,* Winter 1973, 57–62.

McCarty, Daniel E., and William R. McDaniel, "A Note on Expensing versus Depreciating under the Accelerated Cost Recovery System: Comment," *Financial Management,* Summer 1983, 37–39.

For a good reference guide to tax issues, see

Federal Tax Course (Englewood Cliffs, N.J.: Prentice-Hall, published annually).

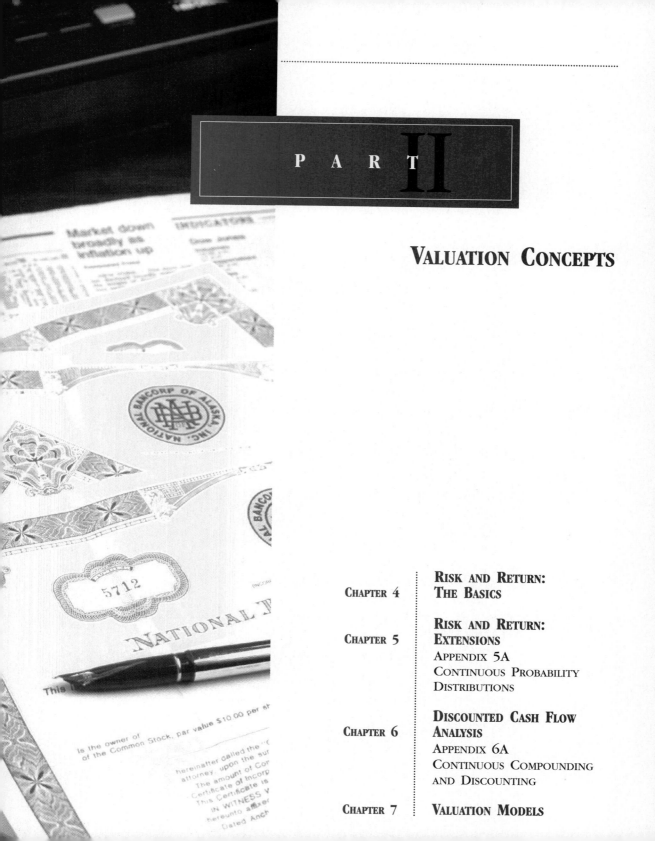

PART II

VALUATION CONCEPTS

CHAPTER 4

RISK AND RETURN: THE BASICS

*T*rue or false? *U.S. Treasury securities are less risky than an average share of stock, and short-term Treasury securities are less risky than long-term T-bonds.*

If you get that one on an exam, be careful — it could be a trick. The "obvious" answer is "true," but the correct answer is more complicated.

To illustrate, The Wall Street Journal *recently carried a story which began, "Treasury bills plunged 37% last year." The article went on to state that the 37 percent drop was in the* income *provided by a T-bill portfolio, not the market value of the portfolio, and it further stated that if risk is measured by the stability of income produced by a portfolio rather than the market value of the portfolio, stocks are the* least *risky investment, bonds are next, and T-bills the riskiest. Further, even if market value rather than income is the criterion, then if inflation is factored in and the holding period examined is 10 years or more, stocks are safer than bonds or bills.*

This point is important, because more and more corporations are shifting from retirement plans in which the companies make all the investment decisions to plans in which employees must make their own investment decisions and then live well or badly depending on how their investments perform. People generally want to invest their retirement funds in "safe" assets, and they assume that T-bills and bonds are safer than stocks. Consequently, they put most of their money in CDs, bonds, or similar investments.

However, as noted in the article, during a recent 12-month period "safe" Treasury bonds provided a total return (interest income plus capital gains or losses) of 2.2 percent, which was more than wiped out by inflation, but "treacherous" stocks provided a hefty 15.2 percent return. Furthermore, as the article noted, this situation is not at all unusual. Therefore, if someone is saving for retirement or college, stocks appear to be less *risky than bonds in most respects.*

Of course, some stocks are riskier than others, and if you put all your money in one risky stock that goes bust, you will be in deep trouble. Business Week *offered several ways for judging relative risk and for limiting it. They recommend that one begin by examining past returns and then calculating the* standard deviation *of those returns. The higher the standard deviation, the greater the risk, assuming the future will be like the past. But* Business Week *noted that the most widely used measure of risk for stocks is the "beta coefficient," which compares a stock's volatility with the S&P 500, a well-known stock market index. If beta equals 1, the stock is about as risky as the average; if beta is less than 1, the stock is less risky; and if beta is greater than 1, the stock is more risky than average.*

According to Business Week, *the single best weapon against risk is diversification:"By spreading your money around, you're not tied to the fickleness of a given market, stock, or industry. . . . Correlation, in portfolio-manager speak, helps you diversify properly because it describes how closely two investments track each other. If they move in tandem, they're likely to suffer from the same bad news. So, you should combine assets with low correlations."*

U.S. investors tend to think of "the stock market" as the U.S. stock market, but, in fact, U.S. stocks amount to only 35 percent of the value of the worldwide market. Foreign markets have been quite profitable, and they are not perfectly correlated with U.S. markets. Therefore, global diversification offers investors an opportunity both to raise returns and to reduce risk. However, foreign investing brings some risks of its own, most notably "currency risk," or the danger that exchange rate shifts will decrease the number of dollars a foreign currency will buy.

Although the central thrust of the Business Week *article was about ways to measure and then reduce risk, it did point out that some newly created instruments which are actually extremely risky have been marketed as low-risk investments to naive investors. For example, several mutual funds have advertised that their portfolios "contain only securities backed by the U.S. government" but then failed to highlight that they are using financial leverage, are investing in "derivatives," or are taking some other action which boosts current yields but at the risk of huge losses.*

When you finish this chapter, you should be able to understand what risk is, how it is measured, and what actions can be taken to minimize it or at least to ensure that you are adequately compensated for bearing it. And, if you get the question which opened this section on an exam, you will know to answer "maybe."[1]

In this chapter, we take an in-depth look at how investment risk should be measured and how it affects returns on investments. Recall that in Chapter 3, when we examined the determinants of interest rates, we defined the real risk-free rate, k*, as the rate of interest on a risk-free security in a world with no inflation. The actual interest rate on a particular debt security was shown to be equal to the real risk-free rate

---

[1]This chapter presents all of the risk and return concepts needed to understand the material presented in the remaining chapters. However, Chapter 4 does not contain the theoretical foundations of risk and return, so you may want to read (or your instructor may assign) Chapter 5 to provide you with a more in-depth understanding of these concepts.

plus several premiums which reflect both inflation and risk. In this chapter, we define more precisely what the term *risk* means as it relates to investments. We also examine procedures managers use to measure risk, and we discuss the relationship between risk and return. Business executives should understand these concepts and use them as they plan the actions which will shape their firms' futures.

As the opening vignette noted, risk can be measured in different ways, and different conclusions about an asset's riskiness can be reached depending on the measure used. This can be confusing, but it will help if you remember the following:

1. All financial assets are expected to produce *cash flows,* and the riskiness of the asset is judged in terms of the riskiness of its cash flows.

2. The riskiness of an asset can be considered in two ways: (1) on a *stand-alone basis,* where the asset's cash flows are analyzed by themselves, or (2) in a *portfolio context,* where the cash flows from a number of assets are combined.[2] There is an important difference between stand-alone and portfolio risk, because an asset which has a great deal of risk if held by itself may be much less risky if it is held as part of a larger portfolio.

3. In a portfolio context, an asset's risk can be divided into two components: (1) a *diversifiable risk component,* which can be diversified away and hence is of little concern to diversified investors, and (2) a *market risk component,* which is caused by broad market movements that cannot be eliminated by diversification and which therefore does concern investors. Only market risk is *relevant* — diversifiable risk is irrelevant because it can be eliminated.

4. An asset with a high degree of relevant (market) risk must provide a relatively high expected rate of return to attract investors. Investors in general are *averse to risk,* so they will not buy risky assets unless these assets have high expected returns.

5. In this chapter, we focus on *financial assets* such as stocks and bonds, but the concepts discussed here also apply to *physical assets* such as machines, trucks, or even whole plants. We apply risk analysis to physical assets in Chapter 11.

STAND-ALONE RISK

Risk is defined in *Webster's* as "a hazard; a peril; exposure to loss or injury." Thus, risk refers to the chance that some unfavorable event will occur. If you engage in skydiving, you are taking a chance with your life—skydiving is risky. If you bet on the horses, you are risking your money. If you invest in speculative stocks (or, really, *any* stock), you are taking a risk in the hope of making an appreciable return.

An asset's risk can be analyzed in two ways: (1) on a stand-alone basis, where the asset is considered in isolation, and (2) on a portfolio basis, where the asset is held

---

[2]A *portfolio* is a collection of investment securities. If you owned some General Motors stock, some Exxon stock, and some IBM stock, you would be holding a three-stock portfolio. Because diversification lowers risk, most securities are held in portfolios.

as one of a number of assets in a portfolio. Thus, an asset's *stand-alone risk* is the risk an investor would face if he or she held only this one asset.

Suppose an investor buys $100,000 of short-term Treasury bills with an expected return of 5 percent. In this case, the rate of return on the investment, 5 percent, can be estimated quite precisely, and the investment is defined as being essentially *risk-free*. However, if the $100,000 were invested in the stock of a company just being organized to prospect for oil in the mid-Atlantic, then the investment's return could not be estimated precisely. One might analyze the situation and conclude that the *expected* rate of return, in a statistical sense, is 20 percent, but the investor should also recognize that the *actual* rate of return could range from, say, +1,000 percent to −100 percent. Because there is a significant danger of actually earning considerably less than the expected return, the stock would be described as being relatively risky.

No investment will be undertaken unless the expected rate of return is high enough to compensate for the perceived risk of the investment. In this example, it is clear that few if any investors would be willing to buy the oil company's stock if its expected return were the same as that of the T-bill.

Naturally, a risky investment might not actually produce its expected rate of return — if assets always produced their expected returns, they would not be risky.

Investment risk, then, is related to the probability of actually earning less than the expected return — the greater the chance of low or negative returns, the riskier the investment. However, risk can be defined more precisely, and it is useful to do so.

PROBABILITY DISTRIBUTIONS

An event's *probability* is defined as the chance that the event will occur. For example, a weather forecaster might state, "There is a 40 percent chance of rain today and a 60 percent chance that it will not rain." If all possible events, or outcomes, are listed, and if a probability is assigned to each event, the listing is called a *probability distribution*. For our weather forecast, we could set up the following probability distribution:

OUTCOME (1)	PROBABILITY (2)	
Rain	0.4 =	40%
No rain	0.6 =	60
	1.0 =	100%

The possible outcomes are listed in Column 1, while the probabilities of these outcomes, expressed both as decimals and as percentages, are given in Column 2. Notice that the probabilities must sum to 1.0, or 100 percent.

Probabilities can also be assigned to the possible outcomes (or returns) from an investment. If you buy a bond, you expect to receive interest on the bond, and those interest payments will provide you with a rate of return on your investment. The possible outcomes from this investment are (1) that the issuer will make the interest payments or (2) that the issuer will default on the payments. The higher the probability of default, the riskier the bond, and the higher the risk, the higher the required rate of return will be. If you invest in a stock instead of buying a bond, you will again expect to earn a return on your money. A stock's return will come from dividends plus capital gains. Again, the riskier the stock — which means the higher the probability that the firm will fail to pay the expected dividends or that the stock price will decline rather than increase — the higher the expected return must be to induce you to invest in the stock.

With this in mind, consider the possible rates of return (dividend yield plus capital gain or loss) that you might earn next year on a $10,000 investment in the stock of either Martin Products Inc. or U.S. Electric Company. Martin manufactures and distributes computer terminals and equipment for the rapidly growing data transmission industry. Because it faces intense competition, and its new products may or may not be competitive in the marketplace, its future earnings could vary widely. Indeed, some new company could develop better products which could literally bankrupt Martin. U.S. Electric, on the other hand, supplies an essential service, and because it has city franchises which protect it from competition, its sales and profits are relatively stable and predictable.

The rate-of-return probability distributions for the two companies are shown in Table 4-1. This type of table is known as a *payoff matrix*. There is a 30 percent chance of strong demand, in which case both companies will have high earnings, pay high dividends, and enjoy capital gains; a 40 percent probability of normal demand and moderate returns; and a 30 percent probability of weak demand, which will mean low earnings and dividends as well as capital losses. Notice, however, that Martin Products' rate of return could vary far more widely than that of U.S. Electric. There is a fairly high probability that the value of Martin's stock will drop substantially, resulting in a loss of 70 percent, while there is no chance of a loss for U.S. Electric.[3]

| PROBABILITY DISTRIBUTIONS (PAYOFF MATRIX) FOR MARTIN PRODUCTS AND U.S. ELECTRIC | | TABLE 4-1 |

		RATE OF RETURN ON STOCK IF THIS STATE OCCURS	
DEMAND FOR THE COMPANY'S PRODUCTS	PROBABILITY OF THIS DEMAND OCCURRING	MARTIN PRODUCTS	U.S. ELECTRIC
Strong	0.3	100%	20%
Normal	0.4	15	15
Weak	0.3	(70)	10
	1.0		

---

[3]It is, of course, completely unrealistic to think that any stock has no chance of a loss. Only in hypothetical examples could this occur. To illustrate, the price of General Public Utilities, the owner of the Three Mile Island (TMI) nuclear plant, dropped from about $18 to $3 after the TMI accident. All investors were reminded that any stock is exposed to some risk of loss, and those investors who bought GPU learned that lesson the hard way.

EXPECTED RATE OF RETURN

If we multiply each possible outcome by its probability of occurrence and then sum these products, as in Table 4-2, we have a *weighted average* of outcomes. The weights are the probabilities, and the weighted average is the *expected rate of return, $\hat{k}$,* called "k-hat."[4] The expected rates of return for both Martin Products and U.S. Electric are shown in Table 4-2 to be 15 percent.

The expected rate of return calculation can also be expressed as an equation which does the same thing as Table 4-2:

$$\text{Expected rate of return} = \hat{k} = P_1 k_1 + P_2 k_2 + \cdots + P_n k_n$$

$$= \sum_{i=1}^{n} P_i k_i. \qquad \text{4-1}$$

Here k_i is the ith possible outcome, P_i is the probability of the ith outcome, and n is the number of possible outcomes. Thus, $\hat{k}$ is a weighted average of the possible outcomes (the k_i values), with each outcome's weight being its probability of occurrence. Using the data for Martin Products, we obtain its expected rate of return as follows:

$$\hat{k} = P_1(k_1) + P_2(k_2) + P_3(k_3)$$

$$= 0.3(100\%) + 0.4(15\%) + 0.3(-70\%)$$

$$= 15\%.$$

U.S. Electric's expected rate of return is also 15 percent:

$$\hat{k} = 0.3(20\%) + 0.4(15\%) + 0.3(10\%)$$

$$= 15\%.$$

| TABLE 4-2 | CALCULATION OF EXPECTED RATES OF RETURN |

		MARTIN PRODUCTS		U.S. ELECTRIC	
DEMAND FOR THE COMPANY'S PRODUCTS (1)	PROBABILITY OF THIS DEMAND OCCURRING (2)	RATE OF RETURN IF THIS DEMAND OCCURS (3)	PRODUCT: (2) × (3) = (4)	RATE OF RETURN IF THIS DEMAND OCCURS (5)	PRODUCT: (2) × (5) = (6)
Stong	0.3	100%	30%	20%	6%
Normal	0.4	15	6	15	6
Weak	0.3	(70)	(21)	10	3
	1.0		$\hat{k} = 15\%$		$\hat{k} = 15\%$

---

[4]In Chapter 7, we will use $\hat{k}_d$ to signify the return on a debt instrument and $\hat{k}_s$ to signify the return on a stock. In this section, however, we discuss only returns on stocks; thus, the subscript s is unnecessary, and we use the term $\hat{k}$ rather than $\hat{k}_s$.

We can graph the rates of return to obtain a picture of the variability of possible outcomes; this is shown in the Figure 4-1 bar charts. The height of each bar signifies the probability that a given outcome will occur. The range of probable returns for Martin Products is from −70 to +100 percent, with an expected return of 15 percent. The expected return for U.S. Electric is also 15 percent, but its range is much narrower.

Thus far, we have assumed that only three situations can exist: strong, normal, and weak demand. Actually, of course, demand could range from a deep depression to a fantastic boom, and there are an unlimited number of possibilities in between. Suppose we had the time and patience to assign a probability to each possible level of demand (with the sum of the probabilities still equaling 1.0) and to assign a rate of return to each stock for each level of demand. We would have a table similar to Table 4-1, except that it would have many more entries in each column. This table could be used to calculate expected rates of return as shown previously, and the probabilities and outcomes could be approximated by continuous curves such as those presented in Figure 4-2. Here we have changed the assumptions so that there is essentially a zero probability that Martin Products' return will be less than −70 percent or more than 100 percent, or that U.S. Electric's return will be less than 10 percent or more than 20 percent, but virtually any return within these limits is possible.

The tighter, or more peaked, the probability distribution, the more likely it is that the actual outcome will be close to the expected value, and, consequently, the less likely it is that the actual return will end up far below the expected return. Thus, the tighter the probability distribution, the lower the risk assigned to a stock. Since

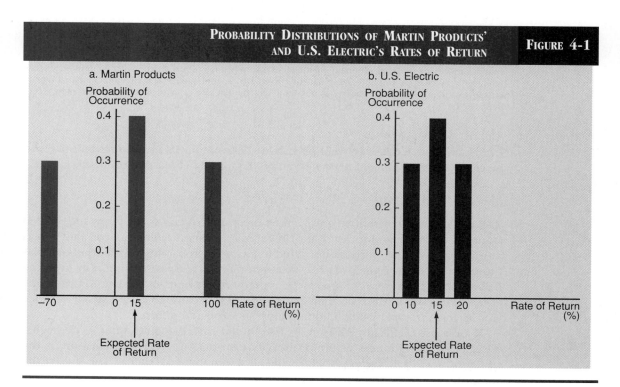

PROBABILITY DISTRIBUTIONS OF MARTIN PRODUCTS' AND U.S. ELECTRIC'S RATES OF RETURN — **FIGURE 4-1**

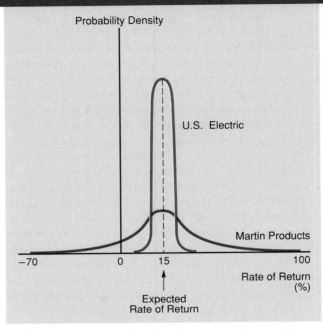

FIGURE 4-2   **CONTINUOUS PROBABILITY DISTRIBUTIONS OF MARTIN PRODUCTS' AND U.S. ELECTRIC'S RATES OF RETURN**

NOTE: The assumptions regarding the probabilities of various outcomes have been changed from those in Figure 4-1. There the probability of obtaining exactly 15 percent was 40 percent; here it is *infinitesimally small* because there are many possible outcomes instead of just three. With continuous distributions, it is more appropriate to ask what the probability is of obtaining at least some specified rate of return than to ask for the probability of obtaining exactly that rate. This topic is covered in more detail in Appendix 5A.

U.S. Electric has a relatively tight probability distribution, its *actual return* is likely to be closer to its 15 percent *expected return* than is that of Martin Products.

MEASURING STAND-ALONE RISK: THE STANDARD DEVIATION

Risk is a difficult concept to grasp, and a great deal of controversy has surrounded attempts to define and measure it. However, a common definition, and one that is satisfactory for many purposes, is stated in terms of probability distributions such as those presented in Figure 4-2: *The tighter the probability distribution of expected future returns, the smaller the risk of a given investment.* According to this definition, U.S. Electric is less risky than Martin Products because there is a smaller chance that its actual return will end up far below its expected return.

To be most useful, any measure of risk should have a definite value — we need a measure of the tightness of the probability distribution. One such measure is the *standard deviation,* the symbol for which is σ, pronounced "sigma." The smaller the standard deviation, the tighter the probability distribution, and, accordingly, the lower the riskiness of the stock. To calculate the standard deviation, we proceed as shown in Table 4-3, taking the following steps:

1. Calculate the expected rate of return:

$$\text{Expected rate of return} = \hat{k} = \sum_{i=1}^{n} P_i k_i.$$

For Martin, we previously found $\hat{k} = 15\%$.

2. Subtract the expected rate of return ($\hat{k}$) from each possible outcome (k_i) to obtain a set of deviations about $\hat{k}$ as shown in Column 1 of Table 4-3:

$$\text{Deviation}_i = k_i - \hat{k}.$$

3. Square each deviation, then multiply the result by the probability of occurrence for its related outcome, and then sum these products to obtain the *variance* of the probability distribution as shown in Columns 2 and 3 of the table:

$$\text{Variance} = \sigma^2 = \sum_{i=1}^{n} (k_i - \hat{k})^2 P_i. \qquad \text{4-2}$$

4. Finally, find the square root of the variance to obtain the standard deviation:

$$\text{Standard deviation} = \sigma = \sqrt{\sum_{i=1}^{n} (k_i - \hat{k})^2 P_i}. \qquad \text{4-3}$$

Thus, the standard deviation is essentially a weighted average of the deviations from the expected value, and it provides an idea of how far above or below the expected value the actual value is likely to be. Martin's standard deviation is seen in Table 4-3

CALCULATING MARTIN PRODUCTS' STANDARD DEVIATION		TABLE 4-3
$k_i - \hat{k}$ (1)	$(k_i - \hat{k})^2$ (2)	$(k_i - \hat{k})^2 P_i$ (3)
$100 - 15 = 85$	7,225	$(7,225)(0.3) = 2,167.5$
$15 - 15 = 0$	0	$(0)(0.4) = 0.0$
$-70 - 15 = -85$	7,225	$(7,225)(0.3) = \underline{2,167.5}$
		$\text{Variance} = \sigma^2 = \underline{4,335.0}$
		$\text{Standard deviation} = \sigma = \sqrt{\sigma^2} = \sqrt{4,335} = 65.84\%.$

to be $\sigma = 65.84\%$. Using these same procedures, we find U.S. Electric's standard deviation to be 3.87 percent. Since Martin Products has a larger standard deviation, which indicates a greater probability of a low or even negative return, it is a riskier investment than U.S. Electric when held alone.

If a probability distribution is normal, the *actual* return will be within ±1 standard deviation of the *expected* return 68.26 percent of the time. Figure 4-3 illustrates this point, and it also shows the situation for ±2σ and ±3σ. For Martin Products, $\hat{k} = 15\%$ and $\sigma = 65.84\%$, whereas $\hat{k} = 15\%$ and $\sigma = 3.87\%$ for U.S. Electric. Thus, *if the two distributions were normal* there would be a 68.26 percent probability that Martin's actual return would be in the range of 15 ± 65.84 percent, or from -50.84 to 80.84 percent. For U.S. Electric, the 68.26 percent range is 15 ± 3.87 percent, or from 11.13 to 18.87 percent. With such a small σ, there is only a small probability that U.S. Electric's return would be significantly less than expected, so the stock is not very risky. For the average firm listed on the New York Stock Exchange, σ has generally been in the range of 35 to 40 percent in recent years.[5]

---

[5]In the example, we described the procedure for finding the mean and standard deviation when the data are in the form of a known probability distribution. If only sample returns data over some past period are available, the standard deviation of returns can be estimated using this formula:

$$\text{Estimated } \sigma = S = \sqrt{\frac{\sum\limits_{t=1}^{n} (\bar{k}_t - \bar{k}_{Avg})^2}{n - 1}}. \tag{4-3a}$$

Here $\bar{k}_t$("k bar t") denotes the past realized rate of return in Period t, and $\bar{k}_{Avg}$ is the average annual return earned during the last n years. Here is an example:

YEAR	$\bar{k}_t$
1994	15%
1995	−5
1996	20

$$\bar{k}_{Avg} = \frac{(15 - 5 + 20)}{3} = 10.0\%.$$

$$\text{Estimated } \sigma \text{ (or S)} = \sqrt{\frac{(15 - 10)^2 + (-5 - 10)^2 + (20 - 10)^2}{3 - 1}}$$

$$= \sqrt{\frac{350}{2}} = 13.2\%.$$

The historical σ is often used as an estimate of the future σ. Much less often, and generally incorrectly, $\bar{k}_{Avg}$ for some past period is used as an estimate of $\hat{k}$, the expected future return. Because past variability is likely to be repeated, σ may be a good estimate of future risk, but it is much less reasonable to expect that the past *level* of return (which could have been as high as +100% or as low as −50%) is the best expectation of what investors think will happen in the future.

Equation 4-3a is built into all financial calculators, and it is very easy to use. We simply enter the rates of return and press the key marked S (or S_x) to get the standard deviation. Note, though, that calculators have no built-in formula for finding σ where probabilistic data are involved; there you must go through the process outlined in Table 4-3 and Equation 4-3.

| PROBABILITY RANGES FOR A NORMAL DISTRIBUTION | FIGURE 4-3 |

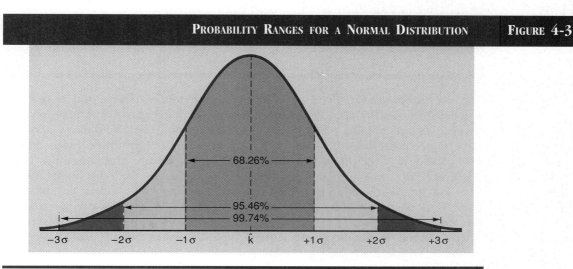

NOTES:

a. The area under the normal curve always equals 1.0, or 100 percent. *Thus, the areas under any pair of normal curves drawn on the same scale, whether they are peaked or flat, must be equal.*

b. Half of the area under a normal curve is to the left of the mean, indicating that there is a 50 percent probability that the actual outcome will be less than the mean, and half is to the right of $\hat{k}$, indicating a 50 percent probability that it will be greater than the mean.

c. Of the area under the curve, 68.26 percent is within $\pm 1\sigma$ of the mean, indicating that the probability is 68.26 percent that the actual outcome will be within the range $\hat{k} - 1\sigma$ to $\hat{k} + 1\sigma$.

d. Procedures exist for finding the probability of other ranges. These procedures are covered in statistics courses.

e. For a normal distribution, the larger the value of σ, the greater the probability that the actual outcome will vary widely from, and hence perhaps be far below, the expected, or most likely, outcome. *Since the probability of having the actual result turn out to be far below the expected result is one definition of risk, and since σ measures this probability, we can use σ as a measure of risk.* This definition may not be a good one, however, if we are dealing with an asset held in a diversified portfolio. This point is covered later in the chapter.

MEASURING STAND-ALONE RISK: THE COEFFICIENT OF VARIATION

If a choice has to be made between two investments which have the same expected returns but different standard deviations, most people would choose the one with the lower standard deviation and, therefore, the lower risk. Similarly, given a choice between two investments with the same risk (standard deviations) but different expected returns, investors would generally prefer the investment with the higher expected return. To most people, this is common sense — return is "good," risk is "bad," and, consequently, investors want as much return and as little risk as possible. But how do we choose between two investments when one has the higher expected return but the other the lower standard deviation? To help answer this question, we use another measure of risk, the *coefficient of variation (CV)*, which is the standard deviation divided by the expected return:

$$\text{Coefficient of variation} = CV = \frac{\sigma}{\hat{k}}. \qquad 4\text{-}4$$

The coefficient of variation shows the risk per unit of return, and it provides a more meaningful basis for comparison when the expected returns on two alternatives are not the same. Since U.S. Electric and Martin Products have the same expected return, the coefficient of variation is not really necessary in this case. The firm with the larger standard deviation, Martin, must have the larger coefficient of variation when the means are equal. In fact, the coefficient of variation for Martin is 65.84/15 = 4.39 and that for U.S. Electric is 3.87/15 = 0.26. Thus, Martin is almost 17 times riskier than U.S. Electric on the basis of this criterion.

For a case where the coefficient of variation is necessary, consider Projects X and Y, which have different expected rates of return and different standard deviations. These projects are graphed in Figure 4-4. Project X has a 60 percent expected rate of return and a 15 percent standard deviation, while Project Y has an 8 percent expected return but only a 3 percent standard deviation. Is Project X riskier, on a relative basis, because it has the larger standard deviation? If we calculate the coefficients of variation for these two projects, we find that Project X has a coefficient of variation of 15/60 = 0.25, and Project Y has a coefficient of variation of 3/8 = 0.375. Thus, we see that Project Y actually has more risk per unit of return than Project X, in spite of the fact that X's standard deviation is larger. Therefore, even though Project Y has the lower standard deviation, according to the coefficient of variation measure it is riskier than Project X.

FIGURE 4-4	**COMPARISON OF PROBABILITY DISTRIBUTIONS AND RATES OF RETURN FOR PROJECTS X AND Y**

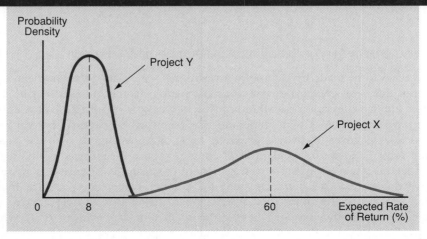

Project Y has the smaller standard deviation, hence the more peaked probability distribution, but it is clear from Figure 4-4 that the chances of a really low return are higher for Y than for X because X's expected return is so high. Because the coefficient of variation captures the effects of both risk and return, it is a better measure for evaluating risk in situations where investments have substantially different expected returns.

RISK AVERSION AND REQUIRED RETURNS

Suppose you have worked hard and saved $1 million, which you now plan to invest. You can buy a 5 percent U.S. Treasury note, and at the end of 1 year you will have a sure $1.05 million, which is your original investment plus $50,000 in interest. Alternatively, you can buy stock in R&D Enterprises. If R&D's research programs are successful, your stock will increase in value to $2.1 million; however, if the research is a failure, the value of your stock will go to zero, and you will be penniless. You regard R&D's chances of success or failure as being 50-50, so the expected value of the stock investment is 0.5($0) + 0.5($2,100,000) = $1,050,000. Subtracting the $1 million cost of the stock leaves an expected profit of $50,000, or an expected (but risky) 5 percent rate of return:

$$\frac{\text{Expected rate}}{\text{of return}} = \frac{\text{Expected ending value} - \text{Cost}}{\text{Cost}}$$

$$= \frac{\$1,050,000 - \$1,000,000}{\$1,000,000}$$

$$= \frac{\$50,000}{\$1,000,000} = 5\%.$$

Thus, you have a choice between a sure $50,000 profit (representing a 5 percent rate of return) on the Treasury note and a risky expected $50,000 profit (also representing a 5 percent expected rate of return) on the R&D Enterprises stock. Which one would you choose? *If you choose the less risky investment, you are risk averse. Most investors are indeed risk averse, and certainly the average investor is risk averse with regard to his or her "serious money." Because this is a well-documented fact, we shall assume risk aversion throughout the remainder of the book.*

What are the implications of risk aversion for security prices and rates of return? The answer is that, other things held constant, the higher a security's risk, the lower its price and the higher its required return. To see how risk aversion affects security prices, consider again U.S. Electric and Martin Products stocks. Suppose each stock sold for $100 per share and each had an expected rate of return of 15 percent. Investors are averse to risk, so under these conditions there would be a general preference for U.S. Electric. People with money to invest would bid for U.S. Electric rather than Martin stock, and Martin's stockholders would start selling their stock and using the money to buy U.S. Electric stock. Buying pressure would drive up the price of U.S. Electric's stock, and selling pressure would simultaneously cause Martin's price to decline.

These price changes, in turn, would cause changes in the expected rates of return on the two securities. Suppose, for example, that the price of U.S. Electric stock was bid up from $100 to $150, whereas the price of Martin's stock declined from $100 to $75. This would cause U.S. Electric's expected return to fall to 10 percent, while Martin's expected return would rise to 20 percent. The difference in returns, 20% − 10% = 10%, is a *risk premium, RP,* which represents the additional compensation investors require for assuming the additional risk of Martin stock.

This example demonstrates a very important principle: *In a market dominated by risk-averse investors, riskier securities must have higher expected returns, as estimated by the average investor, than less risky securities, for if this situation does not hold, buying and selling in the market will force it to occur.* We will consider the question of how much higher the returns on risky securities must be later in the chapter, after we see how diversification affects the way risk should be measured. Then, in Chapter 7, we will see how risk-adjusted rates of return affect the prices investors are willing to pay for different securities.

SELF-TEST QUESTIONS	What does "investment risk" mean?
	Set up an illustrative probability distribution for an investment.
	What is a payoff matrix?
	Which of the two stocks graphed in Figure 4-2 is less risky? Why?
	How does one calculate the standard deviation?
	Which is a better measure of risk if assets have different expected returns: (1) standard deviation or (2) coefficient of variation? Explain.
	Explain the following statement: "Most investors are risk averse."
	How does risk aversion affect rates of return?

RISK IN A PORTFOLIO CONTEXT

In the preceding section, we considered the riskiness of assets held in isolation. Now we analyze the riskiness of assets held in portfolios. As we shall see, an asset held as part of a portfolio usually is less risky than the same asset held in isolation. Accordingly, most financial assets are held as parts of portfolios. Banks, pension funds, insurance companies, mutual funds, and other financial institutions are required by law to hold diversified portfolios. Even individual investors—at least those whose security holdings constitute a significant part of their total wealth—generally hold portfolios, not the stock of only one firm. This being the case, from an investor's standpoint the fact that a particular stock goes up or down is not very important; *what is important is the return on his or her portfolio, and the portfolio's risk. Logically, then, the risk and return of an individual security should be analyzed in terms of how that security affects the risk and return of the portfolio in which it is held.*

To illustrate, Payco American is a collection agency company which operates nationwide through 37 offices. The company is not well known, its stock is not very liquid, its earnings have fluctuated quite a bit in the past, and it doesn't pay a dividend. All this suggests that Payco is risky and that its required rate of return, k, should be relatively high. However, Payco's required rate of return in 1996, and all other years, was quite low in relation to those of most other companies. This indicates that investors regard Payco as being a low-risk company in spite of its uncertain profits. The reason for this counterintuitive fact has to do with diversification and its effect on risk. Payco's earnings and stock price rise during recessions, whereas most other companies' stock prices tend to decline when the economy slumps. Therefore, holding Payco in a portfolio of "normal" stocks tends to stabilize returns on the entire portfolio.

PORTFOLIO RETURNS

The *expected return on a portfolio, $\hat{k}_p$,* is simply the weighted average of the expected returns on the individual assets in the portfolio, with the weights being the fraction of the total portfolio invested in each asset:

$$\hat{k}_p = w_1\hat{k}_1 + w_2\hat{k}_2 + \ldots + w_n\hat{k}_n$$

$$= \sum_{i=1}^{n} w_i\hat{k}_i.$$

4-5

Here the $\hat{k}_i$'s are the expected returns on the individual stocks, the w_i's are the weights, and there are n stocks in the portfolio. Note (1) that w_i is the fraction of the portfolio's dollar value invested in Stock i (that is, the value of the investment in Stock i divided by the total value of the portfolio) and (2) that the w_i's must sum to 1.0.

Assume that in March 1996, a security analyst estimated that the following returns could be expected on the stocks of four large companies:

	EXPECTED RETURN, $\hat{k}$
Microsoft	14%
General Electric	13
Arctic Oil	20
Citicorp	18

If we formed a $100,000 portfolio, investing $25,000 in each stock, the expected portfolio return would be 16.25%:

$$\hat{k}_p = w_1\hat{k}_1 + w_2\hat{k}_2 + w_3\hat{k}_3 + w_4\hat{k}_4$$

$$= 0.25(14\%) + 0.25(13\%) + 0.25(20\%) + 0.25(18\%)$$

$$= 16.25\%.$$

Of course, after the fact and a year later, the actual *realized rates of return* on the individual stocks — the $\bar{k}_i$, or "k-bar," values — will almost certainly be different from their expected values, so $\bar{k}_p$ will be different from $\hat{k}_p = 16.25\%$. For example, Microsoft might double in price and provide a return of +100%, whereas Citicorp stock might have a terrible year, fall sharply, and have a return of −75%. Note, though, that those two events would be somewhat offsetting, so the portfolio's return might still be close to its expected return, even though the individual stocks' actual returns were far from their expected returns.

PORTFOLIO RISK

As we just saw, the expected return on a portfolio is simply the weighted average of the expected returns on the individual assets in the portfolio. However, unlike returns, the riskiness of a portfolio, σ_p, is generally *not* the weighted average of the standard deviations of the individual assets in the portfolio; the portfolio's risk will be *smaller* than the weighted average of the assets' σ's. In fact, it is theoretically possible to combine two stocks which are individually quite risky as measured by their standard deviations and to form a portfolio which is completely riskless, with $\sigma_p = 0$.

To illustrate the effect of combining assets, consider the situation in Figure 4-5. The bottom section gives data on rates of return for Stocks W and M individually, and also for a portfolio invested 50 percent in each stock. The three graphs across the top plot the data in a time series format, and the three graphs in the middle show the probability distributions of returns, assuming that the future is expected to be like the past. The two stocks would be quite risky if they were held in isolation, but when they are combined to form Portfolio WM, they are not risky at all. (Note: These stocks are called W and M because the graphs of their returns in Figure 4-5 resemble a W and an M.)

The reason Stocks W and M can be combined to form a riskless portfolio is that their returns move countercyclically to each other — when W's returns fall, those of M rise, and vice versa. The tendency of two variables to move together is called *correlation,* and the *correlation coefficient, r,* measures this tendency.[6] In statistical terms, we say that the returns on Stocks W and M are *perfectly negatively correlated,* with r = −1.0.

The opposite of perfect negative correlation, with r = −1.0, is *perfect positive correlation,* with r = +1.0. Returns on two perfectly positively correlated stocks (M and M′) move up and down together, and a portfolio consisting of two such stocks would be exactly as risky as the individual stocks. This point is illustrated in Figure 4-6, where we see that the portfolio's standard deviation is equal to that of the individual stocks. *Thus, diversification does nothing to reduce risk if the portfolio consists of perfectly positively correlated stocks.*

Figures 4-5 and 4-6 demonstrate that when stocks are perfectly negatively correlated (r = −1.0), all risk can be diversified away, but when stocks are perfectly positively correlated (r = +1.0), diversification does no good whatsoever. In reality, most stocks are positively correlated, but not perfectly so. On average, the correlation coefficient for the returns on two randomly selected stocks would be about +0.6, and for most pairs of stocks, r would lie in the range of +0.5 to +0.7. *Under such conditions, combining stocks into portfolios reduces risk but does not eliminate it completely.* Figure 4-7 illustrates this point with two stocks whose correlation coefficient is r = +0.67. The portfolio's average return is 15.0 percent, which is exactly the same as the average return for each of the two stocks, but its standard deviation

---

[6]The *correlation coefficient, r,* can range from +1.0, denoting that the two variables move up and down in perfect synchronization, to −1.0, denoting that the variables always move in exactly opposite directions. A correlation coefficient of zero suggests that the two variables are not related to each other — that is, changes in one variable are *independent* of changes in the other.

It is easy to calculate correlation coefficients with a financial calculator. Simply enter the returns on the two stocks and then press a key labeled "r." For W and M, r = −1.0.

FIGURE 4-5	RATE OF RETURN DISTRIBUTIONS FOR TWO PERFECTLY NEGATIVELY CORRELATED STOCKS (r = −1.0) AND FOR PORTFOLIO WM

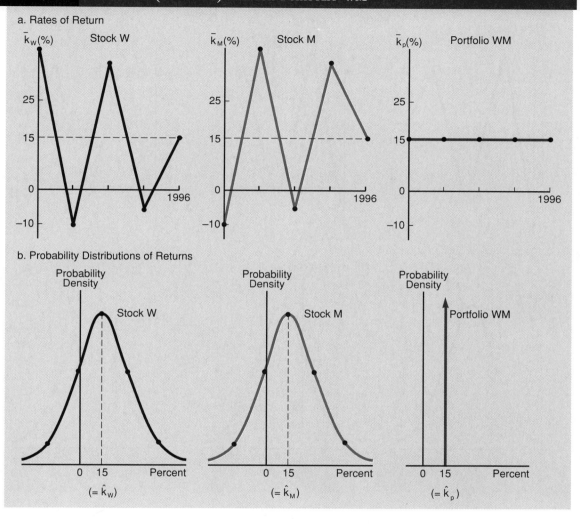

a. Rates of Return

b. Probability Distributions of Returns

YEAR	STOCK W ($\bar{k}_W$)	STOCK M ($\bar{k}_M$)	PORTFOLIO WM ($\bar{k}_p$)
1992	40%	(10%)	15%
1993	(10)	40	15
1994	35	(5)	15
1995	(5)	35	15
1996	15	15	15
Average return	15%	15%	15%
Standard deviation	22.6%	22.6%	0.0%

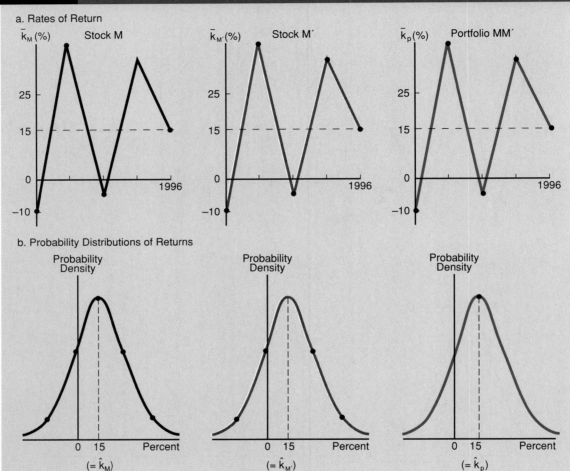

FIGURE 4-6   RATE OF RETURN DISTRIBUTIONS FOR TWO PERFECTLY POSITIVELY CORRELATED STOCKS (r = +1.0) AND FOR PORTFOLIO MM′

a. Rates of Return

b. Probability Distributions of Returns

YEAR	STOCK M ($\bar{k}_M$)	STOCK M′ ($\bar{k}_{M'}$)	PORTFOLIO MM′ ($\bar{k}_P$)
1992	(10%)	(10%)	(10%)
1993	40	40	40
1994	(5)	(5)	(5)
1995	35	35	35
1996	15	15	15
Average return	15%	15%	15%
Standard deviation	22.6%	22.6%	22.6%

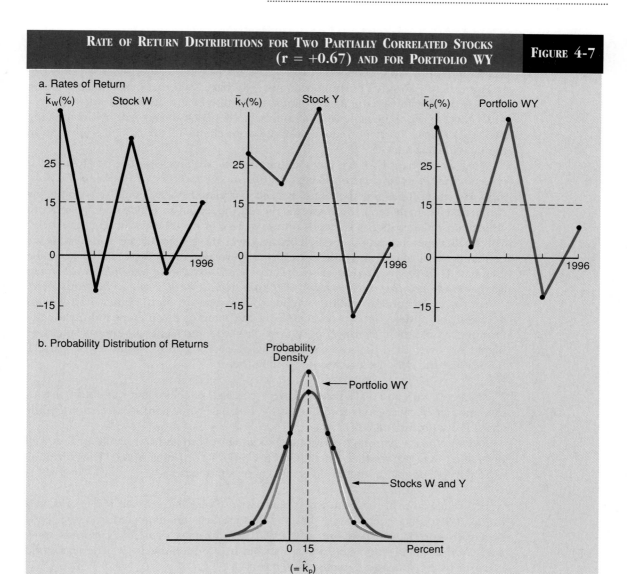

RATE OF RETURN DISTRIBUTIONS FOR TWO PARTIALLY CORRELATED STOCKS (r = +0.67) AND FOR PORTFOLIO WY   FIGURE 4-7

a. Rates of Return

b. Probability Distribution of Returns

YEAR	STOCK W ($\bar{k}_W$)	STOCK Y ($\bar{k}_Y$)	PORTFOLIO WY ($\bar{k}_P$)
1992	40%	28%	34%
1993	(10)	20	5
1994	35	41	38
1995	(5)	(17)	(11)
1996	15	3	9
Average return	15%	15%	15%
Standard deviation	22.6%	22.6%	20.6%

is 20.6 percent, which is less than the standard deviation of either stock. Thus, the portfolio's risk is *not* an average of the risks of its individual stocks — diversification has reduced, but not eliminated, risk.

From these two-stock portfolio examples we have seen that in one extreme case (r = −1.0) risk can be completely eliminated, while in the other extreme case (r = +1.0), diversification does nothing to limit risk. Between these extremes, combining two stocks into a portfolio reduces, but does not eliminate, the riskiness inherent in the individual stocks.

What would happen if we included more than two stocks in the portfolio? *As a rule, the riskiness of a portfolio will decline as the number of stocks in the portfolio increases.* If we added enough partially correlated stocks, could we completely eliminate risk? In general, the answer is no, but the extent to which adding stocks to a portfolio reduces its risk depends on the *degree of correlation* among the stocks: The smaller the correlation coefficient, the lower the risk in a large portfolio. If we could find a set of stocks whose correlations were zero or negative, all risk could be eliminated. *In the real world, where the correlations among the individual stocks are generally positive but less than +1.0, some, but not all, risk can be eliminated.*

To test your understanding, would you expect to find higher correlations between the returns on two companies in the same or in different industries? For example, would the correlation of returns on Ford's and General Motors's stocks be higher or lower than that between Ford and AT&T, and how would those correlations affect the risk of portfolios containing them?

Answer: Ford's and GM's returns have a correlation coefficient of about 0.9 with one another because both are affected by auto sales, but Ford's correlation is only about 0.6 with that of AT&T.

Implications: A two-stock portfolio consisting of Ford and GM would be less well diversified than a two-stock portfolio consisting of Ford plus AT&T. Thus, to minimize risk, portfolios should be diversified across industries.

Before leaving this section, we should issue a warning—in the real world, it is *impossible* to find stocks like W and M, whose returns are expected to be perfectly negatively correlated. *Therefore, it is impossible to form completely riskless stock portfolios.* Diversification can reduce risk, but it cannot eliminate it. The real world is closer to the situation depicted in Figure 4-7).

DIVERSIFIABLE RISK VERSUS MARKET RISK

As noted earlier, it is difficult if not impossible to find stocks whose expected returns are not positively correlated — most stocks tend to do well when the national economy is strong and badly when it is weak.[7] Thus, even very large portfolios end up

---

[7]It is not too hard to find a few stocks that happened to have risen because of a particular set of circumstances in the past while most other stocks were declining, but it is much harder to find stocks that could logically be *expected* to go up in the future when other stocks are falling. Also, note that derivatives can be used to hedge stock market risk, much like our W and M stocks. However, hedging with stock derivatives normally *shifts* risks rather than eliminating them, so stock hedges are expensive. This topic is discussed further in Chapter 23.

with a substantial amount of risk, but not as much risk as if all the money were invested in only one stock.

To see more precisely how portfolio size affects portfolio risk, consider Figure 4-8, which shows how portfolio risk is affected by forming larger and larger portfolios of randomly selected NYSE stocks. Standard deviations are plotted for an average one-stock portfolio, a two-stock portfolio, and so on, up to a portfolio consisting of all 2,000-plus common stocks that were listed on the NYSE at the time the data were graphed. The graph illustrates that, in general, the riskiness of a portfolio consisting of average NYSE stocks tends to decline and to approach some limit as the size of the portfolio increases. According to data accumulated in recent years, σ_1, the standard deviation of a one-stock portfolio (or an average stock), is approximately 35 percent. A portfolio consisting of all stocks, which is called the *market portfolio,* would have a standard deviation, σ_M, of about 18 percent, which is shown as the horizontal dashed line in Figure 4-8.

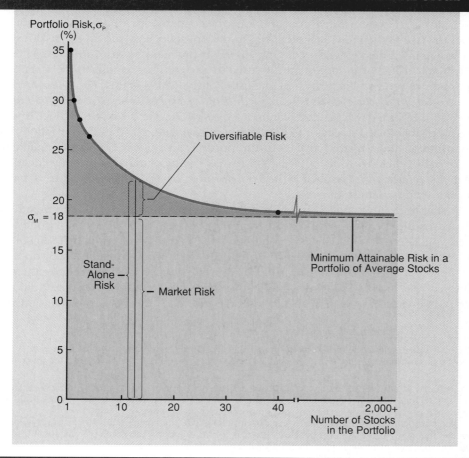

EFFECTS OF PORTFOLIO SIZE ON PORTFOLIO RISK FOR AVERAGE STOCKS | **FIGURE 4-8**

Thus, almost half the riskiness inherent in an average individual stock can be eliminated if the stock is held in a reasonably well-diversified portfolio, which is one containing 40 or more stocks. Some risk always remains, however, so it is virtually impossible to diversify away the effects of broad stock market movements that affect almost all stocks.

That part of the risk of a stock which *can* be eliminated is called *diversifiable risk,* while that part which *cannot* be eliminated is called *market risk.*[8] The fact that a large part of the riskiness of any individual stock can be eliminated is vitally important.

Diversifiable risk is caused by such random events as lawsuits, strikes, successful and unsuccessful marketing programs, winning or losing a major contract, and other events that are unique to a particular firm. Since these events are random, their effects on a portfolio can be eliminated by diversification — bad events in one firm will be offset by good events in another. *Market risk,* on the other hand, stems from factors which systematically affect most firms: war, inflation, recessions, and high interest rates. Since most stocks will tend to be negatively affected by these factors, market risk cannot be eliminated by diversification.

We know that investors demand a premium for bearing risk — the higher the riskiness of a security, the higher its expected return must be to induce investors to buy (or hold) it. However, if investors are primarily concerned with *portfolio risk* rather than the risk of the individual securities in the portfolio, how should the riskiness of an individual stock be measured? One answer is provided by the *Capital Asset Pricing Model (CAPM),* an important tool used to analyze the relationship between risk and rates of return.[9] The primary conclusion of the CAPM is this: *The relevant riskiness of an individual stock is its contribution to the riskiness of a well-diversified portfolio.* In other words, the riskiness of General Electric's stock to a doctor who has a portfolio of 40 stocks or to a trust officer managing a 150-stock portfolio is the contribution the GE stock makes to the portfolio's riskiness. The stock might be quite risky if held by itself, but if half of its risk can be eliminated by diversification, then its *relevant risk,* which is its *contribution to the portfolio's risk,* is much smaller than its stand-alone risk.

A simple example will help make this point clear. Suppose you are offered the chance to flip a coin once; if a head comes up, you win $20,000, but if it comes up tails, you lose $16,000. This is a good bet — the expected return is $0.5(\$20,000) + 0.5(-\$16,000) = \$2,000$. However, it is a highly risky proposition, because you have a 50 percent chance of losing $16,000. Thus, you might well refuse to make the bet. Alternatively, suppose you were offered the chance to flip a coin 100 times, and you would win $200 for each head but lose $160 for each tail. It is possible that you

---

[8]Diversifiable risk is also known as *company-specific,* or *unsystematic,* risk. Market risk is also known as *nondiversifiable,* or *systematic,* or *beta,* risk; it is the risk that remains after diversification.

[9]Indeed, the 1990 Nobel Prize was awarded to the developers of the CAPM, Professors Harry Markowitz and William F. Sharpe. The CAPM is a relatively complex subject, and only its basic elements are presented in this chapter. For a more detailed discussion, see Chapter 5.

    The basic concepts of the CAPM were developed specifically for common stocks, and we examine the theory first in this context. However, it is useful to extend the concepts to capital budgeting and to speak of firms' having "portfolios of tangible assets and projects." In Chapter 11, we discuss the implications of the CAPM for capital budgeting and corporate diversification.

would flip all heads and win $20,000, and it is also possible that you would flip all tails and lose $16,000, but the chances are very high that you would actually flip about 50 heads and about 50 tails, winning a net of about $2,000. Although each individual flip is a risky bet, collectively you have a low-risk proposition because most of the risk has been diversified away. This is the idea behind holding portfolios of stocks rather than just one stock, except that with stocks all of the risk cannot be eliminated by diversification — those risks related to broad, systematic changes in the stock market will remain.

Are all stocks equally risky in the sense that adding them to a well-diversified portfolio would have the same effect on the portfolio's riskiness? The answer is no. Different stocks will affect the portfolio differently, so different securities have different degrees of relevant risk. How can the relevant risk of an individual stock be measured? As we have seen, all risk except that related to broad market movements can, and presumably will, be diversified away. After all, why accept risk that can be easily eliminated? *The risk that remains after diversifying is market risk, or the risk that is inherent in the market, and it can be measured by the degree to which a given stock tends to move up or down with the market.* In the next section, we develop a measure of a stock's market risk, and then, in a later section, we introduce an equation for determining the required rate of return on a stock, given its market risk.

THE CONCEPT OF BETA

The tendency of a stock to move up and down with the market is reflected in its *beta coefficient, b.* An *average-risk stock* is defined as one that tends to move up and down in step with the general market as measured by some index such as the Dow Jones Industrials, the S&P 500, or the New York Stock Exchange Index. Such a stock will, *by definition,* have a beta of 1.0, which indicates that, in general, if the market moves up by 10 percent, the stock will also move up by 10 percent, while if the market falls by 10 percent, the stock will likewise fall by 10 percent. A portfolio of such b = 1.0 stocks will move up and down with the broad market averages, and it will be just as risky as the averages. If b = 0.5, the stock is only half as volatile as the market — it will rise and fall only half as much — and a portfolio of such stocks will be half as risky as a portfolio of b = 1.0 stocks. On the other hand, if b = 2.0, the stock is twice as volatile as an average stock, so a portfolio of such stocks will be twice as risky as an average portfolio. The value of such a portfolio could double — or halve — in a short time, and if you held such a portfolio, you could quickly go from millionaire to pauper.

Figure 4-9 graphs the relative volatility of three stocks. The data below the graph assume that in 1994 the "market," defined as a portfolio consisting of all stocks, had a total return (dividend yield plus capital gains yield) of $k_M = 10\%$, and Stocks H, A, and L (for High, Average, and Low risk) also had returns of 10 percent. In 1995, the market went up sharply, and the return on the market portfolio was $\bar{k}_M = 20\%$. Returns on the three stocks also went up: H soared to 30 percent; A went up to 20 percent, the same as the market; and L only went up to 15 percent. Now suppose the market dropped in 1996, and the market return was $\bar{k}_M = -10\%$. The three stocks' returns also fell, H plunging to −30 percent, A falling to −10 percent, and L going down only to $\bar{k}_L = 0\%$. Thus, the three stocks all moved in the same direction

FIGURE 4-9	RELATIVE VOLATILITY OF STOCKS H, A, AND L

	$\overline{k}_H$	$\overline{k}_A$	$\overline{k}_L$	$\overline{k}_M$
1994	10%	10%	10%	10%
1995	30	20	15	20
1996	(30)	(10)	0	(10)

NOTE: These three stocks plot exactly on their regression lines. This indicates that they are exposed only to market risk. Mutual funds which concentrate on stocks with betas of 2, 1, and 0.5 would have patterns similar to those shown in the graph.

as the market, but H was by far the most volatile, A was just as volatile as the market, and L was less volatile.

Beta measures a stock's volatility relative to an average stock, which by definition has $b = 1.0$, and a stock's beta can be calculated by plotting a line like those in Figure 4-9. The slopes of the lines show how each stock moves in response to a movement in the general market — *indeed, the slope coefficient of such a "regression line" is defined as a beta coefficient.* (Procedures for actually calculating betas are described in Chapter 5.) Betas for literally thousands of companies are calculated and published by Merrill Lynch, Value Line, and numerous other organizations, and the beta coefficients of some well-known companies are shown in Table 4-4. Most stocks have betas in the range of 0.50 to 1.50, and the average for all stocks is 1.0 by definition.

Theoretically, it is possible for a stock to have a negative beta. In this case, the stock's returns would tend to rise whenever the returns on other stocks fall. In practice, we have never seen a stock with a negative beta. For example, *Value Line* follows more than 1,700 stocks, and not one has a negative beta. Keep in mind, though, that a stock in a given year may move counter to the overall market, even though the stock's beta is positive. If a stock has a positive beta, we would *expect* the stock's return to increase whenever the overall stock market rises. However, company-specific factors may cause the stock's realized return to decline, even though the market's return is positive.

If a stock whose beta is greater than 1.0 is added to a b = 1.0 portfolio, then the portfolio's beta, and consequently its riskiness, will increase. Conversely, if a stock whose beta is less than 1.0 is added to a b = 1.0 portfolio, the portfolio's beta and risk will decline. *Thus, since a stock's beta measures its contribution to the riskiness of a portfolio, beta is the theoretically correct measure of the stock's riskiness.*

The preceding analysis of risk in a portfolio context is part of the Capital Asset Pricing Model (CAPM), and we can summarize our discussion to this point as follows:

1. A stock's risk consists of two components, market risk and diversifiable risk.

ILLUSTRATIVE LIST OF BETA COEFFICIENTS	TABLE 4-4

STOCK	BETA
Home Depot	1.45
Apple Computer	1.20
General Electric	1.10
Procter & Gamble	1.05
Anheuser Busch	1.00
Campbell Soup	1.00
Rockwell International	0.95
Hormel Foods	0.80
Pacific Gas & Electric	0.75
Energen Corp.[a]	0.65

SOURCE: *Value Line,* January 5, 1996.
[a]Energen is a gas distribution company. It has a monopoly in much of Alabama, and its rates are adjusted every three months so as to keep its profits relatively constant.

2. Diversifiable risk can be eliminated by diversification, and most investors do indeed diversify, either by holding large portfolios or by purchasing shares in a mutual fund. We are left, then, with market risk, which is caused by general movements in the stock market and which reflects the fact that most stocks are systematically affected by certain overall economic events like war, recessions, and inflation. Market risk is the only relevant risk to a rational, diversified investor because such an investor would eliminate diversifiable risk.

3. Investors must be compensated for bearing risk—the greater the riskiness of a stock, the higher its required return. However, compensation is required only for risk which cannot be eliminated by diversification. If risk premiums existed on stocks due to diversifiable risk, well-diversified investors would start buying those securities (which would not be especially risky to such investors) and bid up their prices, and their final (equilibrium) expected returns would reflect only nondiversifiable market risk.

   If this point is not clear, consider this example. Suppose half of Stock A's risk is market risk (it occurs because Stock A moves up and down with the market), while the other half risk is diversifiable. You hold only Stock A, so you are exposed to all of its risk. As compensation for bearing so much risk, you want a risk premium of 8 percent over the 10 percent T-bond rate. Thus, your required return is $k_A = 10\% + 8\% = 18\%$. But suppose other investors, including your professor, are well diversified. They also hold Stock A, but they have eliminated its diversifiable risk and thus are exposed to only half as much risk as you. Therefore, their risk premium will be only half as large as yours, and their required rate of return will be $k_A = 10\% + 4\% = 14\%$.

   If the stock were yielding your required return of 18 percent in the market, diversified investors, including your professor, would bid its price up and its yield down, hence you could not buy it at a price low enough to provide you with an 18 percent return. In the end, you would have to accept a 14 percent return or else keep your money in the bank. Thus, risk premiums in a market populated by diversified investors can reflect only market risk.

4. The market risk of a stock is measured by its beta coefficient, which is an index of the stock's relative volatility. Some benchmark betas follow:

   b = 0.5: Stock is only half as volatile, or risky, as the average stock.

   b = 1.0: Stock is of average risk.

   b = 2.0: Stock is twice as risky as the average stock.

5. *Since a stock's beta coefficient determines how the stock affects the riskiness of a diversified portfolio, beta is the most relevant measure of any stock's risk.*

Portfolio Beta Coefficients

A portfolio consisting of low-beta securities will itself have a low beta, because the beta of a portfolio is a weighted average of the individual securities' betas:

$$b_p = w_1 b_1 + w_2 b_2 + \cdots + w_n b_n$$

$$= \sum_{i=1}^{n} w_i b_i.$$

4-6

Here b_p is the beta of the portfolio, and it reflects how volatile the portfolio is in relation to the market; w_i is the fraction of the portfolio invested in the ith stock; and b_i is the beta coefficient of the ith stock. For example, if an investor holds a $100,000 portfolio consisting of $33,333.33 invested in each of three stocks, and if each of the stocks has a beta of 0.7, then the portfolio's beta will be $b_p = 0.7$:

$$b_p = 0.3333(0.7) + 0.3333(0.7) + 0.3333(0.7) = 0.7.$$

Such a portfolio will be less risky than the market, so it should experience relatively narrow price swings and have relatively small rate-of-return fluctuations. In terms of Figure 4-9, the slope of its regression line would be 0.7, which is less than that for a portfolio of average stocks.

Now suppose one of the existing stocks is sold and replaced by a stock with $b_i = 2.0$. This action will increase the beta of the portfolio from $b_{p1} = 0.7$ to $b_{p2} = 1.13$:

$$b_{p2} = 0.3333(0.7) + 0.3333(0.7) + 0.3333(2.0)$$

$$= 1.13.$$

Had a stock with $b_i = 0.2$ been added, the portfolio beta would have declined from 0.7 to 0.53. Adding new stocks can, therefore, change the riskiness of a portfolio.

Explain the following statement: "An asset held as part of a portfolio is generally less risky than the same asset held in isolation."

What is meant by *perfect positive correlation, perfect negative correlation,* and *zero correlation?*

In general, can the riskiness of a portfolio be reduced to zero by increasing the number of stocks in the portfolio? Explain.

What is an average-risk stock? What will be its beta?

Why is beta the theoretically correct measure of a stock's riskiness?

If you plotted the returns on a particular stock versus those on the New York Stock Exchange Index over the past 5 years, what would the slope of the regression line you obtained tell you about the stock's market risk?

SELF-TEST QUESTIONS

THE RELATIONSHIP BETWEEN RISK AND RATES OF RETURN

In the preceding section, we saw that under the CAPM theory, beta is the measure of a stock's relevant risk. Now we consider how risk affects required return: For a given level of risk as measured by beta, what rate of return will investors require on a stock to compensate them for bearing that risk? To begin, let us define the following terms:

$\hat{k}_i$ = *expected* rate of return on the ith stock.

k_i = *required* rate of return on the ith stock. Note that if $\hat{k}_i$ is less than k_i, you would not purchase this stock, or you would sell it if you owned it. If $\hat{k}_i$ were greater than k_i, you would want to buy the stock, because it looks like a bargain. You would be indifferent if $\hat{k}_i = k_i$.

k_{RF} = risk-free rate of return. In this context, k_{RF} is generally measured by the return on long-term U.S. Treasury bonds.

b_i = beta coefficient of the ith stock. The beta of an average stock is $b_A = 1.0$.

k_M = required rate of return on a portfolio consisting of all stocks, which is called *the market portfolio*. k_M is also the required rate of return on an average ($b_A = 1.0$) stock.

$RP_M = (k_M - k_{RF})$ = risk premium on "the market," and also on an average ($b = 1.0$) stock. This is the additional return over the risk-free rate required to compensate an investor for assuming an average amount of risk. Average risk means $b_A = 1.0$.

$RP_i = (k_M - k_{RF})b_i = (RP_M)b_i$ = risk premium on the ith stock. The stock's risk premium is less than, equal to, or greater than the premium on an average stock, RP_M, depending on whether its beta is less than, equal to, or greater than 1.0. For example, if Stock i's beta is 0.5 and RPM = 5%, the stock's risk premium is $RP_i = (5\%)(0.5) = 2.5\%$. If b_i had been 2.0, then its RP_i would have been 10%.

The *market risk premium, RP_M*, shows the premium investors require for bearing the risk of an average stock, and it depends on the degree of aversion that investors have to risk.[10] Let us assume that at the current time Treasury bonds yield $k_{RF} = 6\%$, and an average share of stock has a required return of $k_M = 11\%$. Therefore, the market risk premium is 5 percentage points:

$$RP_M = k_M - k_{RF} = 11\% - 6\% = 5\%.$$

It follows that if one stock were twice as risky as another, its risk premium would be twice as high, while if its risk were only half as much, its risk premium would be half

---

[10]This concept, as well as other aspects of the CAPM, is discussed in more detail in Chapter 5. It should be noted that the risk premium of an average stock, $k_M - k_{RF}$, cannot be measured with great precision because it is impossible to obtain precise values for the expected future return on the market, k_M. However, empirical studies suggest that where long-term U.S. Treasury bonds are used to measure k_{RF} and where k_M is an estimate of the expected return on the S&P 400 Industrial Stocks, the market risk premium varies somewhat from year to year, and it has generally ranged from 4 to 8 percent during the last 20 years.

Chapter 5 also discusses the assumptions embodied in the CAPM framework. Some of these are unrealistic, and because of this the theory does not hold exactly.

as large. Further, we can measure a stock's relative riskiness by its beta coefficient. Therefore, if we know the market risk premium, RP_M, and the stock's risk as measured by its beta coefficient, b_i, we can find the stock's risk premium as the product $(RP_M)b_i$. For example, if some low-risk stock has $b_L = 0.5$, and if $RP_M = 5\%$, then RP_L is 2.5 percent:

$$\text{Risk premium for Stock L} = RP_L = (RP_M)b_L \qquad \text{4-7}$$

$$= (5\%)(0.5)$$
$$= 2.5\%.$$

In general, the required return for any investment can be expressed as

$$\text{Required return} = \text{Risk-free return} + \text{Premium for risk.}$$

Here the risk-free return includes a premium for expected inflation, and we assume the assets under consideration have similar maturities and liquidity.

The required return for Stock L can be found using the *Security Market Line (SML)* Equation:

$$\text{SML Equation: } k_i = k_{RF} + (k_M - k_{RF})b_i. \qquad \text{4-8}$$

$$k_L = k_{RF} + (RP_M)b_L$$
$$= 6\% + (11\% - 6\%)(0.5)$$
$$= 6\% + 5\%(0.5)$$
$$= 8.5\%.$$

If you think of the SML as a standard linear equation, $Y = a_0 + a_1x$, then k_{RF} is a_0, the intercept; RP_M is a_1, the slope coefficient; and b_i is x, the variable, so $Y = k_{RF} + RP_Mb_i = 6 + 5b_i$, measured in percentages.

If some other Stock H were riskier than Stock L and had $b_H = 2.0$, then its required rate of return would be 16 percent:

$$k_H = 6\% + (5\%)2.0 = 16\%.$$

An average stock, with $b = 1.0$, would have a required return of 11 percent, the same as the market return:

$$k_A = 6\% + (5\%)1.0 = 11\% = k_M.$$

The SML equation is often expressed in graph form, as in Figure 4-10, which shows the SML when $k_{RF} = 6\%$ and $k_M = 11\%$. Note the following points:

1. Required rates of return are shown on the vertical axis, while risk as measured by beta is shown on the horizontal axis. This graph is quite different from the one shown in Figure 4-9, where the returns on individual stocks were plotted

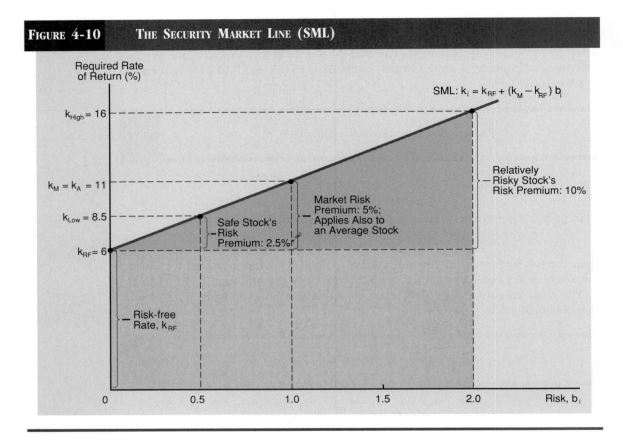

FIGURE 4-10   THE SECURITY MARKET LINE (SML)

on the vertical axis and returns on the market index were shown on the horizontal axis. The slopes of the three lines in Figure 4-9 were used to calculate the three stocks' betas, and those betas were then plotted as points on the horizontal axis of Figure 4-10.

2. Riskless securities have $b_i = 0$; therefore, k_{RF} appears as the vertical axis intercept in Figure 4-10. If we could construct a portfolio with a beta of zero, it would also have an expected return equal to the risk-free rate.

3. The slope of the SML (5% in Figure 4-10) reflects the degree of risk aversion in the economy — the greater the average investor's aversion to risk, then (1) the steeper the slope of the line, (2) the greater the risk premium for all stocks, and (3) the higher the required rate of return on all stocks.[11] These points are discussed further in a later section.

---

[11]Students sometimes confuse beta with the slope of the SML. This is a mistake. The slope of any straight line is equal to the "rise" divided by the "run," or $(Y_1 - Y_0)/(X_1 - X_0)$. Consider Figure 4-10. If we let $Y = k$ and $X = $ beta, and we go from the origin to $b = 1.0$, we see that the slope is $(k_M - k_{RF})/(b_M - b_{RF}) = (11\% - 6\%)/(1 - 0) = 5\%$. Thus, the slope of the SML is equal to $(k_M - k_{RF})$, the market risk premium. In Figure 4-10, $k_i = 6\% + 5\%b_i$, so a doubling of beta (for example, from 1.0 to 2.0) would produce a 5 percentage point increase in k_i.

4. The values we worked out for stocks with $b_i = 0.5$, $b_i = 1.0$, and $b_i = 2.0$ agree with the values shown on the graph for k_{Low}, k_A, and k_{High}.

Both the Security Market Line and a company's position on it change over time due to changes in interest rates, investors' risk aversion, and individual companies' betas. Such changes are discussed in the following sections.

THE IMPACT OF INFLATION

As we saw in Chapter 3, interest amounts to "rent" on borrowed money, or the price of money. Thus, k_{RF} is the price of money to a riskless borrower. We also saw that the risk-free rate as measured by the rate on U.S. Treasury securities consists of two elements: (1) a *real inflation-free rate of return, k**, and (2) an *inflation premium, IP*, equal to the anticipated rate of inflation.[12] Thus, $k_{RF} = k^* + IP$. The real rate on long-term Treasury bonds has historically ranged from 2 to 4 percent, with a mean of about 3 percent. Therefore, if no inflation were expected, long-term Treasury bonds would yield about 3 percent. However, as the expected rate of inflation increases, a premium must be added to the real risk-free rate of return to compensate investors for the loss of purchasing power that results from inflation. Therefore, the 6 percent k_{RF} shown in Figure 4-10 might be thought of as consisting of a 3 percent real risk-free rate of return plus a 3 percent inflation premium: $k_{RF} = k^* + IP = 3\% + 3\% = 6\%$.

If the expected rate of inflation rose by 2 percentage points, to $3\% + 2\% = 5\%$, this would cause k_{RF} to rise to 8 percent. Such a change is shown in Figure 4-11. Notice that under the CAPM, the increase in k_{RF} also causes an *equal* increase in the rate of return on all risky assets, because the same inflation premium is built into the required rate of return of both riskless and risky assets.[13] For example, the rate of return on an average stock, k_M, increases from 11 to 13 percent. Other risky securities' returns also rise by two percentage points.

CHANGES IN RISK AVERSION

The slope of the Security Market Line reflects the extent to which investors are averse to risk — the steeper the slope of the line, the greater the average investor's risk aversion. Suppose investors were indifferent to risk; that is, they were not risk averse. If k_{RF} were 6 percent, then risky assets would also provide an expected return of 6 percent, because if there were no risk aversion, there would be no risk

---

[12]Long-term Treasury bonds also contain a maturity risk premium, MRP. Here we assume that the same MRP is contained in stocks and T-bonds.

[13]Recall that the inflation premium for any asset is equal to the average expected rate of inflation over the life of the asset. Thus, in this analysis we must assume either that all securities plotted on the SML graph have the same life or else that the expected rate of future inflation is constant.

It should also be noted that k_{RF} in a CAPM analysis can be proxied by either a long-term rate (the T-bond rate) or a short-term rate (the T-bill rate). Traditionally, the T-bill rate was used, but in recent years there has been a movement toward use of the T-bond rate because there is a closer relationship between T-bond yields and stocks than between T-bill yields and stocks. See *Stocks, Bonds, Bills, and Inflation; 1996 Yearbook* (Chicago: Ibbotson & Associates, 1996) for a discussion.

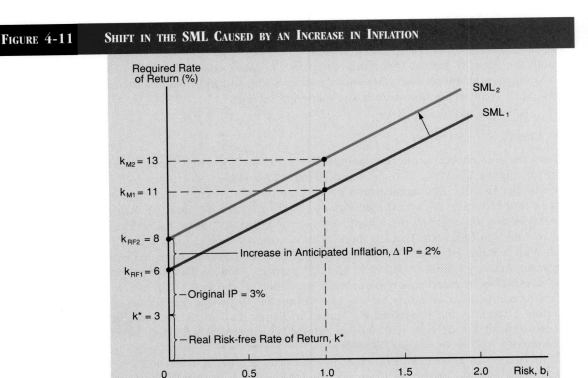

FIGURE 4-11   SHIFT IN THE SML CAUSED BY AN INCREASE IN INFLATION

premium, and the SML would be horizontal. As risk aversion increases, so does the risk premium, and this causes the slope of the SML to become steeper.

Figure 4-12 illustrates an increase in risk aversion. The market risk premium rises from 5 to 7.5 percent, causing k_M to rise from $k_{M1} = 11\%$ to $k_{M2} = 13.5\%$. The returns on other risky assets also rise, and the effect of this shift in risk aversion is more pronounced on riskier securities. For example, the required return on a stock with $b_i = 0.5$ increases by only 1.25 percentage points, from 8.5 to 9.75 percent, whereas that on a stock with $b_i = 1.5$ increases by 3.75 percentage points, from 13.5 to 17.25 percent.

CHANGES IN A STOCK'S BETA COEFFICIENT

As we shall see later in the book, a firm can influence its market risk, hence its beta, by changing the composition of its assets and also through its use of debt. A company's beta can also change as a result of external factors such as increased competition in its industry, the expiration of basic patents, and the like. When such changes occur, the required rate of return also changes, and, as we shall see in Chapter 7, this will affect the price of the firm's stock. For example, consider Allied Food Products, with a beta of 1.40. Now suppose some action occurred which caused Allied's beta to increase from 1.40 to 2.00. If the conditions depicted in Figure 4-10 held, Allied's required rate of return would increase from 13 to 16 percent:

SHIFT IN THE SML CAUSED BY INCREASED RISK AVERSION   FIGURE 4-12

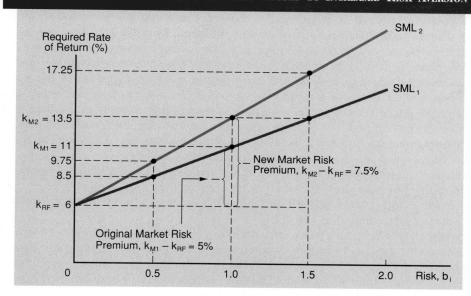

$$k_1 = k_{RF} + (k_M - k_{RF})b_i$$
$$= 6\% + (11\% - 6\%)1.40$$
$$= 13\%$$

to

$$k_2 = 6\% + (11\% - 6\%)2.0$$
$$= 16\%.$$

Any change which affects the required rate of return on a security, such as a change in its beta coefficient or in expected inflation, will have an impact on the price of the security. We will discuss the relationship between a stock's required rate of return and its price in Chapter 7.

SELF-TEST QUESTIONS

Differentiate between the expected rate of return ($\hat{k}$) and the required rate of return (k) on a stock. Which would have to be larger to get you to buy the stock?

What are the differences between the relative volatility graph (Figure 4-9), where "betas are made," and the SML graph (Figure 4-10), where "betas are used"? Discuss how the graphs are constructed and the information they convey.

What happens to the SML graph in Figure 4-10 when inflation increases or decreases?

What happens to the SML graph when risk aversion increases or decreases? What would the SML look like if investors were indifferent to risk, that is, had zero risk aversion?

How can a firm influence its market risk as reflected in its beta?

PHYSICAL ASSETS VERSUS SECURITIES

In a book on financial management for business firms, why do we spend so much time discussing the riskiness of stocks? Why not begin by looking at the riskiness of such business assets as plant and equipment? *The reason is that, for a management whose primary goal is stock price maximization, the overriding consideration is the riskiness of the firm's stock, and the relevant risk of any physical asset must be measured in terms of its effect on the stock's risk as seen by investors.* For example, suppose Goodyear Tire Company is considering a major investment in a new product, recapped tires. Sales of recaps, hence earnings on the new operation, are highly uncertain, so on a stand-alone basis the new venture appears to be quite risky. However, suppose returns in the recap business are negatively correlated with Goodyear's regular operations — when times are good and people have plenty of money, they buy new tires, but when times are bad, they tend to buy more recaps. Therefore, returns would be high on regular operations and low on the recap division during good times, but the opposite situation would occur during recessions. The result might be a pattern like that shown earlier in Figure 4-5 for Stocks W and M. Thus, what appears to be a risky investment when viewed on a stand-alone basis might not be very risky when viewed within the context of the company as a whole.

This analysis can be extended to the corporation's stockholders. Because Goodyear's stock is owned by diversified stockholders, the real issue each time the company makes an asset investment is this: How does this investment affect the risk of our stockholders? Again, the stand-alone risk of an individual project may look quite high, but viewed in the context of the project's effect on stockholders' risk, it may not be very large. We will address this issue again in Chapter 11, where we examine the effects of capital budgeting on companies' beta coefficients and thus on stockholders' risks.

SELF-TEST QUESTIONS

Explain the following statement: "The stand-alone risk of an individual project may look quite high, but viewed in the context of a project's effect on stockholders, the project's risk may not be very large."

How would the correlation between returns on a project and returns on the firm's other assets' returns affect the project's risk?

SOME CAUTIONS ABOUT BETA AND THE CAPM

The Capital Asset Pricing Model (CAPM) is more than just an abstract theory described in textbooks — it is also widely used by analysts, investors, and corporations. Therefore, it is reasonable to ask, "Is the CAPM correct in the sense that stocks with higher betas have higher returns?"

A recent study by two University of Chicago professors, Eugene Fama and Kenneth French, concluded that the answer is no.[14] They found no historical relation-

---

[14]See Eugene F. Fama and Kenneth R. French, "The Cross-Section of Expected Stock Returns," *Journal of Finance,* June 1992, 427–465.

ship between stocks' returns and their betas, confirming a position long held by a number of professors and stock market analysts. Nevertheless, the Fama-French findings surprised many people, and they led some to conclude that "beta is dead."

If beta does not determine returns, what does? Fama and French found two variables which are consistently related to stock returns: (1) the firm's size and (2) its market/book ratio. After adjusting for other factors, they found that smaller firms have provided relatively high returns, and returns are higher on stocks with low market-to-book ratios. By contrast, after controlling for size of firm and market-to-book ratios, they found no relationship between a stock's beta and its return.

Given Fama and French's findings, should you just ignore everything said about beta in this chapter? In other words, is beta really dead? Probably not. Proponents of the CAPM argue that the theory is right, but Fama and French's evidence is flawed. In particular, the CAPM states that there is a relationship between a firm's *expected future* volatility and its *expected future* return. However, Fama and French tested the CAPM using historical instead of expected future data, and they assumed that investors expect the future to be like the past. However, there is no guarantee that investors expect historical relationships to be maintained. Therefore, studies such as Fama-French cannot prove or disprove the CAPM.

Practitioners and academicians have long recognized the limitations of the CAPM, and they are constantly working on ways to improve it. For example, as we discuss in Chapter 8, procedures have been developed to calculate "adjusted" betas, which provide a better indication of a stock's future relative volatility than purely historical betas. Also, people recognize that factors other than market risk (beta) — including the size of the company, oil prices, unemployment, and the like — probably affect returns. Therefore, as we discuss in Chapter 5, "multifactor" CAPM procedures are being developed and used.

Overall, the CAPM is the most logical and intuitively appealing method ever devised to measure risk and relate it to required returns. However, although the CAPM represents a significant step forward in security pricing theory, it does have some potentially serious deficiencies when applied in practice, and estimates of k_i found through use of the SML may be subject to considerable error.

Are there any reasons to question the validity of the CAPM? Explain.

SELF-TEST QUESTION

VOLATILITY VERSUS RISK

Before closing this chapter, we should note that volatility does not necessarily imply risk. For example, suppose a company's sales and earnings fluctuate widely from month to month, or year to year, or in some other manner. Does this imply that the company is risky in either the stand-alone or portfolio sense? If the fluctuations follow seasonal or cyclical patterns, as for an ice cream distributor or a steel company, they can be predicted, hence they would not signify much in the way of risk. If the ice cream company's earnings dropped about as much as they normally did in the winter, this would not concern investors, so the company's stock price would not be affected. Similarly, if the steel company's earnings fell during a recession, this would not be a surprise, so the company's stock price would probably not fall nearly as much as its earnings. Therefore, earnings volatility does not necessarily imply investment risk.

Now consider some other company, say, Wal-Mart. In 1995 Wal-Mart's earnings declined for the first time in its history. That decline worried investors — they were concerned that Wal-Mart's era of rapid growth had ended. The result was a sharp decline in Wal-Mart's stock price. Again, we conclude that a downturn in earnings does not necessarily imply risk, but it could, depending on conditions.

Now let's consider stock price volatility as opposed to earnings volatility. Is stock price volatility more likely to imply risk than earnings volatility? The answer is a loud yes! Stock prices vary because investors are uncertain about the future, especially about future earnings. So, if you see a company whose stock price fluctuates relatively widely, which will normally translate to a high beta, you can bet that its future earnings are relatively unpredictable. Thus, biotech companies have less predictable earnings than electric utilities, biotech's stock prices are volatile, and they have relatively high betas.

To conclude, keep two points in mind: (1) Earnings volatility does not necessarily signify risk. You have to think about the cause of the volatility before reaching any conclusion as to whether earnings volatility indicates risk. (2) Stock price volatility does signify risk (except for stocks that are negatively correlated with the market, and they are few and far between). We will return to the volatility versus risk situation in Chapter 11, when we discuss the risk of capital budgeting projects.

SUMMARY

The primary goals of this chapter were (1) to show how risk is measured in financial analysis and (2) to explain how risk affects rates of return. The key concepts that were covered are listed below.

- ■ *Risk* can be defined as the chance that some unfavorable event will occur.
- ■ The riskiness of an asset's cash flows can be considered on a *stand-alone basis* (each asset by itself) or in a *portfolio context,* where the investment is combined with other assets and its risk is reduced through diversification.
- ■ Most rational investors hold *portfolios of assets,* and they are more concerned with the risks of their portfolios than with the risks of individual assets.
- ■ The *expected return* on an investment is the mean value of its probability distribution of returns.
- ■ The *higher the probability* that the actual return will be far below the expected return, the *greater the stand-alone risk* associated with an asset.

■ The average investor is *risk averse,* which means that he or she must be compensated for holding risky assets. Therefore, riskier assets have higher required returns than less risky assets.

■ An asset's risk consists of (1) *diversifiable risk,* which can be eliminated by diversification, plus (2) *market risk,* which cannot be eliminated by diversification.

■ The *relevant risk* of an individual asset is its contribution to the riskiness of a well-diversified *portfolio,* which is the asset's *market risk.* Since market risk cannot be eliminated by diversification, investors must be compensated for bearing it.

■ A stock's *beta coefficient, b,* is a measure of the stock's market risk. Beta measures the extent to which the stock's returns move relative to the market.

■ A *high-beta stock* is more volatile than an average stock, while a *low-beta stock* is less volatile than an average stock. An *average stock* has b = 1.0.

■ The *beta of a portfolio* is a *weighted average* of the betas of the individual securities in the portfolio.

■ The *Security Market Line (SML)* equation shows the relationship between a security's market risk and its required rate of return. The return required for any security i is equal to the *risk-free rate* plus the *market risk premium* times the *security's beta:* $k_i = k_{RF} + (k_M - k_{RF})b_i$.

■ Even though the expected rate of return on a stock is generally equal to its required return, a number of things can happen to cause the required rate of return to change: (1) *the risk-free rate can change* because of changes in anticipated inflation, (2) *a stock's beta can change,* and (3) *investors' aversion to risk can change.*

In Chapter 5 we will extend our discussion of risk and return, and in Chapter 7 we will see how a security's rate of return affects its value. Then, in the remainder of the book, we will examine the ways in which a firm's management can influence a stock's riskiness and hence its price.

QUESTIONS

4-1   Define the following terms, using graphs or equations to illustrate your answers wherever feasible:

a. Stand-alone risk; risk; probability distribution

b. Expected rate of return, $\hat{k}$

c. Continuous probability distribution

d. Standard deviation, σ; variance, σ^2; coefficient of variation, CV

e. Risk aversion; realized rate of return, $\bar{k}$

f. Risk premium for Stock i, RP_i; market risk premium, RP_M

g. Capital Asset Pricing Model (CAPM)

h. Expected return on a portfolio, $\hat{k}_p$

    i. Correlation coefficient, r

    j. Market risk; diversifiable risk; relevant risk

    k. Beta coefficient, b; average stock's beta, b_A

    l. Security Market Line (SML); SML equation

    m. Slope of SML as a measure of risk aversion

4-2 The probability distribution of a less risky expected return is more peaked than that of a riskier return. What shape would the probability distribution have for (a) completely certain returns and (b) completely uncertain returns?

4-3 Security A has an expected return of 7 percent, a standard deviation of expected returns of 35 percent, a correlation coefficient with the market of −0.3, and a beta coefficient of −0.5. Security B has an expected return of 12 percent, a standard deviation of returns of 10 percent, a correlation with the market of 0.7, and a beta coefficient of 1.0. Which security is riskier? Why?

4-4 Suppose you owned a portfolio consisting of $250,000 worth of long-term U.S. government bonds.

    a. Would your portfolio be riskless?

    b. Now suppose you hold a portfolio consisting of $250,000 worth of 30-day Treasury bills. Every 30 days your bills mature and you reinvest the principal ($250,000) in a new batch of bills. Assume that you live on the investment income from your portfolio and that you want to maintain a constant standard of living. Is your portfolio truly riskless?

    c. Can you think of any asset that would be completely riskless? Could someone develop such an asset? Explain.

4-5 A life insurance policy is a financial asset. The premiums paid represent the investment's cost.

    a. How would you calculate the expected return on a life insurance policy?

    b. Suppose the owner of a life insurance policy has no other financial assets—the person's only other asset is "human capital," or lifetime earnings capacity. What is the correlation coefficient between returns on the insurance policy and returns on the policyholder's human capital?

    c. Life insurance companies have to pay administrative costs and sales representatives' commissions; hence, the expected rate of return on insurance premiums is generally low, or even negative. Use the portfolio concept to explain why people buy life insurance in spite of negative expected returns.

4-6 If investors' aversion to risk increased, would the risk premium on a high-beta stock increase more or less than that on a low-beta stock? Explain.

4-7 If a company's beta were to double, would its required return double?

4-8 Is it possible to construct a portfolio of stocks which has an expected return equal to the risk-free rate?

SELF-TEST PROBLEM

(SOLUTION APPEARS IN APPENDIX C)

ST-1 REALIZED RATES OF RETURN Stocks A and B have the following historical returns:

YEAR	STOCK A'S RETURNS, k_A	STOCK B'S RETURNS, k_B
1992	(10.00%)	(3.00%)
1993	18.50	21.29
1994	38.67	44.25
1995	14.33	3.67
1996	33.00	28.30

a. Calculate the average rate of return for each stock during the period 1992 through 1996. Assume that someone held a portfolio consisting of 50 percent of Stock A and 50 percent of Stock B. What would have been the realized rate of return on the portfolio in each year from 1992 through 1996? What would have been the average return on the portfolio during this period?

b. Now calculate the standard deviation of returns for each stock and for the portfolio. Use Equation 4-3a in Footnote 5.

c. Looking at the annual returns data on the two stocks, would you guess that the correlation coefficient between returns on the two stocks is closer to 0.9 or to −0.9?

d. If you added more stocks at random to the portfolio, which of the following is the most accurate statement of what would happen to σ_p?

(1) σ_p would remain constant.

(2) σ_p would decline to somewhere in the vicinity of 18 percent.

(3) σ_p would decline to zero if enough stocks were included.

PROBLEMS

4-1 EXPECTED RETURNS Suppose you won the Florida lottery and were offered (1) $0.5 million or (2) a gamble in which you would get $1 million if a head were flipped but zero if a tail came up.

a. What is the expected value of the gamble?

b. Would you take the sure $0.5 million or the gamble?

c. If you choose the sure $0.5 million, are you a risk averter or a risk seeker?

d. Suppose you actually take the sure $0.5 million. You can invest it in either a U.S. Treasury bond that will return $537,500 at the end of a year or a common stock that has a 50-50 chance of being either worthless or worth $1,150,000 at the end of the year.

(1) What is the expected dollar profit on the stock investment? (The expected profit on the T-bond investment is $37,500.)

(2) What is the expected rate of return on the stock investment? (The expected rate of return on the T-bond investment is 7.5 percent.)

(3) Would you invest in the bond or the stock?

(4) Exactly how large would the expected profit (or the expected rate of return) have to be on the stock investment to make *you* invest in the stock, given the 7.5 percent return on the bond?

(5) How might your decision be affected if, rather than buying one stock for $0.5 million, you could construct a portfolio consisting of 100 stocks with $5,000 invested in each? Each of these stocks has the same return characteristics as the one stock—that is, a 50-50 chance of being worth either zero or $11,500 at year-end. Would the correlation between returns on these stocks matter?

4-2 **SECURITY MARKET LINE** The Kish Investment Fund, in which you plan to invest some money, has total capital of $500 million invested in five stocks:

STOCK	INVESTMENT	STOCK'S BETA COEFFICIENT
A	$160 million	0.5
B	120 million	2.0
C	80 million	4.0
D	80 million	1.0
E	60 million	3.0

The beta coefficient for a fund like Kish Investment can be found as a weighted average of the fund's investments. The current risk-free rate is 6 percent, whereas market returns have the following estimated probability distribution for the next period:

PROBABILITY	MARKET RETURN
0.1	7%
0.2	9
0.4	11
0.2	13
0.1	15

a. What is the estimated equation for the Security Market Line (SML)? (Hint: First determine the expected market return.)

b. Compute the fund's required rate of return for the next period.

c. Suppose Bridget Nelson, the president, receives a proposal for a new stock. The investment needed to take a position in the stock is $50 million, it will have an expected return of 15 percent, and its estimated beta coefficient is 2.0. Should the new stock be purchased? At what expected rate of return should the fund be indifferent to purchasing the stock?

4-3 **REALIZED RATES OF RETURN** Stocks A and B have the following historical returns:

YEAR	STOCK A'S RETURNS, $\bar{k}_A$	STOCK B'S RETURNS, $\bar{k}_B$
1992	(18.00%)	(14.50%)
1993	33.00	21.80
1994	15.00	30.50
1995	(0.50)	(7.60)
1996	27.00	26.30

a. Calculate the average rate of return for each stock during the period 1992 through 1996.

b. Assume that someone held a portfolio consisting of 50 percent of Stock A and 50 percent of Stock B. What would have been the realized rate of return on the portfolio in each year from 1992 through 1996? What would have been the average return on the portfolio during this period?

c. Calculate the standard deviation of returns for each stock and for the portfolio.

d. Calculate the coefficient of variation for each stock and for the portfolio.

e. If you are a risk-averse investor, would you prefer to hold Stock A, Stock B, or the portfolio? Why?

4-4 **EXPECTED AND REQUIRED RATES OF RETURN** You have observed the following returns over time:

YEAR	STOCK X	STOCK Y	MARKET
1992	14%	13%	12%
1993	19	7	10
1994	−16	−5	−12
1995	3	1	1
1996	20	11	15

Assume that the risk-free rate is 6 percent and the market risk premium is 5 percent.

a. What are the betas of Stocks X and Y? (Hint: Plot the returns on Stocks X and Y versus the market returns.)

b. What are the required rates of return for Stocks X and Y?

c. What is the required rate of return for a portfolio consisting of 80 percent of Stock X and 20 percent of Stock Y?

d. If Stock X's expected return is 22 percent, is Stock X under- or overvalued?

4-5 **EXPECTED RETURNS** The market and Stock J have the following probability distributions:

PROBABILITY	k_M	k_J
0.3	15%	20%
0.4	9	5
0.3	18	12

a. Calculate the expected rates of return for the market and Stock J.

b. Calculate the standard deviations for the market and Stock J.

c. Calculate the coefficients of variation for the market and Stock J.

4-6 **EXPECTED RETURNS** Stocks X and Y have the following probability distributions of expected future returns:

PROBABILITY	X	Y
0.1	(10%)	(35%)
0.2	2	0
0.4	12	20
0.2	20	25
0.1	38	45

a. Calculate the expected rate of return, $\hat{k}$, for Stock Y. ($\hat{k}_X = 12\%$.)

b. Calculate the standard deviation of expected returns for Stock X. (That for Stock Y is 20.35 percent.) Now calculate the coefficient of variation for Stock Y. Is it possible that most investors might regard Stock Y as being *less* risky than Stock X? Explain.

4-7   **REQUIRED RATE OF RETURN** Suppose $k_{RF} = 5\%$, $k_M = 10\%$, and $k_A = 12\%$.

a. Calculate Stock A's beta.

b. If Stock A's beta were 2.0, what would be A's new required rate of return?

4-8   **REQUIRED RATE OF RETURN** Suppose $k_{RF} = 9\%$, $k_M = 14\%$, and $b_i = 1.3$.

a. What is k_i, the required rate of return on Stock i?

b. Now suppose k_{RF} (1) increases to 10 percent or (2) decreases to 8 percent. The slope of the SML remains constant. How would this affect k_M and k_i?

c. Now assume k_{RF} remains at 9 percent but k_M (1) increases to 16 percent or (2) falls to 13 percent. The slope of the SML does not remain constant. How would these changes affect k_i?

4-9   **PORTFOLIO BETA** Suppose you hold a diversified portfolio consisting of a $7,500 investment in each of 20 different common stocks. The portfolio beta is equal to 1.12. Now, suppose you have decided to sell one of the stocks in your portfolio with a beta equal to 1.0 for $7,500 and to use these proceeds to buy another stock for your portfolio. Assume the new stock's beta is equal to 1.75. Calculate your portfolio's new beta.

4-10   **PORTFOLIO REQUIRED RETURN** Suppose you are the money manager of a $4 million investment fund. The fund consists of 4 stocks with the following investments and betas:

STOCK	INVESTMENT	BETA
A	$400,000	1.50
B	600,000	(0.50)
C	1,000,000	1.25
D	2,000,000	0.75

If the market required rate of return is 14 percent and the risk-free rate is 6 percent, what is the fund's required rate of return?

4-11   **PORTFOLIO BETA** You have a $2 million portfolio consisting of a $100,000 investment in each of 20 different stocks. The portfolio has a beta equal to 1.1. You are considering selling $100,000 worth of one stock which has a beta equal to 0.9 and using the proceeds to purchase another stock which has a beta equal to 1.4. What will be the new beta of your portfolio following this transaction?

4-12   **REQUIRED RATE OF RETURN** Stock R has a beta of 1.5, Stock S has a beta of 0.75, the expected rate of return on an average stock is 13 percent, and the risk-free rate of return is 7 percent. By how much does the required return on the riskier stock exceed the required return on the less risky stock?

SPREADSHEET PROBLEM

Using the computerized model, rework Problem 4-3, assuming that a third stock, Stock C, is available for inclusion in the portfolio. Stock C has the following historical returns:

YEAR	STOCK C'S RETURNS, k_C
1992	32.00%
1993	(11.75)
1994	10.75
1995	32.25
1996	(6.75)

a. Calculate (or read from the computer screen) the average return, standard deviation, and coefficient of variation for Stock C.

b. Assume that the portfolio now consists of 33.33 percent of Stock A, 33.33 percent of Stock B, and 33.33 percent of Stock C. How does this affect the portfolio return, standard deviation, and coefficient of variation versus when 50 percent was invested in A and in B?

c. Make some other changes in the portfolio, making sure that the percentages sum to 100 percent. For example, enter 25 percent for Stock A, 25 percent for Stock B, and 50 percent for Stock C. (Note that the program will not allow you to enter a zero for the percentage in Stock C.) Notice that $\hat{k}_p$ remains constant and that σ_p changes. Why do these results occur?

d. In Problem 4-3, the standard deviation of the portfolio decreased only slightly, because Stocks A and B were highly positively correlated with one another. In this problem, the addition of Stock C causes the standard deviation of the portfolio to decline dramatically, even though $\sigma_C = \sigma_A = \sigma_B$. What does this indicate about the correlation between Stock C and Stocks A and B?

e. Would you prefer to hold the portfolio described in Problem 4-3 consisting only of Stocks A and B or a portfolio that also included Stock C? If others react similarly, how might this affect the stocks' prices and rates of return?

SPREADSHEET EXERCISE: FORMULAS

This exercise uses a spreadsheet model to calculate the expected rate of return, standard deviation, and coefficient of variation for individual stocks and portfolios given the forecasted returns distributions on the stocks and portfolio composition. The starting model contains data for two stocks and one portfolio, but students can easily add additional stocks and portfolios to the model. In the exercise, students add one stock and one portfolio.

1. Retrieve the model (Filename SE-04) from the models diskette.

2. Change the probabilities in Column C to see how the probabilities of occurrence affect risk and return on Circuit, Luster, and Portfolio CL. (Be sure that the probabilities of occurrence sum to 1.00.) Note that when extreme economic conditions such as recession and boom have higher probabilities, both the individual stocks and Portfolio CL have more risk. When you are finished, change the probabilities back to their initial values: 0.05, 0.20, 0.50, 0.20, and 0.05.

3. Now change the rates of return for Circuit in Column D to see how the returns distribution affects risk and expected rate of return. Note that when the distribution is "stretched out" by lowering the values in the poor economic states and raising the values in the good economic states, the riskiness of Circuit, as measured by standard deviation, increases. When you are finished, change the returns for Circuit back to −20.0, −5.0, 20.0, 33.0, and 47.0. (Note that the cells are formatted to display percentages, but the values must be entered as decimals. For example, Cell D12, which will display 33.0%, must be entered as 0.33.)

4. To assess the impact of the portfolio mix on Portfolio CL's risk and return, change the percent of Circuit value in Cell C4, starting with 0 and moving to 100 percent. Note that Portfolio CL's standard deviation is the same as Luster when the mix is zero and the same as Circuit when the mix is 1.00, but the portfolio standard deviation is only 1.4 percent when the portfolio contains 30 percent Circuit. Since the returns on Circuit and Luster are negatively correlated, combining them into a portfolio can substantially lower the risk inherent in the lower-risk stock (Luster, which has a standard deviation of 6.6 percent).

5. Fill in the following return values for Apex in the range F9.F13: 6.0, −8.0, 6.0, 30.0, and 12.0. (Again, note that these percentages must be entered as decimals.)

6. Enter the formulas for Apex's expected return, standard deviation, and coefficient of variation in Cells F16, F17, and F18, respectively. For inspiration, look at the formulas for Luster in the adjacent cells in Column E.

7. Finally, fill in the cells in the ranges H9.H13 and H16.H18 to calculate Portfolio CA's returns in each economic state, expected return, standard deviation, and coefficient of variation. Again, look at the formulas in the adjacent cells in Column G to gain some insights into the proper entries. Note that the standard deviation of Portfolio CA is never less than that of Apex. Apex and Circuit are highly positively correlated, so combining them into a portfolio does not reduce the riskiness inherent in the individual stocks. In both Portfolios CL and CA, the expected rate of return is a linear combination of the expected rates of return of the component stocks. Unlike risk, portfolio returns do not depend on the correlations among the components.

MINI CASE

Assume that you recently graduated with a major in finance, and you just landed a job as a financial planner with Merrill Finch Inc., a large financial services corporation. Your first assignment is to invest $100,000 for a client. Because the funds are to be invested in a business at the end of one year, you have been instructed to plan for a one-year holding period. Further, your boss has restricted you to the following investment alternatives, shown with their probabilities and associated outcomes. (Disregard for now the items at the bottom of the data; you will fill in the blanks later.)

RETURNS ON ALTERNATIVE INVESTMENTS

ESTIMATED RATE OF RETURN

STATE OF THE ECONOMY	PROBABILITY	T-BILLS	HIGH TECH	COLLECTIONS	U.S. RUBBER	MARKET PORTFOLIO	2-STOCK PORTFOLIO
Recession	0.1	8.0%	(22.0%)	28.0%	10.0%*	(13.0%)	3.0%
Below average	0.2	8.0	(2.0)	14.7	(10.0)	1.0	
Average	0.4	8.0	20.0	0.0	7.0	15.0	10.0
Above average	0.2	8.0	35.0	(10.0)	45.0	29.0	
Boom	0.1	8.0	50.0	(20.0)	30.0*	43.0	15.0
$\hat{k}$				1.7%	13.8%	15.0%	
σ		0.0		13.4	18.8	15.3	3.3
CV				7.9	1.4	1.0	0.3
b				−0.86	0.68		

*Note that the estimated returns of U.S. Rubber do not always move in the same direction as the overall economy. For example, when the economy is below average, consumers purchase fewer tires than they would if the economy was stronger. However, if the economy is in a flat-out recession, a large number of consumers who were planning to purchase a new car may choose to wait and instead purchase new tires for the car they currently own. Under these circumstances, we would expect U.S. Rubber's stock price to be higher if there is a recession than if the economy was just below average.

Merrill Finch's economic forecasting staff has developed probability estimates for the state of the economy, and its security analysts have developed a sophisticated computer program which was used to estimate the rate of return on each alternative under each state of the economy. High Tech Inc. is an electronics firm; Collections Inc. collects past-due debts; and U.S. Rubber manufactures tires and various other rubber and plastics products. Merrill Finch also maintains an "index fund" which owns a market-weighted fraction of all publicly traded stocks; you can invest in that fund, and thus obtain average stock market results. Given the situation as described, answer the following questions.

a. (1) Why is the T-bill's return independent of the state of the economy? Do T-bills promise a completely risk-free return? (2) Why are High Tech's returns expected to move with the economy whereas Collections' are expected to move counter to the economy?
b. Calculate the expected rate of return on each alternative and fill in the blanks on the row for $\hat{k}$ in the table above.
c. You should recognize that basing a decision solely on expected returns is only appropriate for risk-neutral individuals. Since your client, like virtually everyone, is risk averse, the riskiness of each alternative is an important aspect of the decision. One possible measure of risk is the standard deviation of returns. (1) Calculate this value for each alternative, and fill in the blank on the row for σ in the table above. (2) What type of risk is measured by the standard deviation? (3) Draw a graph which shows *roughly* the shape of the probability distributions for High Tech, U.S. Rubber, and T-bills.
d. Suppose you suddenly remembered that the coefficient of variation (CV) is generally regarded as being a better measure of stand-alone risk than the standard deviation when the alternatives being considered have widely differing expected returns. Calculate the missing CVs and fill in the blanks on the row for CV in the table above. Does the CV produce the same risk rankings as the standard deviation?

e. Suppose you created a 2-stock portfolio by investing $50,000 in High Tech and $50,000 in Collections. (1) Calculate the expected return ($\hat{k}_p$), the standard deviation (σ_p), and the coefficient of variation (CV_p) for this portfolio and fill in the appropriate blanks in the table above. (2) How does the riskiness of this 2-stock portfolio compare to the riskiness of the individual stocks if they were held in isolation?

f. Suppose an investor starts with a portfolio consisting of one randomly selected stock. What would happen (1) to the riskiness and (2) to the expected return of the portfolio as more and more randomly selected stocks were added to the portfolio? What is the implication for investors? Draw two graphs to illustrate your answer.

g. (1) Should portfolio effects impact the way investors think about the riskiness of individual stocks? (2) If you decided to hold a 1-stock portfolio, and consequently were exposed to more risk than diversified investors, could you expect to be compensated for all of your risk; that is, could you earn a risk premium on that part of your risk that you could have eliminated by diversifying?

h. The expected rates of return and the beta coefficients of the alternatives as supplied by Merrill Finch's computer program are as follows:

SECURITY	RETURN ($\hat{k}$)	RISK (BETA)
High Tech	17.4%	1.29
Market	15.0	1.00
U.S. Rubber	13.8	0.68
T-bills	8.0	0.00
Collections	1.7	(0.86)

(1) What is a beta coefficient, and how are betas used in risk analysis? (2) Do the expected returns appear to be related to each alternative's market risk? (3) Is it possible to choose among the alternatives on the basis of the information developed thus far? Use the data given at the start of the problem to construct a graph which shows how the T-bill's, High Tech's, and Collections's beta coefficients are calculated. Then discuss what betas measure and how they are used in risk analysis.

i. (1) Write out the Security Market Line (SML) equation, use it to calculate the required rate of return on each alternative, and then graph the relationship between the expected and required rates of return. (2) How do the expected rates of return compare with the required rates of return? (3) Does the fact that Collections has an expected return which is less than the T-bill rate make any sense? (4) What would be the market risk and the required return of a 50-50 portfolio of High Tech and Collections? Of High Tech and U.S. Rubber?

j. (1) Suppose investors raised their inflation expectations by 3 percentage points over current estimates as reflected in the 8 percent T-bill rate. What effect would higher inflation have on the SML and on the returns required on high- and low-risk securities? (2) Suppose instead that investors' risk aversion increased enough to cause the market risk premium to increase by 3 percentage points. (Inflation remains constant.) What effect would this have on the SML and on returns of high- and low-risk securities?

SELECTED ADDITIONAL REFERENCES AND CASES

Probably the best sources of additional information on probability distributions and single-asset risk measures are statistics textbooks. For example, see

Kohler, Heinz, *Statistics for Business and Economics* (New York: HarperCollins, 1994).

Mendenhall, William, Richard L. Schaeffer, and Dennis D. Wackerly, *Mathematical Statistics with Applications* (Boston: PWS, 1996).

Probably the best place to find an extension of portfolio theory concepts is one of the investments textbooks. These are some good ones:

Francis, Jack C., *Investments: Analysis and Management* (New York: McGraw-Hill, 1991).

Radcliffe, Robert C., *Investment: Concepts, Analysis, and Strategy* (New York: HarperCollins, 1994).

Reilly, Frank K., and Keith C. Brown, *Investment Analysis and Portfolio Management* (Fort Worth, Tex.: Dryden Press, 1997).

Sharpe, William F., *Investments* (Englewood Cliffs, N.J.: Prentice-Hall, 1995).

Those who want to start at the beginning in studying portfolio theory should see

Markowitz, Harry M., "Portfolio Selection," *Journal of Finance,* March 1952, 77–91.

_____, "Foundations of Portfolio Theory," *Journal of Finance,* June 1991, 469–477.

The following case from the Cases in Financial Management: Dryden Request *series covers many of the concepts discussed in this chapter as well as concepts to be covered in Chapter 5:*

Case 2, "Peachtree Securities, Inc. (A)."

CHAPTER 5

RISK AND RETURN: EXTENSIONS*

One of the most useful references for individuals working in investments and portfolio management is Stocks, Bonds, Bills, and Inflation, *published annually by Ibbotson Associates. The latest Ibbotson report presents a history of the total returns realized from 1926 through 1995 in the following six U.S. capital markets:*

1. *Small-company stocks, as represented by the smallest 20 percent of stocks (by market value) listed on the New York Stock Exchange.*

2. *Common stocks, as represented by the Standard and Poor's 500 Stock Composite Index (S&P 500).*

3. *Long-term corporate bonds, as represented by the Salomon Brothers long-term, high-grade corporate bond total return index.*

4. *Long-term government bonds, as represented by a U.S. Treasury bond with a 20-year maturity.*

5. *Intermediate-term government bonds, as represented by a U.S. Treasury bond with a five-year maturity.*

6. *U.S. Treasury bills, as represented by a bill with a maturity of approximately 30 days.*

---

*This chapter may be omitted without loss of continuity.

A long-term perspective of capital market history reveals the general relationship between risk and return across different asset classes, as well as the relationship between nominal and real (inflation-adjusted) returns. By studying the past, one can make inferences about what is likely to happen in the future. Although the specific events that occurred from 1926 through 1995 cannot be repeated, similar events, such as economic recessions and booms, will undoubtedly recur, and such events will probably affect future investment returns in much the same way as they did in the past.

The Ibbotson report presents historical data in many different formats, but perhaps the most widely used is the annual return data. For example, the 1996 Yearbook, which contains data for 70 years (1926 through 1995), provides the following total return information, along with inflation data:

INVESTMENT	AVERAGE ANNUAL RETURN	HIGHEST ANNUAL RETURN	LOWEST ANNUAL RETURN
Small-company stocks	17.4%	142.9%	−58.0%
Common stocks	12.2	54.0	−43.3
Long-term corporate bonds	5.7	43.8	−8.1
Long-term government bonds	5.2	40.4	−9.2
Intermediate-term government bonds	5.2	29.1	−2.3
U.S. Treasury bills	3.7	14.7	0.0
Inflation	3.2	18.2	−10.3

The most striking feature of the historical data is the significant difference in risk and return characteristics among the investments. Although a portfolio of small-company stocks averaged a 17.4 percent annual return, the return on T-bills averaged only 3.7 percent. In fact, the return on T-bills barely kept pace with inflation, earning on average only 50 basis points (0.5 percentage points) above inflation. When taxes are considered, the real average return on T-bills was negative. For example, an investor who paid on average only 20 percent in taxes would have an after-tax average return on T-bills of only 0.8(3.7%) ≈ 3.0%, which means a real loss of about 20 basis points per year.

Why do historical returns vary so widely among investments? The answer is simple: risk. To see this more clearly, note that an investor in small-company stocks would have lost 58 percent of the value of his or her portfolio in one of the past 70 years (to be precise, in 1937), while the worst pre-tax experience for an investor holding T-bills was a breakeven year. In general, we see that a strong relationship exists between risk and return — the higher the risk, the higher the return. Although we have not quantified the riskiness of the listed investments, a numerical analysis would lead to the same conclusion — namely, to obtain higher returns, investors must accept greater risk.

In Chapter 4 we presented the key elements of risk and return analysis. There we saw that much of the risk inherent in a stock can be eliminated by diversification, so rational investors should hold portfolios of stocks rather than single stocks. We also introduced the Capital Asset Pricing Model (CAPM), which links risk and required rates of return, using a stock's beta coefficient as the relevant measure of risk. In this chapter, we extend the Chapter 4 material by presenting an in-depth treatment of portfolio concepts and the CAPM. Additionally, we show how betas are actually calculated, and we discuss an alternative view of the risk/return relationship, the Arbitrage Pricing Theory (APT).

MEASURING PORTFOLIO RISK

In the preceding chapter, we examined portfolio risk at an intuitive level. We now describe how portfolio risk is actually measured and dealt with in practice. First, the riskiness of a portfolio is measured by the standard deviation of its return distribution, and Equation 5-1 is used to calculate this standard deviation:[1]

$$\text{Portfolio standard deviation} = \sigma_p = \sqrt{\sum_{i=1}^{n} (k_{pi} - \hat{k}_p)^2 P_i}. \qquad \textbf{5-1}$$

Here σ_p is the portfolio's standard deviation; k_{pi} is the return on the portfolio under the ith state of the economy; $\hat{k}_p$ is the expected rate of return on the portfolio; P_i is the probability of occurrence of the ith state of the economy; and there are n economic states. This equation is exactly the same as the one for the standard deviation of a single asset, except that here the asset is a portfolio of assets (for example, a mutual fund).

COVARIANCE AND THE CORRELATION COEFFICIENT

Two key concepts in portfolio analysis are (1) *covariance* and (2) the *correlation coefficient.* Covariance is a measure which combines the variance (or volatility) of a stock's returns with the tendency of those returns to move up or down at the same time other stocks move up or down. For example, the covariance between Stocks A and B tells us whether the returns of the two stocks tend to rise and fall together, and how large those movements tend to be. Equation 5-2 defines the covariance (Cov) between Stocks A and B:

$$\text{Covariance} = \text{Cov(AB)} = \sum_{i=1}^{n} (k_{Ai} - \hat{k}_A)(k_{Bi} - \hat{k}_B) P_i. \qquad \textbf{5-2}$$

---

[1]Other risk measures such as the coefficient of variation or semivariance could also be used to measure the risk of a portfolio, but since portfolio returns (1) are approximately normally distributed and (2) have reasonably similar expected values, these refinements are generally not necessary and hence are not used.

The first term in parentheses after the Σ is the deviation of Stock A's return from its expected value under the ith state of the economy; the second term is Stock B's deviation under the same state; and P_i is the probability of the ith state occurring. Before going through an example, note these points:

1. If the returns on A and B tend to move together, the terms in parentheses will both be positive or both be negative for each state of the economy; that is, if k_{Ai} is above its expected value, $\hat{k}_A$, then k_{Bi} generally will be above $\hat{k}_B$, and vice versa. Therefore, if the returns move together, the terms in parentheses will both be positive or both be negative, hence the product $(k_{Ai} - \hat{k}_A)(k_{Bi} - \hat{k}_B)$ will be positive, while if the returns move counter to one another, the products will tend to be negative. However, if the two stocks' returns fluctuate randomly, then the products will sometimes be positive and sometimes be negative, and the sum of the products will be close to zero because the positives and negatives will tend to cancel out. Therefore, if Stocks A and B tend to move together, their covariance, Cov(AB), will be positive, while if they tend to move counter to one another, Cov(AB) will be negative. If they fluctuate randomly, Cov(AB) could be either positive or negative, but, in either event, it will be close to zero.

2. If the return on either A or B is highly uncertain, then it will have a high standard deviation, its deviations as shown in the parenthetical terms will tend to be large, the products will tend to be large, and the absolute size of Cov(AB) will also tend to be large. However, Cov(AB) will be small, even if σ_A and/or σ_B is large, if A and B move randomly, because the plus and minus terms will cancel out.

3. If either stock has a zero standard deviation, hence is riskless, then all of its deviations $(k_i - \hat{k})$ will be zero, and Cov(AB) also will be zero. Similarly, if one asset is not completely riskless, but it has a relatively low risk, then its deviations will tend to be small, and this, too, will hold down the size of Cov(AB).

4. Therefore, Cov(AB) will be large and positive if two assets have large standard deviations and tend to move together; it will be large and negative for two high σ assets which move counter to one another; and it will be small if the two assets' returns move randomly, rather than up or down with one another, or if either of the assets has a small standard deviation.

To illustrate the calculation process, first look at Table 5-1, which presents the probability distributions of the rates of return on four stocks, and at Figure 5-1, which plots scatter diagrams between returns on several pairs of the stocks. We can use Equation 5-2 to calculate the covariance between Stocks F and G as follows:

$$Cov(FG) = \sum_{i=1}^{5} (k_{Fi} - \hat{k}_F)(k_{Gi} - \hat{k}_G)P_i$$

$$= (6 - 10)(14 - 10)(0.1) + (8 - 10)(12 - 10)(0.2)$$
$$+ (10 - 10)(10 - 10)(0.4) + (12 - 10)(8 - 10)(0.2)$$
$$+ (14 - 10)(6 - 10)(0.1)$$

$$= -4.8.$$

The negative sign indicates that the rates of return tend to move in opposite directions, which is consistent with the pattern shown in Panel b of Figure 5-1.

PROBABILITY OF OCCURRENCE	RATE OF RETURN DISTRIBUTION			
	E	F	G	H
0.1	10.0%	6.0%	14.0%	2.0%
0.2	10.0	8.0	12.0	6.0
0.4	10.0	10.0	10.0	9.0
0.2	10.0	12.0	8.0	15.0
0.1	10.0	14.0	6.0	20.0
$\hat{k} =$	10.0%	10.0%	10.0%	10.0%
$\sigma =$	0.0%	2.2%	2.2%	5.0%

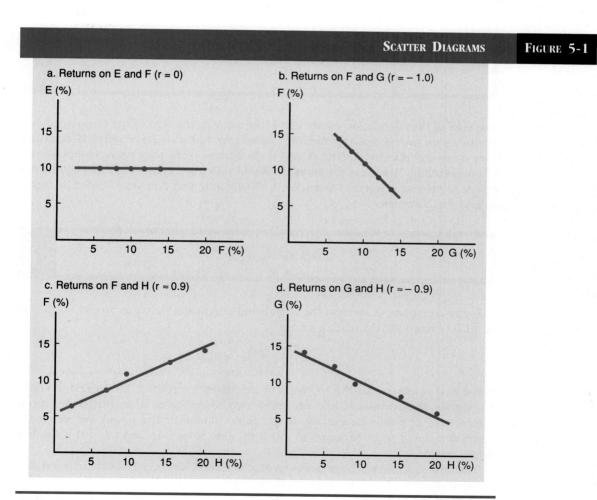

a. Returns on E and F (r = 0)

b. Returns on F and G (r = −1.0)

c. Returns on F and H (r ≈ 0.9)

d. Returns on G and H (r ≈ −0.9)

NOTES:

a. The lines shown in each graph are called *regression lines;* they will be discussed in detail in a later section.

b. These graphs are drawn as if each point had an equal probability of occurrence.

If we calculated the covariance between Stocks F and H, we would find Cov(FH) = +10.8, indicating that these assets tend to move together, as indicated by the positive slope in Panel c. A zero covariance, as between Stocks E and F, indicates that there is no relationship between the variables; that is, the variables are independent. (E's return is always 10 percent, so $\sigma_E = 0\%$, and the covariance of E with any asset must be zero.)

It is difficult to interpret the magnitude of the covariance term, so a related statistic, the correlation coefficient, is often used to measure the degree of comovement between two variables. The correlation coefficient standardizes the covariance by dividing by a product term, which facilitates comparisons by putting things on a similar scale. The correlation coefficient, r, is calculated as follows for variables A and B:

$$\text{Correlation coefficient(AB)} = r_{AB} = \frac{\text{Cov(AB)}}{\sigma_A \sigma_B}. \qquad \text{5-3}$$

The sign of the correlation coefficient is the same as the sign of the covariance, so a positive sign means that the variables move together, a negative sign indicates that they move in opposite directions, and if r is close to zero, they move independently of one another. Moreover, the standardization process confines the correlation coefficient to values between −1.0 and +1.0. Finally, note that Equation 5-3 can be solved to find the covariance:

$$\text{Cov(AB)} = r_{AB} \sigma_A \sigma_B. \qquad \text{5-3a}$$

Using Equation 5-3, we find the correlation coefficient between Stocks F and G to be −1.0 (except for a rounding error):

$$r_{FG} = \frac{-4.8}{(2.2)(2.2)} \approx -1.0.$$

These two stocks are said to be perfectly negatively correlated. As Panel b of Figure 5-1 shows, the regression line for these two assets' rates of return is negatively sloped, and all points lie exactly on the line. Whenever the points are all on the regression line, r must be equal to 1.0 if the line slopes up and to −1.0 if the line slopes down.

The correlation coefficient between Stocks F and H is +0.9. Thus, there is a strong positive relationship — their regression line is upward sloping, but all points are not exactly on the line. Except in the case where one of the assets has zero variance, the closer the points are to the regression line, the higher the absolute value of the correlation coefficient.

THE TWO-ASSET CASE

Under the assumption that the distributions of returns on the individual securities are normal, a complicated looking but operationally simple equation can be used to determine the riskiness of a two-asset portfolio:[2]

$$\text{Portfolio SD} = \sigma_p = \sqrt{x^2\sigma_A^2 + (1-x)^2\sigma_B^2 + 2x(1-x)r_{AB}\sigma_A\sigma_B}. \qquad \text{5-4}$$

Here x is the fraction of the portfolio invested in Security A, so $(1-x)$ is the fraction invested in Security B.

How is the riskiness of a portfolio measured?
What does the correlation coefficient measure?

EFFICIENT PORTFOLIOS

One important use of the statistical relationships we have just discussed is to select *efficient portfolios,* defined as those portfolios which provide the highest expected return for any degree of risk, or the lowest degree of risk for any expected return. To illustrate the concept, assume that two securities, A and B, are available, and we can allocate our funds between them in any proportion. Suppose Security A has an expected rate of return of $\hat{k}_A = 5\%$ and a standard deviation of returns $\sigma_A = 4\%$, while $\hat{k}_B = 8\%$ and $\sigma_B = 10\%$. Our first task is to determine the set of *attainable* portfolios, and then from this attainable set to select the *efficient* subset.

To construct the attainable set, we need data on the degree of correlation between the two securities' expected returns, r_{AB}. Let us work with three different assumed degrees of correlation, $r_{AB} = +1.0$, $r_{AB} = 0$, and $r_{AB} = -1.0$, and using them, develop the portfolios' expected returns, $\hat{k}_p$, and standard deviations, σ_p. (Of course, only one correlation can exist; our example simply shows three alternative situations that might exist.)

To calculate k_p, we use a modified version of Equation 4-5 from Chapter 4, substituting the given values for $\hat{k}_A$ and $\hat{k}_B$, and then solving for $\hat{k}_p$ at different values of x. For example, when x equals 0.75, then $\hat{k}_p = 5.75\%$:

---

[2]Equation 5-4 is derived from Equation 5-1 in standard statistics books. Notice that if x = 1, all of the portfolio is invested in Security A, and Equation 5-4 reduces to σ_A:

$$\sigma_p = \sqrt{\sigma_A^2} = \sigma_A.$$

The portfolio contains but a single asset, so the risk of the portfolio and that of the asset are identical. Equation 5-4 could be expanded to include any number of assets by adding additional terms, but we shall not do so here.

$$\hat{k}_p = x\hat{k}_A + (1 - x)\hat{k}_B \tag{4-5a}$$

$$= 0.75(5\%) + 0.25(8\%) = 5.75\%.$$

Other values of $\hat{k}_p$ were found similarly, and they are shown in the three $\hat{k}_p$ columns of Table 5-2.

Next, we use Equation 5-4 to find σ_p. Substitute the given values for σ_A, σ_B, and r_{AB}, and then solve for σ_p at different values of x. For example, in the case where $r_{AB} = 0$ and $x = 0.75$, then $\sigma_p = 3.9\%$:

$$\sigma_p = \sqrt{x^2\sigma_A^2 + (1 - x)^2\sigma_B^2 + 2x(1 - x)r_{AB}\sigma_A\sigma_B}$$

$$= \sqrt{(0.5625)(16) + (0.0625)(100) + 2(0.75)(0.25)(0)(4)(10)}$$

$$= \sqrt{9.00 + 6.25} = \sqrt{15.25} = 3.9\%.$$

Table 5-2 gives $\hat{k}_p$ and σ_p values for x = 1.00, 0.75, 0.50, 0.25, and 0.00, and Figure 5-2 plots $\hat{k}_p$, σ_p, and the attainable set of portfolios for each correlation. In both the table and the graphs, note the following points:

1. The three graphs across the top row of Figure 5-2 designate Case I, where the two assets are perfectly positively correlated, that is, $r_{AB} = +1.0$. The three graphs in the middle row are for the zero correlation case, and the three in the bottom row are for perfect negative correlation.

2. All three cases are theoretical in the sense that we would rarely encounter $r_{AB} = -1.0$, 0.0, or + 1.0. Generally, in the real world, r_{AB} would be in the range of +0.5 to +0.7 for most stocks. Case II (zero correlation) produces graphs which, pictorially, most closely resemble real-world examples.

3. The left column of graphs shows how the expected portfolio returns vary with different combinations of A and B. We see that these graphs are identical in each of the three cases: The portfolio return, $\hat{k}_p$, is a linear function of x, and it does not depend on the correlation coefficients. This is also seen from the $\hat{k}_p$ columns in Table 5-2.

4. The middle column of graphs shows how risk is affected by the portfolio mix. Starting from the top, we see that portfolio risk, σ_p, increases linearly in Case

| $\hat{k}_p$ AND σ_p UNDER VARIOUS ASSUMPTIONS | | | | | | TABLE 5-2 |

PROPORTION OF PORTFOLIO IN SECURITY A (VALUE OF x)	PROPORTION OF PORTFOLIO IN SECURITY B (VALUE OF 1 − x)	CASE I ($r_{AB} = +1.0$)		CASE II ($r_{AB} = 0$)		CASE III ($r_{AB} = -1.0$)	
		$\hat{k}_p$	σ_p	$\hat{k}_p$	σ_p	$\hat{k}_p$	σ_p
1.00	0.00	5.00%	4.0%	5.00%	4.0%	5.00%	4.0%
0.75	0.25	5.75	5.5	5.75	3.9	5.75	0.5
0.50	0.50	6.50	7.0	6.50	5.4	6.50	3.0
0.25	0.75	7.25	8.5	7.25	7.6	7.25	6.5
0.00	1.00	8.00	10.0	8.00	10.0	8.00	10.0

I, where $r_{AB} = +1.0$; it is nonlinear in Case II; and Case III shows that risk can be completely diversified away if $r_{AB} = -1.0$. Thus σ_p, unlike $\hat{k}_p$, *does* depend on correlation.

5. The right column of graphs shows the *attainable,* or *feasible, set* of portfolios constructed with different mixes of Securities A and B. Each of the three graphs was plotted from pairs of $\hat{k}_p$ and σ_p as shown in Table 5-2. For example, Point A in the upper right graph is the point $\hat{k}_p = 5\%$, $\sigma_p = 4\%$ from the Case I data. All other points on the curves were plotted similarly. With only two securities, the attainable set is a curve or line, and we can achieve each risk/return combination on the relevant curve by some allocation of our investment funds between Securities A and B.

6. Are all portfolios on the attainable set equally good? The answer is no: Only that part of the attainable set from Y to B in Cases II and III is defined to be *efficient.* The part from A to Y is inefficient because for any degree of risk on

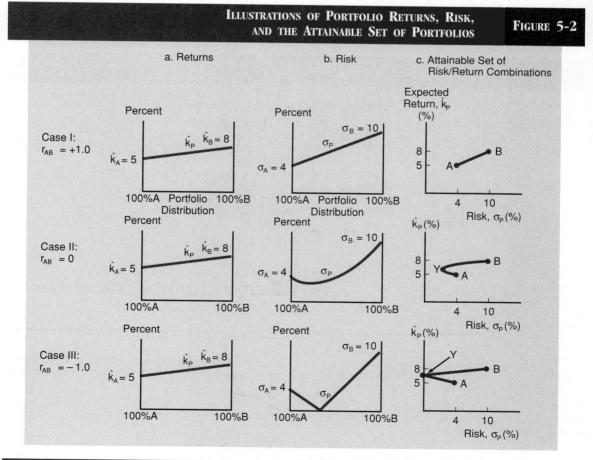

ILLUSTRATIONS OF PORTFOLIO RETURNS, RISK, AND THE ATTAINABLE SET OF PORTFOLIOS

FIGURE 5-2

the line segment AY, a higher return can be found on segment YB. Thus, no rational investor would hold a portfolio that lay on segment AY. In Case I, however, the entire feasible set is also efficient—here no combination of the securities can be ruled out.

From these examples we see that in one extreme case (r = −1.0), risk can be completely eliminated, while in the other extreme case (r = +1.0), diversification does no good whatever. In between these extremes, combining two stocks into a portfolio reduces but does not eliminate the riskiness inherent in the individual stocks.[3]

SELF-TEST   What is meant by the term "attainable, or feasible, set"?
QUESTIONS   Within the attainable set, which portfolios are "efficient"?

CHOOSING THE OPTIMAL PORTFOLIO

With only two assets, the feasible set of portfolios is a line or curve as shown in the third column of graphs back in Figure 5-2. However, if we were to increase the number of assets, we would obtain an area such as the shaded area in Figure 5-3. The

FIGURE 5-3   THE EFFICIENT SET OF INVESTMENTS

---

[3]If we differentiate Equation 5-4, set the derivative equal to zero, and then solve for x, we obtain the fraction of the portfolio that should be invested in Security A if we wish to form the least-risky portfolio. Here is the equation:

$$\text{Minimum risk portfolio:} \quad x = \frac{\sigma_B(\sigma_B - r_{AB}\sigma_A)}{\sigma_A^2 + \sigma_B^2 - 2r_{AB}\sigma_A\sigma_B}.$$

As a rule, we limit x to the range 0 to +1.0; that is, if the solution value is x > 1.0, set x = 1.0, and if x is negative, set x = 0. A negative x would imply short sales, and x > 1.0 would imply borrowing.

points A, H, G, and E represent single securities (or portfolios containing only one security). All the other points in the shaded area, including its boundaries, represent portfolios of two or more securities. The shaded area comprises the *feasible,* or *attainable, set.* Each point in this area represents a particular portfolio with a risk of σ_p and an expected return of $\hat{k}_p$. For example, point X represents one such portfolio's risk and expected return, as do B, C, and D.

Given the full set of potential portfolios that could be constructed from the available assets, which portfolio should actually be held? This choice involves two separate decisions: (1) determining the *efficient set* of portfolios and (2) choosing from the efficient set the single portfolio that is best for the specific investor.

THE EFFICIENT FRONTIER

In Figure 5-3, the boundary line BCDE defines the *efficient set* of portfolios, which is also called the *efficient frontier.*[4] Portfolios to the left of the efficient set are not possible because they lie outside the attainable set. Portfolios to the right of the boundary line (interior portfolios) are inefficient because some other portfolio would provide either a higher return with the same degree of risk or a lower risk for the same rate of return. For example, Portfolio X is dominated by Portfolios C and D.

RISK/RETURN INDIFFERENCE CURVES

Given the efficient set of portfolios, which specific portfolio should an investor choose? To determine the optimal portfolio for a particular investor, we must know the investor's attitude toward risk as reflected in his or her risk/return trade-off function, or *indifference curve.*

An investor's risk/return trade-off function is based on the standard economic concepts of utility theory and indifference curves, which are illustrated in Figure 5-4. The curves labeled I_Y and I_Z represent the indifference curves of Individuals Y and Z. Ms. Y is indifferent with regard to the riskless 5 percent portfolio, a portfolio with an expected return of 6 percent but a risk of $\sigma_p = 1.4\%$, and so on. Mr. Z is equally well satisfied with a riskless 5 percent return, an expected 6 percent return with risk of $\sigma_p = 3.3\%$, and so on.

Notice that Ms. Y requires a higher expected rate of return to compensate for any given amount of risk; thus, Ms. Y is said to be more *risk averse* than Mr. Z. Her higher risk aversion causes Ms. Y to require a higher *risk premium*—defined here as the difference between the 5 percent riskless return and the expected return required to compensate for any specific amount of risk—than does Mr. Z. Thus, Ms. Y requires a risk premium (RP_Y) of 2.5 percent to compensate for a risk of $\sigma_p = 3.3\%$, while Mr. Z's risk premium for this degree of risk is only $RP_Z = 1.0\%$. As a generalization, the steeper the slope of the indifference curve, the more risk averse the investor. Thus, Ms. Y is more risk averse than Mr. Z.

---

[4]A computational procedure for determining the efficient set of portfolios was developed by Harry Markowitz and first reported in his article "Portfolio Selection," *Journal of Finance,* March 1952, 77–91. In this article, Markowitz developed the basic concepts of portfolio theory, and he later won the Nobel Prize in economics for his work.

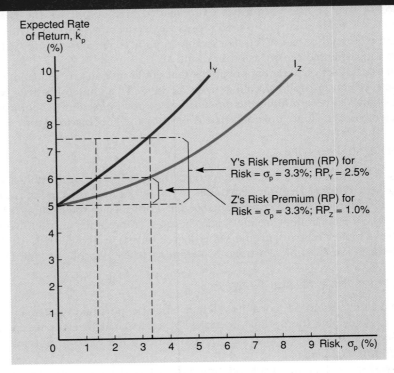

FIGURE 5-4   RISK/RETURN INDIFFERENCE CURVES

Each individual has a "map" of indifference curves; the indifference maps for Ms. Y and Mr. Z are shown in Figure 5-5. The higher curves denote a greater level of satisfaction (or utility). Thus, I_{Z2} is better than I_{Z1} because, for any level of risk, Mr. Z has a higher expected return, hence greater utility. An infinite number of indifference curves could be drawn for each individual, and each individual has a unique set of curves.

THE OPTIMAL PORTFOLIO FOR AN INVESTOR

Figure 5-5 also shows the feasible set of portfolios for the two-asset case, under the assumption that $r_{AB} = 0$, as it was developed in Figure 5-1. The optimal portfolio for each investor is found at the tangency point between the efficient set of portfolios and one of the investor's indifference curves. This tangency point marks the highest level of satisfaction the investor can attain. Ms. Y, who is more risk averse than Mr. Z, chooses a portfolio with a lower expected return (about 6 percent) but a riskiness of only $\sigma_p = 4.2\%$. Mr. Z picks a portfolio that provides an expected return of about 7.2 percent, but it has a risk of about $\sigma_p = 7.1\%$. Ms. Y's portfolio is more heavily

SELECTING THE OPTIMAL PORTFOLIO OF RISKY ASSETS   FIGURE 5-5

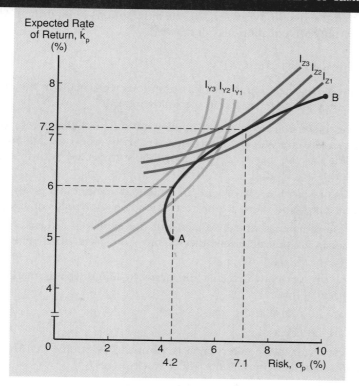

weighted with the less risky security, while Mr. Z's portfolio contains a larger proportion of the more risky security.[5]

What is the efficient frontier?
What are indifference curves?
Conceptually, how does an investor choose his or her optimal portfolio?

SELF-TEST
QUESTIONS

THE CAPITAL ASSET PRICING MODEL

The *Capital Asset Pricing Model (CAPM),* which was introduced in Chapter 4, specifies the relationship between risk and required rates of return on assets when they

---

[5]Ms. Y's portfolio would contain 67 percent of Security A and 33 percent of Security B, whereas Mr. Z's portfolio would consist of 27 percent of Security A and 73 percent of Security B. These percentages can be determined with Equation 4-5a by simply seeing what percentage of the two securities is consistent with $\hat{k}_p = 6.0\%$ and 7.2%. For example, x(5%) + (1 − x)(8%) = 7.2%, and solving for x, we obtain x = 0.27 and (1 − x) = 0.73.

are held in well-diversified portfolios. In Chapter 4, we focused on the Security Market Line equation, because that is the "bottom line" of the CAPM. In this chapter, we expand on that discussion by presenting the assumptions behind the CAPM and by showing how the SML equation was developed.

BASIC ASSUMPTIONS OF THE CAPM

As in all financial theories, a number of assumptions were made in the development of the CAPM; they are summarized in the following list:[6]

1. All investors focus on a single holding period, and they seek to maximize the expected utility of their terminal wealth by choosing among alternative portfolios on the basis of each portfolio's expected return and standard deviation.

2. All investors can borrow or lend an unlimited amount at a given risk-free rate of interest, k_{RF}, and there are no restrictions on short sales of any asset.[7]

3. All investors have identical estimates of the expected returns, variances, and covariances among all assets; that is, investors have homogeneous expectations.

4. All assets are perfectly divisible and perfectly liquid (that is, marketable at the going price).

5. There are no transactions costs.

6. There are no taxes.

7. All investors are price takers (that is, all investors assume that their own buying and selling activity will not affect stock prices).

8. The quantities of all assets are given and fixed.

Theoretical extensions in the literature have relaxed some of these assumptions, and in general these extensions have led to conclusions that are reasonably consistent with the basic theory. However, even the extensions contain assumptions which are both strong and unrealistic, so the validity of the model can only be established through empirical tests. More will be said later about the empirical validity of the CAPM, but first we must discuss its basic properties and conclusions.

SELF-TEST QUESTIONS   What are the key assumptions of the CAPM?
In what sense are these assumptions unrealistic? Explain.

---

[6]The CAPM was originated by William F. Sharpe in his article "Capital Asset Prices: A Theory of Market Equilibrium under Conditions of Risk," which appeared in the September 1964 issue of the *Journal of Finance*. Note that Professor Sharpe won the Nobel Prize in economics for his capital asset pricing work. The assumptions inherent in Sharpe's model were spelled out by Michael C. Jensen in "Capital Markets: Theory and Evidence," *Bell Journal of Economics and Management Science*, Autumn 1972, 357–398.

[7]In a *short sale*, one borrows a stock and then sells it, expecting to buy it back later (at a lower price) in order to repay the person from whom the stock was borrowed. If you sell short and the stock price rises, you lose; you gain if the stock price falls after you go short.

THE CAPITAL MARKET LINE

Figure 5-5 showed the set of portfolio opportunities for the two-asset case, and it illustrated how indifference curves can be used to select the optimal portfolio from the feasible set. In Figure 5-6, we show a similar diagram for the multi-asset case, but here we also include a risk-free asset with a return k_{RF}. The riskless asset by definition has zero risk, hence $\sigma = 0\%$, so it is plotted on the vertical axis.

The figure shows both the feasible set of portfolios of risky assets (the shaded area) and a set of indifference curves (I_1, I_2, I_3) for a particular investor. Point N, where indifference curve I_1 is tangent to the efficient set, represents a possible portfolio choice; it is the point on the efficient set of risky portfolios where the investor obtains the highest possible return for a given amount of risk, σ_p, and the smallest degree of risk for a given expected return, $\hat{k}_p$.

However, the investor can do better than Portfolio N—he or she can reach a higher indifference curve. In addition to the feasible set of risky portfolios, we now have a risk-free asset that provides a riskless return, k_{RF}. Given the risk-free asset, investors can create new portfolios that combine the risk-free asset with a portfolio of risky assets. This enables them to achieve any combination of risk and return on the straight line connecting k_{RF} with M, the point of tangency between that straight

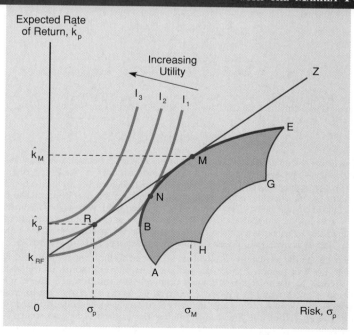

INVESTOR EQUILIBRIUM: COMBINING THE RISK-FREE ASSET WITH THE MARKET PORTFOLIO

FIGURE 5-6

line and the efficient frontier of risky asset portfolios.[8] Some portfolio on the line $k_{RF}MZ$ will be preferred to most risky portfolios on the efficient frontier BNME, so the points on the line $k_{RF}MZ$ now represent the best attainable combinations of risk and return.

Given the new opportunity set $k_{RF}MZ$, our investor will move from Point N to Point R, which is on his or her highest attainable risk/return indifference curve. Note that any point on the old efficient frontier BNME (except the point of tangency M) is dominated by some point along the line $k_{RF}MZ$. In general, since investors can include both the risk-free security and a fraction of the risky portfolio, M, in a portfolio, it will be possible to move to a point such as R. In addition, if the investor can borrow as well as lend (lending is equivalent to buying risk-free debt securities) at the riskless rate, k_{RF}, it is possible to move out on the line segment MZ, and one would do so if his or her indifference curve were tangent to $k_{RF}MZ$ to the right of Point M.[9]

All investors should hold portfolios lying on the line $k_{RF}MZ$ under the conditions assumed in the CAPM. This implies that they should hold portfolios that are combinations of the risk-free security and the risky portfolio M. Thus, the addition of the risk-free asset totally changes the efficient set: The efficient set now lies along line $k_{RF}MZ$ rather than along the curve BNME. Also, note that if the capital market is to be in equilibrium, M must be a portfolio that contains every risky asset in exact pro-

---

[8]The risk/return combinations between a risk-free asset and a risky asset (a single stock or a portfolio of stocks) will always be linear. To see this, consider the following equations, which were developed earlier, for return, $\hat{k}_p$, and risk, σ_p, for any combination x and $(1 - x)$:

$$\hat{k}_p = xk_{RF} + (1 - x)\hat{k}_M, \qquad \text{(4-5a)}$$

and

$$\sigma_p = \sqrt{x^2\sigma_{RF}^2 + (1 - x)^2\sigma_M^2 + 2x(1 - x)r_{RF/M}\sigma_{RF}\sigma_M}. \qquad \text{(5-4a)}$$

Equation 4-5a is linear. From Equation 5-4a, we know that k_{RF} is the risk-free asset, so $\sigma_{RF} = 0$; hence, σ_{RF}^2 is also zero. Using this information, we can simplify Equation 5-4a as follows:

$$\sigma_p = \sqrt{(1 - x)^2\sigma_M^2} = (1 - x)\sigma_M. \qquad \text{(5-4b)}$$

Thus, σ_p is also linear when a riskless asset is combined with a portfolio of risky assets.

If expected returns as measured by $\hat{k}_p$ and risk as measured by σ_p are both linear functions of x, then the relationship between $\hat{k}_p$ and σ_p, when graphed as in Figure 5-6, must also be linear. For example, if 100 percent of the portfolio is invested in k_{RF} with a return of 8 percent, the portfolio return will be 8 percent and σ_p will be 0. If 100 percent is invested in M, with $k_M = 12\%$ and $\sigma_M = 10\%$, then $\sigma_p = 1.0(10\%) = 10\%$, and $\hat{k}_p = 0(8\%) + 1.0(12\%) = 12\%$. If 50 percent of the portfolio is invested in M and 50 percent in the risk-free asset, then $\sigma_p = 0.5(10\%) = 5\%$, and $\hat{k}_p = 0.5(8\%) + 0.5(12\%) = 10\%$. Plotting these points will reveal the linear relationship given as $k_{RF}MZ$ in Figure 5-6.

[9]An investor who is highly averse to risk will have a steep indifference curve and will end up at a point such as R, holding some of the risky market portfolio and some of the riskless asset. An investor only slightly averse to risk will have a relatively flat indifference curve, which will cause him or her to move out beyond M toward Z, borrowing to do so. This investor might buy stocks on *margin*, which means borrowing and using the stocks as collateral. If individuals' borrowing rates are higher than k_{RF}, then the line $k_{RF}MZ$ will tilt down (that is, be less steep) beyond M. This condition would invalidate the basic CAPM, or at least require it to be modified. Therefore, the assumption of equal lending and borrowing rates is crucial to CAPM theory.

portion to that asset's fraction of the total market value of all assets; that is, if Security i is x percent of the total market value of all securities, x percent of the market portfolio M must consist of Security i. (In other words, M is the market-value-weighted portfolio of *all* risky assets in the economy.) Thus, all investors should hold portfolios which lie on the line $k_{RF}MZ$, with the particular location of a given individual's portfolio being determined by the point at which his or her indifference curve is tangent to the line.

The line $k_{RF}MZ$ in Figure 5-6 is called the *Capital Market Line (CML).* It has an intercept of k_{RF} and a slope of $(\hat{k}_M - k_{RF})/\sigma_M$.[10] Therefore, the equation for the Capital Market Line may be expressed as follows:

$$\text{CML:} \quad \hat{k}_p = k_{RF} + \left(\frac{\hat{k}_M - k_{RF}}{\sigma_M} \right)\sigma_p. \qquad \text{5-5}$$

The expected rate of return *on an efficient portfolio* is equal to the riskless rate plus a risk premium, and the risk premium is equal to $(\hat{k}_M - k_{RF})/\sigma_M$ multiplied by the portfolio's standard deviation, σ_p. Thus, the CML specifies a linear relationship between expected return and risk, with the slope of the CML being equal to the expected return on the market portfolio of risky stocks, $\hat{k}_M$, minus the risk-free rate, k_{RF}, which is called the *market risk premium,* all divided by the standard deviation of returns on the market portfolio, σ_M:

$$\text{Slope of the CML} = (\hat{k}_M - k_{RF})/\sigma_M.$$

For example, suppose $k_{RF} = 10\%$, $\hat{k}_M = 15\%$, and $\sigma_M = 15\%$. Then, the slope of the CML would be $(15\% - 10\%)/15\% = 0.33$, and if a particular portfolio had $\sigma_p = 10\%$, then its $\hat{k}_p$ would be

$$\hat{k}_p = 10\% + 0.33(10\%) = 13.3\%.$$

A riskier portfolio with $\sigma_p = 20\%$ would have $\hat{k}_p = 10\% + 0.33(20\%) = 16.6\%$.

Equation 5-5 states that the expected return on an efficient portfolio in equilibrium is equal to a risk-free return plus a risk premium which is equal to the slope of the CML multiplied by the standard deviation of the portfolio's returns. This relationship is graphed in Figure 5-7. The CML is a straight line with an intercept at k_{RF} and a slope equal to the market risk premium $(\hat{k}_M - k_{RF})$ divided by σ_M. The slope of the CML reflects the aggregate attitude of investors toward risk.

In Chapter 4 we saw that the standard deviation (σ_i) of an individual stock should not be used to measure the stock's riskiness, because some of its risk as reflected in σ_i can be eliminated by diversification. Therefore, since its beta reflects risk after taking diversification benefits into account, beta rather than σ_i is used to measure

---

[10]Recall that the slope of any line is measured as $\Delta Y/\Delta X$, or the change in height associated with a given change in horizontal distance. k_{RF} is at 0 on the horizontal axis, so $\Delta X = \sigma_M - 0 = \sigma_M$. The vertical axis difference associated with a change from k_{RF} to $\hat{k}_M$ is $\hat{k}_M - k_{RF}$. Therefore, slope $= \Delta Y/\Delta X = (\hat{k}_M - k_{RF})/\sigma_M$.

FIGURE 5-7	THE CAPITAL MARKET LINE (CML)

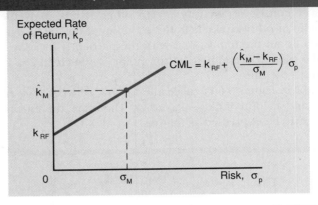

NOTE: We did not draw it in, but you can visualize the shaded space shown in Figure 5-6 in this graph, and the CML as the line formed by connecting k_{RF} with the tangent to the shaded space.

individual stocks' riskiness to investors. The relationship between individual stocks' riskiness and their required returns is set forth in the Security Market Line (SML), so in an SML graph such as that given back in Figure 4-10, we show beta on the horizontal axis. We discuss how betas are calculated in the next section.

Note that an efficient portfolio is one that is well diversified, so unlike individual stocks, all the riskiness of an efficient portfolio is measured by its standard deviation, σ_p. The CML equation specifies the relationship between risk and return for such efficient portfolios, that is, for portfolios that lie on the CML, so in the CML equation and graph, risk is measured by the portfolio standard deviation. For an individual stock, the relevant (market) risk is measured by its beta coefficient, b, and the relationship between risk and return is specified by the Security Market Line (SML) equation. Be sure to keep in mind the distinction between the SML and the CML—and why that distinction exists.

SELF-TEST QUESTIONS

Draw a graph which shows the feasible set of risky assets, the efficient frontier, the risk-free asset, and the CML.

Write out the equation for the CML and explain its meaning.

What is the difference between CML and the SML?

CALCULATING BETA COEFFICIENTS: THE CHARACTERISTIC LINE

As we noted in the preceding section, the relevant measure of risk for use in the Security Market Line (SML) equation is the stock's *beta coefficient,* which measures the volatility of a stock relative to that of a portfolio containing all stocks. In this section, we show how betas are calculated and used, and in the process we explain in more detail the difference between diversifiable risk and market risk.

The market risk of a given stock can be measured by its tendency to move with the general market. The procedure for determining market risk is illustrated in Figure 5-8 and explained in the following paragraphs.[11] First, however, familiarize yourself with the definitions of the terms used in Figure 5-8:

CALCULATING BETA COEFFICIENTS   **FIGURE 5-8**

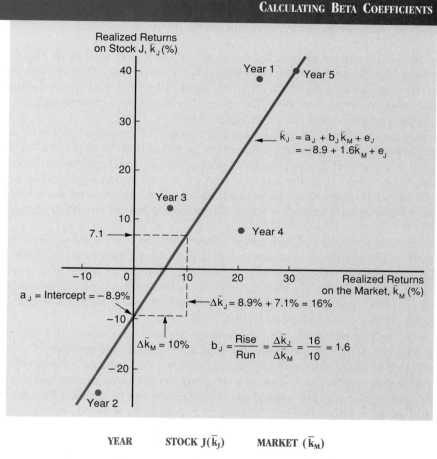

YEAR	STOCK J ($\bar{k}_J$)	MARKET ($\bar{k}_M$)
1	38.6%	23.8%
2	(24.7)	(7.2)
3	12.3	6.6
4	8.2	20.5
5	40.1	30.6
Average $\bar{k}$ =	14.9%	14.9%
$\sigma_{\bar{k}}$ =	26.5%	15.1%

---

[11]It should be noted that beta analysis in practice is somewhat more difficult than our discussion makes it sound. We will see this in Chapter 8.

$\overline{k}_J$ = historical (realized) rate of return on Stock J. (Recall that $\hat{k}_J$ and k_J are defined as Stock J's expected and required returns, respectively.)

$\overline{k}_M$ = historical (realized) rate of return on the market.

a_J = vertical axis intercept term for Stock J.

b_J = slope, or beta coefficient, for Stock J.

e_J = random error, reflecting the difference between the actual return on Stock J in a given year and the return as predicted by the regression line.

The historical returns on Stock J are given in the lower section of Figure 5-8, along with historical returns on the market, $\overline{k}_M$. Notice that when returns on the market are high, returns on Stock J likewise tend to be high, and when the market is down, Stock J's returns are low. This general relationship is expressed more precisely in the regression line shown in Figure 5-8.

Recall what the term *regression equation* means: The equation Y = a + bX + e is the standard form of a simple linear regression. It states that the dependent variable, Y, is equal to a constant, a, plus b times X, where X is the "independent" variable, plus a random error term. Thus, the rate of return on Stock J during a given time period depends on what happens to the general stock market, which is measured by $\overline{k}_M$, plus the effects of random events which affect Stock J but do not affect most other stocks.

In general, the regression equation is obtained by ordinary least squares regression analysis, using either a calculator with statistical functions or a computer with a regression software package such as a spreadsheet's regression function. The plot of the regression equation is called the *regression line*. In his 1964 article which set forth the CAPM, Sharpe called the regression line the stock's *characteristic line*. Thus, a stock's beta is the slope of its characteristic line.

To illustrate the regression process, assume that we have drawn the regression line in Figure 5-8 "by hand" without the benefit of a statistical package. Once the regression, or characteristic, line has been drawn, we can estimate its intercept and slope, the a and b values in Y = a + bX. The intercept, a, is simply the point where the line cuts the vertical axis. The slope coefficient, b, can be estimated by the "rise over run" method. This involves calculating the amount by which $\overline{k}_J$ increases for a given increase in $\overline{k}_M$. For example, we observe (in Figure 5-8) that $\overline{k}_J$ increases from −8.9 to +7.1 percent (the rise) as $\overline{k}_M$ increases from 0.0 to 10.0 percent (the run). Thus, b, the beta coefficient, can be measured as follows:

$$b_J = \frac{\text{Rise}}{\text{Run}} = \frac{\Delta Y}{\Delta X} = \frac{7.1\% - (-8.9\%)}{10.0\% - 0.0\%} = \frac{16.0\%}{10.0\%} = 1.6.$$

Note that rise over run is a ratio, and it would be the same if measured using any two arbitrarily selected points on the line.

Although the "by eye" approach is useful for visualizing what the beta concept is all about, an in-depth understanding and efficient application of the concept require the use of statistics. Basic statistics courses demonstrate that the following equation can be used to calculate the slope of any simple linear regression line, and this formula is also programmed into the statistical functions on calculators and computers:

$$b_J = \frac{\text{Covariance between Stock J and the market}}{\text{Variance of market returns}} = \frac{\text{Cov}(k_J, k_M)}{\sigma_M^2}$$

$$= \frac{r_{JM}\sigma_J\sigma_M}{\sigma_M^2} = r_{JM}\left(\frac{\sigma_J}{\sigma_M}\right).$$

Thus a stock's beta, hence its market risk, depends on (1) its correlation with the stock market as a whole, r_{JM}; (2) its own variability, σ_J; and (3) the variability of the market, σ_M. In the Figure 5-8 example, $r_{JM} = 0.91$, $\sigma_J = 26.5\%$, and $\sigma_M = 15.1\%$. Therefore, $b_J = 0.91(26.5\%/15.1\%) = 1.60$.

Now that we have plotted Stock J's historical rates of return and estimated its beta coefficient, we can note the following points:

1. The *predicted future* returns on Stock J are assumed to bear a linear relationship of the following form to those of the market:

$$\text{Predicted future rate of return} = \hat{k}_J = a_J + b_J\hat{k}_M + e_J$$
$$= -8.9\% + 1.6\hat{k}_M + e_J. \qquad \text{5-6}$$

Here we assume that the historical relationship between Stock J and the market as a whole, as given by its characteristic line, will continue on into the future.[12]

2. In addition to general market movements, each firm also faces events that are unique to it and thus are independent of the general economic climate. Such events cause the returns on Firm J's stock to move somewhat independently of those for the market as a whole, and these random events are accounted for by the random error term, e_J. Before the fact, the expected value of the error term is zero; after the fact, it is generally either positive or negative. This component of total risk is the stock's *diversifiable*, or *company-specific, risk*, and rational investors will eliminate its effects by holding diversified portfolios of stocks.

3. The regression coefficient, b (the beta coefficient), is a market sensitivity index; it measures the relative volatility of a given stock versus the average stock, or "the market." The tendency of an individual stock to move with the market constitutes a risk, because the market does fluctuate, and these fluctuations cannot be diversified away. This part of total risk is the stock's *market*,

---

[12]The characteristic line equation is also called the *Market Model*. The Market Model asserts that the relationship between the returns on individual stocks and the returns on the market is linear and can be expressed by Equation 5-6. The Capital Asset Pricing Model (CAPM), on the other hand, states that, in equilibrium, returns on individual stocks can be expressed by the Security Market Line, Equation 4-8. The two models require different assumptions, so the acceptance of one model does not necessarily imply acceptance of the other. We will use the Market Model, or characteristic line, only to estimate betas for use in the Security Market Line of the CAPM. For more information on the Market Model and the differences between the two models, see Robert C. Radcliffe, *Investment: Concepts, Analysis, Strategy* (Glenview, Ill.: Scott, Foresman, 1996).

or *nondiversifiable, risk*. Even well-diversified portfolios contain some market risk.

4. The relationship between a stock's total risk, market risk, and diversifiable risk can be expressed as follows:

$$\text{Total risk} = \text{Variance} = \text{Market risk} + \text{Diversifiable risk}$$
$$\sigma_J^2 \quad = \quad b_J^2 \sigma_M^2 \quad + \quad \sigma_{e_J}^2.$$

Here σ_J^2 is the variance (or total risk) of Stock J, σ_M^2 is the variance of the market, b_J is Stock J's beta coefficient, and $\sigma_{e_J}^2$ is the variance of Stock J's regression error term.

5. If in Figure 5-8 all the points plotted exactly on the regression line, then the variance of the error term, $\sigma_{e_J}^2$, would be zero, and all of the stock's total risk would be market risk. On the other hand, if the points were widely scattered about the regression line, much of the stock's total risk would be diversifiable. The shares of a large, well-diversified mutual fund would plot very close to the regression line, as would those of a broadly diversified firm such as GE.

6. If the stock market never fluctuated, then stocks would have no market risk. Of course, the market does fluctuate, so market risk is present — even if you hold an extremely well-diversified portfolio, you will still suffer losses if the market falls. In recent years, the standard deviation of annual market returns, σ_M, has been about 18 percent. However, on a single day, October 19, 1987, the market lost about 25 percent of its value.

7. Beta is a measure of relative market risk, but the *actual* market risk of Stock J is $b_J^2 \sigma_M^2$. Market risk can also be expressed in standard deviation form, $b_J \sigma_M$, so Stock J's market risk is $b_J \sigma_M = 1.6(15.1\%) = 24.2\%$, while its total risk is $\sigma_J = 26.5\%$. The higher a stock's beta, the higher its market risk. If beta were zero, the stock would have no market risk, while if beta were 1.0, the stock would be exactly as risky as the market—assuming the stock is held in a diversified portfolio—and the stock's market risk would be σ_M.

8. The diversifiable risk can and should be eliminated by diversification, so the *relevant* risk is market risk, not total risk. If Stock J had b = 0.5, then the stock's relevant risk would be $b_J \sigma_M = 0.5(15.1\%) = 7.55\%$. A portfolio of such low-beta stocks would have a standard deviation of expected returns of $\sigma_p = 7.55\%$, or one-half the standard deviation of expected returns on a portfolio of average (b = 1.0) stocks. Had Stock J been a high-beta stock (b = 2.0), then its relevant risk would have been $b_J \sigma_M = 2.0(15.1\%) = 30.2\%$. A portfolio of b = 2.0 stocks would have $\sigma_p = 30.2\%$, so such a portfolio would be twice as risky as a portfolio of average stocks.

9. A stock's risk premium depends only on its market risk, not its total risk: $RP_J = (k_M - k_{RF})b_J$. Mr. S might own only Stock J, and hence be concerned with its total risk and seek a return based on that risk. However, if other investors hold well-diversified portfolios, they would face less risk from Stock J. Therefore, if Stock J offered a return high enough to satisfy Mr. S, it would represent a bargain for other investors, who would then buy it, pushing its price up and its yield down in the process. Since most financial assets are

held by diversified investors, and since any given security can have only one price and hence only one rate of return, market action drives each stock's risk premium to the level specified by its relevant, or market, risk.

Explain the meaning and significance of a stock's beta coefficient. Illustrate your explanation by drawing, on one graph, the characteristic lines for stocks with low, average, and high risk. (Hint: Let your three characteristic lines intersect at $\bar{k}_i = \bar{k}_M$= 9%, the assumed risk-free rate.)

What is the relationship among total risk, market risk, and diversifiable risk?

SELF-TEST QUESTIONS

EMPIRICAL TESTS OF THE CAPM

As noted earlier, the CAPM was developed on the basis of a set of unrealistic assumptions. If those assumptions were all true, then the CAPM would have to be true. However, since the assumptions are not completely correct, the basic SML equation, $k_i = k_{RF} + (k_M - k_{RF})b_i$, might or might not represent an accurate description of how investors behave and of how rates of return are established in the marketplace. For example, if many investors are not fully diversified, hence have not eliminated all diversifiable risk from their portfolios, then (1) beta would not be an adequate measure of risk and (2) the SML would not explain how required returns are set. Also, if the interest rate that investors must pay to borrow money is greater than the risk-free rate (that is, if the borrowing rate is greater than the lending rate), then the CML would not continue in a straight line beyond Point M as it does in Figure 5-6, and this too would invalidate the SML. And, of course, taxes and brokerage costs do exist, and their presence could also distort the CAPM relationships.

For all these reasons, it is entirely possible that the CAPM is not completely valid, in which case the SML will not produce accurate estimates of k_i. Therefore, the CAPM must be tested empirically and validated before it can be used with real confidence. The literature dealing with empirical tests of the CAPM is quite extensive, so we can give here only a synopsis of some of the key work.

TESTS OF THE STABILITY OF BETA COEFFICIENTS

According to the CAPM, the beta used to estimate a stock's market risk should reflect investors' estimates of the stock's *future* volatility in relation to that of the market. Obviously, we do not know now how a stock will be related to the market in the future, nor do we know how the average investor views this expected future relative volatility. All we have are data on past volatility, which we can use to plot the characteristic line and to calculate *historical betas*. If historical betas are stable over time, then there would seem to be reason for investors to use past betas as estimators of future volatility. For example, if Stock J's beta had been stable in the past, then its historical b_J would probably be a good proxy for its *ex ante*, or expected, beta. By "stable" we mean that if b_J were calculated with data from the period of, say, 1992 to 1996, then this same beta (approximately) should be found from 1997 to 2001.

Robert A. Levy, Marshall E. Blume, and others have studied the question of beta stability in depth.[13] Levy calculated betas for individual securities, as well as for portfolios of securities, over a range of time intervals. He concluded (1) that the betas of individual stocks are unstable, hence that past betas for *individual securities* are *not* good estimators of their future risk, but (2) that betas of portfolios of ten or more randomly selected stocks are reasonably stable, hence that past *portfolio* betas are good estimators of future portfolio volatility. In effect, the errors in individual securities' betas tend to offset one another in a portfolio. The work of Blume and others supports this position.

The conclusion that follows from the beta stability studies is that the CAPM is a better concept for structuring investment portfolios than it is for estimating the cost of capital for individual securities. We will return to this issue in Chapter 8, when we discuss cost of capital estimation procedures.

Tests of the CAPM Based on the Slope of the SML

As we noted in Chapter 4, the CAPM states that a linear relationship exists between a security's required rate of return and its beta. Further, when the SML is graphed, the vertical axis intercept should be k_{RF}, and the required rate of return for a stock (or portfolio) with $b = 1.0$ should be k_M, the required rate of return on the market. Various researchers have attempted to test the validity of the CAPM by calculating betas and realized rates of return, plotting these values in graphs such as that in Figure 5-9, and then observing whether or not (1) the intercept is equal to k_{RF}, (2) the regression line is linear, and (3) the line passes through the point $b = 1.0$, k_M. Monthly historical rates of return are generally used for stocks, and both 30-day Treasury bill rates and long-term Treasury bond rates have been used to estimate the value of k_{RF}. Also, most of the studies actually analyze portfolios rather than individual securities because security betas are so unstable.

Before discussing the results of the tests, it is critical to recognize that although the CAPM is an ex ante, or forward-looking model, the data used to test it are entirely historical. There is no reason to believe that *realized* rates of return over past holding periods are necessarily equal to the rates of return which people *expect* in the future. Also, historical betas may or may not reflect expected future risk. This lack of ex ante data makes it extremely difficult to test the CAPM, but for what it is worth, here is a summary of the key results:

1. The evidence generally shows a significant positive relationship between realized returns and systematic risk. However, the slope of the relationship is usually less than that predicted by the CAPM.

2. The relationship between risk and return appears to be linear. Empirical studies give no evidence of significant curvature in the risk/return relationship.

3. Tests that attempt to assess the relative importance of market and company-specific risk do not yield conclusive results. The CAPM implies that company-

---

[13]See Robert A. Levy, "On the Short-Term Stationarity of Beta Coefficients," *Financial Analysts Journal*, November–December 1971, 55–62, and Marshall E. Blume, "Betas and Their Regression Tendencies," *Journal of Finance*, June 1975, 785–796.

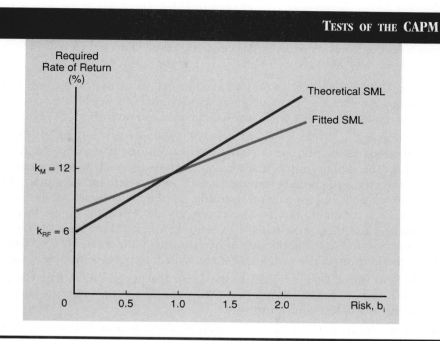

TESTS OF THE CAPM   **FIGURE 5-9**

specific risk should not be relevant, yet both kinds of risk appear to be positively related to security returns; that is, higher returns seem to be required to compensate for diversifiable as well as market risk. However, it may be that the observed relationships reflect statistical problems rather than the true nature of capital markets.

4. Richard Roll has questioned whether it is even conceptually possible to test the CAPM.[14] Roll showed that the linear relationship which prior researchers had observed in graphs like that in Figure 5-9 resulted from the mathematical properties of the models being tested, hence that a finding of linearity proved nothing whatsoever about the validity of the CAPM. Roll's work did not disprove the CAPM theory, but he did show that it is virtually impossible to prove that investors behave in accordance with its predictions.

5. If the CAPM were completely valid, it should apply to all financial assets, including bonds. In fact, when bonds are introduced into the analysis, they *do not* plot on the SML. This is worrisome, to say the least.

CURRENT STATUS OF THE CAPM

The CAPM is extremely appealing at an intellectual level: It is logical and rational, and once someone works through and understands the theory, his or her reaction is

---

[14]See Richard Roll, "A Critique of the Asset Pricing Theory's Tests," *Journal of Financial Economics*, March 1977, 129–176.

usually to accept it without question. However, doubts begin to arise when one thinks about the assumptions upon which the model is based, and these doubts are as much reinforced as reduced by the empirical tests. Our own views as to the current status of the CAPM are as follows:

1. The CAPM framework, with its focus on market as opposed to total risk, is clearly a useful way to think about the riskiness of assets. Thus, as a conceptual model, the CAPM is of truly fundamental importance.

2. Although the CAPM appears to provide neat, precise answers to important questions about risk and required rates of return, the answers are really not clear. The simple truth is that we do not know precisely how to measure any of the inputs required to implement the CAPM. These inputs should all be ex ante, yet only ex post data are available. Further, as we shall see in Chapter 8, historical data on $\overline{k}_M$, k_{RF}, and betas vary greatly depending on the time period studied and the methods used to estimate them. Thus, although the CAPM appears precise, its inputs cannot be estimated with precision, so estimates of k_i found through use of the CAPM are subject to potentially large errors.

3. Because the CAPM is logical in the sense that it represents the way people who want to maximize returns while minimizing risk ought to behave, the model is a useful conceptual tool.

4. As we discussed in Chapter 4, a recent study by Eugene F. Fama and Kenneth R. French of the University of Chicago seriously challenges the CAPM. Fama and French examined the relationships between betas and returns on thousands of stocks over the past 50 years. According to the CAPM, high-beta stocks should provide higher returns than low-beta stocks. However, the Fama–French study revealed no relationship between historical betas and historical returns—low-beta stocks provided about the same returns as high-beta stocks.

   It will take more research to decide whether the Fama–French study truly invalidates the CAPM. At this point, however, our own feeling is that the CAPM is purely an expectational model, and as such, its logic is sound. The problem is that we only have historical data, not expectational data, available for testing. So, the fact that no relationship is found between historical betas and historical returns does not convince us that the CAPM concept is wrong. However, it is difficult to implement the CAPM numerically because expectational data must be estimated.

5. It is appropriate to think about many financial problems in a CAPM framework. However, it is important to recognize the limitations of the CAPM when using it in practice. We will elaborate on this point in Chapters 8 and 11.

SELF-TEST QUESTIONS
What are the two major types of tests that have been performed to test the validity of the CAPM? (Hint: Beta stability and slope of the SML.)
Are there any reasons to question the validity of the CAPM? Explain.

ARBITRAGE PRICING THEORY

The CAPM is a single-factor model. That is, it specifies risk as a function of only one factor, the security's beta coefficient. Perhaps the risk/return relationship is more complex, with a stock's required return a function of more than one factor. For example, what if investors, because personal taxes on capital gains are taxed at a lower rate, value capital gains more highly than dividends? Then, if two stocks had the same market risk, the stock paying the higher dividend would have the higher required rate of return. In that case, required returns would be a function of two factors, market risk and dividend yield.

Further, what if many factors were required to specify the equilibrium risk/return relationship rather than just one or two? Stephen Ross has proposed an approach called the *Arbitrage Pricing Theory (APT)*.[15] The APT can include any number of risk factors, so the required return could be a function of two, three, four, or even more factors. We should note at the outset that the APT is based on complex mathematical and statistical theory which goes far beyond the scope of this text. Although the APT model is widely discussed in the current academic literature, practical usage to date has been limited. However, usage may increase, so students of finance should at least have an intuitive idea of what the APT is all about.

The SML states that each stock's required return is equal to the risk-free rate plus the product of the market risk premium times the stock's beta coefficient:

$$k_i = k_{RF} + (k_M - k_{RF})b_i. \qquad \text{5-7}$$

The realized return, $\bar{k}_i$, will generally be different, and it will actually turn out to be

$$\bar{k}_i = \hat{k}_i + (\bar{k}_M - \hat{k}_M)b_i + e_i. \qquad \text{5-8}$$

That is, the realized return, $\bar{k}_i$, will be equal to the expected return, $\hat{k}_i$, plus an increase or decrease, $(\bar{k}_M - \hat{k}_M)b_i$, which depends jointly on the stock's beta and the realized excess or shortfall in the market return, plus a random error term, e_i.

The market return, $\bar{k}_M$, is in turn determined by a number of factors, including domestic economic activity as measured by gross domestic product (GDP), the strength of the world economy, the level of inflation, changes in tax laws, and so forth. Further, different groups of stocks are affected in different ways by these

---

[15]See Stephen A. Ross, "The Arbitrage Theory of Capital Asset Pricing," *Journal of Economic Theory*, December 1976, 341–360.

fundamental factors. So, rather than specifying a stock's return as a function of one factor (return on the market), one could specify required and realized returns on individual stocks as a function of various fundamental economic factors. If this were done, we would transform Equation 5-8 into 5-9:

$$\bar{k}_i = \hat{k}_i + (\bar{F}_1 - \hat{F}_1)b_{i1} + \ldots + (\bar{F}_j - \hat{F}_j)b_{ij} + e_i. \qquad \text{5-9}$$

Here

$\bar{k}_i$ = realized rate of return on Stock i.

$\hat{k}_i$ = expected rate of return on Stock i.

$\bar{F}_j$ = realized value of economic Factor j.

$\hat{F}_j$ = expected value of Factor j.

b_{ij} = sensitivity of Stock i to economic Factor j.

e_i = effect of unique events on the realized return of Stock i.

Equation 5-9 shows that the realized return on any stock is equal to (1) the stock's expected return, (2) increases or decreases which depend on unexpected changes in fundamental economic factors times the sensitivity of the stock to these changes, and (3) a random term which reflects changes unique to the firm or industry.

Certain stocks or groups of stocks are most sensitive to Factor 1, others to Factor 2, and so forth, and every portfolio's returns depend on what happened to the different fundamental factors. Theoretically, one could construct a portfolio such that (1) the portfolio was riskless and (2) the net investment in it was zero (some stocks would be sold short, with the proceeds from the short sales being used to buy the stocks held long). Such a zero investment portfolio must have a zero expected return, or else arbitrage operations would occur, which, in turn, would cause the prices of the underlying assets to change until the portfolio's expected return was zero. Using some complex mathematics and a set of assumptions including the possibility of short sales, the APT equivalent of the CAPM's Security Market Line can be developed from Equation 5-9:[16]

$$k_i = k_{RF} + (\lambda_1 - k_{RF})b_{i1} + \cdots + (\lambda_j - k_{RF})b_{ij}. \qquad \text{5-10}$$

Here λ_j is the required rate of return on a portfolio that is sensitive only to the *j*th economic factor ($b_j = 1.0$) and zero sensitivity to all other factors. Thus, for exam-

---

[16]See Thomas E. Copeland and J. Fred Weston, *Financial Theory and Corporate Policy* (Reading, Mass.: Addison-Wesley, 1988).

ple, $(\lambda_2 - k_{RF})$ is the risk premium on a portfolio with $b_2 = 1.0$ and all other $b_j = 0.0$. Note that Equation 5-10 is identical in form to the SML, but it permits a stock's required return to be a function of multiple factors.

To illustrate the APT concept, assume that all stocks' returns depend on only three risk factors: inflation, industrial production, and the aggregate degree of risk aversion (the cost of bearing risk, which we assume is reflected in the spread between the yields on Treasury and low-grade bonds). Further, suppose (1) the risk-free rate is 8.0 percent; (2) the required rate of return is 13 percent on a portfolio with unit sensitivity ($b = 1.0$) to inflation and zero sensitivities ($b = 0.0$) to industrial production and degree of risk aversion; (3) the required return is 10 percent on a portfolio with unit sensitivity to industrial production and zero sensitivities to inflation and degree of risk aversion; and (4) the required return is 6 percent on a portfolio (the risk-bearing portfolio) with unit sensitivity to the degree of risk aversion and zero sensitivities to inflation and industrial production. Finally, assume that Stock i has factor sensitivities (betas) of 0.9 to the inflation portfolio, 1.2 to the industrial production portfolio, and -0.7 to the risk-bearing portfolio. Stock i's required rate of return, according to the APT, would be 16.3 percent:

$$k_i = 8\% + (13\% - 8\%)0.9 + (10\% - 8\%)1.2 + (6\% - 8\%)(-0.7)$$
$$= 16.3\%.$$

Note that if the required rate of return on the market was 15.0 percent and Stock i had a CAPM beta of 1.1, then its required rate of return, according to the SML, would be 15.7 percent:

$$k_i = 8\% + (15\% - 8\%)1.1 = 15.7\%.$$

The primary theoretical advantage of the APT is that it permits several economic factors to influence individual stock returns, whereas the CAPM assumes that the impact of all factors, except those unique to the firm, can be captured in a single measure, the volatility of the stock with respect to the market portfolio. Also, the APT requires fewer assumptions than the CAPM and hence is a more general theory. Finally, the APT does not assume that all investors hold the market portfolio, a CAPM requirement that clearly is not met in practice. However, the APT faces several major hurdles in implementation, the most severe being that the APT does not identify the relevant factors. Thus, APT does not tell us what factors influence returns, nor does it even indicate how many factors should appear in the model. There is some empirical evidence that only three or four factors are relevant: perhaps inflation, industrial production, the spread between low- and high-grade bonds, and the term structure of interest rates, but no one knows for sure.

The APT's proponents note that it is not actually necessary to identify the relevant factors. Researchers use a complex statistical procedure called *factor analysis* to develop the APT parameters. Basically, they start with hundreds, or even thousands, of stocks and then create several different portfolios, where the returns on each portfolio are not highly correlated with returns on the other portfolios. Thus, each portfolio is apparently more heavily affected by one of the unknown factors than are the other portfolios. Then, the required rate of return on each portfolio becomes the λ for that unknown economic factor, and the sensitivities of each individual stock's returns to the returns on that portfolio are the factor sensitivities (betas). Unfortunately, the results of factor analysis are not easily interpreted, hence it does not provide significant insights into the underlying economic determinants of risk.

The APT is in an early stage of development, and there are still many unanswered questions. Nevertheless, the basic premise of the APT—that returns can be a function of several factors rather than just one—has considerable intuitive appeal. If the factors can be identified, and if the theory can be satisfactorily explained to practitioners, then the APT might replace the CAPM as the primary model describing the relationship between risk and return. Currently though, CAPM rules.

SELF-TEST What is the primary difference between the APT and the CAPM?
QUESTIONS What are some disadvantages of the APT?

SUMMARY

Chapter 5 completes our discussion of risk and return. The primary goal of this chapter was to extend your knowledge of risk and return concepts. The key concepts covered are listed below:

- The *feasible set* of portfolios represents all portfolios that can be constructed from a given set of assets.

- An *efficient portfolio* is one that offers the most return for a given amount of risk, or the least risk for a given amount of return.

- The *optimal portfolio* for an investor is defined by the tangency point between the *efficient set* of portfolios and the investor's highest *indifference curve*.

- The *Capital Asset Pricing Model (CAPM)* describes the relationship between market risk and required rates of return.

- The CAPM is based on an extensive set of *assumptions.*

- The *Capital Market Line (CML)* describes the risk/return relationship for efficient portfolios; that is, for portfolios that consist of a mix of the market portfolio and a riskless asset.

- The *Security Market Line (SML)* (an integral part of the CAPM) describes the risk/return relationship for individual assets. The required rate of return for any Stock i is equal to the *risk-free rate* plus the *market risk premium* times the stock's *beta coefficient:* $k_i = k_{RF} + (k_M - k_{RF})b_i$.

■ Stock i's *beta coefficient, b_i,* is a measure of the stock's *market risk.* Beta measures the *volatility* of returns on a security *relative to returns on the market,* which is the portfolio of all risky assets.

■ The beta coefficient is measured by the slope of the stock's *characteristic line,* which is found by regressing historical returns on the stock versus the historical returns on the market.

■ Although the CAPM provides a convenient framework for thinking about risk and return issues, it *cannot be proven empirically,* and its parameters are very difficult to estimate. Thus, the CAPM should be used with caution in practice.

■ Deficiencies in the CAPM have motivated theorists to seek other risk/return equilibrium models; the *Arbitrage Pricing Theory (APT)* is one important new model.

In the next two chapters, we will see how a security's required rate of return affects its value. Then, in most of the remainder of the book, we will examine the ways in which a firm's management can influence a stock's riskiness and hence its price.

QUESTIONS

5-1   Define the following terms, using graphs or equations to illustrate your answers wherever feasible:
a. Portfolio
b. Feasible set
c. Efficient portfolio
d. Efficient frontier
e. Indifference curve
f. Optimal portfolio
g. Capital Asset Pricing Model (CAPM)
h. Capital Market Line (CML)
i. Characteristic line
j. Beta coefficient, b; average stock's beta, $b_A = b_M$
k. Arbitrage Pricing Theory (APT)

5-2   Security A has an expected rate of return of 6 percent, a standard deviation of expected returns of 30 percent, a correlation coefficient with the market of −0.25, and a beta coefficient of −0.5. Security B has an expected return of 11 percent, a standard deviation of returns of 10 percent, a correlation with the market of 0.75, and a beta coefficient of 0.5. Which security is more risky? Why?

SELF-TEST PROBLEM

(SOLUTION APPEARS IN APPENDIX C)

ST-1   **RISK AND RETURN** You are planning to invest $200,000. Two securities, A and B, are available, and you can invest in either of them or in a portfolio with some of each. You estimate that the following probability distributions of returns are applicable for A and B:

SECURITY A		SECURITY B	
P_A	k_A	P_B	k_B
0.1	−10%	0.1	−30%
0.2	5	0.2	0
0.4	15	0.4	20
0.2	25	0.2	40
0.1	40	0.1	70
	$\hat{k}_A = ?$		$\hat{k}_B = 20.0\%$
	$\sigma_A = ?$		$\sigma_B = 25.7\%$

a. The expected return for Security B is $\hat{k}_B = 20\%$, and $\sigma_B = 25.7\%$. Find $\hat{k}_A$ and σ_A.

b. Use the equation in Footnote 3 to find the value of w_A that produces the minimum risk portfolio. Assume $r_{AB} = -0.5$ for Parts b and c.

c. Construct a table giving $\hat{k}_p$ and σ_p for portfolios with $w_A = 1.00, 0.75, 0.50, 0.25, 0.0$, and the minimum risk value of w_A. (Hint: For $w_A = 0.75$, $\hat{k}_p = 16.25\%$ and $\sigma_p = 8.5\%$; for $w_A = 0.5$, $\hat{k}_p = 17.5\%$ and $\sigma_p = 11.1\%$; for $w_A = 0.25$, $\hat{k}_p = 18.75\%$ and $\sigma_p = 17.9\%$.)

d. Graph the feasible set of portfolios and identify the efficient frontier of the feasible set.

e. Suppose your risk/return trade-off function, or indifference curve, is tangent to the efficient set at the point where $\hat{k}_p = 18\%$. Use this information, plus the graph constructed in Part d, to locate (approximately) your optimal portfolio. Draw in a reasonable indifference curve, indicate the percentage of your funds invested in each security, and determine the optimal portfolio's σ_p and $\hat{k}_p$. (Hint: Estimate σ_p and $\hat{k}_p$ graphically, and then use the equation for $\hat{k}_p$ to determine w_A.)

f. Now suppose a riskless asset with a return $k_{RF} = 10\%$ becomes available. How would this change the investment opportunity set? Explain why the efficient frontier becomes linear.

g. Given the indifference curve in Part e, would you change your portfolio? If so, how? (Hint: Assume the indifference curves are parallel.)

h. What are the beta coefficients of Stocks A and B? [Hints: (1) Recognize that $k_i = k_{RF} + b_i(k_M - k_{RF})$ and solve for b_i and (2) assume that your preferences match those of most other investors.]

PROBLEMS

5-1 **CHARACTERISTIC LINE AND SECURITY MARKET LINE** You are given the following set of data:

HISTORICAL RATES OF RETURN

YEAR	NYSE	STOCK X
1	(26.5%)	(14.0%)
2	37.2	23.0
3	23.8	17.5
4	(7.2)	2.0
5	6.6	8.1
6	20.5	19.4
7	30.6	18.2

a. Use a calculator with a linear regression function (or a spreadsheet) to determine Stock X's beta coefficient, or plot these data points on a scatter diagram, draw in the regression line, and then estimate the value of the beta coefficient.

b. Determine the arithmetic average rates of return for Stock X and the NYSE over the period given. Calculate the standard deviations of returns for both Stock X and the NYSE.

c. Assuming (1) that the situation during Years 1 to 7 is expected to hold true in the future (that is, $\hat{k}_X = \bar{k}_X$; $\hat{k}_M = \bar{k}_M$; and both σ_X and b_X in the future will equal their past values), and (2) that Stock X is in equilibrium (that is, it plots on the Security Market Line), what is the risk-free rate?

d. Plot the Security Market Line.

e. Suppose you hold a large, well-diversified portfolio and are considering adding to the portfolio either Stock X or another stock, Stock Y, that has the same beta as Stock X but a higher standard deviation of returns. Stocks X and Y have the same expected returns; that is, $\hat{k}_X = \hat{k}_Y = 10.6\%$. Which stock should you choose?

5-2 **CHARACTERISTIC LINE** You are given the following set of data:

HISTORICAL RATES OF RETURN

YEAR	NYSE	STOCK Y
1	4.0%	3.0%
2	14.3	18.2
3	19.0	9.1
4	(14.7)	(6.0)
5	(26.5)	(15.3)
6	37.2	33.1
7	23.8	6.1
8	(7.2)	3.2
9	6.6	14.8
10	20.5	24.1
11	30.6	18.0
	Mean = 9.8%	9.8%
	σ = 19.6%	13.8%

a. Construct a scatter diagram showing the relationship between returns on Stock Y and the market, and then draw a freehand approximation of the regression line. What is the approximate value of the beta coefficient? If you have a calculator with a linear regression function or a spreadsheet, check the approximate value of beta obtained from the graph.

b. Give a verbal interpretation of what the regression line and the beta coefficient show about Stock Y's volatility and relative riskiness as compared with those of other stocks.

c. Suppose the scatter of points had been more spread out, but the regression line was exactly where your present graph shows it. How would this affect (1) the firm's risk if the stock is held in a one-asset portfolio and (2) the actual risk premium on the stock if the CAPM holds exactly?

d. Suppose the regression line had been downward-sloping and the beta coefficient had been negative. What would this imply about (1) Stock Y's relative riskiness, (2) its correlation with the market, and (3) its probable risk premium?

e. Construct an illustrative probability distribution graph of returns on portfolios consisting of (1) only Stock Y, (2) 1 percent each of 100 stocks with beta coefficients similar to that of Stock Y, and (3) all stocks (that is, the distribution of returns on the market). Use as the expected rate of return the arithmetic mean as given previously for both Stock Y and the market and assume that the distributions are normal. Are the expected returns "reasonable"; that is, is it reasonable that $\hat{k}_Y = \hat{k}_M = 9.8\%$?

5-3 **SML AND CML COMPARISON** The beta coefficient of an asset can be expressed as a function of the asset's correlation with the market as follows:

$$b_i = \frac{r_{iM}\sigma_i}{\sigma_M}.$$

a. Substitute this expression for beta into the Security Market Line (SML), Equation 4-8. This results in an alternative form of the SML.

b. Compare your answer to Part a with the Capital Market Line (CML), Equation 5-5. What similarities are observed? What conclusions can be drawn?

SPREADSHEET APPLICATIONS

SPREADSHEET EXERCISE: LINEAR REGRESSION

This exercise uses a spreadsheet model to calculate the beta coefficient of a stock given historical returns data. The starting model contains data for one stock (Circuit) and the market (Index Fund). Students add data and calculate betas for two additional stocks, Luster and Apex.

1. Retrieve the model (Filename SE-05) from the models diskette. Note that this exercise uses data from the Chapter 4 Spreadsheet Exercise but the data are assumed to be historical data, so each year has the same probability of occurrence.

2. One linear regression has been conducted, and the regression output is contained in Rows 13 through 20. On this regression, the constant, or intercept term, is in cell D14, the standard error of the regression is in D15, R^2 is in D16, and so on. Of particular interest is the X coefficient contained in Cell C20 because this value is the beta coefficient for the stock being analyzed, in this case Circuit.

3. Enter the returns data for Luster and Apex. In the Range E5.E9, enter 16.0, 8.0, 2.0, −7.0, and −13.0, and in F5.F9, enter 6.0, −8.0, 6.0, 30.0, and 12.0. (Note that these percentages must be entered as decimals.)

4. Now use your spreadsheet's regression capability to obtain the betas for Luster and Apex. The resulting betas are −0.68 and 0.59, respectively. You can copy Luster's beta coefficient into Cell E11 and Apex's into F11 to fill out the table. Format the cells for two decimal places for consistency.

5. To create a graph of Circuit's characteristic line, it is necessary to first create the points on the line since the historical returns in Cells D5.D9 do not fall on the regression line. The line points are created in Cells H5.H9 by entering the formula +D14+D$11*G5 in Cell H5. This formula creates the regression line point given by Intercept + Slope(X value) when the X value is −10.0 percent. Now copy this formula into Cells H6.H9. The resulting values, when plotted, will produce the regression line.

6. Now use your spreadsheet's graph (chart) capability to graph Circuit's characteristic line. Here, use the values in H5.H9 for the regression line and the values in D5.D9 as the realized return points.

7. If you want to practice graphing (charting), create and graph the characteristic lines for Luster, Apex, and the Market.

MINI CASE

To begin, briefly review the Chapter 4 Mini Case. Then, extend your knowledge of risk and return by answering the following questions:

a. What is the Capital Asset Pricing Model (CAPM)? What are the assumptions that underlie the model?

b. Construct a reasonable, but hypothetical, graph which shows risk, as measured by portfolio standard deviation, on the X axis and expected rate of return on the Y axis. Now add an illustrative feasible (or attainable) set of portfolios, and show what portion of the feasible set is efficient. What makes a particular portfolio efficient? Don't worry about specific values when constructing the graph — merely illustrate how things look with "reasonable" data.

c. Now add a set of indifference curves to the graph created for Part b. What do these curves represent? What is the optimal portfolio for this investor? Finally, add a second set of indifference curves which leads to the selection of a different optimal portfolio. Why do the two investors choose different portfolios?

d. Now add the risk-free asset. What impact does this have on the efficient frontier?

e. Write out the equation for the Capital Market Line (CML) and draw it on the graph. Interpret the CML. Now add a set of indifference curves, and illustrate how an investor's optimal portfolio is some combination of the risky portfolio and the risk-free asset. What is the composition of the risky portfolio?

f. What is a characteristic line? How is this line used to estimate a stock's beta coefficient? Write out and explain the formula that relates total risk, market risk, and diversifiable risk.

g. What are two potential tests that can be conducted to verify the CAPM? What are the results of such tests? What is Roll's critique of CAPM tests?

h. Briefly explain the difference between the CAPM and the Arbitrage Pricing Theory (APT).

SELECTED ADDITIONAL REFERENCES AND CASES

Probably the best place to find more information on CAPM and APT concepts is one of the investments textbooks. These are some good recent ones:

Francis, Jack C., *Investments: Analysis and Management* (New York: McGraw-Hill, 1991).

Radcliffe, Robert C., *Investment: Concepts, Analysis, and Strategy* (New York: HarperCollins, 1994).

Reilly, Frank K., and Keith C. Brown, *Investment Analysis and Portfolio Management* (Fort Worth, Tex.: Dryden Press, 1997).

Sharpe, William F., *Investments* (Englewood Cliffs, N.J.: Prentice-Hall, 1995).

For a thorough discussion of beta stability, see

Kolb, Robert W., and Ricardo J. Rodriguez, "The Regression Tendencies of Betas: A Reappraisal," *The Financial Review,* May 1989, 319–334.

_____, "Is the Distribution of Betas Stationary?" *Journal of Financial Research,* Winter 1990, 279–283.

Those who want to start at the beginning in studying portfolio theory and the CAPM should see

Lintner, John, "Security Prices, Risk, and Maximal Gains from Diversification," *Journal of Finance,* December 1965, 587–616.

Markowitz, Harry M., "Portfolio Selection," *Journal of Finance,* March 1952, 77–91.

Mossin, Jan, "Security Pricing and Investment Criteria in Competitive Markets," *American Economic Review,* December 1969, 749–756.

Sharpe, William F., "Capital Asset Prices: A Theory of Market Equilibrium under Conditions of Risk," *Journal of Finance,* September 1964, 425–442.

————, "Capital Asset Prices with and without Negative Holdings," *Journal of Finance,* June 1991, 489–509.

Literally thousands of articles providing theoretical extensions and tests of the CAPM theory have appeared in finance journals. Some of the more important earlier papers are contained in a book compiled by Jensen:

Jensen, Michael C., ed., *Studies in the Theory of Capital Markets* (New York: Praeger, 1972).

For one challenge to the CAPM, see

Wallace, Anise, "Is Beta Dead?" *Institutional Investor,* July 1980, 23–30.

For a recent article supporting a positive link between market risk and return, see

Marston, Felicia, and Robert S. Hanes, "Risk and Return: A Revisit Using Expected Returns," *Financial Review,* February 1993, 117–137.

For additional discussion of Arbitrage Pricing Theory, see

Bower, Dorothy H., Richard S. Bower, and Dennis E. Logue, "A Primer on Arbitrage Pricing Theory," *Midland Corporate Finance Journal,* Fall 1984, 31–40.

Bubnys, Edward L., "Simulating and Forecasting Utility Stock Returns: Arbitrage Pricing Theory vs. Capital Asset Pricing Model," *The Financial Review,* February 1990, 1–23.

Goldenberg, David H., and Ashok J. Robin, "The Arbitrage Pricing Theory and Cost-of-Capital Estimation: The Case of Electric Utilities," *Journal of Financial Research,* Fall 1991, 181–196.

Robin, Ashok, and Ravi Shukla, "The Magnitude of Pricing Errors in the Arbitrage Pricing Theory," *Journal of Financial Research,* Spring 1991, 65–82.

Additional references concerning the use of the CAPM are given in Chapter 8.

The following case from the Cases in Financial Management: Dryden Request *series covers many of the concepts discussed in this chapter:*

Case 2, "Peachtree Securities, Inc. (A)."

CONTINUOUS PROBABILITY DISTRIBUTIONS

In Chapter 4, we illustrated risk/return concepts using discrete distributions, and we assumed that only three states of the economy could exist. In reality, however, the state of the economy can range from a deep recession to a fantastic boom, and there are an infinite number of possibilities in between. It is inconvenient to work with a large number of outcomes using discrete distributions, but it is relatively easy to deal with such situations with *continuous distributions* since they can be completely specified by only two or three summary statistics such as the mean (or expected value), standard deviation, and a measure of skewness. In the past, financial managers did not have the tools necessary to use continuous distributions in practical risk analyses. Now, however, firms have access to computers and powerful software packages, such as the *Interactive Financial Planning System (IFPS)* and spreadsheet add-ins, which can process continuous distributions. Thus, if financial risk analysis is computerized, as is increasingly the case, it is often preferable to use continuous distributions to express the distribution of outcomes.[1]

UNIFORM DISTRIBUTION One continuous distribution that is often used in financial models is the *uniform distribution,* in which each possible outcome has the same probability of occurrence as any other outcome; hence, there is no clustering of values. Figure 5A-1 shows two uniform distributions.

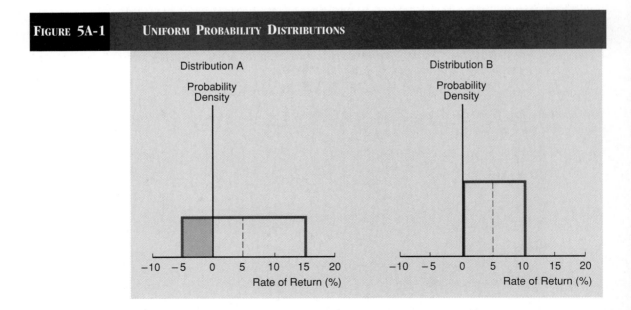

| FIGURE 5A-1 | UNIFORM PROBABILITY DISTRIBUTIONS |

NOTE: The expected rate of return for both distributions is $\hat{k} = 5\%$.

---

[1]Computerized risk analysis techniques are discussed in detail in Chapter 11.

Distribution A of Figure 5A-1 has a range of −5 to +15 percent. Therefore, the absolute size of the range is 20 units. Since the entire area under the density function must equal 1.00, the height of the distribution, h, must be 0.05: 20h = 1.0, so h = 1/20 = 0.05. We can use this information to find the probability of different outcomes. For example, suppose we want to find the probability that the rate of return will be less than zero. The probability is the area under the density function from −5 to 0 percent; that is, the shaded area:

$$\text{Area} = (\text{Right point} - \text{Left point})(\text{Height of distribution})$$
$$= [0 - (-5)][0.05] = 0.25 = 25\%.$$

Similarly, the probability of a rate of return between 5 and 15 is 50 percent:

$$\text{Probability} = \text{Area} = (15 - 5)(0.05) = 0.50 = 50\%.$$

The expected rate of return is the midpoint of the range, or 5 percent, for both distributions in Figure 5A-1. Since there is a smaller probability of the actual return falling very far below the expected return in Distribution B, Distribution B depicts a less risky situation in the stand-alone risk sense.

TRIANGULAR DISTRIBUTION   Another useful continuous distribution is the *triangular distribution*. This type of distribution, which is illustrated in Figure 5A-2, has a clustering of values around the most likely outcome, and the probability of occurrence declines in each direction from the most likely outcome. Distribution C has a range of −5 to +15 percent and a most likely return of +10 percent. Distribution D has a most likely return of 5 percent, but its range is only from 0 to +10 percent. Note that Distribution C is skewed to the left, while Distribution D is symmetric. The expected rate of return for Distribution C is 6.67 percent,

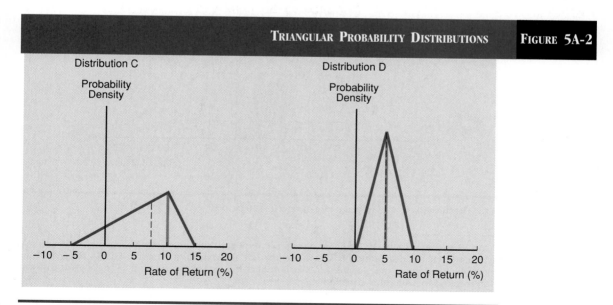

TRIANGULAR PROBABILITY DISTRIBUTIONS   FIGURE 5A-2

NOTE: The most likely rate of return is 10 percent for Distribution C and 5 percent for Distribution D; the expected rates of return are $\hat{k}_C = 6.67\%$ and $\hat{k}_D = 5\%$.

whereas that of D is only 5 percent.[2] However, it is obvious by inspection that Distribution C is riskier; its dispersion about the mean is greater than that for Distribution D, and it has a significant chance of actual losses, whereas losses are not possible in Distribution D.

NORMAL DISTRIBUTION Because it is discussed so much in statistics courses, is so easy to use, and conforms well to so many real-world situations, the most commonly used continuous distribution is the *normal distribution*. It is symmetric about the expected value, and its tails extend out to plus and minus infinity. Figure 5A-3 is a normal distribution with an expected, or mean (μ, pronounced "mu"), rate of return of 10 percent and a standard deviation (σ, or sigma) of 5 percent. Approximately 68.3 percent of the area under any normal curve lies within $\pm 1\sigma$ of its mean, 95.5 percent lies within $\pm 2\sigma$, and 99.7 percent lies within $\pm 3\sigma$. Therefore, the probability of actually achieving a rate of return within the range of 5 to 15 percent ($\mu \pm 1\sigma$) is 68.3 percent, and so forth. Obviously, the smaller the standard deviation, the

FIGURE 5A-3   NORMAL PROBABILITY DISTRIBUTION

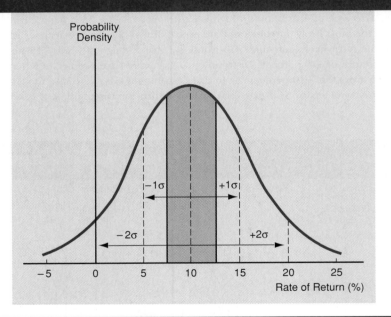

NOTE: The most likely and expected rate of return is 10 percent.

---

[2]Note that the most likely outcome equals the expected outcome only when the distribution is symmetric. If the distribution is skewed to the left, the expected outcome falls to the left of the most likely outcome, and vice versa. Also, note that the expected outcome of a triangular distribution is found by using this equation:

(Lower limit + Most likely outcome + Upper limit)/3.

Thus, the expected rate of return for Distribution C is (−5% + 10% + 15%)/3 = 6.67%.

smaller the probability of the actual outcome deviating very much from the expected value, and hence the smaller the total risk of the investment.

If we want to find the probability that an outcome will fall between 7.5 and 12.5 percent, we must calculate the area beneath the curve between these points, or the shaded area in Figure 5A-3. This area can be determined by integration or, more easily, by the use of statistical tables of the area under the normal curve.[3] To use the tables, we first use the following formula to standardize the distribution:

$$z = \frac{x - \mu}{\sigma}. \qquad \text{5A-1}$$

Here z is the standardized variable, or the number of standard deviations from the mean; x is the outcome of interest; and μ and σ are the mean and standard deviation of the distribution, respectively.[4] In our example, we are interested in the probability that an outcome will fall between 7.5 and 12.5 percent. Since the mean of the distribution is 10, and it is between the two points of interest, we must evaluate and then combine two probabilities, one to the left and one to the right of the mean. We first normalize these points by using Equation 5A-1:

$$z_{\text{Left}} = \frac{7.5 - 10}{5} = -0.5; \quad z_{\text{Right}} = \frac{12.5 - 10}{5} = +0.5.$$

The areas associated with these z values as found in Table 5A-1 are 0.1915 and 0.1915.[5] This means that the probability is 0.1915 that the actual outcome will fall between 7.5 and 10 percent and also 0.1915 that it will fall between 10 and 12.5 percent. Thus, the probability that the outcome will fall between 7.5 and 12.5 percent is 0.1915 + 0.1915 = 0.3830, or 38.3 percent.

Suppose we are interested in determining the probability that the actual outcome will be less than zero. We first determine that the probability is 0.4773 that the outcome will be between 0 and 10 percent and then observe that the probability of an outcome less than the mean, 10, is 0.5000. Thus, the probability of an outcome less than zero is 0.5000 − 0.4773 = 0.0227, or 2.27 percent.

---

[3]The equation for the normal curve is tedious to integrate, thus making the use of tables much more convenient. The equation for the normal curve is

$$f(x) = \frac{1}{\sqrt{2\pi\sigma^2}} e^{-(x-\mu)^2/2\sigma^2}$$

where π and e are mathematical constants; μ and σ denote the expected value, or mean, and standard deviation of the probability distribution, respectively; and x is any possible outcome.

[4]Note that if the point of interest is 1σ away from the mean, then $x - \mu = \sigma$, so $z = \sigma/\sigma = 1.0$. Thus, when z = 1.0, the point of interest is 1σ away from the mean; when z = 2, the deviation is 2σ; and so forth.

[5]Note that the negative sign on z_{Left} is ignored. Since the normal curve is symmetric around the mean, the minus sign merely indicates that the point of interest lies to the left of the mean.

TABLE 5A-1	AREA UNDER THE NORMAL CURVE

z	AREA FROM THE MEAN TO THE POINT OF INTEREST
0.0	0.0000
0.5	0.1915
1.0	0.3413
1.5	0.4332
2.0	0.4773
2.5	0.4938
3.0	0.4987

NOTE: Here z is the number of standard deviations from the mean. Some area tables are set up to indicate the area to the left or right of the indicated z values, but in our table, we indicate the area between the mean and the z value. Thus, the area from the mean to either z = +0.5 or −0.5 is 0.1915, or 19.15 percent of the total area or probability. A more complete set of values can be found in Table A-5 at the end of the book.

USING CONTINUOUS DISTRIBUTIONS Continuous distributions are generally used in financial analysis in the following manner:

1. Someone with a good knowledge of a particular situation is asked to specify the most applicable type of distribution and its parameters. For example, a company's marketing manager might be asked to supply this information for sales of a given product, or an engineer might be asked to estimate the construction costs of a capital project.

2. A financial analyst could then use these input data to help evaluate the riskiness of a given decision. For example, the analyst might conclude that the probability is 50 percent that the actual rate of return on a project will be between 5 and 10 percent, that the probability of a loss (negative rate of return) on the project is 15 percent, or that the probability of a return greater than 10 percent is 25 percent. Generally, such an analysis would be done by using a computer program. We shall return to this topic in Chapter 11.

In theory, we should use the specific distribution that best represents the true situation. Sometimes the true distribution is known, but with most financial data, it is not known. For example, we might think that interest rates could range from 8 to 15 percent next year, with a most likely value of 10 percent. This suggests a triangular distribution. Or we might think that interest rates next year can best be represented by a normal distribution, with a mean of 10 percent and a standard deviation of 2.5 percent. The point is, there is simply no type of distribution that is always "best"; you need to be familiar with different types of distributions and their properties, and then you must select the best distribution for the problem at hand.

CHAPTER 6

DISCOUNTED CASH
FLOW ANALYSIS

he cover story in a recent issue of Fortune *was entitled, "Will You Be Able to Retire?" Although you may laugh when we say the article should be of interest to you, the fact is it should be. The article began with some well-known facts: (1) The savings rate in the United States is the lowest of any major industrial nation. (2) The ratio of workers to retirees, which was 17 to 1 in 1950 and is currently down to 3 to 1, will decline to less than 2 to 1 after the Year 2000. (3) Because of points 1 and 2, the Social Security system is in serious trouble.*

The article went on to present some figures on how much money the "Baby Boom" generation (people born in the post–World War II period from 1946 through 1968) will need when they retire, given projected trends in inflation. Next, it presented statistics on the amount of money members of that generation are saving, and the rates of return savers are getting on their investments. Finally, the article concluded that even relatively affluent Baby Boomers (those with current incomes of about $85,000) will have trouble maintaining a reasonable standard of living when they retire, and that the children of the Boomers (some of you) will probably end up having to support their parents.

What does the retirement plight of the Baby Boomers (and their children) have to do with discounted cash flow analysis? Actually, a great deal. The concepts covered in this chapter are exactly the ones Fortune *used to forecast the Boomers' retirement needs, their probable wealth at retirement, and the resulting shortfall. For example, suppose Ms. Greene, who earned $85,000 in 1996, plans to retire in 2007, currently has savings of $100,000, and expects to live for another 20 years. She would need $68,000 in retirement income (1996 dollars) to meet the suggested standard of 80 percent of preretirement income. Her employer has no retirement plan, and she doubts that she will be able to collect from Social Security. First, note that if inflation averages 5 percent per year in the future, she* *would need an annual income of $110,765 in 10 years, $180,424 in 20 years, and a whopping $293,892 in 30 years. How much wealth would Ms. Greene need when she retires if she is to maintain her standard of living, and how much must she save over each of her remaining working years to amass the required amount? The answers to questions such as these are found using discounted cash flow (DCF) analysis.*

Investors use DCF analysis to evaluate stocks and bonds, and financial managers also deal with DCF concepts every day. For example, DCF analysis is used (1) when new projects are being evaluated, (2) when firms are analyzing whether to purchase or to lease an asset, and (3) when firms are deciding whether to refund a bond issue (sell a new bond and use the proceeds to retire an existing issue). In each of these situations, DCF analysis is used to find the present, or current, value of future cash flows, which is a vital step in the decision process. As you study this chapter, think about how the concepts discussed might be used in real-world financial analyses. Then, as you progress through the remainder of the text, you will understand why discounted cash flow analysis is often called "the cornerstone of finance."

In Chapter 1 we saw that the primary goal of financial management is to maximize the value of the firm's stock. We also saw that stock values depend in part on the timing of the cash flows investors expect to receive from an investment—a dollar expected soon is worth more than a dollar expected in the distant future. Therefore, it is essential that financial managers have a clear understanding of discounted cash flow analysis and its impact on the value of the firm. These concepts are discussed in this chapter, where we show how the timing of cash flows affects asset values and rates of return.

The principles of discounted cash flow analysis have many applications, ranging from setting up schedules for paying off loans to decisions about whether to acquire new equipment. *In fact, of all the concepts used in finance, none is more important than discounted cash flow (DCF) analysis, which is often called time value of money analysis.* Since this concept is used throughout the remainder of the book, it is vital that you understand the material in this chapter before you move on.[1]

TIME LINES

One of the most important tools in DCF analysis is the *time line,* which is used by analysts to help visualize what is happening in a particular problem and then to help set up the problem for solution. To illustrate the time line concept, consider the following diagram:

Time: 0   1   2   3   4   5

[1]This chapter, and indeed the entire book, is written on the assumption that students have financial calculators. As a result, procedures for obtaining financial calculator solutions are set forth in each of the major sections, along with procedures for obtaining solutions by using regular calculators or tables. It is highly desirable for each student to obtain a financial calculator and to learn how to use it, for financial calculators and computers—and not clumsy, rounded, and incomplete tables—are used exclusively in businesses.

Time 0 is today; Time 1 is one period from today, or the end of Period 1; Time 2 is two periods from today, or the end of Period 2; and so on. Thus, the numbers above the tick marks represent end-of-period values. Often the periods are years, but other time intervals such as semiannual periods, quarters, months, or even days are also used. If each period on the time line represents a year, the interval from the tick mark corresponding to 0 to the tick mark corresponding to 1 would be Year 1, the interval from 1 to 2 would be Year 2, and so on. Note that each tick mark corresponds to the end of one period as well as the beginning of the next period. In other words, the tick mark at Time 1 represents the *end* of Year 1, and it also represents the *beginning* of Year 2 because Year 1 has just passed.

Cash flows are placed directly below the tick marks, and interest rates are shown directly above the time line. Unknown cash flows, which you are trying to find in the analysis, are indicated by question marks. Now consider the following time line:

```
Time:    0   5%   1        2        3
         |--------|--------|--------|
Cash Flows:  -100                   ?
```

Here the interest rate for each of the three periods is 5 percent; a single amount (or lump sum) cash *outflow* is made at Time 0; and the Time 3 value is an unknown *inflow.* Since the initial $100 is an outflow (an investment), it has a minus sign. Since the Period 3 amount is an inflow, it does not have a minus sign. Note that no cash flows occur at Times 1 and 2. Note also that we generally do not show dollar signs on time lines to reduce clutter.

Now consider the following situation, where a $100 cash outflow is made today, and we will receive an unknown amount at the end of Time 2:

```
    0   5%   1   10%   2
    |--------|--------|
  -100                ?
```

Here the interest rate is 5 percent during the first period, but it rises to 10 percent during the second period. If the interest rate is constant in all periods, we show it only in the first period, but if it changes, we show all the relevant rates on the time line.

Time lines are essential when you are first learning discounted cash flow concepts, but even experts use time lines to analyze complex problems. We will be using time lines throughout the book, and you should get into the habit of using them when you work problems.

Draw a 3-year time line which illustrates the following situation: (1) An outflow of $10,000 occurs at Time 0. (2) Inflows of $5,000 occur at the end of Years 1, 2, and 3. (3) The interest rate during the three years is 10 percent.

SELF-TEST QUESTION

FUTURE VALUE

A dollar in hand today is worth more than a dollar to be received in the future because, if you had it now, you could invest it, earn interest, and end up with more than one dollar in the future. The process of going from today's values, or present values (PVs), to future values (FVs) is called *compounding*. To illustrate, suppose you deposited $100 in a bank account that paid 5 percent interest each year. How much would you have at the end of one year? To begin, we define the following terms:

PV = present value, or beginning amount, in your account. Here PV = $100.

i = interest rate the bank pays on the account per year. The interest earned is based on the balance at the beginning of each year, and we assume that it is paid at the end of the year. Here i = 5%, or, expressed as a decimal, i = 0.05. Throughout this chapter, we designate the interest rate as i (or I) because that symbol is used on most financial calculators. Note, though, that in later chapters we use the symbol k to denote interest rates because k is used more often in the financial literature.

INT = dollars of interest you earn during the year = Beginning amount × i. Here INT = $100(0.05) = $5.

FV_n = future value, or ending amount, of your account at the end of n years. Whereas PV is the value now, or the *present value*, FV_n is the value n years into the *future*, after the interest earned has been added to the account.

n = number of periods involved in the analysis. Here n = 1.

In our example, n = 1, so FV_n can be calculated as follows:

$$FV_n = FV_1 = PV + INT$$
$$= PV + PV(i)$$
$$= PV(1 + i)$$

$$= \$100(1 + 0.05) = \$100(1.05) = \$105.$$

Thus, the *future value (FV)* at the end of one year, FV_1, equals the present value multiplied by 1 plus the interest rate, so you will have $105 after one year.

What would you end up with if you left your $100 in the account for five years? Here is a time line set up to show the amount at the end of each year:

	0 5%	1	2	3	4	5
Initial deposit:	−100	$FV_1 = ?$	$FV_2 = ?$	$FV_3 = ?$	$FV_4 = ?$	$FV_5 = ?$
Interest earned:		5	5.25	5.51	5.79	6.08
Amount at the end of each period:		105	110.25	115.76	121.55	**127.63**

Note the following points: (1) You start by depositing $100 in the account — this is shown as an outflow at t = 0. (2) You earn $100(0.05) = $5 of interest during the first year, so the amount at the end of Year 1 (or t = 1) is $100 + $5 = $105. (3) You start the second year with $105, earn $5.25 on the now larger amount, and end the second year with $110.25. Your interest during Year 2, $5.25, is higher than the first year's interest, $5, because you earned $5(0.05) = $0.25 interest on the first year's interest. (4) This process continues, and because the beginning balance is higher in each succeeding year, the annual interest earned increases. (5) The total interest earned, $27.63, is reflected in the final balance at t = 5, $127.63.

Note that the value at the end of Year 2, $110.25, is equal to

$$FV_2 = FV_1(1 + i)$$
$$= PV(1 + i)(1 + i)$$
$$= PV(1 + i)^2$$
$$= \$100(1.05)^2 = \$110.25.$$

Continuing, the balance at the end of Year 3 is

$$FV_3 = FV_2(1 + i)$$
$$= PV(1 + i)^3$$
$$= \$100(1.05)^3 = \$115.76,$$

and

$$FV_5 = \$100(1.05)^5 = \$127.63.$$

In general, the future value of an initial lump sum at the end of n years can be found by applying Equation 6-1:

$$FV_n = PV(1 + i)^n. \qquad \text{6-1}$$

Equation 6-1 and most other equations associated with discounted cash flow problems can be solved in four ways: numerically using a regular calculator, with interest tables, with a financial calculator, or with a computer spreadsheet program. Most advanced work in financial management will be done on a computer, but when learning basic concepts it is best to use one (or more) of the other methods.

NUMERICAL SOLUTION

One can use a regular calculator and either multiply (1 + i) by itself n − 1 times or use the exponential function to raise (1 + i) to the nth power. With most calculators, you would enter 1 + i = 1.05 and multiply it by itself four times, or else enter 1.05, then press the y^x (exponential) function key, and then enter 5. In either case, your answer would be 1.2763 (if you set your calculator to display four decimal places), which you would multiply by $100 to get the final answer, $127.63.

In certain problems, it is extremely difficult to arrive at a solution using a regular calculator. We will tell you this when we have such a problem, and in these cases we will not show a numerical solution. Also, at times we show the numerical solution just below the time line, as a part of the diagram, rather than in a separate section.

INTEREST TABLES (TABULAR SOLUTION)

The *Future Value Interest Factor for i and n (FVIF$_{i,n}$)* is defined as $(1 + i)^n$, and these factors can be found by using a regular calculator as discussed above and then put into tables. Table 6-1 is illustrative, while Table A-3 in Appendix A at the back of the book contains FVIF$_{i,n}$ values for a wide range of i and n values.

Since $(1 + i)^n$ = FVIF$_{i,n}$, Equation 6-1 can be rewritten as follows:

$$FV_n = PV(FVIF_{i,n}). \qquad \text{6-1a}$$

To illustrate, the FVIF for our 5-year, 5 percent interest problem can be found in Table 6-1 by looking down the first column to Period 5, and then looking across that row to the 5 percent column, where we see that FVIF$_{5\%,5}$ = 1.2763. Then, the value of $100 after 5 years is found as follows:

$$FV_n = PV(FVIF_{i,n})$$
$$= \$100(1.2763) = \$127.63.$$

Before financial calculators became readily available (in the 1980s), the tables were used extensively, but they are rarely used today in the real world.

FINANCIAL CALCULATOR SOLUTION

Equation 6-1 and a number of other equations have been programmed directly into financial calculators, and such a calculator can be used to find future values. Note that calculators have five keys which correspond to the five most commonly used time value of money variables:

| N | | I | | PV | | PMT | | FV |

TABLE 6-1	FUTURE VALUE INTEREST FACTORS: $FVIF_{i,n} = (1 + i)^n$		
PERIOD (n)	4%	5%	6%
1	1.0400	1.0500	1.0600
2	1.0816	1.1025	1.1236
3	1.1249	1.1576	1.1910
4	1.1699	1.2155	1.2625
5	1.2167	1.2763	1.3382
6	1.2653	1.3401	1.4185

Here

N = the number of periods; some calculators use n rather than N.

I = interest rate per period; again, some calculators use i or I/YR rather than I.

PV = present value.

PMT = payment. This key is used only if the cash flows involve a series of equal, or constant, payments (an annuity). If there are no equal periodic payments in a particular problem, then PMT = 0.

FV = future value.

On some financial calculators, these keys are actually buttons on the face of the calculator, while on others they are shown on a screen after going into the time value of money (TVM) menu.

In this chapter, we will deal with equations which involve only four of the variables at any one time — three of the variables will be known, and the calculator will then solve for the fourth (unknown) variable. In the next chapter, when we deal with bonds, we will use all five variables in the bond valuation equation.[2]

To find the future value of $100 after 5 years at 5 percent interest using a financial calculator, note again that we are dealing with Equation 6-1:

$$FV_n = PV(1 + i)^n. \qquad \text{(6-1)}$$

The equation has four variables, FV_n, PV, i, and n. If we know any three, we can solve for the fourth. In our example, we can enter PV = 100, I = 5, PMT = 0, and N = 5. Then, when we press the FV key, we will get the answer, FV = 127.63 (rounded to two decimal places).[3]

Many financial calculators require that all cash flows be designated as either inflows or outflows, and then outflows must be entered as negative numbers. In our illustration, you deposit, or put in, the initial amount (which is an outflow to you) and you take out, or receive, the ending amount (which is an inflow to you). If your calculator requires that you follow this sign convention, the PV would be entered as −100. (If you entered 100, then the FV would appear as −127.63.) Also, on some calculators you are required to press a "Compute" key before pressing the FV key.

Sometimes the convention of changing signs can be confusing. For example, if you have $100 in the bank now and want to find out how much you will have after

---

[2]The equation programmed into calculators actually has five variables, one for each key. In this chapter, the value of one of the variables is always zero. It is a good idea to get into the habit of inputting a zero for the unused variable (whose value is automatically set equal to zero when you clear the calculator's memory); if you forget to clear your calculator, this procedure will help you avoid trouble.

Note also that we have prepared a *Technology Supplement* which provides instructions for performing all the functions necessary for this book with the leading calculators. The calculator manuals go into a lot of detail on things we never do, hence they are longer and more complex than they need to be for our purposes. See the preface for more information on obtaining the *Technology Supplement*.

[3]Here we assume that compounding occurs once each year. Most calculators have a setting which can be changed. For example, the HP 10B comes preset with payments at 12 per year. You would need to change it to 1 per year to get FV = 127.63. With the HP 10B, you would do this by typing 1, pressing the gold key, and then pressing the P/YR key.

5 years if your account pays 5 percent interest, the calculator will give you a negative answer, in this case −127.63, because the calculator assumes you are going to withdraw the funds. This sign convention should cause you no problem if you understand the process.

We should also note that financial calculators permit you to specify the number of decimal places that are displayed. Twelve significant digits are actually used in the calculations, but we generally use two places for answers when working with dollars or percentages and four places when working with decimals. The nature of the problem dictates how many decimal places should be displayed.

Technology has progressed to the point where the only efficient way to solve most time value of money problems is with a financial calculator or a computer spreadsheet. However, you must understand the concepts behind the calculations and know how to set up time lines in order to work complex problems. This is true for stock and bond valuation, capital budgeting, lease analysis, and many other important types of problems.

PROBLEM FORMAT

To help you understand the various types of discounted cash flow problems, we generally use a standard format in this chapter. First, we state the problem in words. Next, we diagram the problem on a time line. Then, beneath the time line, we show the equation that must be solved. Finally, we present three alternative procedures for solving the equation to obtain the answer: (1) use a regular calculator to obtain a numerical solution, (2) use the tables, or (3) use a financial calculator. Generally, the financial calculator solution is the most efficient.

To illustrate the format, we use the 5-year, 5 percent example:

Time Line:

Time:	0	5%	1	2	3	4	5

−100   FV = ?

Equation:

$$FV_n = PV(1 + i)^n = \$100(1.05)^5.$$

1. Numerical Solution:

Using a regular calculator, raise 1.05 to the 5th power and multiply by $100 to get $FV_5 = \$127.63$.

2. Tabular Solution:

Look up $FVIF_{5\%,5}$ in Table 6-1 or Table A-3 at the end of the book and then multiply by $100:

$$FV_5 = \$100(FVIF_{5\%,5}) = \$100(1.2763) = \$127.63.$$

3. Financial Calculator Solution:

Inputs: 5   5   −100   0

| N | I | PV | PMT | FV |

Output: = 127.63

Note that the calculator diagram tells you to input N = 5, I = 5, PV = −100, and PMT = 0, and then to press the FV key to get the answer, 127.63. Also, note that in this particular problem, the PMT key does not really come into play, as no constant series of payments is involved.[4] Finally, you should recognize that small rounding differences will often occur among the various solution methods because tables use fewer significant digits (4) than do calculators (12) and also because rounding sometimes is done at intermediate steps in long problems.

GRAPHIC VIEW OF THE COMPOUNDING PROCESS: GROWTH

Figure 6-1 shows how $1 (or any other lump sum) grows over time at various interest rates. The data used to plot the curves could be obtained from Table A-3, or it could be generated with a calculator or computer. The higher the rate of interest,

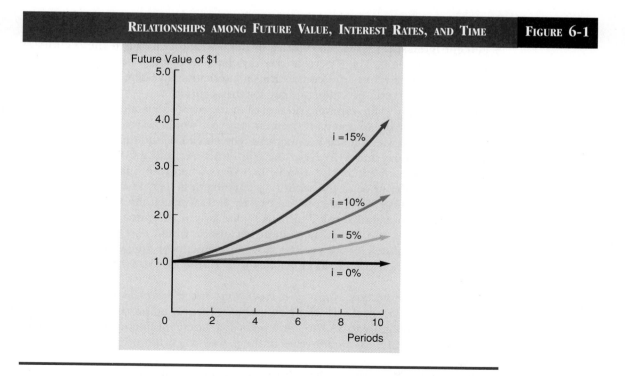

RELATIONSHIPS AMONG FUTURE VALUE, INTEREST RATES, AND TIME   **FIGURE 6-1**

---

[4]We input PMT = 0, but if you cleared the calculator before you started, that would already have been done.

the faster the rate of growth. The interest rate is, in fact, a growth rate: If a sum is deposited and earns 5 percent interest, then the funds on deposit will grow at a rate of 5 percent per period. Note also that the concepts discussed here can be applied to anything that is growing—sales, population, earnings per share, or whatever.

SELF-TEST QUESTIONS

Explain what is meant by the following statement: "A dollar in hand today is worth more than a dollar to be received next year."

What is compounding? What is "interest on interest"?

Explain the following equation: $FV_1 = PV + INT$.

Set up a time line that shows the following situation: (1) Your initial deposit is $100. (2) The account pays 5 percent interest annually. (3) You want to know how much money you will have at the end of 3 years.

What equation could you use to solve the preceding problem?

What are the five TVM (time value of money) keys on a financial calculator?

PRESENT VALUE

Suppose you have some extra cash, and you have a chance to buy a low-risk security which will pay $127.63 at the end of 5 years. Your local bank is currently offering 5 percent interest on 5-year certificates of deposit, and you regard the security as being as safe as a CD. The 5 percent rate is defined as being your *opportunity cost rate,* or the rate of return you could earn on alternative investments of similar risk. How much should you be willing to pay for the security?

From the future value example presented in the previous section, we saw that an initial amount of $100 invested at 5 percent per year would be worth $127.63 at the end of 5 years. As we will see in a moment, you should be indifferent to the choice between $100 today and $127.63 at the end of 5 years, and the $100 is defined as the *present value,* or *PV,* of $127.63 due in 5 years when your opportunity cost rate is 5 percent. If the price of the security is anything less than $100, you should definitely buy it because it would cost you exactly $100 to reach the $127.63 in 5 years if you invested in a similar-risk alternative. Similarly, if the price of the security is greater than $100, you should not buy it because it would cost you only $100 to reach the same future amount on alternative investments of similar risk. If the price is exactly $100, then you could either buy it or turn it down, for $100 is the security's fair value.

In general, *the present value of a cash flow due n years in the future is the amount which, if it were on hand today, would grow to equal the future amount.* Since $100 would grow to $127.63 in 5 years at a 5 percent interest rate, $100 is the present value of $127.63 due 5 years in the future when the opportunity cost rate is 5 percent.

Finding present values is called *discounting,* and it is simply the reverse of compounding—if you know the PV, you can compound to find the FV, while if you know the FV, you can discount to find the PV. When discounting, you would follow these steps:

Time Line:

Equation:

To develop the discounting equation, we begin with Equation 6-1,

$$FV_n = PV(1 + i)^n,$$ (6-1)

and then solve it for PV in several equivalent forms:

$$PV = \frac{FV_n}{(1 + i)^n} = FV_n\left(\frac{1}{1 + i}\right)^n.$$ 6-2

1. Numerical Solution:

Divide \$127.63 by 1.05 five times, or by $(1.05)^5$.

2. Tabular Solution:

Table A-1 in Appendix A contains present value interest factors for selected values of i and n. The present value interest factor, or $PVIF_{i,n}$, for i = 5% and n = 5 is 0.7835, so the present value of \$127.63 to be received after 5 years when the opportunity cost rate is 5 percent equals \$100:

$$PV = \$127.63(PVIF_{5\%,5}) = \$127.63(0.7835) = \$100.$$

3. Financial Calculator Solution:

Inputs:	5	5		0	127.63
	N	I	PV	PMT	FV
Output:			= −100.00		

Enter N = 5, I = 5, PMT = 0, and FV = 127.63, and then press PV to get PV = −100.

GRAPHIC VIEW OF THE DISCOUNTING PROCESS

Figure 6-2 shows how the present value of \$1 (or any other lump sum) to be received in the future diminishes as the years to receipt increases. Again, the data used to plot the curves could be obtained either with a calculator or from Table A-1, and the graph shows (1) that the present value of a sum to be received at some future date decreases and approaches zero as the payment date is extended further into the future and (2) that the rate of decrease is greater the higher the interest

FIGURE 6-2   RELATIONSHIPS AMONG PRESENT VALUE, INTEREST RATES, AND TIME

(discount) rate. At relatively high interest rates, funds due in the future are worth very little today, and even at a relatively low discount rate, the present value of a sum due in the very distant future is quite small. For example, at a 20 percent discount rate, $1 million due in 100 years is worth only 1.207 cents today. (However, 1.207 cents would grow to $1 million in 100 years at 20 percent.)

SELF-TEST QUESTIONS

What is meant by the term "opportunity cost rate"?

What is discounting? How is it related to compounding?

How does the present value of an amount to be received in the future change as the time is extended and as the interest rate increases?

SOLVING FOR INTEREST RATE AND TIME

At this point, you should realize that the compounding and discounting processes are reciprocals of one another, and that we have been dealing with one equation in two different forms:

$$\textbf{FV Form:}\quad FV_n = PV(1 + i)^n. \tag{6-1}$$

$$\textbf{PV Form:}\quad PV = \frac{FV_n}{(1 + i)^n} = FV_n\left(\frac{1}{1 + i}\right)^n. \tag{6-2}$$

There are four variables in these equations — PV, FV, i, and n — and if you know the values of any three, you (or your financial calculator) can find the value of the fourth.

Thus far, we have always given you the interest rate (i) and the number of years (n) plus either the PV or the FV. In many situations, though, you will need to solve for either i or n, as we discuss below.

SOLVING FOR i

Suppose you can buy a security at a price of $78.35 which will pay you $100 after 5 years. Here we know PV, FV, and n, but we do not know i, the interest rate you will earn on your investment. Problems such as this one are solved as follows:

Time Line:

$$-78.35 \qquad\qquad\qquad\qquad\qquad 100$$

Equation:

$$FV_n = PV(1 + i)^n \qquad\qquad (6\text{-}1)$$

$$\$100 = \$78.35(1 + i)^5. \text{ Solve for i.}$$

1. Numerical Solution:

Go through a trial-and-error process in which you insert different values of i into Equation 6-1 until you find a value which "works" in the sense that the right-hand side of the equation equals $100. The solution value is i = 0.05, or 5 percent. The trial-and-error procedure is extremely tedious and inefficient for most time value problems, so no one in the real world uses it.

2. Tabular Solution:

$$FV_n = PV(1 + i)^n = PV(FVIF_{i,n})$$

$$\$100 = \$78.35(FVIF_{i,5})$$

$$FVIF_{i,5} = \$100/\$78.35 = 1.2763.$$

Find the value of the FVIF as shown above, and then look across the Period 5 row in Table A-3 until you find FVIF = 1.2763. This value is in the 5% column, so the interest rate at which $78.35 grows to $100 over 5 years is 5 percent.[5] This procedure can be used only if the interest rate is in the table; therefore, it will not work for fractional interest rates or where n is not a whole number.

---

[5]The solution could also be set up in present value format:

$$PV = FV_n(PVIF_{i,n})$$

$$\$78.35 = \$100(PVIF_{i,5})$$

$$PVIF_{i,5} = \$78.35/\$100 = 0.7835.$$

This value corresponds to i = 5 percent in Table A-1.

3. Financial Calculator Solution:

Inputs: 5   −78.35   0   100

| N | | I | | PV | | PMT | | FV |

Output: = 5.0

Enter N = 5, PV = −78.35, PMT = 0, and FV = 100, and then press I to get I = 5. This procedure can be used for any interest rate or any value of n, including fractional values.

SOLVING FOR n

Suppose you know that the security will provide a return of 5 percent per year, that it will cost $78.35, and that you will receive $100 at maturity, but you do not know when the security matures. Thus, you know PV, FV, and i, but you do not know n, the number of periods. Here is the situation:

Time Line:

```
0     5%    1              2    n − 1       n = ?
|           |              |      |           |
−78.35                                       100
```

Equation:

$$FV_n = PV(1 + i)^n \qquad\qquad (6\text{-}1)$$

$100 = \$78.35(1.05)^n$. Solve for n.

1. Numerical Solution:

Again, you could go through a trial-and-error process wherein you substituted different values for n into the equation. You would find (eventually) that n = 5 "works," so 5 is the number of years it takes for $78.35 to grow to $100 if the interest rate is 5 percent.

2. Tabular Solution:

$$FV_n = PV(1 + i)^n = PV(FVIF_{i,n})$$

$$\$100 = \$78.35(FVIF_{5\%,n})$$

$$FVIF_{5\%,n} = \$100/\$78.35 = 1.2763.$$

Now look down the 5% column in Table A-3 until you find FVIF = 1.2763. This value is in Row 5, which indicates that it takes 5 years for $78.35 to grow to $100 at a 5 percent interest rate.[6]

---

[6]The problem could also be solved as follows:

$$PV = FV_n(PVIF_{i,n})$$

$$\$78.35 = \$100(PVIF_{5\%,n})$$

$$PVIF_{5\%,n} = \$78.35/\$100 = 0.7835.$$

This value corresponds to n = 5 years in Table A-1.

3. Financial Calculator Solution:

Inputs: 5   −78.35   0   100

| N | I | PV | PMT | FV |

Output: = 5.0

Enter I = 5, PV = −78.35, PMT = 0, and FV = 100, and then press N to get N = 5.

SELF-TEST QUESTIONS

Assuming that you are given the PV, FV, and interest rate, i, write out an equation that can be used to determine the time period, n.

Assuming that you are given the PV, FV, and time period, n, write out an equation that can be used to determine the interest rate, i.

Explain how financial calculators can be used to solve for i and n.

FUTURE VALUE OF AN ANNUITY

An *annuity* is a series of equal payments made at fixed intervals for a specified number of periods. For example, $100 at the end of each of the next three years is a 3-year annuity, and $50 at the beginning of each of the next six months is a 6-month annuity. The payments are given the symbol PMT, and they can occur at either the beginning or the end of each period. If the payments occur at the *end* of each period, as they typically do, the annuity is called an *ordinary,* or *deferred, annuity.* If payments are made at the *beginning* of each period, the annuity is an *annuity due.* Since ordinary annuities are more common in finance, when the term "annuity" is used in this book, you should assume that the payments occur at the end of each period unless otherwise noted.

ORDINARY ANNUITIES

An ordinary, or deferred, annuity consists of a series of equal payments made at the *end* of each period. If you deposit $100 at the end of each year for 3 years in a savings account that pays 5 percent interest per year, how much will you have at the end of 3 years? To answer this question, we must find the future value of the annuity, FVA_n. Each payment is compounded out to the end of Period n, and the sum of the compounded payments is the future value of the annuity, FVA_n.

Time Line:

Here we show the regular time line as the top portion of the diagram, but we also show how each cash flow is compounded to produce the value FVA_n in the lower portion of the diagram.

Equation:

$$FVA_n = PMT(1 + i)^0 + PMT(1 + i)^1 + PMT(1 + i)^2 + \ldots + PMT(1 + i)^{n-1}$$

$$= PMT \sum_{t=1}^{n} (1 + i)^{n-t}.$$

6-3

Notice that the first line of Equation 6-3 presents the annuity payments in reverse order of payment, and the superscript in each term indicates the number of periods of interest each payment receives. Because the first annuity payment was made at the end of Period 1, interest would be earned in Period 2 through Period n only; thus, compounding would be for $n - 1$ periods rather than n periods, compounding for the second annuity payment would be for Period 3 through Period n, or $n - 2$ periods, and so on. The last annuity payment is made at the same time the computation is made, so there is no time for interest to be earned. Simplifying the first line produces the last line of Equation 6-3.

1. Numerical Solution:

The lower section of the preceding time line shows the numerical solution. The future value of each cash flow is found, and those FVs are summed to find the FV of the annuity, $315.25. This is a tedious process for long annuities.

2. Tabular Solution:

The summation term in Equation 6-3 is called the *Future Value Interest Factor for an Annuity (FVIFA$_{i,n}$):*[7]

$$FVIFA_{i,n} = \sum_{t=1}^{n} (1 + i)^{n-t} = \frac{(1 + i)^n - 1}{i}.$$

6-3a

FVIFAs have been calculated for various combinations of i and n; Table A-4 in Appendix A contains a set of FVIFA factors. To find the answer to the 3-year, $100 annuity problem, first refer to Table A-4 and look down the 5% column to the third period; the FVIFA is 3.1525. Thus, the future value of the $100 annuity is $315.25:

$$FVA_n = PMT(FVIFA_{i,n})$$

$$FVA_3 = \$100(FVIFA_{5\%,3}) = \$100(3.1525) = \$315.25.$$

---

[7]The third term in Equation 6-3a is found by applying the algebra of geometric progressions. This equation is useful in situations where the required values of i and n are not in the tables and no financial calculator is available.

3. Financial Calculator Solution:

Inputs: 3   5   0   −100

| N | I | PV | PMT | FV |

Output: = 315.25

Note that in annuity problems, the PMT key is used in conjunction with the N and I keys, plus either the PV or the FV key, depending on whether you are trying to find the PV or the FV of the annuity. In our example, you want the FV, so press the FV key to get the answer, $315.25. Since there is no initial payment, we input PV = 0.

ANNUITIES DUE

Had the three $100 payments in the previous example been made at the *beginning* of each year, the annuity would have been an *annuity due*. On the time line, each payment would be shifted to the left one year; therefore, each payment would be compounded for one extra year.

1. Time Line and Numerical Solution:

Again, the regular time line is shown at the top of the diagram, and the values as calculated with a regular calculator are shown in the right column. The payments occur earlier, so more interest is earned. Therefore, the future value of the annuity due is larger, $331.01 versus $315.25 for the ordinary annuity.

2. Tabular Solution:

In an annuity due, each payment is compounded for one additional period, so the future value of the entire annuity is equal to the future value of an ordinary annuity compounded for one additional period. Here is the tabular solution:

$$FVA_n \text{ (annuity due)} = PMT(FVIFA_{i,n})(1 + i) \qquad \text{6-3b}$$

$$= \$100(3.1525)(1.05) = \$331.01.$$

3. Financial Calculator Solution:

Most financial calculators have a switch, or key, marked "DUE" or "BEG" that permits you to switch from end-of-period payments (ordinary annuity) to beginning-of-period payments (annuity due). When the beginning mode is activated, the display will normally show the word "BEGIN." Thus, to deal with annuities due, switch your calculator to "BEGIN" and proceed as before:

$$
\begin{array}{ccccc}
& & & & \text{BEGIN} \\
\text{Inputs:} & 3 & 5 & 0 & -100 \\
& \boxed{\text{N}} & \boxed{\text{I}} & \boxed{\text{PV}} & \boxed{\text{PMT}} \quad \boxed{\text{FV}} \\
\text{Output:} & & & & = 331.01
\end{array}
$$

Enter N = 3, I = 5, PV = 0, PMT = −100, and then press FV to get the answer, $331.01. *Since most problems specify end-of-period cash flows, you should always switch your calculator back to "END" mode after you work an annuity due problem.*

SELF-TEST QUESTIONS

What is the difference between an ordinary annuity and an annuity due?

How do you modify the equation for determining the value of an ordinary annuity in order to determine the value of an annuity due?

Which annuity has the greater *future* value: an ordinary annuity or an annuity due? Why?

Explain how financial calculators can be used to solve future value of annuity problems.

PRESENT VALUE OF AN ANNUITY

Suppose you were offered the following alternatives: (1) a 3-year annuity with payments of $100 or (2) a lump sum payment today. You have no need for the money during the next three years, so if you accept the annuity, you would simply deposit the payments in a savings account that pays 5 percent interest per year. Similarly, the lump sum payment would be deposited into a similar account. How large must the lump sum payment today be to make it equivalent to the annuity?

ORDINARY ANNUITIES

If the payments come at the end of each year, then the annuity is an ordinary annuity, and it would be set up as follows:

Time Line:

The regular time line is shown at the top of the diagram, and the numerical solution values are shown in the left column. The PV of the annuity, PVA_n, is $272.32.

Equation:

Here is the general equation used to find the PV of an ordinary annuity:[8]

$$PVA_n = \frac{PMT}{(1+i)^1} + \frac{PMT}{(1+i)^2} + \cdots + \frac{PMT}{(1+i)^n}$$

$$= \sum_{t=1}^{n} \frac{PMT}{(1+i)^t}.$$

6-4

1. Numerical Solution:

The present value of each cash flow is found and then summed to find the PV of the annuity. This procedure is shown in the lower section of the time line diagram, where we see that the PV of the annuity is $272.32.

2. Tabular Solution:

We could factor out the PMT term in Equation 6-4 to obtain the *Present Value Interest Factor for an Annuity (PVIFA$_{i,n}$)*. Values for the term at different values of i and n are shown in Table A-2 at the back of the book. Thus,

$$PVA_n = PMT(PVIFA_{i,n}).$$

6-4a

To find the answer to the 3-year, $100 annuity problem, simply refer to Table A-2 and look down the 5% column to the third period. The PVIFA is 2.7232, so the present value of the $100 annuity is $272.32:

$$PVA_n = PMT(PVIFA_{i,n})$$
$$PVA_3 = \$100(PVIFA_{5\%,3}) = \$100(2.7232) = \$272.32.$$

3. Financial Calculator Solution:

Inputs:	3	5		−100	0
	N	I	PV	PMT	FV
Output:			= 272.32		

Enter N = 3, I = 5, PMT = −100, and FV = 0, and then press the PV key to find the PV, $272.32.

---

[8]We could factor out the PMT, in which case the summation term is called the *PVIFA*, and, using the geometric progression solution process, its value is found to be

$$\sum_{t=1}^{n} \left(\frac{1}{1+i}\right)^t = \frac{1 - \dfrac{1}{(1+i)^n}}{i} = \frac{1}{i} - \frac{1}{i(1+i)^n}.$$

One especially important application of the annuity concept relates to loans with constant payments, such as mortgages and auto loans. With such loans, called *amortized loans,* the amount borrowed is the present value of an ordinary annuity, and the payments constitute the annuity stream. We will examine constant payment loans in more depth in a later section of this chapter.

ANNUITIES DUE

Had the three $100 payments in the preceding example been made at the beginning of each year, the annuity would have been an annuity due. Each payment would be shifted to the left one year, so each payment would be discounted for one less year. Here is the time line setup:

1. Time Line and Numerical Solution:

```
                        0     5%    1            2            3
                        ├───────────┼────────────┼────────────┤
                        100         100          100
                        95.24  ◄─────┘
                        90.70  ◄──────────────────┘
    PVA₃ (Annuity due) = 285.94
```

Again, we find the PV of each cash flow and then sum these PVs to find the PV of the annuity due. This procedure is illustrated in the lower section of the time line diagram. Since the cash flows occur sooner, the PV of the annuity due exceeds that of the ordinary annuity, $285.94 versus $272.32.

2. Tabular Solution:

In an annuity due, each payment is discounted for one less period. Since its payments come in faster, an annuity due is more valuable than an ordinary annuity, and this higher value is found by multiplying the PV of an ordinary annuity by $(1 + i)$:

$$\text{PVA}_n \text{ (Annuity due)} = \text{PMT}(\text{PVIFA}_{i,n})(1 + i) \qquad \text{6-4b}$$

$$= \$100(2.7232)(1.05) = \$285.94.$$

3. Financial Calculator Solution:

```
                                            BEGIN
        Inputs:      3        5             −100        0
                    ┌───┐   ┌───┐   ┌────┐  ┌─────┐  ┌────┐
                    │ N │   │ I │   │ PV │  │ PMT │  │ FV │
                    └───┘   └───┘   └────┘  └─────┘  └────┘
        Output:                     = 285.94
```

Switch to the beginning-of-period mode, and then enter N = 3, I = 5, PMT = −100, and FV = 0, and then press PV to get the answer, $285.94. *Again, since most problems deal with end-of-period cash flows, don't forget to switch your calculator back to the "END" mode.*

Which annuity has the greater present value: an ordinary annuity or an annuity due? Why?

Explain how financial calculators can be used to find present values of annuities.

PERPETUITIES

Most annuities call for payments to be made over some finite period of time — for example, $100 per year for three years. However, some annuities go on indefinitely, or perpetually, and these annuities are called *perpetuities*. The present value of a perpetuity is found by applying Equation 6-5.[9]

$$\text{PV (Perpetuity)} = \frac{\text{Payment}}{\text{Interest rate}} = \frac{\text{PMT}}{i}. \qquad \text{6-5}$$

Perpetuities can be illustrated by some British securities issued after the Napoleonic Wars. In 1815, the British government sold a huge bond issue and used the proceeds to pay off many smaller issues that had been floated in prior years to pay for the wars. Since the purpose of the bonds was to consolidate past debts, the bonds were called *consols*. Suppose each consol promised to pay $100 per year in perpetuity. (Actually, interest was stated in pounds.) What would each bond be worth if the opportunity cost rate, or discount rate, was 5 percent? The answer is $2,000:

$$\text{PV (Perpetuity)} = \frac{\$100}{0.05} = \$2,000 \text{ if } i = 5\%.$$

Suppose the interest rate rose to 10 percent; what would happen to the consol's value? The value would drop to $1,000:

$$\text{PV (Perpetuity)} = \frac{\$100}{0.10} = \$1,000 \text{ at } i = 10\%.$$

We see that the value of a perpetuity changes dramatically when interest rates change. Perpetuities are discussed further in Chapter 7, where procedures for finding the values of various types of securities are discussed.

What happens to the value of a perpetuity when interest rates increase? What happens when interest rates decrease?

Why do these bonds' prices change when interest rates change?

---

[9]The derivation of Equation 6-5 is given in Appendix 4A of Eugene F. Brigham and Louis C. Gapenski, *Intermediate Financial Management*, 5th ed. (Fort Worth, Tex.: Dryden Press, 1996).

UNEVEN CASH FLOW STREAMS

The definition of an annuity includes the words *constant payment* — in other words, annuities involve payments that are equal in every period. Although many financial decisions do involve constant payments, other important decisions involve uneven, or nonconstant, cash flows; for example, common stocks typically pay an increasing stream of dividends over time, and fixed asset investments such as new equipment normally do not generate constant cash flows. Consequently, it is necessary to extend our time value discussion to include *uneven cash flow streams.*

Throughout the book, we will follow convention and reserve the term *payment (PMT)* for annuity situations where the dollar amounts are constant, and we will use the term *cash flow (CF)* to denote uneven dollar amounts. Financial calculators are set up to follow this convention, so if you are using one and dealing with uneven cash flows, you will need to use the "cash flow register."

PRESENT VALUE OF AN UNEVEN CASH FLOW STREAM

The PV of an uneven cash flow stream is found as the sum of the PVs of the individual cash flows of the stream. For example, suppose we must find the PV of the following cash flow stream, discounted at 6 percent:

0	6%	1	2	3	4	5	6	7
PV = ?		100	200	200	200	200	0	1,000

The PV will be found by applying this general present value equation:

$$PV = CF_1\left(\frac{1}{1+i}\right)^1 + CF_2\left(\frac{1}{1+i}\right)^2 + \cdots + CN_n\left(\frac{1}{1+i}\right)^n$$

$$= \sum_{t=1}^{n} CF_t\left(\frac{1}{1+i}\right)^t = \sum_{t=1}^{n} CF_t(PVIF_{i,t}).$$

6-6

We could find the PV of each individual cash flow using the numerical, tabular, or financial calculator methods, and then sum these values to find the present value of the stream. Here is what the process would look like:

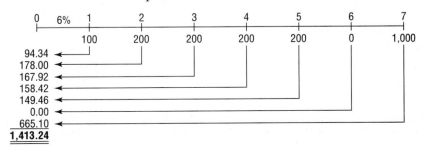

All we did was to apply Equation 6-6, show the individual PVs in the left column of the diagram, and then sum those individual PVs to find the PV of the entire stream.

The present value of a cash flow stream can always be found by summing the present values of the individual cash flows as shown above. However, cash flow regularities within the stream may allow the use of shortcuts. For example, notice that Cash Flows 2 through 5 represent an annuity. We can use that fact to solve the problem in a slightly different manner:

The Year 2–5 cash flows represent an ordinary annuity, so we find its PV at Year 1 (one period before the first payment). This PV ($693.02) must then be discounted back one more period to get its Year 0 value.

Problems involving uneven cash flows can be solved in one step with most financial calculators. First, you input the individual cash flows, in chronological order, into the cash flow register. Cash flows are usually designated CF_0, CF_1, CF_2, CF_3, and so on. Next, you enter the interest rate. At this point, you have substituted in all the known values of Equation 6-6, so you only need to press the NPV key to find the present value of the stream. The calculator has been programmed to find the PV of each cash flow and then to sum these values to find the PV of the entire stream. To input the cash flows for this problem, enter 0 (because $CF_0 = 0$), 100, 200, 200, 200, 200, 0, 1000 in that order into the cash flow register, enter I = 6, and then press NPV to obtain the answer, $1,413.19, which differs slightly from the long-form solution because of rounding differences.

Two points should be noted. First, when dealing with the cash flow register, the calculator uses the term "NPV" rather than "PV." The N stands for "net," so NPV is the abbreviation for "Net Present Value," which is simply the net present value of a series of positive and negative cash flows. Our example has no negative cash flows, but if it did, we would simply input them with negative signs.[10]

The second point to note is that annuities can be entered into the cash flow register more efficiently by using the N_j key. (On some calculators, you are prompted to enter the number of times the cash flow occurs, and on still other calculators the procedures for inputting data, as we discuss next, may be different. You should consult your calculator manual or our *Technology Supplement* to determine the appropriate steps for your specific calculator.) In this illustration, you would enter $CF_0 = 0$, $CF_1 = 100$, $CF_2 = 200$, $N_j = 4$ (which tells the calculator that the 200 occurs 4 times), $CF_6 = 0$, and $CF_7 = 1000$. Then enter I = 6 and press the NPV key, and

---

[10]To input negative numbers, type in the positive number, then press the +/– key to change the sign to negative. If you begin by typing the minus sign, you subtract the negative number from the last number in the calculator.

1,413.19 will appear in the display. Also, note that amounts entered into the cash flow register remain in the register until they are cleared. Thus, if you had previously worked a problem with eight cash flows and then moved to a problem with only four cash flows, the calculator would assume that the cash flows from the first problem belonged to the second problem. Therefore, you must be sure to clear the cash flow register before starting a new problem.

FUTURE VALUE OF AN UNEVEN CASH FLOW STREAM

The future value of an uneven cash flow stream (sometimes called the *terminal value*) is found by compounding each payment to the end of the stream and then summing the future values:

$$FV_n = CF_1(1 + i)^{n-1} + CF_2(1 + i)^{n-2} + \ldots + CF_n(1 + i)^{n-t}$$

$$= \sum_{t=1}^{n} CF_t(1 + i)^{n-t} = \sum_{t=1}^{n} CF_t(FVIF_{i,n-t}).$$

6-7

The future value of our illustrative uneven cash flow stream is $2,124.92:

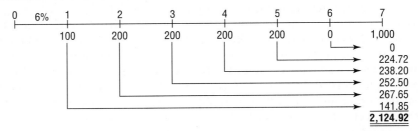

Some financial calculators have a net future value (NFV) key which, after the cash flows and interest rate have been entered into the calculator, can be used to obtain the future value of an uneven cash flow stream. In any event, it is easy enough to compound the individual cash flows to the terminal year and then to sum them to find the FV of the stream. Also, we are generally more interested in the present value of an asset's cash flow stream than in the future value because the present value represents today's value, which we can compare to the price of the asset. Finally, note that the cash flow stream's net present value can be used to find its net future value: NFV = NPV$(1 + i)^n$. Thus, in this example, NFV = $1,413.24(1.06)^7$ = $2,124.99, which, except for a rounding difference, equals the NFV shown on the time line above. (If we had used the calculator-determined NPV of $1,413.19, the NFV would be $2,124.92, exactly the same as our time line solution.)

SOLVING FOR i WITH UNEVEN CASH FLOW STREAMS

It is relatively easy to solve for i numerically or with the tables when the cash flows are lump sums or annuities. However, it is *extremely difficult* to solve for i if the cash flows are uneven, as you would have to go through many tedious trial-and-error calculations. With a financial calculator, though, it is easy to find the value of i. Simply input the CF values into the cash flow register and then press the IRR key. IRR stands for "internal rate of return," which is the percentage return on an investment. We will defer further discussion of this calculation for now, but we will take it up in our discussion of capital budgeting methods in Chapter 9.[11]

SEMIANNUAL AND OTHER COMPOUNDING PERIODS

In all of our examples thus far, we have assumed that interest is compounded once a year, or annually. This is called *annual compounding*. Suppose, however, that you put $100 into a bank which states that it pays a 6 percent annual interest rate but that interest is credited each six months. This is called *semiannual compounding*. How much would you accumulate at the end of one year, two years, or some other period under semiannual compounding?

To illustrate semiannual compounding, assume that $100 is placed into an account at an interest rate of 6 percent and left there for 3 years. First, consider again what happens under annual compounding:

1. Time Line, Equation, and Numerical Solution:

$$FV_n = PV(1 + i)^n = \$100(1.06)^3$$
$$= \$119.10.$$

2. Tabular Solution:

$$FV_3 = \$100(FVIF_{6\%,3}) = \$100(1.1910) = \$119.10.$$

3. Financial Calculator Solution:

Now consider what happens under semiannual compounding. Here we have $n = 2 \times 3 = 6$ semiannual periods, and you will earn $i = 6\%/2 = 3\%$ every six months.

---

[11]To obtain a solution, at least one of the cash flows must have a negative sign, indicating that it is an investment. Since none of the CFs in our example were negative, the cash flow stream has no IRR. However, had we input a cost for CF_0, we could have obtained an IRR, which would be the rate of return earned on the CF_0 investment. For example, if the investment which produced our uneven cash flow stream had a cost of $1,000, then the IRR of that investment would be 13.96 percent.

Note that on most types of contracts, interest is quoted as an annual rate, and if compounding occurs more frequently than once a year, that fact is stated, along with the rate. In our example, the quoted rate is "6 percent, compounded semiannually." Here is how we find the FV after 3 years at 6 percent with semiannual compounding:

Time Line:

1. Equation and Numerical Solution

$$FV_n = PV(1 + i)^n = \$100(1.03)^6$$
$$= \$100(1.1941) = \$119.41.$$

Here i = rate per period = annual rate/compounding periods per year = 6%/2 = 3%, and n = the total number of periods = years × periods per year = 3 × 2 = 6.

2. Tabular Solution:

$$FV_6 = \$100(FVIF_{3\%,6}) = \$100(1.1941) = \$119.41.$$

Look up FVIF for 3%, 6 periods in Table A-3 and complete the arithmetic.

3. Financial Calculator Solution:

Enter N = years × periods per year = 3 × 2 = 6, I = annual rate/periods per year = 6/2 = 3, PV = −100, and PMT = 0, and then press FV to find the answer, $119.41 versus $119.10 under annual compounding. The FV is larger under semiannual compounding because interest on interest is being earned more frequently.

Throughout the world economy, different compounding periods are used for different types of investments. For example, bank accounts generally pay interest daily; most bonds pay interest semiannually; and stocks generally pay dividends quarterly.[12] If we are to properly compare securities with different compounding periods, we need to put them on a common basis. This requires us to distinguish between *nominal,* or *quoted, interest rates* and *effective annual rates.*[13]

---

[12]Some banks and savings and loans even pay interest compounded *continuously.* Continuous compounding is discussed in Appendix 6A.

[13]The term *nominal rate* as it is used here has a different meaning than the way it was used in Chapter 3. There, nominal interest rates referred to stated market rates as opposed to real (zero inflation) rates. In this chapter, the term *nominal rate* means the stated, or quoted, annual rate as opposed to the effective annual rate. Note that in both cases, *nominal* means *stated,* or *quoted,* as opposed to some adjusted rate.

The nominal, or quoted, interest rate in our example is 6 percent. *The effective annual rate (EAR, or EFF% on some calculators) is defined as that rate which would produce the same ending (future) value if annual compounding had been used.* In our example, the effective annual rate is the rate which would produce an FV of $119.41 at the end of Year 3 with annual compounding.

We can determine the effective annual rate, given the nominal rate and the number of compounding periods per year, by solving this equation:

$$\text{Effective annual rate} = \text{EAR or EFF\%} = \left(1 + \frac{i_{Nom}}{m}\right)^m - 1.0. \qquad \text{6-8}$$

Here i_{Nom} is the nominal, or quoted, interest rate, and m is the number of compounding periods per year. For example, to find the effective annual rate if the nominal rate is 6 percent and semiannual compounding is used, we have[14]

$$\text{Effective annual rate} = \text{EAR} = \text{EFF\%} = \left(1 + \frac{0.06}{2}\right)^2 - 1.0$$

$$= (1.03)^2 - 1.0$$

$$= 1.0609 - 1.0 = 0.0609 = 6.09\%.$$

Semiannual compounding (or any nonannual compounding) can be handled in two ways: (1) State everything on a periodic basis rather than on an annual basis. For example, use n = 6 periods rather than n = 3 years, and use i = 3% per period rather than i = 6% per year. (2) Alternatively, find the effective annual rate by applying Equation 6-8, and then use this rate as an annual rate over the given number of years. In our example, use i = 6.09% and n = 3 years. Here are the time lines for the two alternative procedures:

We see that both procedures produce the same result, $119.41. Of course, once you start dealing with noninteger interest rates such as 6.09 percent, the use of a calculator is essential.

The points made about semiannual compounding can be generalized as follows. When compounding occurs more frequently than once a year, we can use a modified version of Equation 6-1 to find the future value of any lump sum:

$$\text{Annual compounding:} \quad FV_n = PV(1 + i)^n. \qquad (6-1)$$

---

[14]Most financial calculators are programmed to find the EAR or, given the EAR, to find the nominal rate. This is called "interest rate conversion," and you simply enter the nominal rate and the number of compounding periods per year and then press the EFF% key to find the EAR.

$$\text{More frequent compounding: } FV_n = PV\left(1 + \frac{i_{Nom}}{m}\right)^{mn}. \qquad \text{6-9}$$

Here i_{Nom} is the nominal, or quoted, rate, m is the number of times compounding occurs per year, and n is the number of years. For example, when banks pay daily interest, the value of m is set at 365 and Equation 6-9 is applied.[15]

To illustrate further the effects of compounding more frequently than annually, consider the interest rate charged on credit cards. Many banks charge 1.5 percent per month, and, in their advertising, they state that the *annual percentage rate (APR)* is 18.0 percent. However, the true rate is the effective annual rate of 19.6 percent:[16]

$$\text{Effective annual rate} = EAR = \left(1 + \frac{0.18}{12}\right)^{12} - 1$$

$$= (1.015)^{12} - 1.0$$

$$= 0.196 = 19.6\%.$$

Semiannual and other compounding periods can also be used for discounting, and for both lump sums and annuities. First, consider the case where we want to find the PV of an ordinary annuity of $100 per year for 3 years when the interest rate is 8 percent, compounded annually:

Time Line:

1. Numerical Solution:

Find the PV of each cash flow and sum them. The PV of the annuity is $257.71.

---

[15]To illustrate, the future value of $1 invested at 10 percent for 1 year under daily compounding is $1.1052:

$$FV_n = \$1\left(1 + \frac{0.10}{365}\right)^{365(1)} = \$1(1.105156) = \$1.1052.$$

Note also that banks sometimes use 360 as the number of days per year for this and other calculations.

[16]The *annual percentage rate (APR)* is the rate often used in bank loan advertisements since it meets the minimum requirements contained in "truth in lending" laws. Typically, the APR is defined as (Periodic rate)(Number of periods in one year). For example, the APR on a credit card with interest charges of 1.5 percent per month is 1.5%(12) = 18.0%. The APR understates the 19.6 percent effective annual rate, so banks tend to use the APR when advertising what they charge on loans, but they use the effective annual rate when advertising rates on savings accounts because they want to make their deposit rates look high.

2. Tabular Solution:

$$PVA_n = PMT(PVIFA_{i,n})$$
$$= \$100(PVIFA_{8\%,3}) = \$100(2.5771) = \$257.71.$$

3. Financial Calculator Solution:

Inputs: 3   8   100   0

N   I   PV   PMT   FV

Output: = −257.71

Now let's change the situation. For example, suppose the annuity calls for payments of $50 each 6 months rather than for $100 per year, and the interest rate is 8 percent, compounded semiannually. Here is the time line:

Time Line:

1. Numerical Solution:

Find the PV of each cash flow by discounting at 4 percent. Treat each tick mark on the time line as a period, so there would be 6 periods. The PV of the annuity is $262.11 versus $257.71 under annual compounding.

2. Tabular Solution:

$$PVA_n = PMT(PVIFA_{i,n})$$
$$= \$50(PVIFA_{4\%,6}) = \$50(5.2421) = \$262.11.$$

3. Financial Calculator Solution:

Inputs: 6   4   50   0

N   I   PV   PMT   FV

Output: = −262.11

The semiannual payments come in sooner, so the $50 semiannual annuity is more valuable than the $100 annual annuity.

SELF-TEST QUESTIONS

What changes must you make in your calculations to determine the future value of an amount that is being compounded at 8 percent semiannually versus one being compounded annually at 8 percent?

Why is semiannual compounding better than annual compounding from a saver's standpoint?

What is meant by the terms "annual percentage rate," "effective annual rate," and "nominal interest rate"?

How does the term "nominal rate" used in this chapter differ from the term as it was used in Chapter 3?

COMPARISON OF DIFFERENT TYPES OF INTEREST RATES

People in finance often work with three types of interest rates: nominal rates, i_{Nom}; periodic rates, i_{Per}; and effective annual rates, EAR or EFF%. Therefore, it is essential that you understand what each one is and when it should be used.

1. **Nominal, or quoted, rate.** This is the rate that is quoted by borrowers and lenders. Practitioners in the stock, bond, mortgage, and bank loan markets express all financial contracts in terms of nominal rates. So, if you talk with a banker, broker, mortgage lender, auto finance company, or student loan officer about rates, the nominal rate is the one he or she will normally quote you. However, to be meaningful, the quoted nominal rate must also include the number of compounding periods per year. For example, a bank might offer 8.5 percent, compounded quarterly, on CDs, or a mutual fund might offer 8 percent, compounded monthly, on its money market account.

   The nominal rate is also called the Annual Percentage Rate (APR). If a credit card issuer quotes an APR rate of 18 percent, monthly, this means an interest rate of 1.5 percent per month, and APR = 12(1.5%) = 18%.

   Nominal rates can be compared with one another, *but only if the instruments being compared use the same number of compounding periods per year.* Thus, you could compare the quoted yields on two bonds if they both pay interest semiannually. However, to compare an 8.5 percent, annual payment CD with an 8 percent, daily payment money market fund, we would need to put both instruments on an *effective (or equivalent) annual rate (EAR)* basis as discussed later in this section.

   Note that the nominal rate is never shown on a time line, and it is never used as an input in a financial calculator (unless compounding occurs only once a year, in which case $i_{Nom} = periodic\ rate = EAR$). If more frequent compounding occurs, you should generally use the periodic rate as discussed below.

2. **Periodic rate, i_{Per}.** This is the rate charged by a lender or paid by a borrower each period. It can be a rate per year, per 6-month period, per quarter, per month, per day, or per any other time interval (usually one year or less). For example, a bank might charge 1.5 percent per month on its credit card loans, or a finance company might charge 3 percent per quarter on consumer loans. We find the periodic rate as follows:

$$\text{Periodic rate, } i_{Per} = i_{Nom}/m, \qquad \text{6-10}$$

which implies that

$$\text{Nominal annual rate} = i_{Nom} = (\text{Periodic rate})(m). \qquad \text{6-11}$$

Here i_{Nom} is the nominal annual rate and m is the number of compounding periods per year. To illustrate, consider a finance company loan at 3 percent per quarter:

$$\text{Nominal annual rate} = i_{Nom} = (\text{Periodic rate})(m) = (3\%)(4) = 12\%,$$

or

$$\text{Periodic rate} = i_{Nom}/m = 12\%/4 = 3\% \text{ per quarter.}$$

If there is only one payment per year, or if interest is added only once a year, then m = 1, and the periodic rate is equal to the nominal rate.

The periodic rate is the rate which is generally shown on time lines and used in calculations. The only exception is in situations where (1) annuities are involved and (2) the payment periods do not correspond to the compounding periods.[17] To illustrate use of the periodic rate, suppose you make the following 8 quarterly payments of $100 each into an account which pays 12 percent, compounded quarterly. How much would you have after two years?

Time Line and Equation:

$$FVA_n = \sum_{t=1}^{n} PMT(1 + i)^{n-t} = \sum_{t=1}^{n} \$100(1.03)^{8-t}.$$

1. Numerical Solution:

Compound each $100 payment at $12/4 = 3$ percent for the appropriate number of periods, and then sum these individual FVs to find the FV of the payment stream, $889.23.

2. Tabular Solution:

Look up FVIFA for 3%, 8 periods, in Table A-4, and complete the arithmetic:

$$FVA_n = PMT(FVIFA_{i,n})$$
$$= \$100(FVIFA_{3\%/8}) = \$100(8.8923) = \$889.23.$$

---

[17]If an annuity is involved, and if its payment periods do not correspond to the compounding periods — for example, if you are making quarterly payments into a bank account to build up a specified future sum, but the bank pays interest on a daily basis — then the calculations are more complicated. For such problems, one can proceed in two alternative ways. (1) Determine the periodic (daily) interest rate by dividing the nominal rate by 360 (or 365 if the bank uses a 365-day year), then compound each payment over the exact number of days from the payment date to the terminal point, and then sum the compounded payments to find the future value of the annuity. This is what would generally be done in the real world. Using a computer, it would be a simple process. (2) Calculate the EAR based on daily compounding, then find the corresponding nominal rate based on quarterly compounding (because the annuity payments are made quarterly), then find the quarterly periodic rate, and then use that rate with standard annuity procedures. The second procedure is faster with a calculator, but hard to explain and generally not used in practice given the ready availability of computers.

3. Financial Calculator Solution:

Inputs: 8   3   0   −100

[N]   [I]   [PV]   [PMT]   [FV]

Output: = 889.23

Input N = 2 × 4 = 8, I = 12/4 = 3, PV = 0, and PMT = −100, and then press the FV key to get FV = $889.23.

3. **Effective (or equivalent) annual rate (EAR).** This is the annual rate which produces the same result as if we had compounded at a given periodic rate m times per year. The EAR is found as follows:

$$\text{EAR (or EFF\%)} = \left(1 + \frac{i_{\text{Nom}}}{m}\right)^m - 1.0. \qquad (6\text{-}8)$$

You could also use the interest conversion feature of a financial calculator.

In the EAR equation, i_{Nom}/m is the periodic rate, and m is the number of periods per year. For example, suppose you could borrow using either a credit card which charges 1 percent per month or a bank loan with a 12 percent quoted nominal interest rate that is compounded quarterly. Which should you choose? To answer this question, the cost rate of each alternative must be expressed as an EAR:

Credit card loan: EAR = $(1 + 0.01)^{12}$ − 1.0 = $(1.01)^{12}$ − 1.0

= 1.126825 − 1.0 = 0.126825 = 12.6825%.

Bank loan: EAR = $(1 + 0.03)^4$ − 1.0 = $(1.03)^4$ − 1.0

= 1.125509 − 1.0 = 0.125509 = 12.5509%.

Thus, the credit card loan is slightly more costly than the bank loan. This result should have been intuitive to you—both loans have the same 12 percent nominal rate, yet you would have to make monthly payments on the credit card versus quarterly payments under the bank loan.

The EAR rate generally is not used in calculations. Rather, it is used to compare the effective cost or rate of return on loans or investments when payment periods differ, as in the credit card versus bank loan example.

SELF-TEST QUESTIONS

Define the nominal (or quoted) rate, the periodic rate, and the effective annual rate.

How are the nominal rate, the periodic rate, and the effective annual rate related? What is the one situation where all three of these rates will be the same?

Which rate should generally be shown on time lines and used in calculations?

FRACTIONAL TIME PERIODS

In all of the examples used thus far in the chapter, we have assumed that payments occur at either the beginning or end of periods but not at some date *within* a period. However, we often encounter situations that require compounding or discounting over fractional periods. For example, suppose you deposited $100 in a bank that pays 10 percent interest, compounded annually. If you leave your money in the bank for 9 months, or 0.75 of the year, how much would you have in your account?

Time Line and Equation:

$$FV_n = PV(1 + i)^n.$$

1. Numerical Solution:

$$FV_n = \$100(1.10)^{0.75} = \$100(1.0741) = \$107.41.$$

2. Financial Calculator Solution:

Inputs: 0.75   10   −100   0

N   I   PV   PMT   FV

Output: = 107.41

Present values, annuities, and problems where you must find interest rates or numbers of periods can all be handled with ease. Note, though, that financial calculators are essential for many fractional year problems—the tables are useless.[18]

Why can't the tables be used if we have fractional time periods?

SELF-TEST
QUESTION

AMORTIZED LOANS

One of the most important applications of compound interest involves loans that are paid off in installments over time. Included are automobile loans, home mortgage loans, student loans, and most business debt other than very short-term loans and long-term bonds. If a loan is to be repaid in equal periodic amounts (monthly, quarterly, or annually), it is said to be an *amortized loan.*[19]

To illustrate, suppose a firm borrows \$1,000, and the loan is to be repaid in 3 equal payments at the end of each of the next 3 years. The lender is to receive 6 percent interest on the loan balance that is outstanding at the beginning of each year. The first task is to determine the amount the firm must repay each year, or the annual payment. To find this amount, recognize that the \$1,000

---

[18]An alternative (different) way to deal with this problem is to divide the interest rate expressed as a decimal by 360 (or 365), multiply by the number of days (0.75 × 360 or 365), and then multiply the result by the beginning amount to find the interest earned, \$7.50 in this case. Banks typically use this calculation to determine the interest on *loans* but not on deposits.

[19]The word *amortized* comes from the Latin *mors,* meaning "death," so an amortized loan is one that is "killed off" over time.

represents the present value of an annuity of PMT dollars per year for 3 years, discounted at 6 percent:

Time Line and Equation:

$$
\begin{array}{ccccccc}
0 & 6\% & 1 & & 2 & & 3 \\
\vdash & & \vdash & & \vdash & & \vdash \\
-1{,}000 & & \text{PMT} & & \text{PMT} & & \text{PMT}
\end{array}
$$

$$
PV = \frac{PMT}{(1+i)^1} + \frac{PMT}{(1+i)^2} + \frac{PMT}{(1+i)^3} = \sum_{t=1}^{3} \frac{PMT}{(1+i)^t}
$$

$$
\$1{,}000 = \sum_{t=1}^{n} \frac{PMT}{(1.06)^t}.
$$

Here we know everything except PMT, so we can solve the equation for PMT.

1. Numerical Solution:

You could follow the trial-and-error procedure, inserting values for PMT in the equation until you found a value that "worked" and caused the right side of the equation to equal $1,000. This would be a tedious process, but you would eventually find PMT = $374.11.

2. Tabular Solution:

Substitute in known values and look up PVIFA for 6%, 3 periods in Table A-2:

$$
PVA_n = PMT(PVIFA_{i,n})
$$

$$
\$1{,}000 = PMT(PVIFA_{6\%,3}) = PMT(2.6730)
$$

$$
PMT = \$1{,}000/2.6730 = \$374.11.
$$

3. Financial Calculator Solution:

$$
\begin{array}{cccccc}
\text{Inputs:} & 3 & 6 & -1000 & & 0 \\
& \boxed{N} & \boxed{I} & \boxed{PV} & \boxed{PMT} & \boxed{FV} \\
\text{Output:} & & & & = 374.11 &
\end{array}
$$

Enter N = 3, I = 6, PV = −1000, and FV = 0, and then press the PMT key to find PMT = $374.11.

Therefore, the firm must pay the lender $374.11 at the end of each of the next 3 years, and the percentage cost to the borrower, which is also the rate of return to the lender, will be 6 percent.

Each payment consists partly of interest and partly of repayment of principal. This breakdown is given in the *amortization schedule* shown in Table 6-2. The interest component is largest in the first year, and it declines as the outstanding balance of the loan decreases. For tax purposes, a business borrower reports the interest component shown in Column 3 as a deductible cost each year, while the lender reports this same amount as taxable income.

Financial calculators are programmed to calculate amortization tables — you simply enter the input data, and then press one key to get each entry in Table 6-2. If you have a financial calculator, it is worthwhile to read the appropriate section of the manual and learn how to use its amortization feature. With a spreadsheet such as *Excel* or *Lotus*, it is quite easy to set up and print out a full amortization schedule.

	BEGINNING AMOUNT	PAYMENT	INTEREST[a]	REPAYMENT OF PRINCIPAL[b]	REMAINING BALANCE
YEAR	**(1)**	**(2)**	**(3)**	**(2) − (3) = (4)**	**(1) − (4) = (5)**
1	$1,000.00	$374.11	$60.00	$314.11	$685.89
2	685.89	374.11	41.15	332.96	352.93
3	352.93	374.11	21.18	352.93	0.00
		$1,122.33	$122.33	$1,000.00	

LOAN AMORTIZATION SCHEDULE, 6 PERCENT INTEREST RATE   **TABLE 6-2**

[a]Interest is calculated by multiplying the loan balance at the beginning of the year by the interest rate. Therefore, interest in Year 1 is $1,000(0.06) = $60; in Year 2 it is $685.89(0.06) = $41.15; and in Year 3 it is $352.93(0.06) = $21.18.

[b]Repayment of principal is equal to the payment of $374.11 minus the interest charge for each year.

To construct an amortization schedule, how do you determine the amount of the periodic payments?

How do you determine the amount of each payment that goes to interest and to principal?

SELF-TEST QUESTIONS

SUMMARY

Financial decisions often involve situations in which someone pays money at one point in time and receives money at some later time. Dollars that are paid or received at two different points in time are different, and this difference is recognized and accounted for by *discounted cash flow (DCF) analysis*. We summarize below the types of DCF analysis and the key concepts covered in this chapter, using the data shown in Figure 6-3 to illustrate the various points. Refer to the figure constantly, and try to find in it an example of the points covered as you go through this summary.

ILLUSTRATION FOR CHAPTER SUMMARY (i = 4%)   **FIGURE 6-3**

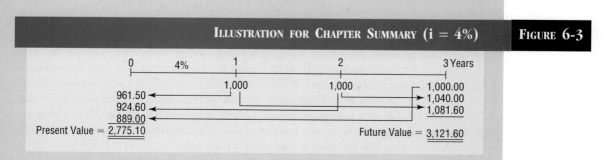

- *Compounding* is the process of determining the *future value (FV)* of a cash flow or a series of cash flows. The compounded amount, or future value, is equal to the beginning amount plus the interest earned.

- Future value: $FV_n = PV(1 + i)^n = PV(FVIF_{i,n})$.
  (single payment)
  Example: $961.50 compounded for 1 year at 4 percent:

$$FV_1 = \$961.50(1.04)^1 = \$1,000.$$

- *Discounting* is the process of finding the *present value (PV)* of a future cash flow or a series of cash flows. Discounting is the reciprocal of compounding.

- Present value: $PV = \dfrac{FV_n}{(1 + i)^n} = FV_n\left(\dfrac{1}{1 + i}\right)^n = FV_n(PVIF_{i,n})$.
  (single payment)

  Example: $1,000 discounted back for 2 years at 4 percent:

$$PV = \frac{\$1,000}{(1.04)^2} = \$1,000(\frac{1}{1.04})^2 = \$1,000(0.9246) = \$924.60.$$

- An *annuity* is defined as a series of equal periodic payments (PMT) for a specified number of periods.

- Future value: $FVA_n = PMT(1 + i)^0 + PMT(1 + i)^1 + PMT(1 + i)^2 + \ldots + PMT(1 + i)^{n-1}$
  (annuity)

$$= PMT \sum_{t=1}^{n} (1 + i)^{n-t} = PMT(FVIFA_{i,n}).$$

  Example: FVA of 3 payments of $1,000 when i = 4%. Enter N = 3, I = 4, PV = 0, and PMT = 1000, and then press FV to find FV = $3,121.60.

- Present value: $PVA_n = \dfrac{PMT}{(1 + i)^i} + \dfrac{PMT}{(1 + i)^2} + \ldots + \dfrac{PMT}{(1 + i)^n}$
  (annuity)

$$= PMT \sum_{t=1}^{n} \left[\frac{1}{1 + i}\right]^t = PMT(PVIFA_{i,n}).$$

  Example: PVA of 3 payments of $1,000 when i = 4%. Enter N = 3, I = 4, PMT = 1000, and FV = 0, and then press PV to find PV = $2,775.09.

- An annuity whose payments occur at the *end* of each period is called an *ordinary annuity.* The formulas above are for ordinary annuities.

- If each payment occurs at the beginning of the period rather than at the end, then we have an *annuity due.* In Figure 6-3, the payments would be shown at Years 0, 1, and 2 rather than at Years 1, 2, and 3. The PV of each payment would be larger because each payment would be discounted back one year less, hence the PV of the annuity would also be larger. Similarly, the FV of the annuity due would also be larger because each payment would be compounded for an extra year. The following formulas can be used to convert the PV and FV of an ordinary annuity to an annuity due:

PVA(annuity due) = PVA of an ordinary annuity $\times$ (1 + i).

FVA(annuity due) = FVA of an ordinary annuity $\times$ (1 + i).

Example: PVA of 3 beginning-of-year payments of $1,000 when i = 4%. Set calculator to "BEGIN," enter values as previously, and press PV to find the present value of the annuity due, PV = $2,886.09. The future value of this same annuity due is $3,246.46.

■ If the time line in Figure 6-3 were extended out forever so that the $1,000 payments went on forever, we would have a *perpetuity* whose value could be found as follows:

$$\text{Value of perpetuity} = \frac{\text{PMT}}{i} = \frac{\$1,000}{0.04} = \$25,000.$$

■ If the cash flows in Figure 6-3 were unequal, we could not use the annuity formulas. To find the PV or FV of an uneven series, find the PV or FV of each individual cash flow and then sum them. However, if some of the cash flows constitute an annuity, then the annuity formula can be used to calculate the present value of that part of the cash flow stream.

■ *Financial calculators* and *computer financial software* have built-in functions which perform all of the operations discussed in this chapter. It would be useful for you to buy such a calculator and to learn how to use it, as well as to learn how to use computer financial software, especially spreadsheet programs. Even with calculators and spreadsheets, though, it is essential that you understand the logical processes involved.

■ DCF calculations generally involve equations which have four variables, so if you know three of the values, you (or your calculator) can solve for the fourth.

■ If you know the cash flows and the PV (or FV) of a cash flow stream, you can *determine the interest rate.* For example, in the Figure 6-3 illustration, if you were given the information that a loan called for 3 payments of $1,000 each, and that the loan had a value today of PV = $2,775.10, then you could find the interest rate that caused the sum of the PVs of the payments to equal $2,775.10. Since we are dealing with an annuity, we could proceed as follows:

a. Set your calculator back to "END" mode, as we are dealing with an ordinary annuity.

b. Enter N = 3, PV = −2775.10, PMT = 1000, and FV = 0. Then press I to find I = 4.00%.

■ Thus far in the summary we have assumed that payments are made, and interest is earned, at the end of each year, or annually. However, many contracts call for more frequent payments; for example, mortgage and auto loans call for monthly payments, and most bonds pay interest semiannually. Similarly, most banks compute interest daily. When compounding occurs more frequently than once a year, this fact must be recognized. We can use the Figure 6-3 example to illustrate the procedures. First, the following formula is used to find an *effective annual rate (EAR)* or EFF%:

$$\text{Effective annual rate} = \text{EAR or EFF\%} = \left(1 + \frac{i_{Nom}}{m}\right)^m - 1.0.$$

For semiannual compounding, the effective annual rate is 4.04 percent:

$$\left(1 + \frac{0.04}{2}\right)^2 - 1.0 = (1.02)^2 - 1.0 = 1.0404 - 1.0 = 0.0404 = 4.04\%.$$

■ This rate would be used in comparisons among loans or investments, but not for doing calculations. If the $1,000 per-year payments were actually payable as $500 each 6 months, you would simply redraw Figure 6-3 to show 6 payments of $500 each, but you would also need to use a *periodic interest rate* of 4%/2 = 2% for determining the PV or FV of the payments.

■ The general equation for finding the future value of a lump sum for any number of compounding periods per year is:

$$FV_n = PV\left(1 + \frac{i_{Nom}}{m}\right)^{mn},$$

where

i_{Nom} = quoted interest rate.

   m = number of compounding periods per year.

   n = number of years.

If you were composing rates of return on securities which had different payment periods, you should compare their EARs.

■ An *amortized loan* is one that is paid off in equal payments over a specified period. An *amortization schedule* shows how much of each payment constitutes interest, how much is used to reduce the principal, and the remaining balance of the loan at each point in time.

The concepts covered in this chapter will be used throughout the remainder of the book. For example, in Chapter 7 we will apply DCF concepts to the process of valuing stocks and bonds, and we will see that the market prices of securities are established by determining the present values of the cash flows they are expected to provide. In later chapters, the same basic concepts are applied to corporate decisions involving both expenditures on capital assets and determining the types of capital that should be used to pay for assets.

6-1 Define each of the following terms:
   a. PV; i; INT; FV_n; PVA_n; FVA_n; PMT; m; i_{Nom}
   b. $FVIF_{i,n}$; $PVIF_{i,n}$; $FVIFA_{i,n}$; $PVIFA_{i,n}$
   c. Opportunity cost rate
   d. Annuity; lump sum payment; cash flow; uneven cash flow stream
   e. Ordinary (deferred) annuity; annuity due
   f. Perpetuity; consol
   g. Outflow; inflow; time line
   h. Compounding; discounting
   i. Annual, semiannual, quarterly, monthly, and daily compounding
   j. Effective annual rate (EAR); nominal (quoted) interest rate; APR; periodic rate
   k. Amortization schedule; principal component versus interest component of a payment; amortized loan
   l. Terminal value

6-2 What is an *opportunity cost rate?* How is this rate used in discounted cash flow analysis, and where is it shown on a time line? Is the opportunity rate a single number which is used in all situations?

6-3 An *annuity* is defined as a series of payments of a fixed amount for a specific number of periods. Thus, $100 a year for 10 years is an annuity, but $100 in Year 1, $200 in Year 2, and $400 in Years 3 through 10 does *not* constitute an annuity. However, the second series *contains* an annuity. Is this statement true or false?

6-4 If a firm's earnings per share grew from $1 to $2 over a 10-year period, the *total growth* would be 100 percent, but the *annual growth rate* would be *less than* 10 percent. True or false? Explain.

6-5 Would you rather have a savings account that pays 5 percent interest compounded semiannually or one that pays 5 percent interest compounded daily? Explain.

6-6 To find the present value of an uneven series of cash flows, you must find the PVs of the individual cash flows and then sum them. Annuity procedures can never be of use, even if some of the cash flows constitute an annuity (for example, $100 each for Years 3, 4, 5, and 6), because the entire series is not an annuity. Is this statement true or false? Explain.

6-7 The present value of a perpetuity is equal to the payment on the annuity, PMT, divided by the interest rate, i: PV = PMT/i. What is the *sum*, or future value, of a perpetuity of PMT dollars per year? (Hint: The answer is infinity, but explain why.)

SELF-TEST PROBLEMS

(SOLUTIONS APPEAR IN APPENDIX C)

ST-1   **FUTURE VALUE**   Assume that it is now January 1, 1997.   On January 1, 1998, you will deposit $1,000 into a savings account that pays 8 percent.

    a. If the bank compounds interest annually, how much will you have in your account on January 1, 2001?

    b. What would your January 1, 2001, balance be if the bank used quarterly compounding rather than annual compounding?

    c. Suppose you deposited the $1,000 in 4 payments of $250 each on January 1 of 1998, 1999, 2000, and 2001. How much would you have in your account on January 1, 2001, based on 8 percent annual compounding?

    d. Suppose you deposited 4 equal payments in your account on January 1 of 1998, 1999, 2000, and 2001. Assuming an 8 percent interest rate, how large would each of your payments have to be for you to obtain the same ending balance as you calculated in Part a?

ST-2   **TIME VALUE OF MONEY**   Assume that it is now January 1, 1997, and you will need $1,000 on January 1, 2001. Your bank compounds interest at an 8 percent annual rate.

    a. How much must you deposit on January 1, 1998, to have a balance of $1,000 on January 1, 2001?

    b. If you want to make equal payments on each January 1 from 1998 through 2001 to accumulate the $1,000, how large must each of the 4 payments be?

    c. If your father were to offer either to make the payments calculated in Part b ($221.92) or to give you a lump sum of $750 on January 1, 1998, which would you choose?

    d. If you have only $750 on January 1, 1998, what interest rate, compounded annually, would you have to earn to have the necessary $1,000 on January 1, 2001?

    e. Suppose you can deposit only $186.29 each January 1 from 1998 through 2001, but you still need $1,000 on January 1, 2001. What interest rate, with annual compounding, must you seek out to achieve your goal?

    f. To help you reach your $1,000 goal, your father offers to give you $400 on January 1, 1998. You will get a part-time job and make 6 additional payments of equal amounts each 6 months thereafter. If all of this money is deposited in a bank which pays 8 percent, compounded semiannually, how large must each of the 6 payments be?

    g. What is the effective annual rate being paid by the bank in Part f?

    h. *Reinvestment rate risk* was defined in Chapter 3 as being the risk that maturing securities (and coupon payments on bonds) will have to be reinvested at a lower rate of interest than they were previously earning. Is there a reinvestment rate risk involved in the preceding analysis? If so, how might this risk be eliminated?

ST-3   **EFFECTIVE ANNUAL RATES**   Bank A pays 8 percent interest, compounded quarterly, on its money market account. The managers of Bank B want its money market account to equal Bank A's effective annual rate, but interest is to be compounded on a monthly basis. What nominal, or quoted, rate must Bank B set?

6-1 **PRESENT AND FUTURE VALUES FOR DIFFERENT PERIODS** Find the following values, *using the equations,* and then work the problems using a financial calculator or the tables to check your answers. Disregard rounding differences. (Hint: If you are using a financial calculator, you can enter the known values and then press the appropriate key to find the unknown variable. Then, without clearing the TVM register, you can "override" the variable which changes by simply entering a new value for it and then pressing the key for the unknown variable to obtain the second answer. This procedure can be used in Parts b and d, and in many other situations, to see how changes in input variables affect the output variable.)

a. An initial $500 compounded for 1 year at 6 percent.

b. An initial $500 compounded for 2 years at 6 percent.

c. The present value of $500 due in 1 year at a discount rate of 6 percent.

d. The present value of $500 due in 2 years at a discount rate of 6 percent.

6-2 **PRESENT AND FUTURE VALUES FOR DIFFERENT INTEREST RATES** Use the tables or a financial calculator to find the following values. See the hint for Problem 6-1.

a. An initial $500 compounded for 10 years at 6 percent.

b. An initial $500 compounded for 10 years at 12 percent.

c. The present value of $500 due in 10 years at a 6 percent discount rate.

d. The present value of $1,552.90 due in 10 years at a 12 percent discount rate and at a 6 percent rate. Give a verbal definition of the term *present value,* and illustrate it using a time line with data from this problem. As a part of your answer, explain why present values are dependent upon interest rates.

6-3 **TIME FOR A LUMP SUM TO DOUBLE** To the closest year, how long will it take $200 to double if it is deposited and earns the following rates? [Notes: (1) See the hint for Problem 6-1. (2) This problem cannot be solved exactly with some financial calculators. For example, if you enter PV = −200, PMT = 0, FV = 400, and I = 7 in an HP-12C, and then press the N key, you will get 11 years for Part a. The correct answer is 10.2448 years, which rounds to 10, but the calculator rounds up. However, the HP-10B and HP-17B give the correct answer. You should look up FVIF = 400/200 = 2 in the tables for Parts a, b, and c, but figure out Part d.]

a. 7 percent.

b. 10 percent.

c. 18 percent.

d. 100 percent.

6-4 **FUTURE VALUE OF AN ANNUITY** Find the *future value* of the following annuities. The first payment in these annuities is made at the *end* of Year 1; that is, they are *ordinary annuities.* (Note: See the hint to Problem 6-1. Also, note that you can leave values in the TVM register, switch to "BEG," press FV, and find the FV of the annuity due.)

a. $400 per year for 10 years at 10 percent.

b. $200 per year for 5 years at 5 percent.

c. $400 per year for 5 years at 0 percent.

d. Now rework Parts a, b, and c assuming that payments are made at the *beginning* of each year; that is, they are *annuities due.*

6-5   PRESENT VALUE OF AN ANNUITY Find the *present value* of the following *ordinary annuities* (see note to Problem 6-4.):

a. $400 per year for 10 years at 10 percent.

b. $200 per year for 5 years at 5 percent.

c. $400 per year for 5 years at 0 percent.

d. Now rework Parts a, b, and c assuming that payments are made at the *beginning* of each year; that is, they are *annuities due.*

6-6   UNEVEN CASH FLOW STREAM

a. Find the present values of the following cash flow streams. The appropriate interest rate is 8 percent. (Hint: It is fairly easy to work this problem dealing with the individual cash flows. However, if you have a financial calculator, read the section of the manual which describes how to enter cash flows such as the ones in this problem. This will take a little time, but the investment will pay huge dividends throughout the course. Note, if you do work with the cash flow register, then you must enter $CF_0 = 0$.)

YEAR	CASH STREAM A	CASH STREAM B
1	$100	$300
2	400	400
3	400	400
4	400	400
5	300	100

b. What is the value of each cash flow stream at a 0 percent interest rate?

6-7   EFFECTIVE RATE OF INTEREST Find the interest rates, or rates of return, on each of the following:

a. You *borrow* $700 and promise to pay back $749 at the end of 1 year.

b. You *lend* $700 and receive a promise to be paid $749 at the end of 1 year.

c. You borrow $85,000 and promise to pay back $201,229 at the end of 10 years.

d. You borrow $9,000 and promise to make payments of $2,684.80 per year for 5 years.

6-8   FUTURE VALUE FOR VARIOUS COMPOUNDING PERIODS Find the amount to which $500 will grow under each of the following conditions:

a. 12 percent compounded annually for 5 years.

b. 12 percent compounded semiannually for 5 years.

c. 12 percent compounded quarterly for 5 years.

d. 12 percent compounded monthly for 5 years.

6-9   PRESENT VALUE FOR VARIOUS COMPOUNDING PERIODS Find the present value of $500 due in the future under each of the following conditions:

a. 12 percent nominal rate, semiannual compounding, discounted back 5 years.

b. 12 percent nominal rate, quarterly compounding, discounted back 5 years.

c. 12 percent nominal rate, monthly compounding, discounted back 1 year.

6-10   FUTURE VALUE OF AN ANNUITY FOR VARIOUS COMPOUNDING PERIODS Find the future values of the following ordinary annuities:

a. FV of $400 each 6 months for 5 years at a nominal rate of 12 percent, compounded semiannually.

b. FV of $200 each 3 months for 5 years at a nominal rate of 12 percent, compounded quarterly.

c. The annuities described in Parts a and b have the same amount of money paid into them during the 5-year period and both earn interest at the same nominal rate, yet the annuity in Part b earns $101.60 more than the one in Part a over the 5 years. Why does this occur?

-11   **EFFECTIVE VERSUS NOMINAL INTEREST RATES** Universal Bank pays 7 percent interest, compounded annually, on time deposits. Regional Bank pays 6 percent interest, compounded quarterly.

a. Based on effective interest rates, in which bank would you prefer to deposit your money?

b. Could your choice of banks be influenced by the fact that you might want to withdraw your funds during the year as opposed to at the end of the year? In answering this question, assume that funds must be left on deposit during the entire compounding period in order for you to receive any interest.

-12   **AMORTIZATION SCHEDULE**

a. Set up an amortization schedule for a $25,000 loan to be repaid in equal installments at the end of each of the next 5 years. The interest rate is 10 percent.

b. How large must each annual payment be if the loan is for $50,000? Assume that the interest rate remains at 10 percent and that the loan is paid off over 5 years.

c. How large must each payment be if the loan is for $50,000, the interest rate is 10 percent, and the loan is paid off in equal installments at the end of each of the next 10 years? This loan is for the same amount as the loan in Part b, but the payments are spread out over twice as many periods. Why are these payments not half as large as the payments on the loan in Part b?

-13   **EFFECTIVE RATES OF RETURN** Assume that AT&T's pension fund managers are considering two alternative securities as investments: (1) Security Z (for zero intermediate-year cash flows), which costs $422.41 today, pays nothing during its 10-year life, and then pays $1,000 after 10 years or (2) Security B, which has a cost today of $1,000 and which pays $80 at the end of each of the next 9 years and then $1,080 at the end of Year 10.

a. What is the rate of return on each security?

b. Assume that the interest rate AT&T's pension fund managers can earn on the fund's money falls to 6 percent immediately after the securities are purchased and is expected to remain at that level for the next 10 years. What would the price of each security change to, what would the fund's profit be on each security, and what would be the percentage profit (profit divided by cost) for each security?

c. Assuming that the cash flows for each security had to be reinvested at the new 6 percent market interest rate, (1) what would be the value attributable to each security at the end of 10 years and (2) what "actual, after-the-fact" rate of return would the fund have earned on each security? (Hint: The "actual" rate of return is found as the interest rate which causes the PV of the compounded Year 10 amount to equal the original cost of the security.)

d. Now assume all the facts as given in Parts b and c except assume that the interest rate *rose* to 12 percent rather than fell to 6 percent. What would happen to the profit figures as developed in Part b and to the "actual" rates of return as determined in Part c? Explain your results.

-14   **REQUIRED ANNUITY PAYMENTS** A father is planning a savings program to put his daughter through college. His daughter is now 13 years old. She plans to enroll at the university in 5 years, and it should take her 4 years to complete her education. Currently, the cost per year (for everything — food, clothing, tuition, books, transportation, and so forth) is $12,500, but a 5 percent inflation rate in these costs is forecasted. The daughter recently received $7,500 from her grandfather's estate; this money, which is invested in a bank account paying 8 percent interest compounded annually, will be used to help meet the costs of the daughter's education. The rest of the costs will be met by money the father will deposit in the savings account. He will make 6 equal deposits to the account — one in each year from now until his daughter starts college. These deposits will begin today and will also earn 8 percent interest.

a. What will be the present value of the cost of four years of education at the time the daughter becomes 18? [Hint: Calculate the future value of the cost (at 5%) for each year of her education, then discount three of these costs back (at 8%) to the year in which she turns 18, then sum the four costs.]

b. What will be the value of the $7,500 which the daughter received from her grandfather's estate when she starts college at age 18? (Hint: Compound for 5 years at 8%.)

c. If the father is planning to make the first of 6 deposits today, how large must each deposit be for him to be able to put his daughter through college?

6-15   **PRESENT VALUE COMPARISON**   Which amount is worth more at 14 percent: $1,000 in hand today or $2,000 due in 6 years?

6-16   **GROWTH RATES**   Hanebury Corporation's 1996 sales were $12 million. Sales were $6 million 5 years earlier (in 1991).

a. To the nearest percentage point, at what rate have sales been growing?

b. Suppose someone calculated the sales growth for Hanebury Corporation in Part a as follows: "Sales doubled in 5 years. This represents a growth of 100 percent in 5 years, so, dividing 100 percent by 5, we find the growth rate to be 20 percent per year." Explain what is wrong with this calculation.

6-17   **EXPECTED RATE OF RETURN**   Washington-Pacific invests $4 million to clear a tract of land and to set out some young pine trees. The trees will mature in 10 years, at which time Washington-Pacific plans to sell the forest at an expected price of $8 million. What is Washington-Pacific's expected rate of return?

6-18   **EFFECTIVE RATE OF INTEREST**   Your broker offers to sell you a note for $13,250 that will pay $2,345.05 per year for 10 years. If you buy the note, what rate of interest (to the closest percent) will you be earning?

6-19   **EFFECTIVE RATE OF INTEREST**   A mortgage company offers to lend you $85,000; the loan calls for payments of $8,273.59 per year for 30 years. What interest rate is the mortgage company charging you?

6-20   **REQUIRED LUMP SUM PAYMENT**   To complete your last year in business school and then go through law school, you will need $10,000 per year for 4 years, starting next year (that is, you will need to withdraw the first $10,000 one year from today). Your rich uncle offers to put you through school, and he will deposit in a bank paying 7 percent interest a sum of money that is sufficient to provide the four payments of $10,000 each. His deposit will be made today.

a. How large must the deposit be?

b. How much will be in the account immediately after you make the first withdrawal? After the last withdrawal?

6-21   **REPAYING A LOAN**   While Mary Corens was a student at the University of Florida, she borrowed $12,000 in student loans at an annual interest rate of 9 percent. If Mary repays $1,500 per year, how long, to the nearest year, will it take her to repay the loan?

6-22   **REACHING A FINANCIAL GOAL**   You need to accumulate $10,000. To do so, you plan to make deposits of $1,250 per year, with the first payment being made a year from today, in a bank account which pays 12 percent annual interest. Your last deposit will be less than $1,250 if less is needed to round out to $10,000. How many years will it take you to reach your $10,000 goal, and how large will the last deposit be?

6-23   **PRESENT VALUE OF A PERPETUITY**   What is the present value of a perpetuity of $100 per year if the appropriate discount rate is 7 percent? If interest rates in general were to double and the appropriate discount rate rose to 14 percent, what would happen to the present value of the perpetuity?

-24 **PV AND EFFECTIVE ANNUAL RATE** Assume that you inherited some money. A friend of yours is working as an unpaid intern at a local brokerage firm, and her boss is selling some securities which call for four payments, $50 at the end of each of the next 3 years, plus a payment of $1,050 at the end of Year 4. Your friend says she can get you some of these securities at a cost of $900 each. Your money is now invested in a bank that pays an 8 percent nominal (quoted) interest rate but with quarterly compounding. You regard the securities as being just as safe, and as liquid, as your bank deposit, so your required effective annual rate of return on the securities is the same as that on your bank deposit. You must calculate the value of the securities to decide whether they are a good investment. What is their present value to you?

-25 **LOAN AMORTIZATION** Assume that your aunt sold her house on December 31 and that she took a mortgage in the amount of $10,000 as part of the payment. The mortgage has a quoted (or nominal) interest rate of 10 percent, but it calls for payments every 6 months, beginning on June 30, and the mortgage is to be amortized over 10 years. Now, one year later, your aunt must inform the IRS and the person who bought the house of the interest that was included in the two payments made during the year. (This interest will be income to your aunt and a deduction to the buyer of the house.) To the closest dollar, what is the total amount of interest that was paid during the first year?

-26 **LOAN AMORTIZATION** Your company is planning to borrow $1,000,000 on a 5-year, 15%, annual payment, fully amortized term loan. What fraction of the payment made at the end of the second year will represent repayment of principal?

-27 **NONANNUAL COMPOUNDING**

a. It is now January 1, 1997. You plan to make 5 deposits of $100 each, one every 6 months, with the first payment being made *today*. If the bank pays a nominal interest rate of 12 percent but uses semiannual compounding, how much will be in your account after 10 years?

b. You must make a payment of $1,432.02 ten years from today. To prepare for this payment, you will make 5 equal deposits, beginning today and for the next 4 quarters, in a bank that pays a nominal interest rate of 12 percent, quarterly compounding. How large must each of the 5 payments be?

-28 **NOMINAL RATE OF RETURN** Anne Lockwood, manager of Oaks Mall Jewelry, wants to sell on credit, giving customers 3 months in which to pay. However, Anne will have to borrow from her bank to carry the accounts payable. The bank will charge a nominal 15 percent, but with monthly compounding. Anne wants to quote a nominal rate to her customers (all of whom are expected to pay on time) which will exactly cover her financing costs. What nominal annual rate should she quote to her credit customers?

-29 **REQUIRED ANNUITY PAYMENTS** Assume that your father is now 50 years old, that he plans to retire in 10 years, and that he expects to live for 25 years after he retires, that is, until he is 85. He wants a fixed retirement income that has the same purchasing power at the time he retires as $40,000 has today (he realizes that the real value of his retirement income will decline year by year after he retires). His retirement income will begin the day he retires, 10 years from today, and he will then get 24 additional annual payments. Inflation is expected to be 5 percent per year from today forward; he currently has $100,000 saved up; and he expects to earn a return on his savings of 8 percent per year, annual compounding. To the nearest dollar, how much must he save during each of the next 10 years (with deposits being made at the end of each year) to meet his retirement goal?

SPREADSHEET APPLICATIONS

SPREADSHEET PROBLEM

Set up an amortization schedule for a $30,000 loan to be repaid in equal installments at the end of each of the next 20 years at an interest rate of 10 percent.

a. What is the annual payment?

b. Set up an amortization schedule for a $60,000 loan to be repaid in 20 equal annual install-ments at an interest rate of 10 percent. What is the annual payment?

c. Set up an amortization schedule for a $60,000 loan to be repaid in 20 equal annual install-ments at an interest rate of 20 percent. What is the annual payment?

MINI CASE

Assume that you are nearing graduation and that you have applied for a job with a local bank. As part of the bank's evaluation process, you have been asked to take an examination which covers several financial analysis techniques. The first section of the test addresses discounted cash flow analysis. See how you would do by answering the following questions.

a. Draw time lines for (a) a $100 lump sum cash flow at the end of Year 2, (b) an ordinary annuity of $100 per year for 3 years, and (c) an uneven cash flow stream of −$50, $100, $75, and $50 at the end of Years 0 through 3.

b. (1) What is the future value of an initial $100 after 3 years if it is invested in an account paying 10 percent annual interest?

(2) What is the present value of $100 to be received in 3 years if the appropriate interest rate is 10 percent?

c. We sometimes need to find how long it will take a sum of money (or anything else) to grow to some specified amount. For example, if a company's sales are growing at a rate of 20 percent per year, how long will it take sales to double?

d. What is the difference between an ordinary annuity and an annuity due? What type of annuity is shown below? How would you change it to the other type of annuity?

e. (1) What is the future value of a 3-year ordinary annuity of $100 if the appropriate inter-est rate is 10 percent?

(2) What is the present value of the annuity?

(3) What would the future and present values be if the annuity were an annuity due?

f. What is the present value of the following uneven cash flow stream? The appropriate inter-est rate is 10 percent, compounded annually.

g. What annual interest rate will cause $100 to grow to $125.97 in 3 years?

h. (1)Will the future value be larger or smaller if we compound an initial amount more often than annually, for example, every 6 months, or *semiannually,* holding the stated interest rate constant? Why?

   (2) Define (a) the stated, or quoted, or nominal rate (i_{Nom}), (b) the periodic rate (i_{Per}), and (c) the effective annual rate (EAR).

   (3) What is the effective annual rate for a nominal rate of 10 percent, compounded semiannually? Compounded quarterly? Compounded daily?

   (4) What is the future value of $100 after 3 years under 10 percent semiannual compounding? Quarterly compounding?

i. Will the effective annual rate ever be equal to the nominal (quoted) rate?

j. (1)What is the value at the end of Year 3 of the following cash flow stream if the quoted interest rate is 10 percent, compounded semiannually?

   (2) What is the PV of the same stream?

   (3) Is the stream an annuity?

   (4) An important rule is that you should *never* show a nominal rate on a time line or use it in calculations unless what condition holds? (Hint: Think of annual compounding, when i_{Nom} = EAR = i_{Per}.) What would be wrong with your answer to questions j (1) and j (2) if you used the nominal rate (10%) rather than the periodic rate ($i_{Nom}/2$ = 10%/2 = 5%)?

k. (1)Construct an amortization schedule for a $1,000, 10 percent annual rate loan with 3 equal installments.

   (2) What is the annual interest expense for the borrower, and the annual interest income for the lender, during Year 2?

l. Suppose on January 1, 1997, you deposit $100 in an account that pays a nominal, or quoted, interest rate of 11.33463 percent, with interest added (compounded) daily. How much will you have in your account on October 1, or after 9 months?

m. Now suppose you leave your money in the bank for 21 months. Thus, on January 1, 1997, you deposit $100 in an account that pays a 12 percent effective annual interest rate. How much will be in your account on October 1, 1998?

n. Suppose someone offered to sell you a note calling for the payment of $1,000 fifteen months from today. They offer to sell it to you for $850. You have $850 in a bank time deposit which pays a 6.76649 percent nominal rate with daily compounding, which is a 7 percent effective annual interest rate, and you plan to leave the money in the bank unless you buy the note. The note is not risky — you are sure it will be paid on schedule. Should you buy the note? Check the decision in three ways: (1) by comparing your future value if you buy the note versus leaving your money in the bank, (2) by comparing the PV of the note with your current bank account, and (3) by comparing the EAR on the note versus that of the bank account.

o. Suppose the note discussed in Part n had a cost of $850, but called for 5 quarterly payments of $190 each, with the first payment due in 3 months rather than $1,000 at the end of 15 months. Would it be a good investment for you?

SELECTED ADDITIONAL REFERENCES

For a more complete discussion of the mathematics of finance, see

Atkins, Allen B., and Edward A. Dyl, "The Lotto Jackpot: The Lump Sum versus the Annuity," *Financial Practice and Education*, Fall/Winter 1995, 107–111.

Cissell, Robert, Helen Cissell, and David C. Flaspohler, *Mathematics of Finance* (Boston: Houghton Mifflin, 1978).

Lindley, James T., "Compounding Issues Revisited," *Financial Practice and Education*, Fall 1993, 127–129.

To learn more about using financial calculators, see the manual which came with your calculator. For example, see

Hewlett-Packard, *HP-10B Business Calculator Owner's Manual*, June 1990.

White, Mark A., *Financial Analysis with an Electronic Calculator*, 2nd edition (Chicago: Irwin, 1995).

———, "Financial Problem Solving with an Electronic Calculator: Texas Instruments' BA II Plus," *Financial Practice and Education*, Fall 1993, 123–126.

APPENDIX 6A

CONTINUOUS COMPOUNDING AND DISCOUNTING

In Chapter 6, we dealt only with situations where interest is added at discrete intervals — annually, semiannually, monthly, and so forth. In some instances, though, it is possible to have instantaneous, or *continuous,* growth. In this appendix, we discuss present value and future value calculations when the interest rate is compounded continuously.

CONTINUOUS COMPOUNDING The relationship between discrete and *continuous compounding* is illustrated in Figure 6A-1. Panel a shows the annual compounding case, where interest is added once a year; Panel b shows the situation when compounding occurs twice a year; and Panel c shows interest being earned continuously. As the graphs show, the more frequent the compounding period, the larger the final compounded amount because interest is earned on interest more often.

Equation 6-9 in the chapter can be applied to any number of compounding periods per year:

$$\text{More frequent compounding: } FV_n = PV \left(1 + \frac{i_{Nom}}{m}\right)^{mn}. \tag{6-9}$$

To illustrate, let PV = $100, i = 10%, and n = 5. At various compounding periods per year, we obtain the following future values at the end of 5 years:

$$\text{Annual: } FV_5 = \$100 \left(1 + \frac{0.10}{1}\right)^{1(5)} = \$100(1.10)^5 = \$161.05.$$

$$\text{Semiannual: } FV_5 = \$100 \left(1 + \frac{0.10}{2}\right)^{2(5)} = \$100(1.05)^{10} = \$162.89.$$

$$\text{Monthly: } FV_5 = \$100 \left(1 + \frac{0.10}{12}\right)^{12(5)} = \$100(1.0083)^{60} = \$164.53.$$

$$\text{Daily: } FV_5 = \$100 \left(1 + \frac{0.10}{365}\right)^{365(5)} = \$100(1.00027)^{1825} = \$164.86.$$

We could keep going, compounding every hour, every minute, every second, and so on. At the limit, we could compound every instant, or *continuously*. The equation for continuous compounding is

$$FV_n = PV(e^{in}). \qquad \text{6A-1}$$

Here e is the value 2.7183. . . .[1] If $100 is invested for 5 years at 10 percent compounded continuously, then FV_5 is calculated as follows:

$$\text{Continuous: } FV_5 = \$100[e^{0.10(5)}] = \$100(2.7183...)^{0.5}$$
$$= \$164.872.$$

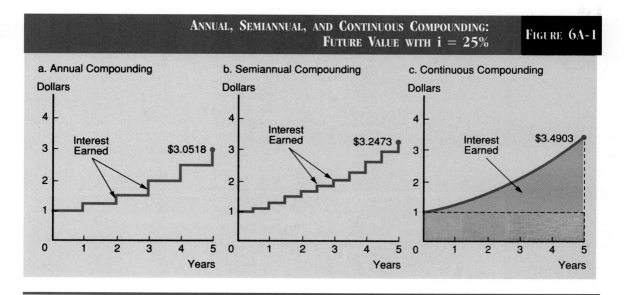

ANNUAL, SEMIANNUAL, AND CONTINUOUS COMPOUNDING: FUTURE VALUE WITH i = 25% **FIGURE 6A-1**

a. Annual Compounding — Interest Earned — $3.0518

b. Semiannual Compounding — Interest Earned — $3.2473

c. Continuous Compounding — Interest Earned — $3.4903

---

[1]Calculators with exponential functions can be used to evaluate Equation 6A-1.

CONTINUOUS DISCOUNTING Equation 6A-1 can be transformed into Equation 6A-2 and used to determine present values under continuous discounting:

$$PV = \frac{FV_n}{e^{in}} = FV_n(e^{-in}).$$

6A-2

Thus, if \$1,649 is due in 10 years, and if the appropriate *continuous* discount rate, i, is 5 percent, then the present value of this future payment is

$$PV = \frac{\$1,649}{(2.7183...)^{0.5}} = \frac{\$1,649}{1.649} = \$1,000.$$

CHAPTER 7

VALUATION MODELS

*I*nterest rates plunged in 1993, and borrowers scrambled to lock in low rates by selling long-term bonds. The longest maturity on corporate bonds had been 40 years — investors were unwilling to bet that companies would be around for longer than that. However, a large pension fund, concerned because declining interest rates had reduced its interest income, wanted to protect itself against further interest rate declines by putting some very long term bonds into its portfolio. The fund approached Morgan Stanley, a leading investment bank, to find out if any of its client companies were interested in issuing 100-year bonds. Morgan Stanley immediately began calling clients who might want to issue such bonds, and within a week, Disney agreed to a $150 million deal at an interest rate of 7.5 percent. Buyers clamored for the bonds, and the offering "flew out the window."

Although Disney's bonds sold well, not all portfolio managers liked them. For example, Glenn Murphy, chief investment officer of Travelers Asset Management, argued that the Disney issue would just be "an historic artifact, a curiosity." And according to William Gross, head of Pacific Investment Management, "It's crazy. Look at the path of Coney Island over the past 50 years to see what can happen to amusement parks." Other analysts noted that even if Disney continues to do well and pays the interest as it comes due, the 100-year bonds would still produce headaches for investors if interest rates rose. Indeed, interest rates did rise just after the bonds were placed, and the 1994 return on these supposedly safe bonds was minus 20 percent.

If Disney's bonds promised a return of 7.5 percent but are exposed to some risk, what about its stock? A $1,000 investment in Disney's stock in 1970 would have grown to more than $40,000 by 1996. That may sound good, but the same $1,000 invested in Wal-Mart's stock would now be worth more than $500,000! However, as any seasoned investor could tell you, stocks can fall just as fast as *they rise. For example, when the October 19, 1987, stock crash occurred, Disney's stock price was sliced in half in just one day.*

All boats may rise and fall with the tide, but the same does not hold for stocks — regardless of the trend in the market, some individual stocks always make huge gains, while others experience terrible losses. For example, the Dow Jones Industrial Average rose by more than 30 percent in 1995. However, during that year U.S. Air gained 212 percent, while L.A. Gear lost 68 percent.

Some stock price movements are easy to understand, but others appear irrational. However, on closer inspection, most price changes can be explained by events at the individual companies or in the economy. After studying this chapter, you should have a good understanding of how bond and stock prices are determined. This knowledge should help you make better personal investment decisions and better business decisions with regard to a firm's choice of securities for use in financing.

In Chapter 1 we noted that the primary goal of financial managers is to maximize the values of their firms' stocks. Then, in Chapter 4, we saw how investors determine the rates of return they require on securities, and in Chapter 6 we examined discounted cash flow (DCF) analysis. Now we use DCF concepts to explain how investors establish the values of stocks and bonds. This is obviously important to investors, and it is equally important to financial managers. *Indeed, since all important corporate decisions should be analyzed in terms of how they will affect the price of the firm's stock, it is essential that managers know how stock prices are determined.*

Direct Claim Securities versus Derivatives

Securities are pieces of paper that represent claims against assets such as land, plant and equipment, commodities, or other securities. There are two basic types of securities: (1) *direct claim securities,* such as bonds and stocks, which have claims against the cash flows produced by real assets, hence values tied directly to those real assets, and (2) *indirect claim, or derivative, securities* such as options and futures whose values are derived from the value of some other asset. For example, the value of IBM's stock is based on the cash flows produced by IBM's assets, and IBM as a corporation backs the stock. A call option on IBM's stock, however, is not an obligation of IBM; rather, it is a contract between the party who wrote the option and the one who purchased it, which gives the holder the right (but not the obligation) to buy a specific amount of IBM stock at a specified price during a specified time period. The value of this option depends on the price of IBM's stock — if IBM's stock goes up, the option is worth more, while if it goes down, the option is worth less.

Stocks, bonds, and most other direct claim securities are valued using discounted cash flow techniques as discussed in Chapter 6. Options, futures, and other derivatives, on the other hand, have values which are based on the current price of the underlying asset and other factors that are not related directly to future cash flows. For example, a call option is more valuable if it has a long time before expiration, because then there is a higher probability that the price of the underlying asset will rise well above the exercise price. Similarly, call options are more valuable if the price of the underlying security fluctuates widely — since the holder will not exercise the option if the price falls below the exercise price but will exercise it if the price rises sharply, there is limited downside risk but unlimited upside potential, and this asymmetry causes the option to be more valuable the greater the uncertainty about the future value of the underlying security.

To understand derivatives, one must have an understanding of how the values of underlying securities are determined. Therefore, this chapter and most of those that follow focus on stocks, bonds, and real assets. Then, with this background, Chapter 23 explains how derivatives are valued and used both as speculative vehicles and to help manage risk.

What are the major differences between direct claim securities and derivatives?　　**SELF-TEST QUESTION**

GENERAL VALUATION MODEL

Since the values of direct claim securities stem from streams of expected cash flows, all such assets are valued in essentially the same way: (1) The cash flow stream must be estimated, which involves finding both the expected cash flow for each period and the riskiness of that cash flow. (2) The required rate of return for each cash flow is established on the basis of its riskiness and the returns available on other investments. (3) Each cash flow is then discounted by its required rate of return to find its present value. (4) Finally, these present values are summed to find the value of the asset. Equation 7-1 formalizes this process.[1]

$$V = \frac{CF_1}{(1 + k_1)^1} + \frac{CF_2}{(1 + k_2)^2} + \cdots + \frac{CF_t}{(1 + k_t)^t} + \cdots + \frac{CF_n}{(1 + k_n)^n}$$

$$= \sum_{t=1}^{n} \frac{CF_t}{(1 + k_t)^t}.$$

7-1

Here V is the current, or present, value of the asset; CF_t is the expected cash flow at Time t; k_t is the required rate of return for each period's cash flow; and n is the number of periods over which cash flows are expected to be generated. If the cash flow stream exhibits certain regularities, and if the required rate of return (k) is constant, then Equation 7-1 can be reduced to a simpler form. We will examine several reduced forms in this chapter.

---

[1]Equation 7-1 is presented in *risk-adjusted discount rate* format. Later, in Chapter 11, we will see that assets can also be valued by the *certainty equivalent* method.

Note that the basic valuation model can be applied to physical assets as well as to direct claim securities. Also, note that direct claim securities are generally broken down into three primary classes: (1) *debt,* which is a contractual obligation calling for specific payments; (2) *preferred stock,* which is also contractual in nature but which has a claim to income and assets after the firm's debt; and (3) *common stock,* which represents ownership and which has a residual claim to all income and assets after the claims of debtholders and preferred stockholders have been satisfied.

There are also variations within each of the primary types of direct claim securities. For example, there is long-term and short-term debt, fixed rate and floating rate debt, debt that may be converted to common stock, secured and unsecured debt, and so forth.

Each of these variations calls for a somewhat different application of Equation 7-1. Indeed, since investment bankers have created an almost limitless variety of securities, with new ones being created every day, one could spend his or her career developing variations of the basic valuation model. At this point, we shall deal only with models for the three basic direct claim securities — bonds, preferred stock, and common stock. We will take up some of the variations in later chapters.

SELF-TEST QUESTIONS

Why is valuation an important concept to financial managers?

Write out the formula for the general valuation model, and then describe its meaning in words.

BOND VALUATION

A *bond* is a long-term debt contract issued by a business or governmental unit. For example, on January 2, 1997, Allied Food Products borrowed $50 million by selling 50,000 individual bonds for $1,000 each. Allied received the $50 million, and it promised to pay the bondholders $7.5 million in annual interest and to repay the $50 million on a specified date. The lenders were willing to give Allied $50 million, so the value of the bond issue was $50 million. But how did the investors decide that the issue was worth $50 million? As a first step in explaining how the values of this and other bonds are determined, we need to define some terms:

1. **Par value.** The *par value* is the stated face value of the bond; it is usually set at $1,000, although multiples of $1,000 (for example, $5,000) are often used. The par value generally represents the amount of money the firm borrows and promises to repay at some future date.

2. **Coupon interest rate.** The bond requires the issuer to pay a specified number of dollars of interest each year (or, more typically, each six months). When this *coupon payment,* as it is called, is divided by the par value, the result is the *coupon interest rate.* For example, Allied's bonds have a $1,000 par value, and they pay $150 in interest each year. The bond's coupon interest is $150, so its coupon interest rate is $150/$1,000 = 15 percent. The $150 is the yearly "rent" on the $1,000 loan. This payment, which is fixed at

the time the bond is issued, remains in force, by contract, during the life of the bond. Incidentally, some time ago, most bonds literally had a number of small (½- by 2-inch) dated coupons attached to them, and on the interest payment date, the owner would clip off the coupon for that date and either cash it at his or her bank or mail it to the company's paying agent, who then mailed back a check for the interest. A 30-year, semiannual bond would start with 60 coupons, whereas a 5-year, annual payment bond would start with only 5 coupons. Such bonds are called *bearer bonds*, because the bearer is entitled to the coupon payment. Today, all newly issued bonds are *registered* — no physical coupons are involved, and interest checks are mailed automatically to the registered owners of the bonds. Even so, people continue to use the terms *coupon* and *coupon interest rate* even when discussing registered bonds.

3. **Maturity date.** Bonds generally have a specified *maturity date* on which the par value must be repaid. Allied's bonds, which were issued on January 2, 1997, will mature on January 1, 2012; thus, they had a 15-year maturity at the time they were issued. Most bonds have *original maturities* (the maturity at the time the bond is issued) of from 10 to 40 years, but any maturity is legally permissible. Of course, the effective maturity of a bond declines each year after it has been issued. Thus, Allied's bonds had a 15-year original maturity, but in 1998 they will have a 14-year maturity, and so on.

4. **Call provisions.** Most bonds have a provision whereby the issuer may pay them off prior to maturity. This feature is known as a *call provision*, and it is discussed in detail in Chapter 17. If a bond is callable, and if interest rates in the economy decline, then the company can sell a new issue of low interest rate bonds and use the proceeds to retire the old, high interest rate issue, just as a homeowner can refinance a home mortgage.

5. **New issues versus outstanding bonds.** As we shall see, a bond's market price is determined primarily by its coupon interest payments — the higher the coupon, other things held constant, the higher the market price of the bond. At the time a bond is issued, the coupon is generally set at a level that will cause the market price of the bond to equal its par value. If a lower coupon were set, investors simply would not be willing to pay $1,000 for the bond, while if a higher coupon were set, investors would clamor for the bond and bid its price up over $1,000. Investment bankers can judge quite precisely the coupon rate that will cause a bond to sell at its $1,000 par value.

A bond that has just been issued is known as a *new issue*. Once the bond has been on the market for a while, it is classified as an *outstanding bond*, also called a *seasoned issue*. Newly issued bonds generally sell very close to par, but the prices of outstanding bonds vary widely from par. Coupon interest payments are constant, so when economic conditions change a bond with a $150 coupon that sold at par when it was issued will sell for more or less than $1,000 thereafter.

THE BASIC BOND VALUATION MODEL

As we noted previously, the values of many assets — stocks, bonds, leases, and even physical assets such as apartment buildings or pieces of machinery — are based on the present value of the cash flows the asset is expected to produce. In the case of a bond, the cash flows consist of interest payments during the life of the bond plus a return of the principal amount borrowed, generally the par value, when the bond matures. In a time line format, here is the situation:

Here

k_d = appropriate interest rate on the bond = 15%. We used the term "i" or "I" to designate the interest rate in Chapter 6 because those terms are used on financial calculators, but "k," with the subscript "d" to designate the rate on a debt security, is normally used in finance.[2]

N = number of years before the bond matures = 15. Note that N declines each year after the bond has been issued, so a bond that had a maturity of 15 years when it was issued (original maturity = 15) will have N = 14 after one year, N = 13 after two years, and so on. Note also that at this point we assume that the bond pays interest once a year, or annually, so N is measured in years. Later on, we will deal with semiannual payment bonds, which pay interest each six months.[3]

INT = dollars of interest paid each year = Coupon rate × Par value = 0.15($1,000) = $150. In calculator terminology, INT = PMT = 150. If the bond had been a semiannual payment bond, the payment would have been $75 each six months.

M = par value of the bond = $1,000. This amount must be paid off at maturity.

We can now redraw the time line to show the numerical values for all variables except the bond's value:

---

[2]The appropriate interest rate on debt securities was discussed in Chapter 3. The bond's riskiness, liquidity, and years to maturity, as well as supply and demand conditions in the capital markets, all influence the interest rate on bonds.

[3]We should note that some bonds, either pay no interest during their lives *(zero coupon bonds)* or else pay very low coupon rates. Such bonds are sold at a discount below par, hence they are called *original issue discount bonds.* The "interest" earned on a zero coupon bond comes at the end, when the company pays off at par ($1,000) a bond which was purchased for, say, $321.97. The discount of $1,000 − $321.97 = $678.03 substitutes for interest. Original issue discount bonds are discussed at length in Chapter 17.

The following general equation can be solved to find the value of any bond:

$$\begin{aligned}
\text{Bond's value} = V_B &= \frac{INT}{(1 + k_d)^1} + \frac{INT}{(1 + k_d)^2} + \cdots + \frac{INT}{(1 + k_d)^N} + \frac{M}{(1 + k_d)^N} \\
&= \sum_{t=1}^{N} \frac{INT}{(1 + k_d)^t} + \frac{M}{(1 + k_d)^N}.
\end{aligned}$$

7-2

Equation 7-2 can also be rewritten for use with the tables:

$$V_B = INT(PVIFA_{k_d,N}) + M(PVIF_{k_d,N}).$$

7-3

Inserting values for our particular bond, we have

$$V_B = \sum_{t=1}^{15} \frac{\$150}{(1.15)^t} + \frac{\$1,000}{(1.15)^{15}}.$$

Notice that the cash flows consist of an annuity of N years plus a lump sum payment at the end of Year N, and this fact is reflected in Equation 7-2. Further, Equation 7-2 can be solved by the three procedures discussed in Chapter 6: (1) numerically, (2) using the tables, and (3) with a financial calculator.

Numerical Solution: Simply discount each cash flow back to the present and sum these PVs to find the value of the bond; see Figure 7-1 for an example. This procedure is not very efficient, especially if the bond has many years to maturity.

Tabular Solution: Simply look up the appropriate PVIFA and PVIF values in Tables A-1 and A-2 at the end of the book, insert them into the equation, and complete the arithmetic:

$$V_B = \$150(5.8474) + \$1,000(0.1229)$$
$$= \$877.11 + \$122.90 \approx \$1,000.$$

There is a one-cent rounding difference, which results from the fact that the tables only go to four decimal places.

Financial Calculator Solution: In Chapter 6 we worked problems where only four of the five time value of money (TVM) keys were used, but all five keys are used with bond problems. Here is the setup:

Inputs:	15	15		150	1000
	N	**I**	**PV**	**PMT**	**FV**
Output:			= −1,000		

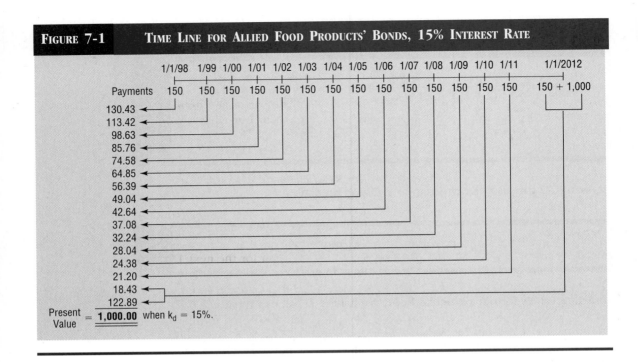

FIGURE 7-1   TIME LINE FOR ALLIED FOOD PRODUCTS' BONDS, 15% INTEREST RATE

Simply input N = 15, I = k = 15, INT = PMT = 150, M = FV = 1000, and then press the PV key to find the value of the bond, $1,000. The calculator finds the PV of the 15-year, $150 annuity and the PV of the $1,000 maturity value, sums them, and shows the total as the PV. Since the PV is an outflow to the investor, it is shown with a negative sign.

CHANGES IN BOND VALUES OVER TIME

If k_d remained constant at 15 percent, what would the value of the bond be 1 year after it was issued? Now the term to maturity is only 14 years — that is, N = 14. With a financial calculator, just override N = 15 with N = 14, press the PV key, and you will see that the value of the bond will remain at $1,000 as long as the appropriate interest rate remains constant at the coupon rate, 15 percent.[4]

---

[4]The bond prices quoted by brokers are calculated as described. However, if you bought a bond between interest payment dates, you would have to pay the basic price plus accrued interest. Thus, if you purchased an Allied bond 6 months after it was issued, your broker would send you an invoice stating that you must pay $1,000 as the basic price of the bond plus $75 interest, representing one-half the annual interest of $150. The seller of the bond would receive $1,075. If you bought the bond the day before its interest payment date, you would pay $1,000 + (364/365)($150) = $1,149.59. Of course, you would receive an interest payment of $150 at the end of the next day. See Self-Test Problem 2 for a detailed discussion of bond quotations between interest payment dates.

Throughout the chapter we assume that the bond is being evaluated immediately after an interest payment date. The more expensive financial calculators such as the HP 17B have a built-in calendar which permits the calculation of exact values between interest payment dates.

Now suppose interest rates in the economy fell after the Allied bonds were issued, and, as a result, k_d *fell below the coupon rate,* decreasing from 15 to 10 percent. Both the coupon interest payments and the maturity value remain constant, but now 10 percent must be used for k_d. With a financial calculator, just change $k_d = I$ from 15 to 10, and then press the PV key to get the answer, $1,368.33. Thus, if k_d fell *below* the coupon rate, the bond would sell above par, or at a *premium.*

The arithmetic of the bond value increase should be clear, but what is the logic behind it? The fact that k_d has fallen to 10 percent means that if you had $1,000 to invest, you could buy new bonds like Allied's (every day some 10 to 12 companies sell new bonds), except that these new bonds would pay $100 of interest each year rather than $150. Naturally, you would prefer $150 to $100, so you would be willing to pay more than $1,000 for Allied's bonds to obtain its higher coupons. All investors would recognize these facts, and, as a result, the Allied bonds would be bid up in price to $1,368.33, at which point they would provide the same rate of return to a potential investor as the new bonds — 10 percent.

Assuming that interest rates remain constant at 10 percent for the next 14 years, what would happen to the value of an Allied bond? It would gradually fall from $1,368.33 at present to $1,000 at maturity, when Allied will redeem each bond for $1,000. This point can be illustrated by calculating the value of the bond 1 year later, when it has 13 years remaining to maturity. With a financial calculator, merely input the values for N, I, PMT, and FV, now using N = 13, and press the PV key to find the value of the bond, $1,355.17. Thus, the value of the bond will have fallen from $1,368.33 to $1,355.21, or by $13.12. If you were to calculate the value of the bond at other future dates, the price would continue to fall as the maturity date approached.

Notice that if you purchased the bond at a price of $1,368.33 and then sold it 1 year later with k_d still at 10 percent, you would have a capital loss of $13.12, or a total return of $150.00 − $13.12 = $136.88. Your percentage rate of return would consist of an *interest yield* (also called a *current yield*) plus a *capital gains yield,* calculated as follows:

$$\text{Interest, or current, yield} = \quad \$150/\$1,368.33 = \quad 0.1096 = 10.96\%$$

$$\text{Capital gains yield} = -\$13.12/\$1,368.33 = -0.0096 = \underline{-0.96\%}$$

$$\text{Total rate of return, or yield} = \$136.88/\$1,368.33 = \quad 0.1000 \approx \underline{10.00\%}$$

Had interest rates risen from 15 to 20 percent during the first year after issue rather than fallen, you could override I = 15 with I = 20, and you would find that the value of the bond would have declined to $769.47. In this case, the bond would sell at a *discount* of $230.53 below its par value:

$$\text{Discount} = \text{Price} - \text{Par value} = \$769.47 - \$1,000.00$$

$$= -\$230.53.$$

The total expected future return on the bond would again consist of a current yield and a capital gains yield, but now the capital gains yield would be *positive.* The total return would be 20 percent. To see this, calculate the price of the bond with 13 years left to maturity, assuming that interest rates remain at 20 percent. With a calculator, enter N = 13, I = 20, PMT = 150, and FV = 1000, and then press PV to obtain the bond's value, $773.37.

Notice that the capital gain for the year is the difference between the bond's value with N = 13 and the bond's value with N = 14, or $773.37 − $769.47 = $3.90. The interest yield, capital gains yield, and total yield are calculated as follows:

$$\text{Interest, or current, yield} = \$150/\$769.47 = 0.1949 = 19.49\%$$

$$\text{Capital gains yield} = \$3.90/\$769.47 = 0.0051 = \underline{0.51\%}$$

$$\text{Total rate of return, or yield} = \$153.90/\$769.47 = 0.2000 = \underline{\underline{20.00\%}}$$

The discount or premium on a bond may also be calculated as the PV of the difference in interest payments, discounted at the new interest rate:

$$\text{Discount or premium} = \sum_{t=1}^{N} \frac{\begin{array}{c}\text{Interest payment}\\\text{on old bond}\end{array} - \begin{array}{c}\text{Interest payment}\\\text{on new bond}\end{array}}{(1 + k_d)^t}.$$

Here N = years to maturity on the old bond and k_d = current rate of interest on a new bond. For example, if interest rates had risen to 20 percent 1 year after the Allied bonds were issued, then N = 14 and the discount would have been calculated as follows:

$$\text{Discount} = \sum_{t=1}^{14} \frac{\$150 - \$200}{(1.20)^t} = -\$230.53.$$

(The minus sign indicates discount.) This value agrees with the −$230.53 value calculated previously. From these calculations, we see that the discount is equal to the present value of the interest payments you would sacrifice if you were to buy a low-coupon old bond rather than a high-coupon new bond. The longer the bond has left to maturity, the greater the sacrifice, hence the greater the discount.

Figure 7-2 graphs the value of the bond over time, assuming that interest rates in the economy (1) remain constant at 15 percent, (2) fall to 10 percent and then remain constant at that level, or (3) rise to 20 percent and remain constant at that level. Of course, if interest rates do *not* remain constant, then the price of the bond will fluctuate. However, regardless of what future interest rates do, the bond's price will approach $1,000 as it nears the maturity date (barring bankruptcy, in which case the bond's value might drop to zero).

Figure 7-2 illustrates the following key points:

1. Whenever the going rate of interest, k_d, is equal to the coupon rate, a bond will sell at its par value. Normally, the coupon rate is set equal to the going interest rate when a bond is issued, so it initially sells at par.

2. Interest rates do change over time, but the coupon rate remains fixed after the bond has been issued. Whenever the going rate of interest is *greater than* the coupon rate, a bond's price will fall *below* its par value. Such a bond is called a *discount bond.*

3. Whenever the going rate of interest is *less than* the coupon rate, a bond's price will rise *above* its par value. Such a bond is called a *premium bond.*

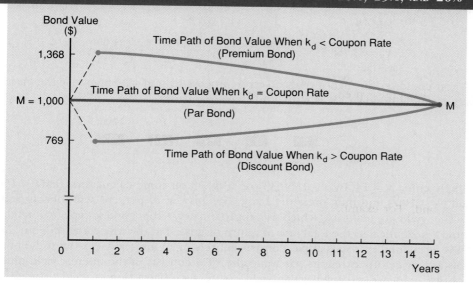

FIGURE 7-2

TIME PATH OF THE VALUE OF A 15% COUPON, $1,000 PAR VALUE BOND WHEN INTEREST RATES ARE 10%, 15%, AND 20%

YEAR	$k_d = 10\%$	$k_d = 15\%$	$k_d = 20\%$
0	—	$1,000	—
1	$1,368.33	1,000	$ 769.47
.	.	.	.
.	.	.	.
.	.	.	.
15	1,000	1,000	1,000

NOTE: The curves for 10% and 20% have a slight bow.

4. Thus, an *increase* in interest rates will cause the price of an outstanding bond to *fall,* whereas a *decrease* in rates will cause it to *rise.* Bond prices move *inversely* to changes in interest rates.

5. The market value of a bond will always approach its par value as its maturity date approaches, provided the firm does not go bankrupt.

These points are very important, for they show that bondholders may suffer capital losses or make capital gains, depending on whether interest rates rise or fall after the bond was purchased. And, as we saw in Chapter 3, interest rates do indeed change over time.

FINDING THE INTEREST RATE ON A BOND: YIELD TO MATURITY

Suppose you were offered a 14-year, 15 percent coupon, $1,000 par value bond at a price of $1,368.33. What rate of interest would you earn on your investment if you bought the bond and held it to maturity? This rate is called the bond's *yield to maturity (YTM),* and it is the interest rate generally discussed by bond traders when they talk about rates of return. To find the yield to maturity, you could solve Equation 7-2 or 7-3 for k_d:

$$V_B = \$1,368.33 = \frac{\$150}{(1 + k_d)^1} + \cdots + \frac{\$150}{(1 + k_d)^{14}} + \frac{\$1,000}{(1 + k_d)^{14}}.$$

You could go through a trial-and-error process to find k_d, but by far the easiest way to find a bond's YTM is with a financial calculator:[5]

Inputs:	14		−1368.33	15	1000
	N	I	PV	PMT	FV
Output:		= 10			

Simply enter N = 14, PV = −1368.33 (or 1368.33 on some calculators), PMT = 150, and FV = 1000, and then press the I key. The answer, 10 percent, will then appear.

The yield to maturity, which is (approximately) the bond's expected rate of return, is identical to the total rate of return discussed in the preceding section.[6] The YTM for a bond that sells at par consists entirely of an interest yield, but if the bond sells at a price other than its par value, the YTM consists of the interest yield plus a positive or negative capital gains yield. Note also that a bond's yield to maturity changes whenever interest rates in the economy change, and this is almost daily. One who purchases a bond and holds it until it matures will receive the YTM that existed on the purchase date, but the bond's calculated YTM will change frequently between the purchase date and the maturity date.

YIELD TO CALL

If you purchased a bond that was callable and the company called it, you would not have the option of holding it until it matured, so the yield to maturity would not be earned. For example, if Allied's 15 percent coupon bonds were callable, and if interest rates fell from 15 percent to 10 percent, then the company could call in the 15 percent bonds, replace them with 10 percent bonds, and save $150 − $100 = $50 interest per bond per year. This would be beneficial to the company, but not to the bondholders.

If current interest rates are well below an outstanding bond's coupon rate, then a callable bond is likely to be called, and investors should estimate the expected rate of return on the bond as the *yield to call (YTC)* rather than as the yield to maturity. To calculate the YTC, solve this equation for k_d:

---

[5]A few years ago, bond traders all had specialized tables called *bond tables* that gave yields on bonds of different maturities selling at different premiums and discounts. Because calculators are so much more efficient (and accurate), bond tables are rarely used anymore.

[6]Actually, a bond's YTM is the *promised rate of return* if it is held to maturity. The YTM is a bond's *expected* rate of return only if (1) the probability of default is zero, (2) the probability of a call is zero, and (3) interest rates are expected to remain at their current level over the life of the bond.

$$\text{Price of callable bond} = \sum_{t=1}^{N} \frac{\text{INT}}{(1 + k_d)^t} + \frac{\text{Call price}}{(1 + k_d)^N}. \qquad \textbf{7-4}$$

Here N is the number of years until the company can call the bond; call price is the price the company must pay in order to call the bond (it is often set equal to the par value plus one year's interest); and k_d is the YTC.

To illustrate the yield-to-call calculation, suppose Allied's bonds had a provision that the company, if it wanted to, could call the bonds 10 years after the issue date at a price of $1,150. Suppose further that interest rates had fallen such that one year after issuance, k_d was 10 percent and the price of the bonds was $1,368.33. Here is the setup for finding the bond's YTC with a financial calculator:

Inputs: 9   −1368.33   150   1150
            N   I   PV   PMT   FV
Output: = 9.78

The YTC is 9.78 percent — this is the return you would earn if you bought the bond at a price of $1,368.33 and it was called 9 years from today at a price of $1,150. (The bond could not be called until 10 years after issuance, and 1 year has gone by, so there are 9 years left until the first call date.)

Do you think Allied *will* call the bonds when they become callable? Allied's action will depend on the going interest rate when the bonds become callable. If the going rate remains at k_d = 10%, then Allied could save 15% − 10% = 5%, or $50 per bond per year, by calling them and replacing the 15 percent bonds with a new 10 percent issue. There would be costs to the company to refund the issue, but the interest savings would probably be worth the cost, so Allied would probably refund the bonds. Therefore, there is a good chance that you would actually end up earning YTC = 9.78% rather than YTM = 10% if you bought the bonds under the indicated conditions.

The analysis used to decide whether or not to call a bond is covered in detail in Appendix 17A. In the balance of this chapter, we assume that bonds are not callable unless otherwise noted, but some of the end-of-chapter problems do deal with yield to call.

BOND VALUES WITH SEMIANNUAL COMPOUNDING

Although some bonds pay interest annually, most actually pay interest semiannually. To evaluate semiannual payment bonds, we must modify the bond valuation model (Equation 7-2) as follows:

1. Divide the annual coupon interest payment by 2 to determine the amount of interest paid each 6 months.
2. Multiply the years to maturity, N, by 2 to determine the number of semiannual periods.

3. Divide the annual interest rate, k_d, by 2 to determine the periodic (semiannual) interest rate.

By making these changes, we obtain the following equation for finding the value of a bond that pays interest semiannually:

$$V_B = \sum_{t=1}^{2N} \frac{INT/2}{(1 + k_d/2)^t} + \frac{M}{(1 + k_d/2)^{2N}}. \qquad \text{7-2a}$$

To illustrate, assume now that Allied Food Products' bonds pay $75 interest each 6 months rather than $150 at the end of each year. Thus, each interest payment is only half as large, but there are twice as many of them. If the annual (nominal) required rate of interest on this 15-year semiannual payment bond is 10 percent, with a financial calculator, enter N = 30, k = I = 5, PMT = 75, FV = 1000, and then press the PV key to obtain the bond's value, $1,384.31:

Inputs:	30	5		75	1000
	N	I	PV	PMT	FV

Output: = −1384.31

The value with semiannual interest payments is slightly larger than $1,380.30, the value when interest is paid annually.

Students sometimes want to discount the maturity value at 10 percent over 15 years rather than at 5 percent over 30 six-month periods. This is incorrect. Logically, all cash flows in a given contract must be discounted at the same periodic rate, the 5 percent semiannual rate in this instance. For consistency, bond traders *must* use the same discount rate for all cash flows, including the cash flow at maturity, and they do.

Note also that when we changed the coupon payments from annual to semiannual, we obtained the discount rate by dividing the 10 percent nominal required rate of interest by 2, which produced a 5 percent semiannual (periodic) discount rate. When we apply this rate, we are actually assuming an effective annual rate (EAR) of interest of 10.25 percent:

$$EAR = (1.05)^2 - 1.0 = 1.1025 - 1.0 = 0.1025 = 10.25\%.$$

In practice, bond professionals work with nominal rates; that is, the required interest rate in our example would be stated as 10 percent, and the actual discount rate applied in the valuation process would be 5 percent per semiannual period. Since bond traders, dealers, and investors all value bonds in this way, we will use this convention throughout the text. Bond professionals generally deal exclusively in semiannual coupon bonds, so this valuation method usually causes no problems. Note, however, that a 10 percent nominal rate (or a 10 percent yield to maturity) under semiannual compounding implies a 10.25 percent effective annual rate, so when bonds are being compared to securities which make payments other than semiannual, it is best to think in terms of the bond's effective annual rate rather than its nominal rate.

INTEREST RATE AND REINVESTMENT RATE RISK

As we saw in Chapter 3, interest rates go up and down over time, and such changes give rise to two types of risk. First, an increase in interest rates leads to a decline in the values of outstanding bonds. Since interest rates can rise, bondholders face the risk of losses in the values of their portfolios. This risk is called *interest rate,* or *price, risk.* Second, many bondholders (including such institutional bondholders as pension funds and life insurance companies) buy bonds to build funds for some future use. These bondholders reinvest the cash flows (interest payments plus repayment of principal when the bonds mature or are called). If interest rates decline, the bondholders will earn a lower rate of return on reinvested cash flows, and this will reduce the future value of their portfolios relative to the values they originally expected. This risk is called *reinvestment rate risk.*

We see, then, that any given change in interest rates has two separate effects on bondholders — it changes the current values of their portfolios (interest rate, or price, risk), and it also changes the rates of return at which the cash flows from their portfolios can be reinvested (reinvestment rate risk). Note that these two risks tend to offset one another. For example, an increase in interest rates will lower the current market value of a bond portfolio, but since the future cash flows produced by the portfolio will then be reinvested at a higher rate of return, the future value of the portfolio will be increased. In this section we show how these two effects operate to affect bondholders' positions.[7]

Suppose you bought some 15 percent Allied bonds at a price of $1,000, and interest rates subsequently rose to 20 percent. As we saw above, the price of the bonds would fall to $769.47, so you would have a loss of $230.53 per bond.[8] One's exposure to interest rate price risk is higher on bonds with long maturities than on those maturing in the near future. This point can be demonstrated by showing how the value of a 1-year bond with a 15 percent coupon fluctuates with changes in k_d and then comparing these changes with those on a 14-year bond as calculated previously. The 1-year bond's values at different interest rates are shown below:

Value at $k_d = 10\%$: Enter N = 1, I = 10, PMT = 150, and FV = 1000, and then press PV to find the value of the bond, $1,045.45.

---

[7]Actually, we will stop short of a full examination of the effects of interest rate changes on bondholders' positions, as such an examination would go well beyond the scope of the text. We can note, though, that a concept called *duration* has been developed to help fixed income investors deal with interest rate risk, and, with a properly structured portfolio (one that has the proper duration), most of the risks of changing interest rates can be eliminated because interest rate risk and reinvestment rate risk can be made to offset one another. We will discuss duration in more depth in Chapter 23.

[8]You would have an *accounting* (and tax) loss only if you sold the bond; if you held it to maturity, you would not have such a loss. However, even if you did not sell, you would still have suffered a *real economic loss in an opportunity cost sense* because you would have lost the opportunity to invest at 20 percent and would be stuck with a 15 percent bond in a 20 percent market. Thus, in an economic sense "paper losses" are just as bad as realized accounting losses.

Value at k_d = 15%: With everything still in your calculator, enter I = 15 to override the old I = 10, and press PV to find the bond's value at k_d = I = 15; it is $1,000.

Value at k_d = 20%: Now enter I = 20 and press the PV key to find the last bond value, $958.33.

The values of the 1-year and 14-year bonds at five current market interest rates are listed and plotted in Figure 7-3. Notice how much more sensitive the price of the

| FIGURE 7-3 | VALUE OF LONG- AND SHORT-TERM 15% ANNUAL COUPON RATE BONDS AT DIFFERENT MARKET INTEREST RATES |

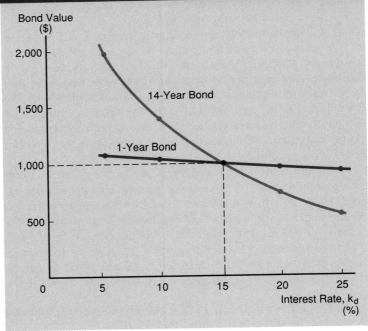

CURRENT MARKET INTEREST RATE, k_d	VALUE OF	
	1-YEAR BOND	14-YEAR BOND
5%	$1,095.24	$1,989.86
10	1,045.45	1,368.33
15	1,000.00	1,000.00
20	958.33	769.47
25	920.00	617.59

NOTE: Bond values were calculated using a financial calculator.

long-term bond is to changes in interest rates. At a 15 percent interest rate, both the long- and the short-term bonds are valued at $1,000. When rates rise to 20 percent, the long-term bond falls to $769.47, but the short-term bond falls only to $958.33.

For bonds with similar coupons, this differential sensitivity to changes in interest rates always holds true — the longer the maturity of the bond, the greater its price changes in response to a given change in interest rates. Thus, even if the risk of default on two bonds is exactly the same, the one with the longer maturity is typically exposed to more interest rate risk from a rise in interest rates.[9]

The logical explanation for this difference in interest rate risk is simple. Suppose you bought a 14-year bond that yielded 15 percent, or $150 a year. Now suppose interest rates on comparable-risk bonds rose to 20 percent. You would be stuck with only $150 of interest for the next 14 years. On the other hand, had you bought a 1-year bond, you would have had a low return for only 1 year. At the end of the year, you would get your $1,000 back, and you could then reinvest it and receive 20 percent, or $200 per year, for the next 13 years. Thus, interest rate risk reflects the length of time one is committed to a given investment.

Although a 1-year bond has less interest rate risk than a 14-year bond, the 1-year bond exposes the buyer to more reinvestment rate risk. Suppose you bought a 1-year bond that yielded 15 percent, and then interest rates on comparable-risk bonds fell to 10 percent. After 1 year, when you got your $1,000 back, you would have to invest it at only 10 percent, so you would lose $150 − $100 = $50 in annual interest. Had you bought the 14-year bond, you would have continued to receive $150 in annual interest payments even if rates fell. If you reinvested those coupon payments, you would have to accept a lower rate of return, but you would still be much better off than if you had been holding the 1-year bond.

BOND PRICES IN RECENT YEARS

We have just seen that the prices of outstanding bonds rise and fall inversely with changes in interest rates. Figure 7-4 shows what has happened to the price of a typical bond, Cleveland Electric's 8.75 percent, 35-year bond which matures in 2005. When this bond was issued in 1970, it was worth $1,000, but at the interest rate peak from 1981 to 1982, it sold for only $605. However, the ensuing drop in interest rates caused the price of the bond to rise, and by 1993 it was back over par at $1,020. The graph also shows that if interest rates remain at the 1995 level, the price of the bond will gradually rise, and it will sell for $1,000 (plus accrued interest) just before it matures in 2005.

---

[9]If a 10-year bond were plotted in Figure 7-3, its curve would lie between those of the 14-year bond and the 1-year bond. The curve of a 1-month bond would be almost horizontal, indicating that its price would change very little in response to an interest rate change, but a perpetuity would have a very steep slope.

We should also note that price sensitivity is also affected by a bond's coupon. The lower the coupon, the larger the maturity value will be relative to the stream of interest payments. Further, as we demonstrate in Chapter 9, distant cash flows are more seriously affected by changes in interest rates. Therefore, a zero coupon bond with a 10-year maturity will have far more price sensitivity to changing rates than will a 10-year, 10 percent coupon bond.

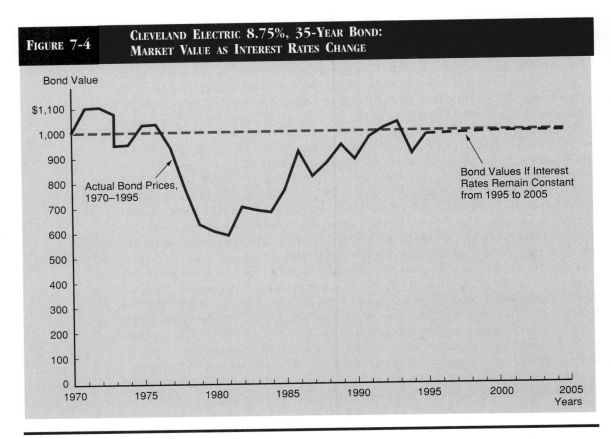

FIGURE 7-4   **CLEVELAND ELECTRIC 8.75%, 35-YEAR BOND: MARKET VALUE AS INTEREST RATES CHANGE**

Bond Value

Actual Bond Prices, 1970–1995

Bond Values If Interest Rates Remain Constant from 1995 to 2005

NOTE: The line from 1995 to 2005 appears linear, but it actually has a slight curve.

BOND MARKETS

Corporate bonds are traded primarily in the over-the-counter market. Most bonds are owned by and traded among the large financial institutions (for example, life insurance companies, mutual funds, and pension funds, all of which deal in very large blocks of securities), and it is relatively easy for the over-the-counter bond dealers to arrange the transfer of large blocks of bonds among the relatively few holders of the bonds. It would be much more difficult to conduct similar operations in the stock market among the literally millions of large and small stockholders, so a higher percentage of stock trades occur on the exchanges.

Information on bond trades in the over-the-counter market is not published, but a representative group of bonds is listed and traded in the bond section of the NYSE. Figure 7-5 gives a section of the bond market page of *The Wall Street Journal* for trading on April 19, 1996. A total of 314 issues were traded on that date, but we show only the bonds of AT&T. Note that AT&T had 10 different bonds that were traded on April 19; the company actually had 16 bond issues outstanding, but some of them did not trade on that date.

NYSE BOND MARKET TRANSACTIONS, APRIL 19, 1996   FIGURE 7-5

Bonds	Cur Yld	Vol	Close	Net Chg.
ATT 4⅜99	4.6	10	94½	...
ATT 6s00	6.1	15	98½	− ¼
ATT 5⅛01	5.4	5	94⅜	+ ½
ATT 7⅛02	7.0	45	102¼	+ ¼
ATT 7s05	7.0	160	100¼	− ¼
ATT 7½06	7.3	10	103⅜	...
ATT 8⅛22	7.8	210	103⅝	+ ⅛
ATT 8⅛24	7.9	115	102¾	...
ATT 8.35s25	7.9	15	105¼	− ⅛
ATT 8⅝31	8.1	12	106⅜	+ ¼

SOURCE: *The Wall Street Journal,* April 22, 1996.

The bonds of AT&T and other companies can have various denominations, but, for convenience, we generally think of each bond as having a par value of $1,000 — this is how much the company borrowed per bond and how much it must someday repay. However, since other denominations are possible, for trading and reporting purposes bonds are quoted as percentages of par. Looking at the first bond listed, we see that there is a 4⅜ just after the company's name; this indicates that the bond is of the series which pays 4⅜ percent interest, or 0.04375($1,000) = $43.75 of interest per year. The 4⅜ percent is the bond's *coupon rate.* The 99 which comes next indicates that this bond matures and must be repaid in the year 1999; it is not shown in the figure, but this bond was issued in 1959, so it had a 40-year original maturity. The 4.6 in the second column is the bond's *current yield,* which is defined as the annual interest payment divided by the closing price of the bond: Current yield = $43.75/$945.00 = 4.63%, rounded to 4.6 percent. The 10 in the third column indicates that 10 of these bonds were traded on April 19, 1996. Since the price shown in the fourth column is expressed as a percentage of par, the bond closed at 94½ percent, which translates to $945.00, which is unchanged from the previous day's close. Note that the second AT&T bond listed, the 6s maturing in 2000, closed down ¼ of 1 percent, or $2.50, from the previous day's close.

Coupon rates are generally set at levels which reflect the "going rate of interest" on the day a bond is issued. If the rates were set lower, investors would simply not buy the bonds at the $1,000 par value, so the company could not borrow the money it needed. Thus, bonds generally sell at their par values on the day they are issued, but bond prices fluctuate thereafter as interest rates change. As seen in Figure 7-5, some of AT&T's bonds sold above par, and some below par, but not one bond closed exactly at par on April 19, 1996.

All bonds traded on the New York Stock Exchange on a given day are listed in the newspaper (hence in Figure 7-5) in alphabetical order by company and in the order of the dates on which they were originally issued, beginning with the earliest bond issued. Thus, the coupon rates shown in Figure 7-5 generally rise as we move down the list, reflecting the fact that interest rates have generally risen over time, except for the past few years.

SELF-TEST
QUESTIONS In what two primary forms do corporations raise capital?
What is meant by the terms "new issue" and "seasoned issue"?
Explain, verbally, the following equation:

$$V_B = \sum_{t=1}^{N} \frac{INT}{(1 + k_d)^t} + \frac{M}{(1 + k_d)^N}.$$

Explain what happens to the price of a bond if (1) interest rates rise above the bond's coupon rate or (2) interest rates fall below the bond's coupon rate.
Write out a formula that can be used to calculate the discount or premium on a bond, and explain it.
Differentiate between interest rate (price) risk and reinvestment rate risk.
How does the calculation of a bond's value differ between a bond that is likely to be called and one that is not?
How must the bond valuation formula shown just above be changed to deal with bonds that have semiannual coupons rather than annual coupons?

PREFERRED STOCK VALUATION

Preferred stock is a *hybrid* — it is similar to bonds in some respects and to common stock in other respects. Preferred dividends are similar to interest payments on bonds in that they are fixed in amount and generally must be paid before common stock dividends can be paid. However, like common dividends, preferred dividends can be omitted without bankrupting the firm, and some preferred issues have no specific maturity date.

Most preferred stocks entitle their owners to regular, fixed dividend payments. If the payments last forever, the issue is a perpetuity whose value V_{ps}, is found as follows:

$$V_{ps} = \frac{D_{ps}}{k_{ps}}.$$

7-5

V_{ps} is the value of the preferred stock, D_{ps} is the preferred dividend, and k_{ps} is the required rate of return. Allied Food Products has preferred stock outstanding which pays a dividend of $10 per year. If the required rate of return on this preferred stock is 10 percent, its value is $100, found by solving Equation 7-5 as follows:

$$V_{ps} = \frac{\$10.00}{0.10} = \$100.00.$$

If we know the current price of a perpetual preferred stock and its dividend, we can solve for the current rate being earned, as follows:

$$k_{ps} = \frac{D_{ps}}{V_{ps}}. \qquad \text{7-5a}$$

Note that if the preferred stock is not perpetual, that is, if it has some finite maturity date, then it will be valued similarly to the way a bond is valued, as we discussed in the previous section. The preferred's dividend payment is equivalent to a bond's coupon payment, while the preferred's par value corresponds to a bond's maturity value. Note too that many preferred stocks pay dividends quarterly or semiannually, in which case we could divide D_{ps} and k_{ps} by payments per year. The yield would, like bond yields, be quoted on a nominal annual basis.

In what way is preferred stock similar to bonds, and in what respect is it similar to common stock?

SELF-TEST QUESTION

COMMON STOCK VALUATION

Common stock represents an ownership interest in a corporation, but to the typical investor, a share of common stock is simply a piece of paper which is expected to provide (1) dividends and (2) capital gains:

1. It entitles its owner to dividends, but only if the company has earnings out of which dividends can be paid and only if management chooses to pay dividends rather than to retain and reinvest all the earnings. Whereas a bond contains a *promise* to pay interest, common stock provides no such promise to pay dividends — if you own a stock, you may *expect* a dividend, but your expectations may not in fact be met. To illustrate, Long Island Lighting Company (LILCO) had paid dividends on its common stock for more than 50 years, and people expected these dividends to continue. However, when the company encountered severe problems a few years ago, it stopped paying dividends. Note, though, that LILCO continued to pay interest on its bonds; if it had not, then it would have been declared bankrupt, and the bondholders could have taken over the company.

2. Stock can be sold at some future date, hopefully at a price greater than the purchase price. If the stock is actually sold at a price above its purchase price, the investor will receive a *capital gain*. Generally, at the time people buy common stocks, they do expect to receive capital gains; otherwise, they would not buy the stocks. However, after the fact, one can end up with capital losses rather than capital gains. LILCO's stock price dropped from $17.50 to $3.75 in one year, so the *expected* capital gains on that stock turned out to be *actual* capital losses.

DEFINITIONS OF TERMS USED IN THE STOCK VALUATION MODELS

Common stocks provide an expected future cash flow stream, and a stock's value is found in the same manner as the values of other financial assets — namely, as the present value of the expected future cash flow stream. The expected cash flows consist of two elements: (1) the dividends expected in each year and (2) the price investors expect to receive when they sell the stock. The expected final stock price includes the return of the original investment plus an expected capital gain.

We saw in Chapter 1 that managers seek to maximize the values of their firms' stocks. A manager's actions affect both the stream of income to investors and the riskiness of that stream. To operate most effectively, managers need to know how alternative actions are likely to affect stock prices, so at this point we develop some models to help show how the value of a share of stock is determined. We begin by defining the following terms:

D_t = dividend the stockholder *expects* to receive at the end of Year t. D_0 is the most recent dividend, which has just been paid; D_1 is the first dividend expected, and it will be paid at the end of this year; D_2 is the dividend expected at the end of 2 years; and so forth. D_1 represents the first cash flow a new purchaser of the stock will receive. Note that D_0, the dividend which has just been paid, is known with certainty. However, all future dividends are expected values, so the estimate of D_t may differ among investors.[10]

P_0 = actual *market price* of the stock today. If you called your broker and asked for a quote, P_0 is the value you would be given. P_0 changes from moment to moment, and large orders to buy or sell can affect P_0, but in this chapter we take P_0 as given.

$\hat{P}_t$ = expected price of the stock at the end of each Year t (pronounced "P hat t"). $\hat{P}_0$ is the *intrinsic,* or *theoretical, value* of the stock today as seen by the particular investor doing the analysis; $\hat{P}_1$ is the price expected at the end of 1 year; and so on. Note that $\hat{P}_0$ is the intrinsic value of the stock today based on a particular investor's estimate of the stock's expected dividend stream and the riskiness of that stream. Hence, whereas P_0 is fixed and is identical for all investors, $\hat{P}_0$ could differ among investors depending on how optimistic they are regarding the company. The caret, or "hat," is used to indicate that $\hat{P}_t$ is an estimated value. $\hat{P}_0$, the individual investor's estimate of the intrinsic value today, could be above or below P_0, the current stock price. The investor would buy the stock only if his or her estimate of $\hat{P}_0$ were equal to or greater than P_0.

Since there are many investors in the market, there can be many values for $\hat{P}_0$. However, we can think of a group of "marginal" investors whose actions actually determine the market price. For these marginal investors, P_0 must equal $\hat{P}_0$; otherwise, a disequilibrium would exist, and buying and selling in the market would change P_0 until $P_0 = \hat{P}_0$ for marginal investors.

---

[10]Stocks generally pay dividends quarterly, so theoretically we should evaluate them on a quarterly basis. However, in stock valuation, most analysts work on an annual basis because the data generally are not precise enough to warrant refinement to a quarterly model. For additional information on the quarterly model, see Charles M. Linke and J. Kenton Zumwalt, "Estimation Biases in Discounted Cash Flow Analysis of Equity Capital Cost in Rate Regulation," *Financial Management,* Autumn 1984, 15-21.

g = expected *growth rate* in dividends. (If we assume that dividends are expected to grow at a constant rate, g is also equal to the expected rate of growth in the stock's price.) Different investors may use different g's to evaluate a firm's stock, but the market price, P_0, is set on the basis of the g as estimated by marginal investors.

k_s = minimum acceptable, or *required, rate of return* on the stock, considering both its riskiness and the returns available on other investments. The determinants of k_s were discussed in detail in Chapter 5.

$\hat{k}_s$ = *expected rate of return* which an investor who buys the stock actually expects to receive. $\hat{k}_s$ (pronounced "k hat s") could be above or below k_s, but one would buy the stock only if $\hat{k}_s$ were equal to or greater than k_s.

$\bar{k}_s$ = *actual, or realized, rate of return* (pronounced "k bar s"). You may *expect* to obtain a return of $\hat{k}_s = 15$ percent if you buy Exxon stock today, but if the market goes down, you may end up next year with an actual realized return that is much lower, perhaps even negative.

D_1/P_0 = expected *dividend yield* on the stock during the coming year. If the stock is expected to pay a dividend of $1 during the next 12 months, and if its current price is $10, then the expected dividend yield is $1/\$10 = 0.10 = 10\%$.

$\dfrac{\hat{P}_1 - P_0}{P_0}$ = expected *capital gains yield* on the stock during the coming year. If the stock sells for $10 today, and if it is expected to rise to $10.50 at the end of 1 year, then the expected capital gain is $\hat{P}_1 - P_0 = \$10.50 - \$10.00 = \$0.50$, and the expected capital gains yield is $\$0.50/\$10 = 0.05 = 5\%$.

Expected total return = $\hat{k}_s$ = expected dividend yield (D_1/P_0) plus expected capital gains yield $[(\hat{P}_1 - P_0)/P_0]$. In our example, the *expected total return* = $\hat{k}_s$ = $10\% + 5\% = 15\%$.

EXPECTED DIVIDENDS AS THE BASIS FOR STOCK VALUES

Stock prices are determined as the present value of a stream of cash flows, and the basic stock valuation equation is similar to the bond valuation equation. What are the cash flows that corporations provide to their stockholders? First, think of yourself as an investor who buys a stock with the intention of holding it (in your family) forever. In this case, all that you (and your heirs) will receive is a stream of dividends, and the value of the stock today is calculated as the present value of an infinite stream of dividends:

$$
\begin{aligned}
\text{Value of stock} = \hat{P}_0 &= \text{PV of expected future dividends} \\[2mm]
&= \frac{D_1}{(1 + k_s)^1} + \frac{D_2}{(1 + k_s)^2} + \cdots + \frac{D_\infty}{(1 + k_s)^\infty} \\[2mm]
&= \sum_{t=1}^{\infty} \frac{D_t}{(1 + k_s)^t}.
\end{aligned}
$$

7-6

What about the more typical case, where you expect to hold the stock for a finite period and then sell it — what will be the value of $\hat{P}_0$ in this case? Unless the company is likely to be liquidated and thus to disappear, *the value of the stock is again determined by Equation 7-6.* To see this, recognize that for any individual investor, the expected cash flows consist of expected dividends plus the expected sale price of the stock. However, the sale price the current investor receives will depend on the dividends some future investor expects. Therefore, for all present and future investors in total, expected cash flows depend on expected future dividends. To put it another way, unless a firm is liquidated or sold to another concern, the cash flows it provides to its stockholders will consist only of a stream of dividends; therefore, the value of a share of its stock must be established as the present value of that expected dividend stream.

The general validity of Equation 7-6 can also be confirmed by asking the following question: Suppose I buy a stock and expect to hold it for 1 year. I will receive dividends during the year plus the value $\hat{P}_1$ when I sell out at the end of the year. But what will determine the value of $\hat{P}_1$? The answer is that it will be determined as the present value of the dividends during Year 2 plus the stock price at the end of that year, which in turn will be determined as the present value of another set of future dividends and an even more distant stock price. This process can be continued ad infinitum, and the ultimate result is Equation 7-6.[11]

Equation 7-6 is a generalized stock valuation model in the sense that the time pattern of D_t can be anything: D_t can be rising, falling, or constant, or it can even be fluctuating randomly, and Equation 7-6 will still hold. Often, however, the projected stream of dividends follows a systematic pattern, in which case we can develop a simplified (that is, easier to evaluate) version of the stock valuation model expressed in Equation 7-6. In the following sections we consider the cases of zero growth, constant growth, and nonconstant growth.

STOCKS WITH ZERO GROWTH

Suppose dividends are not expected to grow at all but to remain constant. Here we have a *zero growth stock,* for which the dividends expected in future years are equal to some constant amount — that is, $D_1 = D_2 = D_3$ and so on. Therefore, we can drop the subscripts on D and rewrite Equation 7-6 as follows:

$$\hat{P}_0 = \frac{D}{(1 + k_s)^1} + \frac{D}{(1 + k_s)^2} + \cdots + \frac{D}{(1 + k_s)^\infty}. \qquad \text{7-6a}$$

---

[11]We should note that investors periodically lose sight of the long-run nature of stocks as investments and forget that in order to sell a stock at a profit, one must find a buyer who will pay the higher price. If you analyzed a stock's value in accordance with Equation 7-6, concluded that the stock's market price exceeded a reasonable value, and then bought the stock anyway, then you would be following the "bigger fool" theory of investment — you think that you may be a fool to buy the stock at its excessive price, but you also think that when you get ready to sell it, you can find someone who is an even bigger fool. The bigger fool theory was widely followed in the summer of 1987, just before the stock market lost about one-quarter of its value in the "Black Monday" crash of October 19, 1987.

As we noted in Chapter 6 in connection with the British consol bond and also in our discussion of preferred stocks, a security that is expected to pay a constant amount each year forever is called a perpetuity. *Therefore, a zero growth stock is a perpetuity.*

Although a zero growth stock is expected to provide a constant stream of dividends into the indefinite future, each dividend has a smaller present value than the preceding one, and as N gets very large, the present value of the future dividends approaches zero. To illustrate, suppose D = $1.15 and k_s = 13.4%. We can rewrite Equation 7-6a as follows:

$$\hat{P}_0 = \frac{\$1.15}{(1.134)^1} + \frac{\$1.15}{(1.134)^2} + \frac{\$1.15}{(1.134)^3} + \cdots + \frac{\$1.15}{(1.134)^{50}} + \cdots + \frac{\$1.15}{(1.134)^{100}} + \cdots$$

$$= \ \$1.01 \ + \ \$0.89 \ + \ \$0.79 \ + \cdots + \ \$0.002 \ + \cdots + \$0.000004 + \cdots$$

We can also show the perpetuity in graph form, as in Figure 7-6. The horizontal line shows the constant dividend stream, D_t = $1.15. The descending step function curve shows the present value of each future dividend. If we extended the analysis on out to infinity and then summed the present values of all the future dividends, the sum would be equal to the value of the stock.

As we saw in Chapter 6, the value of any perpetuity is simply the payment divided by the discount rate, so the value of a zero growth stock reduces to this formula:

$$\hat{P}_0 = \frac{D}{k_s}.$$

7-7

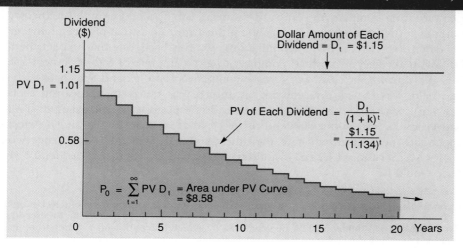

PRESENT VALUES OF DIVIDENDS OF A ZERO GROWTH STOCK (PERPETUITY)   FIGURE 7-6

Therefore, the value of our illustrative stock is $8.58:

$$\hat{P}_0 = \frac{\$1.15}{0.134} = \$8.58.$$

If you extended Figure 7-6 on out forever and then added up the present value of each individual dividend, you would end up with the intrinsic value of the stock, $8.58.[12] The actual market value of the stock, P_0, could be greater than, less than, or equal to $8.58, depending on other investors' perceptions of the dividend pattern and riskiness of the stock.

We could transpose the $\hat{P}_0$ and the k_s in Equation 7-7 and solve for k_s to produce Equation 7-8:

$$\hat{k}_s = \frac{D}{P_0}. \qquad\qquad 7\text{-}8$$

We could then look up the price of the stock and the latest dividend, P_0 and D, in the newspaper, and the value D/P_0 would be the rate of return we could expect to earn if we bought the stock. Since we are dealing with an *expected rate of return,* we put a "hat" on the k value. Thus, if we bought the stock at a price of $8.58 and expected to receive a constant dividend of $1.15, our expected rate of return would be

$$\hat{k}_s = \frac{\$1.15}{\$8.58} = 0.134 = 13.4\%.$$

NORMAL, OR CONSTANT, GROWTH

Although the zero growth model is applicable to a few companies, the earnings and dividends of most companies are expected to increase each year. Expected growth rates vary from company to company, but aggregate dividend growth is expected to continue in the foreseeable future at about the same rate as that of the nominal gross domestic product (real GDP plus inflation). On this basis, one may expect the dividend of an average, or "normal," company to grow at a rate of 6 to 8 percent a year. Thus, if a *normal, or constant, growth* company's last dividend, which has already been paid, was D_0, its dividend in any future Year t may be forecasted as $D_t = D_0(1 + g)^t$, where g is the constant expected rate of growth. For example, if Allied Food Products just paid a dividend of $1.15 (that is, $D_0 = \$1.15$), and if investors expect an 8 percent growth rate, then the estimated dividend 1 year hence would be $D_1 = \$1.15(1.08) = \$1.24$; D_2 would be $1.34; and the estimated dividend 5 years hence would be

---

[12]If you think that having a stock pay dividends forever is unrealistic, then think of it as lasting only for 50 years. Here you would have an annuity of $1.15 per year for 50 years. The PV of a 50-year annuity of $1.15, discounted at 13.4 percent, is $8.57, which differs by only a penny from that of the perpetuity. Thus, the dividends from Years 51 to infinity contribute almost nothing to the value of the stock.

$$D_t = D_0(1 + g)^t = \$1.15(1.08)^5 = \$1.69.$$

Using this method for estimating future dividends, we can determine the current stock value, $\hat{P}_0$, using Equation 7-6 as set forth previously. In other words, we can find the expected future cash flow stream (the dividends), then calculate the present value of each dividend payment, and finally sum these present values to find the value of the stock. Thus, the intrinsic value of the stock is equal to the present value of its expected future dividends.

If g is constant, Equation 7-6 may be rewritten as follows:[13]

$$\hat{P}_0 = \frac{D_0(1 + g)^1}{(1 + k_s)^1} + \frac{D_0(1 + g)^2}{(1 + k_s)^2} + \cdots + \frac{D_0(1 + g)^\infty}{(1 + k_s)^\infty}$$
$$= \frac{D_0(1 + g)}{k_s - g} = \frac{D_1}{k_s - g}.$$

7-9

Inserting values into Equation 7-9, we find the value of our illustrative stock to be $23.00:

$$\hat{P}_0 = \frac{\$1.15(1.08)}{0.134 - 0.08} = \frac{\$1.242}{0.054} = \$23.00.$$

The *constant growth model* as set forth in the last term of Equation 7-9 is often called the Gordon Model, after Myron J. Gordon, who did much to develop and popularize it.

Note that Equation 7-9 is sufficiently general to encompass the zero growth case described earlier: If growth is zero, this is simply a special case of constant growth, and Equation 7-9 is equal to Equation 7-7. Note also that a necessary condition for the derivation of the simplified form of Equation 7-9 is that k_s be greater than g. If the equation is used in situations where k_s is not greater than g, the results will be meaningless.

The concept underlying the valuation process for a constant growth stock is graphed in Figure 7-7. Dividends are growing at the rate g = 8%, but because $k_s > g$, the present value of each future dividend is declining. For example, the dividend in Year 1 is $D_1 = D_0(1 + g)^1 = \$1.15(1.08) = \$1.242$. However, the present value of this dividend, discounted at 13.4 percent, is $PV(D_1) = \$1.242/(1.134)^1 = \$1.095$. The dividend expected in Year 2 grows to $\$1.242(1.08) = \$1.341$, but the present value of this dividend falls to $1.04. Continuing, $D_3 = \$1.449$ and $PV(D_3) = \$0.993$, and so on. Thus, the expected dividends are growing, but the present value of each successive dividend is declining because the dividend growth rate (8%) is less than the rate used for discounting the dividends to the present (13.4%).

---

[13]Equation 7-9 is derived in Appendix 4A of Eugene F. Brigham and Louis C. Gapenski, *Intermediate Financial Management*, 5th ed. (Fort Worth, Tex.: Dryden Press, 1996). In essence, Equation 7-9 is the sum of a geometric progression, and the final result is the solution value of the progression.

FIGURE 7-7	PRESENT VALUES OF DIVIDENDS OF A CONSTANT GROWTH STOCK: $D_0 = \$1.15$, $g = 8\%$, $k_s = 13.4\%$

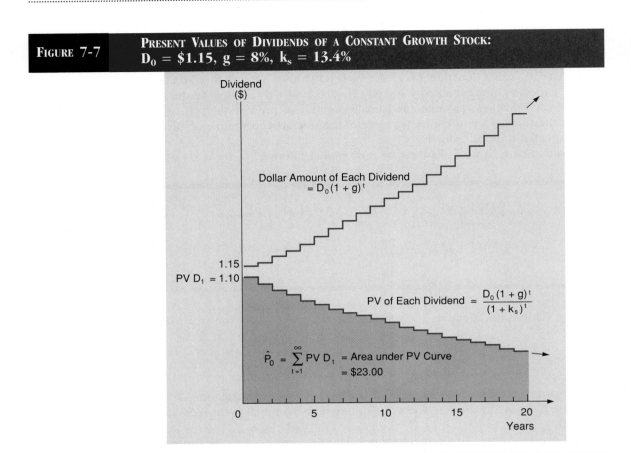

If we summed the present values of each future dividend, this summation would be the value of the stock, $\hat{P}_0$. When g is a constant, this summation is equal to $D_1/(k_s - g)$, as shown in Equation 7-9. Therefore, if we extended the lower step function curve in Figure 7-7 on out to infinity and added up the present values of each future dividend, the summation would be identical to the value given by Equation 7-9, $23.00.

Growth in dividends occurs primarily as a result of growth in *earnings per share (EPS)*. Earnings growth, in turn, results from a number of factors, including (1) inflation, (2) the amount of earnings the company retains and reinvests, and (3) the rate of return the company earns on its equity (ROE). Regarding inflation, if output (in units) is stable and if both sales prices and input costs rise at the inflation rate, then EPS will also grow at the inflation rate. EPS will also grow as a result of the reinvestment, or plowback, of earnings. If the firm's earnings are not all paid out as dividends (that is, if some fraction of earnings is retained), the dollars of investment behind each share will rise over time, which should lead to growth in earnings and dividends.

EXPECTED RATE OF RETURN ON A CONSTANT GROWTH STOCK

We can solve Equation 7-9 for k_s, again using the hat to denote that we are dealing with an expected rate of return:[14]

$$
\begin{array}{ccc}
\text{Expected rate} & \text{Expected} & \text{Expected growth} \\
\text{of return} = & \text{dividend} + & \text{rate, or capital} \\
& \text{yield} & \text{gains yield} \\
\\
\hat{k}_s & = \dfrac{D_1}{P_0} & + \quad g.
\end{array}
$$

7-10

Thus, if you buy a stock at a price $P_0 = \$23$, and if you expect the stock to pay a dividend $D_1 = \$1.242$ one year from now and to grow at a constant rate $g = 8\%$ in the future, then your expected rate of return will be 13.4 percent:

$$
\hat{k}_s = \frac{\$1.242}{\$23} + 8\% = 5.4\% + 8\% = 13.4\%.
$$

In this form, we see that $\hat{k}_s$ is an *expected total return* and that it consists of an *expected dividend yield,* $D_1/P_0 = 5.4\%$, plus an *expected growth rate or capital gains yield,* $g = 8\%$.

Suppose this analysis had been conducted on January 1, 1997, so $P_0 = \$23$ is the January 1, 1997, stock price and $D_1 = \$1.242$ is the dividend expected at the end of 1997. What is the expected stock price at the end of 1997 (or the beginning of 1998)? We would again apply Equation 7-9, but this time we would use the 1998 dividend, $D_2 = D_1(1 + g) = \$1.242(1.08) = \$1.3414$:

$$
\hat{P}_{1/1/1998} = \frac{D_{1998}}{k_s - g} = \frac{\$1.3414}{0.134 - 0.08} = \$24.84.
$$

Now notice that $\$24.84$ is 8 percent greater than P_0, the $23 price on January 1, 1997:

$$
\$23(1.08) = \$24.84.
$$

Thus, we would expect to make a capital gain of $\$24.84 - \$23 = \$1.84$ during 1997, and a capital gains yield of 8 percent:

$$
\text{Capital gains yield}_{1997} = \frac{\text{Capital gain}}{\text{Beginning price}} = \frac{\$1.84}{\$23} = 0.08 = 8\%.
$$

We could extend the analysis on out, and in each future year the expected capital gains yield would always equal g, the expected dividend growth rate.

---

[14]The k_s value of Equation 7-9 is a *required* rate of return, but when we transform it to obtain Equation 7-10, we are finding an *expected* rate of return. Obviously, the transformation requires that $k_s = \hat{k}_s$. This equality holds if the stock market is in equilibrium, a condition that will be discussed later in the chapter.

Continuing, the dividend yield in 1998 could be estimated as follows:

$$\text{Dividend yield}_{1998} = \frac{D_{1998}}{\hat{P}_{1/1/98}} = \frac{\$1.3414}{\$24.84} = 0.054 = 5.4\%.$$

The dividend yield for 1999 could also be calculated, and again it would be 5.4 percent. Thus, *for a constant growth stock,* the following conditions must hold:

1. The dividend is expected to grow forever at a constant rate, g.
2. The stock price is expected to grow at this same rate.
3. The expected dividend yield is a constant.
4. The expected capital gains yield is also a constant, and it is equal to g.
5. The expected total rate of return, $\hat{k}_s$, is equal to the expected dividend yield plus the expected growth rate: $\hat{k}_s$ = dividend yield + g.

The term *expected* should be clarified — it means expected in a probabilistic sense, as the statistically expected outcome. Thus, if we say the growth rate is expected to remain constant at 8 percent, we mean that the best prediction for the growth rate in any future year is 8 percent, not that we literally expect the growth rate to be exactly equal to 8 percent in each future year. In this sense, the constant growth assumption is a reasonable one for many large, mature companies.

NONCONSTANT GROWTH

Firms typically go through *life cycles.* During the early part of their lives, their growth is much faster than that of the economy as a whole; then they match the economy's growth; and finally their growth is slower than that of the economy.[15] Automobile manufacturers in the 1920s and computer software firms such as Microsoft in the 1990s are examples of firms in the early part of the cycle; these firms are called *supernormal growth* firms. Figure 7-8 illustrates supernormal growth and also compares it with normal growth, zero growth, and negative growth.[16]

In the figure, the dividends of the supernormal growth firm are expected to grow at a 30 percent rate for 3 years, after which the growth rate is expected to

---

[15]The life cycle concept could be broadened to *product cycle,* which would include both small, startup companies and large companies like IBM, which periodically introduce new products that give sales and earnings a boost. We should also mention *business cycles,* which alternately depress and boost sales and profits. The growth rate just after a major new product has been introduced, or just after a firm emerges from the depths of a recession, is likely to be much higher than the "expected long-run average growth rate," or "normalized" growth rate, which is the proper number for a DCF constant growth analysis.

[16]A negative growth rate indicates a declining company. A mining company whose profits are falling because of a declining ore body is an example. Someone buying such a company would expect its earnings, and consequently its dividends and stock price, to decline each year, and this would lead to capital losses rather than capital gains. Obviously, a declining company's stock price will be relatively low, and its dividend yield must be high enough to offset the expected capital loss and still produce a competitive total return. Students sometimes argue that they would not be willing to buy a stock whose price was expected to decline. However, if the annual dividends are large enough to *more than offset* the falling stock price, the stock still could provide a good return.

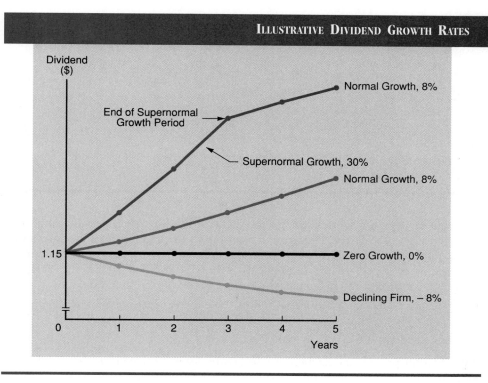

ILLUSTRATIVE DIVIDEND GROWTH RATES | **FIGURE 7-8**

fall to 8 percent, the assumed average for the economy. The value of this firm, like any other, is the present value of its expected future dividends as determined by Equation 7-6. In the case in which D_t is growing at a constant rate, we simplified Equation 7-6 to $\hat{P}_0 = D_1/(k_s - g)$. In the supernormal case, however, the expected growth rate is not a constant—it declines at the end of the period of supernormal growth. To find the value of such a stock, or of any nonconstant growth stock when the growth rate will eventually stabilize, we proceed in three steps:

1. Find the PV of the dividends during the period of nonconstant growth.
2. Find the price of the stock at the end of the nonconstant growth period, at which point it has become a constant growth stock, and discount this price back to the present.
3. Add these two components to find the intrinsic value of the stock, $\hat{P}_0$.

Figure 7-9 can be used to illustrate the process for valuing nonconstant growth stocks, assuming the following five facts exist:

k_s = stockholders' required rate of return = 13.4%. This rate is used to discount the cash flows.

N = years of supernormal growth = 3.

g_s = rate of growth in both earnings and dividends during the supernormal growth period = 30%. (Note: The growth rate during the supernormal growth period could vary from year to year. Also, there could be several different supernormal growth periods, for example, 30% for 3 years, then 20% for 3 years, and then a constant 8%.) This rate is shown directly on the time line.

g_n = rate of normal, constant growth after the supernormal period = 8%. This rate is also shown on the time line, after Year 3.

D_0 = last dividend the company paid = $1.15.

The valuation process as diagrammed in Figure 7-9 is explained in the three steps set forth below. The value of the supernormal growth stock is calculated to be $39.21.

Step 1. Calculate the dividends expected at the end of each year during the supernormal growth period. Calculate the first dividend, $D_1 = D_0(1 + g_s)$ = $1.15(1.30) = $1.4950. Here g_s is the growth rate during the 3-year supernormal growth period, 30 percent. Show the $1.4950 on the time line as the cash flow for Year 1. Now calculate $D_2 = D_1(1 + g_s)$ = $1.4950(1.30) = $1.9435, and then $D_3 = D_2(1 + g_s)$ = $1.9435(1.30) = $2.5266. Show these values on the time line as the cash flows for Years 2 and 3.

Step 2. The price of the stock is the PV of dividends from Year 1 to infinity, so in theory we could project each future dividend, with growth at the normal growth rate, g_n = 8%, used to calculate D_4 and the following dividends. However, we know that after D_3 has been paid, which is at the end of Year 3, the stock becomes a constant growth stock, so we can use the constant growth formula to find $\hat{P}_3$, which is the PV of the dividends from Year 4 to infinity.

First, we determine D_4 = $2.5266(1.08) = $2.7287 for use in the formula, and then we calculate $\hat{P}_3$ as follows:

$$\hat{P}_3 = \frac{D_4}{k_s - g_n} = \frac{\$2.7287}{0.134 - 0.08} = \$50.5310.$$

Now we show this $50.5310 on the time line as a second cash flow at Year 3. The $50.5310 is a Year 3 cash flow in the sense that the owner of the stock could sell it for $50.5310 at Year 3 and also in the sense that $50.5310 is the present value at t = 3 of the dividend cash flows from Year 4 to infinity. Note that the *total cash flow* at Year 3 consists of the sum $D_3 + \hat{P}_3 = \$2.5266 + \$50.5310 = \$53.0576$.

Step 3. Now that the cash flows have been placed on the time line, we can discount each cash flow at the required rate of return, $k_s = 13.4\%$, using the cash flow (CFLO) register of your calculator. You must enter 0 for CF_0 because you get no cash flow at Time 0, then $CF_1 = 1.495$, $CF_2 = 1.9435$, and $CF_3 = 2.5266 + 50.531 = 53.0576$. Then enter I = 13.4, and press the NPV key to find the value of the stock, $39.21.

The example shown in Figure 7-9 assumed that growth would be a constant 30 percent for 3 years and 8 percent thereafter. However, the most likely scenario is often that a company's growth rate will decline steadily over some fairly long period before reaching a constant growth situation. For example, some analysts expect Intel's 1997 growth rate to be about 30 percent, then to decline by about 2 percentage points per year over the next 10 years, and then to level out at about 10 percent per year in 2006 and thereafter. This situation, and any other, can be analyzed using Equation 7-10:

$$
P_0 = \frac{D_0(1 + g_1)}{(1 + k_s)^1} + \frac{D_1(1 + g_2)}{(1 + k_s)^2} + \cdots + \frac{D_{m-1}(1 + g_m)}{(1 + k_s)^m}
$$
$$
+ \left(\frac{D_m(1 + g_n)}{k_s - g_n}\right)\left(\frac{1}{1 + k_s}\right)^m.
$$

7-10

Here we know the last dividend (D_0) and the required return (k_s), and we have estimates of the growth rate for each year (g_t) during the years of supernormal growth, the length of the supernormal growth period (m), and the constant, or "normal," long-run growth rate (g_n). Given these inputs, it is easy to use a computer spreadsheet to find the value of the stock. Note too that projected dividends could be zero for a number of years, as was true for Apple Computer and Intel just after their founding and as is still true for Microsoft, Netscape, and many startup firms which need their earnings to finance growth.

Security analysts evaluate companies such as Apple, Intel, Microsoft, and Netscape using Equation 7-10. The mechanics are simple (with a spreadsheet such as *Excel*), but getting good estimates of the growth rates, the years of supernormal growth, and the appropriate discount rate is not at all simple. That's why good analysts command salaries that go up into the millions.

Explain the following statement: "Whereas a bond contains a promise to pay inter-
est, common stock provides an expectation but no promise of dividends."
What are the two elements of a stock's expected return?
Write out and explain the valuation model for a zero growth stock.
Write out and explain the valuation model for a constant growth stock.
How does one calculate the capital gains yield and the dividend yield of a stock?
Explain how one would find the value of a nonconstant growth stock.

STOCK MARKET EQUILIBRIUM

Recall from Chapter 4 that the required return on Stock X, k_X, can be found using
the Security Market Line (SML) equation:

$$k_X = k_{RF} + (k_M - k_{RF}) b_X.$$

If the risk-free rate of return is 8 percent, if the market risk premium is 4 percent,
and if Stock X has a beta of 2, then the investor will require a return of 16 percent
on Stock X, calculated as follows:

$$k_X = 8\% + (12\% - 8\%) 2.0$$
$$= 16\%.$$

This 16 percent required return is shown as the highest dot on the SML in Figure 7-10.

FIGURE 7-10   EXPECTED AND REQUIRED RETURNS ON STOCK X

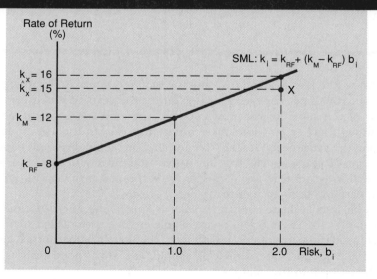

The investor will want to buy Stock X if the expected rate of return is more than 16 percent, will want to sell it if the expected rate of return is less than 16 percent, and will be indifferent, hence will hold but not buy or sell, if the expected rate of return is exactly 16 percent. Now suppose the investor's portfolio contains Stock X, and he or she analyzes the stock's prospects and concludes that its earnings, dividends, and price can be expected to grow at a constant rate of 5 percent per year. The last dividend was $D_0 = \$2.8571$, so the next expected dividend is

$$D_1 = \$2.8571(1.05) = \$3.$$

Our investor observes that the present price of the stock, P_0, is $30. Should he or she purchase more of Stock X, sell the present holdings, or maintain the present position?

The investor can calculate Stock X's *expected rate of return* as follows:

$$\hat{k}_X = \frac{D_1}{P_0} + g = \frac{\$3}{\$30} + 5\% = 15\%.$$

This value is plotted on Figure 7-10 as Point X, which is below the SML. Because the expected rate of return is less than the required return, this investor would want to sell the stock, as would other holders. However, few people would want to buy at the $30 price, so the present owners would be unable to find buyers unless they cut the price of the stock. Thus, the price would decline, and this decline would continue until the stock's price reached $27.27, at which point the market for this security would be in *equilibrium,* because the expected rate of return, 16 percent, would be equal to the required rate of return:

$$\hat{k}_X = \frac{\$3}{\$27.27} + 5\% = 11\% + 5\% = 16\% = k_X.$$

Had the stock initially sold for less than $27.27, say, at $25, events would have been reversed. Investors would have wanted to buy the stock because its expected rate of return would have exceeded its required rate of return, and buy orders would have driven the stock's price up to $27.27.

To summarize, in equilibrium these two related conditions must hold:

1. The expected rate of return as seen by the marginal investor must equal the required rate of return: $\hat{k}_i = k_i$.

2. The actual market price of the stock must equal its intrinsic value as estimated by the marginal investor: $P_0 = \hat{P}_0$.

Of course, some individual investors may believe that $\hat{k}_i > k$ and $\hat{P}_0 > P_0$, and hence they would be eager to buy the stock, while other investors may have an opposite view and would sell all of their shares. However, it is the marginal investor who establishes the actual market price, and for this investor, $\hat{k}_i = k_i$ and $P_0 = \hat{P}_0$, for if these conditions do not hold, trading will occur until they do hold.

CHANGES IN EQUILIBRIUM STOCK PRICES

Stock market prices are not constant — they undergo violent changes at times. For example, on October 19, 1987, the Dow Jones average dropped 508 points, and the average stock lost about 25 percent of its value in just one day. Some stocks, including Disney, lost over half of their value that day. On the other hand, in 1995 the average stock's price increased by about 35 percent, and a number of stocks increased by 200 to 300 percent.

To see how such changes can occur, let us assume that Stock X is in equilibrium, selling at a price of $27.27 per share. If all expectations were exactly met, during the next year the price would gradually rise to $28.63, or by 5 percent. However, many different events could occur to cause a change in the equilibrium price of the stock. To illustrate, consider again the set of inputs used to develop Stock X's price of $27.27, along with a new set of assumed input variables:

	VARIABLE VALUE	
	ORIGINAL	NEW
Risk-free rate, k_{RF}	8%	7%
Market risk premium, $k_M - k_{RF}$	4%	3%
Stock X's beta coefficient, b_X	2.0	1.0
Stock X's expected growth rate, g_X	5%	6%
D_0	$2.8571	$2.8571
Price of Stock X	$27.27	?

Now give yourself a test: How would the change in each variable, by itself, affect the price, and what is your guess as to the new stock price?

Every change, taken alone, would lead to an increase in the price. The first three variables influence k_X, which declines from 16 to 10 percent:

$$\text{Original } k_X = 8\% + 4\%(2.0) = 16\%.$$

$$\text{New } k_X = 7\% + 3\%(1.0) = 10\%.$$

Using these values, together with the new g value, we find that $\hat{P}_0$ rises from $27.27 to $75.71.[17]

$$\text{Original } \hat{P}_0 = \frac{\$2.8571(1.05)}{0.16 - 0.05} = \frac{\$3}{0.11} = \$27.27.$$

$$\text{New } \hat{P}_0 = \frac{\$2.8571(1.06)}{0.10 - 0.06} = \frac{\$3.0285}{0.04} = \$75.71.$$

At the new price, the expected and required rates of return will be equal:[18]

$$\hat{k}_X = \frac{\$3.0285}{\$75.71} + 6\% = 10\% = k_X.$$

---

[17]A price change of this magnitude is by no means rare. The prices of *many* stocks double or halve during a year. For example, during 1995, Continental Airlines increased in value by 370 percent; on the other hand, Smith Corona, a typewriter manufacturer, fell by 96 percent.

[18]It should be obvious by now that *realized* rates of return are not necessarily equal to expected and required returns. Thus, an investor might have *expected* to receive a return of 15 percent if he or she had bought Continental Airlines or Smith Corona stock in early 1995, but, after the fact, the realized return on Continental Airlines was far above 15 percent, whereas that on Smith Corona was far below.

Evidence suggests that stocks, especially those of large companies, adjust rapidly to disequilibrium situations. Consequently, equilibrium ordinarily exists for any given stock, and, in general, required and expected returns are equal. Stock prices certainly change, sometimes violently and rapidly, but this simply reflects changing conditions and expectations. There are, of course, times when a stock continues to react for several months to a favorable or unfavorable development, but this does not signify a long adjustment period; rather, it simply illustrates that as more new pieces of information about the situation become available, the market adjusts to them. The ability of the market to adjust to new information is discussed in the next section.

THE EFFICIENT MARKETS HYPOTHESIS

A body of theory called the *Efficient Markets Hypothesis (EMH)* holds (1) that stocks are always in equilibrium and (2) that it is impossible for an investor to consistently "beat the market." Essentially, those who believe in the EMH note that there are 100,000 or so full-time, highly trained, professional analysts and traders operating in the market, while there are fewer than 3,000 major stocks. Therefore, if each analyst followed 30 stocks (which is about right, as analysts tend to specialize in the stocks in a specific industry), there would on average be 1,000 analysts following each stock. Further, these analysts work for organizations such as Citibank, Merrill Lynch, Prudential Insurance, Fidelity Investments, and the like, which have billions of dollars available with which to take advantage of bargains. In addition, as a result of SEC disclosure requirements and electronic information networks, as new information about a stock becomes available, these 1,000 analysts generally receive and evaluate it at about the same time. Therefore, the price of a stock will adjust almost immediately to any new development.

LEVELS OF MARKET EFFICIENCY

If markets are efficient, stock prices will rapidly reflect all available information. This raises an important question: What types of information are available and, therefore, are incorporated into stock prices? Financial theorists have discussed three forms, or levels, of market efficiency.

WEAK-FORM EFFICIENCY The *weak-form* of the EMH states that all information contained in past price movements is fully reflected in current market prices. If this were true, then information about recent trends in stock prices would be of no use in selecting stocks — the fact that a stock has risen for the past three days, for example, would give us no useful clues as to what it will do today or tomorrow. People who believe that weak-form efficiency exists also believe that "tape watchers" and "chartists" are wasting their time.[19]

For example, after studying the past history of the stock market, a chartist might "discover" the following pattern: If a stock falls on three consecutive days, its price typically rises by 10 percent the following day. The technician would then conclude

---

[19]Tape watchers are people who watch the NYSE tape, while chartists plot past patterns of stock price movements. Both are called "technicians," and both believe that they can tell if something is happening to the stock that will cause its price to move up or down in the near future.

that investors could make money by purchasing a stock whose price has fallen three consecutive days.

But if this pattern truly existed, wouldn't other investors also discover it, and if so, why would anyone be willing to sell a stock after it had fallen three consecutive days? In other words, if a stock is selling at $40 per share after falling three consecutive days, why would investors sell the stock if they expected it to rise to $44 per share one day later? Those who believe in weak-form efficiency argue that if the stock would really rise to $44 per share tomorrow, its price *today* would actually rise to somewhere near $44 per share, thereby eliminating the trading opportunity. In summary, weak-form efficiency implies that any information that comes from past stock prices is rapidly incorporated into the current stock price.

Semistrong-Form Efficiency   The *semistrong-form* of the EMH states that current market prices reflect all *publicly available* information. Therefore, if semistrong-form efficiency exists, it would do no good to pore over annual reports or other published data because market prices would have already adjusted to any good or bad news contained in such reports, back when the news came out. With semistrong-form efficiency, investors should expect to earn the returns predicted by the SML, but they should not expect to do any better unless they have information that is not publicly available. However, insiders (for example, the presidents of companies) who have information which is not publicly available can earn abnormal returns (returns higher than those predicted by the SML) even under semistrong-form efficiency.

Another implication of semistrong-form efficiency is that whenever information is released to the public, stock prices will respond only if the information is different from what had been expected. If, for example, a company announces a 30 percent increase in earnings, and if that increase is consistent with what analysts had been expecting, the announcement should have little or no effect on the company's stock price. On the other hand, the stock price would probably fall if analysts had expected earnings to increase by more than 30 percent, but it would rise if they had expected a significantly smaller increase.

Strong-Form Efficiency   The *strong-form* of the EMH states that current market prices reflect all pertinent information, whether publicly available or privately held. If this form holds, even insiders would find it impossible to earn abnormal returns in the stock market.[20]

Many empirical studies have been conducted to test for the three forms of market efficiency. Most of these studies suggest that the stock market is indeed highly efficient in the weak form and reasonably efficient in the semistrong form, at least for the larger and more widely followed stocks. However, the strong-form EMH does not hold, so abnormal (but illegal) profits can be made by those who possess inside information.

---

[20]Several cases of illegal insider trading have made the news headlines. These cases involved employees of several major investment banking houses and even an employee of the SEC. In the most famous case, Ivan Boesky admitted to making $50 million by purchasing the stock of firms he knew were about to merge. He went to jail, and he had to pay a large fine, but he helped disprove the strong-form EMH.

IMPLICATIONS OF MARKET EFFICIENCY

What bearing does the EMH have on financial decisions? Since stock prices do seem to reflect public information, most stocks appear to be fairly valued. This does not mean that new information could not cause a stock's price to soar or to plummet, but it does mean that stocks in general are neither overvalued nor undervalued — they are fairly priced and in equilibrium. However, there are certainly cases in which corporate insiders have information not known to outsiders.

If the EMH is correct, it is a waste of time for most of us to analyze stocks by looking for those that are undervalued. If stock prices already reflect all publicly available information, hence are fairly priced, one can "beat the market" only by luck. Thus, it is difficult, if not impossible, for anyone to consistently outperform the market averages. Empirical tests have shown that the EMH, in its weak and semistrong forms, is valid. However, people such as corporate officers who have inside information can do better than the averages, and individuals and organizations that are especially good at digging out information on small, new companies also seem to do consistently well. Also, some investors may be able to analyze and react more quickly than others to releases of new information, and these investors may have an advantage over others. However, the buy-sell actions of those investors quickly bring market prices into equilibrium. Therefore, it is generally safe to assume that $\hat{k} = k$, that $\hat{P}_0 = P_0$, and that stocks plot on the SML.

Market efficiency also has important implications for managerial decisions, especially those pertaining to common stock issues, stock repurchases, and tender offers. Stocks appear to be fairly valued, so decisions based on the premise that a stock is undervalued or overvalued must be approached with caution. However, managers do have better information about their own companies than outsiders, and this information can legally be used to the companies' (but not the managers') advantage.

We should also note that some Wall Street pros have consistently beaten the market over many years, which is inconsistent with the EMH. An interesting article in the April 3, 1995, issue of *Fortune* (Terence P. Paré, "Yes, You Can Beat the Market") argued strongly against the EMH. Paré suggested that each stock has a fundamental value, but when good or bad news about it is announced, most investors fail to interpret this news correctly. As a result, stocks are generally priced above or below their long-term values.

Think of a graph with stock price on the vertical axis and years on the horizontal axis. A stock's fundamental value might be moving up steadily over time as it retains and reinvests earnings. However, its actual price might fluctuate about the intrinsic value line, overreacting to good or bad news and indicating departures from equilibrium. Successful value investors, according to the article, use fundamental analysis to identify stocks' intrinsic values as reflected by the trend line, and then they buy stocks that are undervalued and sell those that are overvalued.

Paré's argument implies that the market is systematically out of equilibrium and that investors can act on this knowledge to beat the market. That position may turn out to be correct, but it may also be that the superior performance Paré noted simply demonstrates that some people are better at obtaining and interpreting information than others. However, the fact that most stock mutual fund managers fail to beat "the averages" demonstrates, even if Paré is right, that it is extremely difficult to identify those stocks that are improperly valued.

ACTUAL STOCK PRICES AND RETURNS

Our discussion thus far has focused on *expected* stock prices and *expected* rates of return. Anyone who has ever invested in the stock market knows that there can be, and generally are, large differences between *expected* and *realized* prices and returns.

We can use IBM to illustrate this point. In early 1995, IBM's stock price was about $70 per share. Its 1994 dividend, D_0, had been $1.00, but analysts expected the dividend to grow at a constant rate of about 10 percent in the future. Thus, an average investor who bought IBM at a price of $70 would have expected to earn a return of about 11.6 percent:

$$\hat{k}_s = \frac{\text{Expected dividend}}{\text{yield}} + \frac{\text{Expected growth rate, which is also}}{\text{the expected capital gains yield}}$$

$$= \frac{D_0(1 + g)}{P_0} + g = \frac{\$1.10}{\$70} + 10\%$$

$$= 1.6\% + 10.0\% = 11.6\%.$$

In fact, things worked out much better than expected. IBM's new management, which had been brought in to stem the company's mainframe losses, performed bet-

FIGURE 7-11   S&P 500 INDEX, 1967–1995

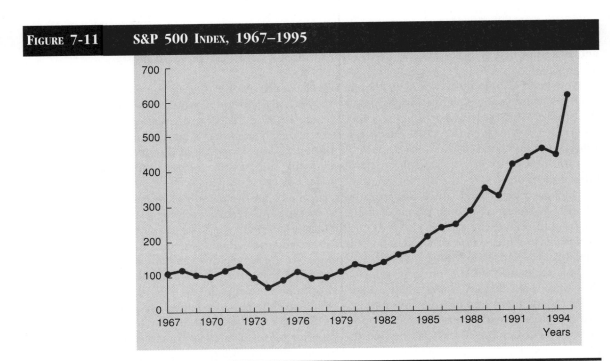

SOURCE: Data taken from various issues of *The Wall Street Journal*, "Stock Market Data Bank" section.

ter than anticipated, and IBM closed the year at $91. Thus, on a beginning-of-the-year investment of $70, the actual return on IBM for 1995 was 31.4 percent, in spite of the fact that the dividend stayed at $1.00:

$$\bar{k}_s = \text{Actual dividend yield} + \text{Actual capital gains yield}$$

$$= \frac{\$1.00}{\$70} + \frac{\$21}{\$70} = 1.4\% + 30.0\% = 31.4\%.$$

Many other stocks performed similarly to IBM's, or better, in 1995.

Figure 7-11 shows how the price of an average share of stock has varied in recent years, and Figure 7-12 shows how total realized returns have varied. The market trend has been strongly up, but it has gone up in some years and down in others, and the stocks of individual companies have likewise gone up and down. We know from theory that expected returns as estimated by a marginal investor are always positive, but in some years, as Figure 7-12 shows, negative returns have been realized. Of course, even in bad years some individual companies do well, so the "name of the game" in security analysis is to pick the winners. Financial managers attempt to take actions which will put their companies into the winners' column, but they don't always succeed. In subsequent chapters, we will examine the actions that managers can take to increase the odds of their firms doing relatively well in the marketplace.

STOCK MARKET REPORTING

Figure 7-13, taken from *The Wall Street Journal,* is a section of the stock market page for stocks listed on the NYSE. For each stock, the NYSE report provides spe-

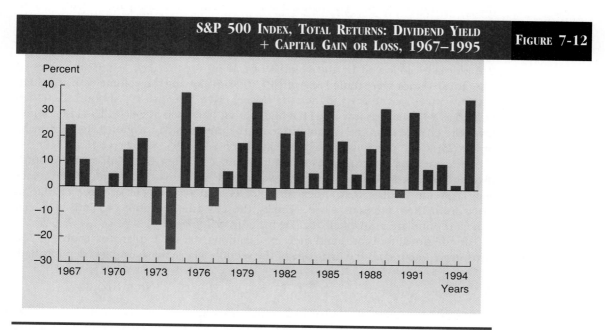

FIGURE 7-12

S&P 500 INDEX, TOTAL RETURNS: DIVIDEND YIELD + CAPITAL GAIN OR LOSS, 1967–1995

SOURCE: *Stocks, Bonds, Bills, and Inflation: 1996 Yearbook,* (Chicago: Ibbotson Associates, 1996).

FIGURE 7-13

FIGURE 7-13   **STOCK MARKET TRANSACTIONS, APRIL 19, 1996**

Quotations as of 5 p.m. Eastern Time
Friday, April 19, 1996

52 Weeks Hi	Lo	Stock	Sym	Div	Yld %	PE	Vol 100s	Hi	Lo	Close	Net Chg

-A-A-A-

50½	36⅜	ASA	ASA	2.00	4.5	...	510	45⅜	44¾	44⅞	– ¼
44½	23⅜ ♣	ATT Cap	TCC	.44	1.1	14	78	38⅜	38⅛	38⅜	+ ⅜
68⅞	47⅞	AT&T Cp	T	1.32	2.2	cc	39203	61¼	60¾	61	+ ⅛
45	11¾	AamesFnl	AAM	.30	.7	19	664	42¼	41⅛	41⅝	+ ½
44¾	36⅛	AbbotLab	ABT	.96f	2.3	19	13057	41⅞	41	41⅝	+ ⅝
19	13	Abitibi g	ABY	.30e	...	...	535	15	14¾	14⅞	– ⅛
17½	13⅛ ♣	AcceptIns	AIF	...	...	56	254	15⅞	15⅝	15¾	+ ⅜
50¾	24⅜	ACE Ltd	ACL	.56	1.3	6	455	44	43½	43½	– ¼
31⅜	15⅞	AcmeCleve	AMT	.52	1.7	7	213	30½	30¼	30½	+ ¼
38¾	**6**	**AcmeElec**	**ACE**	**...**	**dd**	**260**	**7**	**6½**	**7**	**+ ½**	

SOURCE: *The Wall Street Journal,* April 22, 1996.

cific data on the trading that took place the prior trading day. Similar information
is available for stocks listed on the other exchanges as well as for stocks traded
over-the-counter.

Stocks are listed alphabetically, from AAR Industries to Zweig; the data in Figure
7-13 were taken from the top portion of the listing. We will examine the data for
Abbott Laboratories, (AbbotLab), shown about halfway down the table. The two
columns on the left show the highest and lowest prices at which the stocks have sold
during the past year; Abbott Labs has traded in the range from $44¾ to $36⅛ during
the preceding 52 weeks. The figure just to the right of the company's ticker symbol
is the dividend; Abbott Labs had a current indicated annual dividend rate of $0.96 per
share and a dividend yield (which is the dividend divided by the closing stock price)
of 2.3 percent. Next comes the ratio of the stock's price to its annual earnings (the
P/E ratio), 19, followed by the volume of trading for the day: 1,305,700 shares of
Abbott Labs stock were traded on April 19, 1996. Following the volume come the high
and low prices for the day, and then the closing price. On April 19, Abbott Labs traded
as high as $41⅞ and as low as $41, while the last trade was at $41⅝. The last column
gives the change from the closing price on the previous day. Abbott Labs was up ⅝,
or $0.625, so the previous close must have been $45.625 – $0.625 = $45.

There are three other points to note in Figure 7-13. First, the "f" following Abbott's
dividend indicates that the dividend was raised on the last payment. Next, issues
such as Acme Electric that appear in boldface had a 5 percent or more change in
price from their previous close. Finally, the cloverleaf symbol (♣) indicates that
annual reports are available from *The Wall Street Journal*.

For additional footnotes and their explanations, see the explanatory notes in *The
Wall Street Journal* on the first page of the section where these listings are published.

A CLOSING QUESTION: HOW DO INVESTORS "REALLY" PRICE STOCKS?

At this point, readers who have had actual investment experience are likely to ask,
"Are stock prices actually determined as described in the chapter, by forecasting
future dividends, finding the PV of those dividends, and then setting the price equal

to the PV of the dividends?" Our answer is yes, but we admit that, at times, the yes is not very strong. Individual investors do not necessarily operate as the chapter suggests — most actually rely on analysts' recommendations. However, security analysts do evaluate stocks as we indicate, so it is fair to say that most stocks' prices are at most times determined as indicated in the chapter.

We could at this point get some objections. Sophisticated readers might note that during strong bull markets like the one of 1995, investors seem to "chase" stocks, and entrepreneurs with ideas but little money rush to market with initial public offerings (IPOs). These readers might also cite the example of Netscape, a 16-month-old company that sells software used to access the Internet, which went public in August 1995. The company had never earned a penny, and its revenues were only $16 million, yet investors valued the company at $2.7 billion, or 168 times revenues. The investment bankers originally planned to bring the issue out at about $14 per share, but early indications of demand were so great that the issue was priced at $28. It soared to $71 on its first day of trading, later fell back to a low of $45, but within three months had roared back to $124 per share. Were investors really pricing Netscape shares on the basis of a DCF analysis?

We believe the answer is yes, though many would disagree. First, a number of analysts, including those who worked for the underwriters, did indeed forecast Netscape's future revenues, costs, profits, and dividends, and then found a value for the stock using Equation 7-10. However, those analysts all recognized the truth in the old adage, "Garbage In, Garbage Out," or GIGO, and the fact that they could be accused of practicing the SWAG method of analysis, or "Scientific Wild A-- Guess." So, these analysts and the investors whom they represented were following the dictates of the chapter, even though their analyses demonstrated that Netscape's "true" value was highly uncertain.

Others bought Netscape's stock without even knowing how to spell the company's name — they just knew that Internet usage is growing at a phenomenal rate, that such growth is likely to continue, and that successful companies involved with important new technologies are generally quite profitable. These investors, or at least the more sophisticated ones (who are also the ones most likely to be allocated some of the stock at issuance), also know that the investment bankers do not like to bring out stocks that drop shortly after issue. Therefore, the bankers analyze the situation carefully prior to setting the initial offering price.

Our conclusion is that the prices of all stocks, even those like Netscape, are determined by the type of DCF analysis described in this chapter. However, at times, investors who do not practice DCF analysis may simply overwhelm "value investors" and run the price of a stock like Netscape up above any "reasonable" DCF-based value. If this happens, though, chances are good that the stock will eventually fall back to earth. DCF rules!

When a stock is in equilibrium, what two conditions must hold?

What is the major conclusion of the Efficient Markets Hypothesis (EMH)?

What is the difference between the three forms of the EMH: (1) weak form, (2) semi-strong form, and (3) strong form?

If a stock is not in equilibrium, explain how financial markets adjust to bring it into equilibrium.

**SELF-TEST
QUESTIONS**

SUMMARY

Corporate decisions should be analyzed in terms of how alternative courses of action are likely to affect the value of a firm. However, it is necessary to know how bond and stock prices are established before attempting to measure how a given decision will affect a specific firm's value. Accordingly, this chapter showed how bond and stock values are determined as well as how investors go about estimating the rates of return they expect to earn. The key concepts covered in the chapter are summarized below.

■ A *bond* is a long-term promissory note issued by a business or governmental unit. The firm receives the selling price of the bond in exchange for promising to make interest payments and to repay the principal on a specified future date.

■ The *value of a bond* is found as the present value of an *annuity* (the interest payments) plus the present value of a lump sum (the *principal*). The bond is evaluated at the appropriate periodic interest rate over the number of periods for which interest payments are made.

■ The equation used to find the value of an annual coupon bond is:

$$V_B = \sum_{t=1}^{N} \frac{INT}{(1 + k_d)^t} + \frac{M}{(1 + k_d)^N}.$$

An adjustment to the formula must be made if the bond pays interest *semi-annually:* divide INT and k_d by 2, and multiply N by 2.

■ The return earned on a bond held to maturity is defined as the bond's *yield to maturity (YTM)*. If the bond can be redeemed before maturity, it is *callable,* and the return investors will receive if it is called is the *yield to call (YTC)*.

■ The longer the maturity of a bond, the more its price will change in response to a given change in interest rates; this is called *interest rate,* or *price, risk.* Bonds with short maturities, however, expose the investor to high *reinvestment rate risk,* which is the risk that cash flows (interest payments plus maturity value) will have to be reinvested at lower interest rates.

■ Most preferred stocks are *perpetuities,* and the value of a share of perpetual preferred stock is found as the dividend divided by the required rate of return:

$$V_{ps} = \frac{D_{ps}}{k_{ps}}.$$

■ The *value of a share of stock* is calculated as the *present value of the stream of dividends* it is expected to provide in the future.

■ The equation used to find the *value of a constant,* or *normal, growth stock* is

$$\hat{P}_0 = \frac{D_1}{(k_s - g)}.$$

Note that k_s must be greater than g.

■ The *expected total rate of return* from a stock consists of an *expected dividend yield* plus an *expected capital gains yield*. For a constant growth stock, both the expected dividend yield and the expected capital gains yield are constant.

■ The equation for the *expected rate of return on a constant growth stock* can be expressed as follows: $\hat{k}_s = D_1/P_0 + g$.

■ A *zero growth stock* is one whose future dividends are not expected to grow at all, while a *supernormal growth stock* is one whose earnings and dividends are expected to grow much faster than the economy as a whole over some specified time period.

■ To find the *present value of a supernormal growth stock,* (1) find the dividends expected during the supernormal growth period, (2) find the price of the stock at the end of the supernormal growth period, (3) discount the dividends and the projected price back to the present, and (4) sum these PVs to find the current value of the stock, $\hat{P}_0$. The value of any nonconstant growth stock can be found in this manner.

■ The *Efficient Markets Hypothesis (EMH)* holds (1) that stocks are always in equilibrium and (2) that it is impossible for an investor who does not have inside information to consistently "beat the market." Therefore, according to the EMH, stocks are always fairly valued ($\hat{P}_0 = P_0$), the required return on a stock is equal to its expected return ($k = \hat{k}$), and all stocks' expected returns plot on the SML.

■ Finally, in this chapter we saw that differences can and do exist between realized and expected returns in the stock and bond markets, that is, $\bar{k} \neq \hat{k}$. Only for short-term, risk-free assets are expected and actual (or realized) returns generally equal.

QUESTIONS

7-1 Define each of the following terms:

a. Bond

b. Par value; maturity date; call provision

c. Coupon payment; coupon interest rate

d. Premium bond; discount bond

e. Current yield (on a bond); yield to maturity (YTM); yield to call (YTC)

f. Interest rate (or price) risk; reinvestment rate risk

g. Intrinsic value ($\hat{P}_0$); market price (P_0)

h. Required rate of return, k_s; expected rate of return, $\hat{k}_s$; actual, or realized, rate of return, $\bar{k}_s$

i. Capital gains yield; dividend yield; expected total return

j. Zero growth stock; perpetuity

k. Normal, or constant, growth; supernormal, or nonconstant, growth
l. Equilibrium
m. Efficient Markets Hypothesis (EMH); three forms of EMH

7-2   Two investors are evaluating AT&T's stock for possible purchase. They agree on the expected value of D_1 and also on the expected future dividend growth rate. Further, they agree on the riskiness of the stock. However, one investor normally holds stocks for 2 years, while the other normally holds stocks for 10 years. On the basis of the type of analysis done in this chapter, they should both be willing to pay the same price for AT&T's stock. True or false? Explain.

7-3   A bond that pays interest forever and has no maturity date is a perpetual bond. In what respect is a perpetual bond similar to a no-growth common stock, and to a share of perpetual preferred stock?

7-4   Is it true that the following equation can be used to find the value of an N-year bond that pays interest once a year?

$$V_B = \sum_{t=1}^{N} \frac{\text{Annual interest}}{(1 + k_d)^t} + \frac{\text{Par value}}{(1 + k_d)^N}.$$

7-5   "The values of outstanding bonds change whenever the going rate of interest changes. In general, short-term interest rates are more volatile than long-term interest rates. Therefore, short-term bond prices are more sensitive to interest rate changes than are long-term bond prices." Is this statement true or false? Explain.

7-6   The rate of return you would get if you bought a bond and held it to its maturity date is called the bond's yield to maturity. If interest rates in the economy rise after a bond has been issued, what will happen to the bond's price and to its YTM? Does the length of time to maturity affect the extent to which a given change in interest rates will affect the bond's price?

7-7   If you buy a *callable* bond and interest rates decline, will the value of your bond rise by as much as it would have risen if the bond had not been callable? Explain.

7-8   If you bought a share of common stock, you would typically expect to receive dividends plus capital gains. Would you expect the distribution between dividend yield and capital gains to be influenced by the firm's decision to pay more dividends rather than to retain and reinvest more of its earnings?

7-9   Is it true that the following expression can be used to find the value of a constant growth stock?

$$\hat{P}_0 = \frac{D_0}{k_s + g}.$$

SELF-TEST
PROBLEMS

(SOLUTIONS APPEAR IN APPENDIX C)

ST-1   STOCK GROWTH RATES AND VALUATION You are considering buying the stocks of two companies that operate in the same industry; they have very similar characteristics except for their dividend payout policies. Both companies are expected to earn $6 per share this year. However, Company D (for "dividend") is expected to pay out all of its earnings as dividends, while Company G (for "growth") is expected to pay out only one-third of its earnings, or $2 per share. D's stock price is $40. G and D are equally risky. Which of the following is most likely to be true?

a. Company G will have a faster growth rate than Company D. Therefore, G's stock price should be greater than $40.

b. Although G's growth rate should exceed D's, D's current dividend exceeds that of G, and this should cause D's price to exceed G's.

c. An investor in Stock D will get his or her money back faster because D pays out more of its earnings as dividends. Thus, in a sense, D is like a short-term bond, and G is like a long-term bond. Therefore, if economic shifts cause k_d and k_s to increase, and if the expected streams of dividends from D and G remain constant, Stocks D and G will both decline, but D's price should decline further.

d. D's expected and required rate of return is $\hat{k}_s = k_s = 15\%$. G's expected return will be higher because of its higher expected growth rate.

e. On the basis of the available information, the best estimate of G's growth rate is 10 percent.

7-2 BOND VALUATION The Pennington Corporation issued a new series of bonds on January 1, 1971. The bonds were sold at par ($1,000), have a 12 percent coupon, and mature in 30 years, on December 31, 2000. Coupon payments are made semiannually (on June 30 and December 31).

a. What was the YTM of Pennington's bonds on January 1, 1971?

b. What was the price of the bond on January 1, 1976, 5 years later, assuming that the level of interest rates had fallen to 10 percent?

c. Find the current yield and capital gains yield on the bond on January 1, 1976, given the price as determined in Part b.

d. On July 1, 1994, Pennington's bonds sold for $916.42. What was the YTM at that date?

e. What were the current yield and capital gains yield on July 1, 1994?

f. Now assume that you purchased an outstanding Pennington bond on March 1, 1994, when the going rate of interest was 15.5 percent. How large a check must you have written to complete the transaction?

7-3 CONSTANT GROWTH STOCK VALUATION Ewald Company's current stock price is $36, and its last dividend was $2.40. In view of Ewald's strong financial position and its consequent low risk, its required rate of return is only 12 percent. If dividends are expected to grow at a constant rate, g, in the future, and if k_s is expected to remain at 12 percent, what is Ewald's expected stock price 5 years from now?

7-4 SUPERNORMAL GROWTH STOCK VALUATION Snyder Computer Chips Inc. is experiencing a period of rapid growth. Earnings and dividends are expected to grow at a rate of 15 percent during the next 2 years, at 13 percent in the third year, and at a constant rate of 6 percent thereafter. Snyder's last dividend was $1.15, and the required rate of return on the stock is 12 percent.

a. Calculate the value of the stock today.

b. Calculate $\hat{P}_1$ and $\hat{P}_2$.

c. Calculate the dividend yield and capital gains yield for Years 1, 2, and 3.

PROBLEMS

7-1 BOND VALUATION Suppose Ford Motor Company sold an issue of bonds with a 10-year maturity, a $1,000 par value, a 10 percent coupon rate, and semiannual interest payments.

a. Two years after the bonds were issued, the going rate of interest on bonds such as these fell to 6 percent. At what price would the bonds sell?

b. Suppose that, 2 years after the initial offering, the going interest rate had risen to 12 percent. At what price would the bonds sell?

c. Suppose that the conditions in Part a existed — that is, interest rates fell to 6 percent 2 years after the issue date. Suppose further that the interest rate remained at 6 percent for the next 8 years. What would happen to the price of the Ford Motor Company bonds over time?

7-2 PERPETUAL BOND VALUATION The bonds of the McCue Corporation are perpetuities with a 10 percent coupon. Bonds of this type currently yield 8 percent, and their par value is $1,000.

a. What is the price of the McCue bonds?

b. Suppose interest rate levels rise to the point where such bonds now yield 12 percent. What would be the price of the McCue bonds?

c. At what price would the McCue bonds sell if the yield on these bonds were 10 percent?

d. How would your answers to Parts a, b, and c change if the bonds were not perpetuities but had a maturity of 20 years?

7-3 CONSTANT GROWTH STOCK VALUATION Your broker offers to sell you some shares of Stanton & Co. common stock that paid a dividend of $2 *yesterday*. You expect the dividend to grow at the rate of 5 percent per year for the next 3 years, and if you buy the stock you plan to hold it for 3 years and then sell it.

a. Find the expected dividend for each of the next 3 years; that is, calculate D_1, D_2, and D_3. Note that $D_0 = \$2$.

b. Given that the appropriate discount rate is 12 percent and that the first of these dividend payments will occur 1 year from now, find the present value of the dividend stream; that is, calculate the PV of D_1, D_2, and D_3, and then sum these PVs.

c. You expect the price of the stock 3 years from now to be $34.73; that is, you expect $\hat{P}_3$ to equal $34.73. Discounted at a 12 percent rate, what is the present value of this expected future stock price? In other words, calculate the PV of $34.73.

d. If you plan to buy the stock, hold it for 3 years, and then sell it for $34.73, what is the most you should pay for it?

e. Use Equation 7-9 to calculate the present value of this stock. Assume that $g = 5\%$, and it is constant.

f. Is the value of this stock dependent upon how long you plan to hold it? In other words, if your planned holding period were 2 years or 5 years rather than 3 years, would this affect the value of the stock today, $\hat{P}_0$?

7-4 RETURN ON COMMON STOCK You buy a share of Hoffmeister Corporation stock for $21.40. You expect it to pay dividends of $1.07, $1.1449, and $1.2250 in Years 1, 2, and 3, respectively, and you expect to sell it at a price of $26.22 at the end of 3 years.

a. Calculate the growth rate in dividends.

b. Calculate the expected dividend yield.

c. Assuming that the calculated growth rate is expected to continue, you can add the dividend yield to the expected growth rate to get the expected total rate of return. What is this stock's expected total rate of return?

7-5 CONSTANT GROWTH STOCK VALUATION Investors require a 15 percent rate of return on Shipley Company's stock ($k_s = 15\%$).

a. What will be Shipley's stock value if the previous dividend was $D_0 = \$2$ and if investors expect dividends to grow at a constant compound annual rate of (1) $- 5$ percent, (2) 0 percent, (3) 5 percent, and (4) 10 percent?

b. Using data from Part a, what is the Gordon (constant growth) model value for Shipley's stock if the required rate of return is 15 percent and the expected growth rate is (1) 15 percent or (2) 20 percent? Are these reasonable results? Explain.

c. Is it reasonable to expect that a constant growth stock would have $g > k_s$?

7-6 STOCK AND BOND REPORTING Look up the prices of BellSouth's stock and bonds in *The Wall Street Journal* (or some other newspaper which provides this information).

a. What was the stock's price range during the last year?

b. What is BellSouth's current dividend? What is its dividend yield?

c. What change occurred in BellSouth's stock price the day the newspaper was published?

d. If BellSouth were to sell a new issue of $1,000 par value long-term bonds, approximately what coupon interest rate would it have to set on the bonds if it wanted to bring them out at par? (Note: BellSouth bonds trade on the NYSE.)

e. If you had $10,000 and wanted to invest it in BellSouth, what return would you expect to get if you bought the bonds and what return if you bought BellSouth's stock? (Hint: Think about capital gains when you answer the latter part of this question.)

7-7 DISCOUNT BOND VALUATION Assume that in February 1967 the Los Angeles Airport Authority issued a series of 3.4 percent, 30-year bonds. Interest rates rose substantially in the years following the issue, and as they did, the price of the bonds declined. In February 1980, 13 years later, the price of the bonds had dropped from $1,000 to $650. In answering the following questions, assume that the bond requires annual interest payments.

a. Each bond originally sold at its $1,000 par value. What was the yield to maturity of these bonds when they were issued?

b. Calculate the yield to maturity in February 1980.

c. Assume that interest rates stabilized at the 1980 level and stayed there for the remainder of the life of the bonds. What would have been the bonds' price in February 1993 when they had 4 years remaining to maturity?

d. What will the price of the bonds be the day before they mature in 1997? (Disregard the last interest payment.)

e. In 1980 the Los Angeles Airport bonds were classified as "discount bonds." What happens to the price of a discount bond as it approaches maturity? Is there a "built-in capital gain" on such bonds?

f. The coupon interest payment divided by the market price of a bond is called the bond's *current yield.* Assuming the conditions in Part c, what would have been the current yield of a Los Angeles Airport bond (1) in February 1980 and (2) in February 1993? What would have been its capital gains yields and total yields (total yield equals yield to maturity) on those same two dates?

7-8 SUPERNORMAL GROWTH STOCK VALUATION Thompson Technologies Corporation (TTC) has been growing at a rate of 20 percent per year in recent years. This same growth rate is expected to last for another 2 years.

a. If $D_0 = \$1.60$, $k = 10\%$, and $g_n = 6\%$, what is TTC's stock worth today? What are its expected dividend yield and capital gains yield at this time?

b. Now assume that TTC's period of supernormal growth is to last another 5 years rather than 2 years. How would this affect its price, dividend yield, and capital gains yield? Answer in words only.

c. What will be TTC's dividend yield and capital gains yield once its period of supernormal growth ends? (Hint: These values will be the same regardless of whether you examine the case of 2 or 5 years of supernormal growth; the calculations are very easy.)

d. Of what interest to investors is the changing relationship between dividend yield and capital gains yield over time?

7-9 YIELD TO CALL It is now January 1, 1997, and you are considering the purchase of an outstanding Aikman Corporation bond that was issued on January 1, 1995. The Aikman bond has a 9.5 percent annual coupon and a 30-year original maturity (it matures on December 31, 2024). There is a 5-year call protection (until December 31, 1999), after which time the bond can be called at 109 (that is, at 109 percent of par, or $1,090). Interest rates have declined since the bond was issued, and the bond is now selling at 116.575 percent of par, or $1,165.75. You want to determine both the yield to maturity and the yield to call for this bond. (Note: The yield to call considers the effect of a call provision on the bond's probable yield. In the calculation, we assume that the bond will be outstanding until the call date, at which time it will be called. Thus, the investor will have received interest payments for the call-protected period and then will receive the call price — in this case, $1,090 — on the call date.)

a. What is the yield to maturity in 1997 for the Aikman bond? What is its yield to call?

b. If you bought this bond, which return do you think you would actually earn? Explain your reasoning.

c. Suppose the bond had sold at a discount. Would the yield to maturity or the yield to call have been more relevant?

7-10 EQUILIBRIUM STOCK PRICE The risk-free rate of return, k_{RF}, is 11 percent; the required rate of return on the market, k_M, is 14 percent; and The Andrews Company's stock has a beta coefficient of 1.5.

a. If the dividend expected during the coming year, D_1, is $2.25, and if g = a constant 5%, at what price should Andrews's stock sell?

b. Now suppose the Federal Reserve Board increases the money supply, causing the risk-free rate to drop to 9 percent and k_M to fall to 12 percent. What would this do to the price of the stock?

c. In addition to the change in Part b, suppose investors' risk aversion declines; this fact, combined with the decline in k_{RF}, causes k_M to fall to 11 percent. At what price would Andrews's stock sell?

d. Now suppose Andrews has a change in management. The new group institutes policies that increase the expected constant growth rate to 6 percent. Also, the new management stabilizes sales and profits and thus causes the beta coefficient to decline from 1.5 to 1.3. Assume that k_{RF} and k_M are equal to the values in Part c. After all these changes, what is Andrews's new equilibrium price? (Note: D_1 goes to $2.27.)

7-11 BETA COEFFICIENT Suppose Crum Chemical Company's management conducts a study and concludes that if Crum expanded its consumer products division (which is less risky than its primary business, industrial chemicals), the firm's beta would decline from 1.2 to 0.9. However, consumer products have a somewhat lower profit margin, and this would cause Crum's constant growth rate in earnings and dividends to fall from 7 to 5 percent.

a. Should management make the change? Assume the following: k_M = 12%; k_{RF} = 9%; D_0 = $2.

b. Assume all the facts as given above except the change in the beta coefficient. How low would the beta have to fall to cause the expansion to be a good one? (Hint: Set $\hat{P}_0$ under the new policy equal to $\hat{P}_0$ under the the old one, and find the new beta that will produce this equality.)

7-12 BOND VALUATION The Braver company has two bond issues outstanding. Both bonds pay $100 annual interest plus $1,000 at maturity. Bond L has a maturity of 15 years and Bond S a maturity of 1 year.

a. What will be the value of each of these bonds when the going rate of interest is (1) 5 percent, (2) 8 percent, and (3) 12 percent? Assume that there is only one more interest payment to be made on Bond S.

b. Why does the longer-term (15-year) bond fluctuate more when interest rates change than does the shorter-term bond (1-year)?

13 YIELD TO MATURITY The Glasgo Company's bonds have 4 years remaining to maturity. Interest is paid annually; the bonds have a $1,000 par value; and the coupon interest rate is 9 percent.

a. What is the yield to maturity at a current market price of (1) $829 or (2) $1,104?

b. Would you pay $829 for one of these bonds if you thought that the appropriate rate of interest was 12 percent — that is, if $k_d = 12\%$? Explain your answer.

14 PERPETUAL BOND RATE OF RETURN What will be the rate of return on a perpetual bond with a $1,000 par value, an 8 percent coupon rate, and a current market price of (a) $600, (b) $800, (c) $1,000, and (d) $1,400? Assume interest is paid annually.

15 DECLINING GROWTH STOCK VALUATION Miller Mining Company's ore reserves are being depleted, so its sales are falling. Also, its pit is getting deeper each year, so its costs are rising. As a result, the company's earnings and dividends are declining at the constant rate of 5 percent per year. If $D_0 = \$5$ and $k_s = 15\%$, what is the value of Miller Mining's stock?

16 RATES OF RETURN AND EQUILIBRIUM The beta coefficient for Stock C is $b_c = 0.4$, whereas that for Stock D is $b_D = -0.5$. (Stock D's beta is negative, indicating that its rate of return rises whenever returns on most other stocks fall. There are very few, if any, negative beta stocks, although collection agency stocks are sometimes cited as an example.)

a. If the risk-free rate is 9 percent and the expected rate of return on an average stock is 13 percent, what are the required rates of return on Stocks C and D?

b. For Stock C, suppose the current price, P_0, is $25; the next expected dividend, D_1, is $1.50; and the stock's expected constant growth rate is 4 percent. Is the stock in equilibrium? Explain, and describe what will happen if the stock is not in equilibrium.

17 SUPERNORMAL GROWTH STOCK VALUATION Assume that the average firm in your company's industry is expected to grow at a constant rate of 6 percent, and its dividend yield is 7 percent. Your company is about as risky as the average firm in the industry, but it has just successfully completed some R&D work which leads you to expect that its earnings and dividends will grow at a rate of 50 percent $[D_1 = D_0(1 + g) = D_0(1.50)]$ this year and 25 percent the following year, after which growth should match the 6 percent industry average rate. The last dividend paid (D_0) was $1. What is the value per share of your firm's stock?

18 FINANCIAL CALCULATOR NEEDED; EFFECTIVE ANNUAL RATE Assume that as investment manager of Southeastern Electric Company's pension plan (which is exempt from income taxes), you must choose between Wal-Mart bonds and AT&T preferred stock. Assume the bonds have a $1,000 par value, they mature in 20 years, they pay $40 each 6 months, they are callable at Wal-Mart's option at a price of $1,080 after 5 years (ten 6-month periods), and they sell at a price of $897.40 per bond. The preferred stock is a perpetuity; it pays a dividend of $2 each quarter, and it sells for $95 per share. What is the *most likely* effective annual rate of return (EAR) on the *higher*-yielding security?

19 NOMINAL INTEREST RATE Nodine Corporation's 14 percent coupon rate, semiannual payment, $1,000 par value bonds which mature in 30 years are callable at a price of $1,050 five years from now. The bonds sell at a price of $1,353.54, and the yield curve is flat. Assuming that interest rates in the economy are expected to remain at their current level, what is the best estimate of Nodine's nominal interest rate on new bonds?

20 SUPERNORMAL GROWTH STOCK VALUATION Mangan Corporation is expanding rapidly, and it currently needs to retain all of its earnings, hence it does not pay any dividends. However,

investors expect Mangan to begin paying dividends, with the first dividend of $1.00 coming 3 years from today. The dividend should grow rapidly — at a rate of 50 percent per year — during Years 4 and 5. After Year 5, the company should grow at a constant rate of 8 percent per year. If the required return on the stock is 15 percent, what is the value of the stock today?

SPREADSHEET APPLICATIONS

SPREADSHEET PROBLEM

It is now January 1, 1997. Bigbee Electric Inc. has just developed a solar panel capable of generating 200 percent more electricity than any solar panel currently on the market. As a result, Bigbee is expected to experience a 15 percent annual growth rate for the next 5 years. By the end of 5 years, other firms will have developed comparable technology, and Bigbee's growth rate will slow to 5 percent per year indefinitely. Stockholders require a return of 12 percent on Bigbee's stock. The most recent annual dividend (D_0), which was paid yesterday, was $1.75 per share.

a. Calculate Bigbee's expected dividends for 1997, 1998, 1999, 2000, and 2001.

b. Calculate the value of the stock today, $\hat{P}_0$. Proceed by finding the present value of the dividends expected at the end of 1997, 1998, 1999, 2000, and 2001 plus the present value of the stock price which should exist at the end of 2001. The year-end 2001 stock price can be found by using the constant growth equation. Notice that to find the December 31, 2001, price, you use the dividend expected in 2002, which is 5 percent greater than the 2001 dividend.

c. Calculate the expected dividend yield, D_1/P_0, the capital gains yield expected in 1997, and the expected total return (dividend yield plus capital gains yield) for 1997. (Assume that $\hat{P}_0 = P_0$, and recognize that the capital gains yield is equal to the total return minus the dividend yield.) Also calculate these same three yields for 2001.

d. How might an investor's tax situation affect his or her decision to purchase stocks of companies in the early stages of their lives, when they are growing rapidly, versus stocks of older, more mature firms? When does Bigbee's stock become "mature" in this example?

e. Suppose your boss tells you she believes that Bigbee's annual growth rate will be only 12 percent during the next 5 years and that the firm's normal growth rate will be only 4 percent. Without doing any calculations, what general effect would these growth-rate changes have on the price of Bigbee's stock?

f. Suppose your boss also tells you that she regards Bigbee as being quite risky and that she believes the required rate of return should be 14 percent, not 12 percent. Again without doing any calculations, how would the higher required rate of return affect the price of the stock, its capital gains yield, and its dividend yield?

g. Rework Part e to determine what Bigbee's expected dividends and stock price would be under the conditions given.

h. Suppose your boss tells you that she regards Bigbee as being quite risky and that she believes the required rate of return should be higher than the 12 percent originally specified. Rework the problem under the conditions given in Part e, except change the required rate of return to (1) 13 percent, (2) 15 percent, and (3) 20 percent to determine the effects of the higher required rates of return on Bigbee's stock price.

SPREADSHEET EXERCISE: @NPV AND @IRR FUNCTIONS

This exercise uses a spreadsheet model to do bond valuation calculations. The starting model examines annual coupon bonds. Students add a section to the model that deals with semiannual coupon bonds.

1. Retrieve the model (Filename SE-07.WK1) from the models diskette. Note that there are only four inputs to the model: coupon rate, par value, required return, and current price. The model calculates current value based on the input values for coupon rate, par value, and required return. It also calculates yield to maturity based on the input values for coupon rate, par value, and current price. The model is structured to handle six maturities: 1-year, 5-year, 10-year, 20-year, 30-year, and perpetual.

2. To begin, change some of the input values in Cells C6.C9 to see how the inputs affect the output data in Cells C17.D22. (Note that it is easier to see the output if Row 4 is at the top of your screen.) The model allows you to easily see the bond valuation relationships. For example, when the required return increases, the values of the bonds fall, with the values of longer-term bonds affected more than the values of shorter-term bonds.

3. To incorporate semiannual valuation into the model, first fill in each maturity's cash flows in Cells G28.K88. Note that the cash flows in Column G extend down 1 year (2 periods), the flows in Column H extend down 5 years (10 periods), and so on. Be sure to use formulas to pull the correct amounts from the data in Cells E7 and E13 rather than use numerical values. By referencing Cells E7 and E13, the cash flow data will change as inputs are changed.

4. Once the cash flows are entered into the model, the next step is to fill in the formulas in Cells E17.F22. The formulas will use the cash flow data to calculate value and yield to maturity for each bond maturity. Begin with Cell E17, which is the value of a 1-year, semiannual coupon bond. Use the NPV @function, which has the form @NPV (interest, range), where interest is the periodic required rate of return (E8) and range is the range of cash flows (G29.G30). Note that @NPV assumes that the first cash flow occurs in Period 1, an assumption that fits simple bond valuation since the first interest payment is generally assumed to occur one period from today. The formulas in the remaining cells (E18.E22) are similar to the E17 formula, but use the cash flows of different maturities.

5. The next step is to place the correct formulas into Cells E17.F22 to calculate each bond's yield to maturity. Begin with Cell E17, which is the yield to maturity of a 1-year, semiannual coupon bond. Use the IRR @function, which has the form @IRR (guess, range), where guess is your best estimate of the cash flow stream's IRR. (We usually use 0.10 as our guess, unless we believe the IRR to be significantly higher or lower.) Range is the entire range of cash flows, including the price, or G28.G30 in this situation. Finally, note that the value returned by the IRR function is a periodic (semiannual) rate, so it must be multiplied by 2 to obtain the nominal yield to maturity. The formulas in the remaining cells (F18.F22) are similar to the E17 formula, but use the cash flows of different maturities.

6. Finally, you can, if you choose to, calculate the effective annual yields to maturity in Cells G17.G22. To do this, note that the @IRR functions in Cells F17.F22 give the periodic rate, so the formula $(1 + @IRR \text{ function})^2 - 1$ will produce the effective annual yield to maturity.

MINI CASE

Robert Balik and Carol Kiefer are senior vice presidents of the Mutual of Chicago Insurance Company. They are co-directors of the company's pension fund management division, with Balik having responsibility for fixed income securities (primarily bonds) and Kiefer being responsible for equity investments. A major new client, the California League of Cities, has requested that Mutual of Chicago present an investment seminar to the mayors of the represented cities, and Balik and Kiefer, who will make the actual presentation, have asked you to help them by answering the following questions.

SECTION I: BOND VALUATION

a. What are the key features of a bond?

b. How is the value of any asset whose value is based on expected future cash flows determined?

c. How is the value of a bond determined? What is the value of a 1-year, $1,000 par value bond with a 10 percent annual coupon if its required rate of return is 10 percent? What is the value of a similar 10-year bond?

d. (1) What would be the value of the bond described in Part c if, just after it had been issued, the expected inflation rate rose by 3 percentage points, causing investors to require a 13 percent return? Would we now have a discount or a premium bond?

   (2) What would happen to the bond's value if inflation fell, and k_d declined to 7 percent? Would we now have a premium or a discount bond?

   (3) What would happen to the value of the 10-year bond over time if the required rate of return remained at 13 percent or remained at 7 percent?

e. (1) What is the yield to maturity on a 10-year, 9 percent annual coupon, $1,000 par value bond that sells for $887.00? That sells for $1,134.20? What does the fact that a bond sells at a discount or at a premium tell you about the relationship between k_d and the bond's coupon rate?

   (2) What is the current yield, the capital gains yield, and the total return in each case?

f. What is interest rate (price) risk? Which bond in Part c has more price risk, the 1-year bond or the 10-year bond?

g. What is reinvestment rate risk? Which bond in Part c has more reinvestment rate risk, assuming a 10-year investment horizon?

h. Redo Parts c and d, assuming the bonds have semiannual rather than annual coupons.

i. Suppose you could buy, for $1,000, either a 10 percent, 10-year, annual payment bond or a 10 percent, 10-year, semiannual payment bond. They are equally risky. Which would you prefer? If $1,000 is the proper price for the semiannual bond, what is the proper price for the annual payment bond?

j. What is the value of a perpetual bond with an annual coupon of $100 if its required rate of return is 10 percent? 13 percent? 7 percent? Assess the following statement: "Because perpetual bonds match an infinite investment horizon, they have little price risk."

k. Suppose a 10-year, 10 percent, semiannual coupon bond with a par value of $1,000 is currently selling for $1,135.90, producing a yield to maturity of 8 percent. However, the bond can be called after 5 years for a price of $1,050.

   (1) What is the bond's yield to call (YTC)?

   (2) If you bought this bond, do you think you would be more likely to earn the YTM or the YTC?

SECTION II: STOCK VALUATION To illustrate the common stock valuation process, Balik and Kiefer have asked you to analyze the Bon Temps Company, an employment agency that supplies word processor operators and computer programmers to businesses with temporarily heavy workloads. You are to answer the following questions.

a. (1) Write out a formula that can be used to value any stock, regardless of its dividend pattern.
   (2) What is a constant growth stock? How are constant growth stocks valued?
   (3) What happens if the constant $g > k_s$? Will many stocks have $g > k_s$?

b. Assume that Bon Temps has a beta coefficient of 1.2, that the risk-free rate (the yield on T-bonds) is 10 percent, and that the required rate of return on the market is 15 percent. What is the required rate of return on the firm's stock?

c. Assume that Bon Temps is a constant growth company whose last dividend (D_0, which was paid yesterday) was $2.00 and whose dividend is expected to grow indefinitely at a 6 percent rate.
   (1) What is the firm's expected dividend stream over the next 3 years?
   (2) What is the firm's current stock price?
   (3) What is the stock's expected value one year from now?
   (4) What are the expected dividend yield, the capital gains yield, and the total return during the first year?

d. Now assume that the stock is currently selling at $21.20. What is the expected rate of return on the stock?

e. What would the stock price be if its dividends were expected to have zero growth?

f. Now assume that Bon Temps is expected to experience supernormal growth of 30 percent for the next 3 years, then to return to its long-run constant growth rate of 6 percent. What is the stock's value under these conditions? What is its expected dividend yield and capital gains yield in Year 1? In Year 4?

g. Suppose Bon Temps is expected to experience zero growth during the first 3 years and then to resume its steady-state growth of 6 percent in the fourth year. What is the stock's value now? What is its expected dividend yield and its capital gains yield in Year 1? In Year 4?

h. Finally, assume that Bon Temps's earnings and dividends are expected to decline by a constant 6 percent per year, that is, $g = -6\%$. Why would anyone be willing to buy such a stock, and at what price should it sell? What would be the dividend yield and capital gains yield in each year?

i. What does market equilibrium mean?

j. If equilibrium does not exist, how will it be established?

k. What is the Efficient Markets Hypothesis, what are its three forms, and what are its implications?

SELECTED ADDITIONAL REFERENCES AND CASES

Many investment textbooks cover stock and bond valuation models in depth and detail. Some of the better ones are listed in the Chapter 4 references.

The seminal work on stock valuation models is

Williams, John Burr, *The Theory of Investment Value* (Cambridge, Mass.: Harvard University Press, 1938).

The following classic articles extend J. B. Williams' works:

Durand, David, "Growth Stocks and the Petersburg Paradox," *Journal of Finance,* September 1957, 348–363.

Gordon, Myron J., and Eli Shapiro, "Capital Equipment Analysis: The Required Rate of Profit," *Management Science,* October 1956, 102–110.

For some recent works on valuation, see

Bey, Roger P., and J. Markham Collins, "The Relationship between Before- and After-Tax Yields on Financial Assets," *The Financial Review,* August 1988, 313–343.

Brooks, Robert, and Billy Helms, "An N-Stage, Fractional Period, Quarterly Dividend Discount Model," *Financial Review,* November 1990, 651–657.

Taylor, Richard W., "The Valuation of Semiannual Bonds between Interest Payment Dates," *The Financial Review,* August 1988, 365–368.

Tse, K. S. Maurice, and Mark A. White, "The Valuation of Semiannual Bonds between Interest Payment Dates: A Correction," *Financial Review,* November 1990, 659–662.

The following case in the Cases in the Financial Management: Dryden Request *series covers many of the valuation concepts contained in Chapter 7.*

Case 3, "Peachtree Securities, Inc. (B)."

PART III

STRATEGIC INVESTMENT DECISIONS

CHAPTER 8

THE COST OF CAPITAL

*I*n late 1995, AT&T stunned the financial community by announcing that it would voluntarily divide itself into three independent, publicly traded companies. The plan announced by the world's largest telecommunications company comes 11 years after the federal government forced it to spin off its Bell system local phone companies.

The original forced breakup resulted from antitrust considerations — the old AT&T was a monopoly with a stranglehold on local and long-distance telecommunications, and it was thought (correctly) that competition would lead to improved services and lower prices. The 1995 voluntary breakup was triggered by the changing telecommunications environment. AT&T had five major segments: (1) long-distance and cellular services, (2) consulting services, (3) credit card and other financial services, (4) research (Bell Labs) plus telecommunications equipment manufacturing, and (5) computers, primarily its NCR subsidiary. Three separate companies will emerge. First, there will be a new AT&T, which will retain long-distance, cellular services, credit cards, and consulting. Second, a new company named Lucent Technologies will take over equipment manufacturing and the Bell Laboratories. Third, a currently unnamed company will take over the computer division. The new AT&T will have about $50 billion of revenues, the manufacturing company about $20 billion, and the computer company about $8 billion.

AT&T's current structure reflects a type of vertical integration that was once touted as ideal by business strategists. However, (1) sales to local operating telephone companies and to cellular communications companies account for a big chunk of AT&T's equipment business, and (2) the local telcos are about to get permission to compete with AT&T in the long-distance markets, and AT&T is now competing with its equipment customers in the local phone service market. AT&T's equipment customers are naturally reluctant to buy from a rival, so AT&T's management felt that the split-up would boost sales for its *manufacturing company. According to AT&T's chairman, Robert E. Allen, "The complexity of trying to manage different businesses began to overwhelm the advantages of integration. The world has changed. Markets have changed. Conflicts have arisen. Today, each of our businesses has to be able to react more quickly."*

Mr. Allen clearly believes that the restructuring will enhance shareholder value. The three separate companies will each have their own stocks and bonds. This will make it easier to estimate each business's opportunity cost of capital, which, in turn, will facilitate choosing proper strategies and making optimal capital investments. Furthermore, the managers of the three companies will have a more direct control over their stocks' prices, which will better link managerial compensation and stock price.

This chapter will explain how AT&T and other companies estimate the cost of capital used in the analysis of new capital investments. Then, in subsequent chapters, we will see how the cost of capital affects investment decisions.

A firm's cost of capital is critically important for three reasons: (1) Maximizing the value of a firm requires that the costs of all inputs, including capital, be minimized, and to minimize the cost of capital we must be able to estimate it. (2) Capital budgeting decisions require an estimate of the cost of capital. (3) Many other types of decisions, including those related to public utility regulation, leasing, bond refunding, executive compensation, and short-term asset management, require estimates of the cost of capital.

At a recent Annual Meeting of the Financial Management Association, a day-long panel discussion focused on the cost of capital. Financial managers from Hershey Foods and Du Pont, among others, discussed procedures for estimating corporations' cost of capital. All of the panelists agreed that while the task is difficult, it is essential to good decision making, especially in the key capital budgeting area. Further, they agreed that the overall corporate cost-of-capital estimate should be viewed only as the first step in the development of divisional and specific projects' costs of capital. In this chapter, we discuss the actual process of estimating a firm's overall, or weighted average, cost of capital. Then, in Chapter 10, we use this overall cost of capital as a key element in estimates of divisional and project costs of capital.

CAPITAL COMPONENTS AND COSTS

In developing the firm's overall cost of capital, we first identify and then determine the cost of each capital component, after which we combine the component costs to form the *weighted average cost of capital (WACC)*. Capital, as we use the term, represents the funds used to finance the firm's assets and operations. .The sales which produce profits are not possible without the assets that are shown on the left side of the balance sheet, and those assets must be financed from the sources shown on the right side. Thus, capital constitutes the entire right-hand side of the balance sheet, including both short-term and long-term debt, preferred stock, and common equity.

CAPITAL COMPONENTS

Our first task is to decide which capital sources should be included when we estimate the WACC. Since the cost of capital is used primarily in the process of making long-term investment decisions, our discussion will focus on the development of the cost of capital for capital budgeting purposes. First, consider the firm's short-term, non-interest-bearing liabilities: accounts payable, accrued wages, and accrued taxes. All of these items arise from normal operations — if sales increase, then funds are spontaneously (automatically) generated from these sources. In capital budgeting, the dollar amount of the spontaneously generated liabilities associated with a given project is subtracted from the amount that would otherwise be required to finance the project. To illustrate, suppose a potential project has a total cost of $2,000,000, consisting of $1,500,000 of fixed assets and $500,000 of required new current assets, say, inventories. However, if payables and accruals will spontaneously increase by $200,000 if the project is undertaken, then these funds partially offset the increase in current assets. Thus, the project's required net current assets (or net working capital) would be only $300,000, and the net funds required for the project would be only $1,800,000.

Increase in fixed assets		$1,500,000
Increase in current assets	$500,000	
Less: Spontaneous increase in current liabilities	200,000	300,000
Net funds required for project		$1,800,000

It is the cost of this $1,800,000 that concerns us — will the return on the project be high enough to cover the cost of the $1,800,000 of nonspontaneous capital required to undertake it? Since we are concerned only with the cost of the nonspontaneous capital, spontaneously generated current liabilities are not included when the WACC is estimated.

We must also decide how to treat short-term notes payable, often bank loans, which are not generated spontaneously. The answer depends on whether the firm deliberately uses short-term debt to finance long-term investments. If short-term debt is only used as temporary financing to support cyclical or seasonal fluctuations in current assets, it should not be included in the firm's WACC. However, if the firm uses short-term debt as part of its permanent financing, then such debt should be included when the cost of capital is estimated. As we will show in Chapter 21, the use of nonspontaneous short-term debt to finance long-term assets is quite risky, and it is not common among well-managed firms. Therefore, in this chapter we assume that interest-bearing short-term debt is used to support cyclical or seasonal working capital, and since our primary focus is on developing a cost of capital for use in capital budgeting, we exclude short-term debt when we estimate the WACC unless otherwise noted. Long-term debt, preferred stock, and common equity (common stock plus retained earnings) are the primary sources of capital for capital expansion, so they are the components included in the WACC estimate.

In summary, the relevant capital components for cost of capital purposes include (1) that portion of short-term interest-bearing debt that is considered to be permanent financing; (2) all long-term debt; (3) all preferred stock; and (4) all common equity. Non-interest-bearing liabilities such as accounts payable and accruals are netted out in the capital budgeting cash flow estimation process, hence are excluded from the cost of capital calculations.

TAXES

In developing the costs for the different capital components, the issue of taxes arises: Should we use, a before- or an after-tax cost? In considering this question, remember that stockholders are concerned primarily with the cash flows that are available for their use, namely, those cash flows available to common shareholders after corporate taxes have been paid. Therefore, if management is to maximize stockholder well-being and thereby maximize the price of the stock, all analyses must fully reflect the impact of taxes. Although the tax benefits of debt financing, which arise due to the tax deductibility of interest expense, could be accounted for in either the cash flows or the WACC, the most common approach is to include the tax benefits in the WACC. Therefore, we will express all debt component costs on an after-tax basis.

HISTORICAL VERSUS NEW, OR MARGINAL, COSTS

Another issue is this: Is the historical, or embedded, cost of the capital that was raised in the past relevant, or should we focus on the cost of new, marginal funds? Embedded costs are important for some decisions. For example, the average cost of all the capital raised in the past and still outstanding is relevant to regulators who determine the allowed rate of return for a public utility. However, in financial management, the WACC is used primarily to make investment decisions, and these decisions hinge on the cost of new, or marginal, capital. *Thus, for our purposes, the relevant costs are the marginal costs of new funds to be raised during the planning period.*

SELF-TEST QUESTIONS
Which financing sources are typically included, and which are excluded, when a firm estimates its WACC? Explain.

Should the component cost estimates be on a before-tax or after-tax basis? Why?

Should the component cost estimates reflect historical or marginal costs? Why?

COST OF DEBT

As noted in the previous section, the relevant cost of debt is the after-tax cost of new debt. Although estimating this cost is conceptually straightforward, some problems arise in practice. Companies use both fixed and floating rate debt, straight and convertible debt, and debt with and without sinking funds, and each form of debt has a somewhat different cost.

It is unlikely that the financial manager will know at the start of a planning period the exact types and amounts of debt that will be used in the future: The type of debt actually used will depend on the specific assets to be financed and on capital market conditions as they develop over time. Even so, the financial manager does know what types of debt are typical for his or her firm. For example, National Computer Corporation (NCC), a full-line computer manufacturer, typically issues commercial paper to raise short-term money used to finance cyclical working capital needs, and it uses 30-year bonds to raise long-term debt capital. Thus, for planning purposes, NCC's managers include only long-term debt in their WACC estimate, and they assume that this debt will consist of 30-year bonds.

Assume that it is January 1997, and NCC's financial managers are estimating the firm's WACC for the coming year. How should they determine the component cost of debt? Most financial managers would begin by discussing current and prospective interest rates with their firms' investment bankers. Assume that NCC's bankers stated that a new 30-year, noncallable, straight bond issue would require an 11 percent coupon rate with semiannual payments, and that it would be offered to the public at a $1,000 par value. Flotation costs, which are all costs associated with issuing new securities, are estimated to be 1 percent of the issue, or $10 for every $1,000 par value bond. Thus, the net proceeds from each bond would be $1,000 minus a $10 flotation cost, or $990. NCC's marginal federal-plus-state tax rate is 40 percent.

With this information, we could estimate the cost of debt in two steps:

1. Find the *before-tax, flotation-adjusted cost to the company*:

0	1	2	3	4	5	6		59	60 Periods
($990)	$55	$55	$55	$55	$55	$55	•••	$55	$ 55
									1,000

$$\text{Net proceeds of bond} = \sum_{t=1}^{2n} \frac{\text{Semiannual interest payment}}{(1 + k_d/2)^t} + \frac{\text{Par value}}{(1 + k_d/2)^{2n}} \qquad \textbf{8-1}$$

$$\$990 = \sum_{t=1}^{60} \frac{\$55}{(1 + k_d/2)^t} + \frac{\$1,000}{(1 + k_d/2)^{60}}.$$

Using a financial calculator, we find $k_d/2 = 5.56\%$, so the nominal flotation-adjusted cost of debt is $k_d = 11.12\%$.

2. Adjust for taxes using this equation:

$$\begin{aligned}
\text{After-tax cost of debt} &= \text{Pre-tax cost}(1 - T) \\
&= (\text{Flotation-adjusted } k_d)(1 - T) \qquad \textbf{8-2} \\
&= 11.12\%(0.60) = 6.67\%.
\end{aligned}$$

Note that most public offerings of debt have flotation costs of less than one percentage point, and flotation costs are even lower on private placements. Thus, if flotation costs were simply ignored, and the component cost of debt were found as $k_d(1 - T)$, the error would not be very large.[1] In our example, $k_d(1 - T) = 11\%(0.60) = 6.60\%$, hence the error would be only seven basis points.[2]

Because the flotation adjustment for debt is generally so low as to be immaterial, we generally ignore it and calculate the component cost of debt as follows:

$$\text{After-tax cost of debt} = \text{Nominal pre-tax cost } (1 - T) \qquad \textbf{8-2a}$$

$$= 11\% (0.6) = 6.60\%.$$

SELF-TEST QUESTIONS

What effects do flotation costs have on the cost of debt? Are flotation costs generally material?

How is the before-tax cost of debt converted to an after-tax cost?

COST OF PREFERRED STOCK

A number of firms, including National Computer Corporation, use preferred stock as part of their permanent financing mix. To determine this cost, we first note that preferred dividends are not tax deductible, so the company bears their full cost. *Therefore, no tax adjustment is necessary when calculating the cost of preferred stock.* Second, although some preferred stock is issued without a stated maturity date,

---

[1] It is sometimes suggested that the effective annual rate cost of debt should be used in the WACC. In our example, the flotation-adjusted effective annual rate is $(1.0556)^2 - 1.0 = 0.1143 = 11.43\%$. That position would be correct only if the cost of common stock were based on a quarterly compounding model and if, in capital budgeting, an attempt were made to determine exactly when, during the year, cash flows would come in rather than assuming end-of-year flows. In view of the uncertainties inherent in estimating the cost of equity, and the even greater uncertainties about the cash flows produced by projects over their operating lives, we (and most people in industry) think it would be pointless to attempt to estimate effective rates and intra-year cash flows; it would even be misleading in that such calculations would imply greater accuracy than exists in the basic data. Further, it would be inconsistent to combine an effective bond yield with a nominal return on equity—the bond's cost would be inflated vis-à-vis that of the equity. Finally, note that the flotation cost can be amortized over the life of the bond ($10/30 = $0.33 per year, or $0.167 per semiannual period). This saves taxes in the amount of $0.167(T) = $0.167(0.40) = $0.067 per period. Theoretically, we should take this tax savings into account, but ignoring it does not introduce a material error.

[2] A basis point is 1/100 of a percentage point. Investment bankers in particular use this term. Also, note that in our example, we used a marginal tax rate of 40 percent. Therefore, we were implicitly assuming that NCC's marginal tax rate over the next 30 years will remain at 40 percent. However, there are three potential problems with this assumption: (1) The value of the tax deduction depends on the taxable income for each year, and a change in taxable income might lead to a change in the marginal tax rate, hence to a change in the after-tax cost of debt. (2) Tax losses can only be carried back for three years; therefore, several years of consecutive losses would mean that the benefits of tax deductibility could not be realized in the year the interest is paid. Instead, this benefit would be delayed until the firm becomes profitable, and this would raise the after-tax cost of debt. (3) Congress could raise or lower corporate tax rates, which would also have an effect on the after-tax cost of debt. For all these reasons, we should recognize that firms cannot be certain of the true effects of tax deductibility, so the true after-tax cost of debt could be higher or lower than the estimated cost.

much of the preferred issued recently has a call feature, a sinking fund, or both. Finally, although it is not mandatory that preferred dividends be paid, firms generally do have every intention of paying preferred dividends, because if they fail to do so (1) they cannot pay dividends on their common stock, (2) they will find it difficult to raise additional funds in the capital markets, and (3) in some cases preferred stockholders will be able to take control of the firm.

With these points in mind, assume that NCC's investment bankers indicated that the firm could sell *perpetual* preferred stock with a 10 percent yield. If the stock had a par value of $100, then the annual dividend would be $10. Additionally, the investment bankers stated that flotation costs would amount to 2.5 percent of the par value. Thus, the firm would net $97.50 from each share sold, and it would have an obligation to pay $10 of dividends per share per year. We calculate the component cost of perpetual preferred stock as follows:

$$\text{Component cost of perpetual preferred stock} = k_{ps} = \frac{D_{ps}}{P_n}. \qquad \text{8-3}$$

Here D_{ps} is the annual preferred dividend and P_n is the price the firm receives net of flotation costs. Applying Equation 8-3 to our example, we find NCC's cost of preferred stock to be 10.26 percent.[3] Because flotation costs are material for preferred stocks, we generally do adjust for them in the calculation.

$$k_{ps} = \frac{D_{ps}}{P_n} = \frac{\$10}{\$97.50} = 0.1026 = 10.26\%.$$

Describe how the cost of preferred stock is estimated.
Is a tax adjustment required when estimating the cost of preferred stock? Explain.

SELF-TEST QUESTIONS

COST OF RETAINED EARNINGS

A firm can raise common equity capital in two ways: (1) by retaining earnings and (2) by issuing new common stock. Thus, when we consider NCC's component cost

---

[3]Most preferred stocks pay quarterly dividends, so we could calculate an effective return based on quarterly compounding. However, for the same reasons we discussed in Footnote 1 in connection with debt, it would be inappropriate (or at least not worthwhile) to do so. We should also note that firms have begun to issue variable, or floating, rate bonds and preferred stocks. Since future capital market rates are difficult if not impossible to predict, future interest payments and preferred dividends are normally estimated on the basis of current rates, hence the expected costs of floating rate securities are the same as for similar fixed rate securities. However, the realized cost of a floating rate security can be higher or lower than expected, depending on the actual rates over the life of the security, whereas the realized cost of a fixed rate security is known with relative certainty. Note also that current tax laws do not permit either preferred or common stock flotation costs to be expensed against taxable income. Finally, note that many preferred issues have sinking funds, mandatory call provisions, or both. The costs of nonperpetual preferred stocks are estimated similarly to bonds.

of equity, we must consider the costs of two different types of equity. We begin by examining the cost of retained earnings.

First, note that the costs of debt and preferred stock are based on the return that investors require on these securities. The cost of equity obtained by retaining earnings can be defined similarly: *It is k_s, the rate of return stockholders require on the firm's common stock.* The firm's net income after taxes and preferred dividends literally belongs to its common stockholders. Bondholders are compensated by interest payments; preferred stockholders are compensated by fixed dividend payments; and the firm's remaining income belongs to its common stockholders and serves to "pay the rent" on capital supplied by stockholders. Management may either pay out earnings in the form of dividends or else retain earnings for reinvestment in the business. If part of the earnings is retained, an *opportunity cost* is incurred: Stockholders could have received those earnings as dividends and then invested that money in stocks, bonds, real estate, and so on. *Thus, the firm should earn on its retained earnings at least as much as its stockholders themselves could earn on alternative investments of equivalent risk.*

What rate of return can stockholders expect to earn on other investments of equivalent risk? The answer is k_s, because they could earn that return simply by buying the stock of the firm in question or that of a similar firm. Therefore, if our firm cannot earn at least k_s on retained earnings, then it should pay those earnings to its stockholders and let them invest the money themselves in assets that do provide a return of k_s.

Whereas debt and preferred stocks are contractual obligations which have easily determined costs, it is not at all easy to estimate k_s. However, three methods can be used: (1) the Capital Asset Pricing Model (CAPM), (2) the discounted cash flow (DCF) model, and (3) the bond-yield-plus-risk-premium approach. These methods should not be regarded as mutually exclusive — no one dominates the others, and all are subject to error when used in practice. Therefore, when faced with the task of estimating a company's cost of equity, we generally use all three methods and then choose among them on the basis of our confidence in the data used for each in the specific case at hand.

SELF-TEST   What are the two types of common equity whose costs must be estimated?
QUESTIONS   Explain why there is a cost for retained earnings.

THE CAPM APPROACH

As we saw in Chapter 5, the Capital Asset Pricing Model is based on some unrealistic assumptions, and it cannot be empirically verified. Still, because of its logical appeal, the CAPM is generally used in the cost of capital estimation process.

Under the CAPM we assume that the cost of equity is equal to the risk-free rate plus a risk premium that is equal to the stock's beta coefficient times the market risk premium as set forth in the Security Market Line (SML) equation:

$$k_s = \text{Risk-free rate} + \text{Risk premium}$$
$$= k_{RF} + (k_M - k_{RF})b_i.$$

We obtain estimates of (1) the risk-free rate, k_{RF}, (2) the firm's beta, b_i, and (3) the required rate of return on the market, k_M, and then estimate the required rate of return on the firm's stock, k_s. This required return is a measure of the cost of retained earnings.

ESTIMATING THE RISK-FREE RATE

The starting point for the CAPM cost of equity estimate is k_{RF}, the risk-free rate. There is really no such thing as a truly riskless asset in the U.S. economy. Treasury securities are essentially free of default risk, but long-term T-bonds will suffer capital losses if interest rates rise, and a portfolio of short-term T-bills will provide a volatile earnings stream because the rate earned on T-bills varies over time.

Since we cannot in practice find a truly riskless rate upon which to base the CAPM, what rate should we use? Our preference — and this preference is shared by most practitioners — is to use the rate on long-term Treasury bonds. Here are our reasons:

1. Capital market rates include a real, riskless rate (generally thought to vary from 2 to 4 percent) plus a premium for inflation which reflects the expected inflation rate over the life of the security, be it 30 days or 40 years. The expected rate of inflation is likely to be relatively high during booms and low during recessions. Therefore, during booms T-bill rates tend to be high to reflect the high current inflation rate, whereas in recessions T-bill rates are generally low. T-bond rates, on the other hand, reflect expected inflation rates over a long period, so they are far less volatile than T-bill rates.

2. Common stocks are long-term securities, and although a particular stock-holder may not have a long investment horizon, most stockholders do invest on a long-term basis. Therefore, it is reasonable to think that stock returns embody long-term inflation expectations similar to those reflected in bonds rather than the short-term expectations in bills. Therefore, the cost of equity should be more highly correlated with T-bond rates than with T-bill rates.

3. Treasury bill rates are also subject to more random disturbances than are Treasury bond rates. For example, bills are used by the Federal Reserve System to control the money supply, and bills are used by foreign governments, firms, and individuals as a temporary safe haven for money. Thus, if the Fed decides to stimulate the economy, it drives down the bill rate, and the same thing happens if trouble erupts somewhere in the world and money flows into the United States seeking safety. T-bond rates are also influenced by Fed actions and by international money flows, but not to the same extent as T-bill rates. This is another reason why T-bill rates are more volatile than T-bond rates and, most experts agree, more volatile than k_s.

4. T-bills are essentially free of interest rate risk, but they are exposed to a relatively high degree of reinvestment rate risk. Long-term investors such as pension funds and life insurance companies are as concerned about reinvestment rate risk as interest rate risk. Therefore, most long-term investors would feel equally exposed to risk if they held bills or bonds.

5. When the CAPM is used to estimate a particular firm's cost of equity over time, bond rates produce more reasonable results. For example, when T-bill

rates were low in 1977 and 1978, the CAPM produced a cost of equity estimate for Texas Utilities of about 11 percent. T-bill rates then shot up in 1979 and 1980, and the T-bill-based CAPM estimate more than doubled, to 23 percent. The company's bond yields, meanwhile, only rose from 9 to 14 percent. Neither we nor the company's management believed that the cost of equity rose by 12 full percentage points at a time when the cost of long-term debt was rising by only 5 percentage points. CAPM estimates based on T-bond yields produced much more reasonable results.[4]

In light of the preceding discussion, we believe that the cost of common equity is more logically related to Treasury bond rates than to T-bill rates. This leads us to favor T-bonds as the base rate, or k_{RF}, in a CAPM cost of equity analysis. T-bond rates can be found in *The Wall Street Journal* or the *Federal Reserve Bulletin*. Generally, we use the yield on a 20-year T-bond as the proxy for the risk-free rate. Assuming that this rate was 8.0 percent in January 1997, we would use this as our estimate for k_{RF} in a January 1997 CAPM cost of equity estimate.

ESTIMATING THE MARKET RISK PREMIUM

The market risk premium, $RP_M = k_M - k_{RF}$, can be estimated on the basis of (1) ex post, or historical, data or (2) ex ante, or forward-looking, data.

EX POST RISK PREMIUMS   A very complete and accurate ex post risk premium study, updated annually, is available from Ibbotson Associates, who examine market data over long periods of time to find the average annual rates of return on stocks, T-bills, T-bonds, and a set of high-grade corporate bonds.[5] For example, Table 8-1 summarizes some results from their 1996 study, which covers the period 1926–1995.

Note that common stocks provided the highest average return over the 70-year period, while Treasury bills gave the lowest. T-bills barely covered inflation versus a substantial real return for common stocks. However, the superior returns on stocks had its cost — stocks were by far the riskiest of the investments listed as judged by the standard deviation, and they would also rank as riskiest in a CAPM framework. To further illustrate the risk differentials, we note that the range of annual returns on stocks was from −43.3 to 54.0 percent, while the range on T-bills was only 0.0 to 14.7 percent. The Ibbotson study provides strong empirical support for the premise that higher returns can be obtained only by bearing greater risk.

---

[4]All of this can be illustrated by a true but not-very-funny story. A particular state public utility commission hired a professor who used T-bill rates as the base rate in his CAPM analysis to estimate the cost of capital for the state's utilities. Each utility's cost of capital in turn was built into its electric, gas, or telephone rates. Therefore, the lower the cost of capital, the lower the utility service rates, and the less political heat the commission faced. This particular commission was very politically sensitive — so much so that one of its staff members admitted privately that the commission had selected its cost of capital expert on the basis of who could produce the lowest number.

The commission hired the professor in 1978, when T-bill rates, and thus his CAPM cost of equity estimates based on the T-bill rate, were very low. But the rate cases did not come up until 1979, and by then, the bill rate had gone through the roof. As a result, the professor's cost of equity estimates were even higher than the companies were asking permission to earn! At that point, the commission rejected the CAPM approach and sent the professor home.

[5]See *Stocks, Bonds, Bills and Inflation: 1996 Yearbook* (Chicago: Ibbotson Associates, 1996). Also, note that Ibbotson now recommends using the T-bond rate as the proxy for the risk-free rate when using the CAPM. Before 1988, Ibbotson recommended that T-bills be used.

SELECTED IBBOTSON ASSOCIATES DATA, 1926–1995		TABLE 8-1
	ARITHMETIC MEAN	**STANDARD DEVIATION**
AVERAGE RATES OF RETURN		
Common stocks	12.5%	20.4%
Long-term corporate bonds	6.0	8.7
Long-term government bonds	5.5	9.2
Treasury bills	3.8	3.3
Inflation rate	3.2	4.6
RISK PREMIUMS		
Common stocks over T-bills	8.8%	Not reported
Common stocks over T-bonds	7.4	Not reported
T-bonds over T-bills	1.4	Not reported

Table 8-1 also reports the risk premiums, or differences, among the various securities. For example, Ibbotson found the average risk premium of stocks over T-bonds to be 7.4 percentage points.[6] However, these premiums have large standard deviations, so one must use them with caution. Although not reported, we estimate the standard deviation of the stocks over T-bonds premium to be more than 20 percent. Also, it should be noted that the choice of the beginning and ending periods can have a major impact on the calculated risk premiums. Ibbotson Associates used the longest period available to them, but had their data begun some years earlier or later, or ended earlier, their results would have been seriously affected. Indeed, over many periods their data would indicate *negative* risk premiums, which would lead to the conclusion that Treasury securities have a higher required return than common stocks, which is contrary to both financial theory and common sense. All this suggests that historical risk premiums should be approached with caution. As one businessman muttered after listening to a professor give a lecture on the CAPM, "Beware of academicians bearing gifts!"

EX ANTE RISK PREMIUMS The ex post approach to risk premiums used by Ibbotson Associates assumes that investors expect future results, on average, to equal past results. However, as we noted, the estimated risk premium varies greatly depending on the period selected, and, in any event, investors today probably expect results in the future to be different from those achieved during the Great Depression of the 1930s, the World War II years of the 1940s, and the peaceful boom years of the

[6]It is worth noting that Ibbotson Associates calculates average returns in two ways: (1) by taking each of the 70 annual holding period returns and deriving the arithmetic average of these annual returns and (2) by finding the compound annual rate of return over the whole period, which amounts to a geometric average. The stocks over T-bonds risk premium as measured by arithmetic averages is 1.8 percentage points higher than the geometric mean risk premium. This leads to the question of which average to use. The arithmetic average is most consistent with the standard CAPM; under the CAPM, investors are supposed to be concerned with returns during the next period (say, one year) and to focus on the expected return and the standard deviation of this return.

1950s, all of which are included (and given equal weight with more recent results) in the Ibbotson data. The questionable assumption that future expectations are equal to past realizations, together with the sometimes nonsensical results obtained in historical risk premium studies, has led to a search for ex ante risk premiums.

The most common approach to ex ante premiums is to use the discounted cash flow (DCF) model to estimate the expected market rate of return, $\hat{k}_M = k_M$, then to calculate RP_M as $k_M - k_{RF}$, and finally to use this estimate of RP_M in the SML. This procedure recognizes that if markets are in equilibrium, the expected rate of return on the market is also its required rate of return, so when we estimate $\hat{k}_M$, we are also estimating k_M:

$$\text{Expected} \atop \text{rate of return} = \hat{k}_M = \frac{D_1}{P_0} + g = k_{RF} + RP_M = k_M = {\text{Required} \atop \text{rate of return}}.$$

Since D_1 for the market as measured by the S&P 500 or some other index can be predicted quite accurately, and since the current market value of the index (used for P_0) is also known, the major task is to estimate g, the average expected long-term growth rate for the market index. Even here, however, the estimation task is simplified because one can reasonably assume a constant long-term growth rate for a portfolio of mature stocks such as those in the S&P 500.

Financial services companies such as *s* publish, on a regular basis, a forecast based on DCF methodology for the expected rate of return on the market, $\hat{k}_M$. One can subtract the current T-bond rate from such a market forecast to obtain an estimate of the current market risk premium, RP_M. To illustrate, assume that *Value Line's* reported expected return on the market in January 1997 was 14.0 percent. The T-bond rate, as mentioned earlier, is assumed to be 8.0 percent. Thus, *Value Line's* implied market risk premium over T-bonds would be 6.0 percentage points.

Two potential problems arise when we attempt to use data from organizations such as *Value Line*. First, what we really want is *investors'* expectations, not those of security analysts. However, this is probably not a major problem, since several studies have proved beyond much doubt that investors, on average, form their own expectations on the basis of professional analysts' forecasts. The second problem is that there are a number of securities firms besides *Value Line*, and, at any given time, different analysts' forecasts of future market returns are somewhat different. This suggests that it would be most appropriate to obtain a number of forecasts of $\hat{k}_M$ and then to use the average value to estimate RP_M for use in the SML. Several services (including Zacks and Institutional Brokers Estimate System, or IBES) publish data on the forecasts of essentially all widely followed analysts, so one can use the Zacks or IBES aggregate growth rate forecast along with an aggregate dividend yield, to develop a consensus RP_M forecast and thus avoid potential bias from the use of only one organization's estimate. However, we have followed the forecasts of several of the larger organizations over a period of several years, and we have rarely found their $\hat{k}_M$ estimates to differ by more than ±0.3 percentage points from one another. Therefore, for present purposes, the assumed *Value Line* $\hat{k}_M = k_M = 14.0\%$ and $RP_M = 6.0$ percentage points may be considered to be a "reasonable" proxy for the expectations of the marginal investor. Note, though, that ex ante risk premiums are not stable: they vary over time. Therefore, when using the CAPM to estimate the cost of equity, it is best to use a current estimate of the ex ante RP_M.

ESTIMATING BETA

The last parameter needed for a CAPM cost of equity estimate is the beta coefficient. Recall from Chapter 4 that a stock's beta is a measure of its volatility relative to that of an average stock, and that betas are generally estimated from the stock's characteristic line by running a linear regression between past returns on the stock in question and past returns on some market index. We define betas developed in this manner as *historical betas.*

Note, however, that historical betas show how risky a stock was *in the past,* whereas investors are interested in *future* risk. It may be that a given company appeared to be quite safe in the past, but that things have changed, and its future risk is judged to be higher than its past risk, or vice versa. AT&T is a good example. AT&T was among the bluest of the blue chips when it owned the regional telephone companies, but investors now recognize that AT&T as it exists today faces far more intense competition than it ever faced in the past. Chrysler, on the other hand, was practically bankrupt a few years ago, but it now appears to be reasonably healthy. Therefore, one would think that Chrysler's risk had declined while AT&T's had increased.

Now consider the use of beta as a measure of a company's risk. If we use its historical beta in a CAPM framework to measure a firm's cost of equity, we are implicitly assuming that the company's future risk is the same as its past risk. This would be a troublesome assumption for a company like Chrysler or AT&T today. But what about most companies in most years? As a general rule, is future risk sufficiently similar to past risk to warrant the use of historical betas in a CAPM analysis? For individual firms, past risk is often *not* a good predictor of future risk, and historical betas of individual firms are often not very stable.

Since historical betas may not be good predictors of future risk, researchers have sought ways to improve them. This has led to the development of two different types of betas: (1) adjusted betas and (2) fundamental betas. *Adjusted betas* grew largely out of the work of Marshall E. Blume, who showed that true betas tend to move toward 1.0 over time.[7] Therefore, one can begin with a firm's pure historical statistical beta, make an adjustment for the expected future movement toward 1.0, and produce an adjusted beta which will, on average, be a better predictor of the future beta than would the unadjusted historical beta. *Value Line* publishes betas based on approximately this formula:

$$\text{Adjusted beta} = 0.33 \text{ (Historical beta)} + 0.67(1.0).$$

Other researchers have extended the adjustment process to include such fundamental risk variables as financial leverage, sales volatility, and the like. The end product here is a *fundamental beta.*[8] These betas are constantly adjusted to reflect changes in a firm's operations and capital structure, whereas with historical betas

---

[7]See Marshall E. Blume, "Betas and Their Regression Tendencies," *Journal of Finance,* June 1975, 785–796.

[8]See Barr Rosenberg and James Guy, "Beta and Investment Fundamentals," *Financial Analysts Journal,* May–June 1976, 60–72. Rosenberg, a professor at the University of California at Berkeley, later set up a company which calculates fundamental betas by a proprietary procedure and then sells them to institutional investors.

(including adjusted ones), such changes might not be reflected until several years after the company's "true" beta had changed.

Adjusted betas are obviously heavily dependent on unadjusted historical betas, and so are fundamental betas as they are actually calculated. Therefore, the plain old historical beta, calculated as the slope of the characteristic line, is important even if one goes on to develop a more exotic version. With this in mind, it should be noted that several different sets of data can be used to calculate historical betas, and the different data sets produce different results. Here are some points to note:

1. Betas can be based on historical periods of different lengths. For example, data for the past one, two, three, and so on, years may be used. Most people who calculate betas today use five years of data, but this choice is arbitrary, and different lengths of time usually alter significantly the calculated beta for a given company.[9]

2. Returns may be calculated on holding periods of different lengths — a day, a week, a month, a quarter, a year, and so on. For example, if it has been decided to analyze data on NYSE stocks over a 5-year period, then we might obtain $52(5) = 260$ weekly returns on each stock and on the market index. We could also use $12(5) = 60$ monthly returns, or $1(5) = 5$ annual returns. The set of returns on each stock, however large the set turns out to be, would then be regressed on the corresponding market returns to obtain the stock's beta. In statistical analysis, it is generally better to have more rather than fewer observations, because using more observations generally leads to greater statistical confidence. This suggests the use of weekly returns, and, say, five years of data, for a sample size of 260, or even daily returns for a still larger sample size. However, the shorter the holding period, the more likely the data are to exhibit random "noise." Also, the greater the number of years of data, the more likely it is that the company's basic risk position has changed (for example, see the preceding comments on Chrysler and AT&T). Thus, the choice of both the number of years of data and the length of the holding period for calculating rates of return involves trade-offs between a desire to have many observations versus a desire to rely on recent and consequently more relevant data.

3. The value used to represent "the market" is also an important consideration, as the index used can have a significant effect on the calculated beta. Many analysts today use the New York Stock Exchange Composite Index (based on more than 2,000 common stocks, weighted by the value of each company), but others use the S&P 500 Index or some other group, including one (the Wilshire Index) with more than 5,000 stocks. In theory, the broader the index, the better the beta. Indeed, the index should really include returns on all stocks, bonds, leases, private businesses, real estate, and even "human capital." As a practical matter, however, we cannot get accurate returns data on most other types of assets, so measurement problems largely restrict us to stock indexes.

---

[9]A commercial provider of betas once told the authors that his firm, and others, did not know what the right period was, but they all decided to use five years in order to reduce the apparent differences between various services' betas, because large differences reduced everyone's credibility!

The bottom line of all this is that one can calculate betas in many different ways and, depending on the method used, different betas, hence different costs of capital, will result. To illustrate this point, consider Table 8-2, which contains the beta coefficients for five well-known companies as reported in 1996 by Merrill Lynch and Value Line. Merrill Lynch uses the S&P 500 as the market index, while Value Line uses the New York Stock Exchange Composite Index. Further, Value Line betas are adjusted, while the Merrill Lynch betas listed in Table 8-2 are pure historical betas. Merrill Lynch uses five years of monthly returns, or 60 observations; Value Line uses 260 weekly observations.

Where does this leave financial managers regarding the proper beta? They must "pay their money and take their choice." Some managers calculate their own betas, using whichever procedure seems most appropriate under the circumstances. Others use betas calculated by organizations such as Merrill Lynch or *Value Line*, perhaps using one service or perhaps averaging the betas of several services. The choice is a matter of judgment and data availability, for there is no "right" beta. Generally, though, the betas derived from different sources will, for a given company, be reasonably close together. If they are not, then our confidence in the CAPM cost of capital estimate will be diminished.

ILLUSTRATION OF THE CAPM APPROACH

We are now in a position to estimate National Computer's cost of equity from retained earnings by the CAPM method. We use as the risk-free rate the assumed T-bond rate in January 1997, which is 8.0 percent, and *Value Line's* assumed estimate of the expected return on the market, $\hat{k}_M = k_M = 14.0\%$. Thus, we can write the SML equation for January 1997 as follows:

$$k_s = k_{RF} + (k_M - k_{RF})b_i$$
$$= 8.0\% + (14.0\% - 8.0\%)b_i = 8.0\% + (6.0\%)b_i.$$

Therefore, if we know a company's beta, we can insert it into the SML equation and estimate the company's cost of retained earnings, k_s. We have two estimates of NCC's beta, an adjusted beta of 1.10 and an unadjusted beta of 1.20. Using the adjusted beta, we obtain $k_{NCC} = 14.6\%$:

$$k_{NCC} = 8.0\% + (6.0\%)1.1 = 14.6\%.$$

	MERRILL LYNCH	VALUE LINE
BETA COEFFICIENTS FOR FIVE COMPANIES — TABLE 8-2		
Chrysler	1.26	1.20
Polaroid	0.86	0.90
IBM	0.89	0.95
Mobil	0.64	0.70
Southwestern Public Service	0.51	0.65

Using the unadjusted beta, we obtain 15.2 percent. Therefore, on the basis of this CAPM analysis, National Computer Corporation's cost of retained earnings falls in the range of 14.6 to 15.2 percent.

Rather than using single values, we could have developed high and low estimates for the risk-free rate and for the market risk premium. Then, by combining all of the low estimators and all of the high estimators, we could have estimated the extreme low and high values of NCC's cost of retained earnings. Obviously, this range would have been greater than 14.6 to 15.2 percent.

SELF-TEST QUESTIONS What is the best proxy for the risk-free rate when using the CAPM? Why?

Explain the two methods used to estimate the market risk premium.

What are the three types of betas that can be used in the CAPM, and how do they differ?

Should the CAPM estimate of k_s be thought of as a precise point or a range?

THE DCF APPROACH

The second major procedure for estimating the cost of retained earnings is the discounted cash flow (DCF) approach. We know that the intrinsic value of a stock, $\hat{P}_0$, is the present value of its expected dividend stream:

$$\hat{P}_0 = \frac{D_1}{(1 + k_s)^1} + \frac{D_2}{(1 + k_s)^1} + \frac{D_3}{(1 + k_s)^1} + \cdots + \frac{D_\infty}{(1 + k_s)^\infty}.$$

Also, we know that we can recast this equation, given the market price of the stock, P_0, and solve for $\hat{k}_s$, the implied expected return:

$$P_0 = \frac{D_1}{(1 + \hat{k}_s)^1} + \frac{D_2}{(1 + \hat{k}_s)^2} + \frac{D_3}{(1 + \hat{k}_s)^2} + \cdots + \frac{D_\infty}{(1 + \hat{k}_s)^\infty}.$$

Finally, we know that in equilibrium, $\hat{k}_s = k_s$, so if a stock is in equilibrium, as it generally is, then an estimate of the expected rate of return also provides us with an estimate of the required rate of return.

If a stock is expected to grow at a constant rate, we can use the constant growth model to estimate $\hat{k}_s$:

$$\hat{k}_s = \frac{D_1}{P_0} + g.$$

Here P_0 is read from *The Wall Street Journal,* and next year's annual dividend, D_1, can be estimated relatively easily. It is not easy to estimate the growth rate expected by the marginal investor, but three approaches to estimating g are discussed below.

HISTORICAL GROWTH RATES

First, if earnings and dividend growth rates have been relatively stable in the past, and if investors expect these trends to continue, then the past realized growth rate may be used as an estimate of the expected future growth rate. To illustrate, consider Figure 8-1, which gives EPS and DPS data from 1982 to 1996 for NCC, along with a plot of these data on a semilog scale. Note these points:

1. **Time period.** We show 15 years of data in Figure 8-1, but we could have used 25 years, 5 years, or 10 years. There is no rule as to the appropriate number of years to analyze when calculating historical growth rates. However, the

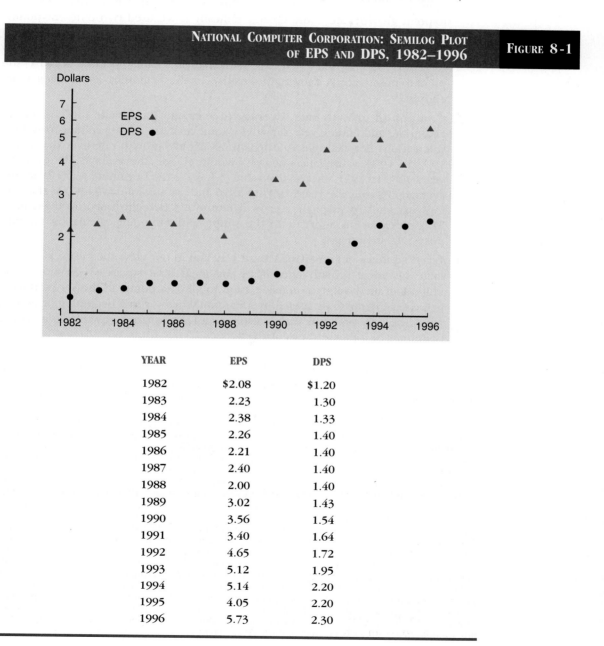

NATIONAL COMPUTER CORPORATION: SEMILOG PLOT OF EPS AND DPS, 1982–1996

FIGURE 8-1

YEAR	EPS	DPS
1982	$2.08	$1.20
1983	2.23	1.30
1984	2.38	1.33
1985	2.26	1.40
1986	2.21	1.40
1987	2.40	1.40
1988	2.00	1.40
1989	3.02	1.43
1990	3.56	1.54
1991	3.40	1.64
1992	4.65	1.72
1993	5.12	1.95
1994	5.14	2.20
1995	4.05	2.20
1996	5.73	2.30

period chosen should reflect, to the extent possible, conditions similar to those expected in the future.

2. **Compound growth rate, point-to-point.** The easiest historical growth rate to calculate is the compound rate between two dates. For example, EPS grew at an annual rate of 7.5 percent from 1982 to 1996, and DPS grew at a 4.8 percent rate during this same period.[10] Note that the point-to-point growth rate could change radically if we used two different points. For example, if we calculated the 5-year EPS growth rate from 1990 to 1995, we would obtain 2.6 percent, but the 5-year rate one year later, from 1991 to 1996, is 11.0 percent. This radical change occurs because the point-to-point rate is extremely sensitive to the beginning and ending years chosen.

3. **Compound growth rate, average-to-average.** To alleviate the problem of beginning and ending year sensitivity, some analysts use an average-to-average calculation. For example, to calculate NCC's EPS growth rate over the period 1990 to 1995, Value Line's analysts would (1) get the average EPS over the years 1989 to 1991 and use this value ($3.33) as the beginning year, (2) get the average EPS over the years 1994 to 1996 and use this value ($4.97) as the ending year, and (3) calculate a growth rate of 8.3 percent based on these data. This procedure is superior to the simple point-to-point calculation for purposes of estimating g.

4. **Least squares regression.** A third way, and in our view the best way, to estimate historical growth rates is by log-linear least squares regression. The regression method gives consideration to all data points in the series; thus, it is the least likely to be biased by a randomly high or low beginning or ending year. The only practical way to estimate a least squares growth rate is with a computer or a financial calculator.[11]

---

[10]To obtain g_{EPS} using a financial calculator, enter −2.08 as PV, 5.73 as FV, 14 as N (because, with 15 data points, we have 14 growth periods: 1996 − 1982 = 14), and then press I to obtain the growth rate, 7.5 percent.

[11]Log-linear regression is a standard time-series linear regression in which the data for the dependent (Y) variable are plotted as natural logarithms. The slope of the regression line is then the average annual growth rate, assuming continuous compounding. In a standard time-series linear regression of EPS or DPS, the slope of the regression line is the average annual dollar change. To find the EPS growth rate with a financial calculator, use the regression routine, entering years as the X variable and ln EPS as the Y variable. Obtain the slope coefficient of the regression, b, which is the annual growth rate assuming continuous compounding. Then find e^b, which produces the value $1 + g$, where g is the effective annual growth rate. For example, using the EPS data in Figure 8-1, we obtain a slope coefficient of b = 0.07607, then find EXP (0.07607) = $e^{0.07607}$ = 1.07903, so g = 7.903%. The exact regression procedures are calculator specific, but with an HP 17B, one would enter the years and the EPS and DPS data, specify an exponential model (EXP), find the slope coefficient m, go into the math menu and press the exponential key (EXP = e^x) to find $1 + g$, and subtract 1.0 to obtain the growth rate. With an HP 10B, one would enter the EPS or DPS data, convert to natural logs (LN), complete the regression and determine the slope coefficient (m), convert to e^x, and then subtract 1.0 to obtain the growth rate. Other calculators require somewhat different procedures. Also, note that the same procedures can be used with a spreadsheet program to find the growth rate — input each value of EPS, run a regression, then find @EXP(regression coefficient), which is $1 + g$. Finally, note that these procedures can be used to find the growth rate of any variable that changes over time, not just EPS or DPS.

5. **Earnings versus dividends.** If earnings and dividends are growing at the same rate, there is no problem, but if these two growth rates are unequal, we do have a problem. First, the DCF model requires the expected *dividend* growth rate. However, if EPS and DPS are growing at different rates, something is going to have to change — these two series cannot indefinitely grow at two different rates. There is no rule for handling differences in historical g_{EPS} and g_{DPS}, and where they differ, this simply demonstrates yet another problem with using historical growth as a proxy for expected future growth. Like many aspects of finance, judgment is required when estimating growth rates.

Table 8-3 summarizes the historical growth rates we have just discussed. It is obvious that one can take a given set of historical data and, depending on the years and the calculation method used, obtain a large number of quite different growth rates. Now recall our purpose in making these calculations: We are seeking the future dividend growth rate that investors expect, and we reasoned that, if past growth rates have been stable, then investors might base future expectations on past trends. This is a reasonable proposition, but, unfortunately, one rarely finds much historical stability. Therefore, the use of historical growth rates in a DCF analysis must be applied with judgment, and also be used (if at all) in conjunction with other growth estimation methods as discussed next.

RETENTION GROWTH MODEL

Another method for estimating the growth rate is to use the *retention growth model:*

$$g = b(r). \qquad \textbf{8-4}$$

Here r is the expected future return on equity (ROE), and b is the fraction of its earnings that a firm is expected to retain (1 − Payout ratio).[12] Equation 8-4 produces a

NATIONAL COMPUTER CORPORATION: HISTORICAL GROWTH RATES			TABLE 8-3
METHOD (PERIOD)	**EPS**	**DPS**	**AVERAGE**
Point-to-point (1991–1996)	11.0%	7.0%	9.0%
Point-to-point (1982–1996)	7.5	4.8	6.2
Average-to-average (1990–1995)	8.3	7.7	8.0
Average-to-average (1983–1995)	6.9	4.7	5.8
Least squares regression (1991–1996)	6.6	7.6	7.1
Least squares regression (1982–1996)	7.9	4.6	6.3

[12]Since there are more terms for which symbols are needed than there are letters in the alphabet, some letters are used to denote several different things. This is one of those instances, and b is standard notation for both the beta coefficient and the retention rate. Note also that the retention rate is the complement of the payout rate, that is, Retention rate = (1 − Payout rate).

constant growth rate, but when we use it we are, by implication, making four important assumptions: (1) We expect the payout rate, and thus the retention rate, $b = 1 -$ Payout, to remain constant; (2) we expect the return on equity on new investment, r, to equal the firm's current ROE, which implies that we expect the return on equity to remain constant; (3) the firm is not expected to issue new common stock, or, if it does, we expect this new stock to be sold at a price equal to its book value; and (4) future projects are expected to have the same degree of risk as the firm's existing assets.

NCC has had an average return on equity of about 15 percent over the past 15 years. The ROE has been relatively steady, but even so it has ranged from a low of 11.0 percent to a high of 17.6 percent. In addition, NCC's dividend payout rate has averaged 0.52 over the past 15 years, so its retention rate, b, has averaged $1.0 - 0.52 = 0.48$. Using Equation 8-4, we estimate g to be 7.2 percent:

$$g = 0.48(15\%) = 7.2\%.$$

This figure, together with the historical EPS and DPS growth rates examined earlier, might lead us to conclude that National Computer's expected growth rate is in the range of 6.5 to 7.5 percent. Therefore, if we forecasted NCC's next annual dividend to be $2.40, and if its current stock price is $32, then its dividend yield would be $D_1/P_0 = \$2.40/\$32 = 0.075$ or 7.5%, and its DCF cost of capital would be in the range of 14.0 to 15.0 percent:

$$\hat{k}_{NCC} = D_1/P_0 + g.$$

$$\text{Lower end: } k_{NCC} = \hat{k}_{NCC} = 7.5\% + 6.5\% = 14.0\%.$$

$$\text{Upper end: } k_{NCC} = \hat{k}_{NCC} = 7.5\% + 7.5\% = 15.0\%.$$

This is reasonably close to the 14.6 to 15.2 percent range found by use of the CAPM method.

ANALYSTS' FORECASTS

A third growth rate estimating technique calls for using security analysts' forecasts. Analysts publish growth rate estimates for most of the larger publicly owned companies. For example, Value Line provides such forecasts on 1,700 companies, and all of the larger brokerage houses provide similar forecasts. Further, several companies compile analysts' forecasts on a regular basis and provide summary information such as the median and range of forecasts on widely followed companies. These growth rate summaries, such as the one compiled by Lynch, Jones & Ryan in its *Institutional Brokers Estimate System (IBES)*, can be ordered for a fee and obtained either in hardcopy format or as on-line computer data.

However, these forecasts often involve nonconstant growth. For example, in January 1997, some analysts were forecasting that NCC would have a 10.4 percent annual growth rate in earnings and dividends over the next 5 years, or from 1997 through 2001, and they were forecasting a steady-state growth rate beyond 2001 of 6.5 percent. On the basis of the current $32 market price and a D_1 of $2.40, we can use the nonconstant growth stock valuation approach developed in Chapter 7 to find the expected rate of return. However, obtaining the solution is no trivial matter — we used a spreadsheet model and found $\hat{k}_s = k_s$ to be 15.0 percent.

As an alternative, a nonconstant growth forecast can be used to develop a proxy constant growth rate. Computer simulations indicate that dividends beyond Year 50 contribute very little to the value of any stock — the present value of dividends beyond Year 50 is virtually zero, so for practical purposes, we can ignore anything beyond 50 years. If we consider only a 50-year horizon, we can develop a weighted average growth rate and use it as a constant growth rate for cost of capital purposes. In the NCC case, we assumed a growth rate of 10.4 percent for 5 years followed by a growth rate of 6.5 percent for 45 years, which produces an average growth rate of $0.10(10.4\%) + 0.90(6.5\%) = 6.9\%$. This constant growth proxy results in $k_s = \hat{k}_s = 14.4\%$:

$$k_s = \hat{k}_s = \frac{\$2.40}{\$32} + 6.9\%$$

$$= 7.5\% + 6.9\% = 14.4\%.$$

These nonconstant growth DCF calculations suggest a range for k_s of 14.4 to 15.0 percent.

SELF-TEST QUESTIONS

What are the three most commonly used methods for estimating the future dividend growth rate?

Briefly describe the retention growth method for estimating the dividend growth rate. What are its underlying assumptions?

Can the DCF model be used to estimate k_s for a nonconstant growth stock? Explain.

BOND-YIELD-PLUS-RISK-PREMIUM APPROACH

A third method for estimating the required rate of return on retained earnings calls for adding an estimated risk premium to the company's own bond yield:

$$k_s = \text{Company's own bond yield} + \text{Risk premium.}$$

As discussed earlier, a corporate treasurer can easily estimate his or her own firm's yield to maturity on long-term bonds if they are publicly traded, or ask an investment banker for k_d if the bonds are not traded. The real problem occurs when trying to estimate the appropriate risk premium.

The average historical risk premium of stocks over corporate bonds as reported by Ibbotson Associates is $12.5 - 6.0 = 6.5$ percentage points. If risk premiums were stable over time, or if they fluctuated randomly about a stable mean, then the average historical premium could be used with confidence to estimate the current risk premium. However, risk premiums are not stable, so some analysts argue that more reliance should be placed on the current level of the risk premium than on its historical average.

There are two common methods for estimating current risk premiums: a survey approach and a DCF-based approach similar to the method we discussed earlier in connection with the market risk premium. One example of the survey approach is the work of Charles Benore, a security analyst with Paine Webber. Benore has for several years surveyed a large number of institutional investors, asking them what premium above the return on the company's bonds would make them indifferent between the stock and the bonds. In one survey, Benore found that most investors required a premium of from 2 to 4 percentage points on stock over the company's bond yield, with an average value of 3.6 percentage points. This average could be used as an estimate of the risk premium. Benore's survey analyzes only public utility companies, but the approach is applicable to any company or industry. Note, though, that in some years Benore found risk premiums as high as 6 percent, but in other years he found values closer to 3 percent. The high premiums occurred during periods of low interest rates, and the low premiums in high-rate periods. Thus, Benore's studies suggest that risk premiums are not stable, hence that using old survey data is questionable.

The second method for estimating risk premiums is based on the DCF model. To illustrate, we assumed earlier that in January 1997 *Value Line*, using the DCF approach, estimated that the required rate of return on the market, as measured by the S&P 500, was 14.0 percent. At the same time, assume that the *Federal Reserve Bulletin* reported that the yield on an average (A-rated) corporate long-term bond was 10.2 percent. Using these data, we would estimate the risk premium of an average stock over an average bond to be 14.0% − 10.2% = 3.8 percentage points, or 380 basis points. However, one should recognize that the figure of 3.8 percentage points is not precise; we would, ourselves, conclude that the risk premium of an average company's stock over its own bonds, in January 1997, was somewhere between 3.3 and 4.3 percentage points.

We can apply the DCF-based risk premium approach to estimate the required rate of return for NCC. The company has been experiencing some problems from lower-cost foreign producers, and its bonds are rated Baa. Therefore, whereas if the *Federal Reserve Bulletin* reported that an average corporate bond yielded 10.2 percent in January 1997, NCC's relatively risky bonds yielded 11.0 percent, ignoring flotation costs. (Our studies indicate that the average NYSE company's bonds are rated A; NCC's bonds are rated below A.) Assuming that every company's required equity return exceeds its own cost of debt by the same risk premium, we would determine the high and low values of NCC's cost of equity as follows:

$$\text{Low: } k_{NCC} = 11.0\% + 3.3\% = 14.3\%.$$

$$\text{High: } k_{NCC} = 11.0\% + 4.3\% = 15.3\%.$$

If NCC had a higher bond rating, its cost of debt and consequently its estimated cost of equity would have been lower.[13]

Note again, however, that risk premiums have not been stable over time, so it may not be appropriate, as a general rule, to add 3.3 to 4.3 percentage points to a company's bond yield to indicate its cost of equity. In recent years, our work suggests that the over-own-debt risk premium has ranged from about 2 to about 5 percentage points. (The low premium occurred when interest rates were quite high and people were reluctant to invest in long-term bonds because of a fear of runaway inflation, further increases in interest rates, and losses on investments in bonds. The high premiums occurred in periods when interest rates were relatively low.) Therefore,

---

[13]Note that if you know a company's bond rating, or if you can estimate from an analysis of its financial statements what rating it would have if its debt were rated, then you can find its approximate k_d in Moody's or Standard & Poor's bond yield publications. This procedure is useful for outsiders analyzing companies that have no publicly traded debt. The company's own treasurer would always know, or could quickly find out, its cost of debt from the firm's investment bankers.

we repeat our earlier warning: Use a current risk premium when estimating equity capital costs by the bond-yield-plus-risk-premium method.

Describe the basic concept underlying the bond-yield-plus-risk-premium approach. How can the risk premium be estimated? | **SELF-TEST QUESTIONS**

COMPARISON OF THE CAPM, DCF, AND RISK PREMIUM METHODS

We have discussed three methods for estimating the required rate of return on retained earnings — CAPM, DCF, and bond yield plus risk premium. Table 8-4 summarizes the results for National Computer. We see that the estimates range from 14.0 to 15.3 percent, that the average highs and average lows produce a range of 14.3 to 15.1 percent, and that the overall average is 14.7 percent. In our view, there is sufficient consistency in the results to warrant the use of 14.7 percent as our estimate of the cost of retained earnings for National Computer. If the methods produced widely varied estimates, then the financial manager would have to use his or her judgment as to the relative merits of each estimate, and then choose the estimate which seemed most reasonable under the circumstances. In general, this choice would be made on the basis of the financial manager's confidence in the input parameters of each approach.

How would you choose between widely different estimates of k_s? | **SELF-TEST QUESTION**

COST OF NEWLY ISSUED COMMON EQUITY

The cost of retained earnings as estimated in the preceding section is appropriate when retained earnings are being used to finance expansion. However, if the firm is expanding so rapidly that its retained earnings have been exhausted, then it must

ESTIMATED REQUIRED RATES OF RETURN ON EQUITY FOR NATIONAL COMPUTER CORPORATION		TABLE 8-4

	ESTIMATE	
METHOD	LOW	HIGH
CAPM	14.6%	15.2%
DCF (constant growth)	14.0	15.0
DCF (nonconstant growth)	14.4	15.0
Bond yield plus risk premium	14.3	15.3
Average	14.3%	15.1%
Overall average	14.7%	

raise equity by selling newly issued common stock, and common equity has a higher cost than retained earnings. The sale of new common equity involves flotation costs, these costs lower the net usable dollars produced by new stock issues, and this, in turn, increases the cost of the funds. We took account of flotation costs in our estimates of the costs of debt and preferred stock, and the same general approach can be used with common equity.

When the firm sells new common stock, it receives a net amount equal to $P_0(1 - F)$, where F is the percentage flotation cost expressed in decimal form. Note that F consists of issuance expenses such as printing costs and investment banker commissions, as well as price effects resulting from market pressure and information asymmetries, topics which are discussed in detail in Chapters 14 and 16.

The constant growth DCF model, modified to include flotation costs, is used to estimate $\hat{k}_e$, the cost of external equity raised by selling new common stock:

$$\text{Net proceeds} = P_0(1 - F) = \frac{D_1}{\hat{k}_e - g}. \qquad \text{8-5}$$

Solving Equation 8-5 for $\hat{k}_e$ produces this expression for the cost of external equity:

$$\text{Cost of external equity} = \hat{k}_e = \frac{D_1}{P_0(1 - F)} + g. \qquad \text{8-5a}$$

This procedure recognizes that the purchaser of a share of newly issued stock will expect the same dividend stream as the holder of an old share, but the company will, because of flotation expenses, receive less money from the sale of the new share than the value of the old share, P_0. Therefore, money raised from the sale of new stock will have to "work harder" to produce the earnings needed to provide the expected dividend stream. As a result, $k_e > k_s$.

Note also that we could rewrite Equation 8-5a as follows:

$$\hat{k}_e = \frac{D_1/P_0}{(1 - F)} + g = \frac{\text{Dividend yield}}{(1 - F)} + g. \qquad \text{8-5b}$$

Equations 8-5a and 8-5b are equivalent, and either can be used, depending on the form of the available data. Using Equation 8-5a and a growth estimate of 6.5 percent, we obtain NCC's DCF cost of new common equity:

$$\hat{k}_e = \frac{\$2.40}{\$32(1 - 0.15)} + 6.5\%$$

$$= 8.8\% + 6.5\% = 15.3\%.$$

The DCF value for $\hat{k}_e$ is 15.3 percent versus the DCF $\hat{k}_s = 14.0\%$ for retained earnings that we estimated earlier, so the flotation cost adjustment is +1.3 percentage points. This means that new outside equity costs 1.3 percentage points more than retained earnings according to the DCF method:

$$\text{Flotation cost adjustment} = \text{DCF } \hat{k}_e - \text{DCF } \hat{k}_s$$

$$= 15.3\% - 14.0\%$$

$$= 1.3\%.$$

Notice that only one method (DCF) is commonly used to estimate the flotation cost adjustment, whereas three methods are used to estimate k_s. In practice, the DCF adjustment factor is also added to the CAPM and risk premium estimates of the cost of retained earnings to find the cost of new stock as estimated by those methods. For National Computer, our final estimate of the cost of retained earnings was 14.7 percent. Thus, NCC's cost of new equity is estimated to be 16.0 percent:

$$k_e = k_s + \text{Flotation cost adjustment}$$

$$= 14.7\% + 1.3\% = 16.0\%.$$

Explain in words why the cost of new common stock is higher than the cost of retained earnings.

How is the flotation cost adjustment factor estimated?

SELF-TEST QUESTIONS

WEIGHTED AVERAGE COST OF CAPITAL

Thus far we have discussed how to estimate the component costs of debt, preferred stock, retained earnings, and new common stock. Now we must combine these elements to form a weighted average cost of capital, WACC. Each firm has a *target capital structure*, defined as management's estimate of the mix of debt, preferred, and common equity that will cause its stock price to be maximized. Further, when the firm raises new capital, it generally tries to finance so as to keep the actual capital structure reasonably close to the target over time. Here is the general formula for the weighted average cost of capital:

$$\text{WACC} = w_d k_d (1 - T) + w_{ps} k_{ps} + w_{ce}(k_s \text{ or } k_e). \qquad \text{8-6}$$

Here w_d, w_{ps}, and w_{ce} are the target weights for debt, preferred stock, and common equity, respectively. The cost of the debt component of the WACC would itself be an average of several items if the firm uses several types of debt for its permanent financing, while the common equity used in the calculation will be either the cost of retained earnings, k_s, or the cost of new common stock, k_e.

One point should be made immediately: The WACC is the weighted average cost of each new dollar of capital raised at the margin — it is not the average cost of all the dollars the firm has raised in the past, nor is it the average cost of all the dollars the firm will raise during the current year. We are primarily interested in obtaining a cost of capital for use in capital budgeting, and for such purposes a *marginal cost* is required.[14] That means, conceptually, that we must estimate the cost of each dollar the firm raises during the year. Each of those dollars will consist of some debt, some preferred, and some common equity, and the equity will be either retained earnings or new common stock.

To illustrate, suppose National Computer has a target capital structure calling for 30 percent debt, 10 percent preferred stock, and 60 percent common equity. As we estimated earlier, the company's before-tax cost of debt, k_d, is 11.0 percent, ignoring flotation costs; its cost of preferred stock, k_{ps}, is 10.3 percent; its cost of common equity from retained earnings, k_s, is 14.7 percent; and its cost of equity from new common stock sales, k_e, is 16.0 percent. Further, the company's marginal tax rate is 40 percent.

Now suppose the firm needs to raise $100. In order to keep its capital structure on target, it must obtain $30 as debt, $10 as preferred, and $60 as common equity. (Common equity can come either from retained earnings or from the sale of new stock.) The weighted average cost of the $100, assuming the common equity is from retained earnings, is calculated as follows:

$$WACC = w_d k_d (1 - T) + w_{ps} k_{ps} + w_{ce} k_s$$

$$= 0.3(11.0\%)(0.6) + 0.1(10.3\%) + 0.6(14.7\%) = 11.8\%.$$

Every dollar of new capital that NCC obtains consists of 30 cents of debt with an after-tax cost of 6.6 percent, 10 cents of preferred with a cost of 10.3 percent, and 60 cents of common equity (retained earnings) with a cost of 14.7 percent. The average cost of each new dollar is 11.8 percent.

The weights could be based on the accounting values shown on the firm's balance sheet (book values), or on the market values of the different securities shown on the balance sheet, or on management's estimation of the firm's optimal capital structure, which becomes the firm's target market value weights. *The correct weights are the firm's target weights*; the rationale for using target weights is discussed in Chapters 13 and 14.

THE MARGINAL COST OF CAPITAL (MCC) SCHEDULE

NCC's optimal capital structure calls for 30 percent debt, 10 percent preferred, and 60 percent equity, so each new (or marginal) dollar will be raised as 30 cents of debt, 10 cents of preferred, and 60 cents of common equity. Otherwise, the capital structure would not stay on target. As long as the firm's debt has an after-tax cost of 6.6 percent, its preferred has a cost of 10.3 percent, and its common equity has a cost of 14.7 percent, then its weighted average cost of capital will be 11.8 percent.

BREAKS, OR JUMPS, IN THE MCC SCHEDULE

Could NCC raise an unlimited amount of new capital at the 11.8 percent cost? The answer is *no*. As companies raise larger and larger sums during a given time period,

---

[14]The only use we can think of for the average cost of all the capital a firm has raised, as opposed to the marginal cost of capital, is in public utility regulation, where utility commissions are supposed to set rates such that customers pay for all costs of service, including the cost of the capital that was used to buy the assets that provide service.

the costs of both debt and equity will eventually begin to rise, and as this occurs, the weighted average cost of new dollars will also begin to rise. Thus, just as corporations cannot hire unlimited numbers of workers at a constant wage, neither can they raise unlimited amounts of capital at a constant cost. At some point, the cost of each new dollar will begin to increase.

Where will this point occur? As a first step to determining the point of increasing costs, recognize that all of NCC's existing capital was raised in the past, and all of it is invested in assets that are used in operations. Now suppose the capital budget calls for net expenditures of $100 million during 1997. This new (or marginal) capital will presumably be raised so as to maintain the 30/10/60 debt/preferred/common equity target capital structure. Therefore, the company will obtain $30 million of debt, $10 million of preferred, and $60 million of common equity.[15] The new common equity could come from two sources: (1) that part of this year's profits which management decides to retain in the business rather than use for dividends (but not from earnings retained in the past, because those dollars will have already been invested) or (2) the sale of new common stock.

The debt will have an interest rate of 11.0 percent, or an after-tax cost of 6.6 percent. The preferred stock will have a cost of 10.3 percent. The cost of common equity will be k_s as long as the equity is obtained from retained earnings, but it will rise to k_e once the company must sell new common stock. Consider first the case where the new equity comes from retained earnings. As we saw above, the company's cost of retained earnings is 14.7 percent, and its weighted average cost of capital when using retained earnings is 11.8 percent.

Now suppose the company has such a large capital budget that its retained earnings for the year are not sufficient to meet its needs for new equity, forcing it to sell new common stock. We previously estimated the cost of new equity, k_e, to be 16.0 percent, so the WACC once the company must use new common stock is

$$WACC = w_d k_d (1 - T) + w_{ps} k_{ps} + w_{ce} k_e$$
$$= 0.3(11.0\%)(0.6) + 0.1(10.3\%) + 0.6(16.0\%) \approx 12.6\%.$$

Thus, we see that the WACC is 11.8 percent as long as retained earnings are used, but it jumps to 12.6 percent once the firm exhausts its retained earnings and is forced to sell new common stock.

How much new capital can NCC raise before it exhausts its retained earnings and must sell new common stock? Assume that the company expects to have total earnings of $20 million for the year, and that it has a policy of paying out 48 percent of its earnings as dividends. Thus, its *payout ratio,* which is the proportion of net income paid out as dividends, is 0.48. The *retention ratio,* which is the proportion of net income retained within the firm, is 1 − Payout ratio = 1 − 0.48 = 0.52. Therefore, the amount of retained earnings available for investment will be 0.52($20,000,000) = $10,400,000.

---

[15]In reality, the company might raise the entire $100 million by issuing new debt, or perhaps by issuing new common stock. By issuing large blocks of securities, there are savings on flotation costs. However, over the long haul the firm will stick to its target capital structure. Thus, a financing deviation in one year will be offset by opposite financing deviations in future years, so the cost of capital remains a function of the target capital structure regardless of year-to-year financing decisions.

How much *total financing* (debt and preferred stock plus the $10.4 million of retained earnings) can be done before the retained earnings are exhausted and the firm must sell new common stock? In effect, we are seeking some amount of capital, X, which is defined as a *break point* and which represents the total financing that can be done before NCC is forced to sell new common stock. We know that 30 percent of X will be debt and 10 percent will be preferred, while 60 percent will be the new retained earnings. Therefore, $0.3X$ = debt, $0.1X$ = preferred, and $0.6X$ = new retained earnings. We also know that retained earnings will amount to $10.4 million. Therefore,

$$0.6X = \text{Retained earnings} = \$10,400,000.$$

Solving for X, which is the *retained earnings break point,* we obtain

$$\text{Break point} = X = \frac{\text{Retained earnings}}{\text{Equity fraction}} = \frac{\$10,400,000}{0.6} = \$17,333,333.$$

Thus, the company can raise a total of $17,333,333, consisting of $10,400,000 of retained earnings along with $5,200,000 of new debt and $1,733.333 of preferred stock supported by these new retained earnings, without altering its capital structure:

New debt supported by retained earnings	$5,200,000	30%
Preferred stock supported by retained earnings	1,733,333	10
Retained earnings	10,400,000	60
Total expansion supported by retained earnings (that is, break point for retained earnings)	$17,333,333	100%

The WACC for each of these dollars would be 11.8 percent.

Now consider the left panel of Figure 8-2, which graphs NCC's first approximation marginal cost of capital schedule. (Disregard the right panel for now.) Each dollar has a weighted average cost of 11.8 percent until the company has raised a total of $17,333,333. However, if the firm raises more than $17,333,333, each additional (or marginal) dollar will contain 60 cents of equity *obtained by selling new common equity at a cost of 16.0 percent,* so the WACC rises from 11.8 to 12.6 percent.

THE MCC SCHEDULE BEYOND THE RETAINED EARNINGS BREAK POINT

There is a jump, or break, in NCC's MCC schedule at $17,333,333 of new capital. Could there be other breaks in the schedule? Yes, there could be. The cost of capital could also rise due to increases in the cost of debt or the cost of preferred stock, or as a result of increases in flotation costs as the firm issues more and more common stock. Some people have argued that the costs of capital components other than common stock should not rise. Their argument is that as long as the capital structure does not change, and assuming that the firm uses new capital to invest in profitable projects with the same degree of risk as its existing projects, investors should be willing to invest unlimited amounts of additional capital at the same rate. However, this argument assumes an infinitely elastic demand for a firm's securities. As we show in Chapter 16, the demand curve of investors for securities is downward sloping, so the more securities sold during a given period, the lower the price

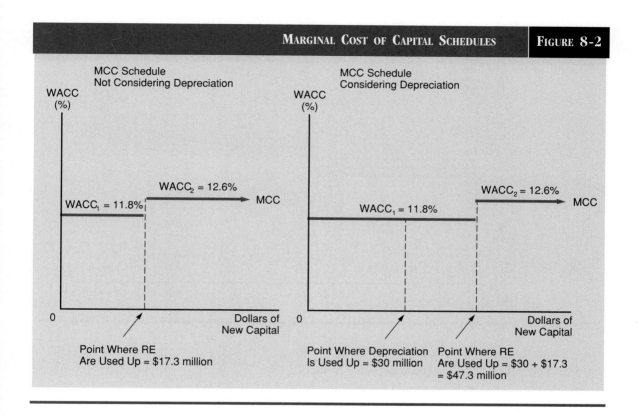

MARGINAL COST OF CAPITAL SCHEDULES   FIGURE 8-2

received for the securities, and the higher the required rate of return. In this situation, the more new financing required, the higher the firm's WACC.

As a result of all this, firms face increasing MCC schedules, such as the one shown in Figure 8-3. Here we have identified a specific retained earnings break point (excluding depreciation), but because of estimation difficulties, we have not attempted to identify precisely any additional break points. However, we have (1) shown the MCC schedule to be upward sloping, reflecting a positive relationship between the amount of capital raised and capital costs, and (2) indicated our inability to precisely measure these costs by using a band of costs rather than a single line. Note that this band exists even at the first dollar of capital raised — our component costs are only estimates, these estimates become more uncertain as the firm requires more and more capital, and thus the band widens as the amount of new capital raised increases. Even the break point could be drawn with a band, because the company does not know it precisely and also because it could alter its capital structure and/or its payout ratio in order to avoid the sharp jump.

In a later section we will show how the MCC schedule is used to help determine a firm's optimal level of new investment. Then, in Chapter 11, we will address this topic in detail.

FIGURE 8-3   MARGINAL COST OF CAPITAL SCHEDULE BEYOND THE RETAINED EARNINGS BREAK POINT

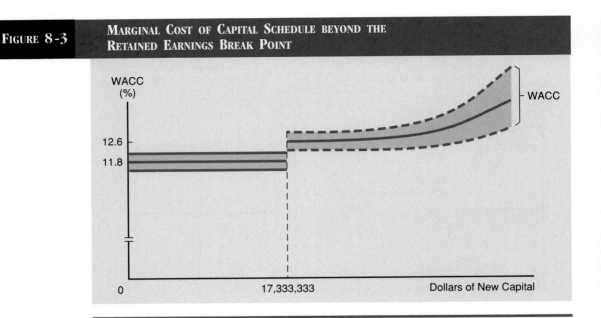

SELF-TEST QUESTIONS

What is the formula for a firm's WACC?

What weights should be used to estimate a firm's WACC? Why?

What is an MCC schedule?

What is the retained earnings break point?

What happens to the MCC schedule beyond the retained earnings break point?

OTHER ISSUES REGARDING THE COST OF CAPITAL

Before concluding this chapter, we will discuss several items that affect the cost of capital. The purpose here is as much to raise questions as to answer them. Still, the material does have important practical implications, so anyone involved with financial management should be aware of the issues and understand how they affect the practical, rule-of-thumb procedures that financial managers are necessarily forced to follow.

THE EFFECTS OF PERSONAL TAXES

We noted earlier that whenever a firm retains a portion of its net income rather than paying all earnings out in dividends, there is an *opportunity cost* to the stockholders. National Computer has a required rate of return on equity (retained earnings) of 14.7 percent. This suggests that shareholders could invest retained earnings, if they were paid out in dividends, in the stock of firms with similar risk and receive a 14.7 percent return. Therefore, NCC should retain and reinvest earnings only if the projects in which the retained earnings are invested yield 14.7 percent or more on the equity invested. The value $k_s = 14.7\%$ is defined as the *opportunity cost* of retained earnings. However, note that we have implicitly assumed that the stockholders (1) pay no income tax on dividends received and (2) incur no brokerage costs when they reinvest dividends. To the extent that these assumptions are not met, the opportunity cost of retained earnings might be lower than the required rate of return, k_s.

Although taxes and brokerage costs are a fact of life, publicly owned firms can repurchase their own stock in the marketplace and earn a return equal to k_s on the investment. Thus, publicly held firms should never invest retained earnings in capital budgeting projects which have expected returns less than k_s. However, personal tax effects are important for closely held firms, and such firms may have a cost of retained earnings that is less than k_s.[16]

COST OF DEPRECIATION-GENERATED FUNDS

The very first increment of internal funds used to finance any year's investments in new assets is normally depreciation-generated funds. Further, in their statements of cash flows, corporations generally show depreciation to be one of their most important sources of funds.[17] Of course, depreciation is an allowance for the annual reduction in value of a firm's fixed assets. Thus, for an ongoing firm, depreciation-generated funds must be used to replace worn-out and obsolete assets, but such replacements are part of the capital budgeting process.

For capital budgeting purposes, should depreciation be considered "free" capital, should it be ignored completely, or should a charge be assessed against it? *The answer is that a charge should indeed be assessed against depreciation-generated funds, and the cost used should be the weighted average cost of capital before out-*

---

[16]For closely held firms, this expression can be used to estimate the cost of retained earnings, k_r:

$$k_r = k_s(1 - T_s)(1 - B).$$

Here k_s is the stockholders' required rate of return, T_s is the *stockholders'* marginal tax rate, and B is the percentage brokerage cost expressed in decimal form. To illustrate, if NCC were a closely held firm, and T_s = 28% and B = 5%, then its cost of retained earnings would be 10.1 percent:

$$k_r = 14.7\%(1 - 0.28)(1 - 0.05) \approx 10.1\%.$$

As a publicly held firm, though, this figure is irrelevant: Because NCC can repurchase its own shares and earn 14.7 percent, 14.7 percent is its opportunity cost of retained earnings.

[17]Depreciation is a noncash charge. To illustrate, suppose a company reports the following income statement:

Sales	$100.0
Cash costs	60.0
Depreciation	20.0
Taxable income	$ 20.0
Taxes (34%)	6.8
Net income	$ 13.2

If sales are all collected during the year, and if all costs except depreciation are paid in cash during the year, then the cash flow from operations available for dividends or reinvestment will be $33.2:

$$\text{Cash flow} = \text{Net income} + \text{Depreciation} = \$13.2 + \$20 = \$33.2.$$

side equity is used. The reasoning here is that the firm could, if it so desired, distribute the depreciation-generated funds to its stockholders and creditors, the parties who financed the assets in the first place, so these funds definitely have an opportunity cost. For example, suppose a firm has $10 million of depreciation-generated funds available. Its equity has a cost of k_s = 15%, and its debt has an after-tax cost of $k_d(1 - T)$ = 12%(0.66) ≈ 7.9%. If it has a 50-50 capital structure, and if it uses no preferred stock, then its WACC would be 0.5(7.9%) + 0.5(15%) ≈ 11.4%.

Now suppose the firm has no projects available to it, not even projects which replace worn-out equipment, that return 11.4 percent or more. It obviously should not raise new capital. Moreover, it should retain no earnings for internal investment, because stockholders would be better off receiving the earnings as dividends and investing the funds themselves at k_s = 15% (or have the company repurchase its stock). Going on, this firm should not even invest its depreciation-generated $10 million. If it did keep and invest this money, it would receive a return of less than 11.4 percent. If it distributed the $10 million to its investors, with $5 million going to stockholders and $5 million to bondholders so as to maintain the target capital structure, then the stockholders could buy the stock of companies with similar risk and earn 15 percent on their money, and bondholders could buy the bonds of companies with similar risk and earn 12 percent. (Such distributions would, under most conditions, be a return of capital, hence not be taxable. If the equity distribution were taxable, then the company could repurchase its shares rather than make a direct distribution to stockholders.) *The conclusion from all this is that depreciation has an opportunity-based cost which is approximately equal to the weighted average cost of capital before external equity is used.*

Since depreciation-generated funds have the same cost as the firm's WACC using retained earnings, it is not necessary to consider them when calculating the WACC. However, depreciation does influence the point at which the WACC increases due to flotation costs on new stock sales. As shown in the right panel of Figure 8-2, presented earlier, NCC's $30 million of depreciation-generated funds extend the point where the WACC increases out to the right by $30 million, to $47.3 million. This topic will be discussed further in Chapter 11.

COST OF DEFERRED TAXES

Most companies show "deferred taxes" as a liability on their balance sheets. Deferred taxes arise principally from the use of accelerated depreciation for tax purposes along with straight line depreciation for stockholder reporting. For example, suppose the XYZ Company uses accelerated depreciation for tax purposes but straight line for book (or stockholder reporting) purposes. Its accelerated depreciation for 1996 might be $20 million versus $10 million had it used straight line. The company's tax and book income statements are given in Table 8-5. As a result of using accelerated depreciation, the company writes off assets for tax purposes over a period which is shorter than the assets' economic lives. Therefore, in the early years of an asset's life, tax depreciation is high, so actual taxes are low. Later on, tax depreciation will be low, so actual taxes will be high relative to the taxes that would have resulted from the use of straight line depreciation. Thus, deferred taxes represent the taxes that do not have to be paid currently but which will have to be paid at some future date.

	ILLUSTRATION OF XYZ COMPANY'S 1996 DEFERRED TAXES (MILLIONS OF DOLLARS)	TABLE 8-5

	TAX BOOKS (1)	STOCKHOLDER BOOKS (2)
Sales	$100.0	$100.0
Costs except depreciation	60.0	60.0
Depreciation (noncash charge)	20.0	10.0
Operating income	$ 20.0	$ 30.0
Taxes:		
Payable this year (34%)	6.8	6.8[a]
Deferred (noncash charge)	—	3.4[b]
Net income	$ 13.2	$ 19.8
Cash flow[c]	$ 33.2	$ 33.2

[a]Taken from tax books.
[b]Deferred taxes represent the difference between taxes actually paid and taxes that would have been paid had straight line depreciation been used for tax purposes:

$$\text{Deferred taxes} = \$30(0.34) - \$6.8 = \$3.4.$$

[c]Cash flow = Net income + Noncash expenses
            = Net income + Depreciation + Deferred taxes.

Companies keep a "running total" of the accumulated deferred taxes that have accrued over time, and the net balance is reported on the balance sheet as "deferred taxes." Thus, XYZ Company would add $3.4 million to the accumulated deferred tax figure reported on its 1995 balance sheet. In later years, when tax depreciation falls below straight line depreciation, the "deferred taxes" account will be drawn down, and a credit will appear on the income statement seen by investors.[18]

Deferred taxes represent a noncash charge, so they constitute a source of funds in a cash flow sense. In effect, deferred taxes represent an interest-free loan from the federal government, so they constitute zero cost capital. However, just like depreciation, deferred taxes have an opportunity cost. The deferred tax cash flow,

---

[18]When we were working on this section, we looked at how several companies reported taxes in their annual reports. Three patterns were noted. First, most industrial companies reported income in their annual reports to stockholders as we show in Column 2 of Table 8-5. However, two other situations were found. First, a few extremely strong firms used accelerated depreciation for book and tax purposes. Thus, in effect, such a company would not have a Column 2 and would simply report Column 1 to stockholders. This is a very conservative accounting practice, as it substantially lowers reported net income for any growing company. At the other extreme, some public utilities reported income as shown in Column 2 but *without subtracting the deferred taxes*. In this case, reported income would be $30.0 − $6.8 = $23.2 million. This treatment is very *unconservative*, since it disregards the fact that future taxes will rise as tax depreciation falls. The regulatory commissions of these utilities forced them to report this way to make their profits look higher without the need to raise utility service rates in the short run. The FASB permits this treatment for utilities but does not permit it for unregulated companies.

We see, then, that otherwise identical companies can report very different levels of earnings. Security analysts and investors need to be aware of the accounting procedures of different companies. A rose is a rose is a rose is a rose, but a dollar of reported profits for one company is not necessarily equal to a dollar reported by another.

$3.4 million for XYZ Company in 1996, could be turned over to the firm's investors. Therefore, deferred taxes, like depreciation, have a cost equal to the firm's WACC using retained earnings as the equity component. Indeed, deferred taxes arise solely because a firm records a different depreciation expense on its tax books and on the books used to report income to shareholders. To see this, note in Table 8-5 that the shareholder books show deferred taxes of $3.4 million and a net income that is $19.8 − $13.2 = $6.6 million greater than shown on the tax books. The deferred taxes and incremental net income sum to $10 million, which is the same as the difference in the depreciation expense between the two sets of books. Thus, the tax books show an additional $10 million in depreciation cash flow, while the shareholder books show an extra $10 million of reported net income plus deferred taxes.

Deferred taxes are treated the same way as depreciation: they are not included when estimating the firm's WACC, but the point at which the WACC increases due to having used up retained earnings must be extended out to the right by the amount of the deferred taxes for the year ($3.4 million in our example).

ALTERNATIVE APPROACH TO FLOTATION COST ADJUSTMENTS

Throughout this chapter, where they were material we have incorporated flotation costs into the component costs of capital. Flotation costs raise component costs, hence increase the firm's WACC. An alternative approach is to ignore flotation costs when estimating the firm's WACC, but then, in the capital budgeting process, to allocate dollar flotation costs to the firm's new projects, hence increasing project costs rather than capital costs.[19]

When flotation costs are added to other project costs, all flotation costs incurred in the current year must be borne by the projects being financed, whether or not the capital raised will be retained within the firm and used for follow-on projects. When flotation costs are incorporated into the firm's WACC, as we recommend, these costs are allocated to both the projects being considered today as well as all future projects. In effect, the conventional method amortizes flotation costs over an infinite life, while the alternative method recovers (amortizes) flotation costs over the life of the projects currently being evaluated. We prefer the WACC adjustment because (1) common equity raised does generally remain in the firm indefinitely, and (2) most flotation costs are associated with common equity.[20]

SELF-TEST QUESTIONS

What are depreciation-generated funds?

Do depreciation-generated funds have a cost? If so, what is it?

What is the cost of deferred taxes?

How do depreciation-generated funds and deferred taxes affect a firm's WACC and the MCC schedule?

---

[19]For a more complete discussion of the alternative approach, see Carl M. Hubbard, "Flotation Costs in Capital Budgeting: A Note on the Tax Effect," *Financial Management,* Summer 1984, 38–40; and John P. Ezzell and R. Burr Porter, "Flotation Costs and the Weighted Average Cost of Capital," *Journal of Financial and Quantitative Analysis,* September 1976, 403–413.

[20]For an in-depth comparison of the two methods, see Eugene F. Brigham and Louis C. Gapenski, "Flotation Cost Adjustments," *Journal of Financial Practice and Education,* Winter 1992, 29–34.

USING THE MCC SCHEDULE IN CAPITAL BUDGETING: A PREVIEW

The cost of capital is a key element in the capital budgeting process. In essence, capital budgeting consists of these steps:

1. Identify the firm's potential investment opportunities.

2. Estimate the future cash flows associated with each project.

3. Find the present value of each future cash flow, discounted at the cost of the capital used to finance the project, and sum these PVs to obtain the total PV of each project.

4. Compare each project's PV with its cost, and accept a project if the PV of its future cash inflows exceeds its cost.

As you learned in earlier chapters, the appropriate discount rate for a given cash flow stream depends on the riskiness of the stream — the riskier the stream (or the riskier the asset), the higher the discount rate. Therefore, the riskier a capital budgeting project, the higher its cost of capital. In this chapter, we were determining the firm's cost of capital for an *average-risk* project. It should be intuitively clear that firms take on different projects with differing degrees of risk. Part of the capital budgeting process involves assessing the riskiness of each project and assigning to it a capital cost based on its relative risk. The cost of capital assigned to an average-risk project should be the marginal cost of capital as determined in this chapter. More risky projects should be evaluated with higher costs of capital, while less risky projects should be evaluated with lower costs of capital. We will examine procedures for dealing with project risk in Chapter 11. Basically, though, firms first measure the marginal cost of capital as we did in this chapter, and then scale it up or down to reflect the individual division's and project's riskiness.

Another issue that arises relates to picking the appropriate point on the marginal cost of capital schedule for use in capital budgeting. As we have seen, every dollar raised by National Computer Corporation is a weighted average which consists of 30 cents of debt, 10 cents of preferred stock, and 60 cents of common equity (with the equity coming from retained earnings until they have been used up, and then from the issuance of new common stock). Further, we saw that the MCC schedule is constant for a while, but after the firm has exhausted its least expensive sources of capital, the MCC schedule rises. Figure 8-2 gave NCC's MCC schedule with and without depreciation.

Since its cost of capital depends on how much capital the firm raises, just which cost rate should we use in capital budgeting? Put another way, which of the WACC values shown in Figure 8-2 should be used to evaluate an average risk project? We could use 11.8 percent or 12.6 percent, but which one *should* we use? The answer is based on the concept of marginal analysis as developed in economics. In economics you learned that firms should expand output to the point where marginal revenue is equal to marginal cost. At that point, the last unit of output exactly covers its cost — further expansion would reduce profits, but the firm would forego profits at any lower production rate. Therefore, the firm should expand to the point where its marginal revenue equals its marginal cost.

This same type of analysis is applied in capital budgeting. We have already developed the marginal cost curve — it is the MCC schedule. Now we need to develop a

FIGURE 8-4	COMBINING THE MCC AND IOS SCHEDULES TO DETERMINE THE OPTIMAL CAPITAL BUDGET

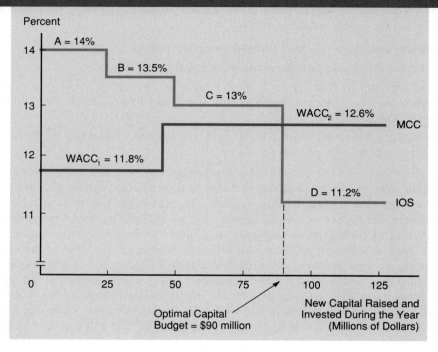

PROJECT	COST (IN MILLIONS)	RATE OF RETURN
A	$25	14.0%
B	25	13.5
C	40	13.0
D	40	11.2

schedule that is analogous to the marginal revenue schedule. This is the *Investment Opportunity Schedule (IOS)*, which shows the rate of return that is expected on each potential investment opportunity. As you will see in the next chapter, rates of return on capital projects are found in essentially the same way as rates of returns on stocks and bonds. Thus, we can calculate an expected rate of return on each potential project, and we can then plot those returns on the same graph that shows our marginal cost of capital. Figure 8-4 gives such a graph for NCC. Projects A, B, and C all have expected rates of return which exceed the cost of the capital that will be used to finance them, but the expected return on Project D is less than its cost of capital. Therefore, Projects A, B, and C should be accepted, and Project D should be rejected.

The WACC at the pont where the Investment Opportunity Schedule intersects the MCC schedule is defined as "the corporate cost of capital"—this point reflects the marginal cost of capital to the corporation. In our example, NCC's corporate cost of capital is 12.6 percent, and that is the cost of capital that NCC would use to evaluate average risk projects and as the basing point for developing "risk-adjusted costs of capital" for the firm's other projects. We will return to the MCC and IOS schedules in Chapter 11, after we have seen how IOS schedules are actually developed.

One final point should be made: Many older, established firms virtually never sell new common stock because retained earnings are sufficient to meet their need for new equity. For such a firm, it is not necessary to calculate the cost of external equity, and the WACC as shown in a graph such as Figure 8-2, 8-3, or 8-4 is simply a horizontal line over the relevant range of capital. Only if the firm is considering an expansion so great that new stock would have to be sold would it have to consider anything other than one corporate WACC, and it would not have to deal with the MCC schedule.

As a general rule, should a firm's cost of capital as determined in this chapter be used to evaluate all of its capital budgeting projects? Explain.

In what respect is marginal analysis in economics analogous to capital budgeting?

Why might it be difficult to identify a firm's cost of capital for use in capital budgeting if you had no idea whatever of how large the capital budget was likely to be?

SUMMARY

This chapter discussed how a firm's cost of capital is estimated. The key concepts covered are listed below:

- The cost of capital to be used in capital budgeting decisions is the *weighted average* of the various types of capital the firm uses, typically debt, preferred stock, and common equity.

- The *component cost of debt,* which is the *after-tax* cost of new debt, is found by multiplying the cost of new debt by $(1 - T)$, where T is the firm's marginal tax rate: $k_d(1 - T)$. Flotation costs for debt are typically quite small, so they are usually ignored.

- The *component cost of perpetual preferred stock* is calculated as the preferred dividend divided by the net issuance price, where the net issuance price is the price the firm receives after deducting flotation costs: $k_{ps} = D_{ps}/P_n$.

- The *cost of common equity* is the cost of retained earnings as long as the firm has retained earnings, but the cost of equity becomes the cost of new common stock once the firm has exhausted its retained earnings.

- The *cost of retained earnings* is the rate of return investors require on the firm's common stock, and it can be estimated in three ways: (1) the *CAPM approach,* (2) the *DCF approach,* and (3) the *bond-yield-plus-risk-premium approach.*

- To use the *CAPM approach,* we (1) estimate the firm's beta, (2) multiply this beta by the market risk premium to determine the firm's risk premium, and

(3) add the firm's risk premium to the risk-free rate to obtain the firm's cost of retained earnings: $k_s = k_{RF} + (k_M - k_{RF})b_i$.

■ The best proxy for the *risk-free rate* is the yield on long-term T-bonds.

■ Three types of betas can be used in the CAPM: (1) *historical,* (2) *adjusted,* and (3) *fundamental.*

■ The market risk premium can be estimated either *historically (ex post)* or *prospectively (ex ante).*

■ To use the *DCF approach,* we solve for $\hat{k}_s$ in the stock valuation equation. Under constant growth, this is done by adding the firm's expected growth rate to its expected dividend yield: $k_s = \hat{k}_s = D_1/P_0 + g$.

■ The growth rate can be estimated from historical data by use of the *retention growth model,* $g = br$, or it can be based on analysts' forecasts.

■ The *bond-yield-plus-risk-premium approach* requires one to add a risk premium to the firm's cost of debt: k_s = Company's own bond yield + RP.

■ The *cost of new common equity,* or *external equity,* is higher than the cost of retained earnings because the firm must incur *flotation expenses* to sell stock. To find the cost of new common equity by the DCF method, the stock price is first reduced by the flotation expense, then the dividend yield is calculated on the basis of the price the firm will actually receive, and then the expected growth rate is added: $k_e = D_1/[P_0(1 - F)] + g$.

■ Each firm has a *target capital structure,* and the target weights are used to estimate the firm's *weighted average cost of capital (WACC):*

$$WACC = w_d k_d (1 - T) + w_{ps} k_{ps} + w_{ce}(k_s \text{ or } k_e).$$

■ The *marginal cost of capital (MCC)* is defined as the cost of the last dollar of new capital the firm raises. The MCC increases as the firm raises more and more capital during a given period. A graph of the MCC plotted against dollars raised is the *MCC schedule.*

The concepts developed in this chapter will be used extensively throughout the book, especially in capital budgeting decisions (Chapters 9 through 11) and capital structure decisions (Chapters 13 and 14).

QUESTIONS

8-1   Define each of the following terms:

a. Weighted average cost of capital, WACC
b. After-tax cost of debt, $k_d(1 - T)$
c. Cost of preferred stock, k_{ps}
d. Cost of retained earnings, k_s
e. Historical beta; adjusted beta; fundamental beta

   f. Cost of new common equity, k_e
   g. Flotation cost, F
   h. Target capital structure
   i. MCC schedule
   j. Cost of depreciation-generated funds
   k. Cost of deferred taxes

8-2 In what sense is the WACC an average cost? A marginal cost?

8-3 How would each of the following affect a firm's cost of debt, $k_d(1 - T)$; its cost of equity, k_s; and its weighted average cost of capital, WACC? Indicate by a plus (+), a minus (−), or a zero (0) if the factor would raise, lower, or have an indeterminate effect on the item in question. Assume other things are held constant. Be prepared to justify your answer, but recognize that several of the parts probably have no single correct answer; these questions are designed to stimulate thought and discussion.

	EFFECT ON		
	$k_d(1 - T)$	k_s	WACC
a. The corporate tax rate is lowered.	_____	_____	_____
b. The Federal Reserve tightens credit.	_____	_____	_____
c. The firm uses more debt.	_____	_____	_____
d. The dividend payout ratio is increased.	_____	_____	_____
e. The firm doubles the amount of capital it raises during the year.	_____	_____	_____
f. The firm expands into a risky new area.	_____	_____	_____
g. The firm merges with another firm whose earnings are countercyclical to those of the first firm and to the stock market.	_____	_____	_____
h. The stock market falls drastically, and our firm's stock price falls along with the rest.	_____	_____	_____
i. Investors become more risk averse.	_____	_____	_____
j. The firm is an electric utility with a large investment in nuclear plants. Several states propose a ban on nuclear power generation.	_____	_____	_____

(SOLUTION APPEARS IN APPENDIX C)

ST-1   **MCC SCHEDULE** Longstreet Communications Inc. (LCI) has the following capital structure, which it considers to be optimal:

Debt	25%
Preferred stock	15
Common stock	60
Total capital	100%

LCI's net income expected this year is $17,142.86; its established dividend payout ratio is 30 percent; its tax rate is 40 percent; and investors expect earnings and dividends to grow at a constant rate of 9 percent in the future. LCI paid a dividend of $3.60 per share last year (D_0), and its stock currently sells at a price of $60 per share. Treasury bonds yield 11 percent; an average stock has a 14 percent expected rate of return; and LCI's beta is 1.51. These terms would apply to new security offerings:

Common: New common stock would have a flotation cost of 10 percent.

Preferred: New preferred could be sold to the public at a price of $100 per share, with a dividend of $11. Flotation costs of $5 per share would be incurred.

Debt: Debt could be sold at an interest rate of 12 percent.

a. Find the component costs of debt, preferred stock, retained earnings, and new common stock.
b. How much new capital can be raised before LCI must sell new equity? (In other words, find the retained earnings break point.)
c. What is the WACC when LCI meets its equity requirement with retained earnings? With new common stock?
d. Construct a graph showing LCI's MCC schedule.
e. Assume that LCI has forecasted $10,000 in depreciation expense for the planning period. What impact does this have on the MCC schedule?

8-1 **COMPONENT COST OF DEBT** Calculate the after-tax cost of debt under each of the following conditions:

   a. Interest rate, 10 percent; tax rate, 0 percent.
   b. Interest rate, 10 percent; tax rate, 20 percent.
   c. Interest rate, 10 percent; tax rate, 40 percent.

8-2 **COST OF RETAINED EARNINGS** The Garvin Company's last dividend per share was $1; that is, $D_0 = \$1$. The stock sells for $20 per share. The expected growth rate is a constant 5 percent. Calculate the firm's cost of retained earnings using the DCF method.

8-3 **WACC ESTIMATION** On January 1, the total market value of the Tysseland Company was $60 million. During the year, the company plans to raise and invest $30 million in new projects. The firm's present market value capital structure, shown below, is considered to be optimal. Assume that there is no short-term debt.

Debt	$30,000,000
Common equity	30,000,000
Total capital	$60,000,000

New bonds will have an 8 percent coupon rate, and they will be sold at par. Common stock, currently selling at $30 a share, can be sold to net the company $27 a share. Stockholders' required rate of return is estimated to be 12 percent, consisting of a dividend yield of 4 percent and an expected constant growth rate of 8 percent. (The next expected dividend is $1.20, so $1.20/$30 = 4%.) Retained earnings for the year are estimated to be $3 million. The marginal corporate tax rate is 40 percent. (Assume no depreciation cash flow.)

   a. To maintain the present capital structure, how much of the new investment must be financed by common equity?
   b. How much of the needed new common equity funds must be generated internally? Externally?
   c. Calculate the cost of each of the common equity components.
   d. At what level of capital expenditures will the firm's WACC increase?
   e. Calculate the firm's WACC using (1) the cost of retained earnings and (2) the cost of new equity.

8-4   **WACC ESTIMATION** The following tabulation gives earnings per share figures for Pappas Manufacturing during the preceding 10 years. The firm's common stock, 140,000 shares outstanding, is now selling for $50 a share, and the expected dividend for the coming year (1997) is 50 percent of EPS for the year. Investors expect past trends to continue, so g may be based on the historical earnings growth rate.

YEAR	EPS
1987	$2.00
1988	2.16
1989	2.33
1990	2.52
1991	2.72
1992	2.94
1993	3.18
1994	3.43
1995	3.70
1996	4.00

The current interest rate on new debt is 8 percent. The firm's marginal federal-plus-state tax rate is 40 percent. The firm's market value capital structure, considered to be optimal, is as follows:

Debt	$ 3,000,000
Common equity	7,000,000
Total capital	$10,000,000

a. Calculate the firm's after-tax cost of new debt and of common equity, assuming new equity comes only from retained earnings. Calculate the cost of equity assuming constant growth; that is, $\hat{k}_s = D_1/P_0 + g = k_s$.
b. Find the firm's WACC, assuming no common stock is sold.
c. How much can be spent for net new capital investments before external equity must be sold? (Assume no depreciation cash flow.)
d. What is the WACC beyond the retained earnings break point if new common stock can be sold to the public at $50 a share to net the firm $45 a share?

8-5   **MARKET VALUE CAPITAL STRUCTURE** Suppose the Schoof Company has this *book value* balance sheet:

Current assets	$30,000,000	Current liabilities	$10,000,000
Fixed assets	50,000,000	Long-term debt	30,000,000
		Common equity:	
		Common stock (1 million shares)	1,000,000
		Retained earnings	39,000,000
Total assets	$80,000,000	Total claims	$80,000,000

The current liabilities consist entirely of notes payable to banks, and the interest rate on this debt is 10 percent, the same as the rate on new bank loans. The long-term debt consists of 30,000 bonds, each of which has a par value of $1,000, carries an annual coupon interest rate of 6 percent, and matures in 20 years. The going rate of interest on new long-term debt, k_d, is 10 percent, and this is the present yield to maturity on the bonds. The common stock sells at a price of $60 per share. Calculate the firm's market value capital structure.

8-6 **COST OF EQUITY** The Tallman Tractor Company's EPS in 1996 was $2.00. EPS in 1991 was $1.3612. The company pays out 40 percent of its earnings as dividends, and the stock currently sells for $21.60. The company expects earnings of $10 million in 1997. Its optimal market value debt/assets ratio is 60 percent, and the firm has no preferred stock outstanding.

a. Calculate the firm's growth rate in earnings.
b. Calculate the firm's dividend per share expected in 1997. Assume that the growth rate calculated in Part a will continue.
c. What is the firm's cost of retained earnings, k_s?
d. What amount of retained earnings is expected in 1997?
e. At what amount of total financing will the firm's cost of equity increase? (Assume no depreciation cash flow.)
f. The sale of new stock would net the company $18.36 per share. What is the firm's percentage flotation cost, F? What is the cost of new common stock, k_e?

8-7 **COST OF EQUITY ESTIMATION METHODS** You have just estimated the cost of equity for Shrieves Shipping Company using all three estimation techniques. The results are summarized in the following table:

METHOD	k_s ESTIMATE
CAPM	12.1%
DCF	14.0
Bond yield plus risk premium	15.4

The inconsistency of the results is worrisome, but you must still develop your equity cost estimate. What factors might you consider as you attempt to place confidence in the above estimates?

8-8 **WACC ESTIMATION** A summary of the balance sheet of Travellers Inn Inc. (TII), a company which was formed by merging a number of regional motel chains and which hopes to rival Holiday Inn on the national scene, is shown in the table:

TRAVELLERS INN: DECEMBER 31, 1996
(MILLIONS OF DOLLARS)

Cash	$ 10	Accounts payable	$ 10
Accounts receivable	20	Accruals	10
Inventories	20	Short-term debt	5
Current assets	$ 50	Current liabilities	$ 25
Net fixed assets	50	Long-term debt	30
		Preferred stock	5
		Common equity:	
		Common stock	$ 10
		Retained earnings	30
		Total common equity	$ 40
Total assets	$100	Total liabilities and equity	$100

These facts are also given for TII:

(1) Short-term debt consists of bank loans which currently cost 10 percent, with interest payable quarterly. These loans are used to finance receivables and inventories on a seasonal basis, so in the off-season, bank loans are zero.

(2) The long-term debt consists of 20-year, semiannual payment mortgage bonds with a coupon rate of 8 percent. Currently, these bonds provide a yield to investors of $k_d = 12\%$. If new bonds were sold, they would yield investors 12 percent, but a flotation cost of 5 percent would be required to sell new bonds.

(3) TII's perpetual preferred stock has a $100 par value, pays a quarterly dividend of $2, and has a yield to investors of 11 percent. New perpetual preferred would have to provide the same yield to investors, and the company would incur a 5 percent flotation cost to sell it.

(4) The company has 4 million shares of common stock outstanding. $P_0 = \$20$, but the stock has recently traded in a range of $17 to $23. $D_0 = \$1$ and $EPS_0 = \$2$. ROE based on average equity was 24 percent in 1996, but management expects to increase this return on equity to 30 percent; however, security analysts are not aware of management's optimism in this regard.

(5) Betas, as reported by security analysts, range from 1.3 to 1.7; the T-bond rate is 10 percent; and k_M is estimated by various brokerage houses to be in the range of 14.5 to 15.5 percent. Brokerage house reports forecast growth rates in the range of 10 to 15 percent over the foreseeable future. However, some analysts do not explicitly forecast growth rates, but they indicate to their clients that they expect TII's historical trends as shown in the table below to continue.

(6) At a recent conference, TII's financial vice-president polled some pension fund investment managers on the minimum rate of return they would have to expect on TII's common to make them willing to buy the common rather than TII bonds, when the bonds yielded 12 percent. The responses suggested a risk premium over TII bonds of 4 to 6 percentage points.

(7) TII is in the 40 percent federal-plus-state tax bracket. Its dominant stockholders are in the 28 percent bracket.

(8) New common stock would have a 10 percent flotation cost.

(9) TII's principal investment banker, Henry, Kaufman & Company, predicts a decline in interest rates, with k_d falling to 10 percent and the T-bond rate to 8 percent, although Henry, Kaufman & Company acknowledges that an increase in the expected inflation rate could lead to an increase rather than a decrease in rates.

(10) The firm expects depreciation expenses of $5 million for the coming year.

(11) Here is the historical record of EPS and DPS:

YEAR	EPS[a]	DPS[a]	YEAR	EPS[a]	DPS[a]
1982	$0.09	$0.00	1990	$0.78	$0.00
1983	−0.20	0.00	1991	0.80	0.00
1984	0.40	0.00	1992	1.20	0.20
1985	0.52	0.00	1993	0.95	0.40
1986	0.10	0.00	1994	1.30	0.60
1987	0.57	0.00	1995	1.60	0.80
1988	0.61	0.00	1996	2.00	1.00
1989	0.70	0.00			

[a]Adjusted for a 2:1 stock split in 1986, a 3:1 split in 1994, and 10 percent stock dividends in 1983 and 1991.

Assume that you are a recently hired financial analyst, and your boss, the treasurer, has asked you to estimate the company's WACC for both retained earnings and new common stock sales. Your cost of capital figures at each level should be appropriate for use in evaluating projects which are in the same risk class as the firm's average assets now on books.

MINI CASE

You have just been hired as a financial analyst by Harry Davis Industries Inc. Your first assignment is to estimate the firm's cost of capital. To get you started, the CFO assembled the following information:

(1) The firm's federal-plus-state tax rate is 40 percent.

(2) The firm has outstanding an issue of 12 percent, semiannual coupon, noncallable bonds with 15 years remaining to maturity. They sell at a price of $1,153.72. The firm does not use short-term debt on a permanent basis.

(3) The current price of the firm's perpetual preferred stock (10 percent, $100 par value, quarterly payment) is $113.10. New perpetual preferred could be sold to the public at this price, but Davis would incur flotation costs of $2.00 per share.

(4) The firm's common stock is currently selling at $50 per share. Its last dividend (D_0) was $4.19, and investors expect the dividend to grow at a constant 5 percent rate into the foreseeable future. The firm's beta is 1.2; the current yield on T-bonds is 7 percent; and the market risk premium is estimated to be 6 percent. When using the bond-yield-plus-risk-premium approach, the managers assume a risk premium of 4 percentage points.

(5) New common stock would involve flotation costs, including market pressure, of 15 percent.

(6) The firm's target capital structure is 30 percent long-term debt, 10 percent preferred stock, and 60 percent common equity.

(7) The company forecasts retained earnings of $300,000 for the coming year.

(8) Depreciation expenses for the coming year are expected to be $500,000.

To structure the task a bit, the CFO asked you to answer the following questions:

a. (1) What sources of capital should be included in the estimate of Davis's WACC?

(2) Should the component cost estimates be on a before-tax or an after-tax basis?

(3) Should the cost estimates reflect historical (embedded) costs or new (marginal) costs?

b. (1) What is the firm's component cost of debt?

(2) Should flotation costs be considered?

(3) Should you use the nominal cost of debt or the effective annual cost?

(4) Would a cost of debt estimate based on 15-year bonds be a valid estimate of k_d if the firm actually planned to issue 30-year bonds?

c. (1) What is the firm's cost of preferred stock?

(2) Is the firm's preferred stock more or less risky to investors than its debt? Why is the yield to investors on the preferred lower than the yield to maturity on the debt?

(3) Now suppose you discovered that the firm's preferred stock had a mandatory redemption provision which specified that the firm must redeem the issue in five years at a price of $110 per share. What would the firm's cost of preferred be in this situation? (Ignore this part in the remainder of the case.)

d. (1) Why is there a cost associated with retained earnings?
   (2) What is the firm's estimated cost of retained earnings based on the CAPM approach?
   (3) Why is the T-bond rate a better estimate of the risk-free rate than is the T-bill rate?
   (4) What is the difference among historical betas, adjusted betas, and fundamental betas?
   (5) Describe two methods which can be used to estimate the market risk premium.
e. (1) What is the estimate of the firm's discounted cash flow (DCF) cost of retained earnings, k_s?
   (2) Suppose the firm has historically earned 15 percent on equity (ROE) and retained 35 percent of earnings, and investors expect this situation to continue in the future. How could you use this information to estimate the future dividend growth rate, and what growth rate would you get? Is this growth rate consistent with the 5 percent given earlier?
   (3) Could DCF methodology be applied if the growth rate was not constant? How?
f. What is the firm's cost of retained earnings based on the bond-yield-plus-risk-premium method?
g. What is your final estimate for k_s?
h. (1) What is the firm's cost of new common stock, k_e?
   (2) Explain in words why new common stock has a higher percentage cost than retained earnings.
i. (1) What is the firm's overall, or weighted average, cost of capital (WACC) when only retained earnings are used as the equity component?
   (2) What is the WACC when new common stock is used as the equity component?
j. (1) At what amount of new investment would the firm be forced to issue new common stock? (For now, ignore the depreciation cash flow.)
   (2) Construct the firm's MCC schedule. Is it reasonable to assume that the firm's MCC schedule would remain constant beyond the retained earnings break point regardless of the amount of capital required? Would what the company planned to do with the money it raised have any effect on the WACC?
k. We know that a firm's annual cash flows are equal to net income plus noncash expenses, typically net income plus depreciation, yet the analysis thus far has ignored the depreciation cash flow. What impact does depreciation have on Davis's MCC schedule? Would a consideration of depreciation affect the acceptability of proposed capital budgeting projects and the size of the total capital budget? Explain.

SELECTED ADDITIONAL REFERENCES AND CASES

The following articles provide some valuable insights into the CAPM approach to estimating the cost of equity:

Beaver, William H., Paul Kettler, and Myron Scholes, "The Association between Market Determined and Accounting Determined Risk Measures," *Accounting Review,* October 1970, 654–682.

Bowman, Robert G., "The Theoretical Relationship between Systematic Risk and Financial (Accounting) Variables," *Journal of Finance,* June 1979, 617–630.

Chen, Carl R., "Time-Series Analysis of Beta Stationarity and Its Determinants: A Case of Public Utilities," *Financial Management,* Autumn 1982, 64–70.

Cooley, Philip L., "A Review of the Use of Beta in Regulatory Proceedings," *Financial Management,* Winter 1981, 75–81.

The weighted average cost of capital as described in this chapter is widely used in both industry and academic circles. It has been criticized on several counts, but to date it has withstood the challenges. See the following articles:

Arditti, Fred D., and Haim Levy, "The Weighted Average Cost of Capital as a Cutoff Rate: A Critical Examination of the Classical Textbook Weighted Average," *Financial Management,* Fall 1977, 24–34.

Beranek, William, "The Weighted Average Cost of Capital and Shareholder Wealth Maximization," *Journal of Financial and Quantitative Analysis,* March 1977, 17–32.

Boudreaux, Kenneth J., and Hugh W. Long; John R. Ezzell and R. Burr Porter; Moshe Ben Horim; and Alan C. Shapiro, "The Weighted Average Cost of Capital: A Discussion," *Financial Management,* Summer 1979, 7–23.

Reilly, Raymond R., and William E. Wacker, "On the Weighted Average Cost of Capital," *Journal of Financial and Quantitative Analysis,* January 1973, 123–126.

Some other works that are relevant include the following:

Alberts, W. W., and Stephen H. Archer, "Some Evidence on the Effect of Company Size on the Cost of Equity Capital," *Journal of Financial and Quantitative Analysis,* March 1973, 229–242.

Amihud, Yakov, and Haim Mendelson, "Liquidity and Cost of Capital: Implications for Corporate Management," *Journal of Applied Corporate Finance,* Fall 1989, 65–73.

Brigham, Eugene F., Dilip K. Shome, and Steve R. Vinson, "The Risk Premium Approach to Measuring a Utility's Cost of Equity," *Financial Management,* Spring 1985, 33–45.

Chen, Andrew, "Recent Developments in the Cost of Debt Capital," *Journal of Finance,* June 1978, 863–883.

Harris, Robert S., "Using Analysts' Growth Forecasts to Estimate Shareholder Required Rates of Return," *Financial Management,* Spring 1986, 58–67.

Harris, Robert S., and Felecia C. Marston, "Estimating Shareholder Risk Premia Using Analysts' Growth Forecasts," *Financial Management,* Summer 1992, 63–70.

Myers, Stewart C., "Interactions of Corporate Financing and Investments Decisions — Implications for Capital Budgeting," *Journal of Finance,* March 1974, 1–25.

Nantell, Timothy J., and C. Robert Carlson, "The Cost of Capital as a Weighted Average," *Journal of Finance,* December 1975, 1343–1355.

Siegal, Jeremy J., "The Application of DCF Methodology for Determining the Cost of Equity Capital," *Financial Management,* Spring 1985, 46–53.

Taggart, Robert A., Jr., "Consistent Valuation and Cost of Capital Expressions with Corporate and Personal Taxes," *Financial Management,* Autumn 1991, 8–20.

Timme, Stephen G., and Peter C. Eisemann, "On the Use of Consensus Forecasts of Growth in the Constant Growth Model: The Case of Electric Utilities," *Financial Management,* Winter 1989, 23–35.

For some insights into the cost of capital techniques used by major firms, see

Gitman, Lawrence J., and Vincent A. Mercurio, "Cost of Capital Techniques Used by Major U.S. Firms: Survey and Analysis of Fortune's 1000," *Financial Management,* Winter 1982, 21–29.

Additional references on the cost of capital are cited in Chapters 5, 10, and 11.

The following cases in the Cases in Financial Management: Dryden Request *series cover concepts related to the cost of capital:*

Case 4, "Silicon Valley Medical Technologies, Inc.," and Case 5, "Telecommunications Services, Inc.," focus on corporate cost of capital issues, while Case 6, "Randolph Corporation," illustrates divisional costs of capital.

CHAPTER 9

THE BASICS OF CAPITAL BUDGETING

few years ago, Chrysler was in trouble. Its stock price had plummeted, its bonds had been downgraded, and its future looked bleak. Indeed, the only thing that kept the company afloat was a government bailout. But what a difference a few years can make! Chrysler's stock, which sold for $12 a share in the early 1990s, was trading at more than $50 in early 1996, and its bond rating had improved from "junk" to investment grade.

How did the "Chrysler Miracle" come about? First, the company developed an innovative concept for designing and producing new models. Whereas most other car makers had separate design and manufacturing teams for each model, Chrysler combined the two groups into one "platform team," which cut design time and lowered manufacturing costs. The new approach allowed the company to get new models on the road quicker and for less money, and the result was world leadership in profit per vehicle.

Chrysler hired Robert Eaton, former head of General Motors's European operations, to replace Lee Iacocca as its chief executive officer in 1992. Eaton is given high marks by most industry analysts, but Chrysler's comeback really began much earlier, during Iacocca's regime. The true test of Eaton's managerial skills will occur in coming years.

Eaton and his staff face many important decisions. Despite the fact that its capital outlays on new plant and equipment have exceeded $4 billion per year, the company had still accumulated more than $8 billion in cash in early 1995. According to Eaton, to maintain its momentum in the very competitive world auto industry, Chrysler must design new autos, modernize its manufacturing processes, and increase research and development of electric and solar-powered cars. Further, those efforts must be continued even when the inevitable next slump occurs and cash flows dry up.

Chrysler's largest shareholder, Kirk Kerkorian, disagreed with Eaton — Kerkorian thought the cash hoard was excessive and that some of it should be returned to stockholders through higher dividends or stock repurchases. When he was unable to convince Eaton, Kerkorian hired Iacocca and launched a hostile takeover attempt. To appease Kerkorian and also to help persuade Chrysler's stockholders to back him rather than Kerkorian, Eaton agreed to buy back $2 billion worth of Chrysler's stock, and he raised the dividend three times during 1994 and 1995, from an annual rate of $0.80 to $2.00.

The decisions regarding the use of Chrysler's remaining cash (more than $6 billion in 1996) will require two types of analysis. First, the company must have a vision about the future of the auto industry and its role in it. Second, it must make investments to implement that strategy. Both types of analysis are based, to a large extent, on the techniques discussed in this chapter. As you read this chapter, think about how Chrysler — or any other company — could use capital budgeting analysis to make sound long-run investment decisions.

In the last chapter, we discussed the cost of capital. Now we turn to investment decisions involving fixed assets, or *capital budgeting.* Here the term *capital* refers to fixed assets used in production, while a *budget* is a plan which details projected inflows and outflows during some future period. Thus, the *capital budget* is an outline of planned expenditures on fixed assets, and *capital budgeting* is the whole process of analyzing projects and deciding which ones to include in the capital budget.

Our treatment of capital budgeting is divided into three chapters. First, Chapter 9 explains the basic techniques used in capital budgeting analysis. Chapter 10 goes on to consider how cash flows are estimated. Finally, Chapter 11 discusses risk analysis in capital budgeting and explains how the optimal capital budget is established.

IMPORTANCE OF CAPITAL BUDGETING

A number of factors combine to make capital budgeting extremely important. First, since the effects of capital budgeting decisions continue over many years, the decision maker loses some of his or her flexibility. For example, the purchase of an asset with an economic life of 10 years often "locks in" the firm for a 10-year period. Further, because asset expansion is fundamentally related to expected future sales, a decision to buy a fixed asset that is expected to last 10 years involves an implicit 10-year sales forecast. Finally, a firm's capital budgeting decisions define its strategic direction, because moves into new products, services, or markets must be preceded by capital expenditures.

An erroneous forecast of asset requirements can have serious consequences. If the firm invests too much, it will incur unnecessarily heavy expenses. If it does not spend enough, two problems will arise. First, its equipment will not be sufficiently modern to enable it to produce competitively. Second, if it has inadequate capacity, it will lose a portion of its market share to rival firms, and regaining lost customers typically requires heavy selling expenses, price reductions, or product improvements, all of which are costly. Of course, if the product or service does not meet customers' needs, the results can be even more serious. For example, Beech Aircraft introduced its Starship corporate propjet in 1989 amid much fanfare. The plane was technologically advanced, roomy, quiet, and beautiful, and it received rave reviews from aviation aficionados. Based on what they saw on the drawing board, the aviation press praised the project, and Beech committed to an initial production run of 53 planes. Unfortunately, the plane offered prop performance at jet prices, so the company could sell only 20 planes. Needless to say, the project had a large, negative impact on Beech's financial condition.

Another aspect of capital budgeting is timing — capital assets must be available when they are needed. Edward Ford, who was recently brought in as president of Western Design, a troubled decorative tile company, gave the authors an illustration of the importance of capital budgeting. His firm tried to operate near capacity most of the time. During a four-year period, Western experienced intermittent spurts in the demand for its products, which forced it to turn away orders. After a sharp increase in demand, the firm would add capacity by renting an additional building, then purchasing and installing the appropriate equipment. It would take six to eight months to get the additional capacity ready, and frequently by that time there was no demand for the increased output — other firms had already expanded and had taken a larger share of the market. If Western had properly forecasted demand and had planned its new capacity six months to a year in advance, it would have been able to maintain or perhaps even increase its market share.

Effective capital budgeting will improve both the timing and the quality of asset additions. A firm which forecasts its needs for capital assets in advance can purchase and install the assets before its sales are at capacity. In practice, though, many firms do not order new plant and equipment until they have approached full capacity, need to replace worn-out equipment, or are adding new product lines. If sales increase because of an increase in general market demand, all firms in the industry will tend to order capital equipment at about the same time. This often results in backlogs, long waiting times for machinery, a deterioration in the quality of the capital assets, and an increase in costs. The firm which anticipates its needs can avoid these problems. Note, though, that if a firm forecasts an increase in demand and expands to meet the anticipated demand, and if sales then do not expand, it will be saddled with excess capacity and abnormally high costs. This can lead to losses or even bankruptcy. Thus, an accurate sales forecast is critical.

Finally, capital budgeting is also important because asset expansion typically involves substantial expenditures, and before a firm spends a large amount of money, it must make the proper plans — large amounts of funds are not available automatically. A firm contemplating a major capital expenditure program may need to arrange its financing several years in advance to be sure of having the funds required for the expansion.

SELF-TEST
QUESTIONS
Why are capital budgeting decisions so important to the success of a firm?
Why is the sales forecast a key element in capital budgeting decisions?

GENERATING IDEAS FOR CAPITAL PROJECTS

The same general concepts that are used in security valuation are also involved in capital budgeting. However, a set of stocks and bonds exists in the securities market and investors select from this set, *but capital budgeting projects are created by the firm.* For example, a sales representative may report that customers are asking for a particular product that the company does not now produce. The sales manager then discusses the idea with the marketing research group to determine the size of the market for the proposed product. If it appears likely that a significant market does exist, cost accountants and engineers will be asked to estimate production costs. If it appears that the product can be produced and sold at a sufficient profit, the project will be undertaken.

A firm's growth, and even its ability to remain competitive and to survive, depends on a constant flow of ideas for new products, for ways to make existing products better, and for ways to produce at a lower cost. Accordingly, a well-managed firm will go to great lengths to develop good capital budgeting proposals. For example, the executive vice-president of one very successful corporation indicated that his company takes the following steps to generate projects:

> Our R&D department is constantly searching for new products and for ways to improve existing products. In addition, our executive committee, which consists of senior executives in marketing, production, and finance, identifies the products and markets in which our company should compete, and the committee sets long-run targets for each division. These targets, which are spelled out in the corporation's *strategic business plan,* provide a general guide to the operating executives who must meet them. The operating executives then seek new products, set expansion plans for existing products, and look for ways to reduce production and distribution costs. Since bonuses and promotions are based on each unit's ability to meet or exceed its targets, these economic incentives encourage our operating executives to seek out profitable investment opportunities.
>
> While our senior executives are judged and rewarded on the basis of how well their units perform, people further down the line are given bonuses for suggestions which lead to profitable investments. Additionally, a percentage of our corporate profit is set aside for distribution to nonexecutive employees, and we have an Employees' Stock Ownership Plan (ESOP) to provide further incentives. Our objective is to encourage employees at all levels to keep an eye out for good ideas, including those that lead to capital investments.

If a firm has capable and imaginative executives and employees, and if its incentive system is working properly, many ideas for capital investment will be advanced. Some ideas will be good ones, but others will not. Therefore, procedures must be established for screening projects, the primary topic of this chapter.

SELF-TEST
QUESTION
What are some ways a firm gets ideas for capital projects?

PROJECT CLASSIFICATIONS

Analyzing capital expenditure proposals is not a costless operation — benefits can be gained from a careful analysis, but such an investigation does have a cost. For certain types of projects, a relatively detailed analysis may be warranted; for others, cost/benefit studies suggest that simpler procedures should be used. Accordingly, firms generally classify projects into the following categories, and they analyze projects in each category somewhat differently:

1. **Replacement: maintenance of business.** Some expenditures are necessary to replace worn-out or damaged equipment used to produce profitable products. These projects are necessary if the firm is to continue in its current businesses. The only issues here are (a) should we continue to produce these products or services, and (b) should we continue to use our existing plant and equipment? Usually, the answers are "yes," so maintenance decisions are normally made without going through an elaborate decision process.

2. **Replacement: cost reduction.** This category includes expenditures to replace serviceable but obsolete equipment. The purpose here is to lower the costs of labor, materials, or other inputs such as electricity. These decisions are somewhat more discretionary, so a more detailed analysis is generally required to support the expenditure.

3. **Expansion of existing products or markets.** Expenditures to increase output of existing products, or to expand outlets or distribution facilities in markets now being served, are included here. These decisions are more complex because they require an explicit consideration of future demand in the firm's product markets. Mistakes are more likely, so a still more detailed analysis is required, and the final decision is made at a higher level within the firm.

4. **Expansion into new products or markets.** These are expenditures necessary to produce a new product or to expand into a geographic area not currently being served. These projects involve strategic decisions that could change the fundamental nature of the business, and they normally require the expenditure of large sums of money over long periods. Invariably, a very detailed analysis is required, and final decisions on new products or markets are generally made by the board of directors as a part of the firm's strategic plan.

5. **Safety and/or environmental projects.** Expenditures necessary to comply with government orders, labor agreements, or insurance policy terms fall into this category. These expenditures are often called *mandatory investments,* or *non-revenue-producing projects.* How they are handled depends on their size, with small ones being treated much like the Category 1 projects described previously.

6. **Research and development.** For many firms, R&D constitutes the largest and most important type of capital expenditure. Although these expenditures can, conceptually, be analyzed in the same way as tangible asset investments, the cash flows they produce are often too uncertain to warrant a standard DCF analysis. What happens, generally, is that managers think in subjective DCF terms about R&D expenditures, then appropriate a certain amount of

money to conduct research on a given project or set of projects. Since R&D results are almost always highly uncertain, and since continuing to fund a project will depend on results at earlier stages, the decision tree analysis discussed in Chapter 11 is often used.

7. **Other.** This catch-all includes office buildings, parking lots, executive aircraft, and so on. How they are handled frequently depends on their size.

In general, relatively simple calculations and only a few supporting documents are required for replacement decisions, especially maintenance-type investments in profitable plants. More detailed analysis is required for cost-reduction replacements, for expansion of existing product lines, and especially for investments in new products or areas. Also, within each category, projects are broken down by their dollar costs: The larger the required investment, the more detailed the analysis, and the higher the level of the officer who must authorize the expenditure. Thus, although a plant manager may be authorized to approve maintenance expenditures up to $10,000 on the basis of a relatively unsophisticated analysis, the full board of directors may have to approve decisions which involve either amounts over $1 million or expansions into new products or markets. Statistical data are generally lacking for new-product and R&D decisions, so here judgments, as opposed to detailed cost data, are a key element in the decision process.

Note too that corporate mergers are essentially a type of capital budgeting expenditure. Companies frequently decide to acquire other firms in order to obtain low-cost production facilities, to increase capacity, or to expand into different markets. The analysis related to such mergers is conceptually similar to that related to regular capital budgeting projects. Thus, when AT&T decided to go into the cellular telephone business, it had the choice of building facilities from the ground up or acquiring an existing business. AT&T chose to acquire McCaw Cellular. Note, though, that proper merger analysis requires an understanding of the techniques of capital budgeting analysis. We discuss mergers in detail in Chapter 25.

SELF-TEST QUESTION   Identify and briefly explain how capital project classifications are used.

SIMILARITIES BETWEEN CAPITAL BUDGETING AND SECURITY VALUATION

Conceptually, capital budgeting involves exactly the same six steps that are used in security analysis:

1. First, the cost of the project must be determined. This is similar to finding the price that must be paid for a stock or bond.

2. Next, management must estimate the expected cash flows from the project, including the value of the asset at a specified terminal date. This is similar to estimating the future dividend or interest payment stream on a stock or bond.

3. Third, the riskiness of the projected cash flows must be estimated. To do this, management needs information about the probability distributions (uncertainty) of the cash flows.

4. Then, given the riskiness of the projected cash flows, management determines the appropriate cost of capital at which the project's cash flows are to be discounted.

5. Next, the expected cash inflows are put on a present value basis to obtain an estimate of the asset's value to the firm. This is equivalent to finding the present value of expected future dividends or interest payments.

6. Finally, the present value of the expected cash inflows is compared to the required outlay, or cost, of the project; if the asset's value exceeds its cost, the project should be accepted. Otherwise, the project should be rejected. (Alternatively, the expected rate of return on the project can be calculated, and if this rate of return exceeds the project's required rate of return, the project is accepted.)

If an individual investor buys a stock or bond whose market price is less than its true value, the value of the investor's portfolio will increase. Similarly, if a firm identifies (or creates) an investment opportunity with a present value greater than its cost, the value of the firm will increase. Thus, as we noted in Chapter 2 when we discussed MVA and EVA, there is a direct link between capital budgeting and stock values: The more effective the firm's capital budgeting procedures, the higher the price of its stock.

List the six steps of the capital budgeting process, and relate them to security valuation.

SELF-TEST QUESTION

CAPITAL BUDGETING DECISION RULES

Six primary methods are used to rank projects and to decide whether or not they should be accepted for inclusion in the capital budget: (1) payback period, (2) discounted payback, (3) net present value (NPV), (4) internal rate of return (IRR), (5) modified IRR (MIRR), and (6) profitability index (PI). We first explain how each ranking criterion is calculated, and then we discuss how well each performs in terms of identifying those projects which will maximize the firm's stock price.[1]

We use the cash flow data shown in Figure 9-1 for Projects S and L to illustrate each method, and throughout this chapter we assume that the projects are equally risky. Note that the cash flows in each year, CF_t, are expected values, and that they are adjusted to reflect taxes, depreciation, and salvage values. Also, since many projects require an investment in both fixed assets and working capital, the investment outlays shown as CF_0 include any necessary increases in net working capital.[2]

---

[1]Another method, the *Accounting Rate of Return (ARR)*, was also used in the past. It does not produce useful results, and it is rarely used today, so we do not discuss it.

[2]The most difficult part of the capital budgeting process is the estimation of the relevant cash flows. For simplicity, the net cash flows are treated as a given in this chapter, which allows us to focus on our main area of concern, the capital budgeting decision rules. However, in Chapter 10 we will discuss cash flow estimation in detail. Also, note that working capital is defined as the firm's current assets, and that net working capital is current assets minus current liabilities.

FIGURE 9-1	NET CASH FLOWS FOR PROJECTS S AND L

		EXPECTED AFTER-TAX NET CASH FLOWS, CF_t	
YEAR (t)		PROJECT S	PROJECT L
0^a		($1,000)	($1,000)
1		500	100
2		400	300
3		300	400
4		100	600

Project S:

0	1	2	3	4
−1,000	500	400	300	100

Project L:

0	1	2	3	4
−1,000	100	300	400	600

$^a CF_0$ represents the net investment outlay, or initial cost.

Finally, we assume that all cash flows occur at the end of the designated year. Incidentally, the S stands for *short* and the L for *long:* Project S is a short-term project in the sense that its cash inflows tend to come in sooner than L's.

PAYBACK PERIOD AND DISCOUNTED PAYBACK

The *payback period,* defined as the expected number of years required to recover the original investment, was the first formal method used to evaluate capital budgeting projects. The payback calculation is diagrammed in Figure 9-2, and it is explained below for Project S.

1. Enter $CF_0 = -1000$ in your calculator. (You do not need to use the cash flow register; just have your display show −1,000.)

2. Now add $CF_1 = 500$ to find the cumulative cash flow at the end of Year 1. This is −500.

3. Now add $CF_2 = 400$ to find the cumulative cash flow at the end of Year 2. This is −100.

4. Now add $CF_3 = 300$ to find the cumulative cash flow at the end of Year 3. This is +200.

5. You see that by the end of Year 3 the cumulative inflows have more than recovered the initial outflow. Thus, the payback occurred during the third year. If the $300 of inflows come in evenly during Year 3, then the exact payback can be found as follows:

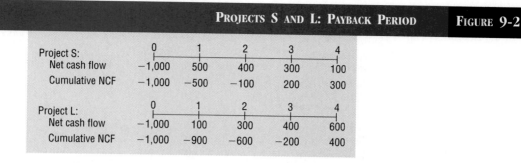

PROJECTS S AND L: PAYBACK PERIOD — **FIGURE 9-2**

Project S:	0	1	2	3	4
Net cash flow	−1,000	500	400	300	100
Cumulative NCF	−1,000	−500	−100	200	300

Project L:	0	1	2	3	4
Net cash flow	−1,000	100	300	400	600
Cumulative NCF	−1,000	−900	−600	−200	400

$$\text{Payback}_S = \text{Year before full recovery} + \frac{\text{Unrecovered cost at start of year}}{\text{Cash flow during year}}$$

$$= 2 + \frac{100}{300} = 2.33 \text{ years.}$$

Applying the same procedure to Project L, we find $\text{Payback}_L = 3.33$ years.

The shorter the payback the better. Therefore, if the firm required a payback of three years or less, Project S would be accepted but Project L would be rejected. If the projects were mutually exclusive, S would be ranked over L because S has the shorter payback. *Mutually exclusive* means that if one project is taken on, the other must be rejected. For example, the installation of a conveyor-belt system in a warehouse and the purchase of a fleet of forklifts for the same warehouse would be mutually exclusive projects — accepting one implies rejection of the other. *Independent projects* are projects whose cash flows are independent of one another.

Some firms use a variant of the regular payback, the *discounted payback period,* which is similar to the regular payback period except that the expected cash flows are discounted by the project's cost of capital.[3] Thus, the discounted payback period is defined as the number of years required to recover the investment from *discounted* net cash flows. Figure 9-3 contains the discounted net cash flows for Projects S and L, assuming both projects have a cost of capital of 10 percent. To construct Figure 9-3, each cash inflow is divided by $(1 + k)^t = (1.10)^t$, where t is the year in which the cash flow occurs and k is the project's cost of capital. After 3 years, Project S will have generated the $1,000 cost plus an extra $11, or $1,011 in discounted cash inflows. Since the cost is $1,000, the discounted payback is just under 3 years, or, to be precise, 2 + ($214/$225) = 2.95 years. Project L's discounted payback is 3.88 years:

Discounted payback$_S$ = 2.0 + $214/$225 = 2.95 years.

Discounted payback$_L$ = 3.0 + $360/$410 = 3.88 years.

---

[3] A project's cost of capital reflects (1) the overall cost of capital to the firm and (2) the differential risk between the firm's existing projects and the project being evaluated. Risk adjustments will be discussed in detail in Chapter 11.

FIGURE 9-3   PROJECTS S AND L: DISCOUNTED PAYBACK PERIOD

Project S:	0	1	2	3	4
Net cash flow	−1,000	500	400	300	100
Discounted NCF	−1,000	455	331	225	68
Cumulative discounted NCF	−1,000	−545	−214	11	79

Project L:	0	1	2	3	4
Net cash flow	−1,000	100	300	400	600
Discounted NCF	−1,000	91	248	301	410
Cumulative discounted NCF	−1,000	−909	−661	−360	50

For Projects S and L, the rankings are the same regardless of which payback method is used; that is, Project S is preferred to Project L, and Project S would still be selected if the firm were to require a discounted payback of three years or less. Often, however, the regular and the discounted paybacks produce conflicting rankings.

Note that the payback is a type of "breakeven" calculation in the sense that if cash flows come in at the expected rate until the payback year, then the project will break even. However, the regular payback does not take account of the cost of capital — no cost for the debt or equity used to undertake the project is reflected in the cash flows or the calculation. The discounted payback does take account of capital costs — it shows the breakeven year after covering debt and equity costs.

An important drawback of both the payback and discounted payback methods is that they ignore cash flows that are paid or received after the payback period. For example, consider two projects, X and Y, each of which requires an up-front cash outflow of $3,000, so $CF_0 = -\$3,000$. The projects are equally risky, and they have a cost of capital of 10 percent. Project X is expected to produce cash inflows of $1,000 in each of the next four years, while Project Y will produce no cash flows the first four years but then generate a cash inflow of $1,000,000 five years from now. Common sense suggests that Project Y would create more value for the firm's shareholders, yet its payback and discounted payback make it look worse than Project X. Consequently, both payback methods have serious deficiencies.

Although the payback method has some serious faults as a ranking criterion, it does provide information on how long funds will be tied up in a project. Thus, the shorter the payback period, other things held constant, the greater the project's *liquidity.* Also, since cash flows expected in the distant future are generally riskier than near-term cash flows, the payback is often used as one indicator of a project's *riskiness.*

NET PRESENT VALUE (NPV)

As the flaws in the payback were recognized, people began to search for ways to improve the effectiveness of project evaluations. One such method is the *net pres-*

ent value (NPV) method, which relies on *discounted cash flow* (DCF) methodology. To implement this approach, we proceed as follows:

1. Find the present value of each period's net cash flow, including both inflows and outflows, discounted at the project's cost of capital.

2. Sum these discounted net cash flows; this sum is defined as the project's NPV.

3. If the NPV is positive, the project should be accepted. If the NPV is negative, it should be rejected. And if two projects are mutually exclusive, the one with the higher positive NPV should be chosen.

The NPV is found using this equation:

$$NPV = \sum_{t=0}^{n} \frac{CF_t}{(1+k)^t}.$$

9-1

Here CF_t is the expected net cash flow at Period t, and k is the project's cost of capital.[4] Cash outflows (expenditures on the project, such as the cost of buying equipment or building factories) are treated as *negative* cash flows. In evaluating Projects S and L, only CF_0 is negative, but for many large projects such as a new automobile model, an electric generating plant, or a new steel mill, outflows occur for several years before operations begin and cash flows turn positive. Also, note that Equation 9-1 is quite general, so inflows and outflows could occur on any time basis, say, quarterly or monthly, in which case t would represent quarters or months rather than years.[5]

At a 10 percent cost of capital, the NPV of Project S is $78.82:

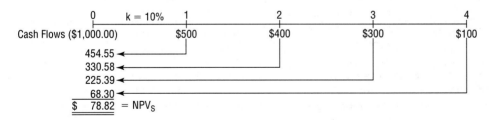

By a similar process, we find $NPV_L = \$49.18$. On this basis, both projects should be accepted if they are independent, but S should be the one chosen if they are mutually exclusive.

---

[4]In Equation 9-1, we assume that the project's cost of capital, k, is constant across all periods. Since changes in capital costs are difficult, if not impossible, to forecast, a constant capital cost is almost always used in practice. However, riskier projects are evaluated using a higher cost of capital than less risky projects.

[5]If t represents any period other than years, then the cost of capital must be adjusted to reflect the periodic rate. For example, if the annual cost of capital were 10 percent, but we were evaluating a project on the basis of quarterly cash flows, the periodic rate would be 10%/4 = 2.5%.

When using a financial calculator, enter the cash flows, in order, into the cash flow register, then enter k = I = 10, and finally push the NPV key (or compute NPV). When entering the cash flows, note that many calculators have a register labelled CF_0 for the initial cash flow, which is usually an outflow, and then registers labelled CF_j for the succeeding cash flows.[6]

RATIONALE FOR THE NPV METHOD

The rationale for the NPV method is straightforward. An NPV of zero signifies that the project's cash flows are exactly sufficient to repay the invested capital and to provide the required rate of return on that capital. If a project has a positive NPV, then its cash flows are generating more than the required return, and, since the return to bondholders is fixed, the extra return accrues solely to the firm's stockholders. Therefore, if a firm takes on a zero-NPV project, the position of the stock-

---

[6]The precise steps for two popular calculators, the HP 10B and the HP 17B, are shown below. If you have another type of financial calculator, see its manual.

HP 10B:

1. Clear the memory.
2. Enter CF_0 as follows: 1000 $\boxed{+/-}$ $\boxed{\text{CF}_j}$.
3. Enter CF_1 as follows: 500 $\boxed{\text{CF}_j}$.
4. Repeat the process to enter the other cash flows. Note that CF 0, CF 1, and so forth flash on the screen as you press the $\boxed{\text{CF}_j}$ key. If you hold the key down, CF 0 and so forth will remain on the screen until you release it.
5. Once the CFs have been entered, enter k = I = 10%: 10 $\boxed{\text{I/YR}}$.
6. Now that all of the inputs have been entered, you can press $\blacksquare$ $\boxed{\text{NPV}}$ to get the answer, NPV = $78.82.
7. If a cash flow is repeated for several years, you can avoid having to enter the CFs for each year. For example, if the $500 cash flow for Year 1 had also been the CF for Years 2 through 10, making 10 of these $500 cash flows, then after entering 500 $\boxed{\text{CF}_j}$ the first time, you could enter 10 $\blacksquare$ $\boxed{\text{N}_j}$. This would automatically enter 10 CFs of 500.

HP 17B:

1. Go to the cash flow (CFLO) menu, clear if FLOW(0) = ? does not appear on the screen.
2. Enter CF_0 as follows: 1000 $\boxed{+/-}$ $\boxed{\text{INPUT}}$.
3. Enter CF_1 as follows: 500 $\boxed{\text{INPUT}}$.
4. Now the calculator will ask you if the 500 is for Period 1 only or if it is also used for several following periods. Since it is only used for Period 1, press $\boxed{\text{INPUT}}$ to answer "1." Alternatively, you could press $\boxed{\text{EXIT}}$ and then $\boxed{\text{#T?}}$ to turn off the prompt for the remainder of the problem. For some problems you will want to use the repeat feature.
5. Enter the remaining CFs, being sure to turn off the prompt or else to specify "1" for each entry.
6. Once the CFs have all been entered, press $\boxed{\text{EXIT}}$ and then $\boxed{\text{CALC}}$.
7. Now enter k = I = 10% as follows: 10 $\boxed{\text{I\%}}$.
8. Now press $\boxed{\text{NPV}}$ to get the answer, NPV = $78.82.

holders remains constant — the firm becomes larger, but the price of its stock remains unchanged. However, if the firm takes on a project with a positive NPV, the position of the stockholders is improved. In our example, shareholders' wealth would increase by $78.82 if the firm takes on Project S, but it would increase by only $49.18 if it takes on Project L. Viewed in this manner, it is easy to see why S is preferred to L, and it is also easy to see the logic of the NPV approach.[7]

There is also a direct relationship between NPV and EVA (economic value added) — if, during a given year, a firm takes on a set of projects which all have positive NPVs, then over time its cumulative EVA should rise by the sum of the projects' NPVs. Things will never work out this way because investors cannot determine the expected NPVs of all the firm's projects. Still, over time positive NPVs should translate into positive EVAs, and to a positive MVA (market value added, or the excess of the firm's market value over its book value). So, a reward system that compensates managers for producing positive EVA will lead to the use of NPV for making capital budgeting decisions.

INTERNAL RATE OF RETURN (IRR)

In Chapter 7 we presented procedures for finding the yield to maturity, or rate of return, on a bond — if you invest in the bond and hold it to maturity, you can expect to earn the YTM on the money you invested. Exactly the same concepts are employed in capital budgeting when the IRR method is used. The IRR is defined as that discount rate which equates the present value of a project's expected cash inflows to the present value of the project's expected costs or, equivalently, forces the NPV to equal zero:

$$NPV = \sum_{t=0}^{n} \frac{CF_t}{(1 + IRR)^t} = 0. \qquad \text{9-2}$$

Here is the setup for Project S:

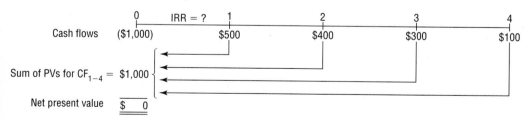

[7]This description of the process is somewhat oversimplified. Both analysts and investors anticipate that firms will identify and accept positive NPV projects, and current stock prices reflect these expectations. Thus, stock prices react to announcements of new capital projects only to the extent that such projects were not already expected. In this sense, we may think of a firm's value as consisting of two parts: (1) the value of its existing assets and (2) the value of its "growth opportunities," or projects with positive NPVs.

$$\text{IRR}_s = 14.5\% = \text{Discount rate which forces the sum of the PVs}$$
$$\text{of } \text{CF}_{1-4} \text{ to equal the project's cost, } \$1,000, \text{ i.e.,}$$
$$\text{which forces the NPV to equal zero.}$$

Internal rates of return can be calculated with financial calculators and computers, and most firms have computerized their capital budgeting processes and can quickly generate IRRs, NPVs, and paybacks for all projects. Thus, business firms have no difficulty whatsoever with the mechanical side of capital budgeting, and a serious business student should have a financial calculator or computer capable of finding IRRs. All IRRs reported in this and the following chapters were obtained using a financial calculator or a computer. By keying in the cash flows and then pressing the IRR button, we used a financial calculator to find that Project S has $\text{IRR}_S = 14.5\%$, while $\text{IRR}_L = 11.8\%$.[8] If both projects have a cost of capital, or *hurdle rate,* of 10 percent, then the internal rate of return rule indicates that if the projects are independent, both should be accepted — they both are expected to earn more than the cost of the capital needed to finance them. If they are mutually exclusive, S ranks higher and should be accepted, while L should be rejected. If the cost of capital is more than 14.5 percent, both projects should be rejected.

Notice that the IRR formula, Equation 9-2, is simply the NPV formula, Equation 9-1, solved for the particular discount rate that forces the NPV to equal zero. Thus, the same basic equation is used for both methods, but in the NPV method the discount rate, k, is specified and the NPV is found, whereas in the IRR method the NPV is specified to equal zero, and the value of IRR that forces this equality is determined.

RATIONALE FOR THE IRR METHOD

Why is the particular discount rate that equates a project's cost with the present value of its receipts (the IRR) so special? In effect, the IRR on a project is its expected rate of return. If the internal rate of return exceeds the cost of the funds used to finance the project, a surplus remains after paying for the capital, and this surplus accrues to the firm's stockholders. Therefore, taking on a project whose IRR exceeds its cost of capital increases shareholders' wealth. On the other hand, if the internal rate of return is less than the cost of capital, then taking on the project imposes a cost on current stockholders. It is this "breakeven" characteristic that makes the IRR useful in evaluating capital projects.

PROFITABILITY INDEX

Another method used to evaluate projects is the *profitability index (PI),* or the *benefit/cost ratio,* as it is sometimes called:

---

[8]To find the IRR with an HP 10B or HP 17B, repeat the steps given in Footnote 6. Then, with an HP 10B, press ■ IRR/YR , and after a pause, 14.49, Project S's IRR, will appear. With the HP 17B, simply press IRR% to get the IRR. With either calculator, you would always want to calculate both the NPV and the IRR after entering the input data, before clearing the cash flow register.

$$PI = \frac{PV \text{ benefits}}{PV \text{ costs}} = \frac{\displaystyle\sum_{t=0}^{n} \frac{CIF_t}{(1+k)^t}}{\displaystyle\sum_{t=0}^{n} \frac{COF_t}{(1+k)^t}}.$$

9-3

Here CIF_t represents the expected cash *inflows,* or benefits, and COF_t represents the expected cash *outflows,* or costs. The PI shows the *relative* profitability of any project, or the present value of benefits per present value dollar of costs. The PI for Project S, based on a 10 percent cost of capital, is 1.079:

$$PI_S = \frac{\$1,078.82}{\$1,000} = 1.079.$$

Thus, on a present value basis, Project S is expected to produce $1.079 for each $1 of investment. Project L, with a PI of 1.049, should produce $1.049 for each dollar invested.

A project is acceptable if its PI is greater than 1.0, and the higher the PI, the higher the project's ranking. Therefore, both S and L would be accepted by the PI criterion if they were independent, and S would be ranked ahead of L if they were mutually exclusive.

Mathematically, the NPV, the IRR, and the PI methods will always lead to the same accept/reject decisions for *independent* projects: If a project's NPV is positive, its IRR will always exceed k and its PI will always be greater than 1.0. However, NPV, IRR, and PI can give conflicting rankings for *mutually exclusive* projects. This point is discussed in more detail in later sections.

Name the six capital budgeting ranking methods discussed in this section. Briefly describe each method, and explain the rationale for its use.

What three methods always lead to the same accept/reject decision for independent projects?

What two pieces of information does the payback period provide that are not provided by the other methods?

SELF-TEST QUESTIONS

COMPARISON OF THE NPV AND IRR METHODS

As we will demonstrate later, the NPV method is better than either the IRR or PI. Therefore, we were tempted to explain only the NPV, to state that it should be used as the acceptance criterion, and then go on to the next topic. However, the IRR and PI are familiar to many corporate executives, they are widely entrenched in industry, and they do provide some useful information. Therefore, it is important that finance students understand the IRR and PI methods and be prepared to explain why, at times, a project with a lower IRR or PI may be preferable to one with a higher IRR or PI.

NPV PROFILES

A graph which relates a project's NPV to the discount rate used to calculate the NPV is defined as the project's *net present value profile;* profiles for Projects L and S are shown in Figure 9-4. To construct the profiles, first note that at a zero discount rate, the NPV is simply the total of the project's undiscounted cash flows. Thus, at a zero discount rate, $NPV_S = \$300$ and $NPV_L = \$400$. These values are plotted as the vertical axis intercepts in Figure 9-4. Next, calculate the projects' NPVs at three discount rates, say, 5, 10, and 15 percent, and plot these values. The four points plotted on our graph for each project are shown at the bottom of the figure.

Finally, recall that the IRR is defined as the discount rate at which a project's NPV equals zero. Therefore, *the point where its net present value profile crosses the hor-*

| FIGURE 9-4 | NET PRESENT VALUE PROFILES: NPVS OF PROJECTS S AND L AT DIFFERENT COSTS OF CAPITAL |

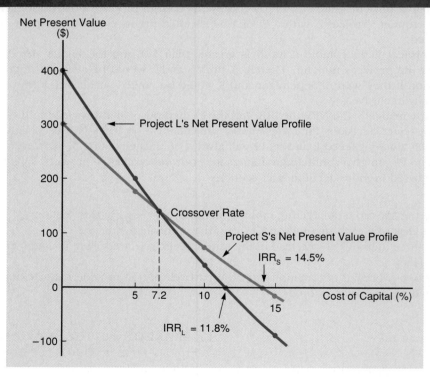

COST OF CAPITAL	NPV$_S$	NPV$_L$
0%	$300.00	$400.00
5	180.42	206.50
10	78.82	49.18
15	(8.33)	(80.14)

izontal axis indicates a project's internal rate of return. Since we calculated IRR$_S$ and IRR$_L$ in an earlier section, we have two other points which we can use in plotting the projects' NPV profiles.

When we connect the plot points, we have the net present value profiles.[9] NPV profiles can be very useful in project analysis, and we will use them often in the remainder of the chapter.

Only NPV Rankings Depend on the Discount Rate

Figure 9-4 shows that the IRRs of Projects L and S are fixed — they do not vary with changes in the discount rate. However, the NPV profiles of both Project L and Project S do vary — they both decline as the discount rate increases. Notice, however, that Project L has the higher NPV at low discount rates, while S's NPV exceeds that of L if the discount rate is above 7.2 percent, the "crossover rate." Notice also that Project L's NPV is "more sensitive" to changes in the discount rate than is NPV$_S$. That is, Project L's net present value profile has the steeper slope, indicating that a given change in k has a larger effect on NPV$_L$ than on NPV$_S$.

To see why L has the greater sensitivity, recall first that the cash flows from S are received faster than those from L — in a payback sense, S is a short-term project, while L is a long-term project. Next, recall the equation for the NPV:

$$NPV = \frac{CF_0}{(1 + k)^0} + \frac{CF_1}{(1 + k)^1} + \frac{CF_2}{(1 + k)^2} + \frac{CF_3}{(1 + k)^3} + \frac{CF_4}{(1 + k)^4}.$$

Notice that the denominators of the terms in this equation increase as k and t increase, and the increase is exponential; that is, the effect of a higher k is more pronounced if t is larger. To understand this point more clearly, consider the following data:

PV of a $100 cash flow due in 1 year, discounted at 5%	$95.24
PV of a $100 cash flow due in 1 year, discounted at 10%	$90.91
Percentage decline in the PV resulting from a 5 percentage point increase in k when t = 1	−4.5%
PV of a $100 cash flow due in 10 years, discounted at 5%	$61.39
PV of a $100 cash flow due in 10 years, discounted at 10%	$38.55
Percentage decline in the PV resulting from a 5 percentage point increase in k when t = 10	−37.2%

A 5 percentage point increase in the discount rate causes only a 4.5 percent decline in the PV of a cash flow due in one year, but the same discount rate increase causes the PV of a Year 10 cash flow to fall by 37.2 percent. Thus, if a project has most of its cash flows coming in the early years, its NPV will not be lowered very much by a discount rate increase, but the NPV of a project whose cash flows come

---

[9]Notice that NPV profiles are curved — they are *not* straight lines. Also, NPV profiles approach the t = 0 cash flow value (the cost of the project) as the discount rate increases without limit. The reason is that, at an infinitely high discount rate, the PVs of the inflows would be zero, so NPV at k = ∞ is CF$_0$, which in our example is −$1,000. We should also note that under certain conditions the NPV profiles can cross the horizontal axis several times, or never cross it. This point is discussed later in the chapter.

later will be severely penalized by high discount rates. Accordingly, the NPV of Project L, which has its largest cash flows in the later years, drops sharply as the discount rate rises, while Project S, which has relatively rapid cash flows, is affected less. Therefore, L's NPV profile has the steeper slope.

INDEPENDENT PROJECTS

If two projects are *independent,* then the NPV and IRR methods always lead to the same accept/reject decision: if NPV says accept, IRR also says accept. To see why this is so, look back at Figure 9-4, focus on Project L's NPV, and notice (1) that the IRR criterion for acceptance is that the project's cost of capital is less than (or to the left of) the IRR, and (2) that whenever the project's cost of capital is less than the IRR, its NPV is positive. Thus, at any cost of capital less than 11.8 percent, Project L is acceptable by both the NPV and the IRR criteria, while both methods reject the project if the cost of capital is greater than 11.8 percent. Project S — and all other independent projects under consideration — could be analyzed similarly, and it will always turn out that if IRR > k, then NPV > 0.

MUTUALLY EXCLUSIVE PROJECTS

Now assume that Projects S and L are *mutually exclusive* rather than independent. That is, we can choose either Project S or Project L, or we can reject both, but we cannot accept both projects. Notice in Figure 9-4 that as long as the cost of capital is *greater than* the crossover rate of 7.2 percent, NPV_S is greater than NPV_L, and IRR_S is greater than IRR_L. Therefore, for k greater than the crossover rate of 7.2 percent, the two methods lead to the selection of the same project. However, if the cost of capital is *less than* the crossover rate, a conflict arises — the NPV method ranks Project L higher, but the IRR method indicates that Project S is better.[10]
    In summary:

1. **Independent projects.** NPV and IRR always lead to the same decision. There is never a conflict.

2. **Mutually exclusive projects.**
    a. Cost of capital *greater than* crossover rate. Never a conflict.
    b. Cost of capital *less than* crossover rate. There is a conflict between NPV and IRR.

Now suppose the cost of capital is less than the crossover rate and a conflict exists. NPV says choose mutually exclusive L, while IRR says take S. Which answer is correct? Logic suggests that the NPV method is better, since it selects that project which adds the most to shareholder wealth.

---

[10]The crossover point is important, and it is easy to calculate. Simply go back to Figure 9-1, where we set forth the two projects' cash flows, and calculate the difference in those flows in each year. The differences are $CF_S - CF_L = \$0, + \$400, + \$100, - \$100$, and $- \$500$, respectively. Enter these values in the cash flow register of a financial calculator, press the IRR button, and the crossover rate, $7.17 \approx 7.2$, appears. Be sure to enter $CF_0 = 0$.

WHY CONFLICTS ARISE   Two basic conditions can cause NPV profiles to cross, and thus can lead to conflicts between NPV and IRR: (1) when *project size (or scale) differences* exist, meaning that the cost of one project is larger than that of the other, or (2) when *timing differences* exist, meaning that the timing of cash flows from the two projects differs such that most of the cash flows from one project come in the early years and most of the cash flows from the other project come in the later years, as occurred with Projects L and S.[11]

When either size or timing differences occur, the firm will have different amounts of funds to invest in the various years, depending on which project it chooses. For example, if one project costs more than the other, then the firm will have more money at t = 0 to invest elsewhere if it selects the smaller project. Similarly, for projects of equal size, the one with the larger early cash inflows provides more funds for reinvestment in the early years. Given this situation, the assumed rate of return at which differential cash flows can be invested is a key consideration.

THE REINVESTMENT RATE   The critical issue in resolving conflicts between mutually exclusive projects is this: What is the value of generating the cash flows earlier rather than later? This value depends on the opportunity cost rate at which we can reinvest differential early years' cash flows. *The NPV method implicitly assumes that the opportunity rate at which cash flows can be reinvested is the cost of capital, whereas the IRR method assumes that the firm has the opportunity to reinvest at the IRR.* These assumptions are inherent in the mathematics of the discounting process: The NPV method discounts cash flows at the cost of capital, while the IRR method discounts cash flows at the project's IRR, whatever that rate happens to be. The cash flows may actually be withdrawn as dividends by the stockholders and spent on beer and pizza, but the assumption of a reinvestment opportunity is still implicit in the NPV and IRR calculations.

RESOLUTION OF CONFLICT   Which is the better assumption, reinvestment at the cost of capital or reinvestment at the project's IRR? We can answer the question as follows:

1. Assume that the firm's cost of capital is 10 percent. Management can obtain all the funds it wants at this rate. This condition is expected to hold in the foreseeable future. Further, assume that all potential projects have the same risk as the firm's existing assets.

2. The capital budgeting process calls for all potential projects to be evaluated at k = 10%. All projects with NPV > 0 are accepted. An unlimited supply of capital is available at k = 10% to finance these projects, both now and in the future.

3. As cash flows come in from past investments, what will be done with them? These cash flows can either (a) be paid out to the equity and debt investors who, on average, require a 10 percent rate of return or (b) be used as a

---

[11]Of course, it is possible for mutually exclusive projects to differ with respect to both scale and timing. Also, if mutually exclusive projects have different lives (as opposed to different cash flow patterns over a common life), this introduces further complications, and for meaningful comparisons, some mutually exclusive projects must be evaluated over a common life. This point will be discussed in detail in the next chapter.

substitute for outside capital that costs 10 percent. Thus, since the cash flows are expected to save the firm 10 percent, this is their value to the firm, that is, their opportunity cost rate.

4. The IRR method implicitly assumes reinvestment at the internal rate of return itself. However, given (a) ready access to capital markets and (b) a constant expected future cost of capital, the appropriate reinvestment rate is the opportunity cost of capital, 10 percent. Even if the firm expects to have projects in the future whose IRRs are high, say, 30 percent, this is irrelevant — those projects could have been financed with new external capital costing 10 percent, so cash flows from past projects have an opportunity cost reinvestment rate which is only equal to the cost of capital.

Therefore, we come to the conclusion that *the better reinvestment rate assumption is the cost of capital, which is built into the NPV method.* This, in turn, leads us to prefer the NPV method, at least for firms willing and able to obtain capital at a cost reasonably close to their current cost of capital. In Appendix 11A, when we discuss capital rationing, we will see that under certain conditions the NPV rule may be questionable, but for most firms at most times, NPV is conceptually better than IRR.

We should reiterate that, when projects are independent, the NPV and IRR methods both lead to exactly the same accept/reject decisions. However, *when evaluating mutually exclusive projects, especially those that differ in scale and/or timing, the NPV method should be used.*

MULTIPLE IRRs

There is one other situation in which the IRR approach may not be usable — this is when non-normal cash flows are involved. A project has *normal* cash flows when one or more cash outflows (costs) are followed by a series of cash inflows. If, however, a project calls for a large cash outflow either sometime during or at the end of its life, then it has *non-normal* cash flows. Non-normal cash flows can present unique difficulties for the IRR method, especially the problem of multiple IRRs.

Consider again Equation 9-2, which we solve to find the IRR:

$$\sum_{t=0}^{n} \frac{CF_t}{(1 + IRR)^t} = 0. \qquad \text{9-2}$$

It is possible to obtain more than one value for IRR, which means that multiple IRRs can occur. Notice that Equation 9-2 is a polynomial of degree n, so it has n different roots, or solutions. All except one of the roots are imaginary numbers when cash flows are normal (one or more cash outflows followed by a series of cash inflows), so in the normal case, only one value of IRR appears. However, the possibility of multiple real roots, hence multiple IRRs, arises when the cash flows are non-normal (negative net cash flows occur during some year after the project has begun generating positive cash flows).

To illustrate this problem, suppose a firm is considering the expenditure of $1.6 million to develop a strip mine (Project M). The mine will produce a cash flow of $10 million at the end of Year 1. Then, at the end of Year 2, $10 million must be expended to restore the land to its original condition. Therefore, the project's expected net cash flows are as follows (in millions of dollars):

$$
\begin{array}{ccc}
0 & 1 & 2 \\
\hline
(\$1.6) & \$10 & (\$10)
\end{array}
$$

These values can be substituted into Equation 9-2 to derive the IRR for the investment:

$$
\text{NPV} = \frac{-\$1.6 \text{ million}}{(1 + \text{IRR})^0} + \frac{\$10 \text{ million}}{(1 + \text{IRR})^1} + \frac{-\$10 \text{ million}}{(1 + \text{IRR})^2} = 0.
$$

When solved, we find that NPV = 0 when IRR = 25% and also when IRR = 400%.[12] Therefore, the IRR of the investment is both 25 and 400 percent. This relationship is depicted graphically in Figure 9-5.[13] Note that no dilemma would arise if the NPV method were used; we would simply use Equation 9-1, find the NPV, and use this to evaluate the project. If Project M's cost of capital is 10 percent, then its NPV is −$0.77 million, and the project should be rejected. If k were between 25 and 400 percent, Project M's NPV would be positive.

The authors encountered another example of multiple internal rates of return when a major bank *borrowed* funds from an insurance company and then used those funds (plus an initial investment of its own) to buy a number of jet engines, which it then leased to an airline. The bank expected to receive positive net cash flows (lease payments minus interest on the insurance company loan) for a number of years, then several large negative cash flows as it repaid the insurance company loan, and, finally, a large inflow from the sale of the engines when the lease expired.[14]

The bank discovered two IRRs and wondered which was correct. It could not ignore the IRR and use the NPV method since the lease was already on the books and the bank's senior loan committee, as well as Federal Reserve bank examiners, wanted to know the return on the lease. We were asked to help devise a solution, and we recommended that the bank compound the cash flows — both positive and negative — at an assumed reinvestment rate of 9 percent, its average return on loans, to arrive at a compounded terminal value for the operation. Then the interest rate

---

[12]If you attempted to find the IRR of Project M with most financial calculators, you would get an error message. However, with many calculators you can enter a "guess" for the IRR, and one of the IRRs will be calculated. If the guess is to the left of the peak in Figure 9-5, the lower IRR will be calculated. The upper IRR will be calculated if the guess is to the right of the peak.

[13]We developed Figure 9-5 using a spreadsheet to find NPVs at a number of discount rates and then plotting the figure. Also, does Figure 9-5 suggest that the firm should try to *raise* its cost of capital to about 100 percent to maximize the NPV of the project? Certainly not. The firm should seek to *minimize* its cost of capital; this will cause the price of its stock to be maximized. Actions taken to raise the cost of capital might make this particular project look good, but those actions would be terribly harmful to the firm's more numerous other projects. Only if the firm's cost of capital is high, in spite of efforts to keep it down, will the illustrative project have a positive NPV.

[14]The situation described here is a *leveraged lease*. See Chapter 18 for more on leveraged leases.

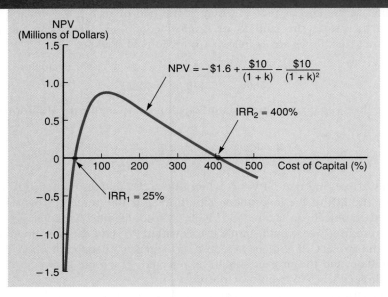

FIGURE 9-5   NPV PROFILE FOR PROJECT M

NPV
(Millions of Dollars)

$$NPV = -\$1.6 + \frac{\$10}{(1 + k)} - \frac{\$10}{(1 + k)^2}$$

$IRR_2 = 400\%$

$IRR_1 = 25\%$

Cost of Capital (%)

that equated this terminal sum to the bank's initial cost was used as the IRR, or the rate of return on the lease. This procedure, which, in essence, is the modified IRR method discussed in the next section, satisfied both the bank's loan committee and its examiners.

The examples just presented illustrate one problem, multiple IRRs, that can arise when the IRR criterion is used with a project that has non-normal cash flows. Use of the IRR method on non-normal cash flow projects could produce other problems such as no IRR or an IRR which leads to an incorrect accept/reject decision. In all such cases, the NPV criterion could be easily applied, and this method would lead to conceptually correct capital budgeting decisions.

**SELF-TEST
QUESTIONS**

Describe how NPV profiles are constructed.

What is a crossover point, and how does it affect the choice when mutually exclusive projects are being considered?

What are the two basic conditions that can lead to conflicts between the NPV and IRR methods?

What is the primary underlying assumption which leads to conflicts between the NPV and IRR methods?

If a conflict exists, should the capital budgeting decision be made on the basis of the NPV or the IRR ranking? Why?

Explain the difference between normal and non-normal cash flows.

What is the "multiple IRR problem," and what condition is necessary for it to occur?

MODIFIED INTERNAL RATE OF RETURN (MIRR)

In spite of a strong academic preference for the NPV method, surveys indicate that business executives prefer IRR over NPV by a margin of 3 to 1. Apparently, many managers find it easier to analyze investments in terms of percentage rates of return than dollars of NPV. Given this fact, can we devise a percentage evaluator that is better than the regular IRR? The answer is yes — we can modify the IRR and make it a better indicator of relative profitability, hence better for use in capital budgeting. The new measure is called the *modified IRR,* or *MIRR,* and it is defined as follows:

$$\text{PV costs} = \text{PV terminal value}$$

$$\sum_{t=0}^{n} \frac{COF_t}{(1+k)^t} = \frac{\sum_{t=0}^{n} CIF_t(1+k)^{n-t}}{(1+MIRR)^n}$$

$$\text{PV costs} = \frac{TV}{(1+MIRR)^n}.$$

9-2a

The equation looks complicated, but it really is not. COF refers to cash outflows, or the cost of the project, and CIF refers to cash inflows. The left term is simply the PV of the investment outlays when discounted at the cost of capital, and the numerator of the right term is the total future value of the inflows, assuming the inflows are reinvested at the cost of capital. The future value of the inflows is also called the *terminal value,* or *TV.* The discount rate that forces the PV of the TV to equal the PV of the costs is defined as the MIRR.[15]

If the investment costs are all incurred at t = 0, and if the first operating inflow occurs at t = 1, as for our illustrative Projects S and L, then this equation may be used:

$$\text{Cost} = \frac{TV}{(1+MIRR)^n} = \frac{\sum_{t=1}^{n} CIF_t(1+k)^{n-t}}{(1+MIRR)^n}.$$

9-2b

---

[15]There are several alternative definitions for the MIRR. The one we present here is effective and relatively simple to use. For a complete discussion, see William R. McDaniel, Daniel E. McCarty, and Kenneth A. Jessell, "Discounted Cash Flow with Explicit Reinvestment Rates: Tutorial and Extension," *The Financial Review,* August 1988, 369–385.

We can illustrate the calculation with Project S:

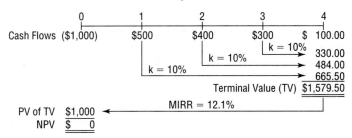

First, find the FV of each cash inflow when compounded at k = 10%, and sum these FVs to find the TV of the inflows. Then, using a financial calculator, enter PV = 1000, FV = 1579.5 (or −1579.5), and n = 4, and press the i button to find $MIRR_S$ = 12.1%. Similarly, we find $MIRR_L$ = 11.3%.

The modified IRR has a significant advantage over the regular IRR. MIRR assumes that cash flows from all projects are reinvested at the cost of capital, while the regular IRR assumes that the cash flows from each project are reinvested at the project's own IRR. Since reinvestment at k is generally a better assumption, the modified IRR is a better indicator of a project's true profitability. MIRR also solves the multiple IRR problem. To illustrate, with k = 10%, Project M (the strip mine project) has MIRR = 5.6%, hence it should be rejected. This is consistent with the decision based on the NPV method, because NPV = −$0.77 million.

Is MIRR as good as NPV for selecting among competing (mutually exclusive) projects? If the two projects are of equal size and have the same life, then NPV and MIRR will always lead to the same project selection decision. Thus, for any projects like our Projects S and L, if $NPV_S > NPV_L$, then $MIRR_S > MIRR_L$, and the kinds of conflicts we encountered between NPV and the regular IRR will not occur. Also, if the projects are of equal size, but differ in lives, the MIRR will always lead to the same decision as the NPV if the MIRRs are both calculated on the basis of the longer project's life. (Just fill in zeros for the shorter project's missing cash flows.) *However, if the projects differ in scale (size), then conflicts can still occur — if we were comparing a large project with a small mutually exclusive one, then we might find $NPV_L > NPV_S$, but $MIRR_S > MIRR_L$.*

Our conclusion is that the modified IRR is superior to the regular IRR as an indicator of a project's "true" rate of return, or "expected long-term rate of return," but the NPV method is still better for choosing among competing projects because it always provides a good indicator of how much each project contributes to the value of the firm.[16]

---

[16]Occasionally, a project will require cash outlays sometime during its life, and when this occurs, the question of how to treat the outlays arises. To illustrate, suppose our Project S involved a process which would require a new pump at a cost of $600 at the end of Year 2. However, operating inflows during that year are expected to be $1,000, so the net cash flow expected for Year 2 is $1,000 − $600 = $400. Now the question arises: Should we calculate the MIRR using the $400 net cash inflow, or should we separate the two flows, compounding the $1,000 operating inflow and discounting the $600 outflow? The generally accepted view is that if the $600 Year 2 outflow will definitely have to be made, even if the project is abandoned after Year 2 but before the end of its expected life, then it should be regarded as a cost. Thus, it would be discounted back to Time 0 and added to the PV of costs, while the $1,000 operating inflow should be compounded and

Briefly describe how the modified IRR (MIRR) is calculated.
What is the primary difference between the MIRR and the regular IRR?
What advantages does the MIRR have over the regular IRR in capital budgeting?
What condition can cause the MIRR and NPV methods to lead to different decisions?

COMPARISON OF THE NPV AND PI METHODS

The PI method measures the present value of benefits per dollar of investment, whereas the NPV measures the total dollars of net present value. These two methods can lead to conflicts when used to evaluate mutually exclusive projects. To illustrate, suppose a firm is comparing Project L (for large), which requires a $5 million investment and returns $6 million after one year, with Project S (for small), which requires an outlay of $100,000 and returns $130,000 at the end of one year. Both projects have average risk and hence will be evaluated at the firm's 10 percent cost of capital. Here are the projects' NPVs and PIs:

$$NPV_L = -\$5,000,000 + \frac{\$6,000,000}{(1.10)^1} = \$454,545.$$

$$NPV_S = -\$100,000 + \frac{\$130,000}{(1.10)^1} = \$18,182.$$

$$PI_L = \frac{\dfrac{\$6,000,000}{(1.10)^1}}{\$5,000,000} = 1.09.$$

$$PI_S = \frac{\dfrac{\$130,000}{(1.10)^1}}{\$100,000} = 1.18.$$

Thus, the NPV method indicates that we should accept Project L because $NPV_L > NPV_S$, but the PI method indicates that Project S is preferable, because $PI_S > PI_L$.

Given this conflict, which project should be accepted? Remembering that shareholders' wealth increases by the NPV of a project, it is clear that Project L contributes more to shareholder wealth, so L should be selected over S. Thus, for a firm

---

included in the TV. If these changes were made in the preceding time line for Project S, its MIRR would fall from 12.1 to 11.4 percent, demonstrating that net-versus-gross treatment does make a difference. If the $600 expenditure were discretionary, then it would be treated as an operating cost, and the $400 net value would be used. Finally, note that the net-versus-gross treatment will never change the accept/reject decision.

Also, note that some financial calculators, for example the HP-17B, make it relatively easy to calculate MIRR. With the 17B, you enter two cash flow streams: (1) an outflow stream with zeroes in place of inflows and (2) an inflow stream with zeroes for costs. Then, the 17B calculates the terminal value of the inflow stream and the present value of the outflow stream. The final step is merely finding the MIRR.

With a 10B, you can use the cash flow register to find the PV of the inflows, discounting at 10 percent, and then find the FV of that PV, compounded at 10 percent, to get the TV. Then, find the MIRR as before.

that seeks to maximize stockholders' wealth, the NPV method is better. Of course, if the projects were independent, both would be chosen, since both projects have positive NPVs and hence PIs greater than 1.0.

In general, the NPV method leads to better decisions than the PI method. However, the PI may be useful when capital rationing exists. We explore this topic in Appendix 11A.

SELF-TEST
QUESTIONS

What condition can lead to conflicts between the NPV and PI methods?

If a conflict exists, should the NPV or the PI method be used to make the decision?

PRESENT VALUE OF FUTURE COSTS

Firms often choose between mutually exclusive projects on the basis of the present value of future costs rather than on the basis of the projects' NPVs. For example, Moët & Chandon, a French champagne producer, recently evaluated several different methods for disposing of grape pulp at its California winery. The disposal system chosen would have no effect on either the prices or the quantity of sparkling wine produced by the plant — these would be set in the competitive marketplace. Therefore, the revenue stream would be the same regardless of which disposal process is used, so revenues are irrelevant to this capital budgeting decision.

Since the revenue stream will be the same, Moët & Chandon could make the decision on the basis of expected future costs alone, choosing the process that does the job for the lowest cost. Table 9-1 contains the expected net costs for the best two processes over their 5-year expected lives. Process A requires a lower expenditure on capital equipment than B, but A is more labor intensive. Therefore, A's Year 0 cost is relatively low, but its operating costs are relatively high.

The company's analysts judged the processes to both have the same risk as the company's average project, and thus they used the firm's overall cost of capital, 12 percent, to discount the flows of each project. As shown in Table 9-1, Process A has a lower present value of future costs, so it was chosen. We will have more to say

---

TABLE 9-1   PRODUCTION COSTS FOR PROCESSES A AND B

	EXPECTED NET COST	
YEAR	PROCESS A	PROCESS B
0	($50,000)	($100,000)
1	(22,000)	(10,000)
2	(22,000)	(10,000)
3	(22,000)	(10,000)
4	(22,000)	(10,000)
5	(22,000)	(10,000)
PV at 12%:	($129,305)	($136,048)

about discounting costs (or outflows) in Chapter 11, where we discuss risk adjustments.

Explain the procedure for evaluating two mutually exclusive projects on the basis of costs alone.

What condition is necessary to use the cost analysis approach? (Hint: Think about revenues, but explain.)

OUR VIEW OF CAPITAL BUDGETING ANALYSIS

We have presented a number of capital budgeting decision methods, and each has its own set of advantages and disadvantages. We purposely compared the methods against one another to highlight their relative strengths and weaknesses. However, in the process we may have created the impression that "sophisticated" firms would use only one method in the decision process, NPV. Today, virtually all capital budgeting decisions of importance are analyzed by computer, so it is easy to calculate and print out all the alternative decision measures. In making the accept/reject decision, most large, sophisticated firms calculate and consider all the measures, because each provides decision makers with a somewhat different piece of relevant information.

Payback and discounted payback provide an indication of both the risk and the liquidity of a project—a long payback means that the investment dollars will be locked up for many years, hence the project is relatively illiquid, and since the project's cash flows must be forecast far out into the future, the project is probably quite risky. A good analogy for this is the bond valuation process. You would never compare the yields to maturity on two bonds without considering their terms to maturity (or durations), because a bond's riskiness is significantly influenced by its maturity.

NPV is important because it gives a direct measure of the dollar benefit (on a present value basis) of the project to the firm's shareholders. Therefore, we regard NPV as the best single measure of *profitability*. IRR also measures profitability, but expressed as a percentage rate of return, which many decision makers, especially nonfinancial managers, seem to prefer. Further, IRR contains information concerning a project's "safety margin" which is not inherent in NPV. To illustrate, consider the following two projects: Project S (for small) costs $10,000 at t = 0 and returns $16,500 at the end of one year, and Project L (for large) costs $100,000 and has a payoff of $115,500 after one year. At a 10 percent cost of capital, both projects have an NPV of $5,000, and, if they were mutually exclusive, the NPV method indicates that we should be indifferent between the two. However, Project S actually provides a much larger margin for error. The realized cash inflow could be almost 40 percent below the $16,500 forecast, and the firm would still recover its $10,000 investment. On the other hand, if the actual inflow from Project L fell by only 14 percent from the forecasted $115,500, the firm would fall short of recovering its investment. Moreover, if no revenues were generated at all, the firm would lose only $10,000 on Project S but $100,000 on Project L. The NPV contains no information about either the "safety margin" inherent in a project's cash flow forecasts or the amount of capital at risk. However, the IRR does provide "safety margin" information — Project S's IRR is a whopping 65.0 percent, while Project L's IRR is only 15.5 percent, so even if its realized return fell substantially, Project S would still be a money-maker.

The profitability index also provides a measure of a project's "safety margin," because it measures the profitability per dollar of investment, or the "bang for the buck." Project S's PI is 1.50 while Project L's PI is 1.05. Thus the PI, like the IRR, indicates that Project S has a greater tolerance for cash flow uncertainty than Project L.[17] Finally, the modified IRR has all the virtues of the IRR, but since it incorporates the correct reinvestment rate assumption, it provides a better estimate of projects' "true" profitability. Also, the MIRR avoids the problems that the IRR can have when applied to non-normal projects.

In summary, the different evaluation methods provide different types of information to decision makers, and since it is so easy to calculate each measure, all should be considered in the decision process. Generally, the most weight should be given to the NPV, but it would be foolish to ignore the information inherent in any of the methods.

SELF-TEST QUESTIONS | Describe the advantages and disadvantages of the six capital budgeting methods described in this chapter.
Should capital budgeting decisions be made solely on the basis of a project's NPV?

THE POST-AUDIT

An important aspect of the capital budgeting process is the *post-audit,* which involves (1) comparing actual results with those predicted by the project's sponsors and (2) explaining why any differences occurred. For example, many firms require that the operating divisions send a monthly report for the first six months after a project goes into operation, and a quarterly report thereafter, until the project's results are up to expectations. From then on, reports on the project are reviewed on a regular basis like those of other operations.

The post-audit has several purposes, including the following:

1. **Improve forecasts.** When decision makers are forced to compare their projections to actual outcomes, there is a tendency for estimates to improve. Conscious or unconscious biases are observed and eliminated; new forecasting methods are sought as the need for them becomes apparent; and people simply tend to do everything better, including forecasting, if they know that their actions are being monitored.

2. **Improve operations.** Businesses are run by people, and people can perform at higher or lower levels of efficiency. When a divisional team has made a forecast about an investment, its members are, in a sense, putting their reputations

---

[17]For an interesting article which supports the use of the profitability index in capital budgeting decision making, see Edward M. Miller, "The Competitive Market Assumption and Capital Budgeting Criteria," *Financial Management,* Winter 1987, 22–28.

on the line. If costs are above predicted levels, sales below expectations, and so on, executives in production, sales, and other areas will strive to improve operations and to bring results into line with forecasts. In a discussion related to this point, an IBM executive made this statement: "You academicians only worry about making good decisions. In business, we also worry about making decisions good."

3. **Identify abandonment/termination opportunities.** Although the decision to undertake a project may be the correct one based on information at hand, things do not always turn out as expected. If initial operating results indicate that a project is not likely to achieve its expected profitability, it may be best for the firm to abandon rather than continue the project. Furthermore, most projects, at some point in their lives, lose their economic viability and should be terminated. Both the post-audit and a continuing review of ongoing operations help identify the optimal point for abandonment or termination of a project.

The post-audit is not a simple process, and a number of factors can cause complications. First, we must recognize that each element of the cash flow forecast is subject to uncertainty, so a percentage of all projects undertaken by any reasonably venturesome firm will necessarily go awry. This fact must be considered when appraising the performances of the operating executives who submit capital expenditure requests. Second, projects sometimes fail to meet expectations for reasons beyond the control of the operating executives and for reasons that no one could realistically be expected to anticipate. For example, the decline in oil prices in the mid-1980s adversely affected many energy-related projects, as well as real estate projects in Texas and other oil-producing areas. Third, it is often difficult to separate the operating results of one investment from those of a larger system. Although some projects stand alone and permit ready identification of costs and revenues, the actual cost savings that result from a new computer system, for example, may be very hard to measure. Fourth, it is often hard to hand out blame or praise, because the executives who were actually responsible for a given decision may have moved on by the time the results of a long-term investment are known.

Because of these difficulties, some firms tend to play down the importance of the post-audit. However, observations of both businesses and governmental units suggest that the best-run and most successful organizations are the ones that put the greatest emphasis on post-audits. Accordingly, we regard the post-audit as one of the most important elements in a good capital budgeting system.

What is done in the post-audit?
Identify several purposes of the post-audit.
What factors can cause complications in the post-audit?

SELF-TEST QUESTIONS

SUMMARY

This chapter discussed the capital budgeting process, and the key concepts covered are listed below:

■ *Capital budgeting* is the process of analyzing potential capital expenditures and deciding which investments the firm should undertake.

■ The capital budgeting process requires that the firm (1) determine the *cost of the project,* (2) estimate the *expected cash inflows* from the project and the riskiness of those cash flows, (3) determine the appropriate *cost of capital* at which to discount the cash flows, and (4) determine the sum of the *present values* of the expected cash flows.

■ The *payback period* is defined as the expected number of years required to recover the original investment. The payback method ignores cash flows beyond the payback period, and it does not consider the time value of money. The payback does, however, provide an indication of a project's risk and liquidity, because it shows how long the original capital will be "at risk."

■ The *discounted payback* is similar to the regular payback except that it discounts cash flows at the project's cost of capital. Like the regular payback, it ignores cash flows beyond the discounted payback period.

■ The *net present value (NPV)* is found by discounting all cash flows (positive and negative) at the project's cost of capital and then summing those cash flows. The project is accepted if the NPV is positive.

■ The *profitability index (PI)* is the ratio of the present value of cash inflows to the present value of cash outflows. The PI shows the profitability of a project per dollar of investment, or its "bang per buck."

■ The *internal rate of return (IRR)* is the discount rate which forces the present value of a project's future cash inflows to equal the present value of its costs. The project is accepted if the IRR is greater than the project's cost of capital.

■ The NPV, PI, and IRR methods make the same accept/reject decisions for *independent projects,* but if projects are *mutually exclusive,* then ranking conflicts can arise. If conflicts arise, the NPV method should generally be given the most weight. The NPV, PI, and IRR methods are all superior to the payback, but NPV is the single best measure of a project's profitability because it shows how much the project adds to shareholder wealth. In a sense, NPV measures the economic value added (EVA) of a project.

■ The NPV method assumes that cash flows will be reinvested at the firm's cost of capital, while the IRR method assumes reinvestment at the project's IRR. Because *reinvestment at the cost of capital is the better assumption,* NPV is superior to IRR.

- The *modified IRR (MIRR) method* corrects some of the problems with the regular IRR. MIRR involves finding the terminal value (TV) of the cash inflows compounded at the firm's cost of capital and then determining the rate (MIRR) which forces the present value of the TV to equal the present value of the outflows. Still, conflicts can arise between MIRR and NPV if projects differ in size, and where conflicts arise, the decision should generally be based on the NPV.

- Firms often choose among mutually exclusive projects on the basis of the *present value of future costs.*

- Sophisticated managers consider all of the project evaluation measures because the different measures provide different elements of information. In particular, if the NPV of Project A is only slightly higher than that of Project B, but B's IRR and/or PI is significantly higher than A's, then B should probably be chosen because of risk considerations.

Although this chapter has presented the basic elements of the capital budgeting process, there are many other aspects of this crucial topic. Some of the more important ones are discussed in the following two chapters.

QUESTIONS

9-1 Define each of the following terms:
   a. Capital budget
   b. Regular payback; discounted payback
   c. Mutually exclusive projects; independent projects
   d. DCF techniques; net present value (NPV)
   e. Internal rate of return (IRR)
   f. Modified internal rate of return (MIRR)
   g. Profitability index (PI)
   h. NPV profile; crossover rate
   i. Non-normal cash flows; multiple IRRs
   j. Project cost of capital, or discount rate
   k. Reinvestment rate assumption
   l. Post-audit

9-2 How is a project classification scheme (for example, replacement or expansion into new markets) used in the capital budgeting process?

9-3 Explain why the NPV of a relatively long-term project, defined as one where a high percentage of its cash flows is expected in the distant future, is more sensitive to changes in the cost of capital than is the NPV of a short-term project.

9-4 Explain why, if two mutually exclusive projects are being compared, the short-term project might have the higher ranking under the NPV criterion if the cost of capital is high, but the long-term project might be deemed better if the cost of capital is low. Would changes in the cost of capital ever cause a change in the IRR ranking of two such projects?

9-5   For independent projects, is it true that if PI > 1.0, then NPV > 0 and IRR > k? Prove it.

9-6   In what sense is a reinvestment rate assumption embodied in the NPV, IRR, and MIRR methods? What is the implicitly assumed reinvestment rate of each method?

SELF-TEST PROBLEM

(SOLUTION APPEARS IN APPENDIX C)

ST-1   PROJECT ANALYSIS You are a financial analyst for the Hittle Company. The director of capital budgeting has asked you to analyze two proposed capital investments, Projects X and Y. Each project has a cost of $10,000, and the cost of capital for both projects is 12 percent. The projects' expected net cash flows are as follows:

	EXPECTED NET CASH FLOW	
YEAR	PROJECT X	PROJECT Y
0	($10,000)	($10,000)
1	6,500	3,500
2	3,000	3,500
3	3,000	3,500
4	1,000	3,500

a. Calculate each project's payback, net present value (NPV), internal rate of return (IRR), modified internal rate of return (MIRR), and profitability index (PI).
b. Which project, or projects, should be accepted if they are independent?
c. Which project should be accepted if they are mutually exclusive?
d. How might a change in the cost of capital produce a conflict between the NPV and IRR rankings of these two projects? At what values of k would this conflict exist? Plot the NPV profiles.
e. Why does the conflict exist?

PROBLEMS

9-1   CAPITAL BUDGETING METHODS Project S has a cost of $10,000 and is expected to produce benefits (cash flows) of $3,000 per year for five years. Project L costs $25,000 and is expected to produce cash flows of $7,400 per year for five years. Calculate the two projects' NPVs, IRRs, MIRRs, and PIs, assuming a cost of capital of 12 percent. Which project would be selected, assuming they are mutually exclusive, using each ranking method? Which should actually be selected?

9-2   TIMING DIFFERENCES The Ewert Exploration Company is considering two mutually exclusive plans for extracting oil on property for which it has mineral rights. Both plans call for the expenditure of $10,000,000 to drill development wells. Under Plan A, all the oil will be extracted in one year, producing a cash flow at t = 1 of $12,000,000, while under Plan B, cash flows will be $1,750,000 per year for 20 years.

a. What are the annual incremental cash flows that will be available to Ewert Exploration if it undertakes Plan B rather than Plan A? (Hint: Subtract Plan A's flows from B's.)

b. If the firm accepts Plan A, then invests the extra cash generated at the end of Year 1, what rate of return (reinvestment rate) would cause the cash flows from reinvestment to equal the cash flows from Plan B?

c. Suppose a company has a cost of capital of 10 percent. Is it logical to assume that it would take on all available independent projects (of average risk) with returns greater than 10 percent? Further, if all available projects with returns greater than 10 percent have been taken, would this mean that cash flows from past investments would have an opportunity cost of only 10 percent, because all the firm could do with these cash flows would be to replace money that has a cost of 10 percent? Finally, does this imply that the cost of capital is the correct rate to assume for the reinvestment of a project's cash flows?

d. Construct NPV profiles for Plans A and B, identify each project's IRR, and indicate the crossover rate of return.

-3 **SCALE DIFFERENCES** The Pinkerton Publishing Company is considering two mutually exclusive expansion plans. Plan A calls for the expenditure of $50 million on a large-scale, integrated plant which will provide an expected cash flow stream of $8 million per year for 20 years. Plan B calls for the expenditure of $15 million to build a somewhat less efficient, more labor-intensive plant which has an expected cash flow stream of $3.4 million per year for 20 years. The firm's cost of capital is 10 percent.

a. Calculate each project's NPV and IRR.

b. Set up a Project Δ by showing the cash flows that will exist if the firm goes with the large plant rather than the smaller plant. What are the NPV and the IRR for this Project Δ?

c. Graph the NPV profiles for Plan A, Plan B, and Project Δ.

d. Give a logical explanation, based on reinvestment rates and opportunity costs, as to why the NPV method is better than the IRR method when the firm's cost of capital is constant at some value such as 10 percent.

-4 **MULTIPLE RATES OF RETURN** The Ulmer Uranium Company is deciding whether or not it should open a strip mine, the net cost of which is $4.4 million. Net cash inflows are expected to be $27.7 million, all coming at the end of Year 1. The land must be returned to its natural state at a cost of $25 million, payable at the end of Year 2.

a. Plot the project's NPV profile.

b. Should the project be accepted if k = 8%? If k = 14%? Explain your reasoning.

c. Can you think of some other capital budgeting situations where negative cash flows during or at the end of the project's life might lead to multiple IRRs?

d. What is the project's MIRR at k = 8%? At k = 14%? Does the MIRR method lead to the same accept/reject decision as the NPV method?

-5 **MULTIPLE RATES OF RETURN** The Durst Development Company (DDC) has many excellent investment opportunities, but it has insufficient cash to undertake them all. Now DDC is offered the chance to borrow $2 million from the Rancho Palisades Retirement Fund at 10 percent, the loan to be repaid at the end of one year. Also, a "consulting fee" of $700,000 will be paid to Rancho Palisades' mayor at the end of one year for helping to arrange the credit. Of the $2 million received, $1 million will be used immediately to buy an old city-owned hotel and to convert it into a gambling casino. The other $1 million will be invested in other lucrative DDC projects that otherwise would have to be foregone because of a lack of capital. For two years, all cash generated by the casino will be plowed back into the casino project. At the end of the two years, the casino will be sold for $2 million.

Assuming that (1) the deal has been worked out in the sunshine and is completely legal and (2) cash from other DDC Company operations will be available to make the required payments at the end of Year 1, under what rate of return conditions should DDC accept the offer? Disregard taxes.

9-6 PRESENT VALUE OF COSTS The Aubey Coffee Company is evaluating the within-plant distribution system for its new roasting, grinding, and packing plant. The two alternatives are (1) a conveyor system with a high initial cost, but low annual operating costs, and (2) several fork-lift trucks, which cost less, but have considerably higher operating costs. The decision to construct the plant has already been made, and the choice here will have no effect on the over-all revenues of the project. The cost of capital for the plant is 8 percent, and the projects' expected net costs are listed in the table:

	EXPECTED NET COST	
YEAR	CONVEYOR	FORKLIFT
0	($500,000)	($200,000)
1	(120,000)	(160,000)
2	(120,000)	(160,000)
3	(120,000)	(160,000)
4	(120,000)	(160,000)
5	(20,000)	(160,000)

a. What is the IRR of each alternative?
b. What is the present value of costs of each alternative? Which method should be chosen?

SPREADSHEET APPLICATIONS

SPREADSHEET PROBLEM

Midwest Manufacturing Company is considering two mutually exclusive investments. The projects' expected net cash flows are as follows:

	EXPECTED NET CASH FLOW	
YEAR	PROJECT A	PROJECT B
0	($300)	($405)
1	(387)	134
2	(193)	134
3	(100)	134
4	600	134
5	600	134
6	850	134
7	(180)	0

a. Construct NPV profiles for Projects A and B.

b. What is each project's IRR?

c. If you were told that each project's cost of capital is 10 percent, which project should be selected? If the cost of capital were 17 percent, what would the proper choice be?

d. What is each project's MIRR at a cost of capital of 10 percent? At k = 17%?

e. What is the crossover rate, and what is its significance?

f. The firm's management is confident of the projects' cash flows in Years 0 to 6 but is uncertain as to what the Year 7 cash flows will be for the two projects. Under a worst-case scenario, Project A's Year 7 cash flow will be −$300 and B's will be −$150, while under a best-case scenario, the cash flows will be −$70 and +$120 for Projects A and B, respectively. Answer Parts b through d using these new cash flows. Which project should be selected under each scenario?

g. Put the Year 7 cash flows back to −$180 for A and zero for B. Now change the cost of capital and observe what happens to NPV at k = 0%, 5%, 20%, and 400% (input as 4.0).

SPREADSHEET EXERCISE: DATA TABLE 1

This exercise uses a spreadsheet model to evaluate two capital investments, Projects S and L. The model is finished except for one data table, which you will complete.

1. Retrieve the model (Filename SE-09.WK1) from the models diskette. The model calculates Payback, NPV, IRR, Profitability Index, and Modified IRR for the two projects.

2. Beginning on Row 21, the model is set up to contain two data tables, one for each project, that are used to construct the NPV profiles. The NPV profile graph is already set up. View the graph now, and you will see that it contains the NPV profile for Project L but not for Project S.

3. To complete the graph, it is necessary to construct the data table for Project S. The first step is to put the output cell designation in Cell D25. In this case, you want the data table to compute and record the NPV for Project S, so +C15 should be entered. Next, the input variable of interest must be entered into Cells C26.C32. Here, we are interested in finding the relationship between NPV and discount rate, so discount rates are entered into the range, starting with 0% and increasing in 5 percentage point intervals. (Hint: The values can be copied from Cells A26.A32.)

4. Now use the Data Table 1 command to fill in the data table that you just created. If everything was set up and run properly, NPV values will fill Cells D26.D32, with the highest value being $60.0 and the lowest being −$11.2.

5. View the graph again, and note that both NPV profiles can now be seen.

6. The "1" in the Data Table 1 command indicates that the data table has one input value, but it may have one or more output values. To see how the Data Table 1 command works with multiple output values, erase the values in Cells C26.C32, and then move Cells D25.D32 left one column, into Column C. Now repeat the Data Table 1 command, but be sure to include the entire range A25.C32 in the data table range. One data table now produces the NPV profiles for both projects.

7. Note that the graph that you created does not change as the model's input data are changed. This is because the graph is tied to the data in the data tables, and these data do not automatically change with input data changes. The advantage to having a single data table is that the F8 function key automatically recalculates the last data table created. Thus, a single keystroke will recalculate the data table when model inputs are changed, and hence the graph can be easily updated. In later exercises, we will show how macros can be used to easily recalculate such tables.

MINI CASE

Your boss, the chief financial officer (CFO) for the Palmer Company, has just handed you the estimated cash flows for two proposed projects. Project L involves adding a new item to the firm's frozen foods line; it would take some time to build up the market for this product, so the cash inflows would increase over time. Project S involves an add-on to an existing line, and its cash flows would decrease over time. Both projects have 3-year lives because Palmer is planning to introduce an entirely new frozen foods line at that time.

Here are the net cash flow estimates (in thousands of dollars):

	EXPECTED NET CASH FLOW	
YEAR	PROJECT L	PROJECT S
0	($100)	($100)
1	10	70
2	60	50
3	80	20

Depreciation, salvage values, net working capital requirements, and tax effects are all included in these flows.

The CFO also made subjective risk assessments of each project, and he concluded that the projects both have risk characteristics which are similar to the firm's average project. Palmer's overall cost of capital is 10 percent. You must now determine whether one or both of the projects should be accepted.

a. What is capital budgeting? Are there any similarities between a firm's capital budgeting decisions and an individual's investment decisions?

b. What is the difference between independent and mutually exclusive projects? Between normal and non-normal cash flows?

c. (1) What is the payback period? Find the paybacks for Projects L and S.
   (2) What is the rationale for the payback? According to the payback criterion, which project or projects should be accepted if the firm's maximum acceptable payback is two years, and Projects L and S were independent? Mutually exclusive?
   (3) What is the difference between the regular payback and the discounted payback?
   (4) What is the main disadvantage of discounted payback? Is the payback method of any real usefulness in capital budgeting decisions?

d. (1) Define the net present value (NPV). What is each project's NPV?
   (2) What is the rationale behind the NPV method? According to NPV, which project or projects should be accepted if they are independent? Mutually exclusive?
   (3) Would the NPVs change if the cost of capital changed?

e. (1) Define the internal rate of return (IRR). What is each project's IRR?
   (2) How is the IRR on a project related to the YTM on a bond?
   (3) What is the logic behind the IRR method? According to IRR, which projects should be accepted if they are independent? Mutually exclusive?
   (4) Would the projects' IRRs change if the cost of capital changed?

f. (1) Define the profitability index (PI). What is each project's PI?

(2) What is the rationale behind the PI method? According to the PI, which project or projects should be accepted if they are independent? Mutually exclusive?

g. (1) Draw the NPV profiles for Projects L and S. At what discount rate do the profiles cross?

(2) Look at the NPV profile graph without referring to the actual NPVs and IRRs. Which project or projects should be accepted if they are independent? Mutually exclusive? Explain. Do your answers here apply for all discount rates less than 23.6 percent?

h. (1) What is the underlying cause of ranking conflicts between NPV and IRR?

(2) Under what conditions can conflicts occur?

(3) Which method is best? Why?

i. (1) Define the modified IRR (MIRR). Find the MIRR for Projects L and S.

(2) What are the MIRR's advantages and disadvantages vis-à-vis the regular IRR? What are the MIRR's advantages and disadvantages vis-à-vis the NPV?

j. As a separate project (Project P), the firm is considering sponsoring a pavilion at the upcoming World's Fair. The pavilion would cost $800,000, and it is expected to result in $5 million of incremental cash inflows during its one year of operation. However, it would then take another year, and $5 million of costs, to demolish the site and return it to its original condition. Thus, Project P's expected net cash flows look like this (in millions of dollars):

YEAR	CASH FLOW
0	($0.8)
1	5
2	(5)

The project is estimated to be of average risk, so its cost of capital is 10 percent.

(1) What is Project P's NPV? What is its IRR? Its MIRR?

(2) Draw Project P's NPV profile. Does Project P have normal or nonnormal cash flows? Should this project be accepted?

SELECTED ADDITIONAL REFERENCES AND CASES

For an in-depth treatment of capital budgeting techniques, see

Bierman, Harold, Jr., and Seymour Smidt, *The Capital Budgeting Decision* (New York: Macmillan, 1993).

Grant, Eugene L., William G. Ireson, and Richard S. Leavenworth, *Principles of Engineering Economy* (New York: John Wiley & Sons, 1990).

Levy, Haim, and Marshall Sarnat, *Capital Investment and Financial Decisions* (Englewood Cliffs, N.J.: Prentice-Hall, 1994).

Seitz, Neil E., and Mitch Ellison, *Capital Budgeting and Long-Term Financing Decisions* (Fort Worth, Tex.: Dryden Press, 1995).

For a discussion of strategic considerations in capital budgeting, see

Crum, Roy L., and Frans G. J. Derkinderen, eds., *Readings in Strategies for Corporate Invest-ments* (New York: Pitman, 1981).

The following articles present interesting comparisons of four different approaches to find-ing NPV:

Brick, Ivan E., and Daniel G. Weaver, "A Comparison of Capital Budgeting Techniques in Iden-tifying Profitable Investments," *Financial Management,* Winter 1984, 29–39.

Greenfield, Robert L., Maury R. Randall, and John C. Woods, "Financial Leverage and Use of the Net Present Value Investment Criterion," *Financial Management,* Autumn 1983, 40–44.

Five articles related directly to the topics in Chapter 9 are

Bacon, Peter W., "The Evaluation of Mutually Exclusive Investments," *Financial Management,* Summer 1977, 55–58.

Chaney, Paul K., "Moral Hazard and Capital Budgeting," *Journal of Financial Research,* Sum-mer 1989, 113–128.

Lewellen, Wilbur G., Howard P. Lanser, and John J. McConnell, "Payback Substitutes for Dis-counted Cash Flow," *Financial Management,* Summer 1973, 17–23.

Miller, Edward M., "Safety Margins and Capital Budgeting Criteria," *Managerial Finance,* Num-ber 2/3, 1988, 1–8.

Woods, John C., and Maury R. Randall, "The Net Present Value of Future Investment Opportu-nities: Its Impact on Shareholder Wealth and Implications for Capital Budgeting Theory," *Financial Management,* Summer 1989, 85–92.

For five recent articles which discuss the capital budgeting methods actually used in prac-tice, see

Kim, Suk H., Trevor Krick, and Seung H. Kim, "Do Executives Practice What Academics Preach?" *Management Accounting,* November 1986, 49–52.

Mukherjee, Tarun K., "Capital Budgeting Surveys: The Past and the Future," *Review of Business and Economic Research,* Spring, 1987, 37–56.

———, "The Capital Budgeting Process of Large U.S. Firms: An Analysis of Capital Budgeting Manuals," *Managerial Finance,* Number 2/3, 1988, 28–35.

Ross, Marc, "Capital Budgeting Practices of Twelve Large Manufacturers," *Financial Manage-ment,* Winter 1986, 15–22.

Weaver, Samuel C., Donald Peters, Roger Cason, and Joe Daleiden, "Capital Budgeting," *Finan-cial Management,* Spring 1989, 10–17.

Additional capital budgeting references are provided in Chapters 10 and 11.

For a case which focuses on capital budgeting decision methods, see

Case 11, "Chicago Valve Company," in the *Cases in Financial Management: Dryden Request* series.

CHAPTER 10

PROJECT CASH FLOW ANALYSIS

ordPerfect Corporation, developer of the widely used word pro-cessing program, recently held an interesting contest — it offered a $25,000 prize to the person who could come the closest to estimating the number of copies of WordPerfect for Windows *shipped during the month following its introduction. Here is an extract from WordPerfect's advertisement:*

> *While we're confident* WordPerfect for Windows *will live up to our standards as the industry leader, we are much less confident about our sales projections. Our vice-president of marketing, Clive Winn, is having trouble predicting how many copies we should produce to meet our first month's orders.*
>
> *Here are some questions he must consider:*
>
> 1. *Of the more than 150,000 people who purchase a copy of* WordPerfect for DOS *each month, how many will prefer a Windows product?*
> 2. *Of the more than 6 million* WordPerfect for DOS *users worldwide, how many will take advantage of our $125 trade-up to* WordPerfect for Windows *during the first month?*
> 3. *Of the 40,000 people who purchase a new personal computer with Windows software included, how many will prefer* WordPerfect for Windows *over competing word pro-cessing programs?*
> 4. *Of the 2 million or so Windows owners who have not purchased a word processor, how many are waiting for WordPerfect to be released?*
>
> *The more we look at all the variables, the more we realize we need your help. So, we're going to do what we do best — listen to what you, our current and potential customers, have to say. Give us your best guess and we'll make it worth your while. Get out your*

calculator, some paper and pencils, and possibly your algebra book, and call us with your estimate.

Although the contest was clearly designed more to sell WordPerfect than to gather information, it does illustrate that sales forecasting can be quite difficult. Further, sales are but one component—albeit the most important one—in a project cash flow analysis. Also, WordPerfect's contest focused on the first month, but in its internal planning, WordPerfect had to worry about a much longer time frame. In addition, the firm must consider "cannibalization," or the impact of the Windows product on sales of its other products. For example, some WordPerfect for Windows *sales will undoubtedly be to customers who would otherwise have bought* WordPerfect for DOS. *On the other hand, sales of* WordPerfect for Windows *may stimulate sales of some of WordPerfect's other products.*

As you study this chapter, think about the difficulties involved in forecasting each of the cash flow elements associated with new projects—unit sales, sales price, operating costs, and capital requirements. For many types of projects the forecasting task is daunting, yet good cash flow forecasts are essential for good capital budgeting decisions. The principles and concepts discussed in this chapter will not guarantee that you won't make forecasting errors, but they can help you avoid many of the pitfalls that lead to avoidable errors.

The basic methods used to evaluate capital budgeting decisions were covered in Chapter 9. However, we assumed that the cash flows were known, so we ignored the most difficult step in capital budgeting—estimating projects' cash flows. Now we examine some key issues related to cash flow analysis, including (1) cash flow estimation, (2) replacement decisions, (3) cash flow estimation bias, (4) option values, (5) mutually exclusive projects with unequal lives, (6) abandonment value, and (7) the effects of inflation. An understanding of these issues is essential to good capital budgeting decisions.

CASH FLOW ESTIMATION

The most important step in analyzing a potential project is estimating its cash flows—the investment outlays that will be required and the net cash inflows the project will produce. Many variables are involved in cash flow forecasting, and many individuals and departments participate in the process. For example, the forecasts of unit sales and sales prices are normally made by marketing people, based on their knowledge of price elasticity, advertising effects, the state of the economy, competitors' reactions, and trends in consumers' tastes. Similarly, the required capital outlays are generally obtained from the engineering and product development staffs, while operating costs are estimated by cost accountants, production experts, personnel specialists, purchasing agents, and so forth.

It is difficult to accurately forecast the costs and revenues associated with a large, complex project, so errors can be quite large. For example, when several major oil companies decided to build the Alaska Pipeline, the original cost forecast was about $700 million, but the final cost was closer to $7 billion. Similar or even worse miscalculations are common in forecasts of product design costs, such as the costs to develop a new pen-based personal computer. Further, as difficult as plant and equipment costs are to estimate, sales revenues and operating costs over the project's life are even more uncertain.

The financial staff's role in the forecasting process includes (1) coordinating the efforts of the other departments, such as engineering and marketing, (2) ensuring that everyone involved uses a consistent set of economic assumptions, and (3) making sure that no biases creep into the forecasts. This last point is extremely important, because managers often become emotionally involved with pet projects, leading to rosy forecasts which make bad projects look good — on paper.

Note also that obtaining unbiased estimates of the key variables is only part of the forecasting process — as we shall see in the next chapter, data on probability distributions or other indicators of risk are also essential.

It is almost impossible to overstate the difficulties one can encounter when forecasting cash flows. It is also difficult to overstate the importance of these forecasts. However, if the principles discussed in the next several sections are observed, forecasting errors can be minimized.

What is the most important step in the capital budgeting process?
What departments are involved in estimating a project's cash flows?
What is the financial staff's role in cash flow estimation?

SELF-TEST QUESTIONS

IDENTIFYING THE RELEVANT CASH FLOWS

Cash flows for a project are defined as the differences in the firm's cash flows for each period if the project is undertaken versus if it is not undertaken:

$$\text{Project CF}_t = \frac{\text{CF}_t \text{ for corporation}}{\text{with project}} - \frac{\text{CF}_t \text{ for corporation}}{\text{without project}}. \qquad \text{10-1}$$

Defined in this way, we see that project cash flows are *incremental*, or *additional*, *cash flows* that occur if the project is accepted. In this section, we discuss how to measure the incremental cash flows attributable to a project.

CASH FLOW VERSUS ACCOUNTING INCOME

Income statements in some respects mix apples and oranges. For example, accountants deduct labor costs, which are cash outflows, from revenues, which may or may not be entirely cash (some sales may be on credit). At the same time, they do not deduct capital outlays, which are cash outflows, but they do deduct depreciation expenses, which are not cash outflows. In capital budgeting, it is critical that we base decisions strictly on cash flows, or the actual dollars that flow into and out of the company during each time period.

As noted above, the *relevant cash flows* for capital budgeting purposes are the *incremental cash flows* attributable to a project. Theoretically, it is possible to construct pro forma cash flow statements with and without a project for each year of the project's life, and then to measure the project's annual cash flows as the differences in cash flows between the two sets of statements.

To illustrate, suppose a firm is considering a new project that has a cost of $1,000 and a 10-year life. If the project is undertaken, the operating cash flow statement in the left column of the following table is expected, while if the project is not undertaken, the firm's operating cash flows will be as shown in the middle column. The third column shows the changes, or incremental cash flows, resulting from the project. The incremental net operating cash flow (NOCF) is $298 per year for 10 years:[1]

	WITH PROJECT	− WITHOUT PROJECT	= INCREMENTAL CASH FLOW
Sales	$1,600	$1,000	$600
Cash operating costs	600	400	200
Depreciation	200	100	100
Pre-tax income	$ 800	$ 500	$300
Taxes (34%)	272	170	102
Net operating income (NOI)	$ 528	$ 330	$198
NOCF = NOI + Depreciation	$ 728	$ 430	$298

TIMING OF CASH FLOW

We must account properly for the timing of cash flows. Accounting income statements are for periods such as years or months, so they do not reflect exactly when during the period cash revenues or expenses occur. Because of the time value of money, capital budgeting cash flows should in theory be analyzed exactly as they occur. Of course, there must be a compromise between accuracy and feasibility. A time line with daily cash flows would in theory be most accurate, but daily cash flow estimates would be costly to construct, unwieldy to use, and probably no more accurate than annual cash flow estimates because we simply cannot forecast well enough to warrant this degree of detail. Therefore, in most cases, we simply assume that all cash flows occur at the end of every year. However, for some projects, it may be useful to assume that cash flows occur at mid-year, or even quarterly or monthly.

INCREMENTAL CASH FLOWS

As noted previously, our concern is with those cash flows that result directly from the decision to undertake a project, or *incremental cash flows.* Three special issues must be addressed when estimating incremental cash flows:

---

[1]Note that we are concentrating solely on operating cash flows. Financing flows (interest expense) are not included because financing costs are dealt with by discounting at the WACC. When we use the WACC as a discount rate to obtain a project's NPV, we are effectively reducing the values of the cash flows to account for capital costs, so we would be double counting if we also reduced the cash flows by deducting interest expenses.

SUNK COSTS   Sunk costs are *not* incremental costs, so they should *not* be included in a capital budgeting analysis. A *sunk cost* refers to an outlay that has already occurred (or been committed). Since the outlay has already occurred, it is not affected by the accept/reject decision under consideration. Suppose, for example, that in 1997 General Motors was evaluating a proposal to build an assembly plant just across the Mexican border from El Paso. As a part of the project, GM had, back in 1996, hired a consulting firm to perform a site analysis at a cost of $100,000, and this $100,000 was expensed for tax purposes in 1996. Is this 1996 expenditure a relevant cost with respect to the 1997 capital budgeting decision? The answer is no. The $100,000 is a sunk cost — GM cannot recover it regardless of whether or not the new plant is built. It often turns out that a particular project looks bad (that is, has a negative NPV or an IRR less than its cost of capital) when all the associated costs, including sunk costs, are considered. However, on an incremental basis, the project may be a good one, because the incremental cash inflows are large enough to produce a positive NPV on the incremental investment. Thus, sunk costs should be disregarded in a capital budgeting analysis.[2]

OPPORTUNITY COSTS   The second potential problem relates to opportunity costs. For example, suppose GM owns a piece of land that is suitable for the plant. When evaluating the prospective project, should the cost of the land be disregarded because no additional cash outlay would be required? The answer is no, because there is an *opportunity cost* inherent in the use of the property. For example, suppose the land could be sold to net $1 million after commissions and taxes. Using the site for the new plant would require forgoing this cash inflow, so the $1 million should be charged as an opportunity cost against the project. Note, though, that the proper land cost in this example would be the $1 million market-determined value, net of any taxes and fees, irrespective of whether GM had paid $500,000 or $2 million for the property when it was acquired.

EFFECTS ON OTHER PROJECTS (EXTERNALITIES)   The third potential problem involves the effects of the project being analyzed on the firm's other projects. For example, suppose Gillette is considering the production of a new titanium-bladed razor. Some of the customers that Gillette predicts will buy the new razor are already using Gillette's other razors. The profits generated by these customers would not be new to the company, but, rather, would represent a shift from an old product line to a new line. Thus, the net cash flows produced by these customers should not be treated as incremental income in the capital budgeting analysis. On the other hand, the new razors may create sales of such related Gillette products as shaving cream and after-shave lotion. In this case, the additional cash flows projected from sales of these existing products should be attributed to the new project.

When a new project takes sales from an existing product, this is often called "cannibalization." Naturally, firms do not like to cannibalize existing products, but it often turns out that if you don't do it, someone else will. To illustrate, IBM for

---

[2]For an old but still excellent example of the improper treatment of sunk costs by a major corporation, see U. E. Reinhardt, "Break-Even Analysis for Lockheed's TriStar: An Application of Financial Theory," *Journal of Finance,* September 1973, 821–838.

years refused to provide full support for its PC division because it did not want to steal sales from its highly profitable mainframe business. That turned out to be a huge strategic error, because it allowed Intel, Microsoft, Compaq, and others to become dominant forces in the computer industry. So, when considering externalities, the full implications of the proposed new project should be taken into account.

Define the term "incremental cash flow."

Briefly describe the meaning and treatment of (1) sunk costs, (2) opportunity costs, (3) externalities, and (4) cannibalization.

TAX EFFECTS

Taxes can have a major impact on cash flows, and in many cases tax effects will make or break a project. Therefore, it is critical that taxes be dealt with correctly. Our tax laws are extremely complex, and they are subject to interpretation and to change. The financial staff can get assistance from the firm's accountants and tax lawyers, but even so, it is necessary for financial analysts to have a working knowledge of the current tax laws and their effects on cash flows.

AN OVERVIEW OF DEPRECIATION

Suppose Blockbuster Entertainment buys a computerized inventory system for $100,000 and uses it for five years, after which it is scrapped. The cost of the video rentals supported by the system must include a charge for the system, and this charge is called *depreciation*. Because depreciation reduces profits as calculated by accountants, the higher a firm's depreciation charges, the lower its reported net income. However, depreciation is not a cash charge, so higher depreciation levels do not reduce cash flows. Indeed, higher depreciation *increases* cash flows, because the higher a firm's depreciation, the lower its tax bill.

Companies generally calculate depreciation one way when figuring taxes and another way when reporting income to investors: most use the *straight line* method for stockholder reporting (or "book" purposes), but they use the fastest rate permitted by law for tax purposes. Under the straight line method as used for reporting purposes, one normally takes the cost of the asset, subtracts its estimated salvage value, and divides the net amount by the asset's economic life. For an asset with a 5-year economic life that costs $100,000 and has a $15,000 salvage value, the annual straight line depreciation charge is ($100,000 − $15,000)/5 = $17,000.

For tax purposes, companies must use the depreciation method specified in our tax laws, which Congress changes from time to time. Prior to 1954, the straight line method was required for tax purposes, but in 1954 *accelerated* methods (double declining balance and sum-of-years'-digits) were permitted. Then, in 1981, the old accelerated methods were replaced by a simpler procedure known as the *Accelerated Cost Recovery System (ACRS,* which is pronounced "acres"). The ACRS system was modified in 1986 as a part of the Tax Reform Act, and it is now called the *Modified Accelerated Cost Recovery System (MACRS)*.

Note that U.S. tax laws are very complicated, and in this text we can only provide an overview of MACRS designed to give you a basic understanding of the impact of depreciation on capital budgeting decisions. Further, the tax laws change so often that the numbers we present may be outdated before the book is even published. Thus, when dealing with tax depreciation in real-world situations, current Internal Revenue Service (IRS) publications or individuals with expertise in tax matters should be consulted.

TAX DEPRECIATION CALCULATIONS

For tax purposes, the cost of an asset is expensed over its depreciable life. Historically, an asset's tax depreciable life was closely related to its economic life; it was intended that an asset would be fully depreciated at approximately the same time that it reached the end of its useful life. However, MACRS created several classes of assets, each with a more or less arbitrarily prescribed life called a *recovery period* that bears only a rough relationship to the expected economic life.

A major effect of the MACRS system has been to shorten the depreciable lives of assets, thus giving businesses larger tax deductions and thereby increasing cash flows. Table 10-1 describes the types of property that fit into the different recovery periods, and Table 10-2 sets forth the MACRS *recovery allowance percentages* (depreciation rates) for various classes of property.

The first column of Table 10-1 gives the MACRS recovery periods, while the second column describes the types of assets which fall into each category. Property in the 27.5- and 39-year categories (real estate) must be depreciated by an alternate MACRS straight line method, but 3-, 5-, 7-, and 10-year property can be depreciated either by the straight line method or by an accelerated method which uses the rates shown in Table 10-2.[3]

MACRS: MOST COMMONLY USED RECOVERY PERIODS	TABLE 10-1

RECOVERY PERIOD	TYPE OF PROPERTY
3 years	Specially designated tools and devices, and tractor units.
5 years	Automobiles, trucks, computers, typewriters, copiers, and other designated equipment.
7 years	Most industrial equipment, office furniture, and fixtures.
10 years	Certain longer-lived types of equipment.
27.5 years	Residential rental real property such as apartment buildings.
39 years	All nonresidential real property, including commercial and industrial buildings.

[3]As a benefit to very small companies, the Tax Code permits companies to *expense,* which is equivalent to depreciating over one year, up to $17,500 of equipment. Thus, if a small company bought assets costing $17,500, it could write the assets off in the year they were acquired. This is called "Section 179 expensing." We shall disregard this provision throughout the book.

| TABLE 10-2 | MACRS RECOVERY ALLOWANCE PERCENTAGES FOR PERSONAL PROPERTY (NOT REAL ESTATE) |

OWNERSHIP YEAR	RECOVERY PERIOD			
	3-YEAR	5-YEAR	7-YEAR	10-YEAR
1	33%	20%	14%	10%
2	45	32	25	18
3	15	19	17	14
4	7	12	13	12
5		11	9	9
6		6	9	7
7			9	7
8			4	7
9				7
10				6
11				3
	100%	100%	100%	100%

NOTES:

a. We developed these recovery allowance percentages based on the 200 percent declining balance method prescribed in the 1986 Tax Act, with a switch to straight line depreciation at some point in the asset's life. For example, consider the 5-year recovery allowance percentages. The straight line percentage would be 20 percent per year, so the 200 percent declining balance multiplier is $2.0(20\%) = 40\% = 0.4$. However, because the half-year convention applies, the MACRS percentage for Year 1 is only 20 percent. For Year 2, there is 80 percent of the depreciable basis remaining, so the recovery allowance percentage is $0.40(80\%) = 32\%$. In Year 3, $20\% + 32\% = 52\%$ of the depreciation has been taken, leaving 48%, so the percentage is $0.4(48\%) \approx 19\%$. In Year 4, the percentage is $0.4(29\%) \approx 12\%$. After 4 years, straight line depreciation exceeds the declining balance depreciation, so a switch is made to straight line (this is permitted under the law). However, the half-year convention must also be applied at the end of the class life, hence the remaining 17 percent of depreciation must be taken (amortized) over 1.5 years. Thus, the percentage in Year 5 is $17\%/1.5 \approx 11\%$, and in Year 6, $17\% - 11\% = 6\%$. We rounded to the nearest whole number for ease of illustration.

b. Residential rental property (apartments) is depreciated over a 27.5-year life, whereas commercial and industrial structures are depreciated over 39 years. In both cases, straight line depreciation must be used. The depreciation allowance for the first year is based, pro rata, on the month the asset was placed in service, with the remainder of the first year's depreciation being taken in the 28th or 40th year.

As we saw earlier, higher depreciation expenses result in lower taxes, hence higher cash flows. Therefore, when a firm has the option of using for tax purposes the straight line method or the accelerated rates shown in Table 10-2, it should generally elect to use the accelerated rates. The yearly *recovery allowance* (or depreciation expense) is determined by multiplying each asset's *depreciable basis* by the applicable recovery percentage given in Table 10-2. Calculations are discussed in the following sections.

HALF-YEAR CONVENTION

Under MACRS, the assumption is generally made that property is placed in service in the middle of the first year. Thus, for 3-year property, depreciation begins in the middle of the year the asset is placed in service and ends three years later. The effect of this *half-year convention* is to extend the depreciation out one more year, so 3-year property is depreciated during four calendar years, 5-year property is depreciated during six calendar years, and so on. This convention is incorporated into Table 10-2's recovery allowance percentages.[4]

DEPRECIABLE BASIS

The *depreciable basis* is a critical element of MACRS, because each year's allowance (depreciation expense) depends jointly on the asset's depreciable basis and its MACRS recovery rate. The depreciable basis under MACRS is equal to the purchase price of the asset plus any shipping and installation costs. The basis is *not* adjusted for *salvage value* (which is the estimated market value of the asset at the end of its useful life) regardless of whether MACRS percentages or the straight line method is used.

SALE OF A DEPRECIABLE ASSET

If a depreciable asset is sold, any profit, defined as the net price received for the asset minus the then-existing tax book value, is taxed at the firm's marginal tax rate. For example, suppose a firm buys a 5-year recovery period asset for $100,000 and sells it at the end of the fourth year for $32,000. After four years, the asset's tax book value is equal to $100,000(0.11 + 0.06) = $100,000(0.17) = $17,000, so $32,000 − $17,000 = $15,000 is added to the firm's operating income and is taxed.

In this case, the tax depreciation charges over the four years exceeded "true" depreciation, and the excess depreciation that was taken is "recaptured." Since depreciation reduces ordinary income, its recapture is taxed as ordinary income. Occasionally, the net price received is less than the book value, and a loss is reported. In such cases, the sale produces a tax cash inflow, because the firm's taxable income and hence its taxes are reduced by the loss.

MACRS ILLUSTRATION

Assume that Blockbuster's $100,000 computerized inventory control system, which has a MACRS 5-year recovery period, is placed into service on March 15, 1997. Blockbuster must pay an additional $20,000 for delivery and installation. Salvage value is not considered, so the asset's depreciable basis is $120,000.

---

[4]The half-year convention also applies if straight line is used, with half of one year's depreciation taken in the first year, a full year's depreciation taken in each of the remaining years of the asset's recovery period, and the remaining half-year's depreciation taken in the year following the end of the recovery period. You should recognize that virtually all companies have computerized depreciation systems. Each asset's depreciation pattern is programmed into the system at the time of its acquisition, and the computer aggregates the depreciation allowances for all assets when the accountants close the books and prepare the financial statements and tax returns.

(Delivery and installation charges must be included in the depreciable basis rather than expensed in the year incurred.) Each year's recovery allowance (tax depreciation expense) is determined by multiplying the depreciable basis by the applicable recovery allowance percentage in Table 10-2. Thus, the depreciation expense for 1997 is 0.20($120,000) = $24,000, and for 1998 it is 0.32($120,000) = $38,400. Similarly, the depreciation expense is $22,800 for 1999, $14,400 for 2000, $13,200 for 2001, and $7,200 for 2002. The total depreciation expense over the 6-year recovery period is $120,000, which is equal to the depreciable basis of the asset.

SELF-TEST QUESTIONS

What do the acronyms ACRS and MACRS stand for?

Briefly describe the tax depreciation system under MACRS.

How does the sale of a depreciable asset affect a firm's cash flows?

CHANGES IN NET WORKING CAPITAL

Normally, additional inventories are required to support a new operation, and the new sales will also generate additional accounts receivable. Since both inventories and receivables increase as a result of capital budgeting decisions, the "investment outlay" for a new project must include working capital as well as fixed assets. However, accounts payable and accruals will also increase spontaneously as a result of the expansion, and this will reduce the need to raise capital to finance the project. The difference between the increase in current assets and that in current liabilities is defined as the *change in net working capital* (ΔNWC). This change is normally positive, so some additional investment, over and above the cost of the fixed assets, is required.[5]

Net working capital may change over several years, so the increase (or decrease) could be reflected in cash flows for several years. However, once the operation has stabilized, net working capital will also stabilize at the new level, and no further changes will occur until the project is terminated. At the end of the project's life, the firm's total working capital requirements should revert to prior levels, so it will receive an end-of-project cash inflow equal to the net investment in working capital. This point is illustrated in the next section.

SELF-TEST QUESTIONS

What is net working capital (NWC)?

How do changes in NWC affect a project's cash flow estimates?

---

[5]Actually, the entire change in net working capital does not require additional investment, because some of the increase in receivables represents profits, hence does not require financing. However, profit margins are normally just a few percentage points, so ignoring this factor does not lead to serious errors. This topic is discussed further in Chapter 20. In the unlikely event that the change in net working capital is negative, then the project would be generating an initial cash inflow from the change in net working capital, which would reduce the project's initital outlay.

EXAMPLE OF CASH FLOW ANALYSIS

In this section, we tie things together by examining a capital budgeting decision that faces Regency Integrated Chips (RIC), a Minneapolis-based technology company. RIC's research and development department has been applying its expertise in chip technology to develop a small microprocessor and sensor system specifically designed to control commercial landscape watering systems. Once programmed, the system would automatically sense the need for watering in each separate watering zone and then provide just the right amount of water to each zone. By eliminating excess watering, the system could save enough to pay for itself in a few years. This project has now reached the stage where a decision must be made on whether to go forward with production.

Investment requirements for the project are itemized in Table 10-3. The firm would need a new plant, which could be built and made ready for production two years after the "go" decision is made. The plant would require a 25-acre site, and RIC currently has an option to purchase a suitable tract of land for $1.2 million; the option could be exercised in late 1997. Building construction would begin in early 1998 and would continue through 1999. The building, which according to a special tax ruling has a MACRS 31.5-year recovery period, would cost an estimated $8 million; a $4 million payment would be made on December 31, 1998, and the remaining $4 million would be paid on December 31, 1999.

The necessary equipment would be installed late in 1999 and would be paid for on December 31, 1999. The equipment has a MACRS 5-year recovery period and would cost $9.5 million, plus another $500,000 for installation.

The project would also require an initial investment in net working capital equal to 12 percent of the estimated sales in the first year. The initial working capital investment would be made on December 31, 1999, and on December 31 of each following year net working capital would be increased by an amount equal to 12 percent of any sales increase expected during the coming year. The project's estimated economic life is six years. At that time, the land is expected to have a market value of $1.7 million, the building a value of $1.0 million, and the equipment a value of $2 million. The marketing vice-president believes that annual sales would be 25,000

			INVESTMENT OUTLAYS, 1997–1999	TABLE 10-3	
FIXED ASSETS	1997	1998	1999	**TOTAL COSTS, 1997–1999**	**DEPRECIABLE BASIS**
Land	$1,200,000	$ 0	$ 0	$ 1,200,000	$ 0
Building	0	4,000,000	4,000,000	8,000,000	8,000,000
Equipment	0	0	10,000,000	10,000,000	10,000,000
Total fixed assets	$1,200,000	$4,000,000	$14,000,000	$19,200,000	
Net working capital[a]	0	0	6,600,000	6,600,000	
Total investment	$1,200,000	$4,000,000	$20,600,000	$25,800,000	

[a]12 percent of first year's sales, or 0.12($55,000,000) = $6,600,000.

units if the systems were priced at $2,200 each. (See Table 10-4.) The production department has estimated that variable manufacturing costs would total 65 percent of dollar sales, and that fixed overhead costs, excluding depreciation, would be $8 million for the first year of operations. Sales prices and fixed overhead costs, other than depreciation, are projected to increase with inflation, which is expected to average 6 percent per year over the 6-year life of the project.

RIC's marginal federal-plus-state tax rate is 40 percent; its weighted average cost of capital is 11.5 percent; and the company's policy, for capital budgeting purposes,

TABLE 10-4 — NET CASH FLOWS, 2000–2005

	2000	2001	2002	2003	2004	2005
Unit sales	25,000	25,000	25,000	25,000	25,000	25,000
Sale price[a]	$ 2,200	$ 2,332	$ 2,472	$ 2,620	$ 2,777	$ 2,944
Net sales[a]	$55,000,000	$58,300,000	$61,800,000	$65,500,000	$69,425,000	$73,600,000
Variable costs[b]	35,750,000	37,895,000	40,170,000	42,575,000	45,126,250	47,840,000
Fixed costs (overhead)[a]	8,000,000	8,480,000	8,988,800	9,528,128	10,099,816	10,705,805
Depreciation (building)[c]	120,000	240,000	240,000	240,000	240,000	240,000
Depreciation (equipment)[c]	2,000,000	3,200,000	1,900,000	1,200,000	1,100,000	600,000
Earnings before taxes	$ 9,130,000	$ 8,485,000	$10,501,200	$11,956,872	$12,858,934	$14,214,195
Taxes (40%)	3,652,000	3,394,000	4,200,480	4,782,749	5,143,574	5,685,678
Projected net operating income	$ 5,478,000	$ 5,091,000	$ 6,300,720	$ 7,174,123	$ 7,715,360	$ 8,528,517
Add back noncash expenses[d]	2,120,000	3,440,000	2,140,000	1,440,000	1,340,000	840,000
Cash flow from operations[e]	$ 7,598,000	$ 8,531,000	$ 8,440,720	$ 8,614,123	$ 9,055,360	$ 9,368,517
Investment in NWC[f]	(396,000)	(420,000)	(444,000)	(471,000)	(501,000)	8,832,000
Net salvage value[g]						5,972,000
Total projected cash flow	$ 7,202,000	$ 8,111,000	$ 7,996,720	$ 8,143,123	$ 8,554,360	$24,172,517

[a]The 2000 estimates are increased by the assumed 6 percent inflation rate.
[b]65 percent of net sales.
[c]MACRS depreciation rates are as follows:

YEAR	1	2	3	4	5	6
Building	1.5%	3%	3%	3%	3%	3%
Equipment	20	32	19	12	11	6

These percentages are multiplied by each asset's depreciable basis to get the depreciation expense for each year. Note that the allowances have been rounded for ease of computation.
[d]In this case, depreciation on building and equipment.
[e]Net operating income plus noncash expenses.
[f]12 percent of next year's increase in sales. For example, 2001 sales are $3.3 million greater than 2000 sales, so the addition to NWC in 2000 required to support 2001 sales is (0.12)($3,300,000) = $396,000. The cumulative working capital investment is recovered when the project ends in 2005.
[g]See Table 10-5 for the net salvage value calculation.

is to assume that cash flows occur at the end of each year. Since the plant would begin operations on January 1, 2000, the first operating cash flows would thus occur on December 31, 2000.

As one of the company's financial analysts, you have been assigned to conduct the capital budgeting analysis. For now, you may assume that the project has the same risk as the firm's existing assets, hence you may use the corporate cost of capital, 11.5 percent, for this project. Later on, we will examine additional information concerning the riskiness of the project, but at this point assume that the project is of average risk.

ANALYSIS OF THE CASH FLOWS

The first step in the analysis is to summarize the investment outlays required for the project; this is done in Table 10-3. Note that the land cannot be depreciated, hence we show its depreciable basis to be $0. Also, since the project will require an increase in net working capital during 1999, this is shown as an investment outlay for that year.

Having estimated the capital requirements, we must now forecast the operating cash flows that will occur once production begins; these are set forth in Table 10-4. The operating cash flows estimates are based on information provided by RIC's various departments. Note that the sales price and fixed costs are projected to increase each year by the 6 percent inflation rate, and since variable costs are 65 percent of dollar sales, they too will rise by 6 percent each year. The changes in net working capital (NWC) represent the additional investments required to support sales increases (12 percent of the next year's sales increase, which in this case results only from inflation) during 2000–2004, and the recovery of the cumulative net working capital investment in 2005. The depreciation amounts were obtained by multiplying each asset's depreciable basis by the MACRS recovery allowance rates set forth in Note c to Table 10-4.

The analysis also requires an estimation of the cash flows generated by salvage values; Table 10-5 summarizes this analysis. First, we compare the projected 2005 market values against the 2005 book values. The land cannot be depreciated, and it has an estimated 2005 salvage value greater than the initial purchase price. Thus, RIC would have to pay taxes on the profit. The building has an estimated salvage value less than its book value — it will be sold at a loss for tax purposes. The loss will reduce the company's taxable income and thus generate a tax savings; in effect, the company has been depreciating the building too slowly, so it would write off the loss against ordinary income. On the other hand, the equipment will be sold for more than book value, so the company would have to pay ordinary taxes on the $2 million difference. In all cases, book value is the depreciable cost less accumulated depreciation, and the total cash flow from salvage values is merely the sum of the land, building, and equipment components.

MAKING THE DECISION

To summarize the data and get it ready for evaluation, we combine all the net cash flows on a time line as shown in Table 10-6. The table also shows the payback period, IRR, MIRR, and NPV (at the 11.5 percent cost of capital). The project appears

TABLE 10-5	AFTER-TAX SALVAGE VALUES, 2005		
	LAND	**BUILDING**	**EQUIPMENT**
Salvage (ending market) value	$1,700,000	$1,000,000	$2,000,000
Initial cost	1,200,000	8,000,000	10,000,000
Depreciable basis (1999)	0	8,000,000	10,000,000
Book value (2005)[a]	1,200,000	6,680,000	0
Capital gains income	$ 500,000	$ 0	$ 0
Ordinary income (loss)[b]	0	(5,680,000)	2,000,000
Taxes[c]	200,000	(2,272,000)	800,000
Net salvage value (Salvage value − Taxes)	$1,500,000	$3,272,000	$1,200,000

Net cash flow from salvage value = $1,500,000 + $3,272,000 + $1,200,000 = $5,972,000.

[a]Book value for the building in 2005 equals depreciable cost minus accumulated MACRS depreciation of $1,320,000. The accumulated depreciation on the equipment is $10,000,000. See Table 10-4.
[b]Building: $1,000,000 market value − $6,680,000 book value = $5,680,000 depreciation shortfall, which is treated as an operating expense in 2005.
Equipment: $2,000,000 market value − $0 book value = $2,000,000 depreciation recapture, which is treated as ordinary income in 2005.
[c]Since corporate capital gains are now taxed at the ordinary income rate, all taxes are based on RIC's 40 percent marginal federal-plus-state rate. The table is set up to differentiate ordinary income from capital gains because Congress may reinstate differential tax rates on those two income sources.

to be acceptable using the NPV, IRR, or MIRR methods, and it would also be acceptable if RIC required a payback of six years or less. Note, however, that the analysis thus far has been based on the assumption that the project has the same degree of risk as the company's average project. If the project is riskier than an average project, then it would be necessary to increase the cost of capital, which in turn might cause the NPV to become negative and the IRR and MIRR to fall below k. In Chapter 11, we extend the evaluation of this project to include the necessary risk analysis. Note also that in practice we would do the analysis using a computer spreadsheet, and the information given in Tables 10-3 through 10-6 would all be generated in the spreadsheet.

TABLE 10-6	TIME LINE OF CONSOLIDATED END-OF-YEAR NET CASH FLOWS, 1997–2005

1997	1998	1999	2000	2001	2002	2003	2004	2005
($1,200,000)	($4,000,000)	($20,600,000)	$7,202,000	$8,111,000	$7,996,720	$8,143,123	$8,554,360	$24,172,517

Payback period: 5.3 years from first outflow.
IRR: 25.1% verus an 11.5% cost of captial.
MIRR: 17.9% verus an 11.5% cost of capital.
NPV: $12,075,384.

How does RIC account for inflation in the cash flow estimation process?
Why was it necessary to include changes in net working capital in the analysis?
Describe how depreciation tax effects were included in the Table 10-4 operating
cash flows.
Explain the meaning of the negative taxes shown for the building in the net salvage
value analysis in Table 10-5.

**SELF-TEST
QUESTIONS**

REPLACEMENT ANALYSIS

RIC's watering system project was used to show how an expansion project is analyzed. All companies also make *replacement decisions,* where cash flows from both
the old and the new assets must be considered. Replacement analysis is illustrated
with an example from RIC's research and development (R&D) division.

A lathe for trimming molded plastics was purchased 10 years ago at a cost of
$7,500. The machine had an expected life of 15 years at the time it was purchased,
and management originally estimated, and still believes, that the salvage value will be
zero at the end of the 15-year life. The machine is being depreciated on a straight
line basis; therefore, its annual depreciation charge is $500, and its present book
value is $2,500.[6]

The R&D manager reports that a new special-purpose machine can be purchased
for $12,000 (including freight and installation) which, over its 5-year life, will reduce
labor and raw materials usage sufficiently to cut operating costs from $7,000 to
$4,000. These cost cuts will cause before-tax profits to rise by $7,000 − $4,000 =
$3,000 per year.

It is estimated that the new machine can be sold for $2,000 at the end of five
years; this is its estimated salvage value. The old machine's actual current market
value is $1,000, which is below its $2,500 book value. If the new machine were
acquired, the old lathe would be sold. The company's marginal federal-plus-state tax
rate is 40 percent, and the replacement project is of average risk. Net working capital requirements will also increase by $1,000 at the time of replacement. Assume
that an IRS ruling places the new machine into the 3-year MACRS recovery period.
If the cost of capital is 11.5 percent, should the replacement be made?

Table 10-7 shows the spreadsheet format the company uses to analyze replacement projects. A line-by-line description of the table follows.

Line 1. The top section, Lines 1 through 5, sets forth the cash flows which occur
at (approximately) t = 0, the time the investment is made. Line 1 shows
the purchase price of the new machine, including any installation and
freight charges.

Line 2. Here we show the price received from the sale of the old equipment.

Line 3. Since the old equipment would be sold at less than its book value,
this creates a loss which reduces the firm's taxable income and thus

---

[6]Since the company had losses when the machine was purchased, it chose to depreciate the lathe
using the MACRS straight line method.

TABLE 10-7   REPLACEMENT ANALYSIS SPREADSHEET

I. NET CASH FLOW AT THE TIME THE INVESTMENT IS MADE

	t = 0
1. Cost of new equipment	($12,000)
2. Market value of old equipment	1,000
3. Tax savings due to loss on old equipment	600
4. Increase in net working capital	(1,000)
5. Total net investment	($11,400)

YEAR:	0	1	2	3	4	5
II. OPERATING INFLOWS OVER THE PROJECT'S LIFE						
6. After-tax cost savings		$1,800	$1,800	$1,800	$1,800	$1,800
7. Depreciation on new machine		$3,960	$5,400	$1,800	$ 840	$0
8. Depreciation on old machine		500	500	500	500	500
9. Change in depreciation		$3,460	$4,900	$1,300	$ 340	($ 500)
10. Tax savings from depreciation		1,384	1,960	520	136	(200)
11. Net operating cash flow (6 + 10)		$3,184	$3,760	$2,320	$1,936	$1,600
III. TERMINAL-YEAR CASH FLOWS						
12. Estimated salvage value of new machine						$2,000
13. Tax on salvage value						(800)
14. Recovery of net working capital						1,000
15. Total termination cash flow						$2,200
IV. NET CASH FLOWS						
16. Net cash flow	($11,400)	$3,184	$3,760	$2,320	$1,936	$3,800

V. RESULTS

Payback period: 4.1 years.

IRR: 10.1% versus an 11.5% cost of capital.

MIRR: 10.7% versus an 11.5% cost of capital.

NPV: −$388.77

---

lowers its next quarterly income tax payment. The tax saving is equal to $(Loss)(T) = (\$1,500)(0.40) = \$600$, where T is the marginal tax rate. The Tax Code defines this loss as an operating loss because it reflects the fact that inadequate depreciation was taken on the old asset. If there had been a profit on the sale (that is, if the sales price had exceeded book value), Line 3 would have shown taxes *paid*, a cash outflow. In the actual case, the equipment would be sold at a loss, so no taxes would be paid, and the company would realize a tax savings of $600.[7]

Line 4. The investment in net working capital (new current asset requirements less increases in accounts payable and accruals) is shown here. This investment will be recovered at the end of the project's life (see Line 14). No taxes are involved.

Line 5. Here we show the total net cash outflow at the time the replacement is made. The company writes a check for $12,000 to pay for the machine, and another $1,000 is invested in net working capital. However, these outlays are partially offset by the sale of the old equipment.

Line 6. Section II of the table shows the *incremental operating cash flows,* or benefits, that are expected if the replacement is made. The first of these benefits is the reduction in operating costs shown on Line 6, which (1) increases cash flows because operating costs are reduced by $3,000, but (2) therefore, also increases taxable income and, hence, income taxes. Therefore, the after-tax benefit is $3,000(1 − T) = $3,000(1 − 0.40) = $3,000(0.60) = $1,800. Note that if the replacement had resulted in an increase in sales in addition to the reduction in costs (if the new machine had been both larger and more efficient), then a new line would be added. Finally, note that the $3,000 cost savings is constant over Years 1 through 5; had the annual savings been expected to change over time, this fact would have to be built into the analysis.

Line 7. The depreciable basis of the new machine, $12,000, is multiplied by the appropriate MACRS recovery allowance for 3-year class property to obtain the depreciation figures shown on Line 7. Note that if you summed Line 7, the total would be $12,000, the depreciable basis.

Line 8. Line 8 shows the $500 straight line depreciation on the old machine.

Line 9. The depreciation expense on the old machine as shown on Line 8 can no longer be taken if the replacement is made, but the new machine's depreciation will be available. Therefore, the $500 depreciation on the old machine is subtracted from that on the new machine to show the *incremental change in annual depreciation*. The change is positive in Years 1 through 4, but negative in Year 5. The Year 5 negative net change signifies that replacing the machine results in a *decrease* in depreciation expense in Year 5.

Line 10. The net change in depreciation results in tax savings equal to the change in depreciation multiplied by the tax rate: Depreciation savings = T(Change in depreciation) = 0.40($3,460) = $1,384 for Year 1. Capital budgeting decisions are based on *incremental* cash flows, and

---

[7]If the old asset were being exchanged for the new asset, rather than being sold to a third party, the tax consequences would be different. In an exchange of similar assets, no gain or loss is recognized. If the market value of the old asset is greater than its book value, the depreciable basis of the new asset is decreased by the gain. Conversely, if the market value of the old asset is less than its book value, the depreciable basis is increased by the loss.

since we lose $500 of depreciation if we replace the old machine, that fact must be taken into account.

Line 11. Here we show the net operating cash flows over the project's 5-year life. These flows are found by adding the after-tax cost savings to the depreciation tax savings, or Line 6 + Line 10.

Line 12. Part III shows the cash flows at the termination of the project. To begin, Line 12 shows the estimated salvage value of the new machine at the end of its 5-year life, $2,000.[8]

Line 13. Since the book value of the new machine at the end of Year 5 is zero, the company will have to pay taxes of $2,000(0.4) = $800.

Line 14. An investment of $1,000 in net working capital was shown as an outflow at t = 0. This investment, like the new machine's salvage value, will be recovered when the project is terminated. Accounts receivable will be collected, inventories will be drawn down and not replaced, and the result will be an inflow of $1,000 at t = 5.

Line 15. Here we show the total cash flow resulting from terminating the project.

Line 16. Part IV shows, on Line 16, the total net cash flows in a time line format suitable for capital budgeting evaluation. Note that these are the firm's *incremental* cash flows for each year, that is, the *difference* in its cash flows if it replaces the machine versus if it does not. If the incremental cash flows over Years 1 through 5 are sufficient to offset the costs of Year 0, then the machine should be replaced.

Part V of the table, "Results," shows the replacement project's payback, IRR, MIRR, and NPV. The project is assumed to be of similar risk to the old project, and the old project is assumed to be about as risky as the company's average project. Therefore, an 11.5 percent project cost of capital is appropriate. At this cost of capital, the project is not acceptable, so the old lathe should not be replaced.

SELF-TEST QUESTIONS
What are the primary differences between the cash flow analysis for a new project and that for a replacement project?
Why is the depreciation tax saving negative in Year 5 in Table 10-7?

CASH FLOW ESTIMATION BIAS

As noted at the beginning of the chapter, cash flow estimation is the most critical, and also the most difficult, part of the capital budgeting process. For most projects,

---

[8]In this analysis, the estimated salvage value of the old machine is zero. However, if the old machine could be sold at the end of five years, then replacing the old machine now would eliminate this cash flow. Thus, the after-tax salvage value of the old machine would represent an opportunity cost to the firm, and it would be included as a Year 5 cash outflow in the terminal cash flow section of the worksheet.

cash flows must be forecasted many years into the future, and estimation errors are bound to occur.[9] Clearly, large errors can and do occur. However, large firms evaluate and accept many projects every year, and if the cash flow estimates are unbiased and the errors are random, estimation errors will tend to cancel each other out. Some projects will have NPV estimates that are too high and others will have estimates that are too low, but the average realized NPV on all the projects accepted should be relatively close to the aggregate NPV estimate.

Unfortunately, several studies indicate that capital budgeting cash flow forecasts are often biased—many managers tend to be overly optimistic, so revenues tend to be overstated and costs understated.[10] The end result is an upward bias in net operating cash flows and thus an upward bias in estimated NPVs. This is most likely to occur if managers are paid on the basis of the size of the company, hence are motivated to maximize size rather than to create wealth. Even when this is not the case, managers can become emotionally attached to their projects and thus fail to objectively assess projects' potential negative factors.

If a bias exists at a particular firm, then accepting a project with a zero estimated NPV will likely result in a loss, hence in a decrease in shareholders' wealth. Recognizing that biases may exist, senior managers at many firms now develop data on divisional managers' forecasting accuracies and then consider this information in the capital budgeting decision process. Some companies lower the cash flow estimates of managers whose track records suggest that their forecasts are too rosy, while other companies increase the cost of capital, or hurdle rate, applied to such project submissions.

The first step in uncovering cash flow estimation bias, especially for projects that are estimated to be highly profitable, is to ask this question: What is the underlying cause of this project's high profitability? If the firm has some inherent advantage such as patent protection, unique marketing expertise, or a well-known brand name, then some of its projects may truly be extraordinarily profitable. However, in the long run above-normal profits generally attract competition and thus are eroded. If there is reason to believe that competition is likely to increase, and if division managers cannot identify any unique factor which would support a project's continued high profitability, then senior management should be concerned about estimation bias.

RIC's top management considered the possibility of estimation bias when they reviewed the watering system project. With an IRR of 25.1 percent and an MIRR of 17.9 percent versus a cost of capital of 11.5 percent, the project is clearly projected to earn above-normal profits. These high profits might attract other firms into the market, and new entry might cause the actual cash flows to fall far below those forecast in Table 10-4. However, RIC's management concluded that competitors would

---

[9]For a discussion of the cash flow estimation practices of some large firms, as well as some estimates of the inaccuracies involved, see Randolph A. Pohlman, Emmanuel S. Santiago, and F. Lynn Markel, "Cash Flow Estimation Practices of Large Firms," *Financial Management*, Summer 1988, 71–79.

[10]For a discussion of cash flow estimation bias, see Stephen W. Pruitt and Lawrence J. Gitman, "Capital Budgeting Forecast Biases: Evidence from the *Fortune* 500," *Financial Management*, Spring 1987, 46–51.

not be able to develop and produce a competing product within the next several years. Further, they noted that the unit sales forecasts were held constant over the life of the project, which is probably conservative. Finally, as we will see in Chapter 11, the project is actually quite risky, and the forecasted returns are not out of line in view of the risks involved.

SELF-TEST QUESTIONS | Why might cash flow estimation bias exist in the capital budgeting decision process? What can be done to counteract such a bias?

OPTION VALUE

Traditional discounted cash flow (DCF) analysis—where an asset's cash flows are estimated and then discounted to obtain the asset's NPV—has been the cornerstone of asset valuation since the 1950s. Accordingly, most of our discussion of capital budgeting focuses on DCF valuation techniques. However, in recent years a growing number of academics and practitioners have demonstrated that DCF valuation techniques do not always tell the complete story about a project's value and that rote use of these techniques can, at times, lead to incorrect capital budgeting decisions.[11]

DCF techniques were originally developed to value securities such as stocks and bonds. These securities are passive investments—once they have been purchased, most investors have no influence over the cash flows the assets produce. However, real assets are not passive investments—managerial actions can influence their results. Furthermore, investing in a new project often brings with it a potential increase in the firm's future opportunities. Opportunities are, in effect, *options*— the right but not the obligation to take some action in the future. As we saw in Chapter 7 and will discuss in detail in Chapter 23, options are valuable, so any project that expands the firm's set of opportunities has positive *option value*. Similarly, any project that reduces the set of future opportunities has negative option value. A project's impact on the firm's opportunities, or its option value, may not be captured by conventional NPV analysis.

To illustrate one type of option value created by projects, consider the decision facing McDonald's when it decided to build a restaurant in Moscow. The company had to get a whole series of permits, set up a supply system, find a site, and train a set of employees who were totally unfamiliar with operations like McDonald's. It would be impossible to justify building the new restaurant on the basis of an NPV analysis—the NPV would be hugely negative. However, McDonald's management felt that setting up the Moscow operation would give it experience in doing business in Russia, and, if the venture were successful, it would open the door to millions

---

[11]For an excellent general discussion of the problems inherent in discounted cash flow valuation techniques as applied to capital budgeting, see Avinash K. Dixit and Robert S. Pindyck, "The Options Approach to Capital Investment," *Harvard Business Review,* May–June 1995, 105–115. For more information on the option value inherent in investment timing decisions, see Stephen A. Ross, "Uses, Abuses, and Alternatives to the Net-Present-Value Rule," *Financial Management,* Autumn 1995, 96–101. Also, the Spring 1987 issue of the *Midland Corporate Finance Journal* contains several interesting articles on the use of option concepts in capital budgeting.

of potential new customers. Thus, the main value expected from the Moscow investment was in the form of an option, not the direct cash flows the Moscow restaurant would produce. Hundreds of other companies are setting up operations in China, Latin America, Africa, and other areas for the strategic options those investments provide, in spite of the negative NPVs produced by conventional NPV analysis.

Compaq Computer provides a somewhat different type of example. Compaq recently invested about $3 million in Intellon Corporation, a small startup company which is attempting to develop a commercially viable system which uses buildings' interior wiring for digital communications. Compaq could not justify its investment on the basis of an NPV analysis, but it wanted to be in on the ground floor if Intellon's technology turns out to be feasible for use in developing "intelligent buildings." Then, Compaq could supply the computers which would control the system. Compaq and hundreds of other companies are spending billions on "strategic investments" in smaller companies like Intellon, primarily for the option value these investments provide.

Another type of option that can add value is the ability to *abandon,* or discontinue, a project, either to cut losses or because the operation is more valuable to some other party and can be sold for more than the present value of the remaining cash flows. Often, capital budgeting analyses are conducted assuming a fixed life for each project. However, if a project can be abandoned, it may be less risky and have a higher expected value than is indicated by conventional fixed-life NPV analysis. We will discuss abandonment options and their effects in more detail later in this chapter and again in Chapter 11.

It should also be noted that a conventional NPV analysis can, at times, overstate the value of a project. This occurs because accepting a certain type of project today "kills off" future opportunities. To illustrate, consider the situation recently faced by Royal Dutch Petroleum when it was deciding whether or not to open a newly discovered oil field. The exploratory work had already been done, so the company knew how much oil was in the field, and it also knew how much it would cost to get it out of the ground and how much it could earn on each barrel produced. The project had a positive NPV, hence conventional discounted cash flow analysis indicated that the field should be developed. However, a conventional analysis implicitly assumes that the project will be undertaken now or never, because the analysis provides only two possible choices—accept or reject.

Yet suppose oil prices are significantly higher five years from now. In that case, each barrel extracted and sold at today's prices would preclude selling that barrel in the future at a higher price. Therefore, the NPV of the project might be higher if Royal Dutch delayed taking it on rather than going forward today. By opening the oil field today, the company is, in effect, "exercising an option" and thus reducing its future opportunities. Put another way, it is giving up some option value. In such cases, a conventional NPV analysis may overstate the value of the project, so decision makers should insist on an NPV that is both positive and also large enough to offset the option value given up by not holding the oil field for future development. Indeed, some companies deliberately set hurdle rates that are above the calculated cost of capital when evaluating projects that contain such *timing options.* By doing so, they recognize that taking on the project today involves some loss of value due to extinguishing an implicit call option.

Our conclusion to all this is that the true values of projects which include embedded options may exceed those shown in a straightforward NPV calculation, while the NPVs of projects which limit future opportunities may be overstated. Therefore, managers should identify such options and take them into account in their capital budgeting decisions. Decision trees, which we discuss in Chapter 11, provide one method for formally dealing with options. Also, option pricing models, which we discuss in Chapter 23, can be used in certain situations. A great deal of work is going on in this area, and we expect to see more widespread use of option analysis as a supplement to discounted cash flow analysis in capital budgeting in the future. For now, you should recognize that as a result of embedded options some projects have more or less value than is indicated by their NPVs, and this value should, at a minimum, be subjectively considered when making capital budgeting decisions.

SELF-TEST QUESTIONS

How might option considerations cause a conventional NPV valuation to produce an incorrect decision recommendation for a project?

What actions can managers take to correct the NPV valuation problem?

EVALUATING PROJECTS WITH UNEQUAL LIVES

Note that a replacement decision involves two mutually exclusive projects: retaining the old asset versus buying a new one. To simplify matters, in the replacement example we presented earlier, we assumed that the new machine had a life equal to the remaining life of the old machine. If, however, we were choosing between two such mutually exclusive alternatives with significantly different lives, an adjustment would be necessary. We now discuss two procedures — (1) the replacement chain method and (2) the equivalent annual annuity method — to illustrate the problem and to show how one can deal with it.

Suppose RIC is planning to modernize its warehouse facilities, and, as a part of the process, it is considering either a conveyor system (Project C) or a fleet of forklift trucks (Project F) for moving materials. Table 10-8 shows both the expected net cash flows and the NPVs for these two mutually exclusive alternatives. We see that Project C, when discounted at an 11.5 percent cost of capital, has the higher NPV and thus appears to be better. Project F's IRR is higher, but since C's NPV is higher, it still appears to be the best choice.

REPLACEMENT CHAIN (COMMON LIFE) APPROACH

Although the analysis in Table 10-8 suggests that Project C should be selected, this analysis is incomplete, and the decision to choose Project C is actually incorrect. If we choose Project F, we will have the opportunity to make a similar investment in 3 years, and if costs and revenues continue at the Table 10-8 levels, this second investment will also be profitable. However, if we choose Project C, we will not have this second investment opportunity. To make a proper comparison of Projects C and F, we could apply the *replacement chain (common life)* approach. This involves finding the NPV of Project F over the shortest common life of the two projects — in this

YEAR	PROJECT C	PROJECT F
	EXPECTED NET CASH FLOWS FOR PROJECTS WITH UNEQUAL LIVES — TABLE 10-8	
0	($40,000)	($20,000)
1	8,000	7,000
2	14,000	13,000
3	13,000	12,000
4	12,000	—
5	11,000	—
6	10,000	—
NPV at 11.5%:	$7,165	$5,391
IRR:	17.5%	25.2%

case 6 years — and then comparing this extended NPV with the NPV of Project C over the same 6 years.

The NPV for Project C, as calculated in Table 10-8, is already over the 6-year common life. For Project F, however, we must assume a second investment that extends the overall life of the combined projects to 6 years. Here we assume that Project F's cost and annual cash inflows will not change if the project is replicated in three years and that RIC's cost of capital will remain at 11.5 percent:

$$\text{NPV for Project F} = \$9,281.$$
$$\text{IRR for Project F} = 25.2\%.$$

The NPV of this extended-life Project F is $9,281, and its IRR is 25.2 percent. (The IRR of two Project Fs is the same as the IRR for one Project F.) Since the extended-life NPV of Project F over the 6-year common life is greater than the $7,165 NPV of Project C, Project F should be chosen.[12]

---

[12]An alternative procedure would produce the same result. We could recognize that the value of the cash flow stream of two consecutive Project Fs can be summarized by two NPVs: one at Year 0 representing the value of the initial project and one at Year 3 representing the value of the replication project:

$$\text{NPV} = \$9,281.$$

The present value of these two flows, when discounted at 11.5 percent, is also $9,281, so we again come to the conclusion that Project F should be selected.

Note that if Project C had a 5-year life and F a 3-year life, then it would have been necessary to extend the analysis out to Year 15, the shortest common life. Then, we would have had three replacements for C and five for F. Obviously, the analysis would have to be modified if costs and revenues were not expected to remain constant.

EQUIVALENT ANNUAL ANNUITY APPROACH

Although the preceding example illustrates why an extended analysis is necessary if we are comparing mutually exclusive projects with different lives, the arithmetic is generally more complex in practice. As we noted, if C had a 5-year life and F a 3-year life, this would require a replacement chain analysis over 15 years, the least common multiple of the two lives. In such a situation, it is often simpler to use a second procedure, the *equivalent annual annuity (EAA)* method, which involves two steps:

1. Find each project's NPV over its initial life. In Table 10-8, we found $NPV_C = \$7,165$ and $NPV_F = \$5,391$.

2. Find the constant annual cash flow over the life of each project that produces the same present value as its NPV. This annual cash flow is called the *equivalent annual annuity (EAA)*. For Project F, here is the time line:

To find the EAA_F, enter 5391 as the PV, $k = i = 11.5$, and $n = 3$ in your calculator and solve for PMT. The answer is $\$2,225$. This cash flow stream, when discounted back 3 years at 11.5 percent, has a present value equal to Project F's original NPV, $\$5,391$. The value $\$2,225$ is called the project's "equivalent annual annuity (EAA)." The EAA for Project C is found similarly to be $\$1,718$. Thus, Project C has an NPV which is equivalent to an annuity of $\$1,718$ per year for 6 years, while Project F's NPV is equivalent to an annuity of $\$2,225$ for 3 years.

The project with the higher EAA will have the higher NPV over any common life, because each project's NPV is equal to the present value of its EAA stream. Since Project F has the higher EAA, it will have the higher NPV so F is preferable to C.

The EAA method is generally easier to apply than the replacement chain method, but the replacement chain method is easier to explain to decision makers. Still, the two methods always lead to the same decision if consistent assumptions are used.

When should we worry about unequal life analysis? As a general rule, the unequal life issue (1) does not arise for independent projects, but (2) it can arise if mutually exclusive projects with significantly different lives are being evaluated. However, even for mutually exclusive projects it is not always appropriate to extend the analysis to a common life. *This should only be done if there is a high probability that the projects can actually be repeated beyond their initial lives.*

We should note several potentially serious weaknesses inherent in unequal life analysis: (1) If inflation is expected, then replacement equipment will have a higher price, and both sales prices and operating costs will probably change. This would invalidate the static conditions built into the analysis. (2) Replacements that occur down the road will probably employ new technology, which, in turn, might change the cash flows. This factor is not built into either replacement chain analysis or the EAA approach. (3) It is difficult enough to estimate the lives of most projects, so estimating the lives of a series of projects is often just a guess. (4) If product markets are efficient, then the profitability of projects will be eroded over time. Therefore, by the time a project reaches the end of its life, the NPV of its replacement may well have fallen to zero. To the extent that this situation holds, we can simply compare projects over their initial lives.

In view of these problems, no experienced financial analyst would be too concerned about comparing mutually exclusive projects with lives of, say, eight years and ten years. Given all the uncertainties in the estimation process, such projects could, for all practical purposes, be assumed to have the same life. Still, it is important to recognize that a problem may exist if mutually exclusive projects have substantially different lives. When we encounter such problems in practice, we build expected inflation and/or possible efficiency gains directly into the cash flow estimates generated with a spreadsheet, then use the replacement chain approach (but not the equivalent annual annuity method). The cash flow estimation is more complicated, but the concepts involved are exactly the same as in our example.

Under what conditions is it necessary to adjust for unequal lives?
Briefly describe the replacement chain (common life) approach.
Briefly describe the equivalent annual annuity (EAA) approach.

SELF-TEST QUESTIONS

ABANDONMENT VALUE

Projects are normally analyzed under the assumption that the firm will operate the asset over its full physical life. However, this may not be the best course of action — it may be best to abandon a project before the end of its potential life, and this possibility can materially affect the project's estimated profitability.[13] The situation in Table 10-9 can be used to illustrate the abandonment value concept and its effects

PROJECT A: INVESTMENT, OPERATING, AND ABANDONMENT CASH FLOWS		TABLE 10-9
YEAR (t)	**INITIAL (YEAR 0) INVESTMENT AND OPERATING CASH FLOWS**	**NET ABANDONMENT VALUE AT END OF YEAR t**
0	($4,800)	$4,800
1	2,000	3,000
2	2,000	1,650
3	1,750	0

[13]The classic work on this subject is Alexander A. Robichek and James C. Van Horne, "Abandonment Value and Capital Budgeting," *Journal of Finance,* December 1967, 577–589.

on capital budgeting. The abandonment values listed in the third column are equivalent to net salvage values, except that they have been estimated for each year of Project A's life.

Using a 10 percent cost of capital, the expected NPV based on three years of operating cash flows and the zero abandonment (salvage) value is −$14.12:

```
0       10%    1              2              3
|--------------|--------------|--------------|
($4,800)      $2,000         $2,000         $1,750
                                             0
```

$$NPV = -\$4,800 + \$2,000/(1.10)^1 + \$2,000/(1.10)^2 + \$1,750/(1.10)^3$$
$$= -\$14.12.$$

Thus, Project A would not be accepted if we assume that it will be operated over its full 3-year life. However, what would its NPV be if the project were abandoned after two years? In this case, we would receive operating cash flows in Years 1 and 2, plus the abandonment value at the end of Year 2, and the project's NPV would be $34.71:

```
0       10%    1              2
|--------------|--------------|
($4,800)      $2,000         $2,000
                             1,650
```

$$NPV = -\$4,800 + \$2,000/(1.10)^1 + \$2,000/(1.10)^2 + \$1,650/(1.10)^2$$
$$= \$34.71.$$

Thus, Project A would be profitable if we operate it for two years and then dispose of it. To complete the analysis, note that if the project were abandoned after one year, its NPV would be −$254.55. Thus, the optimal life for this project is two years. As a general rule, any project should be abandoned if its abandonment value is greater than the present value of all cash flows beyond the abandonment year, discounted to the abandonment decision point.

Abandonment value should be considered in the capital budgeting process because, as our example illustrates, there are cases where recognizing abandonment possibilities can make an otherwise unacceptable project acceptable. Indeed, this type of analysis is required to determine a project's economic life, which is defined as that project life which maximizes the project's NPV and thus maximizes shareholder wealth. For Project A, the *economic life* is actually two years versus the three-year *physical*, or *engineering, life*. Abandonment value also should be considered during routine post-audits of ongoing projects. As time goes by, more information becomes available concerning both a project's current abandonment value and its future operating cash flows. If the abandonment alternative creates more value than continued operation, a project should be terminated.

Two very different types of abandonment occur: (1) sale by the original user of a still-valuable asset to some other party who can obtain greater cash flows from the asset and (2) abandonment of an asset because the project is losing money. The first type of situation can be illustrated by Eastman Kodak's 1994 sale of its Sterling Winthrop pharmaceutical business to Sanofi, a French health care and beauty products company. The business had more value to Sanofi than to Kodak because it gave Sanofi U.S. distribution channels for its current and future drug products. In addition, the sale allowed Kodak to focus on its core film and digital imaging business.

The second type of abandonment—closing down money-losing operations—can cut losses, and this possibility reduces the riskiness of a project. This aspect of abandonment is illustrated by Coca-Cola's termination of its new formula Coke after it became apparent that the product would never become the money-maker the firm had anticipated. We will have more to say about the impact of abandonment on project risk in Chapter 11. The main point to understand now is that the cash flows from a project can be materially different if it is abandoned (or sold off) rather than operated to the end of its initially projected life, and if abandonment possibilities are not considered, then the project's cash flows may be badly misspecified.

Define the economic life of a project (as opposed to its physical life).

Should projects be viewed as having only one life, or should alternative lives be considered in the capital budgeting process?

What are the two main situations in which abandonment may be desirable?

SELF-TEST QUESTIONS

ADJUSTING FOR INFLATION

Inflation is a fact of life in the United States and most other nations, so it must be considered in any sound capital budgeting analysis.[14]

INFLATION-INDUCED BIAS

Note that *in the absence of inflation,* the real rate, k_r, is equal to the nominal rate, k_n. Moreover, the real and nominal expected net cash flows—RCF_t and NCF_t—are also equal. (Remember that *real* interest rates and cash flows do not include inflation effects, while *nominal* rates and flows do reflect the effects of inflation. In particular, an inflation premium, IP, is built into all nominal market interest rates.) In the absence of inflation, NPV can thus be calculated in either of two ways:

$$\text{NPV (no inflation)} = \sum_{t=0}^{n} \frac{RCF_t}{(1 + k_r)^t} = \sum_{t=0}^{n} \frac{NCF_t}{(1 + k_n)^t}. \qquad \textbf{10-2}$$

Now suppose the expected rate of inflation is positive, and we expect *all* of the project's cash flows — including those related to depreciation — to rise at the rate i. Further, assume that this same inflation rate, i, is built into the market cost of capital as

---

[14]For a formal discussion of this subject, see James C. Van Horne, "A Note on Biases in Capital Budgeting Introduced by Inflation," *Journal of Financial and Quantitative Analysis,* January 1971, 653–658; Philip L. Cooley, Rodney L. Roenfeldt, and It-Keong Chew, "Capital Budgeting Procedures under Inflation," *Financial Management,* Winter 1975, 18–27; and "Cooley, Roenfeldt, and Chew vs. Findlay and Frankle," *Financial Management,* Autumn 1976, 83–90.

an inflation premium, IP = i. In this situation, the nominal net cash flow, NCF_t, will increase annually at the rate of i percent, producing this result:

$$NCF_t = RCF_t(1 + i)^t.$$

For example, if we expected a net cash flow of \$100 in Year 5 in the absence of inflation, then with a 5 percent annual rate of inflation, $NCF_5 = \$100(1.05)^5 = \$127.63$.

In general, the cost of capital used as the discount rate in capital budgeting analysis is based on the market-determined costs of debt and equity, so it is a nominal rate. To convert a real interest rate to a nominal rate when the inflation rate is i, we use this formula:

$$(1 + k_n) = (1 + k_r)(1 + i).$$

For example, if the real cost of capital is 7 percent and the inflation rate is 5 percent, then $1 + k_n = (1.07)(1.05) = 1.1235$, so $k_n = 12.35\%$.

Now if net cash flows increase at the rate of i percent per year, and if this same inflation premium is built into the firm's cost of capital, then the NPV would be calculated as follows:

$$\text{NPV (with inflation)} = \sum_{t=0}^{n} \frac{NCF_t}{(1 + k_n)^t} = \sum_{t=0}^{n} \frac{RCF_t\,(1 + i)^t}{(1 + k_r)^t\,(1 + i)^t}. \qquad \textbf{10-3}$$

Since the $(1 + i)^t$ terms in the numerator and denominator cancel, we are left with Equation 10-2:

$$\text{NPV} = \sum_{t=0}^{n} \frac{RCF_t}{(1 + k_r)^t}.$$

Thus, if all costs and also the sales price, hence annual cash flows, are expected to rise at the same inflation rate that investors have built into the cost of capital, then the inflation-adjusted NPV as determined using Equation 10-3 is identical to the real NPV found using Equation 10-2.[15]

However, firms occasionally use base year, or constant (unadjusted), dollars throughout the analysis — say, 1997 dollars if the analysis is done in 1997 — along with a cost of capital as determined in the marketplace as we described in Chapter 8. This is wrong: *If the cost of capital includes an inflation premium, as it typically does, but the cash flows are all stated in constant (unadjusted) dollars, then the calculated NPV will be downward biased.* The denominator will reflect inflation, but the numerator will not, and this will produce a downward biased NPV.

---

[15]To focus on inflation effects, we have simplified the situation somewhat. The actual project cost of capital is made up of debt and equity components, both of which are affected by inflation, but only the debt component is adjusted for tax effects. Thus, the relationship between nominal and real costs of capital is more complex than indicated in our discussion here.

MAKING THE INFLATION ADJUSTMENT

There are two ways to adjust for inflation. First, all project cash flows can be expressed as real (unadjusted) flows, with no consideration of inflation, and then the cost of capital can be adjusted to a real rate by removing the inflation premiums from the component costs. This approach is relatively simple, but to produce an unbiased NPV it requires (1) that all project cash flows, including depreciation, be affected identically by inflation, and (2) that this rate of increase equals the inflation rate built into investors' required returns. Since these assumptions do not necessarily hold in practice, this method is not commonly used.

The second method involves leaving the cost of capital in its nominal form, and then adjusting the individual cash flows to reflect the impact of inflation. This is what we did earlier in our RIC example as summarized in Table 10-4. There we assumed that sales prices, variable costs, and fixed overhead costs would all increase at a rate of 6 percent per year but that depreciation charges would not be affected by inflation. Of course, we could have assumed different rates of inflation for sales prices, for variable costs, and for fixed overheads. For example, RIC might have long-term labor contracts which cause wage rates to rise with the Consumer Price Index (CPI), but its raw materials might be purchased under a fixed price contract, with the net result that variable costs are expected to rise by a smaller percentage than sales prices. In any event, one should build inflation into the cash flow analysis, with the specific adjustment reflecting as accurately as possible the most likely set of circumstances. With a spreadsheet, it is easy to make the adjustments.

Our conclusions about inflation may be summarized as follows. First, inflation is critically important, for it can and does have major effects on businesses. Therefore, it must be recognized and dealt with. Second, the most effective way of dealing with inflation in capital budgeting analyses is to build inflation estimates into each cash flow element, using the best available information on how each element will be affected. Third, since we cannot estimate future inflation rates with precision, errors are bound to be made. Thus, inflation adds to the uncertainty, or riskiness, of capital budgeting as well as to its complexity.

Under what seemingly straightforward method of analysis would inflation cause a bias in a project's estimated NPV? Would the bias be upward or downward?

What is the best way of handling inflation, and how does this procedure eliminate the potential bias?

SELF-TEST QUESTIONS

SUMMARY

This chapter discussed several issues in project cash flow analysis. The key concepts covered are listed below:

- The most important, but also the most difficult, step in capital budgeting is *estimating the incremental after-tax cash flows* a project will produce.

- In determining incremental cash flows, *opportunity costs* (the cash flows foregone by using an asset the company already owns) must be included, but *sunk costs* (cash outlays that have been made and that cannot be recouped) are not included. Any effects of a project on other parts of the firm should also be included in the analysis.

- *Tax laws* affect cash flow analyses in two ways: (1) They reduce operating cash flows, and (2) they determine the depreciation expense that can be taken in each year.

- Capital projects often require an additional investment in *net working capital (NWC),* which must be included in the project's cost and then shown as a cash inflow at the end of the project's life.

- *Replacement analysis* is slightly different from that for *expansion projects* because the cash flows from the old asset must be taken into account.

- Cash flow *estimation bias* will occur if managers are overly optimistic in their forecasts.

- A project may have an *option value* that is not accounted for in a conventional discounted cash flow analysis.

- If mutually exclusive projects have *unequal lives,* it may be necessary to place the projects on an equal life basis. This can be done using either the *replacement chain* approach or the *equivalent annual annuity* approach.

- A project's value may be greater than the NPV of its physical life if it can be *abandoned* at some earlier time.

- *Inflation effects* must be considered. The best procedure is to build inflation directly into the cash flow estimates.

We continue our discussion of capital budgeting analysis in Chapter 11, where we discuss risk analysis and the optimal capital budget.

0-1 Define each of the following terms:
   a. Cash flow; accounting income
   b. Incremental cash flow; sunk cost; opportunity cost
   c. Net working capital changes
   d. Salvage value
   e. Replacement decision
   f. Replacement chain
   g. Equivalent annual annuity
   h. Abandonment value
   i. Real rate of return, k_r, versus nominal rate of return, k_n
   j. Cash flow estimation bias
   k. Option value

0-2 Operating cash flows, rather than accounting profits, are listed in Table 10-4. What is the basis for this emphasis on cash flows as opposed to net income?

0-3 Why is it true, in general, that a failure to adjust expected cash flows for expected inflation biases the calculated NPV downward?

0-4 Suppose a firm is considering two mutually exclusive projects. One has a life of six years and the other a life of ten years. Would the failure to employ some type of replacement chain analysis bias an NPV analysis against one of the projects? Explain.

0-5 Look at Table 10-7 and answer these questions:

   a. Why is the salvage value shown on Line 12 reduced for taxes on Line 13?
   b. Why is depreciation on the old machine deducted on Line 8 to get Line 9?
   c. What would happen if the new machine permitted a *reduction* in net working capital?
   d. Why are the cost savings on Line 6 reduced by multiplying the before-tax figure by $(1 - T)$, whereas the change in depreciation figure on Line 9 is multiplied by T?

(SOLUTIONS APPEAR IN APPENDIX C)

T-1 NEW PROJECT ANALYSIS You have been asked by the president of the Farr Construction Company to evaluate the proposed acquisition of a new earth mover. The mover's basic price is $50,000, and it would cost another $10,000 to modify it for special use. Assume that the mover falls into the MACRS 3-year class, it would be sold after 3 years for $20,000, and it would require an increase in net working capital (spare parts inventory) of $2,000. The earth mover would have no effect on revenues, but it is expected to save the firm $20,000 per year in before-tax operating costs, mainly labor. The firm's marginal federal-plus-state tax rate is 40 percent.
   a. What is the net cost of the earth mover? (That is, what are the Year 0 cash flows?)
   b. What are the operating cash flows in Years 1, 2, and 3?

c. What are the additional (nonoperating) cash flows in Year 3?

d. If the project's cost of capital is 10 percent, should the earth mover be purchased?

ST-2   **REPLACEMENT PROJECT ANALYSIS**   The Erickson Toy Corporation currently uses an injection molding machine that was purchased 2 years ago. This machine is being depreciated on a straight line basis toward a $500 salvage value, and it has 6 years of remaining life. Its current book value is $2,600, and it can be sold for $3,000 at this time. Assume, for ease of calculation, that the annual depreciation expense is $350 per year.

The firm is offered a replacement machine which has a cost of $8,000, an estimated useful life of 6 years, and an estimated salvage value of $800. This machine falls into the MACRS 5-year class. The replacement machine would permit an output expansion, so sales would rise by $1,000 per year; even so, the new machine's much greater efficiency would still cause operating expenses to decline by $1,500 per year. The new machine would require that inventories be increased by $2,000, but accounts payable would simultaneously increase by $500.

The firm's marginal federal-plus-state tax rate is 40 percent, and its cost of capital is 15 percent. Should it replace the old machine?

PROBLEMS

10-1   **DEPRECIATION EFFECTS**   Susan Fischer, great-granddaughter of the founder of Taussig Tile Products and current president of the company, believes in simple, conservative accounting. In keeping with her philosophy, she has decreed that the company shall use alternative straight line depreciation, based on the MACRS class lives, for all newly acquired assets. Your boss, the financial vice-president and the only non-family officer, has asked you to develop an exhibit which shows how much this policy costs the company in terms of market value. Ms. Fischer is interested in increasing the value of the firm's stock because she fears a family stockholder revolt which might remove her from office. For your exhibit, assume that the company spends $50 million each year on new capital projects, that the projects have on average a 10-year class life, that the company has a 10 percent cost of debt, and that its tax rate is 34 percent. (Hint: Show how much the NPV of projects in an average year would increase if Taussig used the standard MACRS recovery allowances. Also, ignore the half-year convention on the straight line calculation.)

10-2   **NEW PROJECT ANALYSIS**   You have been asked by the president of your company to evaluate the proposed acquisition of a new spectrometer for the firm's R&D department. The equipment's basic price is $70,000, and it would cost another $15,000 to modify it for special use by your firm. The spectrometer, which falls into the MACRS 3-year class, would be sold after 3 years for $30,000. Use of the equipment would require an increase in net working capital (spare parts inventory) of $4,000. The spectrometer would have no effect on revenues, but it is expected to save the firm $25,000 per year in before-tax operating costs, mainly labor. The firm's marginal federal-plus-state tax rate is 40 percent.

a. What is the net cost of the spectrometer? (That is, what is the Year 0 net cash flow?)

b. What are the net operating cash flows in Years 1, 2, and 3?

c. What is the additional (nonoperating) cash flow in Year 3?

d. If the project's cost of capital is 10 percent, should the spectrometer be purchased?

)-3 **REPLACEMENT ANALYSIS** The Wingler Equipment Company purchased a machine 5 years ago at a cost of $100,000. It had an expected life of 10 years at the time of purchase and an expected salvage value of $10,000 at the end of the 10 years. It is being depreciated by the straight line method toward a salvage value of $10,000, or by $9,000 per year.

A new machine can be purchased for $150,000, including installation costs. Over its 5-year life, it will reduce cash operating expenses by $50,000 per year. Sales are not expected to change. At the end of its useful life, the machine is estimated to be worthless. MACRS depreciation will be used, and it will be depreciated over its 3-year class life rather than its 5-year economic life.

The old machine can be sold today for $65,000. The firm's tax rate is 34 percent. The appropriate discount rate is 15 percent.

a. If the new machine is purchased, what is the amount of the initial cash flow at Year 0?

b. What incremental operating cash flows will occur at the end of Years 1 through 5 as a result of replacing the old machine?

c. What incremental nonoperating cash flow will occur at the end of Year 5 if the new machine is purchased?

d. What is the NPV of this project? Should the firm replace the old machine?

)-4 **UNEQUAL LIVES** Filkins Fabric Company is considering the replacement of its old, fully depreciated knitting machine. Two new models are available: Machine 190-3, which has a cost of $190,000, a 3-year expected life, and after-tax cash flows (labor savings and depreciation) of $87,000 per year; and Machine 360-6, which has a cost of $360,000, a 6-year life, and after-tax cash flows of $98,300 per year. Knitting machine prices are not expected to rise, because inflation will be offset by cheaper components (microprocessors) used in the machines. Assume that Filkins' cost of capital is 14 percent.

a. Should the firm replace its old knitting machine, and, if so, which new machine should it use?

b. Suppose the firm's basic patents will expire in 9 years, and the company expects to go out of business at that time. Assume further that the firm depreciates its assets using the straight line method, that its marginal federal-plus-state tax rate is 40 percent, and that the used machines can be sold at their book values. Under these circumstances, should the company replace the old machine and, if so, which new model should the company purchase?

)-5 **ABANDONMENT VALUE** The Scampini Supplies Company recently purchased a new delivery truck. The new truck cost $22,500, and it is expected to generate net after-tax operating cash flows, including depreciation, of $6,250 per year. The truck has a 5-year expected life. The expected abandonment values (salvage values after tax adjustments) for the truck are given below. The company's cost of capital is 10 percent.

YEAR	ANNUAL OPERATING CASH FLOW	ABANDONMENT VALUE
0	($22,500)	$22,500
1	6,250	17,500
2	6,250	14,000
3	6,250	11,000
4	6,250	5,000
5	6,250	0

a. Should the firm operate the truck until the end of its 5-year physical life, or, if not, what is its optimal economic life?

b. Would the introduction of abandonment values, in addition to operating cash flows, ever *reduce* the expected NPV and/or IRR of a project?

10-6   INFLATION ADJUSTMENTS The Rodriguez Company is considering an average-risk investment in a mineral water spring project that has a cost of $150,000. The project will produce 1,000 cases of mineral water per year indefinitely. The current sales price is $138 per case, and the current cost per case (all variable) is $105. The firm is taxed at a rate of 34 percent. Both prices and costs are expected to rise at a rate of 6 percent per year. The firm uses only equity, and it has a cost of capital of 15 percent. Assume that cash flows consist only of after-tax profits, since the spring has an indefinite life and will not be depreciated.

a. Should the firm accept the project? (Hint: The project is a perpetuity, so you must use the formula for a perpetuity to find its NPV.)

b. If total costs consisted of a fixed cost of $10,000 per year and variable costs of $95 per unit, and if only the variable costs were expected to increase with inflation, would this make the project better or worse? Continue with the assumption that the sales price will rise with inflation.

S P R E A D S H E E T
A P P L I C A T I O N S

SPREADSHEET PROBLEM 1

McLaughlin Mills is evaluating the proposed acquisition of a new milling machine. The machine's base price is $180,000, and it would cost another $25,000 to modify it for special use by your firm. The machine falls into the MACRS 3-year class, and it would be sold after 3 years for $80,000. The machine would require an increase in net working capital (inventory) of $7,500. The machine would have no effect on revenues, but it is expected to save the firm $75,000 per year in before-tax operating costs, mainly labor. McLaughlin's marginal tax rate is 34 percent.

a. What is the net cost of the machine for capital budgeting purposes? (That is, what is the Year 0 net cash flow?)

b. What are the operating cash flows in Years 1, 2, and 3?

c. What is the additional (nonoperating) cash flow in Year 3?

d. If the project's cost of capital is 10 percent, should the machine be purchased?

e. Determine the NPV if the cost of capital were (1) to rise to 12 percent or (2) to fall to 8 percent.

f. There is some uncertainty about the salvage value. It could be as low as $50,000 or as high as $90,000. What would the NPV be at those two salvage value levels? (Assume k = 10 percent.) Should this uncertainty affect the decision to invest? What salvage value (to the nearest thousand) would make you indifferent to the project?

g. Return to the original salvage value of $80,000. What would be the project's NPV if the corporate tax rate were increased to 46 percent?

h. Return the tax rate to 34 percent. Now assume that the manufacturer of the machine calls you with bad news: The base price of the machine has increased to $200,000. What does this do to the project's NPV? At what cost (to the nearest hundred) would McLaughlin be indifferent to the project?

SPREADSHEET PROBLEM 2

The Orange Fizz Company is contemplating the replacement of one of its bottling machines with a newer and more efficient one. The old machine has a book value of $500,000 and a remaining useful life of 5 years. The firm does not expect to realize any return from scrapping the old machine in 5 years, but it can sell it now to another firm in the industry for $200,000. The old machine is being depreciated toward a zero salvage value, or by $100,000 per year, using the straight line method.

The new machine has a purchase price of $1.2 million, an estimated useful life and MACRS class life of 5 years, and an estimated salvage value of $175,000. It is expected to economize on electric power usage, labor, and repair costs, and also to reduce the number of defective bottles. In total, an annual savings of $275,000 will be realized if it is installed. The company is in the 40 percent federal-plus-state tax bracket, and it has a 10 percent cost of capital.

a. What is the initial cash outlay required for the new machine?
b. Calculate the annual depreciation allowances for both machines, and compute the change in the annual depreciation expense if the replacement is made.
c. What are the operating cash flows in Years 1 to 5?
d. What is the cash flow from the salvage value in Year 5?
e. Should the firm purchase the new machine? Support your answer.
f. In general, how would each of the following factors affect the investment decision, and how should each be treated?
   (1) The expected life of the existing machine decreases.
   (2) The cost of capital is not constant but is increasing.
g. The firm may be able to purchase an alternative new bottling machine from another supplier. Its purchase price would be $1,050,000, and its salvage value would be $250,000. This machine has a lower annual operating savings of $210,000. Should the firm purchase this machine?
h. If the salvage value on the alternative new machine were $200,000 rather than $250,000, how would this affect the decision?
i. With everything as in Part h, assume that the cost of capital declined from 10 percent to 8 percent. How would this affect the decision?

SPREADSHEET PROBLEM 3

The Dalrymple Company is evaluating an average-risk capital project having both a 3-year economic and MACRS class life. The net investment outlay at Time 0 is $18,800. The expected end-of-year cash flows, expressed in Time 0 dollars, are listed below: (Ignore salvage value and Year 4 depreciation.)

	YEAR 1	YEAR 2	YEAR 3
Revenues	$30,000	$30,000	$30,000
Variable costs	15,000	15,000	15,000
Fixed costs	6,500	6,500	6,500
Depreciation	6,204	8,460	2,820

The firm has a marginal federal-plus-state tax rate of 40 percent. Dalrymple's current cost of debt is 12 percent, and its cost of equity is 16 percent. These costs include an estimated inflation premium of 6 percent. The firm's target capital structure is 50 percent debt and 50 percent equity.

a. What is the firm's nominal WACC? Its real WACC?
b. What are the project's relevant real cash flows? What discount rate should be utilized when calculating a project's NPV based upon real cash flows? Why?
c. What is the NPV for this project? Should this project be accepted? What might have occurred if you had used the *nominal* WACC with *real* cash flows?

d. Now assume that all revenues and costs, except depreciation, are expected to increase at the inflation rate of 6 percent. What are the project's nominal cash flows and NPV based on these flows? Why is this NPV different from the NPV calculated in Part c?

e. Assume that the firm's management anticipates a rate of inflation resulting in a 6 percent inflation premium for Year 1 through Year 3. Based upon this assumption, the firm accepts the project. However, suppose the firm actually experiences nonneutral inflation such that revenues increase by only 6 percent, while variable and fixed costs increase by 7.5 percent. What are the actual after-tax cash flows in this case? What effect would the acceptance of the project, coupled with unanticipated nonneutral inflation, have had upon the value of the firm?

f. If a company, in its capital budgeting process, bases its cash flows on sales prices and unit costs at the time it analyzes the project, (1) would this tend to produce systematic errors in its capital budgeting evaluations, (2) would any such error be more serious for long-term or short-term projects, and (3) if you do think that systematic errors are likely to occur, how could they be corrected?

MINI CASE

John Crockett Furniture Company is considering adding a new line to its product mix, and the capital budgeting analysis is being conducted by Joan Samuels, a recently graduated finance MBA. The production line would be set up in unused space in Crockett's main plant. The machinery's invoice price would be approximately $200,000; another $10,000 in shipping charges would be required; and it would cost an additional $30,000 to install the equipment. Further, the firm's inventories would have to be increased by $25,000 to handle the new line, but its accounts payable would rise by $5,000. The machinery has an economic life of 4 years, and Crockett has obtained a special tax ruling which places the equipment in the MACRS 3-year class. The machinery is expected to have a salvage value of $25,000 after 4 years of use.

The new line would generate $125,000 in incremental net revenues (before taxes and excluding depreciation) in each of the next 4 years. The firm's tax rate is 40 percent, and its overall weighted average cost of capital is 10 percent.

a. Set up, without numbers, a time line for the project's cash flows.

b. (1) Construct incremental operating cash flow statements for the project's 4 years of operations.

   (2) Does your cash flow statement include any financial flows such as interest expense or dividends? Why or why not?

c. (1) Suppose the firm had spent $100,000 last year to rehabilitate the production line site. Should this cost be included in the analysis? Explain.

   (2) Now assume that the plant space could be leased out to another firm at $25,000 a year. Should this be included in the analysis? If so, how?

   (3) Finally, assume that the new product line is expected to decrease sales of the firm's other lines by $50,000 per year. Should this be considered in the analysis? If so, how?

d. Disregard the assumptions in Part c. What is Crockett's net investment outlay on this project? What is the net nonoperating cash flow at the time the project is terminated? Based on these cash flows, what are the project's NPV, IRR, MIRR, and payback? Do these indicators suggest that the project should be undertaken?

e. Assume now that the project is a replacement project rather than a new, or expansion, project. Describe how the analysis would differ for a replacement project.

f. Explain what is meant by cash flow estimation bias. What are some steps that Crockett's management could take to eliminate the incentives for bias in the decision process?

g. Do you think it likely that the project being considered here might have option value over and above the indicated NPV? If so, how might this be handled?

h. Assume that inflation is expected to average 5 percent over the next 4 years. Does it appear that Crockett's cash flow estimates are real or nominal? That is, are all the cash flows stated in the Time 0 dollars or have the cash flows been increased to account for expected inflation? Further, would it appear that the 10 percent cost of capital is a nominal or real interest rate? Does it appear that the current NPV is biased because of inflation effects? If so, in what direction, and how could any bias be removed?

i. In an unrelated analysis, Joan was asked to choose between the following two mutually exclusive projects:

	EXPECTED NET CASH FLOW	
YEAR	PROJECT S	PROJECT L
0	($100,000)	($100,000)
1	60,000	33,500
2	60,000	33,500
3	—	33,500
4	—	33,500

The projects provide a necessary service, so whichever one is selected is expected to be repeated into the foreseeable future. Both projects have a 10 percent cost of capital.

(1) What is each project's initial NPV without replication?

(2) Now apply the replacement chain approach to determine the projects' extended NPVs. Which project should be chosen?

(3) Repeat the analysis using the equivalent annual annuity approach.

(4) Now assume that the cost to replicate Project S in 2 years will increase to $105,000 because of inflationary pressures. How should the analysis be handled now, and which project should be chosen?

j. Crockett is also considering another project which has a physical life of 3 years; that is, the machinery will be totally worn-out after 3 years. However, if the project were abandoned prior to the end of 3 years, the machinery would have a positive salvage (or abandonment) value. Here are the project's estimated cash flows:

YEAR	INITIAL INVESTMENT AND OPERATING CASH FLOWS	END-OF-YEAR NET ABANDONMENT VALUE
0	($5,000)	$5,000
1	2,100	3,100
2	2,000	2,000
3	1,750	0

Using the 10 percent cost of capital, what is the project's NPV if it is operated for the full 3 years? Would the NPV change if the company planned to abandon the project at the end of Year 2? At the end of Year 1? What is the project's optimal (economic) life?

SELECTED ADDITIONAL REFERENCES AND CASES

Several articles have been written regarding the implications of the Accelerated Cost Recovery System (ACRS). Among them are the following:

Angell, Robert J., and Tony R. Wingler, "A Note on Expensing versus Depreciating Under the Accelerated Cost Recovery System," *Financial Management,* Winter 1982, 34-35.

McCarty, Daniel E., and William R. McDaniel, "A Note on Expensing versus Depreciating Under the Accelerated Cost Recovery System: Comment," *Financial Management,* Summer 1983, 37-39.

For further information on replacement analysis, as well as other aspects of capital budgeting, see the texts by Bierman and Smidt; by Grant, Ireson, and Leavenworth; by Levy and Sarnat; and by Seitz referenced in Chapter 9.

Three additional papers on the impact of inflation on capital budgeting are the following:

Bailey, Andrew D., and Daniel L. Jensen, "General Price Level Adjustments in the Capital Budgeting Decision," *Financial Management,* Spring 1977, 26-32.

Mehta, Dileep R., Michael D. Curley, and Hung-Gay Fung, "Inflation, Cost of Capital, and Capital Budgeting Procedures," *Financial Management,* Winter 1984, 48-54.

Rappaport, Alfred, and Robert A. Taggart, Jr., "Evaluation of Capital Expenditure Proposals Under Inflation," *Financial Management,* Spring 1982, 5-13.

For additional insights into unequal life analysis, see

Emery, Gary W., "Some Guidelines for Evaluating Capital Investment Alternatives with Unequal Lives," *Financial Management,* Spring 1982, 15-19.

For an interesting discussion on cash flow estimation and abandonment biases, see

Statman, Meir, and David Caldwell, "Applying Behavioral Finance to Capital Budgeting: Project Terminations," *Financial Management,* Winter 1987, 7-13.

Statman, Meir, and Tyzoon T. Tyebjee, "Optimistic Capital Budgeting Forecasts: An Experiment," *Financial Management,* Autumn 1985, 27-33.

The following articles pertain to other topics in this chapter:

Bjerksund, Petter, and Steinar Ekern, "Managing Investment Opportunities Under Price Uncertainty: From 'Last Chance' to 'Wait and See' Strategies," *Financial Management,* Autumn 1990, 65-83.

Chen, Son-Nan, "Optimal Asset Abandonment and Replacement: Tax and Replacement Considerations," *Financial Review,* May 1991, 157-177.

Kroll, Yoram, "On the Differences between Accrual Accounting Figures and Cash Flows: The Case of Working Capital," *Financial Management,* Spring 1985, 75-82.

Kulatilaka, Nalin, and Alan J. Marcus, "Project Valuation under Uncertainty: When Does DCF Fail," *Journal of Applied Corporate Finance,* Fall 1992, 92–100.

Mukherjee, Tarun K., "Reducing the Uncertainty-Induced Bias in Capital Budgeting Decisions — A Hurdle Rate Approach," *Journal of Business Finance & Accounting,* September 1991, 747–753.

Triantis, Alexander J., and James E. Hodder, "Valuing Flexibility as a Complex Option," *Journal of Finance,* June 1990, 549–565.

The Cases in Financial Management: Dryden Request *series contains the following cases which focus on Chapter 9 and 10 material:*

Case 12, "Indian River Citrus Company (A), Case 12A, "Cranfield, Inc. (A)," and Case 14, "Robert Montoya, Inc. (A)," which focus on cash flow estimation but also include capital budgeting decision methods.

CHAPTER 11

Risk Analysis and the Optimal Capital Budget

implesse, *a fat substitute developed by NutraSweet Corporation, was supposed to ensure the company's success and usher in an era of guilt-free gluttony for America's calorie counters and cholesterol watchers. It promised all the taste virtues of real fat but with none of the associated vices. To some, it seemed too good to be true.*

Simplesse is a highly processed mixture of whipped egg whites and skim milk intended to simulate not only the taste of fat but also its rich texture, its so-called "mouthfeel." Fat is what makes mayonnaise slippery and potato chips crunchy; it provides the creaminess in Häagen-Dazs ice cream and the gratifying greasiness in a Big Mac. However, consumers recognize the dark side of fat: It tastes great, but it can cause "spare tires" and heart disease.

As an ingredient, Simplesse is temperamental. It curdles when heated too high, which makes it hard to use in cooking. It requires refrigeration, and its shelf life is short. Still, about $100 million went into the development of Simplesse. To justify the expenditure, NutraSweet's managers estimated that Simplesse would provide $444 million in revenues and $20 million in annual profits. Although most of the profits were expected to come from sales to other food companies for use in various food products, to get the ball rolling NutraSweet decided to develop a Simplesse product itself — Simple Pleasures, an imitation ice cream.

The research team's goal was to produce a product that rivaled Häagen-Dazs's vanilla flavor. During in-house testing, senior managers would give samples to junior managers and ask, "Doesn't it taste like Häagen-Dazs?" Needless to say, everyone replied, "Yes, it tastes just like Häagen-Dazs." In reality, it tasted more like chalk, and early versions of Simple Pleasures melted too slowly and left a scummy ring around the bowl. To add to the problems, NutraSweet badly underestimated how much it would cost to make and market the product and how difficult it would be to move from making small batches in the lab to large-scale production runs.

In the end, Simple Pleasures captured about 8 percent of the nonfat ice cream market. The consensus among consumers seems to be that although Simple Pleasures isn't dreadful, it isn't like real ice cream. It compares favorably in taste and texture with other nonfat ice creams, but it is considerably more expensive.

What do NutraSweet's problems have to do with capital budgeting? It is clear that the cash flows associated with new projects are not known with certainty. Indeed, for most projects, there is much uncertainty, and uncertainty creates risk. In this chapter, we discuss procedures that are used to assess risk and incorporate it into the decision process. As you read the chapter, consider how NutraSweet might have used these procedures in its analysis of the Simplesse/Simple Pleasures project.

Risk analysis is important in all financial decisions, especially those relating to capital budgeting. As we saw in Chapter 4, the higher the risk associated with a security, the higher its required rate of return. This situation is also true for capital projects. In this chapter, we discuss procedures for assessing risk and incorporating it into capital budgeting decisions. Also, we discuss how firms determine their optimal capital budgets.

INTRODUCTION TO PROJECT RISK

Three separate and distinct types of project risk can be defined: (1) *stand-alone risk,* which views a project's risk in isolation, hence without regard to portfolio effects; (2) *within-firm risk,* also called *corporate risk,* which views project risk within the context of the firm's portfolio of assets; and (3) *market risk,* which recognizes that the firm's stockholders hold diversified portfolios of stocks. As we shall see, a particular project might have highly uncertain returns, thus have high stand-alone risk, yet taking it on might not have much effect on either the firm's corporate risk or the risk of its owners, once portfolio effects are taken into account.

Figure 11-1 provides a framework for analyzing the riskiness of a project. The figure is rather formidable, so before going through it in detail, it is useful to explain briefly what it is all about. First, the top section shows that a project's riskiness depends on the uncertainty inherent in its cash flows (σ_P), on the correlation between those flows and returns on the firm's other assets (r_{PF}), and on the correlation between the project's flows and stock market returns (r_{PM}). Projects with highly uncertain flows as measured by σ_P actually may not be very risky if those flows are negatively correlated with returns on other assets or stocks in general. Second, the two middle boxes show how a project's beta coefficient can be calculated and used to help assess its risk. Finally, the graphs in the lower section show that, in general, diversification lowers the riskiness of an individual project vis-à-vis its riskiness if there were no diversification either within the firm or with other stocks.

Exactly how all this works is explained in the remainder of this section, and the ways risk is measured and used in capital budgeting are discussed in later sections. Here is a detailed discussion of the figure:

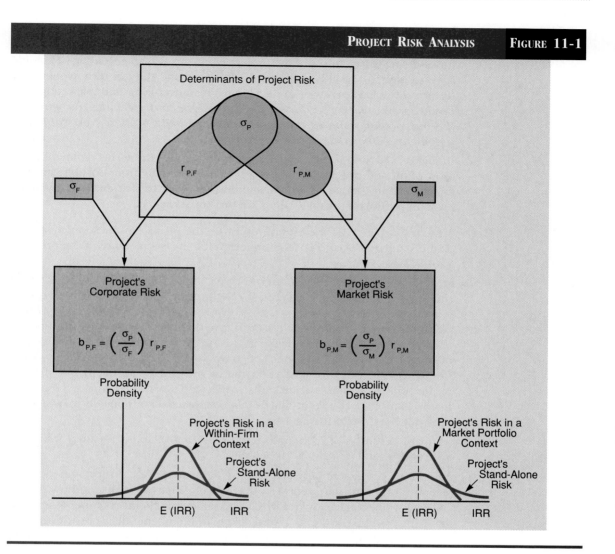

PROJECT RISK ANALYSIS   **FIGURE 11-1**

Determinants of Project Risk

σ_P

$r_{P,F}$

$r_{P,M}$

σ_F

σ_M

Project's
Corporate Risk

$$b_{P,F} = \left(\frac{\sigma_P}{\sigma_F}\right) r_{P,F}$$

Project's
Market Risk

$$b_{P,M} = \left(\frac{\sigma_P}{\sigma_M}\right) r_{P,M}$$

Probability
Density

Project's Risk in a
Within-Firm
Context

Project's
Stand-Alone
Risk

E (IRR)   IRR

Probability
Density

Project's Risk in a
Market Portfolio
Context

Project's
Stand-Alone
Risk

E (IRR)   IRR

1. Risk in Figure 11-1 and throughout the chapter relates to uncertainty about *future* events, and in capital budgeting, this means the *actual* returns on a project as compared with its expected returns. For certain types of projects, it is possible to look back at historical data and get a statistical estimate of the project's riskiness. This is often true when the investment involves an expansion decision. For example, if Sears were opening a new store, if Citibank were opening a new branch, or if GM were expanding its Chevrolet plant, then past experience could be used as a starting point for assessing the project's risk. Similarly, a company that is considering going into a new business might be able to look at historical data on existing firms in that business and get an idea about its riskiness. However, there are times when it is impossible to obtain

historical data regarding proposed investments. For example, if GM were considering the production of an electric auto, not much relevant historical data for assessing the riskiness of the project would be available. Rather, GM would have to rely on the judgment of its executives, and they, in turn, would have to rely on their experience in developing, manufacturing, and marketing new products. *We will try to quantify risk analysis, but you must recognize at the outset that some of the data will necessarily be based on subjective judgments rather than historical statistics.*

2. In Figure 11-1, and in risk analysis generally, we use the terms defined below. Most of these terms and concepts were drawn directly from portfolio analysis as set forth in Chapter 4, so you should refer back to that chapter if you are hazy on portfolio concepts. Here are the key terms:

σ_P = standard deviation of the rate of return on the project in question, measured as the standard deviation of the project's IRR. σ_P is a measure of the project's *stand-alone risk.*

σ_F = standard deviation of the rate of return on the firm's assets before it takes on the project in question, measured as (Net income + Interest)/(Debt + Equity). Note that the firm's average rate of return is, in effect, a rough average of realized IRRs on past projects, and if σ_F is low, then the firm is stable and its *corporate risk* is relatively low, while if σ_F is high, then the firm has a high degree of corporate risk, and its chances of going bankrupt are higher than if σ_F were low. The value of σ_F for past years can be measured statistically, but changes in the firm's situation may make its *expected future corporate riskiness* different from its past risk, in which case a subjectively estimated σ_F would be preferable for use in the analysis.

σ_M = standard deviation of the market's returns. This value is measured using historical data, and it is about 18 percent.

r_{PF} = correlation coefficient between the rate of return on the project and the average rate of return on the firm's other assets. What we want to know is this: Will this project have low returns at the same time the firm's other assets also have low returns, or are its returns likely to be independent of (or even negatively correlated with) returns on the firm's other assets? This correlation can be determined statistically for certain types of projects, but for many others it must be assessed subjectively.

r_{PM} = correlation coefficient between the rate of return on the project and returns on a stock market index, or "the market." If this correlation, which generally must be assessed subjectively on the basis of judgment and experience, is positive, then the project will tend to produce high returns when the economy, and most stocks, are also doing well.

b_{PF} = *corporate beta coefficient* of the project. It is found (conceptually) by regressing the project's expected returns under different economic states against expected returns on the firm's other assets. If you think of the project as a stock, and the firm as the market, then b_{PF} is found (conceptually) the same way stock betas were found back in Chapter 4. Note also that we can use the following formula, which was developed in Chapter 4, to calculate a project's corporate beta:

$$b_{PF} = \left(\frac{\sigma_P}{\sigma_F}\right)r_{PF}.$$

Here we see that the project's corporate beta is a function of its stand-alone risk, σ_P, the riskiness of the firm's other assets, σ_F, and the correlation coefficient between the returns on the project and those on the firm's other assets. Thus, the corporate beta is a measure of the project's contribution to the firm's *corporate risk,* just as a stock's beta is a measure of its contribution to the risk faced by a well-diversified investor who holds a broad portfolio of stocks.

b_{PM} = *market beta coefficient* of the project. This beta could (conceptually) be found by regressing the project's returns against returns on the market under different economic states. Again, we can express b_{PM} as an equation:

$$b_{PM} = \left(\frac{\sigma_P}{\sigma_M}\right)r_{PM}.$$

The project's *market beta* is a measure of the contribution of the project to the risk borne by the firm's stockholders, who are assumed to hold diversified portfolios.

3. Now look carefully at Figure 11-1. The upper box shows that there are three determinants of a project's risk: (1) the standard deviation of the project's forecasted returns, σ_P, (2) the correlation of those returns with the firm's other assets, r_{PF}, and (3) the correlation of the project's returns with the stock market, r_{PM}. As shown in the left-center panel, two of the project's risk attributes, σ_P and r_{PF}, combine with the standard deviation of returns on the firm's other assets, σ_F, to determine the project's corporate risk. Then, as shown in the right-center panel, two of the project's risk attributes, σ_P and r_{PM}, combine with the riskiness of the market, σ_M, to determine the project's contribution to the riskiness of a diversified investor, or the project's *market risk.*

4. We see that the project's stand-alone risk, σ_P, is especially important when assessing a project's riskiness, because that element is used in all three aspects of capital budgeting risk analysis.

5. Most projects are positively correlated with the firm's other assets, with the correlation being highest for projects in the firm's core business and less high (but still positive) for projects outside the core. However, the correlation coefficient is rarely +1.0. This being the case, some of most projects' stand-alone risk will be eliminated by within-firm diversification. Therefore, in the probability distribution graph shown at the lower-left corner of Figure 11-1, we show a flatter distribution for the illustrative project's stand-alone risk than for its risk within the context of the firm's portfolio of assets; this shows that a project's corporate risk is less than its stand-alone risk.

6. Most projects are also positively correlated with other assets in the economy — most corporate assets have high returns when the economy is strong, and vice versa — but again the correlation is usually not perfect, so the typical project's stand-alone risk is greater than its market risk. Hence, in the lower-right graph we drew the probability distribution curve for the project's stand-alone risk flatter than its distribution within a market portfolio context.

7. If a project's corporate beta, b_{PF}, is equal to 1.0, then the project has the same degree of corporate risk as an average project. If b_{PF} is greater than 1.0, the project has more than average corporate risk, and vice versa if b_{PF} is less than 1.0. A higher than average corporate risk would probably lead to the use of a higher than average project cost of capital, but there is no precise formula for specifying how much higher — the adjustment is a matter of judgment.

8. If the project's market beta, b_{PM}, is equal to the firm's market beta, then the project has the same degree of market risk as an average project. If b_{PM} is greater than the firm's beta, then the project has more than average market risk, and vice versa if b_{PM} is less than the firm's beta. Taking on a project with a higher than average market beta, where "average" is defined as the firm's beta, would lead to an increase in the corporate cost of capital, and the CAPM can be used to make the adjustment. We discuss this adjustment process later in the chapter.

9. People occasionally argue that stand-alone and corporate risk as we have defined them are not important — if a firm seeks to maximize shareholders' wealth, the only relevant risk is market risk. We disagree, for the following reasons:

    a. Undiversified stockholders, including the owners of small businesses, are more concerned about corporate risk than about market risk.

    b. Many financial theorists argue that investors, even those who are well diversified, consider factors other than market risk when setting required returns. One such factor is the risk of financial distress, which depends on a firm's corporate risk. Empirical studies of the determinants of required rates of return generally find both market and corporate risk to be important.

    c. The firm's stability is important to other stakeholders, including managers, workers, customers, suppliers, creditors, and the community in which it operates. Firms that are in serious danger of bankruptcy, or even of suffering low profits and reduced output, have difficulty attracting and retaining good managers and workers. Also, both suppliers and customers are reluctant to depend on weak firms, and such firms have difficulty borrowing money except at high interest rates. Finally, risky firms have trouble maintaining R&D programs, marketing programs, and the like. All of these factors tend to reduce risky firms' profitability, hence the prices of their stocks.

For all these reasons, corporate risk is also important, even to well-diversified stockholders.

Can the type of analysis implied in Figure 11-1 actually be applied in practice? The answer is no, because the data that are available are never sufficiently accurate. However, it is useful to keep Figure 11-1 in mind as you think about project risk, because the conceptual framework is extremely important.

What are the three types of project risk, and how are they measured?
How are the three risks related?
Why should managers be concerned with a project's corporate risk as well as its market risk?

**SELF-TEST
QUESTIONS**

STAND-ALONE RISK

A project's *stand-alone risk* is of little interest in and of itself. However, as we saw in Figure 11-1, stand-alone risk as measured by σ_P is an important determinant of both corporate and market risk. Therefore, firms spend a great deal of time and effort assessing stand-alone risk.

The starting point for analyzing a project's stand-alone risk involves determining the uncertainty inherent in its cash flows. This can be handled in a number of ways, ranging from informal judgments to complex economic and statistical analyses. To illustrate what's involved, refer back to the Regency Integrated Chips (RIC) watering system project that we discussed in Chapter 10. Most of the individual cash flows in Tables 10-3, 10-4, and 10-5, which produced the expected net cash flows for the project as set forth back in Table 10-6, are subject to uncertainty. For example, sales for 2000 were projected at 25,000 units to be sold at a price of $2,200 per unit, or $55 million in total. However, actual unit sales would almost certainly be somewhat higher or lower than 25,000, and the sales price would probably be different from $2,200 per unit. The sales quantity and price estimates are really expected values taken from probability distributions, as are many of the other values listed in Tables 10-3 through 10-5. The distributions could be relatively "tight," reflecting small standard deviations and low risk, or they could be "flat," denoting a great deal of uncertainty about the variable in question.

The variables' distributions, and their correlations with one another, determine the project's NPV and IRR distributions, thus its stand-alone risk. In the following sections, we discuss four techniques for assessing stand-alone risk: (1) sensitivity analysis, (2) scenario analysis, (3) Monte Carlo simulation, and (4) decision trees.

SENSITIVITY ANALYSIS

Intuitively, we know that many of the variables which determine a project's net cash flows are subject to some type of probability distribution, hence not known with certainty. We also know that if a key input variable such as units sold changes, so will the project's NPV and IRR. *Sensitivity analysis is a technique which indicates exactly how much the NPV or IRR will change in response to a given change in an input variable, other things held constant.*

Sensitivity analysis begins with a *base case* situation developed using each input's expected value. To illustrate, consider the data given in Table 10-4 in Chapter 10, where projected cash flows for RIC's watering system project are developed. The values for unit sales, sales price, fixed costs, and variable costs are the *expected,* or *base case, values,* and the resulting $12,075,384 NPV shown in Table 10-6 is called the *base case NPV.* Now we ask a series of "what if" questions: "What if unit sales fall

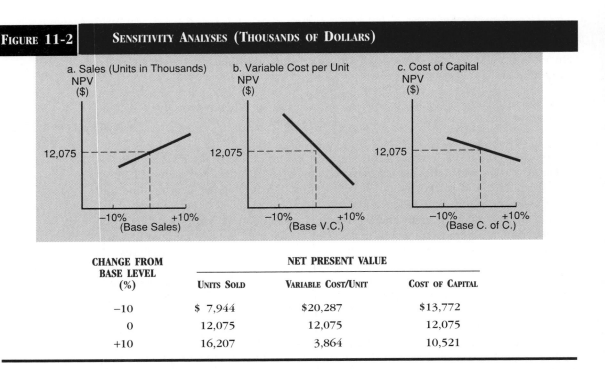

FIGURE 11-2   **SENSITIVITY ANALYSES (THOUSANDS OF DOLLARS)**

CHANGE FROM BASE LEVEL (%)	NET PRESENT VALUE		
	UNITS SOLD	VARIABLE COST/UNIT	COST OF CAPITAL
−10	$ 7,944	$20,287	$13,772
0	12,075	12,075	12,075
+10	16,207	3,864	10,521

20 percent below the expected level?" "What if the sales price per unit falls?" "What if variable costs are 70 percent of dollar sales rather than the expected 65 percent?" *Sensitivity analysis is designed to provide decision makers with answers to questions such as these.*

In a sensitivity analysis, we usually change each variable by specific percentages above and below its expected value, holding other things constant, then calculate new NPVs, and finally plot the new NPVs against the variable that was changed. Figure 11-2 shows the watering system project's sensitivity graphs for three of the key input variables. The table below the graphs gives the NPVs that were used to construct the graphs. The slopes of the lines in the graphs show how sensitive the project's NPV is to changes in each of the inputs: the steeper the slope, the more sensitive the NPV is to a change in the variable. Here we see that the project's NPV is very sensitive to changes in variable costs, fairly sensitive to changes in sales volume, and relatively insensitive to changes in the cost of capital.

If we were comparing two projects, the one with the steeper sensitivity lines would be regarded as riskier because a relatively small error in estimating an input such as the variable cost per unit would produce a large error in the project's projected NPV. Thus, sensitivity analysis can provide useful insights into the riskiness of a project.

Although sensitivity analysis is probably the most widely used risk analysis technique, it does have some limitations. Consider, for example, a proposed coal mine whose NPV is highly sensitive to changes in output and sales prices. However, if a utility company has contracted to buy a fixed amount of coal at an inflation-adjusted price per ton, then the mining venture may be quite safe in spite of its steep sensitivity lines. *In general, a project's stand-alone risk depends on both (1) the sensitivity of its NPV to changes in key variables and (2) the range of likely values of these variables as reflected in their probability distributions.* Because sensitivity analysis considers only the first factor, it is incomplete.

Before we move on, note these four additional points. (1) Computer spreadsheet models are ideally suited for performing sensitivity analyses, because such models automatically recalculate NPV when an input value is changed. We used a spreadsheet model to conduct the analyses represented in Figure 11-2, both to generate the tabular data and to plot the graphs. (2) We could have plotted all the sensitivity lines on one graph; this would have facilitated direct comparisons of the sensitivities among different input variables. (3) Sensitivity analysis provides decision makers with information regarding which input variables have the biggest effect on a project's profitability, hence where forecasting resources should be focused and/or where hedging would be most useful. (4) Sensitivity tables and graphs provide useful break-even information. For example, both the graph on the right and the tabular data in Figure 11-2 show that RIC's watering system project remains highly profitable even if the discount rate is increased by 10 percent, or from 11.5 percent to 11.5%(1.10) = 12.65%. This makes it clear that even a fairly large error in the cost of capital would not lead to an incorrect capital budgeting decision.

SCENARIO ANALYSIS

A stand-alone risk analysis technique that considers both the sensitivity of NPV to changes in key variables and the range of likely input values is *scenario analysis.* Here the financial analyst asks operating managers to pick a "bad" set of circumstances (low unit sales, low sales price, high variable cost per unit, high construction cost, and so on), an average, or "most likely" set, and a "good" set. The NPVs under the "bad" and "good" conditions are then calculated and compared with the "most likely" NPV.

As an example, consider again RIC's watering system project. Assume that RIC's managers are fairly confident of their estimates of all the variables except price and unit sales. Further, suppose they regard a drop in unit sales below 15,000 or a rise above 35,000 units as being extremely unlikely. Similarly, they expect the sales price as set in the marketplace to fall within the range of $1,700 to $2,700. Thus, 15,000 units at a price of $1,700 defines the lower bound, or the *worst case scenario,* while 35,000 units at a price of $2,700 defines the upper bound, or the *best case scenario.* Remember that the most likely values (which are the same as the base case values in this example) are 25,000 units and a price of $2,200. Also, note that the indicated sales prices are for 2000, with future years' prices expected to rise because of inflation.

TABLE 11-1	SCENARIO ANALYSIS					
SCENARIO	SALES VOLUME (UNITS)	SALES PRICE	NPV (THOUSANDS)	PROBABILITY × OF OUTCOME	= PRODUCT
Worst case	15,000	$1,700	($10,079)	0.25	($ 2,520)
Most likely case	25,000	2,200	12,075	0.50	6,038
Best case	35,000	2,700	41,752	0.25	10,438
				Expected NPV =	$13,956
				σ_{NPV} =	$18,421

NOTE: Inputs other than unit sales and sales price were set at their expected values.

To complete the scenario analysis, we set up a spreadsheet model which recalculated Table 10-4 and the other tables related to the project. Then we used the worst case input values to obtain the worst case NPV and the best case input values to obtain the best case NPV.[1] Table 11-1 summarizes the results. We see that the most likely case results in a positive NPV; the worst case produces a negative NPV; and the best case results in a very large positive NPV. The scenario analysis provides RIC's managers with one especially important piece of information — under the worst case assumptions, RIC will lose more than $10 million on the project. Given RIC's size, a loss of this magnitude can be absorbed without dire financial consequences, so the project will not threaten the firm's future. Thus, the watering system project is not a "bet the company" investment.

However, the fact that the project cannot sink the company does not mean that it has low risk. We can take a closer look at the project's stand-alone risk, using the NPV data to determine the expected NPV, standard deviation of NPV, and coefficient of variation of NPV as shown in Table 11-1. For this, we need an estimate of the probabilities of occurrence of the three scenarios. Suppose management estimates that there is a 25 percent probability of the worst case occurring, a 50 percent probability of the most likely case, and a 25 percent probability of the best case. Of course, it is *very difficult* to estimate scenario probabilities accurately.

The expected NPV (in thousands of dollars) is

$$0.25(-\$10,079) + 0.50(\$12,075) + 0.25(\$41,752) = \$13,956.$$

Note that the expected NPV is *not* the same as the base case NPV, $12,075 (in thousands). This is because the two uncertain variables, sales volume and sales price, are multiplied together to get dollar sales, and this process causes the NPV distribution to be skewed to the right. (A big number times another big number produces a very big number, which, in turn, causes the average, or expected value, to be increased.)

---

[1]We could have included worst and best case values for fixed and variable costs, the inflation rate, salvage values, and so on. For illustrative purposes, we limited the changes to only two variables.

The standard deviation of NPV is \$18,421 (in thousands of dollars):[2]

$$\sigma_{NPV} = [0.25(-\$10,079 - \$13,956)^2 + 0.50(\$12,075 - \$13,956)^2$$
$$+ 0.25(\$41,752 - \$13,956)^2]^{1/2} = \$18,421.$$

Finally, the project's coefficient of variation of NPV is 1.3:

$$CV_{NPV} = \frac{\sigma_{NPV}}{E(NPV)} = \frac{\$18,421}{\$13,956} = 1.3.$$

---

[2]If we had a probability distribution for the net cash flows for each year of the project's life, then we could calculate the expected net cash flow for each year, CF_t, and the variance of that cash flow, σ_t^2. We could then calculate the expected NPV as

$$E(NPV) = \sum_{t=0}^{n} \frac{CF_t}{(1 + k)^t}.$$

11-1

If the net cash flow distributions for each year were normal, and if the yearly cash flows were not correlated with one another (intertemporally *independent*), then the standard deviation of the NPV would be calculated as follows:

$$\text{Independent cash flow case: } \sigma_{NPV} = \left[\sum_{t=0}^{n} \frac{\sigma_t^2}{(1 + k)^{2t}}\right]^{1/2}.$$

11-2

If the net cash flow distributions from one year to the next were normal and were completely *dependent* on one another (intertemporally *dependent*) such that the correlation coefficient between them was 1.0, then σ_{NPV} would be calculated as

$$\text{Dependent cash flow case: } \sigma_{NPV} = \sum_{t=0}^{n} \frac{\sigma_t}{(1 + k)^t}.$$

11-3

The independent case would apply in situations where cash flows fluctuated with the business cycle, weather conditions, and the like. The dependent case would apply in situations where customers either liked or disliked the product.

See Frederick S. Hillier, "The Derivation of Probabilistic Information for the Evaluation of Risky Investments," *Management Science,* April 1963, 443–457. Although Hillier's approach to finding projects' standard deviations is relatively simple, it is rarely used in practice because (1) many project cash flow distributions are not normal and (2) most project cash flow distributions over time are neither totally independent nor perfectly positively correlated. Still, Hillier's model does show that if a project's cash flows are independent across time (that is, fluctuate randomly from year to year), the project is less risky than if cash flows are dependent, because for a given set of σ_t, Equation 11-2 produces a lower σ_{NPV} than Equation 11-3.

This coefficient of variation can be compared with the coefficient of variation of an "average" asset to get an idea of the project's relative stand-alone riskiness. Assume that RIC's existing assets have an average coefficient of variation of about 1.0. Thus, on the basis of this stand-alone risk measure, RIC's managers would conclude that the watering system project is 30 percent riskier than an "average" project.

While scenario analysis provides useful information about stand-alone risk, it does have two major limitations. First, it only considers a few discrete outcomes (NPVs) for the project, although there are in reality an infinite number of possibilities. Second, scenario analysis as it is commonly applied assumes that the variables treated as uncertain are perfectly positively correlated, because all inputs are at their worst case or best case levels at the same time. In the RIC scenario analysis, the worst case NPV could only be realized if the lowest unit sales, lowest price, highest cost of capital, highest fixed and variable costs, and so on, all occurred together. In reality, the probability that all worst case and all best case inputs would occur at the same time is extremely low. Therefore, scenario analysis typically overstates the extremes — the worst case NPV is too low, and the best case NPV is too high. In the next section, we describe a method of assessing a project's stand-alone risk which deals with these problems.

MONTE CARLO SIMULATION

Monte Carlo simulation, so named because this type of analysis grew out of work on the mathematics of casino gambling, ties together sensitivities and input probability distributions.[3] The first step in a Monte Carlo simulation is to create a computer model that develops the project's cash flows and NPV. Next, the analyst must specify the probability distribution of each uncertain input such as sales price and sales quantity. Continuous distributions, which allow analysts to specify uncertainty with only a mean and standard deviation, or distributions defined by a lower limit, most likely value, and upper limit, are usually used for this purpose. Once this has been done, the simulation proceeds as follows:

1. The Monte Carlo software chooses at random a value for each uncertain variable, based on its specified probability distribution. For example, a value for unit sales and a value for sales price would be chosen.

2. The value selected for each uncertain variable, along with values for the fixed inputs such as the tax rate and depreciation charges, are then used by the model to determine the net cash flow for each year, and these cash flows are then used to determine the project's NPV for this particular computer run.

3. Steps 1 and 2 are repeated many times, say, 1,000, resulting in 1,000 NPVs, which are then used to form a probability distribution with its own expected value and standard deviation.

Using this procedure, we performed a simulation analysis on RIC's watering system project. As in our scenario analysis, we simplified the illustration by specifying

---

[3]The use of simulation analysis in capital budgeting was first reported by David B. Hertz, "Risk Analysis in Capital Investments," *Harvard Business Review,* January–February 1964, 95–106.

the distributions for only two key variables, unit sales and sales price. For all the other inputs, we merely specified their expected values.

In our simulation analysis, we assumed that sales price can be represented by a continuous normal distribution. Suppose the expected value is $2,200, and the actual sales price is not likely to vary by more than $500 from the expected value, that is, to fall below $1,700 or rise above $2,700. We know that in a normal distribution, the expected value plus or minus three standard deviations will encompass virtually the entire distribution. This implies that $500 represents about three standard deviations of potential sales price changes. Therefore, we assumed that $\sigma_{\text{Sales price}} = \$500/3 = \$166.67 \approx \$167$, so we instructed the computer to assume that the sales price distribution is normal, with an expected value of $2,200 and a standard deviation of $167.

Next, we assumed that the estimated distribution of unit sales has an expected value of 25,000 units, that sales could be as high as 40,000 units, given our production capacity, if demand is strong, but as low as 10,000 units if customers do not like the product. We could have again specified a normal distribution, but in the case of unit sales, we believed that a triangular distribution, with a most likely value of 25,000, a lower limit of 10,000, and an upper limit of 40,000, is most appropriate.

We used these data, plus a spreadsheet add-in program, to conduct the simulation. The output is summarized in Table 11-2, and the resulting NPV probability distribution is plotted in Figure 11-3. From the top part of Table 11-2 we see that there is a 90 percent probability that NPV will be no worse than −$2,114,000. Thus, there is a 10 percent probability of NPV being less than −$2,114,000. There is an 85.7 percent probability that the project would have NPV of at least zero, hence a 14.3 percent probability that the project would be unprofitable. Also, note that the simulation output includes the expected value (mean) and the standard deviation of the NPV.[4] Thus, the project's coefficient of variation of NPV can be calculated and stand-alone risk can be appraised in the same way as in scenario analysis.

In spite of its obvious appeal, Monte Carlo simulation has not been as widely used in industry as one might expect. The major problem is specifying each uncertain variable's probability distribution and the correlations among the distributions. Mechanically, it is easy to incorporate any type of correlation among variables into a simulation analysis; simulation software permits us to specify both intervariable and intertemporal correlations. However, it is *not* easy to determine correlations and probability distributions. Indeed, people who have tried to obtain such relationships

---

[4]Note that the standard deviation of NPV in the simulation is much smaller than the standard deviation we obtained in the scenario analysis. In the scenario analysis, we assumed that the low unit sales figure would be coupled with the low sales price for the worst case, and high values of each for the best case. That is, we assumed that these variables were *dependent* on one another, so high unit sales would mean high price, and vice versa. Thus, we ended up with only 3 NPVs, and a 25 percent probability of the worst (or best) case occurring.

In the simulation, we assumed that unit sales and price are *independent* of one another. Thus, in the simulation a high unit sales could be picked, and in the same run the computer could choose a low sales price. When the two variables are independent, the probability of a very low unit sales coupled with a very low sales price is remote. Further, in a simulation there are many possible values for each uncertain variable, while in a scenario analysis there is a discrete number (3 in our example). These two differences led to a lower standard deviation in the simulation analysis. See Footnote 2 for more on this.

Figure 11-3   NPV Probability Distribution (Thousands of Dollars)

Expected NPV = $12,096.
σ_{NPV} = $10,724.
CV_{NPV} = $10,724/$12,096 = 0.89.

Table 11-2   Summary of Simulation Results (Thousands of Dollars)

PROBABILITY OF NPV BEING EQUAL TO OR GREATER THAN THE INDICATED NPV

	0.90	0.857	0.80	0.70	0.60	0.50	0.40	0.30	0.20	0.10
NPV	($2,114)	$0.0	$2,577	$6,153	$8,993	$11,637	$14,740	$17,797	$21,417	$26,424

NPV DISTRIBUTION STATISTICS

Expected NPV	$12,096
Maximum NPV	$46,755
Minimum NPV	($13,888)
NPV range	$60,643
Probability of NPV > 0	85.7%
Probability of NPV < 0	14.3%
Standard deviation	$10,724
Coefficient of variation	$10,724/$12,096 = 0.89
Skewness	0.15[a]

[a]Positive skewness indicates that the NPV distribution is skewed to the right.

from the operating managers who must estimate them have eloquently emphasized the difficulties involved. Clearly, the problem is not insurmountable, and simulation is being used in business with increasing frequency. Still, it is important not to underestimate the difficulty of obtaining valid estimates of variables' probability distributions, and correlations among the distributions.[5]

Another problem with both scenario and simulation analysis is that even when the analysis has been completed, no clear-cut decision rule emerges. We end up with an expected NPV and a distribution about this expected value, which we can use to judge the project's stand-alone risk. However, the analysis provides no criterion to indicate whether a project's profitability as measured by its expected NPV is sufficient to compensate for its risk as measured by σ_{NPV} or CV_{NPV}.

Finally, scenario and simulation analysis both focus on a project's stand-alone risk — they ignore the effects of diversification, both among projects within the firm and by investors in their personal investment portfolios. Thus, an individual project may have highly uncertain returns when evaluated on a "stand-alone" basis, but if those returns are not correlated with the returns on the firm's other assets or with stocks in general, then the project may not be very risky in terms of either corporate or market risk. Indeed, if the project's returns are negatively correlated with the firm's other assets, then it may decrease the firm's corporate risk, and in this case, the larger its σ_{NPV}, the more it will reduce the firm's overall risk. Similarly, if a project's returns are not positively correlated with the stock market, then even a project with highly variable returns might not be risky to well-diversified stockholders.

DECISION TREES

Up to this point we have focused primarily on techniques for estimating a project's stand-alone risk. Although this is an integral part of capital budgeting, managers are generally more concerned about *reducing* risk than with *measuring* it. Often, project expenditures do not have to be made all at one time, but, rather, can be made over a period of years. This gives managers the opportunity to reevaluate decisions using new information and then either to invest additional funds or to cancel (abandon) the project. Projects that can be structured to permit capital outlays over several years can be evaluated using *decision trees.*

For example, suppose United Robotics is considering the production of an industrial robot for the television manufacturing industry. The net investment for this project can be broken down into three stages, as set forth in Figure 11-4:

Stage 1. At t = 0, which in this case is sometime in the near future, conduct a $500,000 study of the market potential for robots in television assembly lines.

---

[5]For an interesting discussion of the pros and cons of simulation analysis, see Wilbur G. Lewellen and Michael S. Long, "Simulation versus Single-Value Estimates in Capital Expenditure Analysis," *Decision Sciences,* October 1972, 19–33. For more insight into the difficulties involved in estimating probability distributions and correlations in practice, see K. Larry Hastie, "One Businessman's View of Capital Budgeting," *Financial Management,* Winter 1974, 36–43. Hastie was treasurer of Bendix Corporation and later president of the Financial Management Association.

FIGURE 11-4 | UNITED ROBOTICS: DECISION TREE ANALYSIS (THOUSANDS OF DOLLARS)

TIME							JOINT PROBABILITY	NPV	PRODUCT: PROB. × NPV
t = 0	t = 1	t = 2	t = 3	t = 4	t = 5	t = 6			
			$10,000	$10,000	$10,000	$10,000	0.144	$15,250	$2,196
		($10,000)	$4,000	$4,000	$4,000	$4,000	0.192	436	84
	($1,000)		($2,000)	($2,000)	($2,000)	($2,000)	0.144	(14,379)	(2,071)
($500)		Stop					0.320	(1.397)	(447)
	Stop						0.200	(500)	(100)
							1.000	Expected NPV =	($338)

Stage 2. If it appears that a sizable market does exist, then at t = 1 spend $1,000,000 to design and fabricate several prototype robots. These robots would then be evaluated by television engineers, and their reactions would determine whether the firm should proceed with the project.

Stage 3. If reaction to the prototype robots is good, then at t = 2 build a production plant at a net cost of $10,000,000. If this stage were reached, the project would generate high, medium, or low net cash flows over the following 4 years.

A decision tree such as the one in Figure 11-4 can be used to analyze such multistage, or sequential, decisions. Here we assume that one year goes by between decisions. Each circle represents a decision point. The dollar value to the left of each decision point represents the net investment required at that decision point, and the cash flows shown under t = 3 to t = 6 represent the cash inflows if the project is pushed on to completion. Each diagonal line represents a branch of the decision tree, and each branch has an estimated probability. For example, if the firm decides to "go" with the project at Decision Point 1, it will spend $500,000 on a marketing study. Management estimates that there is a 0.8 probability that the study will produce favorable results, leading to the decision to move on to Stage 2, and a 0.2 probability that the marketing study will produce negative results, indicating that the project should be canceled after Stage 1. If the project is canceled, the cost to the company will be $500,000 for the initial marketing study, and it will be a loss.

If the marketing study yields positive results, then United Robotics will spend $1,000,000 on the prototype robot at Decision Point 2. Management estimates (before even making the initial $500,000 investment) that there is a 60 percent probability that the television engineers will find the robot useful and a 40 percent probability that they will not like it.

If the engineers like the robot, the firm will spend the final $10,000,000 to build the plant and go into production. If the engineers do not like the prototype, the project will be dropped. If the firm does go into production, the operating cash flows over the project's 4-year life will depend on how well the market accepts the final product. There is a 30 percent chance that acceptance will be quite good and net cash flows will be $10,000,000 per year, a 40 percent probability of $4,000,000 each year, and a 30 percent chance of losing $2,000,000 per year. These cash flows are shown under Years 3 through 6. Also, for now we assume that United Robotics would be contractually bound to continue production for four years, even if losses occur.

The column of joint probabilities in Figure 11-4 gives the probability of occurrence of each branch, hence each NPV. Each joint probability is obtained by multiplying together all probabilities on a particular branch. For example, the probability that the company will, if Stage 1 is undertaken, move through Stages 2 and 3, and that a strong demand will produce $10,000,000 of inflows, is $(0.8)(0.6)(0.3) = 0.144 = 14.4\%$.

The company has a cost of capital of 11.5 percent, and management assumes initially that the project is of average risk. The NPV of the top (most favorable) branch as shown in the next to last column is $15,250 (in thousands of dollars):

$$NPV = -\$500 - \frac{\$1,000}{(1.115)^1} - \frac{\$10,000}{(1.115)^2} + \frac{\$10,000}{(1.115)^3} + \frac{\$10,000}{(1.115)^4} + \frac{\$10,000}{(1.115)^5} + \frac{\$10,000}{(1.115)^6}$$

$$= \$15,250.$$

The NPVs for other branches were calculated similarly.

The last column in Figure 11-4 gives the product of the NPV for each branch times the joint probability of that branch, and the sum of these products is the project's expected NPV. Based on the expectations set forth in Figure 11-4 and a cost of capital of 11.5 percent, the project's expected NPV is −$338,000.

Since the expected NPV is negative, it would appear that the project should be rejected, but that conclusion is not necessarily correct. First, recall that management assumed that the project is of average risk, hence we used the corporate cost of capital to evaluate it. However, we should now consider whether this project is more, less, or about as risky as an average project. The expected NPV is a negative $338,000, and the standard deviation of that NPV is $7,991,000, so the coefficient of variation is huge. This suggests that the project is extremely risky in terms of stand-alone risk. Note also that there is a $0.144 + 0.320 + 0.200 = 0.664$ probability of incurring a loss. Based on all this, the project appears to be totally unacceptable. However, there are two other considerations: (1) It is possible that the project could be abandoned if sales are poor, and this option could have a considerable impact on the analysis. We discuss this point in the next section. (2) As we discussed in Chapter 10, the project could have a strategic option value that is not captured in the DCF analysis.

Define stand-alone risk.

Briefly describe the mechanics of sensitivity analysis, scenario analysis, Monte Carlo simulation, and decision tree analysis.

What are the advantages and disadvantages of each type of stand-alone risk analysis?

SELF-TEST QUESTIONS

THE IMPACT OF ABANDONMENT ON NPV AND STAND-ALONE RISK

In Chapter 10, we introduced the concept of abandonment value. We now show how the possibility of abandonment can affect a project's risk as well as its expected NPV. Suppose United Robotics is not contractually bound to continue the industrial robot project. Thus, if sales are poor and cash flows are −$2,000 during the first year of operations (Year 3), and a similar cash flow situation is expected for the remainder of the project's life, the firm can abandon the project at the beginning of Year 4. (Here we are assuming that low first-year cash flows signify that the product is not well received in the market, hence that future sales will be poor. In other situations, the cash flows could vary from year to year depending on economic conditions, in which case low first-year sales and cash flows might be followed by high cash flows in subsequent years.)

The ability to abandon the project changes the third branch of the decision tree. It now looks like this:

		JOINT PROBABILITY	NPV	PRODUCT: PROB. × NPV
($2,000) ④	Stop	0.144	(10,883)	(1,567)

Changing this branch to reflect the abandonment alternative eliminates the $2 million cash losses in Years 4, 5, and 6, and thus causes the NPV for the branch to be less negative. This increases the project's expected NPV from −$338,000 to a positive $166,000. Moreover, abandonment lowers the standard deviation from $7,991,000 to $7,157,000. Thus, abandonment possibilities change the project's NPV from negative to positive, and also lower its stand-alone risk as measured by either the standard deviation or the coefficient of variation.

Here are some additional points concerning decision tree analysis and abandonment:

1. Managers can reduce project risk if they can structure the decision process to include several decision points rather than just one. To illustrate, if United Robotics were to make a total commitment at t = 0, signing contracts that would in effect require completion of the project, it might save some money and accelerate the project, but in doing so it would substantially increase the project's riskiness.

2. Once production begins, if the firm can shut down or spin off the operation, this could dramatically reduce its risk. Indeed, firms do this frequently.

3. The cost of abandonment is generally reduced if the firm has alternative uses for the project's assets. If United Robotics could use its TV robot production equipment for an expansion of its auto robot production facilities, then the costs involved in abandoning the TV robot project might be lowered, hence its riskiness would be reduced.

4. Finally, note that capital budgeting is a dynamic process. Virtually all inputs change over time, so firms must periodically review both their capital expenditure plans and their operating assets. In the United Robotics example, con-

ditions might change between Decision Points 1 and 2, and if so, this new information should be used to revise probability and cash flow estimates.

The key concept to remember is that decisions can often be structured with multiple decision points. If so, and if the company has the willpower to admit it when a project is not working out as initially planned and then to abandon it, risks can be reduced and profitability increased.

How can the possibility of abandonment affect a project's profitability and stand-alone risk?

What are the costs and benefits of structuring large capital budgeting decisions in stages rather than as a single go/no-go decision?

SELF-TEST QUESTIONS

CORPORATE RISK

A project's *corporate risk* is the project's contribution to the firm's overall corporate risk, or, put another way, corporate risk reflects the impact of the project on uncertainty about the firm's total cash flows. Corporate risk is a function of (1) the project's standard deviation and (2) its correlation with returns on the firm's other assets. Therefore, a project with a high standard deviation, hence high stand-alone risk, might have relatively low corporate risk if its returns are uncorrelated or negatively correlated with those from the firm's other assets.

Remember that a stock's "market risk characteristic line" is found by plotting the stock's market returns against the returns on some market index, say, the S&P 500. Further, the slope of the characteristic line is the beta coefficient, which measures the stock's market risk. If we consider a firm to be a portfolio of individual assets, then we can think of a project's corporate risk characteristic line as being the plot of the project's returns under alternative economic scenarios versus returns on the entire firm, which are made up of returns on all the firm's individual assets other than the project being evaluated. The slope of such an accounting return characteristic line would be the project's *corporate beta*.

A project with a corporate beta of 1.0 would be as risky as the firm's average asset; a beta greater than 1.0 would signify more than average risk; and a beta less than 1.0 would signify relatively low corporate risk. Note (from Figure 11-1) that the corporate beta can be calculated as $(\sigma_P/\sigma_F)r_{PF}$, where σ_P is the project's standard deviation of returns, σ_F is the firm's standard deviation of returns, and r_{PF} is the correlation coefficient between the two sets of returns. Thus, we see that a project's corporate risk depends on the project's standard deviation, on the standard deviation of the entire firm's returns, and on the correlation coefficient between those returns. A project with a relatively large standard deviation and high correlation will have more corporate risk than a project with a relatively low standard deviation and low, or negative, correlation.

In practice, it is difficult to estimate the returns distribution for a single project, but the distributions for firms and divisions are more easily estimated. Thus, the corporate risk characteristic line is seldom used for individual projects, but it is used to estimate the relative risk of divisions within a firm. Therefore, the transition from a project's stand-alone risk to its corporate risk is usually made subjectively. If the project is in the same line of business as the firm's other projects, which is normally the case, then high stand-alone risk translates into high corporate risk, because the correlation coefficient will also be high. On the other hand, if the project is not in the same line of business, then the correlation may be low, in which case the project's stand-alone risk will overstate its corporate risk. In the final analysis, managers must use informed judgment when assessing projects' riskiness.

SELF-TEST QUESTIONS

Define corporate risk.

Can a project's corporate risk be different from its stand-alone risk?

Briefly describe how a project's corporate risk might be measured, at least in theory.

What are the three primary determinants of a project's corporate risk?

MARKET RISK

The types of risk analysis discussed thus far provide insights into a project's stand-alone and corporate risk. However, these methods do not assess a project's market risk, which, in theory, should be the most relevant risk to stockholders. Further, while the methods described to this point may help assess a project's riskiness, they do not specify which projects should be accepted and which rejected. In this section, we discuss how the CAPM might be used to help overcome those shortcomings. Of course, the CAPM has shortcomings of its own, but it does provide useful insights into capital budgeting risk analysis.

OVERVIEW

To begin, recall that the Security Market Line expresses the risk/return relationship for stocks as follows:

$$k_s = k_{RF} + (k_M - k_{RF})b_i.$$

For example, if RIC's beta = 1.8, k_{RF} = 8%, and k_M = 13%, then the firm's cost of common equity is 17.0 percent:

$$k_s = 8\% + (13\% - 8\%)1.8$$

$$= 8\% + (5\%)1.8 = 17.0\%.$$

Further, if RIC's cost of debt is 10 percent, if its marginal federal-plus-state tax rate is 40 percent, and if its target capital structure calls for 50 percent debt and 50 percent common equity, then its corporate weighted average cost of capital (WACC) is 11.5 percent.[6]

---

[6]As we noted in Chapter 8, RIC would estimate its marginal cost of capital (MCC) schedule and its investment opportunity curve (IOS), and then its corporate cost of capital would be determined by the intersection of the MCC and investment opportunity schedules. Here we assume that the intersection occurs to the left of the retained earnings break point, so RIC's weighted average cost of capital (WACC) using retained earnings as the equity component is the corporate cost of capital.

$$\text{Corporate WACC} = w_d k_d (1 - T) + w_s k_s$$
$$= 0.5(10\%)(0.60) + 0.5(17\%)$$
$$= 3.0\% + 8.5\% = 11.5\%.$$

This suggests that investors would be willing to give money to RIC to invest in average-risk projects if the company could earn 11.5 percent or more on this money. In this case, the term "average risk" means projects which have a *market* risk — which is the risk that concerns stockholders — similar to that of the firm's existing assets.

Now recall that a firm is a portfolio of assets, and its beta as established in the market is an average of its assets' betas. Therefore, if taking on a particular project will cause a change in RIC's 1.8 beta coefficient, then taking on the project will also cause a change in the company's cost of equity.[7] For example, the watering system project might have a beta, if financed at the target capital structure, of 2.5, so taking it on would cause the company's overall beta to rise and to end up somewhere between the original beta of 1.8 and the new project's beta of 2.5. The new company beta will depend on the relative size of the investment in the watering system project versus the company's investment in other assets. If 80 percent of RIC's total funds would be in other assets with an average beta of 1.8, and 20 percent in the new project with a beta of 2.5, then the new company beta would be 1.94, up from 1.8:

$$\text{New b} = 0.8(1.8) + 0.2(2.5) = 1.94.$$

This increase in RIC's market risk would cause the stock price to decline *unless the increased beta were offset by a higher expected overall rate of return.* Specifically, taking on the new project would cause the company's required rate of return on equity to rise from 17.0 to 17.7 percent,

$$k_s = 8\% + (5\%)1.94 = 17.7\%,$$

and the corporate WACC would rise from 11.5 to 11.85 percent:

$$\text{Corporate WACC} = 0.5(10\%)(0.60) + 0.5(17.7\%) = 11.85\%.$$

Therefore, to keep the watering system project from lowering the stock price, RIC's expected overall rate of return would have to rise from 11.5 to 11.85 percent.

If RIC's original assets must earn 11.5 percent, how much must the new project earn in order for the new overall rate of return to equal 11.85 percent? We know that if it completes the new project, RIC would have 80 percent of its assets invested in other assets which must earn 11.5 percent, that 20 percent of its assets would be in the new project which must earn X percent, and that the average required rate of return would be 11.85 percent. Therefore,

$$0.8(11.5\%) + 0.2X = 11.85\%$$
$$0.2X = 11.85\% - 9.20\%$$
$$X = 2.65\%/0.2 = 13.25\%.$$

---

[7]Acceptance of the project would probably also change the firm's cost of debt. However, since debt represents a contractual obligation, while equity is a claim on residual cash flows, the impact on the cost of equity is typically much greater than that on debt. We ignore any impact on the cost of debt.

Thus, the watering system project must have an overall expected return, or IRR, of 13.25 percent if the corporation is to earn its new cost of capital.

In summary, if RIC takes on the new project, its corporate beta would rise from 1.8 to 1.94; its cost of equity would increase from 17.0 to 17.7 percent; its corporate cost of capital would rise from 11.5 to 11.85 percent; and the new project would have to earn at least 13.25 percent to avoid lowering RIC's stock price.

This line of reasoning leads to the conclusion that if the beta coefficient for each project, b_i, could be determined, then each project's cost of capital could be found as follows:

1. Find Project i's required rate of return on equity, k_{si}:

$$k_{si} = k_{RF} + (k_M - k_{RF})b_i.$$

2. Use k_{si} to find the project's cost of capital, Project k_i:

$$\text{Project } k_i = w_d k_d (1 - T) + w_s k_{si}.$$

Applying these two steps to RIC's new project gives this result:

$$k_{si} = 8\% + (5\%)2.5 = 20.5\%,$$

and

$$\text{Project } k_i = 0.5(10\%)(0.60) + 0.5(20.5\%) = 13.25\%.$$

We see that the required rate of return on the watering system project is the same using this "short-cut" method as it was when we developed the project's cost of capital by solving for X in the equation $11.85\% = 0.8(11.5) + 0.2X$. Note, however, that both solutions disregard any effects of the new project on either the firm's capital structure or its cost of debt; implicitly, we assumed that the cost of the debt used to support the new project, and the financing mix, would be the same as for the firm's existing assets.

EQUITY BETAS, ASSET BETAS, AND CAPITAL STRUCTURE

Betas as developed in Chapter 4 show how returns on a firm's stock co-vary with returns on the market. Moreover, the beta of a firm's stock is based on the betas of its individual assets. Therefore, we can think of each project, or asset, as a "minifirm," and of the firm itself as a portfolio of minifirms. If a firm were financed only with common equity, and if it had only one asset, then the beta of the firm and that of the asset (or project) would be identical. In this sense, we can think of a "project beta" as being equal to the beta of an unleveraged, single-asset minifirm.

The beta of a firm with an all-equity capital structure (which means that the firm has zero financial leverage) is defined as an "unlevered beta." If the firm then begins to use debt, the riskiness inherent in its equity, and also its "levered beta," will begin to rise. In Chapter 14, we will discuss in detail Robert Hamada's formula for the relationship between levered and unlevered betas:

Hamada's formula: $b_L = b_U[1 + (1 - T)(D/S)]$. **11-4**

Here b_L is the beta given that the firm uses debt, b_U is the beta it would have if it used no debt, T is its tax rate, D is its dollars of debt, and S is the market value of its stock. If we were dealing with an unlevered, single-project firm, then its beta, b_U, would also be the beta of the firm's single asset. Thus, b_U can be thought of as an unlevered asset's beta.

The beta of the *equity* of a single-asset firm is a function of both the asset's business risk as measured by b_U and how the asset is financed, and it can be approximated by the Hamada equation. We stated earlier that the beta on RIC's stock before it takes on the watering system project (its levered beta) is 1.8. This value was determined by regressing historical returns on the stock against those on the market. RIC's capital structure was already reflected in its 1.8 market-determined stock beta. However, what is the average underlying beta of RIC's existing assets, that is, the beta its stock would have if RIC used no debt? To find this average asset beta, we must remove the financing effect; this can be approximated by solving Equation 11-4, the Hamada formula, for b_U:

$$b_U = \frac{b_L}{1 + (1 - T)(D/S)} . \qquad \text{11-4a}$$

For RIC, with a tax rate of 40 percent and a debt/equity ratio of 0.50/0.50, we obtain an asset beta of 1.125:

$$b_U = \frac{1.8}{1 + (0.60)(0.50/0.50)} = \frac{1.8}{1.6} = 1.125.$$

Thus, the beta of RIC's existing assets if the company used no debt is 1.125. Financial leverage has pushed the stock's beta up from 1.125 to 1.8.

Equations 11-4 and 11-4a enable us to convert asset betas to leveraged stock betas, and vice versa. However, in our discussion in Chapter 14, we will note that Equations 11-4 and 11-4a were derived under some very restrictive assumptions, so results based on those equations must be viewed as rough approximations. Nevertheless, we will use these equations in the next section, when we discuss the "pure play" method for estimating project betas.

TECHNIQUES FOR MEASURING MARKET RISK

In Chapter 8, when we discussed the estimation of firms' betas, we indicated that it is difficult to estimate "true future betas" for common stocks. The estimation of *project* betas is even more difficult and more fraught with uncertainty, primarily because individual operating assets pay no dividends and have no quoted market prices, hence we cannot calculate historical market-return betas for use in the analysis. However, two approaches have been used for estimating the betas of individual assets: (1) the pure play method and (2) the accounting beta method.

THE PURE PLAY METHOD In the *pure play method,* the company tries to find one or more nonintegrated, single-product companies in the same line of business as the project being evaluated.[8] For example, suppose RIC could find several publicly traded firms that produced only watering systems. Further, suppose RIC believes that its new project would be subject to the same risks as those other firms. It could then determine the betas of these firms by the regular regression process, average them, and use this average as a proxy for the project's beta.

To illustrate, assume that RIC's analysts have identified three publicly owned companies engaged only in the production and distribution of watering control systems. Further, assume that the average stock beta of these firms is 2.23; that their average debt-to-equity ratio, D/S, is 0.4/0.6 = 0.67; and that their average federal-plus-state tax rate is 36 percent. We cannot conclude that the project's appropriate leverage-adjusted beta is 2.23, because RIC has a capital structure and tax rate different from those of the proxy firms.

To adjust for differences in financial leverage and tax rates, we can employ Equations 11-4 and 11-4a, using the following four steps:

Step 1. Note that the proxy firms' average stock beta of 2.23 reflects their average D/S ratio of 0.67 and their average tax rate of 36 percent.

Step 2. We can insert these values into Equation 11-4a to determine the three proxy firms' underlying asset beta:

$$b_U = \frac{2.23}{1 + (0.64)(0.67)} = 1.56.$$

Step 3. Now we can use Equation 11-4 to find what the proxy firms' stock betas would be if they had the same capital structure and tax rate as RIC:

$$b_L = 1.56[1 + (0.60)(0.50/0.50)]$$

$$= 2.50.$$

Step 4. Determine the project's cost of equity and its weighted average cost of capital, using 2.5 as the estimate for its beta:

$$k_{si} = 8\% + (13\% - 8\%)2.50 = 20.5\%.$$

$$\text{Project } k_i = 0.5(10\%)(0.60) + 0.5(20.5\%) = 13.25\%.$$

These values are consistent with those we calculated earlier.

The pure play approach is often difficult to implement because it is difficult to find pure play proxy firms. For our illustration, we assumed the existence of three pure play proxies. In reality, there is no pure play manufacturer of watering control systems. In fact, most systems are made by GE, Honeywell, and other large, multidi-

---

[8]One important article on this subject is Russell J. Fuller and Halbert S. Kerr, "Estimating the Divisional Cost of Capital: An Analysis of the Pure-Play Technique," *Journal of Finance,* December 1981, 997–1009. Fuller and Kerr used the method to estimate divisional betas and then tested the results empirically. They concluded that the pure play method is a valid technique for estimating the betas of major subparts of a firm.

visional firms, and their watering system operations are combined with their other operations in a manner that makes it impossible to ascertain market betas for watering system projects. However, there are times when the method is feasible. For example, when the founders of Gateway Computer were considering going into the personal computer business, they were able to get data on Apple, Compaq, Dell, and several other essentially pure play personal computer companies. Similarly, Pillsbury is able to employ this technique when it is considering capital budgeting decisions in its Godfather's Pizza, Steak and Ale, and Bennigan's divisions.

THE ACCOUNTING BETA METHOD If it is not possible to find single-product, publicly traded firms suitable for the pure play approach, then companies can use the *accounting beta method.* As you know, betas are normally found by regressing the returns on a particular company's stock against returns on a stock market index. However, one could run a regression of the company's basic earning power (Earnings before interest and taxes/Total assets) against the average basic earning power for a large sample of companies such as the NYSE or the S&P 500. Such data are readily available from Standard & Poor's Compustat database. Betas determined in this manner, using accounting data rather than stock market data, are called *accounting betas.*

Historical accounting betas can be calculated for companies, divisions, or even certain types of large projects. But how good are accounting betas as proxies for market betas? Many studies have addressed this issue.[9] Although the results vary, most studies support the conclusion that firms with high accounting betas tend to have high market betas, whereas firms with low accounting betas tend to have low market betas. However, the correlations are generally only in the 0.5 to 0.6 range, so accounting-determined betas provide only rough approximations for market-determined betas, market risk, and consequently the cost of capital.

Note that the accounting beta method described here is similar to the procedure discussed earlier to estimate a project's within-firm, or corporate, risk. The only difference is that when measuring corporate risk, the regression is run on the firm's returns rather than on the average accounting return of firms in a stock index. Also, the accounting beta technique can be used to estimate different divisions' within-firm risk. Here the firm's overall accounting rate of return would be used as the index, and the results would reflect the degree of correlation between different divisions.

SELF-TEST QUESTIONS

What is the difference between corporate risk and market risk?

What is meant by the term "unleveraged asset beta," and how does its value differ from a project beta? From the firm's stock beta?

Briefly describe two techniques that can be used to estimate a project's market risk.

---

[9]The original work on this subject was William H. Beaver and James Manegold, "The Association between Market-Determined Measures of Systematic Risk: Some Further Evidence," *Journal of Financial and Quantitative Analysis,* June 1975, 231–284. That study, and many subsequent ones, are summarized in George Foster, *Financial Statement Analysis* (Englewood Cliffs, N.J.: Prentice-Hall, 1986).

INCORPORATING RISK AND CAPITAL STRUCTURE INTO CAPITAL BUDGETING DECISIONS

Thus far, we have seen that capital budgeting decisions can affect a firm's market risk, its corporate risk, or both. We have also seen that it is exceedingly difficult to quantify either type of risk. In other words, it may be possible to reach the general conclusion that one project is riskier than another (in either the market, corporate, or stand-alone sense), but it is difficult to develop a really good *measure* of project risk. Further, this lack of precision in measuring project risk makes it difficult to incorporate risk differentials into capital budgeting decisions.

Nevertheless, two methods have been developed for incorporating project risk into the capital budgeting decision process. One is the *certainty equivalent* method, in which the expected cash flows are adjusted to reflect project risk — risky cash flows are scaled down, and the riskier the flows, the lower their certainty equivalent values. The second procedure is the *risk-adjusted discount rate* method, where differential project risk is dealt with by changing the discount rate — average-risk projects are discounted at the firm's corporate cost of capital, above-average-risk projects are discounted at a higher cost of capital, and below-average-risk projects are discounted at a rate below the corporate cost of capital. Although the risk-adjusted discount rate method is used by most companies, the certainty equivalent approach does have some advantages, so financial managers should be familiar with it.

THE CERTAINTY EQUIVALENT METHOD

The certainty equivalent (CE) method follows directly from the concept of utility theory. Under the CE approach, the decision maker must first evaluate a cash flow's risk and then specify how much money, with certainty, would make him or her indifferent between the riskless and the risky cash flows. To illustrate, suppose a rich eccentric offered you the following two choices:

1. Flip a fair coin. If a head comes up, you receive $1,000,000, but if a tail comes up, you get nothing. The expected value of the gamble is (0.5)($1,000,000) + (0.5)($0) = $500,000, but the actual outcome will be either $0 or $1,000,000, so it is risky.

2. Do not flip the coin and simply pocket $300,000 cash.

If you find yourself indifferent between the two alternatives, then $300,000 is your certainty equivalent for this particular risky $500,000 expected cash flow. The certain (or riskless) $300,000 thus provides you with the same utility as the risky $500,000 expected return.

Now ask yourself this question: In the preceding example, exactly how much cash-in-hand would it actually take to make *you* indifferent between a certain sum and the risky $500,000 expected return? If you are like most people, your certainty equivalent would be significantly less than $500,000, indicating that you are risk averse. In general, risk aversion exists, and the lower the certainty equivalent, the greater the decision maker's risk aversion.

The certainty equivalent concept can be applied to capital budgeting decisions, at least in theory, in the following way:

1. Estimate the certainty equivalent cash flow in each Year t, CE_t, based on the expected cash flow and its riskiness.

2. Given these certainty equivalents, discount by the risk-free rate to obtain the project's NPV.[10]

To illustrate, suppose Project A, whose expected net cash flows are shown in Table 11-3, is to be evaluated using the certainty equivalent method. Assume that the initial net cost, $2,000, is fixed by contract and hence known with certainty. Further, assume that the capital budgeting analyst estimates that the cash inflows in Years 1 through 4 all have average risk, and that the appropriate certainty equivalent is $700. The project's NPV, found using a risk-free discount rate of 5 percent, is $482.17:

$$NPV_A = -\$2,000 + \frac{\$700}{(1.05)^1} + \frac{\$700}{(1.05)^2} + \frac{\$700}{(1.05)^3} + \frac{\$700}{(1.05)^4}$$

$$= \$482.17.$$

Since the risk-adjusted NPV is positive, the project should be accepted.

The certainty equivalent method is simple and neat. Further, it can easily accommodate differential risk among cash flows. For example, if the Year 4 expected net cash flow of $1,000 included a very risky estimated salvage value, we could simply reduce the certainty equivalent, say, from $700 to $500, and recalculate the project's NPV. Unfortunately, there is no practical way to estimate certainty equivalents. Each individual would have his or her own estimate, and these could vary significantly. To further complicate matters, certainty equivalents should reflect shareholders' risk preferences rather than those of management. For these reasons, the certainty equivalent method is not used to any extent in corporate decision making. However, it is conceptually a powerful tool, and in a later section we will use certainty equivalents to help see some assumptions embodied in constant risk-adjusted discount rates.

		PROJECT A: CERTAINTY EQUIVALENT ANALYSIS	TABLE 11-3
YEAR	EXPECTED NET CASH FLOW	DEGREE OF RISK	CERTAINTY EQUIVALENT CASH FLOW
0	($2,000)	Zero	($2,000)
1	1,000	Average	700
2	1,000	Average	700
3	1,000	Average	700
4	1,000	Average	700

[10]Note that the risk-free rate normally does not reflect the tax advantage of debt as does the WACC. Thus, either the certainty equivalent estimates or the risk-free rate should be constructed so that they capture this benefit.

THE RISK-ADJUSTED DISCOUNT RATE METHOD

With the risk-adjusted discount rate method, we use the expected cash flow values, CF_t, and the risk adjustment is made to the denominator of the NPV equation (the discount rate) rather than to the numerator. To illustrate, again consider Project A, whose expected cash flows were given in Table 11-3. Suppose the firm evaluating Project A had a corporate cost of capital of 15 percent. Thus, all average-risk projects would be evaluated using a discount rate of 15 percent. Now assume that a risk analysis of Project A indicated that the project had above-average risk, and a project cost of capital of 22 percent was subjectively assigned to the project. In this situation, the risk-adjusted discount rate method produces an NPV of $493.64:

$$NPV_A = -\$2,000 + \frac{\$1,000}{(1.22)^1} + \frac{\$1,000}{(1.22)^2} + \frac{\$1,000}{(1.22)^3} + \frac{\$1,000}{(1.22)^4}$$

$$= \$493.64.$$

In theory, if managers were able to estimate precisely both a project's certainty equivalent cash flows and its risk-adjusted discount rate (or rates), the two methods would produce the identical NPV. However, the risk-adjusted discount rate method is easier to use in practice because the discount rate for average-risk projects (the firm's corporate cost of capital) can be estimated from observable market data, but no market data are available to help managers estimate certainty equivalent cash flows.

CERTAINTY EQUIVALENTS VERSUS RISK-ADJUSTED DISCOUNT RATES

As noted above, investment risk can be handled by making adjustments either to the numerator of the present value equation (the certainty equivalent, or CE, method) or to the denominator (the risk-adjusted discount rate, or RADR, method). The RADR method dominates in practice because people find it far easier to estimate suitable discount rates based on current market data than to derive certainty equivalent cash flows. Some financial theorists have suggested that the certainty equivalent approach is theoretically superior,[11] but other theorists have shown that if risk increases with time, then using a risk-adjusted discount rate is a valid procedure.[12]

Risk-adjusted rates lump together the pure time value of money as represented by the risk-free rate and a risk premium: $k = k_{RF} + RP$. On the other hand, the CE approach keeps risk and the time value of money separate. This separation gives a theoretical advantage to certainty equivalents, because lumping together the time value of money and the risk premium compounds the risk premium over time. By compounding the risk premium over time, the RADR method automatically assigns more risk to cash flows that occur in the distant future, and the farther into the future, the greater the implied risk. Since the CE method assigns risk to each cash flow individually, it does not impose any assumptions regarding the relationship between risk and time.

---

[11]See Alexander A. Robichek and Stewart C. Myers, "Conceptual Problems in the Use of Risk-Adjusted Discount Rates," *Journal of Finance,* December 1966, 727–730.

[12]See Houng-Yhi Chen, "Valuation under Uncertainty," *Journal of Financial and Quantitative Analysis,* September 1967, 313–326.

IMPLICATIONS

A firm using the RADR approach for its capital budgeting decisions will have a corporate cost of capital that reflects its overall market-determined riskiness. This rate should be used for "average" projects, that is, for projects which have the same risk as the firm's existing assets. Lower rates should be used for less risky projects, and higher rates should be used for riskier projects. To facilitate the decision process, corporate headquarters generally prescribes rates for different classes of investments (for example, replacement, expansion of existing lines, and expansion into new lines). Then, investments of a given class within a given division are analyzed in terms of the prescribed rate. For example, replacement decisions in the retailing division of an oil company might all be evaluated with a 10 percent discount rate, while exploratory drilling projects might be evaluated at a 20 percent rate.

However, a constant k implies that risk increases with time, and it therefore imposes a relatively severe burden on long-term projects. This means that short-payoff projects will tend to be selected over those with longer payoffs when, for example, there are alternative ways of performing a given task. This is often appropriate, but there are projects for which distant returns are *not* more risky than near-term returns. For example, the estimated returns on a water pipeline serving a developing community may be highly uncertain in the short run, because the rate of growth of the community is uncertain. However, the water company may be quite sure that, in time, the community will be fully developed and will utilize the full capacity of the pipeline. Similar situations could exist in many public projects — water projects, highway programs, schools, and so forth, and when industrial firms are building plants or retailers are building stores to serve growing geographic markets.

To the extent that the implicit assumption of rising risk over time reflects the facts, then a constant discount rate may be appropriate. Indeed, in the vast majority of business situations, risk undoubtedly is an increasing function of time, so a constant risk-adjusted discount rate is generally reasonable. However, one should be aware of the relationships described in this section and avoid the pitfall of unwittingly penalizing long-term projects when they are not, in fact, more risky than short-term projects.

IMPLEMENTING RISK ADJUSTMENTS IN PRACTICE

Because of implementation problems with the CE approach, firms generally use the RADR method to incorporate risk into the capital budgeting process — average-risk projects are discounted at the corporate cost of capital, high-risk projects are discounted at a higher cost of capital, and low-risk projects are discounted at a lower rate. Unfortunately, since risk cannot be measured precisely, there is no good way of specifying exactly *how much* higher or lower these discount rates should be — given the present state of the art, risk adjustments are necessarily judgmental, and somewhat arbitrary.

Capital structure must also be taken into account if a firm finances different assets in different ways. For example, one division might have a lot of real estate, which is well suited as collateral for loans, whereas some other division might have most of its capital tied up in special-purpose machinery, which is not good collateral. As a result, the division with the real estate might have a higher *debt capacity* than the machinery division, hence an optimal capital structure which contains a higher percentage of debt. In this case, the division with more real estate contributes more to the overall debt capacity of the firm, and management might calculate its cost of capital using a higher debt ratio than for the other division.

Although the process is not exact, many companies use a two-step procedure to develop risk-adjusted discount rates for use in capital budgeting: (1) *Divisional costs of capital* are established for each of the major operating divisions on the basis of each division's estimated riskiness and debt capacity. (2) Within each division, all projects are classified into three categories — high risk, average risk, and low risk — and then each division uses its divisional cost of capital as the discount rate for average-risk projects, reduces the divisional cost of capital by one or two percentage points when evaluating low-risk projects, and raises the divisional cost of capital by several percentage points for high-risk projects. We will have more to say about risk adjustments in a later section when we discuss our view of project risk analysis.

SELF-TEST QUESTIONS	Describe how the certainty equivalent approach can be used to incorporate risk into the capital budgeting decision.
	Describe how the risk-adjusted discount rate approach is used.
	Which approach dominates in practice?
	If a constant risk-adjusted discount rate is used to evaluate cash flows in all years, what does this imply about the perceived risk of cash flows in different years?
	How do most firms incorporate differences in risk and debt capacity into capital budgeting decisions?

RISKY CASH OUTFLOWS

Projects often have negative cash flows during their lives, and when this occurs, special problems may arise. To illustrate, suppose Duke Power Company has concluded that it needs a new generating plant, and it is choosing between a nuclear plant and a coal-fired plant. Both plants will produce the same amount of electricity, hence have the same revenues. However, the coal plant will have a smaller investment requirement but higher operating costs, hence smaller annual cash flows. Also, the nuclear plant will have to be decommissioned at the end of its 30-year life. At this time, the company knows that the costs of tearing down the plant and removing the radioactive material will be high, but the exact cost is highly uncertain.

Table 11-4 shows the projected cash flows from the two plants. The coal plant has a cost of $2 billion, and it is expected to produce net cash flows of $250 million per year for 30 years. The nuclear plant has a cost of $4 billion, it is expected to produce cash flows of $474 million per year for 30 years, and then the company expects to have to spend $2 billion to decommission the radioactive plant. All of the cash flows except the decommissioning costs have the same risk as Duke Power's other cash flows, hence they are to be discounted at the company's WACC, 10 percent. However, the decommissioning costs are much more uncertain, hence should be discounted at a rate which reflects their higher risks.

| | | EXPECTED CASH FLOWS, COAL VERSUS NUCLEAR POWER PLANTS (MILLIONS OF DOLLARS) | TABLE 11-4 |

		CASH FLOWS FROM:	
YEAR	COAL PLANT	NUCLEAR PLANT	
0	($2,000)	($4,000)	
1	250	474	
2	250	474	
.	.	.	
.	.	.	
.	.	.	
28	250	474	
29	250	474	
30	250	474	
31	0	(2,000)	
NPV coal plant @ 10%		$357	
NPV nuclear plant @10%		$364	
NPV nuclear plant @ 10% for operating CF but 15% for risky decommissioning costs:		$442	
NPV nuclear plant @ 10% for operating CF but 8% for risky decommissioning costs:		$284	

At the bottom of Table 11-4 we show the projects' NPVs. That of the coal plant, discounting at the 10 percent WACC, is $357 million. At the 10 percent WACC, the nuclear plant has a slightly higher NPV, $364 million, but this value does not reflect nuclear's greater risk which results from uncertainty about decommissioning costs. Our first inclination is to discount the operating cash flows at WACC = 10% because those cash flows are assumed to be of average risk, but to discount the decommissioning costs at a higher rate to reflect their greater risk. Using a discount rate of 15 percent for the decommissioning costs, we get an NPV of $442. But note — something is amiss. We applied a higher risk-adjusted discount rate and this *improved* the relative position of the nuclear plant! Something is wrong!

What we conclude is that, whereas it is appropriate to increase the discount rate applied to risky cash *inflows* to adjust for their risk, *we must use a lower discount rate to reflect higher risks for cash outflows*. Therefore, we must discount the decommissioning costs at some lower rate to properly reflect their greater risk. When we discount these costs at an 8 percent rate, the nuclear plant's NPV is lowered, as it should be. When the discount rate problem is properly resolved, we see that the coal plant is the better choice.

Many projects have especially risky cash outflows some time during their lives, and when this occurs it is important to remember the lessons of this section and discount these risky outflows at a relatively low rate. It is easy, in a complex set of cash flows, to forget about this and therefore produce a flawed NPV. This situation also comes up in other types of DCF analyses. For example, in certain leasing problems the salvage value at the end of a lease is more uncertain than the payment stream during the life of the lease. At times, the salvage value must be treated as an outflow (if the lessee plans to continue using the asset, hence must buy if from the lessor). Here too the adjustment for the risky outflow is critical.[13]

SELF-TEST QUESTIONS

Describe some "real-world" situations in which risk adjustments must be applied to cash outflows.

How does the risk adjustment process differ for cash outflows versus cash inflows?

OUR VIEW OF PROJECT RISK ANALYSIS

From our discussion thus far, it should be apparent that project risk analysis is far from precise. First, there are three types of project risk that can be considered, and a project can be highly risky in one sense, say, corporate risk, but not very risky in another, say, market risk. Second, no type of risk can be measured very precisely. Still, managers must deal with risk. To help put things into perspective, we present our views on the process.

To begin, should managers place more emphasis on a project's stand-alone, corporate, or market risk? First, note that stand-alone risk is almost never completely relevant. Thus, in most situations, a project's riskiness is better measured by its corporate risk, which takes into account the firm's whole portfolio of assets, than by its stand-alone risk. Second, well-diversified investors should be concerned primarily with market risk, managers should be concerned primarily with stock price maximization, and these two factors lead to the conclusion that market risk should be given the most weight in capital budgeting decisions. However, stockholders should be concerned about the costs of financial distress, and these costs are not captured by market risk. Further, managers should be and are concerned about the firm's other stakeholders (bondholders, suppliers, employees, customers, and so on), and this implies that corporate risk should be taken into account. Thus, managers should consider both a project's corporate risk and its market risk when making capital budgeting decisions.

In many cases, it is impossible to accurately assess a project's market risk, or even its corporate risk, hence managers are often left with only an estimate of the project's stand-alone risk. In most situations, the project being evaluated is in the same line of business as the firm's other projects, and most firms' profitability is highly correlated

---

[13]For more on the effects of negative cash flows, see Wilbur G. Lewellen, "Some Observations on Risk-Adjusted Discount Rates," *Journal of Finance,* September 1977, 1331–1337; and a comment on that paper by Stephen E. Celec and Richard H. Pettway, plus a reply by Lewellen, in the September 1979 issue of the *Journal,* 1061–1066. Pettway and Celec's analysis leads to a risk-adjustment process similar to the one contained in this section. Lewellen points out that even though an outflow may be risky in the stand-alone risk sense, this outflow may have correlations with the firm's other cash flows and/or the returns on the market such that its corporate and/or market risk is equal to or even less than the firm's average risk.

with the national economy. Therefore, stand-alone, corporate, and market risk are usually highly correlated, so a project with high stand-alone risk will typically have high corporate and market risk. This suggests that managers can get a feel for the relative risk of most projects on the basis of sensitivity, scenario, simulation, and/or decision tree analyses even though these procedures measure only stand-alone risk.

The corporate cost of capital provides the starting point for estimating a project's risk-adjusted discount rate. If all projects had equal risk and equal debt capacity, then all projects would be evaluated at the corporate cost of capital. However, larger firms typically have several divisions that vary in risk, and projects within divisions can also have risk differences. The first step in developing a project's cost of capital calls for adjusting the corporate cost of capital to reflect divisional risk and debt capacity. A division with above-average risk or below-average debt capacity would have a divisional cost of capital above the firm's corporate cost of capital. A division with below-average risk or above-average debt capacity would have a lower-than-average corporate cost of capital. (Of course, the average of the divisional costs of capital must equal the corporate cost of capital.)

Each project is then assigned to a risk category on the basis of its own risk relative to its division's average risk. If it is riskier than average for the division, then its risk-adjusted discount rate is set above the divisional cost of capital, and the opposite holds true if the project has below-average risk. (Remember, though, that the risk adjustment process is reversed for cash outflows.) Also, adjustments should be made when projects have debt capacities which differ widely from the divisional average. The most difficult part of this process is judging how large the divisional and project adjustments should be. If data are available, then the project's beta and the CAPM can be used to estimate the size of the adjustment. However, in most situations the adjustment is judgmental, and often a range of two to five percentage points is used.

This subjective risk-adjustment process is illustrated in Figure 11-5, which shows a firm with three divisions in separate lines of business. The overall (aggregate) risk and

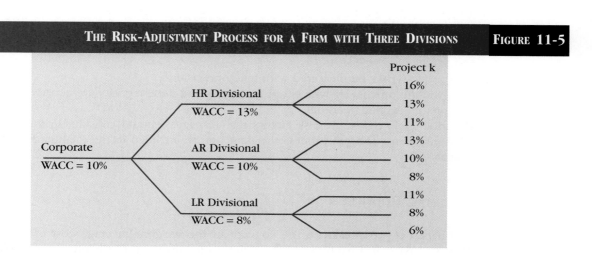

THE RISK-ADJUSTMENT PROCESS FOR A FIRM WITH THREE DIVISIONS   **FIGURE 11-5**

debt capacity of the company is such that the corporate WACC is 10 percent. Division HR is riskier than the corporation as a whole, so it has a divisional cost of capital of 13 percent. Division AR has average risk, so it is assigned a 10 percent divisional cost of capital. Division LR's low relative risk gives it a cost of capital of 8 percent. Within each division, individual project riskiness is assessed *relative to an average project within the division,* and high-risk projects are assigned a project cost of capital three percentage points above the divisional cost of capital, while low-risk projects have a project cost of capital two percentage points below the divisional cost of capital. Thus, high-risk projects in Division HR would have a 16 percent project cost of capital, while that division's low-risk projects would have an 11 percent project cost of capital. Overall, project costs of capital range from a low of 6 percent for a low-risk project in Division LR to 16 percent for a high-risk project in Division HR.

The end result of the process is a project cost of capital and an NPV which incorporates, to the extent possible, the project's debt capacity and at least one aspect of the project's relative riskiness. Managers may also have to consider other risk factors. For example, if the project could lead to litigation against the firm, then it has additional riskiness that should be taken into account — a number of drug, chemical, and asbestos companies have learned this, to their regret. Conversely, if the project can easily be abandoned, or if the assets can easily be converted to other uses within the firm, then it might be less risky than appears in a standard analysis. Such additional factors must be considered subjectively in making the final accept/reject decision. Typically, if the project involves new products and is large relative to the firm's average project, then these additional risk factors will be very important to the final decision — one large mistake can bankrupt a firm, and such "bet the company" decisions are not made lightly. On the other hand, if the project being considered is a small replacement project, then the decision would be made almost exclusively on the basis of a straight numerical analysis.

Ultimately, capital budgeting decisions require a mix of objective and subjective analyses. Nothing is very precise, so there is a temptation to ignore risk considerations because they are so nebulous. However, despite the imprecision and subjectiveness, risk should be assessed and incorporated into the capital budgeting process. Anything less would be tantamount to ignoring one of the basic principles of finance — projects with higher risk require higher returns.

SELF-TEST QUESTIONS

Can projects' risks be measured with much precision?

Describe the process by which a project's risk and debt capacity are considered in capital budgeting decisions.

Describe some qualitative risk factors that managers should consider in the capital budgeting decision process that may not be included in the quantitative risk analysis.

THE OPTIMAL CAPITAL BUDGET

In Chapter 8, we developed the concept of the weighted average cost of capital (WACC). Then, in Chapters 9 and 10, and up to this point in Chapter 11, we have discussed how the cost of capital is used in project evaluations. However, capital budgeting and the cost of capital are actually interrelated — we cannot specify the cost of capital until we know the size of the capital budget, and we cannot determine the capital budget until we specify the cost of capital. Therefore, as we show in the next sections, *the cost of capital and the capital budget must be determined simultaneously.* Swift Foods, a Midwestern grocery wholesaler, is used to illustrate the process.

THE INVESTMENT OPPORTUNITY SCHEDULE (IOS)

Consider first Figure 11-6, which gives some information on Swift's potential capital projects for next year. The tabular data show each project's cash flows, IRR, and payback. The graph is defined as the firm's *investment opportunity schedule (IOS),* which is a plot of each project's IRR, in descending order, versus the dollars of new capital required to finance it. For example, Project A has an IRR of 38.5 percent, shown on the vertical axis, and a cost of $100,000, shown on the horizontal axis.[14] Notice also that Projects A and A′ are mutually exclusive. Thus Swift has two possible IOS schedules: the one defined by the solid line, which contains Project A plus B, C, D, and E, and the one defined by the dotted line, which contains Project A′ plus B, C, D, and E. Beyond $600,000, the two IOS schedules are identical. Thus, the two alternative schedules differ only in that one contains A and has B ranked second, while the other contains A′ and ranks B first because $IRR_B > IRR_{A'}$. For now, we assume that all six projects have the same risk as Swift's "average" project.

THE MARGINAL COST OF CAPITAL (MCC) SCHEDULE

In Chapter 8, we discussed the concept of the weighted average cost of capital (WACC). However, the value of the WACC depends on the amount of new capital raised — the WACC will, at some point, rise if more and more capital is raised during a given year. This increase occurs because (1) flotation costs (including any "signaling" costs associated with stock issues) cause the cost of new equity to be higher than that of retained earnings, and (2) higher rates of return on debt, preferred stock, and common stock may be required to induce additional investors to supply capital to the firm.

Suppose Swift's cost of retained earnings is 15.0 percent, while its cost of new common stock is 16.8 percent. The company's target capital structure calls for 40 percent debt and 60 percent common equity; its marginal federal-plus-state tax rate is 40 percent; and its before-tax cost of debt is 10 percent. Thus, Swift's WACC using retained earnings as the common equity component is 11.4 percent:

$$WACC_1 = w_d(k_d)(1 - T) + w_{ce}k_s$$

$$= 0.4(10\%)(0.6) + 0.6(15\%) = 11.4\%.$$

---

[14]Do not be concerned by the fact that we use IRR in this analysis rather than MIRR or NPV. The fact is, we cannot calculate either MIRR or NPV until we know k, and we are using this analysis to develop a first-approximation estimate of k. Later on, we will switch to MIRR or NPV, but such a switch is not possible at this point.

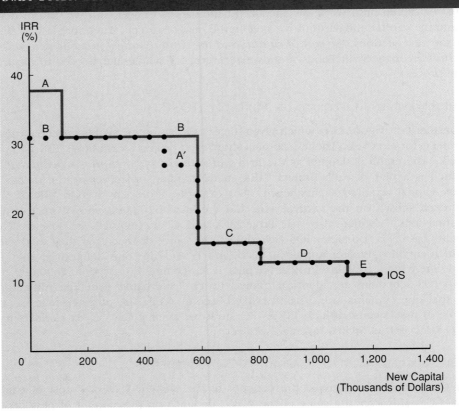

FIGURE 11-6   SWIFT FOODS: IOS SCHEDULES

CASH FLOWS OF POTENTIAL PROJECTS

YEAR	A	A′	B	C	D	E
0	($100,000)	($100,000)	($500,000)	($200,000)	($300,000)	($100,000)
1	90,000	10,000	190,000	52,800	98,800	58,781
2	60,000	70,000	190,000	52,800	98,800	58,781
3	10,000	100,000	190,000	52,800	98,800	—
4	—	—	190,000	52,800	98,800	—
5	—	—	190,000	52,800	—	—
6	—	—	190,000	52,800	—	—
IRR	38.5%	27.0%	30.2%	15.2%	12.0%	11.5%
Payback	1.2	2.2	2.6	3.8	3.0	1.7

[a]Projects A and A′ are mutually exclusive.

Swift is forecasting $240,000 of retained earnings plus $300,000 of depreciation cash flow during the planning period, hence its retained earnings break point is $700,000:

$$\text{Break point} = \$240,000/0.6 + \$300,000 = \$400,000 + \$300,000 = \$700,000.$$

After $700,000 of new capital has been raised, Swift's WACC increases to 12.5 percent:

$$\text{WACC}_2 = 0.4(10\%)(0.6) + 0.6(16.8\%) \approx 12.5\%.$$

Thus, each dollar has a weighted average cost of 11.4 percent until the company has raised a total of $700,000. This $700,000 will consist of $300,000 of depreciation cash flow with a cost of 11.4 percent, $160,000 of new debt with an after-tax cost of 6 percent, and $240,000 of retained earnings with a cost of 15 percent. However, if the company raises $700,001 or more, each additional dollar will contain 60 cents of equity obtained by selling new common stock, so $k_a = \text{WACC}$ rises from 11.4 to 12.5 percent.

COMBINING THE MCC AND IOS SCHEDULES

Now that we have estimated the MCC schedule, we can use it to help determine the base discount rate for the capital budgeting process; *that is, we can use the MCC schedule to find the corporate cost of capital for use in determining an average-risk project's net present value.* To do this, we combine the IOS and MCC schedules on the same graph, as in Figure 11-7, and then analyze this consolidated figure.

FINDING THE CORPORATE COST OF CAPITAL Just how far down its IOS curve should Swift go? That is, which of the firm's available projects should it accept? *First, Swift should accept all independent projects that have rates of return in excess of the cost of the capital that will be used to finance them, and it should reject all others.* Projects D and E should be rejected, because they would have to be financed with capital that has a cost of 12.5 percent, and at that cost of capital, we know that these projects must have negative NPVs (because their IRRs are below their costs of capital). Therefore, Swift's capital budget should consist of either A or A', plus B and C, and the firm should thus raise and invest a total of $800,000.[15]

The preceding analysis, as summarized in Figure 11-7, reveals a very important point: The basic WACC used in the capital budgeting process is actually determined at the intersection of the IOS and MCC schedules. This cost is called the firm's *corporate cost of capital,* and if it is used to evaluate average-risk projects, then the firm will make correct accept/reject decisions, and its level of financing and investment will be optimal. If it uses any other rate for average-risk projects, its capital budget will not be optimal.

If Swift had fewer good investment opportunities, then its IOS schedule would be shifted to the left, possibly causing the intersection to occur at the $\text{WACC}_1 = 11.4\%$ portion of the MCC curve. Then, Swift's corporate cost of capital would be 11.4 percent, and average-risk projects would be evaluated at that rate. Conversely, if the

---

[15]Note that if the MCC schedule cuts through a project, and if that project must be accepted in total or else rejected, then we can calculate the average cost of the capital that will be used to finance the project (some at the higher WACC and some at the lower WACC) and compare that average WACC to the project's IRR.

| FIGURE 11-7 | SWIFT FOODS: COMBINED IOS AND MCC SCHEDULES |

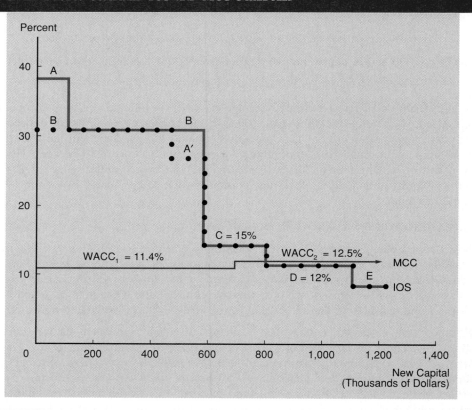

firm had more and better investment opportunities, its IOS would be shifted to the right, and if the shift is very far to the right, then Swift might have to raise its corporate cost of capital above 12.5 percent. Thus, we see that the discount rate used for evaluating average-risk projects is influenced by the set of available projects. We have, of course, abstracted from differential project riskiness in this section, because we assumed that all of Swift's projects are equally risky.

CHOOSING BETWEEN MUTUALLY EXCLUSIVE PROJECTS   We have not, at this point, actually determined Swift's optimal capital budget. We know that it should total $800,000 and that Projects B and C should be included, but we do not know which of the mutually exclusive projects, A or A', should be made part of the final budget. How can we choose between A and A'? We know that in general the final set of projects should be the one which has the highest total NPV, as this set will increase the value of the firm by the largest amount. We also know that Projects B and C should be included in the final set. This narrows our analysis to the NPVs of A and A', and the one with the higher NPV should be chosen.

Notice that Figure 11-6 contained the projects' paybacks and IRRs, but no NPVs or MIRRs. We were not able to determine NPVs or MIRRs at that point because we did not know Swift's marginal cost of capital. Now, in Figure 11-7, we see that the last dollar raised will cost 12.5 percent, so Swift's corporate cost of capital is 12.5 percent. Therefore, assuming the projects both have average risk, we can use a 12.5 percent discount rate to find NPV_A = \$34,431 and $NPV_{A'}$ = \$34,431. Thus, in our example, Swift should be indifferent between the two mutually exclusive projects, according to the NPV criterion. Given a tie, Project A would probably be selected because of its faster payback and higher IRR.

Define a firm's corporate cost of capital.
How should a firm choose between two mutually exclusive projects?

SELF-TEST QUESTIONS

CAPITAL RATIONING

Under ordinary circumstances, capital budgeting is, in essence, an application of a classic economic principle: A firm should expand to the point where its marginal return is just equal to its marginal cost. However, under some circumstances, a firm may deviate from this principle and place an absolute limit on the size of its capital budget. This is called *capital rationing,* which we discuss in Appendix 11A.

Define capital rationing.

SELF-TEST QUESTION

ESTABLISHING THE OPTIMAL CAPITAL BUDGET IN PRACTICE

The process set forth in the preceding sections is conceptually correct, and it is important that you understand the logic of the process. However, Swift Foods (and most other companies) actually uses a more judgmental, less quantitative process for establishing its final capital budget:

Step 1. The financial vice-president obtains a reasonably good idea of the firm's IOS schedule from the director of capital budgeting, and a reasonably good estimate of the MCC schedule from the treasurer. These two schedules are then combined, as in Figure 11-7, to get a reasonably good estimate of the company's corporate cost of capital (the cost of capital at the intersection of the IOS and MCC schedules).

Step 2. The corporate cost of capital is scaled up or down for each division to reflect the division's capital structure and risk characteristics. Swift assigns a factor of 0.9 to its stable, low-risk canned vegetables division but a factor of 1.1 to its more risky gourmet frozen foods group. Therefore, if the corporate WACC is determined to be 12.5 percent, the cost for the canned vegetables division is 0.9(12.5%) = 11.25%, while that for the gourmet frozen foods division is 1.1(12.5%) = 13.75%.

Step 3. Each project within each division is classified into one of three groups — high risk, average risk, and low risk, and the same 0.9 and 1.1 factors are used to adjust the divisional MCCs. For example, a low-risk project in the canned vegetables division would have a cost of capital of 0.9(11.25%) = 10.13%, rounded to 10 percent, if the corporate cost of capital were 12.5 percent, while a high-risk project in the gourmet frozen foods division would have a cost of 1.1(13.75%) = 15.13%, rounded to 15 percent.

Step 4. Each project's NPV is then determined, using its risk-adjusted project cost of capital. The optimal capital budget consists of all independent projects with positive risk-adjusted NPVs plus those mutually exclusive projects with the highest positive risk-adjusted NPVs.

These steps implicitly assume that the projects taken on have, in total, about the same debt capacity and risk characteristics, and consequently the same weighted average cost of capital, as the firm's existing assets. If this were not true, then the corporate cost of capital determined in Step 1 would not be correct, and it would have to be adjusted. However, given all the measurement errors and uncertainties inherent in the entire cost of capital/capital budgeting process, it would be unrealistic to push the adjustment process very far.

This type of analysis may seem more precise than the data warrant. Nevertheless, an understanding of these concepts does help management understand the nature of each division's relative risk, the risk of each project within the divisions, and the relationship between the total amount of capital raised and the cost of that capital. Further, the steps outlined above help the firm to adjust its capital budget to reflect capital market conditions—if the cost of debt and equity rise, this fact will be reflected in the cost of capital used to evaluate projects, and projects that would be marginally acceptable when capital costs were low would (correctly) be ruled unacceptable when capital costs were high.

SELF-TEST QUESTIONS Describe the general procedures that most firms follow when establishing optimal capital budgets.

What assumptions are made about the average of all projects' risk and debt capacity?

SUMMARY

This chapter discussed three issues in capital budgeting: (1) measuring risk, (2) incorporating risk into the capital budgeting decision process, and (3) determining the optimal capital budget. The key concepts are summarized below.

■ A project's *stand-alone risk* is the risk it would have if it were the firm's only asset and if its stockholders held only one stock. Stand-alone risk is measured by uncertainty about the asset's expected returns. Stand-alone risk is often used as a proxy for both market and corporate risk, because (1) market and corporate risk are difficult to measure and (2) the three types of risk are usually highly correlated.

- *Corporate risk* reflects the effects of a project on the firm's risk, and it is measured by the project's effect on the riskiness of the firm's earnings. Stockholder diversification is not taken into account.

- *Market risk* reflects the effects of a project on the riskiness of a well-diversified stockholder's portfolio. In theory, market risk should be the most relevant type of risk.

- *Corporate risk* is important because it influences the firm's ability to use low-cost debt, to maintain smooth operations over time, and to avoid crises that might consume management's energy and also disrupt the firm's employees, customers, suppliers, and community.

- *Sensitivity analysis* is a technique which shows how much an output variable such as NPV will change in response to a given change in an input variable such as unit sales, other things held constant.

- *Scenario analysis* is a risk analysis technique in which the best and worst case NPVs are compared with the project's expected NPV.

- *Monte Carlo simulation* is a risk analysis technique in which a computer is used to simulate future events and thus to estimate the expected NPV and the riskiness of a project.

- Projects where capital outlays are made in stages over several years are often evaluated using *decision trees*. Like sensitivity analysis, scenario analysis, and Monte Carlo simulation, decision trees measure stand-alone risk.

- The ability to *abandon* a project can increase its return and decrease its riskiness.

- The *pure play method* and the *accounting beta method* can be used to estimate betas for large projects or divisions.

- Either *certainty equivalents* or *risk-adjusted discount rates* can be used to incorporate risk into the decision process. In practice, risk-adjusted discount rates dominate.

- A *risk-adjusted discount rate* is the rate which is used to evaluate a given risky project. The discount rate is increased for projects which are riskier than average projects, and it is decreased for less risky projects.

- When evaluating *risky outflows,* the risk-adjustment process is reversed; that is, *lower* rates are used to discount more risky outflows.

- *Capital rationing* occurs when management places a constraint on the size of the capital budget.

- The *investment opportunity schedule (IOS)* is a graph of the firm's investment opportunities, listed in descending order of IRR.

- The *marginal cost of capital (MCC) schedule* is a graph of the firm's weighted average cost of capital versus the amount of funds raised.

- The MCC and IOS schedules are combined, and the intersection defines the firm's *corporate cost of capital.*

This chapter completes our discussion of capital budgeting. In the next chapter, we begin our discussion of strategic financing decisions.

QUESTIONS

11-1 Define each of the following terms:

a. Stand-alone risk; corporate risk; market risk
b. Sensitivity analysis
c. Simulation analysis
d. Scenario analysis
e. Decision tree analysis
f. Coefficient of variation versus standard deviation
g. Project beta versus corporate beta
h. Accounting beta versus stock market beta
i. Pure play method of estimating divisional betas
j. Corporate diversification versus stockholder diversification
k. Certainty equivalent
l. Risk-adjusted discount rate; project cost of capital
m. IOS schedule; MCC schedule; corporate cost of capital

11-2 Differentiate between (a) Monte Carlo simulation analysis, (b) scenario analysis, and (c) sensitivity analysis. If AT&T were considering two investments, one calling for the expenditure of $100 million to develop a satellite communications system and the other involving the expenditure of $5,000 for a new truck, on which one would the company be more likely to use simulation?

11-3 Distinguish between market risk, within-firm (or corporate) risk, and stand-alone risk for a project being considered for inclusion in the capital budget. Which type do you feel should be given the greatest weight in capital budgeting decisions?

11-4 Suppose Lima Locomotive Company, which has a high beta and also a great deal of stand-alone risk, merged with Homestake Mining, which has a low beta but relatively high stand-alone risk. What would the merger do to the cost of capital in the consolidated company's locomotive division and its gold mining division?

11-5 Suppose a firm estimates its MCC and IOS schedules for the coming year and finds that they intersect at the point 10 percent, $10 million. What cost of capital should be used to evaluate average-risk projects, high-risk projects, and low-risk projects?

11-6 The MCC and IOS schedules can be thought of as "bands" rather than as lines to show that they are not known with certainty but, rather, are merely estimates of the true MCC and IOS schedules.

a. Do you think that the bands would be wider for the MCC or for the IOS schedule? In answering this question, visualize each point on the MCC and IOS schedules as being the expected value of a probability distribution.
b. For the IOS schedule, would the band, or confidence interval, associated with each project be identical? If not, what would this imply, and how might it affect the firm's capital budgeting analysis?

(SOLUTIONS APPEAR IN APPENDIX C)

ST-1   **CORPORATE RISK ANALYSIS**   The staff of Porter Manufacturing has estimated the following net cash flows and probabilities for a new manufacturing process:

	NET CASH FLOW		
YEAR	P = 0.2	P = 0.6	P = 0.2
0	($100,000)	($100,000)	($100,000)
1	20,000	30,000	40,000
2	20,000	30,000	40,000
3	20,000	30,000	40,000
4	20,000	30,000	40,000
5	20,000	30,000	40,000
5*	0	20,000	30,000

Line 0 is the cost of the process, Lines 1–5 are operating cash flows, and Line 5* contains the estimated salvage values. The firm's corporate cost of capital is 10 percent.

a. Assume that the project has average risk. Find the project's base case NPV. (Hint: Use expected values for the net cash flow in each year.)

b. Find the best case and worst case NPVs. What is the probability of occurrence of the worst case if the cash flows are perfectly dependent (perfectly positively correlated) over time? If they are independent over time?

c. Assume that all the cash flows are perfectly positively correlated; that is, there are only three possible cash flow streams over time: (1) the worst case, (2) the most likely case, and (3) the best case, with probabilities of 0.2, 0.6, and 0.2, respectively. These cases are represented by each of the columns in the table. Find the expected NPV, its standard deviation, and its coefficient of variation.

d. The coefficient of variation of the firm's average project is in the range 0.8 to 1.0. If the coefficient of variation of a project being evaluated is greater than 1.0, 2 percentage points are added to the firm's corporate WACC. Similarly, if the coefficient of variation is less than 0.8, 1 percentage point is deducted from the corporate WACC. What is the project's cost of capital? Should the firm accept or reject the project?

ST-2   **OPTIMAL CAPITAL BUDGET**   Wolfe Enterprises has the following capital structure, which it considers to be optimal under the present and forecasted conditions:

Debt	30%
Common equity	70
Total capital	100%

For the coming year, management expects to realize net earnings of $56,000, plus $35,000 in depreciation cash flow. The past dividend policy of paying out 50 percent of earnings will continue. Present commitments from its banker will allow the firm to borrow at a rate of 8 percent.

The company's federal-plus-state tax rate is 40 percent; the current market price of its stock is $50 per share; its *last* dividend was $1.85 per share; and its expected constant growth rate is 8 percent. External equity (new common) can be sold at a flotation cost of 15 percent. The firm has the following investment opportunities for the next period:

PROJECT	COST	IRR
A	$50,000	12%
B	15,000	11
C	20,000	10
D	50,000	9

Management asks you to help them determine what projects (if any) should be undertaken. You proceed with this analysis by following these steps:

a. Calculate the WACC using both retained earnings and new common stock.
b. Graph the IOS and MCC schedules.
c. Which projects should the firm accept?
d. What implicit assumptions about project risk are embodied in this problem? If you learned that Projects A and B were of above-average risk, yet the firm chose the projects which you indicated in Part c, how would this affect the situation?
e. The problem stated that the firm pays out 50 percent of its earnings as dividends. How would the analysis change if the payout ratio were changed to 0 percent? To 100 percent?

PROBLEMS

11-1 RISKY CASH OUTFLOWS Suwannee Electric and Gas Company is deciding if it should build an oil or a coal generating plant. Its cost of capital is 8 percent for low-risk projects, 10 percent for projects of average risk, and 12 percent for high-risk projects. Management believes that an oil plant is of average risk, but that a coal plant is of high risk due to the problem of acid rain. The cash *outflows* required to construct each plant are listed here. The revenues, fuel costs, and other operating costs are expected to be the same under both plans:

YEAR	CONSTRUCTION COSTS (THOUSANDS OF DOLLARS)	
	COAL PLANT	OIL PLANT
0	($100)	($400)
1	(500)	(1,000)
2	(1,500)	(1,000)
3	(1,500)	(1,000)
4	(1,500)	(1,500)
5	(1,000)	(1,000)
6	(500)	(200)

Which type of plant should be constructed?

-2   **SEQUENTIAL DECISIONS** The Yoran Yacht Company (YYC), a prominent sailboat builder in Newport, may design a new 30-foot sailboat based on the "winged" keels first introduced on the 12-meter yachts that raced for the America's Cup.

First, YYC would have to invest $10,000 at t = 0 for the design and model tank testing of the new boat. YYC's managers believe that there is a 60 percent probability that this phase will be successful and the project will continue. If Stage 1 is not successful, the project will be abandoned with zero salvage value.

The next stage, if undertaken, would consist of making the molds and producing two prototype boats. This would cost $500,000 at t = 1. If the boats test well, YYC would go into production. If they do not, the molds and prototypes could be sold for $100,000. The managers estimate that the probability is 80 percent that the boats will pass testing, and that Stage 3 will be undertaken.

Stage 3 consists of converting an unused production line to produce the new design. This would cost $1,000,000 at t = 2. If the economy is strong at this point, the net value of sales would be $3,000,000, while if the economy is weak, the net value would be $1,500,000. Both net values occur at t = 3, and each state of the economy has a probability of 0.5. YYC's corporate cost of capital is 12 percent.

a. Assume that this project has average risk. Construct a decision tree and determine the project's expected NPV.

b. Find the project's standard deviation of NPV and coefficient of variation (CV) of NPV. If YYC's average project had a CV of between 1.0 and 2.0, would this project be of high, low, or average stand-alone risk?

-3   **DIVISIONAL MARKET RISK ADJUSTMENTS** SureGrip Rubber Company has two divisions: (1) the tire division, which manufactures tires for new autos, and (2) the recap division, which manufactures recapping materials that are sold to independent tire recapping shops throughout the United States. Since auto manufacturing fluctuates with the general economy, the tire division's earnings contribution to SureGrip's stock price is highly correlated with returns on most other stocks. If the tire division were operated as a separate company, its beta coefficient would be about 1.60. The sales and profits of the recap division, on the other hand, tend to be countercyclical, since recap sales boom when people cannot afford to buy new tires. The recap division's beta is estimated to be 0.40. Approximately 75 percent of SureGrip's corporate assets are invested in the tire division and 25 percent are in the recap division.

Currently, the rate of interest on Treasury bonds is 10 percent, and the expected rate of return on an average share of stock is 15 percent. SureGrip uses only common equity capital, hence it has no debt outstanding.

a. What is the required rate of return on SureGrip's stock?

b. What discount rate should be used to evaluate capital budgeting projects? Explain your answer fully, and in the process, illustrate your answer with a project which costs $100,000, has a 10-year life, and provides expected after-tax net cash flows of $20,000 per year.

-4   **SIMULATION** Singleton Supplies Corporation (SSC) manufactures medical products for hospitals, clinics, and nursing homes. SSC may introduce a new type of X-ray scanner designed to identify certain types of cancers in their early stages. There are a number of uncertainties about the proposed project, but the following data are believed to be reasonably accurate.

	PROBABILITY	VALUE	RANDOM NUMBERS
Developmental costs	0.3	$2,000,000	00–29
	0.4	4,000,000	30–69
	0.3	6,000,000	70–99
Project life	0.2	3 years	00–19
	0.6	8 years	20–79
	0.2	13 years	80–99
Sales in units	0.2	100	00–19
	0.6	200	20–79
	0.2	300	80–99
Sales price	0.1	$13,000	00–09
	0.8	13,500	10–89
	0.1	14,000	90–99
Cost per unit (excluding developmental costs)	0.3	$5,000	00–29
	0.4	6,000	30–69
	0.3	7,000	70–99

SSC uses a cost of capital of 15 percent to analyze average-risk projects, 12 percent for low-risk projects, and 18 percent for high-risk projects. These risk adjustments reflect primarily the uncertainty about each project's NPV and IRR as measured by the coefficients of variation of NPV and IRR. SSC is in the 40 percent federal-plus-state income tax bracket.

a. What is the expected IRR for the X-ray scanner project? Base your answer on the expected values of the variables. Also, assume the after-tax "profits" figure you develop is equal to annual cash flows. All facilities are leased, so depreciation may be disregarded. Can you determine the value of σ_{IRR} short of actual simulation or a fairly complex statistical analysis?

b. Assume that SSC uses a 15 percent cost of capital for this project. What is the project's NPV? Could you estimate σ_{NPV} without either simulation or a complex statistical analysis?

c. Show the process by which a computer would perform a simulation analysis for this project. Use the random numbers 44, 17, 16, 58, 1; 79, 83, 86; and 19, 62, 6 to illustrate the process with the first computer run. Actually calculate the first-run NPV and IRR. Assume that the cash flows for each year are independent of cash flows for other years. Also, assume that the computer operates as follows: (1) A developmental cost and a project life are estimated for the first run. (2) Next, sales volume, sales price, and cost per unit are estimated and used to derive a cash flow for the first year. (3) Then, the next three random numbers are used to estimate sales volume, sales price, and cost per unit for the second year, hence the cash flow for the second year. (4) Cash flows for other years are developed similarly, on out to the first run's estimated life. (5) With the developmental cost and the cash flow stream established, NPV and IRR for the first run are derived and stored in the computer's memory. (6) The process is repeated to generate perhaps 500 other NPVs and IRRs. (7) Frequency distributions for NPV and IRR are plotted by the computer, and the distributions' means and standard deviations are calculated.

d. Does it seem a little strange to conduct a risk analysis such as the one here *after* having already established a cost of capital for use in the analysis? What might be done to improve this situation?

e. In this problem, we assumed that the probability distributions were all independent of one another. It would have been possible to use conditional probabilities where, for example, the probability distribution for cost per unit would vary from trial to trial, depending on the unit sales for the trial. Also, it would be possible to construct a simulation model such that the sales distribution in Year t would depend on the sales level attained in Year t − 1. Had these modifications been made in this problem, do you think the standard deviation of the NPV distribution would have been larger (riskier) or smaller (less risky) than where complete independence is assumed?

f. Name two *major* difficulties not mentioned earlier that occur in the kind of analysis discussed in this problem.

-5 SIMPLE OPTIMAL CAPITAL BUDGET The Teague Corporation's present capital structure, which is also its target capital structure, calls for 50 percent debt and 50 percent common equity. The firm has only one potential project, an expansion program with a 10.2 percent IRR and a cost of $20 million but which is completely divisible; that is, Teague can invest any amount up to $20 million. The firm expects to retain $2 million of earnings next year and to generate $2 million in depreciation cash flow. It can raise up to $5 million in new debt at a before-tax cost of 8 percent, and all debt after the first $5 million will have a cost of 10 percent. The cost of retained earnings is 12 percent and the firm can sell any amount of new common stock desired at a constant cost of new equity of 15 percent. The firm's marginal federal-plus-state tax rate is 40 percent. What is the firm's optimal capital budget?

-6 OPTIMAL CAPITAL BUDGET The management of Flannigan Phosphate Industries (FPI) is planning next year's capital budget. FPI projects its net income at $7,500, and its payout ratio is 40 percent. Depreciation is forecasted at $3,000. The company's earnings and dividends are growing at a constant rate of 5 percent; the last dividend, D_0, was $0.90; and the current stock price is $8.59. FPI's new debt will cost 14 percent. If FPI issues new common stock, flotation costs will be 20 percent. FPI is at its optimal capital structure, which is 40 percent debt and 60 percent equity, and the firm's marginal tax rate is 40 percent. FPI has the following independent, indivisible, and equally risky investment opportunities:

PROJECT	COST	IRR
A	$15,000	17%
B	20,000	14
C	15,000	16
D	12,000	15

What is FPI's optimal capital budget?

-7 RISK-ADJUSTED OPTIMAL CAPITAL BUDGET Refer to Problem 11-6. Management neglected to incorporate project risk differentials into the analysis. FPI's policy is to add 2 percentage points to the cost of capital of those projects significantly more risky than average and to subtract 2 percentage points from the cost of capital of those which are substantially less risky than average. Management judges Project A to be of high risk, Projects C and D to be of average risk, and Project B to be of low risk. No projects are divisible. What is the optimal capital budget after adjustment for project risk?

SPREADSHEET APPLICATIONS

SPREADSHEET PROBLEM

Your firm, Agrico, is considering the purchase of a tractor which will have a net cost of $30,000, will increase pre-tax operating cash flows exclusive of depreciation effects by $10,000 per year, and will be depreciated on a straight line basis to zero over 5 years at the rate of $6,000 per year, beginning the first year. (Annual cash flows will be $10,000, reduced by taxes, plus the tax savings that result from $6,000 of depreciation.) The board of directors, however, is having a heated debate as to whether the tractor will actually last 5 years. Specifically, Hugo Phillips insists that he knows of some that have lasted only 4 years. Joe Copeland agrees with Phillips, but he argues that most tractors do give 5 years of service. Kate Brown, on the other hand, says she has seen some last as long as 8 years.

a. Given this discussion, the board asks you to prepare a scenario analysis to ascertain the importance of the uncertainty about the tractor's life. Assume a 40 percent marginal federal-plus-state tax rate, a zero salvage value, and a marginal cost of capital of 10 percent. (Hint: The MACRS alternate straight line depreciation is based on the class life of the tractor and is not affected by the actual life. Also, ignore the half-year convention for this problem.)

b. The board would also like to know how changes in the cost of capital affect the analysis. Assume that the machine's life is 5 years, and analyze the effects of a change in the cost of capital to 8 percent or to 12 percent. Is the project very sensitive to changes in the cost of capital?

c. The board would like to determine the sensitivity of the project's NPV to changes in certain variables. First, they would like to examine the effect of changes in pre-tax operating revenues upon NPV. Calculate the project's NPV at plus 10, 20, and 30 percent of the estimated $10,000 pre-tax revenues, as well as minus 10, 20, and 30 percent of this figure. (Hold all other variables constant.) Second, calculate the effect upon NPV of various project lives. (Hint: Hold all other variables constant, and try lives ranging from 1 to 10 years.) Finally, examine NPV while changing the cost of capital. (Once again, hold all other variables constant at their original levels.) Plot a separate sensitivity diagram for each variable examined.

SPREADSHEET EXERCISE: GRAPHING

This exercise uses a spreadsheet model to generate the cash flows and evaluate the profitability of a capital project. The model is complete except for graphics. Students will use the model to create a sensitivity analysis graph.

1. Retrieve the model (Filename SE11.WK1) from the models diskette. The model calculates NPV, IRR, and Modified IRR for a 4-year project.

2. The section beginning on Row 62 contains the sensitivity analysis data tables, which show the sensitivity of the project's NPV to changes in unit sales, salvage value, and cost of capital.

3. Your task is to create a single sensitivity analysis graph. Unfortunately, the exact steps to be taken to graph the sensitivity analysis depend on the type of software being used. For example, graph creation using *Lotus 1-2-3* differs between DOS and Windows versions.

4. Create the sensitivity analysis graph. Use a line graph with Cells A26.A32 as the X-axis range, Cells D69.D75 as the A range, Cells F69.F75 as the B range, and Cells H69.H75 as the C range. Place appropriate titles and legends on the graph. Be sure to specify Color to obtain the best possible graph. (Hint: If you are not familiar with spreadsheet graphing, consult your software manual.)

5. View the graph. It is obvious that the project's NPV is most sensitive to changes in unit sales and least sensitive to changes in salvage value. Also, the slope of the cost of capital sensitivity line is negative, indicating that higher-than-expected values of k lead to lower-than-expected NPVs.

6. Note that the graph that you created does not change as the model's input data are changed. This is because the graph is tied to the data in the data tables, and these data do not automatically change with input data changes. In a later exercise, we will show how macros can be used to easily recalculate such tables.

MINI CASE

The Chapter 10 Mini Case contains the details of a new-project capital budgeting evaluation being conducted by Joan Samuels at the John Crockett Furniture Company. However, in the initial analysis the riskiness of the project was not considered. The base case, or expected, cash flow estimates as they were estimated in Chapter 10 (in thousands of dollars) are given next. Crockett's corporate cost of capital (WACC) is 10 percent.

		YEAR			
	0	1	2	3	4
Investment in:					
Fixed assets	($240)				
Net working capital	(20)				
Unit sales		1,250	1,250	1,250	1,250
Sales price (dollars)		$200	$200	$200	$200
Gross revenue		$250	$250	$250	$250
Cash operating costs (50%)		125	125	125	125
Operating profit		$125	$125	$125	$125
Depreciation		79	108	36	17
EBIT		$ 46	$ 17	$ 89	$108
Taxes (40%)		18	7	36	43
Net operating income		$ 28	$ 10	$ 53	$ 65
Add back depreciation		79	108	36	17
Net operating cash flow		$107	$118	$ 89	$ 82
Salvage value					25
Tax on SV (40%)					(10)
Recovery of NWC					20
Net cash flow	($260)	$107	$118	$ 89	$117

NPV at 10% cost of capital = $82.

IRR = 23.8%.

MIRR = 17.8%.

As Joan's assistant, you have been directed to answer the following questions:

a. What does the term "risk" mean in the context of capital budgeting, to what extent can risk be quantified, and when risk is quantified, is the quantification based primarily on statistical analysis of historical data or on subjective, judgmental estimates?

b. (1) What are the three types of risk that are relevant in capital budgeting?
   (2) How is each of these risk types measured, and how do they relate to one another?
   (3) How is each type of risk used in the capital budgeting process?

c. (1) What is sensitivity analysis?
   (2) Perform a sensitivity analysis on the unit sales, salvage value, and cost of capital for the project. Assume that each of these variables can vary from its base case, or expected, value by plus and minus 10, 20, and 30 percent. Include a sensitivity diagram, and discuss the results.
   (3) What is the primary weakness of sensitivity analysis? What is its primary usefulness?

d. Assume that Joan Samuels is confident of her estimates of all the variables that affect the project's cash flows except unit sales: If product acceptance is poor, unit sales would be only 900 units a year, while a strong consumer response would produce sales of 1,600 units. In either case, cash costs would still amount to 50 percent of revenues. Joan believes that there is a 25 percent chance of poor acceptance, a 25 percent chance of excellent acceptance, and a 50 percent chance of average acceptance (the base case).
   (1) What is the worst case NPV? The best case NPV?
   (2) Use the worst, most likely, and best case NPVs and probabilities of occurrence to find the project's expected NPV, standard deviation, and coefficient of variation.

e. (1) Assume that Crockett's average project has a coefficient of variation in the range of 0.2–0.4. Would the new furniture line be classified as high risk, average risk, or low risk? What type of risk is being measured here?
   (2) Based on common sense, how highly correlated do you think that the project would be to the firm's other assets? (Give a correlation coefficient, or range of coefficients, based on your judgment.)
   (3) How would this correlation coefficient and the previously calculated σ combine to affect the project's contribution to corporate, or within-firm, risk? Explain.

f. (1) Based on your judgment, what do you think the project's correlation coefficient would be with the general economy and thus with returns on "the market"?
   (2) How would this correlation affect the project's market risk?

g. (1) Crockett typically adds or subtracts 3 percentage points to the overall cost of capital to adjust for risk. Should the new furniture line be accepted?
   (2) Are there any subjective risk factors that should be considered before the final decision is made?

h. Define scenario analysis and simulation analysis, and discuss their principal advantages and disadvantages.

i. (1) Crockett's target capital structure is 50 percent debt and 50 percent common equity; its cost of debt is 12 percent; the risk-free rate is 10 percent; the market risk premium is 6 percent; and the firm's tax rate is 40 percent. If Joan's estimate of the new project's beta is 1.2, what is the project's market risk, and what is its cost of capital based on the CAPM?
   (2) How does the project's market risk compare with the firm's overall market risk?
   (3) How does the project's market risk compare with its stand-alone risk?
   (4) Briefly describe two methods that Joan could conceivably have used to estimate the project's market beta. How feasible do you think those procedures would actually be in this case?
   (5) What are the advantages and disadvantages of focusing on a project's market risk?

j. As a completely different project, Crockett is also evaluating two different production line systems for its overstuffed furniture line. Plan W requires more workers but less capital, while Plan C requires more capital but fewer workers. Both systems have estimated 3-year lives. Since the production line choice has no impact on revenues, Joan will base her decision on the relative costs of the two systems as set forth next:

	EXPECTED NET COSTS	
YEAR	PLAN W	PLAN C
0	($500)	($1,000)
1	(500)	(300)
2	(500)	(300)
3	(500)	(300)

(1) Assume initially that the two systems are both of average risk. Which one should be chosen?
(2) Now assume that the worker-intensive plan (W) is judged to be riskier than average, because future wage rates are very difficult to forecast. Under this condition, which system should be chosen?
(3) What is Plan W's IRR?

MINI CASE 2

Ron Redwine, financial manager of Blum Industries, is developing the firm's optimal capital budget for the coming year. He has identified the five potential projects shown below. Projects B and B* are mutually exclusive, while the remainder are independent. Neither B nor B* is essential to the firm's operations, so replication is not mandatory.

PROJECT	COST	CF_{1-N}	LIFE (N)	IRR	NPV
A	$400,000	$119,326	5	15%	
B	200,000	56,863	5	13	
B*	200,000	35,397	10	12	
C	100,000	27,057	5	11	
D	300,000	79,139	5	10	

The following information was developed for purposes of determining Blum's weighted average cost of capital (WACC):

Interest rate on new debt	8.0%
Tax rate	40.0%
Debt ratio	60.0%
Current stock price, P_0	$20.00
Last dividend, D_0	$2.00
Expected growth rate, g	6.0%
Flotation cost on common, F	19.0%
Expected addition to retained earnings	$200,000

The firm adjusts for differential project risk by adding or subtracting 2 percentage points to the firm's corporate cost of capital.

a. Calculate the WACC, and then plot the company's IOS and MCC schedules. What is the firm's corporate cost of capital for capital budgeting purposes?

b. Assume initially that all five projects are of average risk. What is Blum's optimal capital budget? Explain your answer fully.

c. Now assume that the retained earnings break point occurred at $900,000 of new capital. What effect would this have on the firm's MCC schedule and its optimal capital budget?

d. Now suppose it was discovered that the firm has $200,000 of depreciation cash flow that had not been included in the analysis thus far. Discuss how this might affect the firm's MCC schedule and its optimal capital budget.

e. Now disregard the $200,000 of depreciation cash flow, and return to the situation in Part a, with the $500,000 break point. Suppose Project A is reexamined, and it is judged to be a high-risk project, while Projects C and D are, upon reexamination, judged to have low risk. Projects B and B* remain average-risk projects. How would these changes affect Blum's optimal capital budget?

f. In reality, companies like Blum have hundreds of projects to evaluate each year, hence it is generally not practical to draw the IOS and MCC schedules which include every potential project. Now suppose this situation exists for Blum. Suppose also that the company has 3 divisions, L, A, and H, with low, average, and high risk, respectively, and that the projects within each division can also be grouped into three risk categories. Describe how Blum might go about structuring its capital budgeting decision process and choosing its optimal set of projects. For this purpose, assume that Blum's corporate WACC is estimated to be 11 percent. As part of your answer, find appropriate divisional and project hurdle rates when differential risk is considered.

SELECTED ADDITIONAL REFERENCES AND CASES

The literature on risk analysis in capital budgeting is vast; here is a small but useful selection of additional references that bear directly on the topics covered in this chapter:

Ang, James S., and Wilbur G. Lewellen, "Risk Adjustment in Capital Investment Project Evaluations," *Financial Management,* Summer 1982, 5–14.

Bower, Richard S., and Jeffrey M. Jenks, "Divisional Screening Rates," *Financial Management,* Autumn 1975, 42–49.

Butler, J. S., and Barry Schachter, "The Investment Decision: Estimation Risk and Risk Adjusted Discount Rates," *Financial Management,* Winter 1989, 13–22.

Fama, Eugene F., "Risk-Adjusted Discount Rates and Capital Budgeting under Uncertainty," *Journal of Financial Economics,* August 1977, 3–24.

Findlay, M. Chapman III, Arthur E. Gooding, and Wallace Q. Weaver, Jr., "On the Relevant Risk for Determining Capital Expenditure Hurdle Rates," *Financial Management,* Winter 1976, 9–16.

Gehr, Adam K., Jr., "Risk-Adjusted Capital Budgeting Using Arbitrage," *Financial Management,* Winter 1981, 14–19.

Gup, Benton E., and S. W. Norwood III, "Divisional Cost of Capital: A Practical Approach," *Financial Management,* Spring 1982, 20–24.

Lessard, Donald R., and Richard S. Bower, "An Operational Approach to Risk Screening," *Journal of Finance,* May 1973, 321–338.

Myers, Stewart C., and Samuel M. Turnbull, "Capital Budgeting and the Capital Asset Pricing Model: Good News and Bad News," *Journal of Finance,* May 1977, 321–333.

Robichek, Alexander A., "Interpreting the Results of Risk Analysis," *Journal of Finance,* December 1975, 1384–1386.

Sick, Gordon A., "A Certainty-Equivalent Approach to Capital Budgeting," *Financial Management,* Winter 1986, 23–32.

Weaver, Samuel C., Peter J. Clemmens III, Jack A. Gunn, and Bruce D. Danneburg, "Divisional Hurdle Rates and the Cost of Capital," *Financial Management,* Spring 1989, 18–25.

Yagil, Joseph, "Divisional Beta Estimation under the Old and New Tax Laws," *Financial Management,* Winter 1987, 16–21.

The Cases in Financial Management: Dryden Request *series contains the following cases which focus on capital budgeting under uncertainty:*

Case 13, "Indian River Citrus (B)," Case 13A, "Cranfield, Inc. (B)," and Case 15, "Robert Montoya, Inc. (B)," which illustrate project risk analysis.

Case 16, "New England Seafood Company " and Case 16A, "Gulf Coast Fisheries," which focus on sequential investments and decision trees.

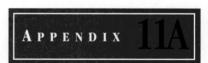

APPENDIX 11A

CAPITAL RATIONING

As we discussed in Chapter 11, under ordinary circumstances a firm should expand to the point where its marginal return is just equal to its marginal cost. A simplified view of the concept is shown in Figure 11A-1. Here we assume that the firm has five equally risky and independent investment opportunities which would cost a total of $23 million. Its cost of capital is assumed to be constant at 10 percent, implying that the firm can raise all the money it wants at a cost of 10 percent. Under these conditions, the firm would accept Projects V, W, and X, since they all have IRRs greater than the cost of capital, hence NPVs greater than zero. It would reject Y and Z because they have IRRs less than k, indicating negative NPVs. This decision would maximize the value of the firm and the wealth of its stockholders.

Firms ordinarily operate in the manner depicted in the graph—they accept all independent projects having positive NPVs, reject those with negative NPVs, and choose between mutually exclusive investments on the basis of the higher NPV. However, some firms set an absolute limit on the size of their capital budgets such that the size of the budget is less than the level of investment called for by the NPV (or IRR) criterion. This is called *capital rationing,* and it is the topic of this appendix.

REASONS FOR CAPITAL RATIONING   The principal reason for capital rationing is that some firms are reluctant to engage in external financing (either borrowing or selling stock). One management, recalling the plight of firms with substantial amounts of debt during recent credit crunches, may simply refuse to use debt. Another management, which has no objection to selling debt, may not want to sell equity capital for fear of losing some measure of voting control. Still others may refuse to use any form of outside financing, considering safety and control to be more important than additional profits. These are all cases of capital rationing, and they result in limiting the rate of expansion to a slower pace than would be dictated by "purely rational wealth-maximizing behavior."

We should make three points here. First, a decision to hold back on expansion is not necessarily irrational. If the owners/managers of a privately held firm have what they consider to be plenty of income and wealth, then it might be quite rational for them to "trim their sails," relax, and concentrate on enjoying what they have already earned rather than on earning still more. Such behavior would not, however, be appropriate for a publicly owned firm.

Second, it is not correct to interpret as capital rationing a situation where the firm is willing to sell additional securities at the going market price but finds that it cannot because the market simply will not absorb more of its issues. Rather, such a situation indicates that the weighted average cost of capital is rising. If more acceptable investments are indicated than can be financed, then the marginal cost of capital being used is too low and should be raised.

Third, firms sometimes set a limit on capital expenditures, not because of a shortage of funds, but because of limitations on other resources, especially managerial talent. A firm might, for example, feel that its personnel development program is sufficient to handle an expansion of no more than 10 percent a year, and then set a limit on the capital budget to ensure that expansion is held to that rate. This is not capital rationing — rather, it involves a downward reevaluation of project returns if growth exceeds some limit; that is, expected rates of return are, after some point, a decreasing function of the level of expenditures.

PROJECT SELECTION UNDER CAPITAL RATIONING   How should projects be selected under conditions of true capital rationing? First, note that if a firm truly rations capital, its value is not being maximized: If management were maximizing, then it would move to the point where the marginal project's NPV was zero, and capital rationing as defined would not exist. So, if a firm uses capital rationing, it has ruled out value maximization. The firm may, however, want to maximize value *subject to the constraint that the capital ceiling not be exceeded.* Constrained maximization behavior will, in general, result in a lower value than following unconstrained maximization, but some type of constrained maximization may produce reasonably satisfactory results. *Linear programming* is one method of constrained maximization that has been applied to capital rationing. Much work has been done in this area, and linear programming may, in the future, be widely applied in capital budgeting.[1]

[1]For further information on mathematical programming solutions to capital rationing, and for a review and analysis of the literature on this issue, see H. Martin Weingarten, "Capital Rationing: n Authors in Search of a Plot," *Journal of Finance,* December 1977, 1403-1431; and Stephen P. Bradley and Sherwood C. Frey, Jr., "Equivalent Mathematical Programming Models of Pure Capital Rationing," *Journal of Financial and Quantitative Analysis,* June 1978, 345-361.

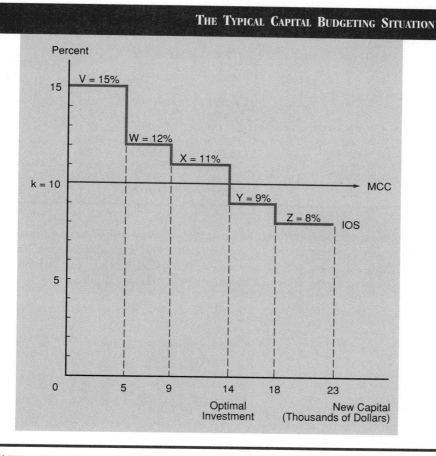

THE TYPICAL CAPITAL BUDGETING SITUATION **FIGURE 11A-1**

NOTE: If IRR > 10%, NPV is positive. Therefore, Projects V, W, and X have NPV > 0, while Y and Z have NPV < 0.

If the firm does face capital rationing, and if the constraint cannot be lifted, what can the financial manager do? The objective should be to select projects, subject to the capital rationing constraint, such that the sum of the projects' NPVs is maximized. Linear programming can be used, or if there are not too many projects involved, the financial manager can simply enumerate all the sets of projects that meet the budget constraint and then select the set with the largest total NPV.

The complexities involved in a capital rationing situation are indicated in Table 11A-1. Here we assume that the firm is considering a total of eight potential projects; all are independent and have average risk. The firm has a 10 percent cost of capital, but management has decided to limit capital expenditures during the year to the amount of money that can be generated internally, $500,000. In the table, the projects are listed in the descending order of their NPVs, but their IRRs and profitability indices (PIs) are also shown.

| TABLE 11A-1 | ILLUSTRATION OF CAPITAL RATIONING |

PROJECT NUMBER	PROJECT COST, OR OUTLAY, AT T = 0	PROJECT LIFE (YEARS)	CASH FLOW PER YEAR	NPV AT THE 10% COST OF CAPITAL	IRR	PROFITABILITY INDEX
1	$400,000	20	$58,600	$98,894	13.5%	1.25
2	250,000	10	55,000	87,951	17.7	1.35
3	100,000	8	24,000	28,038	17.3	1.28
4	75,000	15	12,000	16,273	13.7	1.22
5	75,000	6	18,000	3,395	11.5	1.05
6	50,000	5	14,000	3,071	12.4	1.06
7	250,000	10	41,000	1,927	10.2	1.01
8	250,000	3	99,000	(3,802)	9.1	0.98

If it is to maximize the value of the firm, management must choose the set of projects with the greatest total NPV, subject to the constraint that total expenditures must not exceed $500,000. With only eight projects in total, we can try all different combinations and by "brute force," determine the set which maximizes NPV. This set is optimal:[2]

PROJECT	COST	NPV
2	$250,000	$87,951
3	100,000	28,038
4	75,000	16,273
5	75,000	3,395
	$500,000	$135,657

This analysis seems simple enough, but there are three factors which complicate it greatly in realistic situations:

1. **Number of projects.** In the example, we have only eight projects, so it is easy to simply list all the combinations whose costs do not exceed $500,000 and then see which combination provides the greatest total NPV. For a large firm with thousands of projects, this would be a tedious process, although computer programs are available to solve such problems. However, the other problems listed next are more serious.

2. **Project risk.** In our example, we assumed that the eight projects are equally risky, hence have the same cost of capital. If this was not the case, and if the number of projects was so large as to preclude hand analysis, then it would be difficult, if not impossible, to reach an optimal solution, because the computer programs currently available cannot deal efficiently with projects having differential risks.

---

[2]Note that in capital rationing the goal in project selection is to get the "biggest bang for the buck." Since this is measured by the profitability index (PI), one way to determine the optimal set is by accepting projects in descending order of PIs, but recognizing that some high-PI projects might have to be rejected because insufficient funds are available.

3. **Multiple time constraints.** Our example also assumed a single-time-period capital constraint. Yet, realistically, when capital rationing is practiced, the constraints usually extend for several years. However, the funds available in future years depend on cash throw-offs from investments made in earlier years. Thus, the constraint in Year 2 depends on the investments made in Year 1, and so on. For example, we might have investment funds of $500,000 per year available from external sources for 1997 through 2001 plus the cash flows from investments made in previous years. To solve this type of multiperiod problem, we need information on both investment opportunities and funds availability in future years, and not just on the situation in the current year. Also, the NPV we seek to maximize is the sum of the present values of the NPVs in each year over the time horizon being analyzed, say, 1997 to 2001. In such a situation, we might even choose Project 8 in Table 11A-1, in spite of its negative NPV, because it has rapid cash throw-offs. In fact, if excellent investment opportunities are expected to be available in 1998, 1999, and 2000, taking Project 8 might be part of the best long-run strategy.

A BETTER APPROACH TO CAPITAL RATIONING   Our main conclusion thus far about capital rationing—which means deliberately foregoing projects with positive NPVs—is that practicing it is irrational for any firm which seeks to maximize its stockholders' wealth. Also, while mathematical programming methods are available to help solve the simpler cases of capital rationing so that management can make the best of a bad situation, programming methods are really not capable of dealing with all the complexities encountered in the real world.

Fortunately, there is a better method for handling the types of situations that give rise to capital rationing. Usually, capital rationing occurs when the firm believes that it will encounter severe problems if it attempts to raise capital beyond some specified amount. For example, the interest rate it would have to pay would rise sharply if it attempted to increase its existing lines of credit. Such situations can be rationally handled by increasing the firm's WACC as the amount of capital raised increases. In effect, in terms of Figure 11A-1, the MCC schedule would begin to rise beyond some amount of capital, resulting in a higher corporate cost of capital, and this higher cost should be used as the discount rate when determining a project's NPV.

P A R T IV

STRATEGIC FINANCING DECISIONS

CHAPTER 12

LONG-TERM FINANCIAL PLANNING

*M*itch Leibovitz, CEO of Pep Boys — Manny, Moe, and Jack, the auto parts and service chain, wants to annihilate the competition. When intense competition from Pep Boys forces chains such as Auto Zone, Western Auto, or Genuine Parts to abandon a location, Leibovitz adds a snapshot of the closed store to his collection. "I don't believe in friendly competition. I want to put them out of business," he says. Consolidation is under way in the $125-billion-a-year aftermarket for automotive parts and servicing, so survival demands that Pep Boys be "a killer."

Alone among its competitors, Pep Boys can install what it sells. If customers don't want to do the work themselves, Pep Boys will do everything except body work or replacing engines and transmissions. Nearly all of its 406 stores have ten or more service bays that keep long hours. They stay open 13 hours a day Monday through Saturday, 9 hours on Sunday. No appointment is needed. The company can perform repairs more cheaply than dealers, largely because it charges no markup on parts. Mechanics get paid 32 to 38 percent of the service charge instead of an hourly wage, but, contrary to common practice, no share of the parts they install. If work has to be redone, mechanics must do it at their own expense.

Pep Boys was founded in 1921 by Emmanuel Rosenfield ("Manny"), Maurice Strauss ("Moe"), and W. Graham Jackson ("Jack"). The company grew to more than 100 stores by the early 1960s, after which conservative family management slowed expansion. Pep Boys went public in 1946, but the families kept control until the mid-1980s.

When Leibovitz took the helm in 1986, the company embarked on a major expansion program. Since 1986, Leibovitz has more than doubled the number of stores and more than tripled sales to over $1.6 billion. Pep Boys's success *demonstrates that unswerving dedication to a single concept, no matter how mundane, can create a dynamic, growing business.*

Pep Boys now has more than 400 stores in 28 states. Analysts expect the store count to grow by 10 percent a year into the foreseeable future as the company enters new states and fills holes in existing markets. At this rate, the number of stores will double again in about seven years. Each new unit requires about $2.5 million for fixed assets and inventory, which Pep Boys funds primarily with internally generated equity plus debt.

According to Leibovitz, "If you want to have ho-hum results, have ho-hum goals." Pep Boys will have to do a lot of work to complete its expansion program. It will have to locate unserved markets, select sites, and line up the funds necessary to build the new outlets on schedule. In this chapter, we discuss financial forecasting, with an emphasis on how firms estimate the amount of capital needed to meet their growth targets. As you read the chapter, think about how Mitch Leibovitz might use the concepts presented here as he plans Pep Boys's expansion program. When you consider the potential impact of incorrect forecasting, you will quickly realize how important financial planning is to the success of any business.

Thus far, we have focused on financial decisions. We began with background information on financial statements, financial markets, risk measurement, discounted cash flow analysis, and valuation. Then we examined cost of capital and capital budgeting.

Parts I through III dealt to a large extent with theory and capital budgeting. However, investment decisions are made within guidelines set down in firms' operating and financing plans. Now, in Part IV, we discuss the planning process, with emphasis on long-term financial planning, capital structure decisions, and dividend policy. In this chapter, we discuss long-term planning, which provides managers with a "road map" for the next five to ten years.

STRATEGIC PLANS

Financial plans are developed within the framework of the firm's overall strategic plan. Thus, we begin with an overview of the strategic planning process.[1]

CORPORATE PURPOSE

The long-run strategic plan generally begins with a statement of the *corporate purpose,* or *corporate vision,* which defines the overall mission of the firm. There should be no conflict between a firm's corporate purpose and stockholders' interests, but occasionally there is. For example, Varian Associates Inc., an NYSE company with 1996 sales of almost $2 billion, was for years regarded as one of the most technologically advanced electronics companies. However, Varian's management had been more concerned with developing new technology than with marketing it, and

---

[1]One can take many approaches to corporate planning. For more insights into the corporate planning process, see Benton E. Gup, *Guide to Strategic Planning* (New York: McGraw-Hill, 1980).

the stock price was lower than it had been 10 years earlier. Some of the larger stockholders were intensely unhappy with the state of affairs, and management was faced with the threat of a proxy fight or forced merger. In 1991, management announced a change in policy and stated that it would, in the future, emphasize both technological excellence *and* profitability, rather than focusing primarily on technology. Earnings improved dramatically, and the stock price rose from $6.75 to more than $60 in only four years.

Similarly, IBM was floundering in the late 1980s and early 1990s, as personal computers hurt sales of its profitable mainframe business. Finally, IBM's board decided to replace top management, and Lou Gerstner was brought in as chairman. Early in his tenure, Gerstner was asked about his vision for the company, and he replied, in effect, that he did not have one. Analysts reacted harshly, and the stock dropped. Eventually, after he had a chance to evaluate IBM's strengths and weaknesses, Gerstner did articulate his vision for the company. Analysts and investors reacted positively, and the stock price doubled. It remains to be seen just how good Gerstner's vision turns out to be.

The Varian and IBM examples illustrate both the importance of the corporate purpose and the discipline imposed by the financial markets. Well-run companies must define an area and become competent at meeting the needs of their customers, but they will be forced by the market to translate that competence into earnings.

CORPORATE SCOPE

The *corporate scope* defines a firm's lines of business and geographic area of operations. Again, the corporate scope can be spelled out in great detail or stated in general terms. The steel industry provides a study in contrasts: some companies such as U.S. Steel (now USX Corporation) have diversified widely, from oil to financial services, while other companies have stuck closely to their basic business. Nucor Corporation, an NYSE-listed specialty steel producer, is one which has stuck to its basic business:

> We are a manufacturing company producing primarily steel products. Nucor's major strength is constructing plants economically and operating them efficiently.

A $1,000 investment in Nucor's stock in 1977 would be worth over $20,000 in 1996, while a similar investment in U.S. Steel would be worth less than $2,000. Factors other than scope of operations affected these results, but scope and focus were surely important factors.

CORPORATE OBJECTIVES

The corporate purpose and scope outline the general philosophy of the business, but they do not provide managers with operational objectives. The *corporate objectives* set forth specific goals that management strives to attain. Corporate objectives can be quantitative, such as specifying a target market share, a target ROE, a target earnings per share growth rate, or a target economic value added (EVA), or they can be qualitative, such as "keeping the firm's research and development efforts at the cutting edge of the industry." Multiple objectives are generally established, and they are not static — they are changed as conditions change. The objectives should be challenging, yet realistic, and management's compensation should be based on the extent to which objectives are met.

CORPORATE STRATEGIES

Once a firm has defined its purpose, scope, and objectives, it should develop a strategy to achieve its goals. *Corporate strategies* are broad approaches rather than detailed plans. For example, one airline may have a strategy of offering no-frills service between a limited number of cities, while another may plan to offer "staterooms in the sky." Strategies should be both attainable and compatible with the firm's purpose, scope, and objectives.

Perhaps the most interesting and important set of strategies that has been developed in recent years is that of AT&T and the Bell operating companies in the wake of the forced breakup of AT&T in 1984. The seven regional telephone holding companies which emerged from the breakup all provide basic local telephone service, but beyond that, they have been developing different strategies which will take them in different directions. Some now sell a broad array of telecommunications equipment, while others have more limited offerings. Some are rapidly diversifying into nonregulated lines of business — Bell Atlantic has spent more than $2 billion for this purpose — while others are diversifying at a much slower pace. Others are moving abroad; for example, BellSouth recently won a $220 million contract to build a mobile phone system in Argentina. Even more surprising, two separate mergers between the operating companies — Bell Atlantic with NYNEX and SBC with Pacific Telesis — have recently been announced, so to some extent the breakup is being reversed.

The surviving AT&T has changed its corporate strategy several times since the 1984 breakup. First, it tried to compete with IBM and the other computer companies, and failed. In 1996, AT&T announced plans to break itself up into three separate companies—new AT&T, which will be in the telecommunications business; Lucent Technologies, which will operate the manufacturing segment; and a yet-to-be-named computer company. (See the opening section of Chapter 8 for more about AT&T's strategic plans.)

SELF-TEST QUESTION

Briefly describe the nature and use of the following corporate planning tools:
(1) Corporate purpose
(2) Corporate scope
(3) Corporate objectives
(4) Corporate strategies

OPERATING PLANS

Operating plans can be developed for any time horizon, but most companies use a five-year horizon. A five-year plan is most detailed for the first year, with each succeeding year's plan becoming less specific. The plan is intended to provide detailed implementation guidance, based on the corporate strategy, in order to meet the corporate objectives. The plan explains in considerable detail who is responsible for what particular function, when specific tasks are to be accomplished, and the like.

Table 12-1 contains the annual planning schedule of MicroDrive Incorporated, a manufacturer of disk drives for microcomputers. This schedule illustrates the fact that for larger companies, the planning process is essentially continuous. Next, Table 12-2 outlines the key elements of MicroDrive's five-year plan. A full outline would require several pages, but Table 12-2 does at least provide insights into the format and content of a five-year plan. It should be noted that large, multidivisional companies such as General Electric break down their operating plans by divisions. Thus, each division has its own goals, mission, and plan for meeting its objectives, and these plans are then consolidated to form the corporate plan.

<table>
<tr><td>What is the purpose of a firm's operating plan?
What is the most common time horizon for operating plans?
Briefly describe the contents of a typical operating plan.</td><td>**SELF-TEST**
QUESTIONS</td></tr>
</table>

THE FINANCIAL PLAN

The financial planning process can be broken down into six steps:

1. Set up a system of projected financial statements which can be used to analyze the effects of the operating plan on projected profits and various financial ratios. This system can also be used to monitor operations after the plan has been finalized and put into effect. Rapid awareness of deviations from plans is essential to a good control system, which, in turn, is essential to corporate success in a changing world.

2. Determine the funds needed to support the five-year plan. This includes funds for plant and equipment as well as for inventory and receivables, for R&D programs, and for major advertising campaigns.

MicroDrive Incorporated: Annual Planning Schedule	Table 12-1

MONTHS	ACTION
April–May	Planning department analyzes general economic and industry factors. Marketing department prepares sales forecast for each product group.
June–July	Engineering department prepares cost estimates for new manufacturing facilities and plant modernization programs.
August–September	Financial analysts evaluate proposed capital expenditures, divisional operating plans, and proposed sources and uses of funds.
October–November	Five-year plan is finalized by planning department, reviewed by divisional officers, and put into "semifinal" form.
December	Five-year plan is approved by the executive committee and then submitted to the board of directors for final approval.

TABLE 12-2	MICRODRIVE INCORPORATED: FIVE-YEAR OPERATING PLAN OUTLINE

Part 1.   Corporate purpose

Part 2.   Corporate scope

Part 3.   Corporate objectives

Part 4.   Projected business environment

Part 5.   Corporate strategies

Part 6.   Summary of projected business results

Part 7.   Product line plans and policies
    a.   Marketing
    b.   Manufacturing
    c.   Finance
        1.   Working capital
            (a) Overall working capital policy
            (b) Cash and marketable securities
            (c) Inventory management
            (d) Credit policy and receivables management
        2.   Dividend policy
        3.   Capital structure policy
        4.   Financial forecast
            (a) Capital budget
            (b) Cash budget
            (c) Pro forma financial statements
            (d) External financing requirements
            (e) Financial condition analysis
        5.   Accounting plan
        6.   Control plan
    d.   Administrative and personnel
    e.   Research and development
    f.   New products

3. Forecast funds availability over the next five years. This involves estimating the funds to be generated internally as well as those to be obtained from external sources. Any constraints on operating plans imposed by financial restrictions should be incorporated into the plan; examples include restrictions on the debt ratio, the current ratio, and the coverage ratios.

4. Establish and maintain a system of controls governing the allocation and use of funds within the firm. In essence, this involves making sure that the basic plan is carried out properly.

5. Develop procedures for adjusting the basic plan if the economic forecasts upon which the plan was based do not materialize. For example, if the economy turns out to be stronger than was forecasted, then these new conditions must be recognized and reflected in higher production schedules, larger marketing quotas, and the like, and as rapidly as possible. Thus, Step 5 is really a "feedback loop" which triggers modifications to the financial plan.

6. Establish a performance-based management compensation system. It is critically important that such a system be used, and that it rewards managers for doing what stockholders want them to do—maximize share prices. The EVA system is generally regarded as one, indeed perhaps the best, of the procedures for this critical task.

In the remainder of this chapter, we focus on three key elements of the strategic plan, the sales forecast, pro forma financial statements, and the external financing plan.

What are the six steps of the financial planning process?

SELF-TEST QUESTION

SALES FORECASTS

The *sales forecast* generally starts with a review of sales during the past five to ten years, expressed in a graph such as that in Figure 12-1. The graph shows five years of historical sales for MicroDrive. The graph could have contained ten years of sales data, but MicroDrive typically focuses on sales figures for the latest five years because future growth is more closely related to the recent than to the distant past.

MicroDrive had its ups and downs during the period from 1992 to 1996. In 1994, poor performance of one of its drives led to bad publicity, which caused sales to fall below the 1993 level. Then, a banner year of microcomputer sales in 1995 pushed MicroDrive's sales up by 15 percent, an unusually high growth rate for the company. Based on a regression study, MicroDrive's forecasters determined that the average annual growth rate in sales over the past 5 years was 9.1 percent. On the basis of this historical sales trend, on new product introductions, and on MicroDrive's forecast for the economy, the firm's planning committee projects 10 percent sales growth during 1997, to $3,300 million. Here are some of the factors that MicroDrive considered in its sales forecast:

1. MicroDrive has two divisions: standard drives and custom drives. The standard drive division produces large quantities of standardized disk drives, generally having capacities of less than 1,000 megabytes (1 gigabyte) and selling for less than $1,000. The custom division manufactures high-capacity, super-fast drives with capacities greater than 1 gigabyte; they sell for as much as $3,000 and are produced in relatively small quantities. Sales growth is seldom the same for each division, so to begin the forecasting process, independent divisional forecasts are made on the basis of historical growth, and then the divisional forecasts are combined to produce a "first approximation" corporate sales forecast.

2. Next, the level of economic activity and the overall demand for microcomputers are forecasted. Here, MicroDrive's planners must recognize that the firm's products are sold in two vastly different markets. Most drives are sold directly to personal computer manufacturers such as Packard-Bell, Gateway 2000, and Zeos. Such sales are high volume, and their prices are negotiated. In addition, a significant percentage of sales is made through wholesalers to

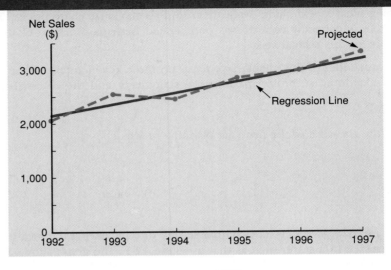

FIGURE 12-1   MICRODRIVE INCORPORATED: 1997 SALES PROJECTION (MILLIONS OF DOLLARS)

YEAR	SALES
1992	$2,058
1993	2,534
1994	2,472
1995	2,850
1996	3,000
1997	3,300 (Projected)

individuals or small firms who are either making their own microcomputers or replacing disk drives that have failed.

3. Then, the forecasters must estimate MicroDrive's market share for each product line in each market, considering both the overall demand for disk drives and the competition among the major manufacturers. Consideration must be given to the firm's production capacity, to its competitors' capacities, and to new product introductions both by microcomputer manufacturers and disk drive producers. Pricing strategies must also be considered—for example, should the company raise prices to boost margins, or should it lower prices to build market share and gain economies of scale in production?

4. MicroDrive sells all over the world. Its European sales represent about 20 percent of total sales, and Asian sales, which are currently only 4 percent of the total, are growing rapidly. MicroDrive's foreign sales present unique forecasting problems. In particular, its planners must consider how exchange rate

fluctuations would impact sales. MicroDrive must also consider the effects of trade agreements, governmental policies, and the like.

5. Inflation will also affect the firm's prices. Over the next five years, the inflation rate is expected to average 3 to 4 percent, and MicroDrive plans to increase prices, on average, by a like amount. In addition, the firm expects to expand its market share in certain products, resulting in a 4 percent growth rate in unit sales. The combination of unit sales growth and increases in sales prices has resulted in historical revenue growth rates in the 8 to 10 percent range, and this same situation is expected in the future.

6. Advertising campaigns, promotional discounts, credit terms, and the like, also affect sales, so developments in these areas must be factored in.

7. Forecasts are made for each division both in total and on an individual product basis. The individual product sales forecasts are summed, and this sum is compared with the overall divisional forecasts. Differences are reconciled, and the end result is a sales forecast for the company as a whole but with breakdowns by the two divisions and by individual products.

If the sales forecast is off, the consequences can be serious. First, if the market expands *more* than MicroDrive has geared up for, the company will not be able to meet demand. Its customers will end up buying competitors' products, and Micro-Drive will lose market share. On the other hand, if its projections are overly optimistic, MicroDrive could end up with too much plant, equipment, and inventory. This would mean low turnover ratios, high costs for depreciation and storage, and, possibly, write-offs of obsolete inventory. All of this would result in a low rate of return on equity, which in turn would depress the company's stock price. If Micro-Drive had financed an unnecessary expansion with debt, its problems would be compounded. Thus, an accurate sales forecast is critical to the well-being of the firm.[2]

SELF-TEST QUESTIONS

How do past trends affect a sales forecast?

List some factors that should be considered when developing a sales forecast.

Explain why an accurate sales forecast is critical to profitability.

FINANCIAL STATEMENT FORECASTING: THE CONSTANT RATIO METHOD

Once sales have been forecasted, we must forecast future balance sheets and income statements. The simplest technique, and the one that is most useful for explaining the mechanics of financial statement forecasting, is the *constant ratio method*. The steps in this procedure are described below for MicroDrive.

---

[2]A sales forecast is actually the *expected value of a probability distribution* with many possible levels of sales. Because any sales forecast is subject to uncertainty, financial planners are just as interested in the degree of uncertainty inherent in the sales forecast, as measured by the standard deviation, as in the expected level of sales.

STEP 1.   FORECASTED INCOME STATEMENT

The income statement for the coming year is forecasted in order to obtain an estimate of reported income and the amount of retained earnings the company will generate during the year. This requires assumptions about the operating cost ratio, the tax rate, interest charges, and the dividend payout ratio. In the simplest case, the assumption is made that all costs will increase at the same rate as sales; in more complicated situations, specific costs will be forecasted separately. Still, the primary objective of this part of the forecast is to determine how much income the company will earn and retain for reinvestment during the forecasted year.

Table 12-3 shows MicroDrive's actual 1996 and forecasted 1997 income statements. To begin, we assume that sales and costs grow by 10 percent in 1997 over the 1996 levels. Therefore, we show the factor $(1 + g) = 1.10$ in the first three rows of Column 2, and in the same rows of Column 3 we show the forecasted 1997 sales, operating costs, and depreciation. EBIT is found by subtraction, while the interest charges in Column 3 are simply carried over from Column 1. Note, though, that interest charges will change once we know how much additional debt will be required.

Earnings before taxes (EBT) are then calculated, as is net income before preferred dividends. Preferred dividends are carried over from the 1996 column, and they will

						TABLE 12-3
MICRODRIVE INCORPORATED: ACTUAL 1996 AND PROJECTED 1997 INCOME STATEMENTS (MILLIONS OF DOLLARS)						

			1997 FORECAST			
	ACTUAL 1996 (1)	**FORECAST BASIS (2)**	**FIRST PASS (3)**	**FEEDBACK (4)**	**SECOND PASS (5)**	**FINAL (6)**
1. Sales	$3,000	×1.10[a]	$3,300		$3,300	$3,300
2. Costs except depreciation	$2,616	×1.10	$2,878		$2,878	$2,878
3. Depreciation	100	×1.10	110		110	110
4. Total operating costs	$2,716		$2,988		$2,988	$2,988
5. EBIT	$ 284		$ 312		$ 312	$ 312
6. Less interest	88		88[b]	+5	93	93
7. Earnings before taxes (EBT)	$ 196		$ 224		$ 219	$ 219
8. Taxes (40%)	78		89	−1	88	88
9. NI before preferred dividends	$ 118		$ 135		$ 131	$ 131
10. Dividends to preferred	4		4[b]		4	4
11. NI available to common	$ 114		$ 131		$ 127	$ 127
12. Dividends to common	$ 58		$ 63[c]	+3	$ 66	$ 66
13. Addition to retained earnings	$ 56		$ 68	−7	$ 61	$ 61

[a]×1.10 indicates "times $1 + g$"; used for items which grow proportionally with sales.
[b]Indicates a 1996 amount carried over for first-pass forecast.
[c]Indicates a projected amount. See text for explanation.

remain constant unless MicroDrive decides to issue additional preferred stock. Net income available to common is calculated, and then the 1997 initial dividends are forecasted as follows: the 1996 dividend per share is $1.15, and this dividend is expected to be increased by about 8 percent, to $1.25. Since there are 50 million shares outstanding, the initially projected dividends are $1.25(50,000,000) = $62.5 million, rounded to $63 million. (Again, like interest, this figure will be increased later in the analysis to reflect additional shares sold.)

As the last part of the first-pass forecasted income statement, the $63 million projected dividends are subtracted from the $131 million projected net income to determine the first-pass projection of retained earnings, $131 − $63 = $68 million. *Note, though, that this $68 million forecast for retained earnings will turn out to be too high because it understates the actual amount of interest and common stock dividends for 1997. MicroDrive will have to borrow as well as sell additional common stock to finance its asset requirements, and these actions will change the first-pass forecasted income statement.* Those modifications will be made after we know how much additional financing will be required.

STEP 2. FORECAST THE BALANCE SHEET

If MicroDrive's sales are to increase, then its assets must also grow. Since the company was operating at full capacity in 1996, each asset account must increase if the higher sales level is to be attained: more cash will be needed, higher sales will lead to higher receivables, additional inventory will have to be stocked, and new plant and equipment must be added.

Further, if MicroDrive's assets are to increase, its liabilities and equity must also increase — the additional assets must be financed. *Spontaneously generated funds* will be provided by accounts payable and accruals. For example, as sales increase, so will MicroDrive's purchases of raw materials, and these larger purchases will spontaneously lead to higher levels of accounts payable. Similarly, a higher level of operations will require more labor, while higher sales will result in higher taxable income. Therefore, accrued wages and accrued taxes will increase. In general, these spontaneous liability accounts will increase at the same rate as sales.

Retained earnings will also increase, but not at the same rate as sales: the new level of retained earnings will be the old level plus the addition to retained earnings, which we calculated in Step 1. Also, notes payable, long-term bonds, preferred stock, and common stock will not rise spontaneously with sales — rather, the projected levels of these accounts will depend on financing decisions that will be made later.

In summary, (1) higher sales must be supported by higher asset levels, (2) some of the asset increases will be financed by spontaneous increases in accounts payable and accruals and by retained earnings, and (3) any shortfall must be financed from external sources, using some combination of debt, common stock, and preferred stock.

Table 12-4 contains MicroDrive's 1996 actual and its projected 1997 balance sheets. The mechanics of the balance sheet forecast are similar to those used to develop the forecasted income statement. First, those balance sheet accounts that are expected to increase directly with sales are multiplied by 1.10 to obtain the initial 1997 forecasts. Thus, 1997 cash is projected to be $10(1.10) = $11 million,

| TABLE 12-4 | MicroDrive Incorporated: Actual 1996 and Projected 1997 Balance Sheets (Millions of Dollars) |

| | ACTUAL 1996 (1) | FORECAST BASIS (2) | 1997 FORECAST | | | |
			FIRST PASS (3)	AFN[a] (4)	SECOND PASS (5)	FINAL (6)
Cash	$ 10	×1.10[b]	$ 11			
Accounts receivable	375	×1.10	412			
Inventories	615	×1.10	677			
Total current assets	$1,000		$1,100			
Net plant and equipment	1,000	×1.10	1,100			
Total assets	$2,000		$2,200		$2,200	$2,200
Accounts payable	$ 60	×1.10	$ 66		$ 66	$ 66
Notes payable	110		110[c]	+ 28	138	140
Accruals	140	×1.10	154		154	154
Total current liabilities	$ 310		$ 330		$ 358	$ 360
Long-term bonds	754		754[c]	+ 28	782	784
Total debt	$1,064		$1,084		$1,140	$1,144
Preferred stock	$ 40		$ 40[c]		$ 40	$ 40
Common stock	$ 130		$ 130[c]	+ 56	$ 186	$ 189
Retained earnings	766	+68[d]	834		827	827
Total common equity	$ 896		$ 964		$1,013	$1,016
Total liabilities and equity	$2,000		$2,088	+112	$2,193	$2,200
Additional funds needed (AFN) this pass			$ 112		$ 7	$ 0
Cumulative AFN			$ 112		$ 119	$ 119

[a]AFN stands for "Additional Funds Needed." This figure is determined at the bottom of Column 3, and Column 4 shows how the required $112 of AFN will be raised.
[b]×1.10 indicates "times $1 + g$"; used for items which grow proportionally with sales.
[c]Indicates a 1996 amount carried over as the first-pass forecast.
[d]From Column 3 of Table 12-3.

accounts receivable are projected to be $375(1.10) \approx$ $412 million, and so on. Note that MicroDrive was operating its fixed assets at full capacity in 1996, so its net plant and equipment must also increase by the 10 percent sales growth rate.

Once the individual asset accounts have been forecasted, they can be summed to complete the asset side of the balance sheet. For example, the total current assets forecasted for 1997 are $11 + $412 + $677 = $1,100 million, and total assets equal $2,200 million.

Next, the spontaneously increasing liabilities (accounts payable and accruals) are forecasted and shown in Column 3, the first-pass forecast. Then, those liability accounts whose values reflect conscious management decisions—notes payable, long-term bonds, preferred stock, and common stock—are initially set at their 1996 levels. Thus, 1997 notes payable are initially set at $110 million, the long-term bond account is forecasted at $754 million, and so on. The 1997 value for the retained earnings (RE) account is obtained by adding the projected addition to retained earnings as developed in the 1997 income statement (see Table 12-3) to the 1996 ending balance:

$$1997 \text{ RE} = 1996 \text{ RE} + 1997 \text{ forecasted addition to RE}$$

$$= \$766 + \$68 = \$834 \text{ million on first pass.}$$

The forecast of total assets as shown in the first-pass forecast of Table 12-4 is $2,200 million, which indicates that MicroDrive must add $200 million of new assets in 1997 to support the higher sales level. However, the forecasted liability and equity accounts as shown in the lower portion of Column 3 total to only $2,088 million. Since the balance sheet must balance, MicroDrive must raise an additional $2,200 − $2,088 = $112 million, which we designate as *Additional Funds Needed (AFN)*. The AFN will be raised by borrowing from the bank as notes payable, by issuing long-term bonds, and by selling new common stock.

STEP 3. RAISING THE ADDITIONAL FUNDS NEEDED

MicroDrive's financial manager will base the financing mix on several factors, including the firm's target capital structure, conditions in the debt and equity markets, and restrictions imposed by existing debt agreements. MicroDrive's financial manager, after considering all of the relevant factors, decided on the following financing mix to raise the $112 million of additional funds:

	AMOUNT OF NEW CAPITAL		
TYPE OF CAPITAL	PERCENT	DOLLARS (MILLIONS)	INTEREST RATE
Notes payable	25%	$ 28	8%
Long-term bonds	25	28	10
Common stock	50	56	—
	100%	$112	

These amounts, which are shown in Column 4 of Table 12-4, are added to the initially forecasted account totals as shown in Column 3 to generate the second-pass balance sheet. Thus, in Column 5 the notes payable account increases to $110 + $28 = $138 million, long-term bonds rise to $754 + $28 = $782 million, and common stock increases to $130 + $56 = $186 million.

If there were no changes in any other income statement or balance sheet account, the forecast would be complete—the initial shortfall was $112 million, and MicroDrive would raise that amount as shown above. However, when MicroDrive takes on new debt, its interest expenses will rise, and the additional shares of common stock will cause dividend payments to increase. These changes will affect the amount of retained earnings, as we discuss in the next section.

STEP 4.   FINANCING FEEDBACKS

One complexity that arises in financial forecasting relates to *financing feedbacks:* The external funds raised to pay for new assets create additional expenses which must be reflected in the income statement, and that lowers the initially forecasted addition to retained earnings. To handle financing feedbacks, we first forecast the additional interest expense and dividends that result from external financings. New short-term debt costs 8 percent, so the $28 million of new notes payable will increase MicroDrive's projected 1997 interest expense by 0.08($28) = $2.24 million. Similarly, new long-term bonds will add 0.10($28) = $2.80 million in interest expense, so the total increase in interest expense will be $5.04 million. When these feedbacks are considered, interest expense as shown in the projected 1997 second-pass income statement in Column 5 of Table 12-3 increases to $88 + $5 = $93 million. These higher interest charges will, of course, also affect the remainder of the income statement.

The financing plan also calls for issuing $56 million of new common stock. MicroDrive's stock price was $23 at the end of 1996, and if we assume that new shares would be sold at this price, then $56/$23 = 2.4 million shares of new stock will have to be sold. Further, MicroDrive's 1997 dividend payment is projected to be $1.25 per share, so the 2.4 million shares of new stock will require 2.4($1.25) = $3 million of additional dividend payments. Thus, dividends to common stockholders as shown in the second-pass income statement increase to $63 + $3 = $66 million.

The net effect of the financing feedbacks is to reduce the addition to retained earnings by $7 million, from $68 million to $61 million. This reduces the balance sheet forecast of retained earnings by a like amount, so in Table 12-4 the second-pass 1997 balance sheet projection for retained earnings becomes $766 + $61 = $827 million, or $7 million less than in the initial forecast. Thus, a shortfall of $7 million will still exist as a result of financing feedback effects. This amount is shown toward the bottom of Column 5 in Table 12-4.

How would the second-pass shortfall be financed? In MicroDrive's case, 25 percent of the $7 million would be obtained as short-term debt, 25 percent as long-term bonds, and 50 percent as new common stock.

We could create a third-pass balance sheet by using this financing mix to add another $7 million to the liabilities and equity side. Would the third pass balance? No, because the additional $7 million in capital would require another increase in interest and dividend payments, and this would affect the third-pass income statement. There would still be a shortfall, although it would be much smaller than the $7 million shortfall on the second pass. We could then construct a fourth-pass forecasted income statement and balance sheet, fifth-pass statements, and so on. In each iteration, the additional financing would become smaller and smaller, and after about five iterations, the AFN would become so small that we could consider the forecast to be completed. We do not show the additional iterations, but the final results are shown in Column 6 of Tables 12-3 and 12-4.[3]

---

[3]It is rather tedious to make financial forecasts by hand. Fortunately, it is easy to make a model using a spreadsheet program which can do the iterations and arrive at the final forecast.

ANALYSIS OF THE FORECAST

The 1997 forecast as developed above is only the first part of MicroDrive's total forecasting process. Now we must analyze the projected statements to determine whether the forecast meets the firm's financial targets laid down in the five-year plan. If the statements do not meet the targets, then elements of the forecast must be changed.

Table 12-5 shows MicroDrive's key ratios for 1996, plus the projected 1997 ratios and the latest industry average ratios. (The table also shows some "Revised" data which we will discuss later.) The firm's financial condition at the close of 1996 was weak, with many ratios being well below the industry averages. The preliminary forecast for 1997 (after financing feedbacks are considered), which assumes that MicroDrive's past practices will continue into the future, is also relatively weak, and this condition will persist unless management takes action to improve things.

MicroDrive actually plans to take three steps to improve its financial condition: (1) Management plans to lay off some workers and to close certain operations. These steps should lower operating costs (excluding depreciation) from the current 87.2 percent of sales to 86 percent. (2) By screening credit customers more closely and by being more aggressive in collecting past-due accounts, the days sales outstanding on receivables will be reduced from 45 to 42.5 days. (3) Finally, management thinks that the inventory turnover ratio can be increased from 4.9 to 6 times through tighter inventory controls.[4]

These proposed operational changes were then used to create a revised set of forecasted statements for 1997. We do not show the new financial statements, but their impact on the key ratios is shown in Table 12-5 in the Revised 1997 column. Here are the highlights:

	ACTUAL 1996	PROJECTED AFN AND KEY RATIOS **TABLE 12-5**		
	ACTUAL 1996	PRELIMINARY 1997[a]	INDUSTRY AVERAGE	REVISED 1997[a]
AFN		$119		($64)
Current ratio	3.2	3.1	4.2	3.6
Inventory turnover	4.9	4.9	9.0	6.0
Days sales outstanding	45.0	45.0	36.0	42.5
Total assets turnover	1.5	1.5	1.8	1.6
Debt ratio[b]	55.2%	53.8%	40.0%	51.6%
Profit margin	3.8%	3.8%	5.0%	4.8%
Return on assets	5.7%	5.8%	9.0%	7.7%
Return on equity	12.7%	12.5%	15.0%	15.9%

[a]The 1997 data reflect all financing feedbacks.
[b]Includes preferred stock.

---

[4]We will discuss inventory and receivables management in Chapter 20.

1. By decreasing operating costs from 87.2 to 86 percent of sales, MicroDrive's forecasted cost figures on Rows 2 and 4 of Table 12-3 were lowered. These changes worked on through the income statement, and as a result the profit margin improves from 3.8 to 4.8 percent, which is close to the industry average.

2. The increase in the profit margin results in an increase in projected retained earnings. Further, by tightening inventory controls and reducing the days sales outstanding, MicroDrive projects a reduction in the forecasted levels of inventories and receivables. Taken together, these actions result in a *negative* AFN of $64 million, which means that MicroDrive would actually generate $64 million more from internal operations than it needs for new assets. This $64 million of surplus funds would be used to reduce short-term debt, which would lead to a decrease in the forecasted debt ratio from 53.8 to 51.6 percent. The debt ratio would still be well above the industry average, but this would be a step in the right direction.

3. The indicated changes would also affect MicroDrive's current ratio, which would improve from 3.1 to 3.6.

4. These actions also lead to an improvement in the rate of return on assets from 5.8 to 7.7 percent, and they boost the return on equity from 12.5 to 15.9 percent, which even exceeds the industry average.

Although MicroDrive's managers believe that the revised forecast is achievable, they cannot be sure of this. Accordingly, they also want to know how variations in sales would affect the forecast. A spreadsheet model was run using alternative sales growth rates, and the results were analyzed to see how the firm's financial condition would change under alternative growth scenarios. To illustrate, if the sales growth rate forecast increased from 10 to 20 percent, the additional funding requirement would change dramatically, from a $64 million surplus to an $83 million shortfall.

The spreadsheet model was also used to evaluate dividend policy. If MicroDrive decided to reduce its dividend growth rate, then additional funds would be available, and these funds could be invested in plant, equipment, and inventories, used to reduce debt, or used to repurchase stock.

The model was also used to evaluate financing alternatives. For example, Micro-Drive could use the forecasted $64 million of surplus funds to retire long-term bonds rather than to reduce short-term debt. Under this scenario, the current ratio would drop from 3.6 to 2.9, but the debt ratio would decline and interest coverage would be improved.

Forecasting is an iterative process, both in the way the financial statements are generated and the way the financial plan is developed. For planning purposes, the financial staff develops a preliminary forecast based on a continuation of past policies and trends. This provides the executives with a starting point, or "straw man" forecast. Next, the model is modified to see how alternative operating plans affect earnings and the financial ratios. This generally leads to a revised forecast. In addition, alternative operating plans are examined under different sales growth rate scenarios, and the model is used to evaluate both dividend policy and capital structure decisions.

The model can also be used to analyze alternative short-term policies — that is, to see how changes in cash management, credit policy, inventory policy, and the use of different types of short-term credit affect things. We will examine short-term policy decisions in Chapter 20, but in the remainder of this chapter we consider some other aspects of the financial forecasting process.

SELF-TEST QUESTIONS

What is the AFN, and how is it estimated?

What is a financing feedback, and how do financing feedbacks affect the estimate of AFN?

THE FORMULA METHOD FOR FORECASTING AFN

Although forecasts of capital requirements are made by constructing pro forma income statements and balance sheets as described above, the following formula can be used to obtain an initial rough estimate of financial requirements:

$$
\begin{array}{llll}
\text{Additional} & \text{Required} & \text{Spontaneous} & \text{Increase in} \\
\text{funds} & = \text{increase} & - \text{increase in} & - \text{retained} \\
\text{needed} & \text{in assets} & \text{liabilities} & \text{earnings}
\end{array}
$$

$$
\text{AFN} = (A^*/S)\Delta S - (L^*/S)\Delta S - MS_1(1 - d).
$$

12-1

Here

AFN = additional funds needed.

A^*/S = assets that must increase if sales are to increase, expressed as a percentage of sales, or the required dollar increase in assets per $1 increase in sales. A^*/S = $2,000/$3,000 = 0.6667 for MicroDrive. Thus, for every $1 increase in sales, assets must increase by about 67 cents. Note that A designates total assets and A^* designates those assets that must increase if sales are to increase. When the firm is operating at full capacity, as is the case here, $A^* = A$. Often, though, A^* and A are not equal, and the equation must be modified.

L^*/S = liabilities that increase spontaneously with sales as a percentage of sales, or spontaneously generated financing per $1 increase in sales. L^*/S = ($60 + $140)/$3,000 = 0.0667 for MicroDrive. Thus, every $1 increase in sales generates about 7 cents of spontaneous financing. Again, L^* represents liabilities that increase spontaneously, and L^* is normally less than L, the firm's total liabilities.

S_1 = total sales projected for next year. Note that S_0 designates last year's sales. S_1 = $3,300 million for MicroDrive.

ΔS = change in sales = $S_1 - S_0$ = $3,300 million - $3,000 million = $300 million for MicroDrive.

M = profit margin, or rate of profit per $1 of sales. M = $114/$3,000 = 0.0380 for MicroDrive.

> d = fraction of earnings paid out in common dividends, or the dividend payout ratio; d = \$58/\$114 = 0.5088 for MicroDrive.

Inserting values for MicroDrive into Equation 12-1, we find the additional funds needed to be \$118 million:

$$AFN = 0.667(\Delta S) - 0.067(\Delta S) - 0.038(S_1)(1 - 0.509)$$

$$= 0.667(\$300 \text{ million}) - 0.067(\$300 \text{ million}) - 0.038(\$3,300 \text{ million})(0.491)$$

$$= \$200 \text{ million} - \$20 \text{ million} - \$62 \text{ million}$$

$$= \$118 \text{ million.}$$

To increase sales by \$300 million, the formula suggests that MicroDrive must increase assets by \$200 million. The \$200 million of new assets must be financed in some manner. Of the total, \$20 million will come from a spontaneous increase in liabilities, while another \$62 million will be obtained from retained earnings. The remaining \$118 million must be raised from external sources. This value is only an approximation, and it is slightly different from the \$119 we developed in Table 12-4.

Inherent in the formula are the assumptions (1) that each asset item must grow at the same rate as sales, (2) that designated liability accounts also grow at the same rate as sales, and (3) that the profit margin and dividend payout are constant. Obviously, these assumptions do not always hold, so the formula does not always produce reliable results. Therefore, the formula is used primarily for a rough-and-ready forecast of financial requirements, and as a supplement to the projected financial statement method.

RELATIONSHIP BETWEEN GROWTH AND FINANCIAL REQUIREMENTS

The faster a firm's growth in sales, the greater its need for additional financing; we can use Equation 12-1, a variant of which is plotted in Figure 12-2, to demonstrate this relationship. The data given below the graph show MicroDrive's additional financial requirements at various growth rates, and these data are plotted in the graph. The figure illustrates the following four points:

1. **Financial feasibility.** At low growth rates MicroDrive needs no external financing, and it even generates surplus cash. However, if the company grows faster than 3.21 percent, it must raise capital from outside sources.[5] Further, the faster its growth rate, the greater its capital requirements. If management forcasts a high growth rate but foresees difficulties in raising the required capital, it should reconsider its expansion plans.

2. **Effect of dividend policy on financing needs.** Dividend policy as reflected in the payout ratio (d in Equation 12-1) also affects external capital requirements — the higher the payout ratio, the smaller the addition to retained earnings, hence the greater the requirements for external capital. Therefore, if MicroDrive foresees difficulties in raising capital, it might want to consider reducing its dividend payout ratio. This would lower (or shift to the

---

[5]We found the 3.21 percent growth rate by setting AFN equal to zero, substituting gS_0 for ΔS and $S_0 + g(S_0)$ for S_1 in the AFN equation, and then solving the equation $0 = 0.667(g)(S_0) - 0.067(g)(S_0) - 0.038(S_0 + gS_0)(1 - 0.509)$ for g. The g that solved this equation was about 0.0321, or 3.21 percent. This growth rate can also be read from the graph in Figure 12-2.

right) the line in Figure 12-2, indicating smaller external capital requirements at all growth rates. However, before changing its dividend policy, management should consider the effects of such a decision on stock prices, a topic we take up in Chapter 15.

Notice that the line in Figure 12-2 does *not* pass through the origin. Therefore, at low growth rates (below 3.21 percent), surplus funds will be produced, because retained earnings plus spontaneous funds will exceed the required asset increases. Only if the dividend payout ratio were 100 percent, meaning that the firm did not retain any of its earnings, would the "funds needed" line pass through the origin.

MICRODRIVE INCORPORATED: RELATIONSHIP BETWEEN GROWTH IN SALES AND FINANCIAL REQUIREMENTS, ASSUMING $S_0 = \$3,000$ (MILLIONS OF DOLLARS)

FIGURE 12-2

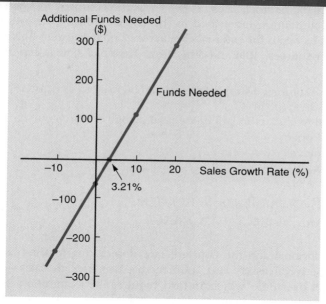

GROWTH RATE IN SALES (1)	INCREASE (DECREASE) IN SALES, ΔS (2)	FORECASTED SALES, S_1 (3)	ADDITIONAL FUNDS NEEDED (4)
(10%)	($300)	$2,700	($230)
0	0	3,000	(56)
3.21	96	3,096	0
10	300	3,300	118
20	600	3,600	293

Explanation of Columns:
Column 1: Assumed growth rate in sales, g.
Column 2: Increase (decrease) in sales, $\Delta S = g(S_0) = g(\$3,000)$.
Column 3: Forecasted sales, $S_1 = S_0 + g(S_0) = S_0(1 + g) = \$3,000(1 + g)$.
Column 4: Additional funds needed = $0.667(\Delta S) - 0.067(\Delta S) - 0.019(S_1)$.

3. **Capital intensity.** The amount of assets required per dollar of sales, A^*/S in Equation 12-1, is often called the *capital intensity ratio.* This ratio has a major effect on capital requirements per unit of sales growth. If the capital intensity ratio is low, sales can grow rapidly without much outside capital. However, if the firm is capital intensive, even a small growth in output will require a great deal of new capital.

4. **Profit margin.** The profit margin, M, is also an important determinant of AFN — the higher the margin, the lower the funds requirements, other things held constant. In terms of the graph, an increase in the profit margin would cause the line to shift down, and its slope would also become less steep. Because of the relationship between profit margins and additional capital requirements, some very rapidly growing firms do not need much external capital. For example, for many years Xerox grew at a rapid rate with very little borrowing or stock sales. However, as the company lost patent protection and as competition intensified in the copier industry, Xerox's profit margin declined, its needs for external capital rose, and it began to borrow from banks and other sources. IBM and other firms have had similar experiences.

SELF-TEST QUESTIONS

Under certain conditions, a simple formula can be used to forecast AFN. Give the formula and briefly explain it.

How do the following factors affect external capital requirements?
(1) Dividend policy
(2) Capital intensity
(3) Profit margin

FORECASTING FINANCIAL REQUIREMENTS WHEN THE BALANCE SHEET RATIOS ARE SUBJECT TO CHANGE

Both the AFN formula and the constant ratio forecasting method assume that the relationships between assets and spontaneous liabilities to sales (A^*/S and L^*/S) remain constant over time, which, in turn, requires the assumption that each "spontaneous" asset and liability item increases at the same rate as sales. In graph form, this implies the type of relationship shown in Panel a of Figure 12-3, a relationship that is (1) linear and (2) passes through the origin. Under those conditions, if the company's sales increase from $200 million to $400 million, inventory must increase at the same rate, from $100 million to $200 million.

The assumption of constant ratios, which implies identical growth rates, is appropriate at times, but there are times when it is incorrect. Three such conditions are described in the following sections.

ECONOMIES OF SCALE

There are economies of scale in the use of many assets, and when economies occur, the ratios are likely to change over time as the size of the firm increases. For example, firms often need to maintain base stocks of different inventory items even if cur-

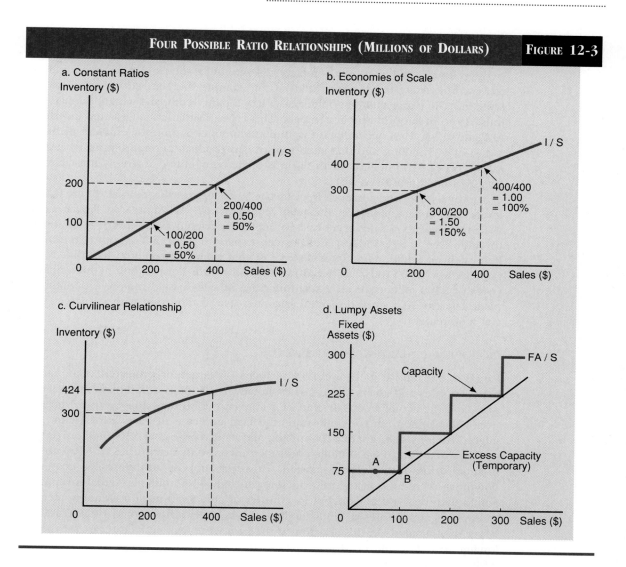

FOUR POSSIBLE RATIO RELATIONSHIPS (MILLIONS OF DOLLARS)   FIGURE 12-3

rent sales are quite low. As sales expand, inventories grow less rapidly than sales, so the ratio of inventory to sales declines. This situation is depicted in Panel b of Figure 12-3. Here we see that the inventory/sales ratio is 1.5, or 150 percent, when sales are $200 million, but the ratio declines to 1.0 when sales climb to $400 million.

The relationship shown in Panel b is linear, but nonlinear relationships often exist. Indeed, as we shall see in Chapter 22, if the firm uses one popular model for establishing inventory levels, the EOQ model, its inventories will rise with the square root of sales. In this situation, which is shown in Panel c, the graph is a curved line whose slope decreases at higher sales levels.

Lumpy Assets

In many industries, technological considerations dictate that if a firm is to be competitive, it must add fixed assets in large, discrete units; such assets are often referred to as *lumpy assets*. In the paper industry, for example, there are strong economies of scale in basic paper mill equipment, so when a paper company expands capacity, it must do so in large, lumpy increments. This type of situation is depicted in Panel d of Figure 12-3. Here we assume that the minimum economically efficient plant has a cost of $75 million and that such a plant can produce enough output to attain a sales level of $100 million. If the firm is to be competitive, it simply must have at least $75 million of fixed assets.

Lumpy assets have a major effect on the fixed assets/sales ratio at different sales levels, and consequently on financial requirements. At Point A in Figure 12-3d, which represents a sales level of $50 million, the fixed assets are $75 million, so the ratio FA/S = $75/$50 = 1.5. Sales can expand by $50 million, out to $100 million, with no additions to fixed assets. At that point, represented by Point B, the ratio FA/S = $75/$100 = 0.75. However, if the firm is operating at full capacity (sales of $100 million), even a small increase in sales would require a doubling of plant capacity, so a small projected sales increase would bring with it a large financial requirement.[6]

Nonoptimal Starting Point Ratios

Panels a, b, c, and d of Figure 12-3 all focus on target, or projected, relationships between sales and assets. Actual sales, however, are often different from projected sales, and the actual asset/sales ratio for a given period may thus be quite different from the planned ratio. To illustrate, the firm depicted in Panel b of Figure 12-3 might, when its sales are at $200 million and its inventories at $300 million, project a sales expansion to $400 million and then increase its inventories to $400 million in anticipation of the sales expansion. However, suppose an unforeseen economic downturn were to limit the sales increase to only $300 million. Actual inventories would then be $400 million, but inventories of only $350 million would be needed to support actual sales of $300 million. Thus, inventories would be $50 million larger than needed. In this situation, if the firm were making its forecast for the following year, it would need to recognize that sales could expand by $100 million with no increase whatever in inventories, but that any sales expansion beyond $100 million would require additional financing to carry inventories.

---

[6]Several other points should be noted about Panel d of Figure 12-3. First, if the firm is operating at a sales level of $100 million or less, any expansion that calls for a sales increase above $100 million will require a *doubling* of the firm's fixed assets. A much smaller percentage increase would be involved if the firm were large enough to be operating a number of plants. Second, firms generally go to multiple shifts and take other actions to minimize the need for new fixed asset capacity as they approach Point B. However, these efforts can go only so far, and eventually a fixed asset expansion will be required. Third, firms often make arrangements to share excess capacity with other firms in their industry. For example, consider the situation in the electric utility industry, which is very much like that depicted in Panel c. Electric companies often build jointly owned plants, or else they "take turns" building plants, and then they buy power from or sell power to other utilities to avoid building new plants that may be underutilized.

EXCESS CAPACITY ADJUSTMENTS

Consider again the MicroDrive example set forth in Tables 12-3 and 12-4. Now assume that excess capacity exists in fixed assets. Specifically, assume that fixed assets in 1996 were being utilized to only 96 percent of capacity. If fixed assets had been used to full capacity, 1996 sales could have been as high as $3,125 million, versus the $3,000 million in actual sales:

$$\text{Full capacity sales} = \frac{\text{Actual sales}}{\text{Percentage of capacity at which fixed assets were operated}} \qquad \text{12-2}$$

$$= \frac{\$3,000 \text{ million}}{0.96} = \$3,125 \text{ million.}$$

This suggests that MicroDrive's Target fixed assets/Sales ratio should be 32 percent:

$$\text{Target fixed assets/Sales ratio} = \frac{\text{Actual fixed assets}}{\text{Full capacity sales}} \qquad \text{12-3}$$

$$= \frac{\$1,000}{\$3,125} = 0.32 = 32\%.$$

Therefore, if sales are to increase to $3,300 million, then fixed assets would have to increase to $1,056 million:

$$\text{Required level of fixed assets} = \text{Target fixed assets to sales ratio (Projected sales)} \qquad \text{12-4}$$

$$= 0.32(\$3,300) = \$1,056 \text{ million.}$$

We had previously forecasted that MicroDrive would need to increase fixed assets at the same rate as sales, or by 10 percent, which meant an increase from $1,000 million to $1,100 million, or by $100 million. Now we see that the actual required increase is only from $1,000 million to $1,056 million, or by $56 million. Thus, the capacity-adjusted forecast of AFN is $100 million − $56 million = $44 million less than the earlier forecast. Therefore, the projected AFN would decline from an estimated $112 million (before financing feedback effects) to $112 million − $44 million = $68 million.

Note also that when excess capacity exists, sales growth up to the capacity sales as determined above can occur with no increase whatever in fixed assets and that sales beyond that growth will require fixed asset additions as calculated in our example. The same situation could occur with respect to inventories, and the required additions would be determined in exactly the same manner as for fixed assets. Theoretically, the same situation could occur with other types of assets, but as a practical matter, substantial excess capacity normally exists only with respect to fixed assets and inventories.

SELF-TEST QUESTIONS   Describe three conditions under which the assumption that each "spontaneous" asset and liability item increases at the same rate as sales is *not* correct.

Explain how excess capacity adjustments are handled.

OTHER TECHNIQUES FOR FORECASTING FINANCIAL STATEMENT VARIABLES

If any of the conditions noted above applies (economies of scale, excess capacity, nonoptimal starting ratios, or lumpy assets), the A*/S ratio will not be a constant, and the constant ratio technique should not be used. Rather, other techniques must be used to forecast income statement and balance sheet accounts, hence additional financing requirements. Several methods are discussed in the following sections.

SIMPLE LINEAR REGRESSION

If we assume that the relationship between an asset account and sales is linear, then we can use simple linear regression techniques to estimate the account level for any given sales increase. For example, MicroDrive's levels of sales, inventories, and receivables during the last five years are shown in the lower section of Figure 12-4, and each current asset item is plotted in the upper section as a scatter diagram versus sales. Regression equations found with a spreadsheet are also shown with each graph. For example, the estimated relationship between inventories and sales (in millions of dollars) is

$$\text{Inventories} = -\$35.7 + 0.186(\text{Sales}).$$

The plotted points are not very close to the regression line, which indicates a low degree of correlation. In fact, the correlation coefficient between inventories and sales is 0.71, indicating a moderate positive relationship between these two variables. Still, management regards the regression relationship as providing a reasonable basis for forecasting target inventory levels, and they have more confidence in it than they do in the constant ratio forecast.

We can use the estimated relationship between inventories and sales to forecast 1997 inventory levels. Since 1997 sales are projected to be $3,300 million, 1997 inventories should be $578 million:

$$\text{Inventories} = -\$35.7 + 0.186(\$3,300) = \$578 \text{ million.}$$

This is $99 million less than the preliminary forecast based on the constant ratio method as shown in Table 12-4. The difference occurs because the constant ratio method assumed that the ratio of inventories to sales would remain constant, when in fact it will probably decline due to economies of scale. Note also that although

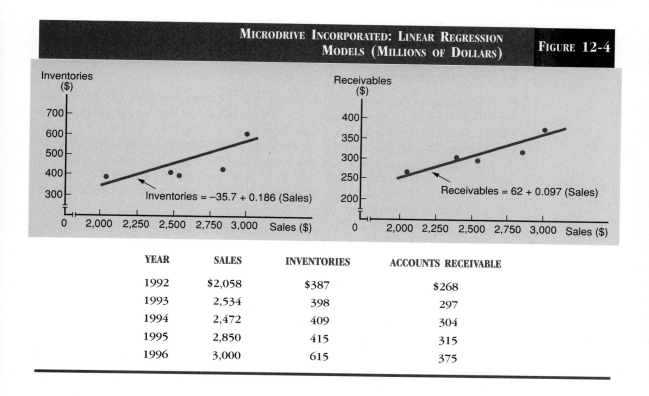

MICRODRIVE INCORPORATED: LINEAR REGRESSION MODELS (MILLIONS OF DOLLARS)   **FIGURE 12-4**

YEAR	SALES	INVENTORIES	ACCOUNTS RECEIVABLE
1992	$2,058	$387	$268
1993	2,534	398	297
1994	2,472	409	304
1995	2,850	415	315
1996	3,000	615	375

our graphs show linear relationships, we could have easily used a nonlinear regression model had such a relationship been indicated.

After analyzing the regression results, MicroDrive's managers directed that a new forecast of AFN be developed in which a lower days sales outstanding and a higher inventory turnover ratio are assumed. Management recognized that the 1996 levels of these accounts were above the industry averages, hence that the preliminary results projected for 1997 were also too high. When simple linear regression was used to forecast the receivables and inventories accounts, the 1997 levels reflect both the average relationships of these accounts to sales over the five-year period and the trend in the variables' values. The constant ratio method assumed that the nonoptimal 1996 levels would remain constant in 1997 and beyond. The new preliminary 1997 forecast for MicroDrive, based on the Figure 12-4 linear regression relationships for receivables and inventories, projected a 1997 funds surplus of $17 million.

CURVILINEAR REGRESSION

The constant ratio method may be used for forecasting balance sheet accounts when the relationship between those accounts and sales is linear and passes through the origin, as in Figure 12-3a. Linear regression is appropriate when the relationship is linear but does not pass through the origin, as in Figure 12-3b. If the relationship is as shown in Figure 12-3c, then *curvilinear regression* should be used to make the forecast.

MULTIPLE REGRESSION

If the relationship between a variable such as inventories and sales has points that are widely scattered about the regression line, hence a low correlation, then there is a good chance that other factors, in addition to sales, affect that variable. For example, inventory might be a function of both sales and the number of different items stocked. In that case, the best forecast for inventories might be obtained using *multiple regression,* whereby inventories were regressed against both sales and the number of items being stocked. Many spreadsheets can perform multiple regression, so the statistical tools are right at hand.

SPECIFIC VARIABLE FORECASTING

A final approach to forecasting is to develop a specific model for each income statement and balance sheet variable to be forecasted. For example, receivables could be forecasted using historical collections experience, inventories might be projected using curvilinear regression, operating costs using linear regression, gross fixed assets by the capital budget, depreciation by the tax department's consolidated depreciation schedule, and so on. Also, our company's asset/sales ratios could be based on industry averages, in which case the forecast would show our company's AFN assuming it was operated like an average firm in the industry. Of course, projected sales demand is still the driving force behind each specific variable forecast, but given the sales forecast, each variable would be analyzed and forecasted by its own unique technique. This method is called *specific variable forecasting,* and each income statement item and balance sheet account is forecasted independently, given the sales forecast.

COMPARISON OF THE FORECASTING METHODS

The constant ratio method of forecasting financial statements assumes that most income statement and balance sheet variables vary directly (proportionally) with sales. It is the easiest method to use, but its forecasts are often of questionable value. As we move down the list from the constant ratio method to specific variable forecasting, accuracy usually increases, but so does the cost of the forecast. The need to employ more complicated, and consequently more costly, forecasting methods varies from situation to situation. As in all decisions, the costs of using more refined techniques must be balanced against the benefits of increased accuracy.

SELF-TEST QUESTIONS

Describe each of the following forecasting methods, its assumptions, and the situations under which it might be used:
(1) Constant ratio (or constant growth) method
(2) Simple linear regression
(3) Curvilinear regression
(4) Multiple regression
(5) Specific variable forecasting
In what sense does financial statement forecasting involve a cost/benefit trade-off?

COMPUTERIZED FINANCIAL PLANNING MODELS

Although the types of financial forecasting described in this chapter can be done with a hand calculator, virtually all corporate forecasts are made using computerized forecasting models, often based on a spreadsheet program. Such models have two major advantages over pencil-and-paper calculations. First, it is much faster to construct a spreadsheet model than to make a "by-hand" forecast if the forecast period extends beyond two or three years. Second, and more important, a spreadsheet model can instantaneously recompute the projected financial statements and ratios when one of the input variables is changed, thus making it feasible for managers to determine the effects of changes in variables such as sales.

We developed forecasts for MicroDrive using a five-year financial planning spreadsheet model. The model began with five years of historical data, which were used to establish basic relationships. Other input data included forecasted sales growth rates, the financing mix to apply to any additional funds needed, the cost rates on incremental debt financing, and the tax rate. The model calculated projected financial statements for five years, including financing feedback effects, along with some key financial ratios. We used the spreadsheet's linear regression capability to develop MicroDrive's historical sales growth rate and the historical relationships between accounts receivable, inventories, and sales. Thus, it was quite easy to examine the effects of alternative assumptions on MicroDrive's forecasts.[7]

Why are computerized planning models playing an increasingly important role in corporate management?   **SELF-TEST QUESTION**

FINANCIAL CONTROLS

Financial forecasting and planning is vital to corporate success, but planning is for nought unless the firm has a control system that (1) ensures implementation of the planned policies, and (2) provides a feedback loop which permits rapid adjustments if the conditions upon which the plan is based change. In a financial control system,

---

[7]It is becoming increasingly easy for companies to develop planning models as a result of the dramatic improvements that have been made in computer hardware and software in recent years. Spreadsheet programs are the most widely used forecasting tool, although many companies also employ more complex and elaborate modeling systems. Increasingly, a knowledge of spreadsheet programs is becoming a requirement for getting even an entry-level job in many corporations. Indeed, surveys indicate that the probability of a business student getting an attractive job offer increases dramatically if he or she has a working knowledge of spreadsheets. In addition, starting salaries are materially higher for those students who have such a knowledge.

Note also that we have concentrated on long-run, or strategic, financial planning. Within the framework of the long-run strategic plan, firms also develop short-run financial plans. For example, suppose that MicroDrive's final forecast called for $20 million in new external capital, and that it planned to raise this capital by using short-term debt, long-term debt, and common stock. However, we do not know when during the year the funds will be needed or when MicroDrive will obtain each of its different types of capital. To address these issues, the firm must develop a short-run financial plan, the centerpiece of which is the cash budget, which is a projection of cash inflows and outflows on a daily, weekly, or monthly basis during the coming year (or other budget period). We will discuss cash budgeting in Chapter 20, where we continue our discussion of financial planning and control.

the key question is not "How is the firm doing in 1997 as compared with 1996?" Rather, it is "How is the firm doing in 1997 as compared with our forecasts for 1997, and if actual results differ from the budget, what can we do to get back on track?"

The basic tools of financial control are *budgets* and *pro forma financial statements*. These documents set forth expected performance, hence they express management's targets. These targets are then compared with actual corporate performance — on a daily, weekly, or monthly basis — to determine the variances, which are defined here as the difference between actual values and target values. The control system should identify those areas where performance is not meeting target levels. If a division's actuals are better than its targets, this could signify that its manager should be given a raise, but it could also mean that the targets were set too low and thus should be raised in the future. Conversely, failure to meet the financial targets could mean that market conditions are changing, that some managers are not performing up to par, or that the targets were set initially at unrealistic levels. In any event, some action should be taken, and quickly if the situation is deteriorating rapidly. By focusing on variances, managers can "manage by exception," concentrating on those things that are most in need of improvement and leaving alone those operations that are running smoothly.[8]

SELF-TEST QUESTIONS

What are the purposes of a financial control system?

What are the basic financial control tools, and how do they work?

---

[8]Of course, entire textbooks have been written on financial controls, and financial control overlaps with managerial, or cost, accounting. We must also add that financial control systems are not costless. Thus, managers must balance the cost of a control system against the savings it is intended to produce.

SUMMARY

This chapter described in broad outline how firms project their financial statements and determine their capital requirements. The key concepts are listed below.

- The primary planning documents are *strategic plans, operating plans,* and *financial plans.*

- *Financial forecasting* generally begins with a forecast of the firm's sales, in terms of both units and dollars.

- *Projected,* or *pro forma, financial statements* are used to forecast financial requirements.

- A firm can determine the amount of *additional funds needed (AFN)* by estimating the amount of new assets necessary to support the forecasted level of sales and then subtracting from that amount the funds that will be generated from operations. The firm can then plan to raise the AFN through bank borrowing, by issuing securities, or both.

■ The *higher a firm's sales growth rate,* the *greater* its need for additional financing. Similarly, the *larger a firm's dividend payout ratio,* the *greater* its need for additional funds.

■ Adjustments must be made if *economies of scale* exist in the use of assets, if *excess capacity exists,* or if assets must be added in *lumpy increments.*

■ Many balance sheet accounts can be projected using the *constant ratio method,* which assumes that the accounts will grow at the same rate as sales.

■ *Linear regression* can be used to forecast assets in situations where they are not expected to grow at the same rate as sales.

■ Even the smallest firms now use *computerized financial planning models* to forecast both their financial statements and their external financing needs.

The type of forecasting described in this chapter is important for several reasons. First, if the projected operating results are unsatisfactory, management can "go back to the drawing board," reformulate its plans, and develop more reasonable targets for the coming year. Second, it is possible that the funds required to meet the sales forecast simply cannot be obtained. If so, it is obviously better to know this in advance and to scale back the projected level of operations than to suddenly run out of cash and have operations grind to a halt. And third, even if the required funds can be raised, it is desirable to plan for their acquisition well in advance.

QUESTIONS

2-1 Define each of the following terms:
    a. Operating plan; five-year plan
    b. Financial plan
    c. Sales forecast
    d. Constant ratio method
    e. Spontaneously generated funds
    f. Dividend payout ratio
    g. Pro forma financial statement
    h. Additional funds needed (AFN); AFN formula
    i. Capital intensity ratio
    j. Lumpy assets
    k. Financing feedback
    l. Simple linear regression
    m. Computerized financial planning model

2-2 Certain liability and net worth items generally increase spontaneously with increases in sales. Put a check (✓) by those items that typically increase spontaneously:

Accounts payable	_____
Notes payable to banks	_____
Accrued wages	_____
Accrued taxes	_____
Mortgage bonds	_____
Common stock	_____
Retained earnings	_____

12-3 The following equation can, under certain assumptions, be used to forecast financial requirements:

$$AFN = (A^*/S)(\Delta S) - (L^*/S)(\Delta S) - MS_1(1 - d).$$

Under what conditions does the equation give satisfactory predictions, and when should it not be used?

12-4 Assume that an average firm in the office supply business has a 6 percent after-tax profit margin, a 40 percent debt/assets ratio, a total assets turnover of 2 times, and a dividend payout ratio of 40 percent. Is it true that if such a firm is to have *any* sales growth (g > 0), it will be forced either to borrow or to sell common stock (that is, it will need some nonspontaneous, external capital even if g is very small)?

12-5 Is it true that computerized corporate planning models were a fad during the 1980s but, because of a need for flexibility in corporate planning, they have been dropped by most firms?

12-6 Suppose a firm makes the following policy changes. If the change means that external, nonspontaneous financial requirements (AFN) will increase, indicate this by a (+); indicate a decrease by a (−); and indicate indeterminate or no effect by a (0). Think in terms of the immediate, short-run effect on funds requirements.

a. The dividend payout ratio is increased.   _____

b. The firm contracts to buy, rather than make, certain components used in its products.   _____

c. The firm decides to pay all suppliers on delivery, rather than after a 30-day delay, to take advantage of discounts for rapid payment.   _____

d. The firm begins to sell on credit (previously all sales had been on a cash basis).   _____

e. The firm's profit margin is eroded by increased competition; sales are steady.   _____

f. Advertising expenditures are stepped up.   _____

g. A decision is made to substitute long-term mortgage bonds for short-term bank loans.   _____

h. The firm begins to pay employees on a weekly basis (previously it had paid at the end of each month).   _____

(SOLUTIONS APPEAR IN APPENDIX C)

-1 **MAXIMUM GROWTH RATE** Weatherford Industries Inc. has the following ratios: A*/S = 1.6; L*/S = 0.4; profit margin = 0.10; and dividend payout ratio = 0.45, or 45 percent. Sales last year were $100 million. Assuming that these ratios will remain constant, use the AFN formula to determine the maximum growth rate Weatherford can achieve without having to employ nonspontaneous external funds.

-2 **ADDITIONAL FUNDS NEEDED** Suppose Weatherford's financial consultants report (1) that the inventory turnover ratio is sales/inventory = 3 times versus an industry average of 4 times and (2) that Weatherford could reduce inventories and thus raise its turnover to 4 without affecting sales, the profit margin, or the other asset turnover ratios. Under these conditions, use the AFN formula to determine the amount of additional funds Weatherford would require during each of the next 2 years if sales grew at a rate of 20 percent per year.

-3 **EXCESS CAPACITY** Van Auken Lumber's 1996 financial statements are shown below.

**VAN AUKEN LUMBER:
BALANCE SHEET AS OF DECEMBER 31, 1996
(THOUSANDS OF DOLLARS)**

Cash	$ 1,800	Accounts payable	$ 7,200
Receivables	10,800	Notes payable	3,472
Inventories	12,600	Accruals	2,520
Total current assets	$25,200	Total current liabilities	$13,192
Net fixed assets	21,600	Mortgage bonds	5,000
		Common stock	2,000
		Retained earnings	26,608
Total assets	$46,800	Total liabilities and equity	$46,800

**VAN AUKEN LUMBER:
INCOME STATEMENT FOR DECEMBER 31, 1996
(THOUSANDS OF DOLLARS)**

Sales	$36,000
Operating costs	30,783
Earnings before interest and taxes	$ 5,217
Interest	1,017
Earnings before taxes	$ 4,200
Taxes (40%)	1,680
Net income	$ 2,520
Dividends (60%)	$1,512
Addition to retained earnings	$1,008

a. Assume that the company was operating at full capacity in 1996 with regard to all items *except* fixed assets; fixed assets in 1996 were being utilized to only 75 percent of capacity.

By what percentage could 1997 sales increase over 1996 sales without the need for an increase in fixed assets?

b. Now suppose 1997 sales increase by 25 percent over 1996 sales. How much additional external capital will be required? Assume that Van Auken cannot sell any fixed assets. (Hint: Use the constant ratio method to develop a pro forma balance sheet and income statement as in Tables 12-3 and 12-4.) Assume that any required financing is borrowed as notes payable. Do not include any financing feedbacks, and use a pro forma income statement to determine the addition to retained earnings. (Another hint: Notes payable = $6,021.)

c. Use the financial statements developed in Part b to incorporate the financing feedback which results from the addition to notes payable. (That is, do the next financial statement iteration.) For purposes of this part, assume that the notes payable interest rate is 12 percent. What is the AFN for this iteration?

d. Suppose the industry average DSO and inventory turnover ratio are 90 days and 3.33, respectively, and that Van Auken Lumber matches these figures in 1997 and then uses the funds released to reduce equity. (It pays a special dividend out of retained earnings.) What would this do to the rate of return on year-end 1997 equity? Use the second-pass balance sheet and income statement as developed in Part c, and assume that the additional AFN amount calculated in that iteration is added to notes payable. (Hint: Notes payable is now $6,094.)

PROBLEMS

12-1   PRO FORMA STATEMENTS AND RATIOS Upton Computers makes bulk purchases of small computers, stocks them in conveniently located warehouses, and ships them to its chain of retail stores. Upton's balance sheet as of December 31, 1996, is shown here (millions of dollars):

Cash	$ 3.5	Accounts payable	$ 9.0
Receivables	26.0	Notes payable	18.0
Inventories	58.0	Accruals	8.5
Total current assets	$ 87.5	Total current liabilities	$ 35.5
Net fixed assets	35.0	Mortgage loan	6.0
		Common stock	15.0
		Retained earnings	66.0
Total assets	$122.5	Total liabilities and equity	$122.5

Sales for 1996 were $350 million, while net income for the year was $10.5 million. Upton paid dividends of $4.2 million to common stockholders. The firm is operating at full capacity. Assume that all ratios remain constant.

a. If sales are projected to increase by $70 million, or 20 percent, during 1997, use the AFN equation to determine Upton's projected external capital requirements.

b. Construct Upton's pro forma balance sheet for December 31, 1997. Assume that all external capital requirements are met by bank loans and are reflected in notes payable. Do not consider any financing feedback effects.

c. Now calculate the following ratios, based on your projected December 31, 1997, balance sheet. Upton's 1996 ratios and industry average ratios are shown here for comparison:

	UPTON COMPUTERS		INDUSTRY AVERAGE
	12/31/97	12/31/96	12/31/96
Current ratio	_____	2.5×	3×
Debt/total assets	_____	33.9%	30%
Rate of return on equity	_____	13%	12%

d. Now assume that Upton grows by the same $70 million but that the growth is spread over 5 years — that is, that sales grow by $14 million each year. Do not consider any financing feedback effects.

(1) Calculate total additional financial requirements over the 5-year period. (Hint: Use 1996 ratios, ΔS = $70, but total sales for the 5-year period.)

(2) Construct a pro forma balance sheet as of December 31, 2001, using notes payable as the balancing item.

(3) Calculate the current ratio, total debt/total assets ratio, and rate of return on equity as of December 31, 2001.[Hint: Be sure to use *total sales*, which amount to $1,960 million, to calculate retained earnings but 2001 profits to calculate the rate of return on equity — that is, return on equity = (2001 profits)/(12/31/00 equity).]

e. Do the plans outlined in Parts b and/or d seem feasible to you? That is, do you think Upton could borrow the required capital, and would the company be raising the odds on its bankruptcy to an excessive level in the event of some temporary misfortune?

2 ADDITIONAL FUNDS NEEDED Stevens Textile's 1996 financial statements are shown below.

STEVENS TEXTILE:
BALANCE SHEET AS OF DECEMBER 31, 1996
(THOUSANDS OF DOLLARS)

Cash	$ 1,080	Accounts payable	$ 4,320
Receivables	6,480	Accruals	2,880
Inventories	9,000	Notes payable	2,100
Total current assets	$16,560	Total current liabilities	$ 9,300
Net fixed assets	12,600	Mortgage bonds	3,500
		Common stock	3,500
		Retained earnings	12,860
Total assets	$29,160	Total liabilities and equity	$29,160

STEVENS TEXTILE:
INCOME STATEMENT FOR DECEMBER 31, 1996
(THOUSANDS OF DOLLARS)

Sales	$36,000
Operating costs	32,440
Earnings before interest and taxes	$ 3,560
Interest	560
Earnings before taxes	$ 3,000
Taxes (40%)	1,200
Net income	$ 1,800
Dividends (45%)	$ 810
Addition to retained earnings	$ 990

a. Suppose 1997 sales are projected to increase by 15 percent over 1996 sales. Determine the additional funds needed. Assume that the company was operating at full capacity in 1996, that it cannot sell off any of its fixed assets, and that any required financing will be borrowed as notes payable. Also, assume that assets, spontaneous liabilities, and operating costs are expected to increase by the same percentage as sales. Use the constant ratio method to develop a pro forma balance sheet and income statement for December 31, 1997. (Do not incorporate any financing feedback effects. Use the pro forma income statement to determine the addition to retained earnings.)

b. Use the financial statements developed in Part a to incorporate the financing feedback as a result of the addition to notes payable. (That is, do the next financial statement iteration.) For the purpose of this part, assume that the notes payable interest rate is 10 percent. What is the AFN for this iteration?

12-3   ADDITIONAL FUNDS NEEDED Garlington Technologies Inc.'s 1996 financial statements are shown below.

GARLINGTON TECHNOLOGIES INC.:
BALANCE SHEET AS OF DECEMBER 31, 1996

Cash	$ 180,000	Accounts payable	$ 360,000
Receivables	360,000	Notes payable	156,000
Inventories	720,000	Accruals	180,000
Total current assets	$1,260,000	Total current liabilities	$ 696,000
Fixed assets	1,440,000	Common stock	1,800,000
		Retained earnings	204,000
Total assets	$2,700,000	Total liabilities and equity	$2,700,000

GARLINGTON TECHNOLOGIES INC.: INCOME STATEMENT FOR DECEMBER 31, 1996

Sales	$3,600,000
Operating costs	3,279,720
EBIT	$ 320,280
Interest	20,280
EBT	$ 300,000
Taxes (40%)	120,000
Net income	$ 180,000

PER SHARE DATA

Common stock price	$24.00
Earnings per share (EPS)	$1.80
Dividends per share (DPS)	$1.08

a. Suppose that in 1997 sales increase by 10 percent over 1996 sales and that 1997 DPS will increase to $1.12. Construct the pro forma financial statements using the constant ratio method. How much additional capital will be required? Assume the firm operated at full capacity in 1996. Do not include any financing feedbacks.

b. Now assume that 50 percent of the additional capital required will be financed by selling common stock and the remainder by borrowing as notes payable. Assume that the interest rate on notes payable is 13 percent. Do the next iteration of financial statements incorporating financing feedbacks. What is the AFN for this iteration?

c. If the profit margin were to remain at 5 percent and the dividend payout rate were to remain at 60 percent, at what growth rate in sales would the additional financing requirements be exactly zero? (Hint: Set AFN equal to zero and solve for g.)

-4 **EXTERNAL FINANCING REQUIREMENTS** The 1996 balance sheet and income statement for the Damon Company are shown below.

DAMON COMPANY: BALANCE SHEET AS OF DECEMBER 31, 1996 (THOUSANDS OF DOLLARS)

Cash	$ 80	Accounts payable	$ 160
Accounts receivable	240	Accruals	40
Inventories	720	Notes payable	252
Total current assets	$1,040	Total current liabilities	$ 452
Fixed assets	3,200	Long-term debt	1,244
		Total debt	$1,696
		Common stock	1,605
		Retained earnings	939
Total assets	$4,240	Total liabilities and equity	$4,240

DAMON COMPANY:
INCOME STATEMENT FOR DECEMBER 31, 1996
(THOUSANDS OF DOLLARS)

Sales	$8,000
Operating costs	7,450
EBIT	$ 550
Interest	150
EBT	$ 400
Taxes (40%)	160
Net income	$ 240

PER SHARE DATA

Common stock price	$16.96
Earnings per share (EPS)	$1.60
Dividends per share (DPS)	$1.04

a. The firm operated at full capacity in 1996. It expects sales to increase by 20 percent during 1997 and expects 1997 dividends per share to increase to $1.10. Use the constant ratio method to determine how much outside financing is required, developing the firm's pro forma balance sheet and income statement, and use AFN as the balancing item.

b. If the firm must maintain a current ratio of 2.3 and a debt ratio of 40 percent, how much financing, after the first pass, will be obtained using notes payable, long-term debt, and common stock?

c. Make the second-pass financial statements incorporating financing feedbacks, using the ratios in Part b. Assume that the interest rate on debt averages 10 percent.

12-5 **LONG-TERM FINANCING NEEDED** At year-end 1996, total assets for Bertin Inc. were $1.2 million and accounts payable were $375,000. Sales, which in 1996 were $2.5 million, are expected to increase by 25 percent in 1997. Total assets and accounts payable are proportional to sales and that relationship will be maintained. Bertin typically uses no current liabilities other than accounts payable. Common stock amounted to $425,000 in 1996, and retained earnings were $295,000. Bertin plans to sell new common stock in the amount of $75,000. The firm's profit margin on sales is 6 percent; 40 percent of earnings will be paid out as dividends.

a. What was Bertin's total debt in 1996?

b. How much new, long-term debt financing will be needed in 1997? (Hint: AFN − New stock = New long-term debt.) Do not consider any financing feedback effects.

-6 **ADDITIONAL FUNDS NEEDED** The Booth Company's sales are forecasted to increase from $1,000 in 1996 to $2,000 in 1997. Here is the December 31, 1996 balance sheet:

Cash	$ 100	Accounts payable	$ 50
Accounts receivable	200	Notes payable	150
Inventories	200	Accruals	50
Net fixed assets	500	Long-term debt	400
		Common stock	100
		Retained earnings	250
Total assets	$1,000	Total liabilities and equity	$1,000

Booth's fixed assets were used to only 50 percent of capacity during 1996, but its current assets were at their proper levels. All assets except fixed assets increase at the same rate as sales, and fixed assets would also increase at the same rate if the current excess capacity did not exist. Booth's after-tax profit margin is forecasted to be 5 percent, and its payout ratio will be 60 percent. What is Booth's additional funds needed (AFN) for the coming year? Ignore financing feedback effects.

SPREADSHEET APPLICATIONS

SPREADSHEET PROBLEM

Roussakis Industries' 1996 financial statements are shown below.

ROUSSAKIS INDUSTRIES:
BALANCE SHEET AS OF DECEMBER 31, 1996
(MILLIONS OF DOLLARS)

Cash	$ 4.0	Accounts payable	$ 8.0
Receivables	12.0	Notes payable	5.0
Inventories	16.0	Total current liabilities	$13.0
Total current assets	$32.0	Long-term debt	12.0
Net fixed assets	40.0	Common stock	20.0
		Retained earnings	27.0
Total assets	$72.0	Total liabilities and equity	$72.0

ROUSSAKIS INDUSTRIES:
INCOME STATEMENT FOR DECEMBER 31, 1996
(MILLIONS OF DOLLARS)

Sales	$80.0
Operating costs	71.3
EBIT	$ 8.7
Interest	2.0
EBT	$ 6.7
Taxes (40%)	2.7
Net income	$ 4.0
Dividends (40%)	$1.60
Addition to retained earnings	$2.40

Assume that the firm has no excess capacity in fixed assets, that the average interest rate for debt is 12 percent, and that the projected annual sales growth rate for the next 5 years is 15 percent.

a. Roussakis plans to finance its additional funds needed with 50 percent short-term debt and 50 percent long-term debt. Using the constant ratio method, prepare the pro forma financial statements for 1997 through 2001, and then determine (1) additional funds needed, (2) the current ratio, (3) the debt ratio, and (4) the return on equity.

b. Sales growth could be 5 percentage points above or below the projected 15 percent. Determine the effect of such variances on AFN and the key ratios.

c. Perform an analysis to determine the sensitivity of AFN and the key ratios for 2001 to changes in the dividend payout ratio as specified in the following, assuming sales grow at a constant 15 percent. What happens to AFN if the dividend payout ratio (1) is raised from 40 to 70 percent or (2) is lowered from 40 to 20 percent?

MINI CASE

Sue Wilson, the new financial manager of Northwest Chemicals (NWC), an Oregon producer of specialized chemicals for use in fruit orchards, must prepare a financial forecast for 1997. NWC's 1996 sales were $2 billion, and the marketing department is forecasting a 25 percent increase for 1997. Sue thinks the company was operating at full capacity in 1996, but she is not sure about this. The 1996 financial statements, plus some other data, are given in Table MC 12-1.

FINANCIAL STATEMENTS AND OTHER DATA ON NWC (MILLIONS OF DOLLARS)	TABLE MC12-1

A. 1996 BALANCE SHEET

Cash and securities	$ 20	Accounts payable and accruals	$ 100
Accounts receivable	240	Notes payable	100
Inventories	240	Total current liabilities	$ 200
Total current assets	$ 500	Long-term debt	100
Net fixed assets	500	Common stock	500
		Retained earnings	200
Total assets	$1,000	Total liabilities and equity	$1,000

B. 1996 INCOME STATEMENT

Sales	$2,000.00
Variable costs	1,200.00
Fixed costs	700.00
Earnings before interest and taxes	$ 100.00
Interest	16.00
Earnings before taxes	$ 84.00
Taxes (40%)	33.60
Net income	$ 50.40
Dividends (30%)	15.12
Addition to retained earnings	$ 35.28

C. KEY RATIOS

	NWC	INDUSTRY
Basic earning power	10.00%	20.00%
Profit margin	2.52	4.00
Return on equity	7.20	15.60
Days sales outstanding (360 days)	43.20 days	32.00 days
Inventory turnover	8.33×	11.00×
Fixed assets turnover	4.00	5.00
Total assets turnover	2.00	2.50
Debt/assets	30.00%	36.00%
Times interest earned	6.25×	9.40×
Current ratio	2.50	3.00
Payout ratio	30.00%	30.00%

Assume that you were recently hired as Sue's assistant, and your first major task is to help her develop the forecast. She asked you to begin by answering the following set of questions.

a. Assume (1) that NWC was operating at full capacity in 1996 with respect to all assets, (2) that all assets must grow proportionally with sales, (3) that accounts payable and accruals will also grow in proportion to sales, and (4) that the 1996 profit margin and dividend payout will be maintained. Under these conditions, what will the company's financial requirements be for the coming year? Use the AFN equation to answer this question.

b. Now estimate the 1997 financial requirements using the constant ratio approach, making an initial forecast plus one additional "pass" to determine the effects of "financing feedbacks." Assume (1) that each type of asset, as well as payables, accruals, and fixed and variable costs, grow at the same rate as sales; (2) that the payout ratio is held constant at 30 percent; (3) that external funds needed are financed 50 percent by notes payable and 50 percent by long-term debt (no new common stock will be issued); and (4) that all debt carries an interest rate of 8 percent.

c. Why do the two methods produce somewhat different AFN forecasts? Which method provides the more accurate forecast?

d. Calculate NWC's forecasted ratios, and compare them with the company's 1996 ratios and with the industry averages. How does NWC compare with the average firm in its industry, and is the company expected to improve during the coming year?

e. Suppose you now learn that NWC's 1996 receivables and inventories were in line with required levels, given the firm's credit and inventory policies, but that excess capacity existed with regard to fixed assets. Specifically, fixed assets were operated at only 75 percent of capacity.
  (1) What level of sales could have existed in 1996 with the available fixed assets? What would the fixed assets/sales ratio have been if NWC had been operating at full capacity?
  (2) How would the existence of excess capacity in fixed assets affect the additional funds needed during 1997?

f. Without actually working out the numbers, how would you expect the ratios to change in the situation where excess capacity in fixed assets exists? Explain your reasoning.

g. Based on comparisons between NWC's days sales outstanding (DSO) and inventory turnover ratios with the industry average figures, does it appear that NWC is operating efficiently with respect to its inventories and accounts receivable? If the company were able to bring these ratios into line with the industry averages, what effect would this have on its AFN and its financial ratios? (Note: Inventories and receivables will be discussed in detail in Chapter 20.)

h. The relationship between sales and the various types of assets is important in financial forecasting. The constant ratio approach, under the assumption that each asset item grows at the same rate as sales, leads to an AFN forecast that is reasonably close to the forecast using the AFN equation. Explain how each of the following factors would affect the accuracy of financial forecasts based on the AFN equation: (1) excess capacity, (2) base stocks of assets, such as shoes in a shoe store, (3) economies of scale in the use of assets, and (4) lumpy assets.

i. (1) How could regression analysis be used to detect the presence of the situations described above and then to improve the financial forecasts? Plot a graph of the following data, which is for a typical well-managed company in NWC's industry, to illustrate your answer.

YEAR	SALES	INVENTORIES
1994	$1,280	$118
1995	1,600	138
1996	2,000	162
1997 (est.)	2,500	192

(2) On the same graph that plots the above data, draw a line which shows how the regression line must appear to justify the use of the AFN formula and the constant ratio forecasting procedure. As a part of your answer, show the growth rate in inventories that results from a 10 percent increase in sales from a sales level of (a) $200 and (b) $2,000 based on both the actual regression line and a *hypothetical* regression line which is linear and which goes through the origin.

j. How would changes in these items affect the AFN? (1) The dividend payout ratio, (2) the profit margin, (3) the capital intensity ratio, and (4) NWC begins buying from its suppliers on terms which permit it to pay after 60 days rather than after 30 days. (Consider each item separately and hold all other things constant.)

SELECTED ADDITIONAL REFERENCES AND CASES

The heart of successful financial planning is the sales forecast. On this key subject, see

Pan, Judy, Donald R. Nichols, and O. Maurice Joy, "Sales Forecasting Practices of Large U.S. Industrial Firms," *Financial Management,* Fall 1977, 72–77.

Hirschey, Mark, and James L. Pappas, *Managerial Economics* (Fort Worth, Tex.: Dryden Press, 1996).

Computer modeling is becoming increasingly important. For general references, see

Carleton, Willard T., Charles L. Dick, Jr., and David H. Downes, "Financial Policy Models: Theory and Practice," *Journal of Finance,* December 1973, 691–709.

Francis, Jack Clark, and Dexter R. Rowell, "A Simultaneous Equation Model of the Firm for Financial Analysis and Planning," *Financial Management,* Spring 1978, 29–44.

Grinyer, P. H., and J. Wooller, *Corporate Models Today — A New Tool for Financial Management* (London: Institute of Chartered Accountants, 1978).

Pappas, James L., and George P. Huber, "Probabilistic Short-Term Financial Planning," *Financial Management,* Autumn 1973, 36–44.

Traenkle, J. W., E. B. Cox, and J. A. Bullard, *The Use of Financial Models in Business* (New York: Financial Executives' Research Foundation, 1975).

Considerable effort has been expended to develop integrated financial planning models that identify optimal policies. For one example, see

Myers, Stewart C., and Gerald A. Pogue, "A Programming Approach to Corporate Financial Management," *Journal of Finance,* May 1974, 579–599.

For a recent article on control, see

Bierman, Harold, "Beyond Cash Flow ROI," *Midland Corporate Finance Journal,* Winter 1988, 36–39.

The Dryden Press Cases in Financial Management: Dryden Request *series contains the following applicable cases:*

Case 37, "Space-Age Materials, Inc.," Case 38, "Automated Banking Mangement, Inc.," Case 38A, "Expert Systems," and Case 38B, "Medical Management Systems, Inc.," which all focus on using the percentage of sales forecasting method to forecast future financing requirements.

CAPITAL STRUCTURE
DECISIONS: THE BASICS

*T*o open its doors, a new business requires capital, and additional capital is needed for expansion. The required funds can come from many different sources, and it can take many different forms, but all capital can be classified into two basic types — debt and equity.

Raising capital as debt has several advantages. First, interest is tax deductible, which lowers the effective cost of debt. Second, debtholders are limited to a fixed return, so stockholders do not have to share the profits if the business is extremely successful. Finally, debtholders do not have voting rights, so stockholders can control a business with less money than would otherwise be required.

However, financing with debt also has some disadvantages. First, the higher the debt ratio, the greater the risk and thus the higher the interest rate. At some point, rising interest rates overwhelm the advantages of debt. Second, if a company falls on hard times, and if its operating income is insufficient to cover interest charges, then stockholders will have to make up the shortfall, and if they cannot, the company may be forced into bankruptcy. Good times may be just around the corner, but too much debt can keep the company from getting there and can wipe out stockholders in the process.

Crown Cork & Seal Company, a $4.5 billion NYSE company, is a good example of a firm that used debt to good advantage. Over an eight-year period, from 1988 to 1996, Crown increased its long-term debt from a minuscule $9 million to $800 million, or by more than 8,000 percent. This pushed its debt ratio up to a still-reasonable 42 percent. Crown used the proceeds of the debt issues to acquire other companies, and, since it earned more on the acquired assets than its cost of debt, that pushed up its ROE and, consequently, its stock price. Indeed, the stock price rose from $10 to more than $50 over the eight-year period.

On the other hand, debt financing is causing severe problems for many airlines, including U.S. Air. In 1996, U.S. Air had a long-term debt to capitalization ratio of almost 100 percent, i.e., it was financed almost entirely by debt. Further, its annual interest expense was more than $200 million, considerably more than the company's operating income during most of the 1990s. U.S. Air cannot pay dividends on its common stock, and its very survival is at stake. The airline industry is extremely cyclical, and large amounts of debt put tremendous pressures on a company when earnings turn south.

Companies can use either debt or equity capital. Is one form better than the other? If so, should firms be financed either with all debt or all equity? If the best solution is some mix of debt and equity, what is the optimal mix? In this chapter, we discuss the key facets of the debt-versus-equity, or capital structure, decision. As you read the chapter, think about Crown Cork & Seal and U.S. Air, and the ways the concepts discussed might aid the managers of these and other companies as they make capital structure decisions.[1]

One of the most perplexing issues facing financial managers is the relationship between *capital structure,* which is the mix of debt and equity financing, and stock prices. Does capital structure affect stock prices and corporate costs of capital? Should different industries and different firms within industries have different capital structures, and, if so, what factors lead to these differences? Although the optimal capital structure decision is generally not crystal clear, an understanding of this chapter will help you deal with the issues involved.

BUSINESS AND FINANCIAL RISK

In Chapter 4, when we examined risk from the viewpoint of the individual investor, we distinguished between *market risk,* which is measured by the firm's beta coefficient, and *stand-alone risk,* which includes both market risk and an element of risk which can be eliminated by diversification. Now we introduce two new dimensions of risk: (1) *business risk,* or the riskiness of the firm's assets if it uses no debt, and (2) *financial risk,* which is the additional risk placed on the common stockholders as a result of the firm's decision to use debt.[2]

Conceptually, the firm has a certain amount of risk inherent in its operations: this is its business risk. If it uses debt, then, in effect, it partitions its investors into two groups and concentrates most of its business risk on one class of investors — the common stockholders. However, the common stockholders generally demand compensation for assuming more risk and thus set a higher required rate of return. In

---

[1] We have divided the material on capital structure into two chapters. Chapter 13 covers the basics, while Chapter 14 provides some extensions related primarily to the theory of capital structure. Both chapters are useful, but Chapter 13 does cover all of the concepts (including theory) needed to understand the material presented in succeeding chapters. Therefore, if time pressures preclude coverage of both chapters, Chapter 14 can be omitted.

[2] Preferred stock also adds to financial risk. To simplify matters somewhat, we concentrate on debt and common equity in this chapter.

this section, we examine business and financial risk within a stand-alone risk framework, which ignores the benefits of stockholder diversification.

BUSINESS RISK

Business risk, in a stand-alone sense, is a function of the uncertainty inherent in projections of a firm's future rate of return on assets (ROA). We could measure ROA in several ways, but for purposes of capital structure analysis, the following definition is most appropriate:

$$\frac{\text{Return on assets}}{\text{(ROA)}} = \frac{\text{Return to investors}}{\text{Assets}} = \frac{\text{Net income to}}{\text{common stockholders} + \text{Interest payments}}{\text{Assets}}.$$

If a firm uses no debt, then its interest payments will be zero, its assets will be all-equity financed, and its return on assets will equal its return on equity, ROE:

$$\text{ROA (zero debt)} = \text{ROE} = \frac{\text{Net income to common stockholders}}{\text{Common equity}}.$$

Therefore, the business risk of a *leverage-free* firm can be measured by the standard deviation of its expected ROE, σ_{ROE}.

To illustrate, consider Strasburg Electronics Company, a *debt-free (unlevered)* firm. Figure 13-1 gives some clues about the company's business risk. The top graph shows the trend in ROE from 1986 through 1996; this graph gives both security analysts and Strasburg's management an idea of the degree to which ROE has varied in the past and might vary in the future.

The lower graph shows the beginning-of-year subjectively estimated probability distribution of Strasburg's ROE for 1996, based on the trend line in the top section of Figure 13-1. As both graphs indicate, Strasburg's actual ROE in 1996 was only 8 percent, well below the expected value of 12 percent — 1996 was a bad year.

Strasburg's past fluctuations in ROE were caused by many factors — booms and recessions in the national economy, successful new products introduced both by Strasburg and by its competitors, labor strikes, price controls, a fire in Strasburg's main plant, and so on. Similar events will doubtless occur in the future, and when they do, the realized ROE will be higher or lower than the projected level. Further, there is always the possibility that a long-term disaster might strike, permanently depressing the company's earning power; for example, a competitor might introduce a new product that would permanently lower Strasburg's earnings. This uncertainty regarding Strasburg's future ROE, *assuming the firm uses no debt financing,* is defined as the company's *basic business risk.*

Business risk varies not only from industry to industry but also among firms in a given industry. Further, business risk can change over time. For example, the electric utilities were regarded for years as having little business risk, but a combination of events in recent years altered the utilities' situation, producing sharp declines in their ROEs and greatly increasing the industry's business risk. Now, food processors and grocery retailers are frequently given as examples of industries with low

| FIGURE 13-1 | STRASBURG ELECTRONICS: TREND IN ROE, 1986–1996, AND SUBJECTIVE PROBABILITY DISTRIBUTION OF ROE, 1996 |

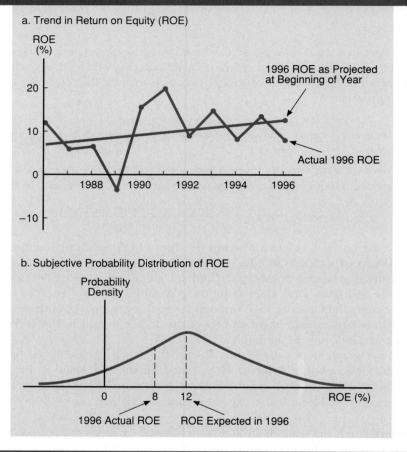

a. Trend in Return on Equity (ROE)

1996 ROE as Projected at Beginning of Year

Actual 1996 ROE

b. Subjective Probability Distribution of ROE

1996 Actual ROE   ROE Expected in 1996

business risk, while cyclical manufacturing industries such as autos and steel, as well as many small startup companies, are regarded as having especially high business risk.[3]

Business risk depends on a number of factors, the more important of which are listed below:

1. **Demand variability.** The more stable the demand for a firm's products, other things held constant, the lower its business risk.

---

[3]We have avoided any discussion of market versus company-specific risk in this section. We note now (1) that any action which increases business risk in the stand-alone risk sense will generally also increase a firm's beta coefficient, and (2) that a part of business risk as we define it will generally be company-specific, hence subject to elimination by diversification by the firm's stockholders. This point is discussed at some length in Chapter 14.

2. **Sales price variability.** Firms whose products are sold in highly volatile markets are exposed to more business risk than similar firms whose output prices are more stable.

3. **Input cost variability.** Firms whose input costs are highly uncertain are exposed to a high degree of business risk.

4. **Ability to adjust output prices for changes in input costs.** Some firms are better able than others to raise their own output prices when input costs rise. The greater the ability to adjust output prices to reflect cost conditions, the lower the degree of business risk.

5. **Ability to develop new products in a timely, cost-effective manner.** Firms in such high-tech industries as drugs and computers depend on a constant stream of new products. The faster its products become obsolete, the greater a firm's business risk.

6. **The extent to which costs are fixed: operating leverage.** If a high percentage of costs are fixed, hence do not decline when demand falls off, then the firm is exposed to a relatively high degree of business risk. This factor is called *operating leverage,* and it is discussed at length in the next section.

Each of these factors is determined partly by the firm's industry characteristics, but each of them is also controllable to some extent by management. For example, most firms can, through their marketing policies, take actions to stabilize both unit sales and sales prices. However, this stabilization may require spending a great deal on advertising and/or price concessions to get commitments from customers to purchase fixed quantities at fixed prices in the future. Similarly, firms such as Strasburg Electronics can reduce the volatility of future input costs by negotiating long-term labor and materials supply contracts, but they may have to pay prices above the current spot price to obtain these contracts.

OPERATING LEVERAGE

As noted above, business risk depends in part on the extent to which a firm builds fixed costs into its operations — if fixed costs are high, even a small decline in sales can lead to a large decline in ROE. So, other things held constant, the higher a firm's fixed costs, the greater its business risk. Higher fixed costs are generally associated with more highly automated, capital intensive firms and industries. However, businesses that employ highly skilled workers who must be retained and paid even during recessions also have relatively high fixed costs, as do firms with high product development costs, because the amortization of development costs is an element of fixed costs.

If a high percentage of total costs are fixed, then the firm is said to have a high degree of *operating leverage.* In physics, leverage implies the use of a lever to raise a heavy object with a small force. In politics, if people have leverage, their smallest word or action can accomplish a lot. *In business terminology, a high degree of operating leverage, other factors held constant, implies that a relatively small change in sales results in a large change in ROE.*

Figure 13-2 illustrates the concept of operating leverage by comparing the results that Strasburg could expect if it used different degrees of operating leverage. Plan A

FIGURE 13-2   STRASBURG ELECTRONICS: ILLUSTRATION OF OPERATING LEVERAGE

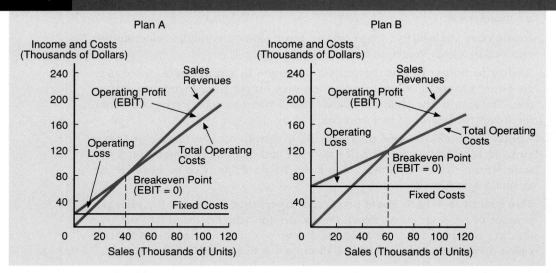

Selling price = $2.00	Selling price = $2.00
Fixed costs = $20,000	Fixed costs = $60,000
Variable costs = $1.50 per unit	Variable costs = $1.00 per unit

			PLAN A					PLAN B		
PROB-ABILITY	UNITS SOLD, Q	SALES	OPERATING COSTS	OPERATING EBIT	NI	ROE	COSTS	EBIT	NI	ROE
0.03	0	$ 0	$ 20,000	($20,000)	($12,000)	(6.9%)	$60,000	($60,000)	($36,000)	(20.6%)
0.07	40,000	80,000	80,000	0	0	0.0	100,000	(20,000)	(12,000)	(6.9)
0.15	60,000	120,000	110,000	10,000	6,000	3.4	120,000	0	0	0.0
0.50	110,000	220,000	185,000	35,000	21,000	12.0	170,000	50,000	30,000	17.1
0.15	160,000	320,000	260,000	60,000	36,000	20.6	220,000	100,000	60,000	34.3
0.07	180,000	360,000	290,000	70,000	42,000	24.0	240,000	120,000	72,000	41.1
0.03	220,000	440,000	350,000	90,000	54,000	30.9	280,000	160,000	96,000	54.9
Expected value				$35,000	$21,000	12.0%		$50,000	$30,000	17.1%
Standard deviation				$23,249	$13,949	8.0%		$46,497	$27,898	15.9%

NOTES:
a. Strasburg Electronics has a 40 percent federal-plus-state tax rate.
b. The firm uses no debt financing.
c. For simplicity, we assume assets = equity = $175,000 under both plans.

calls for a relatively small amount of fixed costs, $20,000. Here the firm would not have much automated equipment, so its depreciation, maintenance, property taxes, and so on would be low, but the total operating costs line has a relatively steep slope, indicating that variable costs per unit are higher than they would be if the firm used more operating leverage. Plan B calls for a higher level of fixed costs, $60,000. Here the firm uses automated equipment (with which one operator can turn out a few or many units at the same labor cost) to a much larger extent. The breakeven point is higher under Plan B—breakeven occurs at 60,000 units under Plan B versus only 40,000 units under Plan A.

We can calculate the breakeven quantity by recognizing that breakeven occurs when ROE = 0, and, hence, when earnings before interest and taxes (EBIT) = 0:

$$EBIT = 0 = PQ - VQ - F.$$

Here P is average sales price per unit of output, Q is units of output, V is variable cost per unit, and F is fixed operating costs.[4] If we solve for the breakeven quantity, Q_{BE}, we get this expression:

$$Q_{BE} = \frac{F}{P - V}.$$

Thus for Plan A,

$$Q_{BE} = \frac{\$20,000}{\$2.00 - \$1.50} = 40,000 \text{ units},$$

and for Plan B,

$$Q_{BE} = \frac{\$60,000}{\$2.00 - \$1.00} = 60,000 \text{ units}.$$

How does operating leverage affect business risk? *Other things held constant, the higher a firm's operating leverage, the higher its business risk.* This point is demonstrated in Figure 13-3, where we develop probability distributions for ROE under Plans A and B.

The left-hand section of Figure 13-3 graphs the probability distribution of sales that was presented in tabular form in Figure 13-2. The sales probability distribution depends on how demand for the product varies, not on whether the product is

---

[4]This definition of breakeven does not include any fixed financial costs because Strasburg is an unlevered firm. If there were fixed financial costs, the firm would suffer an accounting loss at the operating breakeven point. Thus, Equation 13-1 defines the *operating* breakeven level of sales. We will introduce financial costs shortly.

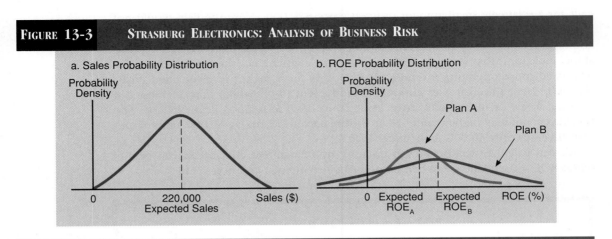

FIGURE 13-3   STRASBURG ELECTRONICS: ANALYSIS OF BUSINESS RISK

a. Sales Probability Distribution

b. ROE Probability Distribution

NOTE: We are using continuous distributions to approximate the discrete distributions contained in Figure 13-2. Using data from Figure 13-2, we calculate σ_{Sales} = $92,995.

manufactured by Plan A or by Plan B. Therefore, the same sales probability distribution applies to both production plans; this distribution has expected sales of $220,000, and it ranges from zero to about $450,000, with σ_{Sales} = $92,995.

We use the sales probability distribution, together with the operating costs at each sales level, to develop graphs of the ROE probability distributions under Plans A and B. These are shown in the right-hand section of Figure 13-3. Plan B has a higher expected ROE, but this plan also entails a much higher probability of large losses. Clearly, Plan B, the one with more fixed costs and a higher degree of operating leverage, is riskier. *In general, holding other factors constant, the higher the degree of operating leverage, the greater the firm's business risk.*

To what extent can firms control their operating leverage? To a large extent, operating leverage is determined by technology. Electric utilities, telephone companies, airlines, steel mills, and chemical companies simply *must* have large investments in fixed assets; this results in high fixed costs and operating leverage. Similarly, drug, auto, computer, and similar companies must spend heavily to develop new products, and product-development costs increase operating leverage. Grocery stores, on the other hand, generally have significantly lower fixed costs, hence lower operating leverage. Still, although industry factors do exert a major influence, all firms have some control over their operating leverage. For example, an electric utility can expand its generating capacity by building either a gas-fired or a coal-fired plant. The coal plant would require a larger investment and would have higher fixed costs, but its variable operating costs would be relatively low. The gas-fired plant, on the other hand, would require a smaller investment and would have lower fixed costs, but the variable costs (for gas) would be high. Thus, by its capital budgeting decisions, a utility (or any other company) can influence its operating leverage, hence its business risk.

The concept of operating leverage was originally developed for use in capital budgeting. Mutually exclusive projects which involve alternative methods for producing a given product often have different degrees of operating leverage, thus different breakeven points and different degrees of risk. Strasburg Electronics and many other companies regularly undertake a type of breakeven analysis (the sensitivity analysis discussed in Chapter 11) for each proposed project as a part of their regular capital budgeting process. Still, once a corporation's operating leverage has been established, this factor exerts a major influence on its capital structure decision.

FINANCIAL RISK

Financial risk is the additional risk placed on the common stockholders as a result of the decision to finance with debt. Conceptually, stockholders face a certain amount of risk which is inherent in a firm's operations—this is its business risk, which is defined as the uncertainty inherent in projections of future ROE, assuming the firm is financed solely with common stock. If a firm uses debt (financial leverage), this concentrates the business risk on common stockholders. To illustrate, suppose ten people decide to form a corporation to manufacture disk drives. There is a certain amount of business risk in the operation. If the firm is capitalized only with common equity, and if each person buys 10 percent of the stock, then each investor shares equally in the business risk. However, suppose the firm is capitalized with 50 percent debt and 50 percent equity, with five of the investors putting up their capital as debt and the other five putting up their money as equity. In this case, the five investors who put up the equity will have to bear all of the business risk, so the common stock will be twice as risky as it would have been had the firm been financed only with equity. Thus, the use of debt, or *financial leverage,* concentrates the firm's business risk on its stockholders.

To illustrate the concentration of business risk, again consider Strasburg Electronics. Strasburg has $175,000 in assets and is all-equity financed.[5] If the firm were using Plan A from Figure 13-2, then its expected ROE would be 12.0 percent with a standard deviation of 8.0 percent. Now suppose the firm decides to change its capital structure by issuing $87,500 of debt at $k_d = 10\%$ and using these funds to replace $87,500 of equity. Its expected return on equity (which would now be only $87,500) would rise from 12 to 18 percent:

	NEW (LEVERAGED) SITUATION	OLD (UNLEVERAGED) SITUATION (SEE FIGURE 13-2)
Expected EBIT (unchanged)	$35,000	$35,000
Interest (10% on $87,500 of debt)	8,750	0
Earnings before taxes	$26,250	$35,000
Taxes (40%)	10,500	14,000
Net income	$15,750	$21,000
Expected ROE:	$15,750/$87,500 = 18%	$21,000/$175,000 = 12%

[5] A firm in business for at least ten years would likely have far more than $175,000 in assets. We are purposely keeping Strasburg Electronics small so that we may focus on the concepts without being overwhelmed by the numbers. Also note that, to be consistent with capital structure theory, we should be working with market values of securities rather than book values of assets. We are using book values at this point to simplify the illustration, but we will discuss market value relationships later in the chapter. In this regard, see Haim Levy and Robert Brooks, "Financial Break-Even Analysis and the Value of the Firm," *Financial Management,* Autumn 1986, 22–26.

Thus, the use of debt would "leverage up" the expected ROE from 12 percent to 18 percent.

Note that the total dollar return to all investors (both bondholders and stockholders) is Net income = $21,000 when no debt is used, but Net income + Interest = $15,750 + $8,750 = $24,500 when $87,500 of debt is used. Thus, the use of debt allows more of the $35,000 of EBIT to flow through to investors. The additional dollar return to investors, $24,500 − $21,000 = $3,500, in the leveraged situation results from interest tax savings—the interest expense of $8,750 saved the company T(Interest) = 0.40($8,750) = $3,500 in taxes. Thus, the use of debt financing shields a portion of a company's earnings from the tax collector.

Since raising half of its capital as debt would increase the expected dollar return to investors and leverage up the ROE to stockholders, should the firm use this amount, or even more, debt financing? The answer would definitely be yes except for one problem: The use of financial leverage also increases the risk faced by the equity investors, and this higher risk may offset the benefits of debt. To illustrate, suppose EBIT actually turned out to be $5,000 rather than the expected $35,000. If the firm used no debt, then ROE would decline from 12.0 percent to 1.7 percent. However, with debt financing, ROE would fall from 18.0 to −2.6 percent:

	$87,500 OF DEBT	ZERO DEBT
Actual EBIT	$5,000	$5,000
Interest (10%)	8,750	0
Earnings before taxes	−$3,750	$5,000
Taxes (40%)	− 1,500	2,000
Net income	−$2,250	$3,000
Actual ROE	− 2.6%	1.7%
Expected ROE	18.0%	12.0%

A more complete analysis of the effects of leverage on Strasburg's ROE is illustrated in Figure 13-4. The two lines in the top graph show the ROE that would exist at different levels of EBIT under the two different capital structures. The greater the use of financial leverage, the more sensitive ROE is to changes in EBIT.

The lower panel of Figure 13-4 shows the effects of leverage on the firm's ROE probability distribution. With zero debt, expected ROE is 12 percent, with a relatively tight distribution. With 50 percent debt, the expected ROE rises to 18 percent, but the ROE distribution is flatter, indicating a more risky situation. In fact, the standard deviation of ROE is 8.0 percent at zero debt, but exactly twice as high, 16.0 percent, at 50 percent debt.

Our conclusions from this analysis are as follows:

1. The use of debt generally increases a firm's expected ROE; this situation occurs whenever the expected return on assets (measured by EBIT/Total assets) exceeds the interest rate on debt.

2. The standard deviation of ROE if the firm uses zero financial leverage, $\sigma_{ROE(U)}$, is a measure of the firm's business risk, and σ_{ROE} at any debt level is a measure of the stand-alone risk borne by stockholders. $\sigma_{ROE} = \sigma_{ROE(U)}$ if the firm

STRASBURG ELECTRONICS: EFFECTS OF FINANCIAL LEVERAGE ON ROE | FIGURE 13-4

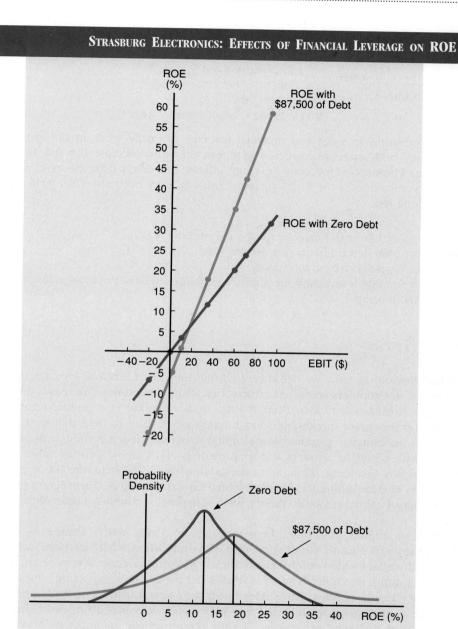

does not use any financial leverage. However, if the firm does use debt, then $\sigma_{ROE} > \sigma_{ROE(U)}$, because business risk is being concentrated on the stockholders.

3. The difference between σ_{ROE} and $\sigma_{ROE(U)}$ is a measure of the risk-increasing effects of financial leverage:

$$\text{Stand-alone risk} = \sigma_{ROE}.$$

$$\text{Business risk} = \sigma_{ROE(U)}.$$

$$\text{Financial risk} = \sigma_{ROE} - \sigma_{ROE(U)}.$$

In our example,

$$\text{Financial risk} = 16.0\% - 8.0\% = 8.0\%.$$

4. Operating leverage and financial leverage normally work in the same way; they both increase expected ROE, but they also increase the risk borne by stockholders.[6] Operating leverage affects the firm's business risk, financial leverage affects the firm's financial risk, and they both affect the firm's stand-alone risk.

SELF-TEST QUESTIONS

Conceptually, how can business risk be measured?

What are some determinants of business risk?

How can financial risk be measured?

What is operating leverage? What are the similarities between operating leverage and financial leverage?

CAPITAL STRUCTURE THEORY

In the previous section, we demonstrated that the use of financial leverage typically increases stockholders' expected returns, but, at the same time, it increases their risk. The question managers face, then, is this: Is the increase in expected return sufficient to compensate stockholders for the increase in risk? To help answer this question, it is necessary to examine some capital structure theory. Although theory does not provide all of the answers, it does provide useful insights into the value of debt versus equity financing. Thus, an understanding of capital structure theory will aid managers in establishing their firms' optimal capital structures. This section provides the basics of capital structure theory, while Chapter 14 contains a more detailed discussion.

Modern capital structure theory began in 1958, when Professors Franco Modigliani and Merton Miller (hereafter MM) published what has been called the most influential finance article ever written.[7] MM proved, under a very restrictive set of assumptions, that a firm's value is unaffected by its capital structure. Put another way, MM's results suggest that it does not matter how a firm finances its operations because capital structure is irrelevant. MM's study was based on some unrealistic assumptions, including zero taxes. Despite the unrealistic assumptions, MM's irrele-

---

[6]Note that for operating leverage to benefit shareholders, the firm must be operating at a sales level above the breakeven point, and for financial leverage to be of benefit, the cost of debt must be less than the return on assets as measured by EBIT/Total assets. Normally, when managers make operating and financing decisions, they expect the firm to be operating above the breakeven point, and they also expect the return on assets to exceed the cost of debt.

[7]Franco Modigliani and Merton H. Miller, "The Cost of Capital, Corporation Finance, and the Theory of Investment," *American Economic Review,* June 1958. Modigliani and Miller both won Nobel Prizes for their work.

vance result is extremely important. By indicating the conditions under which capital structure is irrelevant, MM also provided us with some clues about what is required for capital structure to be relevant and hence to affect a firm's value.

THE EFFECT OF TAXES

MM published a follow-up paper in which they relaxed the assumption that there are no corporate taxes.[8] The tax code allows corporations to deduct interest payments as an expense, but dividend payments to stockholders are not deductible. This differential treatment encourages corporations to use debt in their capital structures. Indeed, MM demonstrated that if all their other assumptions hold, this differential treatment leads to a situation which calls for 100 percent debt financing.

Several years later, Merton Miller (this time without Modigliani) extended the analysis to include personal taxes.[9] He noted that all of the income from bonds generally comes as interest, which is taxed as personal income at rates going up to 39.6 percent, while income from stocks generally comes partly from dividends and partly from capital gains. Further, capital gains are taxed at a maximum rate of 28 percent, and this tax is deferred until the stock is sold and the gain realized. If stock is held until the owner dies, no capital gains tax whatever must be paid. So, on balance, common stocks are taxed at significantly lower effective rates than debt.

Because of the tax situation, investors are willing to accept relatively low before-tax returns on stock vis-à-vis the before-tax returns on bonds. For example, an investor might require a return of 10 percent on Firm B's bonds, and if stock income were taxed at the same rate as bond income, the required rate of return on Firm B's stock might be 16 percent because of the stock's greater risk. However, in view of the favorable treatment of returns on the stock, investors might be willing to accept a before-tax return of only 14 percent on the stock.

Thus, as Miller pointed out, (1) the *deductibility of interest* favors the use of debt, but (2) the *favorable tax treatment of income from stocks* lowers the required rate of return on stock and thus favors the use of equity financing. It is difficult to say what the net effect of these two factors is. Most observers believe that interest deductibility has the stronger effect, hence that our tax system still favors the corporate use of debt, but that effect is reduced by the lower capital gains tax rate.

One can observe changes in corporate financing patterns following major changes in tax rates. For example, in 1993 the top personal tax rate on interest and dividends was raised sharply, but the capital gains tax rate was not increased. This has resulted in a greater reliance on equity financing.

THE EFFECT OF BANKRUPTCY COSTS

MM's irrelevance results also depended on the assumption that there are no bankruptcy costs. However, in practice bankruptcy can be quite costly. Firms in bankruptcy have very high legal and accounting expenses, and they also have a hard time

---

[8]Franco Modigliani and Merton H. Miller, "Corporate Income Taxes and the Cost of Capital: A Correction," *American Economic Review* 53, June 1963, 433–443.
[9]Merton H. Miller, "Debt and Taxes," *Journal of Finance* 32, May 1977, 261–275.

retaining customers, suppliers, and employees. Moreover, bankruptcy often forces a firm to liquidate and sell assets for less than they would be worth if the firm were to continue operating. Assets such as plant and equipment are often illiquid because they are configured to a company's individual needs and also because they are difficult to disassemble and move.

Note, too, that the *threat of bankruptcy,* not just bankruptcy per se, brings about problems. Key employees jump ship, suppliers refuse to grant credit, customers seek more stable suppliers, and lenders demand higher interest rates or even refuse to extend credit.

Bankruptcy-related problems are most likely to arise when a firm has a lot of debt in its capital structure. Therefore, bankruptcy costs discourage firms from pushing their use of debt to excessive levels.

Bankruptcy-related costs depend on three things: (1) the probability of bankruptcy, (2) the costs the firm will incur given that financial distress has arisen, and (3) the adverse effects that the potential for bankruptcy has on current operations. Firms whose earnings are more volatile, all else equal, face a greater chance of bankruptcy and, therefore, should use less debt than more stable firms. This is consistent with our earlier point that firms with a high degree of operating leverage, and thus greater business risk, should limit their use of financial leverage. Likewise, firms which would face high costs in the event of financial distress should rely less heavily on debt. For example, firms whose assets are illiquid and thus would have to be sold at "fire sale" prices should limit their use of debt financing. Finally, firms such as airlines, whose current sales are affected by anything that worries potential customers, should limit their use of debt.

TRADE-OFF THEORY

Work related to the MM papers has led to "the trade-off theory of leverage," in which firms trade off the benefits of debt financing (favorable corporate tax treatment) against higher interest rates and bankruptcy costs. A summary of the trade-off theory is expressed graphically in Figure 13-5. Here are some observations about the figure:

1. The fact that interest is deductible makes debt less expensive than common or preferred stock. In effect, the government pays part of the cost of debt capital, or, to put it another way, debt provides *tax shelter benefits.* As a result, using debt causes more of the firm's operating income (EBIT) to flow through to investors, so the more debt a company uses, the higher its value and stock price. Under the assumptions of the Modigliani-Miller with-taxes paper, a firm's stock price will be maximized if it uses 100 percent debt, and the line labeled "MM Result Incorporating the Effects of Corporate Taxation" in Figure 13-5 expresses their 1963 idea of the relationship between stock prices and debt.

2. In the real world, firms rarely use 100 percent debt. One reason is because of the favorable treatment of income from stocks, but the primary reason is that firms limit their use of debt to reduce the probability of financial distress (bankruptcy). Also, the interest rate on debt becomes prohibitively high at high debt levels.

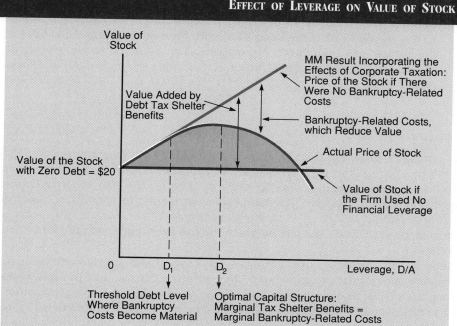

EFFECT OF LEVERAGE ON VALUE OF STOCK — **FIGURE 13-5**

Value of
Stock

MM Result Incorporating the
Effects of Corporate Taxation:
Price of the Stock if There
Were No Bankruptcy-Related
Costs

Value Added by
Debt Tax Shelter
Benefits

Bankruptcy-Related Costs,
which Reduce Value

Actual Price of Stock

Value of the Stock
with Zero Debt = $20

Value of Stock if
the Firm Used No
Financial Leverage

0   D₁   D₂   Leverage, D/A

Threshold Debt Level
Where Bankruptcy
Costs Become Material

Optimal Capital Structure:
Marginal Tax Shelter Benefits =
Marginal Bankruptcy-Related Costs

3. There is some threshold level of debt, labeled D_1 in Figure 13-5, below which the probability of bankruptcy is so low as to be immaterial. Beyond D_1, however, bankruptcy-related costs and rising interest rates become increasingly important, and they reduce the tax benefits of debt at an increasing rate. In the range from D_1 to D_2, bankruptcy-related costs reduce but do not completely offset the tax bene-fits of debt, so the firm's stock price rises (but at a decreasing rate) as its debt ratio increases. However, beyond D_2, bankruptcy-related costs exceed the tax benefits, so from this point on increasing the debt ratio lowers the value of the stock. Therefore, D_2 is the optimal capital structure.

4. Although not indicated in Figure 13-5, there is a relationship between the firm's stock price and its weighted average cost of capital. As a firm uses more and more debt, its weighted average cost of capital decreases, reaches a minimum, and then begins to rise. Moreover, the minimum weighted average cost of capital occurs where the stock price is maximized—at Point D_2 in Figure 13-5. Thus, the same capital structure that maximizes the stock price also minimizes the overall cost of capital.

5. Both theoretical and empirical evidence support the preceding discussion. However, statistical problems prevent us from identifying Points D_1 and D_2. So, while theoretical and empirical work supports the general shape of the curves in Figure 13-5, these curves must be taken as approximations, not as precisely defined functions.

6. Another disturbing aspect of capital structure theory as expressed in Figure 13-5 is the fact that many large, successful firms such as Apple and Microsoft use far less debt than the theory suggests. This point led to the development of a second theory of capital structure, "signaling theory," which is discussed below.

SIGNALING THEORY

MM assumed that investors and managers have exactly the same information about a firm's prospects — this is called *symmetric information.* However, managers often have better information than outside investors. This is called *asymmetric information,* and it has an important effect on capital structure. To see why, consider two situations, one in which a company's managers know that its prospects are extremely good (Firm G) and one in which the managers know that the future looks bad (Firm B).

Suppose, for example, that Firm G's R&D labs have just discovered a non-patentable cure for the common cold. They want to keep the new product a secret as long as possible to delay competitors' entry into the market. New plants must be built to make the new product, so capital must be raised. How should Firm G's management raise the needed capital? If the firm sells stock, then, when profits from the new product start flowing in, the price of the stock would rise sharply, and the purchasers of the new stock would make a bonanza. The current stockholders (including the managers) would also do well, but not as well as they would have done if the company had not sold stock before the price increased, because then they would not have had to share the benefits of the new product with the new stockholders. *Therefore, one would expect a firm with very favorable prospects to try to avoid selling stock and, rather, to raise any required new capital by other means, including using debt beyond the normal optimal capital structure.*[10]

Now let's consider Firm B. Suppose its managers have information that new orders are off sharply because a competitor has installed new technology which has improved its products' quality. Firm B must upgrade its own facilities, at a high cost, just to maintain its current sales. As a result, its return on investment will fall (but not by as much as if it took no action, which would lead to a 100 percent loss through bankruptcy). How should Firm B raise the needed capital? Here the situation is just the reverse of that facing Firm G, which did not want to sell stock so as to avoid having to share the benefits of future developments. *A firm with unfavorable prospects would want to sell stock, which would mean bringing in new investors to share the losses!*[11]

---

[10]It would be illegal for Firm G's managers to personally purchase more shares on the basis of their inside knowledge of the new product. They could be sent to jail if they did.

[11]Of course, Firm B would have to make certain disclosures when it offered new shares to the public, but it might be able to meet the legal requirements without fully disclosing management's worst fears.

The conclusion from all this is that firms with extremely good prospects prefer to finance with debt, whereas firms with poor prospects like to finance with stock. How should you, as an investor, react to this conclusion? You ought to say, "If I see that a company plans to issue stock, this should worry me because I know that management would not want to issue stock if future prospects looked good, but it would want to issue stock if things looked bad. Therefore, I should lower my estimate of the firm's value, other things held constant." The negative reaction should be stronger if the stock sale were by a large, established company such as GM or IBM, which has many financing options, than if it were by a small, unlisted company such as GeneSplicer. For GeneSplicer, a stock sale might signify truly extraordinary investment opportunities that cannot be exploited without raising new equity.

If you gave the above answer, your views are consistent with those of sophisticated portfolio managers of institutions such as Morgan Guaranty Trust, Fidelity Investments, Prudential Insurance, and so forth. *So, in a nutshell, the announcement of a stock offering by a mature firm that has financing alternatives is taken as a signal that the firm's prospects as seen by its management are not bright.* This, in turn, suggests that when a mature firm announces a new stock offering, the price of its stock should decline. Empirical studies have shown that this situation does indeed exist.[12]

What are the implications of all this for capital structure decisions? The answer is that firms should, in normal times, maintain a *reserve borrowing capacity* which can be used in the event that some especially good investment opportunity comes along. *This means that firms should, in normal times, use less debt than is suggested by the tax benefit/bankruptcy cost trade-off model expressed in Figure 13-5.*

Signaling/asymmetric information concepts also have implications for the marginal cost of capital (MCC) curve as discussed in Chapter 11. There we saw that the weighted average cost of capital (WACC) jumped when retained earnings were exhausted and the firm was forced to sell new common stock to raise equity. The jump in the WACC, or the break in the MCC schedule, was attributed only to flotation costs. However, if the announcement of a stock sale causes a decline in the price of the stock, then k as measured by $k = D_1/P_0 + g$ will rise because of the decline in P_0. This factor reinforces the effects of flotation costs, and it is perhaps an even more important explanation for the jump in the MCC schedule at the point at which new stock must be issued. For example, assume that $P_0 = \$10$, $D_1 = \$1$, $g = 5\%$, and $F = 10\%$. Therefore, $k_s = 10\% + 5\% = 15\%$, and k_e, the cost of external equity, is 16.1 percent:

$$k_e = \frac{D_1}{P_0(1 - F)} + g = \frac{\$1}{\$10(1.0 - 0.10)} + 5\% = 16.1\%.$$

Suppose, however, that the announcement of a stock sale causes the market price of the stock to fall from $P_0 = \$10$ to $P_0 = \$8$. This will produce an increase in the costs of both retained earnings (k_s) and external equity:

[12]Paul Asquith and David W. Mullins, Jr., "The Impact of Initiating Dividend Payments on Shareholders' Wealth," *Journal of Business,* January 1983, 77–96.

$$\text{New } k_s = \frac{D_1}{P_0} + g = \frac{\$1}{\$8} + 5\% = 17.5\%.$$

$$\text{New } k_e = \frac{D_1}{P_0(1 - F)} + g = \frac{\$1}{\$8(0.9)} + 5\% = 18.9\%.$$

This would, of course, have further implications for capital budgeting. Specifically, it would make it even more difficult for a marginal project to show a positive NPV if taking on the project required the firm to issue stock.

USING DEBT FINANCING TO CONSTRAIN MANAGERS

In Chapter 1 we stated that agency problems may arise if managers and shareholders have different objectives. Such conflicts are particularly likely when the firm's managers have too much cash at their disposal. Managers often use such cash to finance their pet projects or for perquisites such as nicer offices, corporate jets, and tickets to sporting events, all of which may do little to maximize stock prices.[13] By contrast, managers with limited "free cash flow" are less able to make wasteful expenditures.

Firms can reduce excess cash flow in a variety of ways. One way is to funnel it back to shareholders through higher dividends or stock repurchases. Another alternative is to shift the capital structure toward more debt in the hope that higher debt service requirements will force managers to become more disciplined. If debt is not serviced as required, the firm will be forced into bankruptcy, and its managers would likely lose their jobs. Therefore, a manager is less likely to buy that expensive new corporate jet if the firm has large debt service requirements which could cost the manager his or her job.

Leveraged buyouts (LBOs) reduce excess cash flow. In an LBO debt is used to finance the purchase of a company's shares, after which the firm "goes private." Many leveraged buyouts, which were especially common during the late 1980s, were designed specifically to reduce corporate waste.

Of course, increasing debt and reducing free cash flow has its downside: It increases the risk of bankruptcy, which can be costly. One observer has argued that adding debt to a firm's capital structure is like putting a dagger pointing at the driver into the steering wheel of a car.[14] The dagger motivates you to drive more carefully, but you may get stabbed if someone runs into you, even if you are being careful. The analogy applies to corporations in the following sense: Higher debt forces managers to be more careful with shareholders' money, but even well-run firms could face bankruptcy (get stabbed) if some event beyond their control occurs. To continue the analogy, the capital structure decision comes down to deciding how big a dagger stockholders should employ to keep managers in line.

If you find our discussion of capital structure theory imprecise and somewhat confusing, you are not alone. In truth, no one knows how to identify precisely a

---

[13]If you don't believe corporate managers can waste money, read Bryan Burrough, *Barbarians at the Gate* (New York: Harper & Row, 1990), the story of the takeover of RJR-Nabisco.

[14]Ben Bernake, "Is There Too Much Corporate Debt?" Federal Reserve Bank of Philadelphia *Business Review,* September/October 1989, 3–13.

firm's optimal capital structure, or how to measure exactly the effects of capital structure on stock prices and the cost of capital. In practice, capital structure decisions must be made by combining judgment and numerical analysis. Still, an understanding of the theoretical issues presented here can help you make better judgments on capital structure issues.[15]

In what sense did MM's original theory produce an "irrelevance result"?

How do corporate and personal taxes affect firms' capital structure decisions?

Explain how "asymmetric information" and "signals" affect capital structure decisions.

What is meant by *reserve borrowing capacity,* and why is it important to firms?

How can the use of debt serve to discipline firms' managers?

SETTING THE TARGET CAPITAL STRUCTURE WHEN CASH FLOWS ARE PERPETUITIES

Capital structure theory suggests that each firm has an optimal capital structure, one that maximizes its value and minimizes its overall cost of capital. However, research on capital structure theory also points out that there are many contradictory issues regarding capital structure decisions, and that theory cannot enable us to specify a precisely optimal structure for any firm. In this section, we illustrate how a firm with perpetual cash flows might go about setting its target capital structure. The example will reinforce many of the concepts discussed in previous sections, as well as help you understand how managers deal with real-world capital structure decisions.

HILL SOFTWARE SYSTEMS

Hill Software Systems (HSS) was founded in 1980 to develop and market a new type of graphics software for personal computers. The basic program was written and patented by Mark Hill, HSS's founder. Hill owns a majority of the stock, although a significant portion is held by institutional investors. The company has no debt, and HSS's key financial data are shown in Table 13-1. Assets are carried at a book value of $1 million; hence, the common equity also has a balance sheet value of $1 million. However, these balance sheet figures are not very meaningful because (1) the asset figures do not include the value of patents and (2) the fixed assets were purchased several years ago at prices lower than today's.

Mark Hill plans to retire shortly, and he wants to sell a major part of his stock to the public, using the proceeds to diversify his personal portfolio. As a part of the planning process, the question of capital structure has arisen. Should the firm con-

---

[15]One of the authors can report firsthand the usefulness of financial theory in the actual establishment of corporate capital structures. In recent years, he has served as a consultant to several of the regional telephone companies established after the breakup of AT&T, as well as to several large electric utilities. On the basis of finance theory and computer models which simulated results under a range of conditions, the companies were able to specify "optimal capital structure ranges" with at least a reasonable degree of confidence. Without finance theory, setting a target capital structure would have amounted to little more than throwing darts.

TABLE 13-1	DATA ON HILL SOFTWARE SYSTEMS

BALANCE SHEET AS OF DECEMBER 31, 1996

Current assets	$ 500,000	Debt	$ 0
Net fixed assets	500,000	Common equity (1.0 million shares outstanding)	1,000,000
Total assets	$1,000,000	Total claims	$1,000,000

INCOME STATEMENT FOR 1996

Sales		$20,000,000
Fixed operating costs	$ 4,000,000	
Variable operating costs	12,000,000	16,000,000
Earnings before interest and taxes (EBIT)		$ 4,000,000
Interest		0
Taxable income		$ 4,000,000
Taxes (40% federal-plus-state)		1,600,000
Net income		$ 2,400,000

OTHER DATA

1. Earnings per share = EPS = $2,400,000/1,000,000 shares = $2.40.
2. Dividends per share = DPS = $2,400,000/1,000,000 shares = $2.40. Thus, the company has a 100 percent payout ratio.
3. Book value per share = $1,000,000/1,000,000 shares = $1.
4. Market price per share = P_0 = $20. Thus, the stock sells at 20 times its book value.
5. Price/earnings ratio = P/E = $20/2.40 = 8.33 times.
6. Dividend yield = DPS/P_0 = $2.40/$20 = 12%.

tinue its policy of using no debt, or should it recapitalize? And if it does decide to substitute some debt for equity, how far should it go? As in all such decisions, the correct answer is that *it should choose that capital structure which maximizes the value of the stock.* If the stock price is maximized, then the cost of capital will simultaneously be minimized.[16]

To simplify the analysis, we assume that the long-run demand for HSS's products is not expected to grow, so *its EBIT is expected to continue at $4 million indefinitely.* (However, future sales may turn out to be different from the expected level, so realized EBIT may be more or less than the expected $4 million.) Also, since the company has no need for new capital, *all of its income will be paid out as dividends.*

---

[16]In general, a firm's stock price is maximized when the firm's total market value is maximized. However, in some relatively rare situations, a firm's stock price is greatest when the firm's total value is less than maximum. To reach such a situation, the firm's bondholders must lose some value, and a portion of this loss is transferred to the firm's stockholders.

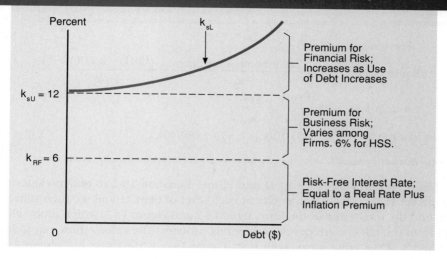

HSS's COSTS OF DEBT AND EQUITY AND BETA | **FIGURE 13-6**

AMOUNT BORROWED[a] (1)	INTEREST RATE ON ALL DEBT, k_d (2)	ESTIMATED BETA COEFFICIENT, OF STOCK, b[b] (3)	REQUIRED RATE OF RETURN ON STOCK, k_s (4)
$ 0	—	1.50	12.0%
2,000,000	8.0%	1.55	12.2
4,000,000	8.3	1.65	12.6
6,000,000	9.0	1.80	13.2
8,000,000	10.0	2.00	14.0
10,000,000	12.0	2.30	15.2
12,000,000	15.0	2.70	16.8
14,000,000	18.0	3.25	19.0

[a]HSS is unable to borrow more than $14 million because of limitations on interest coverage in its corporate charter.
[b]Note that the beta coefficient estimates do not correspond to Hamada's equation. The betas given here are subjective estimates furnished by investment bankers.
[c]We assume here that k_{RF} = 6% and k_M = 10%. Therefore, at zero debt, k_s = 6% + (10% − 6%)1.5 = 12%. Other values of k_s are calculated similarly.

Now assume that HSS's treasurer consults with the firm's investment bankers and learns that debt can be sold, but the more debt used, the riskier the debt and, of course, the higher its interest rate, k_d. Also, the bankers state that the more debt HSS uses, the greater the riskiness of its stock, hence the higher its required rate of return on equity, k_s. Estimates of k_d, beta, and k_s at different debt levels are given in Figure 13-6, along with a graph of the relationship between k_s and debt level.

Given the data in Table 13-1, along with those in Figure 13-6, we can determine HSS's total market value, V, at different capital structures, and we can then use this information to establish the company's stock price as a function of its capital structure. These equations are used in the analysis:[17]

Firm value:	$V = D + S.$	13-1
Equity value:	$S = \dfrac{\text{Net income after taxes}}{k_s} = \dfrac{(\text{EBIT} - k_d D)(1 - T)}{k_s}.$	13-2
Stock price:	$P_0 = \dfrac{\text{DPS}}{k_s} = \dfrac{\text{EPS}}{k_s}.$	13-3
Cost of capital:	$\text{WACC} = (D/V)(k_d)(1 - T) + (S/V)(k_s).$	13-4

We first substitute values for k_d, D, and k_s into Equation 13-2 to obtain values for S, the market value of common equity, at each level of debt, D, and we then sum S and D to find the total value of the firm. Table 13-2 and Figure 13-7, which plots selected data from the table, were developed by this process. The values shown in Columns 1, 2, and 3 of the table were taken from Figure 13-6, while those in Column 4 were obtained by solving Equation 13-2 at different debt levels. The values given in Column 5 were obtained by summing Columns 1 and 4, D + S = V.

To see how the stock prices shown in Column 6 were developed, visualize this series of events:

1. Initially, HSS has no debt. The firm's value is $20 million, or $20 for each of its 1 million shares. (See the top line of Table 13-2.)

2. Management announces a decision to change the capital structure; legally, the firm *must* make an explicit announcement or run the risk of having stockholders sue the directors.

3. The values shown in Columns 1 through 5 of Table 13-2 are estimated as described previously. The major institutional investors, and the large brokerage companies which advise individual investors, have analysts just as capable of making these estimates as the firm's management. These analysts would start making their own estimates as soon as HSS announced the planned change in leverage, and they would presumably reach conclusions similar to those of the HSS analysts.

4. HSS's stockholders initially own the entire company. (There are not yet any bondholders.) They see, or are told by their advisor-analysts, that very shortly the value of the enterprise will rise from $20 million to some higher amount, presumably the maximum attainable, which is $21,727,000. Thus, they anticipate that the value of the firm will increase by $1,727,000.

5. This additional $1,727,000 will accrue to the firm's current stockholders. Since there are 1 million shares of stock, each share will rise in value by $1.73, or from $20 to $21.73.

[17]Note that Equations 13-1 through 13-4 do not stem from a particular capital structure theory—they do not require acceptance of MM, Miller, or any other theory. Rather, they are definitions and basic DCF valuation equations for perpetual cash flows.

| HSS's VALUE, STOCK PRICE, AND COST OF CAPITAL AT DIFFERENT DEBT LEVELS | | | | | | | | TABLE 13-2 |

VALUE OF DEBT, D (IN MILLIONS) (1)	k_d (2)	k_s (3)	VALUE OF STOCK, S (IN MILLIONS) (4)	VALUE OF FIRM, V (IN MILLIONS) (1) + (4) = (5)	STOCK PRICE, P_0 (6)	D/V (7)	WACC (8)
$ 0.0	—	12.0%	$20.000	$20.000	$20.00	0.0%	12.0%
2.0	8.0%	12.2	18.885	20.885	20.89	9.6	11.5
4.0	8.3	12.6	17.467	21.467	21.47	18.6	11.2
6.0	**9.0**	**13.2**	**15.727**	**21.727**	**21.73**	**27.6**	**11.0**
8.0	10.0	14.0	13.714	21.714	21.71	36.8	11.1
10.0	12.0	15.2	11.053	21.053	21.05	47.5	11.4
12.0	15.0	16.8	7.857	19.857	19.86	60.4	12.1
14.0	18.0	19.0	3.158	17.158	17.16	81.6	12.3

NOTES:
a. The data in Columns 1 through 3 were taken from Figure 13-6.
b. The values for S in Column 4 were found by use of Equation 13-2.

$$S = \frac{\text{Net income}}{k_s} = \frac{(\text{EBIT} - k_dD)(1 - T)}{k_s}.$$

For example, at D = $0,

$$S = \frac{(\$4.0 - 0)(0.6)}{0.12} = \frac{\$2.4}{0.12} = \$20.0 \text{ million},$$

and at D = $6.0,

$$S = \frac{[\$4.0 - 0.09(\$6.0)](0.6)}{0.132} = \frac{\$2.076}{0.132} = \$15.727 \text{ million}.$$

c. The values for V in Column 5 were obtained as the sum of D + S. For example, at D = $6.0, V = $6.0 + $15.727 = $21.727 million.
d. The stock prices shown in Column 6 are equal to the value of the firm as shown in Column 5 divided by the original number of shares outstanding, which, in this case, is 1 million. The logic behind this procedure is explained in the text.
e. Column 7 is found by dividing Column 1 by Column 5. For example, at D = $6.0, D/V = $6.0/$21.727 = 27.6%.
f. Column 8 is found by use of Equation 13-4. For example, at D = $6.0,

$$\text{WACC} = (D/V)(k_d)(1 - T) + (S/V)(k_s)$$

$$= (0.276)(9\%)(0.6) + (0.724)(13.2\%) = 11.0\%.$$

g. At $14.0 million of debt, EBIT declines from $4 million to $3.52 million.
h. The row in boldface indicates the optimal amount of debt.

| FIGURE 13-7 | RELATIONSHIP BETWEEN HSS'S CAPITAL STRUCTURE, COST OF CAPITAL, AND STOCK PRICE |

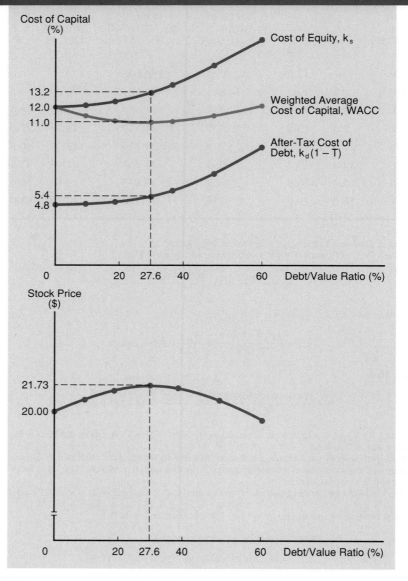

6. This price increase will occur *before* the transaction is completed. To see why, suppose the stock price remained at $20 after the announcement of the recapitalization plan. Shrewd investors would immediately recognize that the stock's price will soon go up to $21.73, and they would place orders to buy at any price below $21.73. This buying pressure would quickly run the price up to $21.73, at which point it would remain constant. Thus, $21.73 is the *equilibrium stock price* for HSS once the decision to recapitalize is announced.

7. The firm sells $6 million of bonds at an interest rate of 9 percent. This money is used to buy stock at the market price, which is now $21.73, so 276,116 shares are repurchased:

$$\text{Shares repurchased} = \frac{\$6,000,000}{\$21.73} = 276,116.$$

8. The value of the equity after the 276,116 shares have been repurchased is $15,727,000, as shown in Column 4 of Table 13-2. There are 1,000,000 − 276,116 = 723,884 shares still outstanding, so the value per share of the remaining stock is

$$\text{Value per share} = \frac{\$15,727,000}{723,884} = \$21.73.$$

This confirms our earlier calculation of the equilibrium stock price.

9. The same process was used to find stock prices at other capital structures; these prices are given in Column 6 of Table 13-2 and plotted in the lower graph of Figure 13-7. *Since the maximum price occurs when HSS uses $6 million of debt, its optimal capital structure calls for $6 million of debt.* Note also that $6 million of debt corresponds to a firm value of $21.727 million. Thus, the optimal market value capital structure, D/V*, is $6/$21.727 = 27.6%.

10. *In this example, we assumed that EBIT would decline from $4 million to $3.52 million if the firm's debt rose to $14 million.* The reason for the decline is that, at this very high level of debt, managers and employees would be worried about the firm's failing and about losing their jobs; suppliers would not sell to the firm on normal credit terms; orders would be lost because of customers' fears that the company might go bankrupt and thus be unable to deliver; and so on. EBIT is independent of financial leverage at "reasonable" debt levels, but at extreme degrees of leverage, EBIT is adversely affected.

11. Quite obviously, the situation in the real world is much more complex, and less exact, than this example suggests. Most important, different investors will have different estimates for EBIT and k_s, hence they will form different expectations about the equilibrium stock price. This means that HSS might have to pay more than $21.73 to repurchase its shares, or perhaps that the shares could be bought at a lower price. These changes would cause the optimal amount of debt to be somewhat higher or lower than $6 million. Still, $6 million represents our best estimate of the optimal debt level, so it is the level we should use as our target capital structure.

12. The WACC for the various levels of debt is shown in Column 8 of Table 13-2. It can be seen that the minimum cost of capital, 11.0 percent, corresponds to the level of debt at which the value of the firm and its stock price are maximized, $6.0 million.

TABLE 13-3	HSS's EPS AT DIFFERENT AMOUNTS OF DEBT (MILLIONS OF DOLLARS EXCEPT PER-SHARE FIGURES)		
OPERATING INCOME (EBIT)			
Probability of indicated sales	0.2	0.6	0.2
Sales	$10.00	$20.00	$30.00
Fixed operating costs	4.00	4.00	4.00
Variable costs (60% of sales)	6.00	12.00	18.00
Total costs (except interest)	$10.00	$16.00	$22.00
Earnings before interest and taxes (EBIT)	$ 0.00	$ 4.00	$ 8.00
ZERO DEBT			
Less interest	0.00	0.00	0.00
Earnings before taxes	$ 0.00	$ 4.00	$ 8.00
Less taxes (40%)	0.00	1.60	3.20
Net income	$ 0.00	$ 2.40	$ 4.80
Earnings per share on 1 million shares (EPS)	$ 0.00	$ 2.40	$ 4.80
Expected EPS		$ 2.40	
Standard deviation of EPS[a]		$ 1.52	
Coefficient of variation of EPS[a]		0.63	

The stock price and cost of capital relationships developed in Table 13-2 are graphed in Figure 13-7. Here we see that HSS's stock price is maximized, and its weighted average cost of capital is minimized, at the same D/V ratio, 27.6 percent.

THE EFFECT OF FINANCIAL LEVERAGE ON EPS

Thus far we have focused on the impact of leverage on a firm's total value and stock price. Before we leave the HSS illustration, we should also take a look at how leverage affects earnings per share (EPS); this is done in Table 13-3. The top third of the table gives operating income data. It begins by recognizing that HSS's future EBIT is not known with certainty. Expected EBIT is $4 million, but the realized EBIT could be less than or greater than $4 million. To simplify matters, we have assumed a discrete distribution of sales, so EBIT has only three possible outcomes. Notice also that EBIT is assumed not to depend on financial leverage.[18]

The middle third of Table 13-3 shows the situation that would exist if HSS continues to use no debt. Net income after taxes is divided by the 1 million shares outstanding to calculate EPS. If sales were as low as $10 million, EPS would be zero, but EPS would rise to $4.80 at sales of $30 million.

---

[18]As we discussed earlier, capital structure does affect EBIT at very high debt levels. For example, we assumed that HSS's EBIT would fall from $4 million to $3.52 million if the level of debt rose to $14 million. However, debt in Table 13-3 is limited to $10 million, so the "excessive leverage effect on EBIT" is not present in this particular example.

		CONTINUED	Table 13-3

$10 MILLION OF DEBT

Less interest (0.12 × $10,000,000)	1.20	1.20	1.20
Earnings before taxes	($1.20)	$ 2.80	$ 6.80
Less taxes (40%)[b]	(0.48)	1.12	2.72
Net income	($0.72)	$ 1.68	$ 4.08
Earnings per share on 524,940 shares (EPS)[c]	($1.37)	$ 3.20	$ 7.77
Expected EPS		$ 3.20	
Standard deviation of EPS[a]		$ 2.90	
Coefficient of variation of EPS[a]		0.91	

[a]Procedures for calculating the standard deviation and the coefficient of variation were discussed in Chapter 4.

[b]Assume tax credit on losses. If credits were not available, expected EPS would be lower, and risk higher, at high debt levels.

[c]Shares outstanding is determined as follows:

$$\text{Shares} = \text{Original shares} - \frac{\text{Debt}}{\text{Stock price}} = 1,000,000 - \frac{\text{Debt}}{\text{Stock price}},$$

where the stock price is taken from Table 13-2, Column 6. With $10 million of debt, P = $21.05. After the recapitalization, 524,940 shares will remain outstanding:

$$\text{Shares} = 1,000,000 - \frac{\$10,000,000}{\$21.05} = 524,940.$$

EPS figures can also be calculated using this formula:

$$\text{EPS} = \frac{(\text{EBIT} - k_dD)(1 - T)}{\text{Original shares} - \text{Debt/Price}}.$$

For example, at D = $10 million,

$$\text{EPS} = \frac{[\$4,000,000 - (0.12)(\$10,000,000)](0.6)}{1,000,000 - \$10,000,000/\$21.05} = \frac{\$1,680,000}{524,940} = \$3.20.$$

The EPS at each sales level is next multiplied by the probability of that sales level to obtain the expected EPS, which is $2.40 if HSS uses no debt. We also calculate the standard deviation of EPS and its coefficient of variation to get an idea of the firm's stand-alone risk at a zero debt ratio: σ_{EPS} = $1.52, and CV_{EPS} = 0.63.

The lower third of Table 13-3 shows the financial results that would occur if the company decided to use $10 million of debt. The interest rate on the debt, 12 percent, is taken from Figure 13-6. With $10 million of 12 percent debt outstanding, the company's interest expense is $1.2 million per year. This is a fixed cost, and it is deducted from EBIT as calculated in the top section. Next, taxes are taken out, and we work on down to the EPS figures that would result at each sales level. With $10 million of debt, EPS would be −$1.37 if sales were as low as $10 million; it would rise to $3.20 if sales were $20 million; and it would soar to $7.77 if sales were as high as $30 million.

Continuous approximations of the EPS distributions under the two financial structures are graphed in Figure 13-8. Although expected EPS is much higher if the firm uses financial leverage, the graph makes it clear that the risk of low, or even negative, EPS is also higher if debt is used. Figure 13-8 thus shows that using leverage involves a risk/return trade-off—higher leverage increases expected earnings per share, but it also increases the firm's risk. It is this increasing risk that causes k_s and k_d to increase at higher amounts of financial leverage.[19]

The relationship between expected EPS and financial leverage is plotted in the top section of Figure 13-9. Here we see that expected EPS first rises as the use of debt increases—interest charges rise, but the decreasing number of shares outstanding as debt is substituted for equity still causes EPS to increase. However, EPS peaks when $12 million of debt is used. Beyond this amount, interest rates rise rapidly, and EBIT begins to fall, so EPS is depressed in spite of the falling number of shares outstanding. Risk as measured by the coefficient of variation of EPS shown in the fourth column of the data in Figure 13-9 rises continuously, and at an increasing rate, as debt is substituted for equity.

Does the same amount of debt maximize both price and EPS? The answer is *no.* As we can see from the lower graph in Figure 13-9, HSS's stock price is maximized with $6 million of debt, while the upper graph shows that expected EPS is maximized by using $12 million of debt. *Since management is primarily interested in*

| FIGURE 13-8 | PROBABILITY DISTRIBUTION OF EPS FOR HSS WITH DIFFERENT AMOUNTS OF FINANCIAL LEVERAGE |

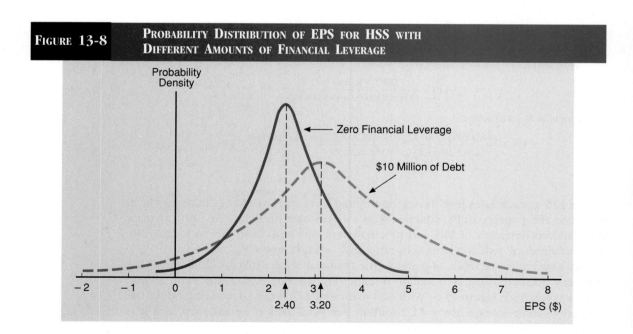

---

[19]Note that financial leverage has similar effects on the risk of both EPS and ROE. Thus, Figure 13-8 is similar in appearance to the lower part of Figure 13-4.

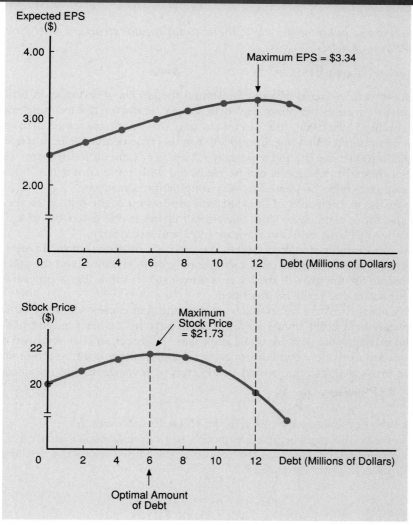

DEBT	EXPECTED EPS	STANDARD DEVIATION OF EPS	COEFFICIENT OF VARIATION	STOCK PRICE[b]
$ 0	$2.40[a]	$1.52[a]	0.63[a]	$20.00
2,000,000	2.55	1.68	0.66	20.89
4,000,000	2.70	1.87	0.69	21.47
6,000,000	2.87	2.09	0.73	21.73
8,000,000	3.04	2.40	0.80	21.71
10,000,000	3.20[a]	2.90[a]	0.91[a]	21.05
12,000,000	3.34	3.83	1.15	19.86
14,000,000	3.26	5.20	1.60	17.16

[a]These values are taken from Table 13-3. Values at other debt levels were calculated similarly.
[b]Stock prices are from Table 13-2.

maximizing the value of the stock, the optimal capital structure calls for the use of $6 million of debt.

PROBLEMS WITH THE HSS ANALYSIS

The Hill Software Systems example illustrated the effects of leverage on firm value, stock prices, earnings per share, and debt values. However, the example was obviously simplified to facilitate the discussion, and we cannot overemphasize the difficulties encountered when one attempts to use this type of analysis in practice. First, the capitalization rates (k_d and especially k_s) are very difficult to estimate. The cost of debt at different debt levels can be estimated with some confidence, but cost of equity estimates must be viewed as very rough approximations.[20]

Second, the mathematics of the valuation process make the outcomes very sensitive to the input estimates. Thus, fairly small errors in the estimates of k_d, k_s, and EBIT can lead to large errors in estimated EPS and stock price.

Third, our example was restricted to the case of a no-growth firm. In view of the input requirements to model even a simple no-growth situation, and the still greater requirements for the growth model, it is unrealistic to think that a precise optimal capital structure can really be identified.

Finally, many firms are not publicly owned, and that causes still more difficulties. If a privately held firm's owner never plans to have his or her firm go public, then potential market value data are really irrelevant. However, an analysis based on market values for a privately owned firm is useful if the owner is interested in knowing how the firm's market value would be affected by leverage should the decision be made to go public.

SELF-TEST
QUESTIONS

What are the key assumptions used in the Hill Software example?

Briefly describe the steps involved in finding Hill's optimal capital structure.

What problems occur when the Hill example procedures are used to estimate real-world optimal capital structures?

SOME CONSIDERATIONS IN THE CAPITAL STRUCTURE DECISION

Since firms cannot determine their precise optimal capital structures, managers must apply judgment to their quantitative analyses. The judgmental analysis involves several different factors. In one situation a particular factor might have great importance. In another, that factor might be relatively unimportant. This section discusses some of the more important judgmental issues that should be taken into account.

---

[20]The statistical relationship between k_s and financial leverage has been studied extensively using both cross-sectional and time series data. In the cross-sectional studies, a sample of firms is analyzed, with multiple regression techniques used in an attempt to "hold constant" all factors other than financial leverage that might influence k_s. The general conclusion of these studies is that k_s rises as leverage increases, but statistical problems preclude us from specifying the functional relationship with much confidence.

In the time series studies, a single firm's k_s is analyzed over time in an attempt to see how k_s changes in response to changes in its debt ratio. Here again, "other factors" do not remain constant, so it is impossible to specify exactly how k_s is affected by financial leverage.

LONG-RUN VIABILITY

Managers of large firms, especially those providing vital services such as electricity or telephone service, have a responsibility to provide *continuous* service, so they must refrain from using leverage to the point where the firm's long-run viability is endangered. Long-run viability may conflict with stock price maximization and cost of capital minimization.[21]

MANAGERIAL CONSERVATISM

Well-diversified investors have eliminated most, if not all, of the diversifiable risk from their portfolios. Therefore, the typical investor can tolerate some chance of financial distress, because a loss on one stock would probably be offset by gains on another. However, managers generally view financial stability as being quite important—they are typically not well diversified, and their careers, and thus the present value of their expected earnings, can be seriously affected by financial distress. Thus, it is not difficult to imagine that managers might be more "conservative" in their use of leverage than the average stockholder would desire. If this is true, then managers would set somewhat lower target debt ratios than the ones which maximize stock prices. The managers of a publicly owned firm would never admit this, for unless they owned voting control, they would quickly be removed from office. However, in view of the uncertainties about what constitutes the value-maximizing structure, management could always say that the target capital structure employed is, in its judgment, the value-maximizing structure, and it would be difficult to prove otherwise.[22]

LENDER AND RATING AGENCY ATTITUDES

Regardless of a manager's own analysis of the proper leverage for his or her firm, there is no question but that lenders' and rating agencies' attitudes are frequently important determinants of financial structures. Generally, management will discuss the firm's financial structure with lenders and rating agencies and give much weight to their advice. However, if a particular firm's management is so confident of the

---

[21]Recognizing this fact, most public service commissions require utilities to obtain their approval before issuing long-term securities, and Congress has empowered the SEC to supervise the capital structures of public utility holding companies. However, both managers and regulators recognize a need to keep all costs as low as possible, including the cost of capital. Since a firm's capital structure affects its cost of capital, regulatory commissions and utility managers try to select capital structures that minimize utilities' cost of capital, subject to the constraint that a firm's ability to finance needed construction projects is not endangered.

[22]It is, of course, possible for a particular manager to be less conservative than his or her firm's average stockholder. However, this condition is less likely to occur than is excessive managerial conservatism, which is just another manifestation of the agency problem. If excessive conservatism exists, then managers, as agents of the stockholders, are not acting in the best interests of their principals. However, when managers become the primary owners of a company, such as in managerial buyouts (MBOs), they often become very aggressive in their use of financial leverage. By using extreme amounts of debt, they take on a great deal of risk, but, in the process, they open the door for big payoffs. Note too that the threat of takeovers motivates underleveraged firms' managers to use more debt than they otherwise would.

future that it seeks to use leverage beyond the norms for its industry, its lenders may be unwilling to accept such debt increases, or may do so only at a high price.

Coverage ratios are often used by lenders and rating agencies to measure the risk of financial distress. Accordingly, managements give considerable weight to such ratios as the *times-interest-earned (TIE) ratio,* which is defined as EBIT divided by total interest charges. The lower this ratio, the higher the probability that a firm will encounter financial distress.

Table 13-4 shows how HSS's expected TIE ratio declines as its use of debt increases. At zero debt, the TIE ratio is undefined, but it is almost infinitely high at very low debt levels. When $2 million of debt is used, the expected TIE is a high 25 times, but the interest coverage ratio declines rapidly as debt rises. Note, however, that these coverages are expected values — the actual TIE will be higher if sales exceed the expected $20 million level, but lower if sales fall below $20 million.

The variability of the TIE ratio is highlighted in Figure 13-10, which shows the probability distributions of the ratio at $8 million and $12 million of debt. The expected TIE is much higher if only $8 million of debt is used. Even more important, with less debt there is a much lower probability of a TIE of less than 1.0, the level at which the firm is not earning enough to meet its required interest payments.

Another coverage ratio that is often used by lenders and rating agencies is the *fixed charge coverage (FCC) ratio.* This ratio recognizes that there are fixed financial charges other than interest payments which could lead to financial distress. The FCC ratio is defined as follows:

$$FCC = \frac{EBIT + Lease\ payments}{Interest + \left(\begin{array}{c} Lease \\ payments \end{array}\right) + \left(\dfrac{Sinking\ fund\ payments}{1 - T}\right)}.$$

Note that sinking fund payments reduce the debt — they are not deductible interest payments — hence sinking fund payments must be "grossed up" in recognition of the

TABLE 13-4	HSS's Expected Times-Interest-Earned Ratio at Different Amounts of Debt

AMOUNT OF DEBT (IN MILLIONS)	EXPECTED TIE[a]
$ 0	Undefined
2	25.0
4	12.1
6	7.4
8	5.0
10	3.3
12	2.2

[a]TIE = EBIT/Interest. Example: TIE = $4,000,000/$1,200,000 = 3.3 at $10 million of debt. Data are from Table 13-1 and Figure 13-6.

fact that they must be made with after-tax dollars (net income). Interest and lease payments are fully deductible, hence they do not need to be grossed up.

If HSS had $1 million of lease payments and $1 million of sinking fund payments, its FCC ratio at a debt level of $10 million would be 1.3:

$$FCC = \frac{\$4,000,000 + \$1,000,000}{\$1,200,000 + \$1,000,000 + \dfrac{\$1,000,000}{0.6}}$$

$$= \frac{\$5,000,000}{\$3,866,667} = 1.3.$$

Thus, the coverage of total fixed charges is considerably less than the 3.3 times-interest-earned coverage at the same debt level.

RESERVE BORROWING CAPACITY AND FINANCING FLEXIBILITY

When we discussed asymmetric information and signaling, we noted that firms should maintain some reserve borrowing capacity, which preserves their ability to issue debt on favorable terms. For example, suppose Biotechnics Inc. had just successfully completed an R&D program, and its internal projections are for much higher earnings in the immediate future. However, the new earnings are not yet anticipated by investors, hence are not reflected in the price of its stock. Biotechnics would not want to issue stock — it would prefer to finance with debt until the higher earnings materialized and were reflected in the stock price, at which time it could sell an issue of common stock, retire the debt, and return to its target capital structure. Similarly, if the financial manager felt that interest rates were temporarily low, but were likely to rise fairly soon, he or she might want to issue long-term bonds and thus "lock in" the low rates for many years. To obtain this *financing flexibility*, firms generally use less debt under "normal" conditions, thus presenting a stronger financial picture than they would otherwise have. This is not suboptimal from a long-run standpoint, although it might appear so if viewed strictly on a short-run basis.

Note too that firms' debt contracts often specify that no new debt can be issued unless certain ratios exceed minimum levels. Very frequently, the TIE ratio is required to exceed 2 or 2.5 times as a condition for the issuance of additional debt. With this in mind, look back at Figure 13-10 and note that, if it used $12 million of debt, HSS's TIE would be less than 2.0 almost half the time, whereas the probability of a coverage less than 2.0 would be quite small if it used only $8 million of debt. Thus, if HSS sets a relatively high target debt ratio, its financing flexibility would be reduced in the sense that it could not count on using whatever type of capital it wanted to use at all times.

CONTROL

The effect of debt on a management's control position may also influence the capital structure decision. If management just barely has majority control (just over 50 percent of the stock), but it is not in a position to buy any more stock, debt may be the choice for new financings. On the other hand, a management group that is not concerned about voting control may decide to use equity rather than debt if the financial situation is so weak that the use of debt might subject the company to serious risk of default. If the firm gets into serious difficulties, creditors (through covenants in the debt agreements) may assume control and perhaps force a management change. This has happened to Chrysler, Navistar International (formerly International Harvester), Braniff, Continental Illinois Bank, and a number of other companies in recent years. However, if too little debt is used, management runs the risk of a takeover, where some other company or management group persuades stockholders to turn over control to the new group, which plans to boost earnings and stock prices by using financial leverage. This happened to Lenox, the china company, and to many other firms in the 1980s. Control considerations do not necessarily suggest the use of debt or of equity, but if management does not have majority control, the effects of financing decisions on control will certainly be taken into account.

ASSET STRUCTURE

Firms whose assets are suitable as security for loans tend to use debt rather heavily. Thus, real estate companies tend to be highly leveraged. However, companies involved in technological research employ relatively little debt. Also, if the firm's assets are subject to high business risk, then it will be less able to use financial leverage than a firm with low business risk. Accordingly, factors such as sales stability and operating leverage, which influence business risk, also influence capital structure decisions.

GROWTH RATE

Other factors the same, faster-growing firms must rely more heavily on external capital — slow growth can be financed with retained earnings, but rapid growth generally requires the use of external funds. For reasons set forth in our discussion of information asymmetry theory, and also because the flotation costs involved in selling common stock exceed those incurred when selling debt, firms first turn to debt financing to meet external funding needs. Thus, rapidly growing firms tend to use somewhat more debt than slower-growth companies.

PROFITABILITY

One often observes that firms with very high rates of return on investment use relatively little debt. This behavior is consistent with the information asymmetry theory, and the practical reason seems to be that highly profitable firms such as Merck, 3M, and Microsoft simply do not need to do much debt financing—their high profits enable them to do most of their financing with retained earnings.

TAXES

Interest is a deductible expense, while dividends are not deductible, so the higher a firm's corporate tax rate, the greater the advantage of using debt.

Is the capital structure decision mostly objective (made on the basis of numerical analysis) or mostly subjective (judgmental, with many factors considered)?

Briefly discuss some of the factors that managers consider when setting the firm's target capital structure.

SELF-TEST QUESTIONS

AN APPROACH TO SETTING THE TARGET CAPITAL STRUCTURE

Thus far in the chapter, we have discussed (1) the basics of business and financial risks, (2) several theories of capital structure, (3) a method of analysis based on perpetual cash flows, and (4) a number of factors which influence the capital structure decision. In this section, we describe a pragmatic approach to setting the target capital structure. Our approach requires judgmental assumptions, but it also requires managers to consider how alternative capital structures would affect future profitability, coverage, and external financing requirements under a variety of assumptions.

The starting point for the analysis is a forecasting model set up to test the effects of capital structure changes. Here is a brief description of the spreadsheet model we use in consulting assignments. Basically, the model generates forecasted data based on inputs supplied by the firm's financial staff. Each data item can be fixed, or it can be allowed to vary from year to year. The required data include the most recent balance sheet and income statement, plus the following items, all of which represent either expectations or management-determined policy variables:

1. Annual growth rates in unit sales
2. Annual inflation rates
3. Corporate tax rate
4. Variable costs as a percentage of sales

5. Fixed costs

6. Interest rates on already outstanding (or embedded) debt

7. Marginal component costs of capital

8. Capital structure percentages

9. Dividend growth rate

10. Long-term dividend payout ratio

The model uses the input data to forecast balance sheets and income statements for future years, and it calculates and displays other information such as external financing requirements, ROE, EPS, DPS, times interest earned, stock price, WACC, and a set of key ratios for projected future years.

The financial manager begins by entering base year balance sheet and income statement values plus data on expected unit sales growth rates, expected inflation rates, and so on. These inputs are used by the model to forecast operating income and asset requirements. Next, the model brings in the financing mix. It uses as inputs both the debt/equity mix and the debt maturity structure. By debt maturity structure, we mean the proportion of short-term versus long-term debt. Further, the manager must estimate as best he or she can the effects of the firm's capital structure on its component costs — a higher debt ratio will lead to increases in the costs of all components, and vice versa if less debt is used. With all inputs entered, the model then forecasts financial statements and generates projected stock prices.

The model is then used to analyze alternative scenarios. This analysis takes two forms: (1) changing the financing inputs to get an idea about how the financing mix affects the key outputs and (2) changing the operating inputs to see how economic conditions affect the key outputs under various financing strategies. Finally, the model's output must be reviewed and analyzed, and a decision must be made as to the best capital structure. We pay particular attention to the forecasted EPS, interest coverage, external funding requirements, and projected stock price.

The model can generate output "answers" quite easily, but it is up to the financial manager to assign input values, to interpret the output, and, finally, to set the target capital structure. The final decision is based on all the factors we have discussed, and the decision maker must judge which factors are most relevant to his or her firm. Reaching a decision is not easy, but a capital structure forecasting model such as the one we use does help managers to analyze the effects of alternative courses of action, which is essential in good decision making.

It should be noted that *while capital structure decisions do affect stock prices, those effects are generally small in comparison to the effects of operating decisions*. A company's ability to identify (or create) market opportunities, and to produce and sell products or services efficiently, is the primary determinant of success. Financial arrangements can facilitate or hamper operations, but the best of financial plans cannot overcome deficiencies in the operations area. This statement is supported by empirical studies, which generally find a weak statistical relationship between capital structure and stock prices. It is also supported by runs of our computer model, which show stock prices to be affected significantly by changes in unit sales, sales prices, fixed costs, and variable costs, but only slightly affected by changes in capital structure. This last point can also be seen from the HSS example discussed earlier. Refer again to Table 13-2. Hill Software Systems' stock price is maximized at a D/V ratio of 27.6 percent. However, at a D/V of 18.6 percent, which is one-third lower, the firm's stock price drops only from $21.73 to $21.47, or by 1.2 percent, while if D/V rises to 36.8 percent, HSS's stock price hardly drops at all. Thus, HSS could set its target D/V ratio anywhere in the range from 18.6 to 36.8 percent and still come very close to maximizing the stock price.

Briefly describe the elements of a financial forecasting model designed to help set the target capital structure.

How critical is the optimal capital structure decision to the financial performance of the firm; that is, how important are small deviations from the optimal structure?

Should the target capital structure be thought of as a single point or as a range?

SELF-TEST QUESTIONS

SOME ADDITIONAL INSIGHTS INTO CAPITAL STRUCTURE DECISIONS

At this point, one might have an uneasy feeling regarding both how to establish the target capital structure and its effect on risk, profitability, and stock prices. We can construct models which generate projected earnings, stock prices, coverage ratios, and so on, under different capital structures. However, our confidence in these results is limited, because we do not know for sure how k_d and k_s, hence stock prices, will really change with changes in the capital structure. We also know that in practice many more or less subjective factors also influence the decision. Therefore, to gain more insights into capital structure decisions, it is useful to look at how managers say they actually establish target capital structures.

Professors David Scott and Dana Johnson surveyed a group of firms to find out how managers attempt to estimate the optimal capital structure, and whether managers really believe that one can be determined.[23] Scott and Johnson sent questionnaires to the chief financial officer (CFO) of each Fortune 1000 firm. Although only 212 financial managers replied, the sample was still large enough to provide useful insights into the operational decision process.

First, the respondents agreed that capital structure decisions do matter — in general, financial managers believe that the prudent use of debt can lower the firm's overall cost of capital, and that an excessive use of debt will increase the required rate of return on equity. Second, the most popular measures of financial leverage are (1) the long-term debt to total capitalization ratio,[24] (2) the times-interest-earned (TIE) ratio, and (3) the long-term debt to common equity ratio. However, when computing these ratios, accounting (or book) values rather than market values were virtually always used. Third, 64 percent of the responding managers indicated that their target long-term debt to total capitalization ratios were in the range of 26 to 40 percent, and the most popular reported target range was 26 to 30 percent. (Because

---

[23]See David F. Scott and Dana J. Johnson, "Financing Policies and Practices in Large Corporations," *Financial Management*, Summer 1982, 51–59.

[24]Total capitalization is defined as long-term debt plus preferred stock plus common equity. Therefore, current liabilities and deferred taxes are excluded.

stock market values generally exceed book values, the debt ratio measured in market value terms would be quite a bit lower than these reported book value figures.)

The survey also provided data on how various parties influence the capital structure decision. The data indicate that managers give the greatest weight to their own internal analyses, but that investment bankers and bond rating agencies also have a significant influence. Additionally, firms consider industry averages when setting their target capital structures, but they are willing to depart from these averages if their own conditions suggest that a departure is warranted.

Note that the Scott-Johnson survey was taken in 1982. Since then, many MBAs have graduated, gone into the work force, and now make important financial decisions. Our guess—supported by our own observations—is that if the survey were repeated today more companies would report that they give weight to market value as well as book value capital structures.

SELF-TEST
QUESTIONS

Do practicing financial managers believe that capital structures matter?

Do investment bankers and rating agencies influence the capital structure decision?

SUMMARY

This chapter discussed capital structure decisions. The key concepts covered are listed below:

- *Business risk* is the inherent riskiness in a firm's operations if it uses no debt. *Financial risk* is the additional risk that is concentrated on the shareholders when debt financing is used.

- Within a *stand-alone risk framework,* business risk can be measured by $\sigma_{ROE(U)}$, stand-alone risk can be measured by σ_{ROE}, and financial risk can be measured by Stand-alone risk − Business risk = $\sigma_{ROE} - \sigma_{ROE(U)}$.

- In 1958, *Franco Modigliani and Merton Miller (MM)* startled the academic community by proving, under a restrictive set of assumptions including zero taxes, that capital structure is irrelevant; that is, according to the original MM article, a firm's value is not affected by its financing mix.

- When *corporate taxes are added* to the MM model, the results indicate that firms should use 100 percent debt financing. However, later work by Miller demonstrated that *personal taxes* reduce, but do not eliminate, the value of debt financing.

- The addition of financial distress and agency costs to either the MM corporate tax model or the Miller model results in a *trade-off model.* Here the marginal costs and benefits of debt financing are balanced against one another, and the result is an optimal capital structure that falls somewhere between zero and 100 percent debt.

■ Unfortunately, capital structure theory does not provide neat, clean answers to the question of the optimal capital structure. Thus, many factors must be considered when actually choosing a target capital structure, and the final decision will be based on both analysis and judgment.

■ If a firm has *perpetual cash flows,* then a relatively simple model can be used to value the firm at different capital structures. In theory, this model can be used to find the capital structure that maximizes stock price. However, the inputs to the model are very difficult, if not impossible, to estimate. Further, most firms are growing, so they do not have constant cash flows.

■ Since one cannot determine the optimal capital structure with quantitative models, managers must also consider *qualitative factors* including long-run viability, managerial conservatism, lender and rating agency attitudes, reserve borrowing capacity, control, asset structure, profitability, and taxes.

■ Firms generally have *computerized planning models* which are used in the financial planning process. These models can be used to get a feel for the impact of capital structure changes on a firm's financial condition.

In the next chapter, we will examine some additional issues which provide further insights into the capital structure decision.

QUESTIONS

13-1 Define each of the following terms:
a. Capital structure
b. Business risk
c. Financial risk
d. Operating leverage
e. Financial leverage
f. Breakeven point
g. Capital structure theory
h. Perpetual cash flow analysis
i. Reserve borrowing capacity

13-2 What term refers to the uncertainty inherent in projections of future ROE(U)?

13-3 Firms with relatively high nonfinancial fixed costs are said to have a high degree of what?

13-4 "One type of leverage affects both EBIT and EPS. The other type affects only EPS." Explain this statement.

13-5 Why is the following statement true? "Other things being the same, firms with relatively stable sales are able to carry relatively high debt ratios."

13-6 Why do public utility companies usually have capital structures that are different from those of retail firms?

13-7 Some economists believe that swings in business cycles will not be as wide in the future as they have been in the past. Assuming that they are correct, what effect might this added stability have on the types of financing used by firms in the United States? Would your answer be true for all firms?

13-8   Why is EBIT generally considered to be independent of financial leverage? Why might EBIT actually be influenced by financial leverage at high debt levels?

13-9   If a firm with no debt could buy back and retire its stock at the pre-announcement price, would its final stock price be higher than that resulting from the procedure outlined in the chapter? Would it be fair for a firm to buy back its stock without telling stockholders that stock was being repurchased?

13-10   How might increasingly volatile inflation rates, interest rates, and bond prices affect the optimal capital structure for corporations?

13-11   If a firm went from zero debt to successively higher levels of debt, why would you expect its stock price to first rise, then hit a peak, and then begin to decline?

13-12   The stock of Gentech Company is currently selling at its low for the year, but management feels that the stock price is only temporarily depressed because of investor pessimism. The firm's capital budget this year is so large that the use of new outside equity is contemplated. However, management does not want to sell new stock at the current low price and is therefore considering a temporary departure from the firm's "optimal" capital structure by borrowing the funds it would otherwise have raised in the equity markets. Does this seem to be a wise move? Does this action conform to any of the theories presented in the chapter?

13-13   Why is the debt level that maximizes a firm's expected EPS generally higher than the debt level that maximizes its stock price?

SELF-TEST PROBLEM

(SOLUTION APPEARS IN APPENDIX C)

ST-1   OPTIMAL CAPITAL STRUCTURE The Rogers Company is currently in this situation: (1) EBIT = $4 million; (2) tax rate, T = 35%; (3) value of debt, D = $2 million; (4) k_d = 10%; (5) k_s = 15%; and (6) shares of stock outstanding, n = 600,000. The firm's market is stable, and it expects no growth, so all earnings are paid out as dividends. The debt consists of perpetual bonds.

a. What is the total market value of the firm's stock, S, its price per share, P_O, and the firm's total market value, V?

b. What is the firm's weighted average cost of capital?

c. The firm can increase its debt by $8 million, to a total of $10 million, using the new debt to buy back and retire some of its shares. Its interest rate on all debt will be 12 percent (it will have to call and refund the old debt), and its cost of equity will rise from 15 to 17 percent. EBIT will remain constant. Should the firm change its capital structure?

-1 OPERATING LEVERAGE AND BREAKEVEN Schweser Satellites Inc. produces satellite earth stations which sell for $100,000 each. The firm's fixed costs, F, are $2 million; 50 earth stations are produced and sold each year; profits total $500,000; and the firm's assets (all equity financed) are $5 million. The firm estimates that it can change its production process, adding $4 million to investment and $500,000 to fixed operating costs. This change will (1) reduce variable costs per unit by $10,000 and (2) increase output by 20 units, but (3) the sales price on all units will have to be lowered to $95,000 to permit sales of the additional output. The firm has tax loss carry-forwards that cause its tax rate to be zero, its cost of equity is 15 percent, and it uses no debt.

a. Should the firm make the change?

b. Would the firm's operating leverage increase or decrease if it made the change? What about its breakeven point?

c. Would the new situation expose the firm to more or less business risk than the old one?

-2 BUSINESS AND FINANCIAL RISK Here are the estimated ROE distributions for Firms A, B, and C:

	PROBABILITY				
	0.1	0.2	0.4	0.2	0.1
Firm A: ROE_A	0.0%	5.0%	10.0%	15.0%	20.0%
Firm B: ROE_B	(2.0)	5.0	12.0	19.0	26.0
Firm C: ROE_C	(5.0)	5.0	15.0	25.0	35.0

a. Calculate the expected value and standard deviation for Firm C's ROE. $ROE_A = 10.0\%$, $\sigma_A = 5.5\%$; $ROE_B = 12.0\%$, $\sigma_B = 7.7\%$.

b. Discuss the relative riskiness of the three firms' returns. (Assume that these distributions are expected to remain constant over time.)

c. Now suppose all three firms have the same standard deviation of basic earning power (EBIT/Total assets), $\sigma_A = \sigma_B = \sigma_C = 5.5\%$. What can we tell about the financial risk of each firm?

-3 CAPITAL STRUCTURE ANALYSIS The following data reflect the current financial conditions of the Levine Corporation:

Value of debt (book = market)	$1,000,000
Market value of equity	$5,257,143
Sales, last 12 months	$12,000,000
Variable operating costs (50% of sales)	$6,000,000
Fixed operating costs	$5,000,000
Tax rate, T (federal-plus-state)	40%

At the current level of debt, the cost of debt, k_d, is 8 percent and the cost of equity, k_s, is 10.5 percent. Management questions whether or not the capital structure is optimal, so the financial vice-president has been asked to consider the possibility of issuing $1 million of additional debt and using the proceeds to repurchase stock. It is estimated that if the leverage were increased by raising the level of debt to $2 million, the interest rate on new debt would rise to 9 percent and k_s would rise to 11.5 percent. The old 8 percent debt is senior to the new debt, and it would remain outstanding, continue to yield 8 percent, and have a market value of $1 million. The firm is a zero-growth firm, with all of its earnings paid out as dividends.

a. Should the firm increase its debt to $2 million?

b. If the firm decided to increase its level of debt to $3 million, its cost of the additional $2 million of debt would be 12 percent and k_s would rise to 15 percent. The original 8 percent of debt would again remain outstanding, and its market value would remain at $1 million. What level of debt should the firm choose: $1 million, $2 million, or $3 million?

c. The market price of the firm's stock was originally $20 per share. Calculate the new equilibrium stock prices at debt levels of $2 million and $3 million.

d. Calculate the firm's earnings per share if it uses debt of $1 million, $2 million, and $3 million. Assume that the firm pays out all of its earnings as dividends. If you find that EPS increases with more debt, does this mean that the firm should choose to increase its debt to $3 million, or possibly higher?

e. What would happen to the value of the old bonds if the firm uses more leverage and the old bonds are not senior to the new bonds?

13-4   CAPITAL STRUCTURE ANALYSIS   The Rivoli Company has no debt outstanding, and its financial position is given by the following data:

Assets (book = market)	$3,000,000
EBIT	$500,000
Cost of equity, k_s	10%
Stock price, P_0	$15
Shares outstanding, n	200,000
Tax rate, T (federal-plus-state)	40%

The firm is considering selling bonds and simultaneously repurchasing some of its stock. If it uses $900,000 of debt, its cost of equity, k_s, will increase to 11 percent to reflect the increased risk. Bonds can be sold at a cost, k_d, of 7 percent. Rivoli is a no-growth firm. Hence, all its earnings are paid out as dividends, and earnings are expectationally constant over time.

a. What effect would this use of leverage have on the value of the firm?

b. What would be the price of Rivoli's stock?

c. What happens to the firm's earnings per share after the recapitalization?

d. The $500,000 EBIT given previously is actually the expected value from the following probability distribution:

PROBABILITY	EBIT
0.10	($ 100,000)
0.20	200,000
0.40	500,000
0.20	800,000
0.10	1,100,000

What is the probability distribution of EPS with zero debt and with $900,000 of debt? Which EPS distribution is riskier?

e. Determine the probability distributions of times interest earned for each debt level. What is the probability of not covering the interest payment at the $900,000 debt level?

3-5   **CAPITAL STRUCTURE ANALYSIS** Pettit Printing Company has a total market value of $100 million, consisting of 1 million shares selling for $50 per share and $50 million of 10 percent perpetual bonds now selling at par. The company's EBIT is $13.24 million, and its tax rate is 15 percent. Pettit can change its capital structure by either increasing its debt to $70 million or decreasing it to $30 million. If it decides to *increase* its use of leverage, it must call its old bonds and issue new ones with a 12 percent coupon. If it decides to *decrease* its leverage, it will call in its old bonds and replace them with new 8 percent coupon bonds. The company will sell or repurchase stock at the new equilibrium price to complete the capital structure change.

The firm pays out all earnings as dividends; hence, its stock is a zero growth stock. If it increases leverage, k_s will be 16 percent. If it decreases leverage, k_s will be 13 percent.

a. What is the firm's cost of equity at present?

b. Should the firm change its capital structure?

c. Suppose the tax rate is changed to 34 percent. This would lower after-tax income and also cause a decline in the price of the stock and the total value of the equity, other things held constant. Calculate the new stock price (at $50 million of debt).

d. Continue the scenario of Part c, but now re-examine the question of the optimal amount of debt. Does the tax rate change affect your decision about the optimal use of financial leverage?

e. Go back to Part b; that is, assume T = 15%. How would your analysis of the capital structure change be modified if the firm's presently outstanding debt could not be called, and it did not have to be replaced; that is, if the $50 million of 10 percent debt continued even if the company issued new 12 percent bonds?

f. Suppose these probabilities for EBIT exist: P[EBIT = $5 million] = 0.2; P[EBIT = $15 million] = 0.6; and P[EBIT = $25 million] = 0.2. Under the assumptions of Part e, what are (1) expected EPS and σ_{EPS} and (2) expected TIE and σ_{TIE}, assuming an increase in book value of debt to $70 million?

3-6   **SUBJECTIVE ANALYSIS** You have been hired as a financial consultant by two firms, Alpha Industries (Firm A) and Zed Corporation (Firm Z). Firm A is in the fast-growing microcomputer retail sales industry, while Firm Z manufactures office equipment such as pencil sharpeners, staplers, and tape dispensers. Your task is to recommend the optimal capital structure for the two firms. Discuss the factors that would influence your decision, and specifically how each of these factors apply to each firm. Here are some additional points about the two firms:

(1) Firm A generally leases its stores, while Firm Z purchases its plants.

(2) Firm A's stock is widely held, while the family of Firm Z's founder holds 40 percent of its stock.

(3) Firm Z has a significant amount of accelerated depreciation expense each year, while Firm A has almost none.

(4) Firm A has demonstrated high growth and profitability over the last few years. On the other hand, Firm Z's growth has averaged a modest 5 percent per year, and its profit margins and ROEs have been unspectacular.

SPREADSHEET APPLICATIONS

SPREADSHEET PROBLEM

The Norman Corporation is currently all-equity financed, but the firm is considering a change to 50 percent debt financing. The debt would cost 12 percent, and would be used to repurchase shares currently selling at $25 per share. Norman now has 40,000 shares outstanding and $1,000,000 in total assets. Its pro forma income statement for 1997, assuming zero debt usage, is as follows:

Sales	$900,000
Operating costs	750,000
EBIT	$150,000
Taxes (40%)	60,000
Net income	$ 90,000

a. What is the firm's expected EPS for 1997 using zero debt? At a debt level of $500,000?

b. Assume that operating costs remain at 83.33 percent of sales over a wide range of sales levels. Further, the 1997 pro forma income statement is based on expected sales of $900,000, but the actual sales distribution is as follows:

PROBABILITY	SALES
0.10	$500,000
0.15	700,000
0.50	900,000
0.15	1,100,000
0.10	1,300,000

Find the EPS at each sales level for both zero debt and 50 percent debt financing.

c. Make a plot of EPS versus sales level for both financing alternatives. Place the plots on the same set of axes. Interpret this graph.

d. At a zero debt level, Norman's expected ROE = $90,000/$1,000,000 = 9.0%, while at $500,000 of debt, expected ROE = $54,000/$500,000 = 10.8%. Determine the firm's ROE at each debt level for every possible sales level. Plot the two ROE distributions.

e. Now, assume that the $500,000 debt financing would cost 15 percent. Repeat the Part d analysis. Is there a significant difference? Why?

SPREADSHEET EXERCISE: MACROS

This exercise uses a spreadsheet model to calculate the optimal capital structure for a firm with perpetual cash flows. The model is complete including graphics. Students will add macros to the model to make it easier to switch among low, average, and high business risk scenarios.

1. Retrieve the model (Filename SE-13. WK1) from the models diskette. The key inputs include cost of debt and equity estimates at alternative capital structures. The model calculates total market values, stock price, and WACC at each debt level. In addition, the model has a graph of market value versus capital structure.

2. The section beginning on Row 21 contains the input costs of debt and equity for three levels of business risk: low, average, and high. To access the impact of differing business risk, the costs from this section must be copied into the input data section in Cells B7.C11. One way to accomplish this is to simply reenter the data. A more efficient way is to use the copy command, but the most efficient way is to build three macros that use the copy command to move the data with just a single keystroke.

3. Note that Cells A35, A37, and A39 are logical places to construct the macros. In fact, Cells D35, D37, and D39 contain labels to designate the macros. To begin, place the cursor in Cell A35. Note that this cell is next to the \A label, so you will enter the macro to copy the average business risk cost data. Enter '/CF27.G31{GOTO}B7. Since the first character is ', the entry will be a label. If you did not first type ', the entry would be interpreted as a command. The tilde (~), when part of a macro, means Enter, while the entry {GOTO} moves the cursor to the cell address that follows. Thus, the keystrokes in Cell A35 tell the spreadsheet to copy the component cost data from Cells F27.G31 to the range beginning in Cell B7.

4. Now you must tell the spreadsheet that the label in Cell A35 is a macro and also what key must be pressed to run the macro. The Range Name command is used to accomplish this. Press /RNC to create the range name, then \A to designate the range to be named as a macro, and name it A for average. Then, with the highlighter on Cell A35, press Enter. To run the macro, simultaneously press ALT A.

5. Now create macros in Cells A37 and A39 to copy the low and high business risk component cost data, respectively. With all three macros completed, you will be able to easily change the input data to reflect varying business risk conditions. Try it, and view the graph after each input data change.

6. Finally, note that newer releases of spreadsheets have a feature called Learn or Record that allows you to create a macro by executing the keystrokes you wish to perform, rather than typing the keystrokes as labels. The advantage here is that you can see on the screen exactly what the macro does as you are creating it.

MINI CASE

Assume you have just been hired as business manager of PizzaPalace, a pizza restaurant located adjacent to campus. The company's EBIT was $500,000 last year, and since the university's enrollment is capped, EBIT is expected to remain constant (in real terms) over time. Since no expansion capital will be required, PizzaPalace plans to pay out all earnings as dividends. The management group owns about 50 percent of the stock, and the stock is traded in the over-the-counter market.

The firm is currently financed with all equity; it has 100,000 shares outstanding; and $P_0 = \$20$ per share. When you took your MBA corporate finance course, your instructor stated that most firms' owners would be financially better off if the firms used some debt. When you suggested this to your new boss, he encouraged you to pursue the idea. As a first step, assume that you obtained from the firm's investment banker the following estimated costs of debt and equity for the firm at different debt levels (in thousands of dollars):

AMOUNT BORROWED	k_d	k_s
$ 0	—	15.0%
250	10.0%	15.5
500	11.0	16.5
750	13.0	18.0
1,000	16.0	20.0

If the company were to recapitalize, debt would be issued, and the funds received would be used to repurchase stock. PizzaPalace is in the 40 percent state-plus-federal corporate tax bracket.

a. (1) What is business risk? What factors influence a firm's business risk?
   (2) What is operating leverage, and how does it affect a firm's business risk?
b. (1) What is meant by financial leverage and financial risk?
   (2) How does financial risk differ from business risk?
c. How are financial and business risk measured in a stand-alone risk framework?
d. Now, to develop an example that can be presented to PizzaPalace's management to illustrate the effects of financial leverage, consider two hypothetical firms: Firm U, which uses no debt financing, and Firm L, which uses $10,000 of 12 percent debt. Both firms have $20,000 in assets and a 40 percent tax rate, and the following EBIT distribution applies to both for the coming year:

PROBABILITY	EBIT
0.25	$2,000
0.50	3,000
0.25	4,000

(1) Construct partial income statements, which start with EBIT, for the two firms at each level of EBIT.
(2) Now calculate the ratio of EBIT to total assets (the basic earning power ratio); ROI [(Net income + Interest) / (Debt + Equity)]; ROE; and the times-interest-earned (TIE) ratio for both firms at each level of EBIT.
(3) What does this example illustrate about the impact of financial leverage on risk and expected rate of return?
e. What does capital structure theory attempt to do? What lessons can be learned from capital structure theory?
f. With the above points in mind, now consider the optimal capital structure for PizzaPalace.
   (1) What valuation equations can you use in the analysis?
   (2) Could either the MM or the Miller capital structure theories be applied directly in this analysis, and if you presented an analysis based on these theories, how do you think the owners would respond?
g. (1) Describe briefly, without using any numbers, the sequence of events that would take place if PizzaPalace does recapitalize.
   (2) What would be the new stock price if PizzaPalace recapitalized and used these amounts of debt: $250,000; $500,000; $750,000?
   (3) How many shares would remain outstanding after recapitalization under each debt scenario?
   (4) Considering only the levels of debt discussed, what is PizzaPalace's optimal capital structure?
h. (1) Assume now that the firm has recapitalized with $250,000 of debt, and that currently S = $1,839,000, D = $250,000, P = $20.89, and n = 88,030. The debt has a "poison put" which requires that it be paid off if additional debt is issued. What would PizzaPalace's stock price be if it now increased its debt to $500,000 by issu-

ing $500,000 of new debt and using half to refund the old issue and half to repurchase stock? [Hint: Use the formula $P_1 = (V_1 - D_0)/n_0$.]

(2) Now assume that PizzaPalace issues an additional $250,000 of debt, but it does not have to refund the old issue. What would happen to its stock price? Assume also that the new and old issues have the same priority of claims.

i. It is also useful to determine the effect of any proposed recapitalization on EPS. Calculate the EPS at debt levels of $0, $250,000, $500,000, and $750,000, assuming that the firm begins at zero debt and recapitalizes to each level in a single step. Is EPS maximized at the same level that maximizes stock price?

j. Calculate the firm's WACC at each debt level. What is the relationship between the WACC and the stock price?

k. Suppose you discovered that PizzaPalace had more business risk than you originally estimated. Describe how this would affect the analysis. What if the firm had less business risk than originally estimated?

l. Would it make sense to do an analysis similar to the PizzaPalace analysis for most firms? Why or why not? What type of analysis do you think a firm should actually use to help set its optimal, or target, capital structure? What other factors should managers consider when setting the target capital structure?

SELECTED ADDITIONAL REFERENCES AND CASES

Chapter 14 provides references that focus on the theory of capital structure; the references listed here are oriented more toward applications than theory.

Donaldson's work on the setting of debt targets is old but still relevant:

Donaldson, Gordon, "New Framework for Corporate Debt Capacity," *Harvard Business Review,* March–April 1962, 117–131.

———, "Strategy for Financial Emergencies," *Harvard Business Review,* November–December 1969, 67–79.

For an article on signaling, see

Baskin, Jonathon, "An Empirical Investigation of the Pecking Order Hypothesis," *Financial Management,* Spring 1989, 26–35.

Definitive references on the empirical relationships between capital structure and (1) the cost of debt, (2) the cost of equity, (3) earnings, and (4) the price of a firm's stock are virtually nonexistent—statistical problems make the precise estimation of these relationships extraordinarily difficult, if not impossible. One good way to get a feel for the issues involved is to obtain a set of the cost of capital testimonies filed in a major utility rate case—such testimony is available from state public utility commissions, the Federal Communications Commission, the Federal Energy Regulatory Commission, and utility companies themselves. For an academic discussion of the issues, see

Caks, John, "Corporate Debt Decisions: A New Analytical Framework," *Journal of Finance,* December 1978, 1297–1315.

Gordon, Myron J., *The Cost of Capital to a Public Utility* (East Lansing, Mich.: Division of Research, Graduate School of Business Administration, Michigan State University, 1974).

Hamada, Robert S., "The Effect of the Firm's Capital Structure on the Systematic Risk of Common Stocks," *Journal of Finance,* May 1972, 435–452.

Masulis, Ronald W., "The Impact of Capital Structure Change on Firm Value: Some Estimates," *Journal of Finance,* March 1983, 107–126.

Piper, Thomas R., and Wolf A. Weinhold, "How Much Debt Is Right for Your Company?" *Harvard Business Review,* July–August 1982, 106–114.

Shalit, Sol S., "On the Mathematics of Financial Leverage," *Financial Management,* Spring 1975, 57–66.

Shiller, Robert J., and Franco Modigliani, "Coupon and Tax Effects on New and Seasoned Bond Yields and the Measurement of the Cost of Debt Capital," *Journal of Financial Economics,* September 1979, 297–318.

For some insights into how practicing financial managers view the capital structure decision, see

Norton, Edgar, "Factors Affecting Capital Structure Decisions," *Financial Review,* August 1991, 431–446.

Pinegar, J. Michael, and Lisa Wilbricht, "What Managers Think of Capital Structure Theory: A Survey," *Financial Management,* Winter 1989, 82–91.

Scott, David F., and Dana J. Johnson, "Financing Policies and Practices in Large Corporations," *Financial Management,* Summer 1982, 51–59.

To learn more about the link between market risk and operating and financial leverage, see

Callahan, Carolyn M., and Rosanne M. Mohr, "The Determinants of Systematic Risk: A Synthesis," *The Financial Review,* May 1989, 157–181.

Gahlon, James M., and James A. Gentry, "On the Relationship between Systematic Risk and the Degrees of Operating and Financial Leverage," *Financial Management,* Summer 1982, 15–23.

Prezas, Alexandros P., "Effects of Debt on the Degrees of Operating and Financial Leverage," *Financial Management,* Summer 1987, 39–44.

Here are some additional articles which relate to this chapter:

Easterwood, John C., and Palani-Rajan Kadapakkam, "The Role of Private and Public Debt in Corporate Capital Structures," *Financial Management,* Autumn 1991, 49–57.

Garvey, Gerald T., "Leveraging the Underinvestment Problem: How High Debt and Management Shareholdings Solve the Agency Costs of Free Cash Flow," *Journal of Financial Research,* Summer 1992, 149–166.

Harris, Milton, and Artur Raviv, "Capital Structure and the Informational Role of Debt," *Journal of Finance,* June 1990, 321–349.

Israel, Ronen, "Capital Structure and the Market for Corporate Control: The Defensive Role of Debt Financing," *Journal of Finance,* September 1991, 1391–1409.

See the following three articles for additional insights into the relationship between industry characteristics and financial leverage:

Bowen, Robert M., Lane A. Daley, and Charles C. Huber, Jr., "Evidence on the Existence and Determinants of Inter-Industry Differences in Leverage," *Financial Management,* Winter 1982, 10–20.

Long, Michael, and Ileen Malitz, "The Investment-Financing Nexus: Some Empirical Evidence," *Midland Corporate Finance Journal,* Fall 1985, 53–59.

Scott, David F., Jr., and John D. Martin, "Industry Influence on Financial Structure," *Financial Management,* Spring 1975, 67–73.

For a more thorough discussion of the international implications of capital structure, see

Rutterford, Janette, "An International Perspective on the Capital Structure Puzzle," *Midland Corporate Finance Journal,* Fall 1985, 60-72.

The Dryden Press Cases in Financial Management: Dryden Request *series contains many of the concepts we present in Chapters 13 and 14.*

Case 9, "Home Security Systems, Inc.," Case 10, "Kleen Kar, Inc.," Case 10A, "Mountain Springs, Inc.," and Case 10B, "Greta Cosmetics, Inc.," which present a situation similar to the Hill Software Systems example in the text.

CHAPTER 14

CAPITAL STRUCTURE DECISIONS: EXTENSIONS*

*A*t a recent meeting of the Financial Management Association, a professional organization that includes both academics and practitioners, a panel session focused on how firms actually set their target capital structures. The participants included financial managers from Hershey Foods, Bell Atlantic, EG&G (a high-tech firm), and a number of other firms in various industries. Although there were minor differences in philosophy and procedures among the companies, several themes emerged.

First, in practice it is impossible to specify a point value as a firm's optimal capital structure — indeed, managers even feel uncomfortable about specifying an optimal capital structure range. Thus, financial managers worry primarily about whether their firms are using too little or too much debt, not about the precise optimal amount of debt. Second, even if a firm's actual capital structure varies widely from the theoretical optimum, this might not have much impact on the firm's stock price. Thus, financial managers believe that capital structure decisions are secondary in importance to operating decisions, especially those relating to capital budgeting and the strategic direction of the firm.

In general, financial managers focus more on identifying a "prudent" level of debt than on setting a precise optimal level. A prudent level of debt is defined as one that captures most of the benefits of debt yet (1) keeps financial risk at a manageable level, (2) ensures future financing flexibility, and (3) allows the firm to maintain a desirable credit rating. Thus, a prudent level of debt will protect the company against financial distress under all but the most unlikely pessimistic economic scenarios and will assure access to money and capital markets.

---

*This chapter may be omitted without loss of continuity.

As you read this chapter, think about how you would make capital structure decisions if you were the financial manager at Hershey, Bell Atlantic, or EG&G. At the same time, don't forget the very important message from the panel session: Establishing the right capital structure is an imprecise process at best, and it should be based on both informed judgment and quantitative analyses.

Chapter 13 presented the basic material on capital structure, including a brief introduction to capital structure theory. We saw that debt concentrates a firm's business risk on its stockholders, but debt also increases the expected return on equity. We also saw that there is some optimal level of debt that maximizes a company's stock price, but that it is very difficult to identify the optimal capital structure. Now we go into more detail on capital structure theory, which will give you a better understanding of the benefits and costs associated with debt financing.

CAPITAL STRUCTURE THEORY: THE MODIGLIANI-MILLER MODELS

Until 1958, capital structure theory consisted of loose assertions about investor behavior rather than carefully constructed models which could be tested by formal statistical analysis. In what has been called the most influential set of financial papers ever published, Franco Modigliani and Merton Miller (MM) addressed capital structure in a rigorous, scientific fashion, and they set off a chain of research that continues to this day.[1]

ASSUMPTIONS

To begin, MM made the following assumptions, some of which were later relaxed:

1. Business risk can be measured by σ_{EBIT}, and firms with the same degree of business risk are said to be in a *homogeneous risk class.*

2. All present and prospective investors have identical estimates of each firm's future EBIT; that is, investors have *homogeneous expectations* about expected future corporate earnings and the riskiness of those earnings.

3. Stocks and bonds are traded in *perfect capital markets.* This assumption implies, among other things, (a) that there are no brokerage costs and (b) that investors (both individuals and institutions) can borrow at the same rate as corporations.

---

[1]See Franco Modigliani and Merton H. Miller, "The Cost of Capital, Corporation Finance and the Theory of Investment," *American Economic Review,* June 1958, 261-297; "The Cost of Capital, Corporation Finance and the Theory of Investment: Reply," *American Economic Review,* September 1958, 655-669; "Taxes and the Cost of Capital: A Correction," *American Economic Review,* June 1963, 433-443; and "Reply," *American Economic Review,* June 1965, 524-527. In a 1979 survey of Financial Management Association members, the original MM article was judged to have had the greatest impact on the field of finance of any work ever published. See Philip L. Cooley and J. Louis Heck, "Significant Contributions to Finance Literature," *Financial Management,* Tenth Anniversary Issue 1981, 23-33. Note that both Modigliani and Miller won Nobel prizes—Modigliani in 1985 and Miller in 1990.

4. The debt of firms and individuals is riskless, so the interest rate on debt is the risk-free rate. Further, this situation holds regardless of how much debt a firm (or individual) uses.

5. All cash flows are perpetuities; that is, the firm is a zero-growth firm with an "expectationally constant" EBIT, and its bonds are perpetuities. "Expectationally constant" means that investors expect EBIT to be constant, but, after the fact, the realized level could be different from the expected level.

MM WITHOUT TAXES

MM first analyzed leverage under the added assumption that there are no corporate or personal income taxes. On the basis of the preceding assumptions, and in the absence of corporate taxes, MM stated and algebraically proved two propositions:[2]

PROPOSITION I   The value of any firm is established by capitalizing its expected net operating income (EBIT) at a constant rate based on the firm's risk class:

$$V_L = V_U = \frac{EBIT}{WACC} = \frac{EBIT}{k_{sU}}. \qquad \text{14-1}$$

Here the subscript L designates a levered firm and U designates an unlevered firm. Both firms are assumed to be in the same risk class, and k_{sU} is the required rate of return for an unlevered, or all-equity, firm. (For our purposes, it is easiest to think in terms of a single firm that has the option of either financing with all equity or using some combination of debt and equity.)

Since V as established by Equation 14-1 is a constant, *then under the MM model, when there are no taxes, the value of the firm is independent of its leverage.* As we shall see, this also implies (1) that the weighted average cost of capital to any firm is completely independent of its capital structure, and (2) that the WACC for any firm, regardless of the amount of debt it uses, is equal to the cost of equity it would have if it used no debt.

PROPOSITION II   The cost of equity to a levered firm, k_{sL}, is equal to (1) the cost of equity to an unlevered firm in the same risk class, k_{sU}, plus (2) a risk premium whose size depends on both the differential between an unlevered firm's costs of debt and equity and the amount of debt used:

$$k_{sL} = k_{sU} + \text{Risk premium} = k_{sU} + (k_{sU} - k_d)(D/S). \qquad \text{14-2}$$

---

[2]MM actually stated and proved three propositions, but the third one is not material to our discussion here.

Here D = market value of the firm's debt, S = market value of the firm's equity, and k_d = constant cost of debt. *Proposition II states that as the firm's use of debt increases, its cost of equity also rises, and in a mathematically precise manner.*

Taken together, the two MM propositions imply that the inclusion of more debt in the capital structure will not increase the value of the firm, because the benefits of cheaper debt will be exactly offset by an increase in the riskiness, hence in the cost, of its equity. *Thus, MM state that in a world without taxes, both the value of a firm and its overall cost of capital are unaffected by its capital structure.*

MM's Arbitrage Proof

MM used an *arbitrage proof* to support their propositions.[3] They showed that, under their assumptions, if two companies differed only (1) in the way they are financed and (2) in their total market values, then investors would sell shares of the higher-valued firm, buy those of the lower-valued firm, and continue this process until the companies had exactly the same market value. To illustrate, assume that two firms, L (for levered) and U (for unlevered), are identical in all important respects except financial structure. Firm L has $4,000,000 of 7.5 percent debt, while Firm U uses only equity. Both firms have EBIT = $900,000, and σ_{EBIT} is the same for both firms, so they are in the same risk class.

MM assumed that all firms are in a zero-growth situation; that is, EBIT is expected to remain constant, and all earnings are paid out as dividends. Under this assumption, the total market value of a firm's common stock, S, is the present value of a perpetuity, which is found as follows:

$$S = \frac{\text{Dividends}}{k_s} = \frac{\text{Net income}}{k_s} = \frac{(\text{EBIT} - k_d D)(1 - T)}{k_s}. \qquad 14\text{-}3$$

Equation 14-3 is merely the value of a perpetuity whose numerator is the net income available to common stockholders, which is all paid out as dividends, and whose denominator is the cost of common equity. In MM's zero-tax world, the tax rate, T, is zero, so Equation 14-3 becomes simply $(\text{EBIT} - k_d D)/k_s$.

Assume that in the initial situation, before any arbitrage occurs, both firms have the same equity capitalization rate: $k_{sU} = k_{sL} = 10\%$. Under this condition, according to Equation 14-3, the following situation would exist:

---

[3]By *arbitrage* we mean the simultaneous buying and selling of essentially identical assets at different prices. The buying increases the price of the undervalued asset, and the selling decreases the price of the overvalued asset. Arbitrage operations will continue until prices have been adjusted to the point where the arbitrageur can no longer earn a profit, at which point the markets are in equilibrium.

Firm U:

$$\begin{array}{l} \text{Value of} \\ \text{Firm U's} \\ \text{stock} \end{array} = S_U = \frac{\text{EBIT} - k_dD}{k_{sU}} = \frac{\$900,000 - \$0}{0.10} = \$9,000,000.$$

$$\begin{array}{l} \text{Total market} \\ \text{value of} \\ \text{Firm U} \end{array} = V_U = D_U + S_U = \$0 + \$9,000,000 = \$9,000,000.$$

Firm L:

$$\begin{array}{l} \text{Value of} \\ \text{Firm L's} \\ \text{stock} \end{array} = S_L = \frac{\text{EBIT} - k_dD}{k_{sL}}$$

$$= \frac{\$900,000 - 0.075(\$4,000,000)}{0.10} = \$6,000,000.$$

$$\begin{array}{l} \text{Total market} \\ \text{value of} \\ \text{Firm L} \end{array} = V_L = D_L + S_L = \$4,000,000 + \$6,000,000 = \$10,000,000.$$

Thus, before arbitrage, and assuming that $k_{sU} = k_{sL}$ (hence that capital structure has no effect on the cost of equity), the value of the levered Firm L exceeds that of unlevered Firm U.

MM argued that this is a disequilibrium situation which cannot persist. To see why, suppose you owned 10 percent of L's stock, so the market value of your investment was 0.10($6,000,000) = $600,000. According to MM, you could increase your income without increasing your exposure to risk. For example, suppose you (1) sold your stock in L for $600,000, (2) borrowed an amount equal to 10 percent of L's debt ($400,000), and then (3) bought 10 percent of U's stock for $900,000. Notice that you would receive $1,000,000 from the sale of your 10 percent of L's stock plus your borrowing, and you would be spending only $900,000 on U's stock, so you would have an extra $100,000, which MM assumed you would invest in riskless debt to yield 7.5 percent, or $7,500 annually.

Now consider your income positions:

OLD INCOME:	10% of L's $600,000 equity income		$60,000
NEW INCOME:	10% of U's $900,000 equity income	$90,000	
	Less 7.5% interest on $400,000 loan	(30,000)	$60,000
	Plus 7.5% interest on extra $100,000		7,500
	Total new income		$67,500

Thus, your net income from common stock would be exactly the same as before, $60,000, but you would have $100,000 left over for investment in riskless debt, which would increase your income by $7,500. Therefore, the total return on your $600,000 net worth would rise to $67,500. Further, your risk, according to MM, would be the same as before; you would have simply substituted $400,000 of "homemade" leverage for your 10 percent share of Firm L's $4 million of corporate leverage, hence neither your "effective" debt nor your risk would have changed. Thus, you would have increased your income without raising your risk, which is obviously a desirable thing to do.

MM argued that this arbitrage process would actually occur, with sales of L's stock driving its price down, and purchases of U's stock driving its price up, until the market values of the two firms were equal. Until this equality was established, gains could be obtained by switching from one stock to the other, so the profit motive would force the equality to be reached. When equilibrium is established, the values of Firms L and U, and their weighted average costs of capital, would be equal. Thus, according to Modigliani and Miller, both a firm's value and its WACC must be independent of capital structure.

Note that each of the assumptions listed at the beginning of this section is necessary for the arbitrage proof to work. For example, if the companies do not have identical business risk, then the arbitrage process cannot be invoked. We will discuss further implications of the assumptions later in the chapter.

MM with Corporate Taxes

MM's original work, published in 1958, assumed zero taxes. In 1963, they published a second article which included corporate tax effects. With corporate income taxes, they concluded that leverage will increase a firm's value. This occurs because interest on debt is a tax-deductible expense, hence more of a leveraged firm's operating income flows through to investors. Here are the MM propositions when corporations are subject to income taxes:

Proposition I   The value of a levered firm is equal to the value of an unlevered firm in the same risk class (V_U) *plus* the gain from leverage. The gain from leverage is the value of the tax savings, found as the product of the corporate tax rate (T) times the amount of debt the firm uses (D):

$$V_L = V_U + TD. \tag{14-1a}$$

The important point here is that when corporate taxes are introduced, the value of the levered firm exceeds that of the unlevered firm by the amount TD. Note also that the gain from leverage increases as the firm's debt increases, so in theory a firm's value is maximized at 100 percent debt financing.

The value of the unlevered firm can be found by using Equation 14-4. With zero debt, then D = $0, and the value of the firm is its equity value. Thus,

$$S = V_U = \frac{EBIT(1 - T)}{k_{sU}}. \tag{14-4}$$

PROPOSITION II   The cost of equity to a levered firm is equal to (1) the cost of equity to an unlevered firm in the same risk class plus (2) a risk premium whose size depends on the differential between the costs of equity and debt to an unlevered firm, the amount of financial leverage used, and the corporate tax rate:

$$k_{sL} = k_{sU} + (k_{sU} - k_d)(1 - T)(D/S). \qquad \text{14-2a}$$

Notice that Equation 14-2a is identical to the corresponding without-tax equation, 14-2, except for the term $(1 - T)$ in 14-2a. Since $(1 - T)$ is less than 1, the imposition of corporate taxes causes the cost of equity to rise less rapidly than was true in the absence of taxes. Still, the fact that taxes reduce the effective cost of debt produces the Proposition I result, namely, the firm's value increases as its leverage increases.

ILLUSTRATION OF THE MM MODELS

To illustrate the without-tax and with-tax MM models, assume that the following data and conditions hold for Fredrickson Water Company, an old, established firm that supplies water to business and residential customers in several no-growth upstate New York metropolitan areas.

1. Fredrickson currently has no debt; it is an all-equity company.
2. Expected EBIT = $2,400,000. EBIT is not expected to increase over time, so Fredrickson is in a no-growth situation.
3. Fredrickson pays out all of its income as dividends.
4. If Fredrickson begins to use debt, it can borrow at a rate k_d = 8%. This borrowing rate is constant—it does not increase regardless of the amount of debt used. Any money raised by selling debt would be used to retire common stock, *so Fredrickson's assets would remain constant.*
5. The business risk inherent in Fredrickson's assets, and thus in its EBIT, is such that its required rate of return, k_{sU}, is 12 percent if no debt is used.

WITH ZERO TAXES   To begin, assume that there are no taxes, so T = 0%. At any level of debt, Proposition I (Equation 14-1) can be used to find Fredrickson's value in an MM world, $20 million:

$$V_L = V_U = \frac{\text{EBIT}}{k_{sU}} = \frac{\$2.4 \text{ million}}{0.12} = \$20.0 \text{ million}.$$

If Fredrickson uses $10 million of debt, its stock value must be $10 million:

$$S = V - D = \$20 \text{ million} - \$10 \text{ million} = \$10 \text{ million}.$$

We can also find Fredrickson's cost of equity, k_{sL}, and its WACC at a debt level of $10 million. First, we use Proposition II (Equation 14-2) to find k_{sL}, Fredrickson's leveraged cost of equity:

$$k_{sL} = k_{sU} + (k_{sU} - k_d)(D/S)$$
$$= 12\% + (12\% - 8\%)(\$10 \text{ million}/\$10 \text{ million})$$
$$= 12\% + 4.0\% = 16.0\%.$$

Now we can find the company's weighted average cost of capital:

$$WACC = (D/V)(k_d)(1 - T) + (S/V)k_s$$
$$= (\$10/\$20)(8\%)(1.0) + (\$10/\$20)(16.0\%) = 12.0\%.$$

Fredrickson's value and cost of capital based on the MM model with zero taxes at various debt levels are shown in Panel a of Figure 14-1. Here we see that in an MM world without taxes, financial leverage does not matter: The value of the firm and its overall cost of capital are independent of the amount of debt financing.

WITH CORPORATE TAXES   To illustrate the MM model with corporate taxes, assume that all of the previous assumptions hold except these two:

1. Expected EBIT = $4,000,000.
2. Fredrickson has a 40 percent federal-plus-state tax rate, so T = 40%.

Note that, other things held constant, the introduction of corporate taxes would lower Fredrickson's net income, hence its value, so we increased EBIT from $2.4 million to $4 million to make the comparison between the two models easier.

When Fredrickson has zero debt but pays taxes, Equation 14-4 can be used to find its value, $20 million:[4]

$$V_U = \frac{EBIT (1 - T)}{k_{sU}} = \frac{\$4 \text{ million } (0.6)}{0.12} = \$20.0 \text{ million.}$$

With $10 million of debt in a world with taxes, we see by Proposition I (Equation 14-1a) that Fredrickson's total market value rises to $24 million:

$$V_L = V_U + TD = \$20 \text{ million} + 0.4(\$10 \text{ million}) = \$24 \text{ million.}$$

Therefore, the value of Fredrickson's stock must be $14 million:

$$S = V - D = \$24 \text{ million} - \$10 \text{ million} = \$14 \text{ million.}$$

---

[4]Note that we increased Fredrickson's EBIT to $4.0 million. If we had left its EBIT at $2.4 million, the introduction of corporate taxes would have reduced the firm's value from $20 million to $12 million:

$$V_U = \frac{EBIT (1 - T)}{k_{sU}} = \frac{\$2.4 \text{ million } (0.6)}{0.12} = \$12.0 \text{ million.}$$

Corporate taxes reduce the amount of operating income available to investors in an unlevered firm by the factor (1 − T), so the value of the firm is reduced by a like amount.

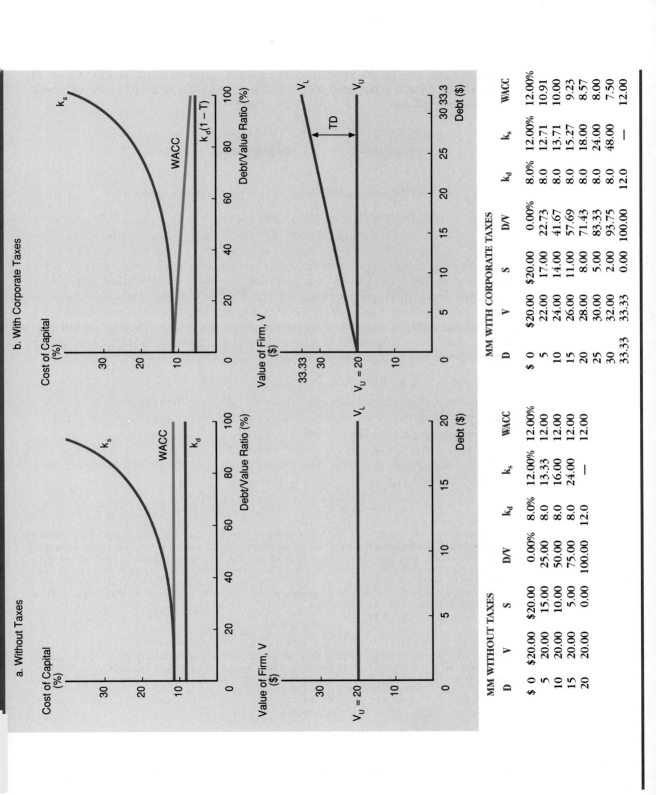

a. Without Taxes

b. With Corporate Taxes

MM WITHOUT TAXES

D	V	S	D/V	k_d	k_s	WACC
$0	$20.00	$20.00	0.00%	8.0%	12.00%	12.00%
5	20.00	15.00	25.00	8.0	13.33	12.00
10	20.00	10.00	50.00	8.0	16.00	12.00
15	20.00	5.00	75.00	8.0	24.00	12.00
20	20.00	0.00	100.00	12.0	—	12.00

MM WITH CORPORATE TAXES

D	V	S	D/V	k_d	k_s	WACC
$0	$20.00	$20.00	0.00%	8.0%	12.00%	12.00%
5	22.00	17.00	22.73	8.0	12.71	10.91
10	24.00	14.00	41.67	8.0	13.71	10.00
15	26.00	11.00	57.69	8.0	15.27	9.23
20	28.00	8.00	71.43	8.0	18.00	8.57
25	30.00	5.00	83.33	8.0	24.00	8.00
30	32.00	2.00	93.75	8.0	48.00	7.50
33.33	33.33	0.00	100.00	12.0	—	12.00

We can also find Fredrickson's cost of equity, k_{sL}, and its WACC at a debt level of $10 million. First, we use Proposition II (Equation 14-2a) to find k_{sL}, the leveraged cost of equity:

$$k_{sL} = k_{sU} + (k_{sU} - k_d)(1 - T)(D/S)$$

$$= 12\% + (12\% - 8\%)(0.6)(\$10 \text{ million}/\$14 \text{ million})$$

$$= 12\% + 1.71\% = 13.71\%.$$

Now we can find the company's weighted average cost of capital:

$$WACC = (D/V)(k_d)(1 - T) + (S/V)k_s$$

$$= (\$10/\$24)(8\%)(0.6) + (\$14/\$24)(13.71\%) = 10.0\%.$$

Fredrickson's value and cost of capital at various debt levels with corporate taxes are shown in Panel b of Figure 14-1. Here we see that in an MM world with corporate taxes, financial leverage does matter: The value of the firm is maximized, and its overall cost of capital is minimized, if it uses 100 percent debt financing. Further, we see that the increase in value is due solely to the tax deductibility of interest payments, which lowers both the cost of debt and the increase in the cost of equity with leverage by $(1 - T)$.[5]

SELF-TEST QUESTIONS

What is the optimal capital structure under the MM zero-tax model?

What is the optimal capital structure under the MM model with corporate taxes?

How does Proposition I differ in the two models?

How does Proposition II differ in the two models?

How do taxes result in a "gain from leverage" in the MM model with corporate taxes?

---

[5]In the limiting case, where the firm used 100 percent debt financing, the bondholders would own the entire company; thus, they would have to bear all the business risk. (Up until this point, MM assume that the stockholders bear all the risk.) If the bondholders bear all the risk, then the capitalization rate on the debt should be equal to the equity capitalization rate at zero debt, $k_d = k_{sU} = 12\%$.

The income stream to the stockholders in the all-equity case was $4,000,000(1 - T) = $2,400,000, and the value of the firm was

$$V_U = \frac{\$2,400,000}{0.12} = \$20,000,000.$$

With all debt, the entire $4,000,000 of EBIT would be used to pay interest charges — k_d would be 12 percent, so $I = 0.12(\text{Debt}) = \$4,000,000$. Taxes would be zero, and investors (bondholders) would get the entire $4,000,000 of operating income; they would not have to share it with the government. Thus, at 100 percent debt, the value of the firm would be

$$V_L = \frac{\$4,000,000}{0.12} = \$33,333,333 = D.$$

There is, of course, a transition problem in all this — MM assume that $k_d = 8\%$ regardless of how much debt the firm has until debt reaches 100 percent, at which point k_d jumps to 12 percent, the cost of equity. As we shall see later in the chapter, k_d realistically rises as the use of financial leverage increases.

Business and Financial Risk: A Market Risk Perspective

In our discussion of business and financial risk in Chapter 13, we focused on stand-alone risk, using $\sigma_{ROE(U)}$ as the measure of business risk and σ_{ROE} as the measure of the stand-alone risk borne by stockholders. Thus, in the stand-alone risk sense, $\sigma_{ROE(L)} - \sigma_{ROE(U)}$ is a measure of financial risk. Recall, though, that part of stand-alone risk can be eliminated if stockholders diversify their own portfolios. Therefore, we need to consider business and financial risk from a *market risk* standpoint.

Robert Hamada combined the Capital Asset Pricing Model (CAPM) presented in Chapter 4 with the MM after-tax model to obtain this expression for k_{sL}, the cost of equity to a leveraged firm:[6]

$$
\begin{aligned}
k_{sL} &= \begin{matrix} \text{Risk-free} \\ \text{rate} \end{matrix} + \begin{matrix} \text{Business risk} \\ \text{premium} \end{matrix} + \begin{matrix} \text{Financial risk} \\ \text{premium} \end{matrix} \\
&= k_{RF} + (k_M - k_{RF})b_U + (k_M - k_{RF})b_U(1 - T)(D/S).
\end{aligned}
$$

14-5

Here b_U is the beta coefficient the firm would have if it used no financial leverage, and the other terms are as defined previously. In effect, Equation 14-5 partitions the required rate of return on a stock into three components: k_{RF}, the risk-free rate, which compensates shareholders for the time value of money; a premium for business risk as reflected by the term $(k_M - k_{RF})b_U$; and a premium for financial risk as reflected by the third term, $(k_M - k_{RF})b_U (1 - T)(D/S)$. If a firm has no financial leverage (D = $0), then the financial risk premium term would be zero (the third term would drop out) and equity investors would be compensated only for business risk.

As we will see, the MM model with corporate taxes does not hold exactly, and we also know that the CAPM does not fully describe investor behavior. Therefore, Equation 14-5 must be regarded as an approximation. Nevertheless, Equation 14-5 can provide financial managers with some useful insights. As an illustration, assume that Firm U, an unlevered company with $b_U = 1.5$ and $100,000 of equity (S = $100,000), is considering replacing $20,000 of equity with debt. Assuming also that $k_{RF} = 10\%$, $k_M = 15\%$, and T = 34%, then Firm U's current unlevered required rate of return on equity would be 17.5 percent:

$$k_{sU} = 10\% + (15\% - 10\%)1.5$$
$$= 10\% + 7.5\% = 17.5\%.$$

This shows that the business risk premium is 7.5 percentage points. If the firm were to add $20,000 of debt to its capital structure, then its new value, according to MM,

---

[6]See Robert S. Hamada, "Portfolio Analysis, Market Equilibrium, and Corporation Finance," *Journal of Finance,* March 1969, 13–31. Note that Thomas Conine and Maurry Tamarkin have extended Hamada's work to include risky debt. See "Divisional Cost of Capital Estimation: Adjusting for Leverage," *Financial Management,* Spring 1985, 54–58.

would be $V_L = V_U + TD = \$100{,}000 + 0.34(\$20{,}000) = \$106{,}800$, and its k_s, using Equation 12-6, would rise to 18.64 percent:

$$k_{sL} = 10\% + (15\% - 10\%)1.5 + (15\% - 10\%)1.5(1 - 0.34)(\$20{,}000/\$86{,}800)$$
$$= 10\% + 7.5\% + 1.14\% = 18.64\%.$$

Thus, adding \$20,000 of debt to the capital structure would result in a financial risk premium on the stock of 1.14 percentage points, which would be added to the business risk premium of 7.5 percentage points.

Hamada also showed that Equation 14-5 can be used to analyze the effect of financial leverage on beta. We know that the SML can be used to estimate a firm's required rate of return on equity:

$$\text{SML: } k_s = k_{RF} + (k_M - k_{RF})b.$$

Now, by equating the SML equation with Equation 14-5, we obtain:

$$k_{RF} + (k_M - k_{RF})b = k_{RF} + (k_M - k_{RF})b_U + (k_M - k_{RF})b_U(1 - T)(D/S)$$
$$(k_M - k_{RF})b = (k_M - k_{RF})b_U + (k_M - k_{RF})b_U(1 - T)(D/S)$$
$$b = b_U + b_U(1 - T)(D/S), \tag{14-6}$$

or

$$b = b_U[1 + (1 - T)(D/S)]. \tag{14-6a}$$

Thus, under the MM and CAPM assumptions, the beta of any firm is equal to the beta the firm would have if it used zero debt, adjusted upward by a factor that depends on (1) the corporate tax rate and (2) the amount of financial leverage employed.[7] Therefore, the firm's market risk, which is measured by b, depends on both the firm's business risk as measured by b_U and its financial risk as measured by $b - b_U = b_U(1 - T)(D/S)$.

To continue our illustration, if Firm U were to replace \$20,000 of equity with debt, its beta would increase from 1.5 to 1.728, according to Equation 14-6a:

$$b = b_U[1 + (1 - T)(D/S)]$$
$$= 1.5[1 + (1 - 0.34)(20{,}000/\$86{,}800)]$$
$$= 1.5(1.152) = 1.728.$$

---

[7]If a firm uses preferred stock financing, then Equation 14-6 becomes

$$b = b_U + b_U(P/S) + b_U(1 - T)(D/S),$$

where P = market value of preferred stock. Here the unlevered beta is adjusted upward by the preferred stock as well as the debt.

We can confirm the Equation 14-5 value of $k_{sL} = 18.64\%$ by using $b = 1.728$ in the SML:

$$k_s = k_{RF} + (k_M - k_{RF})b$$
$$= 10\% + (15\% - 10\%)1.728 = 18.64\%.$$

These relationships can be used to help estimate a company's or a division's cost of equity. In both instances, we proceed by obtaining betas for similar publicly traded firms and then "lever them up or down" to make them consistent with our own firm's (or division's) capital structure and tax rate. The result is an estimate of our firm's (or division's) beta, given (1) its business risk as measured by the betas of other firms in the same line of business and (2) its financial risk as measured by its own capital structure and tax rate.

According to Hamada, the required rate of return on a stock consists of three elements. What are they?

How is business risk measured within a market risk framework?

How is financial risk measured within a market risk framework?

What is the relationship between levered and unlevered betas according to Hamada?

SELF-TEST QUESTIONS

CAPITAL STRUCTURE THEORY: THE MILLER MODEL

Although MM included *corporate* taxes in the second version of their model, they did not extend the model to include *personal* taxes. However, in his presidential address to the American Finance Association, Merton Miller did introduce a model designed to show how leverage affects firms' values when both personal and corporate taxes are taken into account.[8] To explain Miller's model, let us begin by defining T_c as the corporate tax rate, T_s as the personal tax rate on income from stocks, and T_d as the personal tax rate on income from debt. Note that stocks' returns come partly as dividends and partly as capital gains, so T_s is a weighted average of the effective tax rates on dividends and capital gains, while essentially all debt income comes from interest, which is effectively taxed at investors' top rates.

With personal taxes included, *and under the same set of assumptions used in the earlier MM models,* the value of an unlevered firm is found as follows:

$$V_U = \frac{EBIT(1 - T_c)(1 - T_s)}{k_{sU}}. \qquad \text{14-7}$$

The $(1 - T_s)$ term takes account of personal taxes. Therefore, the numerator shows how much of the firm's operating income is left after the unlevered firm pays corporate income taxes and its stockholders subsequently pay personal taxes on their

---

[8]See Merton H. Miller, "Debt and Taxes," *Journal of Finance,* May 1977, 261-275.

equity income. Since the introduction of personal taxes lowers the income available to investors, personal taxes reduce the value of the unlevered firm, other things held constant.

Miller's results can be supported by an arbitrage proof similar to the one we presented earlier. However, the alternative proof shown below is easier to follow. To begin, we partition the levered firm's annual cash flows, CF_L, into those going to the stockholders and those going to the bondholders, after both corporate and personal taxes:

$$CF_L = \text{Net CF to stockholders} \quad + \text{Net CF to bondholders}$$
$$= (EBIT - I)(1 - T_c)(1 - T_s) + \qquad I(1 - T_d). \tag{14-8}$$

Here I is the annual interest payment. Equation 14-8 can be rearranged as follows:

$$CF_L = [EBIT(1 - T_c)(1 - T_s)] - [I(1 - T_c)(1 - T_s)] + [I(1 - T_d)]. \tag{14-8a}$$

The first term in Equation 14-8a is identical to the after-tax cash flow of an unlevered firm as shown in Equation 14-7, and its present value is found by discounting the perpetual cash flow by k_{sU}. The second and third terms, which reflect leverage, result from the cash flows associated with interest payments, and these two cash flows are assumed to have a risk equal to that of the basic interest payment stream, hence their present values are obtained by discounting at the cost of debt, k_d. (Remember, these are all perpetual cash flows, so the basic perpetuity valuation model, $V = CF/k$, applies.) Combining the present values of the three terms, we obtain this value for the levered firm:

$$V_L = \frac{EBIT(1 - T_c)(1 - T_s)}{k_{sU}} - \frac{I(1 - T_c)(1 - T_s)}{k_d} + \frac{I(1 - T_d)}{k_d}. \tag{14-9}$$

The first term in Equation 14-9 is identical to V_U as set forth in Equation 14-7, and when we consolidate the second two terms we obtain this equation:

$$V_L = V_U + \frac{I(1 - T_d)}{k_d} \left[1 - \frac{(1 - T_c)(1 - T_s)}{(1 - T_d)} \right]. \tag{14-9a}$$

Now recognize that the after-tax perpetual interest payment divided by the required rate of return on debt, $I(1 - T_d)/k_d$, equals the market value of the debt, D. Substituting D into the preceding equation, and rearranging, we obtain this very important expression, called the Miller model:

$$\text{Miller model: } V_L = V_U + \left[1 - \frac{(1 - T_c)(1 - T_s)}{(1 - T_d)}\right]D. \qquad \textbf{14-10}$$

The Miller model provides an estimate of the value of a levered firm in a world with both corporate and personal taxes.

The Miller model has several important implications:

1. The term in brackets,

$$\left[1 - \frac{(1 - T_c)(1 - T_s)}{(1 - T_d)}\right],$$

    when multiplied by D, represents the gain from leverage. The bracketed term thus replaces the factor T in the earlier MM model with corporate taxes, $V_L = V_U + TD$.

2. If we ignore all taxes, that is, if $T_c = T_s = T_d = 0$, then the bracketed term is zero, so in that case Equation 14-10 is the same as the original MM model without taxes.

3. If we ignore personal taxes, that is, if $T_s = T_d = 0$, then the bracketed term reduces to $[1 - (1 - T_c)] = T_c$, so Equation 14-10 is the same as the MM model with corporate taxes.

4. If the effective personal tax rates on stock and bond incomes were equal, that is, if $T_s = T_d$, then $(1 - T_s)$ and $(1 - T_d)$ would cancel, and the bracketed term would again reduce to T_c.

5. If $(1 - T_c)(1 - T_s) = (1 - T_d)$, then the bracketed term would go to zero, and the value of using leverage would also be zero. This implies that the tax advantage of debt to the firm would be exactly offset by the personal tax advantage of equity. Under this condition, capital structure would have no effect on a firm's value or its cost of capital, so we would be back to MM's original zero-tax theory.

6. Because taxes on capital gains are lower at the top personal rate and can also be deferred, the effective tax rate on stock income is normally less than that on bond income. This being the case, what would the Miller model predict as the gain from leverage? To answer this question, assume that the tax rate on corporate income is $T_c = 34\%$, the effective rate on bond income is $T_d = 28\%$, and the effective rate on stock income is $T_s = 20\%$.[9] Using these values in the

---

[9]In a 1978 article, Miller and Scholes described how investors could, theoretically, shelter or delay income from stock to the point where the effective personal tax rate on such income is essentially zero. See Merton H. Miller and Myron S. Scholes, "Dividends and Taxes," *Journal of Financial Economics,* December 1978, 333–364. However, the 1986 changes in the tax law eliminated most of the shelters Miller and Scholes discussed.

Miller model, we find that a levered firm's value increases over that of an unlevered firm by 27 percent of the market value of corporate debt:

$$\text{Gain from leverage} = \left[1 - \frac{(1 - T_c)(1 - T_s)}{(1 - T_d)} \right] D$$

$$= \left[1 - \frac{(1 - 0.34)(1 - 0.20)}{(1 - 0.28)} \right] D$$

$$= [1 - 0.73]D = 0.27(D).$$

Note that the MM model with corporate taxes would indicate a gain from leverage of $T_c(D) = 0.34D$, or 34 percent of the amount of corporate debt. Thus, with these assumed tax rates, adding personal taxes to the model lowers but does not eliminate the benefit from corporate debt. In general, whenever the effective tax rate on income from stock is less than the effective rate on income from bonds, the Miller model produces a lower gain from leverage than is produced by the MM with-tax model.

In his paper, Miller argued that firms in the aggregate would issue a mix of debt and equity securities such that the before-tax yields on corporate securities and the personal tax rates of the investors who bought these securities would adjust until an equilibrium was reached. At the equilibrium, $(1 - T_d)$ would equal $(1 - T_c)(1 - T_s)$, so, as we noted earlier in Point 5, the tax advantage of debt to the firm would be exactly offset by personal taxation, and capital structure would have no effect on a firm's value or its cost of capital. Thus, according to Miller, the conclusions derived from the original Modigliani-Miller zero-tax model are correct!

Others have extended and tested Miller's analysis. Generally, these extensions question Miller's conclusion that there is no advantage to the use of corporate debt. In the United States, the effective tax rate on income from stock is less than on income from bonds. Thus, it appears that $(1 - T_c)(1 - T_s)$ is less than $(1 - T_d)$, hence there is an advantage to the use of corporate debt. Still, Miller's work does show that personal taxes offset some of the benefits of corporate debt, so the tax advantages of corporate debt are less than were implied by the earlier MM model, where only corporate taxes were considered.

As we note in the next section, there are a number of problems with both the MM and the Miller models, so one should regard our examples as indicating the general effects of leverage on firms' value, not a precise relationship.

SELF-TEST QUESTIONS

How does the Miller model differ from the MM model with corporate taxes?

What are the implications of the Miller model if $T_c = T_s = T_d = 0$?

What are the implications if $T_s = T_d = 0$?

Considering the current tax structure in the United States, what is the primary implication of the Miller model?

CRITICISMS OF THE MM AND MILLER MODELS

The conclusions of the MM and Miller models follow logically from their initial assumptions. However, both academicians and financial executives have voiced concern over the validity of the MM and Miller models, and virtually no one believes they hold precisely. The MM zero-tax model leads to the conclusion that capital structure doesn't matter, yet we observe systematic capital structure patterns within industries. Further, when used with "reasonable" tax rates, both the MM model with corporate taxes and the Miller model lead to the conclusion that firms should use 100 percent debt financing, but virtually no firms deliberately go to that extreme.

People who disagree with the MM and Miller theories generally attack them on the grounds that their assumptions are not correct. Here are the main objections:

1. Both MM and Miller assume that personal and corporate leverage are perfect substitutes. However, an individual investing in a levered firm has less loss exposure as a result of corporate *limited liability* than if he or she used "home-made" leverage. For example, in our earlier illustration of the MM arbitrage argument, it should be noted that only the $600,000 our investor had in Firm L would be lost if that firm went bankrupt. However, if the investor engaged in arbitrage transactions and employed "homemade" leverage to invest in Firm U, then he or she could lose $900,000 — the original $600,000 investment plus the $400,000 loan less the $100,000 investment in riskless bonds. This increased personal risk exposure would tend to restrain investors from engaging in arbitrage, and that could cause the equilibrium values of V_L, V_U, k_{sL}, and k_{sU} to be different from those specified by MM. Restrictions on institutional investors, who dominate capital markets today, may also retard the arbitrage process, because many institutional investors cannot legally borrow to buy stocks, hence are prohibited from engaging in homemade leverage.

2. Brokerage costs were assumed away by MM and Miller, making the switch from L to U costless. However, brokerage and other transaction costs (including "market pressure") do exist, and they too impede the arbitrage process.

3. MM initially assumed that corporations and investors can borrow at the risk-free rate. Although risky debt has been introduced into the analysis by others, to reach the MM and Miller conclusions it is still necessary to assume that both corporations and investors can borrow at the same rate. While major institutional investors probably can borrow at the corporate rate, many institutions are not allowed to borrow to buy securities. Further, most individual investors must borrow at higher rates than those paid by large corporations.

4. In his article, Miller concluded that an equilibrium would be reached, but to reach his equilibrium the tax benefit from corporate debt must be the same for all firms, and it must be constant for an individual firm regardless of the amount of leverage used. However, we know that tax benefits vary from firm to firm: Highly profitable companies gain the maximum tax benefit from leverage, while the benefits to firms that are struggling are much smaller. Further, some firms have other tax shields such as high depreciation, pension plan contributions, and operating loss carry-forwards, and these shields reduce the tax savings from interest payments.[10] It also appears simplistic to assume that the

---

[10]For a discussion of the impact of tax shields other than debt financing, see Harry DeAngelo and Ronald W. Masulis, "Optimal Capital Structure under Corporate and Personal Taxation," *Journal of Financial Economics,* March 1980, 3–30.

expected tax shield is unaffected by the amount of debt used. Higher leverage increases the probability that the firm will not be able to use the full tax shield in the future, because higher leverage increases the probability of future unprofitability and consequently lower tax rates. All things considered, it appears likely that the interest tax shield from corporate debt is more valuable to some firms than to others.

5. MM and Miller assume that there are no costs associated with financial distress, and they ignore agency costs. Further, they assume that all market participants have identical information about firms' prospects, which is also incorrect. These topics are discussed in the next section.

SELF-TEST QUESTIONS

Should we accept that one of the models presented thus far (MM with zero taxes, MM with corporate taxes, or Miller) is correct? Why or why not?

Are any of the assumptions used in the models worrisome to you, and what does "worrisome" mean in this context?

CAPITAL STRUCTURE THEORY: THE TRADE-OFF MODELS

If some of the assumptions inherent in the MM and Miller models are relaxed, this does not alter the basic MM/Miller conclusions.[11] However, as we discuss next, when financial distress and agency costs are considered, the MM and Miller results are altered significantly.

COSTS OF FINANCIAL DISTRESS

Financial distress includes, but is not restricted to, bankruptcy, and when financial distress occurs, several things can happen:

1. Arguments between claimants often delay the liquidation of assets. Bankruptcy cases can take many years to settle, and during this time machinery rusts, buildings are vandalized, inventories become obsolete, and the like.

2. Lawyer's fees, court costs, and administrative expenses can absorb a large part of the firm's value. Together, the costs of physical deterioration plus legal fees and administrative expenses are called the *direct costs* of financial distress.

3. Managers and other employees generally lose their jobs when a firm fails. Knowing this, the management of a firm that is in financial distress may take actions which keep it alive in the short run but which also dilute long-run value. For example, the firm may defer maintenance of machinery, sell off valuable assets at bargain prices to raise cash, or cut costs so much that the quality of its products or services is impaired and the firm's long-run market position is eroded.

---

[11]For example, see Robert A. Haugen and James L. Pappas, "Equilibrium in the Pricing of Capital Assets, Risk-Bearing Debt Instruments, and the Question of Optimal Capital Structure," *Journal of Financial and Quantitative Analysis,* June 1971, 943–954; Joseph Stiglitz, "A Re-Examination of the Modigliani-Miller Theorem," *American Economic Review,* December 1969, 784–793; and Mark E. Rubenstein, "A Mean-Variance Synthesis of Corporate Financial Theory," *Journal of Finance,* March 1973, 167–181.

4. Both customers and suppliers are aware of the problems that can arise, and they often take "evasive action" that further damages the troubled firm. For example, Eastern Airlines, as it struggled to deal with its unions and to avoid liquidation, was having trouble selling tickets because potential customers were worried about buying a seat for a future flight and then having the company shut down before they could take the trip. Some potential customers were also worried that the company might cut back on maintenance, and its suppliers were reluctant to grant normal credit terms or to gear up to supply Eastern with parts and other materials on a long-term basis. Finally, Eastern had trouble attracting and retaining the highest-quality workers, as most workers with a choice preferred employment with a more stable airline to one that might go out of business at any time.

5. Nonoptimal managerial actions associated with financial distress, as well as the costs imposed by customers, suppliers, and capital providers, are called the *indirect costs* of financial distress. Of course, these costs may be incurred by a firm in financial distress even if it does not go into bankruptcy: Bankruptcy is just one point on the continuum of financial distress.

All things considered, the direct and indirect costs associated with financial distress are high.[12] Further, financial distress typically occurs only if a firm has debts — debt-free firms do not usually experience financial distress. *Therefore, the greater the use of debt financing, and the larger the fixed interest charges, the greater the probability that a decline in earnings will lead to financial distress, hence the higher the probability that the costs of financial distress will be incurred.*

An increase in the probability of future financial distress lowers the current value of a firm and raises its cost of capital. To see why, suppose we estimate that Fredrickson Water will incur costs of $7 million if it fails at some future date, and that the *present value* of this possible future cost is $5 million. Further, the probability of financial distress increases with leverage, causing the expected present value of the cost of financial distress to rise from zero at zero debt to $4.75 million at $30 million of debt as shown in Table 14-1.

These expected costs must be subtracted from the values we previously calculated in Part b of Figure 14-1 to find the firm's value at various amounts of leverage: They would reduce the values of V and S and, as a result, would raise k_s and the WACC. For example, at $20 million of debt, we would obtain the values in Table 14-2.[13] These changes would, of course, then have carry-through effects on the

---

[12]See Edward I. Altman, "A Further Empirical Investigation of the Bankruptcy Cost Question," *Journal of Finance,* September 1984, 1067–1089. On the basis of a sample of 26 bankrupt companies, Altman found that bankruptcy costs often exceed 20 percent of firm value.

[13]To find k_s and the WACC in Table 14-2, simply transpose Equation 14-3 and then apply the definition for the WACC:

$$k_s = \frac{(EBIT - k_dD)(1 - T)}{S} = \frac{[\$4 - 0.08(\$20)](1 - 0.4)}{\$5.5} = 26.18\%.$$

$$WACC = (D/V)(k_d)(1 - T) + (S/V)(k_s)$$

$$= (\$20/\$25.5)(8\%)(0.6) + (\$5.5/\$25.5)(26.18\%)$$

$$= 3.76\% + 5.65\% = 9.41\%.$$

TABLE 14-1	FREDRICKSON WATER COMPANY: EXPECTED COSTS OF FINANCIAL DISTRESS				

		AMOUNT OF DEBT			
	$0	$5 MILLION	$10 MILLION	$20 MILLION	$30 MILLION
Probability of financial distress	0.0	0.05	0.15	0.50	0.95
PV of expected costs of financial distress[a]	$0	$250,000	$750,000	$2,500,000	$4,750,000

[a]$5 million times the indicated probability.

graphs in Panel b of Figure 14-1. Most important, they would (1) reduce the decline of the WACC line and (2) reduce the slope of the V_L line.

The effects of financial distress are also felt by a firm's bondholders. Firms experiencing financial distress have a higher probability of defaulting on debt payments, so the higher the probability of financial distress, the higher the required return on debt. Thus, as a firm uses more and more debt, hence increasing the probability of distress, the value of k_d also increases, causing several elements in Panel b of Figure 14-1 to change.

AGENCY COSTS

We introduced the concept of agency costs in Chapter 1. One agency relationship is between a firm's stockholders and its bondholders. In the absence of any restrictions, management would be tempted to take actions that would benefit stockholders at the expense of bondholders. For example, if Fredrickson Water were to issue only a small amount of debt, then this debt would have relatively little risk, a high bond rating, and a low interest rate. After it issued the low-risk debt, Fredrickson might issue more debt secured by the same assets as the original debt. This would raise the risks faced by *all bondholders,* cause k_d to rise, and consequently cause the original bondholders to suffer capital losses. Similarly, after issuing debt

TABLE 14-2	FREDRICKSON WATER COMPANY: EFFECTS OF FINANCIAL DISTRESS (MILLIONS OF DOLLARS)	

	VALUES AT D = $20 MILLION WITH FINANCIAL DISTRESS EFFECTS IGNORED: PURE MM	VALUES AT D = $20 MILLION WITH FINANCIAL DISTRESS EFFECTS CONSIDERED: MODIFIED MM
V	$28.00	$28.00 − $2.5 = $25.5
S	$8.00	$8.00 − $2.5 = $5.5
k_s	18.00%	26.18%
WACC	8.57%	9.41%

Fredrickson might decide to restructure its assets, selling off assets with low business risk and acquiring assets that were more risky but that also had higher expected rates of return. If things worked out well, the stockholders would get all of the benefit, but if things went sour, much of the loss would fall on the bondholders. So, stockholders would be playing a game of "heads, I win; tails, you lose" with bondholders.

Because stockholders might try to take advantage of bondholders in these and other ways, bonds are protected by restrictive covenants. These covenants hamper the corporation's legitimate operations to some extent. Further, the company must be monitored to ensure that the covenants are being obeyed, and the costs of monitoring are passed on to the stockholders in the form of higher debt costs. The lost efficiency plus monitoring are an important type of *agency cost,* which increases the cost of debt and thus reduces its advantage.[14]

VALUE AND COST OF CAPITAL CONSIDERING FINANCIAL DISTRESS AND AGENCY COSTS

If the MM model with corporate taxes were correct, a firm's value would rise continuously as it moved from zero debt toward 100 percent debt: The equation $V_L = V_U + TD$ shows that TD, hence V_L, is maximized if D is at a maximum. Recall that the increasing component of value, TD, arises as a direct result of the tax shelter provided by interest on the debt. However, as noted above, financial distress and agency costs could cause V_L to decline as the level of debt rises. Therefore, the relationship between a firm's value and its use of leverage should look like this:

$$V_L = V_U + TD - \begin{pmatrix} \text{PV of} \\ \text{expected} \\ \text{costs of} \\ \text{financial} \\ \text{distress} \end{pmatrix} - \begin{pmatrix} \text{PV of} \\ \text{agency} \\ \text{costs} \end{pmatrix}. \qquad \text{14-11}$$

The relationship expressed in Equation 14-11 is graphed in Figure 14-2. The tax shelter effects totally dominate until the amount of debt reaches Point A. After Point A, financial distress and agency costs become increasingly important, offsetting some of the tax advantages. At Point B, the marginal tax shelter benefit of additional debt is exactly offset by the disadvantages of debt, and beyond Point B, the disadvantages outweigh the tax benefit.

---

[14]Michael C. Jensen and William H. Meckling point out that there are also agency costs between outside equityholders and management. See "Theory of the Firm: Managerial Behavior, Agency Costs, and Ownership Structure," *Journal of Financial Economics,* October 1976, 305–360. Their study further suggests that (1) bondholder agency costs increase as the debt ratio increases, but (2) outside stockholder agency costs move in reverse fashion, falling with increased use of debt.

FIGURE 14-2   NET EFFECTS OF LEVERAGE ON THE VALUE OF THE FIRM

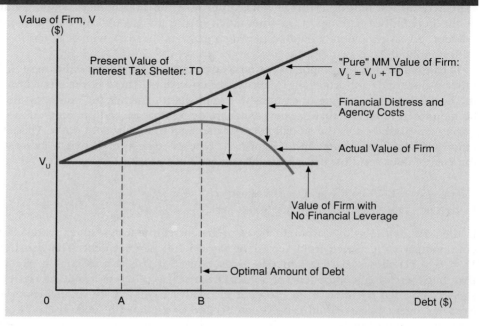

Equation 14-10, the Miller model, can also be modified to reflect financial distress and agency costs. The equation would be identical to Equation 14-11, except that the gain from leverage term, TD, would reflect the addition of personal taxes. In either the MM or Miller models, the gain from leverage can at least be roughly estimated, but the value reduction resulting from potential financial distress and agency costs is almost entirely subjective. We know that these costs must increase as leverage rises, but we do not know the specific functional relationships.

The addition of financial distress and agency costs to either the MM tax model or the Miller model results in a *trade-off model* of capital structure. In such a model, the optimal capital structure can be visualized as a trade-off between the benefit of debt (the interest tax shelter) and the costs of debt (financial distress and agency costs).

IMPLICATIONS OF THE TRADE-OFF MODELS

The trade-off models cannot be used to specify a precise optimal capital structure, but they do enable us to make three statements about leverage:

1. Firms with more business risk ought to use less debt than lower-risk firms, other things being equal, because the greater the business risk, the greater the probability of financial distress at any level of debt, hence the greater the expected costs of distress. Thus, firms with lower business risk can borrow

more before the expected costs of distress offset the tax advantages of borrowing (Point B in Figure 14-2).

2. Firms that have tangible, readily marketable assets such as real estate can use more debt than firms whose value is derived primarily from intangible assets such as patents and goodwill. The costs of financial distress depend not only on the probability of incurring distress but also on what happens if distress occurs. Specialized assets and intangible assets are more likely to lose value if financial distress occurs than are standardized, tangible assets.

3. Firms that are currently paying taxes at the highest rate, and that are likely to do so in the future, should use more debt than firms with lower tax rates. High corporate taxes lead to greater benefits from debt, other factors held constant, so more debt can be used before the tax shield is offset by financial distress and agency costs.

According to the trade-off models, each firm should set its target capital structure such that the costs and benefits of leverage are balanced at the margin, because such a structure will maximize its value. If the trade-off models are correct, we should find actual target structures that are consistent with the three points just noted. Further, we should find that firms within a given industry have similar capital structures, because such firms should have roughly the same types of assets, business risk, and profitability.

THE EMPIRICAL EVIDENCE

The trade-off models have intuitive appeal because they lead to the conclusion that both no-debt and all-debt are bad, while a "moderate" debt level is good. However, we must ask ourselves whether these models explain actual behavior. If they do not, then we must search for other explanations.

In fact, the trade-off models have only limited empirical support.[15] It does turn out that firms which invest primarily in tangible assets do tend to borrow more heavily than firms whose value stems from intangibles. However, empirical evidence refutes other aspects of the trade-off models. First, several studies have examined models of financing behavior to see if firms' financing decisions are consistent with a target capital structure. There is some evidence that this occurs, but the explanatory power of the models is very low, suggesting that trade-off models capture only a part of actual behavior. Second, studies have not consistently demonstrated that a firm's tax rate has a predictable, material effect on its capital structure. Also, firms used about as much debt before corporate income taxes even existed as they do today. Finally, actual debt ratios tend to vary widely across apparently similar firms within given industries, whereas the trade-off models suggest that similar firms should have similar debt ratios.

---

[15]For examples of the empirical research in this area, see Robert A. Taggart, Jr., "A Model of Corporate Financing Decisions," *Journal of Finance,* December 1977, 1467–1484; and Paul Marsh, "The Choice between Equity and Debt: An Empirical Study," *Journal of Finance,* March 1982, 121–144.

All in all, the empirical support for the trade-off models is weak, which suggests that factors not incorporated into these models are also at work. In other words, the trade-off models do not tell the full story.

SELF-TEST QUESTIONS

Describe some types of financial distress and agency costs.

How are these costs related to the use of financial leverage?

How are the basic MM with corporate taxes and Miller models affected by the inclusion of financial distress and agency costs?

What is a trade-off model of capital structure?

What implications do the trade-off models have regarding capital structure?

Does the empirical evidence support the trade-off models?

CAPITAL STRUCTURE THEORY: THE ASYMMETRIC INFORMATION MODEL

Some time ago, Professor Gordon Donaldson of Harvard University conducted an extensive study of how corporations actually establish their capital structures.[16] Here is a summary of his findings:

1. Firms prefer to finance with internally generated funds, that is, with retained earnings and depreciation cash flow.

2. Firms set target dividend payout ratios based on their expected future investment opportunities and their expected future cash flows. The target payout ratio is set at a level such that retained earnings plus depreciation will cover capital expenditures under normal conditions.

3. Dividends are "sticky" in the short run — firms are reluctant to raise dividends unless they are confident that the higher dividend can be maintained, and they are especially reluctant to cut the dividend. Indeed, they generally do not reduce the dividend unless things are so bad they simply have to.

4. If a firm has more internal cash flow than is needed to cover its capital expenditures, then it will invest in marketable securities, use the funds to retire debt, increase dividends, or repurchase stock. On the other hand, if it has insufficient internal cash flow to finance nonpostponable new projects, it will first draw down its marketable securities portfolio, then go to the external capital markets, first issuing debt, then convertible bonds, and then common stock as a last resort. *Thus, Donaldson observed that there is a "pecking order" of financing, not the balanced approach that would result if the trade-off models accurately described real-world behavior.*

Professor Stewart Myers noted the inconsistency between Donaldson's findings and the trade-off models, and that inconsistency led Myers to propose a new the-

---

[16]Gordon Donaldson, *Corporate Debt Capacity: A Study of Corporate Debt Policy and the Determination of Corporate Debt Capacity* (Boston: Harvard Graduate School of Business Administration, 1961).

ory.[17] First, Myers noted that Donaldson's pecking-order findings led away from, rather than toward, a well-defined capital structure. Equity is raised in two forms — retained earnings and new stock. Retained earnings are at the top of the pecking order, while new common stock is at the bottom. Therefore, if retained earnings are high relative to investment requirements, the equity ratio will increase, while if investment requirements are relatively high, the firm will borrow rather than issue stock, causing the debt ratio to increase. The trade-off models, on the other hand, regard equity from the sale of stock as being identical to that from retained earnings, and they suggest that the debt/equity ratio should remain constant over time.

Next, Myers noted that the trade-off models assume that all market participants have homogeneous expectations, which implies (1) that all participants have the same information and (2) that any changes in operating income are purely random as opposed to being anticipated by some but not all parties. Myers had the insight to see that if the homogeneous expectations assumption is relaxed, and if different groups of market participants have asymmetric (or different) information, then Donaldson's results can be explained in a logical manner. Myers's work resulted in what is now called the *asymmetric information theory* of capital structure.

To illustrate, assume that a firm has 10,000 common shares outstanding. They sell at a price of $19 per share, so the market value of its equity is $190,000. However, its managers have better information regarding the firm's future than stockholders, and the managers believe that the actual value per share based on existing assets is $21, giving the equity a total "intrinsic" value of $210,000. Such an information asymmetry could easily exist, for managers often know more about their firms' prospects than do current and potential investors.[18]

Suppose further that management now identifies a new project which would require $100,000 of external financing and which has an estimated NPV of $5,000. [Remember that a project's NPV represents economic value added (EVA), and that it accrues to the shareholders.] This project is unanticipated by the firm's investors, so the $5,000 NPV has not been incorporated into the $190,000 equity market value. Should the firm accept the project? To begin, suppose the firm issues new stock to raise the $100,000 to finance the project. Several possibilities exist:

1. **Symmetric information.** First, as a point of departure, consider the situation in which management can convey all the information to the public, hence all investors have the same information as management regarding existing asset values. Under these conditions, the stock would rise to the $21 intrinsic value. Then, when the new project comes along and is financed, the firm would have to sell $100,000/$21 = 4,762 new shares. Acceptance of the project would then increase the stock price from $21 to $21.34:

---

[17]Stewart C. Myers, "The Capital Structure Puzzle," *Journal of Finance,* July 1984, 575–592. It is interesting to note that, like the Miller model, Myers's paper was first presented as a presidential address to the American Finance Association.

[18]This assumption is contrary to the strong-form efficient markets hypothesis (EMH) presented in Chapter 7, but as we noted there, few observers — including people who strongly support weak-form and semistrong-form efficiency — are willing to accept strong-form efficiency.

$$\text{New stock price} = \frac{\text{Original market value} + \text{New money raised} + \text{NPV}}{\text{Original shares} + \text{New shares}}$$

$$= \frac{\$210,000 + \$100,000 + \$5,000}{10,000 + 4,762} = \$21.34.$$

Both old and new shareholders would benefit if the project were accepted; each group would gain $21.34 − $21.00 = $0.34 per share as a result of the new project.

2. **Asymmetric information prior to stock issue.** Now suppose management is unable to inform investors about the stock's intrinsic value. Perhaps it is necessary to hold back such information to maintain a competitive edge, or perhaps SEC regulations cause management to refrain from "touting" the stock prior to the new issue (if things did not work out as expected, new shareholders might sue the managers who had provided the rosy forecast). In this situation, new stock would fetch the current price, $19 per share, so the company would have to sell $100,000/$19 = 5,263 shares in order to raise the required $100,000. If this were done, this new price would result after the project was accepted and the information asymmetry was removed:

$$\text{New stock price} = \frac{\text{New market value} + \text{New money raised} + \text{NPV}}{\text{Original shares} + \text{New shares}}$$

$$= \frac{\$210,000 + \$100,000 + \$5,000}{10,000 + 5,263} = \$20.64.$$

Under this condition, the project should not be undertaken. If the project were not accepted, so no new shares were sold, then the price of the stock would rise to its $21 intrinsic value when the information asymmetry was eventually removed. The sale of new stock at $19 per share would lead to a $0.36 per share loss to the firm's existing shareholders. There would be a $1.64 gain to the new shareholders, but management wants to maximize the value of *current* stockholders, not new ones.

3. **A more profitable project.** Now suppose the project had an NPV of $20,000 rather than $5,000, the stock sold for $19, and other conditions in Scenario 2 were unchanged. Now the firm's stock price would rise to $21.62 if it undertook the project:

$$\text{New stock price} = \frac{\$210,000 + \$100,000 + \$20,000}{10,000 + 5,263} = \$21.62.$$

Under these conditions, the firm should take on the project. Note, though, that most of the positive NPV would go to the new stockholders, who would pay $19 per share and thus enjoy a capital gain of $2.62 versus a gain of only $0.62 for the original stockholders.

4. **Dark clouds on the horizon.** Now suppose an entirely different — and bad — situation faced the firm. Stockholders think the firm is worth $19 per share, but managers think (a) that outside investors are entirely too optimistic about growth opportunities, (b) that investors have not factored in proposed legislation which will require large, nonearning investments in pollution control equipment, and (c) that the current stock price does not reflect the need

for new R&D expenditures which are required to keep the firm's products competitive. If all of these bad events materialize, profit margins will be under pressure, cash flows will be down, and the company may have difficulty servicing its debt.

Faced with these conditions, management might well conclude that the stock's intrinsic value is only $17 per share, and then decide to sell a new issue of 10,000 shares at the current price of $19, raising $190,000 and using the funds to retire debt or to support this year's capital budget. This action would increase the intrinsic value of the stock from $17 to $18:

$$\text{New intrinsic value} = \frac{\text{Old intrinsic market value} + \text{New money}}{\text{Original shares} + \text{New shares}}$$

$$= \frac{\$170,000 + \$190,000}{10,000 + 10,000} = \$18.00.$$

Current stockholders will, if management's expectations come true, suffer a loss when the bad news becomes known, but the sale of new stock would reduce that loss. (Note: Management would have to carefully word the prospectus for the new issue, pointing out the potential problems. However, virtually all prospectuses are filled with cautionary language, so investors have difficulty telling from them what management really expects.)

5. **Finance the original $5,000 NPV project with debt.** If the firm used debt to finance the original $100,000 project, *and then the information asymmetry were removed,* the new stock price would be $21.50 versus the $20.64 we found under Scenario 2:

$$\text{New stock price} = \frac{\text{New market value} + \text{NPV}}{\text{Original shares}}$$

$$= \frac{\$210,000 + \$5,000}{10,000} = \$21.50.$$

Thus, if debt were used, all of the intrinsic value of the firm's existing assets, plus the NPV of the new project, would accrue to the original shareholders. If stock were used, we saw earlier that the value of the original stock would end up at $20.64 rather than $21, the intrinsic value without the new investment.[19]

What does all this suggest about corporate financial policy? First, in a world where asymmetric information exists, corporations should issue new shares only in the unlikely event that they have extraordinarily profitable investments that cannot be postponed, signaled to investors, or financed by debt, or if management thinks the shares are overvalued. Second, investors recognize this situation, so selling pressure drives down a company's share price when it announces plans to issue new

---

[19]If the additional debt were not proportionally matched with retained earnings, issuing new debt would increase the firm's risk and consequently its required rate of return on equity. Similarly, the issuance of new equity in the previous scenarios might reduce risk and thus lower the cost of equity. We abstract from these effects because (1) they are of second order importance and (2) incorporating them into the analysis would unnecessarily complicate the examples.

shares. Third, the pecking order that Donaldson observed is rational when asymmetric information exists — it pays to retain a large fraction of earnings, and to keep the equity ratio up and the debt ratio down, so as to maintain a "reserve borrowing capacity" which can be used to support the capital budget if and when an unusually large number of positive NPV projects come along, or if problems arise which require outside capital.[20]

Note that information asymmetry, and its impact on investors' perceptions, differs substantially across firms. To illustrate, asymmetry is typically much greater in the drug and semiconductor industries than in the retailing and trucking industries, because success in the biotech and semiconductor industries depends on secretive proprietary research and development. Thus, managers in these industries have significantly more information about their firms' prospects than do outside investors. Also, emerging firms with limited capital but good growth opportunities are recognized as having to use external financing, so the announcement of new stock offerings by a new company is not viewed with as much concern by investors as are offerings by mature firms with limited growth opportunities. Thus, although asymmetric information affects all firms, its impact varies from firm to firm.

SELF-TEST   Briefly explain the asymmetric information theory.
QUESTIONS   What does this theory suggest about capital structure decisions?
Is the asymmetric information theory equally applicable to all firms?

CAPITAL STRUCTURE THEORY: OUR VIEW

The great contribution of the trade-off models developed by MM, Miller, and their followers is that these models identified the specific benefits and costs of using debt — the tax benefits, financial distress costs, and so on. Prior to MM, no capital structure theory existed, so we had no systematic way of analyzing the effects of debt financing.

The trade-off models are summarized graphically in Figure 14-3. The top graph shows the relationships between the debt ratio and the cost of debt, the cost of equity, and the WACC. Both k_s and $k_d(1 - T_c)$ rise steadily with increases in leverage, but the rate of increase accelerates at higher debt levels, reflecting agency costs and the increased probability of financial distress. The WACC first declines, then hits a minimum at D/V^*, and then begins to rise. Note that the value of D in D/V^* in the upper graph is D^*, the level of debt in the lower graph that maximizes the firm's value. Thus, a firm's WACC is minimized and its value is maximized at the same capital structure. Note also that the general shapes of the curves apply regardless of whether we are using the modified MM with corporate taxes model, the Miller model, or a variant of these models.

---

[20]Flotation costs also play a role in capital structure theory. In general, flotation costs are smaller on debt issues than on equity issues, and this provides an additional rationale for using debt rather than outside equity. We will discuss this issue in more detail in Chapter 16.

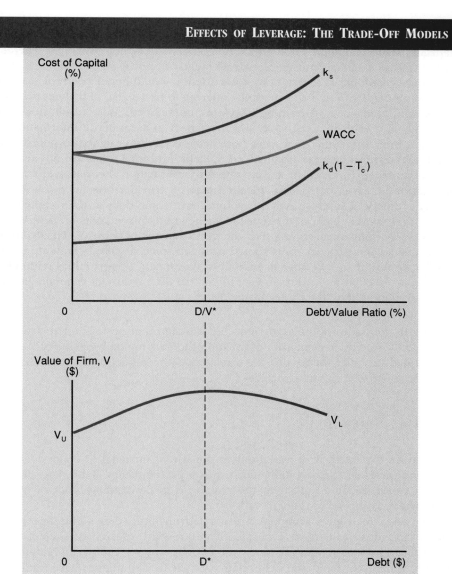

EFFECTS OF LEVERAGE: THE TRADE-OFF MODELS   FIGURE 14-3

Unfortunately, it is impossible to quantify accurately the costs and benefits of debt financing, so it is impossible to pinpoint D/V*, the capital structure that maximizes a firm's value. Most experts believe such a structure exists for every firm, but that it changes over time as firms' operations and investors' preferences change. Most experts also believe that, as shown in Figure 14-3, the relationship between value and leverage is relatively flat over a fairly broad range, so large deviations from the optimal capital structure can occur without materially affecting the stock price.

Now consider the asymmetric information theory. Because of asymmetric information, investors know less about a firm's prospects than its managers know. Further, managers try to maximize value for *current* stockholders, not new ones. Therefore, if the firm has excellent prospects, management will not want to issue new shares, but if things look bleak, then a new stock offering would benefit current stockholders. Consequently, investors take a stock offering to be a signal of bad news, so stock prices tend to decline when new issues are announced. As a result, new equity financings are relatively expensive. The net effect of asymmetric information is to motivate firms to maintain a reserve borrowing capacity designed to permit future investment opportunities to be financed by debt if internal funds are not available.

By combining the trade-off and asymmetric information theories, we obtain this explanation for firms' behavior: (1) Debt financing provides benefits because of the tax deductibility of interest, so firms should have some debt in their capital structures. (2) However, financial distress and agency costs place limits on debt usage — beyond some point, these costs offset the tax advantage of debt. (3) Finally, because of asymmetric information, firms should maintain some reserve borrowing capacity in order to be able to take advantage of good investment opportunities without having to issue stock at low prices, hence the actual debt ratio will generally be lower than that suggested by the trade-off models.

SELF-TEST QUESTIONS

Summarize the trade-off and asymmetric information theories of capital structure.

Are the trade-off and asymmetric information theories mutually exclusive?

Does capital structure theory provide managers with a model that can be used to set a precise optimal capital structure?

VARIATIONS IN CAPITAL STRUCTURES

As might be expected, wide variations in the use of financial leverage occur both across industries and among individual firms in each industry. Table 14-3 illustrates differences for selected industries; the ranking is in descending order of common equity ratios, as shown in Column 1.[21]

Drug and electronics companies use relatively little debt — the uncertainties inherent in industries that are cyclical, oriented toward research, or subject to huge product liability suits render the heavy use of debt unwise. Utility and retailing companies, on the other hand, use debt relatively heavily. The utilities have traditionally used large amounts of debt, particularly long-term debt — their fixed assets make good security for mortgage bonds, and their relatively stable sales has made it safe for them to carry more debt than would be true for firms with more business risk. Note, though, that the utilities are rapidly being deregulated, hence they face rapidly increasing competition. As a result, virtually every utility has revised its target capi-

---

[21]Information on capital structures and financial strength is available from a multitude of sources. We used the *Compustat* data tapes to develop Table 14-3, but published sources include *The Value Line Investment Survey, Robert Morris Association Annual Studies,* and *Dun & Bradstreet Key Business Ratios.*

| | CAPITAL STRUCTURE PERCENTAGES, 1995: FOUR INDUSTRIES RANKED BY COMMON EQUITY RATIOS | | | | | | TABLE 14-3 |

INDUSTRY	COMMON EQUITY (1)	PREFERRED STOCK (2)	TOTAL DEBT (3)	LONG-TERM DEBT (4)	SHORT-TERM DEBT (5)	TIMES-INTEREST-EARNED RATIO (6)	RETURN ON EQUITY (7)
Drugs	74.4%	0.0%	25.6%	18.7%	6.9%	17.1×	26.4%
Electronics	68.4	0.0	31.6	24.5	7.1	6.4	11.7
Retailing	53.6	1.0	45.4	39.4	6.0	5.1	16.2
Utilities	46.9	5.3	47.8	43.8	4.0	2.5	5.6
Composite (average of all industries, not just those listed above)	37.7%	1.5%	60.8%	38.7%	22.1%	3.2×	11.7%

NOTE: These ratios are based on accounting (or book) values. Stated on a market-value basis, the equity percentages would rise, because most stocks sell at prices that are two to three times higher than their book values.
SOURCE: *Compustat* Industrial Data Tape, 1995.

tal structure to include less debt. This demonstrates that firms change their target capital structures as their business risks change.

Particular attention should be given to the times-interest-earned (TIE) ratio because it gives an indication of how safe the debt is and how vulnerable the company is to financial distress. TIE ratios depend on three factors: (1) the percentage of debt, (2) the interest rate on the debt, and (3) the company's profitability. Generally, the least leveraged industries, such as the drug industry, have the highest coverage ratios, whereas the utility industry, which finances heavily with debt, has a low average coverage ratio. Again, it should be noted that both Moody's and Standard & Poor recently changed their "guidelines" for the utility industry, raising the coverage ratios (and lowering the debt ratios) that are necessary to receive bond ratings such as AA, A, and so forth.

Wide variations also exist among firms within given industries. For example, although the average common equity ratio in 1995 for the drug industry was 74.4 percent, Merck's ratio was 93 percent, while that of American Home Products was only 38 percent. Thus, factors unique to individual firms, including managerial attitudes, play an important role in setting target capital structures.

Why do wide variations in the use of financial leverage occur both across industries and among the individual firms in each industry?

SELF-TEST QUESTION

BOOK WEIGHTS VERSUS MARKET WEIGHTS

In Chapter 8, we calculated the weighted average cost of capital with market value rather than book value weights. Further, in our discussions of capital structure thus far in Chapters 13 and 14, we have focused primarily on market values, not book values. However, survey data indicate that financial managers generally focus on book value structures. Thus, there seems to be a conflict between academic theory and business practice. Here are some thoughts on this issue:

1. If stocks and bonds do not sell exactly at book value — and they almost never do — then it would be impossible for a growing firm to establish and maintain at constant levels both a target book value and a target market value capital structure. The firm could stay on its book value target or on its market value target, but not on both. To illustrate, assume that a company has, at book value, $50 million of debt and $50 million of equity, for a total book value of $100 million. However, its stock sells at 2.0 times book. Here is the capital structure situation, with dollars in millions:

	BOOK VALUE		MARKET VALUE	
Debt	$ 50	50%	$ 50	33%
Equity	50	50	100	67
Total	$100	100%	$150	100%

Now suppose the company needs to raise an additional $100 million. If it sells $50 million of debt and $50 million of common stock, it will add these amounts to its balance sheet, so its book value capital structure will remain constant. However, adding $50 million to both debt and equity will cause its market value capital structure to change. On the other hand, if it raises $33 million as debt and $67 million as equity, its market value capital structure will remain constant, but its book value structure will change. Thus, it can maintain either its book value or its market value capital structure, but not both.

2. Book values as reported on balance sheets reflect the historical costs of assets. At times, historical costs have little to do with the actual value of assets or with their ability to produce cash flows. Market values would almost always better reflect cash generation and debt service ability.

3. As we have repeatedly noted throughout this chapter and the last one, the point of capital structure analysis is to find that capital structure which maximizes the firm's market value, hence its stock price. Since this optimum is defined in terms of stock prices, it can only be determined by an analysis of market values.

4. Now suppose a firm found its optimal market value structure, but then financed so as to maintain a constant book value structure. This would lead to a departure from value maximization. Therefore, if a firm is growing, it must finance so as to hold constant its market value structure. That will, as we saw above, normally lead to a change in the book value structure.

5. Since the firm should, to keep its value at a maximum, finance so as to hold its market value structure constant, the weighted average cost of capital, WACC, should be found using market value weights.

6. Business executives prefer stability and predictability to volatility and uncertainty. Book values are far more predictable than market values. Further, a

financial manager can set a target book value capital structure and then attain it, right on the money. It would be virtually impossible to stay at a target market value structure because of bond and stock price fluctuations. This is one reason executives focus on book value structures rather than on the more logical market value structures. Also, many financial executives have accounting backgrounds, and accountants focus on accounting numbers. However, as financial executives gain a knowledge of financial (as opposed to accounting) theory, the focus is shifting more toward market values.

7. For purposes of developing the weighted average cost of capital, we strongly recommend the use of market value weights. However, if a company focuses on a book value capital structure, seeks to maintain that structure, and finances in accordance with book value weights, then its weighted average cost of capital should be based on book weights.

8. Some executives have argued against the use of market value weights on the grounds that as stock prices change, so would capital structure weights, with the result being a volatile cost of capital. This argument is incorrect. The cost of capital should be based on *target* weights, not on the actual capital structure, and there is no reason to think that a target market value structure would be any less stable than a target book value structure. In fact, as we discuss in Point 9 below, target market value weights are probably more stable than target book weights.

9. Now consider a fairly typical situation. Firm X currently has a 50/50 debt/equity ratio at book, and a 33/67 ratio at market. It targets on the book value ratio. Several years go by. The company takes on projects with positive NPVs, and that raises its market value above its book value. Also, inflation occurs, so new assets cost more. Output prices are based on marginal costs, which have risen because of inflation. With the new, higher prices, the rate of return on old assets increases, as does the value of the old assets, and the firm's stock price rises. Book values per share are relatively stable, so the increasing stock price leads to an increase in the market/book ratio. Debt values, on the other hand, remain close to book. Rising stock prices, when combined with stable bond prices, could cause the market value debt/equity ratio to remain constant at the 33/67 level, or even to increase, even though the firm finances on a 50/50 book basis.

10. Note also that, under our scenario, the rising ROE will lead to improved coverage ratios. This fact, together with analysts' knowledge that the firm's book values are understated, will support an increase in the debt ratio measured at book.

What can we conclude from all this? We are absolutely convinced that the procedures we recommend are correct — namely, firms should focus on market value capital structures and base their cost of capital calculations on target market value weights. Because market values do change, it would be impossible to keep the actual capital structure on target at all times, but this fact in no way detracts from the validity of market value targets.

Should the target capital structure be expressed in book value or market value weights?

Why do practicing financial managers prefer to work with book weights?

SUMMARY

In this chapter, we discussed a variety of topics related to capital structure decisions. The key concepts covered are listed below:

- In 1958, *Franco Modigliani and Merton Miller (MM)* startled the academic community by proving, under a restrictive set of assumptions including zero taxes, that capital structure is irrelevant; that is, according to the original MM article, a firm's value is not affected by its financing mix.

- *MM* later added *corporate taxes* to their model and reached the conclusion that capital structure does matter, and that firms should use 100 percent debt financing in order to maximize value.

- MM's model with corporate taxes demonstrated that the benefits of debt stem solely from the *tax deductibility of interest payments*.

- Much later, Miller extended the theory to include *personal taxes*. The introduction of personal taxes reduces, but does not eliminate, the benefits of debt financing. Thus, the *Miller model* also leads to 100 percent debt financing.

- The addition of financial distress and agency costs to either the MM corporate tax model or the Miller model results in a *trade-off model*. Here the marginal costs and benefits of debt financing are balanced against one another, and the result is an optimal capital structure that falls somewhere between zero and 100 percent debt.

- The *Hamada equation* combines the CAPM with MM (with corporate taxes):

$$k_{SL} = k_{RF} + (k_M - k_{RF})b_U + (k_M - k_{RF})b_U(1 - T)(D/S).$$

  This equation shows that the required rate of return on a levered company's stock is equal to the risk-free rate, which compensates investors for the time value of money, plus premiums for business risk and financial risk.

- Within a *market risk framework,* business risk can be measured by b_U, market risk can be measured by b, and financial risk can be measured by $b - b_U = b_U(1 - T)(D/S)$.

- The *asymmetric information theory,* which recognizes that managers have better information than most investors, postulates that there is a preferred "pecking order" of financing: first retained earnings (and depreciation), then debt, and as a last resort only, new common stock.

■ The asymmetric information theory leads to the conclusion that firms should maintain a *borrowing capacity reserve* so that they can always issue debt on reasonable terms rather than have to issue new equity at the wrong time.

■ There are clearly benefits to debt financing, but firms use different amounts of debt depending on their tax rates, asset structures, and business risks.

■ Wide variations in capital structure exist, both across industries and among individual firms within industries. The variations across industries can be explained to a large extent by the economic fundamentals of the industry. Variations within industries also reflect fundamental differences, but they additionally reflect differences in managers' attitudes toward debt.

■ The optimal capital structure should be thought of in market value rather than book value terms, even though managers often seem to focus on book values.

QUESTIONS

14-1 Define each of the following terms.
  a. MM Proposition I without taxes; with corporate taxes
  b. MM Proposition II without taxes; with corporate taxes
  c. Miller model
  d. Financial distress costs
  e. Agency costs
  f. Trade-off model
  g. Asymmetric information theory
  h. Hamada equation
  i. Reserve borrowing capacity

14-2 Explain why agency costs would probably be more of a problem for a large, publicly owned firm that uses both debt and equity capital than for a small, unleveraged, owner-managed firm.

14-3 Explain, verbally, how MM use the arbitrage process to prove the validity of Proposition I. Also, list the major MM assumptions and explain why each of these assumptions is necessary in the arbitrage proof.

14-4 A utility company is supposed to be allowed to charge prices high enough to cover all costs, including its cost of capital. Public service commissions are supposed to take actions to stimulate companies to operate as efficiently as possible in order to keep costs, hence prices, as low as possible. Some time ago, AT&T's debt ratio was about 33 percent. Some people (Myron J. Gordon in particular) argued that a higher debt ratio would lower AT&T's cost of capital and permit it to charge lower rates for telephone service. Gordon thought an optimal debt ratio for AT&T was about 50 percent. Do the theories presented in the chapter support or refute Gordon's position?

SELF-TEST PROBLEM

(SOLUTION APPEARS IN APPENDIX C)

ST-1   **MM WITH FINANCIAL DISTRESS COSTS** B. Gibbs Inc. is an unleveraged firm, and it has constant expected operating earnings (EBIT) of $2 million per year. The firm's tax rate is 40 percent, and its market value is V = S = $12 million. Management is considering the use of some debt financing. (Debt would be issued and used to buy back stock, so the size of the firm would remain constant.) Since interest expense is tax deductible, the value of the firm would tend to increase as debt is added to the capital structure, but there would be an offset in the form of a rising risk of financial distress. The firm's analysts have estimated, as an approximation, that the present value of any future financial distress costs is $8 million, and that the probability of distress would increase with leverage according to the following schedule:

VALUE OF DEBT	PROBABILITY OF FINANCIAL DISTRESS
$ 2,500,000	0.00%
5,000,000	1.25
7,500,000	2.50
10,000,000	6.25
12,500,000	12.50
15,000,000	31.25
20,000,000	75.00

a. What is the firm's cost of equity and weighted average cost of capital at this time?
b. According to the "pure" MM with-tax model, what is the optimal level of debt?
c. What is the optimal capital structure when financial distress costs are included?
d. Plot the value of the firm, with and without distress costs, as a function of the level of debt.

PROBLEMS

14-1   **BUSINESS AND FINANCIAL RISK: MARKET** Air Tampa has just been incorporated, and its board of directors is currently grappling with the question of optimal capital structure. The company plans to offer commuter air services between Tampa and smaller surrounding cities. Jaxair has been around for a few years, and it has about the same basic business risk as Air Tampa would have. Jaxair's market-determined beta is 1.8, and it has a current market value debt ratio (total debt/total assets) of 50 percent and a federal-plus-state tax rate of 40 percent. Air Tampa expects only to be marginally profitable at start up, hence its tax rate would only be 25 percent. Air Tampa's owners expect that the total book and market value of the firm's stock, if it uses zero debt, would be $10 million.

a. Estimate the beta of an unleveraged firm in the commuter airline business based on Jax-air's market-determined beta. (Hint: Jaxair's market-determined beta is a leveraged beta. Use Equation 14-6a and solve for b_U.)

b. Now assume that $k_{RF} = 10\%$ and $k_M = 15\%$. Find the required rate of return on equity for an unleveraged commuter airline. What is the business risk premium for this industry?

c. Air Tampa is considering three capital structures: (1) $2 million debt, (2) $4 million debt, and (3) $6 million debt. Estimate Air Tampa's k_s for these debt levels. What is the financial risk premium at each level?

d. Calculate Air Tampa's k_s and financial risk premium at $6 million debt assuming its federal-plus-state tax rate is now 40 percent. Compare this with your corresponding answer to Part c. (Hint: The increase in the tax rate causes V_U to drop to $8 million.)

-2 **MM WITHOUT TAXES** Companies U and L are identical in every respect except that U is unleveraged while L has $10 million of 5 percent bonds outstanding. Assume (1) that all of the MM assumptions are met, (2) that there are no corporate or personal taxes, (3) that EBIT is $2 million, and (4) that the cost of equity to Company U is 10 percent.

a. What value would MM estimate for each firm?

b. What is k_s for Firm U? For Firm L?

c. Find S_L, and then show that $S_L + D = V_L = 20 million.

d. What is the WACC for Firm U? For Firm L?

e. Suppose $V_U = 20 million and $V_L = 22 million. According to MM, do these values represent an equilibrium? If not, explain the process by which equilibrium would be restored.

-3 **MM WITH CORPORATE TAXES** Refer to Problem 14-2. Assume that all the facts hold, except that both firms are subject to a 40 percent federal-plus-state corporate tax rate.

a. What value would MM now estimate for each firm? (Use Proposition I.)

b. What is k_s for Firm U? Firm L?

c. Find S_L, and then show that $S_L + D = V_L$ results in the same value as obtained in Part a.

d. What is the WACC for Firm U? For Firm L?

-4 **MILLER MODEL** Refer to Problems 14-2 and 14-3. Assume that all facts hold, except that both corporate and personal taxes apply. Assume that both firms must pay a federal-plus-state corporate tax rate of $T_c = 40\%$, and that investors in both firms face a tax rate of $T_d = 28\%$ on debt income and $T_s = 20\%$, on average, on stock income.

a. What is the value of the unleveraged firm, V_U? (Note that V_U is now reduced by the personal tax on stock income, hence $V_U \neq 12 million as in Problem 14-3.)

b. What is the value of V_L?

c. What is the gain from leverage in this situation? Compare this with the gain from leverage in Problem 14-3.

d. Set $T_c = T_s = T_d = 0$. What is the value of the leveraged firm? The gain from leverage?

e. Now suppose $T_s = T_d = 0$. What are the value of the leveraged firm and the gain from leverage?

f. Assume that $T_d = 28\%$, $T_s = 28\%$, and $T_c = 40\%$. Now what are the value of the leveraged firm and the gain from leverage?

-5 **MM WITH AND WITHOUT TAXES** International Associates (IA) is just about to commence operations as an international trading company. The firm will have book assets of $10 million, and it expects to earn a 16 percent return on these assets before taxes. However, because of certain tax arrangements with foreign governments, IA will not pay any taxes; that is, its tax rate will be zero. Management is trying to decide how to raise the required $10 million. It is known that the capitalization rate for an all-equity firm in this business is 11 percent, that is, $k_{sU} = 11\%$. Further, IA can borrow at a rate $k_d = 6\%$. Assume that the MM assumptions apply.

a. According to MM, what will be the value of IA if it uses no debt? If it uses $6 million of 6 percent debt?

b. What are the values of the WACC and k_s at debt levels of D = $0, D = $6 million, and D = $10 million? What effect does leverage have on firm value? Why?

c. Assume the initial facts of the problem (k_d = 6%, EBIT = $1.6 million, k_{sU} = 11%), but now assume that a 40 percent federal-plus-state corporate tax rate exists. Find the new market values for IA with zero debt and with $6 million of debt, using the MM formulas.

d. What are the values of the WACC and k_s at debt levels of D = $0, D = $6 million, and D = $10 million, assuming a 40 percent corporate tax rate? Plot the relationships between the value of the firm and the debt ratio, and between capital costs and the debt ratio.

e. What is the maximum dollar amount of debt financing that can be used? What is the value of the firm at this debt level? What is the cost of this debt?

f. How would each of the following factors tend to change the values you plotted in your graph?

(1) The interest rate on debt increases as the debt ratio rises.

(2) At higher levels of debt, the probability of financial distress rises.

14-6   AGENCY COSTS Until recently, the Prestopino Company carried a triple-A bond rating and was strong in every respect. However, a series of problems has afflicted the firm: It is currently in severe financial distress, and its ability to make future payments on outstanding debt is questionable. If the firm were forced into bankruptcy at this time, the common stockholders would almost certainly be wiped out. Although the firm has limited financial resources, its cash flows (primarily from depreciation) are sufficient to support one of two mutually exclusive investments, each costing $150 million and having a 10-year expected life. These projects have the same market risk, but different total risk as measured by the variance of returns. Each project has the following after-tax cash inflows for 10 years:

	ANNUAL CASH INFLOWS	
PROBABILITY	PROJECT A	PROJECT B
0.5	$30,000,000	$10,000,000
0.5	35,000,000	50,000,000

Assume that both projects have the same market risk as the firm's "average" project. The firm's weighted average cost of capital is 15 percent.

a. What is the expected annual cash inflow from each project?

b. Which project has the greater total risk?

c. Which project would you choose if you were a stockholder? Why?

d. Which project would the bondholders prefer to see management select? Why?

e. If the choices conflict, what "protection" do the bondholders have against the firm's making a decision that is contrary to their interests?

f. Who bears the cost of this "protection"? How is this cost related to leverage and the optimal capital structure?

14-7   MM WITH FINANCIAL DISTRESS COSTS The Boisjoly Company currently has no debt. An in-house research group has just been assigned the job of determining whether the firm should change its capital structure. Because of the importance of the decision, management has also hired the investment banking firm of Stanley Morgan & Company to conduct a parallel analysis of the situation. Mr. Harris, the in-house analyst, who is well versed in modern finance theory, has decided to carry out the analysis using the MM framework. Ms. Broske, the Stanley Morgan consultant, who has a good knowledge of capital market conditions and is confident of her ability to predict the firm's debt and equity costs at various levels of debt, has decided to estimate the optimal capital structure as that structure which minimizes the firm's weighted average cost of capital. The following data are relevant to both analyses:

$$\text{EBIT} = \$4 \text{ million per year, in perpetuity.}$$

Federal-plus-state tax rate = 40%.

Dividend payout ratio = 100%.

Current required rate of return on equity = 12%.

The cost of capital schedule predicted by Mr. Harris follows:

	AT A DEBT LEVEL OF (MILLIONS OF DOLLARS)							
	$0	$2	$4	$6	$8	$10	$12	$14
Interest rate (%)	—	8.0	8.3	9.0	10.0	11.0	13.0	16.0
Cost of equity (%)	12.0	12.25	12.75	13.0	13.15	13.4	14.65	17.0

Ms. Broske estimated the present value of financial distress costs at $8 million. Additionally, she estimated the following probabilities of financial distress:

	AT A DEBT LEVEL OF (MILLIONS OF DOLLARS)							
	$0	$2	$4	$6	$8	$10	$12	$14
Probability of financial distress	0	0	0.05	0.07	0.10	0.17	0.47	0.90

a. What level of debt would Mr. Harris and Ms. Broske recommend as optimal?
b. Comment on the similarities and differences in their recommendations.

SPREADSHEET APPLICATIONS

SPREADSHEET PROBLEM

The Brandt Corporation is an unleveraged firm, and it has constant expected operating earnings (EBIT) of $2 million per year. Brandt's federal-plus-state tax rate is 40 percent, its cost of equity is 10 percent, and its market value is V = S = $12 million. Management is considering the use of debt which would cost the firm 8 percent regardless of the amount used. (Debt would be issued and used to buy back stock, so the size of the firm would remain constant.) Since interest expense is tax deductible, the value of the firm would tend to increase as debt is added to the capital structure, but there would be an offset in the form of rising risk of financial distress. The firm's analysts have estimated, as an approximation, that the present value of any future financial distress costs is $8 million, and that the probability of distress would increase with leverage according to the following schedule:

VALUE OF DEBT	PROBABILITY OF DISTRESS
$ 0	0.0%
2,500,000	2.5
5,000,000	5.0
7,500,000	10.0
10,000,000	25.0
12,500,000	50.0
15,000,000	75.0

a. According to the "pure" MM with corporate taxes model, what is the optimal level of debt? (Consider only those debt values listed in the table.)

b. What is the optimal capital structure when financial distress costs are included?

c. Plot the value of the firm, with and without financial distress costs, as a function of the level of debt.

d. Assume that the firm's unleveraged cost of equity is 8 percent. What is the firm's optimal capital structure now? (From this point on, include financial distress costs in all your analyses.)

e. Return to the base case k_{sU} of 10 percent. Now assume that the firm's tax rate increases to 60 percent. What effect does this change have on the firm's optimal capital structure?

f. Return to the base case tax rate of 40 percent. Assume that the estimated present value of financial distress costs is only $5 million. Now what is the firm's optimal capital structure?

SPREADSHEET EXERCISE: MACROS

This exercise uses a spreadsheet model to calculate security values and capital costs for a firm at different capital structures, assuming the MM assumptions hold. The model is complete including graphics. Students will add macros to the model to make it easier to display the graphs, especially with DOS spreadsheets.

1. Retrieve the model (Filename SE-14.WK1) from the models diskette. The model calculates V_L, V_U, gain from leverage, S_L, K_{sL}, $WACC_U$, and $WACC_L$ according to the MM propositions.

2. The section beginning on Row 21 contains the data that are used to create the MM graphs. To view the graphs, type /GNU and then move the highlighter with the Arrow keys to highlight either MM58 or MM63, and press Enter. The chosen graph will then be displayed. Hit any key to return to the spreadsheet. View both graphs.

3. You can see that it is not easy to view the graphs because a series of keystrokes is required. Even if you are using a Windows spreadsheet, several steps must be taken with the mouse to display each graph.

4. To make it easier to view the graphs, you are going to create two macros. In essence, a macro is a preestablished set of keystrokes that are executed on command. If we can record the keystrokes necessary to view each graph and then execute the keystrokes with a simple keystroke, the graphs can be more easily viewed.

5. To begin, place the cursor in Cell F23. Then enter '/GNU~Q. Since the first character is ', the entry will be a label. If you did not first type ', the entry would be interpreted as a command. The tilde (~), when part of a macro, means Enter. Thus, the keystrokes in Cell F23 first invoke the graph menu (/G), then tell the spreadsheet to Name Use (NU), and finally invoke Enter while the highlighter is on the first named graph, MM58. The final character in the macro, Q, exits the Graph menu after the graph has been viewed and any key is pressed.

6. Now you must tell the spreadsheet that the label in Cell F23 is a macro and also what key must be pressed to run the macro. The Range Name command is used to accomplish this. Press /RNC to create the range name, then \M to designate the range to be named as a macro and name it M, and then, with the highlighter on Cell F23, press Enter.

7. You now have a macro named M that will display the MM58 graph when it is run. To run the macro, simultaneously press ALT M. Try it, and if you have done everything correctly, the MM58 graph should be displayed.

8. To test your macro skills, create a macro in Cell F41 named N to display the graph named MM63. (Hint: Within a macro, the characters {RIGHT} move the highlighter one space to the right.) Now, with both macros completed, you should be able to easily view each graph.

9. Finally, note that newer releases of spreadsheets have a feature called Learn or Record that allows you to create a macro by executing the keystrokes you wish to perform rather than typing the keystrokes as labels. The advantage here is that you can see on the screen exactly what the macro does as you are creating it.

MINI CASE

Donald Cheney, the CEO of Cheney Electronics, is concerned about his firm's level of debt financing. The company uses short-term debt to finance its temporary working capital needs, but it does not use any permanent (long-term) debt. Other electronics companies average about 30 percent debt, and Mr. Cheney wonders why the difference occurs, and what its effects are on stock prices. To gain some insights into the matter, he poses the following questions to you, his recently hired assistant:

a. *Business Week* recently ran an article on companies' debt policies, and the names Modigliani and Miller (MM) were mentioned several times as leading researchers on the theory of capital structure. Briefly, who are MM, and what assumptions are embedded in the MM and Miller models?

b. Assume that Firms U and L are in the same risk class, and that both have EBIT = $500,000. Firm U uses no debt financing, and its cost of equity is $k_{sU} = 14\%$. Firm L has $1 million of debt outstanding at a cost of $k_d = 8\%$. There are no taxes. Assume that the MM assumptions hold, and then:
   (1) Find V, S, k_s, and WACC for Firms U and L.
   (2) Graph (a) the relationships between capital costs and leverage as measured by D/V, and (b) the relationship between value and D.

c. Using the data given in Part b, but now assuming that firms L and U are both subject to a 40 percent corporate tax rate, repeat the analysis called for in b(1) and b(2) under the MM with-tax model.

d. Now suppose investors are subject to the following tax rates: $T_d = 30\%$ and $T_s = 25\%$.
   (1) What is the gain from leverage according to the Miller model?
   (2) How does this gain compare to the gain in the MM model with corporate taxes?
   (3) What does the Miller model imply about the effect of corporate debt on the value of the firm, that is, how do personal taxes affect the situation?

e. What capital structure policy recommendations do the three theories (MM without taxes, MM with corporate taxes, and Miller) suggest to financial managers? Empirically, do firms appear to follow any one of these guidelines?

f. What are financial distress and agency costs? How does the addition of these costs change the MM and Miller models? (Express your answer in words, in equation form, and in graphical form.)

g. How are financial and business risk measured in a market risk framework?

SELECTED ADDITIONAL REFERENCES AND CASES

The body of literature on capital structure — and the number of potential references — is huge. Therefore, only a sampling can be given here. For an extensive review of the recent literature, as well as a detailed bibliography, see

Beranek, William, "Research Directions in Finance," *Quarterly Review of Business and Economics,* Spring 1981, 6–24.

The major theoretical works on capital structure theory are discussed in an integrated framework in

Copeland, Thomas E., and J. Fred Weston, *Financial Theory and Corporate Policy* (Reading, Mass.: Addison-Wesley, 1988).

Harris, Milton, and Artur Raviv, "The Theory of Capital Structure," *Journal of Finance,* March 1991, 297–355.

The Fall 1988 issue of The Journal of Economic Perspectives *and the Summer 1989 issue of* Financial Management *each contain several interesting and very readable articles which review the MM propositions after 30 years of debate and testing.*

In addition to Miller's work, the effect of personal taxes on capital structure decisions has been addressed by

Gordon, Myron J., and Lawrence I. Gould, "The Cost of Equity Capital with Personal Income Taxes and Flotation Costs," *Journal of Finance,* September 1978, 1201–1212.

Some other references of relevance include the following:

Ben-Horim, Moshe, Shalom Hochman, and Oded Palmon, "The Impact of the 1986 Tax Reform Act on Corporate Financial Policy," *Financial Management,* Autumn 1987, 29–35.

Bradley, Michael, Gregg A. Jarrell, and E. Han Kim, "On the Existence of an Optimal Capital Structure: Theory and Evidence," *Journal of Finance,* July 1984, 857–878.

Conine, Thomas E., Jr., "Debt Capacity and the Capital Budgeting Decision: Comment," *Financial Management,* Spring 1980, 20–22.

Crutchley, Claire E., and Robert S. Hansen, "A Test of the Agency Theory of Managerial Ownership, Corporate Leverage, and Corporate Dividends," *Financial Management,* Winter 1989, 36–46.

Dugan, Michael T., and Keith A. Shriver, "An Empirical Comparison of Alternative Methods for Estimating the Degree of Operating Leverage," *Financial Review,* May 1992, 309–321.

Ferri, Michael, and Wesley H. Jones, "Determinants of Financial Structure: A New Methodological Approach," *Journal of Finance,* June 1979, 631–644.

Flath, David, and Charles R. Knoeber, "Taxes, Failure Costs, and Optimal Industry Capital Structure," *Journal of Finance,* March 1980, 89–117.

Ghosh, Dilip K, "Optimum Capital Structure Redefined," *Financial Review,* August 1992, 411–429.

Kelly, William A., Jr., and James A. Miles, "Capital Structure Theory and the Fisher Effect," *The Financial Review,* February 1989, 53–73.

Lee, Wayne Y., and Henry H. Barker, "Bankruptcy Costs and the Firm's Optimal Debt Capacity: A Positive Theory of Capital Structure," *Southern Economic Journal,* April 1977, 1453–1465.

Mackie-Mason, Jeffrey K., "Do Taxes Affect Corporate Financing Decisions," *Journal of Finance,* December 1990, 1471–1493.

Martin, John D., and David F. Scott, "Debt Capacity and the Capital Budgeting Decision: A Revisitation," *Financial Management,* Spring 1980, 23–26.

Miller, Merton H., "The Modigliani-Miller Propositions after Thirty Years," *Journal of Applied Corporate Finance,* Spring 1989, 6–18.

———, "Leverage," *Journal of Finance,* June 1991, 479–488.

Pinegar, J. Michael, and Lisa Wilbricht, "What Managers Think of Capital Structure Theory: A Survey," *Financial Management,* Winter 1989, 82–91.

Scherr, Frederick C., "A Multiperiod Mean-Variance Model of Optimal Capital Structure," *The Financial Review,* February 1987, 1–31.

Schneller, Meir I., "Taxes and the Optimal Capital Structure of the Firm," *Journal of Finance,* March 1980, 119–127.

Taggart, Robert A., Jr., "Taxes and Corporate Capital Structure in an Incomplete Market," *Journal of Finance,* June 1980, 645–659.

Thakor, Anjan V., "Strategic Issues in Financial Contracting: An Overview," *Financial Management,* Summer 1989, 39–58.

There has been considerable discussion in the literature concerning a financial leverage clientele effect. Many theorists postulate that firms with low leverage are favored by high-tax-bracket investors and vice versa. Two articles on this subject are

Harris, John M., Jr., Rodney L. Roenfeldt, and Philip L. Cooley, "Evidence of Financial Leverage Clienteles," *Journal of Finance,* September 1983, 1125–1132.

Kim, E. Han, "Miller's Equilibrium, Shareholder Leverage Clienteles, and Optimal Capital Leverage," *Journal of Finance,* May 1982, 301–319.

For a very readable discussion of the many issues involved in capital structure theory, see

"A Discussion of Corporate Capital Structure," *Midland Corporate Finance Journal,* Fall 1985, 19–48.

The Dryden Press Cases in Financial Management: Dryden Request *series has the following cases that apply to this chapter:*

Case 7, "Seattle Steel Products," focuses on capital structure theory.

Case 8, "Johnson Window Company," and Case 8A, "Isle Marine Boat Company," cover operating and financial leverage.

CHAPTER 15

DIVIDEND POLICY

A *t 9:02 on the morning of January 26, 1993, the financial news wire carried this one-sentence announcement: "IBM slashes the quarterly dividend on its common from $1.21 to 54¢." A later story provided this additional information:*

> *The Board of Directors took this action only after serious deliberation and careful consideration of both IBM's earnings and the investment required for the long-term development of the Company's businesses, as well as IBM's intention to pay an appropriate return to shareholders. After weighing all factors, and taking into account the need to maintain IBM's strong financial position, the Board decided to act now in the best long-term interests of the Company and its shareholders.*

IBM's dividend cut — the first ever for the company — reduced the annual dividend from $4.84 to $2.16. The $4.84 amount had been established in 1989, and the dividend growth rate prior to 1989 had averaged 7 percent per year.

Many analysts and investors had been expecting a dividend cut because IBM had not adequately anticipated the shift from mainframe computing to personal computers, and it was not prepared for the slowdown in the mainframe computer market. So, IBM was trapped with massive resources devoted to poor-selling products. Meanwhile, nimbler companies such as Microsoft and Intel earned record profits from the software and microchip businesses that IBM, in effect, gave them in the 1980s. The end result was that IBM set a record for U.S. corporate losses in 1992, saw a 60 percent drop in its stock price, and suffered a 53 percent dividend cut.

IBM's problems mounted in 1993, and it cut the dividend again, from $2.16 to $1.00. However, in 1994 a new management team began to turn things around, and earnings per share improved from a loss in 1993 to $4.92 in 1994, and then to $11.00 in 1995. With profitability restored, IBM now faces two related questions: (1) How much of its free cash flow should it pass on to stockholders, and (2) should it increase the pass-through by raising the dividend or by repurchasing stock? Thus far, IBM's board has authorized a $5.0 billion common stock buyback *and has raised the dividend to $1.40. Further, most analysts expect to see the dividend continue to increase as earnings grow. For example, Value Line forecasts a dividend of $3 on earnings of $15.50 in 1999. These prospects lifted the stock price from a 1993 low of $40.75 to a recent high of $128. IBM is still a long way from its 1987 high of $176, but Value Line forecasts a price of more than $200 by 1999. What really happens remains to be seen.*

This chapter discusses the many facets of dividend policy. As you read the material, put yourself in the shoes of an IBM board member. If the board saw the company's problems on the horizon a few years earlier, why didn't it cut the dividend then? Also, if things looked so bleak, why didn't the board eliminate the dividend instead of just cutting it? Finally, if IBM continues to improve, should the dividend be raised, should more shares be repurchased, or should the company do some of each? By the end of the chapter, you should have a good idea of how dividend policy decisions are made and a better appreciation of the dilemma faced by IBM's board.

Successful companies earn income (and have positive cash flows). Income can be reinvested in operating assets, used to acquire securities, used to retire debt, or distributed to stockholders. If the decision is made to distribute income to stockholders, three key issues arise: (1) What percentage of net income should we distribute? (2) Should the distribution be as cash dividends, or should the cash be passed on to shareholders by buying back some of the stock they hold? (3) How stable should the distribution be; that is, should the funds paid out from year to year be stable and dependable, which stockholders would probably prefer, or be allowed to vary with the firm's cash flows and investment requirements, which would probably be better from an operating standpoint? These three issues are the primary focus of this chapter, but we also consider two related isssues, stock dividends and stock splits.

DIVIDENDS VERSUS CAPITAL GAINS: WHAT DO INVESTORS PREFER?

The target payout ratio — defined as the percentage of net income to be paid out as cash dividends — should be based in large part on investors' preferences for dividends versus capital gains: do investors prefer (1) to have the firm distribute its income as cash dividends or (2) to have it either repurchase stock or else plow the earnings back into the business, both of which should result in capital gains? This preference can be considered in terms of the constant growth stock valuation model:

$$\hat{P}_0 = \frac{D_1}{k_s - g}.$$

This equation shows that if the company increases the payout ratio and thus raises D_1, this increase in the numerator, taken alone, would cause the stock price to rise. However, if D_1 is raised, then less money will be available for reinvestment, the expected growth rate will decline, and that would tend to depress the stock's price.

Thus, any change in payout policy will have two opposing effects, and the firm should strike that balance between current dividends and future growth which maximizes the price of the stock.

In this section we examine three theories of investor preference: (1) the dividend irrelevance theory, (2) the "bird-in-the-hand" theory, and (3) the tax differential theory.

ARE DIVIDENDS IRRELEVANT? MODIGLIANI AND MILLER'S POSITION

In an important theoretical article on dividend policy, Merton Miller and Franco Modigliani (MM) argued that dividend policy has no effect on either the price of a firm's stock or its cost of capital—MM argued that dividend policy is *irrelevant*.[1] They reasoned that the value of a firm is determined by its basic earning power and its business risk. Therefore, a firm's value depends on the earning power of its assets rather than on how the assets are financed or how earnings are split between dividends and retained earnings. MM demonstrated, under a specific set of assumptions, that if a firm pays higher dividends, then it must sell more stock to new investors, and the value of the stock given up to new investors is exactly equal to the dividends paid out. For example, if IBM's capital budget calls for $1 billion of equity financing in 1997, and if the company expects $1 billion of earnings, then (1) it could pay all of its earnings out as dividends and finance the equity requirement by selling $1 billion of new stock; (2) it could retain the entire $1 billion of earnings, pay no dividends, sell no new stock, and provide stockholders with a capital gain having a present value of $1 billion; or (3) it could pick a payout anywhere between 0 and 100 percent and thus provide stockholders with a total return of $1 billion consisting of some dividends and some capital gains.

MM proved that their proposition holds in theory, but their proof requires these five assumptions: (1) There are no personal or corporate income taxes. (2) There are no stock flotation or transaction costs. (3) Investors are indifferent between dividends and capital gains. (4) The firm's capital investment policy is independent of its dividend policy. (5) Investors and managers have the same set of information (symmetric information) regarding future investment opportunities.

The MM assumptions are not realistic, and they obviously do not hold precisely. Firms and investors do pay income taxes, firms do incur flotation costs, and investors do incur transactions costs. Further, managers often have better information than outside investors, and dividend policy can affect capital budgeting through its effect on free cash flow. Thus, MM's theoretical conclusions on dividend irrelevance may not be valid under real-world conditions.

DO INVESTORS PREFER DIVIDENDS? THE "BIRD-IN-THE-HAND" THEORY

In some respects, the most critical assumption in MM's dividend irrelevance theory is that investors are indifferent between dividends and capital gains. This issue has been hotly debated in academic circles. Myron Gordon and John Lintner, on the one

---

[1]Merton H. Miller and Franco Modigliani, "Dividend Policy, Growth, and the Valuation of Shares," *Journal of Business,* October 1961, 411–433.

hand, argued that k_s increases as the dividend payout is reduced, because investors can be more sure of receiving dividend payments than the capital gains which are expected to result from retaining earnings.[2] They say, in effect, that investors prefer a dollar of expected dividends to a dollar of expected capital gains because the expected dividend is less risky than the expected capital gain. Put another way, the dividend yield component, D_1/P_0, is less risky than the g component in the total expected return equation, $\hat{k}_s = D_1/P_0 + g$.

MM called the Gordon-Lintner argument the "bird-in-the-hand fallacy" because, in MM's view, most investors simply reinvest their dividends in the same or similar firms anyway, and, in any event, the riskiness of the firm's cash flows to investors in the long run is determined by the riskiness of its cash flows from operating assets, not by its dividend payout policy.[3]

DO INVESTORS PREFER RETAINED EARNINGS? THE TAX PREFERENCE THEORY

A third theory, based on tax effects, was advanced by Litzenberger and Ramaswamy.[4] Figure 15-1 gives the top tax rates on dividend (and interest) income and on long-term capital gains from 1960 through 1996. There was a very wide differential in 1960, and although the differential has narrowed since then, it has continued to exist, except for 1988 and 1989. Currently (May 1996), the maximum tax rate on long-term capital gains is 28 percent, while the top marginal rate on dividend income is 39.6 percent (and over 40 percent when limitations on deductions and personal exemptions are considered). Thus, an investor in the 40 percent marginal tax bracket would pay a 40 percent tax rate on his or her dividend income but only 28 percent on long-term capital gains. Further, by delaying the sale of his or her stock, the investor could defer realization of the capital gains and thus payment of the tax, and since a dollar paid in the future is less valuable than a dollar paid today, the tax deferral feature provides another important advantage to capital gains.

To illustrate the tax advantage of capital gains, suppose an individual investor in the 40 percent tax bracket is considering the purchase of two stocks: Stock G, which is a "growth stock" with a 10 percent capital gains yield and a 5 percent dividend yield, and Stock I, which is an "income stock" with a 5 percent capital gains yield and a 10 percent dividend yield. Both stocks sell for $10, have the same risk, and are constant-growth stocks; thus, $\hat{k}_G = \hat{k}_I$ = Dividend yield + Capital gains yield = 15% total return on a before-tax basis.

---

[2]See Myron J. Gordon, "Optimal Investment and Financing Policy," *Journal of Finance,* May 1963, 264–272; John Lintner, "Dividends, Earnings, Leverage, Stock Prices, and the Supply of Capital to Corporations," *Review of Economics and Statistics,* August 1962, 243–269; and Myron J. Gordon and Lawrence I. Gould, "The Cost of Equity Capital: A Reconsideration, *Journal of Finance,* June 1979, 849–861.

[3]Academicians other than MM have also rebutted the "bird-in-the-hand" theory. For example, see Michael Brennan, "A Note on Dividend Irrelevance and the Gordon Valuation Model," *Journal of Finance,* December 1971, 1115–1121.

[4]Robert H. Litzenberger and Krishna Ramaswamy, "The Effects of Personal Taxes and Dividends on Capital Asset Prices," *Journal of Financial Economics,* June 1979, 163–196.

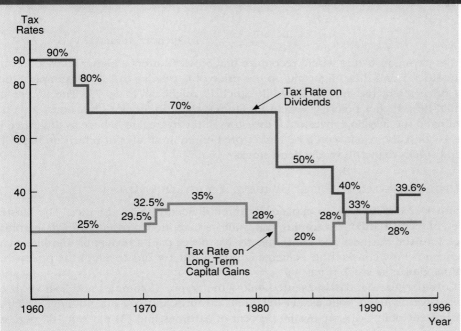

TOP FEDERAL INCOME TAX RATES ON DIVIDENDS (AND INTEREST) AND LONG-TERM CAPITAL GAINS

FIGURE 15-1

SOURCE: *Fortune,* February 6, 1995, 116–117.

If the investor holds the stocks for just over a year and thus is subject to the long-term capital gains tax, the after-tax returns on the two stocks would be as follows:

		DIVIDEND YIELD	+	CAPITAL GAIN	=	TOTAL RETURN
Stock I:	Before-tax return	10.0%		5.0%		15.0%
	Tax (40% and 28%)	− 4.0		− 1.4		− 5.4
	After-tax return	6.0%		3.6%		9.6%
Stock G:	Before-tax return	5.0%		10.0%		15.0%
	Tax (40% and 28%)	− 2.0		− 2.8		− 4.8
	After-tax return	3.0%		7.2%		10.2%

Thus, the after-tax total return on the growth stock is higher than that on the high-dividend (income) stock.

Note too that the after-tax return differential would increase as the holding period increased, because taxes on capital gains are not paid until the gains are realized. At the extreme, when the stocks are kept (in the family) forever, their capital gains taxes are never paid, and the return differential is 2.0 percentage points:

	AFTER-TAX DIVIDEND YIELD	+	AFTER-TAX CAPITAL GAIN	=	AFTER-TAX TOTAL RETURN
Stock I	6.0%		5.0%		11.0%
Stock G	3.0%		10.0%		13.0%
				Difference: Advantage to G =	2.0%

Tax-paying investors would recognize that Stock G offers a higher after-tax return than Stock I, and thus might bid up the price of G relative to I. For example, Stock G's price might rise to $10.25, while Stock I's might fall to $9.75. The end result would be a higher before-tax yield on Stock I than on Stock G, but equal after-tax returns to the marginal investor. If investors in the aggregate behave as described in this section, the result would be higher pre-tax required rates of return on high dividend stocks than on low dividend stocks.

ILLUSTRATION OF THE THREE DIVIDEND POLICY THEORIES

Figure 15-2 can be used to explain the three dividend policy theories. The illustrative company, Hardin Electronics, has from its inception plowed all of its earnings back into the business and consequently has never paid a dividend. Hardin's management is now considering a change in policy, and it wants to adopt the policy that will maximize its stock price.

Consider first the data presented below the graph. Columns 1 and 2 show three alternative dividend policies: (1) Retain all earnings and pay out nothing, which is the present policy, (2) pay out 50 percent of earnings, and (3) pay out 100 percent of earnings. In the example, we assume that the company will have a 15 percent ROE regardless of which payout policy it follows, so with a book value per share of $30, EPS will be 0.15($30) = $4.50 under all payout policies.[5] Given an EPS of $4.50, dividends per share are shown in Column 3 under each payout policy.

Under the assumption of a constant ROE, the growth rate shown in Column 4 will be g = b(ROE) = (% Retained)(ROE), and it will vary from 15 percent at a zero payout to zero at a 100 percent payout. If Hardin pays out 50 percent of its earnings, then its dividend growth rate will be 7.5 percent.

Columns 5, 6, and 7 show how the situation would look if MM's irrelevance theory were correct. Under this theory, neither the stock price nor the cost of equity would be affected by the payout policy — the stock price would remain constant at $30, and k_s would be stable at 15 percent. Note that k_s is found as the sum of the growth rate in Column 4 plus the dividend yield in Column 6.

Columns 8, 9, and 10 show how the situation would look if the bird-in-the-hand theory were true. Under this theory, investors prefer dividends, and the more dividends the company pays out, the higher its stock price and the lower its cost of equity. In this example, the bird-in-the-hand argument indicates that adopting a 100

---

[5]When the three theories were developed, it was assumed that a company's investment opportunities would be held constant and that if the company increased its dividends, its capital budget could be funded by selling common stock. Conversely, if a high-payout company lowered its payout to the point where retained earnings exceeded good investment opportunities, it was assumed that the company would repurchase shares. Transactions costs were assumed to be zero. We maintain those assumptions in our example.

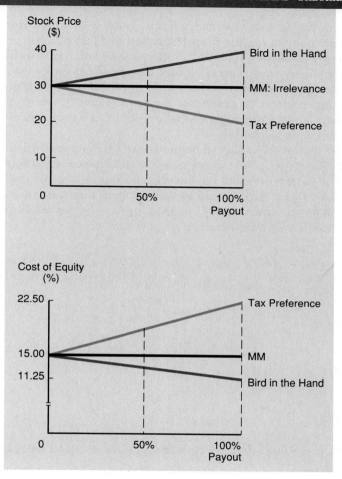

				POSSIBLE SITUATIONS								
				MM			BIRD-IN-THE-HAND			TAX PREFERENCE		
PERCENT PAYOUT (1)	PERCENT RETAINED (2)	DPS (3)	g (4)	P_0 (5)	D/P_0 (6)	k_s (7)	P_0 (8)	D/P_0 (9)	k_s (10)	P_0 (11)	D/P_0 (12)	k_s (13)
0%	100%	$0.00	15.0%	$30	0.0%	15.0%	$30	0.00%	15.00%	$30	0.0%	15.0%
50	50	2.25	7.5	30	7.5	15.0	35	6.43	13.93	25	9.0	16.5
100	0	4.50	0.0	30	15.0	15.0	40	11.25	11.25	20	22.5	22.5

NOTES:
1. Book value = Initial market value = $30 per share.
2. ROE = 15%.
3. EPS = $30(0.15) = $4.50.
4. g = b(ROE) = (% retained)(ROE).
5. k_s = Dividend yield + Growth rate.

percent payout policy would cause the stock price to rise from $30 to $40 and the cost of equity to decline from 15 percent to 11.25 percent.

Finally, Columns 11, 12, and 13 show the situation that would exist if the tax preference theory were correct. Under this theory, investors want companies to retain earnings and thus provide returns in the form of lower-taxed capital gains rather than higher-taxed dividends. If the tax preference theory were correct, then an increase in the dividend payout ratio would cause the stock price to decline and the cost of equity to rise.

The data in the table can be plotted to produce the two graphs shown in Figure 15-2. The upper graph shows how the stock price reacts to dividend policy under each of the theories, and the lower graph shows how the cost of equity is affected. Thus, the three theories lead to very different conclusions. However, we cannot at this point say which theory is most correct—before reaching any conclusions, we must examine the available empirical evidence.

SELF-TEST QUESTIONS

Differentiate between the dividend irrelevance theory, the bird-in-the-hand theory, and the tax preference theory. Use a graph such as Figure 15-2 to illustrate your answer.

List the assumptions Modigliani and Miller used to "prove" their dividend irrelevance theory.

How did the bird-in-the-hand theory get its name?

In what sense does MM's theory represent a middle ground between the other two theories?

TESTS OF THE DIVIDEND THEORIES

In the preceding section, we presented three dividend theories:

1. MM argued that dividend policy is irrelevant; that is, it does not affect a firm's value or its cost of capital. Thus, according to MM, there is no optimal dividend policy—one dividend policy is as good as any other. MM's position is called the *irrelevance theory*.

2. Gordon and Lintner disagreed with MM, arguing that dividends are less risky than capital gains, so a firm should set a high dividend payout ratio and offer a high dividend yield in order to maximize its stock price. This is called the *bird-in-the-hand theory*.

3. A third position is that investors prefer retained earnings to dividends because of the tax preference given to capital gains. This *tax preference theory* suggests that companies should hold dividend payments to low levels if they want to maximize stock prices.

The three theories offer contradictory advice to corporate managers. MM say dividend policy doesn't matter, Gordon-Lintner say set a high payout, and the tax differential advocates say set a low payout. Which theory should we believe?

Two types of empirical tests have been conducted in an attempt to determine the true relationship between dividend policy and required returns. In theory, one could take a sample of companies which have different dividend policies, thus different dividend yield and growth rate components, and plot them in graphs such as those shown in Figure 15-3. Here we show three possible results. Only one result could actually exist, but we show three possibilities on one graph. If the plot resembled the center line in the graph, then, for the sample of firms, $\hat{k}_s = k_s = D_1/P_0 + g =$ a constant 13.3% regardless of the dividend payout. Both the X and Y axes have an intercept of 13.3 percent, and in this case, the total return would be a constant whether it comes entirely as a dividend yield (the Y axis intercept), entirely as expected capital gains (the X axis intercept), or as any combination of the two. The line has a slope of −1.0, and if the test actually resulted in this line, then it would support the MM irrelevance hypothesis.

If the plot looked like the upper line in Figure 15-3, with a slope less negative (less steep) than −1.0 (say, −0.8), then the test would support the Gordon-Lintner bird-in-the-hand hypothesis. Here investors would require a larger total return if the company provided a larger capital gains component, g, than dividend yield, D_1/P_0. An all-dividend stock would have $k_s = 13.3\%$, while a stock which provides only capital gains would have $k_s = 15.0\%$. Thus, more than 1 percent of additional high-risk g is required to offset a 1 percent reduction in the low-risk dividend yield.

Finally, if the tax differential theory were correct, the plot would resemble the lower line in Figure 15-3, with a slope more negative (steeper) than −1.0 (say, −1.2). Here the tax rate advantage coupled with the deferral of capital gains taxes causes investors to favor capital gains over dividends. In this situation, a 100 percent payout stock might have $k_s = 13.3\%$, while a similar stock whose returns all come as capital gains might have $k_s = 11.5\%$. Thus, less than 1 percent of lightly taxed g would be required to offset a 1 percent reduction in highly taxed dividend yield.

ALTERNATIVE THEORIES OF THE EFFECTS OF DIVIDEND POLICY FIGURE 15-3

In fact, when such tests have been conducted, the slope of the regression line is found to be about -1.0. This seems to refute both bird-in-the-hand and tax differential advocates and to support MM. However, statistical problems prevent us from saying that these tests *prove* that MM are right and that dividend policy does not affect k_s. The two statistical problems are these: (1) For a valid statistical test, things other than dividend policy must be held constant; that is, the sample companies must differ only in their dividend payout policies. (2) We must be able to measure with a high degree of accuracy the expected growth rates for the sample firms.[6] Neither of these conditions actually holds: we cannot find a set of publicly owned firms that differ only in their dividend policies, nor can we obtain precise estimates of the growth rates which the marginal investor expects. Therefore, we cannot determine with much precision what effect, if any, dividend policy has on the cost of equity. Our conclusion is that this particular type of test is not capable of resolving the dividend policy riddle.

Academic researchers have also studied the dividend issue from a CAPM perspective. These studies hypothesize that required returns are a function of both market risk as measured by beta and dividend yield. If so, then a stock's required return, k_i, could be expressed as follows:

$$k_i = k_{RF} + (k_M - k_{RF})b_i + (DY_i - DY_A)\lambda_i. \qquad \text{15-1}$$

Here DY_i is the dividend yield of Stock i, DY_A is the dividend yield of an average stock, and λ_i is the dividend impact coefficient. Researchers have tested Equation 15-1 by regressing historical values of k_{RF}, k_M, DY_i, and DY_A against historical values of k_i. If the coefficient of λ_i turns out to be zero, dividend yield would not appear to affect required returns and MM would be supported. If λ_i were positive, then investors would appear to require a higher return on stocks with high dividend yields, as the tax preference theory predicts. If λ_i were negative, this would support the bird-in-the-hand theory.

The results of this line of research have been mixed. Litzenberger and Ramaswamy showed, using NYSE data from 1936 through 1977, that stocks with high dividend yields did have higher total returns than did stocks with low dividend yields, after adjusting for market risk.[7] Their study indicated that the required rate of return increased by about 0.24 percentage points for every percentage point increase in dividend yield. However, other studies have reached contradictory conclusions, namely, that the λ_i term is zero and consequently that dividend yield has no effect on required returns.[8]

---

[6]Also, the expected future growth rate must be constant, or we must measure g as an average of expected future growth rates.

[7]See Litzenberger and Ramaswamy, "Effects of Personal Taxes," 163–196.

[8]For example, see Fischer Black and Myron Scholes, "The Effects of Dividend Yield and Dividend Policy on Common Stock Prices and Returns," *Journal of Financial Economics,* May 1974, 1–22.

The major problem with the CAPM studies is that they used historical earned rates of return as proxies for expected future returns, and with such a poor proxy, the tests are almost bound to have mixed results. *Thus, these CAPM empirical tests, like the DCF-based tests, have not led to definitive conclusions as to which dividend theory is most correct. The issue is still unresolved.*

What are the two types of empirical tests that have been used to try to identify the correct dividend policy theory?

What are the results of the empirical tests?

OTHER DIVIDEND POLICY ISSUES

Before we discuss dividend policy in practice, we need to examine three other issues that could affect our views toward the three theories. These issues are (1) the information content, or signaling, hypothesis, (2) the clientele effect, and (3) the relationship between dividend policy and agency costs.

INFORMATION CONTENT, OR SIGNALING, HYPOTHESIS

When MM set forth their dividend irrelevance theory, they assumed, among other things, that everyone — investors and managers alike — has identical information regarding the firm's future earnings and dividend stream. In reality, however, investors have conflicting views on both the level of future dividend payments and the degree of uncertainty inherent in those payments, and managers often have better information about future prospects than public stockholders. This is the same sort of *asymmetric information* situation that we discussed in Chapter 14 in connection with the announcement of new stock issues.

It has been observed that an increase in its dividend is often accompanied by an increase in the price of a stock, while a dividend cut generally leads to a stock price decline. This could indicate that investors, in the aggregate, prefer dividends to capital gains. However, MM argued differently. They noted the well-established fact that corporations are reluctant to cut dividends, hence do not raise dividends unless they anticipate high earnings in the future. Thus, MM argued that a higher-than-expected dividend increase is a "signal" to investors that the firm's management forecasts good future earnings.[9] Conversely, a dividend reduction, or a smaller-than-expected increase, is a signal that management is forecasting poor earnings in the future. Thus, MM argued that investors' reactions to changes in dividend policy do not

---

[9]Stephen Ross has suggested that managers can use capital structure as well as dividends to give signals concerning firms' future prospects. For example, a firm with good earnings prospects can carry more debt than a similar firm with poor earnings prospects. This theory, called *incentive signaling,* rests on the premise that signals with cash-based variables (either debt interest or dividends) cannot be mimicked by unsuccessful firms because such firms do not have the future cash-generating power to maintain the announced interest or dividend payment. Thus, investors are more likely to believe a glowing verbal report when it is accompanied by a dividend increase or a debt-financed expansion program. See Stephen A. Ross, "The Determination of Financial Structure: The Incentive-Signaling Approach," *The Bell Journal of Economics,* Spring 1977, 23–40.

necessarily show that investors prefer dividends to retained earnings. Rather, the fact that price changes follow dividend actions simply indicated to MM that there is an important *information*, or *signaling, content* in dividend announcements.

Like most other aspects of dividend policy, empirical studies of signaling have had mixed results. There is clearly some information content in dividend announcements. However, it is difficult to tell whether the stock price changes that follow increases or decreases in dividends reflect only signaling effects or both signaling and dividend preference effects. Still, signaling effects should be considered when a firm is contemplating a change in dividend policy.

CLIENTELE EFFECT

Different groups, or *clienteles,* of stockholders prefer different dividend payout policies. For example, retired individuals and university endowment funds generally prefer current income, so they may want the firm to pay out a high percentage of its earnings. Such investors (and also pension funds) are often in a low or even zero tax bracket, so taxes are of no concern. On the other hand, stockholders in their peak earning years might prefer reinvestment, because they have less need for current investment income and would simply reinvest any dividends received, after first paying income taxes on the dividend income.

If a firm retains and reinvests income rather than paying dividends, those stockholders who need current income would be disadvantaged. The value of their stock might increase, but they would still be forced to go to the trouble and expense of selling off some of their shares to obtain cash. Also, some institutional investors (or trustees for individuals) would be precluded from selling stock and then "spending capital." On the other hand, stockholders who are saving rather than spending dividends, might favor the low dividend policy, for the less the firm pays out in dividends, the less these stockholders will have to pay in current taxes, and the less trouble and expense they will have to go through to reinvest their after-tax dividends. Therefore, investors who want current investment income should own shares in high dividend payout firms, while investors with no need for current investment income should own shares in low dividend payout firms. For example, investors seeking high current income might invest in electric utilities, which averaged a 79 percent payout from 1991 through 1995, while those favoring growth could invest in the semiconductor industry, which averaged a low 7 percent payout.

To the extent that stockholders can switch firms, a firm can change from one dividend payout policy to another and then let stockholders who do not like the new policy sell to other investors who do. However, switching may be inefficient because of (1) brokerage costs, (2) the likelihood that stockholders who are selling will have to pay capital gains taxes (the "lock-in effect"), and (3) a possible shortage of investors who like the firm's newly adopted dividend policy. Thus, management might be reluctant to change its dividend policy, because a change might cause current shareholders to sell their stock, forcing the stock price down. Such a price decline might be temporary, but it might also be permanent — if few new investors are attracted by the new dividend policy, then the stock price would remain depressed. Of course, the new policy might attract an even larger clientele than the firm had before, in which case the stock would rise.

Evidence from several studies suggests that there is in fact a clientele effect.[10] MM and others have argued that one clientele is as good as another, so the existence of a clientele effect does not necessarily imply that one dividend policy is better than any other. MM may be wrong, though, and neither they nor anyone else has offered proof that the aggregate makeup of investors permits firms to disregard clientele effects. This issue, like most others in the dividend arena, is still up in the air.

DIVIDEND POLICY AND AGENCY COSTS

One of the most perplexing issues in dividend policy is why firms pay dividends and almost simultaneously issue new securities. Since the cost of issuing securities can be substantial, total corporate costs would be minimized by paying dividends only if investment opportunities were so poor that the full amount of net income could not be productively reinvested within the firm.[11]

One potential answer to this puzzle is the signaling value inherent in dividends. However, it is hard to imagine that the value produced by signaling is greater than the costs associated with new security issues. A second potential explanation for paying dividends relates to agency costs.[12] As we discussed in Chapter 1, an agency conflict exists between stockholders and managers — stockholders, as owners of the firm, want managers to maximize shareholders' value, but managers may be more motivated to act in their own best interests.

Because of this potential agency conflict, stockholders need to incur agency costs to monitor managerial actions. However, for large, publicly held corporations, it is difficult for stockholders to act collectively to monitor managerial actions, hence it is likely that too little monitoring will take place. In this situation, the most efficient way to monitor managerial actions is to have some third party, similar to the trustee who monitors managerial actions on behalf of bondholders, act on shareholders' behalf. (The board of directors is supposed to perform this function, but board members often side with managers when conflicts arise.)

The monitoring problem is substantially reduced when firms must frequently raise external capital. When a firm issues stocks or bonds, its operating and financial decisions are scrutinized by the investment bankers who underwrite the issue, by analysts at rating agencies, by security analysts at retail brokerage houses, and, ultimately, by investors before they purchase the new securities. Whereas a firm's existing investors can influence managerial actions only by voting or selling their securities, new investors can examine managerial behavior and then refuse to buy the new securities if they detect questionable managerial actions. In effect, new investors are more efficient than old investors in monitoring managerial behavior, so agency problems are reduced when firms must continuously raise external capital.

The role of dividend policy in capital market monitoring should be apparent. For any given level of investment, the higher the dividend payout, the more frequently

---

[10]For example, see R. Richardson Pettit, "Taxes, Transactions Costs and the Clientele Effect of Dividends," *The Journal of Financial Economics,* December 1977, 419-436.

[11]We will discuss this concept, called the *residual dividend policy,* in a later section.

[12]For an example of this literature, see Frank H. Easterbrook, "Two Agency-Cost Explanations of Dividends," *American Economic Review,* September 1984, 650-659.

the firm must issue new securities. A higher payout thus forces firms to undergo the frequent scrutiny of the capital markets, and this appraisal process mitigates the agency problem. If the costs involved in paying dividends, including the tax effects on stockholders and the flotation costs associated with security issues, are less than the value inherent in the additional monitoring, then large dividend payouts make sense.

Before leaving this section, we should note another agency issue that has been raised in support of higher dividend payouts — the argument that managers with high levels of free cash flow are likely to make unprofitable investments at stockholders' expense. This is undoubtedly a correct position, but we regard it as more of an investment policy problem than a dividend policy decision. In other words, if proper capital budgeting procedures are followed, the right investment choices will be made, regardless of the firm's dividend policy.

SELF-TEST QUESTIONS

Briefly describe the information content, or signaling, hypothesis.

What is the clientele effect?

How could the signaling hypothesis and the presence of dividend clienteles affect the dividend policy decision?

How might agency considerations justify a high dividend payout policy?

DIVIDEND STABILITY

As we noted at the beginning of the chapter, the decision as to how stable a firm's dividend should be is important. Profits and cash flows vary over time, as do investment opportunities. Taken alone, this suggests that corporations should vary their dividends over time, increasing them when cash flows are large and the need for funds is low and lowering them when cash is in short supply relative to investment opportunities. However, many stockholders rely on dividends to meet expenses, and they would be seriously inconvenienced if the dividend stream were unstable. Further, reducing dividends to make funds available for capital investment could send incorrect signals, and that could drive down stock prices. Thus, maximizing its stock price requires a firm to balance its internal needs for funds against the needs and desires of its stockholders.

How should this balance be struck; that is, how stable and dependable should a firm attempt to make its dividends? It is impossible to give a definitive answer to this question, but the following points are relevant:

1. Virtually every publicly owned company makes a five- to ten-year financial forecast of earnings and dividends. Such forecasts are not made public — they are used for internal planning purposes. However, security analysts construct similar forecasts and make them available to investors; see *Value Line* for an example. Further, every internal five- to ten-year corporate forecast we have seen for a "normal" company projects a trend of higher earnings and dividends. Both managers and investors know that economic conditions may cause actual results to differ from forecasted results, but "normal" companies expect to grow.

2. Years ago, when inflation was not persistent, the term "stable dividend policy" meant a policy of paying the same dollar dividend year after year. AT&T was a prime example of a company with a stable dividend policy — it paid $9 per year ($2.25 per quarter) for 25 straight years. Today, though, most companies and stockholders expect earnings to grow over time as a result of earnings retention and inflation. Further, dividends are normally expected to grow more or less in line with earnings. Thus, today a "stable dividend policy" generally means increasing the dividend at a reasonably steady rate. For example, Rubbermaid made this statement in a recent annual report:

> Dividends per share were increased . . . for the 34th consecutive year. . . . Our goal is to increase sales, earnings, and earnings per share by 15% per year, while achieving a 21% return on beginning shareholders' equity. It is also the Company's objective to pay approximately 30% of current year's earnings as dividends, which will permit us to retain sufficient capital to provide for future growth.

Rubbermaid used the word "approximately" in discussing its payout ratio, because even if earnings vary a bit from the target level, the company still planned to increase the dividend by the target growth rate. Even though Rubbermaid did not mention the dividend growth rate in the statement, analysts can calculate the growth rate and see that it is the same 15 percent as indicated for sales and earnings:

$$g = b \text{ (ROE)}$$
$$= (1 - \text{Payout}) \text{ (ROE)}$$
$$= 0.7(21\%) \approx 15\%.$$

Here b is the fraction of earnings that is retained, or 1.0 minus the payout ratio.

Companies with volatile earnings and cash flows would be reluctant to make a commitment to increase the dividend each year, so they would not make such a detailed statement. Even so, most companies would like to be able to exhibit the kind of stability Rubbermaid has shown, and they try to come as close to it as they can.

Dividend stability has two components: (1) How dependable is the growth rate, and (2) can we count on at least receiving the current dividend in the future? The most stable policy, from an investor's standpoint, is that of a firm whose dividend growth rate is predictable—such a company's total return (dividend yield plus capital gains yield) would be relatively stable over the long run, and its stock would be a good hedge against inflation. The second most stable policy is where stockholders can be reasonably sure that the current dividend will not be reduced—it may not grow at a steady rate, but management will probably be able and willing to avoid cutting the dividend. The least stable situation is where earnings and cash flows are so volatile that investors cannot even count on the company to maintain the current dividend over a typical business cycle.

3. Most observers believe that dividend stability is desirable, even though statistical problems prevent empirical tests from proving the point. If this position

is correct, investors prefer stocks that pay more predictable dividends to stocks expected to pay the same average amount of dividends but to pay them in a more erratic manner. This means that the cost of equity will be minimized, and the stock price maximized, if a firm stabilizes its dividends as much as possible.

SELF-TEST   What does the term "stable dividend policy" mean?
QUESTIONS   What are the two components of dividend stability?

ESTABLISHING THE DIVIDEND POLICY IN PRACTICE

In the preceding sections we saw that investors may or may not prefer dividends to capital gains, but they do prefer predictable to unpredictable dividends. Given this situation, how should firms set their basic dividend policies? For example, how should a company like Rubbermaid establish the specific percentage of earnings it will pay out? Rubbermaid's target is 30 percent, but why not 40 percent, 50 percent, or some other percentage? In this section, we describe how firms actually set their dividend policies.

SETTING THE TARGET PAYOUT RATIO: THE RESIDUAL DIVIDEND MODEL[13]

The optimal payout ratio is a function of four factors: (1) investors' preferences for dividends versus capital gains, (2) the firm's investment opportunities, (3) its target capital structure, and (4) the availability and cost of external capital. The last three elements are combined in what we call the *residual dividend model,* under which a firm follows these four steps when deciding its target payout ratio: (1) It determines the optimal capital budget; (2) it determines the amount of equity needed to finance that budget, given its target capital structure; (3) it uses retained earnings to supply this equity to the extent possible; and (4) it pays dividends only if more earnings are available than are needed to support the optimal capital budget. The word *residual* implies "leftover," and the residual policy implies that dividends are paid out of "leftover" earnings.

We saw in Chapter 8 that the cost of retained earnings is an *opportunity cost* which reflects rates of return available to equity investors. If a firm's stockholders could buy other stocks of equal risk and obtain a 12 percent dividend-plus-capital-gains yield, then 12 percent is the firm's cost of retained earnings. The cost of new outside equity raised by selling common stock is higher because of flotation costs, including both underwriting costs and any downward price pressure resulting from "negative signals" when the stock offering is announced.

---

[13]The term "payout ratio" can be interpreted in two ways: (1) the conventional way, where the payout ratio means the percentage of net income to common paid out as cash dividends, or (2) the percentage of net income distributed to stockholders as dividends and through share repurchases. In this section, we assume that no repurchases occur. Increasingly, though, firms are using the residual model to determine "distributions to shareholders" and then making a separate decision as to the form of that distribution. Further, an increasing percentage of the distribution is in the form of repurchases.

Most firms have a target capital structure that calls for at least some debt, so new financing is done partly with debt and partly with equity. As long as the firm finances with the optimal mix of debt and equity, and provided it uses only internally generated equity (retained earnings), then its marginal cost of each new dollar of capital will be minimized. Internally generated equity is available for financing a certain amount of new investment, but beyond that amount, the firm must turn to new common stock. At the point where new stock must be sold, the cost of equity, and consequently the weighted average cost of capital (WACC), rises.

These concepts, which were developed in Chapters 8 and 11, are illustrated in Figure 15-4 with data from the Dallas Oil Company. Dallas has a WACC of 10 percent as long as its equity is from retained earnings, but its MCC schedule begins to rise at the point where new stock must be sold. Dallas has $60 million of earnings and a 40 percent optimal debt ratio. Provided it does not pay any cash dividends, Dallas can make net investments (investments in addition to asset replacements financed from depreciation) of $100 million, consisting of $60 million from retained earnings plus $40 million of new debt supported by the retained earnings, at a 10 percent cost of capital. Therefore, its WACC is *potentially* constant at 10 percent up to $100 million of capital. Beyond $100 million, the WACC must increase because the firm must use more expensive new common stock.

Of course, if Dallas does not retain all of its earnings, its WACC will begin to rise before $100 million. For example, if Dallas retained only $30 million, then its WACC would begin to rise at $30 million retained earnings + $20 million debt = $50 million.

Now suppose Dallas's director of capital budgeting constructs several investment opportunity schedules and plots them on a graph. In Figure 15-5, we combine these investment opportunity schedules with the cost of capital schedule. The point

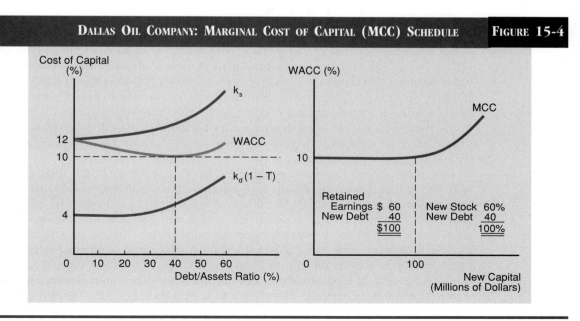

DALLAS OIL COMPANY: MARGINAL COST OF CAPITAL (MCC) SCHEDULE   FIGURE 15-4

| FIGURE 15-5 | DALLAS OIL COMPANY: COMBINED IOS AND MCC SCHEDULES |

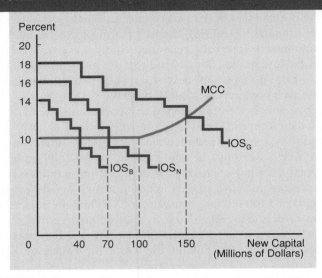

where the relevant IOS curve cuts the MCC curve defines the firm's corporate cost of capital and its optimal level of new investment. When investment opportunities are relatively bad (IOS$_B$), the optimal level of investment is $40 million; when opportunities are normal (IOS$_N$), $70 million should be invested; and when opportunities are relatively good (IOS$_G$), Dallas should make new investments in the amount of $150 million.

If IOS$_G$ is the appropriate schedule, the company should raise and invest $150 million. Dallas has $60 million in earnings and a 40 percent target debt ratio. Thus, it can finance $100 million, consisting of $60 million of retained earnings plus $40 million of new debt, at an average cost of 10 percent if it retains all of its earnings. The remaining $50 million will include external equity and thus have a higher cost. If Dallas pays out part of its earnings in dividends, it will have to begin to use costly new common stock earlier than need be, so its MCC schedule will rise earlier than it otherwise would. *This suggests that, under the conditions of IOS$_G$, Dallas should retain all of its earnings. According to the residual policy, Dallas's payout ratio should be zero if IOS$_G$ applies.*

Under the normal conditions represented by IOS$_N$, however, Dallas should invest only $70 million. How should this investment be financed? First, notice that if Dallas retained all of its earnings, $60 million, it would need to sell only $10 million of new debt. However, if Dallas retained $60 million and sold only $10 million of new debt, it would move away from its target capital structure. To stay on target, Dallas must finance 60 percent of the required $70 million by equity — retained earnings — and 40 percent by debt; this means Dallas must retain $42 million and sell $28 million of new debt. If Dallas retains only $42 million of its $60 million total earnings, it must distribute the residual, $18 million, to its stockholders. Thus, its optimal payout ratio under IOS$_N$ is $18/$60 = 30%.

Under the conditions shown in IOS$_B$, Dallas should invest only $40 million. Because it has $60 million in earnings, it could finance the entire $40 million out of retained earnings and still have $20 million available for dividends. Should this be done? Under our assumptions, this would not be a good decision, because Dallas would move away from its optimal capital structure. To stay at the 40 percent target debt/assets ratio, Dallas must retain $24 million of earnings and sell $16 million of debt. When the $24 million of retained earnings is subtracted from the $60 million total earnings, Dallas is left with a residual of $36 million, the amount that should be paid out in dividends. Thus, the payout ratio as prescribed by the residual policy is $36/$60 = 60%.

Since both the IOS schedule and the earnings level will surely vary from year to year, strict adherence to the residual dividend policy would result in dividend variability — one year the firm might declare zero dividends because investment opportunities were good, but the next year it might pay a large dividend because investment opportunities were poor. Similarly, fluctuating earnings would also lead to variable dividends even if investment opportunities were stable over time. As we noted earlier, variable dividend payments are less desirable than stable dividends, and varying the dividend payments could also lead to false signals and a loss of investor confidence in the firm. *Therefore, the residual model can be used as a guide for establishing the long-run target payout ratio, but the model should not be adhered to strictly on a year-to-year basis.*

Companies use the residual dividend model as discussed above to gain an understanding of the determinants of an optimal dividend policy, but they typically use a computerized financial forecasting model as the basis for the target payout ratio. Most larger corporations forecast their financial statements over the next five or ten years. Information on projected capital expenditures and working capital requirements is entered into the model, along with sales forecasts, profit margins, depreciation, and the other elements required to forecast cash flows. The target capital structure is also specified, and the model shows the amount of debt and equity that will be required to meet the forecasted capital requirements while maintaining the target capital structure.

Then, dividend payments are introduced. Naturally, the higher the payout ratio, the greater the required external equity. Most companies then use the model to find a dividend pattern over the forecast period (generally five years) that will provide sufficient equity to support the capital budget without having to sell new common stock or to move the capital structure ratios outside the optimal range. The end result might include a statement, in a memo from the financial vice-president to the chairman of the board, such as the following:

> We have forecasted the total market demand for our products, what our share of the market is likely to be, and our required investments in capital assets and working capital. Using this information, we have developed projected balance sheets and income statements for the period 1997–2001.
>
> Our 1996 dividends totalled $50 million, or $2 per share. On the basis of projected earnings, cash flows, and capital requirements, we can increase the dividend by 8 percent per year. This is consistent with a payout ratio of 42 percent, on average, over the forecast period. Any faster dividend growth rate (or higher payout) would require us to sell common stock, cut the capital budget, or raise the debt ratio. Any slower growth rate would

lead to a buildup of the common equity ratio. Therefore, I recommend that the Board increase the dividend for 1997 by 8 percent, to $2.16, and that it plan for similar increases in the future.

Events over the next 5 years will undoubtedly lead to differences between our forecasts and actual results. If and when changes occur, we will want to reexamine our position. However, I am confident that we can meet any random cash shortfalls by increasing our borrowings — we have unused debt capacity which gives us flexibility in this regard.

We ran the corporate model under several recession scenarios. If the economy really crashes, our earnings will not cover the dividend. However, in all "reasonable" scenarios cash flows do cover the dividend. I know the Board does not want to push the dividend up to a level where we would have to cut it under bad economic conditions. Our model runs indicate, though, that the $2.16 dividend can be maintained under any reasonable set of forecasts. Only if we increased the dividend to over $3 would we be seriously exposed to the danger of having to cut the dividend.

I might also note that *Value Line* and most other analysts' reports are forecasting that our dividends will grow in the 6 to 8 percent range. Thus, if we go to $2.16, we will be at the high end of the range, which should give our stock a boost. With takeover rumors so widespread, getting the stock up a bit would make us all breathe a little easier.

Finally, we considered a stock repurchase program, under which we would reduce the dividend payout ratio (and the dividend growth rate) and use the funds so generated to buy our stock on the open market. Such a program has several advantages, but it would also have drawbacks. I do not recommend that we institute a stock repurchase program at this time. However, if our free cash flows exceed our forecasts, I would recommend that we use these surpluses to buy back stock. Also, we plan to continue looking into a regular repurchase program, and I may recommend such a program in the future.

This company, like Rubbermaid, has very stable operations, so it can plan its dividends with a fairly high degree of confidence. Other companies, especially those in cyclical industries, have difficulty maintaining in bad times a dividend that is really too low in good times. Such companies set a very low "regular" dividend and then supplement it with an "extra" dividend when times are good. General Motors, Ford, and other auto companies have followed this *low-regular-dividend-plus-extras* policy in the past. Each company announced a low regular dividend that it was sure could be maintained "through hell or high water," and stockholders could count on receiving this dividend under all conditions. Then, when times were good and profits and cash flows were high, each company paid a clearly designated extra dividend. Investors recognized that the extras might not be maintained in the future, so they did not interpret them as a signal that the companies' earnings were going up permanently, nor did they take the elimination of the extra as a negative signal. In recent years, however, the auto companies have replaced the "extras" in their low-regular-dividend-plus-extras policy with stock repurchases.

EARNINGS, CASH FLOWS, AND DIVIDENDS

We normally think of earnings as being the primary determinant of dividends, but in reality cash flows are even more important. This situation is revealed in Figure 15-6, which gives data for Chevron Corporation from 1972 through 1996. Chevron's dividends increased steadily from 1972 to 1981; during that period both earnings and

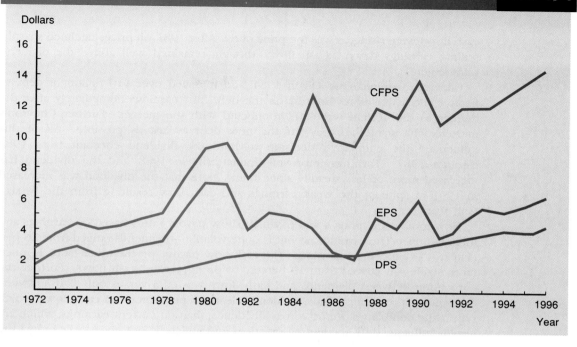

CHEVRON: EARNINGS, CASH FLOWS, AND DIVIDENDS, 1972–1996   FIGURE 15-6

YEAR (1)	DIVIDENDS PER SHARE (2)	EARNINGS PER SHARE (3)	EARNINGS PAYOUT (4)	CASH FLOW PER SHARE (5)	CASH FLOW PAYOUT (6)
1972	$0.73	$1.61	45%	$ 2.72	27%
1973	0.78	2.49	31	3.68	21
1974	0.96	2.86	34	4.36	22
1975	1.00	2.28	44	4.00	25
1976	1.08	2.59	42	4.22	26
1977	1.18	2.98	40	4.68	25
1978	1.28	3.24	40	5.06	25
1979	1.45	5.22	28	7.29	20
1980	1.80	7.02	26	9.26	19
1981	2.20	6.96	32	9.61	23
1982	2.40	4.03	60	7.35	33
1983	2.40	5.15	47	8.93	27
1984	2.40	4.94	49	9.00	27
1985	2.40	4.19	57	12.76	19
1986	2.40	2.63	91	9.86	24
1987	2.40	2.13	113	9.47	25
1988	2.55	4.86	52	11.97	21
1989	2.80	4.16	67	11.33	25
1990	2.95	6.02	49	13.75	21
1991	3.25	3.69	88	11.14	29
1992	3.30	4.70	70	12.88	26
1993	3.50	5.60	62	13.12	27
1994	3.70	5.20	71	12.66	29
1995	3.70	6.20	60	13.80	27
1996 (est.)	4.00	7.00	57	15.00	27

NOTE: For consistency, data have not been adjusted for a two-for-one split in 1994.

cash flows were rising, as was the price of oil. After 1981, oil prices declined sharply, pulling earnings down. Cash flows, though, remained well above the dividend requirement.

Chevron acquired Gulf Oil in 1984, and it issued over $10 billion of debt to finance the acquisition. Interest on the debt hurt earnings immediately after the merger, as did certain write-offs connected with the merger. Further, Chevron's management wanted to pay off the new debt as fast as possible. All of this influenced the company's decision to hold the dividend constant from 1982 through 1987. Earnings improved dramatically in 1988, and the dividend has increased more or less steadily since then. Note that the dividend was increased in 1991 in spite of the weak earnings and cash flow resulting from the Persian Gulf War.

Now look at Columns 4 and 6, which show payout ratios based on earnings and on cash flows. The earnings payout is quite volatile — dividends ranged from 26 percent to 113 percent of earnings. The cash flow payout, on the other hand, is much more stable — it ranged from 19 percent to 33 percent of cash flows. Further, the correlation between dividends and cash flows was 0.93 versus only 0.48 between dividends and earnings. Thus, dividends clearly depend more on cash flows, which reflect the company's *ability* to pay dividends, than on current earnings, which are heavily influenced by accounting practices and which do not necessarily reflect the ability to pay dividends.

PAYMENT PROCEDURES

Dividends are normally paid quarterly, and if conditions permit, the dividend is increased once each year. For example, Randolph Controls paid $0.50 per quarter in 1996, or at an annual rate of $2.00. In common financial parlance, we say that Randolph's *regular quarterly dividend* was $0.50, and its *annual dividend* was $2.00.

The actual payment procedure is as follows:

1. **Declaration date.** On the declaration date — say, on November 15 — the directors meet and declare the regular dividend, issuing a statement similar to the following: "On November 15, 1996, the directors of Randolph Controls met and declared the regular quarterly dividend of 50 cents per share, payable to holders of record on December 13, payment to be made on January 3, 1997. For accounting purposes, the declared dividend becomes an actual liability on the declaration date, and if a balance sheet were constructed, the amount $0.50 \times$ (Number of shares outstanding) would appear as a current liability, and retained earnings would be reduced by a like amount.

2. **Holder-of-record date.** At the close of business on the holder-of-record date, December 13, the company closes its stock transfer books and makes up a list of shareholders as of that date. If Randolph Controls is notified of the sale and transfer of some stock before 5 P.M. on December 13, then the new owner receives the dividend. However, if notification is received on or after December 14, the previous owner gets the dividend check.

3. **Ex-dividend date.** Suppose Jean Buyer buys 100 shares of stock from John Seller on December 11. Will the company be notified of the transfer in time to list Buyer as the new owner and thus pay the dividend to her? To avoid conflict, the securities industry has set up a convention of declaring that the right to the dividend remains with the stock until four business days prior to the holder-of-record date. The date when the right to the dividend leaves the stock — four days before the holder-of-record date — is called the *ex-dividend date.* In this case, the ex-dividend date is December 9:

	Friday,	December 6, Buyer would receive dividend
Ex-dividend date:	Monday,	December 9, Seller will receive dividend
	Tuesday,	December 10
	Wednesday,	December 11
	Thursday,	December 12
Holder-of-record date:	Friday,	December 13

Therefore, if Buyer is to receive the dividend, she must buy the stock on or before December 6. If she buys it on December 9 or later, Seller will receive the dividend.

Randolph Controls's dividend amounts to $0.50, so the ex-dividend date is important. Barring fluctuations in the stock market, one would normally expect the price of a stock to drop by approximately the amount of the dividend on the ex-dividend date. Thus, if Randolph Controls closed at $30½ on Friday, December 6, it would probably open at about $30 on Monday, December 9.

4. **Payment date.** The company actually mails the checks to the holders of record on January 3, the payment date.

Explain the residual dividend model.
How do firms use planning models to help set dividend policy?
Which are more critical to the dividend decision, earnings or cash flows?
Explain the procedures used to actually pay the dividend.

SELF-TEST QUESTIONS

CHANGING DIVIDEND POLICIES

From our previous discussion, it is obvious that firms should try to establish a rational dividend policy and then stick with it. Dividend policy can be changed, but this can cause problems because such changes can inconvenience the firm's existing stockholders, send unintended signals, and convey the impression of dividend instability, all of which can have negative implications for stock prices. Still, economic circumstances do change, and occasionally such changes dictate that a firm alter its dividend policy.

One of the most striking examples of a dividend policy change occurred in May 1994, when the FPL Group, a utility holding company whose primary subsidiary is

Florida Power & Light, announced it would cut its regular quarterly dividend from $0.62 per share to $0.42. At the same time, though, FPL stated it would buy back 10 million of its common shares over the next three years to bolster its stock price.[14] Here is the text of the letter to its stockholders in which FPL announced these changes:

> Dear Shareholder,
>
> Over the past several years, we have been working hard to enhance shareholder value by aligning our strategy with a rapidly changing business environment. . . . The Energy Policy Act of 1992 has brought permanent changes to the electric industry. Although we have taken effective and sometimes painful steps to prepare for these changes, one critical problem remains. Our dividend payout ratio of 90 percent — the percentage of our earnings paid to shareholders as dividends — is far too high for a growth company. It is well above the industry average, and has limited the growth in the price of our stock.
>
> To meet the challenges of this competitive marketplace and to ensure the financial strength and flexibility necessary for success, the Board of Directors has announced a change in our financial strategy that includes the following milestones:
>
> ■ A new dividend policy that provides for paying out 60 to 65 percent of prior years' earnings. This means a reduction in the quarterly dividend from 62 to 42 cents per share beginning with the next payment.
>
> ■ The authorization to repurchase 10 million shares of common stock over the next three years, including at least 4 million shares in the next year.
>
> ■ An earlier dividend evaluation beginning in February 1995 to more closely link dividend rates to annual earnings.
>
> We believe this financial strategy will enhance long-term share value and will facilitate both earnings per share and dividend growth to about 5 percent per year over the next several years.
>
> Adding to shareholder wealth in this manner should be increasingly significant given recent changes in the tax law, which have made capital gains more attractive than dividend income.
>
> . . . We take this action from a position of strength. We are not being forced into a defensive position by expectations of poor financial performance. Rather, it is a strategic decision to align our dividend policy and your total return as a shareholder with the growth characteristics of our company.
>
> We appreciate your understanding and support, and we will continue to provide updates on our progress in forthcoming shareholder reports.

Several analysts called the FPL decision a watershed event for the electric utility industry. Furthermore, many analysts believe that other utilities will follow FPL's lead. FPL saw its circumstances changing — its core electric business is moving from a regulated monopoly environment to one of increasing competition, and the new environment requires a stronger balance sheet and more financial flexibility than is consistent with a 90 percent payout policy.

---

[14]For a complete discussion of the FPL decision, see Dennis Soter, Eugene Brigham, and Paul Evanson, "The Dividend Cut Heard 'Round the World: The Case of FPL," *Journal of Applied Corporate Finance*, Spring 1996, 4–15. Also, note that stock repurchases are discussed in a later section.

What did the market think about FPL's dividend policy change? The company's stock price fell by 14 percent the day the announcement was made. Dozens of dividend cuts followed by sharply lower earnings had conditioned investors to think the worst when a company reduces its dividend — this is the signaling effect discussed earlier. However, over the next few months, as they understood it better, analysts began to praise the decision and to recommend the stock. As a result, FPL's stock outperformed the average utility and soon exceeded the pre-announcement price. The policy change was painful to FP&L's stockholders in the short run, but it was clearly the proper move, and it is proving to be beneficial to stockholders in the longer run.

Why do companies change their dividend policies?
What is the best strategy for announcing dividend policy changes?

**SELF-TEST
QUESTIONS**

DIVIDEND REINVESTMENT PLANS

During the 1970s, most large companies instituted *dividend reinvestment plans (DRPs or DRIPs),* whereby stockholders can automatically reinvest their dividends in the stock of the paying corporation.[15] Today most larger companies offer DRIPs, and although participation rates vary considerably, about 25 percent of the average firm's shareholders are enrolled. There are two types of DRIPs: (1) plans which involve only "old stock" that is already outstanding and (2) plans which involve newly issued stock. In either case, the stockholder must pay taxes on the amount of the dividends, even though stock rather than cash is received.

Under both types of DRIP, stockholders choose between continuing to receive dividend checks or having the company use the dividends to buy more stock in the corporation. Under the "old stock" type of plan, if a stockholder elects reinvestment, a bank, acting as trustee, takes the total funds available for reinvestment, purchases the corporation's stock on the open market, and allocates the shares purchased to the participating stockholders' accounts on a pro rata basis. The transactions costs of buying shares (brokerage costs) are low because of volume purchases, so these plans benefit small stockholders who do not need cash dividends for current consumption.

The "new stock" type of DRIP invests the dividends in newly issued stock, hence these plans raise new capital for the firm. AT&T, Xerox, Union Carbide, and many other companies have had new stock plans in effect in recent years, using them to raise substantial amounts of new equity capital. No fees are charged to stockholders, and many companies offer stock at a discount of 3 to 5 percent below the actual market price. The companies offer discounts as a trade-off against flotation costs that would be incurred if stocks were sold through investment bankers rather than through the dividend reinvestment plans.

---

[15]See Richard H. Pettway and R. Phil Malone, "Automatic Dividend Reinvestment Plans," *Financial Management,* Winter 1973, 11–18, for an excellent discussion of the subject.

One interesting aspect of DRIPs is that they are forcing corporations to reexamine their basic dividend policies. A high participation rate in a DRIP suggests that stockholders might be better off if the firm simply reduced cash dividends, which would save stockholders some personal income taxes. Quite a few firms are surveying their stockholders to learn more about their preferences and to find out how they would react to a change in dividend policy. A more rational approach to basic dividend policy decisions may emerge from this research.

Note that companies start or stop using new stock DRIPs depending on their need for equity capital. Thus, both Union Carbide and AT&T recently stopped offering a new stock DRIP with a 5 percent discount because their needs for equity capital declined, but Xerox began such a plan about the same time.

Some companies have expanded their DRIPs by moving to "open enrollment," whereby anyone can purchase the firm's stock directly and thus bypass brokers' commissions. Exxon not only allows investors to buy their initial shares at no fee but also lets them pick up additional shares through automatic bank account withdrawals. Several plans, including Mobil's, offer dividend reinvestment for individual retirement accounts, and some, such as U.S. West, allow participants to invest weekly or monthly rather than on the quarterly dividend schedule. In all of these plans, and many others, stockholders can invest more than the dividends they are foregoing — they simply send a check to the company and buy shares without a brokerage commission. According to First Chicago Trust, which handles the paperwork for 13 million shareholder DRIP accounts, at least half of all DRIPs will offer open enrollment, extra purchases, and other expanded services within five years.

SELF-TEST What are dividend reinvestment plans?
QUESTIONS What are their advantages and disadvantages from both the stockholders' and the firm's perspectives?

OTHER FACTORS THAT INFLUENCE DIVIDEND POLICY

In earlier sections, we described both the major theories of investor preference and some issues concerning the effect of dividend policy on the value of a firm. We also discussed the residual dividend model for setting a firm's long-run target payout ratio. In this section, we discuss several other factors that affect the dividend decision.

1. **Bond indentures.** Debt contracts often restrict dividend payments to earnings generated after the loan was granted. Also, debt contracts frequently stipulate that no dividends can be paid unless the current ratio, the times-interest-earned ratio, and other safety ratios exceed stated minimums.

2. **Preferred stock restrictions.** Typically, common dividends cannot be paid if the company has omitted its preferred dividend. The preferred arrearages must be satisfied before common dividends can be resumed.

3. **Impairment of capital rule.** Dividend payments cannot exceed the balance sheet item "retained earnings." This legal restriction, known as the "impairment of capital rule," is designed to protect creditors. (*Liquidating dividends* can be paid out of capital, but they must be indicated as such and they must not reduce capital below limits stated in the firm's debt contracts.)

4. **Availability of cash.** Cash dividends can only be paid with cash. Thus, a shortage of cash in the bank can restrict dividend payments. However, unused borrowing capacity can offset this factor.

5. **Penalty tax on improperly accumulated earnings.** To prevent wealthy individuals from using corporations to avoid personal taxes, the Tax Code provides for a special surtax on improperly accumulated income. Thus, if the IRS can demonstrate that the dividend payout ratio is being deliberately held down to help stockholders avoid personal taxes, heavy penalties will be imposed on the firm. However, as a practical matter, the penalty has been applied only to privately owned firms.

6. **Control.** If management is concerned about maintaining control, it may be reluctant to sell new stock, hence it may retain more earnings than it otherwise would. This factor is especially important for small, closely held firms.

7. **Signaling.** As we noted earlier, managers can and do use dividends to signal the firm's situation. For example, if management thinks that investors do not fully understand how well the firm is doing, and how good its prospects are, it may increase the dividend by more than was anticipated in an effort to boost the stock price.

What are some factors that influence a firm's dividend policy decision?   **SELF-TEST QUESTION**

OUR VIEW OF THE DIVIDEND POLICY DECISION

In many ways, our discussion of dividend policy parallels our discussion of capital structure: We have presented the relevant theories and issues, and we have listed some additional factors that influence dividend policy, but we have not come up with any hard-and-fast guidelines that managers should follow. It should be apparent from our discussion that dividend policy decisions are exercises in informed judgment, not decisions that can be based on a precise mathematical model.

In practice, dividend policy is not an independent decision—the dividend decision is made jointly with capital structure and capital budgeting decisions. The underlying reason for this joint decision process is asymmetric information, which influences managerial actions in two ways:

1. In general, managers do not want to issue new common stock. First, new common stock involves issuance costs—commissions, fees, and so on—and those costs can be avoided by using retained earnings to finance the firm's equity needs. Also, as we discussed in Chapter 14, asymmetric information

causes investors to view new common stock sales as negative signals and thus to lower their expectations regarding the firm's future prospects. The end result is that the announcement of a new stock issue usually leads to a decrease in the stock price. Considering the total costs involved, including both issuance and asymmetric information costs, managers strongly prefer to use retained earnings as their primary source of new equity.

2. Dividend changes provide signals about managers' beliefs about their firms' future prospects. Thus, dividend reductions, or, worse yet, omissions, generally have a significant negative effect on a firm's stock price. Since managers recognize this, they try to set dollar dividends low enough so that there is only a remote chance that the payment will have to be reduced in the future. Of course, unexpectedly large dividend increases can be used to provide positive signals.

The effects of asymmetric information suggest that, to the extent possible, managers should avoid both new common stock sales and dividend cuts, because both actions tend to lower stock prices. Thus, in setting dividend policy, managers should begin by considering the firm's future investment opportunities relative to its projected internal sources of funds. The firm's target capital structure also plays a part, but because the optimal capital structure is a *range,* firms can vary their actual capital structures somewhat from year to year. Since it is best to avoid issuing new common stock, the target long-term payout ratio should be designed to permit the firm to meet all its equity capital requirements with retained earnings. In effect, managers should use the residual dividend model to set dividends, but in a long-term framework. Finally, the current dollar dividend should be set so that there is an extremely low probability that the dividend, once set, will ever have to be lowered or omitted.

Of course, the dividend decision is made during the planning process, so there is uncertainty about future investment opportunities and operating cash flows. Thus, the actual payout ratio in any year may be above or below the firm's long-range target. However, the dollar dividend should be maintained, or increased as planned, unless the firm's financial condition deteriorates to the point where the planned policy simply cannot be maintained. A steady or increasing stream of dividends over the long run signals that the firm's financial condition is under control. Further, investor uncertainty is decreased by stable dividends, so a steady dividend stream reduces the negative effect of a new stock issue, should one become absolutely necessary.

In general, firms with superior investment opportunities should set lower payouts, hence retain more earnings, than firms with poor investment opportunities. The degree of uncertainty also influences the decision. If there is a great deal of uncertainty in the forecasts of *free cash flows,* which are defined here as the firm's operating cash flows minus mandatory equity investment requirements, then it is best to be conservative and to set a lower current dollar dividend. Also, firms with postponable investment opportunities can afford to set a higher dollar dividend, because, in times of stress, investments can be postponed for a year or two, thus increasing the cash available for dividends. Finally, firms which have a flat WACC curve, when WACC is plotted against the debt ratio as in the left panel of Figure 15-4, can also afford to set a higher payout ratio, because they can, in times of stress, more easily issue additional debt to maintain the capital budgeting program without having to cut dividends or issue stock.

Firms have only one opportunity to set the dividend payment from scratch, hence today's dividend decisions are constrained by policies that were set in the past. Therefore, setting a policy for the next five years necessarily begins with a review of the current situation.

Although we have outlined a rational process for managers to use when setting their firms' dividend policies, dividend policy still remains one of the most judgmental decisions that firms must make. For this reason, dividend policy is always set by the board of directors — the financial staff analyzes the situation and makes a recommendation, but the board makes the final decision.

Describe the dividend policy decision process. Be sure to discuss all the factors that influence the decision.

SELF-TEST QUESTION

STOCK REPURCHASES

We noted earlier that both IBM and FPL recently cut their dividends but simultaneously instituted programs to repurchase shares of their stocks. Thus, they substituted share repurchases for cash dividends as a way to distribute income to stockholders. IBM and FPL are not alone — during 1995 Philip Morris, GE, Disney, Citicorp, Merck, and more than 800 other companies took similar actions, and the dollars used to repurchase shares approximately matched the amount paid out as dividends.

Why are stock repurchase programs becoming so popular? The short answer is that they enhance shareholder value. A more complete answer is given in the remainder of this section.

THE MECHANICS OF STOCK REPURCHASES

The effects of stock repurchases can be illustrated with data on American Development Corporation (ADC). The company expects to earn $4.4 million in 1997, and 50 percent of this amount, or $2.2 million, will be available for distribution to shareholders. There are 1,100,000 shares outstanding. ADC could use the $2.2 million to repurchase 100,000 of its shares through a tender offer for $22 a share, or it could pay a cash dividend of $2 a share.[16] The current stock price is $20 per share.

---

[16]Stock repurchases are commonly made in four ways. First, a publicly owned firm can simply buy its own stock through a broker on the open market. Second, it can issue a *fixed price tender,* under which it permits stockholders to send in (that is, "tender") their shares to the firm in exchange for a specified price per share. When tender offers are made, the firm generally indicates that it will buy up a specified number of shares within a particular time period (usually one month); if more shares are tendered than the company wishes to purchase, then purchases are made on a pro rata basis. Third, the firm can use a *Dutch-auction tender,* where it announces that it will spend, say, $10 million to repurchase stock, and it then sets a range of prices at which shares can be tendered, say, from $20 to $25 per share if the stock currently sells for $20. Stockholders who elect to tender can choose a price anywhere in the specified range, but the lower the price chosen, the higher the probability of getting cash. The company completes the Dutch-auction tender by using the lowest price which spends the allocated money. All stockholders who tendered at or below the selected price will get that price for their shares, while all others will have their shares returned. Finally, the firm can purchase a block of shares from one or more large holders on a negotiated basis. If a negotiated purchase is employed, care should be taken to ensure that these stockholders do not receive preferential treatment not available to other stockholders.

The effect of the repurchase on ADC's EPS and stock price can be determined in the following way:

1. Current EPS $= \dfrac{\text{Total earnings}}{\text{Number of shares}} = \dfrac{\$4.4 \text{ million}}{1.1 \text{ million}} = \$4$ per share.

2. Current P/E ratio $= \dfrac{\$20}{\$4} = 5$, assumed to remain constant.

3. EPS after repurchase of 100,000 shares $= \dfrac{\$4.4 \text{ million}}{1 \text{ million}} = \$4.40$ per share.

4. Expected stock price after repurchase = (P/E)(EPS) = (5)($4.40) = $22 per share.

5. Expected capital gains per remaining share = $22 − $20 = $2.00.

It should be noticed from this example that investors will receive benefits of $2 per share, either in the form of a $2 cash dividend or a $2 increase in the stock price. This result occurs because we assumed (1) that shares could be repurchased at exactly $22 a share and (2) that the P/E ratio would remain constant. If shares could be bought for less than $22, the repurchase would be even better for *remaining* stockholders, but the reverse would hold if ADC paid more than $22 a share. Furthermore, the P/E ratio might change as a result of the repurchase, rising if investors viewed the repurchase favorably and falling if they viewed it unfavorably. Some factors that might affect P/E ratios are considered next.

ADVANTAGES OF REPURCHASES

The advantages of repurchases are as follows:

1. Repurchase announcements are generally viewed as positive signals by investors because repurchases are often motivated by managements' belief that their shares are undervalued.

2. The stockholders have a choice when a firm repurchases stock — to sell or not to sell. However, stockholders must accept a dividend payment and pay the tax. If a firm elects to distribute excess cash by repurchasing stock, those stockholders who need cash can sell back some of their shares, while those who do not want additional cash can simply retain their stock. From a tax standpoint, in a repurchase both types of stockholders get what they want.

3. A third advantage of a repurchase is that it removes those stockholders who are least favorably impressed with the company, and that tends to benefit the stock's future price performance.

4. Dividends are "sticky" in the short run because managements are reluctant to raise the dividend if the increase cannot be maintained in the future — managements dislike cutting cash dividends. Hence, if the excess cash flow is from a one-time event such as the sale of a division, management may distribute the excess cash through a share repurchase rather than a cash dividend that cannot be maintained.

5. Companies can use the residual model to set a *target cash distribution* level, then divide the distribution into a *dividend component* and a *repurchase component*. The dividend payout ratio will be relatively low, but the dividend

itself will be relatively secure, and it will grow as a result of the declining number of shares outstanding. The company has more flexibility in adjusting the total distribution than it would if the entire distribution were in the form of cash dividends, because repurchases can be varied from year to year without giving off adverse signals. This procedure, which is what FPL did, has much to recommend it, and it is the primary reason for the dramatic increase in the volume of share repurchases.

6. Repurchases can also be used to produce large-scale changes in capital structures. For example, Consolidated Edison recently decided to increase its target debt ratio, so it issued bonds and then used the proceeds to repurchase $400 million of its common stock. The repurchase was necessary to get to the new target debt ratio because even if the company financed its capital budget only with debt, it would still have taken years to get the debt ratio up to the target level.

DISADVANTAGES OF REPURCHASES

Disadvantages of repurchases include the following:

1. Stockholders may not be indifferent between dividends and capital gains, and the price of the stock might benefit more from cash dividends than from repurchases. Cash dividends are generally dependable, but repurchases are not. Still, if a stockholder badly needs cash, he or she can always sell some shares.

2. The *selling* stockholders may not be fully aware of all the implications of a repurchase, or they may not have all pertinent information about the corporation's present and future activities. However, firms generally announce repurchase programs before embarking on them to avoid potential stockholder suits.

3. The corporation may pay too high a price for the repurchased stock, to the detriment of remaining stockholders. If its shares are inactively traded, and if the firm seeks to acquire a relatively large amount of the stock, then the price may be bid above its equilibrium level and then fall after the firm ceases its repurchase operations. This factor was a problem at one time, but it is not today, at least for most firms. Repurchase programs are generally conducted over a long period (three to five years), and a designated investment banking firm buys shares over that time in a manner specifically designed not to disrupt the market.

CONCLUSIONS ON STOCK REPURCHASES

When all the pros and cons have been totaled, where do we stand? Our conclusions may be summarized as follows:

1. Because of the lower capital gains tax rate and the deferred tax on capital gains, repurchases have a significant tax advantage over dividends as a way to distribute income to stockholders. This advantage is reinforced by the fact

that repurchases provide cash to stockholders who want cash but allow those who do not need current cash to delay its receipt. On the other hand, dividends are more dependable and are thus better for those who need a steady source of income.

2. Because of signaling effects, companies should not pay varying dividends — this would lower investors' confidence in a company and adversely affect its cost of equity and its stock price. However, cash flows vary over time, as do investment opportunities, so the "proper" dividend payout ratio in the residual model sense varies. To get around this problem, a company can set its dividend payout ratio at a level low enough to keep dividend payments from constraining operations and then use repurchases on a more or less regular basis to distribute additional cash. Such a procedure would provide regular, dependable dividends plus additional cash flow to those stockholders who want it.

3. Repurchases are also useful to a firm that wants to make a large shift in its capital structure within a short period of time, or to a firm that wants to distribute cash from a one-time event such as the sale of a division without building an increase into its dollar dividend.

On balance, companies probably ought to be doing more repurchasing and distributing less cash as dividends than they are. However, increases in the size and frequency of repurchases in recent years suggest that companies are rapidly reaching this same conclusion.

SELF-TEST QUESTIONS

Explain how repurchases can (1) help stockholders hold down taxes and (2) help firms change their capital structures.

What are the three ways a firm can make repurchases?

What are the key advantages and disadvantages of stock repurchases?

How can stock repurchases help a company operate in accordance with the residual dividend model?

STOCK DIVIDENDS AND STOCK SPLITS

The rationale for stock dividends and splits can best be explained through an example; we will use the Nashville Company, an entertainment company specializing in country and western music, in our illustrations.

Nashville's markets are expanding, and as the company continues to grow and to retain earnings, its book value per share should also grow. More important, its earnings per share and stock price should also rise. The company began its life with only a few thousand shares outstanding. After some years of growth, each share had a very high EPS and DPS. When a "normal" P/E ratio was applied to the stock, the derived market price was so high that few people could afford to buy a "round lot" of 100 shares. This limited demand for the stock, thus keeping the total market value of the firm below what it would have been if more shares, at lower prices, were outstanding. To correct this situation, Nashville "split its stock" as described next.

STOCK SPLITS

Although there is little empirical evidence to support the contention, there is nevertheless a widespread belief in financial circles that an *optimal price range* exists for stocks. "Optimal" means that if the price is in this range, the price/earnings ratio, hence the value of the firm, will be maximized.   Many observers, including Nashville's management, believe that the best range for most New York Stock Exchange stocks is from $20 to $80 per share. Companies whose shares are owned largely by institutions tend to move toward the high end of the range, while those owned largely by individuals, such as the public utilities, generally operate in the lower end of the range.   Companies with average institutional ownership, like Nashville, cluster in the $30 to $50 range.   Accordingly, if the price of Nashville's stock rose to $80, management would probably declare a two-for-one stock split, thus doubling the number of shares outstanding, halving the earnings and dividends per share, and thereby lowering the price of the stock. Each stockholder would have more shares, but each share would be worth less. If the post-split price were $40, Nashville's stockholders would be exactly as well off as they were before the split. If the price of the stock were to stabilize above $40, stockholders would be better off. Stock splits can be of any size. For example, the stock could be split two-for-one, three-for-one, 1.5-for-one, or in any other way.[17]

Stock splits can also be used to increase the "float," or the number of shares held by outsiders. For example, Care Corporation, a nursing home operator, recently declared a four-for-one split, in large part because about 60 percent of the company's 500,000 shares outstanding were controlled by insiders, leaving only 200,000 shares for trading by others. The split increased the float to 800,000 which, according to the firm's management, increased trading activity. Note, though, that academic studies have suggested that stock splits may lower trading volume when measured on a proportional basis, primarily because brokerage commissions are increased.[18]

STOCK DIVIDENDS

Stock dividends are similar to stock splits in that they divide the pie into smaller slices without affecting the fundamental position of the current stockholders. On a 5 percent stock dividend, the holder of 100 shares would receive an additional 5 shares (without cost); on a 20 percent stock dividend, the same holder would receive 20 new shares; and on a 100 percent stock dividend, the holder would receive 100 shares, the same as in a two-for-one split. So, the total number of shares is increased, but earnings, dividends, and price per share all decline.

---

[17] *Reverse splits,* which reduce the shares outstanding, can even be used. For example, a company whose stock sells for $5 might employ a one-for-five reverse split, exchanging one new share for five old shares and raising the value of the shares to about $25, which is within the "acceptable" range. LTV Corporation did this after several years of losses had driven its stock price down below the optimal range.

[18] Commissions are generally higher on a trade of, say, 500 shares at $10 per share than on a trade of 100 shares at $50 a share, even though the dollar value of the trades is the same. For a further discussion of the effects of stock splits on market liquidity, see Thomas E. Copeland, "Liquidity Changes Following Stock Splits," *Journal of Finance,* March 1979, 115–141.

If a firm wants to reduce the price of its stock, should a stock split or a stock dividend be used? Stock splits and large stock dividends are generally used after a sharp price run-up, when a large price reduction is sought. Small stock dividends are occasionally used on a regular annual basis to keep the stock price more or less constrained. For example, if a firm's earnings and dividends are growing at 10 percent per year, the price would tend to go up at about that same rate, and the price would soon be outside the desired trading range. In this case, a 10 percent annual stock dividend would maintain the stock price within the optimal trading range.

Although the economic effects of stock splits and stock dividends are virtually identical, accountants treat them somewhat differently. For a discussion of the accounting treatment, see any financial accounting text.

Price Effects

If a company splits its stock or declares a stock dividend, will this increase the market value of its stock? Several empirical studies have sought to answer this question, and here is a summary of their findings.[19]

1. On average, the price of a company's stock rises shortly after it announces a stock split or dividend.

2. However, these price increases are more the result of the fact that investors take stock splits/dividends as signals of higher future earnings and dividends than of a desire for stock dividends/splits per se. Since only companies whose managements think things look good tend to use stock splits/dividends, the announcement of a stock split is taken as a signal that earnings and cash dividends are likely to rise. Thus, the price increases associated with stock splits/dividends are probably the result of signals of favorable prospects for earnings and dividends, not a desire for stock splits/dividends per se.

3. If a company announces a stock split or dividend, its price will tend to rise. However, if during the next few months it does not announce an increase in earnings and dividends, then its stock price will drop back to the earlier level.

4. As we noted earlier, brokerage commissions are generally higher in percentage terms on lower-priced stocks. This means that it is more expensive to trade low-priced than high-priced stocks, and this, in turn, means that stock splits may reduce the liquidity of a company's shares. This particular piece of evidence suggests that stock splits/dividends might actually be harmful, although a lower price does mean that more investors can afford to trade in round lots (100 shares), which carry lower commissions than do odd lots (less than 100 shares).

---

[19]See Eugene F. Fama, Lawrence Fisher, Michael C. Jensen, and Richard Roll, "The Adjustment of Stock Prices to New Information," *International Economic Review,* February 1969, 1–21; Mark S. Grinblatt, Ronald M. Masulis, and Sheridan Titman, "The Valuation Effects of Stock Splits and Stock Dividends," *Journal of Financial Economics,* December 1984, 461–490; C. Austin Barker, "Evaluation of Stock Dividends," *Harvard Business Review,* July–August 1958, 99–114; and Copeland, op.cit, 115–141.

What do we conclude from all this? From a pure economic standpoint, stock dividends and splits are just additional pieces of paper. However, they provide management with a relatively low-cost way of signaling that the firm's prospects look good. Further, we should note that since few large, publicly owned stocks sell at prices above several hundred dollars, we simply do not know what the effect would be if Microsoft, Xerox, Hewlett-Packard, and other highly successful firms had never split their stocks, and consequently had sold at prices in the thousands or even tens of thousands of dollars. All in all, it probably makes sense to employ stock dividends/splits when a firm's prospects are favorable, especially if the price of its stock has gone beyond the normal trading range.[20]

SELF-TEST QUESTIONS

What are stock dividends and stock splits?

What impact do stock dividends and splits have on stock prices? Why?

In what situations should managers consider the use of stock dividends?

In what situations should they consider the use of stock splits?

---

[20]It is interesting to note that Berkshire Hathaway, which is controlled by billionaire Warren Buffett, one of the most successful financiers of the twentieth century, has never had a stock split, and its stock sold on the NYSE for more than $30,000 per share in early 1996. But, in response to investment trusts that were being formed to sell fractional units of the stock, Buffet created a new class of Berkshire Hathaway stock (Class B) worth about $1/30$ of a Class A (regular) share.

SUMMARY

Dividend policy involves the decision to pay out earnings versus retaining them for reinvestment in the firm. The key factors influencing dividend policy are listed below:

■ The *dividend policy decision* involves three questions: (1) What fraction of earnings should be distributed, on average, over time? (2) Should the distribution be in the form of cash dividends or stock repurchases? (3) Should the firm maintain a steady, stable dividend growth rate?

■ Miller and Modigliani developed the *dividend irrelevance theory,* which holds that a firm's dividend policy has no effect either on the value of the firm or on its cost of capital.

■ The *"bird-in-the-hand" theory,* advocated by Gordon and Lintner, holds that the value of the firm will be maximized by a high dividend payout ratio, because investors regard actual dividends as being less risky than potential capital gains.

■ The *tax preference theory,* advocated by Litzenberger and Ramaswamy, holds that the value of the firm will be maximized by a low dividend payout, because investors pay lower effective taxes on capital gains than on dividends.

■ Because *empirical tests* of the three theories *have been inconclusive,* academicians cannot tell corporate managers with any degree of precision how a change in dividend policy will affect stock prices and capital costs. Thus, actually determining the optimal dividend policy is extremely difficult.

■ The *information content,* or *signaling, hypothesis* states that investors regard dividend changes as a signal of management's forecast of future earnings. The *clientele effect* suggests that a firm will attract investors who like the firm's dividend policy, hence a change in dividend policy will lead to a change in the set of stockholders.

■ A high dividend payout policy may reduce *agency costs,* because it forces firms to go to the capital markets more often, hence to undergo periodic outside scrutiny.

■ In practice, most firms try to follow a policy of paying a *steadily increasing dividend.* This policy provides investors with a stable, dependable income, and if the signaling theory is correct, it also gives investors information about management's expectations for earnings growth.

■ Most firms use the *residual dividend model* to set a long-run target payout ratio which permits the firm to satisfy its equity requirements with retained earnings.

■ Other factors, including *legal constraints, investment opportunities, availability and cost of funds from other sources,* and *taxes,* are considered by managers when they establish dividend policies.

■ A *dividend reinvestment plan (DRP or DRIP)* allows stockholders to have the company automatically use their dividends to purchase additional shares of the firm's stock. DRIPs are popular with investors who do not need current income because the plans allow stockholders to acquire additional shares without incurring normal brokerage fees.

■ Under a *stock repurchase plan,* a firm buys back some of its outstanding stock, thereby decreasing the number of shares, which, in turn, increases both EPS and the stock price. Repurchases are useful for making major changes in a firm's capital structure, as well as for distributing temporary excess cash.

■ Increasingly, firms are using the residual model to determine how much cash to distribute, then setting a *distribution target* which includes some cash dividends and some stock repurchases. The cash dividend component is then held steady (or increased steadily) over time, and the repurchases component is varied, depending on cash flows and investment requirements.

■ A *stock split* is an action taken by a firm to increase the number of shares outstanding. Normally, splits reduce the price per share in proportion to the increase in shares because splits merely "divide the pie into smaller slices." A *stock dividend* is a dividend paid in additional shares of stock rather than in cash. Both stock dividends and splits are used to keep stock prices within an "optimal" range.

5-1 Define each of the following terms:
  a. Dividend policy
  b. Dividend irrelevance theory
  c. "Bird-in-the-hand" theory
  d. Tax preference theory
  e. Residual dividend model
  f. Constraints on dividend policy
  g. Clientele effect
  h. Information content of dividends; signaling
  i. Extra dividend
  j. Ex-dividend date
  k. Dividend reinvestment plans (each of two types)
  l. Stock split; stock dividend
  m. Stock repurchase

15-2 As an investor, would you rather invest in a firm that has a policy of maintaining (a) a constant payout ratio, (b) a constant dollar dividend per share, (c) a target dividend growth rate, or (d) a constant regular quarterly dividend plus a year-end extra (or stock repurchase) when earnings are sufficiently high or corporate investment needs are sufficiently low? Explain your answer, stating how these policies would affect your k_s.

15-3 How would each of the following changes probably affect aggregate (that is, the average for all corporations) payout ratios? Explain your answers.
  a. An increase in the personal income tax rate. An increase in the corporate tax rate.
  b. A liberalization in depreciation for federal income tax purposes, that is, faster tax write-offs.
  c. A rise in interest rates.
  d. An increase in corporate profits.
  e. A decline in investment opportunities.
  f. Reinstatement of a differential (lower) capital gains tax rate.

15-4 Discuss the pros and cons of having the directors formally announce what a firm's dividend policy will be in the future.

15-5 Most firms would like to have their stock selling at a high P/E ratio and also have an extensive public ownership (many different shareholders). Explain how stock dividends or stock splits may help achieve these goals.

15-6 What is the difference between a stock dividend and a stock split? As a stockholder, would you prefer to see your company declare a 100 percent stock dividend or a two-for-one split? Assume that either action is feasible.

15-7 "The cost of retained earnings is less than the cost of new outside equity capital. Consequently, it is totally irrational for a firm to sell a new issue of stock and to pay dividends during the same year." Discuss this statement.

15-8 Would it ever be rational for a firm to borrow money in order to pay dividends? Explain.

15-9 Union representatives have presented arguments similar to the following: "Corporations such as General Motors retain about half of their profits for financing needs. If they financed by selling stock instead of by retaining earnings, they could substantially raise wages and still earn enough to pay the same dividend to their shareholders. Therefore, their profits are too high." Evaluate this statement.

15-10   "Executive salaries have been shown to be more closely correlated to the size of the firm than to its profitability. If a firm's board of directors is controlled by management instead of by outside directors, this might result in the firm's retaining more earnings than can be justified from the stockholders' point of view." Discuss the statement, being sure (a) to use Figure 15-5 in your answer and (b) to explain the implied relationship between dividend policy and stock prices.

15-11   Explain why a high dividend payout policy might encourage managers to act in the best interests of the firm's investors.

PROBLEMS

15-1   DIVIDEND THEORIES Modigliani and Miller (MM), on the one hand, and Gordon and Lintner (GL), on the other, have expressed strong views regarding the effect of dividend policy on a firm's cost of capital and value.
   a. In essence, what are the MM and the GL views regarding the effect of dividend policy on cost of capital and value? Illustrate your answer with a graph.
   b. How does the tax preference model differ from the views of MM and GL?
   c. According to the text, which position (MM, GL, or tax preference) has received statistical confirmation from empirical tests?
   d. How could GL use the fact that dividend increase announcements are often followed by stock price increases to support their "bird-in-the-hand" theory? How could MM use the information content, or signaling, hypothesis to counter these arguments?
   e. How could MM's opponents use the clientele effect concept to counter MM's arguments? If you were debating MM's opponents, how would you counter them?

15-2   RESIDUAL DIVIDEND MODEL One position expressed in the literature is that firms should set their dividends as a residual, after using income to support new investment.
   a. Explain what the residual dividend model implies, illustrating your answer with a graph showing how different conditions could lead to different dividend payout ratios.
   b. Could the residual dividend model be consistent with (1) a constant dividend growth rate policy, (2) a constant payout policy, and/or (3) a low-regular-plus-extras policy? Explain.
   c. In Chapter 13, we considered the relationship between capital structure and the cost of capital. If the WACC versus debt ratio plot were shaped like a sharp V, would this have a different implication for the importance of setting dividends according to the residual model than if the ratio relationship were shaped like a shallow bowl (or a U)?
   d. Companies A and B both have IOS schedules which intersect their MCC schedules at a point which, under the residual policy, calls for a 20 percent payout. In both cases, a 20 percent payout would require a cut in the annual dividend from $2 to $1. One company cut its dividend and accepted all projects, while the other did not cut its dividend and accepted less than the optimal number of projects. One company had a relatively steep IOS curve, while the other had a relatively flat IOS. Explain which company had the steep, and which the flat, IOS.

5-3 STOCK DIVIDENDS AND SPLITS More NYSE companies had stock dividends and stock splits during 1983 and 1984 than ever before. What events in these years could have made stock splits and dividends so popular? Explain the rationale that a financial vice-president might give the board of directors to support a stock split/dividend recommendation.

5-4 RESIDUAL DIVIDEND MODEL Magee Manufacturing Corporation (MMC) has an all-equity capital structure which includes no preferred stock. It has 200,000 shares of $2 par value common stock outstanding.

When MMC's founder, who was also its research director and most successful inventor, died unexpectedly in early 1997, MMC was left suddenly and permanently with materially lower growth expectations and relatively few attractive new investment opportunities. Unfortunately, there was no way to replace the founder's contributions to the firm. Previously, MMC had found it necessary to plow back most of its earnings to finance growth, which has been averaging 12 percent per year. Future growth at a 5 percent rate is considered realistic, but that level would call for an increase in the dividend payout. Further, it now appears that new investment projects with at least the 14 percent rate of return required by MMC's stockholders ($k_s = 14\%$) would amount to only $800,000 for 1997 in comparison with a projected $2,000,000 of net income. If the existing 20 percent dividend payout were continued, retained earnings would be $1.6 million in 1997, but as noted, investments which yield the 14 percent cost of capital amount to only $800,000.

The one encouraging thing is that the high earnings from existing assets are expected to continue and net income of $2 million is still expected for 1997. Given the dramatically changed circumstances, MMC's management is reviewing the firm's dividend policy.

a. Assuming that the acceptable 1997 investment projects would be financed entirely by earnings retained during the year, calculate DPS in 1997 assuming MMC uses the residual payment model.

b. What payout ratio does this imply for 1997?

c. If the increased payout ratio is maintained for the foreseeable future, what should be the present intrinsic value of the common stock? How does this compare with the price that should have prevailed under the assumptions existing just prior to the news about the death of the founder? If the two values of $\hat{P}_0$ are different, comment on why.

5-5 STOCK REPURCHASES Sure Thing Inc. has earnings this year of $16.5 million, 50 percent of which is required to take advantage of the firm's excellent investment opportunities. The firm has 2,062,500 shares outstanding, selling currently at $32 per share. Susan Long, a major stockholder (187,500 shares), has expressed displeasure with a great deal of managerial policy. Management has approached her about selling her holdings back to the firm, and she has expressed a willingness to do this at a price of $32 a share. Assuming that the market uses a constant P/E ratio of 4 in valuing the stock, should the firm buy Long's shares? Assume that dividends will not be paid on Long's shares if they are repurchased. (Hint: Calculate the ex-dividend price of the stock with and without the repurchase, and add to these values the dividends received to determine the remaining shareholders' value per share.)

SPREADSHEET APPLICATIONS

SPREADSHEET PROBLEM

The Tennessee Bourbon Company (TBC) has for many years enjoyed a moderate but stable growth in sales and earnings. However, bourbon consumption has been falling recently, primarily because of an increasing use of lighter alcoholic beverages such as vodka and wines. Anticipating further declines in sales for the future, TBC's management hopes eventually to move almost entirely out of the liquor business and into a newly developed, diversified product line in growth-oriented industries. The company is especially interested in the prospects for pollution-control devices, because its research department has already done much work in this area. Right now the company estimates that an investment of $24 million is necessary to purchase new facilities and to begin operations on these products, but the investment could be earning a return of about 18 percent within a short time. The only other available investment opportunity totals $9.6 million, is expected to return about 11.2 percent, and is indivisible, that is, it must be accepted in its entirety or else be rejected.

The company is expected to pay a $2.00 dividend on its 7 million outstanding shares, the same as its dividend last year. The directors might, however, change the dividend if there are good reasons for doing so. Net income for the year is expected to be $22.5 million; the common stock is currently selling for $45; the firm's target debt ratio (debt/assets ratio) is 45 percent; and its tax rate is 34 percent. The costs of various forms of financing are listed below:

New bonds: $k_d = 11\%$. This is a before-tax rate.

New common stock sold at $45 per share will net $41.

Required rate of return on retained earnings: $k_s = 14\%$.

a. Calculate TBC's expected payout ratio, the break point where its MCC schedule rises, and its marginal cost of capital above and below the point of exhaustion of retained earnings at the current payout. (Hint: k_s is given, and D_1/P_0 can be found. Then, knowing k_s and D_1/P_0, and assuming constant growth, g can be determined.)

b. How large should TBC's capital budget be for the year?

c. What is an appropriate dividend policy for the firm? How should the capital budget be financed?

d. How might risk factors influence TBC's cost of capital, capital structure, and dividend policy?

e. What assumptions, if any, do your answers to Questions a-d make about investors' preferences for dividends versus capital gains, that is, their preferences regarding the D_1/P_0 and g components of k_s?

f. Assume that TBC's management is considering a change in its capital structure to include more debt, and thus it would like to analyze the effects of an increase in the debt ratio to 60 percent. However, the treasurer believes that such a move would cause lenders to increase the required rate of return on new bonds to 12 percent and k_s would rise to 14.5 percent. How would this change affect the optimal capital budget? If k_s rose to 16 percent, would the low-return project be acceptable? Would the project selection be affected if the dividend were reduced to $1.25 from $2.00, still assuming $k_s = 16$ percent?

Information Systems Inc. (ISI) was founded five years ago by Michael Taylor and Karen Black, who are still its only stockholders. ISI has now reached the stage where outside equity capital is necessary if the firm is to grow with the industry and still maintain its target capital structure of 60 percent equity and 40 percent debt. Therefore, Taylor and Black have decided to take the company public. Until now, Taylor and Black have routinely invested all earnings in the firm, so dividend policy had not been an issue. However, since ISI will soon be a publicly owned firm, they will have to decide on a dividend policy.

Assume that you were recently hired by Arthur Adamson & Company, a national consulting firm which has been asked to help ISI prepare its public offering. Tom Nickols, the senior consultant in your group, has asked you to make a presentation to Taylor and Black in which you review the theory of dividend policy and discuss the following questions.

a. (1) What is meant by the term "dividend policy"?
   (2) What are the three elements of dividend policy?
b. (1) What are the three major theories regarding stockholders' preferences for dividends versus capital gains?
   (2) What do the three theories indicate regarding the actions management should take regarding dividend policy?
c. Explain the relationships between dividend policy and (1) stock price and (2) the cost of equity under each dividend policy theory by constructing two graphs, such as those shown in Figure 15-2. Dividend policy should be placed on the X axis. Assume, for purposes of this part only, that if the company paid out all earnings as dividends, it would have a required rate of return of 15 percent and a stock price of $30.
d. Has empirical testing been able to prove which theory, if any, is most correct?
e. What is the information content, or signaling, hypothesis, and how does it constrain dividend policy?
f. What is the clientele effect, and how does it constrain dividend policy?
g. What impact might dividend policy have on agency costs?
h. (1) What is the residual dividend model? Assume that ISI plans to spend $800,000 on capital investments during the coming year; its optimal capital structure calls for 60 percent equity and 40 percent debt; and its net income is forecasted at $600,000. Construct a graph which shows what the total dollar dividend and the payout ratio would be if the firm used the residual model.
   (2) How would a change in net income affect the dividend?
   (3) How would a change in investment opportunities affect the dividend?
   (4) Assume that the firm also forecasts $100,000 of depreciation cash flow. How would these funds impact the residual analysis, still assuming $600,000 in net income?
   (5) What are the advantages and disadvantages of the residual model? (Hint: Think about both signaling and the clientele effect.)
i. What is a dividend reinvestment plan? What are the two major types of plans, and when should each type be used?
j. Describe how most firms set their dividend policies in practice.
k. What is a stock repurchase? Discuss the advantages and disadvantages of stock repurchases.
l. What is a stock dividend, and how does it differ from a stock split? When should a firm consider issuing a stock dividend? When should a firm consider splitting its stock?

SELECTED ADDITIONAL REFERENCES AND CASES

Dividend policy has been studied extensively by academicians. The first major academic work, and still a classic that we recommend highly, is Lintner's analysis of the way corporations actually set their dividend payment policies.

Lintner, John, "Distribution of Incomes of Corporations among Dividends, Retained Earnings, and Taxes," *American Economic Review,* May 1956, 97–113.

The effects of dividend policy on stock prices and capital costs have been examined by many researchers. The classic theoretical argument that dividend policy is important, and that stockholders like dividends, was set forth by Gordon, while Miller and Modigliani (MM) developed the notion that dividend policy is not important. Many researchers have extended both Gordon's and MM's theoretical arguments, and have attempted to test the effects of dividend policy in a variety of ways. Although statistical problems have precluded definitive conclusions, the following articles, among others, have helped to clarify the issues:

Brennan, Michael, "Taxes, Market Valuation, and Corporate Financial Policy," *National Tax Journal,* Spring 1975, 417–427.

Hayes, Linda S., "Fresh Evidence That Dividends Don't Matter," *Fortune,* May 4, 1981, 351–354.

Lewellen, Wilbur G., Kenneth L. Stanley, Ronald C. Lease, and Gary G. Schlarbaum, "Some Direct Evidence on the Dividend Clientele Phenomenon," *Journal of Finance,* December 1978, 1385–1399.

Mukherjee, Tarun, and Larry M. Austin, "An Empirical Investigation of Small Bank Stock Valuation and Dividend Policy," *Financial Management,* Spring 1980, 27–31.

On stock dividends and stock splits, see

Baker, H. Kent, and Patricia L. Gallagher, "Management's View of Stock Splits," *Financial Management,* Summer 1980, 73–77.

Baker, H. Kent, Aaron L. Phillips, and Gary E. Powell, "The Stock Distribution Puzzle: A Synthesis of the Literature on Stock Splits and Stock Dividends," *Financial Practice and Education,* Spring/Summer 1995, 24–37.

Copeland, Thomas E., "Liquidity Changes Following Stock Splits," *Journal of Finance,* March 1979, 115–141.

McNichols, Maureen, and Ajay Dravid, "Stock Dividends, Stock Splits, and Signaling," *Journal of Finance,* July 1990, 857–879.

On repurchases, see

Denis, David J., "Defensive Changes in Corporate Payout Policy: Share Repurchases and Special Dividends," *Journal of Finance,* December 1990, 1433–1456.

Finnerty, Joseph E., "Corporate Stock Issue and Repurchase," *Financial Management,* Autumn 1975, 62–71.

Gay, Gerald D., Jayant R. Kale, and Thomas H. Noe, "Share Repurchase Mechanisms: A Comparative Analysis of Efficacy, Shareholder Wealth and Corporate Control Effects," *Financial Management,* Spring 1991, 44–59.

Klein, April, and James Rosenfeld, "The Impact of Targeted Share Repurchases on the Wealth of Non-Participating Shareholders," *Journal of Financial Research,* Summer 1988, 89–97.

Netter, Jeffry M., and Mark L. Mitchell, "Stock-Repurchase Announcements and Insider Transactions after the October 1987 Stock Market Crash," *Financial Management,* Autumn 1989, 84–96.

Pugh, William, and John S. Jahera, Jr., "Stock Repurchases and Excess Returns: An Empirical Examination," *The Financial Review,* February 1990, 127–142.

Stewart, Samuel S., Jr., "Should a Corporation Repurchase Its Own Stock?" *Journal of Finance,* June 1976, 911–921.

Wansley, James W., William R. Lane, and Salil Sarkar, "Managements' View on Share Repurchase and Tender Offer Premiums," *Financial Management,* Autumn 1989, 97–110.

Woolridge, J. Randall, and Donald R. Chambers, "Reverse Splits and Shareholder Wealth," *Financial Management,* Autumn 1983, 5–15.

For surveys of managers' views on dividend policy, see

Baker, H. Kent, Gail E. Farrelly, and Richard B. Edelman, "A Survey of Management Views on Dividend Policy," *Financial Management,* Autumn 1985, 78–84.

Pruitt, Stephen W., and Lawrence J. Gitman, "The Interactions between the Investment, Financing, and Dividend Decisions of Major U.S. Firms," *Financial Review,* August 1991, 409–430.

Other pertinent articles include

Asquith, Paul, and David W. Mullins, Jr., "Signalling with Dividends, Stock Repurchases, and Equity Issues," *Financial Management,* Autumn 1986, 27–44.

Born, Jeffrey A., "Insider Ownership and Signals — Evidence from Dividend Initiation Announcement Effects," *Financial Management,* Spring 1988, 38–45.

Brealey, Richard A., "Does Dividend Policy Matter?" *Midland Corporate Finance Journal,* Spring 1983, 17–25.

Brennan, Michael J., and Anjan V. Thakor, "Shareholder Preferences and Dividend Policy," *Journal of Finance,* September 1990, 993–1018.

Chang, Rosita P., and S. Ghon Rhee, "The Impact of Personal Taxes on Corporate Dividend Policy and Capital Structure Decisions," *Financial Management,* Summer 1990, 21–31.

DeAngelo, Harry, and Linda DeAngelo, "Dividend Policy and Financial Distress: An Empirical Investigation of Troubled NYSE Firms," *Journal of Finance,* December 1990, 1415–1432.

DeAngelo, Harry, Linda DeAngelo, and Douglas J. Skinner, "Dividends and Losses," *Journal of Finance,* December 1992, 1837–1863.

Dempsey, Stephen J., and Gene Laber, "Effects of Agency and Transactions Costs on Dividend Payout Ratios: Further Evidence of the Agency-Transaction Cost Hypothesis," *Journal of Financial Research,* Winter 1992, 317–321.

Fehrs, Donald H., Gary A. Benesh, and David R. Peterson, "Evidence of a Relation between Stock Price Reactions Around Cash Dividend Changes and Yields," *Journal of Financial Research,* Summer 1988, 111–123.

Ghosh, Chinmoy, and J. Randall Woolridge, "An Analysis of Shareholder Reaction to Dividend Cuts and Omissions," *Journal of Financial Research,* Winter 1988, 281–294.

Healy, Paul M., and Krishna G. Palepu, "How Investors Interpret Changes in Corporate Financial Policy," *Journal of Applied Corporate Finance,* Fall 1989, 59–64.

Impson, C. Michael, and Imre Karafiath, "A Note on the Stock Market Reaction to Dividend Announcements," *The Financial Review,* May 1992, 259–271.

Kale, Jayant R., and Thomas H. Noe, "Dividends, Uncertainty, and Underwriting Costs Under Asymmetric Information," *Journal of Financial Research,* Winter 1990, 265–277.

Manakyan, Herman, and Carolyn Carroll, "An Empirical Examination of the Existence of a Signaling Value Function for Dividends," *Journal of Financial Research,* Fall 1990, 201–210.

Miller, Merton H., "Behavioral Rationality in Finance: The Case of Dividends," *Midland Corporate Finance Journal,* Winter 1987, 6–15.

Peterson, David R., and Pamela P. Peterson, "A Further Understanding of Stock Distributions: The Case of Reverse Stock Splits," *Journal of Financial Research,* Fall 1992, 189–205.

Peterson, Pamela P., David R. Peterson, and Norman H. Moore, "The Adoption of New-Issue Dividend Reinvestment Plans and Shareholder Wealth," *Financial Review,* May 1987, 221–232.

Talmor, Eli, and Sheridan Titman, "Taxes and Dividend Policy," *Financial Management,* Summer 1990, 32–35.

Wansley, James W., C. F. Sirmans, James D. Shilling, and Young-jin Lee, "Dividend Change Announcement Effects and Earnings Volatility and Timing," *Journal of Financial Research,* Spring 1991, 37–49.

Woolridge, J. Randall, and Chinmoy Ghosh, "Dividend Cuts: Do They Always Signal Bad News?" *Midland Corporate Finance Journal,* Summer 1985, 20–32.

The following cases from The Dryden Press Cases in Financial Management: Dryden Request series focus on the issues contained in this chapter:

Case 19, "Georgia Atlantic Company," Case 19A, "Floral Fragrance, Inc.," and Case 19B, "Cook Transportation, Inc.," which examine many dividend policy issues.

Case 20, "Bessemer Steel Products, Inc.," which illustrates the dividend policy decision.

P A R T V

SOURCES OF LONG-TERM FINANCING

CHAPTER **16**

COMMON STOCK AND THE INVESTMENT BANKING PROCESS

*I*n early 1993 Chrysler announced plans to sell 40 million new shares of common stock, which would raise about $1.46 billion. With its shares selling at about $36, Chrysler's stock price had more than tripled from its 1992 low of $11.50. The major reason for the sale was to bolster the balance sheet, which had been weakened by low sales caused by the poor economy. Chrysler planned to use some of the funds to beef up its pension fund, which had about $4 billion in unfunded liabilities. In addition, some of the proceeds would be used to help fund the company's planned 1993–1997 $17.5 billion capital investment program and to pay down some of Chrysler's $3.8 billion debt.

The decision to issue new stock came at the crest of a wave of good news for Chrysler, which just two years before had been one of industrial America's walking wounded. Because of its ongoing cost-cutting efforts, Chrysler had lowered its breakeven point to about 1.7 million vehicles in 1992, down from 1.9 million in 1991. Also, initial sales of the company's trio of new LH sedans — the Chrysler Concorde, Dodge Intrepid, and Eagle Vision — had been so strong that Chrysler planned to increase production.

"The best time to ask people for more money is when they like you," said analyst John Casesa of Wertheim Schroder & Co. "Right now the market feels that Chrysler can do no wrong." The rating agencies also liked the announcement. Both Moody's and Standard & Poor's upgraded Chrysler's debt, and both firms cited the equity issue as well as Chrysler's profitable new products as keys to the upgrade.

As you read this chapter, imagine yourself as a Chrysler executive and think about the pros and cons of its new equity issue. In particular, consider the impact of the stock issue on the firm's debt rating, and the signals the issue announcement might send to the market. When you finish this chapter, you should have a *better appreciation of the advantages and disadvantages of new equity sales, the various ways firms can issue new common stock, and the investment banking process.*

In Part III we saw how financial managers analyze potential investments in long-term (or fixed) assets, and in Part IV we discussed capital structure and dividend policy. Now we turn to specific types of long-term capital. Any decision to acquire new assets necessitates raising new capital, and, generally, long-term assets are financed with long-term capital. In this chapter, we consider in some detail the decisions financial managers must make regarding common stock financings. As a part of this analysis, we also examine in detail the procedures used to raise new long-term capital, or the investment banking process.

BALANCE SHEET ACCOUNTS AND DEFINITIONS

Legal and accounting terminology is vital to both investors and financial managers if they are to avoid misinterpretations and costly mistakes. Therefore, we begin our analysis of common stock with a discussion of accounting and legal issues. Consider first Table 16-1, which shows the common equity section of American Chemical Company's balance sheet. American's owners, its stockholders, have authorized management to issue a total of 30 million shares, and management has thus far actually issued (or sold) 25 million shares. Each share has a *par value* of $1; this is the minimum amount for which new shares can be issued.[1]

American Chemical is an old company — it was established back in 1920. Its initial equity capital consisted of 3,000 shares sold at the $1 par value, so on its first balance sheet the total stockholders' equity was $3,000. The initial paid-in capital and retained earnings accounts showed zero balances. Over the years American has retained some of its earnings, and the firm has issued new stock to raise capital from time to time. During 1996, American earned $60 million, paid $50 million in dividends, and retained $10 million. The $10 million was added to the $365 million accumulated *retained earnings* that appeared on the year-end 1995 balance sheet to produce the $375 million retained earnings at year-end 1996. Thus, since its inception in 1920, American has retained, or plowed back, a total of $375 million. This is money that belongs to the stockholders and that they could have received in the form of dividends. Instead, the stockholders chose to let management reinvest the $375 million in the business.

---

[1]A stock's par value is an arbitrary figure that indicates the minimum amount of money stockholders have put up, or must put up, in the event of bankruptcy. Actually, the firm could legally sell new shares at below par, but any purchaser would be liable for the difference between the issue price and the par value in the event the company went bankrupt. Thus, if American sold an investor 10,000 shares at 40 cents per share, for $4,000, then the investor would have to put up an additional $6,000 if the company later went bankrupt. This contingent liability effectively precludes the sale of new common stock at prices below par.

Also, we should point out that firms are not required to establish a par value for their stock. Thus, American could have elected to use "no par" stock, in which case the common stock and additional paid-in capital accounts could have been consolidated under one account called *common stock,* which would show a 1996 balance of $75 million.

AMERICAN CHEMICAL COMPANY: STOCKHOLDERS' EQUITY ACCOUNTS AS OF DECEMBER 31, 1996	TABLE 16-1

Common stock (30 million shares authorized, 25 million shares outstanding, $1 par)	$ 25,000,000
Additional paid-in capital	50,000,000
Retained earnings	375,000,000
Total common stockholders' equity (or common net worth)	$450,000,000

$$\text{Book value per share} = \frac{\text{Total common stockholders' equity}}{\text{Shares outstanding}} = \frac{\$450,000,000}{25,000,000} = \$18.$$

Now consider the $50 million *additional paid-in capital.* This account shows the difference between the stock's par value and what stockholders paid when they bought newly issued shares. As we noted, American was formed in 1920 with 3,000 shares issued at the $1 par value; thus, the first balance sheet showed a zero balance for additional paid-in capital. By 1925, the company had demonstrated its profitability and was earning 50 cents per share. Further, it had built up the retained earnings account to a total of $6,000, so the total stockholders' equity was $3,000 of par value plus $6,000 of retained earnings = $9,000, and the *book value per share* was $9,000/3,000 shares = $3. American had also borrowed heavily, and, even though it had retained most of its earnings, the company's debt ratio had risen to an unacceptable level, precluding further use of debt without an infusion of equity.

The company had profitable investment opportunities, so in order to take advantage of them, management decided to issue another 2,000 shares of stock. The market price at the time was $4 per share, which was eight times the 50 cents earnings per share (the price/earnings ratio was 8×). This $4 market value per share was well in excess of the $1 par value and also higher than the $3 book value per share, demonstrating that par value, book value, and market value are not necessarily equal. Had the company lost money since its inception, it would have had negative retained earnings, the book value would have been below par, and the market price might well have been below book.

Table 16-2 shows how the 1925 stock sale affected American's common equity accounts. A total of 2,000 new shares were sold to investors at the market price of $4 per share. Each share brought in $4, of which $1 represented the par value, and $3 represented the excess of the sale price above par. Since 2,000 shares were involved, a total of $2,000 was added to common stock, and $6,000 was entered in additional paid-in capital. Notice also that book value per share rose from $3 to $3.40; whenever stock is sold at a price above book, the book value increases, and vice versa if stock is sold below book.[2] Similar transactions have taken place down through the years to produce the current situation, as shown earlier in Table 16-1.[3]

---

[2]The effects of stock sales on book value are not important for industrial firms, but they are *very* important for utility companies, whose allowable earnings per share are in effect determined by regulators as a percentage of book value.

[3]Stock dividends, stock splits, and stock repurchases (the reverse of stock issues) also affect the capital accounts. These topics were discussed in Chapter 15.

TABLE 16-2	EFFECTS OF 1925 STOCK SALE ON AMERICAN CHEMICAL'S EQUITY ACCOUNTS

BEFORE SALE OF STOCK

Common stock (3,000 shares outstanding, $1 par)	$ 3,000
Additional paid-in capital	0
Retained earnings	6,000
Total stockholders' equity	$ 9,000
Book value per share = $9,000/3,000 =	$ 3.00

AFTER SALE OF STOCK

Common stock (5,000 shares outstanding, $1 par)	$5,000
Additional paid-in capital ($4 − $1) × 2,000 shares	6,000
Retained earnings	6,000
Total stockholders' equity	$17,000
Book value per share = $17,000/5,000 =	$ 3.40

SELF-TEST QUESTIONS

Explain how the balance sheet is affected when a company issues new common stock.

Does it really matter if new common stock is sold for more or less than its par value? Than its book value?

LEGAL RIGHTS AND PRIVILEGES OF COMMON STOCKHOLDERS

The common stockholders are the owners of a corporation, and as such they have certain rights and privileges. The most important of these rights are discussed in this section.

CONTROL OF THE FIRM

The stockholders have the right to elect the firm's directors, who, in turn, elect the officers who will manage the business. In a small firm, the major stockholder typically assumes the positions of president and chairman of the board of directors. In a large, publicly owned firm, the managers typically have some stock, but their personal holdings are insufficient to allow them to exercise voting control. Thus, the managements of most publicly owned firms can be removed by the stockholders if they decide a management team is not effective.

Various state and federal laws stipulate how stockholder control is to be exercised. First, corporations must periodically hold an election of directors, usually once a year, with the vote taken at the annual meeting. Frequently, one-third of the directors are elected each year for a three-year term. Each share of stock has one vote; thus, the owner of 1,000 shares has 1,000 votes. Stockholders can appear at the annual meeting and vote in person, but typically they transfer their right to vote to a second party by means of a *proxy.* Management always solicits stockholders' proxies and usually gets them. However, if earnings are poor and stockholders are dissatisfied, an outside group may solicit the proxies in an effort to overthrow management and take control of the business. This is known as a *proxy fight.*

The question of control has become a central issue in finance in recent years. The frequency of proxy fights has increased, as have attempts by one corporation to take over another by purchasing a majority of the outstanding stock. This latter action, which is called a *takeover,* is discussed in detail in Chapter 25. Managers who do not have majority control (over 50 percent) of their firms' stocks are very concerned about proxy fights and takeovers, and many of them are attempting to get stockholder approval for changes in their corporate charters that would make takeovers more difficult. Managements seeking such changes generally cite a fear that the firm will be picked up at a bargain price, but it often appears that managers' concern over their own positions is an even more important consideration.

THE PREEMPTIVE RIGHT

Common stockholders often have the right, called the *preemptive right,* to purchase any new shares sold by the firm. In some states the preemptive right is mandatory; in others it is absent unless specifically inserted into the charter.

The purpose of the preemptive right is twofold. First, it protects the present stockholders' power of control. If it were not for this safeguard, the management of a corporation under criticism from stockholders could secure its position by issuing a large number of additional shares and purchasing these shares itself or getting a group of "friendly" investors to purchase them. Management could thereby gain control of the corporation and frustrate the current stockholders.

The second, and by far the more important, reason for the preemptive right is that it protects stockholders against a dilution of value. For example, suppose 1,000 shares of common stock, each with a price of $100, were outstanding, making the total market value of the firm $100,000. If an additional 1,000 shares were sold at $50 a share, or for $50,000, this would raise the total market value of the firm to $150,000. When the total market value is divided by the new total shares outstanding, a value of $75 a share is obtained. The old stockholders thus lose $25 per share, and the new stockholders have an instant profit of $25 per share. Therefore, selling common stock at a price below the market value would dilute its price and transfer wealth from the present stockholders to those who purchased the new shares. The preemptive right prevents such wealth transfers.

How do shareholders exercise their right of control?
What is the preemptive right, and what is its purpose?

SELF-TEST QUESTIONS

TYPES OF COMMON STOCK

Although most firms have only one type of common stock, in some instances *classified stock* is used to meet the special needs of the company. Generally, when special classifications of stock are used, one type is designated *Class A,* another *Class B,* and so on. Small, new companies seeking to obtain funds from outside sources frequently use different types of common stock. For example, when Genetic Research went public in 1996, its Class A stock was sold to the public and paid a dividend, but carried no voting rights for five years. Its Class B stock was retained by the organizers and carried full voting rights for five years, but dividends could not be paid on the Class B stock until the company had established its earning power and built up retained earnings to a designated level. Because of the classified stock, the public was able to take a position in a conservatively financed growth company without sacrificing income, while the founders retained absolute control during the crucial early stages of the firm's development. At the same time, outside investors were protected against excessive withdrawals of funds by the original owners. As is often the case in such situations, the Class B stock was also called *founders' shares.*

Note that "Class A," "Class B," and so on, have no standard meanings. Most firms have no classified shares, but a firm that does could designate its Class B shares as founders' shares and its Class A shares as those sold to the public, while another could reverse these designations. Other firms could use the A and B designations for entirely different purposes.

General Motors recently introduced yet another type of common stock. When GM acquired Hughes Aircraft for $5 billion, it paid in part with a new Class H common, GMH, which had limited voting rights and whose dividends were tied to Hughes's performance as a GM subsidiary. The reasons for the new stock were reported to be that: (1) GM wanted to limit voting privileges on the new classified stock because of management's concern about a possible takeover, and (2) Hughes employees wanted to participate more directly in Hughes's own performance than would have been possible through regular GM stock. Later, GM created yet another class of stock, Class E, when it acquired Electronic Data Systems. Now (early 1996), GM is considering spinning off its EDS subsidiary.

GM's deals posed a problem for the NYSE, which had a rule against listing any company's common stock if the company had any nonvoting common stock outstanding. GM made it clear that it was willing to delist if the NYSE did not change its rules. The NYSE concluded that arrangements like that of GM were logical and were likely to be made by other companies in the future, so it changed its rules to accommodate GM. In reality, the NYSE had little choice. In recent years the over-the-counter (OTC) market has proven that it can provide a deep, liquid market for common stocks, and the defection of GM would have severely crippled the NYSE's reputation.

SELF-TEST QUESTION   What are some types of common stock, and what are some reasons for their use?

THE MARKET FOR COMMON STOCK

Some companies are so small that their common stock is not actively traded — it is owned by only a few people, usually the companies' managers. Such companies are said to be *privately held*, or *closely held*, and the stock is said to be *closely held stock.* On the other hand, the stocks of most larger companies are owned by many investors, most of whom are not active in management. Such companies are said to be *publicly owned,* and their stock is said to be *publicly held stock.*

The stocks of smaller publicly owned firms are not listed on an exchange; they trade in the *over-the-counter (OTC)* market. The companies and their stocks are said to be *unlisted.* However, most larger publicly owned companies apply for listing on an exchange. These companies and their stocks are said to be *listed.* As a general rule, companies are first listed on a regional exchange, such as the Pacific Coast or Midwest, then they move up to the American (AMEX), and finally, if they grow large enough, to the "Big Board," the New York Stock Exchange (NYSE). Thousands of stocks are traded in the OTC market, but in terms of market value and number of shares traded, the NYSE and the OTC markets are about even. As we discuss next, electronic communication links between OTC market participants are giving them many of the advantages formerly enjoyed solely by the organized exchanges, so the OTC market has been growing more rapidly than the exchanges in recent years.

Institutional investors such as pension funds, insurance companies, and mutual funds own about 55 percent of all common stocks. However, the institutions buy and sell relatively actively, so they account for over 80 percent of all transactions. Thus, the institutions have a heavy influence on the prices of individual stocks — in a real sense, institutional investors determine the price levels of stocks.

We can classify stock market transactions into three categories:

1. Initial public offerings by privately held firms: the new issue market. As we mentioned in the opening vignette for Chapter 1, in 1995 Netscape Communications sold 5 million shares of common stock to the general public. At the time, the company was owned by its management and a small group of venture capital investors. Whenever stock in a closely held company is offered to the public, the company is said to be *going public.* The market for stocks of companies that are going public is called the *new issue market,* and the issue is called an *initial public offering (IPO).* After going public, Netscape's shares were traded in the over-the-counter market. Note that in many IPOs, the company's managers, as well as the company itself, sell shares, so IPOs can raise funds for the issuing corporation as well as put cash into the hands of the founders.

The volume of new issues in the IPO market varies widely from year to year, depending on the general level of stock prices and investors' willingness to buy IPO stocks. For example, there were about 550 initial public offerings completed in 1995, approximately the same as in 1994. However, a surging stock market in 1993 resulting in a record year for IPOs, with 820 issues raising almost $60 billion in capital. Sometimes, deals that are announced never make it to completion. For example, Computerland Corporation, a leading computer retailer, canceled a planned IPO because of poor market conditions. Said a company spokesman, "We realized the stock wasn't going to command the price we thought it deserved."

Firms can go public without raising any additional capital. For example, in its early days the Ford Motor Company was owned exclusively by the Ford family. When Henry Ford died, he left a substantial part of his stock to the

Ford Foundation. When the Foundation later sold some of this stock to the general public, the Ford Motor Company went public, even though the company raised no capital in the transaction.

2. **Additional shares sold by established, publicly owned companies: the primary market.** In 1995, General Motors raised $1.14 billion by issuing new common stock. Since the shares sold were newly created, GM's issue was defined as a *primary market* offering, but since the firm was already publicly held, the offering was not an IPO. As we discussed in Chapters 13 and 14, firms prefer to obtain equity by retaining earnings because of the flotation costs and market pressure associated with the sale of new common stock. Thus, only 12 percent of the dollar value of new securities issued in 1995 were common stock. Still, if a company requires more equity than can be generated from retained earnings, a stock sale may be required.

3. **Outstanding shares of established, publicly owned companies: the secondary market.** If the owner of 100 shares of GM sells his or her stock, the trade is said to have occurred in the *secondary market.* Thus, the market for outstanding shares, or *used shares,* is defined as the secondary market. Over 579 million shares of GM were bought and sold on the NYSE in 1995, and GM did not receive a dime from these transactions.

SELF-TEST QUESTIONS

What is an initial public offering (IPO)?

What are the key differences when GM sells shares in the primary market versus when its shares are traded in the secondary market?

THE DECISION TO GO PUBLIC

Most businesses begin life as proprietorships or partnerships, and then, as the more successful ones grow, at some point they find it desirable to convert into corporations. Generally, new corporations' stocks are owned by the firm's officers, key employees, and/or a very few investors who are not actively involved in management. However, if growth continues, at some point the company may decide to go public. As described earlier, Netscape and hundreds of other companies took this step in 1995. The advantages and disadvantages of public ownership are discussed next.

ADVANTAGES OF GOING PUBLIC

1. **Permits founder diversification.** As a company grows and becomes more valuable, its founders often have most of their wealth tied up in the company. By selling some of their stock in a public offering, they can diversify their holdings, thereby reducing the riskiness of their personal portfolios.

2. **Increases liquidity.** The stock of a closely held firm is illiquid: it has no ready market. If one of the owners wants to sell some shares to raise cash, it is hard to find a ready buyer, and even if a buyer is located, there is no established price on which to base the transaction. These problems do not exist with publicly owned firms.

3. **Facilitates raising new corporate cash.** If a privately held company wants to raise cash by a sale of new stock, it must either go to its existing owners, who may not have any money or not want to put any more eggs in this particular basket, or else shop around for wealthy investors. However, it is usually quite difficult to get outsiders to put money into a closely held company, because if the outsiders do not have voting control (over 50 percent of the stock), the inside stockholders/managers can run roughshod over them. The insiders can pay or not pay dividends, pay themselves exorbitant salaries, have private deals with the company, and so on. For example, the president might buy a warehouse and lease it to the company at a high rental, get the use of a Rolls Royce, and enjoy frequent "all-the-frills" travel to conventions. The insiders can even keep the outsiders from knowing the company's actual earnings, or its real worth. There are few positions more vulnerable than that of an outside stockholder in a closely held company, and for this reason, it is hard for closely held companies to raise new equity capital. Going public, which brings with it both public disclosure of information and regulation by the Securities and Exchange Commission (SEC), greatly reduces these problems, makes people more willing to invest in the company, and thus makes it easier for the firm to raise capital.

4. **Establishes a value for the firm.** For a number of reasons, it is often useful to establish a firm's value in the marketplace. For one thing, when the owner of a privately owned business dies, state and federal tax appraisers must set a value on the company for estate tax purposes. Often, these appraisers set too high a value, which creates an obvious problem. However, a company that is publicly owned has an established value. Similarly, if a company wants to give incentive stock options to key employees, it is useful to know the exact value of those options, and employees much prefer to own stock, or options on stock, that is publicly traded and therefore liquid.

DISADVANTAGES OF GOING PUBLIC

1. **Cost of reporting.** A publicly owned company must file quarterly and annual reports with the SEC and/or with various state agencies. These reports can be a costly pain, especially for small firms.

2. **Disclosure.** Management may not like the idea of reporting operating data, because such data will then be available to competitors. Similarly, the owners of the company may not want people to know their net worth, and since a publicly owned company must disclose the number of shares owned by its officers, directors, and major stockholders, it is easy enough for anyone to multiply shares held by price per share to estimate the net worth of the insiders.

3. **Self-dealings.** The owners/managers of closely held companies have many opportunities for various types of questionable but legal self-dealings, including the payment of high salaries, nepotism, personal transactions with the business (such as a leasing arrangement), and not-truly-necessary fringe benefits. Such self-dealings, which are often designed to minimize taxes, are much harder to arrange if a company is publicly owned.

4. **Inactive market/low price.** If the firm is very small, and if its shares are not traded with much frequency, its stock will not really be liquid, and the market price may not be representative of the stock's true value. Security analysts and stockbrokers simply will not follow the stock, because there will not be sufficient trading activity to generate enough brokerage commissions to cover the costs of following the stock.

5. **Control.** Because of the recent dramatic increase in tender offers and proxy fights, the managers of publicly owned firms who do not have voting control must be concerned about maintaining control. Further, there is pressure on such managers to produce annual earnings gains, even when it might be in the shareholders' best long-term interests to adopt a strategy that reduces short-term earnings but raises them in future years. These factors have led a number of public companies to "go private" in "leveraged buyout" deals where the managers borrow the money to buy out the nonmanagement stockholders. We discuss the decision to go private in a later section.

CONCLUSIONS ON GOING PUBLIC

There are no hard-and-fast rules regarding if or when a company should go public. This is an individual decision that should be made on the basis of the company's and stockholders' own unique circumstances. If a company does decide to go public, either by selling newly issued stock to raise new capital or by the sale of stock by the current owners, the key issue is setting the price at which shares will be offered to the public. The company and its current owners want to set the price as high as possible — the higher the offering price, the smaller the fraction of the company the current owners will have to give up to obtain any specified amount of money. On the other hand, potential buyers want the price set as low as possible. We will return to the establishment of the offering price later in the chapter, after we have described some other aspects of common stock financing.

SELF-TEST QUESTIONS : What are the major advantages of going public?
What are the major disadvantages?

THE DECISION TO LIST

The decision to go public is truly a milestone in a company's life — it marks a major change in the relationship between the firm and its owners. The decision to *list* the stock and have it trade on an exchange rather than in the over-the-counter market, on the other hand, is not a major event. The company will have to file a few new reports and abide by the rules of the exchange; stockholders will generally purchase or sell shares through a stockbroker who acts as an *agent* rather than a *dealer;* and the stock's price will be quoted in the newspaper under a stock exchange rather than in the over-the-counter section. These are not significant differences.

In order to have its stock listed, a company must apply to an exchange, pay a relatively small fee, and meet the exchange's minimum requirements. These requirements relate to the size of the company's net income and the number of shares outstanding and in the hands of outsiders (as opposed to the number held by insiders, who generally do not trade their stock very actively). Also, the company must agree to disclose certain information to the exchange; this information is designed to help the exchange track trading patterns and thus to try to ensure that no one is attempting to manipulate the price of the stock.[4] The size qualifications increase as one moves from the regional exchanges to the AMEX and on to the NYSE.

Assuming a company qualifies, many people believe that listing is beneficial both to it and to its stockholders. Listed companies receive a certain amount of free advertising and publicity, and their status as a listed company may enhance their prestige and reputation. This may have a beneficial effect on the sales of the firm's products. Investors respond favorably to increased information, increased liquidity, and confidence that the quoted price is not being manipulated. By providing investors with these benefits in the form of listing their companies' stocks, financial managers may be able to lower their firms' cost of equity and increase the value of their stock.

However, due to improvements in telecommunications and computer technologies, the differences between the OTC market and the exchanges have become less distinct. As a result, some very large companies such as MCI, Microsoft, Intel, and Apple, which almost certainly would have been listed on the NYSE in earlier days, have elected to remain in the OTC market. Today, corporate CFOs are more conscious than ever that alternative markets have benefits that may exceed the prestige of a NYSE listing.

What are the major advantages and disadvantages to a company listing its stock on an exchange?	**SELF-TEST QUESTION**

PROCEDURES FOR SELLING NEW COMMON STOCK

If a company plans to sell stock to raise new capital, the new shares may be sold in one of five ways: (1) on a pro rata basis to existing stockholders through a rights offering, (2) through investment bankers to the general public in a public offering, (3) to a single buyer (or a very small number of buyers) in a private placement, (4) to employees through employee stock purchase plans, or (5) through a dividend reinvestment plan. We discussed dividend reinvestment plans in Chapter 15; the other procedures are considered in the following sections.

RIGHTS OFFERINGS

As discussed earlier, common stockholders often have the *preemptive right* to purchase any additional shares sold by the firm. If the preemptive right is contained in

---

[4]It is illegal for anyone to attempt to manipulate the price of a stock. During the 1920s, and earlier, syndicates would buy and sell stocks back and forth at rigged prices so the public would believe that a particular stock was worth more or less than its true value. The exchanges, with the encouragement and support of the SEC, utilize sophisticated computer programs to help spot any irregularities that suggest manipulation, and they require disclosures to help identify manipulators. This same system helps to identify illegal insider trading.

a particular firm's charter, the company must offer any newly issued common stock to existing stockholders. If the charter does not prescribe a preemptive right, the firm can sell to its existing stockholders or to the public at large. If it sells to the existing stockholders, the issue is called a *rights offering*. Each stockholder is issued an option to buy a certain number of new shares, and the terms of the option are listed on a certificate called a *stock purchase right*, or simply a *right*. If a stockholder does not wish to purchase any additional shares, then he or she can sell the rights to some other person who does want to buy the stock.[5]

PUBLIC OFFERINGS

If the preemptive right exists in a company's charter, it must sell new stock through a rights offering. If the preemptive right does not apply, the company can choose between a rights offering and a *public offering*. We discuss procedures for public offerings later in the chapter.

PRIVATE PLACEMENTS

In a *private placement*, securities are sold to one or a few investors, generally institutional investors. Private placements are most common with bonds, but they also occur with stocks. The primary advantages of private placements are (1) lower flotation costs and (2) greater speed, since the shares do not have to go through the SEC registration process.

The most common type of private placement occurs when a company places securities directly with a financial institution, often an insurance company or a mutual fund. In fact, Prudential Insurance Company has begun sending salespeople to call on businesses — not to sell them policies, but to sell them on raising funds privately from Prudential. To illustrate a private placement, AT&T recently sold 6.3 million shares of common stock worth about $650 million to Capital Group Inc., a Los Angeles institutional investor that manages both mutual and pension funds. The transaction was a blow to three Wall Street firms, Morgan Stanley, Dillon Reed, and Goldman Sachs, which wanted to sell the stock in a conventional public offering. AT&T's treasurer said selling the stock in a private placement saved about 2.5 percent, or $16.3 million, in underwriting expenses.

One type of private placement that is occurring with increasing frequency is where a large company makes an equity investment in a smaller supplier. For example, Compaq Computer and AMP Corporation each recently invested several million in Intellon Corporation, a telecommunications equipment manufacturer. Intellon needed capital for expansion, and Compaq and AMP were both engaged in joint development ventures with Intellon and wanted it to be financially strong. Similar arrangements are quite common, and some of them go back many years. For example, Sears, Roebuck has for many years supplied equity capital to some of its major suppliers, including Johnson Controls, which furnishes Sears with "Die-

---

[5]For more details on the mechanics of a rights offering, see Eugene F. Brigham and Louis C. Gapenski, *Intermediate Financial Management,* 5th Ed. (Forth Worth, Tex.: Dryden Press, 1996), Chapter 14.

Hard" batteries, and with DeSoto Chemical, which supplies most of the paints that Sears sells.

The primary disadvantage of a private placement is that the securities generally do not go through the SEC registration process, so they cannot be sold except to another large, "sophisticated" purchaser in the event the original buyer wants to sell them. However, the SEC recently ruled that any institution with a portfolio of $100 million or more can buy and sell private placement securities. Since there are many institutions with assets that exceed this limit, private placements are becoming increasingly popular, and today they constitute almost 40 percent of all nonbank debt financing.

EMPLOYEE PURCHASE PLANS AND ESOPs

Many companies have plans that allow employees to purchase stock on favorable terms. Under executive stock option plans, key managers are given options to purchase stock. These managers generally have a direct, material influence on the company's fortunes, so if they perform well, the stock will go up, and the options will become valuable. There are also plans for lower-level employees. For example, IBM permits employees who are not participants in its stock option plan to allocate up to 10 percent of their salaries to its stock purchase plan, and the funds are then used to buy newly issued shares at 85 percent of the market value on the purchase date. Often, the company's contribution (in IBM's case, the 15 percent discount) is not vested in an employee until five years after the purchase date. This type of plan is designed both to improve employee performance and to reduce turnover.

Another type of plan calls for the stock bought for employees to be purchased out of a share of the company's profits. Congress has sought to encourage such plans through tax policy — under an *Employee Stock Ownership Plan (ESOP)*, companies can claim a tax credit equal to a percentage of wages, provided that the funds are used to buy newly issued stock for the benefit of employees. The amount of the credit varies from year to year, depending on the whims of Congress: currently it is ½ of 1 percent of total wages.

ESOPs have been hailed by some as a miracle tonic that will invigorate a tiring manufacturing economy. Critics claim that ESOPs represent a desperate move by managers who would rather give the company to employees than succumb to raiders. Others call ESOPs tax dodges, or socialistic, or "people's capitalism." All parties can muster evidence to support their claims, but the ESOP trend is too new for anyone to be sure who is right.

To start a typical ESOP, a company borrows money to buy its own stock, either from newly issued stock or on the open market, and places the stock in the hands of the ESOP trustee, who then allocates the stock ownership to the firm's employees on the basis of relative salaries. Then, after the ESOP is initially funded, additional stock is bought and paid for out of annual earnings. Often, ESOPs are set up to supplement or to replace entirely employee retirement programs. ESOPs generally have one thing in common with leveraged buyouts (LBOs) — they increase debt, hence result in higher financial leverage. However, the similarity ends there. While an LBO usually makes owners out of a small group of managers, an ESOP makes owners out of practically everyone on the payroll.

The advantages of ESOPs are as follows:

1. **Tax breaks.** Companies get a triple tax deduction on ESOPs — they can deduct (1) the interest on the debt used to buy stock for the ESOP, (2) some of the principal payments on the ESOP-funding debt, and (3) the dividends they pay on the ESOP-held shares.

2. **Anti-takeover defense.** The more of a company's stock the ESOP holds, the better able a company is to fend off a raider, because the ESOP's trustee will generally support current management over a raider who may be planning to fire many of the current employees.

3. **Pension cost control.** When a company uses an ESOP to reduce or even replace its conventional pension plan, it can save heavily. Some companies drop their retirement medical benefits, telling employees that they can dip into their ESOP accounts to buy medical coverage.

4. **Productivity enhancement.** Once the employees are owners as well as workers, they are presumably motivated to become more productive and more concerned about product quality.

Although their advantages are very real, ESOPs have some disadvantages:

1. **Balance of power.** ESOPs transform workers into a large bloc of shareholders with intimate knowledge about the company. If a firm's managers alienate the employee-owners, workers could vote their shares in favor of a raider.

2. **Legal considerations.** The Labor Department and the courts are on the lookout for ESOP abuses. If they perceive an ESOP to be a hastily constructed takeover defense, designed primarily to protect current management, they could reject the ESOP plan. Also, ESOP laws could be changed by Congress at any time to make them less favorable to the firm.

3. **Retiree benefits.** The more retirees' benefits are tied to an ESOP, the more dependent retirees become on the price of the company's stock. That leaves retirees vulnerable to both the whims of Wall Street and management mistakes, and it puts a lot of employees' retirement eggs into one basket.

4. **Obligation to repurchase stock.** Private companies with ESOPs must repurchase stock at the current appraised value when employees leave the company or retire. If a large number of employees quit or retire in a given year, the repurchases can put a significant strain on the company's cash position.

Although employee purchase plans are designed more to provide incentives to improve employee performance than to raise capital, these plans do produce a surprisingly large amount of new equity. Note, though, that a company may choose to purchase shares for its ESOP on the open market rather than issue new shares. The decision to use newly issued shares or repurchased shares depends upon the company's need for funds in a given year. Still, employee purchase plans have the potential for raising a great deal of equity capital.

What is a rights offering?

What is a private placement? What are its primary advantages over a public offering?

Briefly describe employee purchase plans.

What is an Employee Stock Ownership Plan (ESOP)? What are its major advantages and disadvantages?

ADVANTAGES AND DISADVANTAGES OF COMMON STOCK

In this section we briefly discuss the advantages and disadvantages of financing with common stock.

ADVANTAGES OF COMMON STOCK

1. Common stock does not entail fixed charges. If the company does not generate enough earnings, it does not have to pay common stock dividends. If the firm uses debt, it must make interest and principal payments regardless of the level of earnings.

2. Common stock has no fixed maturity date — it is permanent capital which does not have to be "paid back."

3. Since common stock strengthens the position of creditors, its use helps bond ratings and lowers the cost of debt.

4. Common stock can, at times, be sold more easily than debt. It appeals to certain investor groups because (1) it typically carries a higher expected return than does preferred stock or debt, (2) it provides investors with a better hedge against inflation than does preferred stock or bonds, and (3) most of the returns are taxed as capital gains, and taxes can be deferred until the gains are realized.

DISADVANTAGES OF COMMON STOCK

1. The sale of common stock normally gives voting rights, and perhaps even control, to the new investors who are brought into the company. For this reason, equity financing is often avoided by small firms, whose owner-managers may be unwilling to share control with outsiders. Note, though, that firms can use special classes of common stock that do not carry voting rights.

2. Debt enables the firm to acquire funds at a fixed cost, whereas common stock means that more stockholders will share in the firm's future profits.

3. The costs of underwriting and distributing common stock are higher than those for preferred stock or debt.

4. The sale of new common stock may be perceived by investors as a negative signal, hence may cause the stock to fall.

What are the advantages of common stock?

What are some disadvantages of common stock?

THE DECISION TO GO PRIVATE

In a *going private* transaction, the entire equity of a publicly held firm is purchased by a small group of investors which usually includes the firm's current senior management.[6] In some transactions, the current management acquires all of the stock. In others, current management participates in the ownership with a small group of outside investors who arrange for the financing needed to purchase the publicly held stock. Such deals almost always involve substantial borrowing, often up to 90 percent, and thus are commonly known as *leveraged buyouts (LBOs)* or *leveraged managerial buyouts (MBOs)*.

Regardless of the structure of the deal, going private initially affects the right-hand side of the balance sheet, the liabilities and capital, but not necessarily the assets — going private simply rearranges the ownership structure. Going private involves no obvious operating economies, yet the new owners are generally willing to pay a large premium over the stock's current price in order to take the firm private. For example, the managers of Hospital Corporation of America (HCA) paid $51 a share to outside (public) shareholders although the stock was only selling for $31 before the LBO offer was made. The managers of a company, who have the best information about its potential profitability, would not knowingly pay too much for the firm. Thus, HCA's management must have regarded the firm as being grossly undervalued or else thought that they could significantly boost the firm's value under private ownership. This suggests that going private can increase the value of some firms by enough to enrich both managers and public stockholders. The primary advantages to going private are (1) administrative cost savings, (2) increased managerial incentives, (3) increased managerial flexibility, (4) increased shareholder participation, and (5) increased use of financial leverage, which of course reduces taxes. We will discuss each of these advantages in more detail in the following paragraphs.

1. **Administrative cost savings.** Because going private takes the stock out of public hands, it saves on costs associated with securities registration, annual reports, SEC and exchange reporting, responding to stockholder inquiries, and so on. More important, the top managers of private firms are free from meetings with security analysts, government bodies, and other outside parties. Byron C. Radaker, CEO of Congoleum Corporation, a company that went private, estimated the administrative cost savings to his company from going private at between $6 million and $8 million per year.

2. **Increased managerial incentives.** An even larger potential gain comes from the improvement in incentives for high-level managerial performance. Their increased ownership means that the firm's managers will benefit more directly from their own efforts, hence efficiency tends to increase after a firm goes private. If the firm is highly successful, its managers can easily see their personal net worth increase 10- to 20-fold, while if the firm fails, its managers

---

[6]See Harry DeAngelo, Linda DeAngelo, and Edward M. Rice, "Going Private: The Effects of a Change in Corporate Ownership," *Midland Corporate Finance Journal,* Summer 1984, 35–43, for a more complete discussion of going private. The discussion in this section draws heavily from their work.

will end up with nothing. Further, a highly leveraged position will tend to drive the firm toward the extremes—large losses or large profits. The managers of companies that have gone through LBOs state that large interest payments, combined with a knowledge that success will bring great wealth, do much to improve both decisions and effort levels.

3. **Increased managerial flexibility.** A third source of value stems from the increased flexibility enjoyed by managers of private firms. These managers do not have to worry about what a drop in next quarter's earnings will do to the firm's stock price, hence they can focus on long-term, strategic actions that ultimately increase the firm's value. Managerial flexibility concerning asset sales is also greater in a private firm, since such sales do not have to be justified to a large number of shareholders with potentially diverse interests.

4. **Increased shareholder participation.** Going private typically results in replacing a dispersed, largely passive group of public shareholders with a small group of investors who play a much more active role. These new equity investors have a substantial stake in the private firm, hence they are more motivated to monitor management and to provide incentives to management than are the typical stockholders of a public corporation. Further, the new nonmanagement equity investors, such as Kohlberg, Kravis, Roberts & Company (KKR), are typically represented on the board, and they bring both sophisticated financial expertise and hard-nosed attitudes to the new firm. These outsiders don't have good friends running money-losing operations, so they are more willing to force major operating changes than are entrenched managers. For example, a few weeks after KKR won the battle for RJR Nabisco, the much touted but unprofitable Premier "smokeless" cigarette project was abandoned.

5. **Increased financial leverage.** Going private usually entails a drastic increase in the firm's use of debt, which has two effects. First, taxes are reduced because of the increase in deductible interest payments, so more of the operating income flows through to investors. Second, the increased debt servicing requirements force managers to increase revenues and/or reduce costs to ensure that the firm has sufficient cash flow to meet its obligations—a highly leveraged firm simply cannot afford any fat.

One might ask why all firms are not privately held. The answer is that, while there are real benefits to private ownership, there are also benefits to being publicly owned. Most notably, public corporations have access to large amounts of equity capital on advantageous terms, and for most companies, the advantage of access to public capital markets dominates the advantages of going private. Also, note that most companies which go private end up going public again after several years of operation as private firms. For example, HCA, which went private in 1987, again went public in 1992. During the private phase, management typically sheds inefficient businesses, cuts costs throughout the corporation, and, generally, rationalizes operations. These actions increase the value of the firm. Once the company has been "straightened up," going public allows the private equityholders to recover their investment, take their profit, and move on to new ventures.

Note too that the examples set by LBO companies are not lost on companies that maintain their publicly owned status. Thus, companies such as Phillips Petroleum and Union Carbide, under pressure from raiders, changed their operations to the point where they resemble LBO companies. This increased their value and made them less attractive to KKR and other LBO specialists, and thus benefitted both managements and shareholders.

SELF-TEST QUESTIONS

What is meant by the term "going private"?

What are the main benefits of going private?

Why don't all firms go private to capture these benefits?

REGULATION AND THE INVESTMENT BANKING PROCESS

In this section, we describe the regulation of securities markets, the way securities are issued, and the role of investment bankers in the process.

REGULATION OF SECURITIES MARKETS

Sales of new securities, and also sales in the secondary markets, are regulated by the *Securities and Exchange Commission (SEC)* and, to a lesser extent, by each of the 50 states. Here are the primary elements of SEC regulation:

1. The SEC has jurisdiction over all interstate public offerings in amounts of $1.5 million or more.

2. Newly issued securities (stocks and bonds) must be registered with the SEC at least 20 days before they are publicly offered. The *registration statement* provides financial, legal, and technical information about the company to the SEC, and the *prospectus* summarizes this information for investors. The SEC's lawyers and accountants analyze both the registration statement and the prospectus; if the information is inadequate or misleading, the SEC will delay or stop the public offering.

3. After the registration has become effective, new securities may be offered, but all sales solicitations must be accompanied by the prospectus. Preliminary, or *"red herring," prospectuses* may be distributed to potential buyers during the 20-day waiting period, but no sales may be finalized during this time. The "red herring" prospectus contains all the key information that will appear in the final prospectus except the price, which is generally set after the market closes the day before the new securities are actually offered to the public.

4. If the registration statement or prospectus contains misrepresentations or omissions of material facts, any purchaser who suffers a loss may sue for damages. Severe penalties may be imposed on the issuer or its officers, directors, accountants, engineers, appraisers, underwriters, and all others who participated in the preparation of the registration statement or prospectus.

5. The SEC also regulates all national stock exchanges, and companies whose securities are listed on an exchange must file annual reports similar to the registration statement with both the SEC and the exchange.

6. The SEC has control over trading by corporate *insiders.* Officers, directors, and major stockholders must file monthly reports of changes in their holdings of the stock of the corporation. Any short-term profits from such transactions must be turned over to the corporation.

7. The SEC has the power to prohibit manipulation by such devices as pools (large amounts of money used to buy or sell stocks to artificially affect prices) or wash sales (sales between members of the same group to record artificial transaction prices).

8. The SEC has control over the proxy statement and the way the company uses it to solicit votes.

Control over the flow of credit into security transactions is exercised by the Federal Reserve Board through *margin requirements,* which specify the maximum percentage of the purchase price someone can borrow. If a great deal of margin borrowing has been going on, then a decline in stock prices can result in inadequate coverages. This could force stockbrokers to issue *margin calls,* which, in turn, require investors either to put up more money or have their margined stock sold to pay off their loans. Such forced sales further depress the stock market and thus can set off a downward spiral. The margin requirement has been 50 percent since 1974.

States also have some control over the issuance of new securities within their boundaries. This control is usually exercised by a "corporation commissioner" or someone with a similar title. State laws relating to security sales are called *blue sky laws,* because they were put into effect to keep unscrupulous promoters from selling securities that offered the "blue sky" but which actually had little or no asset backing.

The securities industry itself realizes the importance of stable markets, sound brokerage firms, and the absence of stock manipulation. Therefore, the various exchanges work closely with the SEC to police transactions and to maintain the integrity and credibility of the system. Similarly, the *National Association of Securities Dealers (NASD)* cooperates with the SEC to police trading in the OTC market. These industry groups also cooperate with regulatory authorities to set net worth and other standards for securities firms, to develop insurance programs to protect the customers of brokerage houses, and the like.

In general, government regulation of securities trading, as well as industry self-regulation, is designed to ensure that investors receive information that is as accurate as possible, that no one artificially manipulates the market price of a given stock, and that corporate insiders do not take advantage of their position to profit in their companies' stocks at the expense of other stockholders. Neither the SEC, the state regulators, nor the industry itself can prevent investors from making foolish decisions or from having "bad luck," but they can and do help investors obtain the best data possible for making sound investment decisions.

THE INVESTMENT BANKING PROCESS

The investment banking process takes place in two stages.

STAGE I DECISIONS   At Stage I, the firm itself makes some initial, preliminary decisions, including the following:

1. **Dollars to be raised.** How much new capital is needed?

2. **Type of securities used.** Should common, preferred, bonds, or hybrid securities, or a combination, be used? Further, if common stock is to be issued, should it be done as a rights offering or by a direct sale to the general public?

3. **Competitive bid versus a negotiated deal.** Should the company simply offer a block of its securities for sale to the highest bidder, or should it negotiate a deal with an investment banker? These two procedures are called *competitive bids* and *negotiated deals,* respectively. Only about 100 of the largest firms listed on the NYSE, whose securities are already well known to the investment banking community, are in a position to use the competitive bidding process. The investment banks must do a great deal of investigative work ("due diligence") in order to bid on an issue unless they are already quite familiar with the firm, and such costs would be too high to make it worthwhile unless the bank was sure of getting the deal. Therefore, except for the largest firms, offerings of stock and bonds are generally on a negotiated basis.

4. **Selection of an investment banker.** If the issue is to be negotiated, the firm must select an investment banker. This can be an important decision for a firm that is going public. On the other hand, an older firm that has already "been to market" will have an established relationship with an investment banker. However, it is easy to change bankers if the firm is dissatisfied. Different investment banking houses are better suited for different companies. The older, larger "establishment houses" such as Morgan Stanley deal mainly with companies such as AT&T, IBM, and Exxon. Other bankers handle more speculative issues. Some houses specialize in new issues, while others are not well suited to handle such issues because their brokerage clients are relatively conservative. (Investment banking houses sell new issues largely to their own regular brokerage customers, so the nature of these customers has a major effect on the ability of the house to do a good job for a corporate client.) Table 16-3 lists the top ten U.S. underwriters for 1995 as measured by the dollar amount of securities underwritten.

STAGE II DECISIONS   Stage II decisions, which are made jointly by the firm and its selected investment banker, include the following:

1. **Reevaluating the initial decisions.** The firm and its banker will reevaluate the initial decisions regarding the size of the issue and the type of securities to use. For example, the firm may have decided initially to raise $50 million by selling common stock, but the investment banker may convince management that it would be better off, in view of current market conditions, to limit the stock issue to $25 million and to raise the other $25 million as debt.

TOP TEN UNDERWRITERS OF U.S. DEBT AND EQUITY	TABLE 16-3

	TOTAL AMOUNT MANAGED (IN BILLIONS OF DOLLARS)
1. Merrill Lynch	122.3
2. Lehman Brothers	70.3
3. Goldman Sachs	68.5
4. Morgan Stanley	68.5
5. Salomon Brothers	68.1
6. CS First Boston	64.6
7. J. P. Morgan	40.2
8. Bear Stearns	25.4
9. Donaldson, Lufkin & Jenrette	22.2
10. Smith Barney	20.7

SOURCE: *The Wall Street Journal*, January 2, 1996, p. R38. Reprinted by permission of *The Wall Street Journal*, © 1996. Dow Jones & Company, Inc. All Rights Reserved Worldwide.

2. **Best efforts or underwritten issues.** The firm and its investment banker must decide whether the banker will work on a *best efforts* basis or will *underwrite* the issue. In a best efforts sale, the banker does not guarantee that the securities will be sold or that the company will get the cash it needs, only that it will put forth its best efforts to sell the issue. On an underwritten issue, the company does get a guarantee, because the banker agrees to buy the entire issue and then resell the stock to its customers. Therefore, the banker bears significant risks in underwritten offerings. For example, on one IBM bond issue, interest rates rose sharply, and bond prices fell, after the deal had been set but before the investment bankers could sell the bonds to ultimate purchasers. The bankers lost somewhere between $10 million and $20 million. Had the offering been on a best efforts basis, IBM would have been the loser.

3. **Banker's compensation and other expenses.** The investment banker's compensation must be negotiated. Also, the firm must estimate the other underwriting expenses it will incur in connection with the issue — lawyers' fees, accountants' costs, printing and engraving, and so on. In an underwritten issue, the banker will buy the issue from the company at a discount below the price at which the securities are to be offered to the public, with this "spread" being set to cover the banker's costs and to provide a profit.

Table 16-4 gives an indication of the issuance costs associated with public issues of straight bonds, convertible bonds, and common stock. As the table shows, costs as a percentage of the proceeds are higher for stocks than for bonds, and costs are higher for small than for large issues. The relationship between size of issue and flotation cost is due primarily to the existence of

TABLE 16-4	ISSUANCE COSTS FOR UNDERWRITTEN, NONRIGHTS OFFERINGS (EXPRESSED AS PERCENTAGE OF GROSS PROCEEDS)					

SIZE OF ISSUE (MILLIONS OF DOLLARS)	STRAIGHT BONDS			CONVERTIBLE BONDS		
	UNDERWRITING COMMISSION	OTHER EXPENSES	TOTAL COSTS	UNDERWRITING COMMISSION	OTHER EXPENSES	TOTAL COSTS
Under 1.0	10.0%	4.0%	14.0%	9.0%	7.1%	16.1%
1.0–1.9	8.0	3.0	11.0	8.2	6.8	15.0
2.0–4.9	4.0	2.2	6.2	6.9	3.4	10.3
5.0–9.9	2.4	0.8	3.2	5.7	3.3	9.0
10.0–19.9	1.5	1.4	2.9	5.5	3.2	8.7
20.0–49.9	1.5	0.9	2.4	3.7	1.4	5.1
50.0 and over	1.5	0.5	2.0	2.2	0.2	2.4

NOTES:

a. In the last edition of this book we reported the costs of issuing preferred stock. In this edition we replaced preferred stock with convertible bonds because more convertibles are issued than preferred stocks.

b. Flotation costs tend to rise somewhat when interest rates are cyclically high, indicating that money is in relatively tight supply, hence investment bankers will have a relatively hard time placing issues with permanent investors. Thus, the figures shown in this table represent averages, as flotation costs actually vary somewhat over time.

c. Underpricing is shown as a separate cost component for initial public offerings because it has been measured and is reasonably predictable. Underpricing also exists for common stock offerings by companies that already have publicly traded stock, but the effects are unstable and difficult to measure; these effects are discussed later in the chapter.

fixed costs — certain costs must be incurred regardless of the size of the issue, so the percentage flotation cost is quite high for small issues.

Also, it should be noted that when companies go public to raise new capital, the new shares are typically underpriced, so the stock often closes on the first day of trading at a price above the issue price. For example, Boston Chicken's stock soared from its $20 offering price to close the first day at $51. Underpricing represents a potentially large cost to existing shareholders, as shown in the initial public offerings section of Table 16-4. Further, the investment bankers frequently take part of their compensation in the form of options to buy stock in the firm. For example, Glasgo Technologies recently went public with a $10 million issue by selling 1 million shares at a price of $10 per share. Its investment bankers bought the stock from the company at a price of $9.75 per share, so the direct underwriting fee was only 1,000,000($10.00 − $9.75) = $250,000, or 2.5 percent, but they also received a five-year option to buy 200,000 shares at a price of $10 per share. If the stock should go up to $15 per share, which the bankers expected it to do, then the investment banking firm would make a $1 million profit, which would in effect be an additional underwriting fee.

4. **Setting the offering price.** If the company is already publicly owned, the offering price will be based upon the existing market price of the stock. Typ-

COMMON STOCK: ADDITIONAL SHARES			COMMON STOCK: INITIAL PUBLIC OFFERINGS			
UNDERWRITING COMMISSION	OTHER EXPENSES	TOTAL COSTS	UNDERWRITING COMMISSION	OTHER EXPENSES	UNDERPRICING COSTS	TOTAL COSTS
13.0%	9.0%	22.0%	9.8%	9.6%	12.3%	31.7%
11.0	5.9	16.9	9.8	9.6	12.3	31.7
8.6	3.8	12.4	9.4	6.6	6.9	22.9
7.2	2.1	9.3	8.0	4.3	5.5	17.8
6.4	2.5	8.9	7.2	4.4	6.6	18.2
5.3	1.1	6.4	6.5	2.5	7.4	16.4
4.1	0.3	4.4	6.2	0.9	5.8	12.9

SOURCES: Inmoo Lee, Scott Lochhead, Jay Ritter, and Quanshui Zhao, "The Costs of Raising Capital," University of Illinois Working Paper dated July 25, 1995, and informal surveys of security offerings conducted by the authors.

ically, the investment banker buys the securities at a prescribed number of points below the closing price on the last day of registration. For example, suppose that in October 1996, the stock of Microwave Telecommunications Inc. (MTI) had a current price of $28.60 per share, and the stock had traded between $25 and $30 per share during the previous three months. Suppose further that MTI and its underwriter agreed that the investment banker would buy 10 million new shares at $1 per share below the closing price on the last day of registration. If the stock closed at $25 on the day the SEC released the issue, MTI would receive $24 per share. Typically, such agreements have an escape clause that provides for the contract to be voided if the price of the securities drops below some predetermined figure. In the illustrative case, this "upset" price might be set at $24 per share. Thus, if the closing price of the shares on the last day of registration had been $23.50, MTI would have had the option of withdrawing from the agreement.

The investment banker will have an easier job if the issue is priced relatively low, but the issuer naturally wants as high a price as possible. A conflict of interest on price therefore arises between the investment banker and the issuer. If the issuer is financially sophisticated and makes comparisons with similar security issues, the investment banker will be forced to price close to the market.

As we discussed in Chapter 13, the announcement of a new stock offering by a mature firm is often taken as a negative signal — if the firm's prospects were good, management would not want to issue new stock and thus share the rosy future with new stockholders. Therefore, the announcement of a new offering is taken as bad news. Consequently, the price will probably fall when the announcement is made, so the offering price will probably have to be set at a price substantially below the pre-announcement market price. Consider Figure 16-1, in which d_0 is the estimated market demand curve for MTI's stock and S_0 is the number of shares currently outstanding. Initially, there are 50 million shares outstanding, and the equilibrium price is $28.60 per share, determined as follows:

$$\hat{P}_0 = \frac{D_1}{k_s - g} = \frac{\$2.00}{0.12 - 0.05} \approx \$28.60.$$

The values shown for D_1, k_s, and g are the *estimates of the marginal investor.* Investors who do not now own MTI's stock probably, on average, regard the stock as being riskier and thus assign it a higher k_s, or perhaps they estimate the company's growth rate as being lower than do people who now own the stock, and they use g < 5 percent when calculating the stock's intrinsic value. In any event, people who do not now own the stock think the stock is worth less than $28.60.

When MTI announces that it plans to sell another 10 million shares, this is taken as a negative signal. Consequently, the demand curve for the stock drops from d_0 to d_1, and the price falls. The new equilibrium price, if 50 million shares were outstanding and if the marginal investor now expects MTI's growth rate to be 4.2 percent, would be about $25.60:

$$\hat{P}_0 = \frac{\$2.00}{0.12 - 0.042} \approx \$25.60.$$

FIGURE 16-1   **MICROWAVE TELECOMMUNICATIONS INC.: ESTIMATED COMMON STOCK DEMAND CURVES**

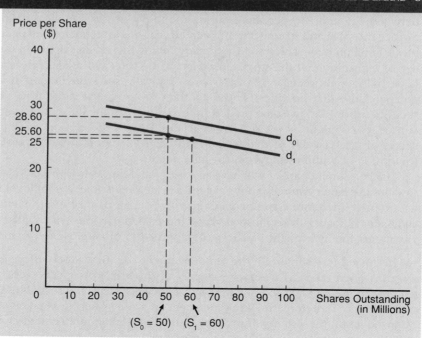

However, if MTI is to sell another 10 million shares of stock, it will either have to attract investors who would not be willing to own the stock at the $25.60 per share price or else induce present stockholders to buy additional shares. There are two ways this can be accomplished: (1) by reducing the offering price of the stock or (2) by "promoting" or "advertising" the company and thus shifting the demand curve for its stock back to the right.[7] If the demand curve does not shift at all from d_1, we see from Figure 16-1 that the only way the 10 million additional shares could be sold would be by setting the offering price at about $25 per share. However, if the investment banker could promote the stock sufficiently to shift the demand curve back up to d_0, then the offering price could be set much closer to the preannouncement equilibrium price of $28.60 per share.[8]

The extent to which the demand curve can be shifted depends primarily on two factors: (1) what investors think the company can do with the money brought in by the stock sale and (2) how effectively the brokers promote the issue. If investors can be convinced that the new money will be invested in highly profitable projects that will raise earnings and the earnings growth rate, then the demand curve shift will occur, and the stock price might actually go above $28.60. Even if investors do not radically change their expectations about the company's fundamental factors, the fact that MTI's stock is brought to the attention of new investors may shift the demand curve. The extent to which this promotion campaign is successful in shifting the demand curve depends, of course, upon the effectiveness of the investment banking firm. Therefore, the effectiveness of different investment bankers, as perceived by MTI's financial manager, will be an important factor in the choice of an underwriter.

One final point is that *if pressure from the new shares and/or negative signaling effects drives down the price of the stock, all shares outstanding, not just the new shares, are affected.* Thus, if MTI's stock should fall from $28.60 to $25 per share as a result of the financing, and if the price should remain at that new level, then the company would incur a loss of $3.60 on each of the 50 million shares previously outstanding, or a total market value loss of $180 million. This loss, like underwriting expenses, is a flotation cost, and it should be considered as a cost associated with the stock issue. However, if the company's prospects really were poorer than investors thought, then the price decline would have occurred sooner or later anyway. On the other hand, if the company's prospects are really not all that bad (the signal was incorrect), then over time MTI's demand curve will move back to d_0, or

---

[7]It should be noted that investors can buy newly issued stock without paying normal brokerage commissions, and brokers are quick to point this out to potential purchasers. Thus, if an investor were to buy MTI's stock at $28 per share in the regular market, the commission would be about 1 percent, or 28 cents per share. If the stock were purchased in an underwriting, this commission would be avoided.

It should also be noted that for years many academicians argued that the demand curve for a firm's stock is either horizontal or has an extremely slight downward slope, and that signaling effects are minimal. Most corporate treasurers, on the other hand, have long felt that both effects exist for mature companies, and empirical studies confirm the treasurers' position. For example, see Andrei Shleifer, "Do Demand Curves for Stocks Slope Down?" *Journal of Finance*, July 1986, 579–590.

[8]Note that the supply curve is a vertical line, first at 50 million and then, after the new issue, at 60 million.

even above d_0, so the company would not suffer a permanent loss anywhere close to $180 million.

If the company is "going public," there will be no established price or demand curve, so the bankers will have to estimate the *equilibrium price* at which the stock will sell after issue. Note that if the offering price is set below the true equilibrium price, as with Boston Chicken and most other IPOs, the stock will rise sharply after the issue, and the company and its selling stockholders will have given away too many shares to raise the required capital. If the offering price is set above the true equilibrium price, either the issue will fail or, if the bankers succeed in selling the stock to their retail clients, these clients will be unhappy when the stock subsequently falls to its equilibrium level. Therefore, it is important that the equilibrium price be closely approximated, although it is hard to estimate this price.[9]

SELLING PROCEDURES   Once the company and its investment bankers have decided how much money to raise, the types of securities to issue, and the basis for pricing the issue, they will prepare and file an SEC *registration statement* and a *prospectus.* It generally takes about 20 days for the issue to be approved by the SEC. The final price of the stock (or the interest rate on a bond issue) is set at the close of business the day the issue clears the SEC, and the securities are offered to the public the following day.

Investors are required to pay for securities within 10 days, and the investment banker must pay the issuing firm within four days of the official commencement of the offering. Typically, the banker sells the stock within a day or two after the offering begins, but on occasion, the banker miscalculates, sets the offering price too high, and thus is unable to move the issue. At other times, the market declines during the offering period, forcing the banker to reduce the price of the stock or bonds. In either instance, on an underwritten offering the firm receives the price that was agreed upon, so the banker must absorb any losses that are incurred.

Because they are exposed to large potential losses, investment bankers typically do not handle the purchase and distribution of issues single-handedly unless the issue is a very small one. If the sum of money involved is large, investment bankers form *underwriting syndicates* in an effort to minimize the risk each banker carries. The banking house which sets up the deal is called the *lead,* or *managing, underwriter.*

In addition to the underwriting syndicate, on larger offerings still more investment bankers are included in a *selling group,* which handles the distribution of securities to individual investors. The selling group includes all members of the underwriting syndicate plus additional dealers who take relatively small percentages

---

[9] IPOs are almost always underpriced; in the period 1990–1994, Lee, Lochhead, Ritter, and Zhao (*op. cit*) found that underpricing averaged more than 12 percent. Various theories have been put forth to explain this phenomenon. The best explanation seems to be that (1) both the company and the investment bankers want to create excitement, and a price run-up does that; (2) a small percentage of the company's stock is generally offered to the public, so current stockholders give away less due to underpricing than appears at first glance; and (3) IPO companies generally plan to have further offerings in the future, and the best way to ensure future success is to have a successful IPO, which underpricing guarantees.

of the total issue from the members of the underwriting syndicate. Thus, the underwriters act as *wholesalers,* while members of the selling group act as *retailers.* The number of houses in a selling group depends partly upon the size of the issue. For example, the one set up when Communications Satellite Corporation (Comsat) went public consisted of 385 members.

A new selling procedure has recently emerged which does not require an underwriting syndicate. In this type of sale, called an *unsyndicated stock offering,* the managing underwriter, acting alone, sells the issue entirely to institutional investors, thus bypassing both retail stockbrokers and individual investors. In recent years, about 50 percent of all stock sold has been by unsyndicated offerings. Behind this phenomenon is a simple motivating force: money. The fees that issuers pay on a syndicated offering, which includes commissions paid to retail brokers, can run at least a full percentage point higher than those on unsyndicated offerings. Further, although total fees are lower if there is no syndicate, managing underwriters usually come out ahead because they do not have to share the fees with an underwriting syndicate. Recent issuers of unsyndicated stock include Transamerica Corporation and Public Service Company of New Mexico. However, some types of stock do not appeal to institutional investors, so not all firms can use unsyndicated offers.

SHELF REGISTRATIONS   The selling procedures described previously, including the 20-day waiting period after registration with the SEC, apply to most security sales. However, under the SEC's Rule 415, large, well-known public companies which issue securities frequently may file a *master registration statement* with the SEC and then update it with a *short-form statement* just prior to each individual offering. Under this procedure, the company can decide at 10 A.M. to sell securities and have the sale completed before noon. This procedure is known as *shelf registration* because, in effect, the company puts its new securities "on the shelf" and then sells them to investors when it feels the market is "right." Firms with less than $150 million in stock held by outside investors cannot use shelf registrations. The rationale for this distinction is to protect investors who may not be able to get adequate financial data about a little-known company in the short time between announcement of a shelf issue and its sale. Shelf registrations have two advantages over standard registrations: (1) lower flotation costs and (2) more control over the timing of the issue.

MAINTENANCE OF THE SECONDARY MARKET   In the case of a large, established firm such as IBM or GM, the investment banking firm's job is finished after it has disposed of the stock and turned the net proceeds over to the issuing firm. However, in the case of a small company going public for the first time, the investment banker is under some obligation to maintain a market in the shares after the issue has been completed. Such stocks are typically traded in the over-the-counter market, and the lead underwriter generally agrees to "make a market" in the stock so as to keep it reasonably liquid. The company wants a good market to exist for its stock, as do the stockholders. Therefore, if the banking house wants to do business with the company in the future, to keep its own brokerage customers happy, and to have future referral business, it will hold an inventory and help to maintain an active secondary market in the stock.

What are the key features of security market regulations?

What is the difference between Stage I and Stage II decisions?

What is the difference between a best efforts and an underwritten issue?

What are some potential problems encountered when setting the offering price on a stock issue?

Briefly explain the selling procedures used on a new securities issue.

What is a shelf registration? What are the advantages of shelf registrations over standard registrations?

SUMMARY

This chapter is more descriptive than analytical, but a knowledge of the issues discussed here is essential to an understanding of corporate finance. The key concepts covered are listed below.

■ *Stockholders' equity* consists of common stock, additional paid-in capital (funds received in excess of the par value), and retained earnings (earnings not paid out as dividends).

■ *Book value per share* is equal to stockholders' equity divided by the number of shares of stock outstanding. A stock's book value is often different from its par value and its market value.

■ A *proxy* is a document which gives one person the power to act for another person, typically the power to vote shares of common stock. A *proxy fight* occurs when an outside group solicits stockholders' proxies in order to vote a new management team into office.

■ Stockholders often have the right to purchase any additional shares sold by the firm. This right, called the *preemptive right*, protects the control position of the present stockholders and prevents dilution of the value of their stock.

■ Although most firms use only one type of common stock, in some instances several *classes of stock* are issued.

■ The major *advantages of common stock* are as follows: (1) there is no obligation to make fixed payments, (2) common stock never matures, (3) the use of common stock increases the creditworthiness of the firm, (4) stock can often be sold more easily than debt, and (5) using stock helps the firm maintain its reserve borrowing capacity.

■ The major *disadvantages of common stock* are (1) it extends voting rights to new stockholders, (2) new stockholders share in the firm's profits, (3) the costs of issuing stock are high, (4) using stock can raise the firm's cost of capital, and (5) dividends paid on common stock are not tax deductible.

■ A *closely held corporation* is one that is owned by a few individuals who are typically associated with the firm's management.

■ A *publicly owned corporation* is one that is owned by a relatively large number of individuals who are not actively involved in management.

■ *Going public* facilitates stockholder diversification, increases liquidity of the firm's stock, makes it easier for the firm to raise capital, and establishes a value for the firm. However, reporting costs are high, operating data must be disclosed, management self-dealings are harder to arrange, the price may sink to a low level if the stock is not traded actively, and public ownership may make it harder for management to maintain control.

■ The decision to *list* the stock on a major exchange is not as critical as the decision to go public.

■ New common stock may be sold in five ways: (1) on a pro rata basis to existing stockholders through a *rights offering*, (2) through investment bankers to the general public in a *public offering*, (3) to a single buyer, or a small number of buyers, in a *private placement*, (4) to employees through an *employee purchase plan*, and (5) to shareholders through a *dividend reinvestment plan*.

■ Securities markets are regulated by the *Securities and Exchange Commission (SEC)*.

■ An *investment banker* assists in the issuing of securities by helping the firm determine the size of the issue and the type of securities to be used, by establishing the selling price, by selling the issue, and, in some cases, by maintaining an after-market for the stock.

QUESTIONS

16-1 Define each of the following terms:
a. Common equity; additional paid-in capital; retained earnings
b. Par value; book value per share; market value per share
c. Proxy; proxy fight
d. Preemptive right
e. Classified stock; founders' shares
f. Closely held corporation; publicly owned corporation
g. Over-the-counter (OTC) market; organized security exchange
h. Primary market; secondary market
i. Going public; new issue market; initial public offering (IPO)
j. Rights offering
k. Public offering; private placement
l. Employee purchase plan; ESOP
m. Securities and Exchange Commission (SEC); registration statement; shelf registration; "blue sky" laws; margin requirement; insiders
n. Prospectus; "red herring" prospectus
o. National Association of Securities Dealers (NASD)
p. Best efforts arrangement; underwritten arrangement

q. Spread; flotation costs; offering price

r. Underwriting syndicate; lead, or managing, underwriter; selling group

16-2   Examine Table 16-1. Suppose American Chemical sold 2 million shares, with the company netting $25 per share. Construct a pro forma statement of the equity accounts to reflect this sale.

16-3   Is it true that the "flatter," or more nearly horizontal, the demand curve for a particular firm's stock, and the less important investors regard the signaling effect of the offering, the more important the role of investment bankers when the company sells a new issue of stock?

16-4   The SEC attempts to protect investors who are purchasing newly issued securities by making sure that the information put out by a company and its investment bankers is correct and is not misleading. However, the SEC does not provide an opinion about the real value of the securities; hence, an investor might pay too much for some new stock and consequently lose heavily. Do you think the SEC should, as a part of every new stock or bond offering, render an opinion to investors on the proper value of the securities being offered? Explain.

16-5   How do you think each of the following items would affect a company's ability to attract new capital and the flotation costs involved in doing so?

a. A decision to list a company's stock; the stock now trades in the over-the-counter market.

b. A decision of a privately held company to go public.

c. The increasing institutionalization of the "buy side" of the stock and bond markets.

d. The trend toward "financial conglomerates" as opposed to stand-alone investment banking houses.

e. Elimination of the preemptive right.

f. The introduction of "shelf registrations" in 1981.

16-6   Before entering a formal agreement, investment bankers carefully investigate the companies whose securities they underwrite; this is especially true of the issues of firms going public for the first time. Since the bankers do not themselves plan to hold the securities but intend to sell them to others as soon as possible, why are they so concerned about making careful investigations?

16-7   It is frequently stated that the primary purpose of the preemptive right is to allow individuals to maintain their proportionate share of the ownership and control of a corporation.

a. How important do you suppose this consideration is for the average stockholder of a firm whose shares are traded on the New York or American Stock Exchanges?

b. Is the preemptive right likely to be of more importance to stockholders of publicly owned or closely held firms? Explain.

c. Is a firm likely to get a wider distribution of shares if it sells new stock through a preemptive rights offering to existing stockholders or directly to underwriters?

d. Why would management be interested in getting a wider distribution of its shares?

6-1 **BOOK VALUE PER SHARE** The Morrissey Music Company had the following balance sheet at the end of 1996.

MORRISSEY MUSIC COMPANY: BALANCE SHEET AS OF DECEMBER 31, 1996

	Accounts payable	$ 48,000
	Notes payable	54,000
	Long-term debt	108,000
	Common stock (30,000 shares authorized, 20,000 shares outstanding)	270,000
	Retained earnings	225,000
Total assets $705,000	Total liabilities and equity	$705,000

a. What is the book value per share of the firm's common stock?
b. Suppose the firm sold the remaining authorized shares and netted $22.50 per share from the sale. What would be the new book value per share?

6-2 **PROFIT OR LOSS ON NEW STOCK ISSUE** Security Brokers Inc. specializes in underwriting new issues by small firms. On a recent offering of Beedles Inc., the terms were as follows:

Price to public:	$5 per share
Number of shares:	3 million
Proceeds to Beedles:	$14,000,000

The out-of-pocket expenses incurred by Security Brokers in the design and distribution of the issue were $300,000. What profit or loss would Security Brokers incur if the issue were sold to the public at an average price of
a. $5 per share?
b. $6 per share?
c. $4 per share?

6-3 **UNDERWRITING AND FLOTATION EXPENSES** The Beranek Company, whose stock price is now $25, needs to raise $20 million in common stock. Underwriters have informed the firm's management that they must price the new issue to the public at $22 per share because of a downward-sloping demand curve. The underwriters' compensation will be 5 percent of the issue price, so Beranek will net $20.90 per share. The firm will also incur expenses in the amount of $150,000.

How many shares must the firm sell to net $20 million after underwriting and flotation expenses?

6-4 **NEW STOCK ISSUE** The Edelman Gem Company, a small jewelry manufacturer, has been successful and has enjoyed a good growth trend. Now Edelman is planning to go public with an issue of common stock, and it faces the problem of setting an appropriate price on the stock. The company and its investment bankers believe that the proper procedure is to select several similar firms with publicly traded common stock and to make relevant comparisons.

Several jewelry manufacturers are reasonably similar to Edelman with respect to product mix, asset composition, and debt/equity proportions. Of these companies, Kennedy Jewelers and Strasburg Fashions are most similar. When analyzing the following data, assume that 1991 and 1996 were reasonably "normal" years for all three companies — that is, these years were neither especially good nor especially bad in terms of sales, earnings, and dividends. At the time of the analysis, k_{RF} was 8 percent and k_M was 12 percent. Kennedy is listed on the AMEX and Strasburg on the NYSE, while Edelman will be traded in the OTC market.

	KENNEDY	STRASBURG	EDELMAN (TOTALS)
Earnings per share			
1996	$ 4.50	$ 7.50	$1,200,000
1991	3.00	5.50	816,000
Price per share			
1996	$36.00	$65.00	—
Dividends per share			
1996	$ 2.25	$ 3.75	$ 600,000
1991	1.50	2.75	420,000
Book value per share, 1996	$30.00	$55.00	$ 9 million
Market/book ratio, 1996	120%	118%	—
Total assets, 1996	$28 million	$ 82 million	$20 million
Total debt, 1996	$12 million	$ 30 million	$11 million
Sales, 1996	$41 million	$140 million	$37 million

a. Assume that Edelman has 100 shares of stock outstanding. Use this information to calculate earnings per share (EPS), dividends per share (DPS), and book value per share for Edelman. (Hint: Edelman's 1996 EPS = $12,000.)

b. Calculate earnings and dividend growth rates for the three companies. (Hint: Edelman's EPS growth rate is 8 percent.)

c. On the basis of your answer to Part a, do you think Edelman's stock would sell at a price in the same "ballpark" as that of Kennedy and Strasburg, that is, in the range of $25 to $100 per share?

d. Assuming that Edelman's management can split the stock so that the 100 shares could be changed to 1,000 shares, 100,000 shares, or any other number, would such an action make sense in this case? Why?

e. Now assume that Edelman did split its stock and has 400,000 shares. Calculate new values for EPS, DPS, and book value per share. (Hint: Edelman's new 1996 EPS is $3.00.)

f. Return on equity (ROE) can be measured as EPS/book value per share or as total earnings/total equity. Calculate ROEs for the three companies for 1996. (Hint: Edelman's 1996 ROE = 13.3%.)

g. Calculate dividend payout ratios for the three companies for both years. (Hint: Edelman's 1996 payout ratio is 50%.)

h. Calculate debt/total assets ratios for the three companies for 1993. (Hint: Edelman's 1996 debt ratio is 55%.)

i. Calculate the P/E ratios for Kennedy and Strasburg for 1996. Are these P/Es reasonable in view of relative growth, payout, and ROE data? If not, what other factors might explain them? (Hint: Kennedy's P/E = 8×).

j. Now determine a range of values for Edelman's stock price, with 400,000 shares outstanding, by applying Kennedy's and Strasburg's P/E ratios, price/dividends ratios, and price/book value ratios to your data for Edelman. For example, one possible price for Edelman's stock is (P/E Kennedy)(EPS Edelman) = 8($3) = $24 per share. Similar calculations would produce a range of prices based on both Kennedy's and Strasburg's data. (Hint: Our range was $24 to $27.)

k. Using the equation $k_s = D_1/P_0 + g$, find approximate k_s values for Kennedy and Strasburg. Then use these values in the constant growth stock price model to find a price for Edelman's stock. (Hint: We averaged the EPS and DPS g's for Edelman.)

l. At what price do you think Edelman's shares should be offered to the public? You will want to select a price that will be low enough to induce investors to buy the stock but not so low that it will rise sharply immediately after it is issued. Think about relative growth rates, ROEs, dividend yields, and total returns ($k_s = D_1/P_0 + g$).

MINI CASE

Randy's, a family-owned restaurant chain operating in Alabama, has grown to the point where expansion throughout the entire Southeast is feasible. The proposed expansion would require the firm to raise about $15 million in new capital. Because Randy's currently has a debt ratio of 50 percent, and also because the family members already have all their personal wealth invested in the company, the family would like to sell common stock to the public to raise the $15 million. However, the family does want to retain voting control. You have been asked to brief the family members on the issues involved by answering the following questions:

a. What are the primary advantages of financing with common stock rather than bonds? What are the disadvantages to financing with stock?

b. Is the stock of Randy's currently publicly held or privately owned? Would this situation change if the stock sale were made?

c. What is classified stock? Would there be any advantages to the family in designating the stock currently outstanding as "founders' shares"? What type of common stock should Randy's sell to the public to allow the family to retain control of the business?

d. Would the stock sale be an initial public offering (IPO)? What would be the advantages to the family members of having the firm go public? Would there be any disadvantages? If you were a key employee, but not a family member, or a potential key employee being interviewed as a part of the expansion process, how would the decision affect you?

e. What does it mean for a stock to be listed? Do you think that Randy's stock would be listed shortly after the company goes public? If not, where would the stock trade?

f. What is a rights offering? Would it make sense for Randy's to use a rights offering to raise the $15 million? Even if you do not think a rights offering should be employed, could one be used?

g. What is the difference between a private placement and a public offering? What are the advantages and disadvantages of each type of placement? Which type would be most suitable for Randy's?

h. What is meant by going private? Assume for the sake of this question that Randy's previously went public. What are the advantages and disadvantages of the firm's going private?

i. (1) Would Randy's be likely to sell the $15 million of stock by itself or through an investment banker?

   (2) If an investment banker were used, would the sale most likely be on the basis of a competitive bid or a negotiated deal?

   (3) If it were a negotiated deal, would it most likely be done on a best efforts or an underwritten basis? In each case, explain your answer.

j. Without doing any calculations, describe the procedure by which the company and its investment banker would determine the price at which the stock would be offered to the public.

k. Suppose the decision were made to issue 1.5 million shares at $10 per share. What would be the approximate flotation cost on the issue? Would the cost be higher or lower if the firm were already publicly owned? Would there be a difference in costs between a best efforts and an underwritten offering?

l. If some of the family members wanted to sell some of their own shares in order to diversify their holdings at the same time the company was selling new shares to raise capital, would this be feasible?

SELECTED ADDITIONAL REFERENCES AND CASES

For a wealth of facts and figures on a major segment of the stock market, see New York Stock Exchange, Fact Book (New York: published annually).

For both a description of the stock markets and some further facts and figures, see the investment textbooks referenced in Chapter 3. For a discussion of the current state of investment banking and trends in the industry, see

Auerbach, Joseph, and Samuel L. Hayes III, *Investment Banking and Diligence: What Price Deregulation* (Boston: HBS Press, 1986).

Eccles, Robert G., and Dwight B. Crane, *Doing Deals: Investment Bankers at Work* (Boston: HBS Press, 1988).

Hayes, S. L., "The Transformation of Investment Banking," *Harvard Business Review,* January–February 1979, 153–170.

Rogowski, Robert, and Eric Sorensen, "The New Competitive Environment of Investment Banking: Transactional Finance and Concession Pricing of New Issues," *Midland Corporate Finance Journal,* Spring 1986, 64–71.

For additional insights on the benefits of listing, see

Baker, H. Kent, and Richard B. Edelman, "AMEX-to-NYSE Transfers, Market Microstructure, and Shareholder Wealth," *Financial Management,* Winter 1992, 60–72.

Edelman, Richard B., and H. Kent Baker, "Liquidity and Stock Exchange Listing," *The Financial Review,* May 1990, 231–249.

Other good references on specific aspects of equity financing include the following:

Aggarwal, Reena, and Pietra Rivoli, "Fads in the Initial Public Offering Market?" *Financial Management,* Winter 1990, 45–57.

Block, Stanley, and Marjorie Stanley, "The Financial Characteristics and Price Movement Patterns of Companies Approaching the Unseasoned Securities Market in the Late 1970s," *Financial Management,* Winter 1980, 30–36.

Bowyer, John W., and Jess B. Yawitz, "Effect of New Equity Issues on Utility Stock Prices," *Public Utilities Fortnightly,* May 22, 1980, 25–28.

Brickley, James A., and Kathleen T. Hevert, "Direct Employee Stock Ownership: An Empirical Investigation," *Financial Management,* Summer 1991, 70–84.

Carter, Richard, and Steven Manaster, "Initial Public Offerings and Underwriter Reputation," *Journal of Finance,* September 1990, 1045–1067.

Denis, David J., "The Costs of Equity Issues Since Rule 415: A Closer Look," *Journal of Financial Research,* Spring 1993, 77–88.

Fabozzi, Frank J., "Does Listing on the AMEX Increase the Value of Equity?" *Financial Management,* Spring 1981, 43–50.

Hansen, Robert S., and John M. Pinkerton, "Direct Equity Financing: A Resolution to a Paradox," *Journal of Finance,* June 1982, 651–665.

Ibbotson, Roger G., Jody L. Sindelar, and Jay R. Ritter, "Initial Public Offerings," *Journal of Applied Corporate Finance,* Summer 1988, 37–45.

_____, "The Market's Problems with the Pricing of Initial Public Offerings," *Journal of Applied Corporate Finance*, Spring 1994, 66–74.

Jurin, Bruce, "Raising Equity in an Efficient Market," *Midland Corporate Finance Journal,* Winter 1988, 53–60.

Loderer, Claudio, John W. Cooney, and Leonard D. Van Drunen, "The Price Elasticity of Demand for Common Stock," *Journal of Finance,* June 1991, 621–651.

Logue, Dennis, and Robert A. Jarrow, "Negotiation versus Competitive Bidding in the Sale of Securities by Public Utilities," *Financial Management,* Autumn 1978, 31–39.

Lucas, Deborah, J., and Robert L. McDonald, "Equity Issues and Stock Price Dynamics," *Journal of Finance,* September 1990, 1019–1043.

Michaely, Roni, and Wayne H. Shaw, "The Choice of Going Public: Spin-offs vs. Carve-outs," *Financial Management*, Autumn 1995, 5–21.

Muscarella, Chris J., and Michael R. Vetsuypens, "The Underpricing of 'Second' Initial Public Offerings," *Journal of Financial Research,* Fall 1989, 183–192.

Ritter, Jay R., "The Long-Run Performance of Initial Public Offerings," *Journal of Finance,* March 1991, 3–27.

For more information on shelf registration, see

Bhagat, Sanjai, "The Evidence on Shelf Registration," *Midland Corporate Finance Journal,* Spring 1984, 6–12.

For an excellent discussion of the various procedures used to raise capital, see

Smith, Clifford W., Jr., "Raising Capital: Theory and Evidence," *Midland Corporate Finance Journal,* Spring 1986, 6–22. Also, pages 72–76 of the Spring 1986 issue of the *Midland Corporate Finance Journal* contain a bibliography of recent articles pertaining to investment banking and capital acquisition.

The Spring 1990 issue of Financial Management *is devoted to Employee Stock Ownership Plans (ESOPs).*

The Spring 1993 issue of Financial Management *contains several articles on IPOs and LBOs.*

The Winter 1993 issue of the Journal of Applied Corporate Finance *is devoted to the SEC and securities regulation.*

The following cases from the Cases in Financial Management: Dryden Request *case series focus on the issues contained in this chapter:*

Case 21, "Sun Coast Savings Bank," which illustrates the decision to go public.

Case 22, "Precision Tool Company," which emphasizes the investment banking process.

Case 23, "Art Deco Reproductions, Inc.," which focuses on the analysis of a rights offering.

CHAPTER 17

LONG-TERM DEBT

On any given day, corporations go to the markets for vast amounts of debt capital. One good way to become familiar with the many facets of debt financing is to read the debt announcements in The Wall Street Journal. The following debt-related actions are among the thousands that occurred during one recent week:

1. *Georgia Power Company issued $100 million of 7⅜ percent first mortgage bonds due March 1, 2023. The bonds were priced at 99.2 ($992 per $1,000 par value) to yield 7.69 percent. These A-rated bonds, which are callable after 5 years, yielded 95 basis points above the 30-year T-bond.*

2. *Pacific Bell issued $625 million of 7¼ percent debentures due March 15, 2026. These bonds were priced at 98.11 to yield 7.28 percent. The AA-rated bonds, which are noncallable, yielded 55 basis points above the nearest (30-year) Treasury issue.*

3. *Scotia Pacific Holdings, a subsidiary of Pacific Lumber Company, issued $385 million of timber-collateralized notes due July 2015. Due to early principal payments, the notes have a weighted average life of less than 10 years. The issue, which is rated BBB, was priced at par to yield 7.95 percent, a spread of 188 basis points above the 10-year T-note.*

4. *General Motors Acceptance Corporation issued $1.3 billion of automobile loan asset-backed one-year certificates. The certificates, which are rated AAA and have a coupon rate of 4.15 percent, were priced at 99⅞ to yield 4.28 percent.*

5. *Standard & Poor's Corporation raised its rating on $5 billion of debt of Columbia/HCA Healthcare, the largest hospital company, from BBB+ to A−. S&P cited improved earnings and interest coverage.*

6. *ABN Bank of the Netherlands issued $100 million of subordinated collared floating rate Euronotes due 2005. Interest on the notes floats at ⅛ percent below the London Interbank Offered Rate with a minimum of 5⅛ percent and a maximum of 8 percent.*

7. *Navajo County Arizona announced the sinking fund call of randomly selected bonds from its 1977 Series A Pollution Control Revenue Bond issue. The selected bonds will be redeemed at 100 percent (par value).*

8. *Keisei Electric Railway Company of Japan issued $200 million of 1⅝ percent Eurobonds due April 2, 1997. The bonds, which were priced at par, contained warrants which permit bondholders to purchase the company's stock at a stated price until March 19, 1997. Because investors expect the firm's stock price to increase above the price stated in the warrants, the company was able to issue the bonds at a very low coupon rate.*

Why did these companies use so many different types of debt? Are there still other types? How are bond ratings determined, and how do they affect a firm's cost of debt? How does a company decide when to call a bond, or, at time of issue, whether to make a bond callable? After you read this chapter, you will have a good understanding of these and other issues related to debt financing.

As noted in Chapter 13, the use of debt is generally required to maximize the value of a firm. In this chapter, we discuss the many types of long-term debt, typical provisions in debt contracts, securitization, bond ratings, refunding operations, and the various factors that influence a firm's decision to use debt financing at a particular point in time.

TRADITIONAL DEBT INSTRUMENTS

There are many types of long-term debt: amortized and nonamortized, publicly issued and privately placed, secured and unsecured, marketable and nonmarketable, callable and noncallable, convertible and nonconvertible, and so on. In this section, we review the traditional long-term debt instruments and then, in the next section, we discuss some important recent innovations in long-term debt financing.

TERM LOANS

A *term loan* is a contract under which a borrower agrees to make a series of interest and principal payments, on specific dates, to a lender.[1] Investment bankers are generally not involved: Term loans are negotiated directly between the borrowing firm and a financial institution — generally a bank, an insurance company, or a pension fund. Although the maturities of term loans vary from 2 to 30 years, most are in the 3- to 15-year range.

---

[1]If the interest and maturity payments required under a term loan agreement are not met on schedule, the borrowing firm is said to have *defaulted,* and it can then be forced into bankruptcy.

Term loans have three major advantages over public offerings — *speed, flexibility,* and *low issuance costs.* Also, because they are negotiated directly between the lender and the borrower, formal documentation is minimized. The key provisions of the loan can be worked out much more quickly, and with more flexibility, than can those for a public issue, and it is not necessary to go through the Securities and Exchange Commission registration process. A further advantage of term loans over publicly traded debt has to do with future flexibility: If a bond issue is held by many different bondholders, it is virtually impossible to alter the terms of the agreement, even though new economic conditions may make such changes desirable. With a term loan, the borrower can negotiate with the lender to work out modifications in the contract.

The interest rate on a term loan can be either fixed for the life of the loan or variable (floating). If it is fixed, the rate used will be close to the rate on bonds of equivalent maturity for companies of comparable risk. If the rate is variable, it is usually set at a certain number of percentage points over the prime rate, the commercial paper rate, the T-bill rate, or the London Interbank Offered Rate (LIBOR). Then, when the index rate goes up or down, so does the rate on the outstanding balance of the term loan. In 1996, about 60 percent of the dollar amount of term loans made by banks had floating rates, up from virtually zero in 1970. Most of the money banks lend to corporations is "bought" in the certificate of deposit market, and if CD rates rise, banks need to raise the rates they earn in order to meet their own interest costs. With the increased volatility of interest rates in recent years, banks are rightly reluctant to make long-term, fixed rate loans.

Term loans are actually private placements of debt (as we discussed in Chapter 16), as opposed to public offerings of bonds. Typically, bonds are sold by large, well-known companies with strong financial positions. Thus, bond buyers do not need to spend much time and effort gathering information about the issuer. Further, most bonds are not amortized, that is, no principal payments are made during the life of the issue. On the other hand, private placements usually involve smaller companies whose credit conditions must be analyzed. Credit assessment can be done easily by large banks, insurance companies, and the like, but individual investors and small institutional investors do not have this capability. Also, private placements (term loans) are usually amortized in equal installments over the life of the loan. Private placements are often called *story credit,* because each placement has a "story" which explains the company's need for funds.

BONDS

Like a term loan, a bond is a long-term contract under which a borrower agrees to make interest and principal payments, on specific dates, to the holder of the bond. Although bonds are similar to term loans, a bond issue is generally advertised, offered to the public, and actually sold to many different investors. Indeed, thousands of individual and institutional investors may participate when a firm such as New York Telephone sells a bond issue, but there is generally only one lender in the case of a term loan.[2] Bonds are generally issued with maturities in the range of 20 to

---

[2]However, for very large term loans, 20 or more financial institutions may form a syndicate to grant the credit. Also, it should be noted that a bond issue can be sold to one lender (or to just a few); in this case, the issue would be a private placement.

30 years. However, shorter maturities, such as 7 to 10 years, are sometimes used, and Coca-Cola and Disney recently sold 100-year issues. Unlike interest rates on term loans, a bond's interest rate is generally fixed, although in recent years there has been an increase in the use of floating rate bonds.

MORTGAGE BONDS   Under a *mortgage bond,* the corporation pledges certain real assets as security for the bond. To illustrate, suppose McLaughlin Container Company needs $10 million in 1996 to purchase land and to build a plant. Bonds in the amount of $4 million, secured by a mortgage on the property, are issued. If McLaughlin defaults on the bonds, the bondholders could foreclose on the plant and sell it to satisfy their claims.

McLaughlin could, if it so chose, also issue *second mortgage bonds* secured by the same $10 million plant. In the event of liquidation, the holders of these second mortgage bonds would have a claim against the property only after the first mortgage bondholders had been paid off in full. Thus, second mortgages are sometimes called *junior mortgages,* or *junior liens,* because they are junior in priority to claims of *senior mortgages,* or *first mortgage bonds.*

Most major corporations' first mortgage indentures (discussed in detail later in the chapter) were written 20, 30, 40, or more years ago. These indentures are generally "open ended," meaning that new bonds may be issued from time to time under the existing indenture. However, the amount of new bonds that can be issued is virtually always limited to a specified percentage of the firm's total "bondable property," which generally includes all plant and equipment. For example, Savannah Electric Company can issue first mortgage bonds which total up to 60 percent of its fixed assets. If fixed assets totaled $100 million, and if Savannah Electric had $50 million of first mortgage bonds outstanding, then it could, by the 60 percent of property test, issue another $10 million of bonds.

At times, Savannah Electric has been unable to issue new first mortgage bonds because of another indenture provision: Its times-interest-earned (TIE) ratio was below 2.5, the minimum coverage that it must maintain in order to sell new bonds. Thus, Savannah Electric passed the property test but failed the coverage test, so it could not issue first mortgage bonds, and it had to finance with other securities. Since first mortgage bonds carry lower interest rates than junior long-term debt, this restriction was a costly one.

Savannah Electric's neighbor, Georgia Power Company, has more flexibility under its indenture; its interest coverage requirement is only 2.0 versus Savannah's 2.5 requirement. In hearings before the Georgia Public Service Commission, it was suggested that Savannah Electric should change its indenture coverage to 2.0 so that it could issue more first mortgage bonds. However, this was not possible — the holders of the outstanding bonds would have to approve the change, and it is inconceivable that they would vote for a change that would seriously weaken their position.

DEBENTURES   A *debenture* is an unsecured bond, and as such it has no lien against specific property as security for the obligation. Debenture holders are, therefore, general creditors whose claims are protected by property not otherwise pledged. In practice, the use of debentures depends on the nature of the firm's assets and its general credit strength. If its credit position is exceptionally strong, the firm can issue debentures — it simply does not need specific security. AT&T and General Electric have both financed mainly through debentures; they are such strong corporations that they do not have to put up property as security for their debt issues. Debentures are also issued by companies in industries where it would not be practical to provide security through a mortgage on fixed assets. Examples of such industries are the large mail-order houses and commercial banks, which characteristically hold most of their assets in the form of inventory or loans, neither of which is good security for a mortgage bond. Finally, companies that have used up their capacity to borrow in the mortgage market may be forced to use debentures. These companies' debentures are generally quite risky, and their interest rates are correspondingly high.

SUBORDINATED DEBENTURES The term *subordinate* means "below," or "inferior." Thus, *subordinated debt* has a claim on assets in the event of bankruptcy only after senior debt has been paid off. Debentures may be subordinated either to designated notes payable — usually bank loans — or to all other debt. In the event of liquidation or reorganization, holders of subordinated debentures cannot be paid until senior debt as named in the debentures' indenture has been paid. The subordinated debenture of a company that has used up its ability to employ mortgage bonds is normally quite risky, and these debentures carry interest rates that are up to six percentage points above the rate on top quality debt. Precisely how subordination works, and how it strengthens the position of senior debtholders, is discussed in Chapter 24.

OTHER TYPES OF BONDS Several other types of bonds are used often enough to warrant mention. First, *convertible bonds* are securities that are convertible into shares of common stock, at a fixed price, at the option of the bondholder. Basically, convertibles provide their holders with a chance for capital gains in exchange for a lower coupon rate, while the issuing firm gets the advantage of a low coupon rate. Bonds issued with *warrants* are similar to convertibles. Warrants are options which permit the holder to buy stock for a stated price. Therefore, if the price of the stock rises, the holder of the warrant will earn a capital gain. Bonds that are issued with warrants, like convertibles, carry lower coupon rates than straight bonds. Both warrants and convertibles are discussed in detail in Chapter 19.

Income bonds pay interest only when the interest is earned, so these securities cannot bankrupt a company. From a corporation's standpoint, they are less risky than "regular" bonds, but from an investor's standpoint, they are riskier. Another type of bond that has been discussed in the United States, but which has not yet been used here to any extent, is the *indexed,* or *purchasing power, bond,* which is popular in Brazil, Israel, and a few other countries long plagued by high inflation. The interest rate paid on these bonds is based on an inflation index such as the Consumer Price Index, and the interest paid rises when the inflation rate rises, thus protecting bondholders against inflation. As this book was going to press, the U.S. Treasury announced that it will begin issuing indexed bonds. No specifics were given, but by the time you read this, indexed Treasury bonds will probably exist. These bonds would, for all intents and purposes, be truly riskless securities.

Some companies may be in a position to benefit from the sale of either *development bonds* or *pollution control bonds.* State and local governments may set up both *industrial development agencies* and *pollution control agencies.* These agencies are allowed, under certain circumstances, to sell *tax-exempt bonds,* then to make the proceeds available to corporations for specific uses deemed (by Congress) to be in the public interest. Thus, an industrial development agency in Florida might sell bonds to provide funds for a paper company to build a plant in the Florida Panhandle, where unemployment is high. Similarly, a Detroit pollution control agency might sell bonds to provide Ford with funds to be used to purchase pollution control equipment. In both cases, the income from the bonds would be tax exempt to the holders, so the bonds would sell at relatively low interest rates. Note, however, that these bonds are guaranteed by the corporation that will use the funds, not by a governmental unit, so their rating reflects the credit strength of the corporation using the funds.

SELF-TEST QUESTION	**Describe the primary features of the following debt instruments:**
	(1) Term loan; bond
	(2) Mortgage bond; first mortgage bond; junior mortgage
	(3) Debenture; subordinated debenture
	(4) Convertible bond; bond with warrants; income bond
	(5) Indexed bond; development bond; pollution control bond

RECENT INNOVATIONS IN BOND FINANCING

The last 15 years witnessed many innovations in long-term debt financing. We will discuss six in this section. The first three — zero coupon bonds, floating rate bonds, and bonds that are redeemable at par — are a result of the extreme volatility in interest rates which has characterized the period. The fourth, so called "junk bonds," gained popularity (some might say notoriety) as a source of takeover financing. The fifth and sixth, project financing and securitization, permit a firm to tie a debt issue to a specific asset.

ZERO (OR VERY LOW) COUPON BONDS

Some bonds pay no interest but are offered at a substantial discount below their par values and hence provide capital appreciation rather than interest income. These securities are called *zero coupon bonds ("zeros")*, or *original issue discount bonds (OIDs)*. Corporations first used zeros in a major way in 1981. In recent years IBM, Alcoa, JCPenney, ITT, Cities Service, GMAC, Martin-Marietta, and many other companies have used them to raise billions of dollars. Municipal governments also sell "zero munis," and investment bankers have created zero coupon Treasury bonds.

To understand how zeros are used and analyzed, consider the zeros of Vandenberg Corporation, a shopping center developer. Vandenberg is developing a new shopping center in Orange County, California, and it needs $50 million. The company does not anticipate major cash flows from the project for about 5 years. However, Pieter Vandenberg, the president, plans to sell the center once it is fully developed and rented, which should take about 5 years. Therefore, Vandenberg wants to use a financing vehicle that will not require cash outflows for 5 years, and he has decided on a 5-year zero coupon bond, with a maturity value of $1,000.

Vandenberg Corporation is an A-rated company, and A-rated zeros with 5-year maturities yield 9 percent at this time (5-year coupon bonds also yield 9 percent). The company is in the 40 percent federal-plus-state tax bracket. Pieter Vandenberg wants to know the firm's after-tax cost of capital if it uses 9 percent, 5-year maturity zeros, and he also wants to know what the bond's cash flows will be. Table 17-1 provides an analysis of the situation, and the following numbered paragraphs explain the table itself.

1. The information in the "Basic Data" section, except the issue price, was given in the preceding paragraph, and the information in the "Analysis" section was calculated using the known data. The maturity value of the bond is always set at $1,000 or some multiple thereof.

2. The issue price is the PV of $1,000, discounted back 5 years at the rate k_d = 9%. Using a financial calculator, we input N = 5, I = 9, and FV = 1000, then press the PV key to find PV = $649.93. Note that $649.93, compounded annually for 5 years at 9 percent, will grow to $1,000 as shown on the time line in Table 17-1.

3. The accrued values as shown on Line 1 in the analysis section represent the compounded value of the bond at the end of each year. The accrued value for Year 0 is the issue price; the accrued value for Year 1 is found as $649.93 $(1.09)^1$ = $708.42; the accrued value at the end of Year 2 is $649.93(1.09)^2$ = $772.18; and, in general, the value at the end of any Year n is

---

ANALYSIS OF A ZERO COUPON BOND   TABLE 17-1

BASIC DATA:

Maturity value	$1,000
k_d	9.00%
Maturity	5 years
Corporate tax rate	40.00%
Issue price	$649.93

ANALYSIS:

Years

	0	1	2	3	4	5
(1) Year-end accrued value	649.93	708.42	772.18	841.68	917.43	1000.00
(2) Interest deduction		58.49	63.76	69.50	75.75	82.57
(3) Tax savings (40%)		23.40	25.50	27.80	30.30	33.03
(4) Cash flow	+649.93	+23.40	+25.50	+27.80	+30.30	−966.97

After-tax cost of debt = 5.40%.
Number of $1,000 zeros the company must issue to raise $50 million = Amount needed/Price per bond
= $50,000,000/$649.93
= 76,931 bonds.
Face amount of bonds: (76,931)($1,000) = $76,931,000.

$$\text{Accrued value at the end of Year n} = \text{Issue price} \times (1 + k_d)^n.$$

4. The interest deduction as shown on Line 2 represents the increase in accrued value during the year. Thus, interest in Year 1 = \$708.42 − \$649.93 = \$58.49. In general,

$$\text{Interest in Year n} = \text{Accrued value}_n - \text{Accrued value}_{n-1}.$$

This method of calculating taxable interest is specified in the Tax Code.

5. The company can take a tax deduction for interest each year, even though the payment is not made in cash. This deduction lowers the taxes that would otherwise be paid, producing the following savings:

$$\text{Tax savings} = (\text{Interest deduction})(T)$$

$$= \$58.49(0.4)$$
$$= \$23.40 \text{ in Year 1.}$$

6. Line 4 represents a cash flow time line; it shows the cash flow at the end of Years 0 through 5. At Year 0, the company receives the \$649.93 issue price. The company then has positive cash inflows equal to the tax savings during Years 1 through 4. Finally, in Year 5, it must pay the \$1,000 maturity value, but it gets one more interest tax saving for that year. Therefore, the net cash flow in Year 5 is −\$1,000 + \$33.03 = −\$966.97.

7. We can find the IRR of the cash flows shown on Line 4 using the IRR function of a financial calculator by simply inputting the annual cash flows in the cash flow register. The IRR is 5.4 percent, and it is the after-tax cost of zero coupon debt to the company. Conceptually, here is the situation:

$$\sum_{t=0}^{n} \frac{CF_n}{(1 + k_{d(AT)})^n} = 0$$

$$\frac{\$649.93}{(1 + k_{d(AT)})^0} + \frac{\$23.40}{(1 + k_{d(AT)})^1} + \frac{\$25.50}{(1 + k_{d(AT)})^2} + \frac{\$27.80}{(1 + k_{d(AT)})^3} + \frac{\$30.30}{(1 + k_{d(AT)})^4} + \frac{-\$966.97}{(1 + k_{d(AT)})^5} = 0.$$

The value $k_{d(AT)} = 0.054 = 5.4\%$, found with a financial calculator, produces the equality, and it is the after-tax cost of the zero coupon bond.

8. Note that $k_d(1 - T) = 9\%(0.6) = 5.4\%$. As we saw in Chapter 8, the cost of capital for regular coupon debt is found using the formula $k_d(1 - T)$. Thus, there is symmetrical treatment for tax purposes for zero coupon and regular coupon debt, that is, both types of debt have the same tax implications. This was Congress's intent, and it is why the Tax Code specifies the treatment set forth in Table 17-1.[3]

Not all original issue discount bonds (OIDs) have zero coupons. For example, Vandenberg might have sold an issue of 5-year bonds with a 5 percent coupon at a time when other bonds with similar ratings and maturities were yielding 9 percent. Such a bond would have had a value of $844.41:

$$\text{Bond value} = \sum_{t=1}^{5} \frac{\$50}{(1.09)^t} + \frac{\$1,000}{(1.09)^5} = \$844.41.$$

If an investor had purchased these bonds at a price of $844.41, the yield to maturity would have been 9 percent. The discount of $1,000 − $844.41 = $155.59 would have been amortized over the bond's 5-year life, and it would have been handled by both Vandenberg and the bondholders exactly as the discount on the zeros was handled.

Thus, zero coupon bonds are just one type of original issue discount bond. Any nonconvertible bond whose coupon rate is set below the going market rate at the time of its issue will sell at a discount, and it will be classified (for tax and other purposes) as an OID bond.

Shortly after corporations began to issue zeros, investment bankers figured out a way to create zeros from U.S. Treasury bonds, which are issued only in coupon form. In 1983 Salomon Brothers bought $1 billion of 7 percent, 30-year Treasuries. Each bond had 60 coupons worth $35 each, which represented the interest payments due every 6 months. Salomon then in effect clipped the coupons and placed them in 60 piles; the last pile also contained the now "stripped" bond itself, which represented a promise of $1,000 in the year 2013. These 60 piles of U.S. Treasury promises were then placed with the trust department of a bank and used as collateral for "zero coupon U.S. Treasury Trust Certificates," which are, in essence, zero coupon Treasury bonds. A pension fund that expected to need money in 2004 could have bought

---

[3]The purchaser of a zero coupon bond must calculate interest income on the bond in the same manner as the issuer calculates the interest deduction. Thus, in Year 1, a buyer of a bond would report interest income of $58.49 and would pay taxes in the amount of T(Interest income), even though no cash was received. T, of course, would be the bondholder's personal tax rate. Because of the tax situation, most zero coupon bonds are bought by pension funds and other tax-exempt entities. Individuals do, however, buy taxable zeros for their Individual Retirement Accounts (IRAs). Also, state and local governments issue "tax exempt muni zeros," which are purchased by individuals in high tax brackets.

Note too that we have analyzed the bond as if the cash flows accrued annually. Generally, to facilitate comparisons with semiannual payment coupon bonds, the analysis is conducted on a semiannual basis.

21-year certificates backed by the interest the Treasury will pay in 2004. Treasury zeros are, of course, safer than corporate zeros, so they are very popular with pension fund managers.

Corporate (and municipal) zeros are generally callable at the option of the issuer, just like coupon bonds, after some stated call protection period. The call price is set at a premium over the accrued value at the time of the call. Stripped U.S. Treasury bonds (Treasury zeros) generally are not callable because the Treasury normally sells noncallable bonds. Thus, Treasury zeros are completely protected against reinvestment risk (the risk of having to invest cash flows from a bond at a lower rate because of a decline in interest rates).

FLOATING RATE DEBT

In the early 1980s, inflation pushed interest rates up to unprecedented levels, causing sharp declines in the prices of long-term bonds. Even some supposedly "risk-free" U.S. Treasury bonds lost fully half their value, and a similar situation occurred with corporate bonds, mortgages, and other fixed-rate, long-term securities. As a result, many lenders became reluctant to lend money at fixed rates on a long-term basis, and they would do so only at extraordinarily high rates.

There is normally a *maturity risk premium* embodied in long-term interest rates; this premium is designed to offset the risk of declining bond prices if interest rates rise. Prior to the 1970s, the maturity risk premium on 30-year bonds was about one percentage point, meaning that under normal conditions, a firm might expect to pay about one percentage point more to borrow on a long-term than on a short-term basis. However, in the early 1980s, the maturity risk premium is estimated to have jumped to about three percentage points, which made long-term debt very expensive relative to short-term debt. Lenders were able and willing to lend on a short-term basis, but corporations were correctly reluctant to borrow on a short-term basis to finance long-term assets — such an action is extremely dangerous. Therefore, there was a situation in which lenders did not want to lend on a long-term basis, but corporations needed long-term money. The problem was solved by the introduction of long-term, floating rate debt.

A typical *floating rate bond* works as follows. The coupon rate is set for, say, the initial six-month period, after which it is adjusted every six months based on some market rate. Some corporate issues have been tied to the Treasury bond rate, while other issues have been tied to short-term rates. Many additional provisions can be included in floating rate issues; for example, some are convertible to fixed rate debt, whereas others have limits ("caps," "floors," and "collars") on how high or low the yield can go.

Floating rate debt is advantageous to investors because the interest rate moves up if market rates rise. This causes the market value of the debt to be stabilized, and it also provides lenders such as banks with income which is better geared to their own obligations. (Banks' deposit costs rise with interest rates, so the income on floating rate loans rises just when banks' deposit costs are rising.) Moreover, floating rate debt is advantageous to corporations because by using it, firms can issue debt with a long maturity without committing themselves to paying a high rate of interest for the entire life of the loan. Of course, if interest rates were to move even higher after a floating rate note had been signed, the borrower would have been better off issuing conventional, fixed rate debt.

BONDS THAT ARE REDEEMABLE AT PAR

Bonds that are *redeemable at par* at the holder's option also protect the holder against a rise in interest rates. If rates rise, the price of fixed-rate debt declines. However, if the holders have the option of turning their bonds in and having them redeemed at par, they are protected against rising rates. Examples of such debt include Transamerica's $50 million issue of 25-year, 8½ percent bonds. The bonds are not callable by the company, but holders can turn them in for redemption at par five years after the date of issue. If interest rates have risen, holders will turn in the bonds and reinvest the proceeds at a higher rate. This feature enabled Transamerica to sell the bonds with an 8½ percent coupon at a time when other similarly rated bonds had yields of 9 percent.

In late 1988, the corporate bond markets were sent into turmoil by the leveraged buyout of RJR Nabisco. RJR's bonds dropped in value by 20 percent within days of the LBO announcement, and the prices of many other corporate bonds also plunged, because investors feared that a boom in LBOs would load up many companies with excessive debt, leading to lower bond ratings and declining bond prices. All this led to a resurgence of concern about *event risk,* which is the risk that some sudden action, such as an LBO, will occur and increase the credit risk of the company, hence lower the firm's bond rating and the value of its outstanding bonds. Investors' concern over event risk meant that those firms deemed most likely to face events that could harm bondholders suddenly had to pay dearly to raise new debt capital, if they could raise it at all. In an attempt to control debt costs, a new type of protective covenant devised to minimize event risk was developed. This covenant, called a *super poison put,* enables a bondholder to turn in, or "put" a bond back to the issuer at par in the event of a takeover, merger, or major recapitalization.

Poison puts had actually been around since 1986, when the leveraged buyout trend took off. However, the earlier puts proved to be almost worthless because they allowed investors to "put" their bonds back to the issuer at par value only in the event of an *unfriendly* takeover. But since almost all takeovers are eventually approved by the target firm's board, mergers that started as hostile generally ended as friendly. Also, the earlier poison puts failed to protect investors from voluntary recapitalizations, in which a company loads up on debt to pay a big, one-time dividend to stockholders or to buy back its own stock. The "super" poison puts that were used following the RJR buyout announcement protected against both of these actions. This is a good illustration of how quickly the financial community reacts to changes in the marketplace.

JUNK BONDS

Prior to the 1980s, fixed income investors such as pension funds and insurance companies were generally unwilling to buy risky bonds, so it was almost impossible for risky companies to raise capital in the public bond markets. These companies, if they could raise debt capital at all, had to do so in the term loan market, where the loan could be tailored to satisfy the lender. Then, in the late 1970s, Michael Milken of the investment banking firm Drexel Burnham Lambert, relying on historical studies which showed that risky bonds yielded more than enough to compensate for their risk, began to convince certain institutional investors of the merits of purchasing risky debt. Thus was born the *junk bond,* a high-risk, high-yield bond issued to finance a leveraged buyout, a merger, or a troubled company.[4] For example, when Ted Turner attempted to buy CBS, he planned to finance the acquisition by issuing junk bonds to CBS's stockholders in exchange for their shares. Similarly, Public Service of New Hampshire financed construction of its troubled Seabrook nuclear plant with junk bonds, and junk bonds were used in the RJR Nabisco LBO. In junk bond deals, the debt ratio is generally extremely high, so the bondholders must bear as much risk as stockholders normally would. The bonds' yields reflect this fact — a yield of 25 percent was required to sell the Public Service of New Hampshire bonds.

The emergence of junk bonds as an important type of debt is another example of how the investment banking industry adjusts to and facilitates new developments in capital markets. In the 1980s, mergers and takeovers increased dramatically. People like T. Boone Pickens and Ted Turner thought that certain old-line, established companies were run inefficiently and were financed too conservatively, and they wanted to take these companies over and restructure them. Michael Milken and his staff at Drexel Burnham Lambert began an active campaign to persuade certain institutions (often S&Ls) to purchase high-yield bonds. Milken developed expertise in putting together deals that were attractive to the institutions yet feasible in the sense that projected cash flows were sufficient to meet the required interest payments. The fact that interest on the bonds was tax deductible, combined with the much higher debt ratios of the restructured firms, also increased after-tax cash flows and helped make the deals appear feasible.

The development of junk bond financing has done as much as any single factor to reshape the U.S. financial scene. The existence of these securities led directly to the loss of independence of Gulf Oil and hundreds of other companies, and it led to major shakeups in such companies as CBS, Union Carbide, and USX (formerly U.S. Steel). It also caused Drexel Burnham Lambert to leap from essentially nowhere in the 1970s to become the most profitable investment banking firm during the 1980s.

The phenomenal growth of the junk bond market was impressive, but controversial. In early 1989, Drexel Burnham Lambert was forced into bankruptcy, and "junk bond king" Michael Milken was jailed. These events badly tarnished the junk bond market, which also came under severe criticism for fueling takeover fires and adding to the cost of the S&L bailout. Additionally, the realization that high leverage can spell trouble slowed the growth in the junk bond market.

Do junk bonds have a future role in corporate finance aside from takeovers and LBOs? The answer is yes. In Chapter 13, we discussed the signaling theory of capital structure, which implies that companies should first use retained earnings plus debt supported by retained earnings, then use "reserve borrowing capacity" debt, and only issue new common stock as a last resort, after all the debt capacity has

---

[4]For an excellent discussion of junk bonds, see Kevin J. Perry and Robert A. Taggart, Jr., "The Growing Role of Junk Bonds in Corporate Finance," *Journal of Applied Corporate Finance,* Spring 1988, 37–45. This section draws heavily from their work.

been exhausted. The development of the junk bond market has effectively extended the bounds of firms' debt capacities beyond the earlier limits.

Although the junk bond market was depressed for several years, it roared back with a vengeance in the 1990s. In 1993 alone, companies with below-investment-grade ratings issued a record $54 billion of publicly traded bonds, equaling the total value of junk bonds issued from 1982 through 1986. Well over half of all recent junk bond issues have been used to finance normal expansion rather than to finance mergers and acquisitions. Increasingly, medium-sized companies that formerly looked to insurance companies for private placement financing are turning to the junk bond market as their primary source of debt capital.

PROJECT FINANCING

In recent years, many large projects such as the Alaska pipeline have been financed by what is called *project financing*.[5] We can only present an overview of the concept, for, in practice, it involves very complicated provisions and can take many forms.

Project financing has been used to finance energy explorations, oil tankers, refineries, and electric generating plants. Generally, one or more firms will sponsor the project, putting up the required equity capital, while the remainder of the financing is furnished by lenders or lessors.[6] Most often, a separate legal entity is formed to operate the project. Normally, the project's creditors do not have full recourse against the sponsors. In other words, the lenders and lessors must be paid from the project's cash flows, plus the sponsors' equity in the project, because the creditors have no claims against the sponsors' other assets or cash flows. Often the sponsors write "comfort" letters, giving general assurances that they will strive diligently to make the project successful, but these letters are not legally binding. Therefore, in project financing the lenders and lessors must focus their analysis on the inherent merits of the project plus the equity cushion provided by the sponsors.[7]

Project financing is not a new development. Indeed, back in 1299, the English Crown negotiated a loan with Florentine merchant bankers that was to be repaid with one year's output from the Devon silver mines. Essentially, the Italians were allowed to operate the mines for one year, paying all the operating costs and mining

---

[5]For an excellent discussion of project financing, see John W. Kensinger and John D. Martin, "Project Finance: Raising Money the Old-Fashioned Way," *Journal of Applied Corporate Finance*, Fall 1988, 69–81.

[6]A lessor is an individual or firm that owns buildings and equipment and then leases them to another firm. Leasing is discussed in Chapter 18.

[7]In another type of project financing, each sponsor guarantees its share of the project's debt obligations. Here the creditors would also consider the creditworthiness of the sponsors in addition to the project's own prospects. It should be noted that project financing with multiple sponsors in the electric utility industry has led to problems when one or more of the sponsors has gotten into financial trouble. For example, Long Island Lighting, one of the sponsors in the Nine Mile Point nuclear project, became unable to meet its commitments to the project, which forced other sponsors to shoulder an additional burden or else see the project cancelled and lose all their investment up to that point. Utility executives have stated that this default, and others, will make companies reluctant to enter into similar projects in the future.

as much ore as they could. The Crown made no guarantees as to how much ore could be mined, or the value of the refined silver. A more current example involved GE Capital, the credit arm of General Electric, which recently arranged a $72 million project financing to build an aluminum can plant. The plant is owned by several beverage makers, but it is operated independently, and GE Capital must depend on the cash flows from the plant to repay the loan. About half of all project financings in recent years have been for electric generating plants, including both plants owned by electric utilities and cogeneration plants operated by industrial companies. Project financings are generally characterized by large size and a high degree of complexity. However, since project financing is tied to a specific project, it can be tailored to meet the specific needs of both the creditors and the sponsors. In particular, the financing can be structured so that both the funds provided during the construction phase and the subsequent repayments match the timing of the project's projected cash outflows and inflows.

Project financing offers several potential benefits over conventional debt financing. For one, project financing usually restricts the usage of the project's cash flows, which means that the lenders, rather than the managers, can decide whether to reinvest excess cash flows or to use them to reduce the loan balance by more than the minimum required. Conferring this power on the lenders reduces their risks. Project financings also have advantages for borrowers. First, because risks to the lenders are reduced, the interest rate built into a project financing deal may be relatively low. Second, since suppliers of project financing capital have no recourse against the sponsoring firms' other assets and cash flows, project financings insulate the firm's other assets from risks associated with the project being financed. Managers may be more willing to take on a very large, risky project if they know that the company's existence would not be threatened if it fails.

Project financings increase the number and type of investment opportunities, hence they make capital markets "more complete." At the same time, project financings reduce the costs to investors of obtaining information and monitoring the borrower's operations. To illustrate, consider an oil and gas exploration project that is funded using project financing. If the project were financed as an integral part of the firm's normal operations, investors in all the firm's outstanding securities would need information on the project. By isolating the project, the need for information is confined to the investors in the project financing, and they need to monitor only the project's operations, and not those of the entire firm.

Project financings also permit firms whose earnings are below the minimum requirements specified in their existing bond indentures to obtain additional debt financing. In such situations, lenders look only at the merits of the new project, and its cash flows may support additional debt even though the firm's existing assets would not. Project financings also permit managers to reveal proprietary information to a smaller group of investors, hence project financings increase the ability of a firm to maintain confidentiality. Finally, project financings can improve incentives for key managers by enabling them to take direct ownership stakes in the operations under their control. By establishing separate projects, companies can provide incentives that are much more directly based upon individual performance than is typically possible within a large corporation.

SECURITIZATION

As the term is generally used, a *security* refers to a publicly traded financial instrument, as opposed to a privately placed instrument. Thus, securities have greater liquidity than otherwise similar instruments that are not traded in an open market. In recent years, procedures have been developed to *securitize* various types of debt instruments, thus increasing their liquidity, lowering the cost of capital to borrowers, and generally increasing the efficiency of the financial markets.[8]

Securitization has occurred in two major ways. First, some debt instruments that were formerly rarely traded are now actively traded, with the change being due to decisions by certain financial institutions to "make a market," which means to stand willing to buy or sell the security, and to hold an inventory of the security in order to balance buy and sell orders. This occurred many years ago in the case of common stocks and investment-grade bonds. More recently, it occurred in the commercial paper market, in which large, financially strong firms issue short-term, unsecured debt in lieu of obtaining bank loans. The commercial paper market has grown from about $50 billion outstanding in the mid-1970s to over $350 billion today, and this market permits large firms to finance their working capital needs at lower cost than with bank loans.

Another example of securitization is the junk bond market. Before this market developed, firms with high credit risk were forced to obtain debt financing on a private placement basis, typically from the firm's bank. It was difficult for firms to shop around for the best rate, because lenders who were not familiar with them were unwilling to spend the time and money necessary to determine the feasibility of the loan, and lenders were also concerned about (and hence charged a higher rate for) the illiquidity of privately placed debt. Then, Michael Milken developed procedures for analyzing the repayment feasibility of junk bonds, and Drexel Burnham Lambert put its reputation and credibility behind these issues and made a market for them in case a purchaser needed to cash out. Subsequently, Morgan Stanley, Merrill Lynch, Salomon Brothers, and the other major investment bankers entered the junk bond market, and today it has "securitized" much of the old private placement market for below-investment-grade debt.

The second major development in securitization involves the pledging of specific assets, *asset securitization,* or the creation of *asset-backed securities.* The oldest type of asset securitization is the mortgage-backed bond. Here, individual home mortgages are combined into pools, and then bonds are created which use the pool of mortgages as collateral. The financial institution that originated the mortgage generally continues to act as collection agent, but the mortgage itself is sold to other investors. The securitization of mortgages has created a national mortgage market with many players, hence it has benefited borrowers. The development has also benefited lenders, for the original lending institution, often a savings and loan, no longer owns the relatively long-term mortgage, hence it is better able to match the maturity of its assets (loans) with its liabilities (savings accounts and certificates of deposit).

---

[8]The Fall 1988 issue of the *Journal of Applied Corporate Finance* is devoted to securitization. For additional discussion, see any of its excellent articles.

Today, many different types of assets are being used as collateral, including auto loans and credit card balances.

The asset securitization process involves the pooling and repackaging of loans secured by relatively homogeneous, small-dollar assets into liquid securities. In the past, such financing was provided by a single lending institution, which would write the loan, structure the terms, absorb the credit and interest rate risk, provide the capital, and service the collections. Under securitization, several different institutions are involved, with each playing a different functional role. A savings and loan might originate the loan, an investment banker might pool the loans and structure the security, a federal agency might insure against credit risk, a second investment banker might sell the securities, and a pension fund might be the investor which supplies the final capital.

The process of securitization has, in general, lowered costs and increased the availability of funds to borrowers, decreased risks to lenders, and created new investment opportunities for many investors. With these potential benefits, we predict that securitization will continue to expand in the future.

SELF-TEST QUESTIONS

What are zero coupon bonds? What are their advantages and disadvantages for issuers and purchasers?

What is the difference between fixed rate and floating rate debt? What are the advantages and disadvantages of floating rate debt for issuers and purchasers?

What are super poison puts, and how do they lower event risk?

Briefly describe the characteristics and role of junk bonds.

What is project financing? What are its advantages and disadvantages?

What is meant by securitization? What are the advantages of securitization to borrowers? What are the advantages to lenders?

DEBT CONTRACT PROVISIONS

A firm's managers are most concerned about (1) the effective cost of its debt and (2) any provisions which might restrict the firm's future actions. In this section, we discuss features which could have an effect on either the cost of the firm's debt or its future flexibility.

BOND INDENTURES

An *indenture* is a legal document that spells out the rights of both bondholders and the issuing corporation, and a *trustee* is an official (usually a bank) who represents the bondholders and makes sure that the terms of the indenture are carried out. The indenture may be several hundred pages in length, and it will include *restrictive covenants* that cover such points as the conditions under which the issuer can pay off the bonds prior to maturity, the level at which the issuer's times-interest-earned ratio must be maintained if the company is to issue additional debt, and restrictions against the payment of dividends unless earnings meet certain specifications.

The trustee is responsible for monitoring the covenants and for taking appropriate action if a violation does occur. What constitutes "appropriate action" varies with the circumstances. It might be that to insist on immediate compliance would result in bankruptcy and possibly large losses on the bonds. In such a case, the trustee might decide that the bondholders would be better served by giving the company a chance to work out its problems and thus avoid forcing it into bankruptcy.

The Securities and Exchange Commission (1) approves indentures and (2) makes sure that all indenture provisions are met before allowing a company to sell new securities to the public. Also, it should be noted that the indentures of many larger corporations were actually written in the 1930s or 1940s, and that many issues of new bonds sold since then were covered by the same indenture. The interest rates on the bonds, and perhaps also the maturities, varied depending on market conditions at the time of each issue, but bondholders' protection as spelled out in the indenture was the same for all bonds of the same type.[9]

CALL PROVISIONS

A *call provision* gives the issuing corporation the right to call a bond (or preferred stock) for redemption. If it is used, the call provision generally states that the company must pay an amount greater than the par value for the bond. The additional payment, defined as the *call premium,* is sometimes set equal to one year's interest if the bond is called during the first year, with the premium declining by a constant amount of I/n each year thereafter, where I = annual interest and n = original maturity in years. For example, the call premium on a $1,000 par value, 20-year, 10 percent bond would generally be $100 if it were called during the first year, $95 during the second year (calculated by reducing the $100, or 10 percent, premium by one-twentieth), and so on.

When a callable bond is issued, its coupon rate will probably be set some 20 to 70 basis points above the coupon rate on a similar noncallable bond. Here is the logic:

1. Typically, the coupon rate when a bond is issued is set at a rate which will cause the bond to initially sell at par, that is, at the "going rate" for bonds of similar risk and maturity.

2. If interest rates never fluctuated, or at least never fell below the level which existed at the time of issue, then a callable bond would remain outstanding until it matured, and investors would earn the yield to maturity.

3. However, interest rates do fluctuate, and if a bond has a 30-year maturity, there is a high probability that rates will drop below the coupon rate sometime during its life, in which case callable bonds will be refunded, and the holder will be required to reinvest at a lower rate.

4. Therefore, the expected rate of return on funds invested in a new callable bond, over the bond's original life, will be below its coupon rate. (If the bond were not callable, hence would remain outstanding until it matured, the

---

[9]A firm will have different indentures for each of the major types of bonds it issues. For example, one indenture will cover its first mortgage bonds, another its debentures, and a third its convertible bonds.

expected return would equal the coupon rate, assuming the bond was issued at par and was not expected to default.)[10]

5. The expected rates of return on callable and noncallable bonds *of a given risk class* should be equal. To increase the expected return on the callable bond to that of the noncallable bond, we must raise the callable bond's coupon rate. There is some coupon rate which, when combined with expectations about future interest rate levels and the bond's call premium, would equalize expected rates of return. Note that, *for a given company,* callable bonds will have higher expected rates of return than similar noncallable bonds, because the uncertainty regarding the call makes callable bonds riskier.

6. Investment bankers and sophisticated fixed-income investors actually analyze these factors and determine how much higher callable bonds' coupon rates should be. Generally, the "adder" is 20 to 70 basis points, with the lower number applying (a) to bonds with shorter maturities, hence less time for rates to drop; (b) if the call premium is relatively large, because this will increase the investor's return and also lower the probability of a call; (c) if interest rates are low by historical standards; and (d) if the bond is noncallable for some period of time, which is known as a *deferred call.*

For example, on February 1, 1996, Great Falls Timber Company sold an issue of A-rated bonds, which were callable immediately, and which yielded 8.375 percent. On the same day, Midwest Milling Company sold an issue of A-rated bonds that yielded only 8.0 percent, but that were noncallable for 10 years. Investors were apparently willing to accept a 0.375 percent lower interest rate on Midwest's bonds for the assurance that the rate would be earned for at least 10 years. Great Falls, on the other hand, had to pay a 0.375 percent higher interest rate to obtain the option of calling the bonds in the event of a subsequent decline in interest rates during the first 10 years.

We will discuss when to call a bond in Appendix 17A.

SINKING FUNDS

A *sinking fund* is a provision that provides for the systematic retirement of a bond issue (or an issue of preferred stock). Typically, the sinking fund provision requires a firm to call and retire a portion of its bonds each year. On some occasions, the firm may be required to deposit money with a trustee, who invests the funds and then uses the accumulated sum to retire the entire bond issue when it matures. Sometimes the stipulated sinking fund payment is tied to the sales or earnings of the current year, but usually it is a mandatory fixed amount. If it is mandatory, a failure to

---

[10]The expected return on a newly issued callable bond is actually higher than its coupon rate, because, if the bond is called, then the bondholder will earn the call premium, and that will force the earned rate of return above the coupon rate. However, the proceeds must then be reinvested at a rate below the coupon rate (otherwise the bond would not have been called). If one estimates the expected rate of return over the entire period, from when the bond was issued to its scheduled maturity date, then the expected return on a callable bond will be less than its coupon rate.

meet the sinking fund requirement causes the bond issue to be thrown into default, which may force the company into bankruptcy.

In most cases, the firm is given the right to handle the sinking fund in either of two ways:

1. It may call in for redemption (at par value) a certain percentage of the bonds each year — for example, it might be able to call 2 percent of the total original amount of the issue at a price of $1,000 per bond. The bonds are numbered serially, and the ones called for redemption are determined by a lottery. (For bonds issued in denominations of $100,000 or more, the specified percentage of the holder's par value is called.)

2. It may buy the required amount of bonds on the open market.

The firm will choose the least cost method. Therefore, if interest rates have risen, causing bond prices to fall, the company will elect to buy bonds in the open market at a discount. Otherwise, it will call them. Note that a call for sinking fund purposes is quite different from a refunding call. A sinking fund call requires no call premium, but only a small percentage of the issue is callable in any one year.

Although the sinking fund is designed to protect the bondholders by assuring that the issue is retired in an orderly fashion, the sinking fund at times works to the detriment of bondholders. If, for example, the bond carries a 10 percent interest rate, and if yields on similar securities have fallen to 8 percent, then the bond will sell above par. A sinking fund call at par would thus greatly disadvantage those bondholders whose bonds were called. On balance, however, securities that provide for a sinking fund and continuing redemption are safer than bonds without sinking funds, so adding a sinking fund provision to a bond issue will lower the interest rate on the bond.

<table>
<tr><td>

What is a bond indenture? A restrictive covenant?

What is a call provision? What impact does a call provision have on an issue's required rate of return?

What is a sinking fund? How are bonds retired for sinking fund purposes?

What impact does a sinking fund have on an issue's required rate of return? How do sinking funds differ from call provisions?

</td><td>

SELF-TEST QUESTIONS

</td></tr>
</table>

BOND RATINGS

Since the early 1900s, bonds have been assigned quality ratings that reflect their probability of default. The two major rating agencies are Moody's Investors Service (Moody's) and Standard & Poor's Corporation (S&P). These agencies' rating designations are shown in Table 17-2.[11]

---

[11]In the discussion to follow, reference to the S&P code is intended to imply the Moody's code as well. Thus, for example, triple B bonds means both BBB and Baa bonds; double B bonds, both BB and Ba bonds.

TABLE 17-2	COMPARISON OF BOND RATINGS	
MOODY'S	**S&P**	
Aaa	AAA	Highest quality
Aa	AA	High quality
A	A	Upper medium grade
Baa	BBB	Medium grade
Ba	BB	Lower medium grade/some speculative elements
B	B	Speculative
Caa	CCC	
Ca	CC	More speculative; higher risk of default
C	C	
—	D	In default

NOTE: Both Moody's and S&P use "modifiers" for bonds rated below triple A. S&P uses a plus and minus system; thus, A+ designates the strongest A rated bonds and A − the weakest. Moody's uses a 1, 2, or 3 designation, with 1 denoting the strongest and 3 the weakest; thus, within the double A category, Aa1 is the best, Aa2 is average, and Aa3 is the weakest. Triple A bonds have no modifiers in either system.

The triple and double A bonds are extremely safe. Single A and triple B bonds are strong enough to be called "investment grade," and they are the lowest rated bonds that many banks and other institutional investors are permitted by law to hold. Double B and lower bonds are speculations; they are junk bonds with a fairly high probability of going into default, and many financial institutions are prohibited from buying them.

BOND RATING CRITERIA

Although the rating assignments are subjective, they are based on both qualitative characteristics such as "quality of management" and quantitative factors such as the debt ratio, the coverage ratio, and so forth. Analysts at the rating agencies have consistently stated that no precise formula is used to set a firm's rating — many factors are taken into account, but not in a mathematically precise manner. Statistical studies have borne out this contention. Researchers who have tried to predict bond ratings on the basis of quantitative data have had only limited success, indicating that the agencies do indeed use a good deal of subjective judgment to establish a firm's rating.[12]

IMPORTANCE OF BOND RATINGS

Bond ratings are important to both firms and investors. First, a bond's rating is an indicator of its default risk, so the rating has a direct, measurable influence on the

[12]See Robert S. Kaplan and Gabriel Urwitz, "Statistical Models of Bond Ratings: A Methodological Inquiry," *Journal of Business,* April 1979, 231–261; and Ahmed Belkaoui, *Industrial Bonds and the Rating Process* (London: Quorum Books, 1983).

bond's interest rate and the firm's cost of debt. Second, most bonds are purchased by institutional investors, not by individuals, and many of these institutions are restricted to investment-grade securities. Thus, if a firm's bonds fall below BBB, it will have a hard time selling new bonds, since many potential purchasers will not be allowed to buy them.

As a result of their higher risk and more restricted market, lower-grade bonds have much higher required rates of return, k_d, than do high-grade bonds. This point is highlighted in Figure 17-1, which gives the yields on three types of bonds, and the risk premiums for AAA and BBB bonds, in June 1963, in June 1975, and again in April 1989.[13] Note first that the riskless rate, or vertical axis intercept, rose 5.17 percentage points from 1963 to 1989, reflecting the increase in realized and anticipated inflation. Second, the slope of the line also rose, indicating increased investor risk aversion from 1963 to 1989, but risk aversion declined from 1975 to 1989. Thus, the penalty for having a low credit rating varies over time. Occasionally, as in 1963, it is not too severe, but at other times, as in 1975, it is quite large.[14]

CHANGES IN RATINGS

A change in a firm's bond rating will have a significant effect on its ability to borrow long-term capital, and on the cost of that capital. Rating agencies review outstanding bonds on a periodic basis, occasionally upgrading or downgrading a bond as a result of its issuer's changed circumstances. With the vast quantity of bond issues outstanding, it is not surprising that a large number are either upgraded or downgraded each year. For example, in the first quarter of 1995, S&P raised its rating on 85 issues and lowered its rating on another 156 issues. By comparing the number of upgrades to downgrades, analysts can get a feel for the economic trends occurring both within the economy as a whole and within industry groups.

---

[13]The term *risk premium* ought to reflect only the difference in the expected (and required) returns between two securities that results from differences in their risk. However, the difference between *yields to maturity* on different types of bonds consists of (1) a true risk premium; (2) a liquidity premium, which reflects the fact that U.S. Treasury bonds are more readily marketable than most corporate bonds; (3) a call premium, because most Treasury bonds are not callable, while corporate bonds are; and (4) an expected loss differential, which reflects the probability of loss on the corporate bonds. As an example of the fourth point, suppose the yield to maturity on a BBB bond were 10 percent versus 7 percent on government bonds, but there is a 5 percent probability of total default loss on the corporate bond. In this case, the expected return on the BBB bond would be 0.95(10%) + 0.05(0%) = 9.5%, and the risk premium would be 2.5 percent, not the full 3.0 percentage point difference in "promised" yields to maturity. Therefore, the risk premiums given in Figure 17-1 overstate somewhat the true (but unmeasurable) risk premiums.

[14]The relationship graphed here is akin to the Security Market Line developed in Chapter 4, but with bond ratings rather than beta coefficients used to measure risk. A word about the scaling of the horizontal axis and about the placement of the points is in order. (1) We have shown a linear fit, although there is no theoretical reason to think that yields plotted against bond ratings are necessarily linear. (2) We have shown the interval on the horizontal axis between AAA and BBB to be equal to that between U.S. Government bonds and AAA, but this is an arbitrary scaling. (3) Finally, on an accurate, large-scale graph, it would be clear that the plotted points for the AAA and BBB bonds are not precisely on straight lines as they appear in the graph; however, they are sufficiently close to warrant our analysis.

Attempts have been made to calculate beta coefficients for bonds and to plot bonds on the same SML that is used for common stocks. However, these results have not been successful — bonds do not plot on the same linear SML as stocks.

FIGURE 17-1   **RELATIONSHIP BETWEEN BOND RATINGS AND BOND YIELDS, 1963, 1975, AND 1989**

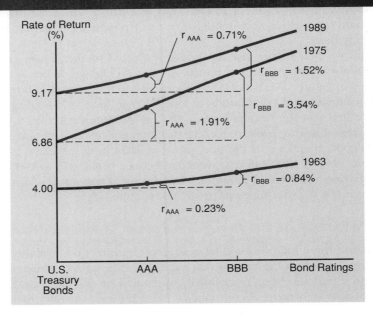

r_{AAA} = risk premium on AAA bonds.
r_{BBB} = risk premium on BBB bonds.

	LONG-TERM GOVERNMENT BONDS (DEFAULT-FREE) (1)	AAA CORPORATE BONDS (2)	BBB CORPORATE BONDS (3)	RISK PREMIUMS	
				AAA (4) = (2) − (1)	BBB (5) = (3) − (1)
June 1963	4.00%	4.23%	4.84%	0.23%	0.84%
June 1975	6.86	8.77	10.40	1.91	3.54
April 1989	9.17	9.88	10.69	0.71	1.52

SOURCES: *Federal Reserve Bulletin*, December 1963 and December 1975; *Federal Reserve Statistical Release*, April 1989.

An announcement that a company plans to sell a new debt issue, or to merge with another company and to pay for the acquisition with bonds, will trigger an agency review and possibly lead to a rating change. For example, when Texaco and financier Carl Icahn reached an agreement which precluded him from making a bid for Texaco, S&P placed Texaco's bonds on "CreditWatch" with "positive implications." CreditWatch is an S&P publication which lists bonds that it is actively reviewing for a possible rating change in response to some development, and investors are warned that the rating may be changed upon completion of the review. CreditWatch listings are published in *The Wall Street Journal,* and the publication itself is available in many libraries. It spells out in detail what S&P sees as going on, and it is updated frequently.[15]

If a firm's situation has deteriorated somewhat, but its bonds have not been reviewed and downgraded, then it may choose to use a term loan or short-term debt rather than to finance through a public bond issue. This will perhaps postpone a rating agency review until the situation has improved. For example, a number of public utilities delayed bond issues in the 1980s, financing with short-term debt until electric rate increases could be obtained to raise interest coverage ratios to acceptable levels. After rate increases were put into effect and coverages improved, the companies sold bonds and used the proceeds to retire the excess short-term debt.

What are the two major rating agencies?
What are some criteria the rating agencies use when they assign ratings?
What impact does its bond rating have on the cost of debt to the issuing firm?

**SELF-TEST
QUESTIONS**

ADVANTAGES AND DISADVANTAGES OF LONG-TERM DEBT

From the issuer's viewpoint, there are several advantages and disadvantages to long-term debt. The major advantages are as follows:

1. The cost of debt is independent of earnings, so debtholders do not participate if profits soar. There is, however, a flip side to this argument — if profits fall, the company must still pay the interest on its debt.

2. Because of the tax deductibility of interest payments, the risk-adjusted component cost of debt is lower than that of common stock.

3. The owners of the corporation do not have to share control when debt financing is used.

The major disadvantages are as follows:

1. Since debt service (interest plus scheduled principal repayments) is a fixed charge, a decline in operating income may result in insufficient cash flow to meet debt service requirements. This can lead to bankruptcy.

2. As discussed in Chapter 13, financial leverage increases the firm's riskiness, hence raises its cost of both debt and equity.

3. Debt normally has a fixed maturity date at which time the firm must repay the principal.

---

[15]Rating agencies do review ratings without being prompted by the company. However, most reviews associated with new issues are actually requested by the company, not because the company wants a review but because the investment bankers make such a review a condition of their handling the offering. Note also that a company must pay the agency to have its bonds rated. It has been suggested that such payments might lead to a favorable bias in ratings. However, there is no evidence of any bias on the part of the major rating agencies. The value of their service, hence the rating agencies' incomes, depends almost entirely on their credibility, so there is every reason to expect the agencies to maintain strict objectivity.

4. In a long-term contractual relationship, it is necessary for the indenture provisions to be much more stringent than in a short-term credit agreement. Thus, the firm will be subject to more restrictions than if it had borrowed on a short-term basis or had issued common stock.

5. There is a limit to the amount of funds which can be raised at a "reasonable" rate. Widely accepted lending standards dictate that the debt ratio should not exceed certain limits (which vary from industry to industry), and when debt goes beyond these limits, its cost becomes prohibitive.

SELF-TEST | What are the major advantages to long-term debt financing?
QUESTIONS | What are the major disadvantages?

FACTORS THAT INFLUENCE LONG-TERM FINANCING DECISIONS

As we show in this section, many factors influence a firm's long-term financing decisions. Their relative importance varies among firms at any point in time and also for any given firm over time, but all should be considered when a firm raises capital.

CAPITAL STRUCTURE CONSIDERATIONS

One of the most important factors in any financing decision is the relationship between the firm's actual capital structure and its target capital structure. Remember that firms establish an optimal, or target, capital structure (or at least a range) and, over time, finance in accordance with this target. Of course, in any one year, few firms finance exactly in accordance with their target capital structures, primarily because of flotation costs: Smaller issues of new securities have proportionally larger flotation costs, so firms tend to issue common stock and long-term debt sporadically, while retained earnings are generated continuously.

Note that having fewer, but larger, security offerings causes a firm's capital structure to fluctuate about its optimal level rather than stay right on target. However, (1) small fluctuations about the optimal capital structure have little effect on the weighted average cost of capital, (2) investors recognize that this procedure is prudent, and (3) the firm saves substantial amounts of flotation costs by financing in this manner. So, while over the long haul firms finance in accordance with their target capital structures, flotation costs plus the factors discussed in the following sections influence the specific financing decisions in any given year.

We should also point out that firms can, and often do, arrange financings in advance. Thus, if a firm concluded that it would need $8 million of debt over a two-year period, it might arrange with an insurance company to lend it $4 million in each of the next two years, with the second $4 million being firmly committed at the time the first $4 million is borrowed. Such financings can reduce flotation costs, because the lender needs to make only one detailed credit analysis. Similarly, larger firms can use shelf registrations, which we discussed in Chapter 16, to hold down financing costs even though they sell relatively small blocks of securities. Both commitment financings and shelf registrations make it possible for firms to adhere reasonably closely to their optimal capital structures without incurring unduly high flotation costs.

MATURITY MATCHING

Assume that Consolidated Tools, a Cincinnati machine tool manufacturer, made the decision to float a $25 million nonconvertible bond issue to help finance its 1997 capital budget. It must choose a maturity for the issue, taking into consideration the shape of the yield curve, management's own expectations about future interest rates, and the maturity of the assets being financed. To illustrate how asset maturities affect the choice of debt maturities, suppose Consolidated's capital projects consist primarily of new, automated milling and stamping machinery for its Cincinnati plant. This machinery has an expected economic life of 10 years (even though it falls into the MACRS 5-year class life). Should Consolidated use debt with a 5-year, 10-year, 20-year, or 30-year, or some other, maturity?

Note that some of the new capital for the machinery will come from common stock, which is permanent capital. On the other hand, debt maturities can be specified at the time of issue. If Consolidated financed its capital budget with 10-year sinking fund bonds, it would be matching asset and liability maturities. The cash flows resulting from the new machinery could be used to make the interest and sinking fund payments on the issue, so the bonds would be retired as the machinery wore out. If Consolidated used one-year debt, it would have to pay off this debt with cash flows derived from assets other than the machinery in question. Conversely, if it used 20-year or 30-year debt, it would have to service the debt long after the assets that were purchased with the funds raised had been scrapped and had ceased providing cash flows. This would worry the lenders.

Of course, the one-year debt could probably be rolled over year after year, out to the 10-year asset maturity. However, if interest rates rose, Consolidated would have to pay a higher rate when it rolled over its debt, or if the company experienced difficulties, it might not be able to refund the debt at any reasonable rate. On the other hand, if Consolidated financed 10-year assets with 20-year or 30-year bonds, (1) it would still have a liability after the 10-year life of the asset, but (2) it would have generated some excess cash from the assets over their 10-year life. The question then would be this: Can we reinvest the accumulated cash flows at a rate which will enable us to pay off the bonds over their remaining 20-year or 30-year life? This strategy clearly imposes uncertainty on the firm, since it cannot know at the time it sells the bonds if profitable capital investment opportunities will be available 10 years later.

For all these reasons, the best all-around financing strategy is to match debt maturities with asset maturities. In recognition of this fact, firms generally do place great emphasis on maturity matching, and this factor often dominates the debt portion of the financing decision.

EFFECTS OF INTEREST RATE LEVELS AND FORECASTS

Financial managers also consider interest rate levels and forecasts, both absolute and relative, when making financing decisions. For example, if long-term interest rates are high by historical standards and are expected to fall, managers will be reluctant to issue long-term debt and thus lock in those costs for long periods. We already know that one solution to this problem is for firms to use a call provision — callability permits refunding should interest rates drop, but there is a cost, because the firm must set a higher coupon on callable debt. Alternatively, the firm could finance with short-term debt whenever long-term rates were historically high, and then, assuming that interest rates subsequently fall, sell a long-term issue to replace the short-term debt. Of course, this strategy has its risks: If interest rates move even higher, the firm will be forced to renew its short-term debt at higher and higher rates, or to replace the short-term debt with a long-term bond which costs even more than it would have when the original decision was made.

One could argue that capital markets are efficient, hence that it is impossible to predict what future interest rates will be because these rates will be determined by information which is not now known. Thus, under the efficient markets hypothesis, it would be unproductive for firms to try to "beat the market" by forecasting future capital costs and then acting on these forecasts. According to this view, financial managers ought to arrange their capital structures in such a manner that they can ride out almost any economic storm, and this generally calls for (1) using some "reasonable" mix of debt and equity and (2) using debt with maturities which more or less match the maturities of the assets being financed.

Although we personally support the view dictated by the efficient markets hypothesis, there is no question that many managers disagree. They are influenced by current cost levels and forecasts, and they act accordingly. One manifestation of this behavior is the heavy use of shelf registrations. Some firms use shelf registrations because managers believe that financing "windows" exist. In the volatile interest rate environment that has characterized recent years, a company might decide to issue bonds when the rate is 8 percent but then find, six weeks later when it has SEC approval to go ahead with the issue, that rates are up to 9 percent. If it had "bonds on the shelf," it could have gone ahead and sold the issue while the low-cost window was open. (Another way to protect against rising rates is to hedge against this possibility with interest rate futures. We discuss futures markets and the use of futures for hedging in Chapter 23.)

A few years ago, the interest rate on AAA corporate bonds was about 12.5 percent. Exxon's investment bankers advised the company to tap the Eurobond market for relatively cheap fixed-rate financing.[16] At the time, Exxon could issue its bonds in London at 0.4 percentage points *below* comparable maturity U.S. Treasury bonds. However, one of Exxon's officers was quoted as saying, "I say so what. The absolute level of rates is too high. Our people would rather wait." The managers of Exxon, as well as many other companies, were betting that the next move in interest rates would be down. Since interest rates are now much lower, it turned out that Exxon was right.

These attitudes confirm that many firms base their financing decisions on expectations about future interest rates. It is easy to be right on one interest rate call — if you predict a decline in interest rates, you have a 50-50 chance of being correct. However, the success of a strategy based on forecasting rates requires that those forecasts be right more often than they are wrong, and it is very difficult to find

---

[16]See Chapter 26 for a discussion of Eurobonds.

someone with a long-term track record which is better than 50-50. Finance would be easy if we could accurately predict future interest rates. Unfortunately, predicting future interest rates with consistent accuracy is somewhere between difficult and impossible — people who make a living selling interest rate forecasts say it is difficult; many others say it is impossible.

INFORMATION ASYMMETRIES

Earlier in the chapter, we discussed bond ratings and the effects of changes in ratings on the cost and availability of capital. If a firm's current financial condition is poor, its managers may be reluctant to issue new long-term debt because (1) a new debt issue would probably trigger a review by the rating agencies, and (2) debt issued when a firm is in poor financial shape would probably cost more and be subject to more severe restrictive covenants than debt issued from strength. Further, in Chapter 13 we pointed out that firms are reluctant to use new common stock financing, especially when this might be taken as a negative signal. Thus, a firm that is in a weakened condition, but which is forecasting a better time in the future, would be inclined to delay permanent financing of any type until things improved. Such a firm would be motivated to use short-term debt even to finance long-term assets, with the expectation of replacing the short-term debt in the future with cheaper, higher-rated long-term debt.

Conversely, a firm that is strong now, but which forecasts a potentially bad time in the period just ahead, would be motivated to finance long term now rather than to wait. Each of these scenarios implies either that the capital markets are inefficient or that investors do not have the same information regarding the firm's future as does its financial manager. The second situation is undoubtedly true at times, and the first one possibly is too at times.

The firm's earnings outlook, and the extent to which forecasted higher earnings per share are reflected in stock prices, also has an effect on the choice of securities. If a successful R&D program has just been concluded, and as a result management forecasts higher earnings than do most investors, then the firm would not want to issue common stock. It would use debt and then, once earnings rise and push up the stock price, sell common to restore the capital structure to its target level.

AMOUNT OF FINANCING REQUIRED

Obviously, the amount of financing required will influence the financing decision. This is mainly due to flotation costs. A $5 million debt financing would most likely be done with a term loan or a privately placed bond issue, while a firm seeking $100 million of new debt would most likely use a public offering.

AVAILABILITY OF COLLATERAL

Generally, secured debt will be less costly than unsecured debt. Thus, firms with large amounts of fixed assets which have a ready resale value are likely to use a relatively large amount of debt, especially mortgage bonds. Additionally, each year's financing decision would be influenced by the amount of qualified assets available as security for new bonds.

What are some factors that financial managers should consider when making long-term financing decisions?

How do information asymmetries affect financing decisions?

SUMMARY

This chapter described the characteristics, advantages, and disadvantages of the major types of long-term debt securities. The key concepts covered are listed next.

■ *Term loans* and *bonds* are long-term debt contracts under which a borrower agrees to make a series of interest and principal payments on specific dates to the lender. A term loan is generally sold to one (or a few) lenders, while a bond is typically offered to the public and sold to many different investors.

■ There are many different types of bonds, including *mortgage bonds, debentures, convertibles, bonds with warrants, income bonds, putable bonds,* and *purchasing power (indexed) bonds.* The return required on each type of bond is determined by the bond's riskiness.

■ A bond's *indenture,* which is a legal document that spells out the rights of the bondholders and the issuing corporation, contains *restrictive covenants* designed to protect bondholders' interests. A *trustee* is assigned to make sure that the terms of the indenture are carried out.

■ A *call provision* gives the issuing corporation the right to redeem bonds prior to maturity under specified terms, usually at a price greater than the maturity value (the difference is a *call premium*). A firm will typically call a bond and refund it if interest rates fall substantially.

■ A *sinking fund* is a provision which requires the corporation to retire a portion of the bond issue each year. The purpose of the sinking fund is to provide for the orderly retirement of the issue. No call premium is paid to the holders of bonds called for sinking fund purposes.

■ Recent innovations in long-term financing include *zero coupon bonds,* which pay no annual interest but which are issued at a discount; *floating rate debt,* whose interest payments fluctuate with changes in the general level of interest rates; and *junk bonds,* which are high-risk, high-yield instruments used by firms which are poor credit risks. Other innovations include *project financing, bonds that are redeemable at par,* and *securitization.*

■ Bonds are assigned *ratings* which reflect the probability of their going into default. The higher a bond's rating, the lower its interest rate.

■ A firm's long-term financing decisions are influenced by its *target capital structure,* the *maturity of its assets,* its current and forecasted *financial condition,* the suitability of its *assets for use as collateral,* and current and forecasted *interest rate levels.*

If a bond has a call provision, the issuer may refund (call) the bond prior to maturity. We discuss refunding analysis in detail in Appendix 17A. Also, firms may issue bonds (or preferred stocks) that are convertible into common stock. Convertible bonds are discussed in detail in Chapter 19.

QUESTIONS

7-1 Define each of the following terms:
a. Story credit
b. Term loan; bond
c. Mortgage bond
d. Debenture; subordinated debenture
e. Convertible bond; warrant; income bond; indexed, or purchasing power, bond
f. Indenture; restrictive covenant
g. Trustee
h. Call provision; sinking fund
i. Zero coupon bond; original issue discount bond (OID)
j. Floating rate bond
k. Junk bond
l. Project financing
m. Securitization
n. Poison put; super poison put
o. Bond rating; rating agency; investment-grade bonds
p. Maturity matching

7-2 What effect would each of the following items have on the interest rate a firm must pay on a new issue of long-term debt? Indicate whether each factor would tend to raise, lower, or have an indeterminate effect on the interest rate, and then explain *why*.
a. The firm uses bonds rather than a term loan.
b. The firm uses nonsubordinated debentures rather than first mortgage bonds.
c. The firm makes its bonds convertible into common stock.
d. The firm makes its debentures subordinate to its bank debt. What will the effect be
  (1) On the cost of the debentures?
  (2) On the cost of the bank debt?
  (3) On the average cost of total debt?
e. The firm sells income bonds rather than debentures.
f. The firm must raise $100 million, all of which will be used to construct a new plant, and is debating the sale of first mortgage bonds or debentures. If it decides to issue $50 million of each type, as opposed to $75 million of first mortgage bonds and $25 million of debentures, how will this affect
  (1) The cost of debentures?
  (2) The cost of mortgage bonds?
  (3) The average cost of the $100 million?
g. The firm puts a call provision on its new issue of bonds.
h. The firm uses zero coupon bonds rather than coupon bonds.
i. The firm includes a sinking fund on its new issue of bonds.

      j. The firm's bonds are downgraded from A to BBB.

      k. The firm adds a super poison put provision on its new bond issue.

17-3   Rank the following securities from lowest (1) to highest (9) in terms of their riskiness for an investor. All securities (except the government bond) are for a given firm. If you think two or more securities are equally risky, indicate so.

      a. Income bond   _____

      b. Subordinated debentures — noncallable   _____

      c. First mortgage bond — no sinking fund   _____

      d. Common stock   _____

      e. U.S. Treasury bond   _____

      f. First mortgage bond — with sinking fund   _____

      g. Subordinated debentures — callable   _____

      h. Amortized term loan   _____

      i. Nonamortized term loan   _____

17-4   A sinking fund can be set up in one of two ways:

      (1) The corporation makes annual payments to the trustee, who invests the proceeds in securities (frequently government bonds) and uses the accumulated total to retire the bond issue at maturity.

      (2) The trustee uses the annual payments to retire a portion of the issue each year, either calling a given percentage of the issue by a lottery and paying a specified price per bond or buying bonds on the open market, whichever is cheaper.

Discuss the advantages and disadvantages of each procedure from the viewpoint of both the firm and the bondholders.

17-5   Draw an SML graph. Put dots on the graph to show (approximately) where you think a particular company's (a) common stock and (b) bonds would lie. Now put on dots to represent a riskier company's stock and bonds.

17-6   Suppose you work for the treasurer of a large, profitable corporation. Your company has some surplus funds to invest. You can buy these securities:

      (1) Aaa-rated Exxon 20-year bonds which sell at par and yield 9 percent.

      (2) Aa-rated Exxon preferred stock which yields 7 percent.

      (3) Ca-rated Continental Airlines bonds which yield 13 percent.

      (4) C-rated Continental Airlines preferred stock which yields 14 percent.

      (5) A-rated Alabama Power floating rate preferred stock which currently yields 5 percent.

      (6) Treasury bills which yield 4 percent.

      a. Does it appear that these securities are in equilibrium?

      b. If these were your only choices, which would you recommend? Why?

SELF-TEST PROBLEM

(SOLUTION APPEARS IN APPENDIX C)

ST-1   **SINKING FUNDS** The California Development Commission has just issued a $100 million, 10-year, 12 percent bond with semiannual coupon payments. A sinking fund will retire the issue over its life. Sinking fund payments are of equal amounts and will be made *semiannually*, and the proceeds will be used to retire bonds as the payments are made. Assume that the bonds will be called at par for sinking fund purposes.

a. How large must each semiannual sinking fund payment be?

b. What will happen, under the conditions of the problem thus far, to the company's debt service requirements per year for this issue over time?

c. Now suppose the Commission had set its sinking fund so that *equal annual amounts,* payable at the end of each year, were paid into a sinking fund trust held by a bank, with the proceeds being used to buy government bonds that pay 9 percent interest. The payments, plus accumulated interest, must total $100 million at the end of 10 years, and the proceeds will be used to retire the bonds at that time. How large must the annual sinking fund payment now be?

d. What are the annual cash requirements for covering bond service costs under the trusteeship arrangement described in Part c? (Note: Interest must be paid on the outstanding bonds but not on bonds that have been retired.)

e. Now assume that the Commission has the option of buying the bonds on the open market. What would have to happen to interest rates to cause the company to buy bonds on the open market rather than call them under the original sinking fund plan?

PROBLEMS

17-1 LOAN AMORTIZATION Suppose a firm is setting up an amortized term loan. What are the annual payments for a $10 million loan under the following terms:

a. 9 percent, 5 years?

b. 9 percent, 10 years?

c. 12 percent, 5 years?

d. 12 percent, 10 years?

17-2 AMORTIZATION SCHEDULE Set up an amortization schedule for a $1 million, 3-year, 10 percent loan.

17-3 YIELD TO CALL Five years ago Wachowicz Company sold a 20-year bond issue with a 17 percent coupon rate and a 10 percent constant call premium. Today the firm called the bonds. The bonds originally were sold at their face value of $1,000. Compute the realized rate of return for investors who purchased the bonds when they were issued and will surrender them today in exchange for the call price.

17-4 PERPETUAL BOND ANALYSIS In 1936 the Canadian government raised $55 million by issuing bonds at a 3 percent annual rate of interest. Unlike most bonds issued today, which have a specific maturity date, these bonds can remain outstanding forever; they are, in fact, perpetuities.

At the time of issue, the Canadian government stated in the bond indenture that cash redemption was possible at face value ($100) on or after September 1966; in other words, the bonds were callable at par after September 1966. Believing that the bonds would in fact be called, many investors purchased these bonds in 1965 with expectations of receiving $100 in 1966 for each perpetual bond they had. In 1965 the bonds sold for $55, but a rush of buyers drove the price to just below the $100 par value by 1966. Prices fell dramatically, however, when the Canadian government announced that these perpetual bonds were indeed perpetual and would not be paid off. A new, 30-year supply of coupons was sent to each bondholder.

The bonds' market price declined to $42 in December 1966. Because of their severe losses, hundreds of Canadian bondholders formed the Perpetual Bond Association to lobby for face value redemption of the bonds, claiming that the government had reneged on an implied promise to redeem the bonds. Government officials in Ottawa insisted that claims for face value payment were nonsense, for the bonds were and always had been clearly identified as perpetuals. One Ottawa official stated, "Our job is to protect the taxpayer. Why should we pay $55 million for less than $25 million worth of bonds?"

The issue heats up again every few years, and it recently resurfaced once more. Here are some questions relating to the Canadian issue that will test your understanding of bonds in general:

a. Would it make sense for a business firm to issue bonds such as the Canadian bonds described here? Would it matter whether the firm were a proprietorship or a corporation?

b. Suppose the U.S. government today sold $100 million each of these four types of bonds: 5-year bonds, 50-year bonds, "regular" perpetuities, and Canadian-type (callable) perpetuities. What do you think the relative order of interest rates would be? In other words, rank the bonds from the one with the lowest to the one with the highest rate of interest. Explain your answer.

c. (1) Suppose that because of pressure by the Perpetual Bond Association you believe that the Canadian government will redeem this particular perpetual bond issue in 3 years. Which course of action would be more advantageous to you if you owned the bonds: (a) sell your bonds today at $42, or (b) wait 3 years and have them redeemed? Assume that similar-risk bonds earn 8 percent today and that interest rates are expected to remain at this level for the next 3 years.

   (2) If you had the opportunity to invest your money in bonds of similar risk, at what rate of return would you be indifferent to the choice of selling your perpetuals today or having them redeemed in 3 years — that is, what is the expected yield to maturity on the Canadian bonds?

d. Show mathematically the perpetuities' value if they yield 7.15 percent, pay $3 interest annually, and are considered "regular" perpetuities. Show what would happen to the price of bonds if the going interest rate fell to 2 percent.

e. Are the Canadian bonds more likely to be valued as "regular" perpetuities if the going rate of interest is above or below 3 percent? Why?

f. Do you think the Canadian government would have taken the same action with regard to retiring the bonds if the interest rate had fallen rather than risen after they were issued?

g. Do you think the Canadian government was "fair" or "unfair" in its actions? Give the pros and cons, and justify your reason for thinking that one outweighs the other. Would it matter if the bonds had been sold to "sophisticated" as opposed to "naive" purchasers?

SPREADSHEET APPLICATIONS

SPREADSHEET PROBLEM

Suppose Southern States Insurance Company needs to raise $400 million, and its investment bankers have indicated that 10-year zero coupon bonds could be sold at a YTM of 12 percent while a 14 percent yield would be required on *annual* payment coupon bonds sold at par. Southern States's tax rate is 34 percent. (Assume that the discount can be amortized by the issuer using the straight line method. This cannot be done under current tax laws, but assume it anyway.)

a. How many $1,000 par value bonds would Southern States have to sell under each plan?

b. What would be the after-tax YTM on each type of bond (1) to a holder who is tax exempt and (2) to a taxpayer in the 50 percent federal-plus-state bracket?

c. What would be the after-tax cost of each type of bond to Southern States?

d. Why would investors be willing to buy the zero coupon bonds?

e. Why might Southern States turn down the offer to issue zero coupon bonds?

f. Redo Parts a, b, and c assuming that the YTM on zero coupon bonds falls to 10 percent and that on annual coupon bonds falls to 12 percent. As in the previous analysis, the after-tax yield to investors on the annual coupon bond exceeds that of the zero coupon bond. Has the differential between the annual and zero coupon bond yields changed? Would investors be more willing to purchase the zero coupon bond under the original assumptions or under the new assumptions? If the before-tax YTM were 10 percent on each type of bond, what would the after-tax YTMs be to zero and to 50 percent taxpayers, what would the after-tax cost be to the company, and what type of investors would be likely to hold the zeros and what type the regular coupon bonds?

SPREADSHEET EXERCISE: PROTECTING CELLS

This exercise uses a spreadsheet model to conduct a bond refunding analysis. The model is complete including graphics. Students will use the model to learn the advantages and disadvantages of protecting cells.

1. Retrieve the model (Filename SE-17.WK1) from the models diskette. The key inputs include data on the old and new bond issues, while the key output is the refunding NPV. The model has a graph that shows the sensitivity of refunding NPV to changes in the current interest rate.

2. The section beginning on Row 42 contains the data table that generates the data for the graph. To check the functioning of the data table, change the flotation cost on the new issue in Cell C15 from 2 percent to 5 percent. Note that the refunding NPV is reduced to $1,541,943.

3. Scroll down to the data table. The value for NPV when the interest rate is 12 percent remains at $2,765,481, so the data table did not recalculate when the flotation cost input was changed. To recalculate the data table, press the F8 key, which automatically repeats the last data table command used. Note that the table changes, and the NPV value at 12 percent is now $1,541,943. Return the model to its original data by changing Cell C15 back to 2 percent and pressing the F8 key.

4. Now suppose that you created this model and you want to give it to a friend. However, your friend is not very experienced with spreadsheets, and you are worried that he will inadvertently change one of the formulas and ruin the spreadsheet. You can guard against this event by protecting the spreadsheet. Type /WGPE, which enables the spreadsheet protection feature. Now try to enter something into Cell E27. The spreadsheet will not allow you to change the formula in the cell; instead, the computer beeps and an error message is displayed. Thus, by enabling the spreadsheet protection feature, you can prevent inadvertent changes from being made. Also, note that the letters PR appear in the control panel when the cursor is on the cell, telling users that the cell is protected.

5. Now go to Cell C18 and change the tax rate to 30 percent. The spreadsheet permits you to make this change because Cell C18 has been unprotected. The control panel indicates this with the letter U. When we created the spreadsheet, we unprotected this cell by placing the cursor on it and typing /RU Enter. All cells that were unprotected are displayed in

green, while the remaining cells, which were not unprotected and which were subsequently protected by the global protection enable command, are displayed in white. We use the range unprotect feature to color certain entries even if we do not intend to protect the entire worksheet. These cells stand out, and make it easier to spot input data cells and spreadsheet headings. However, the true purpose of the unprotect feature is to allow some cells to be changed while the remainder of the spreadsheet is protected from change. Change Cell C18 back to 40 percent.

6. Again change the flotation cost on the new issue in Cell C15 from 2 percent to 5 percent. Note that the refunding NPV is again reduced to $1,541,943. Press the F8 key to update the data table. Oops! The data table cannot recalculate because its cells are protected. Place the cursor in Cell A44, type /RU, highlight the entire data table, and then press Enter. The data table turns green because it is now unprotected. Now press F8, and the data table recalculates. The moral of the story is that data tables that will be recalculated must be unprotected, or else the recalculation will not work.

7. Finally, if you have protected a worksheet and then want to make changes to a formula without unprotecting the cell, the global protection must be disabled, the change made, and then the protection reenabled. Suppose we want to change the formula in Cell E27 from +E23+E24+E25 to @SUM(E23.E25). The new formula does the same calculation as the old formula. If you just try to enter the @SUM function, the global protection will stop you. Thus, first type /WGPD, then enter the @SUM function, and finally reprotect the spreadsheet by typing /WGPE.

MINI CASE

Hospital Development Corporation (HDC) needs $10 million to build a regional testing laboratory in Birmingham, Alabama. Once the lab is completed and fully operational, which should take about 5 years, HDC will sell it to a health maintenance organization (HMO). HDC tentatively plans to raise the $10 million by selling 5-year bonds, and its investment bankers have stated that either regular or zero coupon bonds can be used. Regular coupon bonds would have annual payment coupons of 12 percent, and zero coupon bonds would also be priced to yield 12 percent. Either bond would be callable after 3 years, on the anniversary date of the issue, at a premium of 6 months' interest for regular bonds or 5 percent over the accrued value on the call date for zero coupon bonds. HDC's federal-plus-state tax rate is 40 percent.

As assistant to HDC's treasurer, you have been assigned the task of making a recommendation as to which type of bonds to issue. As part of your analysis, you have been asked to answer the following questions.

a. What is the difference between a bond and a term loan? What are the advantages of a term loan over a bond?

b. Suppose HDC issues bonds and uses the medical center as collateral for the issue. What type of bond would this be? Suppose that instead of using a secured bond, HDC had decided to sell debentures. How would this affect the interest rate that HDC would have to pay on the debt?

c. What is a bond indenture? What are some examples of provisions the bondholders would probably require HDC to include in its indenture?

d. HDC's bonds will be callable after 3 years. If the bonds were not callable, would the interest rate required be higher or lower than 12 percent? What would be the effect on the rate if the bonds were callable immediately? What are the advantages to HDC of making the bonds callable?

e. (1) If its indenture included a sinking fund provision which required HDC to retire one-fifth of the bonds each year, would this provision raise or lower the interest rate required on the bonds?

   (2) How would the sinking fund operate?

   (3) Why might HDC's investors require it to use a sinking fund? For this particular issue, would it make sense to include a sinking fund?

f. If HDC were to issue zero coupon bonds, what initial price would cause the zeros to yield 12 percent? How many $1,000 par value zeros would HDC have to sell to raise the needed $10 million? How many regular 12 percent coupon bonds would HDC have to sell?

g. Set up a time line which shows the accrued value of the zeros at the end of each year, along with the annual after-tax cash flows from the zeros to an investor in the 28 percent tax bracket and to HDC.

h. What would the after-tax yield to maturity be on each type of bond to an investor in the 28 percent tax bracket? What would the after-tax cost of debt be to HDC?

i. If interest rates were to fall, causing HDC to call the bonds (either the coupon or the zero) at the end of Year 3, what would be the after-tax yield to call on each type of bond to an investor in the 28 percent tax bracket?

j. HDC is an A-rated firm. Suppose HDC's bond rating was (1) lowered to triple B or (2) raised to double A. What would be the effect of these changes on the interest rate required on HDC's new long-term debt and on the market value of the company's outstanding debt?

k. What are some of the factors a firm such as HDC should consider when deciding whether to issue long-term debt, short-term debt, or equity? Why might long-term debt be HDC's best choice in this situation?

l. Describe the key features of the following securities and transactions:

   (1) Junk bonds

   (2) Project financing

   (3) Securitization

   (4) Bonds that are redeemable at par

SELECTED ADDITIONAL REFERENCES AND CASES

The investment textbooks listed in the Chapter 4 references provide useful information on bonds, as well as the markets in which they are traded. In addition, the following articles offer useful insights:

Allen, David S., Robert E. Lamy, and G. Rodney Thompson, "Agency Costs and Alternative Call Provisions: An Empirical Investigation," *Financial Management,* Winter 1987, 37–44.

Altman, Edward I., "Revisiting the High-Yield Bond Market," *Financial Management,* Summer 1992, 78–92.

Arak, Marcelle, Arturo Estrella, Laurie Goodman, and Andrew Silver, "Interest Rate Swaps: An Alternative Explanation," *Financial Management,* Summer 1988, 12–18.

Backer, Morton, and Martin L. Gosman, "The Use of Financial Ratios in Credit Downgrade Decisions," *Financial Management,* Spring 1980, 53–56.

Bae, Sung C., Daniel P. Klein, and Raj Padmaraj, "Event Risk Bond Covenants, Agency Costs of Debt and Equity, and Stockholder Wealth," *Financial Management,* Winter 1994, 28–41.

Barrett, W. Brian, Andrea J. Heuson, and Robert W. Kolb, "The Differential Effects of Sinking Funds on Bond Risk Premia," *Journal of Financial Research,* Winter 1986, 303–312.

Chen, Chao, and Philip Fanara, Jr., "The Choice Among Long-Term Financing Instruments for Public Utilities," *The Financial Review,* August 1992, 431–465.

Clark, John J., with Brenton W. Harries, "Some Recent Trends in Municipal and Corporate Securities Markets: An Interview with Brenton W. Harries, President of Standard & Poor's Corporation," *Financial Management,* Spring 1976, 9–17.

Crabbe, Leland, "Event Risk: An Analysis of Losses to Bondholders and 'Super Poison Put' Bond Covenants," *Journal of Finance,* June 1991, 689–706.

Easterwood, John C., and Palani-Rajan Kadapakkam, "The Role of Private and Public Debt in Corporate Capital Structures," *Financial Management,* Autumn 1991, 49–57.

Emerick, Dennis, and William White, "The Case for Private Placements: How Sophisticated Investors Add Value to Corporate Debt Issuers," *Journal of Applied Corporate Finance,* Fall 1992, 83–91.

Ferri, Michael G., "An Empirical Examination of the Determinants of Bond Yield Spreads," *Financial Management,* Autumn 1978, 40–46.

Fridson, Martin S., "The State of the High Yield Bond Market: Overshooting or Return to Normalcy?" *Journal of Applied Corporate Finance,* Spring 1994, 85–97.

Gentry, James A., David T. Whitford, and Paul Newbold, "Predicting Industrial Bond Ratings with a Profit Model and Funds Flow Components," *The Financial Review,* August 1988, 269–286.

Hand, John R. M., Robert W. Holthausen, and Richard W. Leftwich, "The Effect of Bond Rating Agency Announcements on Bond and Stock Prices," *Journal of Finance,* June 1992, 733–752.

Hsueh, L. Paul, and David S. Kidwell, "Bond Ratings: Are Two Better than One?" *Financial Management,* Spring 1988, 46–53.

Johnson, James M., Robert A. Pari, and Leonard Rosenthal, "The Impact of In-Substance Defeasance on Bondholder and Shareholder Wealth," *Journal of Finance,* September 1989, 1049–1057.

Kalotay, Andrew J. "Sinking Funds and the Realized Cost of Debt," *Financial Management,* Spring 1982, 43–54.

———, "Innovations in Corporation Finance: Deep Discount Private Placements," *Financial Management,* Spring 1982, 55–57.

Kao, Chihwa, and Chunchi Wu, "Sinking Funds and the Agency Costs of Corporate Debt," *The Financial Review,* February 1990, 95–113.

Laber, Gene, "Bond Covenants and Foregone Opportunities: The Case of Burlington Northern Railroad Company," *Financial Management,* Summer 1992, 71–77.

Litzenberger, Robert H., "Swaps: Plain and Fanciful," *Journal of Finance,* July 1992, 831–850.

Longstaff, Francis A., and Bruce A. Tuckman, "Calling Nonconvertible Debt and the Problem of Related Wealth Transfer Effects," *Financial Management,* Winter 1994, 21–27.

Pinches, George E., J. Clay Singleton, and Ali Jahankhani, "Fixed Coverage as a Determinant of Electric Utility Bond Ratings," *Financial Management,* Summer 1978, 45–55.

Roach, Stephen S., "Living with Corporate Debt," *Journal of Applied Corporate Finance,* Spring 1989, 19–29.

Smith, Clifford W., and J. B. Warner, "On Financial Contracting: An Analysis of Bond Covenants," *Journal of Financial Economics,* June 1979, 117–161.

Szewczyk, Samuel H., and Raj Varma, "Raising Capital with Private Placements of Debt," *Journal of Financial Research,* Spring 1991, 1–13.

Thompson, G. Rodney, and Peter Vaz, "Dual Bond Ratings: A Test of the Certification Function of Rating Agencies," *Financial Review,* August 1990, 457–471.

Weinsten, Mark I., "The Seasoning Process of New Corporate Bond Issues," *Journal of Finance,* December 1978, 1343–1354.

Zwick, Burton, "Yields on Privately Placed Corporate Bonds," *Journal of Finance,* March 1980, 23–29.

References on bond refunding include the following:

Ang, James S., "The Two Faces of Bond Refunding," *Journal of Finance,* June 1975, 869–874.

_____, "The Two Faces of Bond Refunding: Reply," *Journal of Finance,* March 1978, 354–356.

Chiang, Raymond C., and M. P. Narayanan, "Bond Refunding in Efficient Markets: A Dynamic Analysis with Tax Effects," *Journal of Financial Research,* Winter 1991, 287–302.

Dyl, Edward A. and Michael D. Joehnk, "Refunding Tax Exempt Bonds," *Financial Management,* Summer 1976, 59–66.

Emery, Douglas R., "Overlapping Interest in Bond Refunding: A Reconsideration," *Financial Management,* Summer 1978, 19–20.

Finnerty, John D., "Refunding High-Coupon Debt," *Midland Corporate Finance Journal,* Winter 1986, 59–74.

Harris, Robert S., "The Refunding of Discounted Debt: An Adjusted Present Value Analysis," *Financial Management,* Winter 1980, 7–12.

Kalotay, Andrew J., "On the Advanced Refunding of Discounted Debt," *Financial Management,* Summer 1978, 14–18.

_____, "On the Structure and Valuation of Debt Refundings," *Financial Management,* Spring 1982, 41–42.

Kraus, Alan, "An Analysis of Call Provisions and the Corporate Refunding Decision," *Midland Corporate Finance Journal,* Spring 1983, 46–60.

Laber, Gene, "The Effect of Bond Refunding of Discounted Debt," *Financial Management,* June 1979, 795–799.

_____, "Implications of Discount Rates and Financing Assumptions for Bond Refunding Decisions," *Financial Management,* Spring 1979, 7–12.

_____, "Repurchases of Bonds through Tender Offers: Implications for Shareholder Wealth," *Financial Management,* Summer 1978, 7–13.

Livingston, Miles, "The Effect of Bond Refunding on Shareholder Wealth: Comment," *Journal of Finance,* June 1979, 801–804.

_____, "Bond Refunding Reconsidered: Comment," *Journal of Finance,* March 1980, 191–196.

Mauer, David C., "Optimal Bond Call Policies under Transactions Costs," *Journal of Financial Research,* Spring 1993, 23–37.

Mayor, Thomas H., and Kenneth G. McCoin, "Bond Refunding: One or Two Faces?" *Journal of Finance,* March 1978, 349–353.

Ofer, Aharon R., and Robert A. Taggart, Jr., "Bond Refunding: Reconsidered: Reply," *Journal of Finance,* March 1980, 197–200.

Riener, Kenneth D., "Financial Structure Effects of Bond Refunding," *Financial Management,* Summer 1980, 18–23.

Thatcher, Janet S., and John G. Thatcher, "An Empirical Test of the Timing of Bond-Refunding Decisions," *Journal of Financial Research,* Fall 1992, 219–230.

Yawitz, Jess B., and James A. Anderson, "The Effect of Bond Refunding on Shareholder Wealth," *Journal of Finance,* December 1977, 1738–1746.

———, "The Effect of Bond Refunding on Shareholder Wealth: Reply," *Journal of Finance,* June 1979, 805–809.

Zeise, Charles H., and Roger K. Taylor, "Advance Refunding: A Practitioner's Perspective," *Financial Management,* Summer 1977, 73–76.

The following cases from Cases in Financial Management: Dryden Request *series focus on the topic covered in Appendix 17A:*

Case 24, "Bay Area Telephone Company," Case 24A, "Shenandoah Power Company," and Case 24B, "Tucson Entertainment, Inc.," which illustrate the bond refunding decision.

APPENDIX 17A

REFUNDING OPERATIONS

A great deal of long-term corporate debt was sold during the late 1980s at interest rates in the 9 to 12 percent range. Because the period of call protection on much of this debt has ended or is about to end, and because interest rates have fallen since the debt was issued, many companies are analyzing the pros and cons of bond refundings. Refunding decisions actually involve two separate questions: (1) Is it profitable to call an outstanding issue in the current period and replace it with a new issue; and (2) even if refunding is currently profitable, would the value of the firm be increased even more if the refunding were postponed to a later date? We consider both questions in this section.

Note that the decision to refund a security is analyzed in much the same way as a capital budgeting expenditure. The costs of refunding (the investment outlays) are (1) the call premium paid for the privilege of calling the old issue, (2) the tax savings from writing off the unexpensed flotation costs on the old issue, and (3) the net interest that must be paid while both issues are outstanding (the new issue is often sold one month before the refunding to ensure that the funds will be available). The annual cash flows, in a capital budgeting sense, are the interest payments that are saved each year plus the net tax savings which the firm receives for amortizing the flotation expenses. For example, if the interest expense on the old issue is $1,000,000 whereas that on the new issue is $700,000, the $300,000 reduction in interest savings constitutes an annual benefit.[1]

The net present value method is used to analyze the advantages of refunding: the future cash flows are discounted back to the present, and then this discounted value is compared with the cash outlays associated with the refunding. The firm should refund the bond if the present value of the savings exceeds the cost—that is, if the NPV of the refunding operation is positive.

In the discounting process, the after-tax cost of the new debt should be used as the discount rate. The reasons for this are (1) there is relatively little risk to the savings — cash flows in a refunding are known with relative certainty, which is quite unlike the situation with cash flows in most capital budgeting decisions, and (2) the cash outlay required to refund the old issue is generally obtained by increasing the amount of the new issue (see Footnote 4).

The easiest way to examine the refunding decision is through an example. Microchip Computer Company has outstanding a $60 million bond issue which has a 15 percent annual coupon and 20 years remaining to maturity. This issue, which was sold 5 years ago, had flotation costs of $3 million, which the firm has been amortizing on a straight line basis over the 25-year original life of the issue. The bond has a call provision which makes it possible for the company to retire the bonds at this time by calling them in at a 10 percent call premium. Investment bankers have assured the company that it could sell an additional $60 million to $70 million worth of new annual coupon 20-year bonds at an interest rate of 12 percent. To ensure that the funds required to pay off the old debt will be available, the new bonds would be sold one month before the old issue is called, so for one month, interest would have to be paid on both issues. Current short-term interest rates are 11 percent; for the one-month overlap period, proceeds from the new issue will be invested in short-term securities. Predictions are that long-term interest rates are unlikely to fall below 12 percent.[2] Flotation costs on a new refunding issue would amount to $2,650,000. Microchip's marginal tax rate is 34 percent. Should the company refund the $60 million of 15 percent bonds?

The following steps outline the decision process; the steps are summarized in worksheet form in Table 17A-1.

Step 1. **Determine the investment outlay required to refund the issue.**
    a. Call premium

$$\text{Before tax: } 0.10(\$60,000,000) = \$6,000,000.$$

$$\text{After tax: } \$6,000,000(1 - T) = \$6,000,000(0.66)$$

$$= \$3,960,000$$

Although Microchip must expend $6 million on the call premium, this is a tax deductible expense in the year the call is made. Since the company is in the 34

---

[1]During the early 1980s, there was a flurry of work on the pros and cons of refunding bond issues that had fallen to deep discounts as a result of rising interest rates. At such times, the company could go into the market, buy its debt at a low price, and retire it. The difference between the bonds' par value and the price the company paid would be reported as income, and taxes would have to be paid on it. The results of the research on the refunding of discount issues suggest that bonds should not, in general, be refunded after a rise in rates. See Andrew J. Kalotay, "On the Structure and Valuation of Debt Refundings," *Financial Management,* Spring 1982, 41–42; and Robert S. Harris, "The Refunding of Discounted Debt: An Adjusted Present Value Analysis," *Financial Management,* Winter 1980, 7–12.

[2]The firm's management has estimated that there is a 75 percent probability that interest rates will remain at their present level of 12 percent or else rise; there is only a 25 percent probability that they will fall further.

| TABLE 17A-1 | BOND REFUNDING DECISION WORKSHEET |

INVESTMENT OUTLAY: t = 0	AMOUNT BEFORE TAX	AMOUNT AFTER TAX	PRESENT VALUE AT 7.92%
1. Call premium on old issue	($6,000,000)	($3,960,000)	($3,960,000)
2. Flotation costs on new issue	(2,650,000)	(2,650,000)	(2,650,000)
3. Tax savings on old issue flotation costs	2,400,000	816,000	816,000
4. Extra interest cost on old issue	(750,000)	(495,000)	(495,000)
5. Interest earned on short-term investment	550,000	363,000	363,000
6. Net investment outlay at t = 0			($ 5,926,000)
ANNUAL FLOTATION COST TAX EFFECTS: t = 1 − 20			
7. Annual benefit from new issue flotation costs	$132,500	$45,050	$444,953
8. Annual lost benefit from old issue flotation costs	(120,000)	(40,800)	(402,976)
9. PV of amortization tax effects			$ 41,977
SAVINGS DUE TO REFUNDING: t = 1 − 20			
10. Interest payment on old issue	$9,000,000	$5,940,000	
11. Interest payment on new issue	7,200,000	4,752,000	
12. Net interest savings		$1,188,000	$11,733,727
NPV OF REFUNDING DECISION			$ 5,849,704

percent tax bracket, it saves $6,000,000 − $3,960,000 = $2,040,000 in taxes. Therefore, the after-tax cost of the call is only $3.96 million. This amount is shown as a cost, or outflow, on Line 1 of Table 17A-1.

b. Flotation costs on new issue

Flotation costs on the new issue are $2,650,000, as shown on Line 2 of the worksheet. For tax purposes, flotation costs must be amortized over the life of the new bond, or 20 years. Therefore, the annual tax deduction is

$$\frac{\$2,650,000}{20} = \$132,500.$$

Since Microchip is in the 34 percent tax bracket, it has a tax savings of $132,500(0.34) = $45,050 a year for 20 years. This is an annuity of $45,050 for 20 years. In a refunding analysis, all cash flows should be discounted at the after-tax cost of new debt, in this case 12%(1 − T) = 12%(0.66) = 7.92%. The present value of the tax savings, discounted at 7.92 percent, is $444,953, which is shown on Line 7 as an inflow.

c. Flotation costs on old issue

The old issue has an unamortized flotation cost of (20/25)($3,000,000) = $2.4 million at this time. If the issue is retired, the unamortized flotation cost may be recognized immediately as an expense, thus creating an after-tax savings of

$2,400,000(0.34) = $816,000, which is shown on Line 3 of the worksheet. The firm will, however, no longer receive a tax deduction of $120,000 a year for 20 years, or an after-tax benefit of $40,800 a year. The present value of this tax savings, discounted at 7.92 percent, is $402,976, which is shown on Line 8 as an opportunity cost of the refunding. It is important to note that because of the refunding, the old flotation costs provide an immediate tax saving rather than annual savings over the next 20 years. Thus, the $816,000 − $402,976 = $413,024 net savings simply reflects the difference between the present value of benefits received in the future without the refunding versus an immediate benefit if the refunding occurs.

d. Additional interest

One month "extra" interest on the old issue, after taxes, costs $495,000:

$$(\text{Dollar amount})(1/12 \text{ of } 15\%)(1 - T) = \text{Interest cost}$$

$$(\$60,000,000)(0.0125)(0.66) = \$495,000.$$

However, the proceeds from the new issue can be invested in short-term securities for one month. Thus, $60 million invested at a rate of 11 percent will return $363,000 in after-tax interest:

$$(\$60,000,000)(1/12 \text{ of } 11\%)(1 - T) = \text{Interest earned}$$

$$(\$60,000,000)(0.009167)(0.66) = \$363,000.$$

These figures are reflected in Lines 4 and 5.

e. Total after-tax investment outlay

The total investment outlay required to refund the bond issue, which will be financed by debt, is thus $5,926,000.[3] This is shown on Line 6 of Table 17A-1.

Step 2. Calculate the PV of the flotation cost tax effects.

The net effect of the amortization of the flotation costs on the old and new issues is $41,977 in savings on a present value basis. This amount is shown on Line 9.

Step 3. Calculate the PV of the annual interest savings.

a. Interest on old bond, after tax

The annual after-tax interest on the old issue is $5,940,000:

$$(\$60,000,000)(0.15)(0.66) = \$5,940,000.$$

This is shown on Line 10.

b. Interest on new bond, after tax

The new issue has an annual after-tax cost of $4,752,000.

---

[3]The net cash investment outlay (in this case, about $6 million) is usually obtained by increasing the amount of the new bond issue. Thus, the new issue would be about $66 million. However, the interest on the additional debt *should not* be deducted at Step 2 because the net investment outlay itself will be deducted at Step 3. If additional interest on the $6 million were deducted at Step 2, then interest would, in effect, be deducted twice. The situation here is exactly like that in regular capital budgeting decisions. Even though some debt may be used to finance a project, interest on that debt is not subtracted when developing the annual cash flows. Rather, the annual cash flows are discounted by the project's cost of capital.

$$(\$60,000,000)(0.12)(0.66) = \$4,752,000.$$

This is shown on Line 11.

c. **Annual savings**

Thus, the annual after-tax savings is $1,188,000:

Interest on old bond, after tax	$5,940,000
Interest on new bond, after tax	(4,752,000)
Annual net savings	$1,188,000

This is shown on Line 12.

d. **PV of annual savings**

The PV of $1,188,000 per year at 7.92 percent for 20 years is $11,733,727. This is also shown on Line 12.

Step 4. Determine the NPV of the refunding.

Net investment outlay	($5,926,000)
Amortization tax effects	41,977
Interest savings	11,733,727
NPV from refunding	$ 5,849,704

Since the net present value of the refunding is positive, it would benefit stockholders to refund the old bond issue.

Several other points should be noted. First, since the cash flows are based on differences between contractual obligations, their risk is the same as that of the underlying obligations. Therefore, the present values of the cash flows should be found by discounting at the firm's least risky rate — its after-tax cost of marginal debt. Second, since the refunding operation is advantageous to the firm, it must be disadvantageous to bondholders; they must give up their 15 percent bonds and reinvest in new ones that yield 12 percent. This points out the danger of the call provision to bondholders, and it also explains why bonds without a call provision command higher prices than callable bonds. Third, although it is not emphasized in the example, we assumed that the firm raises the investment required to undertake the refunding operation (the $5,926,000 shown on Line 6 of Table 17A-1) as debt. This should be feasible, since the refunding operation will improve the interest coverage ratio even though, if the investment outlay is raised as debt, a larger amount of debt will be outstanding.[4] Fourth, we set up our example in such a way that the new issue had the same maturity as the remaining life of the old issue. Often, the old bonds have only a relatively short time to maturity (say, 5 to 10 years), while the new bonds would have a longer maturity (say, 25 to 30 years). In this situa-

---

[4]See Aharon R. Ofer and Robert A. Taggart, Jr., "Bond Refunding: A Clarifying Analysis," *Journal of Finance,* March 1977, 21–30, for a discussion of how the method of financing the refunding affects the analysis. Ofer and Taggart prove that (1) if the refunding investment outlay is to be raised as debt, the after-tax cost of debt is the proper discount rate, while (2) if these funds are to be raised as common equity, then the before-tax cost of debt is the proper rate. Since a profitable refunding will virtually always raise the firm's debt-carrying capacity (because total interest charges after the refunding will be lower than before the refunding), it is more logical to use debt than either equity or a combination of debt and equity to finance the operation. Therefore, firms generally do use additional debt to finance refunding operations, so we assume debt financing for the costs of refunding and discount at the after-tax cost of debt.

tion, a replacement chain analysis is required. Although the interest savings benefit occurs over a much shorter period, refunding now pushes future flotation costs out further into the future, and this value can most easily be captured by a replacement chain analysis. Fifth, refunding decisions are well suited for analysis with a spreadsheet program. A refunding spreadsheet is easy to set up, and once it is, it is easy to vary the assumptions, especially the assumption about the interest rate on the new issue, and to see the way such changes affect the NPV.

One final point should be addressed: Although our analysis shows that the refunding would increase the value of the firm, would refunding *at this time* truly maximize the firm's expected value? Note that if interest rates continue to fall, then the company might be better off waiting, for this could increase the NPV of the refunding operation even more. The mechanics of calculating the NPV of a refunding are simple, but the decision on *when* to refund is not a simple one at all, because it requires a forecast of future interest rates. Thus, refund now versus waiting for a possibly more favorable future refunding is a judgmental decision.

To illustrate the timing decision, assume that Microchip's managers forecast that long-term interest rates have a 50 percent probability of remaining at their present level of 12 percent over the next year. However, there is a 25 percent probability that rates could fall to 10 percent, and a 25 percent probability that they could rise to 14 percent. Further, assume that short-term rates are expected to remain one percentage point below long-term rates, and that the call premium would be reduced by one-twentieth if the call were delayed for one year.

The refunding analysis could then be repeated, as previously, but assuming it would take place one year from now. Thus, the old bonds would have only 19 years remaining to maturity. We performed the analysis and found the NPV distribution of refunding one year from now:

PROBABILITY	LONG-TERM INTEREST RATE	NPV OF REFUNDING ONE YEAR FROM NOW
25%	10%	$15,328,674
50	12	5,770,191
25	14	(2,158,208)

At first blush, it would seem reasonable to calculate the expected NPV of refunding next year in terms of the probability distribution. However, that would not be correct. If interest rates did rise to 14 percent, Microchip would not refund the issue; therefore, the actual NPV if rates rise to 14 percent would be zero. The expected NPV from refunding one year hence is, therefore, 0.25($15,328,674) + 0.50($5,770,191) + 0.25($0) = $6,717,264 versus $5,849,704 if refunding occurred today.

Even though the expected NPV of refunding in one year is higher, Microchip's managers would probably decide to refund today. The $5,849,704 represents a certain increase in firm value, whereas the $6,717,264 is only an expected increase, plus proper comparison requires that the $6,717,264 be discounted back one year to today. Microchip's managers should opt to delay refunding only if the expected NPV from later refunding is sufficiently above today's certain NPV to compensate for the risk and time value involved.

Clearly, the decision to refund now versus refund later is complicated by the fact that there would be numerous opportunities to refund in the future rather than just a single opportunity one year from now. Furthermore, the decision must be based on a large set of interest rate forecasts, a daunting task in itself. Fortunately, financial managers making bond refunding decisions can now use the values of derivative securities to estimate the value of the bond issue's embedded call option. If the call option is worth more than the NPV of refunding today, the issue should not be immediately refunded. Rather, the issuer should either delay the refunding to take advantage of the information obtained from the derivative market or actually create a derivative transaction to lock in the value of the call option.[5]

---

[5]For more information on derivatives in general, see Chapter 23. For more information on the use of derivatives to help make call decisions, see Andrew J. Kalotay and George O. Williams, "How to Succeed in Derivatives without Really Buying," *Journal of Applied Corporate Finance,* Fall 1993, 100–103.

CHAPTER 18

LEASE FINANCING

*S*ome of the biggest players in the airline business have never issued a ticket, lost a passenger's luggage, or landed a plane in bad weather. They are the aircraft lease companies — the merchant bankers of aviation — and their role is to help finance aircraft and thus help cash-strapped airlines respond more quickly to market changes. Among the major players in aircraft leasing are GPA Group, a closely held company based in Shannon, Ireland, and International Lease Finance of Beverly Hills.

Aircraft leasing companies purchase airplanes from manufacturers such as Boeing, Airbus Industrie, and McDonnell Douglas and then lease them, often on a relatively short-term basis, to carriers such as American, British Airways, Delta, Lufthansa, and United. Currently, leasing companies buy about 50 percent of all new commercial aircraft sold. Leasing separates the risks and rewards of owning aircraft from those of operating them.

The airline industry is currently undergoing major changes due to deregulation. The highly competitive nature of the industry has forced both TWA and Continental to seek bankruptcy protection twice and has caused many airlines to fail, including Braniff, Eastern, Midway, and Pan Am. In the days of regulation, airlines knew precisely the routes they would serve and also that prices could be raised to cover whatever costs were incurred. Thus, airlines could buy planes confident that route structures would be relatively stable and that revenues would cover financing costs. Now, however, airlines are constantly dropping and adding routes in response to changing competitive conditions and travel patterns. Because different types of aircraft are better suited for some routes than others, airlines must restructure their fleets frequently to optimize their aircraft mix for *the routes being flown. Leasing provides this needed flexibility. If an airline had purchased all of its aircraft, it would be hampered in its ability to respond quickly to changing conditions. The leasing companies, on the other hand, lease all types of aircraft to all types of airlines, so there is usually some airline somewhere interested in leasing an aircraft when its lease is dropped by another airline.*

Interestingly, Airbus Industrie, the European aircraft consortium, has adopted short-term leases as a sales tool. In recent years, Delta and United "bought" aircraft from Airbus on "walkaway" leases, whereby the aircraft could be returned to the manufacturer in less than a year. U.S. manufacturers complain that Airbus can offer such terms only because it is subsidized by the four European countries that back the consortium. The Clinton administration is reportedly lobbying to force Airbus to discontinue its short-term lease program, which would help Boeing and McDonnell Douglas but would potentially hurt U.S. airlines.

As you read this chapter, think about the airline industry and why leasing can be more attractive than buying, at least for some portion of an airline's fleet. Also, think about the leasing companies and manufacturers, and why they may be able to offer attractive lease rates. When you finish the chapter, you should have a good appreciation of how leases are analyzed and, just as important, in what situations leasing is likely to be attractive to both the user of the equipment and the leasing firm.

Firms generally own fixed assets and report them on their balance sheets, but it is the *use* of assets that is important, not their ownership per se. One way of obtaining the use of facilities and equipment is to buy them, but an alternative is to lease them. Prior to the 1950s, leasing was generally associated with real estate—land and buildings. Today, however, it is possible to lease virtually any kind of fixed asset, and currently over 30 percent of all new capital equipment acquired by businesses is financed through lease arrangements.[1]

TYPES OF LEASES

Leasing takes several different forms, the four most important being (1) operating leases, (2) financial, or capital, leases, (3) sale-and-leaseback arrangements, and (4) combination leases.

OPERATING LEASES

Operating leases, sometimes called *service leases,* generally provide for both *financing* and *maintenance.* IBM was one of the pioneers of the operating lease contract, and computers and office copying machines, together with automobiles, trucks, and

---

[1]For a detailed treatment of leasing, see James S. Schallheim, *Lease or Buy? Principles for Sound Decision Making* (Boston: Harvard Business School Press, 1994).

aircraft, are the primary types of equipment involved in operating leases. The owner of the property is called the *lessor,* while the user is called the *lessee.* (The term *lessee* is pronounced "less-ee," not "lease-ee," and *lessor* is pronounced "less-or.") Ordinarily, operating leases require the lessor to maintain and service the leased equipment, and the cost of the maintenance is built into the lease payments.

Another important characteristic of operating leases is the fact that they are *not fully amortized.* In other words, the payments required under the lease contract are not sufficient to recover the full cost of the asset. However, the lease contract is written for a period considerably less than the expected economic life of the asset, and the lessor expects to recover all costs either by subsequent renewal payments, by re-leasing the asset to other lessees, or by sale of the asset.

A final feature of operating leases is that they often contain a *cancellation clause* which gives the lessee the right to cancel the lease and to return the asset before the expiration of the basic lease agreement. This is an important consideration to the lessee, for it means that the asset can be returned if it is rendered obsolete by technological developments or if it is no longer needed because of a change in the lessee's business.

FINANCIAL, OR CAPITAL, LEASES

Financial leases, sometimes called *capital leases,* are differentiated from operating leases in that (1) they *do not* provide for maintenance service, (2) they *are not* cancellable, and (3) they *are* fully amortized (that is, the lessor receives rental payments equal to the full price of the leased equipment plus a return on investment). In a typical arrangement, the firm that will use the equipment (the lessee) selects the specific items it requires, and then it negotiates the price and delivery terms with the manufacturer. The user firm then arranges to have a leasing company (the lessor) buy the equipment from the manufacturer or the distributor, and the user firm simultaneously executes an agreement to lease the equipment from the financial institution. The terms of the lease generally call for full amortization of the lessor's investment, plus a rate of return on the unamortized balance which is close to the percentage rate the lessee would have paid on a secured term loan. For example, if the lessee would have to pay 10 percent for a term loan, then a rate of about 10 percent would be built into the lease contract.

The lessee is generally given an option to renew the lease at a reduced rate upon expiration of the basic lease. However, the basic lease usually cannot be cancelled unless the lessor is completely paid off. Also, the lessee generally pays the property taxes and insurance on the leased property. Since the lessor receives a return *after,* or *net of,* these payments, this type of lease is often called a "net, net" lease.

SALE-AND-LEASEBACK ARRANGEMENTS

Under a *sale-and-leaseback arrangement,* a firm that owns land, buildings, or equipment sells the property to another firm and simultaneously executes an agreement to lease the property back for a stated period under specific terms. The capital supplier could be an insurance company, a commercial bank, a specialized leasing company, the finance arm of an industrial firm, or an individual investor. The sale-and-leaseback plan is an alternative to a mortgage.

Note that the seller immediately receives the purchase price put up by the buyer. At the same time, the seller-lessee retains the use of the property. The parallel to borrowing is carried over to the lease payment schedule. Under a mortgage loan arrangement, the lender would normally receive a series of equal payments just sufficient to amortize the loan and to provide a specified rate of return on the outstanding loan balance. Under a sale-and-leaseback arrangement, the lease payments are set up exactly the same way—the payments are just sufficient to return the full purchase price to the investor, plus a stated return on the lessor's investment.

Sale-and-leaseback arrangements are almost the same as financial leases, the major difference being that the leased equipment is used and the lessor buys it from the user-lessee instead of from a manufacturer or a distributor. A sale and leaseback may, then, be thought of as a special type of financial lease.

COMBINATION LEASES

Many lessors now offer leases under a wide variety of terms. Therefore, in practice, leases often do not fit exactly into the operating lease or financial lease category, but, rather, combine some features of each. Such leases are called *combination leases.* To illustrate, cancellation clauses are normally associated with operating leases, but many of today's financial leases also contain cancellation clauses. However, in financial leases these clauses generally include prepayment provisions whereby the lessee must make penalty payments sufficient to enable the lessor to recover the unamortized cost of the leased property.

SELF-TEST QUESTIONS

What is the difference between an operating lease and a financial, or capital, lease?

What is a sale-and-leaseback transaction?

What is a combination lease?

TAX EFFECTS

The full amount of the lease payments is a tax-deductible expense for the lessee *provided that the Internal Revenue Service agrees that a particular contract is a genuine lease and not simply an installment loan called a lease.* This makes it important that a lease contract be written in a form acceptable to the IRS. A lease that complies with all IRS requirements is called a *guideline,* or *tax-oriented, lease,* and the tax benefits of ownership (depreciation and investment tax credits when they are available) belong to the lessor. The main provisions of the tax guidelines are as follows:[2]

1. The lease term (including any extensions or renewals at a fixed rental rate) must not exceed 80 percent of the estimated useful life of the equipment at

---

[2]See Schallheim, *op. cit.*, Chapter 3, for more on taxes and leasing.

the commencement of the lease transaction. Thus, at the end of the lease the equipment must have an estimated remaining life equal to at least 20 percent of its original life. Further, the remaining useful life must not be less than one year. This requirement limits the maximum term of a guideline lease to 80 percent of the asset's useful life. Note that an asset's useful life is normally much longer than its MACRS depreciation class life.

2. The equipment's estimated residual value (in constant dollars without adjustment for inflation) at the expiration of the lease must equal at least 20 percent of its value at the start of the lease. This requirement can have the effect of limiting the maximum lease term.

3. Neither the lessee nor any related party can have the right to purchase the property at a fixed price predetermined at the lease's inception. However, the lessee can be given an option to buy the asset at its fair market value.

4. Neither the lessee nor any related party can pay or guarantee payment of any part of the price of the leased equipment. Simply put, the lessee cannot make any investment in the equipment, other than through the lease payments.

5. The leased equipment must not be "limited use" property, defined as equipment that can only be used by the lessee or a related party at the end of the lease.

The reason for the IRS's concern about lease terms is that, without restrictions, a company could set up a "lease" transaction calling for very rapid payments, which would be tax deductions. The effect would be to depreciate the equipment over a much shorter period than its MACRS class life. For example, suppose a firm planned to acquire a $2,000,000 computer which had a 3-year MACRS class life. The annual depreciation allowances would be $660,000 in Year 1, $900,000 in Year 2, $300,000 in Year 3, and $140,000 in Year 4. If the firm were in the 40 percent federal-plus-state tax bracket, the depreciation would provide a tax saving of $264,000 in Year 1, $360,000 in Year 2, $120,000 in Year 3, and $56,000 in Year 4, for a total savings of $800,000. At a 6 percent discount rate, the present value of these tax savings would be $757,441.

Now suppose the firm could acquire the computer through a one-year lease arrangement with a leasing company for a payment of $2 million, with a 1-dollar purchase option. If the $2,000,000 payment were treated as a lease payment, it would be fully deductible, so it would provide a tax savings of 0.4($2,000,000) = $800,000 versus a present value of only $757,441 for the depreciation shelters. Thus, the lease payment and the depreciation would both provide the same total amount of tax savings (40% of $2,000,000, or $800,000), but the savings would come in faster, hence have a higher present value, with the one-year lease. Therefore, if just any type of contract could be called a lease and given tax treatment as a lease, then the timing of the tax shelters could be speeded up as compared with ownership depreciation tax shelters. This speedup would benefit companies, but it would be costly to the government. For this reason, the IRS has established the rules described above for defining a lease for tax purposes.

Even though leasing can be used only within limits to speed up the effective depreciation schedule, there are still times when very substantial tax benefits can be derived from a leasing arrangement. For example, if a firm like Tucson Electric has a very large construction program which has generated so many investment tax credits and so much accelerated depreciation that it has no current tax liabilities, then depreciation shelters are not very useful. In this case, a leasing company set up by profitable companies like GE or Philip Morris can buy the equipment, receive the depreciation shelters, and then share these benefits with the lessee by charging lower lease payments. This point will be discussed in detail later in the chapter, but the point to be made now is that if firms are to obtain tax benefits from leasing, the lease contract must be written in a manner that will qualify it as a true lease under IRS guidelines. If there is any question about the legal status of the contract, the financial manager must be sure to have the firm's lawyers and accountants check the latest IRS regulations.[3]

Note that a lease which does not meet the tax guidelines is called a *non-tax-oriented lease.* For this type of lease, the lessee (1) is the effective owner of the leased property, (2) can depreciate it for tax purposes, and (3) can deduct only the interest portion of each lease payment.

SELF-TEST QUESTIONS

What is the difference between a tax-oriented lease and a non-tax-oriented lease?

What are some lease provisions that would cause a lease to be classified as a non-tax-oriented lease?

Why is it necessary for the IRS to place limits on lease provisions?

FINANCIAL STATEMENT EFFECTS[4]

Under certain conditions, neither the leased assets nor the liabilities under the lease contract appear on the firm's balance sheet. For this reason, leasing is often called *off-balance sheet* financing. This point is illustrated in Table 18-1 by the balance sheets of two hypothetical firms, B and L. Initially, the balance sheets of both firms are identical, and they both have debt ratios of 50 percent. Next, each firm decides to acquire a fixed asset costing $100. Firm B borrows $100 and buys the asset, so both an asset and a liability go on its balance sheet, and its debt ratio rises from 50 to 75 percent. Firm L leases the equipment. The lease may call for fixed charges as high or even higher than the loan, and the obligations assumed under the lease may be equally or more dangerous from the standpoint of potential bankruptcy, but the firm's debt ratio remains at only 50 percent.

---

[3]In 1981, Congress relaxed the normal IRS rules to permit *safe harbor leases,* which had virtually no IRS restrictions and which were explicitly designed to permit the transfer of tax benefits from low-profit companies which could not use them to high-profit companies which could. The point of safe harbor leases was to provide incentives for capital investment to companies which had little or no tax liability — under safe harbor leasing, companies with a low tax liability could sell the benefit to companies in a high marginal tax bracket. In 1981 and 1982, literally billions of dollars were paid by such profitable firms as IBM and Philip Morris for the tax shelters of such unprofitable ones as Ford and Eastern Airlines. However, in 1983, Congress sharply curtailed the use of safe harbor leases.

[4]FASB Statement 13, "Accounting for Leases," spells out in detail both the conditions under which the lease must be capitalized and the procedures for capitalizing it. Also, see Schallheim, *op. cit.,* Chapter 4, for more on the accounting treatment of leases.

BALANCE SHEET EFFECTS OF LEASING	TABLE 18-1

BEFORE ASSET INCREASE				AFTER ASSET INCREASE							
	FIRMS B AND L			FIRM B, WHICH BORROWS AND BUYS				FIRM L, WHICH LEASES			
Current assets	$ 50	Debt	$ 50	Current assets	$ 50	Debt	$150	Current assets	$ 50	Debt	$ 50
Fixed assets	50	Equity	50	Fixed assets	150	Equity	50	Fixed assets	50	Equity	50
	$100		$100		$200		$200		$100		$100
Debt/assets ratio:			50%				75%				50%

To correct this problem, the Financial Accounting Standards Board issued FASB Statement 13, which requires that, for an unqualified audit report, firms that enter into financial (or capital) leases must restate their balance sheets to report the leased asset as a fixed asset and the present value of the future lease payments as a liability. This process is called capitalizing the lease, and its net effect is to cause Firms B and L to have similar balance sheets, both of which will, in essence, resemble the one shown for Firm B.

The logic behind Statement 13 is as follows. If a firm signs a financial lease contract, its obligation to make lease payments is just as binding as if it had signed a loan agreement—the failure to make lease payments can bankrupt a firm just as fast as the failure to make principal and interest payments on a loan. Therefore, for all intents and purposes, a financial lease is identical to a loan.[5] This being the case, if a firm signs a financial lease agreement, this has the effect of raising its true debt ratio, and thus its true capital structure is changed. Therefore, if the firm had previously established a target capital structure, and if there is no reason to think that the optimal capital structure has changed, then using lease financing requires additional equity support exactly like debt financing.

If disclosure of the lease in our Table 18-1 example were not made, then Firm L's investors could be deceived into thinking that its financial position is stronger than it really is. Thus, even before FASB Statement 13 was issued, firms were required to disclose the existence of long-term leases in footnotes to their financial statements. At that time, it was debated as to whether or not investors recognized fully the impact of leases and, in effect, would see that Firms B and L were in essentially the

---

[5]There are, however, certain legal differences between loans and leases. In the event of liquidation in bankruptcy, a lessor is entitled to take possession of the leased asset, and if the value of the asset is less than the required payments under the lease, the lessor can enter a claim (as a general creditor) for one year's lease payments. Also, after bankruptcy has been declared but before the case has been resolved, lease payments may be continued, whereas all payments on debts are stopped. In a reorganization, the lessor receives the asset plus three years' lease payments if needed to cover the value of the lease. The lender under a secured loan arrangement has a security interest in the asset, meaning that if it is sold, the lender will be given the proceeds, and the full unsatisfied portion of the lender's claim will be treated as a general creditor obligation. It is not possible to state, as a general rule, whether a supplier of capital is in a stronger position as a secured creditor or as a lessor. However, in certain situations, lessors may bear less risk than secured lenders if financial distress occurs.

same financial position. Some people argued that leases were not fully recognized, even by sophisticated investors. If this were the case, then leasing could alter the capital structure decision in a really significant manner—a firm could increase its true leverage through a lease arrangement, and this procedure would have a smaller effect on its cost of conventional debt, k_d, and on its cost of equity, k_s, than if it had borrowed directly and reflected this fact on its balance sheet. These benefits of leasing would accrue to existing investors at the expense of new investors who would, in effect, be deceived by the fact that the firm's balance sheet did not reflect its true liability situation.

The question of whether investors were truly deceived was debated but never resolved. Those who believed strongly in efficient markets thought that investors were not deceived and that footnotes were sufficient, while those who questioned market efficiency thought that all leases should be capitalized. Statement 13 represents a compromise between these two positions, though one that is tilted heavily toward those who favor capitalization.

A lease is classified as a capital lease, hence is capitalized and shown directly on the balance sheet, if one or more of the following conditions exist:

1. Under the terms of the lease, ownership of the property is effectively transferred from the lessor to the lessee.

2. The lessee can purchase the property at less than its true market value when the lease expires.

3. The lease runs for a period equal to or greater than 75 percent of the asset's life. Thus, if an asset has a 10-year life and the lease is written for 8 years, the lease must be capitalized.

4. The present value of the lease payments is equal to or greater than 90 percent of the initial value of the asset.[6]

These rules, together with strong footnote disclosure rules for operating leases, are sufficient to ensure that no one will be fooled by lease financing; thus, leases are regarded as debt for capital structure purposes, and they have the same effects as debt on k_d and k_s. Therefore, leasing is not likely to permit a firm to use more financial leverage than could be obtained with conventional debt.[7]

SELF-TEST QUESTIONS

Why is lease financing sometimes referred to as off-balance sheet financing?

What is the intent of FASB Statement 13?

What is the difference in the balance sheet treatment of a lease that is capitalized and one that is not?

---

[6]The discount rate used to calculate the present value of the lease payments must be the lower of (1) the rate used by the lessor to establish the lease payments (this rate is discussed later in the chapter) or (2) the rate of interest which the lessee would have to pay for new debt with a maturity equal to that of the lease. Also, note that any maintenance payments embedded in the lease payment must be stripped out prior to checking this condition.

[7]Schallheim, *op. cit.*, in Chapter 5, argues that leases and debt may not be strict substitutes. The evidence on this point is not conclusive. However, the lease analysis models are based on the assumption that leasing is a substitute for borrowing, and that assumption is probably valid in most situations.

EVALUATION BY THE LESSEE

Leases are evaluated by both the lessee and the lessor. The lessee must determine whether leasing an asset is less costly than buying it, and the lessor must decide the size of the lease payments required to produce a target rate of return on the invested funds. This section focuses on the analysis by the lessee.

In the typical case, the events leading to a lease arrangement follow the sequence described below. We should note that a degree of uncertainty exists regarding the theoretically correct way to evaluate lease-versus-purchase decisions, and some very complex decision models have been developed to aid in the analysis. However, the simple analysis given here leads to the correct decision in all the cases we have ever encountered.

1. The firm decides to acquire a particular building or piece of equipment; this decision is based on regular capital budgeting procedures. Whether or not to acquire the asset is *not* part of the typical lease analysis — in a lease analysis, we are concerned simply with whether to obtain the use of the machine by lease or by purchase. However, if the effective cost of capital obtained by leasing is substantially lower than the cost of debt, then the cost of capital used in capital budgeting would have to be recalculated, and perhaps projects formerly deemed unacceptable might become acceptable.

2. Once the firm has decided to acquire the asset, the next question is how to finance its acquisition. Well-run businesses do not have excess cash lying around, so capital to finance new assets must be obtained from some source.

3. Funds to purchase the asset could be obtained by borrowing, by retaining earnings, or by selling new equity. Alternatively, the asset could be leased. Because of the capitalization/disclosure provision for leases, leasing normally has the same capital structure effect as borrowing.

As indicated earlier, a lease is comparable to a loan in the sense that the firm is required to make a specified series of payments and a failure to meet these payments could result in bankruptcy. Thus, the most appropriate comparison is the cost of lease financing versus the cost of debt financing.[8]

To illustrate the basic elements of lease analysis, consider this simplified example. The Thompson-Grammatikos Company (TGC) requires the use of a 2-year asset that costs $100, and the company must choose between leasing and buying the asset. If the asset is purchased, the bank would lend TGC the $100 at a rate of 10 percent on a 2-year, simple interest loan. Thus, the firm would have to pay the bank $10 in interest at the end of each year, plus return the $100 of principal at the end of Year 2. For simplicity, assume that TGC could depreciate the asset over 2 years for tax purposes by the straight line method if it is purchased, resulting in tax depreciation of $50 in

---

[8]Note that the analysis should compare the cost of leasing with the cost of debt financing *regardless* of how the asset purchase is actually financed. The asset may be purchased with available cash if not leased, but since leasing is a substitute for debt financing, and has the same capital structure effect, the appropriate comparison would still be with debt financing.

each year. Also for simplicity, assume the asset's value at the end of 2 years (the residual value) is estimated to be $0.

Alternatively, TGC could lease the asset under a guideline lease for 2 years for a payment of $55 at the end of each year. TGC's tax rate is 40 percent. The analysis for the lease-versus-borrow decision consists of (1) estimating the cash flows associated with borrowing and buying the asset, that is, the flows associated with debt financing, (2) estimating the cash flows associated with leasing the asset, and (3) comparing the two financing methods to determine which has the lower cost. Here are the borrow-and-buy flows:

CASH FLOWS IF TGC BUYS	YEAR 0	YEAR 1	YEAR 2
Equipment cost	($100)		
Loan amount	100		
Interest expense		($10)	($ 10)
Tax savings from interest		4	4
Principal repayment			(100)
Tax savings from depreciation		20	20
Net cash flow	$ 0	$14	($ 86)

The net cash flow is zero in Year 0, positive in Year 1, and negative in Year 2. The operating cash flows are not shown, but they must, of course, be positive or else TGC would not want to acquire the asset. Since the operating cash flows will be the same regardless of whether the asset is leased or purchased, they can be ignored.

Here are the cash flows associated with the lease:

CASH FLOWS IF TGC LEASES	YEAR 0	YEAR 1	YEAR 2
Lease payment		($55)	($55)
Tax savings from payment		22	22
Net cash flow	$0	($33)	($33)

Note that the two sets of cash flows reflect the tax deductibility of either interest expense and depreciation or the lease payments, as appropriate. Thus, the net cash flows include the tax savings from these items. If the lease had not met IRS guidelines, then ownership would effectively reside with the lessee, and TGC would depreciate the asset for tax purposes whether it was leased or purchased. However, only the implied interest portion of the lease payment would be tax deductible. Thus, the analysis for a nonguideline lease would consist of simply comparing the after-tax financing flows on the loan with the after-tax lease payment stream.

To compare the cost streams of buying versus leasing, we must put them on a present value basis. As we explain later, the correct discount rate is the after-tax cost of debt, which for TGC is $10\%(1 - 0.4) = 6.0\%$. Applying this rate, we find the present value cost of buying to be $63.33, and the present value cost of leasing to be $60.50. Since leasing has the lower present value of costs, the company should lease this particular asset.

The example shows the general approach that we use in lease analysis, and it also illustrates a concept that can simplify the cash flow estimation process. Look back at the loan-related cash flows if TGC buys the asset. The after-tax principal and interest payments are −$6 in Year 1 and −$106 in Year 2. When these flows are discounted to Year 0 at the 6.0 percent after-tax cost rate, their present value is −$100, the negative of the loan amount. This equality results because we first used the cost of debt to estimate the future financing flows, and we then used this same rate to discount the flows back to the present, all on an after-tax basis. The net result is that the financing flows cancel one another out.

Here is the cash flow stream after the Year 0 loan amount and the related Year 1 and Year 2 flows have been removed:

CASH FLOWS IF TGC BUYS	YEAR 0	YEAR 1	YEAR 2
Cost of asset	($100)		
Tax savings from depreciation		$20	$20
Net cash flow	($100)	$20	$20

The present value cost of buying here is, of course, $63.33, the same number we found earlier. This result will always occur regardless of the specific terms of the debt financing — as long as the discount rate is the after-tax cost of debt, the cash flows associated with the loan can be ignored.

Now we examine a more realistic example, one for the Anderson Equipment Company, which is conducting a lease analysis on some assembly line equipment that it will procure in the coming year. The following data have been developed:

1. Anderson plans to acquire automated assembly line equipment with a 10-year life and a cost of $10 million, delivered and installed. However, Anderson plans to use the equipment for only 5 years, for it will discontinue the product line at that time.

2. Anderson can borrow the required $10 million at a before-tax cost of 10 percent.

3. The equipment's estimated scrap value is $50,000 after 10 years of use, but its estimated salvage value after only 5 years of use is $1,000,000. Thus, if Anderson buys the equipment, it would expect to receive $1,000,000 before taxes when the equipment is sold in 5 years. Note that in leasing, the asset's value at the end of the lease period is generally called its *residual value*.

4. Anderson can lease the equipment for 5 years at a rental charge of $2,750,000, payable at the beginning of each year, but the lessor will own the equipment upon the expiration of the lease. (The lease payment schedule is established by the potential lessor, as described in the next major section, and Anderson can accept it, reject it, or negotiate.)

5. The lease contract stipulates that the lessor will maintain the equipment at no additional charge to Anderson. However, if Anderson borrows and buys, it will

have to bear the cost of maintenance, which will be performed by the equipment manufacturer at a fixed contract rate of $500,000 per year, payable at the beginning of each year.

6. The equipment falls in the MACRS 5-year class life, Anderson's marginal tax rate is 40 percent, and the lease qualifies as a guideline lease.

NPV Analysis

Table 18-2 shows the steps involved in a complete NPV lease analysis. Part I of the table is devoted to the costs of borrowing and buying. Line 1 gives the

---

TABLE 18-2   ANDERSON EQUIPMENT COMPANY: NPV ANALYSIS (THOUSANDS OF DOLLARS)

I. COST OF OWNING (BORROWING AND BUYING)

	YEAR 0	YEAR 1	YEAR 2	YEAR 3	YEAR 4	YEAR 5
1. Net purchase price	($10,000)					
2. Maintenance cost	(500)	($500)	($ 500)	($500)	($500)	
3. Maintenance tax savings	200	200	200	200	200	
4. Depreciation tax savings		800	1,280	760	480	$ 440
5. Residual value						1,000
6. Tax on residual value						(160)
7. Net cash flow	($10,300)	$ 500	$ 980	$ 460	$ 180	$1,280
8. PV cost of owning = $7,471						

II. COST OF LEASING

	YEAR 0	YEAR 1	YEAR 2	YEAR 3	YEAR 4	YEAR 5
9. Lease payment	($2,750)	($2,750)	($2,750)	($2,750)	($2,750)	
10. Payment tax savings	1,100	1,100	1,100	1,100	1,100	
11. Net cash flow	($1,650)	($1,650)	($1,650)	($1,650)	($1,650)	$0
12. PV cost of leasing = $7,367						

III. COST COMPARISON

13. Net advantage to leasing (NAL) = PV cost of owning – PV cost of leasing = $7,471 – $7,367 = $104.

NOTES: a. The net cash flows shown in Lines 7 and 11 are discounted at the lessee's after-tax cost of debt, 6.0 percent.
b. The MACRS depreciation allowances are 0.20, 0.32, 0.19, 0.12, and 0.11 in Years 1 through 5, respectively. Thus, the depreciation expense is 0.20($10,000) = $2,000 in Year 1, and so on. The depreciation tax savings in each year is 0.4 (Depreciation).
c. The residual value is $1,000 while the book value is $600. Thus, Anderson would have to pay 0.4($1,000 – $600) = $160 in taxes, producing a net after-tax residual value of $1,000 – $160 = $840. These amounts are shown in Lines 5 and 6 in the cost of owning analysis.
d. In practice, a lease analysis such as this would be done using a spreadsheet model.
e. In the NAL equation on Line 13, the PV costs are stated as positive values. If the PV costs are treated as negative values, or outflows, the NAL must be redefined as follows: NAL = PV cost of leasing – PV cost of owning = –$7,367 – (–$7,471) = $104.

equipment's cost. Line 2 shows the maintenance expense. Line 3 gives the maintenance tax savings. Line 4 contains the depreciation tax savings, which is the depreciation expense times the tax rate. Lines 5 and 6 contain the residual value cash flows. Note that the tax is on the excess of the residual value over the asset's book value, not on the full amount of the residual value. Line 7 contains the net cash flows. And Line 8 shows the net present value of these flows, discounted at 6 percent.

Part II of Table 18-2 contains an analysis of the cost of leasing. The lease payments, shown on Line 9, are $2,750,000 per year; this rate, which includes maintenance, was established by the prospective lessor and offered to Anderson Equipment. If Anderson accepts the lease, the full amount will be a deductible expense, so the tax savings, shown on Line 10, is 0.40(Lease payment) = 0.40($2,750,000) = $1,100,000. Thus, the after-tax cost of the lease payment is Lease payment − Tax savings = $2,750,000 − $1,100,000 = $1,650,000. This amount is shown on Line 11, Years 0 through 4.

The next step is to compare the net cost of owning with the net cost of leasing. However, we must first put the annual cash flows of leasing and borrowing on a common basis. This requires converting them to present values, which brings up the question of the proper rate at which to discount the costs. We know that the riskier the cash flows, the higher will be the discount rate used to find present values. This same principle was observed in our discussion of capital budgeting, and it also applies in lease analysis. Just how risky are the cash flows under consideration here? Most of them are relatively certain, at least when compared with the types of cash flow estimates that were developed in capital budgeting. For example, the loan payment schedule is set by contract, as is the lease payment schedule. The depreciation expenses are also established by law and not subject to change, and the $500,000 annual maintenance cost is fixed by contract as well. The tax savings are somewhat uncertain, but they will be as projected so long as Anderson's marginal tax rate remains at 40 percent. The residual value is the least certain of the cash flows, but even here, Anderson's management is fairly confident about the asset's value.

Since the cash flows under the lease and under the borrow-and-purchase alternatives are both relatively certain, they should be discounted at a relatively low rate. Most analysts recommend that the company's cost of debt be used, and this rate seems reasonable in our example. Further, since the interest on the loan would be tax deductible, *the after-tax cost of debt, which is 6.0 percent, should be used.* Accordingly, we discount the net cash flows on Lines 7 and 11 using a rate of 6.0 percent. The resulting present values are $7,471,000 for the cost of owning and $7,367,000 for the cost of leasing, as shown on Lines 8 and 12. The financing method that produces the smaller present value of costs is the one that should be selected. We define the net advantage to leasing (NAL) as follows (see Note e to Table 18-2):

$$
\begin{aligned}
\text{NAL} &= \text{PV cost of owning} - \text{PV cost of leasing} \\
&= \quad \$7,471,000 \quad - \quad \$7,367,000 \\
&= \quad \$104,000.
\end{aligned}
$$

The PV cost of owning exceeds the PV cost of leasing, so the NAL is positive. Therefore, Anderson should lease the equipment.[9]

IRR ANALYSIS

Anderson's lease-versus-purchase decision could also be analyzed using the IRR approach. Here we know the after-tax cost of debt, 6.0 percent, so we can find the *after-tax cost rate implied in the lease contract* and compare it with the cost of the loan. Signing a lease is similar to signing a loan contract — the firm has the use of equipment, but it must make a series of payments under either type of contract. We know the rate built into the loan; it is 6.0 percent after taxes for Anderson. There is an equivalent cost rate built into the lease. If the equivalent after-tax cost rate in the lease is less than the after-tax interest rate on the debt, then there is an advantage to leasing.

Table 18-3 sets forth the cash flows needed to determine the equivalent loan cost. Here is an explanation of the table:

1. The net cost to purchase the equipment, which is avoided if Anderson leases, is shown on Line 1 as a positive cash flow (an inflow) at Year 0. If Anderson leases, it avoids having to pay the net purchase price for the equipment—the lessor pays that cost — so Anderson saves $10 million. That is a positive cash flow at Year 0.

2. Next, we must determine what Anderson must give up (or "pay back") if it leases. As we saw in the last section, Anderson must make annual lease pay-

---

[9]The more complicated methods which exist for analyzing leasing generally focus on the issue of the discount rate that should be used to discount the cash flows. Conceptually, we could assign a separate discount rate to each individual cash flow component, then find the present values of each of the cash flow components, and finally sum these present values to determine the net advantage or disadvantage to leasing. This approach has been taken by Stewart C. Myers, David A. Dill, and Alberto J. Bautista (MDB) in "Valuation of Financial Lease Contracts," *Journal of Finance,* June 1976, 799–819, among others. MDB correctly note that procedures like the one presented in this chapter are valid only if (1) leases and loans are viewed by investors as being equivalent and (2) all cash flows are equally risky, hence appropriately discounted at the same rate. The first assumption is probably valid for most financial leases, and even where it is not, no one knows how to adjust properly for any capital structure effects that leases might have. (MDB, and others, have presented an adjustment formula, but it is based on the assumption that the Modigliani-Miller leverage argument, with no financial distress costs, is correct. Since even MM do not regard the pure MM model as being correct, the MDB formula cannot be correct.) Regarding the second assumption, it is generally believed that all of the cash flows in Table 18-2 except the residual value are of about the same degree of risk, at least to the extent that we are able to evaluate risk. Therefore, the procedures used in Table 18-2 normally meet the MDB assumption; hence, the Table 18-2 analysis is usually correct.

Regarding the residual value, advocates of multiple discount rates often point out that the residual value is less certain than are the other cash flows and thus recommend discounting it at a higher rate. However, there is no way of knowing precisely how much to increase the after-tax cost of debt to account for the increased riskiness of the residual value cash flow. Further, in a market risk sense, all cash flows could be equally risky even though individual items such as the residual value might have more or less total variability than others. To complicate matters even more, the market risk of the residual value will usually be different than the firm's market risk. For more on residual value risk, see Schallheim, *op. cit.,* Chapter 8.

	YEAR 0	YEAR 1	YEAR 2	YEAR 3	YEAR 4	YEAR 5
ANDERSON EQUIPMENT COMPANY: IRR ANALYSIS (THOUSANDS OF DOLLARS) TABLE 18-3						
1. Avoided net purchase price	$10,000					
2. After-tax lease payment	(1,650)	($1,650)	($1,650)	($1,650)	($1,650)	
3. Lost depreciation tax savings		(800)	(1,280)	(760)	(480)	($ 440)
4. Avoided after-tax maintenance cost	300	300	300	300	300	
5. Lost after-tax residual value						(840)
6. Net cash flow	$ 8,650	($2,150)	($2,630)	($2,110)	($1,830)	($1,280)

$$NPV = \sum_{t=0}^{5} \frac{NCF_t}{(1 + k_L)^t} = 0 \text{ when } k_L = IRR = 5.5\%.$$

ments of $2,750,000, which amount to $1,650,000 on an after-tax basis. These amounts are reported as cash outflows on Line 2, Years 0 through 4.

3. If Anderson elects to lease, it will give up the right to depreciate the asset. The lost depreciation tax savings, which represent an opportunity cost of leasing, are shown as outflows on Line 3, Years 1 through 5.

4. If Anderson decides to lease rather than borrow and buy, it will avoid the maintenance cost of $500,000 per year, or $300,000 after taxes. This is shown on Line 4 as an inflow, or benefit of leasing.

5. Finally, if Anderson leases the equipment, it will give up the net after-tax residual value of $840,000. This is also an opportunity cost of leasing, and it is shown on Line 5 as an outflow in Year 5.

6. Line 6 is a time line of the annual net cash flows. If Anderson leases, there is an inflow at Year 0 followed by outflows in Years 1 to 5. Note that the Line 6 net cash flows are simply the net cash flows of leasing rather than buying, or Line 11 minus Line 7 in Table 18-2.

By entering the cash flows on Line 6 into the cash flow register of a calculator and then pressing the IRR button, we can find the IRR for the stream; it is 5.5 percent, and this is the equivalent after-tax cost rate implied in the lease contract. If Anderson leases, it is using up $10 million of its debt capacity, and the implied cost rate is 5.5 percent. Since this cost rate is less than the 6.0 percent after-tax cost of a regular loan, this IRR analysis confirms the NPV analysis: Anderson should lease rather than buy the equipment. The NPV and IRR approaches will always lead to the same decision. Thus, one method is as good as the other from a decision standpoint.[10]

---

[10]Note that the net cash flows shown on Line 6 are the incremental cash flows to Anderson if it leases rather than borrows and buys. Thus, the NPV of these flows is the net advantage to leasing. When discounted at a rate of 6.0 percent, the NPV of the Line 6 flows is $103,389, which, except for a rounding difference, is the same as we obtained in the Table 18-2 NPV analysis.

FEEDBACK EFFECT ON CAPITAL BUDGETING

Up to now, we have assumed that the potential lessee has already made a firm decision to acquire the new equipment. Thus, the lease analysis was conducted only to determine whether the equipment should be leased or purchased. However, if the cost of leasing is less than the cost of debt, it is possible for projects formerly deemed unacceptable to become acceptable.

To illustrate this point, assume that Anderson's target capital structure calls for 50 percent debt and 50 percent common equity, that Anderson's cost of debt, k_d, is 10 percent, and that its cost of equity, k_s, is 15 percent. Thus, Anderson's weighted average cost of capital is

$$WACC = 0.5(10\%)(0.60) + 0.5(15\%)$$
$$= 0.5(6.0\%) + 0.5(15\%) = 10.5\%.$$

Further, assume that the firm's initial capital budgeting analysis on this equipment, using a 10.5 percent project cost of capital for average-risk projects, resulted in an NPV of −$50,000. As we saw in the preceding section, the after-tax cost of leasing for this project is 5.5 percent, compared with Anderson's after-tax cost of debt of 6.0 percent. Thus, this project can be financed at a lower cost than other projects which involve equipment that cannot be leased.

What should we do now? There are two possible polar positions, depending on Anderson's opportunity to substitute lease financing for regular debt financing:

1. **The debt component of all projects can be financed by leasing on similar terms.** In this case, Anderson should never borrow — all "debt" financing should come from leasing. If it had a capital budget of $100 million, and if its optimal capital structure called for 50 percent debt, then it should lease assets with a cost of $50 million and finance the remainder with equity. All projects should be evaluated at a WACC based on the debt cost implied in the lease contracts, 5.5 percent in our example. Thus for all average-risk projects,

$$\frac{\text{WACC for use in}}{\text{capital budgeting}} = 0.5(5.5\%) + 0.5(15\%) = 10.25\%.$$

Anderson's capital budgeting director should now recalculate the project's NPV using a cost of capital of 10.25 percent versus the average project cost of capital, ignoring leasing, of 10.5 percent. Assume that the project's NPV is now +$20,000. The availability of lease financing has made the project acceptable.

2. **The project under consideration is unique—it is the only one for which favorable lease terms are available.** In this case, with the further assumption that the cost of the project does not exceed the company's incremental debt capacity, the NPV of the project for capital budgeting purposes should be determined as follows:

$$\text{Adjusted NPV} = \frac{\text{NPV based on}}{\text{"regular" WACC}} + \frac{\text{NAL from}}{\text{Table 18-2}}$$
$$= -\$50,000 + \$104,000 = \$54,000.$$

Here the firm has enough debt capacity to finance the project entirely by leasing, so the firm will get the entire NAL. (If all projects were suitable for leasing, they still could not all be leased because some equity would be required. Therefore, under the conditions of the preceding paragraph, this procedure would not be appropriate.) The entire NAL should be allocated to this project. All other projects should be evaluated on the basis of the WACC with "regular" debt.

If neither polar position holds, or if different projects can be leased on different lease terms with different equivalent loan rates, then no simple rule can be used. Note, though, that as a practical matter we rarely need to go into the feedback effects of leasing on capital budgeting in the first place, because few projects that are not acceptable under one financing method would be acceptable under another. Given all the uncertainties about capital budgeting cash flows, few managers would change their minds about the acceptability of a project as a result of a few basis points change in the WACC. Still, for certain types of businesses the availability of lease financing could make the difference in the go/no-go decision. Therefore, it is important for financial managers to know how leasing might affect capital budgeting analysis.

We have looked at two different ways of analyzing a lease from the lessee's perspective: (1) the NPV (or NAL) method and (2) the IRR method. Both methods are equivalent, and it is only necessary to apply one method in practice. However, both methods are used in practice, so it is useful to be familiar with both of them.

Explain how the cash flows are structured when estimating the net advantage to leasing.

What discount rate should be used in the lessee's analysis? Why?

Define the term "net advantage to leasing, NAL."

What is the economic significance of a lease's IRR?

Can the ability to lease an asset ever affect the capital budgeting decision? Explain.

SELF-TEST QUESTIONS

EVALUATION BY THE LESSOR

Thus far we have considered leasing only from the lessee's viewpoint. It is also useful to analyze the transaction as the lessor sees it: Is the lease a good investment for the party who must put up the money? The lessor will generally be a specialized leasing company, a bank or bank affiliate, an individual or group of individuals, or a manufacturer such as IBM that uses leasing as a sales tool. The specialized leasing companies are often owned by profitable companies such as General Electric, which owns General Electric Capital, the largest leasing company in existence. Investment banking houses such as Merrill Lynch also set up and/or work with specialized leasing companies, where brokerage clients' money is made available to leasing customers in deals which permit the investors to share in the tax shelters provided by the lease.

Any potential lessor needs to know the rate of return on the capital invested in the lease, and this information is also useful to the prospective lessee: Lease terms on large leases are generally negotiated, so the lessor and the lessee should know one another's position. The lessor's analysis involves (1) determining the net cash outlay, which is usually the invoice price of the leased equipment less any lease payments made in advance; (2) determining the periodic cash inflows, which consist of the lease payments minus both income taxes and any maintenance expense the lessor must bear; (3) estimating the after-tax residual value of the property when the lease expires; and (4) determining whether the rate of return on the lease exceeds the lessor's opportunity cost of capital or, equivalently, whether the NPV of the lease exceeds zero.

To illustrate the lessor's analysis, we assume the same facts as for the Anderson Equipment Company lease, as well as this situation: (1) The potential lessor is a wealthy individual whose current income is in the form of interest, and whose marginal federal-plus-state income tax rate, T, is 40 percent. (2) The investor can buy bonds that have a 9 percent yield to maturity, providing an after-tax yield of $(9\%)(1 - T) = (9\%)(0.6) = 5.4\%$. This is the after-tax return that the investor can obtain on alternative investments of similar risk. (3) The before-tax residual value is $1,000,000. Since the asset will be depreciated to a book value of $600,000 at the end of the 5-year lease, $400,000 of this $1 million will be taxable at the 40 percent rate because of the recapture of depreciation rule, so the lessor can expect to receive $840,000 after taxes from the sale of the equipment after the lease expires.

The NPV of the lease from the lessor's standpoint is developed in Table 18-4. Here we see that the lease as an investment has a net present value of $26,000. On a present value basis, the investor who invests in the lease rather than in the 9 percent bonds (5.4 percent after taxes) is better off by $26,000, indicating that the investor should be willing to write the lease. Since we saw earlier that the lease is

TABLE 18-4	LEASE ANALYSIS FROM THE LESSOR'S VIEWPOINT (THOUSANDS OF DOLLARS)					
	YEAR 0	YEAR 1	YEAR 2	YEAR 3	YEAR 4	YEAR 5
1. Net purchase price	($10,000)					
2. Maintenance cost	(500)	($ 500)	($ 500)	($ 500)	($ 500)	
3. Maintenance tax savings	200	200	200	200	200	
4. Depreciation tax savings		800	1,280	760	480	$ 440
5. Lease payment	2,750	2,750	2,750	2,750	2,750	
6. Tax on lease payment	(1,100)	(1,100)	(1,100)	(1,100)	(1,100)	
7. Residual value						1,000
8. Tax on residual value						(160)
9. Net cash flow	($ 8,650)	$2,150	$2,630	$2,110	$1,830	$1,280

$$NPV = \sum_{t=0}^{5} \frac{NCF_t}{(1+k)^t} = \$26 \text{ when } k = 5.4\%.$$

$$IRR: NPV = 0 = \sum_{t=0}^{5} \frac{NCF_t}{(1+IRR)^t}. \quad IRR = 5.5\%.$$

also advantageous to Anderson Equipment Company, the transaction should be completed.

The investor can also calculate the lease investment's IRR based on the net cash flows shown on Line 9 of Table 18-4. The IRR of the lease, which is that discount rate which forces the NPV of the lease to zero, is 5.5 percent. Thus, the lease provides a 5.5 percent after-tax return to this 40 percent tax rate investor. This exceeds the 5.4 percent after-tax return on 9 percent bonds. So, using either the IRR or the NPV method, the lease would appear to be a satisfactory investment.[11]

SETTING THE LEASE PAYMENT

In the preceding sections we evaluated the lease assuming that the lease payments had already been specified. However, in large leases the parties generally sit down and work out an agreement on the size of the lease payments, with these payments being set so as to provide the lessor with some specific required rate of return. In situations where the lease terms are not negotiated, which is often the case for small leases, the lessor must still go through the same type of analysis, setting terms which provide a target rate of return, and then offering these terms to the potential lessee on a take-it-or-leave-it basis.

Competition among leasing companies forces lessors to build market-related returns into their lease payment schedules. To illustrate all this, suppose the potential lessor described earlier, after examining other alternative investment opportunities, decides that the 5.5 percent return on the Anderson Equipment Company lease is too low, and that the lease should provide an after-tax return of 6.0 percent. What lease payment schedule would provide this return?

To answer this question, note again that Table 18-4 contains the lessor's cash flow analysis. If the basic analysis is computerized, it is very easy to first change the discount rate to 6 percent, and then change the lease payment until the lease's NPV = $0 or, equivalently, its IRR = 6.0 percent. We did this with a spreadsheet lease evaluation model, and found that the lessor must set the lease payment at $2,788,591.50 to obtain an expected after-tax rate of return of 6.0 percent. However, if this lease payment is not acceptable to the lessee, Anderson Equipment Company, then it may not be possible to strike a deal.

Note that a lease payment of $2,788,591.50 would drive Anderson's NAL down to exactly zero. Thus, both the lessee and the lessor would have NAL = NPV = $0. Leasing is not always a zero sum game, but if the inputs to the lessee and the lessor are identical, as in this case, then a positive NAL to the lessee implies an equal but negative NPV to the lessor. However, conditions are often such that leasing can provide net benefits to both parties. This situation arises because of differentials, generally in taxes, in estimated residual values, or in the ability to bear the residual value risk. We will explore this issue in detail in a later section.

---

[11]Note that the lease investment is actually slightly more risky than the alternative bond investment because the residual value cash flow is less certain than a principal repayment. Thus, the lessor might require an expected return somewhat above the 5.4 percent promised on a bond investment.

LEVERAGED LEASE ANALYSIS

When leasing began, only two parties were involved in a lease transaction — the lessor, who put up the money, and the lessee. In recent years, however, a new type of lease, the *leveraged lease,* has come into widespread use. Under a leveraged lease, the lessor arranges to borrow part of the required funds, generally giving the lender a first mortgage on the plant or equipment being leased. The lessor still receives the tax benefits associated with accelerated depreciation. However, the lessor now has a riskier position, because of the use of financial leverage.

Such leveraged leases, often with syndicates of wealthy individuals seeking tax shelters acting as owner-lessors, are an important part of the financial scene today. Incidentally, whether or not a lease is leveraged is not important to the lessee; from the lessee's standpoint, the method of analyzing a proposed lease is unaffected by whether or not the lessor borrows part of the required capital.

The example in Table 18-4 is not set up as a leveraged lease. However, it would be easy enough to modify the analysis if the lessor borrows all or part of the required $10 million, making the transaction a leveraged lease. First, we would add a set of lines to Table 18-4 to show the financing cash flows. The interest component would represent another tax deduction, while the loan repayments would constitute additional cash outlays. The initial cost of the asset would be reduced by the amount of the loan. With these changes made, a new NPV and IRR could be calculated and used to evaluate whether or not the lease represents a good investment.

To illustrate, assume that the lessor can borrow $5 million of the $10 million net purchase price at a rate of 9 percent on a 5-year simple interest loan. Table 18-5 contains the lessor's leveraged lease NPV analysis. The NPV of the leveraged lease investment based on the net cash flows shown on Line 3 is $26,000, which is the same as the $26,000 NPV for the unleveraged lease. Note, though, that the lessor has spent only $3.65 million on this lease. Therefore, the lessor could invest in a total of 2.37 similar leveraged leases for the same $8.65 million investment required to finance a single unleveraged lease, producing a total net present value of 2.37($26,000) = $61,620.

TABLE 18-5	LEVERAGED LEASE ANALYSIS (THOUSANDS OF DOLLARS)					
	YEAR 0	YEAR 1	YEAR 2	YEAR 3	YEAR 4	YEAR 5
1. Net cash flow from Table 18-4	($8,650)	$2,150	$2,630	$2,110	$1,830	$1,280
2. Leveraging cash flows[a]	5,000	(270)	(270)	(270)	(270)	(5,270)
3. Net cash flow	($3,650)	$1,880	$2,360	$1,840	$1,560	($3,990)

$$NPV = \sum_{t=0}^{5} \frac{NCF_t}{(1+k)^t} = \$26 \text{ when } k = 5.4\%.$$

[a]The lessor borrows $5 million at t = 0 and repays it at t = 5. Interest expense, payable at the end of each year, is 0.09($5,000) = $450, but it is tax deductible, so the after-tax interest cash flow is −$450(1 − T) = −$450(0.6) = −$270.

The effect of leverage on the lessor's return is also reflected in the leveraged lease's IRR. The IRR is that discount rate which equates the sum of the present values of the Line 3 cash flows to zero. We find the IRR of the leveraged lease to be about 8.5 percent, which is substantially higher than the 5.5 percent after-tax return on the unleveraged lease.[12]

Typically, leveraged leases provide lessors with higher expected rates of return (IRRs) and higher NPVs per dollar of invested capital than unleveraged leases. However, such leases are also riskier for the same reason that any leveraged investment is riskier. Since leveraged leases are a relatively new development, no standard methodology has been developed for analyzing them in a risk/return framework. However, sophisticated lessors are now developing Monte Carlo simulations similar to those described in Chapter 11. Then, given the apparent riskiness of the lease investment, the lessor can decide whether the returns built into the contract are sufficient to compensate for the risk involved.

What discount rate is used in a lessor's NPV analysis?

What is the economic interpretation of the lessor's IRR?

What is a leveraged lease? What is the usual impact of leveraging on the lessor's expected return? On the lessor's risk?

SELF-TEST QUESTIONS

OTHER ISSUES IN LEASE ANALYSIS

The basic methods of analysis used by lessees and lessors were presented in the previous sections. However, some other issues warrant discussion.

ESTIMATED RESIDUAL VALUE

It is important to note that the lessor owns the property upon expiration of a lease; thus, the lessor has claim to the asset's residual value. Superficially, it would appear that if residual values are expected to be large, owning would have an advantage over leasing. However, this apparent advantage does not hold up. If expected residual values are large — as they may be under inflation for certain types of equipment and also if real property is involved — competition between leasing companies and other financing sources, as well as competition among leasing companies themselves, will force leasing rates down to the point where potential residual values are fully recognized in the lease contract. Thus, the existence of large residual values on equipment is not likely to result in materially higher costs for leasing.

---

[12]Note two additional points concerning the leveraged lease analysis. First, in this situation, leveraging had no impact on the lessor's per-lease NPV. This is because the cost of the loan to the lessor (5.4 percent after taxes) equals the discount rate, and hence the leveraging cash flows are netted out on a present value basis. Second, the leveraged lease has multiple IRRs, one at 0.0 percent and another at approximately 8.5 percent. Leveraged leases frequently have two IRRs.

INCREASED CREDIT AVAILABILITY

As noted earlier, leasing is sometimes said to have an advantage for firms that are seeking the maximum degree of financial leverage. First, it is sometimes argued that firms can obtain more money, and for longer terms, under a lease arrangement than under a loan secured by a specific piece of equipment. Second, since some leases do not appear on the balance sheet, lease financing has been said to give the firm a stronger appearance in a *superficial* credit analysis and thus to permit the firm to use more leverage than would be possible if it did not lease.

There may be some truth to these claims for smaller firms, but now that firms are required to capitalize financial leases and to report them on their balance sheets, this point is of questionable validity for any firm large enough to have audited financial statements. However, leasing can be a way to circumvent existing loan covenants. If restrictive covenants prohibit a firm from issuing more debt but fail to restrict lease payments, then the firm could effectively increase its leverage by leasing additional assets. Also, firms that are in very poor financial condition and facing possible bankruptcy may be able to obtain lease financing at a lower cost than comparable debt financing, because lessors often have a more favorable position than lenders should the lessee actually go bankrupt.

REAL ESTATE LEASES

Most of our examples have focused on equipment leasing. However, leasing originated with real property, and real estate leases still constitute a huge segment of total lease financing. (We distinguish between housing rentals and business leases; our concern is with business leases.) Retailers lease many of their stores. In some situations, retailers have no choice but to lease — this is true of locations in malls and certain buildings. In other situations, they have a choice of building and owning versus leasing. The same situation exists for business firms' offices and other facilities. Law firms and accounting firms, for example, can choose between buying their own facilities or leasing on a long-term basis (up to 20 or more years).

The type of lease-versus-purchase analysis we discussed in this chapter is just as applicable for real estate as for equipment — conceptually, there is no difference. Of course, such things as maintenance, who the other tenants will be, what alterations can be made, who will pay for alterations, and the like, become especially important with real property, but the analytical procedures upon which the lease-versus-buy decision is based are no different from any other lease analysis.

AUTO LEASES

Auto leasing is very popular today, both for large corporations and for individuals, especially professionals such as doctors, lawyers, and accountants. For corporations, the key factor is often maintenance and disposal of used vehicles — the leasing companies are specialists here, and many businesses prefer to "outsource" services related to autos. For individuals, leasing is often more convenient, and it may be easier to justify tax deductions on leased than owned vehicles. Also, most auto leasing to individuals is through dealers. These dealers (and manufacturers) use leasing as a sales tool, and they often make the terms quite attractive, especially when it comes to the down payment, which may be nonexistent in the case of a lease.

The analysis for an auto lease is exactly like the examples we have used throughout the chapter. One simply employs standard DCF techniques and compares the present value of the costs of owning versus the costs of leasing.

COMPUTER MODELS

Lease analysis, like capital budgeting analysis, is particularly well suited for computer analysis. Both the lessee and lessor can create computer models for their analyses. Setting the analysis up on a computer is especially useful when negotiations are under way, and when investment banking houses such as Merrill Lynch are working out a leasing deal between a group of investors and a company, the analysis is always computerized.

LEASING AND TAX LAWS[13]

The ability to structure leases that are advantageous to both lessor and lessee depends in large part on tax laws. The four major tax factors that influence leasing are (1) investment tax credits, (2) depreciation rules, (3) tax rates, and (4) the alternative minimum tax. In this section, we briefly discuss each of these factors and how they influence leasing decisions.

The investment tax credit (ITC), when it is allowed, is a direct reduction of taxes that occurs when a firm purchases new capital equipment. Prior to 1987 firms could immediately deduct up to 10 percent of the cost of new capital investments from their corporate tax bills. Thus, a company that bought a $1,000,000 mainframe computer system would get a $100,000 reduction in current-year taxes. Since the ITC goes to the owner of the capital asset, low-tax-bracket companies that could not otherwise use the ITC could use leasing as a vehicle to pass immediate tax savings to high-tax-bracket lessors. Congress eliminated the ITC in 1986, but the ITC could be reinstated in the future. If the ITC is put back into law, leasing would become more attractive to low-tax-bracket firms.

Owners recover their investments in capital assets through depreciation, which is a tax-deductible expense. Because of the time value of money, the faster an asset can be depreciated, the greater the tax advantages of ownership. Recent tax laws have tended to slow depreciation write-offs and, hence, reduce the value of ownership. This has also reduced the advantage to leasing by low-tax-bracket lessees from high-tax-bracket lessors. Any move to liberalize depreciation rules would tend to make leasing more desirable in many situations. The value of depreciation also depends on the firm's tax rate, because the depreciation tax savings equal the amount of depreciation multiplied by the tax rate. Thus, higher corporate tax rates mean greater ownership tax savings, hence more incentive for tax-driven leases.

Finally, the alternative minimum tax (AMT) also impacts leasing activity. Corporations are permitted to use accelerated depreciation and other tax shelters on their tax books but then use straight line depreciation for reporting results to

---

[13]See Schallheim, *op. cit.*, Chapters 3 and 6, for an in-depth discussion of tax effects on leasing.

shareholders. Thus, some firms report to the IRS that they are doing poorly and hence pay little or no taxes, but report high earnings to shareholders. The AMT, which is roughly computed by applying a 20 percent tax rate to the profits reported to shareholders, is designed to force highly profitable companies to pay at least some taxes even if they have tax shelters that push their taxable income to zero. In effect, all firms (and individuals) must compute the "regular" tax and the AMT tax, and then pay the higher of the two.

Companies that have large AMT liabilities look for ways to reduce their tax bills by lowering reported income. Leasing can be beneficial here — a relatively short-term lease with high annual payments will increase reported expenses and hence lower reported profits. Note that the lease does not have to qualify as a guideline lease and be deducted for regular tax purposes — all that is needed is to lower reported income as shown on the income statement.

We see that tax laws and differential tax rates between lessors and lessees can be a motivating force for leasing. However, as we discuss in the next section, there are some other reasons why firms lease plant and equipment.

SELF-TEST QUESTIONS   Does leasing lead to increased credit availability?

What impact do tax laws have on leasing?

WHY FIRMS LEASE

Up to this point, we have noted that tax rate or other differentials are generally necessary to make leasing attractive to both the lessee and lessor. If the lessee and lessor are facing different tax situations, including the alternative minimum tax, then it is often possible to structure a lease that is beneficial to both parties. However, there are other reasons firms might want to lease an asset rather than buy it.

As discussed in the opening section, over half of the commercial aircraft coming into service today are leased, and smaller airlines, especially in developing nations, lease an even higher percentage of their planes. One of the reasons for the high lease usage is that airlines can reduce their risks by leasing. If an airline purchases all its aircraft, it would be hampered in its ability to respond to changing market conditions. Because they have become specialists at matching airlines with available aircraft, the aircraft lessors are quite good at managing the changing demand for different types of aircraft. This permits them to offer attractive lease terms. In this situation, leasing provides operating flexibility. Leasing is not necessarily less expensive than buying, but the operating flexibility is worth the extra costs.

Leasing is also an attractive alternative for many high-technology items that are subject to rapid and unpredictable technological obsolescence. Say a small rural hospital wants to buy a magnetic resonance imaging (MRI) device. If it buys the MRI equipment, it is exposed to the risk of technological obsolescence. In a short time some new technology might make the current system almost worthless and thus render the project unprofitable. Since it does not use much equipment of this nature, the hospital would bear a great deal of risk if it bought the MRI device. Conversely, a lessor that specializes in state-of-the-art medical equipment would be exposed to significantly less risk. By purchasing and then leasing many different items, the lessor benefits from diversification. Of course, over time some items will probably lose more value than the lessor expected, but this will be offset by other items that retained more value than was expected. Also, since such a leasing company will be especially familiar with the market for used medical equipment, it can refurbish the equipment and then get a better price in the resale market than could a remote rural hospital. For these reasons, leasing can reduce the risk of technological obsolescence.

Leasing can also be attractive when a firm is uncertain about the demand for its products or services, and thus about how long the equipment will be needed. Again, consider the hospital industry. Hospitals often offer services that are dependent on a single staff member — for example, a physician who does liver transplants. To support the physician's practice, the hospital might have to invest millions of dollars in equipment that can be used only for this particular procedure. The hospital will charge for the use of the equipment, and if things go as expected, the investment will be profitable. However, if the physician leaves the hospital staff, and if no replacement can be recruited, then the project is dead, and the equipment becomes useless to the hospital. In this case, a lease with a cancellation clause would permit the hospital to simply return the equipment. The lessor would charge something for the cancellation clause, and this would lower the expected profitability of the project, but it would provide the hospital with an option to abandon the equipment, and such an option could have a value that exceeds the incremental cost of the cancellation clause. The leasing company would be willing to write this option because it is in a better position to remarket the equipment, either by writing another lease or by selling it outright.

The leasing industry recently introduced a type of lease that even transfers some of a project's operating risk from the lessee to the lessor, and also motivates the lessor to maintain the leased equipment in good working order. Instead of making a fixed rental payment, the lessee pays a fee each time the leased equipment is used. This type of lease originated with copy machines, where the lessee pays so much per month plus an additional amount per copy made. If the machine breaks down, no copies are made, and the lessor's rental income declines. This motivates the lessor to repair the machine quickly.

This type of lease is also used in the health care industry, where it is called a "per procedure lease." For example, a hospital might lease an X-ray machine for a fixed fee per X-ray, say, $5. If demand for the machine's X rays is less than expected by the hospital, revenues will be lower than expected, but so will the machine's capital costs. Conversely, high demand would lead to higher-than-expected lease costs, but these would be offset by higher-than-expected revenues. By using a per-procedure lease, the hospital is converting a fixed cost for the equipment into a variable cost, hence reducing the machine's operating leverage and breakeven point. The net effect is to reduce the project's risk. Of course, the expected cost of a per-procedure lease might be more than the cost of a conventional lease, but the risk reduction benefit could be worth the cost. Note too that if the lessor writes a large number of per-procedure leases, much of the riskiness inherent in such leases could be eliminated by diversification, so the risk premiums that lessors build into per-procedure lease payments could be low enough to attract potential lessees.

Some companies also find leasing attractive because the lessor is able to provide services on favorable terms. For example, Virco Manufacturing, a company that makes school desks and other furniture, recently leased 25 truck tractors and 140 trailers which it uses to ship furniture from its plant. The lease agreement, with a large leasing company which specializes in purchasing, maintaining, and then reselling trucks, permitted the replacement of an aging fleet that Virco had built up over seven years. "We are pretty good at manufacturing furniture, but we aren't very good at maintaining a truck fleet," said Virco's CFO.

There are other reasons that might influence a firm to lease an asset rather than buy it. Often, these reasons are difficult to quantify, hence they cannot be easily incorporated into an NPV or IRR analysis. Nevertheless, a sound lease decision must begin with a quantitative analysis, and then qualitative factors can be considered before making the final lease-or-buy decision.

SELF-TEST QUESTION Describe some economic factors which might provide an advantage to leasing.

SUMMARY

In the United States, more than 30 percent of all equipment is leased, as is a great deal of real estate. Consequently, leasing is a very important financing vehicle. In this chapter, we discussed the leasing decision from the standpoints of both the lessee and lessor. The key concepts covered are listed below:

- The four most important types of lease agreement are (1) *operating lease,* (2) *financial,* or *capital, lease,* (3) *sale and leaseback,* and (4) *combination lease.*

- The IRS has specific guidelines that apply to lease arrangements. A lease that meets these guidelines is called a *guideline,* or *tax-oriented, lease,* because the IRS permits the lessor to deduct the asset's depreciation and allows the lessee to deduct the lease payments. A lease that does not meet the IRS guidelines is called a *non-tax-oriented lease.* In these leases, ownership effectively resides with the lessee rather than the lessor.

- *FASB Statement 13* spells out the conditions under which a lease must be *capitalized* (shown directly on the balance sheet) as opposed to shown only in the notes to the financial statements. Generally, leases that run for a period equal to or greater than 75 percent of the asset's life must be capitalized.

- The lessee's analysis consists basically of a comparison of the PV of costs associated with leasing the asset versus the PV of costs associated with owning. There are two analytical techniques that can be used: (1) the *net advantage to leasing (NAL, or PV of costs) method,* and (2) the *internal rate of return (IRR) method.*

■ One of the key issues in the lessee's analysis is the appropriate discount rate. Since the cash flows in a lease analysis are known with relative certainty, the appropriate discount rate is the *lessee's after-tax cost of debt.* A higher discount rate may be used on the *residual value* if it is substantially riskier than the other flows.

■ The lessor evaluates the lease as an *investment.* If the lease's NPV is greater than zero, or if its IRR is greater than the lessor's opportunity cost, then the lease should be written.

■ In a *leveraged lease,* the lessor borrows part of the funds required to buy the asset. Generally, the asset is pledged as collateral for the loan.

■ Leasing is motivated by differentials between lessees and lessors. Some of the more common reasons for leasing are (1) *tax rate differentials,* (2) leases in which the lessee faces the *alternative minimum tax (AMT),* (3) leases in which the lessor is better able to bear the *residual value risk* than the lessee, and (4) situations where the lessor can maintain the leased equipment more efficiently than can the lessee.

In the next chapter, the last in our discussion of long-term financing, we discuss three hybrid securities: preferred stock, warrants, and convertibles.

QUESTIONS

8-1 Define each of the following terms:
  a. Lessee; lessor
  b. Operating lease; financial lease; sale and leaseback; combination lease; leveraged lease
  c. "Off-balance sheet" financing; capitalizing
  d. FASB Statement 13
  e. Guideline lease
  f. Residual value
  g. Lessee's analysis; lessor's analysis
  h. Alternative minimum tax (AMT)

8-2 Distinguish between operating leases and financial leases. Would you be more likely to find an operating lease employed for a fleet of trucks or for a manufacturing plant?

8-3 Would you be more likely to find that lessees are in high or low income tax brackets as compared with lessors?

8-4 Commercial banks moved heavily into equipment leasing during the early 1970s, acting as lessors. One major reason for this invasion of the leasing industry was to gain the benefits of accelerated depreciation and the investment tax credit on leased equipment. During this same period, commercial banks were investing heavily in municipal securities, and they were also making loans to real estate investment trusts (REITs). In the mid-1970s, these REITs got into such serious difficulty that many banks suffered large losses on their REIT loans. Explain how its investments in municipal bonds and REITs could reduce a bank's willingness to act as a lessor.

18-5   One alleged advantage of leasing voiced in the past is that it kept liabilities off the balance sheet, thus making it possible for a firm to obtain more leverage than it otherwise could have. This raised the question of whether or not both the lease obligation and the asset involved should be capitalized and shown on the balance sheet. Discuss the pros and cons of capitalizing leases and related assets.

18-6   Suppose there were no IRS restrictions on what constituted a valid lease. Explain, in a manner that a legislator might understand, why some restrictions should be imposed. Illustrate your answer with numbers.

18-7   What are the advantages and disadvantages of leveraged leases from the standpoint of (a) the lessee, (b) the equity investor in the lease, and (c) the supplier of the debt capital?

18-8   Suppose Congress enacted new tax law changes that would (1) permit equipment to be depreciated over a shorter period, (2) lower corporate tax rates, and (3) reinstate the investment tax credit. Discuss how each of these potential changes would affect the relative volume of leasing versus conventional debt in the U.S. economy.

18-9   In our Anderson Equipment Company example, we assumed that the lease could not be cancelled. What effect would a cancellation clause have on the lessee's analysis? On the lessor's analysis?

SELF-TEST PROBLEM

(SOLUTION APPEARS IN APPENDIX C)

ST-1   **LEASE VERSUS BUY** The Randolph Teweles Company (RTC) has decided to acquire a new truck. One alternative is to lease the truck on a 4-year guideline contract for a lease payment of $10,000 per year, with payments to be made at the *beginning* of each year. The lease would include maintenance. Alternatively, RTC could purchase the truck outright for $40,000, financing the purchase by a bank loan for the net purchase price and amortizing the loan over a 4-year period at an interest rate of 10 percent per year. Under the borrow-to-purchase arrangement, RTC would have to maintain the truck at a cost of $1,000 per year, payable at year end. The truck falls into the MACRS 3-year class. It has a residual value of $10,000, which is the expected market value after 4 years, when RTC plans to replace the truck irrespective of whether it leases or buys. RTC has a marginal federal-plus-state tax rate of 40 percent.

     a. What is RTC's PV cost of leasing?

     b. What is RTC's PV cost of owning? Should the truck be leased or purchased?

     c. The appropriate discount rate for use in the analysis is the firm's after-tax cost of debt. Why?

     d. The residual value is the least certain cash flow in the analysis. How might RTC incorporate differential riskiness of this cash flow into the analysis?

8-1 **BALANCE SHEET EFFECTS** Two companies, Energen and Hastings Corporation, began operations with identical balance sheets. A year later, both required additional manufacturing capacity at a cost of $50,000. Energen obtained a 5-year, $50,000 loan at an 8 percent interest rate from its bank. Hastings, on the other hand, decided to lease the required $50,000 capacity for 5 years, and an 8 percent return was built into the lease. The balance sheet for each company, before the asset increases, follows:

		Debt	$ 50,000
		Equity	100,000
Total assets	$150,000	Total claims	$150,000

a. Show the balance sheets for both firms after the asset increases and calculate each firm's new debt ratio. (Assume that the lease is not capitalized.)
b. Show how Hastings's balance sheet would look immediately after the financing if it capitalized the lease.
c. Would the rate of return (1) on assets and (2) on equity be affected by the choice of financing? How?

18-2 **LEASE VERSUS BUY** A. Sadik Industries must install $1 million of new machinery in its Texas plant. It can obtain a bank loan for 100 percent of the required amount. Alternatively, a Texas investment banking firm which represents a group of investors believes that it can arrange for a lease financing plan. *Assume* that these facts apply:

(1) The equipment falls in the MACRS 3-year class.
(2) Estimated maintenance expenses are $50,000 per year.
(3) The firm's tax rate is 34 percent.
(4) If the money is borrowed, the bank loan will be at a rate of 14 percent, amortized in 3 equal installments at the end of each year.
(5) The tentative lease terms call for payments of $320,000 at the end of each year for 3 years. The lease is a guideline lease.
(6) Under the proposed lease terms, the lessee must pay for insurance, property taxes, and maintenance.
(7) Sadik must use the equipment if it is to continue in business, so it will almost certainly want to acquire the property at the end of the lease. If it does, then under the lease terms it can purchase the machinery at its fair market value at that time. The best estimate of this market value is $200,000, but it could be much higher or lower under certain circumstances.

To assist management in making the proper lease-versus-buy decision, you are asked to answer the following questions:

a. Assuming that the lease can be arranged, should the firm lease or borrow and buy the equipment? Explain. (Hint: In this situation, the firm plans to use the asset beyond the term of the lease. Thus, the residual value becomes a *cost* to leasing in Year 3. Also, there is no Year 3 residual value tax consequence, as the firm cannot immediately deduct the Year 3 purchase price from taxable income.)
b. Consider the $200,000 estimated residual value. Is it appropriate to discount it at the same rate as the other cash flows? What about the other cash flows—are they all equally

risky? (Hint: Riskier cash flows are normally discounted at higher rates, but when the cash flows are *costs* rather than *inflows,* the normal procedure must be reversed.)

SPREADSHEET APPLICATIONS

SPREADSHEET PROBLEM 1

The Dorfman Company has decided to acquire some new R&D equipment. One alternative is to lease the equipment on a 4-year guideline contract for a lease payment of $11,500 per year, payments to be made at the *beginning* of each year. The lease, which would include maintenance, is being offered by Bankston Credit Corporation, a local leasing company. Bankston would purchase the equipment outright for $40,000, and would have to pay the local dealer $1,000 at the beginning of each year to provide maintenance service. The equipment falls into the MACRS 3-year class; and it has a residual value of $10,000, which is the expected market value after 4 years. The lessor's marginal state-plus-federal tax rate is 40 percent. The analysts at Bankston compare the returns on potential leases with returns available on comparable maturity commercial loans which the firm also writes. Currently, Bankston is charging 9 percent on 4-year commercial loans.

a. What is the NPV on the lease investment?
b. Should Bankston write the lease? Why or why not?
c. Assume that interest rates rise, and Bankston can now earn 16 percent (before taxes) on its commercial loans. How does this affect the lease analysis?
d. What lease payment must Bankston charge to be indifferent between writing the lease and loaning at 16 percent?
e. Return to the original situation. Suppose there is a 25 percent chance that the residual value will be only $5,000, and another 25 percent probability that the residual value will be $15,000. There is a 50 percent probability that the residual value will be $10,000. What is Bankston's best-case and worst-case NPV? Suppose that the Bankston analysts account for differential risk by increasing the residual value discount rate. What residual value discount rate forces NPV = $0 when the residual value is $10,000?
f. Now suppose that Bankston can leverage the lease. Bankston could borrow up to $30,000 using the truck as collateral on a term loan at an 8 percent rate. Should Bankston leverage the lease? Should Bankston leverage the lease at 9 percent?
g. Refer back to Part f. Suppose that the loan for $30,000 may only be obtained at a rate of 16 percent. What is the new NPV to the lessor of the leveraged lease? Should Bankston leverage the lease under these circumstances? Why?
h. If Bankston were able to borrow only $15,000 for this project due to restrictive covenants contained in a previous loan agreement, would it be beneficial to leverage the lease at 8 percent? At 9 percent? At 16 percent?

SPREADSHEET PROBLEM 2

As part of its overall plant modernization and cost reduction program, Western Fabrics' management has decided to install a new automated weaving loom. In the capital budgeting analysis of this equipment, the IRR of the project was found to be 29 percent versus a project required return of 14 percent.

The loom has an invoice price of $100,000, including delivery and installation charges. The funds needed could be borrowed from the bank through a 4-year amortized loan at a 15 percent interest rate, with payments to be made at the end of each year. In the event the loom is purchased, the manufacturer will contract to maintain and service it for a fee of $8,000 per year paid at the end of each year. The loom falls in the MACRS 5-year class, and Western's marginal federal-plus-state tax rate is 40 percent.

Aubey Automation Inc., maker of the loom, has offered to lease the loom to Western for $30,500 upon delivery and installation (at t = 0) plus 4 additional annual lease payments of $30,500 to be made at the end of Years 1 to 4. (Note that there are 5 lease payments in total.) The lease agreement includes maintenance and servicing. Actually, the loom has an expected life of 8 years, at which time its expected salvage value is zero; however, after 4 years, its market value is expected to equal its book value. Western plans to build an entirely new plant in 4 years, so it has no interest in either leasing or owning the proposed loom for more than that period.

a. Should the loom be leased or purchased?

b. Western's managers disagree on the appropriate discount rate to be used in the analysis. What effect would a discount rate change have on the lease-versus-purchase decision?

c. The salvage value is clearly the most uncertain cash flow in the analysis. What effect would a salvage value risk adjustment have on the analysis? (Assume that the appropriate salvage value pre-tax discount rate is 18 percent.)

d. The original analysis assumed that the firm would not need the loom after 4 years. Now assume that the firm will continue to use it after the lease expires. Thus, if it leased, Western would have to buy the asset after 4 years at the then existing market value, which is assumed to equal the book value. What effect would this requirement have on the basic analysis?

e. Under the original lease terms, it was to Western's advantage to purchase the loom. However, if you had analyzed the lease from the lessor's viewpoint, you would have found that it was more profitable for Aubey Automation to lease the machine than to sell it — in fact, the manager of Aubey has found that the company can lower the lease payment to $30,000 and still make more by leasing the machine than by selling it. With an annual lease payment of $30,000, should the loom be leased or bought?

f. Perform the lease analysis assuming that Western's marginal tax rate is (1) 0 percent and (2) 50 percent. Assume a lease payment of $30,500 and a 15 percent pre-tax discount rate. What effect, if any, would the lessee's tax rate have on the lease-buy decision?

SPREADSHEET EXERCISE: STATISTICAL AND DATE FUNCTIONS

The spreadsheet model for this exercise is not directly related to the Mini Case. Rather, the model is a simple listing of bids for a lease contract, which students will use to learn about statistical functions. Students will also work with date functions.

1. Retrieve the model (Filename SE-18.WK1) from the models diskette. Note that Cells B6.B15 contain a list of bids from leasing companies regarding the monthly lease payment on a particular piece of equipment. The analyst at the company considering the bids (the lessee) wants to develop some basic statistics describing the distribution of bids.

2. The labels for the statistical data are contained in Cells D6.D12. Your task is to place the proper @functions into Cells E6.E12.

3. To begin, enter the @function for the mean, or average, into Cell E6. The entry is @AVG(List), where list is the argument, or input, into the @function. List is defined as one or more single values or ranges. For example, the function @AVG(A1,B3.B9,C3.C9) would determine the mean of the values contained in Cell A1, Cells B3.B9, and Cells C3.C9. Thus,

the correct entry for Cell E6 is @AVG(B6.B15). When the correct @function is entered, Cell E6 will display $2,495, the mean of the 10 lease bids. Blank cells within the list are ignored; they are not treated as zeroes. Thus, if the bids from Vendors 3 and 6 had not yet been received, and Cells B8 and B11 were blank, the average would be based on 8 values even though the list contained 10 cells. Note, however, that labels in a cell are treated as zeroes rather than ignored in statistical calculations.

4. Now place the appropriate statistical functions into Cells E7.E12. Here are their formats:

@MAX(List)

@MIN(List)

@VAR(List)

@SQRT(List)

@STD(List)

@COUNT(List)

Note that the results displayed in Cells E10 and E11 are identical, because standard deviation is the square root of the variance. Also, note that the @STD function calculates the standard deviation of the list, assuming the list is a population (divides by n), while another function, @STDS, assumes that the list is a sample (divides by n − 1). Finally, note that @COUNT, which merely counts the number of cells in the list, counts all cells, whether filled or blank, acting somewhat unlike the other statistical functions.

5. Spreadsheets have several built-in date functions that have many uses. For example, date functions can be used to determine the number of days between two dates to determine the amount of interest earned on a bond or bank account. Here we illustrate two of the date functions.

6. We will use Cell E14 to demonstrate the date functions. To begin, enter @NOW in Cell E14 to display the current date (assuming the current date is stored in the computer's clock/calendar). Surprise! A number is displayed rather than a date because spreadsheets use a numbering system for dates and times. For example, in *Lotus,* January 1, 1900, is Day 1; December 31, 2099, is Day 73050; and each day in between has its own unique serial number, running consecutively from Day 1. The number to the right of the decimal point is the proportion of the day that has already past, so noon on December 13, 1994, would be displayed as 34681.5000.

7. The serial number displayed can be changed to a more useful format by using the format command. With the cursor on Cell E14, type /RFD to get the date format menu. Now type 1 and press Enter to get the DD-MMM-YY format. Try the various date formats to see how the date display changes. To return to the serial number display, just reformat the cell to the fixed format.

8. The @DATE(Year,Month,Day) function produces the serial number that matches the indicated date. For example, move the cursor to Cell E15 and enter @DATE(94,1,1), and then move to Cell E16 and enter @DATE(94,12,31). Finally, in Cell E17, enter +E16−E15, and 364, the number of days between the two dates, is displayed. You can visualize how the date function could be used in bond valuation or interest calculations.

Lewis Securities Inc. has decided to acquire a new market data and quotation system for its Richmond home office. The system receives current market prices and other information from several on-line data services, then either displays the information on a screen or stores it for later retrieval by the firm's brokers. The system also permits customers to call up current quotes on terminals in the lobby.

The equipment costs $1,000,000, and, if it were purchased, Lewis could obtain a term loan for the full purchase price at a 10 percent interest rate. The equipment is classified as a special-purpose computer, so it falls into the MACRS 3-year class. If the system were purchased, a 4-year maintenance contract could be obtained at a cost of $20,000 per year, payable at the *beginning* of each year. The equipment would be sold after 4 years, and the best estimate of its residual value at that time is $100,000. However, since real-time display system technology is changing rapidly, the actual residual value is uncertain.

As an alternative to the borrow-and-buy plan, the equipment manufacturer informed Lewis that Consolidated Leasing would be willing to write a 4-year guideline lease on the equipment, including maintenance, for payments of $280,000 at the *beginning* of each year. Lewis's marginal federal-plus-state tax rate is 40 percent. You have been asked to analyze the lease-versus-purchase decision, and in the process to answer the following questions:

a. (1) Why is leasing sometimes referred to as "off-balance sheet" financing?
   (2) What is the difference between a capital lease and an operating lease?
   (3) What impact does leasing have on a firm's capital structure?
b. (1) What is the present value cost of owning the equipment? (Hint: Set up a time line which shows the net cash flows over the period t = 0 to t = 4, and then find the PV of these net cash flows, or the PV cost of owning.)
   (2) Explain the rationale for the discount rate you used to find the PV.
c. What is Lewis's present value cost of leasing the equipment? (Hint: Again, construct a time line.)
d. What is the net advantage to leasing (NAL)? Does your analysis indicate that Lewis should buy or lease the equipment? Explain.
e. What is the IRR of the lease from the lessee's standpoint? What is the economic meaning of this IRR?
f. Now assume that the equipment's residual value could be as low as $0 or as high as $200,000, but that $100,000 is the expected value. Since the residual value is riskier than the other cash flows in the analysis, this differential risk should be incorporated into the analysis. Describe how this could be accomplished. (No calculations are necessary, but explain how you would modify the analysis if calculations were required.) What effect would increased uncertainty about the residual value have on Lewis's lease-versus-purchase decision?
g. The lessee compares the cost of owning the equipment with the cost of leasing it. Now put yourself in the lessor's shoes. In a few sentences, how should you analyze the decision to write or not write the lease?
h. (1) Assume that the lease payments were actually $300,000 per year, that Consolidated Leasing is also in the 40 percent tax bracket, and that it also forecasts a $100,000 residual value. Also, to furnish the maintenance support, Consolidated would have to purchase a maintenance contract from the manufacturer at the same $20,000 annual cost, again paid in advance. Consolidated Leasing can obtain an expected 10 percent

pre-tax return on investments of similar risk. What would Consolidated's NPV and IRR of leasing be under these conditions?

(2) What do you think the lessor's NPV would be if the lease payment were set at $280,000 per year? (Hint: The lessor's cash flows would be a "mirror image" of the lessee's cash flows.)

i. Now assume that the lessor can leverage the $300,000 payment lease by borrowing $500,000 of the $1,000,000 purchase price on a 4-year simple interest note having a 10 percent interest rate. The lender requires only interest payments (at the end of each year) during the life of the note, with the full $500,000 principal to be repaid at maturity. What is the NPV of the leveraged lease? What is its rate of return? What factors, besides the NPV and the IRR, should the lessor consider before deciding to leverage the lease? Should it be leveraged?

j. Lewis's management has been considering moving to a new downtown location, and they are concerned that these plans may come to fruition prior to the expiration of the lease. If the move occurs, Lewis would buy or lease an entirely new set of equipment, and hence management would like to include a cancellation clause in the lease contract. What impact would such a clause have on the riskiness of the lease from Lewis's standpoint? From the lessor's standpoint? If you were the lessor, would you insist on changing any of the lease terms if a cancellation clause were added? Should the cancellation clause contain any restrictive covenants and/or penalties of the type contained in bond indentures or provisions similar to call premiums?

SELECTED ADDITIONAL REFERENCES AND CASES

For a description of lease analysis in practice, as well as a comprehensive bibliography of the leasing literature, see

Mukherjee, Tarun K., "A Survey of Corporate Leasing Analysis," *Financial Management,* Autumn 1991, 96–107.

O'Brien, Thomas J., and Bennie H. Nunnally, Jr., "A 1982 Survey of Corporate Leasing Analysis," *Financial Management,* Summer 1983, 30–36.

Many of the theoretical issues surrounding lease analysis are discussed in the following articles:

Finucane, Thomas J., "Some Empirical Evidence on the Use of Financial Leases," *The Journal of Financial Research,* Fall 1988, 321–333.

Hochman, Shalom, and Ramon Rabinovitch, "Financial Leasing under Inflation," *Financial Management,* Spring 1984, 17–26.

Levy, Haim, and Marshall Sarnat, "Leasing, Borrowing, and Financial Risk," *Financial Management,* Winter 1979, 47–54.

Lewellen, Wilbur G., Michael S. Long, and John J. McConnell, "Asset Leasing in Competitive Capital Markets," *Journal of Finance,* June 1976, 787–798.

Miller, Merton H., and Charles W. Upton, "Leasing, Buying, and the Cost of Capital Services," *Journal of Finance,* June 1976, 761–786.

Schall, Lawrence D., "The Evaluation of Lease Financing Opportunities," *Midland Corporate Finance Journal*, Spring 1985, 48–65.

Leveraged lease analysis is discussed in these articles:

Athanasopoulos, Peter J., and Peter W. Bacon, "The Evaluation of Leveraged Leases," *Financial Management*, Spring 1980, 76–80.

Dyl, Edward A., and Stanley A. Martin, Jr., "Setting Terms for Leveraged Leases," *Financial Management*, Winter 1977, 20–27.

Grimlund, Richard A., and Robert Capettini, "A Note on the Evaluation of Leveraged Leases and Other Investments," *Financial Management*, Summer 1982, 68–72.

Perg, Wayne F., "Leveraged Leasing: The Problem of Changing Leverage," *Financial Management*, Autumn 1978, 47–51.

For a discussion of realized returns on lease contracts, see

Lease, Ronald C., John J. McConnell, and James S. Schallheim, "Realized Returns and the Default and Prepayment Experience of Financial Leasing Contracts," *Financial Management*, Summer 1990, 11–20.

The Summer 1987 issue of Financial Management *contains articles by H. Martin Weingartner, Roger L. Cason, and Lawrence D. Schall which focus on the impact of asset life uncertainty on lease analysis.*

The Option Pricing Model (OPM) has been used in lease analysis by

Copeland, Thomas E., and J. Fred Weston, "A Note on the Evaluation of Cancellable Operating Leases," *Financial Management*, Summer 1982, 60–67.

Lee, Wayne Y., John D. Martin, and Andrew J. Senchack, "The Case for Using Options to Evaluate Salvage Values in Financial Leases," *Financial Management*, Autumn 1982, 33–41.

For a discussion of the impact of the AMT on lease decisions, see

"The Effect of the Corporate Alternative Minimum Tax: Amount, Duration, and Effect on the Lease versus Buy Decision," *The Journal of Equipment Lease Financing*, Spring 1989, 7–26.

The Cases in Financial Management: Dryden Request *series contains the following cases which deal with lease analysis:*

Case 25, "Environmental Sciences, Inc.," Case 25A, "Agro Chemical Corporation," and Case 25B, "Friendly Food Stores, Inc.," which examine the lease decision from the perspectives of both the lessee and lessor.

Case 26, "Prudent Solutions, Inc.," which examines the same issues as Case 25.

CHAPTER 19

HYBRID FINANCING: PREFERRED STOCK, WARRANTS, AND CONVERTIBLES

*T*he use of convertible securities — generally bonds or preferred stocks that can be exchanged for common stock of the issuing corporation — has soared during the last decade. In 1995, U.S. firms issued $125 billion of convertibles, a fourfold increase from ten years earlier.

Why do companies use convertibles so heavily? To answer this question, recognize that convertibles virtually always have coupon rates that are lower than would be required on straight, nonconvertible bonds or preferred stocks. Therefore, if a company raises $100 million by issuing convertible bonds, its interest expense is lower than if it financed with nonconvertible debt. But why would investors be willing to buy convertibles with their substandard cash payments? The answer lies in the conversion feature — if the price of the issuer's stock rises, the holder of the convertible can exchange it for stock and realize a capital gain. So, convertibles hold down the cash costs of financing and give investors an opportunity for capital gains which can more than offset the low cash returns.

Convertibles can work out well or badly for investors and companies alike. To illustrate, in 1989 MCI issued $1.3 billion of convertible bonds at a rate 4 percentage points lower than its cost would have been on nonconvertible debt. Investors who purchased the issue expected MCI's stock price to rise, at which point they could exchange the debt for stock and earn a capital gain. However, MCI's stock price didn't rise to the point where it was attractive to convert, and when the issue became callable in 1993, MCI called the bonds and refunded them at the very low rate of interest which existed at the time.

An example with a different result is Hercules Inc.'s $68 million 1990 issue of convertible bonds. The coupon rate was set at 8 percent, 3.5 percentage points *less than the 11.5 percent required on the company's nonconvertible debt. Even at such a low rate, the issue was well received by investors. Hercules's stock has since soared, and by 1996 a $1,000 investment in the convertibles was worth $2,530, giving investors a rate of return of 22.5 percent.*

Convertibles are attractive to investors because they offer the opportunity to earn the higher returns associated with stocks, but if things don't go well for the company, the convertibles still have the stability associated with debt. However, things can go awry. For example, in 1994 Boston Chicken, a company whose stock price had recently gone from $20 to $51 in one day, issued $130 million of convertible bonds. However, the issue was hit with a "double whammy" — the stock price fell, and interest rates rose. This lowered the value of both the underlying bond and the conversion option, and, as a result, the convertibles lost 30 percent of their value.

So, like all securities, convertibles are risky to both issuers and investors. When you finish this chapter, you should have a much better understanding of convertibles, how they are valued, and why a firm might choose to issue a convertible bond rather than either straight debt or common stock.

In the three preceding chapters, we examined common stock, various types of long-term debt, and leasing. In this chapter, we examine three other sources of long-term capital: preferred stock, which is a hybrid security that represents a cross between debt and common equity; warrants, which are derivative (option) securities that are issued by firms; and convertibles, which are hybrids between debt (or preferred stock) and warrants.

PREFERRED STOCK

Preferred stock is a hybrid — it is similar to bonds in some respects and to common stock in other ways. Accountants classify preferred stock as equity, hence show it on the balance sheet as an equity account. However, financial managers view preferred stock as being somewhere between debt and common equity — it imposes a fixed charge and thus increases the firm's financial leverage, yet omitting the preferred dividend does not force a company into bankruptcy. We first describe the basic features of preferred, after which we describe some recent innovations in preferred stock financing.

BASIC FEATURES

Preferred stock has a par (or liquidating) value, often either $25 or $100. The dividend is indicated either as a percentage of par or as so many dollars per share, or sometimes both ways. For example, several years ago Klondike Power Company sold 150,000 shares of $100 par value perpetual preferred stock for a total of $15 million. This preferred had a stated annual dividend of $12 per share, so the preferred dividend yield was $12/$100 = 0.12, or 12 percent, at the time of issue. The dividend was set when the stock was issued; it will not be changed in the future. Therefore, if the required rate of return on preferred, k_{ps}, changes from 12 percent after the issue date — as it did — then the market price of the preferred stock will go up or down. Currently, k_{ps} for Klondike Power's preferred is 9 percent, and the price of the preferred has risen from $100 to $12/0.09 = $133.33.

If the preferred dividend is not earned, the company does not have to pay it. However, most preferred issues are *cumulative,* meaning that the cumulative total of all unpaid preferred dividends must be paid before dividends can be paid on the common stock. Unpaid preferred dividends are called *arrearages.* Dividends in arrears do not earn interest; thus, arrearages do not increase in a compound interest sense — they only grow from continued nonpayment of the preferred dividend. Also, many preferred stocks accrue arrearages for only a limited number of years, not indefinitely. Often, only three years of arrearages accrue, meaning that the cumulative feature ceases after three years. However, the dividends in arrears up until that point continue in force.

Preferred stock normally has no voting rights. However, most preferred issues stipulate that the preferred stockholders can elect a minority of the directors — say, three out of ten — if the preferred dividend is passed (omitted). Jersey Central Power & Light, one of the companies that owned a share of the Three Mile Island (TMI) nuclear plant, had preferred stock outstanding which could elect a *majority* of the directors if the preferred dividend was passed for four successive quarters. Jersey Central kept paying its preferred dividends even during the dark days following the TMI accident. Had the preferred only been entitled to elect a minority of the directors, the dividend would probably have been passed.

Even though nonpayment of preferred dividends will not bankrupt a company, corporations issue preferred with every intention of paying the dividend. Even if passing the dividend does not give the preferred stockholders control of the company, failure to pay a preferred dividend precludes payment of common dividends. In addition, passing the dividend makes it difficult for a firm to raise capital by selling bonds, and virtually impossible to sell more preferred or common stock. However, having preferred stock outstanding does give a firm the chance to overcome its difficulties — if bonds had been used instead of preferred stock, the company might have been forced into bankruptcy before it could straighten out its problems. Thus, from the viewpoint of the issuing corporation, preferred stock is less risky than bonds.

Investors, on the other hand, regard preferred stock as being riskier than bonds for two reasons: (1) Preferred stockholders' claims are subordinated to those of bondholders in the event of liquidation, and (2) bondholders are more likely to continue receiving income during hard times than are preferred stockholders. Accordingly, investors require a higher after-tax rate of return on a given firm's preferred stock than on its bonds. However, since 70 percent of preferred dividends is exempt from the corporate tax, preferred stock is attractive to corporate investors. In recent years, high-grade preferred stock, on average, has sold on a lower pre-tax yield basis than have high-grade bonds. As an example, recently Du Pont's preferred stock had a market yield of about 7.0 percent, whereas its bonds provided a yield of 8.3 percent, or 1.3 percentage points *more* than its preferred. The tax treatment accounted for this differential; the *after-tax yield* to corporate investors was greater on the preferred stock than on the bonds.[1]

About half of all preferred stock issued in recent years has been convertible into common stock. For example, Enron Corporation issued preferred stock which stipulated that one share of preferred could be converted into three shares of common, at the option of the preferred stockholder. Convertibles are discussed at length in a later section.

Some preferred stocks are similar to perpetual bonds in that they have no maturity date. However, many preferred shares do have a sinking fund provision, often one which calls for the retirement of 2 percent of the issue each year, meaning that the issue will "mature" in a maximum of 50 years. Also, many preferred issues are callable by the issuing corporation. This feature, if exercised, can also limit the life of the preferred.[2]

Nonconvertible preferred stock is virtually all owned by corporations, which can take advantage of the 70 percent dividend exclusion to obtain a higher after-tax yield on preferred stock than on bonds. Individuals should not own preferred stocks (except convertible preferreds)—they can get higher yields on safer bonds, so it is not logical for them to hold preferreds. As a result of this ownership pattern, the volume of preferred stock financing is geared to the supply of money in the hands of insurance companies and other corporate investors who are looking for tax-favored investments. When the supply of such money is plentiful, the prices of preferred stocks are bid up, their yields fall, and investment bankers suggest to companies that they consider issuing preferred stock.

For issuers, preferred stock has a tax disadvantage relative to debt because interest expense is tax deductible while preferred dividends are not. On the other hand, omitting a preferred dividend has less serious consequences than defaulting on an interest payment. Even though preferred stock provides no tax benefits to issuing firms, firms with low tax rates have an incentive to issue preferred stock which can be bought by corporate investors with high tax rates who can take advantage of the 70 percent dividend exclusion. If a firm has an expected tax rate which is less than 80 percent of the expected tax rate of potential corporate buyers, the firm might be better off issuing preferred stock than comparable-risk debt. In essence, firms with low tax rates have an incentive to issue, and firms with high tax rates an incentive to buy, preferred stock. With differential tax rates between corporate issuers and

---

[1]The after-tax yield on an 8.3 percent bond to a corporate investor in the 34 percent marginal tax rate bracket is 8.3%(1 − T) = 8.3%(0.66) = 5.48%. The after-tax yield on a 7.0 percent preferred stock is 7.0%(1 − Effective T) = 7.0%[1 − (0.30)(0.34)] = 7.0%(0.898) = 6.29%. Also, note that tax law prohibits firms from issuing debt and then using the proceeds to purchase another firm's preferred or common stock. If debt is used for stock purchases, then the 70 percent dividend exclusion is reduced. This provision is designed to prevent firms from engaging in "tax arbitrage," or the use of tax-deductible debt to purchase largely tax-exempt preferred stock.

[2]Prior to the late 1970s, virtually all preferred stock was perpetual, and almost no issues had sinking funds or call provisions. Then, insurance company regulators, worried about the unrealized losses the companies had been incurring on preferred holdings as a result of rising interest rates, put into effect some regulatory changes which essentially mandated that insurance companies buy only limited life preferreds. From that time on, virtually no new preferred has been perpetuities. This example illustrates the way the nature of securities changes as a result of changes in the economic environment.

corporate buyers, preferred stock has a place in the optimal capital structure of many low tax rate companies.[3]

RECENT INNOVATIONS

Several important innovations in preferred stock financing have occurred in recent years. We discuss two of these here: (1) floating, or adjustable rate, preferred, and (2) money market, or market auction, preferred.

Adjustable rate preferred stocks (ARPs) were introduced in 1982. Instead of paying fixed dividends, these stocks have their dividends tied to the rate on Treasury securities. The ARPs, which are issued mainly by utilities and large commercial banks, were touted as nearly perfect short-term corporate investments since (1) only 30 percent of the dividends are taxable to corporations, and (2) the floating rate feature was supposed to keep the issue trading at near par. The new security proved to be so popular as a short-term investment for firms with idle cash that new mutual funds designed just to invest in these securities sprouted like weeds (shares of the funds, in turn, were purchased by corporations). However, the ARPs still had some price volatility due (1) to changes in the riskiness of the issues (some big banks which had issued ARPs, such as Continental Illinois, ran into serious loan default problems) and (2) to the fact that Treasury yields exhibited significant fluctuations between dividend rate adjustments dates. Thus, the ARPs had too much price instability for the liquid asset portfolios of many corporate investors.

In 1984, investment bankers introduced *money market,* or *market auction, preferred.* Here the underwriter conducts an auction on the issue every seven weeks (to get the 70 percent exclusion from taxable income, buyers must hold the stock at least 46 days). Holders who want to sell their shares can put them up for auction at par value. Buyers then submit bids in the form of the yields they are willing to accept over the next seven-week period. The yield set on the issue for the coming period is the lowest yield sufficient to sell all the shares being offered at that auction. The buyers pay the sellers the par value, hence holders are virtually assured that their shares can be sold at par. The issuer then must pay a dividend rate over the seven-week period as determined by the auction. From the holder's standpoint, market auction preferred is a low-risk, largely tax-exempt, seven-week maturity security which can be sold between auction dates at close to par. However, if there are not enough buyers to match the sellers (in spite of the high yield), then the auction can fail. This has occurred several times recently. For example, an auction of MCorp (a Texas bank holding company) recently failed. Analysts attributed the failure to the downgrading of MCorp's preferred stock from double A to single B, which caused potential buyers to think (correctly, as it turned out) that the company would go bankrupt and not pay any dividends.

Adjustable rate and market auction preferreds are also now being issued by many nonfinancial corporations. For example, Texas Instruments recently issued $225 million of market auction preferred. About the only thing investors do not seem to like

---

[3]For a more rigorous treatment of the tax hypothesis of preferred stock, see Iraj Fooladi and Gordon S. Roberts, "On Preferred Stock," *Journal of Financial Research,* Winter 1986, 319–324. For an example of an empirical test of the hypothesis, see Arthur L. Houston, Jr., and Carol Olson Houston, "Financing with Preferred Stock," *Financial Management,* Autumn 1990, 42–54.

about ARPs and auction market preferreds is that, as stock, they are more vulnerable to an issuer's financial problems than debt would be, as evidenced by the MCorp example.

ADVANTAGES AND DISADVANTAGES OF PREFERRED STOCK

There are both advantages and disadvantages to financing with preferred stock. Here are the major advantages from the issuers' standpoint:

1. In contrast to bonds, the obligation to pay preferred dividends is not contractual in nature, and the passing (omission) of preferred dividends cannot force a firm into bankruptcy.

2. By issuing preferred stock, the firm avoids the dilution of common equity that occurs when common stock is sold.

3. Since preferred stock sometimes has no maturity, and since preferred sinking fund payments, if present, are typically spread over a long period, preferred issues avoid the cash flow drain from repayment of principal that is inherent in debt issues.

There are two major disadvantages:

1. Preferred stock dividends are not deductible as a tax expense to the issuer, hence the after-tax cost of preferred is typically higher than the after-tax cost of debt. However, the tax advantage of preferreds to corporate purchasers lowers the effective cost to issuers.

2. Although preferred dividends can be passed, investors expect them to be paid, and firms intend to pay the dividends if conditions permit. Thus, preferred dividends are considered to be a fixed cost, hence their use, like that of debt, increases the financial risk of the firm and thus its cost of common equity.

SELF-TEST QUESTIONS

Should preferred stock be considered as equity or debt? Explain.

Who are the major purchasers of nonconvertible preferred stock? Why?

Briefly explain the mechanics of adjustable rate and market auction preferred stock.

What are the advantages and disadvantages of preferred stock to the issuer?

WARRANTS

A *warrant* is a certificate issued by a company which gives the holder the right to buy a stated number of shares of the company's stock at a specified price for some specified length of time. Generally, warrants are distributed with debt, and they are used to induce investors to buy a firm's long-term debt at a lower interest rate than would otherwise be required. For example, when Infomatics Corporation, a rapidly growing high-tech company, wanted to sell $50 million of 20-year bonds in 1996, the company's investment bankers informed the financial vice-president that the bonds would be difficult to sell, and that an interest rate of 10 percent would be required. However, as an alternative the bankers suggested that investors might be willing to buy the bonds with a coupon rate of only 8 percent if the company would offer 20 warrants with each $1,000 bond, each warrant entitling the holder to buy one share of common stock at the *exercise price* of $22 per share. The stock was selling for $20 per share at the time, and the warrants would expire in the year 2006 if they had not been exercised previously.

Why would investors be willing to buy Infomatics Corporation's bonds at a yield of only 8 percent in a 10 percent market just because warrants were also offered as part of the package? It is because the warrants are long-term *call options* which have value because holders can buy the firm's common stock at a fixed price regardless of how high the stock price climbs. This option value offsets the low interest rate on the bonds and makes the package of low-yield bonds plus warrants attractive to investors. (See Chapter 23 for a more complete discussion of options.)

INITIAL MARKET PRICE OF BOND WITH WARRANTS

The Infomatics bonds, if they had been issued as straight debt, would have carried a 10 percent interest rate. However, with warrants attached, the bonds were sold to yield 8 percent. Someone buying the bonds at their $1,000 initial offering price would thus be receiving a package consisting of an 8 percent, 20-year bond plus 20 warrants. Since the going interest rate on bonds as risky as those of Infomatics was 10 percent, we can find the straight-debt value of the bonds, assuming an annual coupon for ease of illustration, as follows:

$$\text{Value} = \sum_{t=1}^{20} \frac{\$80}{(1.10)^t} + \frac{\$1,000}{(1.10)^{20}}$$

$$= \$681.09 + \$148.64 = \$829.73.$$

Thus, a person buying the bonds in the initial underwriting would pay $1,000 and receive in exchange a straight bond worth about $830 plus 20 warrants presumably worth about $1,000 − $830 = $170:

$$\frac{\text{Price paid for}}{\text{bond with warrants}} = \frac{\text{Straight-debt}}{\text{value of bond}} + \frac{\text{Value of}}{\text{warrants}}$$

$$\$1,000 \quad = \quad \$830 \quad + \quad \$170.$$

Since investors receive 20 warrants with each bond, each warrant has an implied value of $170/20 = $8.50.

The key issue in setting the terms of a bond-with-warrants offering is valuing the warrants. The straight-debt value of the bond can be estimated quite accurately. However, it is much more difficult to estimate the value of the warrants. Even the Black-Scholes Option Pricing Model (OPM), which we discuss in Chapter 23, provides only a rough estimate because its parameters are not easily estimated and because the OPM assumes no dividends on the underlying stock, which is not generally a reasonable assumption for a warrant. Further, when options are exercised, the stock provided to the optionholder comes from the secondary market, but stock provided when warrants are exercised are newly issued shares, so the exercise of warrants dilutes the value of the underlying equity, which could affect the value of the original warrant.

If, when the issue is originally priced, the warrants are overvalued relative to their true market value, then the coupon rate on the bonds will be set too low, and it will be difficult to sell the bonds-with-warrants package at its par value. Conversely, if the warrants are undervalued, then the coupon rate will be set too high, and investors who subscribe to the issue will receive a windfall profit from Infomatics's stockholders.

USE OF WARRANTS IN FINANCING

Warrants are generally used by small, rapidly growing firms as "sweeteners" when they sell debt or preferred stock. Such firms are frequently regarded by investors as being highly risky. Their bonds can be sold only at extremely high rates of interest and with very restrictive indenture provisions. To avoid this, firms such as Infomatics often offer warrants along with the bonds. However, some years ago, AT&T raised $1.57 billion by selling bonds with warrants. This was the largest financing of any type ever undertaken by a business firm, and it marked the first use ever of warrants by a large, strong corporation.[4]

Getting warrants along with bonds enables investors to share in the company's growth, if it does in fact grow and prosper; therefore, investors are willing to accept a lower bond interest rate and less restrictive indenture provisions. A bond with warrants has some characteristics of debt and some characteristics of equity. It is a hybrid security that provides the financial manager with an opportunity to expand the firm's mix of securities and thus to appeal to a broader group of investors.

Virtually all warrants today are *detachable*. Thus, after a bond with attached warrants is sold, the warrants can be detached and traded separately from the bond. Further, even after the warrants have been exercised, the bond (with its low coupon rate) remains outstanding, so the warrants bring in additional funds while leaving interest costs relatively low.

The exercise price on warrants is generally set at from 10 to 30 percent above the market price of the stock on the date the bond is issued. If the firm grows and prospers, and if its stock price rises above the exercise price at which shares may be purchased, warrant holders could exercise their warrants and buy stock at the stated price. However, without some incentive, warrants would never be exercised prior to maturity — their value in the open market would be greater than their value if exercised, so holders would sell rather than exercise. There are three conditions

---

[4]It is interesting to note that before the AT&T issue, the New York Stock Exchange's stated policy was that warrants could not be listed because they were "speculative" instruments rather than "investment" securities. When AT&T issued warrants, however, the Exchange changed its policy, agreeing to list warrants that met certain requirements. Many other warrants have since been listed.

It is also interesting to note that, prior to the sale, AT&T's treasury staff, working with Morgan Stanley analysts, estimated the value of the warrants as a part of the underwriting decision. The package was supposed to sell for a total price in the neighborhood of $1,000. The bond value could be determined accurately, so the trick was to estimate the equilibrium value of the warrant under different possible exercise prices and years to expiration, and then to use an exercise price and life which would cause Bond value + Warrant value ≈ $1,000. Using the option pricing model, the AT&T/Morgan Stanley analysts set terms which caused the warrant to sell on the open market at a price that was only 35¢ off from the estimated price.

which encourage holders to exercise their warrants: (1) Warrant holders will surely exercise warrants and buy stock if the warrants are about to expire and the market price of the stock is above the exercise price. (2) Warrant holders will exercise voluntarily and buy stock if the company raises the dividend on the common stock by a sufficient amount. No dividend is earned on the warrant, so it provides no current income. However, if the common stock pays a high dividend, it provides an attractive dividend yield. This induces warrant holders to exercise their option to buy the stock. (3) Warrants sometimes have *stepped-up exercise prices,* which prod owners into exercising them. For example, Williamson Scientific Company has warrants outstanding with an exercise price of $25 until December 31, 2000, at which time the exercise price rises to $30. If the price of the common stock is over $25 just before December 31, 2000, many warrant holders will exercise their options before the stepped-up price takes effect and the market value of the warrants falls.

Another desirable feature of warrants is that they generally bring in funds only if funds are needed. If the company grows, it will probably need new equity capital. At the same time, growth will cause the price of the stock to rise and the warrants to be exercised, hence the firm will obtain additional cash. If the company is not successful and cannot profitably employ additional money, the price of its stock will probably not rise sufficiently to induce exercise of the warrants.

THE COMPONENT COST OF BONDS WITH WARRANTS

When Infomatics issued its debt with warrants, the firm received $50 million, or $1,000 for each bond. Simultaneously, the company assumed an obligation to pay $80 interest for 20 years plus $1,000 at the end of 20 years. The cost of the money would have been 10 percent if no warrants had been attached, but each Infomatics bond had 20 warrants, each of which entitles its holder to buy one share of Infomatics stock for $22. What is the percentage cost of the $50 million? As we shall see, the cost is well above the 8 percent coupon rate on the bonds.

Assume that Infomatics's stock price, which is now $20, is expected to grow, and does grow, at 10 percent per year. When the warrants expire 10 years from now, the stock price would be $20(1.10)^{10} = \$51.87$. Assuming the warrants had not been exercised during the 10-year period, the company would then have to issue one share of stock worth $51.87 for each warrant exercised and, in return, Infomatics would receive the exercise price, $22. Thus, a purchaser of the bonds, if he or she holds the complete package, will make a profit in Year 10 of $51.87 - \$22 = \$29.87$ for each common share issued. Since each bond has 20 warrants attached, investors would have a gain of $20(\$29.87) = \$597.40$ per bond at the end of Year 10. Here is a time line of the cash flow stream to an investor:

0	1		9	10	11		20
−$1,000	+$80	...	+$80	+$ 80.00	+$80	...	+ $ 80
				+ 597.40			+ 1,000
				+$677.40			+ $1,080

The IRR of this stream is 10.7 percent, which is the investor's overall rate of return on the issue. This return is 70 basis points higher than the return on straight debt, which reflects the fact that the issue is riskier to investors than a straight-debt issue because some of the return is expected to come in the form of stock price appreciation, and that part of the return is relatively risky.

The expected rate of return to investors is, of course, also the before-tax cost of the issue to the company — this was true of common stocks, straight bonds, and preferred stocks, and it is also true of bonds sold with warrants. In thinking about this, note that the investor's Year 10 gain of $597.40 does not just appear out of thin air — the company is giving the warrant holders the right to buy for $22 a share stock with a market value of $51.87. That obviously dilutes the value of the stock, so Infomatics's existing shareholders are incurring a dilution cost which is exactly equal to the warrant holders' gain.

The cost of warrants can also be illustrated in terms of the effect on earnings per share (EPS). Suppose Infomatics had 1,000,000 common shares outstanding just prior to the expiration of the warrants. Further, assume that the company earns 13.5 percent on its market value equity, so earnings per share are 0.135($51.87) = $7, and total earnings are 1,000,000($7) = $7,000,000. Now, if there were 100,000 warrants outstanding at expiration, exercise of these warrants would bring in 100,000($22) = $2,200,000 of new equity funds, and the number of shares would increase by 100,000. Assuming that the earning power of the $2.2 million of new assets was also 13.5 percent, then 0.135($2,200,000) = $297,000 of new earnings would be produced, making the new total earnings $7,000,000 + $297,000 = $7,297,000. When that new total earnings figure is divided by the new total shares outstanding (1,000,000 + 100,000 = 1,100,000), we get a new EPS of $6.63:

$$\text{New EPS} = \$7,297,000/1,100,000 = \$6.63.$$

Thus, exercise of the warrants results in a dilution of EPS from $7 to $6.63, or by $0.37. This $0.37 EPS dilution is a real cost, it is borne by Infomatics's original shareholders, and it must be considered when calculating the cost of the bonds with warrants.

A WARRANT ISSUE THAT WENT AWRY

Although warrant issues are bought by investors with the expectation of receiving a total return commensurate with the overall riskiness of the securities package being purchased, things do not always work out as expected. For example, in 1989 Sony paid $3.4 billion for Columbia Pictures, a U.S. movie studio. To help finance the deal, in 1990 Sony sold $470 million of four-year bonds with warrants at an incredibly low 0.3 percent coupon interest rate. The rate was so low because the warrants, which also had a maturity of four years, allowed investors to purchase Sony stock at 7,670 yen per share, only 2.5 percent above the share price at the time the bonds with warrants were issued.

Investors snapped up the issue, and many of the warrants were "peeled off" and sold separately on the open market. The warrant buyers obviously believed that Sony's stock would climb well above the exercise price. From Sony's point of view, the bonds-with-warrants package provided a very low-cost "bridge loan" (the bonds) that would be replaced with equity financing when the warrants were exercised, presumably in four years when the bonds became due. Sony also issued $2.2 billion in convertible bonds with a coupon rate of only 1.4 percent to help finance the

Columbia deal. (We will discuss convertible issues in the next section.) This very low-cost capital encouraged Japanese firms to acquire foreign companies and to invest huge amounts in new plant and equipment.

However, the willingness of investors to buy Japanese warrants and convertibles suffered a severe blow when the Japanese stock market fell by 40 percent. At mid-1992, Sony's stock price stood at 4,110 yen, 46 percent below the exercise price on the warrants, and the warrants that were intended to sweeten the bonds were trading at less than 20 percent of their original price. By 1994, when the warrants expired, Sony's stock sold for only 5,950 yen, so the warrants were not exercised. Thus, Sony's planned infusion of equity capital never materialized, and it had to refinance the four-year bond issue at much higher rates.

Sony and the investors both lost on the deal. The investors, other than those who sold off the warrants quickly, lost because they did not get the return that they expected on the issue. Sony lost because it had to alter its financing plans due to the fact that the warrants were not exercised. In spite of presumably good planning by both the company and investors, this bond-with-warrants issue, and many like it, did not work out as anticipated.

What is a warrant?

Describe how a new bond issue with warrants is valued.

How are warrants used in corporate financing?

The use of warrants lowers the coupon rate on the corresponding debt issue. Does this mean that the component cost of a debt-plus-warrants package is less than the cost of straight debt? Explain.

CONVERTIBLES

Convertible securities are bonds or preferred stocks which, under specified terms and conditions, can be exchanged for common stock at the option of the holder. Unlike the exercise of warrants, which brings in additional funds to the firm, conversion does not provide capital: debt (or preferred stock) is simply replaced on the balance sheet by common stock. Of course, reducing the debt or preferred stock will improve the firm's financial strength and make it easier to raise additional fixed charge capital, but that requires a separate action.

CONVERSION RATIO AND CONVERSION PRICE

One of the most important provisions of a convertible security is the *conversion ratio, CR,* defined as the number of shares of stock a bondholder will receive upon conversion. Related to the conversion ratio is the *conversion price, P_c,* which is the effective price investors will pay for the common stock when conversion occurs. The relationship between the conversion ratio and the conversion price can be illustrated by the Silicon Valley Software Company's convertible debentures, issued at their $1,000 par value in July of 1996. At any time prior to maturity on July 15, 2016, a debenture holder can exchange a bond for 20 shares of common stock; therefore, the conversion ratio, CR, is 20. The bond has a par value of $1,000, so the holder would be relinquishing the right to receive $1,000 at maturity if he or she converts. Dividing the $1,000 par value by the 20 shares received gives a conversion price of $P_c = \$50$ a share:

$$\text{Conversion price} = P_c = \frac{\text{Par value of bond given up}}{\text{Shares received}}$$

$$= \frac{\$1,000}{\text{CR}} = \frac{\$1,000}{20} = \$50.$$

Conversely, by solving for CR, we obtain the conversion ratio:

$$\text{Conversion ratio} = \text{CR} = \frac{\$1,000}{P_c} = \frac{\$1,000}{\$50} = 20 \text{ shares.}$$

Once CR is set, the value of P_c is established, and vice versa.

Like a warrant's exercise price, the conversion price is typically set at from 10 to 30 percent above the prevailing market price of the common stock at the time the convertible issue is sold. Exactly how the conversion price is established can best be understood after examining some of the reasons firms use convertibles.

Generally, the conversion price and conversion ratio are fixed for the life of the bond, although sometimes a stepped-up conversion price is used. For example, the 1996 convertible debentures for Breedon Industries are convertible into 12.5 shares until 2006; into 11.76 shares from 2006 until 2016; and into 11.11 shares from 2016 until maturity in 2026. The conversion price thus starts at $80, rises to $85, and then goes to $90. Breedon's convertibles, like most, have a 10-year call-protection period.

Another factor that may cause a change in the conversion price and ratio is a standard feature of almost all convertibles — the clause protecting the convertible against dilution from stock splits, stock dividends, and the sale of common stock at prices below the conversion price. The typical provision states that if common stock is sold at a price below the conversion price, then the conversion price must be lowered (and the conversion ratio raised) to the price at which the new stock was issued. Also, if the stock is split, or if a stock dividend is declared, the conversion price must be lowered by the percentage amount of the stock dividend or split. For example, if Breedon Industries were to have a two-for-one stock split during the first 10 years of its convertible's life, the conversion ratio would automatically be adjusted from 12.5 to 25, and the conversion price lowered from $80 to $40. If this protection were not contained in the contract, a company could completely thwart conversion by the use of stock splits and stock dividends. Warrants are similarly protected against dilution.

The standard protection against dilution from selling new stock at prices below the conversion price can, however, get a company into trouble. For example, assume that Breedon's stock was selling for $65 per share in 1996 at the time of the convertible issue. Further, suppose the market went sour, and Breedon's stock price dropped to $50 per share. If Breedon needed new equity to support operations, a new common stock sale would require the company to lower the conversion price on the convertible debentures from $80 to $50. That would raise the value of the convertibles and, in effect, transfer wealth from current shareholders to the convertible holders. This transfer would, de facto, amount to an additional flotation cost on the new common stock issue. Potential problems such as this must be kept in mind by firms considering the use of convertibles or bonds with warrants.

CONVERTIBLE BOND MODEL

In the spring of 1996, Silicon Valley Software was evaluating the use of the convertible bond issue described earlier. The issue would consist of 20-year convertible bonds which would sell at a price of $1,000 per bond; this $1,000 would also be the bond's par (and maturity) value. The bonds would pay a 10 percent annual coupon interest rate, or $100 per year. Each bond would be convertible into 20 shares of stock, so the conversion price would be $1,000/20 = $50. The stock was expected to pay a dividend of $2.80 during the coming year, and it sold at $35 per share. Further, the stock price was expected to grow at a constant rate of 8 percent per year. Therefore, $k_s = \hat{k}_s = D_1/P_0 + g = \$2.80/\$35 + 8\% = 8\% + 8\% = 16\%$. If the bonds were not made convertible, they would have to offer a yield of 13 percent, given their riskiness and the general level of interest rates. The convertible bonds would not be callable for 10 years, after which they could be called at a price of $1,050, with this price declining by $5 per year thereafter. If, after 10 years, the conversion value exceeds the call price by at least 20 percent, management would probably call the bonds.

Figure 19-1 shows the expectations of both an average investor and the company.[5]

1. The horizontal line at M = $1,000 represents the par (and maturity) value. Also, $1,000 is the price at which the bond is initially offered to the public.

2. The bond is protected against call for 10 years. It is initially callable at a price of $1,050, and the call price declines thereafter by $5 per year. Thus, the call price is represented by the solid section of the line V_0M''.

3. Since the convertible has a 10 percent coupon rate, and since the yield on a nonconvertible bond of similar risk was stated to be 13 percent, the expected "straight-bond" value of the convertible, B_t, must be less than par. At the time of issue, assuming an annual coupon, B_0 is $789:

$$B_0 = \sum_{t=1}^{20} \frac{\$100}{(1.13)^t} + \frac{\$1,000}{(1.13)^{20}} = \$789.$$

Note, however, that the bond's straight-debt value must be $1,000 just prior to maturity, so the bond's expected straight-debt value rises over time. B_t follows the line B_0M'' in the graph.

4. The bond's initial conversion value, or the value of the stock the investor would receive if the bonds were converted at t = 0, is $700: the bond's conversion value is $P_t(CR)$, so at t = 0, conversion value = $P_0(CR) = \$35(20$ shares) = $700. Since the stock's price is expected to grow at an 8 percent

[5]For a more complete discussion of how this model can be used to structure the terms of a convertible offering, see M. Wayne Marr and G. Rodney Thompson, "The Pricing of New Convertible Bond Issues," *Financial Management*, Summer 1984, 31–37.

FIGURE 19-1   SILICON VALLEY SOFTWARE: CONVERTIBLE BOND MODEL

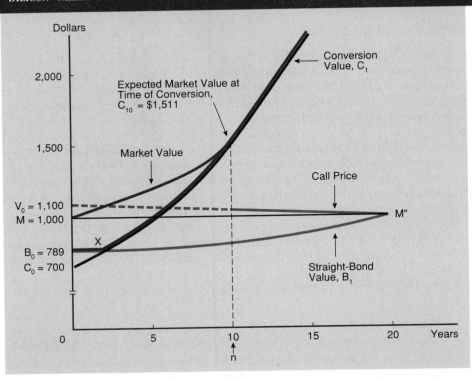

rate, the conversion value of the bond should rise over time. For example, in Year 5 it should be $P_5(CR) = \$35(1.08)^5(20) = \$1,029$. The expected conversion value over time is given by the line C_t in Figure 19-1.

5. The actual market price of the bond can never fall below the higher of its straight-debt value or its conversion value. If the market price were below the straight-bond value, those who wanted bonds would recognize the bargain and buy the convertible as a bond. If the market price were below the conversion value, people would buy the convertibles, exercise them to get the stock, and then sell the stock at a profit. Therefore, the higher of the bond value and conversion value curves in the graph represents a *floor price* for the bond. In Figure 19-1, the floor price is represented by the thicker shaded line B_0XC_t.

6. In fact, the bond's market value will typically exceed its floor value. It will exceed the straight-bond value because the option to convert is worth something — a 10 percent bond with conversion possibilities is worth more than a 10 percent bond without this option. The actual price will also exceed the conversion value because holding the convertible is equivalent to holding a call option, and, prior to expiration, the option's true value is higher than its

expiration (or conversion) value. We cannot say exactly where the market value line will lie, but it will typically be above the floor set by the straight-bond and conversion value lines.

7. At some point, the market value line will hit the conversion value line. This convergence will occur for two reasons. First, the stock should pay higher and higher dividends as the years go by, but the interest payments on the convertible are fixed. For example, Silicon's convertibles would pay $100 in interest annually, while the dividends on the 20 shares received upon conversion would initially be 20($2.80) = $56. However, at an 8 percent growth rate, the dividends after 10 years would be up to $120.90, while the interest would still be $100. Thus, at some point, rising dividends could be expected to push against the fixed interest payments, causing the premium to disappear and investors to convert voluntarily. Second, once the bond becomes callable, its market value cannot get very far above the higher of the conversion value and the call price without exposing investors to the danger of a call. For example, suppose that 10 years after issue (when the bonds were callable), the market value of the bonds was $1,600, the conversion value was $1,500, and the call price was $1,050. If the company called the bonds the day after you bought 10 bonds for $16,000, you would be forced to convert into stock worth only $15,000, so you would suffer a loss of $100 per bond, or $1,000, in one day. Recognizing this danger, you and other investors would simply not pay much of a premium over the higher of the call price or the conversion value once the bond becomes callable. Therefore, in Figure 19-1, we assume that the market value line hits the conversion value line in Year 10, when the bond becomes callable.

8. We can let n represent the year when investors expect conversion to occur, either voluntarily because of rising dividends or because the company calls the convertibles to strengthen its balance sheet by substituting equity for debt. In our example, we assume that n = 10, the first call date. Had the company used a lower initial conversion value, or if we expected a lower growth rate for the stock, such that C_{10} was less than V_{10}, n would have been greater than 10, the first call date.

9. Since n = 10, the expected market value at Year 10 is $35(1.08)^{10}(20) = $1,511. An investor can find the expected rate of return on the convertible bond, k_c, by finding the IRR of the following cash flow stream:

```
 0              1                        9            10
 |              |            . . .       |            |
 -$1,000       +$100                   +$100       +$   100
                                                   +  1,511
                                                   ---------
                                                   +$ 1,611
```

The solution is k_c = IRR = 12.8 percent.

10. The return on a convertible is expected to come partly from interest income and partly from capital gains; in this case, the total return is 12.8 percent, with 10 percent representing interest income and 2.8 percent representing the expected capital gain. The interest component is relatively assured,

while the capital gain component is more risky. On a new straight bond, all of the return is in the form of interest. Therefore, a convertible's expected return is more risky than that of a straight bond, so k_c should be larger than the cost of straight debt, k_d. Thus, it would seem that the expected rate of return on Silicon's convertibles, k_c, should lie between its cost of straight debt, $k_d = 13\%$, and its cost of common stock, $k_s = 16\%$.

Investment bankers use the type of model described here, plus a knowledge of the market, to set the terms on convertibles (the conversion ratio and the coupon interest rate) such that the security will just "clear the market" at its $1,000 offering price. In this example, the required conditions do not seem to hold — the calculated rate of return on the convertible is only 12.8 percent, which is less, rather than more, than the 13 percent cost of straight debt. Therefore, it would appear that the terms on the bond must be made more attractive to investors. Silicon Valley Software would have to increase the coupon interest rate on the convertible above 10 percent, raise the conversion ratio above 20 (and thereby lower the conversion price from $50 to a level closer to the current $35 market price of the stock), or use a combination of these two such that the expected rate of return on the convertible ends up between 13 and 16 percent.[6]

USE OF CONVERTIBLES IN FINANCING

Convertibles have two important advantages from the issuer's standpoint. (1) Convertibles, like bonds with warrants, offer a company the chance to sell debt with lower interest rates and less restrictive covenants in exchange for a chance to participate in the company's success if it does well. (2) In a sense, convertibles provide a way to sell common stock at prices higher than those currently prevailing. Some companies actually want to sell common stock, not debt, but feel that the price of their stock is temporarily depressed. Management may know, for example, that earnings are depressed because of startup costs associated with a new project, but they expect earnings to rise sharply during the next year or so, pulling the price of the stock up with them. Thus, if the company sold stock now, it would be giving up more shares than necessary to raise a given amount of money. However, if it set the conversion price 20 to 30 percent above the present market price of the stock, then 20 to 30 percent fewer shares would be given up when the bonds were converted than if stock were sold directly at the current time. Notice, however, that management is counting on the stock's price to rise above the conversion price to make the bonds attractive in conversion. If earnings do not rise and pull the stock price up, hence conversion does not occur, then the company will be saddled with debt in the face of low earnings, which could be disastrous.

How can the company be sure that conversion will occur if the price of the stock rises above the conversion price? Typically, convertibles contain a call provision that enables the issuing firm to force bondholders to convert. Suppose the conversion

---

[6]In this discussion, we ignore the tax advantages to investors associated with capital gains. This factor could explain why k_c is less than k_d.

price is $50, the conversion ratio is 20, the market price of the common stock has risen to $60, and the call price on the convertible bond is $1,050. If the company calls the bond, bondholders can either convert into common stock with a market value of 20($60) = $1,200 or allow the company to redeem the bond for $1,050. Naturally, bondholders prefer $1,200 to $1,050, so conversion occurs. The call provision therefore gives the company a way to force conversion, provided the market price of the stock is greater than the conversion price. Note, however, that most convertibles have a fairly long period of call protection — 10 years is typical. Therefore, if the company wants to be able to force conversion fairly early, then it will have to set a short call-protection period. This will, in turn, require that it set a higher coupon rate or a lower conversion price.

From the standpoint of the issuer, convertibles have three important disadvantages. (1) Although the use of a convertible security gives the issuer the opportunity to sell stock at a price higher than the price at which it could be sold currently, if the stock greatly increases in price, the firm would probably find that it would have been better off if it had used straight debt in spite of its higher cost and then later sold common stock and refunded the debt. (2) Convertibles typically have a low coupon interest rate, and the advantage of this low-cost debt will be lost when conversion occurs. (3) If the company truly wants to raise equity capital, and if the price of the stock does not rise sufficiently after the bond is issued, then the company will be stuck with debt. This debt will, however, have a low coupon rate.

CONVERTIBLES AND AGENCY COSTS

One of the potential agency problems between bondholders and stockholders discussed in Chapter 1 is asset substitution. Stockholders have an "option-related" incentive to take on projects with high upside potential but which increase the riskiness of the firm. When such an action is taken, there is potential for a wealth transfer between bondholders and stockholders. However, when convertible debt is issued, actions which increase the riskiness of the company may also increase the value of the convertible debt. Thus, some of the gains to shareholders from taking on high-risk projects may be shared with convertible bondholders. This sharing of benefits lowers agency costs. The same general logic applies to warrants.

What is a conversion ratio? A conversion price? A straight-bond value?   **SELF-TEST**
What is meant by a convertible's floor value?   **QUESTIONS**
What are the advantages and disadvantages of convertibles to issuers? To investors?
What is the relationship between convertibles and agency costs?

A FINAL COMPARISON OF WARRANTS AND CONVERTIBLES

Convertible debt can be thought of as straight debt with nondetachable warrants. Thus, at first blush, it might appear that debt with warrants and convertible debt are more or less interchangeable. However, a closer examination reveals one major and several minor differences between these two securities.[7] First and foremost, as we discussed previously, the exercise of warrants brings in new equity capital, while the conversion of convertibles results only in an accounting transfer.

A more subtle difference involves flexibility. Most convertible issues contain a call provision that allows the issuer either to refund the debt or to force conversion, depending on the relationship between the conversion value and call price. However, most warrants are not callable, so firms generally must wait until maturity for the warrants to generate new equity capital. Generally, maturities also differ between warrants and convertibles. Warrants typically have much shorter maturities than convertibles, and warrants typically have much shorter maturities than their accompanying debt. Further, warrants usually provide for fewer future common shares than do convertibles. Together, these facts suggest that debt-plus-warrant issuers are actually more interested in selling debt than in selling equity.

In general, firms that issue debt with warrants are smaller and riskier than those that issue convertibles. One possible rationale for the use of option securities, especially the use of debt with warrants by small firms, is the difficulty investors have assessing the risk of small companies. If a startup with a new, untested product seeks debt financing, it is very difficult for potential lenders to assess the riskiness of the venture, hence it is difficult to set a fair interest rate. Under these circumstances, many potential investors will be reluctant to invest, making it necessary to set very high interest rates to attract debt capital. By issuing debt with warrants, investors obtain a package that offers upside potential to offset the risks of loss.

Finally, there is a significant difference in issuance costs between debt with warrants and convertible debt. Bonds with warrants typically require issuance costs that are about 120 basis points more than the flotation costs for convertibles. In general, bond-with-warrant financings have underwriting fees that closely reflect the weighted average of the fees associated with debt and equity issues, while underwriting costs for convertibles are substantially below the weighted average issuance costs of debt and equity financings.

SELF-TEST QUESTIONS

What are some of the differences between debt-with-warrant financing and convertible debt?

Explain how bonds with warrants might help firms with uncertain risk sell debt securities.

REPORTING EARNINGS WHEN WARRANTS OR CONVERTIBLES ARE OUTSTANDING

If warrants or convertibles are outstanding, a firm could theoretically report earnings per share in one of three ways:

---

[7]For a more detailed comparison of warrants and convertibles, see Michael S. Long and Stephen E. Sefcik, "Participation Financing: A Comparison of the Characteristics of Convertible Debt and Straight Bonds Issued in Conjunction with Warrants," *Financial Management,* Autumn 1990, 23–34.

1. *Simple EPS,* where earnings available to common stockholders are divided by the average number of shares actually outstanding during the period.

2. *Primary EPS,* where earnings available are divided by the average number of shares that would have been outstanding if warrants and convertibles "likely to be converted in the near future" had actually been exercised or converted. In calculating primary EPS, earnings are first adjusted by "backing out" the interest on the convertibles, after which the adjusted earnings are divided by the adjusted number of shares. Accountants have a formula which basically compares the conversion or exercise price with the actual market value of the stock to determine the likelihood of conversion when deciding on the need to use this adjustment procedure.

3. *Fully diluted EPS,* which is similar to primary EPS except that *all* warrants and convertibles are assumed to be exercised or converted, regardless of the likelihood of exercise or conversion.

Simple EPS is virtually never reported by firms which have warrants or convertibles likely to be exercised or converted, but the SEC requires that primary and fully diluted earnings be shown. For firms with large amounts of option securities, there can be a substantial difference between the primary and fully diluted EPS figures. The purpose of the provision is, of course, to give investors a more accurate picture of the firm's true profit position.

SELF-TEST QUESTIONS

What are the three possible methods for reporting EPS when warrants and convertibles are outstanding?

Which methods are most used in practice?

Why should investors be concerned about a firm's outstanding warrants and convertibles?

SECURITIES INNOVATION

In recent years, an avalanche of new types of securities has hit the markets, and the trend shows no sign of letting up. Each new offering is heralded by the investment bank that developed it as a boon to both issuers and investors. Yet there are critics who contend that the development of new securities has contributed little, if any, economic gain to anyone except the investment banks that sell them.

Two primary factors have fueled the rush to innovation. First, the investment banking business has become increasingly competitive, and the development of a successful new security means increased business and profits, both for the firm and for the individuals who developed it. Second, we are in an era of unprecedented volatility: interest rates, tax laws, and regulation are now changing much more rapidly than in the past, and new financial products are needed to cope with the changing economic environment. For example, adjustable rate preferred stock was specifically developed to eliminate investors' exposure to losses in principal as interest rates change, and at the same time to provide a tax shelter to corporate investors in high tax brackets.

The development of new securities has presented an almost overwhelming number of financial alternatives to financial managers, and it is necessary for managers to evaluate the merits of each alternative before making a decision. It is not enough that a security be different — it must also enable issuers or investors to do something that they could not previously do, or permit them to do the same things in a more cost-effective way.[8] Value is created in new securities in a number of ways. For example, value can be created if the new security reallocates risk from one class of investors to another class that is less risk sensitive and thus requires a smaller risk premium. Interest rate swaps are an example of this type of value creation.[9] Value can also be created if a new security reduces transactions costs paid to third parties, or increases liquidity to investors. The development of the junk bond market illustrates these points. Taxes also present an opportunity for value creation. If taxes can be reduced to investors without increasing the corporate tax liability, or vice versa, then value can be created (or at least transferred). Leasing provides a good example of this point.

Undoubtedly, many opportunities remain for innovation, and new ones will arise as the economy continues to change. Such innovation will offer opportunities for financial managers to lower their companies' costs of capital, hence to increase their shareholders' wealth. However, the increase in the number of financing possibilities, and the increasing complexity of the new securities, makes it more important than ever that corporate decision makers keep up with developments in the financial world, and learn how to use (or when to avoid using) the new products.

SELF-TEST
QUESTIONS

What is meant by securities innovation?

What are some factors that can create value in new types of securities?

---

[8]For a more complete discussion of securities innovation, see John D. Finnerty, "Securities Innovation: Where Is the Value Added?" *Financial Management Collection*, Winter 1988, 1–7.

[9]Swaps are discussed in Chapter 23.

SUMMARY

In this chapter, we first discussed preferred stock, then warrants, and finally convertibles. The key concepts are listed below:

- *Preferred stock* is a hybrid — it is similar to bonds in some respects and to common stock in other ways.
- The 1980s spawned two innovations in preferred stock financing: (1) *floating,* or *adjustable rate, preferred,* and (2) *money market,* or *market auction, preferred.*

■ A *warrant* is a long-term call option issued along with a bond. Warrants are generally detachable from the bond, and they trade separately in the markets. When warrants are exercised, the firm receives additional equity capital, and the original bonds remain outstanding.

■ A *convertible* security is a bond or preferred stock which can be exchanged for common stock at the option of the holder. When a security is converted, debt or preferred stock is replaced with common stock, and no money changes hands.

■ Warrants and convertibles are *"sweeteners"* which are used to make the underlying debt or preferred stock issue more attractive to investors. Although the coupon rate on the debt or the dividend yield on the preferred stock is lower when options are part of the issue, the overall cost of the issue is higher than the cost of straight debt or preferred, because the addition of warrants or convertibility makes the issue riskier.

■ In recent years, a large number of new securities have been introduced. Such *securities innovation* provides opportunities for financial managers to lower their firms' costs of capital.

This concludes our discussion of stock, bond, and hybrid financing. In Part VI, we turn our attention to working capital management and financing.

QUESTIONS

-1 Define each of the following terms:
   a. Preferred stock; floating rate preferred
   b. Cumulative dividends; arrearages
   c. Warrant; detachable warrant
   d. Stepped-up price
   e. Convertible security
   f. Conversion ratio; conversion price; conversion value
   g. "Sweetener"
   h. Simple EPS; primary EPS; fully diluted EPS
   i. Securities innovation

-2 Is preferred stock more like bonds or common stock? Explain.

-3 What effect does the trend in stock prices (subsequent to issue) have on a firm's ability to raise funds through (a) convertibles and (b) warrants?

-4 If a firm expects to have additional financial requirements in the future, would you recommend that it use convertibles or bonds with warrants? What factors would influence your decision?

-5 How does a firm's dividend policy affect each of the following?
   a. The value of its long-term warrants.
   b. The likelihood that its convertible bonds will be converted.
   c. The likelihood that its warrants will be exercised.

19-6 Evaluate the following statement: "Issuing convertible securities represents a means by which a firm can sell common stock at a price above the existing market."

19-7 Why do corporations often sell convertibles on a rights basis?

19-8 Suppose a company simultaneously issues $50 million of convertible bonds with a coupon rate of 10 percent and $50 million of straight bonds with a coupon rate of 14 percent. Both bonds have the same maturity. Does the fact that the convertible issue has the lower coupon rate suggest that it is less risky than the straight bond? Is the cost of capital lower on the convertible than on the straight bond? Explain.

PROBLEMS

19-1 **WARRANTS** Maese Industries Inc. has warrants outstanding that permit the holders to purchase 1 share of stock per warrant at a price of $25.

    a. Calculate the theoretical value of the firm's warrants if the common sells at each of the following prices: (1) $20, (2) $25, (3) $30, (4) $100. (Hint: A warrant's theoretical value is the difference between the stock price and the purchase price specified by the warrant.)

    b. At what approximate price do you think the warrants would actually sell under each condition indicated above? What premium above theoretical value is implied in your price? Your answer is a guess, but your prices and premiums should bear reasonable relationships to one another.

    c. How would each of the following factors affect your estimates of the warrants' prices and premiums in Part b?

        (1) The life of the warrant.

        (2) Expected variability (σ_p) in the stock's price.

        (3) The expected growth rate in the stock's EPS.

        (4) The company announces a change in dividend policy: whereas it formerly paid no dividends, henceforth it will pay out *all* earnings as dividends.

    d. Assume the firm's stock now sells for $20 per share. The company wants to sell some 20-year, annual interest, $1,000 par value bonds. Each bond will have attached 50 warrants, each exercisable into 1 share of stock at an exercise price of $25. The firm's straight bonds yield 12 percent. Regardless of your answer to Part b, assume that each warrant will have a market value of $3 when the stock sells at $20. What coupon interest rate, and dollar coupon, must the company set on the bonds with warrants if they are to clear the market?

19-2 **CONVERTIBLE PREMIUMS** The Tsetsekos Company was planning to finance an expansion in the summer of 1996. The principal executives of the company all agreed that an industrial company such as theirs should finance growth by means of common stock rather than by debt. However, they felt that the price of the company's common stock did not reflect its true worth, so they decided to sell a convertible security. They considered a convertible debenture but feared the burden of fixed interest charges if the common stock did not rise in price to make conversion attractive. They decided on an issue of convertible preferred stock, which would pay a dividend of $2.10 per share.

    The common stock was selling for $42 a share at the time. Management projected earnings for 1996 at $3 a share and expected a future growth rate of 10 percent a year in 1997 and beyond. It was agreed by the investment bankers and the management that the common stock would sell at 14 times earnings, the current price/earnings ratio.

a. What conversion price should be set by the issuer? The conversion ratio will be 1.0; that is, each share of convertible preferred can be converted into 1 share of common. Therefore, the convertible's par value (and also the issue price) will be equal to the conversion price, which, in turn, will be determined as a percentage over the current market price of the common. Your answer will be a guess, but make it a reasonable one.

b. Should the preferred stock include a call provision? Why?

-3 CONVERTIBLE BOND ANALYSIS In June 1976, U.S. Steel (now USX Corporation) sold $400 million of convertible bonds. The bonds had a 25-year maturity, a $5\frac{3}{4}$ percent coupon rate, and were sold at their $1,000 par value. The conversion price was set at $62.75 against a current price of $55 per share of common. The bonds were subordinated debentures, and they were given an A rating; straight nonconvertible debentures of the same quality yielded about $8\frac{3}{4}$ percent at the time.

a. Calculate the premium on the bonds, that is, the percentage excess of the conversion price over the current stock price.

b. What is U.S. Steel's annual interest savings on the convertible issue versus a straight-debt issue?

c. Look up U.S. Steel's (USX's) current stock price in the paper. On the basis of this price, do you think it likely that the bonds would have been converted? (Calculate the value of the stock one would receive by converting a bond.)

d. The bonds originally sold for $1,000. If interest rates on A-rated bonds had remained constant at $8\frac{3}{4}$ percent, what do you think would have happened to the price of the convertible bonds?

e. Now suppose the price of U.S. Steel's common stock had fallen from $55 on the day the bonds were issued to $32.75 at present. (At the time this problem was written, that is exactly what had happened.) Suppose also that the rate of interest had fallen from $8\frac{3}{4}$ to $5\frac{3}{4}$ percent. (This had not happened when the problem was being written — the interest rate on A-rated bonds was about 10 percent.) Under these conditions, what do you think would have happened to the price of the bonds?

f. Set up a graphic model to illustrate how investors valued the U.S. Steel convertibles in 1976. How well were these expectations realized?

-4 WARRANT/CONVERTIBLE DECISIONS The Howland Carpet Company has grown rapidly during the past 5 years. Recently, its commercial bank urged the company to consider increasing its permanent financing. Its bank loan under a line of credit has risen to $250,000, carrying an 8 percent interest rate. Howland has been 30 to 60 days late in paying trade creditors.

Discussions with an investment banker have resulted in the decision to raise $500,000 at this time. Investment bankers have assured the firm that the following alternatives are feasible (flotation costs will be ignored):

■ *Alternative 1:* Sell common stock at $8.

■ *Alternative 2:* Sell convertible bonds at an 8 percent coupon, convertible into 100 shares of common stock for each $1,000 bond (that is, the conversion price is $10 per share).

■ *Alternative 3:* Sell debentures at an 8 percent coupon, each $1,000 bond carrying 100 warrants to buy common stock at $10.

John L. Howland, the president, owns 80 percent of the common stock and wishes to maintain control of the company. One hundred thousand shares are outstanding. The following are extracts of Howland's latest financial statements:

BALANCE SHEET

		Current liabilities	$400,000
		Common stock, par $1	100,000
		Retained earnings	50,000
Total assets	$550,000	Total claims	$550,000

INCOME STATEMENT

Sales	$1,100,000
All costs except interest	990,000
EBIT	$ 110,000
Interest	20,000
EBT	$ 90,000
Taxes (40%)	36,000
Net income	$ 54,000
Shares outstanding	100,000
Earnings per share	$0.54
Price/earnings ratio	15.83×
Market price of stock	$8.55

a. Show the new balance sheet under each alternative. For Alternatives 2 and 3, show the balance sheet after conversion of the bonds or exercise of the warrants. Assume that half of the funds raised will be used to pay off the bank loan and half to increase total assets.

b. Show Mr. Howland's control position under each alternative, assuming that he does not purchase additional shares.

c. What is the effect on earnings per share of each alternative, if it is assumed that profits before interest and taxes will be 20 percent of total assets?

d. What will be the debt ratio under each alternative?

e. Which of the three alternatives would you recommend to Howland, and why?

19-5 **CONVERTIBLE BOND MODEL** Niendorf Incorporated needs to raise $25 million to construct production facilities for a new model diskette drive. The firm's straight nonconvertible debentures currently yield 14 percent. Its stock sells for $30 per share; the last dividend was $2; and the expected growth rate is a constant 9 percent. Investment bankers have tentatively proposed that the firm raise the $25 million by issuing convertible debentures. These convertibles would have a $1,000 par value, carry a coupon rate of 10 percent, have a 20-year maturity, and be convertible into 20 shares of stock. The bonds would be noncallable for 5 years, after which they would be callable at a price of $1,075; this call price would decline by $5 per year in Year 6 and each year thereafter. Management has called convertibles in the past (and presumably it will call them again in the future), once they were eligible for call, when the bonds' conversion value was about 20 percent above the bonds' par value (not their call price).

a. Draw an accurate graph similar to Figure 19-1 representing the expectations set forth above. (Assume an annual coupon.)

b. What is the expected rate of return on the proposed convertible issue?

c. Do you think that these bonds could be successfully offered to the public at par? That is, does $1,000 seem to be an equilibrium price in view of the stated terms? If not, suggest the type of change that would have to be made to cause the bonds to trade at $1,000 in the secondary market, assuming no change in capital market conditions.

d. Suppose the projects outlined here work out on schedule for 2 years, but then the firm begins to experience extremely strong competition from Japanese firms. As a result, Niendorf's expected growth rate drops from 9 percent to zero. Assume that the dividend at the time of the drop is $2.38. The company's credit strength is not impaired, and its value of k_s is also unchanged. What would happen (1) to the stock price, and (2) to the convertible bond's price? Be as precise as you can.

S P R E A D S H E E T
A P P L I C A T I O N S

SPREADSHEET EXERCISE: PROTECTING FILES

The spreadsheet model for this exercise examines the expected cost of a convertible bond issue. The model is complete including graphics. Students will use the model to learn about protecting files.

1. Retrieve the model (Filename SE-19.WK1) from the models diskette. The key inputs include data on the convertible bond, including expected time to conversion, while the key output is the expected before-tax cost to the issuer. The model has a graph that shows the convertible bond model.

2. Suppose you were an investment banker who was working on structuring a convertible bond issue for a corporate client. You want to send the spreadsheet model to your client on a diskette, but you want to ensure that no one has access to the model, and hence your recommendations, except the company's CFO. The best way to ensure confidentiality is to protect the file. When an entire file is protected, access is restricted to those individuals who know the password.

3. To protect the file, first type /FS to save the file. Now type the file name, in this case SE-19. But, *before you press Enter,* press the Space Bar, type P, and then press Enter. The spreadsheet will prompt you to enter a password, which can be up to 15 characters. For now, type cfo. As you type the password, three little boxes will appear on the screen. Press Enter, and you will be asked to verify the password. To make the verification, reenter cfo. Since you are saving an existing file, you will be asked whether you want to replace the existing file or cancel the save command. Choose replace.

4. Now that the file has been protected, you will never be able to retrieve it without knowing the password, so be sure that the password is either committed to memory or recorded in a safe place. Try to retrieve the file. Instead of the file appearing on the screen, you are asked to enter the password. At this point, type cfo, press Enter, and the file will be retrieved.

5. If you want to change the password, the file must first be retrieved. Then, start the save process with /FS. Note that the filename is followed by the [PASSWORD PROTECTION] indicator. Press Backspace and the indicator is removed. Now press the Spacebar, type P, and press Enter. Finally, enter the new password, proceeding as before. Try it using your own password. *Be sure to write down or remember the password being used.*

6. To unprotect the file, repeat the procedure outlined above in Paragraph 5, but press Enter immediately after pressing Backspace. This procedure will remove the [PASSWORD PROTECTION] indicator without replacing the password, so the file will be saved in the unprotected mode.

MINI CASE

Paul Duncan, financial manager of EduSoft Inc., is facing a dilemma. The firm was founded 5 years ago to provide educational software for the rapidly expanding primary and secondary school markets. Although EduSoft has done well, the firm's founder believes that an industry shakeout is imminent. To survive, EduSoft must grab market share now, and this will require a large infusion of new capital.

Because he expects earnings to continue rising sharply and looks for the stock price to follow suit, Mr. Duncan does not think it would be wise to issue new common stock at this time. On the other hand, interest rates are currently high by historical standards, and with the firm's B rating, the interest payments on a new debt issue would be prohibitive. Thus, he has narrowed his choice of financing alternatives to two securities: (1) bonds with warrants, or (2) convertible bonds. As Duncan's assistant, you have been asked to help in the decision process by answering the following questions:

a. How does preferred stock differ from both common equity and debt? Briefly describe the features of floating rate (or adjustable rate) preferred stock.

b. What is a call option? How can a knowledge of call options help a financial manager to better understand warrants and convertibles?

c. One of the firm's alternatives is to issue a bond with warrants attached. EduSoft's current stock price is $20, and its investment banker estimates that the cost of a 20-year, annual coupon bond without warrants would be 12 percent. The bankers suggest attaching 50 warrants, each with an exercise price of $25, to each $1,000 bond. It is estimated that each warrant, when detached and traded separately, would have a value of $3.

   (1) What coupon rate should be set on the bond with warrants if the total package is to sell for $1,000?

   (2) Suppose the bonds were issued and the warrants immediately traded on the open market for $5 each. What would this imply about the terms of the issue? Did the company "win" or "lose"?

   (3) When would you expect the warrants to be exercised? Assume they have a 10-year life; that is, they expire 10 years after issue.

   (4) Will the warrants bring in additional capital when exercised? If so, how much, and what type of capital?

   (5) Since warrants lower the cost of the accompanying debt issue, shouldn't all debt be issued with warrants? What is the expected return to the holders of the bond with warrants (or the expected cost to the company) if the warrants are expected to be exercised in 5 years, when EduSoft's stock price is expected to be $36.75? How would you expect the cost of the bond with warrants to compare with the cost of straight debt? With the cost of common stock?

d. As an alternative to the bond with warrants, Mr. Duncan is considering convertible bonds. The firm's investment bankers estimate that EduSoft could sell a 20-year, 10.5 percent annual coupon, callable convertible bond for its $1,000 par value, whereas a straight-debt issue would require a 12 percent coupon. The convertibles would be call protected for 5 years, the call price would be $1,100, and the company would probably call the bonds as soon as possible after their conversion value exceeds $1,200. Note, though, that the call must occur on an issue date anniversary. EduSoft's current stock price is $20, its last dividend was $1.48, and the dividend is expected to grow at a constant 8 percent rate. The convertible could be converted into 40 shares of EduSoft stock at the owner's option.

(1) What conversion price is built into the bond?

(2) What is the convertible's straight-debt value? What is the implied value of the convertibility feature?

(3) What is the formula for the bond's expected conversion value in any year? What is its conversion value at Year 0? At Year 10?

(4) What is meant by the "floor value" of a convertible? What is the convertible's expected floor value at Year 0? At Year 10?

(5) Assume that EduSoft intends to force conversion by calling the bond as soon as possible after its conversion value exceeds 20 percent above its par value, or 1.2($1,000) = $1,200. When is the issue expected to be called? (Hint: Recall that the call must be made on an anniversary date of the issue.)

(6) What is the expected cost of capital for the convertible to EduSoft? Does this cost appear to be consistent with the riskiness of the issue?

e. EduSoft's market value capital structure is as follows (in millions of dollars):

Debt	$ 50
Equity	50
	$100

If the company raises $20 million in additional capital by selling (1) convertibles or (2) bonds with warrants, what would its WACC be, and how would those figures compare with its current WACC? EduSoft's tax rate is 40 percent.

f. Mr. Duncan believes that the costs of both the bond with warrants and the convertible bond are close enough to one another to call them even, and also consistent with the risks involved. Thus, he will make his decision based on other factors. What are some of the factors which he should consider?

SELECTED ADDITIONAL REFERENCES AND CASES

For additional discussions on preferred stock, see

Alderson, Michael J., and Donald R. Fraser, "Financial Innovations and Excesses Revisited: The Case of Auction Rate Preferred Stock," *Financial Management,* Summer 1993, 61–75.

Alderson, Michael J., Keith C. Brown, and Scott L. Lummer, "Dutch Auction Rate Preferred Stock," *Financial Management,* Summer 1987, 68–73.

Fooladi, Iraj, and Gordon S. Roberts, "On Preferred Stock," *Journal of Financial Research,* Winter 1986, 319–324.

Wansley, James W., Fayez A. Elayan, and Brian A. Maris, "Preferred Stock Returns, CreditWatch, and Preferred Stock Rating Changes," *The Financial Review,* May 1990, 265–285.

Winger, Bernard J., et al., "Adjustable Rate Preferred Stock," *Financial Management,* Spring 1986, 48–57.

Quite a bit of work has been done on warrant pricing. Some of the more prominent articles include

Galai, Dan, and Mier I. Schneller, "The Pricing of Warrants and the Value of the Firm," *Journal of Finance,* December 1978, 1333–1342.

Lauterbach, Beni, and Paul Schultz, "Pricing Warrants: An Empirical Study of the Black-Scholes Model and Its Alternatives," *Journal of Finance,* September 1990, 1181–1209.

Leonard, David C., and Michael E. Solt, "On Using the Black-Scholes Model to Value Warrants," *Journal of Financial Research,* Summer 1990, 81–92.

Phelps, Katherine L., William T. Moore, and Rodney L. Roenfeldt, "Equity Valuation Effects of Warrant-Debt Financing," *Journal of Financial Research,* Summer 1991, 93–103.

Schwartz, Eduardo S., "The Valuation of Warrants: Implementing a New Approach," *Journal of Financial Economics,* January 1977, 79–93.

For more insights into convertible pricing and use, see

Alexander, Gordon J., and Roger D. Stover, "Pricing in the New Issue Convertible Debt Market," *Financial Management,* Fall 1977, 35–39.

Alexander, Gordon J., Roger D. Stover, and D. B. Kuhnau, "Market Timing Strategies in Convertible Debt Financing," *Journal of Finance,* March 1979, 143–155.

Asquith, Paul, and David W. Mullins, Jr., "Convertible Debt: Corporate Call Policy and Voluntary Conversion," *Journal of Finance,* September 1991, 1273–1289.

Brennan, Michael, "The Case for Convertibles," *Issues in Corporate Finance* (New York: Stern Stewart Putnam & Macklis, 1983), 102–111.

Emery, Douglas R., Mai E. Iskandor-Datta, and Jong-Chul Rhim, "Capital Structure Management as a Motivation for Calling Convertible Debt," *Journal of Financial Research,* Spring 1994, 91–104.

Harikumar, T., P. Kadapakkam, and Ronald F. Singer, "Convertible Debt and Investment Incentives," *Journal of Financial Research,* Spring 1994, 15–29.

Ingersoll, Jonathan E., "A Contingent Claims Valuation of Convertible Securities," *Journal of Financial Economics,* May 1977, 289–322.

Janjigian, Vahan, "The Leverage Changing Consequences of Convertible Debt Financing," *Financial Management,* Autumn 1987, 15–21.

The following case from the Cases in Financial Management: Dryden Request *series covers many of the issues presented in this chapter:*

Case 27, "Virginia May Chocolate Company," which illustrates convertible bond valuation.

PART VI

WORKING CAPITAL MANAGEMENT AND FINANCING

CHAPTER 20

CURRENT ASSET MANAGEMENT

*C*ore Industries Inc. is a $200 million electrical equipment man-ufacturer whose stock is listed on the NYSE. The stock traded in the range of $12 to $17 per share during most of the 1980s, but during the recession of 1990, earnings plunged and the stock dropped to $4. Then Core's directors made sev-eral key managerial changes, including replacing the chief financial officer (CFO), and things improved dramatically.

At Core's 1994 annual meeting of stockholders, the new CFO, Ray Steben, kicked off the presentations, informing stockholders that 1993 sales had increased by 12 percent, while profits had risen 29 percent and the stock price 79 percent.

What caused this dramatic improvement? According to Steben, the improve-ment resulted primarily from the company's renewed focus on stockholder value:

> Shareholder value will continue to be focused upon, and your management will be stewards of the capital entrusted to it. Return on equity jumped from 7.2 percent to 13.3 percent, a level not exceeded since 1981. As you know, our stated objective is to better 15 percent. Return on capital improved almost 50 percent, from 4.5 percent to 6.8 percent. And the company was considerably more efficient in its use of working capital. As a direct result of a companywide program, working capital was reduced from $0.50 to $0.40 per dollar of sales. Working capital is basically receivables and inventory less payables and accruals. The cash freed up by this program was used to reduce debt and to invest in operations and acquisitions that will return more than our cost of capital.

Following Steben's address, Core's president, Dave Zimmer, elaborated on Core's 1993 improvement and the ways management planned to keep the momentum going in the coming years. Like Steben, Zimmer stressed the improve-ment in working capital management, and the fact that capital previously locked up in excessive inventories and receivables had been freed up and was now earn-ing returns for stockholders. Zimmer also informed the stockholders, "Your top *management has placed a significant portion of its compensation at risk both through the annual bonus plan and the new, long-term incentive plan." He then explained that management's future compensation will be tied directly to stock price performance, so managers will do well only if stockholders do well.*

A year later, Zimmer reported both good news and bad news. The good news was that sales and earnings had continued to increase, and working capital had been lowered even further. The bad news was that "in spite of all that we accomplished in 1994, the stock market treated the company poorly—an obvious disappointment to investors in Core Industries." Actually, the decline in Core's stock price was similar to that of other small capitalization firms during 1994, and despite the decline, the stock still traded at a level substantially higher than the level that existed before the company's turnaround.

Zimmer was not discouraged, and he was resolute in his desire to improve operations. The company plans to continue shrinking working capital. In addition, Zimmer announced that Core has adopted the Economic Value Added (EVA) concept, discussed in Chapter 2, under which employees throughout the corporation will see their overall compensation tied to the EVA levels in their divisions.

Core Industries has taken some important steps to improve its operations. However, it remains to be seen how things will turn out. If the steps taken are successful, they should propel the stock price upward.

About 60 percent of a typical financial manager's time is devoted to working capital management, and many students' first jobs will involve working capital. This is particularly true in smaller businesses, where the most new jobs are being created.

Working capital policy involves two basic questions: (1) What is the appropriate amount of current assets for the firm to carry, both in total and for each specific account, and (2) how should current assets be financed? This chapter addresses the first question, and Chapter 21 takes up the second.

WORKING CAPITAL TERMINOLOGY

We begin our discussion of working capital policy by reviewing some basic definitions and concepts:

1. *Working capital,* sometimes called *gross working capital,* simply refers to current assets.

2. *Net working capital* is defined as current assets minus current liabilities.

3. The *current ratio,* which was discussed in Chapter 2, is calculated by dividing current assets by current liabilities, and it is intended to measure a firm's liquidity. However, a high current ratio does not ensure that a firm will have the cash required to meet its needs. If inventories cannot be sold, or if receivables cannot be collected in a timely manner, then the apparent safety reflected in a high current ratio could be illusory.

4. The *quick ratio,* or *acid test,* also attempts to measure liquidity, and it is found by subtracting inventories from current assets and then dividing by current lia-

bilities. The quick ratio removes inventories from current assets because they are the least liquid of current assets, so the quick ratio is an "acid test" of a company's ability to meet its current obligations.

5. The best and most comprehensive picture of a firm's liquidity position is revealed by its *cash budget*. This statement, which forecasts cash inflows and outflows, focuses on what really counts, the firm's ability to generate sufficient cash inflows to meet its required cash outflows. We will discuss cash budgeting in detail later in the chapter.

6. *Working capital policy* refers to the firm's policies regarding (1) target levels for each category of current assets and (2) how current assets will be financed.

7. *Working capital management* involves the administration, within policy guidelines, of current assets and current liabilities.

The term *working capital* originated with the old Yankee peddler, who would load up his wagon with goods and then go off on his route to peddle his wares. The merchandise was called "working capital" because it was what he actually sold, or "turned over," to produce his profits. The wagon and horse were his fixed assets. He generally owned the horse and wagon, so they were financed with "equity" capital, but he borrowed the funds to buy the merchandise. These borrowings were called *working capital loans,* and they had to be repaid after each trip to demonstrate to the bank that the credit was sound. If the peddler was able to repay the loan, then the bank would make another loan, and banks that followed this procedure were said to be employing "sound banking practices."

Why is the quick ratio also called an acid test?
Where did the term "working capital" originate?

SELF-TEST QUESTIONS

ALTERNATIVE CURRENT ASSET INVESTMENT POLICIES

Figure 20-1 shows three alternative policies regarding the total amount of current assets carried. These policies differ with regard to the amount of current assets carried to support any given level of sales, hence in the turnover of those assets. The line with the steepest slope represents a *relaxed current asset investment* (or "fat cat") *policy,* where relatively large amounts of cash, marketable securities, and inventories are carried, and where sales are stimulated by the use of a credit policy that provides liberal financing to customers and a corresponding high level of receivables. Conversely, under the *restricted current asset investment* (or "lean-and-mean") *policy,* the holdings of cash, securities, inventories, and receivables are minimized. Under the restricted policy, current assets are turned over more frequently, so each dollar of current assets is forced to "work harder." The *moderate current asset investment policy* is between the two extremes.

If sales, costs, lead times, payment periods, and so on, could be predicted with certainty, firms would hold only minimal levels of current assets. Any larger amounts

FIGURE 20-1	ALTERNATIVE CURRENT ASSET INVESTMENT POLICIES (MILLIONS OF DOLLARS)

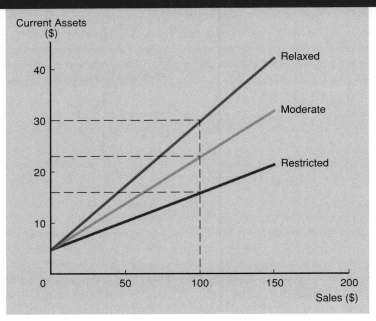

POLICY	CURRENT ASSETS TO SUPPORT $100 OF SALES	TURNOVER OF CURRENT ASSETS
Relaxed	$30	3.3×
Moderate	23	4.3×
Restricted	16	6.3×

NOTE: The sales/current assets relationship is shown here as being linear, but the relationship is often curvilinear.

would increase the need for external funding without a corresponding increase in profits, while any smaller holdings would involve late payments to labor and suppliers, and lost sales due to inventory shortages and an overly restrictive credit policy.

However, the picture changes when uncertainty is introduced. Here the firm requires some minimum amount of cash and inventories which depend on expected payments, expected sales, expected order lead times, and so on, plus additional amounts, or *safety stocks,* which enable it to deal with departures from the expected values. Similarly, accounts receivable levels are determined by credit terms, and the tougher the credit terms, the lower the receivables for any given level of sales. With a restricted current asset investment policy, the firm would hold minimal levels of cash and inventories, and it would have a tight credit policy even though this would mean running the risk of losing sales. A restricted, lean-and-mean current asset investment policy generally provides the highest expected return on this investment, but it entails the greatest risk, while the reverse is true under a relaxed policy. The moderate policy falls in between the two extremes in terms of expected risk and return.

Changing technology can lead to dramatic changes in the optimal current asset investment policy. For example, if new technology makes it possible for a manufacturer such as Core Industries to speed up the production of a given product from 10 days to 5 days, then its work-in-progress inventory can be cut in half. Similarly, retailers such as Wal-Mart or Home Depot have installed systems under which bar codes on all merchandise are read at the cash register. The information on the sale is electronically transmitted to a computer which maintains a record of the inventory of each item, and the computer automatically transmits orders to suppliers' computers when stocks fall to prescribed levels. With such a system, inventories will be held at optimal levels; orders will reflect exactly what styles, colors, and sizes consumers are buying; and the firm's profits will be maximized.

Working capital consists of four main components: cash, marketable securities, inventory, and accounts receivable. The bulk of this chapter will focus on the issues involved with managing each of these components. As you will see in the next section, a common thread underlies all current asset management. For each type of asset, firms face a fundamental trade-off: current assets (that is, working capital) are necessary to conduct business, and the greater the holdings of current assets, the smaller the danger of running out, hence the lower the firm's operating risk. However, holding working capital is costly — if inventories are too large, then the firm will have assets which earn a zero or even negative return if storage and spoilage costs are high. And, of course, firms must acquire capital to buy assets such as inventory, and this capital has a cost, which increases the downward drag from excessive inventories (or receivables or even cash). So, there is pressure to hold the amount of working capital carried to the minimum consistent with running the business without interruption.

Economic Value Added (EVA) methodology provides a useful way of thinking about working capital — this is the approach taken by Core Industries, the company discussed at the beginning of this chapter. The EVA formula is as follows:

$$EVA = [\text{Net operating income} \times (1 - T)] - (\text{WACC} \times \text{Total capital}).$$

If a company like Core can reduce inventories, cash holdings, or receivables without seriously affecting operating income, then cash will be freed up. This cash can then be used to pay off debt or to repurchase stock, that is, to reduce capital. If capital is reduced, the financing costs will decline, and this will raise EVA. Many firms have reported that when division managers and other operating people think about working capital in these terms, they find ways to use working capital more effectively, especially when their compensation depends on their divisions' EVAs.

We can also think of working capital management in terms of ROE and the Du Pont equation:

$$ROE = \quad \text{Profit margin} \quad \times \text{Total assets turnover} \times \text{Leverage factor}$$

$$= \text{Net income/Sales} \times \quad \text{Sales/Total assets} \quad \times \quad \text{Assets/Equity}.$$

If working capital can be reduced without seriously affecting the profit margin, and if the cash released is used to reduce equity, then total assets will decline and the turnover and, consequently, ROE will be increased.

Identify and explain three alternative current asset investment policies.

What are the principal components of working capital?

What are the reasons for not wanting to hold too little working capital? For not wanting to hold too much?

How can the EVA concept be used in working capital management?

THE ZERO WORKING CAPITAL CONCEPT

At first glance, it might seem that working capital management is not as important as capital budgeting, dividend policy, and other decisions that chart firms' long-term directions. However, in today's world of intense global competition, working capital management is receiving increasing attention from managers striving for peak efficiency. In fact, the goal of many leading companies today — including American Standard, Campbell Soup, General Electric, Quaker Oats, and Whirlpool — is *zero working capital*. Proponents of the zero working capital concept claim that a movement toward this goal not only generates cash but also speeds up production and helps businesses make more timely deliveries and operate more efficiently. The concept has its own definition of working capital: Inventories + Receivables − Payables. The rationale here is that inventories and receivables are the keys to making sales, and that inventories can be financed by suppliers through accounts payable.

On average, companies use 20 cents of working capital for each dollar of sales, so, on average, working capital is turned over five times per year. Reducing working capital, and thus increasing turnover, has two major financial benefits. First, every dollar freed up by reducing inventories or receivables, or generated by increasing payables, results in a one-time one dollar contribution to cash flow. Second, a movement toward zero working capital permanently raises a company's earnings. Like all capital, working capital costs money, so reducing it yields permanent savings in capital costs. In addition to the financial benefits, reducing working capital forces a company to produce and deliver faster than its competitors, which helps it gain new business and charge premium prices for filling rush orders. As inventories disappear, warehouses can be sold off, both labor and handling equipment needs are reduced, and obsolete and/or out-of-style goods are minimized.

To illustrate the benefits of striving for zero working capital, in just one year Campbell Soup pared its working capital by $80 million. It used the cash to develop new products and to buy companies in Britain, Australia, and other countries. Equally important, the company expects to increase profits by $50 million over the next few years by lowering overtime labor and storage costs, and these profits will continue year after year.

The most important factor in moving toward zero working capital is increased speed. If the production process is fast enough, companies can produce items as they are ordered rather than having to forecast demand and build up large inventories that are managed by bureaucracies. The best companies are able to start production after an order is received yet still meet customer delivery requirements. This system is known as *demand flow,* or *demand-based management,* and it builds on the just-in-time method of inventory control which we will discuss later in this chapter. However, demand flow management is much broader, because it requires that all elements of a production system operate quickly and efficiently.

Achieving zero working capital requires that every order and part move at maximum speed, which generally means replacing paper with electronic data. Then, orders streak from the processing department to the plant, flexible production lines produce each product every day, and finished goods flow directly from the production line onto waiting trucks or rail cars. Instead of cluttering plants or warehouses with inventories, products move directly into the pipeline. As velocity rises, working capital dwindles.

Clearly, actually achieving zero working capital and infinitely efficient production is not possible for most firms. Still, focusing on minimizing receivables and inventories while maximizing payables will help a firm lower its working capital, reduce its cash conversion cycle (discussed in Chapter 22), and achieve financial and production economies.

What is the basic idea of zero working capital, and how is working capital defined in this concept?

SELF-TEST QUESTION

CASH MANAGEMENT

Cash, defined as demand deposits plus currency, is a "nonearning asset." It is needed to pay for labor and raw materials, to buy fixed assets, to pay taxes, to service debt, to pay dividends, and so on. However, cash itself (and also commercial checking accounts) earns no interest. Thus, the goal of the cash manager is to minimize the amount of cash the firm must hold for use in conducting its normal business activities, yet, at the same time, to have sufficient cash (1) to take trade discounts, (2) to maintain its credit rating, and (3) to meet unexpected cash needs. We begin our analysis with a discussion of the reasons for holding cash.

RATIONALE FOR HOLDING CASH

Firms hold cash for two primary reasons:

1. **Transactions.** Cash balances are necessary in business operations. Payments must be made in cash, and receipts are deposited in the cash account. Cash balances associated with routine payments and collections are known as *transactions balances.*

2. **Compensation to banks for providing loans and services.** A bank makes money by lending out funds that have been deposited with it, so the larger its deposits, the better the bank's profit position. In addition, if a bank is providing services to a customer, it may require the customer to leave a minimum balance on deposit to help offset the costs of providing the services. This type of balance, defined as a *compensating balance,* is discussed in detail later in this chapter.

Two other reasons for holding cash have been noted in the finance and economics literature: for *precaution* and for *speculation*. Cash inflows and outflows are somewhat unpredictable, with the degree of predictability varying among firms and industries. Therefore, firms need to hold some cash in reserve for random, unforeseen fluctuations in inflows and outflows. These "safety stocks" are called *precautionary balances,* and the less predictable the firm's cash flows, the larger such balances should be. However, if the firm has easy access to borrowed funds — that is, if it can borrow on short notice — its need for precautionary balances is reduced. Also, as we note later in this chapter, firms that would otherwise need large precautionary balances tend to hold highly liquid marketable securities rather than cash per se; marketable securities serve many of the purposes of cash, but they provide greater interest income than bank deposits.

Some cash balances may be held to enable the firm to take advantage of bargain purchases; these funds are called *speculative balances.* However, firms today are more likely to rely on reserve borrowing capacity and/or marketable securities portfolios than on cash per se for speculative purposes.

Although the cash accounts of most firms can be thought of as consisting of transactions, compensating, precautionary, and speculative balances, we cannot calculate the amount needed for each purpose, sum them, and produce a total desired cash balance because the same money often serves more than one purpose. For instance, precautionary and speculative balances can also be used to satisfy compensating balance requirements. Firms do, however, consider all four factors when establishing their target cash positions.

ADVANTAGES OF HOLDING ADEQUATE CASH AND NEAR-CASH ASSETS

In addition to the four motives just discussed, sound working capital management requires that an ample supply of cash and near-cash assets be maintained for several specific reasons:

1. It is essential that the firm have sufficient cash and near-cash assets to take *trade discounts.* Suppliers frequently offer customers discounts for early payment of bills. As we will see in the next chapter, the cost of not taking discounts is very high, so firms should have enough cash and near-cash assets to permit payment of bills in time to take discounts.

2. Adequate holdings of cash and near-cash assets can help the firm maintain its credit rating by keeping its current and acid test ratios in line with those of other firms in its industry. A strong credit rating enables the firm both to purchase goods from suppliers on favorable terms and to maintain an ample line of credit with its bank.

3. Cash and near-cash assets are useful for taking advantage of favorable business opportunities, such as special offers from suppliers or the chance to acquire another firm.

4. The firm should have sufficient cash and near-cash assets to meet such emergencies as strikes, fires, or competitors' marketing campaigns, and to weather seasonal and cyclical downturns.

THE CASH BUDGET

The firm estimates its needs for cash as a part of its general budgeting, or forecasting, process. First, it forecasts sales, its fixed asset and inventory requirements, and the times when payments must be made. This information is combined with projections about the delay in collecting accounts receivable, tax payment dates, dividend and interest payment dates, and so on. All of this information is summarized in the *cash budget,* which shows projected cash inflows and outflows over some specified period. Generally, firms use a monthly cash budget forecasted over the next year, plus a more detailed daily or weekly cash budget for the coming month. The monthly cash budgets are used for planning purposes, and the daily or weekly budgets for actual cash control.

The cash budget provides much more detailed information concerning a firm's future cash flows than do the forecasted financial statements. In Chapter 12, we developed MicroDrive Incorporated's 1997 forecasted financial statements. Micro-Drive's projected 1997 sales were $3,300 million, resulting in a net income of $127 million. When all expenditures and financing flows are considered, MicroDrive's cash account is projected to increase by $1 million in 1997. Does this mean that MicroDrive will not have to worry about cash shortages during 1997? To answer this question, we must construct MicroDrive's cash budget for 1997.

To simplify the example, we will only consider the cash budget for the last half of 1997. Further, we will not list every cash flow but rather focus on the operating cash flows. MicroDrive's sales peak is in September, when personal computer manufacturers are beginning their peak sales season. All sales are made on terms of 2/10, net 40, meaning that a 2 percent discount is allowed if payment is made within 10 days, and, if the discount is not taken, the full amount is due in 40 days. However, like most companies, MicroDrive finds that some of its customers delay payment up to 90 days. Experience has shown that payment on 20 percent of MicroDrive's dollar sales is made during the month in which the sale is made — these are the discount sales. On 70 percent of sales, payment is made during the month immediately following the month of sale, and on 10 percent of sales payment is made in the second month following the month of sale.

The costs of component parts and packaging materials average 70 percent of the sales prices of the finished products. These purchases are generally made 1 month before the firm expects to sell the finished products, but MicroDrive's purchase terms with its suppliers allow it to delay payments for 30 days. Accordingly, if July sales are forecasted at $300 million, then purchases during June will amount to $210 million, and this amount will actually be paid in July.

Such other cash expenditures as wages and rent are also built into the cash budget, and MicroDrive must make estimated tax payments of $30 million on September 15 and $20 million on December 15, while a $100 million payment for a new plant

TABLE 20-1	MICRODRIVE INCORPORATED: CASH BUDGET (MILLIONS OF DOLLARS)							
	MAY	JUN	JUL	AUG	SEP	OCT	NOV	DEC
I. COLLECTIONS AND PURCHASES WORKSHEET								
(1) Sales (gross)[a]	$200	$250	$300	$400	$500	$350	$250	$200
COLLECTIONS								
(2) During month of sale: (0.2)(0.98)(month's sales)			59	78	98	69	49	39
(3) During first month after sale: 0.7 (previous month's sales)			175	210	280	350	245	175
(4) During second month after sale: 0.1 (sales 2 months ago)			20	25	30	40	50	35
(5) Total collections (2 + 3 + 4)			$254	$313	$408	$459	$344	$249
PURCHASES								
(6) 0.7(next month's sales)		$210	$280	$350	$245	$175	$140	
(7) Payments (1-month lag)			$210	$280	$350	$245	$175	$140
II. CASH GAIN OR LOSS FOR MONTH								
(8) Collections (from Section I)			$254	$313	$408	$459	$344	$249
(9) Payments for purchases (from Section I)			$210	$280	$350	$245	$175	$140
(10) Wages and salaries			30	40	50	40	30	30
(11) Rent			15	15	15	15	15	15
(12) Other expenses			10	15	20	15	10	10

must be made in October. Assuming the *target cash balance* is $10 million, and $15 million is projected to be on hand on July 1, 1997, what will the firm's monthly cash surpluses or shortfalls be for the period from July to December?

The monthly cash flows are shown in Table 20-1. Section I of the table provides a worksheet for calculating both collections and payments. Line 1 gives the sales forecast for the period from May through December. (May and June sales are necessary to determine collections for July and August.) Next, Lines 2 through 5 show cash collections. Line 2 shows that 20 percent of the sales during any given month are collected during that month. Customers who pay in the first month, however, typically take the discount, so the cash collected in the month of sale is reduced by 2 percent; for example, collections during July for the $300 million of sales in that month will be 20 percent times sales times 1.0 minus the 2 percent discount = $(0.20)(\$300)(0.98) \approx \$59$ million. Line 3 shows collections on the previous month's sales, or 70 percent of sales in the preceding month; for example, in July, 70 percent of the $250 million June sales, or $175 million, will be collected. Line 4 gives collections from sales 2 months earlier, or 10 percent of sales in that month; for example, the July collections for May sales are $(0.10)(\$200) = \$20$ million. The collections during each month are summed and shown on Line 5; thus, the July collections rep-

	MAY	JUN	JUL	AUG	SEP 30	OCT	NOV	DEC 20
					CONTINUED		**TABLE 20-1**	
(13) Taxes								
(14) Payment for plant construction						100		
(15) Total payments			$265	$350	$465	$415	$230	$215
(16) Net cash gain (loss) during month (Line 8 – Line 15)			($ 11)	($ 37)	($ 57)	$ 44	$114	$ 34

III. CASH SURPLUS OR LOAN REQUIREMENT

	MAY	JUN	JUL	AUG	SEP	OCT	NOV	DEC
(17) Cash at start of month if no borrowing is done[b]			$ 15	$ 4	($ 33)	($ 90)	($ 46)	$ 68
(18) Cumulative cash (cash at start, + gain or – loss = Line 16 + Line 17)			$ 4	($33)	($ 90)	($ 46)	$ 68	$102
(19) Target cash balance			10	10	10	10	10	10
(20) Cumulative surplus cash (or loans outstanding) to maintain $10 target cash balance (Line 18 – Line 19)[c]			($ 6)	($ 43)	($100)	($ 56)	$ 58	$ 92

[a]Although the budget period is July through December, sales and purchases data for May and June are needed to determine collections and payments during July and August.

[b]The amount shown on Line 17 for July, the $15 balance (in millions), is assumed to be on hand initially. The values shown for each of the following months on Line 17 are equal to the cumulative cash as shown on Line 18 for the preceding month; for example, the $4 shown on Line 17 for August is taken from Line 18 in the July column.

[c]When the target cash balance of $10 (Line 19) is deducted from the cumulative cash balance (Line 18), a resulting negative figure on Line 20 represents a required loan, whereas a positive figure represents surplus cash. Loans are required from July through October, and surpluses are expected during November and December. Note also that firms can borrow or pay off loans on a daily basis, so the $6 borrowed during July would be done on a daily basis, as needed, and during October the $100 loan that existed at the beginning of the month would be reduced daily to the $56 ending balance, which in turn would be completely paid off during November.

resent 20 percent of July sales (minus the discount) plus 70 percent of June sales plus 10 percent of May sales, or $254 million in total.

Next, payments for purchases of raw materials are shown. July sales are forecasted at $300 million, so MicroDrive will purchase $210 million of materials in June (Line 6) and pay for these purchases in July (Line 7). Similarly, the company will purchase $280 million of materials in July to meet August's forecasted sales of $400 million.

With Section I completed, Section II can be constructed. Cash from collections is shown on Line 8. Lines 9 through 14 list payments made during each month, and these payments are summed on Line 15. The difference between cash receipts and cash payments (Line 8 minus Line 15) is the net cash gain or loss during the month; for July there is a net cash loss of $11 million, as shown on Line 16.

In Section III, we first determine the cash balance at the start of each month, assuming no borrowing is done; this is shown on Line 17. We assume that $15 million will be on hand on July 1. The beginning cash balance (Line 17) is then added to the net cash gain or loss during the month (Line 16) to obtain the cumulative cash that would be on hand if no financing were done (Line 18); at the end of July, we see a forecasted cumulative cash balance of $4 million in the absence of borrowing.

The target cash balance, $10 million, is then subtracted from the cumulative cash balance to determine the firm's borrowing requirements, shown in parentheses, or its surplus cash. Because we expect to have cumulative cash, as shown on Line 18, of only $4 million in July, we must borrow $6 million to bring the cash account up to the target balance of $10 million. Assuming that this amount is indeed borrowed, loans outstanding will total $6 million at the end of July. (No loans were outstanding on July 1.) The cash surplus or required loan balance is given on Line 20; a positive value indicates a cash surplus, whereas a negative value indicates a loan requirement. Note that the surplus cash or loan requirement shown on Line 20 is a *cumulative amount.* Thus, MicroDrive must borrow $6 million in July; it has an additional cash shortfall during August of $37 million as reported on Line 16, so its total loan requirement at the end of August is $6 + $37 = $43 million, as reported on Line 20. MicroDrive's arrangement with the bank permits it to increase its outstanding loans on a daily basis, up to a prearranged maximum, just as you could increase the amount you owe on a credit card. Any surplus funds can be used to pay off loans, and because the loan can be paid down at any time, on a daily basis, the firm will never have both a cash surplus and an outstanding loan balance.

This same procedure is used in the following months. Sales will peak in September, accompanied by increased payments for purchases, wages, and other items. Receipts from sales will also go up, but there will still be a $57 million net cash outflow during the month. The total loan requirement at the end of September will hit a peak of $100 million, the cumulative cash plus the target cash balance. This amount is also equal to the $43 million needed at the end of August plus the $57 million cash deficit for September.

Sales, purchases, and payments will fall sharply in October, but collections will be the highest of any month because they will reflect the high September sales. As a result, MicroDrive will enjoy a healthy $44 million net cash gain during October. This net gain can be used to pay off borrowings, so loans outstanding will decline by $44 million, to $56 million.

There will be an even larger cash surplus in November, which will permit MicroDrive to pay off all of its loans. In fact, the company is expected to have $58 million in surplus cash by the month's end, and another cash surplus in December will swell the excess cash to $92 million. With such a large amount of unneeded funds, the treasurer will certainly want to invest in interest-bearing securities or to put the funds to use in some other way.

Before concluding our discussion of the cash budget, we should make some additional points:

1. For simplicity, our illustrative budget omitted many important cash flows that are anticipated for 1997, such as dividends, proceeds from stock and bond sales, and fixed asset additions. Some of these are projected to occur in the first half of the year, but those that are projected for the July–December period could easily be added to the example. The final cash budget should contain all projected cash inflows and outflows, and it would be consistent with the forecasted financial statements.

2. Our cash budget example does not reflect interest on loans or income from investing surplus cash. This refinement could easily be added.

3. If cash inflows and outflows are not uniform during the month, we could seriously understate the firm's peak financing requirements. The data in Table 20-1 show the situation expected on the last day of each month, but on any given day during the month, it could be quite different. For example, if all payments had to be made on the fifth of each month, but collections came in uniformly throughout the month, the firm would need to borrow much larger amounts than those shown in Table 20-1. In this case, we would prepare a cash budget which determined requirements on a daily basis.

4. Since depreciation is a noncash charge, it does not appear on the cash budget other than through its effect on taxable income, hence on taxes paid.

5. Since the cash budget represents a forecast, all the values in the table are *expected* values. If actual sales, purchases, and so on, are different from the forecasted levels, then the projected cash deficits and surpluses will also be different. Thus, MicroDrive might end up needing to borrow larger amounts than are indicated on Line 20. Therefore, the company should arrange a line of credit in excess of that amount. For example, if monthly sales turn out to be only 80 percent of their forecasted levels, the firm's maximum cumulative borrowing requirement will turn out to be $126 million rather than $100 million.

6. Spreadsheet programs are particularly well suited for constructing and analyzing cash budgets, especially with respect to the sensitivity of cash flows to changes in sales levels, collection periods, and the like. We could change any assumption, say, the projected monthly sales or the lag before customers pay, and the cash budget would automatically and instantly be recalculated. This would show us exactly how the firm's borrowing requirements would change if other things changed. Also, with a spreadsheet model, it is easy to add features such as interest paid on loans, interest earned on marketable securities, and so on. We have written such a model for the spreadsheet problem at the end of the chapter.

7. Finally, we should note that the target cash balance probably will be adjusted over time, rising and falling with seasonal patterns and with long-term changes in the scale of the firm's operations. Thus, MicroDrive will probably plan to maintain larger cash balances during August and September than at other times, and as the company grows so will its required cash balance. Also, the firm might even set the target cash balance at zero — this could be done if it carried a portfolio of marketable securities which could be sold to replenish the cash account, or if it had an arrangement with its bank that permitted it to borrow any funds needed on a daily basis. In that event, the cash budget would simply stop with Line 18, and the amounts on that line would represent projected loans outstanding or surplus cash. Note, though, that most firms would find it difficult to operate with a zero-balance bank account, just as you would, and the costs of such an operation would in most instances offset the costs associated with maintaining a positive cash balance. Therefore, most firms do set a positive target cash balance.

Statistics are not available on whether transactions balances or compensating balances actually control most firms' target cash balances, but compensating balance requirements do often dominate, especially during periods of high interest rates and tight money.[1]

SELF-TEST
QUESTIONS

What is the purpose of a cash budget?

What are the three major sections of a cash budget?

Suppose a firm's cash flows do not occur uniformly throughout the month. What impact would this have on the accuracy of the forecasted borrowing requirements?

How could uncertainty be handled in a cash budget?

Does depreciation appear in a cash budget? Explain.

CASH MANAGEMENT TECHNIQUES

Cash management has changed significantly over the last 20 years. First, from the early 1970s to the mid-1980s, there was an upward trend in interest rates which increased the opportunity cost of holding cash and, therefore, encouraged financial managers to search for more efficient ways of managing the firm's cash. Second, technological developments, particularly computerized electronic funds transfer mechanisms, improved the cash management process.

Most cash management activities are performed jointly by the firm and its primary bank. Effective cash management encompasses efficient processing of both inflows and outflows, which entails (1) synchronizing cash flows, (2) using float, (3) accelerating collections, (4) getting available funds to where they are needed, and (5) controlling disbursements. Most business is conducted by large firms, many of which operate regionally, nationally, or even globally. They collect cash from many sources and make payments from a number of different cities or even countries. For example, IBM, General Motors, and Hewlett-Packard have manufacturing plants all around the world, even more sales offices, and bank accounts in virtually every city where they do business. Their collection points are located to follow sales patterns. Some disbursements are made from local offices, but most disbursements are made in the cities where manufacturing occurs, or else from the home office (dividend and interest payments, taxes, debt repayments, and the like). Thus, a major corporation might have hundreds or even thousands of bank accounts, and since there is no reason to think that inflows and outflows will balance in each account, a system must be in place to transfer funds from where they happen to be to where they are needed, to arrange loans to cover net corporate shortfalls, and to invest net corpo-

---

[1]This point was underscored by an incident that occurred at a professional finance meeting. A professor presented a scholarly paper that used statistical techniques to determine "optimal cash balances" for a sample of firms. He then reported that the firms' actual cash balances greatly exceeded their optimal balances, suggesting inefficiency and the need for more refined techniques. The discussant of the paper made her comments short and sweet. She reported that she had written each of the sample firms and asked them why they had so much cash. They had uniformly replied that their cash holdings were set by compensating balance requirements. Thus, the model might have been useful to determine the optimal cash balance in the absence of compensating balance requirements, but it was precisely those requirements that determined actual balances.

rate surpluses without delay. We discuss the most commonly used techniques for accomplishing these tasks in the following sections.

CASH FLOW SYNCHRONIZATION

If you as an individual received income once a year, you would probably put it in the bank, draw down your account periodically, and have an average balance during the year equal to about half your annual income. If you received income monthly instead of once a year, you would operate similarly, but now your average balance would be much smaller. If you could arrange to receive income daily and to pay rent, tuition, and other charges on a daily basis, and if you were quite confident of your forecasted inflows and outflows, then you could hold a very small average cash balance.

Exactly the same situation holds for business firms — by improving their forecasts and by arranging things so that cash receipts coincide with cash requirements, firms can reduce their transactions balances to a minimum. Recognizing all this, utility companies, oil companies, credit card companies, and so on, arrange to bill customers, and to pay their own bills, on regular "billing cycles" throughout the month. This improves the *synchronization of cash flows,* which, in turn, enables firms to reduce their cash balances, decrease their bank loans, lower interest expenses, and boost profits.

CHECK-CLEARING PROCESS

When a customer writes and mails a check, this *does not* mean that the funds are immediately available to the receiving firm. Most of us have been told by someone that "the check is in the mail," and we have also deposited a check in our account and then been told that we cannot write our own checks against that deposit until the *check-clearing* process has been completed. Our bank must first make sure the check we deposited is good and then receive funds itself before it will give us cash.

In practice, it may take a long time for a firm to process incoming checks and obtain the use of the money. A check must first be delivered through the mail and then be cleared through the banking system before the money can be put to use. Checks received from customers in distant cities are especially subject to delays because of mail time and also because more parties are involved. For example, assume that we receive a check and deposit it in our bank. Our bank must send the check to the bank on which it was drawn. Only when this latter bank transfers funds to our bank are the funds available for us to use. Checks are generally cleared through the Federal Reserve System or through a clearinghouse set up by the banks in a particular city. Of course, if the check is deposited in the same bank on which it was drawn, that bank merely transfers funds by bookkeeping entries from one depositor to another. The length of time required for checks to clear is thus a function of the distance between the payer's and the payee's banks. In the case of private clearinghouses, it can range from one to three days. The maximum time required for checks to clear through the Federal Reserve System is two days, but mail delays can slow down things on each end of the Fed's involvement in the process.

USING FLOAT

Float is defined as the difference between the balance shown in a firm's (or individual's) checkbook and the balance on the bank's records. Suppose a firm writes, on average, checks in the amount of $5,000 each day, and it takes six days for these checks to clear and be deducted from the firm's bank account. This will cause the firm's own checkbook to show a balance $30,000 smaller than the balance on the bank's records; this difference is called *disbursement float*, and it is good from the firm's standpoint. Now suppose the firm also receives checks in the amount of $5,000 daily, but it loses four days while they are being deposited and cleared. This will result in $20,000 of *collections float*, which is bad. In total, the firm's *net float*—the difference between $30,000 positive disbursement float and the $20,000 negative collections float—will be $10,000.

If the firm's own collection and clearing process is more efficient than that of the recipients of its checks—which is generally true of larger, more efficient firms—then the firm could actually show a *negative* balance on its own books but have a *positive* balance on the records of its bank. Some firms indicate that they *never* have positive book cash balances. One large manufacturer of construction equipment stated that while its account, according to its bank's records, shows an average cash balance of about $20 million, its *book* cash balance is *minus* $20 million—it has $40 million of net float. Obviously, the firm must be able to forecast its disbursements and collections accurately in order to make such heavy use of float.

E. F. Hutton provides an example of pushing cash management too far. Hutton, a leading brokerage firm at the time, did business with banks across the country, and it had to keep compensating balances in these banks. The sizes of the required compensating balances were known, and any excess funds in these banks were sent electronically, on a daily basis, to New York and San Francisco banks, where they were immediately invested in interest-bearing securities. However, rather than waiting to see what the end-of-day balances actually were, Hutton began estimating inflows and outflows, and it transferred out for investment the *estimated* end-of-day excess. But then Hutton got greedy and began *kiting* checks. Hutton deliberately overestimated its deposits and underestimated clearings of its own checks, thereby deliberately overstating its estimated end-of-day balances. As a result, Hutton was chronically overdrawn at its local banks, and it was in effect earning interest on funds which really belonged to those banks. It is entirely proper to forecast what your bank will have recorded as your balance and then to make decisions based on the estimate, even if that balance is different from the balance your own books show. However, it is illegal to forecast an overdrawn situation but then to tell the bank that you expect to have a positive balance.[2]

---

[2]A question raised during the Hutton investigation was this: "Why didn't the banks recognize that Hutton was systematically overdrawing its account and call the company to task?" The answer is that some banks, with tight controls, did exactly that—they refused to let Hutton get away with the practice. Other banks were lax. Still other banks apparently let Hutton get away with being chronically overdrawn out of fear of losing its business: Hutton used its economic muscle to force the banks to let it get away with an illegal act. In many people's opinion, the banks were as much at fault as Hutton. Still, in business dealings, honesty is presumed, and Hutton was dishonest in its dealings with the banks. This dishonesty severely damaged Hutton's reputation, cost the company profits totaling hundreds of millions of dollars, cost its top managers their jobs, and contributed to the ultimate demise of the company.

Delays that cause float arise because it takes time for checks (1) to travel through the mail (mail float), (2) to be processed by the receiving firm (processing float), and (3) to clear through the banking system (clearing, or availability, float). Basically, the size of a firm's net float is a function of its ability to speed up collections on checks received and to slow down collections on checks written. Efficient firms go to great lengths to speed up the processing of incoming checks, thus putting the funds to work faster, and they try to stretch their own payments out as long as possible.

ACCELERATION OF RECEIPTS

Financial managers have searched for ways to collect receivables faster since credit transactions began. Several techniques are used both to speed collections and to get funds where they are needed. Included are (1) lockbox plans established close to customers and (2) requiring large customers to pay by wire.

LOCKBOXES   A *lockbox* is one of the oldest cash management tools. In a lockbox system, incoming checks are sent to post office boxes rather than to corporate headquarters. For example, a firm headquartered in New York City might have its West Coast customers send their payments to a box in San Francisco, its customers in the Southwest send their checks to Dallas, and so on, rather than having all checks sent to New York City. Several times a day a local bank will collect the contents of the lockbox and deposit the checks into the company's local account. The bank would then provide the firm with a daily record of the receipts collected, usually via an electronic data transmission system in a format that permits on-line updating of the firm's receivables accounts.

A lockbox system reduces the time required for a firm to receive incoming checks, to deposit them, and to get them cleared through the banking system so that the funds are available for use. Lockbox services can often increase the availability of funds by two to five days over the "regular" system.

PAYMENT BY WIRE   Firms are increasingly demanding payments of larger bills by wire, or even by automatic electronic debits, whereby funds are automatically deducted from one account and added to another. These are, of course, the ultimate in a speeded-up collection process, and computer technology is making such processes increasingly feasible and efficient.

What is float? How do firms use float to increase cash management efficiency? What are some methods firms can use to accelerate receipts?

SELF-TEST QUESTIONS

MARKETABLE SECURITIES

Realistically, the management of cash and the handling of marketable securities go together — management of one implies management of the other. In prior sections, we focused on cash management. Now, we turn to *marketable securities*.

Marketable securities typically provide much lower yields than operating assets. For example, in 1995 Chrysler held a $7.3 billion portfolio of short-term marketable securities that yielded about 6 percent, but its operating assets provided a return of about 14 percent. Why would a company such as Chrysler have such large holdings of low-yielding assets?

In many cases, companies hold marketable securities for the same reasons they hold cash. Although these securities are not as liquid as cash, in most cases they can be converted to cash in a very short period of time (often just a few minutes) with a single telephone call. Moreover, while cash and commercial checking accounts yield nothing, marketable securities provide at least a modest return. For this reason, many firms hold at least some marketable securities in lieu of larger cash balances, liquidating part of the portfolio to increase the cash account when cash outflows exceed inflows.

A few years ago, Chrysler had essentially no cash — it was incurring huge losses, and those losses had drained its cash account. Then a new management team took over, improved operations, and began generating positive cash flows. By 1995, Chrysler's cash (and marketable securities) was up to $7.3 billion, and analysts were forecasting a further buildup over the next two years to more than $10 billion. Management indicated, in various statements, that the cash hoard was necessary to enable the company to weather the next downturn in auto sales.

Although setting the target cash balance is, to a large extent, judgmental, analytical rules can be applied to help formulate better judgments. For example, years ago William Baumol recognized that the trade-off between cash and marketable securities is similar to the one firms face when setting the optimal level of inventory.[3] Baumol then applied the EOQ inventory model to determine the optimal level of cash balances.[4] His model suggests that cash holdings should be higher if costs are high and the time to liquidate marketable securities is long, but that those holdings should be lower if interest rates are low. His logic was that if it is expensive and time consuming to convert securities to cash, and if securities do not earn much because interest rates are low, then it does not pay to hold securities as opposed to cash. It does pay to hold securities if interest rates are high and the securities can be converted to cash quickly and cheaply.

SELF-TEST QUESTIONS   Why might a company hold low-yielding marketable securities when it could earn a much higher return on operating assets?
Why might a low interest rate environment lead to larger cash balances?
How might improvements in telecommunications technology affect the level of corporations' holding of cash?

INVENTORY

Inventories, which may be classified as (1) *raw materials,* (2) *work-in-process,* and (3) *finished goods,* are an essential part of business operations. Inventory levels

---

[3]William J. Baumol, "The Transactions Demand for Cash: An Inventory Theoretic Approach," *Quarterly Journal of Economics,* November 1952, 545–556.

[4]A more complete description of the Baumol and Economic Ordering Quantity (EOQ) models can be found in Chapter 22.

depend heavily upon sales, and inventory must be acquired *ahead* of sales. This makes it necessary to forecast sales before establishing target inventory levels, and that makes inventory management a difficult task. Also, since errors in the establishment of inventory levels quickly lead either to lost sales or to excessive carrying costs, inventory management is as important as it is difficult.

Inventory management techniques are covered in depth in production management courses. Still, since financial managers have a responsibility both for raising the capital needed to carry inventory and for the overall profitability of the firm, they must be concerned with the financial aspects of inventory management. Two examples will make clear the types of issues involved in inventory management, and the financial problems poor inventory control can cause.

TYPICAL INVENTORY DECISIONS

RETAIL CLOTHING STORE

Chicago Discount Clothing Company (CDCC) must order swimsuits for summer sales in January, and it must take delivery by April to be sure of having enough suits to meet the heavy May–June demand. Bathing suits come in many styles, colors, and sizes, and if CDCC stocks incorrectly, either in total or in terms of the style-color-size distribution, then the store will have trouble. It will lose potential sales if it stocks too few suits, and it will be forced to lower prices and take losses if it stocks too many or the wrong types.

The effects of inventory changes on the balance sheet are important. For simplicity, assume that CDCC has a $10,000 base stock of inventory which is financed by common stock. Its balance sheet is as follows:

Inventory (base stock)	$10,000	Common stock	$10,000
Total assets	$10,000	Total claims	$10,000

Now it anticipates that it will sell $5,000 worth of swimsuit inventory this summer. Dollar sales will actually be greater than $5,000, since CDCC makes about $200 in profits for every $1,000 of inventory sold. CDCC finances its seasonal inventory with bank loans, so its pre-summer balance sheet would look like this:

Inventory (seasonal)	$ 5,000	Notes payable to bank	$ 5,000
Inventory (base stock)	10,000	Common stock	10,000
Total assets	$15,000	Total claims	$15,000

If everything works out as planned, sales will be made, inventory will be converted to cash, the bank loan will be retired, and the company will earn a profit. The balance sheet, after a successful season, might look like this:

Cash	$ 1,000	Notes payable to bank	$ 0
Inventory (seasonal)	0	Common stock	10,000
Inventory (base stock)	10,000	Retained earnings	1,000
Total assets	$11,000	Total claims	$11,000

The company is now in a highly liquid position and is ready to begin a new season.

But suppose the season had not gone well, and CDCC had only sold $1,000 of its inventory. As fall approached, the balance sheet would look like this:

Cash	$ 200	Notes payable to bank	$ 4,000
Inventory (seasonal)	4,000	Common stock	10,000
Inventory (base stock)	10,000	Retained earnings	200
Total assets	$14,200	Total claims	$14,200

Now suppose the bank insists on repayment of the $4,000 outstanding on the loan, and it wants cash, not swimsuits. But if the swimsuits did not sell well in the summer, how will out-of-style suits sell in the fall? Assume that CDCC is forced to mark the suits down to half their cost (not half the selling price) in order to sell them to raise cash to repay the bank loan. The result will be as follows:

Cash	$ 2,200	Notes payable to bank	$ 4,000
Inventory (base stock)	10,000	Common stock	10,000
		Retained earnings	(1,800)
Total assets	$12,200	Total claims	$12,200

At this point, CDCC is in serious trouble. It does not have the cash to pay off the loan, and the firm's shareholders have lost $1,800 of their equity. If the bank will not extend the loan, and if other sources of cash are not available, CDCC will have to mark down its base stock prices in an effort to stimulate sales, and if that does not work, CDCC could be forced into bankruptcy. Clearly, poor inventory decisions can spell trouble.

APPLIANCE MANUFACTURER

Now consider a different type of situation, that of Housepro Corporation, an appliance manufacturer whose inventory position, in millions of dollars, follows:

Raw materials	$ 200
Work-in-process	200
Finished goods	600
Total inventory	$1,000

Suppose Housepro anticipates that the economy is about to get much stronger and that the demand for appliances will rise sharply. If it is to share in the expected boom, Housepro will have to increase production. This means it will have to increase inventory, and, since the inventory buildup must precede sales, additional financing will be required — some liability account, perhaps notes payable, will have to be increased in order to support the additional inventory.

Proper inventory management requires close coordination among the sales, purchasing, production, and finance departments. The sales/marketing department is generally the first to spot changes in demand. These changes must be worked into the purchasing and manufacturing schedules, and the financial manager must arrange any financing needed to support the inventory buildup. Lack of coordination among departments, poor sales forecasts, or both, can lead to disaster.

Why is good inventory managment essential to a firm's success?
What departments should be involved in inventory decisions?

**SELF-TEST
QUESTIONS**

INVENTORY COSTS

The goal of inventory management is to ensure that the inventories needed to sustain operations are available, but to hold the costs of ordering and carrying inventories to the lowest possible level. Table 20-2 gives a listing of the typical costs associated with inventory, divided into three categories: carrying costs, ordering and receiving costs, and the costs that are incurred if the firm runs short of inventory.

Inventory is costly to store; therefore, there is always pressure to reduce inventory holdings. A recent article in *Fortune* highlights the fact that an increasing number of corporations are taking drastic steps to control inventory costs.[5] For example,

COSTS ASSOCIATED WITH INVENTORY	TABLE 20-2

	APPROXIMATE ANNUAL COST AS A PERCENTAGE OF INVENTORY VALUE
I. CARRYING COSTS	
Cost of capital tied up	12.0%
Storage and handling costs	0.5
Insurance	0.5
Property taxes	1.0
Depreciation and obsolescence	12.0
Total	26.0%
II. ORDERING, SHIPPING, AND RECEIVING COSTS	
Cost of placing orders, including production and set-up costs	Varies
Shipping and handling costs	2.5%
III. COSTS OF RUNNING SHORT	
Loss of sales	Varies
Loss of customer goodwill	Varies
Disruption of production schedules	Varies

NOTE: These costs vary from firm to firm, from item to item, and also over time. The figures shown are U.S. Department of Commerce estimates for an average manufacturing firm. Where costs vary so widely that no meaningful numbers can be assigned, the term "Varies" is reported.

[5]Shawn Tully, "Raiding a Company's Hidden Cash," *Fortune,* August 22, 1994, 82–87.

Trane Corporation, which makes air conditioners, recently adopted the just-in-time inventory procedure which is described in more detail in the next section.

In the past, Trane produced parts on a steady basis, stored them as inventory, and had them ready whenever the company received an order for a batch of air conditioners. However, the company reached the point where its inventory covered an area equal to three football fields, and it sometimes took as long as 15 days to find the necessary parts and to complete an order. To make matters worse, occasionally some of the necessary components simply could not be located, while in other instances the components were located but found to have been damaged from long storage.

Then Trane adopted a new inventory policy — it began producing components only after an order is received, and then sending the parts directly from the machines which make them to the final assembly line. The net effect: Inventories fell nearly 40 percent even as sales increased by 30 percent.

Trane recognized, though, that as Table 20-2 indicates, there are costs associated with holding too little inventory, and these costs can be severe. Usually, if a firm carries small inventories, it must reorder frequently. This increases ordering costs. Even more important, it could face large costs (for example, an immediate loss of sales and a loss of goodwill which can lead to lower sales in the future) if it does not have the inventory on hand to meet customer demands.

SELF-TEST QUESTIONS

What are the three categories of inventory costs?

What are some components of inventory carrying costs?

What are some components of inventory ordering costs?

INVENTORY CONTROL SYSTEMS

Inventory management also involves the establishment of an *inventory control system*. Inventory control systems run the gamut from very simple to extremely complex, depending on the size of the firm and the nature of its inventory. One simple control procedure is the *red-line method* — inventory items are stocked in a bin, a red line is drawn around the inside of the bin at the level of the reorder point, and the inventory clerk places an order when the red line shows. The *two-bin method* has inventory items stocked in two bins. When the working bin is empty, an order is placed and inventory is drawn from the second bin. These procedures work well for parts such as bolts in a manufacturing process, or for many items in retail businesses.

COMPUTERIZED SYSTEMS

Larger companies employ *computerized inventory control systems*. The computer starts with an inventory count in memory. As withdrawals are made, they are recorded by the computer, and the inventory balance is revised. When the reorder point is reached, the computer automatically places an order, and when the order is received, the recorded balance is increased. As we noted earlier, retailers such as Wal-Mart have carried this system quite far — each item has a bar code, and, as an item is checked out, the code is read, a signal is sent to the computer, and the inventory balance is adjusted. When the balance drops to the reorder point, an order is placed. In Wal-Mart's case, the order goes directly from its computers to those of its suppliers.

A good inventory control system is dynamic, not static. A company such as Wal-Mart or General Motors stocks hundreds of thousands of different items. The sales (or use) of these various items can rise or fall quite separately from rising or falling overall corporate sales. As the usage rate for an individual item begins to rise or fall, the inventory manager must adjust its balance to avoid running short or ending up with obsolete items. If the change in the usage rate appears to be permanent, the safety stock level should be reconsidered, and the computer model used in the control process should be reprogrammed.

JUST-IN-TIME SYSTEMS

A relatively new approach to inventory control called the *just-in-time (JIT) system* has been developed by Japanese firms and is gaining popularity throughout the world. Toyota provides a good example of the just-in-time system. Eight of Toyota's ten factories, along with most of Toyota's suppliers, dot the countryside around Toyota City. Delivery of components is tied to the speed of the assembly line, and parts are generally delivered no more than a few hours before they are used. The just-in-time system reduces the need for Toyota and other manufacturers to carry large inventories, but it requires a great deal of coordination between the manufacturer and its suppliers, in both the timing of deliveries and the quality of the parts. If the component parts are not perfect, bad parts could stop the entire production line. Therefore, JIT inventory management has been developed in conjunction with total quality management (TQM).

Not surprisingly, U.S. automobile manufacturers were among the first domestic firms to move toward just-in-time systems. Ford has been restructuring its production system with a goal of increasing its inventory turnover from 20 times a year to 30 or 40 times. Of course, just-in-time systems place considerable pressure on suppliers. GM formerly kept a 10-day supply of seats and other parts made by Lear Siegler; now GM sends in orders at four- to eight-hour intervals and expects immediate shipment. A Lear Siegler spokesman stated, "We can't afford to keep things sitting around either," so Lear Siegler has had to be tougher on its own suppliers.

Just-in-time systems are also being adopted by smaller firms. In fact, some production experts say that small companies are better positioned than large ones to use just-in-time methods, because it is easier to redefine job functions and to educate people in small firms. One small-firm example is Fireplace Inc., a manufacturer of prefabricated fireplaces. The company was having cash flow problems, and it was carrying $1.1 million in inventory to support annual sales of about $8 million. The company went to a just-in-time system and trimmed its raw material and work-in-process inventory to $750,000, freeing up $350,000 of cash, even as sales doubled.

It has been argued that just-in-time inventory controls do not really increase overall economic efficiency because they merely shift inventory responsibility to other firms further up the supply chain. However, this view is incorrect — the close coordination required between the parties has led to an overall reduction of inventory throughout the production-distribution system, hence to a general improvement in efficiency. This point is made by companies such as Wal-Mart and Toyota. It is also borne out by economic statistics, which indicate that inventory as a percentage of sales has declined since the use of just-in-time procedures began.

OUT-SOURCING

Another important development related to inventory is *out-sourcing,* which is the practice of purchasing components rather than making them in-house. Thus, if GM arranged to buy radiators, axles, and other parts from suppliers rather than making them itself, it would be increasing its use of out-sourcing. Out-sourcing is often combined with just-in-time systems to reduce inventory levels. However, perhaps the major reason for out-sourcing has nothing to do with inventory policy — a bureaucratic, unionized company like GM can often buy parts from a smaller, nonunionized supplier at a lower cost than if it made them itself.

THE RELATIONSHIP BETWEEN PRODUCTION SCHEDULING AND INVENTORY LEVELS

A final point relating to inventory levels is *the relationship between production scheduling and inventory levels.* For example, a greeting card manufacturer has highly seasonal sales. Such a firm could produce on a steady, year-round basis, or it could let production rise and fall with sales. If it established a level production schedule, its inventory would rise sharply during periods when sales were low and then would decline during peak sales periods, and its average inventory holdings would be substantially higher than if production rose and fell with sales.

Our discussions of just-in-time systems, out-sourcing, and production scheduling all point out the necessity of coordinating inventory policy with manufacturing/procurement policies. Companies try to minimize *total production and distribution costs,* and inventory costs are just one part of total costs. Still, they are an important part, so financial managers should be aware of the determinants of inventory costs and how they can be minimized.

SELF-TEST QUESTIONS

Describe some inventory control systems that are used in practice.

What are just-in-time systems? What are their advantages? Why is quality especially important if a JIT system is used?

What is out-sourcing?

Describe the relationship between production scheduling and inventory levels.

RECEIVABLES MANAGEMENT

Firms would, in general, rather sell for cash than on credit, but competitive pressures force most firms to offer credit. Thus, goods are shipped, inventories are reduced, and an *account receivable* is created.[6] Eventually, the customer will pay the account,

---

[6]Whenever goods are sold on credit, two accounts are created — an asset item entitled *accounts receivable* on the books of the selling firm, and a liability item called *accounts payable* on the books of the purchaser. At this point, we are analyzing the transaction from the viewpoint of the seller, so we concentrate on the variables under its control. We will examine the transaction from the viewpoint of the purchaser in Chapter 21, where we discuss accounts payable as a source of funds and consider their cost relative to the cost of funds obtained from other sources.

at which time (1) the firm will receive cash and (2) its receivables will decline. Carrying receivables has both direct and indirect costs, but it also has an important benefit — granting credit will increase sales.

Receivables management begins with the decision of whether or not to grant credit. In this section, we discuss the manner in which receivables build up, and we also discuss several alternative ways to monitor receivables. A monitoring system is important, because without it receivables will build up to excessive levels, cash flows will decline, and bad debts will offset the profits on sales. Corrective action is often needed, and the only way to know whether the situation is getting out of hand is with a good receivables control system.

THE ACCUMULATION OF RECEIVABLES

Total accounts receivable outstanding at any given time is determined by two factors: (1) the volume of credit sales and (2) the average length of time between sales and collections. For example, suppose the Boston Lumber Company (BLC), a wholesale distributor of lumber products, opens a warehouse on January 1 and, starting the first day, makes sales of $1,000 each day. For simplicity, we assume that all sales are on credit, and customers are given 10 days in which to pay. At the end of the first day, accounts receivable will be $1,000; they will rise to $2,000 by the end of the second day; and by January 10, they will have risen to 10($1,000) = $10,000. On January 11, another $1,000 will be added to receivables, but payments for sales made on January 1 will reduce receivables by $1,000, so total accounts receivable will remain constant at $10,000. In general, once the firm's operations have stabilized, this situation will exist:

$$\frac{\text{Accounts}}{\text{receivable}} = \frac{\text{Credit sales}}{\text{per day}} \times \frac{\text{Length of}}{\text{collection period}}$$ 20-1

$$= \$1,000 \times 10 \text{ days} = \$10,000.$$

If either credit sales or the collection period changes, such changes will be reflected in accounts receivable.

Notice that the $10,000 investment in receivables must be financed. To illustrate, suppose that when the warehouse opened on January 1, BLC's shareholders had put up $800 as common stock and used this money to buy the goods sold the first day. The $800 worth of inventory will be sold for $1,000; thus, BLC's gross profit on the $800 investment is $200, or 25 percent. In this situation, the initial balance sheet would be as follows:[7]

---

[7]Note that the firm would need other assets such as cash, fixed assets, and a permanent stock of inventory. Also, overhead costs and taxes would have to be deducted, so retained earnings would be less than the figures shown here. We abstract from these details here so that we may focus on receivables.

| Inventories | $ 800 | Common equity | $ 800 |
| Total assets | $ 800 | Total liabilities and equity | $ 800 |

At the end of the day, the balance sheet would look like this:

Accounts receivable	$1,000	Common equity	$ 800
Inventories	0	Retained earnings	200
Total assets	$1,000	Total liabilities and equity	$1,000

In order to remain in business, BLC must replenish inventories. To do so requires that $800 of goods be purchased, and this requires $800 in cash. Assuming that BLC borrows the $800 from the bank, the balance sheet at the start of the second day will be as follows:

Accounts receivable	$1,000	Notes payable to bank	$ 800
Inventories	800	Common equity	800
		Retained earnings	200
Total assets	$1,800	Total liabilities and equity	$1,800

At the end of the second day, the inventories will have been converted to receivables, and the firm will have to borrow another $800 to restock for the third day.

This process will continue, provided the bank is willing to lend the necessary funds, until the beginning of the 11th day, when the balance sheet reads as follows:

Accounts receivable	$10,000	Notes payable to bank	$ 8,000
Inventories	800	Common equity	800
		Retained earnings	2,000
Total assets	$10,800	Total liabilities and equity	$10,800

From this point on, $1,000 of receivables will be collected every day, and $800 of these funds can be used to purchase new inventories.

This example should make it clear (1) that accounts receivable depend jointly on the level of credit sales and the collection period, (2) that any increase in receivables must be financed in some manner, but (3) that the entire amount of receivables does not have to be financed because the profit portion ($200 of each $1,000 of sales) does not represent a cash outflow. In our example, we assumed bank financing, but, as we demonstrate in Chapter 21, there are many alternative ways to finance current assets.

MONITORING THE RECEIVABLES POSITION

Investors—both stockholders and bank loan officers—should pay close attention to accounts receivable management, for, as we shall see, one can be misled by reported financial statements and as a result suffer serious losses on an investment.

When a credit sale is made, the following events occur: (1) Inventories are reduced by the cost of goods sold, (2) accounts receivable are increased by the sales price, and (3) the difference is profit, which is added to retained earnings. If the sale is for cash, then the cash from the sale has actually been received by the firm, but if the sale is on credit, the firm will not receive the cash unless and until the account is collected. Firms have been known to encourage "sales" to very weak customers in order to report high profits. This could boost the firm's stock price, at least until credit losses begin to lower earnings, at which time the stock price will fall. Analyses along the lines suggested in the following sections will detect any such questionable practice, as well as any unconscious deterioration in the quality of accounts receivable. Such early detection could help both investors and bankers avoid losses.[8]

DAYS SALES OUTSTANDING (DSO) Suppose Super Sets Inc., a television manufacturer, sells 200,000 television sets a year at a price of $198 each. Further, assume that all sales are on credit, with terms of 2/10, net 30. Finally, assume that 70 percent of the customers take discounts and pay on Day 10, while the other 30 percent pay on Day 30.

Super Sets' *days sales outstanding (DSO),* sometimes called the *average collection period (ACP),* is 16 days:

$$DSO = ACP = 0.7(10 \text{ days}) + 0.3(30 \text{ days}) = 16 \text{ days}.$$

Super Sets' *average daily sales (ADS),* assuming a 360-day year, is $110,000:

$$ADS = \frac{\text{Annual sales}}{360} = \frac{(\text{Units sold})(\text{Sales price})}{360} \qquad \textbf{20-2}$$

$$= \frac{200,000(\$198)}{360} = \frac{\$39,600,000}{360} = \$110,000.$$

Super Sets' accounts receivable, assuming a constant, uniform rate of sales throughout the year, will at any point in time be $1,760,000:

$$\text{Receivables} = (ADS)(DSO) \qquad \textbf{20-3}$$

$$= (\$110,000)(16) = \$1,760,000.$$

Note that its DSO, or average collection period, is a measure of the average length of time it takes Super Sets' customers to pay off their credit purchases. Super Sets' DSO can be compared with the industry average DSO. For example, if all television manufacturers sell on the same credit terms, and if the industry average DSO is 25 days versus Super Sets' 16 days, then Super Sets either has a higher percentage of discount customers or else its credit department is exceptionally good at obtaining prompt payment.

---

[8]Accountants are increasingly interested in these matters. Investors have sued several of the major accounting firms for substantial damages when (1) profits were overstated and (2) it could be shown that the auditors should have conducted an analysis along the lines described here and then reported the results to stockholders in their audit opinion.

Finally, note that if you know both the annual sales and the receivables balance, you can calculate DSO as follows:

$$DSO = \frac{Receivables}{Sales\ per\ day} = \frac{\$1,760,000}{\$110,000} = 16\ days.$$

The DSO can also be compared with the firm's own credit terms. For example, suppose Super Sets' DSO had been running at a level of 35 days versus its 2/10, net 30 credit terms. With a 35-day DSO, some customers would obviously be taking more than 30 days to pay their bills. In fact, if many customers were paying within 10 days to take advantage of the discount, the others must, on average, be taking much longer than 35 days. One way to check this possibility is to use an aging schedule as described in the next section.

AGING SCHEDULES   An *aging schedule* breaks down receivables by age of account. Table 20-3 contains the December 31, 1996, aging schedules of two television manufacturers, Super Sets and Wonder Vision. Both firms offer the same credit terms, 2/10, net 30, and both show the same total receivables. However, Super Sets' aging schedule indicates that all of its customers pay on time — 70 percent pay on Day 10 while 30 percent pay on Day 30. Wonder Vision's schedule, which is more typical, shows that many of its customers are not abiding by its credit terms — some 27 percent of its receivables are more than 30 days past due, even though Wonder Vision's credit terms call for full payment by Day 30.

Aging schedules cannot be constructed from the summary data reported in financial statements; they must be developed from the firm's accounts receivable ledger. However, well-run firms have computerized their accounts receivable records, so it is easy to determine the age of each invoice, to sort electronically by age categories, and thus to generate an aging schedule.

Management should constantly monitor both the DSO and the aging schedule to detect trends, to see how the firm's collection experience compares with its credit terms, and to see how effectively the credit department is operating in comparison with other firms in the industry. If the DSO starts to lengthen, or if the aging schedule begins to show an increasing percentage of past-due accounts, then the firm's credit policy may need to be tightened.

TABLE 20-3	AGING SCHEDULES				
	SUPER SETS			**WONDER VISION**	
AGE OF ACCOUNT (DAYS)	VALUE OF ACCOUNT	PERCENTAGE OF TOTAL VALUE		VALUE OF ACCOUNT	PERCENTAGE OF TOTAL VALUE
0–10	$1,232,000	70%		$825,000	47%
11–30	528,000	30		460,000	26
31–45	0	0		265,000	15
46–60	0	0		179,000	10
Over 60	0	0		31,000	2
Total receivables	$1,760,000	100%		$1,760,000	100%

Although a change in the DSO or the aging schedule should signal the firm to investigate its credit policy, a deterioration in these measures does not necessarily indicate that the firm's collection policy has deteriorated. In fact, if a firm experiences sharp seasonal variations, or if it is growing rapidly, then both the aging schedule and the DSO may be distorted. To see this point, note that the DSO is calculated as follows:

$$DSO = \frac{\text{Accounts receivable}}{\text{Sales}/360}.$$

Since receivables at a given point in time reflect sales in the last month or so but sales as shown in the denominator are for the last 12 months, a seasonal increase in sales will increase the numerator more than the denominator, hence will raise the DSO. This will occur even if customers are still taking exactly as long to pay as before. Similar problems arise with the aging schedule if sales fluctuate widely. Therefore, a change in either the DSO or the aging schedule should be taken as a signal to investigate further, but not necessarily as a sign that the firm's credit policy has weakened. Still, days sales outstanding and the aging schedule represent the starting point for reviewing the credit department's performance.[9]

Explain how a new firm's receivables balance is built up over time.
Define days sales outstanding (DSO). What can be learned from it?
What is an aging schedule? What can be learned from it?

SELF-TEST
QUESTIONS

CREDIT POLICY

The success or failure of a business depends primarily on the demand for its products — as a rule, the higher its sales, the larger its profits and the higher the value of its stock. Sales, in turn, depend on a number of factors, some exogenous but others under the control of the firm. The major controllable determinants of demand are sales prices, product quality, advertising, and the firm's *credit policy.* Credit policy, in turn, consists of these four variables:

1. *Credit period,* which is the length of time buyers are given to pay for their purchases.

2. *Credit standards,* which refer to the financial strength of acceptable credit customers and the amount of credit available to different customers.

3. *Collection policy,* which is measured by its toughness or laxity in following up on slow-paying accounts.

4. *Discounts* given for early payment, including the discount percentage and how rapidly payment must be made to qualify for the discount.

The credit manager has the responsibility for administering the firm's credit policy. However, because of the pervasive importance of credit, the credit policy itself

---

[9]See Chapter 22 for a more complete discussion of the problems with the DSO and aging schedule, and ways to correct for them.

is normally established by the executive committee, which usually consists of the president plus the vice-presidents in charge of finance, marketing, and production.

SELF-TEST QUESTION : What are the four credit policy variables?

SETTING CREDIT TERMS

A firm's regular *credit terms*, which include the *credit period* and *discount*, might call for sales on a 2/10, net 30 basis to all "acceptable" customers. Here customers who paid within 10 days would be given a 2 percent discount, and others would be required to pay within 30 days. Its *credit standards* would be applied to determine which customers are qualified for the regular credit terms, and the amount of credit available to each customer.

CREDIT STANDARDS

Credit standards refer to the strength and creditworthiness a customer must exhibit in order to qualify for credit. If a customer does not qualify for the regular credit terms, it can still purchase from the firm, but under more restrictive terms. For example, a firm's "regular" credit terms might call for payment after 30 days, and these terms might be extended to all qualified customers. The firm's credit standards would be applied to determine which customers qualified for the regular credit terms and how much credit each customer should receive. The major factors considered when setting credit standards relate to the likelihood that a given customer will pay slowly or perhaps even end up as a bad debt loss.

Setting credit standards implicitly requires a measurement of *credit quality*, which is defined in terms of the probability of a customer's default. The probability estimate for a given customer is, to some extent, a subjective judgment. Nevertheless, credit evaluation is a well-established practice, and a good credit manager can make reasonably accurate judgments of the probability of default by different classes of customers.

Managing a credit department requires fast, accurate, up-to-date information, and to help get such information, the National Association of Credit Management (a group with 43,000 member firms) persuaded TRW, a large credit-reporting agency, to develop a computer-based telecommunications network for the collection, storage, retrieval, and distribution of credit information. A typical business credit report would include the following pieces of information:

1. A summary balance sheet and income statement.
2. A number of key ratios, with trend information.
3. Information obtained from the firm's suppliers telling whether it has been paying promptly or slowly, and whether it has recently failed to make any payments.
4. A verbal description of the physical condition of the firm's operations.

5. A verbal description of the backgrounds of the firm's owners, including any previous bankruptcies, lawsuits, divorce settlement problems, and the like.

6. A summary rating, ranging from A for the best credit risks down to F for those that are deemed likely to default.

Although a great deal of credit information is available, it must still be processed in a judgmental manner. Computerized information systems can assist in making better credit decisions, but, in the final analysis, most credit decisions are really exercises in informed judgment.[10]

COLLECTION POLICY

Collection policy refers to the procedures the firm uses to collect past-due accounts. For example, a letter might be sent to customers when a bill is 10 days past due; a more severe letter, followed by a telephone call, would be sent if payment is not received within 30 days; and the account would be turned over to a collection agency after 90 days.

The collection process can be expensive in terms of both out-of-pocket expenditures and lost goodwill — customers dislike being turned over to a collection agency. However, at least some firmness is needed to prevent an undue lengthening of the collection period and to minimize outright losses. A balance must be struck between the costs and benefits of different collection policies.

Changes in collection policy influence sales, the collection period, and the bad debt loss percentage. The effects of a change in collection policy, along with changes in the other credit policy variables, will be analyzed in Chapter 22.

CASH DISCOUNTS

The last element in the credit policy decision, the use of *cash discounts* for early payment, is analyzed by balancing the costs and benefits of different cash discounts. For example, a firm might decide to change its credit terms from "net 30," which means that customers must pay within 30 days, to "2/10, net 30." This change should produce two benefits: (1) It should attract new customers who consider the discount to be a price reduction, and (2) the discount should cause a reduction in the days sales outstanding, because some existing customers will pay more promptly in order to take advantage of the discount. Offsetting these benefits is the dollar cost of the discounts. The optimal discount percentage is established at the point where the marginal costs and benefits are exactly offsetting.

---

[10]Credit analysts use procedures ranging from highly sophisticated, computerized "credit-scoring" systems, which actually calculate the statistical probability that a given customer will default, to informal procedures, which involve going through a checklist of factors that should be considered when processing a credit application. The credit-scoring systems use various financial ratios such as the current ratio and the debt ratio (for businesses) and income, years with the same employer, and the like (for individuals) to determine the statistical probability of default. Credit is then granted to those with low default probabilities. The informal procedures often involve examining the "5 C's of Credit": character, capacity, capital, collateral, and conditions. Character is obvious; capacity is a subjective estimate of ability to repay; capital means how much net worth the borrower has; collateral means assets pledged to secure the loan; and conditions refer to business conditions, which affect ability to repay.

If sales are seasonal, a firm may use *seasonal dating* on discounts. For example, Slimware Inc., a swimsuit manufacturer, sells on terms of 2/10, net 30, May 1 dating. This means that the effective invoice date is May 1, even if the sale was made back in January. The discount may be taken up to May 10; otherwise, the full amount must be paid on May 30. Slimware produces throughout the year, but retail sales of bathing suits are concentrated in the spring and early summer, and by offering seasonal dating, the company induces some of its customers to stock up early, saving Slimware storage costs and also "nailing down sales."

SELF-TEST QUESTIONS

What is credit quality, and how is it assessed?

How can cash discounts be used to influence both sales and the DSO?

What is seasonal dating?

OTHER FACTORS INFLUENCING CREDIT POLICY

In addition to the factors discussed in the previous sections, several other points should be made regarding credit policy.

PROFIT POTENTIAL

We have emphasized the costs of granting credit. *However, if it is possible to sell on credit and also to impose a carrying charge on the receivables that are outstanding, then credit sales can actually be more profitable than cash sales.* This is especially true for consumer durables (autos, appliances, and so on), but it is also true for certain types of industrial equipment. Thus, GM's General Motors Acceptance Corporation (GMAC) unit, which finances automobiles, is highly profitable, as is Sears's credit subsidiary.[11] Some encyclopedia companies are even reported to lose money on cash sales but to more than make up these losses from the carrying charges on their credit sales. Obviously, such companies would rather sell on credit than for cash!

The carrying charges on outstanding credit are generally about 18 percent on a nominal basis: 1.5 percent per month, so $1.5\% \times 12 = 18\%$. This is equivalent to an effective annual rate of $(1.015)^{12} - 1.0 = 19.6\%$. Having receivables outstanding that earn more than 18 percent is highly profitable.

LEGAL CONSIDERATIONS

It is illegal, under the Robinson-Patman Act, for a firm to charge prices that discriminate between customers unless these differential prices are cost-justified. The same holds true for credit — it is illegal to offer more favorable credit terms to one customer or class of customers than to another, unless the differences are cost-justified.

SELF-TEST QUESTION

How do profit potential and legal considerations affect a firm's credit policy?

---

[11]Companies that do a large volume of sales financing typically set up subsidiary companies called *captive finance companies* to do the actual financing. Thus, General Motors, Chrysler, and Ford all have captive finance companies, as do Sears, Montgomery Ward, and General Electric.

SUMMARY

This chapter discussed the management of current assets: cash, marketable securities, inventory, and receivables. The key concepts are listed below.

- *Working capital* refers to current assets, and *net working capital* is defined as current assets minus current liabilities. *Working capital policy* refers to decisions relating to the level of and the financing of current assets.

- Under a *relaxed current asset investment policy,* a firm would hold relatively large amounts of each type of current asset. Under a *restricted current asset investment policy,* the firm would hold minimal amounts of these items.

- Both the EVA and Du Pont equations can be used to highlight the effects of working capital management on profitability.

- The *primary goal of cash management* is to reduce the amount of cash held to the minimum necessary to conduct business.

- The *transactions balance* is the cash necessary to conduct day-to-day business, whereas the *precautionary balance* is a cash reserve held to meet random, unforeseen needs. A *compensating balance* is a minimum checking account balance that a bank requires as compensation either for services provided or as part of a loan agreement. Firms also hold *speculative balances,* which allow them to take advantage of bargain purchases. Note, though, that borrowing capacity and marketable security holdings reduce the need for both precautionary and speculative balances.

- A *cash budget* is a schedule showing projected cash inflows and outflows over some period. The cash budget is used to predict cash surpluses and shortages, and thus it is the primary cash management planning tool.

- *Cash management techniques* generally fall into five categories: (1) synchronizing cash flows, (2) using float, (3) accelerating collections, (4) determining where and when funds will be needed, and (5) controlling disbursements.

- *Disbursement float* is the amount of funds associated with checks written by a firm that are still in process and hence have not yet been deducted from the firm's bank account. This is "good" float from the firm's standpoint.

- *Collections float* is the amount of funds associated with checks written to a firm that have not been cleared, hence are not yet available for the firm's use. This is "bad" float.

- *Net float* is the difference between disbursement float and collections float, and it also is equal to the difference between the balance in the firm's own checkbook and the balance on the bank's records. The larger the net float, the smaller the cash balance the firm must maintain, so net float is good.

- Two techniques that can be used to speed up collections are (1) *lockboxes* and (2) *wire transfers.*

■ Firms can reduce their cash balances by holding *marketable securities,* which can be sold on short notice at close to their quoted prices. Marketable securities serve both as a substitute for cash and as a temporary investment for funds that may be needed in the near future. Safety is the primary consideration when selecting marketable securities.

■ *Inventory management* involves determining how much inventory to hold, when to place orders, and how many units to order.

■ *Inventory* can be grouped into three categories: (1) raw materials, (2) work-in-process, and (3) finished goods.

■ *Inventory costs* can be divided into three types: carrying costs, ordering costs, and stock-out costs. Carrying costs increase with inventory, but ordering costs and stock-out costs decline with larger inventory holdings.

■ Firms use inventory control systems such as the *red-line method* and the *two-bin method,* as well as *computerized inventory control systems,* to help them keep track of actual inventory levels and to ensure that inventory levels are adjusted as sales change. *Just-in-time (JIT) systems* are also used to hold down inventory costs and, simultaneously, to improve the production process.

■ The *basic objective* of the credit manager is to increase profitable sales by extending credit to worthy customers and therefore adding value to the firm.

■ When a firm sells goods on credit, an *account receivable* is created.

■ Firms can use *aging schedules* and *days sales outstanding (DSO)* to help monitor their receivables positions and to help avoid increases in bad debts.

■ A firm's *credit policy* consists of four elements: (1) credit period, (2) discounts given for early payment, (3) credit standards, and (4) collection policy. The first two, when combined, are called the *credit terms.*

■ Additional factors that influence a firm's overall credit policy are (1) *profit potential* and (2) *legal considerations.*

As we demonstrated in this chapter, working capital policy involves two basic issues. The first, determining the appropriate level for each current asset, was addressed in this chapter. The second, how current assets should be financed, will be taken up in Chapter 21. Then, in Chapter 22, we explore in more depth some special issues in working capital management.

QUESTIONS

20-1   Define each of the following terms:
  a. Working capital; net working capital; working capital policy
  b. Relaxed current asset investment policy; restricted current asset investment policy; moderate current asset investment policy
  c. Transactions balance; compensating balance; precautionary balance; speculative balance

   d. Cash budget; target cash balance
   e. Trade discounts
   f. Synchronized cash flows
   g. Check clearing; net float; disbursement float; collections float
   h. Lockbox plan
   i. Marketable securities
   j. Red-line method; two-bin method; computerized inventory control system
   k. Just-in-time system; out-sourcing
   l. Account receivable; days sales outstanding
   m. Aging schedule
   n. Credit policy; credit period; credit standards; collection policy; credit terms
   o. Cash discounts
   p. Seasonal dating

2. Assuming the firm's sales volume remained constant, would you expect it to have a higher cash balance during a tight-money period or during an easy-money period? Why?

3. What are the two principal reasons for holding cash? Can a firm estimate its target cash balance by summing the cash held to satisfy each of the two?

4. Explain how each of the following factors would probably affect a firm's target cash balance if all other factors were held constant.
   a. The firm institutes a new billing procedure which better synchronizes its cash inflows and outflows.
   b. The firm develops a new sales forecasting technique which improves its forecasts.
   c. The firm reduces its portfolio of U.S. Treasury bills.
   d. The firm arranges to use an overdraft system for its checking account.
   e. The firm borrows a large amount of money from its bank and also begins to write far more checks than it did in the past.
   f. Interest rates on Treasury bills rise from 5 percent to 10 percent.

5. Why would a lockbox plan make more sense for a firm that makes sales all over the United States than for a firm with the same volume of business but concentrated in its home city?

6. Is it true that when one firm sells to another on credit, the seller records the transaction as an account receivable while the buyer records it as an account payable and that, disregarding discounts, the receivable typically exceeds the payable by the amount of profit on the sale?

7. What are the four elements of a firm's credit policy? To what extent can firms set their own credit policies as opposed to having to accept policies that are dictated by "the competition"?

8. Suppose that a firm makes a purchase and receives the shipment on February 1. The terms of trade as stated on the invoice read "2/10, net 40, May 1 dating." What is the latest date on which payment can be made and the discount still be taken? What is the date on which payment must be made if the discount is not taken?

9. a. What is the days sales outstanding (DSO) for a firm whose sales are $2,880,000 per year and whose accounts receivable are $312,000? (Use 360 days per year.)
   b. Is it true that if this firm sells on terms of 3/10, net 40, its customers probably all pay on time?

10. Is it true that if a firm calculates its days sales outstanding, it has no need for an aging schedule?

11. Firm A had no credit losses last year, but 1 percent of Firm B's accounts receivable proved to be uncollectible and resulted in losses. Should Firm B fire its credit manager and hire A's?

12. Indicate by a (+), (−), or (0) whether each of the following events would probably cause accounts receivable (A/R), sales, and profits to increase, decrease, or be affected in an indeterminant manner:

	A/R	SALES	PROFITS
The firm tightens its credit standards.	_____	_____	_____
The terms of trade are changed from 2/10, net 30, to 3/10, net 30.	_____	_____	_____
The terms are changed from 2/10, net 30, to 3/10, net 40.	_____	_____	_____
The credit manager gets tough with past-due accounts.	_____	_____	_____

20-13   A firm can reduce its investment in inventory by having its suppliers hold raw materials inventory and its customers hold finished goods inventory. Explain actions a firm can take which would result in larger inventory for its suppliers and customers and smaller inventory for itself. What are the limitations of such actions?

SELF-TEST PROBLEMS

(SOLUTIONS APPEAR IN APPENDIX C)

ST-1   **WORKING CAPITAL POLICY** The Calgary Company is attempting to establish a current assets policy. Fixed assets are $600,000, and the firm plans to maintain a 50 percent debt-to-assets ratio. The interest rate is 10 percent on all debt. Three alternative current asset policies are under consideration: 40, 50, and 60 percent of projected sales. The company expects to earn 15 percent before interest and taxes on sales of $3 million. Calgary's effective federal-plus-state tax rate is 40 percent. What is the expected return on equity under each alternative?

ST-2   **FLOAT** The Upton Company is setting up a new checking account with Howe National Bank. Upton plans to issue checks in the amount of $1 million each day and to deduct them from its own records at the close of business on the day they are written. On average, the bank will receive and clear the checks at 5 P.M. the third day after they are written; for example, a check written on Monday will be cleared on Thursday afternoon. The firm's agreement with the bank requires it to maintain a $500,000 average compensating balance; this is $250,000 greater than the cash balance the firm would otherwise have on deposit. It makes a $500,000 deposit at the time it opens the account.

a. Assuming that the firm makes deposits at 4 P.M. each day (and the bank includes them in that day's transactions), how much must it deposit daily in order to maintain a sufficient balance once it reaches a steady state? Indicate the required deposit on Day 1, Day 2, Day 3, if any, and each day thereafter, assuming that the company will write checks for $1 million on Day 1 and each day thereafter.

b. How many days of float does Upton have?

c. What ending daily balance should the firm try to maintain (1) on the bank's records and (2) on its own records?

WORKING CAPITAL POLICY The Rentz Corporation is attempting to determine the optimal level of current assets for the coming year. Management expects sales to increase to approximately $2 million as a result of an asset expansion presently being undertaken. Fixed assets total $1 million, and the firm wishes to maintain a 60 percent debt ratio. Rentz's interest cost is currently 8 percent on both short-term and longer-term debt (which the firm uses in its permanent structure). Three alternatives regarding the projected current asset level are available to the firm: (1) a tight policy requiring current assets of only 45 percent of projected sales, (2) a moderate policy of 50 percent of sales in current assets, and (3) a relaxed policy requiring current assets of 60 percent of sales. The firm expects to generate earnings before interest and taxes at a rate of 12 percent on total sales.

a. What is the expected return on equity under each current asset level? (Assume a 40 percent effective federal-plus-state tax rate.)

b. In this problem, we have assumed that the level of expected sales is independent of current asset policy. Is this a valid assumption?

c. How would the overall riskiness of the firm vary under each policy?

NET FLOAT The Stendardi-Stephens Company (SSC) is setting up a new checking account with National Bank. SSC plans to issue checks in the amount of $1.6 million each day and to deduct them from its own records at the close of business on the day they are written. On average, the bank will receive and clear (that is, deduct from the firm's bank balance) the checks at 5 P.M. the fourth day after they are written; for example, a check written on Monday will be cleared on Friday afternoon. The firm's agreement with the bank requires it to maintain a $1.2 million average compensating balance; this is $400,000 greater than the cash balance the firm would otherwise have on deposit. It makes a $1.2 million deposit at the time it opens the account.

a. Assuming that the firm makes deposits at 4 P.M. each day (and the bank includes them in that day's transactions), how much must it deposit daily in order to maintain a sufficient balance once it reaches a steady state? Indicate the required deposit on Day 1, Day 2, Day 3, Day 4, if any, and each day thereafter, assuming that the company will write checks for $1.6 million on Day 1 and each day thereafter.

b. How many days of float does SSC carry?

c. What ending daily balance should the firm try to maintain (1) on the bank's records and (2) on its own records?

d. Explain how net float can help increase the value of the firm's common stock.

LOCKBOX SYSTEM The Hardin-Gehr Corporation (HGC) began operations 5 years ago as a small firm serving customers in the Detroit area. However, its reputation and market area grew quickly, so that today HGC has customers throughout the entire United States. Despite its broad customer base, HGC has maintained its headquarters in Detroit and keeps its central billing system there. HGC's management is considering an alternative collection procedure to reduce its mail time and processing float. On average, it takes 5 days from the time customers mail payments until HGC is able to receive, process, and deposit them. HGC would like to set up a lockbox collection system, which it estimates would reduce the time lag from customer mailing to deposit by 3 days — bringing it down to 2 days. HGC receives an average of $1,400,000 in payments per day.

a. How many days of collection float now exist (HGC's customers' disbursement float) and what would it be under the lockbox system? What reduction in cash balances could HGC achieve by initiating the lockbox system?

b. If HGC has an opportunity cost of 10 percent, how much is the lockbox system worth on an annual basis?

c. What is the maximum monthly charge HGC should pay for the lockbox system?

20-4   **CASH BUDGETING**   Dorothy Koehl recently leased space in the Southside Mall and opened a new business, Koehl's Doll Shop. Business has been good, but Koehl has frequently run out of cash. This has necessitated late payment on certain orders, which, in turn, is beginning to cause a problem with suppliers. Koehl plans to borrow from the bank to have cash ready as needed, but first she needs a forecast of just how much she must borrow. Accordingly, she has asked you to prepare a cash budget for the critical period around Christmas, when needs will be especially high.

Sales are made on a cash basis only. Koehl's purchases must be paid for during the following month. Koehl pays herself a salary of $4,800 per month, and the rent is $2,000 per month. In addition, she must make a tax payment of $12,000 in December. The current cash on hand (on December 1) is $400, but Koehl has agreed to maintain an average bank balance of $6,000 — this is her target cash balance. (Disregard till cash, which is insignificant because Koehl keeps only a small amount on hand in order to lessen the chances of robbery.)

The estimated sales and purchases for December, January, and February are shown below. Purchases during November amounted to $140,000.

	SALES	PURCHASES
December	$160,000	$40,000
January	40,000	40,000
February	60,000	40,000

a. Prepare a cash budget for December, January, and February.

b. Now, suppose Koehl were to start selling on a credit basis on December 1, giving customers 30 days to pay. All customers accept these terms, and all other facts in the problem are unchanged. What would the company's loan requirements be at the end of December in this case? (Hint: The calculations required to answer this question are minimal.)

20-5   **CASH BUDGETING**   Helen Bowers, owner of Helen's Fashion Designs, is planning to request a line of credit from her bank. She has estimated the following sales forecasts for the firm for parts of 1997 and 1998:

May 1997	$180,000
June	180,000
July	360,000
August	540,000
September	720,000
October	360,000
November	360,000
December	90,000
January 1998	180,000

Collection estimates obtained from the credit and collection department are as follows: collections within the month of sale, 10 percent; collections the month following the sale, 75 percent; collections the second month following the sale, 15 percent. Payments for labor and raw materials are typically made during the month following the one in which these costs have been incurred. Total labor and raw materials costs are estimated for each month as follows:

May 1997	$ 90,000
June	90,000
July	126,000
August	882,000
September	306,000
October	234,000
November	162,000
December	90,000

General and administrative salaries will amount to approximately $27,000 a month; lease payments under long-term lease contracts will be $9,000 a month; depreciation charges will be $36,000 a month; miscellaneous expenses will be $2,700 a month; income tax payments of $63,000 will be due in both September and December; and a progress payment of $180,000 on a new design studio must be paid in October. Cash on hand on July 1 will amount to $132,000, and a minimum cash balance of $90,000 will be maintained throughout the cash budget period.

a. Prepare a monthly cash budget for the last 6 months of 1997.

b. Prepare an estimate of the required financing (or excess funds) — that is, the amount of money Bowers will need to borrow (or will have available to invest) — for each month during that period.

c. Assume that receipts from sales come in uniformly during the month (that is, cash receipts come in at the rate of $\frac{1}{30}$ each day), but all outflows are paid on the fifth of the month. Will this have an effect on the cash budget — in other words, would the cash budget you have prepared be valid under these assumptions? If not, what can be done to make a valid estimate of peak financing requirements? No calculations are required, although calculations can be used to illustrate the effects.

d. Bowers produces on a seasonal basis, just ahead of sales. Without making any calculations, discuss how the company's current ratio and debt ratio would vary during the year assuming all financial requirements were met by short-term bank loans. Could changes in these ratios affect the firm's ability to obtain bank credit?

LOCKBOX SYSTEM I. Malitz and Associates Inc. operates a mail-order firm doing business on the West Coast. Malitz receives an average of $325,000 in payments per day. On average, it takes 4 days from the time customers mail checks until Malitz receives and processes them. Malitz is considering the use of a lockbox system to reduce collection and processing float. The system will cost $6,500 per month and will consist of 10 local depository banks and a concentration bank located in San Francisco. Under this system, customers' checks should be received at the lockbox locations 1 day after they are mailed, and daily totals will be transferred to San Francisco using wire transfers costing $9.75 each. Assume that Malitz has an opportunity cost of 10 percent and that there are $52 \times 5 = 260$ working days, hence 260 transfers from each lockbox location, in a year.

a. What is the total annual cost of operating the lockbox system?

b. What is the benefit of the lockbox system to Malitz?

c. Should Malitz initiate the system?

20-7　RECEIVABLES MANAGEMENT McDowell Industries sells on terms of 3/10, net 30. Total sales for the year are $900,000. Forty percent of the customers pay on the 10th day and take discounts; the other 60 percent pay, on average, 40 days after their purchases.

a. What is the days sales outstanding?

b. What is the average amount of receivables?

c. What would happen to average receivables if McDowell toughened up on its collection policy with the result that all nondiscount customers paid on the 30th day?

SPREADSHEET APPLICATIONS

SPREADSHEET PROBLEM

a. Refer back to Problem 20-5. Suppose that by offering a 2 percent cash discount for paying within the month of sale, the credit manager of Helen's Fashion Designs has revised the collection percentages to 50 percent, 35 percent, and 15 percent, respectively. How will this affect the loan requirements?

b. Return the payment percentages to their base-case values: 10 percent, 75 percent, and 15 percent, respectively, and the discount to zero percent. Now suppose sales fall to only 70 percent of the forecasted level. Production is maintained, so cash outflows are unchanged. How does this affect Bowers's financial requirements?

c. Return sales to the forecasted level (100%), and suppose collections slow down to 3 percent, 10 percent, and 87 percent for the 3 months, respectively. How does this affect financial requirements? If Bowers went to a cash-only sales policy, how would that affect requirements, other things held constant?

SPREADSHEET EXERCISE: LOOKUP FUNCTIONS

The spreadsheet model for this exercise is not directly related to the Mini Case. Rather, the model contains a hypothetical tax rate table that students can use to learn about lookup functions.

1. Retrieve the model (Filename SE-20.WK1) from the models diskette. Cells A8.C14 contain the tax table, while Cells F8.F15 contain the tax and income calculation. Note that salary, bonus, and deductions are inputs.

2. The problem facing you is how to get the appropriate tax rate from the tax table into the income calculation.

3. To begin, note that it is first necessary to match the taxable income in Cell F12 to the appropriate row in the tax table. Once this is done, the tax on the base amount and marginal tax rate can be determined. You will use a Lookup function to make the match. There are two Lookup functions: @VLOOKUP is used for a table that has been set up vertically and @HLOOKUP is used for a table that has been set up horizontally. Since the tax table has been set up vertically, you will use the @VLOOKUP function, which has this format:

@VLOOKUP(Test value, Table range, Column number).

Here, the test value is the entry value for the table lookup, in this case taxable income in Cell F12; the table range is the range of the table, A8.C14; and the column number designates how many columns from the left-hand column to move to pick up the value that is inserted into the cell containing the lookup function.

4. Move the cursor to Cell C16. The appropriate entry for this cell is

$$@VLOOKUP(F12,A8.C14,1).$$

Enter this function and the cell should display $17,750, which is the base tax amount for $105,000 of taxable income. Here is how the VLOOKUP function works. The first column of the lookup table is called the "comparison column," and it must be arranged in ascending order. The VLOOKUP function moves down the left-most column of the table range until it finds a value that exceeds the test value, then it backs up one row. Thus, the VLOOKUP ends up on the $100,000 row. The value returned to Cell C16 is the value one column over, or $17,750 from the Tax Amount on Base column.

5. Move the cursor to Cell C18 and enter the appropriate VLOOKUP function. Note that you are doing the same thing here, except you want to return the marginal tax rate, which is two columns from the comparison column.

6. The model is now complete. Enter different amounts for salary, bonus, and deductions to see how the taxes calculated change with these input values. Also, look at the formula in Cell F13. It has a long nested @If statement to calculate taxes. The nested @If statement is necessary because the amount of income above the base level must be multiplied by the marginal tax rate, so it is necessary to identify the relevant base income.

MINI CASE

Dan Barnes, financial manager of Ski Equipment Inc. (SKI), is excited, but apprehensive. The company's founder recently sold his 51 percent controlling block of stock to Kent Koren, who is a big fan of EVA (Economic Value Added). EVA is found by taking the after-tax operating profit and then subtracting the dollar cost of all the capital the firm uses:

$$EVA = Sales\ revenues - Operating\ costs - Taxes - Capital\ costs$$
$$= Sales - Operating\ costs - Taxes - WACC\ (Capital\ employed).$$

If EVA is positive, then the firm is creating value. On the other hand, if EVA is negative, the firm is not covering its cost of capital, and stockholders' value is being eroded. Koren rewards managers handsomely if they create value, but those whose operations produce negative EVAs are soon looking for work. Koren frequently points out that if a company can generate its current level of sales with less assets, it would need less capital. That would, other things held constant, lower capital costs and increase its EVA.

Shortly after he took control of SKI, Kent Koren met with SKI's senior executives to tell them of his plans for the company. First, he presented some EVA data which convinced everyone that SKI had not been creating value in recent years. He then stated, in no uncertain terms, that this situation must change. He noted that SKI's designs of skis, boots, and clothing are acclaimed throughout the industry, but something is seriously amiss elsewhere in the company. Costs are too high, prices are too low, or the company employs too much capital, and he wants SKI's managers to correct the problem or else.

Barnes has long felt that SKI's working capital situation should be studied — the company may have the optimal amounts of cash, securities, receivables, and inventories, but it may also have too much or too little of these items. In the past, the production manager resisted Dan's efforts to question his holdings of raw materials inventories, the marketing manager resisted questions about finished goods, the sales staff resisted questions about credit policy (which affects accounts receivable), and the treasurer did not want to talk about her cash and securities balances. Koren's speech made it clear that such resistance would no longer be tolerated.

Dan also knows that decisions about working capital cannot be made in a vacuum. For example, if inventories could be lowered without adversely affecting operations, then less capital would be required, the dollar cost of capital would decline, and EVA would increase. However, lower raw materials inventories might lead to production slowdowns and higher costs, while lower finished goods inventories might lead to the loss of profitable sales. So, before inventories are changed, it will be necessary to study operating as well as financial effects. The situation is the same with regard to cash and receivables.

a. Dan plans to use the ratios in Table MC20-1 as the starting point for discussions with SKI's operating executives. He wants everyone to think about the pros and cons of changing each type of current asset and how changes would interact to affect profits and EVA. Based on the Table MC20-1 data, does SKI seem to be following a conservative, moderate, or aggressive working capital policy?

b. How can one distinguish between a conservative but rational working capital policy and a situation where a firm simply has a lot of current assets because it is inefficient? Does SKI's working capital policy seem appropriate?

c. What might SKI do to reduce its cash and securities without harming operations?

d. What is "float," and how is it affected by the firm's cash manager (treasurer)?

In an attempt to better understand SKI's cash position, Dan developed a cash budget. Data for the first two months of the year are shown in Table MC20-2. (Note that Dan's preliminary cash budget does not account for interest income or interest expense.) He has the figures for the other months, but they are not shown in Table MC20-2.

e. Should depreciation expense be explicitly included in the cash budget? Why or why not?

TABLE MC20-1	SELECTED RATIOS: SKI AND INDUSTRY AVERAGE		
		SKI	INDUSTRY
	Current	1.75	2.25
	Quick	0.83	1.20
	Debt/assets	58.76%	50.00%
	Turnover of cash and securities	16.67	22.22
	Days sales outstanding	45.00	32.00
	Inventory turnover	4.82	7.00
	Fixed assets turnover	11.35	12.00
	Total assets turnover	2.08	3.00
	Profit margin on sales	2.07%	3.50%
	Return on equity (ROE)	10.45%	21.00%

		SKI's CASH BUDGET FOR JANUARY AND FEBRUARY				TABLE MC20-2

	NOV	DEC	JAN	FEB	MAR	APR
I. COLLECTIONS AND PURCHASES WORKSHEET						
(1) Sales (gross)	$71,218	$68,212	$65,213	$52,475	$42,909	$30,524
COLLECTIONS						
(2) During month of sale (0.2) (0.98)(month's sales)			$12,781.75	$10,285.10		
(3) During first month after sale (0.7)(previous month's sales)			47,748.40	45,649.10		
(4) During second month after sale (0.1)(sales 2 months ago)			7,121.80	6,821.20		
(5) Total collections (Lines 2 + 3 + 4)			$67,651.95	$62,755.40		
PURCHASES						
(6) (0.85)(forecasted sales 2 months from now)		$44,603.75	$36,472.65	$25,945.40		
(7) Payments (1-month lag)			$44,603.75	$36,472.65		
II. CASH GAIN OR LOSS FOR MONTH						
(8) Collections (from Section I)			$67,651.95	$62,755.40		
(9) Payments for purchases (from Section I)			$44,603.75	$36,472.65		
(10) Wages and salaries			6,690.56	5,470.90		
(11) Rent			2,500.00	2,500.00		
(12) Taxes						
(13) Total payments			$53,794.31	$44,443.55		
(14) Net cash gain (loss) during month (Line 8 − Line 13)			$13,857.64	$18,311.85		
III. CASH SURPLUS OR LOAN REQUIREMENT						
(15) Cash at beginning of month if no borrowing is done			$3,000.00	$16,857.64		
(16) Cumulative cash (cash at start, + gain or − loss = Line 14 + Line 15)			$16,857.64	$35,169.49		
(17) Target cash balance			1,500.00	1,500.00		
(18) Cumulative surplus cash or loans outstanding to maintain $1,500 target cash balance (Line 16 − Line 17)			$15,357.64	$33,669.49		

f. In his preliminary cash budget, Dan has assumed that all sales are collected and, thus, that SKI has no bad debts. Is this realistic? If not, how would bad debts be dealt with in a cash budgeting sense? (Hint: Bad debts will affect collections but not purchases.)

g. Dan's cash budget for the entire year, although not given here, is based heavily on his forecast for monthly sales. Sales are expected to be extremely low between May and September but then increase dramatically in the fall and winter. November is typically the firm's best month, when SKI ships equipment to retailers for the holiday season. Interestingly, Dan's forecasted cash budget indicates that the company's cash holdings will exceed the targeted cash balance every month except for October and November, when shipments will be high but collections will not be coming in until later. Based on the ratios in Table MC20-1, does it appear that SKI's target cash balance is appropriate? In addition to possibly lowering the target cash balance, what actions might SKI take to better improve its cash management policies, and how might that affect its EVA?

h. What reasons might SKI have for maintaining a relatively high amount of cash?

i. What are the three categories of inventory costs? If the company takes steps to reduce its inventory, what effect would this have on the various costs of holding inventory?

j. Is there any reason to think that SKI may be holding too much inventory? If so, how would that affect EVA and ROE?

k. If the company reduces its inventory without adversely affecting sales, what effect should this have on the company's cash position (1) in the short run and (2) in the long run? Explain in terms of the cash budget and the balance sheet.

l. Dan knows that SKI sells on the same credit terms as other firms in its industry. Use the ratios presented in Table MC20-1 to explain whether SKI's customers pay more or less promptly than those of its competitors. If there are differences, does that suggest that SKI should tighten or loosen its credit policy? What four variables make up a firm's credit policy, and in what direction should each be changed by SKI?

m. Does SKI face any risks if it tightens its credit policy?

n. If the company reduces its DSO without seriously affecting sales, what effect would this have on its cash position (1) in the short run and (2) in the long run? Answer in terms of the cash budget and the balance sheet. What effect should this have on EVA in the long run?

SELECTED ADDITIONAL REFERENCES AND CASES

The following books focus on short-term financial management:

Gallinger, George W., and P. Basil Healy, *Liquidity Analysis and Management* (Reading, Mass.: Addison-Wesley, 1991).

Hill, Ned C., and William L. Sartoris, *Short-Term Financial Management* (New York: Prentice-Hall, 1995).

Maness, Terry S., and John T. Zietlow, *Short-Term Financial Management: Text, Cases, and Readings* (Minneapolis/St. Paul: West, 1993).

The following articles provide more information on short-term financial management:

Gentry, James A., "State of the Art of Short-Run Financial Management," *Financial Management,* Summer 1988, 41–57.

Gentry, James A., and Jesus M. De La Garza, "Monitoring Accounts Payables," *Financial Review*, November 1990, 559-576.

Gentry, James A., R. Vaidyanathan, and Hei Wai Lee, "A Weighted Cash Conversion Cycle," *Financial Management*, Spring 1990, 90-99.

Lambrix, R. J., and S. S. Singhvi, "Managing the Working Capital Cycle," *Financial Executive*, June 1979, 32-41.

Maier, Steven F., and James H. Vander Weide, "A Practical Approach to Short-Run Financial Planning," *Financial Management*, Winter 1978, 10-16.

Merville, Larry J., and Lee A. Tavis, "Optimal Working Capital Policies: A Chance-Constrained Programming Approach," *Journal of Financial and Quantitative Analysis*, January 1973, 47-60.

Mitchell, Karlyn, "The Debt Maturity Choice: An Empirical Investigation," *Journal of Financial Research*, Winter 1993, 309-320.

Smith, Keith V., and Brian Belt, "Working Capital Management in Practice: An Update," Krannert Graduate School of Management Working Paper Number 951, March 1989.

Yardini, Edward E., "A Portfolio-Balance Model of Corporate Working Capital," *Journal of Finance*, May 1979, 535-552.

Perhaps the best way to get a good feel for the current state of the art in cash management is to look through recent issues of The Journal of Cash Management, *a relatively new publication aimed at professionals in the field.*

For more information on transfer systems, see

Summers, Bruce J., "Clearing and Payment Systems: The Role of the Central Bank," *Federal Reserve Bulletin*, February 1991, 81-91.

Wood, John C., and Dolores D. Smith, "Electronic Transfer of Government Benefits," *Federal Reserve Bulletin*, April 1991, 204-207.

For more information on float management, see

Batlin, C. A., and Susan Hinko, "Lockbox Management and Value Maximization," *Financial Management*, Winter 1981, 39-44.

Gitman, Lawrence J., D. Keith Forrester, and John R. Forrester, Jr., "Maximizing Cash Disbursement Float," *Financial Management*, Summer 1976, 32-41.

Nauss, Robert M., and Robert E. Markland, "Solving Lockbox Location Problems," *Financial Management*, Spring 1979, 21-31.

The following articles provide more information on cash concentration systems:

Stone, Bernell K., and Ned C. Hill, "Cash Transfer Scheduling for Efficient Cash Concentration," *Financial Management*, Autumn 1980, 35-43.

_____, "The Design of a Cash Concentration System," *Journal of Financial and Quantitative Analysis*, September 1981, 301-322.

Stone, Bernell K., and Tom W. Miller, "Daily Cash Forecasting with Multiplicative Models of Cash Flow Patterns," *Financial Management*, Winter 1987, 45-54.

For greater insights into compensating balance requirements, see

Campbell, Tim S., and Leland Brendsel, "The Impact of Compensating Balance Requirements on the Cash Balances of Manufacturing Corporations," *Journal of Finance*, March 1977, 31-40.

Frost, Peter A., "Banking Services, Minimum Cash Balances, and the Firm's Demand for Money," *Journal of Finance,* December 1970, 1029-1039.

For more information on marketable securities, see

Brown, Keith C., and Scott L. Lummer, "A Reexamination of the Covered Call Option Strategy for Corporate Cash Management," *Financial Management,* Summer 1986, 13-17.

Kamath, Ravindra R., et al., "Management of Excess Cash: Practices and Developments," *Financial Management,* Autumn 1985, 70-77.

Stigum, M., *The Money Market: Myth, Reality, and Practice* (Homewood, Ill.: Dow Jones-Irwin, 1978).

Van Horne, J. C., *Financial Market Rates and Flows* (Englewood Cliffs, N.J.: Prentice-Hall, 1984).

Zivney, Terry L., and Michael J. Alderson, "Hedged Dividend Capture with Stock Index Options," *Financial Management,* Summer 1986, 5-12.

The following articles and books provide additional insights into the problems of inventory management:

Arvan, L., and L. N. Moses, "Inventory Management and the Theory of the Firm," *American Economic Review,* March 1982, 186-193.

Bierman, H., Jr., C. P. Bonini, and W. H. Hausman, *Quantitative Analysis for Business Decisions* (Homewood, Ill.: Irwin, 1977).

Brooks, L. D., "Risk-Return Criteria and Optimal Inventory Stocks," *Engineering Economist,* Summer 1980, 275-299.

Followill, Richard A., Michael Schellenger, and Patrick H. Marchand, "Economic Order Quanties, Volume Discounts, and Wealth Maximization," *The Financial Review,* February 1990, 143-152.

Kallberg, Jarl G., and Kenneth L. Parkinson, *Current Asset Management: Cash, Credit, and Inventory* (New York: Wiley, 1984).

Magee, John F., "Guides to Inventory Policy, I," *Harvard Business Review,* January–February 1956, 49-60.

_____, "Guides to Inventory Policy, II," *Harvard Business Review,* March–April 1956, 103-116.

_____, "Guides to Inventory Policy, III," *Harvard Business Review,* May–June 1956, 57-70.

Mehta, Dileep R., *Working Capital Management* (Englewood Cliffs, N.J.: Prentice-Hall, 1974).

Shapiro, A., "Optimal Inventory and Credit Granting Strategies under Inflation and Devaluation," *Journal of Financial and Quantitative Analysis,* January 1973, 37-46.

Smith, Keith V., *Guide to Working Capital Management* (New York: McGraw-Hill, 1979).

Recent articles which address credit policy and receivables management include the following:

Atkins, Joseph C., and Yong H. Kim, "Comment and Correction: Opportunity Cost in the Evaluation of Investment in Accounts Receivable," *Financial Management,* Winter 1977, 71-74.

Ben-Horim, Moshe, and Haim Levy, "Management of Accounts Receivable under Inflation," *Financial Management,* Spring 1983, 42-48.

Dyl, Edward A., "Another Look at the Evaluation of Interest in Accounts Receivable," *Financial Management,* Winter 1977, 67-70.

Gallinger, George W., and A. James Ifflander, "Monitoring Accounts Receivable Using Variance Analysis," *Financial Management,* Winter 1986, 69–76.

Gentry, James A., and Jesus M. De La Garza, "A Generalized Model for Monitoring Accounts Receivable," *Financial Management,* Winter 1985, 28–38.

Hill, Ned C., and Kenneth D. Riener, "Determining the Cash Discount in the Firm's Credit Policy," *Financial Management,* Spring 1979, 68–73.

Kim, Yong H., and Joseph C. Atkins, "Evaluating Investments in Accounts Receivable: A Wealth Maximizing Framework," *Journal of Finance,* May 1978, 403–412.

Mian, Shehzad L., and Clifford W. Smith, "Extending Trade Credit and Financing Receivables," *Journal of Applied Corporate Finance,* Spring 1994, 75–84.

Oh, John S., "Opportunity Cost in the Evaluation of Investment in Accounts Receivables," *Financial Management,* Summer 1976, 32–36.

Roberts, Gordon S., and Jeremy A. Viscione, "Captive Finance Subsidiaries: The Manager's View," *Financial Management,* Spring 1981, 36–42.

Sachdeva, Kanwal S., and Lawrence J. Gitman, "Accounts Receivable Decisions in a Capital Budgeting Framework," *Financial Management,* Winter 1981, 45–49.

Walia, Tinlochan S., "Explicit and Implicit Cost of Changes in the Level of Accounts Receivable and the Credit Policy Decision of the Firm," *Financial Management,* Winter 1977, 75–78.

Weston, J. Fred, and Pham D. Tuan, "Comment on Analysis of Credit Policy Changes," *Financial Management,* Winter 1980, 59–63.

The following cases from the Cases in Financial Management: Dryden Request *casebook focus on the credit policy decision:*

Case 29, "Office Mates, Inc.," which illustrates how changes in current asset policy affect expected profitability and risk.

Case 32, "Alpine Wear, Inc.," which illustrates the mechanics of the cash budget and the rationale behind its use.

Two new cash budgeting cases, Case 32A, "Toy World, Inc.," and Case 32B, "Sorenson Stove Company," have been added to the Dryden case set.

Case 33, "Upscale Toddlers, Inc.," which deals with credit policy changes.

Case 34, "Texas Rose Company," which focuses on receivables management.

CHAPTER 21

SHORT-TERM FINANCING

*I*n the last chapter we discussed steps Core Industries has taken to improve its working capital management. Core reduced its cash, receivables, and inventories, and, as a result, lowered its operating costs and raised its profits. Even so, Core still has substantial holdings of current assets, and the funds invested in these assets must be obtained from some source. This involves "working capital financing policy," the focus of the current chapter.

Most firms use several types of short-term funds to finance their working capital requirements. Included are bank loans, trade credit, commercial paper, and accruals. Companies structure their current liabilities differently depending on the nature of their business. For example, the sales of Toys 'R' Us are very seasonal — nearly half of its sales occur in the final three months of the year. To meet holiday demands, Toys 'R' Us must dramatically increase its inventories during the summer and early fall. This inventory buildup must be financed until after Christmas, when collections bring cash into the till and debts can be reduced. Toys 'R' Us relies on trade credit, loans from U.S. and foreign banks, and commercial paper, and it obtains additional cash by selling off marketable securities built up during the prior year.

Short-term credit is generally cheaper than long-term capital, and it is easier to obtain. However, it is a riskier, less dependable source of financing. Interest rates can increase dramatically, and changes in a company's financial position can affect both the cost and availability of short-term credit.

In recent years, Core Industries has financed its working capital very conservatively. It uses trade credit and accruals because such credit is essentially free, but it has virtually no short-term bank debt. The company was able to pay off its bank debt as a result of its reduction of receivables and inventories, which freed up cash. Currently, Core is highly liquid, and it is in a good position to finance internal growth, to acquire other companies, or both.

After you have completed this chapter, you will have a better understanding of the various ways corporations can finance their current assets, and of the costs associated with each type of financing.

In the previous chapter, we discussed the first step in working capital management — determining the optimal level for each type of current asset. Now we turn to the second step — financing current assets. We begin with a discussion of alternative financing policies.

ALTERNATIVE CURRENT ASSET FINANCING POLICIES

Most businesses experience seasonal and/or cyclical fluctuations. For example, construction firms peak in the spring and summer, retailers peak around Christmas, and the manufacturers who supply both construction companies and retailers follow similar patterns. Similarly, virtually all businesses must build up current assets when the economy is strong, but they sell off inventories and reduce receivables when the economy slacks off. Still, current assets rarely drop to zero, and this has led to the idea of *permanent current assets,* which are the current assets on hand at the low point of the cycle. Then, as sales increase during the upswing, current assets must likewise increase, and these additional current assets are defined as *temporary current assets.* The manner in which the permanent and temporary current assets are financed is called the firm's *current asset financing policy.*

MODERATE, OR MATURITY MATCHING, APPROACH

The *moderate,* or *maturity matching, approach* calls for matching asset and liability maturities as shown in Panel a of Figure 21-1. This strategy minimizes the risk that the firm will be unable to pay off its maturing obligations. To illustrate, suppose a company borrows on a 1-year basis and uses the funds to build and equip a plant. Cash flows from the plant (profits plus depreciation) would not be sufficient to pay off the loan at the end of only 1 year, so the loan would have to be renewed. If for some reason the lender refused to renew the loan, then the company would have problems. Had the plant been financed with long-term debt, however, the required loan payments would have been better matched with cash flows from profits and depreciation, and the problem of renewal would not have arisen.

At the limit, a firm could attempt to match exactly the maturity structure of its assets and liabilities. Inventory expected to be sold in 30 days could be financed with a 30-day bank loan; a machine expected to last for 5 years could be financed by a 5-year loan; a 20-year building could be financed by a 20-year mortgage bond; and so forth. Actually, of course, two factors prevent this exact maturity matching: (1) there is uncertainty about the lives of assets, and (2) some common equity must be used, and common equity has no maturity. To illustrate the uncertainty factor, a firm might finance inventories with a 30-day loan, expecting to sell the inventories and to use the cash generated to retire the loan. But if sales were

a. Moderate Approach (Maturity Matching)

Dollars

Temporary
Current Assets

Short-Term,
Nonspontaneous Debt
Financing

Temporary
Current Assets

Permanent Level
of Current Assets

Long-Term
Debt plus Equity
plus Spontaneous
Current Liabilities

Total
Permanent
Assets

Fixed Assets

1 2 3 4 5 6 7 8
Time Period

b. Relatively Aggressive Approach

Dollars

Temporary
Current Assets

Short-Term,
Nonspontaneous Debt
Financing

Permanent Level
of Current Assets

Long-Term
Debt plus Equity
plus Spontaneous
Current Liabilities

Fixed Assets

1 2 3 4 5 6 7 8
Time Period

c. Conservative Approach

Short-Term Financing
Requirements

Dollars

Marketable
Securities

Permanent Level
of Current Assets

Long-Term
Debt plus Equity
plus Spontaneous
Current Liabilities

Fixed Assets

1 2 3 4 5 6 7 8
Time Period

slow, the cash would not be forthcoming, and the use of short-term credit could end up causing a problem. Still, if a firm makes an attempt to match asset and liability maturities, we would define this as a moderate current asset financing policy.

AGGRESSIVE APPROACH

Panel b of Figure 21-1 illustrates the situation for a relatively aggressive firm which finances all of its fixed assets with long-term capital and part of its permanent current assets with short-term, nonspontaneous credit. Note that we used the term "relatively" in the title for Panel b because there can be different *degrees* of aggressiveness. For example, the dashed line in Panel b could have been drawn *below* the line designating fixed assets, indicating that all of the permanent current assets and part of the fixed assets were financed with short-term credit; this would be a highly aggressive, extremely nonconservative position, and the firm would be very much subject to dangers from rising interest rates as well as to loan renewal problems. However, short-term debt is often cheaper than long-term debt, and some firms are willing to sacrifice safety for the chance of higher profits.

CONSERVATIVE APPROACH

In Panel c of Figure 21-1, we show the dashed line *above* the line designating permanent current assets, indicating that permanent capital is being used to finance all permanent asset requirements and also to meet some or all of the seasonal needs. In this situation, the firm uses a small amount of short-term, nonspontaneous credit to meet its peak requirements, but it also meets a part of its seasonal needs by "storing liquidity" in the form of marketable securities. The humps above the dashed line represent short-term financing, while the troughs below the dashed line represent short-term security holdings. Panel c represents a very safe, conservative current asset financing policy.

Chrysler, which in early 1996 had more than $7 billion of cash and marketable securities, fits the Panel c pattern. Its chairman, Robert Eaton, stated that these liquid assets will be needed during the next recession, and he cited as evidence the fact that Chrysler had an operating cash deficit of more than $4 billion during the 1991–1992 recession. However, some of Chrysler's stockholders, notably Lee Iacocca and Kirk Kerkorian, argued that only $2 billion was necessary—since Chrysler could borrow funds in the future if need be, the extra $5+ billion should be redeployed to earn more than 3 percent after taxes. This example illustrates the fact that there is no clear, precise answer to the question of how much cash and securities a firm should hold.

SELF-TEST QUESTIONS

What is meant by the term "current asset financing policy"?
What are three alternative current asset financing policies? Is one best?
What is meant by the term "permanent current assets"?
What is meant by the term "temporary current assets"?

ADVANTAGES AND DISADVANTAGES OF SHORT-TERM FINANCING

The three possible financing policies described above were distinguished by the relative amounts of short-term debt used under each policy. The aggressive policy called for the greatest use of short-term debt, while the conservative policy called for the least. Maturity matching fell in between. Although using short-term credit is generally riskier than using long-term credit, short-term credit does have some significant advantages. The pros and cons are considered in this section.

SPEED

A short-term loan can be obtained much faster than long-term credit. Lenders will insist on a more thorough financial examination before extending long-term credit, and the loan agreement will have to be spelled out in considerable detail because a lot can happen during the life of a 10- to 20-year loan. Therefore, if funds are needed in a hurry, the firm should look to the short-term markets.

FLEXIBILITY

If its needs for funds are seasonal or cyclical, a firm may not want to commit itself to long-term debt for three reasons: (1) Flotation costs are generally high when raising long-term debt but trivial for short-term credit. (2) Although long-term debt can be repaid early if the loan agreement includes a prepayment provision, prepayment penalties can be expensive. Accordingly, if a firm thinks its need for funds will diminish in the near future, it should choose short-term debt. (3) Long-term loan agreements always contain provisions, or covenants, which constrain the firm's future actions. Short-term credit agreements are generally much less onerous in this regard.

COST OF LONG-TERM VERSUS SHORT-TERM DEBT

The yield curve is normally upward sloping, indicating that interest rates are normally lower on short-term than on long-term debt. Thus, under normal conditions, the interest rate at the time the funds are obtained will be lower if the firm borrows on a short-term rather than a long-term basis.

RISK OF LONG-TERM VERSUS SHORT-TERM DEBT

Even though short-term debt is often less expensive than long-term debt, short-term credit is riskier to the borrower for two reasons: (1) If a firm borrows on a long-term basis, its interest costs will be relatively stable over time, but if it uses short-term credit, its interest expense will fluctuate widely, at times going quite high. For example, the rate banks charge large corporations for short-term debt more than tripled over a two-year period in the 1980s, rising from 6.25 to 21 percent. Many firms that had borrowed heavily on a short-term basis simply could not meet their rising interest costs, and, as a result, bankruptcies hit record levels. (2) If a firm borrows heavily on a short-term basis, it may find itself unable to repay this debt, and it may be in such a weak financial position that the lender will not extend the loan;

this too could force the firm into bankruptcy. Braniff Airlines, which failed during a credit crunch in the 1980s, is an example.

Another good example of the riskiness of short-term debt is provided by Transamerica Corporation, a major financial services company. Transamerica's chairman, Mr. Beckett, described how his company was moving to reduce its dependency on short-term loans whose costs vary with short-term interest rates. According to Beckett, Transamerica had reduced its variable-rate (short-term) loans by about $450 million over a two-year period after the company's earnings fell sharply when money rates rose to record highs. "We were almost entirely in variable-rate debt," he said, but currently "about 65 percent is fixed rate and 35 percent variable. We've come a long way, and we'll keep plugging away at it." Transamerica's earnings were badly depressed by the increase in short-term rates, but other companies were even less fortunate — they simply could not pay the rising interest charges, and this forced them into bankruptcy.

SELF-TEST QUESTION What are some advantages and disadvantages of short-term debt over long-term debt?

SOURCES OF SHORT-TERM FINANCING

Statements about the flexibility, cost, and riskiness of short-term versus long-term debt depend, to a large extent, on the type of short-term credit that is actually used. There are numerous sources of short-term funds. In the following sections, we describe four major types: (1) accruals, (2) accounts payable (trade credit), (3) bank loans, and (4) commercial paper. In addition, we discuss the cost of bank loans and the factors that influence a firm's choice of a bank.

ACCRUALS

Firms generally pay employees on a weekly, biweekly, or monthly basis, so the balance sheet will typically show some *accrued wages*. Similarly, the firm's own estimated income taxes, the Social Security and income taxes withheld from employee payrolls, and the sales taxes collected are generally paid on a weekly, monthly, or quarterly basis, hence the balance sheet will typically show some *accrued taxes* along with accrued wages. Together, accrued wages and taxes are called *accruals*.

Accruals increase automatically, or spontaneously, as a firm's operations expand. Further, this type of debt is "free" in the sense that no explicit interest is paid on funds raised through accruals. However, a firm cannot ordinarily control its accruals: The timing of wage payments is set by economic forces and industry custom, while tax payment dates are established by law. Thus, firms use all the accruals they can, but they have little control over the levels of these accounts.

SELF-TEST QUESTIONS What types of short-term credit are classified as accruals?
What is the cost of accruals?
How much control do financial managers have over the dollar amount of accruals?

ACCOUNTS PAYABLE (TRADE CREDIT)

Firms generally make purchases from other firms on credit, recording the debt as an *account payable*. Accounts payable, or *trade credit,* is the largest single category of short-term debt, representing about 40 percent of the current liabilities of the average nonfinancial corporation. The percentage is somewhat larger for smaller firms: Because small companies often do not qualify for financing from other sources, they rely especially heavily on trade credit.[1]

Trade credit is a spontaneous source of financing in the sense that it arises from ordinary business transactions. For example, suppose a firm makes average purchases of $2,000 a day on terms of net 30, meaning that it must pay for goods 30 days after the invoice date. On average, it will owe 30 times $2,000, or $60,000, to its suppliers. If its sales, and consequently its purchases, were to double, then its accounts payable would also double, to $120,000. So, simply by growing, the firm would have spontaneously generated an additional $60,000 of financing. Similarly, if the terms under which it bought were extended from 30 to 40 days, its accounts payable would expand from $60,000 to $80,000. Thus, lengthening the credit period, as well as expanding sales and purchases, generates additional financing.

THE COST OF TRADE CREDIT

Firms that sell on credit have a *credit policy* that includes certain *terms of credit.* For example, Microchip Electronics sells on terms of 2/10, net 30, meaning that a 2 percent discount is given if payment is made within 10 days of the invoice date, with the full invoice amount being due and payable within 30 days if the discount is not taken.

Note that the true price of Microchip's products is the net price, or 0.98 times the list price, because any customer can purchase an item at a 2 percent "discount" as long as the customer pays within 10 days. Now consider Personal Computer Company (PCC), which buys its memory chips from Microchip. One commonly used memory chip is listed at $100, so the "true" price to PCC is $98. Now, if PCC wants an additional 20 days of credit beyond the 10-day discount period, it must incur a finance charge of $2 per chip for that credit. Thus, the $100 list price can be thought of as follows:

List price = $98 true price + $2 finance charge.

The question PCC must ask before it turns down the discount to obtain the additional 20 days of credit from Microchip is whether it could obtain similar credit under better terms from some other lender, say, a bank. In other words, could 20 days of credit be obtained for less than $2 per chip?

---

[1]In a credit sale, the seller records the transaction as a receivable, the buyer as a payable. We examined accounts receivable as an asset investment in Chapter 20. Our focus in this chapter is on accounts payable, a liability item. We might also note that if a firm's accounts payable exceed its receivables, it is said to be *receiving net trade credit,* whereas if its receivables exceed its payables, it is *extending net trade credit.* Smaller firms frequently receive net credit; larger firms generally extend it.

PCC buys an average of $11,760,000 of memory chips from Microchip each year at the net, or true, cost of $11,760,000/360 = $32,666.67 per day. For simplicity, assume that Microchip is PCC's only supplier. If PCC decides not to take the additional trade credit — that is, if it pays on the 10th day and takes the discount — its payables will average 10($32,666.67) = $326,667. Thus, PCC will be receiving $326,667 of credit from its only supplier, Microchip.

Now suppose PCC decides to take the additional 20 days credit and thus must pay the finance charge. Since PCC will now pay on the 30th day, its accounts payable will increase to 30($32,666.67) = $980,000.[2] Microchip will now be supplying PCC with an additional $980,000 − $326,667 = $653,333 of credit, which it could use to build up its cash account, to pay off debt, to expand inventories, or even to extend more credit to its own customers, hence increasing its own receivables.

The additional trade credit has a cost — PCC must pay the finance charge by forgoing the 2 percent discount on its purchases from Microchip. Since PCC buys $11,760,000 of chips at a true price of 0.98(list price), the added finance charge increases the total cost to PCC to $11,760,000/0.98 = $12 million, so the annual financing cost is $12,000,000 − $11,760,000 = $240,000. Dividing the $240,000 financing cost by the $653,333 of additional credit, we find the nominal annual cost rate of the additional trade credit to be 36.7 percent:

$$\text{Nominal annual cost} = \frac{\$240,000}{\$653,333} = 36.7\%.$$

Assuming that PCC can borrow from its bank (or from other sources) at an interest rate less than 36.7 percent, it should take discounts and forgo the additional trade credit.

The following equation can be used to calculate the nominal cost, on an annual basis, of not taking discounts, illustrated with terms of 2/10, net 30:

$$\begin{array}{c}\text{Nominal} \\ \text{annual} \\ \text{cost}\end{array} = \frac{\text{Discount percent}}{100 - \begin{array}{c}\text{Discount} \\ \text{percent}\end{array}} \times \frac{360}{\begin{array}{c}\text{Days credit is} \\ \text{outstanding}\end{array} - \begin{array}{c}\text{Discount} \\ \text{period}\end{array}} \qquad \text{21-1}$$

$$= \frac{2}{98} \times \frac{360}{20} = 2.04\% \times 18 = 36.7\%.$$

---

[2] A question arises here: Should accounts payable reflect gross purchases or purchases net of discounts? Generally accepted accounting principles permit either treatment if the difference is not material, but if the discount is material, then the transaction must be recorded net of discounts, or at "true" prices. Then, the higher payments that result from not taking discounts is reported as an additional expense called "discounts lost." *Thus, we show accounts payable net of discounts even if the company does not expect to take the discount.*

The numerator of the first term, Discount percent, is the cost per dollar of credit, while the denominator, 100 − Discount percent, represents the funds made available by not taking the discount. Thus, the first term, 2.04%, is the periodic cost of the trade credit. The denominator of the second term is the number of days of extra credit obtained by not taking the discount, so the entire second term shows how many times each year the cost is incurred, 18 times in this example.

The nominal annual cost formula does not take account of compounding, and in effective annual interest terms, the cost of trade credit can be much higher. The discount amounts to interest, and with terms of 2/10, net 30, the firm gains use of the funds for 30 − 10 = 20 days, so there are 360/20 = 18 "interest periods" per year. Remember that the first term in Equation 21-1, (Discount percent)/(100 − Discount percent) = 0.02/0.98 = 0.0204, is the periodic interest rate. This rate is paid 18 times each year, so the effective annual cost rate of trade credit is

$$\text{Effective annual rate} = (1.0204)^{18} - 1.0 = 1.439 - 1.0 = 43.9\%.$$

Thus, the 36.7 percent nominal cost calculated with Equation 21-1 understates the true cost of trade credit.

Notice, however, that the cost of trade credit can be reduced by paying late. Thus, if PCC could get away with paying in 60 days rather than in the specified 30 days, then the effective credit period would become 60 − 10 = 50 days, the number of times the discount would be lost would fall to 360/50 = 7.2, and the nominal cost would drop from 36.7 percent to 2.04% × 7.2 = 14.7%. The effective annual rate would drop from 43.9 to 15.7 percent:

$$\text{Effective annual rate} = (1.0204)^{7.2} - 1.0 = 1.157 - 1.0 = 15.7\%.$$

In periods of excess capacity, firms may be able to get away with late payments, but they will also suffer a variety of problems associated with *stretching accounts payable* and being branded a "slow payer." These problems are discussed later in the chapter.

The costs of the additional trade credit under some other credit terms are shown below:

CREDIT TERMS	COST OF ADDITIONAL CREDIT IF THE CASH DISCOUNT IS NOT TAKEN	
	NOMINAL COST	EFFECTIVE COST
1/10, net 20	36.4%	43.6%
1/10, net 30	18.2	19.8
2/10, net 20	73.5	106.9
3/15, net 45	37.1	44.1

As these figures show, the cost of not taking discounts can be substantial. Incidentally, throughout the chapter, we assume that payments are made either on the *last day* for taking discounts or on the *last day* of the credit period, unless otherwise noted. It would be foolish to pay, say, on the fifth day or on the twentieth day if the credit terms were 2/10, net 30.

EFFECTS OF TRADE CREDIT ON THE FINANCIAL STATEMENTS

A firm's policy with regard to taking or not taking discounts can have a significant effect on its financial statements. To illustrate, let us assume that PCC is just beginning its operations. On the first day, it makes net purchases of $32,666.67. This amount is recorded on its balance sheet under accounts payable.[3] The second day it buys another $32,666.67. The first day's purchases are not yet paid for, so at the end of the second day, accounts payable total $65,333.34. Accounts payable increase by another $32,666.67 on the third day, for a total of $98,000, and after 10 days, accounts payable are up to $326,667.

If PCC takes discounts, then on the 11th day it will have to pay for the $32,666.67 of purchases made on the first day, which will reduce accounts payable. However, it will buy another $32,666.67, which will increase payables. Thus, after the 10th day of operations, PCC's balance sheet will level off, showing a balance of $326,667 in accounts payable, assuming it pays on the 10th day in order to take discounts.

Now suppose PCC decides not to take discounts. In this case, on the 11th day it will add another $32,666.67 to payables, but it will not pay for the purchases made on the 1st day. Thus, its accounts payable will rise to 11($32,666.67) = $359,333.37. This buildup will continue through the 30th day, at which point payables will total 30($32,666.67) = $980,000. On the 31st day, PCC will buy another $32,666.67 of goods, which will increase accounts payable, but it will also pay for the purchases made the 1st day, which will reduce payables. Thus, its accounts payable will stabilize at $980,000 after 30 days if it does not take discounts.

The upper section of Table 21-1 shows PCC's balance sheet, after it reaches a steady state, under the two trade credit policies. Total assets are unchanged by this policy decision, and we also assume that the accruals and common equity accounts are unchanged. The differences show up in accounts payable and notes payable; when PCC elects to take discounts and thus gives up some of the trade credit it otherwise could have obtained, it will have to raise $653,333 from some other source. It could have sold more common stock, or it could have used long-term bonds, but it chose to use bank credit, which has a 10 percent cost and is reflected in the notes payable account.

The lower section of Table 21-1 shows PCC's income statements. If the company does not take discounts, then its interest expense will be zero, but it will have a $240,000 expense for discounts lost. If it borrows and takes discounts, it will incur an interest expense of $65,333, but it will avoid the cost of discounts lost. Since discounts lost exceed the interest expense, taking discounts results in a higher net income and, thus, in a higher stock price.

COMPONENTS OF TRADE CREDIT: FREE VERSUS COSTLY

On the basis of the preceding discussion, trade credit can be divided into two components: (1) *free trade credit,* which is the credit received during the discount period and which for PCC amounts to 10 days' net purchases, or $326,667, and (2) *costly*

---

[3]Inventories also increase by $32,666.67, but we are not now concerned with inventories. Again note that both inventories and receivables are recorded net of discounts regardless of whether discounts are taken.

	TAKE DISCOUNTS; BORROW FROM BANK (1)	**DO NOT TAKE DISCOUNTS; USE MAXIMUM TRADE CREDIT** (2)	**DIFFERENCE** (1) − (2)

PCC's FINANCIAL STATEMENTS WITH DIFFERENT TRADE CREDIT POLICIES — **TABLE 21-1**

I. BALANCE SHEETS

	(1)	(2)	(1) − (2)
Cash	$ 500,000	$ 500,000	$ 0
Receivables	1,000,000	1,000,000	0
Inventories	2,000,000	2,000,000	0
Fixed assets	2,980,000	2,980,000	0
Total assets	$ 6,480,000	$ 6,480,000	$ 0
Accounts payable	$ 326,667	$ 980,000	$ −653,333
Notes payable (10%)	653,333	0	+653,333
Accruals	500,000	500,000	0
Common equity	5,000,000	5,000,000	0
Total claims	$ 6,480,000	$ 6,480,000	$ 0

II. INCOME STATEMENTS

	(1)	(2)	(1) − (2)
Sales	$15,000,000	$15,000,000	$0
Less: Purchases	11,760,000	11,760,000	0
Labor	2,000,000	2,000,000	0
Interest	65,333	0	+65,333
Discounts lost	0	240,000	−240,000
Earnings before taxes (EBT)	$ 1,174,667	$ 1,000,000	$ +174,667
Taxes (40%)	469,867	400,000	−69,867
Net income	$ 704,800	$ 600,000	$ +104,800

trade credit, which is the credit in excess of the free trade credit and whose cost is the forgone discounts.[4] PCC could obtain $653,333, or 20 days' net purchases, of non-free trade credit at a nominal cost of 37 percent. *Financial managers should always use the free component, but they should use the costly component only after analyzing the cost of this capital to make sure that it is less than the cost of funds which could be obtained from other sources.* Under the terms of trade found in most industries, the costly component is relatively expensive, so stronger firms will avoid using it.

We noted earlier that firms sometimes can and do deviate from the stated credit terms, thus altering the percentage cost figures cited earlier. For example, a California manufacturing firm that buys on terms of 2/10, net 30, makes a practice of

---

[4]There is some question as to whether any credit is really "free," because the supplier will have a cost of carrying receivables which must be passed on to the customer in the form of higher prices. Still, if suppliers sell on standard terms such as 2/10, net 30, and if the base price cannot be negotiated downward for early payment, then for all intents and purposes the 10 days of trade credit is indeed "free."

paying in 15 days (rather than 10), but it still takes discounts. Its treasurer simply waits until 15 days after receipt of the goods to pay, then writes a check for the invoiced amount less the 2 percent discount. The company's suppliers want its business, so they tolerate this practice. Similarly, a Wisconsin firm that also buys on terms of 2/10, net 30, does not take discounts, but it pays in 60 rather than in 30 days, thus "stretching" its trade credit. As we saw earlier, both practices reduce the calculated cost of trade credit. Neither of these firms is "loved" by its suppliers, and neither could continue these practices in times when suppliers were operating at full capacity and had order backlogs, but these practices can and do reduce the costs of trade credit during times when suppliers have excess capacity.

SELF-TEST QUESTIONS

What is trade credit?

What is the difference between free trade credit and costly trade credit?

What is the formula for finding the nominal annual cost of trade credit? What is the formula for the effective, or equivalent, annual cost rate of trade credit?

How does the cost of costly trade credit generally compare with the cost of short-term bank loans?

SHORT-TERM BANK LOANS

Commercial banks, whose loans appear on firms' balance sheets as notes payable, are second in importance to trade credit as a source of short-term financing.[5] The banks' influence is actually greater than the dollar amounts suggest, because banks provide *nonspontaneous* funds. As a firm's financing needs increase, it requests additional funds from its bank. If the request is denied, the firm may be forced to abandon attractive growth opportunities. The key features of bank loans are discussed in the following paragraphs.

MATURITY

Although banks do make longer-term loans, *the bulk of their lending is on a short-term basis* — about two-thirds of all bank loans mature in a year or less. Bank loans to businesses are frequently written as 90-day notes, so the loan must be repaid or renewed at the end of 90 days. If a borrower's financial position has deteriorated, the bank may well refuse to renew the loan. This can mean serious trouble for the borrower.

PROMISSORY NOTE

When a bank loan is approved, the agreement is executed by signing a *promissory note*. The note specifies (1) the amount borrowed; (2) the percentage interest rate;

---

[5]Although commercial banks remain the primary source of short-term loans, other sources are available. For example, GE Capital Corporation (GECC) had several billion dollars in commercial loans outstanding. Firms such as GECC, which was initially established to finance consumers' purchases of GE's durable goods, often find business loans to be more profitable than consumer loans.

(3) the repayment schedule, which can call for either a lump sum or a series of installments; (4) any collateral that might have to be put up as security for the loan; and (5) any other terms and conditions to which the bank and the borrower have agreed. When the note is signed, the bank credits the borrower's checking account with the funds, so on the borrower's balance sheet, both cash and notes payable increase.

COMPENSATING BALANCES

Banks sometimes require borrowers to maintain an average demand deposit (checking account) balance equal to from 10 to 20 percent of the face amount of the loan. This is called a *compensating balance (CB)*, and such balances raise the effective interest rate on the loans. For example, if a firm needs $80,000 to pay off outstanding obligations, but if it must maintain a 20 percent compensating balance, then it must borrow $100,000 to obtain a usable $80,000. If the stated annual interest rate is 8 percent, the effective cost is actually 10 percent: $8,000 interest divided by $80,000 of usable funds equals 10 percent.[6]

INFORMAL LINE OF CREDIT

A *line of credit* is an informal agreement between a bank and a borrower indicating the maximum credit the bank will extend to the borrower. For example, on December 31, a bank loan officer might indicate to a financial manager that the bank regards the firm as being "good" for up to $80,000 during the forthcoming year, provided the borrower's financial condition does not deteriorate. If on January 10 the financial manager signs a promissory note for $15,000 for 90 days, this would be called "taking down" $15,000 of the total line of credit. This amount would be credited to the firm's checking account at the bank, and before repayment of the $15,000, the firm could borrow additional amounts up to a total of $80,000 outstanding at any one time.

REVOLVING CREDIT AGREEMENT

A *revolving credit agreement* is a formal line of credit. To illustrate, in 1996, Texas Petroleum Company negotiated a revolving credit agreement for $100 million with a group of banks. The banks were formally committed for 4 years to lend the firm up to $100 million if the funds were needed. Texas Petroleum, in turn, paid an annual commitment fee of ¼ of 1 percent on the unused balance of the commitment to compensate the banks for making the commitment. Thus, if Texas Petroleum did not take down any of the $100 million commitment during a year, it would still be required to pay a $250,000 annual fee, normally in monthly installments of $20,833.33. If it borrowed $50 million on the first day of the agreement, the unused

---

[6]Note, however, that the compensating balance may be set as a minimum monthly *average,* and if the firm would maintain this average anyway, the compensating balance requirement would not raise the effective interest rate. Also, note that these *loan* compensating balances are added to any compensating balances that the firm's bank may require for *services performed,* such as clearing checks.

portion of the line of credit would fall to $50 million, and the annual fee would fall to $125,000. Of course, interest would also have to be paid on the money Texas Petroleum actually borrowed. As a general rule, the interest rate on "revolvers" is pegged to the prime rate, the T-bill rate, or some other market rate, so the cost of the loan varies over time as interest rates change.[7] Texas Petroleum's rate was set at prime plus 0.5 percentage points.

Note that a revolving credit agreement is very similar to a line of credit, but with an important difference: The bank has a *legal obligation* to honor a revolving credit agreement, and it may receive a commitment fee. Neither the legal obligation nor the fee exists under the informal line of credit.

SELF-TEST QUESTION : Explain how a firm that expects to need funds during the coming year might make sure the needed funds will be available.

THE COST OF BANK LOANS

The cost of bank loans varies for different types of borrowers at any given point in time and for all borrowers over time. Interest rates are higher for riskier borrowers, and rates are also higher on smaller loans because of the fixed costs involved in making and servicing loans. If a firm can qualify as a "prime credit" because of its size and financial strength, it can borrow at the *prime rate,* which has traditionally been the lowest rate banks charge. Rates on other loans are generally scaled up from the prime rate, but loans to very large, strong customers are made at rates below prime. Thus, loans to smaller, riskier borrowers are generally stated to carry an interest rate of "prime *plus* some number of percentage points," but loans to larger, less risky borrowers may have a rate stated as "prime *minus* some percentage points."

Bank rates vary widely over time depending on economic conditions and Federal Reserve policy. When the economy is weak, then (1) loan demand is usually slack, (2) inflation is low, and (3) the Fed also makes plenty of money available to the system. As a result, rates on all types of loans are relatively low. Conversely, when the economy is booming, loan demand is typically strong, the Fed restricts the money supply, and the result is high interest rates. As an indication of the kinds of fluctuations that can occur, the prime rate during 1980 rose from 11 percent to 21 percent in just four months, and it rose from 6 to 9 percent during 1994. Interest rates on other bank loans also vary, generally moving with the prime rate.

The terms on a short-term bank loan to a business are spelled out in the promissory note. Here are the key elements contained in most promissory notes:

1. **Interest only versus amortized.** Loans are either *interest-only*, meaning that only interest is paid during the life of the loan with the principal amount

---

[7]Each bank sets its own prime rate, but, because of competitive forces, most banks' prime rates are identical. Further, most banks follow the rate set by the large New York City banks.

In recent years many banks have been lending to the very strongest companies at rates below the prime rate. As we discuss later in this chapter, larger firms have ready access to the commercial paper market, and if banks want to do business with large, strong companies, they must match, or at least come close to, the commercial paper rate.

being repaid when the loan matures, or *amortized*, meaning that some principal is repaid on each payment date. Amortized loans are called *installment loans*.

2. **Collateral.** If the loan is secured by some specific collateral, generally accounts receivable or inventories in the case of short-term loans, this fact is indicated in the note. If the collateral is to be kept on the premises of the borrower, then a form called a *UCC-1* (Uniform Commercial Code-1) is filed with the secretary of the state in which the collateral resides, along with a *Security Agreement* (also part of the Uniform Commercial Code) which describes the nature of the agreement. These filings prevent the borrower from using the same collateral to secure loans from different lenders, and they spell out conditions under which the lender can seize the collateral.

3. **Loan guarantees.** If the borrower is a small corporation, its bank will probably insist that the larger stockholders *personally guarantee* the loan. Banks have had many situations in which a troubled company's owner diverted assets from the company business to some other entity he or she owned, so banks protect themselves by insisting on personal guarantees. However, stockholder guarantees are virtually impossible to get in the case of larger corporations with many stockholders. Also, guarantees are unnecessary for proprietorships or partnerships because, with these forms of organization, the owners are personally liable for the business's debts anyway.

4. **Nominal, or stated, interest rate.** The interest rate can be either *fixed* or *floating*. If it floats, it is generally indexed to the bank's prime rate, to the T-bill rate, or to the London Inter-Bank Offer Rate (LIBOR). Most loans of any size ($25,000 and up) have floating rates if their maturities are greater than 90 days. The note will also indicate whether the bank uses a *360-* or *365-day year* for purposes of calculating interest; most banks use a 360-day year.

5. **Frequency of interest payments.** If the note is on an interest-only basis, it will indicate *how frequently interest must be paid*. Interest is typically calculated on a daily basis but paid monthly.

6. **Maturity.** Long-term loans always have specific maturity dates. A short-term loan may or may not have a specified maturity. For example, a loan may mature in 30 days, 90 days, 6 months, or 1 year, or it may call for "payment on demand," in which case the loan can remain outstanding as long as the borrower wants to continue using the funds and the bank agrees. Banks virtually never call demand notes unless the borrower's credit worthiness deteriorates, so some "short-term loans" remain outstanding for years, with the interest rate floating with rates in the economy.

7. **Discount interest.** Most loans call for interest to be paid after it has been earned, but *discount loans* require that interest be paid in advance. If the loan is on a discount basis, the borrower actually receives less than the face amount of the loan, and this increases the loan's effective cost.

8. **Add-on basis installment loans.**   Auto loans and other types of consumer installment loans are generally set up on an "add-on basis," which means that interest charges over the life of the loan are calculated and then added to the face amount of the loan.   Thus, the borrower signs a note for the funds received plus the interest. The add-on feature also raises the effective cost of a loan.

9. **Other cost elements.**   As noted above, some loans require compensating balances, and revolving credit agreements often require commitment fees. Both of these conditions will be spelled out in the loan agreement, and both raise the effective cost of a loan above its stated nominal rate.

REGULAR, OR SIMPLE, INTEREST

In this and the following sections, we explain how to calculate the effective cost of a bank loan.   For illustrative purposes, we assume a loan of $10,000 at a nominal interest rate of 12 percent, with a 365-day year.

For business loans, the most common procedure is called *regular,* or *simple, interest*, based on an interest-only loan. We begin by dividing the nominal interest rate, 12 percent in this case, by 365 (or 360 in some cases) to get the rate per day:

$$\text{Interest rate per day} = \frac{\text{Nominal rate}}{\text{Days in year}} \qquad \text{21-2}$$

$$= 0.12/365 = 0.00032876712.$$

This rate is then multiplied by the actual number of days during the specific payment period, and then times the amount of the loan. For example, if the loan is interest-only, with monthly payments, then the interest payment for January would be $101.92:

$$\text{Interest charge for period} = (\text{Days in period})(\text{Rate per day})(\text{Amount of loan}) \qquad \text{21-3}$$

$$= (31 \text{ days})(0.00032876712)(\$10,000) = \$101.92.$$

If interest were payable quarterly, and if there were 91 days in the particular quarter, then the interest payment would be $299.18. The annual interest would be 365 × 0.00032876712 × $10,000 = $1,200.00. Note that if the bank had based the interest calculation on a 360-day year, as most banks do, the interest charges would have been slightly higher, and the annual charge would have been $1,216.67. Obviously, banks use a 360-day year to boost their earnings.

The effective interest rate on a loan depends on how frequently interest must be paid—the more frequently, the higher the effective rate. We demonstrate this point with two time lines, one for interest paid once a year and one for quarterly payments:

Interest paid annually:

0	0.25	0.5	0.75	1.0
10,000	0	0	0	−1,200.00
				−10,000.00
				−11,200.00

The borrower gets $10,000 at t = 0 and pays $11,200 at t = 1. With a financial calculator, enter N = 1, PV = 10000, PMT = 0, and FV = −11200, and then press I to get the effective cost of the loan, 12 percent. Had the bank used a 360-day year, the effective rate would have been 12.17 percent.

Interest paid quarterly:

0	0.25	0.5	0.75	1.0
10,000	−299.18	−299.18	−302.47	−299.18
				−10,000.00
				−10,299.18

Note that the third quarter has 92 days. We enter the data in the cash flow register of a financial calculator (being sure to use the +/− key to enter −299.18), and we find the periodic rate to be 2.9999 percent. The effective annual rate is 12.55 percent:

$$\text{Effective annual rate, quarterly} = \left(1 + \frac{0.029999}{4}\right)^4 - 1 = 12.55\%.$$

Had the loan called for interest to be paid monthly, the effective rate would have been 12.68 percent, and if interest had been paid daily, the rate would have been 12.75 percent. These rates would be higher if the bank used a 360-day year.

In these examples, we assumed that the loan was written for a period of one year but that interest was paid at various times during the year. The calculated rates would have been exactly the same had the loan been written for periods corresponding to the interest payment periods. In other words, the effective rate on a monthly payment loan would be 12.68 percent regardless of whether it matured after 1 month, 6 months, 1 year, or 10 years.

DISCOUNT INTEREST

In a *discount interest* loan, the bank deducts the interest in advance (*discounts* the loan). Thus, the borrower receives less than the face value of the loan. On a 1-year, $10,000 loan with a 12 percent (nominal) rate, discount basis, the interest is $10,000(0.12) = $1,200, so the borrower obtains the use of only $10,000 − $1,200 = $8,800. If the loan were for less than a year, the interest charge (the discount) would be lower; in our example, it would be $600 if the loan were for 6 months, hence the amount received would be $9,400.

The effective rate on a discount loan is always higher than the rate on an otherwise similar simple interest loan. To illustrate, consider the situation for a discounted 12 percent loan for 1 year:

Discount interest, paid annually:

With a financial calculator, enter N = 1, PV = 8800, PMT = 0, and FV = −10000, and then press I to get the effective cost of the loan, 13.64 percent.[8]

If a discount loan matures in less than a year, say, after one quarter, we have this situation:

Discount interest, one quarter:

```
0                 0.25              0.5               0.75              1.0
├─────────────────┼─────────────────┼─────────────────┼─────────────────┤
10,000          −10,000             0                 0                 0
 −300
 9,700
```

Enter N = 1, PV = 9700, PMT = 0, and FV = −10000, and then press I to find the periodic rate, 3.092784 percent per quarter, which corresponds to an effective annual rate of 12.96 percent. Thus, shortening the period of a discount loan lowers the effective rate of interest. This occurs because there is a delay in paying interest relative to a longer-term discount loan ($300 paid each quarter rather than $1,200 paid up front).

EFFECTS OF COMPENSATING BALANCES

If the bank requires a compensating balance, and if the amount of the required balance exceeds the amount the firm would normally hold on deposit, then the excess must be deducted at t = 0 and then added back when the loan matures. This has the effect of raising the effective rate on the loan. To illustrate, here is the setup for a 1-year discount loan, with a 20 percent compensating balance which the firm would not otherwise hold on deposit:

---

[8]Note that the firm actually receives less than the face amount of the loan:

$$\text{Funds received} = \text{Face amount of loan } (1.0 - \text{Nominal interest rate}).$$

We can solve for the face amount as follows:

$$\text{Face amount of loan} = \frac{\text{Funds received}}{1.0 - \text{Nominal rate (decimal)}}.$$

Therefore, if the borrowing firm actually requires $10,000 of cash, it must borrow $11,363.64:

$$\text{Face value} = \frac{\$10,000}{1.0 - 0.12} = \frac{\$10,000}{0.88} = \$11,363.64.$$

Now, the borrower will receive $11,363.64 − 0.12($11,363.64) = $10,000. Increasing the face value of the loan does not change the effective rate of 13.64 percent on the $10,000 of usable funds.

Discount interest, paid annually, with 20 percent compensating balance:

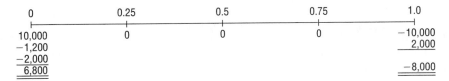

Note that the bank initially gives, and the borrower gets, $10,000 at time 0. However, the bank takes out the $1,200 of interest in advance, and the company must leave $2,000 in the bank as a compensating balance, hence the borrower's effective net cash flow at t = 0 is $6,800. At t = 1, the borrower must repay the $10,000, but $2,000 is already in the bank (the compensating balance), so the company must repay a net amount of $8,000.

With a financial calculator, enter N = 1, PV = 6800, PMT = 0, and FV = –8000, and then press I to get the effective cost of the discount loan with a compensating balance, 17.65 percent.

INSTALLMENT LOANS: ADD-ON INTEREST

Lenders typically charge *add-on interest* on automobile and other types of installment loans. The term "add-on" means that the interest is calculated and then added to the amount received to determine the loan's face value. To illustrate, suppose you borrow $10,000 on an add-on basis at a nominal rate of 12 percent to buy a car, with the loan to be repaid in 12 monthly installments. At a 12 percent add-on rate, you will pay a total interest charge of $10,000(0.12) = $1,200. However, since the loan is paid off in monthly installments, you have the use of the full $10,000 for only the first month, and the outstanding balance declines until, during the last month, only $\frac{1}{12}$ of the original loan will still be outstanding. Thus, you are paying $1,200 for the use of only about half the loan's face amount, as the average usable funds is only about $5,000. Therefore, we can calculate the approximate annual rate as follows:

$$\text{Approximate annual rate}_{\text{Add-on}} = \frac{\text{Interest paid}}{(\text{Amount received})/2} \qquad \boxed{21\text{-}4}$$

$$= \frac{\$1,200}{\$10,000/2} = 24.0\%.$$

To determine the effective rate of an add-on loan, we proceed as follows:

1. The total amount to be repaid is $10,000 of principal, plus $1,200 of interest, or $11,200.

2. The monthly payment is $11,200/12 = $933.33.

3. You are, in effect, paying off a 12-period annuity of $933.33 in order to receive $10,000 today, so $10,000 is the present value of the annuity. Here is the time line:

4. With a financial calculator, enter N = 12, PV = 10000, PMT = −933.33, FV = 0, and then press I to obtain 1.7880%. However, this is a monthly rate.

5. The effective annual rate is found as follows:[9]

$$\text{Effective annual rate}_{\text{Add-on}} = (1 + k_d)^n - 1.0$$
$$= (1.01788)^{12} - 1.0$$
$$= 1.2370 - 1.0 = 23.7\%.$$

The *annual percentage rate (APR),* which by law the bank would be required not only to tell you, because this is a "consumer loan," but also to state in bold print on the loan agreement, would be 21.46 percent:

$$\text{APR rate} = (\text{Periods per year})(\text{Rate per period})$$
$$= 12(1.7880\%) = 21.46\%.$$

Prior to the passage of the truth in lending laws in the 1970s, most banks would have called this a 12 percent loan, period. The truth in lending laws apply primarily to consumer as opposed to business loans.

SELF-TEST QUESTIONS   What are some different ways that banks can calculate interest on loans?
What is a compensating balance? What effect does a compensating balance requirement have on the effective interest rate on a loan?

CHOOSING A BANK

Individuals whose only contact with their bank is through the use of its checking services generally choose a bank for the convenience of its location and the competitive cost of its services. However, a business that borrows from banks must look at other criteria, and a potential borrower seeking a banking relationship should recognize that important differences exist among banks. Some of these differences are considered next.

WILLINGNESS TO ASSUME RISKS

Banks have different basic policies toward risk. Some are inclined to follow relatively conservative lending practices, while others engage in what are properly termed "creative banking practices." These policies reflect partly the personalities of bank officers and partly the characteristics of the bank's deposit liabilities. Thus, a bank with fluctuating deposit liabilities in a static community will tend to be a conservative lender, while a bank whose deposits are growing with little interruption

---

[9]Note that if an installment loan is paid off ahead of schedule, additional complications arise. For a discussion of this point, see Dick Bonker, "The Rule of 78," *Journal of Finance,* June 1976, 877–888.

may follow more liberal credit policies. Similarly, a large bank with broad diversification over geographic regions and across industries can obtain the benefit of combining and averaging risks. Thus, marginal credit risks that might be unacceptable to a small or specialized bank can be pooled by a branch banking system to reduce the overall risk of a group of marginal accounts.[10]

ADVICE AND COUNSEL

Some bank loan officers are active in providing counsel and in stimulating development loans to firms in their early and formative years. Certain banks have specialized departments which make loans to firms expected to grow and thus to become more important customers. The personnel of these departments can provide valuable counseling to customers: The bankers' experience with other firms in growth situations may enable them to spot, and then to warn their customers about, developing problems.

LOYALTY TO CUSTOMERS

Banks differ in their support of borrowers in bad times. This characteristic is referred to as the degree of *loyalty* of the bank. Some banks may put great pressure on a business to liquidate its loans when the firm's outlook becomes clouded, whereas others will stand by the firm and work diligently to help it get back on its feet. An especially dramatic illustration of this point was Bank of America's bailout of Memorex Corporation. The bank could have forced Memorex into bankruptcy, but instead it loaned the company additional capital and helped it survive a bad period. Memorex's stock price subsequently rose on the New York Stock Exchange from $1.50 to $68, so Bank of America's help was indeed beneficial.

SPECIALIZATION

Banks differ greatly in their degrees of loan specialization. Larger banks have separate departments that specialize in different kinds of loans — for example, real estate loans, farm loans, and commercial loans. Within these broad categories, there may be a specialization by line of business, such as steel, machinery, cattle, or textiles. The strengths of banks are also likely to reflect the nature of the business and the economic environment in which they operate. For example, some California banks have become specialists in lending to electronics companies, while many Midwestern banks are agricultural specialists. A sound firm can obtain more creative cooperation and more active support by going to a bank that has experience and familiarity with its particular type of business. Therefore, a bank that is excellent for one firm may be unsatisfactory for another.

---

[10]Bank deposits are insured by a federal agency, and banks are required to pay premiums to cover the cost of this insurance. Logically, riskier banks should pay higher premiums, but to date political forces have limited the use of risk-based insurance premiums. As an alternative, banks with riskier loan portfolios are required to have more equity capital per dollar of deposits than less risky banks. The savings and loan industry, until the 1980s, had federal insurance, no differential capital requirements, and lax regulations. As a result, some S&L operators wrote very high interest rate, but very risky, loans using low-cost, insured deposits. If the loans paid off, the S&L owners would get rich. If they went into default, the taxpayers would have to pay off the deposits. Those government policies ended up costing taxpayers more than $100 billion.

MAXIMUM LOAN SIZE

The size of a bank can be an important factor. Since the maximum loan a bank can make to any one customer is limited to 15 percent of the bank's capital accounts (capital stock plus retained earnings), it is generally not appropriate for large firms to develop borrowing relationships with small banks.

MERCHANT BANKING

The term *merchant bank* was originally applied to banks which not only loaned depositors' money but also provided customers with equity capital and financial advice. Prior to 1933, U.S. commercial banks performed all types of merchant banking functions. However, about one-third of the U.S. banks failed during the Great Depression, in part because of these activities, so in 1933 the Glass-Steagall Act was passed in an effort to reduce banks' exposure to risk. In recent years, commercial banks have been attempting to get back into merchant banking, in part because their foreign competitors offer such services, and U.S. banks need to be able to compete with their foreign counterparts for multinational corporations' business. Currently, the larger banks, often through holding companies, are being permitted to get back into merchant banking, at least to a limited extent. This trend will probably continue, and, if it does, corporations will need to consider a bank's ability to provide a full range of commercial and merchant banking services when choosing a bank.

OTHER SERVICES

Banks can also provide cash management services, assist with electronic funds transfers, help firms obtain foreign exchange, and the like, and the availability of such services should be taken into account when selecting a bank. Also, if the firm is a small business whose manager owns most of its stock, the bank's willingness and ability to provide trust and estate services should be considered as well.

SELF-TEST QUESTION : What are some of the factors that should be considered when choosing a bank?

COMMERCIAL PAPER

Commercial paper is a type of unsecured promissory note issued by large, strong firms and sold primarily to other business firms, to insurance companies, to pension funds, to money market mutual funds, and to banks. Although the amount of commercial paper outstanding is smaller than bank loans outstanding, this form of financing has grown rapidly in recent years. In the fall of 1994, there was approximately $575 billion of commercial paper outstanding, versus about $635 billion of regular business loans.

MATURITY AND COST

Maturities of commercial paper generally vary from one to nine months, with an average of about five months.[11] The interest rate on commercial paper fluctuates with supply and demand conditions — it is determined in the marketplace, varying daily as conditions change. Recently, commercial paper rates have ranged from $1\frac{1}{2}$ to 3 percentage points below the stated prime rate, and about $\frac{1}{8}$ to $\frac{1}{2}$ of a percentage point above the T-bill rate. For example, in May 1996, the average rate on 3-month commercial paper was 5.4 percent, the stated prime rate was 8.25 percent, and the 3-month T-bill rate was about 5.0 percent.

USE OF COMMERCIAL PAPER

The use of commercial paper is restricted to a comparatively small number of very large concerns that are exceptionally good credit risks. Dealers prefer to handle the paper of firms whose net worth is $100 million or more and whose annual borrowing exceeds $10 million. One potential problem with commercial paper is that a debtor who is in temporary financial difficulty may receive little help because commercial paper dealings are generally less personal than are bank relationships. Thus, banks are generally more able and willing to help a good customer weather a temporary storm than is a commercial paper dealer. On the other hand, using commercial paper permits a corporation to tap a wide range of credit sources, including financial institutions outside its own area and industrial corporations across the country, and this can reduce interest costs.

What is commercial paper?

What types of companies can use commercial paper to meet their short-term financing needs?

How does the cost of commercial paper compare with the cost of short-term bank loans? With the cost of Treasury bills?

SELF-TEST
QUESTIONS

USE OF SECURITY IN SHORT-TERM FINANCING

Thus far, we have not addressed the question of whether or not short-term loans should be secured. Commercial paper is never secured, but all other types of loans can be secured if this is deemed necessary or desirable. Given a choice, it is ordinarily better to borrow on an unsecured basis, since the bookkeeping costs of secured loans are often high. However, weak firms may find that they can borrow only if they put up some type of collateral to protect the lender, or that by using security they can borrow at a much lower rate.

Several different kinds of collateral can be employed, including marketable stocks or bonds, land or buildings, equipment, inventory, and accounts receivable. Marketable

---

[11]The maximum maturity without SEC registration is 270 days. Also, commercial paper can only be sold to "sophisticated" investors; otherwise, SEC registration would be required even for maturities of 270 days or less.

securities make excellent collateral, but few firms that need loans also hold portfolios of stocks and bonds. Similarly, real property (land and buildings) and equipment are good forms of collateral, but they are generally used as security for long-term loans rather than for working capital loans. Therefore, most secured short-term business borrowing involves the use of accounts receivable and inventories as collateral.

To understand the use of security, consider the case of a Chicago hardware dealer who wanted to modernize and expand his store. He requested a $200,000 bank loan. After examining his business's financial statements, the bank indicated that it would lend him a maximum of $100,000 and that the interest rate would be 10 percent, discount interest, for an effective rate of 11.1 percent. The owner had a substantial personal portfolio of stocks, and he offered to put up $300,000 of high-quality stocks to support the $200,000 loan. The bank then granted the full $200,000 loan, and at the prime rate of only 8.25 percent, simple interest. The store owner might also have used his inventories or receivables as security for the loan, but processing costs would have been high. Procedures for using accounts receivable and inventories as security for short-term credit are described in Chapter 22.[12]

<table>
<tr><td>SELF-TEST
QUESTIONS</td><td>What is a secured loan?
What are some types of current assets that are pledged as security for short-term loans? ·</td></tr>
</table>

---

[12] The term "asset-based financing" is often used as a synonym for "secured financing." In recent years, accounts receivable have been used as security for long-term bonds, and this permits corporations to borrow from lenders such as pension funds rather than being restricted to banks and other traditional short-term lenders.

SUMMARY

This chapter examined the financing of current assets. The key concepts covered are listed below.

- *Permanent current assets* are those current assets that the firm holds even during slack times, whereas *temporary current assets* are the additional current assets that are needed during seasonal or cyclical peaks. The methods used to finance permanent and temporary current assets define the firm's *current asset financing policy.*

- A *moderate* approach to current asset financing involves matching, to the extent possible, the maturities of assets and liabilities, so that temporary current assets are financed with short-term nonspontaneous debt, and permanent current assets and fixed assets are financed with long-term debt or equity, plus spontaneous debt. Under an *aggressive* approach, some permanent current assets, and perhaps even some fixed assets, are financed with short-term debt. A *conservative* approach would be to use long-term capital to finance all permanent assets and some of the temporary current assets.

■ The advantages of short-term credit are (1) the *speed* with which short-term loans can be arranged, (2) their *flexibility,* and (3) the fact that short-term *interest rates* are generally *lower* than long-term rates. The principal disadvantage of short-term credit is the *extra risk* that the borrower must bear because (1) the lender can demand payment on short notice and (2) the cost of the loan will increase if interest rates rise.

■ *Short-term credit* is defined as any liability originally scheduled for payment within one year. The four major sources of short-term credit are (1) accruals, (2) accounts payable, (3) loans from commercial banks and finance companies, and (4) commercial paper.

■ *Accruals,* which are continually recurring short-term liabilities, represent free, spontaneous credit.

■ *Accounts payable,* or *trade credit,* is the largest category of short-term debt. Trade credit arises spontaneously as a result of credit purchases. Firms should use all the *free trade credit* they can obtain, but they should use *costly trade credit* only if it is less expensive than other forms of short-term debt. Suppliers often offer discounts to customers who pay within a stated discount period. The following equation may be used to calculate the nominal cost, on an annual basis, of not taking discounts:

$$\frac{\text{Nominal}}{\text{cost}} = \frac{\text{Discount percent}}{100 - \frac{\text{Discount}}{\text{percent}}} \times \frac{360}{\frac{\text{Days credit}}{\text{is outstanding}} - \frac{\text{Discount}}{\text{period}}}.$$

■ *Bank loans* are an important source of short-term credit. Interest on bank loans may be quoted as *simple interest, discount interest,* or *add-on interest.* The effective rate on a discount or add-on loan always exceeds the quoted nominal rate.

■ When a bank loan is approved, a *promissory note* is signed. It specifies: (1) the amount borrowed, (2) the percentage interest rate, (3) the repayment schedule, (4) the collateral, and (5) any other conditions to which the parties have agreed.

■ Banks sometimes require borrowers to maintain *compensating balances,* which are deposit requirements set at between 10 and 20 percent of the loan amount. Compensating balances raise the effective interest rate on bank loans.

■ A *line of credit* is an understanding between the bank and the borrower indicating the maximum amount of credit the bank will extend to the borrower.

■ A *revolving credit agreement* is a formal line of credit often used by large firms; it involves a *commitment fee.*

■ *Commercial paper* is unsecured short-term debt issued by large, financially strong corporations. Although the cost of commercial paper is lower than the cost of bank loans, commercial paper's maturity is limited to 270 days, and it can be used only by large firms with exceptionally strong credit ratings.

■ Sometimes a borrower will find that it is necessary to borrow on a *secured basis,* in which case the borrower pledges assets such as real estate, securities, equipment, inventories, or accounts receivable as collateral for the loan.

This concludes our discussion of the basics of working capital management and short-term financing. In Chapter 22, we discuss some elements of working capital management in greater detail.

QUESTIONS

21-1 Define each of the following terms:
   a. Permanent current assets; temporary current assets
   b. Moderate current asset financing policy; aggressive current asset financing policy; conservative current asset financing policy
   c. Maturity matching approach
   d. Accruals
   e. Trade credit; stretching accounts payable; free trade credit; costly trade credit
   f. Promissory note; line of credit; revolving credit agreement
   g. Prime rate
   h. Simple interest; discount interest; add-on interest
   i. Compensating balance (CB)
   j. Commercial paper
   k. Secured loan

21-2 How does the seasonal nature of a firm's sales influence its decision regarding the amount of short-term credit to use in its financial structure?

21-3 What are the advantages of matching the maturities of assets and liabilities? What are the disadvantages?

21-4 From the standpoint of the borrower, is long-term or short-term credit riskier? Explain. Would it ever make sense to borrow on a short-term basis if short-term rates were above long-term rates?

21-5 If long-term credit exposes a borrower to less risk, why would people or firms ever borrow on a short-term basis?

21-6 "Firms can control their accruals within fairly wide limits; depending on the cost of accruals, financing from this source will be increased or decreased." Discuss.

21-7 Is it true that both trade credit and accruals represent a spontaneous source of capital for financing growth? Explain.

21-8 Is it true that most firms are able to obtain some free trade credit and that additional trade credit is often available, but at a cost? Explain.

21-9 The availability of bank credit is often more important to a small firm than to a large one. Why?

21-10 What kinds of firms use commercial paper? Could Mama and Papa Gus's Corner Grocery borrow using this form of credit?

Given that commercial paper interest rates are generally lower than bank loan rates to a given borrower, why might firms which are capable of selling commercial paper also use bank credit?

Suppose a firm can obtain funds by borrowing at the prime rate or by selling commercial paper.

a. If the prime rate is 9 percent, what is a reasonable estimate for the cost of commercial paper?

b. If a substantial cost differential exists, why might a firm like this one actually borrow some of its funds in each market?

SELF-TEST PROBLEM

(SOLUTION APPEARS IN APPENDIX C)

CURRENT ASSET FINANCING Vanderheiden Press Inc. and the Herrenhouse Publishing Company had the following balance sheets as of December 31, 1996 (thousands of dollars):

	VANDERHEIDEN PRESS	HERRENHOUSE PUBLISHING
Current assets	$100,000	$ 80,000
Fixed assets (net)	100,000	120,000
Total assets	$200,000	$200,000
Current liabilities	$ 20,000	$ 80,000
Long-term debt	80,000	20,000
Common stock	50,000	50,000
Retained earnings	50,000	50,000
Total liabilities and equity	$200,000	$200,000

Earnings before interest and taxes for both firms are $30 million, and the effective federal-plus-state tax rate is 40 percent.

a. What is the return on equity for each firm if the interest rate on current liabilities is 10 percent and the rate on long-term debt is 13 percent?

b. Assume that the short-term rate rises to 20 percent. While the rate on new long-term debt rises to 16 percent, the rate on existing long-term debt remains unchanged. What would be the return on equity for Vanderheiden Press and Herrenhouse Publishing under these conditions?

c. Which company is in a riskier position? Why?

PROBLEMS

21-1 **CASH DISCOUNTS** Suppose a firm makes purchases of $3.6 million per year under terms of 2/10, net 30, and takes discounts.
   a. What is the average amount of accounts payable net of discounts? (Assume that the $3.6 million of purchases is net of discounts — that is, gross purchases are $3,673,469, discounts are $73,469, and net purchases are $3.6 million. Also, use 360 days in a year.)
   b. Is there a cost of the trade credit the firm uses?
   c. If the firm did not take discounts but it did pay on the due date, what would be its average payables and the cost of this nonfree trade credit?
   d. What would its cost of not taking discounts be if it could stretch its payments to 40 days?

21-2 **TRADE CREDIT VERSUS BANK CREDIT** The Thompson Corporation projects an increase in sales from $1.5 million to $2 million, but it needs an additional $300,000 of current assets to support this expansion. The money can be obtained from the bank at an interest rate of 13 percent, discount interest; no compensating balance is required. Alternatively, Thompson can finance the expansion by no longer taking discounts, thus increasing accounts payable. Thompson purchases under terms of 2/10, net 30, but it can delay payment for an additional 35 days — paying in 65 days and thus becoming 35 days past due — without a penalty because of its suppliers' current excess capacity problems.
   a. Based strictly on effective, or equivalent, annual interest rate comparisons, how should Thompson finance its expansion?
   b. What additional qualitative factors should Thompson consider before reaching a decision?

21-3 **BANK FINANCING** The Raattama Corporation had sales of $3.5 million last year, and it earned a 5 percent return, after taxes, on sales. Recently, the company has fallen behind in its accounts payable. Although its terms of purchase are net 30 days, its accounts payable represent 60 days' purchases. The company's treasurer is seeking to increase bank borrowings in order to become current in meeting its trade obligations (that is, to have 30 days' payables outstanding). The company's balance sheet is as follows (thousands of dollars):

Cash	$ 100	Accounts payable	$ 600
Accounts receivable	300	Bank loans	700
Inventory	1,400	Accruals	200
Current assets	$1,800	Current liabilities	$1,500
Land and buildings	600	Mortgage on real estate	700
Equipment	600	Common stock, $0.10 par	300
		Retained earnings	500
Total assets	$3,000	Total liabilities and equity	$3,000

   a. How much bank financing is needed to eliminate the past-due accounts payable?
   b. Would you as a bank loan officer make the loan? Why?

21-4 **COST OF BANK LOANS** Gifts Galore Inc. borrowed $1.5 million from National City Bank. The loan was made at a simple annual interest rate of 9 percent a year for 3 months. A 20 percent compensating balance requirement raised the effective interest rate.
   a. The nominal interest rate on the loan was 11.25 percent. What is the true effective rate?
   b. What would be the effective cost of the loan if the note required discount interest?

c. What would be the nominal annual interest rate on the loan if National City Bank required Gifts Galore to repay the loan and interest in 3 equal monthly installments?

SHORT-TERM FINANCING ANALYSIS Malone Feed and Supply Company buys on terms of 1/10, net 30, but it has not been taking discounts and has actually been paying in 60 rather than 30 days. Malone's balance sheet follows (thousands of dollars):

Cash	$ 50	Accounts payable[a]	$ 500
Accounts receivable	450	Notes payable	50
Inventory	750	Accruals	50
Current assets	$1,250	Current liabilities	$ 600
Fixed assets	750	Long-term debt	150
		Common equity	1,250
Total assets	$2,000	Total liabilities and equity	$2,000

[a]Stated net of discounts.

Now, Malone's suppliers are threatening to stop shipments unless the company begins making prompt payments (that is, paying in 30 days or less). The firm can borrow on a 1-year note (call this a current liability) from its bank at a rate of 15 percent, discount interest, with a 20 percent compensating balance required. (Malone's $50,000 of cash is needed for transactions; it cannot be used as part of the compensating balance.)

a. Determine what action Malone should take by calculating (1) the cost of nonfree trade credit and (2) the cost of the bank loan.

b. Assume that Malone forgoes discounts and then borrows the amount needed to become current on its payables from the bank. How large will the bank loan be?

c. Based on your conclusion in Part b, construct a pro forma balance sheet. (Hint: You will need to include an account entitled "prepaid interest" under current assets.)

ALTERNATIVE FINANCING ARRANGEMENTS Suncoast Boats Inc. estimates that because of the seasonal nature of its business, it will require an additional $2 million of cash for the month of July. Suncoast Boats has the following 4 options available for raising the needed funds:

(1) Establish a 1-year line of credit for $2 million with a commercial bank. The commitment fee will be 0.5 percent per year on the unused portion, and the interest charge on the used funds will be 11 percent per annum. Assume that the funds are needed only in July, and that there are 30 days in July and 360 days in the year.

(2) Forgo the trade discount of 2/10, net 40, on $2 million of purchases during July.

(3) Issue $2 million of 30-day commercial paper at a 9.5 percent per annum interest rate. The total transactions fee, including the cost of a backup credit line, on using commercial paper is 0.5 percent of the amount of the issue.

(4) Issue $2 million of 60-day commercial paper at a 9 percent per annum interest rate, plus a transactions fee of 0.5 percent. Since the funds are required for only 30 days, the excess funds ($2 million) can be invested in 9.4 percent per annum marketable securities for the month of August. The total transactions cost of purchasing and selling the marketable securities is 0.4 percent of the amount of the issue.

a. What is the dollar cost of each financing arrangement?

b. Is the source with the lowest expected cost necessarily the one to select? Why or why not?

COST OF TRADE CREDIT Calculate the nominal annual cost of nonfree trade credit under each of the following terms. Assume payment is made either on the due date or on the discount date.

a. 1/15, net 20.

b. 2/10, net 60.

c. 3/10, net 45.

d. 2/10, net 45.

e. 2/15, net 40.

21-8   Cost of Trade Credit

a. If a firm buys under terms of 3/15, net 45, but actually pays on the 20th day and *still takes the discount,* what is the nominal cost of its nonfree trade credit?

b. Does it receive more or less credit than it would if it paid within 15 days?

21-9   Cost of Bank Loans Del Hawley, owner of Hawley's Hardware, is negotiating with First City Bank for a $50,000, 1-year loan. First City has offered Hawley the following alternatives. Calculate the effective annual interest rate for each alternative. Which alternative has the lowest effective annual interest rate?

a. A 12 percent annual rate on a simple interest loan, with no compensating balance required and interest due at the end of the year.

b. A 9 percent annual rate on a simple interest loan, with a 20 percent compensating balance required and interest again due at the end of the year.

c. An 8.75 percent annual rate on a discounted loan, with a 15 percent compensating balance.

d. Interest is figured as 8 percent of the $50,000 amount, *payable at the end of the year,* but the $50,000 is repayable in monthly installments during the year.

21-10   Cost of Trade Credit Grunewald Industries sells on terms of 2/10, net 40. Gross sales last year were $4.5 million, and accounts receivable averaged $437,500. Half of Grunewald's customers paid on the 10th day and took discounts. What are the nominal and effective costs of trade credit to Grunewald's nondiscount customers? (Hint: Calculate sales/day based on a 360-day year; then get average receivables of discount customers; then find the DSO for the nondiscount customers.)

21-11   Effective Cost of Short-Term Credit The D. J. Masson Corporation needs to raise $500,000 for 1 year to supply working capital to a new store. Masson buys from its suppliers on terms of 3/10, net 90, and it currently pays on the 10th day and takes discounts, but it could forego discounts, pay on the 90th day, and get the needed $500,000 in the form of costly trade credit. Alternatively, Masson could borrow from its bank on a 12 percent discount interest rate basis. What is the effective annual interest rate of the lower-cost source?

21-12   Effective Cost of Short-Term Credit Yonge Corporation must arrange financing for its working capital requirements for the coming year. Yonge can (a) borrow from its bank on a simple interest basis (interest payable at the end of the loan) for 1 year at a 12 percent nominal rate; (b) borrow on a 3-month, but renewable, loan at an 11.5 percent nominal rate; (c) borrow on an installment loan basis at a 6 percent add-on rate with 12 end-of-month payments; or (d) obtain the needed funds by no longer taking discounts and thus increasing its accounts payable. Yonge buys on terms of 1/15, net 60. What is the effective annual cost (*not* the nominal cost) of the *least expensive* type of credit, assuming 360 days per year?

SPREADSHEET PROBLEM

Three companies — Aggressive, Moderate, and Conservative — have different working capital management policies as implied by their names. For example, Aggressive employs only minimal current assets, and it finances almost entirely with current liabilities plus equity. This restricted approach has a dual effect. It keeps total assets low, which tends to increase return on assets; but because of stock-outs and credit rejections, total sales are reduced, and because inventory is ordered more frequently and in smaller quantities, variable costs are increased. Condensed balance sheets for the three companies follow:

	AGGRESSIVE	MODERATE	CONSERVATIVE
Current assets	$225,000	$300,000	$450,000
Fixed assets	300,000	300,000	300,000
Total assets	$525,000	$600,000	$750,000
Current liabilities (12%)	$300,000	$150,000	$ 75,000
Long-term debt (10%)	0	150,000	300,000
Total debt	$300,000	$300,000	$375,000
Equity	225,000	300,000	375,000
Total liabilities and equity	$525,000	$600,000	$750,000
Current ratio	0.75:1	2:1	6:1

The cost of goods sold functions for the three firms are as follows:

Cost of goods sold = Fixed costs + Variable costs.

Aggressive: Cost of goods sold = $300,000 + 0.70(Sales).

Moderate: Cost of goods sold = $405,000 + 0.65(Sales).

Conservative: Cost of goods sold = $577,500 + 0.60(Sales).

Because of the working capital differences, sales for the three firms under different economic conditions are expected to vary as follows:

	AGGRESSIVE	MODERATE	CONSERVATIVE
Strong economy	$1,800,000	$1,875,000	$1,950,000
Average economy	1,350,000	1,500,000	1,725,000
Weak economy	1,050,000	1,200,000	1,575,000

a. Construct income statements for each company for strong, average, and weak economies using the following format:

> Sales
>
> Less cost of goods sold
>
> Earnings before interest and taxes (EBIT)
>
> Less interest expense
>
> Earnings before taxes (EBT)
>
> Less taxes (40%)
>
> Net income

b. Compare the basic earning power (EBIT/Assets) and return on equity for the companies. Which company is best in a strong economy? In an average economy? In a weak economy?

c. Suppose that, with sales at the average-economy level, short-term interest rates rose to 20 percent. How would this affect the three firms?

d. Suppose that because of production slowdowns caused by inventory shortages, the aggressive company's variable cost ratio rose to 80 percent. What would happen to its ROE? Assume a short-term interest rate of 12 percent.

e. What considerations for management of working capital are indicated by this problem?

SPREADSHEET EXERCISE: DATABASE MANAGEMENT

The spreadsheet model for this exercise is not directly related to the Mini Case. Rather, the model contains a listing of historical returns on 10 stocks over holding periods of 1, 2, 3, 5, and 10 years. Students will use the table to learn about database management.

1. Retrieve the model (Filename SE-21.WK1) from the models diskette. Cells A6.F15 contain the historical returns on each stock, and Row 17 contains the average return for each holding period, assuming all 10 stocks were held in equal proportions.

2. Perhaps the first task that an analyst might want to do is sort the stocks by rate of return, from the highest to the lowest. The Data Sort command is used to reorder the listings in a data base. To start the sort process, type /DS to enter the Data Sort menu. Since the first element that must be specified is the data range, or the set of data that will be sorted, press D for Data-Range or press Enter. The database is contained in the range A6 to F15, so either mark the range with the cursor or Enter A6.F15. *Note two very important points:* (1) Do not include column or row headings in the data range. (2) The range must include the entire set of data even if you will be focusing only on one, or just a few, columns. If you do not include the entire set of data when you sort, the horizontal relationships among the data will be destroyed.

3. The next task in the data sort command sequence is to specify the primary key, which is the column on which the sort is made. Assume that we want to order the stocks on the basis of returns over the past year, or 1-year returns. Press P or move the cursor to Primary-Key and press Enter. Now either enter B6.B15 or use the cursor to mark the range and then press Enter. The spreadsheet now gives a prompt asking if you want to sort in ascending (A) or descending (D) order, with D as the default choice. Since you want the highest return at the top of the table, press Enter. Note that a secondary sort can also be done, which would serve as a "tiebreaker" if two stocks had the same 1-year return, but disregard this feature and just execute the sort by pressing G for Go. The entire table is now reordered, with Stock C at the top and Stock E at the bottom.

4. Another useful database management command is the Query command. The word *query* means to ask, and the Query command allows you to identify entries in a database that meet a specified criterion. To illustrate, assume that you want to identify all stocks that have a 10-year average return greater than 10 percent. In our small file, we can easily scan

the data and see that 5 stocks meet this requirement. However, if the database had 2,000 stocks, the task would be too difficult to do by sight.

5. To start the query process, type /DQ to get into the Data Query menu. Press Enter or I for Input, then enter (or mark with the cursor and press Enter) the range A5.F15. Note that with the Query command, the column headers, which must be on the row directly above the data entries, must be included in the table range. Now press C for Criterion, and enter H5.H6 to designate the criterion range. For now, type Q to leave the Query menu because the specific criterion must be entered in the criterion range. The top cell, H5, must contain the header from the column that you want to query. Since you want to identify those stocks having superior 10-year returns, enter "10 Year" in Cell H5. Now in Cell H6, enter +F6>0.1. F6 is the topmost cell containing 10-year returns, and you want to identify all stocks that have returns that exceed 10 percent, or 0.1. Now that the input and criterion ranges have been identified, and the criterion has been specified, you can type /DQF, for Data Query Find, and the spreadsheet will highlight all stocks that have 10-year returns greater than 10 percent. Note that the entries are not simultaneously highlighted, but rather the down and up arrows must be used to move from one highlighted entry to another.

6. The stocks identified in the Data Query also can be extracted and printed in a different section of the worksheet. To accomplish this, you must first specify an output range. The top row of the output range must be the headers from the table (input range), so first escape from the Data Query menu, and then copy the headings from Row 5 into Row 22. Then go back into the Data Query menu, press O for Output, and enter A22.F45. This designates an output range with the first row being the table headers and enough blank rows to contain the entire table, should all stocks be selected. Finally, press EQ to extract the stocks and quit the Data Query menu. Move the cursor down to the extract range and, if everything worked properly, you will see the 5 stocks listed that have 10-year returns that exceed 10 percent.

MINI CASE

Bats and Balls (B&B) Inc., a baseball equipment manufacturer, is a small company with seasonal sales. Each year before the baseball season, B&B purchases inventory which is financed through a combination of trade credit and short-term bank loans. At the end of the season, B&B uses sales revenues to repay its short-term obligations. The company is always looking for ways to become more profitable, and senior management has asked one of its employees, Ann Taylor, to review the company's current asset financing policies. Putting together her report, Ann is trying to answer each of the following questions:

a. B&B tries to match the maturity of its assets and liabilities. Describe how B&B could adopt either a more aggressive or more conservative financing policy.

b. What are the advantages and disadvantages of using short-term credit as a source of financing?

c. Is it likely that B&B could make significantly greater use of accruals?

d. Assume that B&B buys on terms of 1/10, net 30, but that it can get away with paying on the 40th day if it chooses not to take discounts. Also, assume that it purchases $3 million of components per year, net of discounts. How much free trade credit can the company get, how much costly trade credit can it get, and what is the percentage cost of the costly credit? Should B&B take discounts?

e. Would it be feasible for B&B to finance with commercial paper?

f. Suppose B&B decided to raise an additional $100,000 as a one-year loan from its bank, for which it was quoted a rate of 8 percent. What is the effective annual cost rate assuming (1) simple interest, (2) discount interest, (3) discount interest with a 10 percent compensating balance, and (4) add-on interest on a 12-month installment loan? For the first three of these assumptions, would it matter if the loan were for 90 days, but renewable, rather than for a year?

g. How large would the loan actually be in each of the cases in Part f?

h. What are the pros and cons of borrowing on a secured versus an unsecured basis? If inventories or receivables are to be used as collateral, how would the loan be handled?

SELECTED ADDITIONAL REFERENCES

For more on trade credit, see

Adams, Paul D., Steve R. Wyatt, and Yong H. Kim, "A Contingent Claims Analysis of Trade Credit," *Financial Management,* Autumn 1992, 104–112.

Brosky, John J., *The Implicit Cost of Trade Credit and Theory of Optimal Terms of Sale* (New York: Credit Research Foundation, 1969).

Schwartz, Robert A., "An Economic Analysis of Trade," *Journal of Financial and Quantitative Analysis,* September 1974, 643–658.

For more on bank lending and commercial credit in general, see

Campbell, Tim S., "A Model of the Market for Lines of Credit," *Journal of Finance,* March 1978, 231–243.

Stone, Bernell K., "Allocating Credit Lines, Planned Borrowing, and Tangible Services over a Company's Banking System," *Financial Management,* Summer 1975, 65–78.

For a discussion of effective yields, see

Finnerty, John D., "Bank Discount, Coupon Equivalent, and Compound Yields: Comment," *Financial Management,* Summer 1983, 40–44.

Glasgo, Philip W., William J. Landes, and A. Frank Thompson, "Bank Discount, Coupon Equivalent, and Compound Yields," *Financial Management,* Autumn 1982, 82–84.

OTHER TOPICS IN WORKING CAPITAL MANAGEMENT[*]

*F*or many Americans, the mention of baseball cards brings to mind the name of Topps Company, the father of the sports card industry. For many years, Topps had the sports card market to itself, but competitors rushed into the market in the 1980s, when news of collectors' paying thousands of dollars for a single classic card helped create a new interest among both serious and casual collectors. Today, about 100 companies vie for a share of the $1.5 billion annual sales generated by sports and entertainment cards. With more than 30 percent of the market, Topps remains the biggest player. Its current line includes the traditional packs of cards covering baseball and three other sports, plus premium packs with fancier pictures, more statistics, and higher prices.

The sports card business is inherently risky because "sales" to wholesalers and retailers — which account for 75 percent of the business — can be returned to manufacturers. Thus, a sale can be "undone" by merely returning the merchandise. Topps records its sales, less a reserve for returns, when it ships its products. Customers have 21 days to pay for cards, but Topps must refund the full price of all cards returned. At the end of each year (but not at the end of each quarter), Topps compares the dollar amount of returned merchandise with the amount placed in reserve. If the actual dollar amount of returned merchandise exceeds the reserve, the difference is subtracted from earnings. On the other hand, if returns are less than the amount built into the reserve, earnings are boosted.

After covering Chapters 20 and 21, it should be apparent that Topps's sales and returns policy creates special problems for its inventory and receivables

---

[*]All or parts of this chapter may be omitted without loss of continuity.

managers. For all practical purposes, the bulk of the finished goods inventory is held by wholesalers and retailers, not by the manufacturer. Accordingly, the quantity in stock is not known, so Topps is somewhat in the dark concerning production requirements. A production run on a particular set of cards would be wasted if a large number of returns were to materialize on that set. A similar problem occurs with receivables, because receivables may be paid off with returned cards rather than cash. Indeed, given its returns policy, a sale by Topps is not really a sale until the cards are sold by the retailer. This keeps both Topps's managers and outside analysts in the dark until the company tabulates end-of-year results. Without interim information on returns, outside analysts cannot get a good grasp on true sales until the reserve account is reconciled and the ending balance reported.

In Chapters 20 and 21, we presented the basic elements of current asset management and short-term financing. Now, in Chapter 22, we present a more in-depth treatment of several working capital topics, including (1) the cash conversion cycle, (2) the target cash balance, (3) accounting for inventory, (4) the EOQ model, (5) monitoring the receivables position, and (6) secured financing.

THE CASH CONVERSION CYCLE

As we noted in Chapter 20, the concept of working capital management originated with the old Yankee peddler, who would borrow to buy inventory, sell the inventory to pay off the bank loan, and then repeat the cycle. That general concept has been applied to more complex businesses, and the cash flow cycle concept is used for analyzing the effectiveness of a firm's working capital management.

We can illustrate the concept with data from Real Time Computer Corporation (RTC), which in early 1996 received an order from a government agency for 100 of its new super-minicomputers. The contract price was $250,000 each, and the effects of the order on RTC's working capital position were analyzed in terms of the following five steps:

1. RTC will order and then receive the materials it needs to produce the 100 computers. Because RTC and most other firms purchase materials on credit, this transaction will create an account payable, but there will be no immediate cash flow effect.

2. Labor will be used to convert the materials into finished computers. However, wages will not be fully paid at the time the work is done, so accrued wages will build up.

3. The finished computers will be shipped, but shipment will create receivables, not immediate cash inflows.

4. At some point during the cycle, RTC must pay off its accounts payable and accrued wages. Because these payments will be made before RTC has collected cash from its receivables, a net cash outflow will occur, and this outflow must be financed.

5. The cycle will be completed when RTC's receivables have been collected. At that time, the company will be in a position to pay off the credit that was used to finance production, and it can then repeat the cycle.

The *cash conversion cycle* model, which focuses on the length of time between when the company makes payments and when it receives cash inflows, formalizes the steps outlined above.[1] The following terms are used in the model:

1. *Inventory conversion period,* which is the average length of time required to convert materials into finished goods and then to sell those goods. Note that the inventory conversion period is calculated by dividing inventory on hand by sales per day. For example, if average inventories are $2 million and annual sales are $10 million, then the inventory conversion period is 72 days:

$$\text{Inventory conversion period} = \frac{\text{Inventory}}{\text{Sales per day}} = \frac{\text{Inventory}}{\text{Sales}/360}$$

$$= \frac{\$2,000,000}{\$10,000,000/360} = 72 \text{ days.}$$

Thus, it takes an average of 72 days to convert raw materials into finished goods and then to sell those goods.

2. *Receivables collection period,* which is the average length of time required to convert receivables into cash, that is, to collect cash following a sale. The receivables collection period is also called the days sales outstanding (DSO), and it is calculated by dividing accounts receivable by the average credit sales per day. If receivables average $666,667 and sales are $10 million, the receivables collection period is

$$\frac{\text{Receivables}}{\text{collection period}} = \text{DSO} = \frac{\text{Receivables}}{\text{Sales}/360}$$

$$= \frac{\$666,667}{\$10 \text{ million}/360} = 24 \text{ days.}$$

Thus, it takes 24 days after a sale to convert the receivables into cash.

3. *Payables deferral period,* which is the average length of time between the purchase of materials and labor and the payment of cash for them. For example, if the firm on average has 30 days to pay for labor and materials, if its cost

---

[1]See Verlyn D. Richards and Eugene J. Laughlin, "A Cash Conversion Cycle Approach to Liquidity Analysis," *Financial Management,* Spring 1980, 32–38. A similar approach was set forth earlier by Lawrence J. Gitman, "Estimating Corporate Liquidity Requirements: A Simplified Approach," *The Financial Review,* 1974, 79–88.

of goods sold is $8 million per year, and if its accounts payable average $666,667, then its payables deferral period can be calculated as follows:

Payables deferral period = Payables/Credit purchases per day
= Payables/(Cost of goods sold/360)

$$= \$666,667/(\$8,000,000/360) = 30 \text{ days.}$$

The calculated figure is consistent with the stated 30-day payment period.

4. *Cash conversion cycle,* which nets out the three periods just defined and thus equals the length of time between the firm's actual cash expenditures to pay for productive resources and its own cash receipts from the sale of products. The cash conversion cycle equals the average length of time a dollar is tied up in current assets.

We can now use these definitions to analyze the cash conversion cycle. First, the concept is diagrammed in Figure 22-1. Each component is given a number, and the cash conversion cycle can be expressed by the following equation:

(1)	+	(2)	−	(3)	=	(4)	
Inventory conversion period	+	Receivables collection period	−	Payables deferral period	=	Cash conversion cycle	22-1

FIGURE 22-1   THE CASH CONVERSION CYCLE MODEL

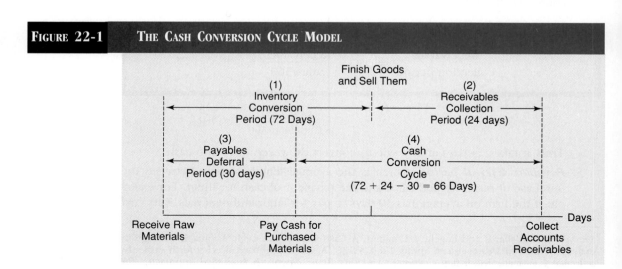

To illustrate, suppose it takes RTC an average of 72 days to convert raw materials to computers and then sell them, and another 24 days to collect on receivables. However, 30 days normally elapse between receipt of raw materials and payment for them. In this case, the cash conversion cycle would be 66 days:

$$72 \text{ days} + 24 \text{ days} - 30 \text{ days} = 66 \text{ days}.$$

To look at it another way,

$$\begin{array}{ccc} \text{Receipts delay} & - \text{ Payment delay} = \text{Net delay} \\ (72 \text{ days} + 24 \text{ days}) - & 30 \text{ days} & = 66 \text{ days}. \end{array}$$

Given these data, RTC knows when it starts producing a computer that it will have to finance its outlays for a 66-day period. The firm's goal should be to shorten its cash conversion cycle as much as possible without hurting operations. This would improve profits, because the longer the cash conversion cycle, the greater the need for external financing, and such financing has a cost.

The cash conversion cycle can be shortened (1) if the firm can reduce the inventory conversion period by processing and selling goods more quickly, (2) if it can reduce the receivables collection period by speeding up collections, or (3) if it can lengthen the payables deferral period by slowing down its own payments. To the extent that these actions can be taken *without increasing costs or depressing sales,* they should be carried out.

To illustrate, suppose RTC must spend $200,000 on materials and labor to produce one computer, and it takes 3 days to produce a computer. Thus, it must invest $200,000/3 = $66,667 for each day's production. This investment must be financed for 66 days—the length of the cash conversion cycle. Therefore, the company's working capital financing needs will be 66 × $66,667 = $4.4 million. Since RTC does not have $4.4 million of idle cash, it will have to line up $4.4 million of financing before it accepts the order. However, if RTC could reduce the cash conversion cycle to 56 days by deferring payment of its accounts payable an additional 10 days, or by speeding up either the production process or the collection of its receivables, it could reduce its working capital financing requirements by about $667,000. We see, then, that actions which affect the inventory conversion period, the receivables collection period, and the payables deferral period all affect the cash conversion cycle, hence they influence the firm's need for current assets and current asset financing.

Firms can use the cash conversion cycle analysis to consider their "regular, ongoing" business operations, or when they are analyzing special orders such as RTC's sale of the 100 computers. Both types of usages are important. Analysis of regular operations can lead to dramatic reductions in working capital and corresponding improvements in EVA and MVA as discussed in Chapter 2. Analysis of new, incremental business can be used to determine the effects of this business on financial requirements, and it can also be used when negotiating price and payment terms, and when discussing things with suppliers. You should keep the cash conversion cycle concept in mind as you go through the remainder of this chapter.

SELF-TEST QUESTIONS
What steps are involved in estimating the cash conversion cycle?

What do the following terms mean?

   (1) Inventory conversion period

   (2) Receivables collection period

   (3) Payables deferral period

What is the cash conversion cycle model? How can it be used to improve current asset management?

Setting the Target Cash Balance

In Chapter 20, when we discussed MicroDrive Incorporated's cash budget, we took as a given the $10 million target cash balance. We also discussed how lockboxes, synchronizing inflows and outflows, and float can reduce the required cash balance. Now we consider how target cash balances are set in practice.

Note (1) that cash per se earns no return, (2) that it is an asset which appears on the left side of the balance sheet, (3) that cash holdings must be financed by raising either debt or equity, and (4) that both debt and equity capital have a cost. If cash holdings could be reduced without hurting sales or other aspects of a firm's operations, this reduction would permit a reduction in either debt or equity, or both, which would increase the return on capital and thus boost the value of the firm's stock. *Therefore, the general operating goal of the cash manager is to minimize the amount of cash held subject to the constraint that enough cash be held to enable the firm to operate efficiently.*

For most firms, cash as a percentage of assets and/or sales has declined sharply in recent years as a direct result of technological developments in computers and telecommunications. Years ago, it was difficult to move money from one location to another, and it was also difficult to forecast exactly how much cash would be needed in different locations at different points in time. As a result, firms had to hold relatively large "safety stocks" of cash to be sure they had enough when and where it was needed. Also, they held relatively large amounts of short-term securities as a backup, and they also had backup lines of credit which permitted them to borrow on short notice to build up the cash account if it became depleted.

Now think how computers and telecommunications affect the situation. With a good computer system, tied together with good telecommunications links, a company can get real-time information on its cash balances, whether it operates in a single location or has facilities all over the world. Further, it can use statistical procedures to forecast cash inflows and outflows, and good forecasts reduce the need for safety stocks. Finally, improvements in telecommunications systems make it possible for a treasurer to replenish his or her cash accounts within minutes by simply calling a lender and stating that the firm wants to borrow a given amount under its line of credit. The lender then wires the funds to the desired location. Similarly, marketable securities can be sold with close to the same speed and with the same minimal transactions costs.

General Telephone can be used to illustrate this. Gen Tel knows exactly how much it must pay and when, and it can forecast quite accurately when it will receive checks. For example, the treasurer of Gen Tel's Florida operation knows when the major employers in Tampa pay their workers and how long after that people generally pay their phone bills. Armed with this information, Gen Tel's Florida treasurer can forecast with great accuracy any cash surpluses or deficits on a daily basis. Of course, no forecast will be exact, so slight overages or underages will occur. But this presents no problem. The treasurer knows by 11 A.M. the checks that must be covered by 4 P.M. that day, how much cash has come in, and consequently how much of a cash surplus or deficit will exist. Then a simple phone call is made, and the company borrows to cover any deficit or buys securities (or pays off outstanding loans) with any surplus. Thus, Gen Tel can maintain cash balances that are very close to zero, a situation that would have been impossible a few years ago.

Today, cash management in reasonably sophisticated firms is largely a job for systems people, and, except for the very largest firms, it is generally most efficient to have a bank handle the actual operations of the cash management system. Banks do this for a living, and there are economies of scale in operating cash management systems. Also, many banks are willing and able to offer such services, so competition has driven the cost of cash management down to a reasonable level. Still, it is essential that corporate treasurers know enough about cash management procedures to be able to negotiate and then work with the banks to ensure that they get the best price (interest rate) on credit lines, the best yield on short-term investments, and a reasonable cost for other banking services. To provide perspective on these issues, we discuss next a theoretical model for cash balances plus a practical approach to setting the target cash balance.

THE BAUMOL MODEL

William Baumol first noted that cash balances are, in many respects, similar to inventories, and that the EOQ inventory model, which will be developed in a later section, can be used to establish a target cash balance.[2] Baumol's model assumes that the firm uses cash at a steady, predictable rate — say, $1 million per week — and that the firm's cash inflows from operations also occur at a steady, predictable rate — say, $900,000 per week. Therefore, the firm's net cash outflows, or net need for cash, also occur at a steady rate — in this case, $100,000 per week.[3] Under these steady-state assumptions, the firm's cash position will resemble the situation shown in Figure 22-2.

If our illustrative firm started at Time 0 with a cash balance of C = $300,000, and if its outflows exceeded its inflows by $100,000 per week, then its cash balance would drop to zero at the end of Week 3, and its average cash balance would be C/2 = $300,000/2 = $150,000. Therefore, at the end of Week 3 the firm would have to replenish its cash balance, either by selling marketable securities, if it had any, or by borrowing.

If C were set at a higher level, say, $600,000, then the cash supply would last longer (6 weeks), and the firm would have to sell securities (or borrow) less frequently.

---

[2]William J. Baumol, "The Transactions Demand for Cash: An Inventory Theoretic Approach," *Quarterly Journal of Economics,* November 1952, 545–556.

[3]Our hypothetical firm is experiencing a $100,000 weekly cash shortfall, but this does not necessarily imply that it is headed for bankruptcy. The firm could, for example, be highly profitable and be enjoying high earnings, but be expanding so rapidly that it is experiencing chronic cash shortages that must be made up by borrowing or by selling common stock. Or, the firm could be in the construction business and therefore receive major cash inflows at wide intervals, but have net cash outflows of $100,000 per week between major inflows.

Figure 22-2   Cash Balances under the Baumol Model's Assumptions

However, its average cash balance would rise from $150,000 to $300,000. Brokerage or some other type of transactions cost must be incurred to sell securities (or to borrow), so holding larger cash balances will lower the transactions costs associated with obtaining cash. On the other hand, cash provides no income, so the larger the average cash balance, the higher the opportunity cost, which is the return that could have been earned on securities or other assets held in lieu of cash. Thus, we have the situation that is graphed in Figure 22-3. The optimal cash balance is found by using the following variables and equations:

C = amount of cash raised by selling marketable securities or by borrowing. $C/2$ = average cash balance.

C^* = optimal amount of cash to be raised by selling marketable securities or by borrowing. $C^*/2$ = optimal average cash balance.

F = fixed costs of selling securities or of obtaining a loan.

T = total amount of net new cash needed for transactions during the entire period (usually a year).

k = opportunity cost of holding cash, set equal to either the rate of return forgone on marketable securities or the cost of borrowing to hold cash.

The total costs of cash balances consist of holding (or opportunity) costs plus transactions costs:[4]

---

[4]Total costs can be expressed on either a before-tax or an after-tax basis. Both methods lead to the same conclusions regarding target cash balances and comparative costs. For simplicity, we present the model here on a before-tax basis.

$$\text{Total costs} = \text{Holding costs} + \text{Transactions costs}$$

$$= \left(\begin{array}{c}\text{Average cash}\\\text{balance}\end{array}\right)\left(\begin{array}{c}\text{Opportunity}\\\text{cost}\end{array}\right) + \left(\begin{array}{c}\text{Number of}\\\text{transactions}\end{array}\right)\left(\begin{array}{c}\text{Cost per}\\\text{transaction}\end{array}\right) \qquad 22\text{-}2$$

$$= \frac{C}{2}(k) + \frac{T}{C}(F).$$

The minimum total costs are achieved when C is set equal to C*, the optimal cash transfer. C* is found as follows:[5]

$$C^* = \sqrt{\frac{2(F)(T)}{k}}. \qquad 22\text{-}3$$

DETERMINATION OF THE TARGET CASH BALANCE   **FIGURE 22-3**

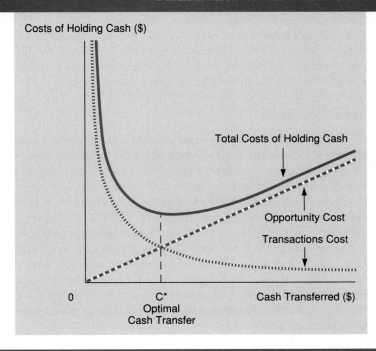

Costs of Holding Cash ($)

Total Costs of Holding Cash

Opportunity Cost

Transactions Cost

0   C*   Cash Transferred ($)
        Optimal
      Cash Transfer

---

[5]Equation 22-2 is differentiated with respect to C. The derivative is set equal to zero, and we then solve for C = C* to derive Equation 22-3. This model, applied to inventories and called the EOQ model, is discussed further in a later section.

Equation 22-3 is the *Baumol model* for determining optimal cash balances. To illustrate its use, suppose F = $150; T = 52 weeks × $100,000/week = $5,200,000; and k = 15% = 0.15. Then

$$C^* = \sqrt{\frac{2(\$150)(\$5,200,000)}{0.15}} = \$101,980.$$

Therefore, the firm should sell securities (or borrow if it does not hold securities) in the amount of $101,980 when its cash balance approaches zero, thus building its cash balance back up to $101,980. If we divide T by C*, we have the number of transactions per year: $5,200,000/$101,980 = 50.99 ≈ 51, or about once a week. The firm's average cash balance is $101,980/2 = $50,990 ≈ $51,000.

Notice that the optimal cash balance increases less than proportionately with increases in the amount of cash needed for transactions. For example, if the firm's size, and consequently its net new cash needs, doubled from $5,200,000 to $10,400,000 per year, average cash balances would increase by only 41 percent, from $51,000 to $72,000. This suggests that there are economies of scale in holding cash balances, and this, in turn, gives larger firms an edge over smaller ones.[6]

Of course, the firm would probably want to hold a safety stock of cash designed to reduce the probability of a cash shortage. However, if the firm is able to sell securities or to borrow on short notice — and most larger firms can do so in a matter of minutes simply by making a telephone call — the safety stock can be quite low.

The Baumol model is obviously simplistic. Most important, it assumes relatively stable, predictable cash inflows and outflows, and it does not take into account seasonal or cyclical trends. Other models have been developed to deal both with uncertainty and with trends, but all of them have limitations and are more useful as conceptual models than for actually setting target cash balances.

Monte Carlo Simulation

Although the Baumol model and other theoretical models provide insights into the optimal cash balance, they are generally not practical for actual use. Rather, firms generally set their target cash balances based on some "safety stock" of cash that holds the risk of running out of money to some acceptably low level. One commonly used procedure is Monte Carlo simulation.[7] To illustrate, consider the cash budget for MicroDrive Incorporated presented in Table 20-1 in Chapter 20. Sales and collections are the driving forces in the cash budget and, of course, are subject to uncertainty. In the cash budget, we used expected values for sales and collections, as well as for all other cash flows. However, it would be relatively easy to use Monte Carlo simulation, first discussed in Chapter 11, to introduce uncertainty. If the cash budget were constructed using a spreadsheet program with Monte Carlo add-in software, then the key uncertain variables could be specified as continuous probability distributions rather than point values.

---

[6]This edge may, of course, be more than offset by other factors — after all, cash management is only one aspect of running a business.

[7]See Eugene M. Lerner, "Simulating a Cash Budget," in *Readings on the Management of Working Capital,* 2d ed., Keith V. Smith, ed. (St. Paul, Minn.: West, 1980).

The end result of the simulation would be a distribution for each month's net cash gain or loss instead of the single values shown on Line 16 of Table 20-1. Suppose September's net cash loss distribution looked like this (in millions):

SEPTEMBER CASH LOSS	PROBABILITY OF THIS AMOUNT OR HIGHER
($83)	90%
(75)	80
(68)	70
(62)	60
(57)	50
(52)	40
(46)	30
(39)	20
(31)	10

Now suppose MicroDrive's managers want to be 90 percent confident that the firm will not run out of cash during September. They would set the beginning-of-month balance at $93 million, well above the current $10 million, because there is only a 10 percent probability that September's cash flow will be worse than an $83 million outflow. With a balance of $83 million at the beginning of the month, there would be only a 10 percent chance that MicroDrive would run out of cash during September. Of course, Monte Carlo simulation could be applied to the remaining months in the Table 20-1 cash budget, and the amounts obtained to meet some confidence level could be used to set each month's target cash balance instead of using a fixed target across all months.

The same type of analysis could be used to determine the amount of short-term securities to hold, or the size of a requested line of credit. Of course, as in all simulations, the hard part is estimating the probability distributions for sales, collections, and the other highly uncertain variables. If these inputs are not good representations of the actual uncertainty facing the firm, then the resulting target balances will not offer the protection against cash shortages implied by the simulation. There is no substitute for experience, and cash managers will adjust the target balances obtained by Monte Carlo simulation to reflect actual results.

How has technology changed the way target cash balances are set?
What is the Baumol model, and how is it used?
Explain how Monte Carlo simulation can be used to set a firm's target cash balance.

SELF-TEST QUESTIONS

ACCOUNTING FOR INVENTORY

When finished goods are sold, the firm must assign a cost of goods sold. The cost of goods sold appears on the income statement as an expense for the period, and the balance sheet inventory account is reduced by a like amount. Four methods can be used to value the cost of goods sold, and hence to value the remaining inventory:

(1) specific identification, (2) first-in, first-out (FIFO), (3) last-in, first-out (LIFO), and (4) weighted average.

SPECIFIC IDENTIFICATION

Under *specific identification,* a unique cost is attached to each item in inventory. Then, when an item is sold the inventory value is reduced by that specific amount. This method is used only when the items are high cost and move relatively slowly, such as would be the case for an automobile dealer.

FIRST-IN, FIRST-OUT (FIFO)

In the *FIFO* method, the units sold during a given period are assumed to be the first units that were placed in inventory. As a result, the cost of goods sold is based on the cost of the oldest inventory items, and the remaining inventory consists of the newest goods.

LAST-IN, FIRST-OUT (LIFO)

LIFO is the opposite of FIFO. The cost of goods sold is based on the last units placed in inventory, while the remaining inventory consists of the first goods placed in inventory. Note that this is purely an accounting convention — the actual physical units sold could be either the earlier or the later units placed in inventory, or some combination. For example, Del Monte has in its LIFO inventory accounts catsup bottled in the 1920s, but all the catsup in its warehouses was bottled in 1995 or 1996.

WEIGHTED AVERAGE

The *weighted average* method involves calculating the weighted average unit cost of goods available for sale from inventory, and this average is then used to determine the cost of goods sold. This method results in a cost of goods sold and an ending inventory that falls somewhere between the FIFO and LIFO methods.

COMPARISON OF INVENTORY ACCOUNTING METHODS

To illustrate these methods and their effects on financial statements, assume that Custom Furniture Inc. manufactured five identical antique reproduction dining tables during a one-year accounting period. During the year, a new labor contract plus dramatically increasing mahogany prices caused manufacturing costs to almost double, resulting in the following inventory costs:

Table Number:	1	2	3	4	5	Total
Cost:	$10,000	$12,000	$14,000	$16,000	$18,000	$70,000

There were no tables in stock at the beginning of the year, and Tables 1, 3, and 5 were sold during the year.

If Custom used the specific identification method, the cost of goods sold would be reported as $10,000 + $14,000 + $18,000 = $42,000, while the end-of-period inventory value would be $70,000 − $42,000 = $28,000. If Custom used the FIFO method, its cost of goods sold would be $10,000 + $12,000 + $14,000 = $36,000, and ending inventory would be $70,000 − $36,000 = $34,000. If Custom used the LIFO method, its cost of goods sold would be $48,000, and its ending inventory would be $22,000. Finally, if Custom used the weighted average method, its average cost per unit of inventory would be $70,000/5 = $14,000, its cost of goods sold would be 3($14,000) = $42,000, and its ending inventory would be $70,000 − $42,000 = $28,000.

If Custom's actual sales revenues from the tables were $80,000, or an average of $26,667 per unit sold, and if its other costs were minimal, the following is a summary of the effects of the four methods:

METHOD	SALES	COST OF GOODS SOLD	REPORTED PROFIT	ENDING INVENTORY VALUE
Specific identification	$80,000	$42,000	$38,000	$28,000
FIFO	80,000	36,000	44,000	34,000
LIFO	80,000	48,000	32,000	22,000
Weighted average	80,000	42,000	38,000	28,000

Ignoring taxes, Custom's cash flows would not be affected by its choice of inventory methods, yet its balance sheet and reported profits would vary with each method. In an inflationary period such as in our example, FIFO gives the lowest cost of goods sold and thus the highest net income. FIFO also shows the highest inventory value, so it produces the strongest apparent liquidity position as measured by net working capital or the current ratio. On the other hand, LIFO produces the highest cost of goods sold, the lowest reported profits, and the weakest apparent liquidity position. However, when taxes are considered, LIFO provides the greatest tax deductibility, and thus it results in the lowest tax burden. Consequently, after-tax cash flows are highest if LIFO is used.

Of course, these results apply only to periods when costs are increasing. If costs were constant, all four methods would produce the same cost of goods sold, ending inventory, taxes, and cash flows. However, inflation has been a fact of life in recent years, so most firms use LIFO to take advantage of its greater tax and cash flow benefits.

What are the four methods used to account for inventory?

What impact does the method used have on the firm's reported profits? On ending inventory levels?

Which method should be used if management anticipates a period of inflation? Why?

SELF-TEST QUESTIONS

THE ECONOMIC ORDERING QUANTITY (EOQ) MODEL

As discussed in Chapter 20, inventories are obviously necessary, but it is equally obvious that a firm's profitability will suffer if it has too much or too little inventory. Most firms use a pragmatic approach to setting inventory levels, in which past experience plays a major role. However, as a starting point in the process, it is useful for managers to consider the insights provided by the *economic ordering (EOQ) quantity* model. The EOQ model first specifies the costs of ordering and carrying inventories and then combines these costs to obtain the total costs associated with inventory holdings. Finally, optimization techniques are used to find that order quantity, hence inventory level, that minimizes total costs. Note that a third category of inventory costs, the costs of running short (stock-out costs), are not considered in our initial discussion. These costs are dealt with by adding safety stocks, as we will discuss later. Similarly, we shall discuss quantity discounts in a later section. The costs that remain for consideration at this stage are carrying costs and ordering, shipping, and receiving costs.

CARRYING COSTS

Carrying costs generally rise in direct proportion to the average amount of inventory carried. Inventories carried, in turn, depend on the frequency with which orders are placed. To illustrate, if a firm sells S units per year, and if it places equal-sized orders N times per year, then S/N units will be purchased with each order. If the inventory is used evenly over the year, and if no safety stocks are carried, then the average inventory, A, will be:

$$A = \frac{\text{Units per order}}{2} = \frac{S/N}{2} . \qquad \text{22-4}$$

For example, if S = 120,000 units in a year, and N = 4, then the firm will order 30,000 units at a time, and its average inventory will be 15,000 units:

$$A = \frac{S/N}{2} = \frac{120,000/4}{2} = \frac{30,000}{2} = 15,000 \text{ units.}$$

Just after a shipment arrives, the inventory will be 30,000 units; just before the next shipment arrives, it will be zero; and on average, 15,000 units will be carried.

Now assume the firm purchases its inventory at a price P = $2 per unit. The average inventory value is thus (P)(A) = $2(15,000) = $30,000. If the firm has a cost of capital of 10 percent, it will incur $3,000 in financing charges to carry the inventory for one year. Further, assume that each year the firm incurs $2,000 of storage costs (space, utilities, security, taxes, and so forth), that its inventory insurance costs are $500, and that it must mark down inventories by $1,000 because of depreciation and obsolescence. The firm's total cost of carrying the $30,000 average inventory is thus $3,000 + $2,000 + $500 + $1,000 = $6,500, and the annual percentage cost of carrying the inventory is $6,500/$30,000 = 0.217 = 21.7%.

Defining the annual percentage carrying cost as C, we can, in general, find the annual total carrying cost, TCC, as the percentage carrying cost, C, times the price per unit, P, times the average number of units, A:

$$TCC = \text{Total carrying cost} = (C)(P)(A). \qquad \text{22-5}$$

In our example,

$$\text{TCC} = (0.217)(\$2)(15,000) \approx \$6,500.$$

ORDERING COSTS

Although we assume that carrying costs are entirely variable and rise in direct pro-portion to the average size of inventories, ordering costs are often fixed. For exam-ple, the costs of placing and receiving an order — interoffice memos, long-distance telephone calls, setting up a production run, and taking delivery — are essentially fixed regardless of the size of an order, so this part of inventory cost is simply the fixed cost of placing and receiving orders times the number of orders placed per year.[8] We define the fixed costs associated with ordering inventories as F, and if we place N orders per year, the total ordering cost is given by Equation 22-6:

$$\text{Total ordering cost} = \text{TOC} = (F)(N). \qquad \textbf{22-6}$$

Here TOC = total ordering cost, F = fixed costs per order, and N = number of orders placed per year.

Equation 22-4 may be rewritten as N = S/2A, and then substituted into Equation 22-6:

$$\text{Total ordering cost} = \text{TOC} = F\left(\frac{S}{2A}\right). \qquad \textbf{22-7}$$

To illustrate the use of Equation 22-7, if F = $100, S = 120,000 units, and A = 15,000 units, then TOC, the total annual ordering cost, is $400:

$$\text{TOC} = \$100\left(\frac{120,000}{30,000}\right) = \$100(4) = \$400.$$

---

[8]Note that in reality both carrying and ordering costs can have variable and fixed cost elements, at least over certain ranges of average inventory. For example, security and utilities charges are prob-ably fixed in the short run over a wide range of inventory levels. Similarly, labor costs in receiving inventory could be tied to the quantity received, and hence could be variable. To simplify matters, we treat all carrying costs as variable and all ordering costs as fixed. However, if these assumptions do not fit the situation at hand, the cost definitions can be changed. For example, one could add another term for shipping costs if there are economies of scale in shipping, such that the cost of shipping a unit is smaller if shipments are larger. However, in most situations shipping costs are not sensitive to order size, so total shipping costs are simply the shipping cost per unit times the units ordered (and sold) during the year. Under this condition, shipping costs are not influenced by inventory policy, hence they may be disregarded for purposes of determining the optimal inventory level and the optimal order size.

TOTAL INVENTORY COSTS

Total carrying cost, TCC, as defined in Equation 22-5, and total ordering cost, TOC, as defined in Equation 22-7, may be combined to find total inventory costs, TIC, as follows:

$$\text{Total inventory costs} = \text{TIC} = \text{TCC} + \text{TOC}$$
$$= (C)(P)(A) + F\left(\frac{S}{2A}\right). \qquad \textbf{22-8}$$

Recognizing that the average inventory carried is A = Q/2, or one-half the size of each order quantity, Q, we may rewrite Equation 22-8 as follows:

$$\text{TIC} = \text{TCC} + \text{TOC}$$
$$= (C)(P)\left(\frac{Q}{2}\right) + (F)\left(\frac{S}{Q}\right). \qquad \textbf{22-9}$$

Here we see that total carrying cost equals average inventory in units, Q/2, multiplied by unit price, P, times the percentage annual carrying cost, C. Total ordering cost equals the number of orders placed per year, S/Q, multiplied by the fixed cost of placing and receiving an order, F. Finally, total inventory costs equal the sum of total carrying cost plus total ordering cost. We will use this equation in the next section to develop the optimal inventory ordering quantity.

DERIVATION OF THE EOQ MODEL

Figure 22-4 illustrates the basic premise on which the EOQ model is built, namely, that some costs rise with larger inventories while other costs decline, and there is an optimal order size (and associated average inventory) which minimizes the total costs of inventories. First, as noted earlier, the average investment in inventories depends on how frequently orders are placed and the size of each order — if we order every day, average inventories will be much smaller than if we order once a year. Further, as Figure 22-4 shows, the firm's carrying costs rise with larger orders: larger orders mean larger average inventories, so warehousing costs, interest on funds tied up in inventory, insurance, and obsolescence costs will all increase. However, ordering costs decline with larger orders and inventories: the cost of placing orders, suppliers' production set-up costs, and order handling costs will all decline if we order infrequently and consequently hold larger quantities.

If the carrying and ordering cost curves in Figure 22-4 are added, the sum represents total inventory costs, TIC. The point where the TIC is minimized represents the *economic ordering quantity (EOQ),* and this, in turn, determines the optimal average inventory level.

DETERMINATION OF THE OPTIMAL ORDER QUANTITY **FIGURE 22-4**

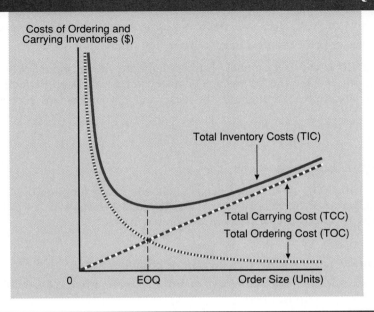

The EOQ is found by differentiating Equation 22-9 with respect to ordering quantity, Q, and setting the derivative equal to zero:

$$\frac{d(\text{TIC})}{dQ} = \frac{(C)(P)}{2} - \frac{(F)(S)}{Q^2} = 0.$$

Now, solving for Q we obtain:

$$\frac{(C)(P)}{2} = \frac{(F)(S)}{Q^2}$$

$$Q^2 = \frac{2(F)(S)}{(C)(P)}$$

$$\text{EOQ} = \sqrt{\frac{2(F)(S)}{(C)(P)}}. \qquad \text{22-10}$$

Here

EOQ = economic ordering quantity, or the optimal quantity to be ordered each time an order is placed.

F = fixed costs of placing and receiving an order.

S = annual sales in units.

C = annual carrying costs expressed as a percentage of average inventory value.

P = purchase price the firm must pay per unit of inventory.

Equation 22-10 is the EOQ model.[9] The assumptions of the model, which will be relaxed shortly, include the following: (1) sales can be forecasted perfectly, (2) sales are evenly distributed throughout the year, and (3) orders are received when expected.

EOQ MODEL ILLUSTRATION

To illustrate the EOQ model, consider the following data supplied by Cotton Tops Inc., a distributor of budget-priced, custom-designed T-shirts which it sells to concessionaires at various theme parks in the United States:

S = annual sales = 26,000 shirts per year.

C = percentage carrying cost = 25 percent of inventory value.

P = purchase price per shirt = $4.92 per shirt. (The sales price is $9, but this is irrelevant for our purposes here.)

F = fixed cost per order = $1,000. Cotton Tops designs and distributes the shirts, but the actual production is done by another company. The bulk of this $1,000 cost is the labor cost for setting up the equipment for the production run, which the manufacturer bills separately from the $4.92 cost per shirt.

Substituting these data into Equation 22-10, we obtain an EOQ of 6,500 units:

$$EOQ = \sqrt{\frac{2(F)(S)}{(C)(P)}} = \sqrt{\frac{(2)(\$1,000)(26,000)}{(0.25)(\$4.92)}}$$

$$= \sqrt{42,276,423} \approx 6,500 \text{ units.}$$

With an EOQ of 6,500 shirts and annual usage of 26,000 shirts, Cotton Tops will place 26,000/6,500 = 4 orders per year. Notice that average inventory holdings depend directly on the EOQ. This relationship is illustrated graphically in Figure 22-5, where we see that average inventory = EOQ/2. Immediately after an order is received, 6,500 shirts are in stock. The usage rate, or sales rate, is 500 shirts per week (26,000/52 weeks), so inventories are drawn down by this amount each week. Thus, the actual number of units held in inventory will vary from 6,500 shirts just

---

[9]The EOQ model can also be written as

$$EOQ = \sqrt{\frac{2(F)(S)}{C^*}},$$

where C^* is the annual carrying cost per unit expressed in *dollars*.

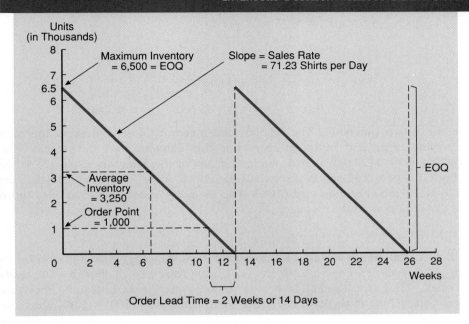

INVENTORY POSITION WITHOUT SAFETY STOCK   FIGURE 22-5

after an order is received to zero just before a new order arrives. With a 6,500 beginning balance, a zero ending balance, and a uniform sales rate, inventories will average one-half the EOQ, or 3,250 shirts, during the year. At a cost of $4.92 per shirt, the average investment in inventories will be (3,250)($4.92) ≈ $16,000. If inventories are financed by bank loans, the loan will vary from a high of $32,000 to a low of $0, but the average amount outstanding over the course of a year will be $16,000.

Notice that the EOQ, hence average inventory holdings, rises with the square root of sales. Therefore, a given increase in sales will result in a less-than-proportionate increase in inventories, so the inventory/sales ratio will tend to decline as a firm grows. For example, Cotton Tops's EOQ is 6,500 shirts at an annual sales level of 26,000, and the average inventory is 3,250 shirts, or $16,000. However, if sales were to increase by 100 percent, to 52,000 shirts per year, the EOQ would rise only to 9,195 units, or by 41 percent, and the average inventory would rise by this same percentage. This suggests that there are economies of scale in holding inventories.[10]

---

[10]Note, however, that these scale economies relate to each particular item, not to the entire firm. Thus, a large distributor with $500 million of sales might have a higher inventory/sales ratio than a much smaller distributor if the small firm has only a few high-sales-volume items while the large firm distributes a great many low-volume items.

Finally, look at Cotton Tops's total inventory costs for the year, assuming that the EOQ is ordered each time. Using Equation 22-9, we find total inventory costs are $8,000:

$$
\begin{aligned}
\text{TIC} &= \quad\quad \text{TCC} \quad\quad + \quad\quad \text{TOC} \\
&= \quad (\text{C})(\text{P})\left(\frac{Q}{2}\right) \quad + \quad (\text{F})\left(\frac{S}{Q}\right) \\
&= 0.25(\$4.92)\left(\frac{6,500}{2}\right) + (\$1,000)\left(\frac{26,000}{6,500}\right) \\
&\approx \quad\quad \$4,000 \quad\quad + \quad\quad \$4,000 \quad\quad = \$8,000.
\end{aligned}
$$

Note these two points: (1) The $8,000 total inventory cost represents the total of carrying costs and ordering costs, but this amount does *not* include the 26,000($4.92) = $127,920 annual purchasing cost of the inventory itself. (2) As we see both in Figure 22-4 and in the calculation above, at the EOQ, total carrying cost (TCC) equals total ordering cost (TOC). This property is not unique to our Cotton Tops illustration; it always holds.

SETTING THE ORDER POINT

If a 2-week lead time is required for production and shipping, what is Cotton Tops's order point level? If we use a 52-week year, Cotton Tops sells 26,000/52 = 500 shirts per week. Thus, if a 2-week lag occurs between placing an order and receiving goods, Cotton Tops must place the order when there are 2(500) = 1,000 shirts on hand. During the 2-week production and shipping period, the inventory balance will continue to decline at the rate of 500 shirts per week, and the inventory balance will hit zero just as the order of new shirts arrives.

If Cotton Tops knew for certain that both the sales rate and the order lead time would never vary, it could operate exactly as shown in Figure 22-5. However, sales do change, and production and/or shipping delays are sometimes encountered; to guard against these events, the firm must carry additional inventories, or safety stocks, as discussed in the next section.

SELF-TEST QUESTIONS

What are some specific inventory carrying costs? As defined here, are these costs fixed or variable?

What are some inventory ordering costs? As defined here, are these costs fixed or variable?

What are the components of total inventory costs?

What is the concept behind the EOQ model?

What is the relationship between total carrying cost and total ordering cost at the EOQ?

What assumptions are inherent in the EOQ model as presented here?

EOQ MODEL EXTENSIONS

The basic EOQ model was derived under several restrictive assumptions. In this section, we relax some of these assumptions and, in the process, extend the model to make it more useful.

THE CONCEPT OF SAFETY STOCKS

The concept of a *safety stock* is illustrated in Figure 22-6. First, note that the slope of the sales line measures the expected rate of sales. The company *expects* to sell 500 shirts per week, but let us assume that the maximum likely sales rate is twice this amount, or 1,000 units each week. Further, assume that Cotton Tops sets the safety stock at 1,000 shirts, so it initially orders 7,500 shirts, the EOQ of 6,500 plus the 1,000-unit safety stock. Subsequently, it reorders the EOQ whenever the inventory level falls to 2,000 shirts, the safety stock of 1,000 shirts plus the 1,000 shirts expected to be used while awaiting delivery of the order.

Notice that the company could, over the 2-week delivery period, sell 1,000 units a week, or double its normal expected sales. This maximum rate of sales is shown by the steeper dashed line in Figure 22-6. The condition that makes this higher sales rate possible is the safety stock of 1,000 shirts.

The safety stock is also useful to guard against delays in receiving orders. The expected delivery time is 2 weeks, but with a 1,000-unit safety stock, the company could maintain sales at the expected rate of 500 units per week for an additional 2 weeks if something should delay an order.

However, carrying a safety stock has a cost. The average inventory is now EOQ/2 plus the safety stock, or 6,500/2 + 1,000 = 3,250 + 1,000 = 4,250 shirts, and the average inventory value is now (4,250)($4.92) = $20,910. This increase in average inventory causes an increase in annual inventory carrying costs equal to (Safety stock)(P)(C) = 1,000($4.92)(0.25) = $1,230.

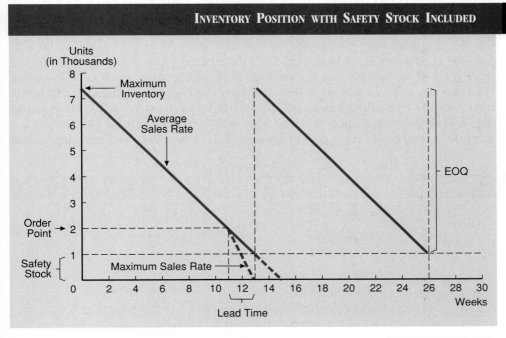

INVENTORY POSITION WITH SAFETY STOCK INCLUDED   **FIGURE 22-6**

The optimal safety stock varies from situation to situation, but, in general, it *increases* (1) with the uncertainty of demand forecasts, (2) with the costs (in terms of lost sales and lost goodwill) that result from inventory shortages, and (3) with the probability that delays will occur in receiving shipments. The optimal safety stock *decreases* as the cost of carrying this additional inventory increases.

SETTING THE SAFETY STOCK LEVEL

The critical question with regard to safety stocks is this: How large should the safety stock be? To answer this question, first examine Table 22-1, which contains the probability distribution of Cotton Tops's unit sales for an average 2-week period, the time it takes to receive an order of 6,500 T-shirts. Note that the expected sales over an average 2-week period is 1,000 units. Why do we focus on a 2-week period? Because shortages can occur only during the 2 weeks it takes an order to arrive.

Cotton Tops's managers have estimated that the annual carrying cost is 25 percent of inventory value. Since each shirt has an inventory value of $4.92, the annual carrying cost per unit is 0.25($4.92) = $1.23, and the carrying cost for each 13-week inventory period is $1.23(13/52) = $0.308 per unit. Even though shortages can occur only during the 2-week order period, safety stocks must be carried over the full 13-week inventory cycle. Next, Cotton Tops's managers must estimate the cost of shortages. Assume that when shortages occur, 50 percent of Cotton Tops's buyers are willing to accept back orders, while 50 percent of its potential customers simply cancel their orders. Remember that each shirt sells for $9.00, so each one-unit shortage produces expected lost profits of 0.5($9.00 − $4.92) = $2.04. With this information, the firm can calculate the costs of different safety stock levels. This is done in Table 22-2.

For each safety stock level, we determine the expected cost of a shortage based on the sales probability distribution in Table 22-1. There is an expected shortage cost of $408 if no safety stock is carried; $102 if the safety stock is set at 500 units; and no expected shortage, hence no shortage cost, with a safety stock of 1,000 units. The cost of carrying each safety level is merely the cost of carrying a unit of inventory over the 13-week inventory period, $0.308, times the safety stock; for example, the cost of carrying a safety stock of 500 units is $0.308(500) = $154. Finally, we sum the expected shortage cost in Column 6 and the safety stock carrying cost in

TABLE 22-1   TWO-WEEK SALES PROBABILITY DISTRIBUTION

PROBABILITY	UNIT SALES
0.1	0
0.2	500
0.4	1,000
0.2	1,500
0.1	2,000
1.0	Expected sales = 1,000

| | | | | SAFETY STOCK ANALYSIS | | | TABLE 22-2 |

SAFETY STOCK (1)	SALES DURING TWO-WEEK DELIVERY PERIOD (2)	PROBABILITY (3)	SHORTAGE[a] (4)	SHORTAGE COST (LOST PROFITS): $2.04 \times (4)$ = (5)	EXPECTED SHORTAGE COST: $(3) \times (5)$ = (6)	SAFETY STOCK CARRYING COST: $0.308 \times (1)$ = (7)	EXPECTED TOTAL COST: $(6) + (7)$ = (8)
0	0	0.1	0	$ 0	$ 0		
	500	0.2	0	0	0		
	1,000	0.4	0	0	0		
	1,500	0.2	500	1,020	204		
	2,000	0.1	1,000	2,040	204		
		1.0		Expected shortage cost = $408		$ 0	$408
500	0	0.1	$0	$ 0	$ 0		
	500	0.2	0	0	0		
	1,000	0.4	0	0	0		
	1,500	0.2	0	0	0		
	2,000	0.1	500	1,020	102		
		1.0		Expected shortage cost = $102		$154	$256
1,000	0	0.1	0	$ 0	$ 0		
	500	0.2	0	0	0		
	1,000	0.4	0	0	0		
	1,500	0.2	0	0	0		
	2,000	0.1	0	0	0		
		1.0		Expected shortage cost = $ 0		$308	$308

[a]Shortage = Actual sales − (1,000 Stock at order point + Safety stock); positive values only.

Column 7 to obtain the total cost figures given in Column 8. Since the 500-unit safety stock has the lowest expected total cost, Cotton Tops should carry this safety level.

Of course, the optimal safety level is highly sensitive to the estimates of the sales probability distribution and shortage costs. Errors here could result in incorrect safety stock levels. Note also that in calculating the $2.04 per unit shortage cost, we implicitly assumed that a lost sale in one period would not result in lost sales in future periods. If shortages cause customer ill will, this could lead to permanent sales reductions. Then the situation would be much more serious, stock-out costs would be far higher, and the firm should consequently carry a larger safety stock.

The stock-out example is just one example of the many judgments required in inventory management — the mechanics are relatively simple, but the inputs are judgmental and difficult to obtain.

QUANTITY DISCOUNTS

Now suppose the T-shirt manufacturer offered Cotton Tops a *quantity discount* of 2 percent on large orders. If the quantity discount applied to orders of 5,000 or more, then Cotton Tops would continue to place the EOQ order of 6,500 shirts and take the quantity discount. However, if the quantity discount required orders of 10,000 or more, then Cotton Tops would have to compare the savings in purchase price that would result if its ordering quantity were increased to 10,000 units with the increase in total inventory costs caused by the departure from the 6,500-unit EOQ.

First, consider the total costs associated with Cotton Tops's EOQ of 6,500 units. We found earlier that total inventory costs are $8,000:

$$\text{TIC} = \text{TCC} + \text{TOC}$$

$$= (C)(P)\left(\frac{Q}{2}\right) + (F)\left(\frac{S}{Q}\right)$$

$$= 0.25(\$4.92)\left(\frac{6,500}{2}\right) + (\$1,000)\left(\frac{26,000}{6,500}\right)$$

$$\approx \$4,000 + \$4,000 = \$8,000.$$

Now, what would total inventory costs be if Cotton Tops ordered 10,000 units instead of 6,500? The answer is $8,625:

$$\text{TIC} = 0.25(\$4.82)\left(\frac{10,000}{2}\right) + (\$1,000)\left(\frac{26,000}{10,000}\right)$$

$$= \$6,025 + \$2,600 = \$8,625.$$

Notice that when the discount is taken, the price, P, is reduced by the amount of the discount; the new price per unit would be 0.98($4.92) = $4.82. Also note that when the ordering quantity is increased, carrying costs increase because the firm is carrying a larger average inventory, but ordering costs decrease since the number of orders per year decreases. If we were to calculate total inventory costs at an ordering quantity of 5,000, we would find that carrying costs would be less than $4,000, and ordering costs would be more than $4,000, but the total inventory costs would be more than $8,000, since they are at a minimum when 6,500 units are ordered.[11]

Thus, inventory costs would increase by $8,625 − $8,000 = $625 if Cotton Tops were to increase its order size to 10,000 shirts. *However, this cost increase must be compared with Cotton Tops's savings if it takes the discount.* Taking the discount would save 0.02($4.92) = $0.0984 per unit. Over the year, Cotton Tops orders 26,000 shirts, so the annual savings is $0.0984(26,000) ≈ $2,558. Here is a summary:

---

[11]At an ordering quantity of 5,000 units, total inventory costs are $8,275:

$$\text{TIC} = (0.25)(\$4.92)\left(\frac{5,000}{2}\right) + (\$1,000)\left(\frac{26,000}{5,000}\right)$$

$$= \$3,075 + \$5,200 = \$8,275.$$

Reduction in purchase price = 0.02($4.92)(26,000) = $2,558
Increase in total inventory cost   =   625
Net savings from taking discounts $1,933

Obviously, the company should order 10,000 units at a time and take advantage of the quantity discount.

INFLATION

Moderate inflation — say, 3 percent per year — can largely be ignored for purposes of inventory management, but higher rates of inflation must be explicitly considered. If the rate of inflation in the types of goods the firm stocks tends to be relatively constant, it can be dealt with quite easily — simply deduct the expected annual rate of inflation from the carrying cost percentage, C, in Equation 22-10, and use this modified version of the EOQ model to establish the ordering quantity. The reason for making this deduction is that inflation causes the value of the inventory to rise, thus offsetting somewhat the effects of depreciation and other carrying costs. Since C will now be smaller, the calculated EOQ, and the average inventory, will increase. However, the higher the rate of inflation, the higher are interest rates, and this factor will cause C to increase, thus lowering the EOQ and average inventories.

On balance, there is no evidence that inflation either raises or lowers the optimal inventories of firms in the aggregate. Inflation should still be explicitly considered, however, for it will raise the individual firm's optimal holdings if the rate of inflation for its own inventories is above average (and is greater than the effects of inflation on interest rates), and vice versa.

SEASONAL DEMAND

For most firms, it is unrealistic to assume that the demand for an inventory item is uniform throughout the year. What happens when there is seasonal demand, as would hold true for an ice cream company? Here the standard annual EOQ model is obviously not appropriate. However, it does provide a point of departure for setting inventory parameters, which are then modified to fit the particular seasonal pattern. We divide the year into the seasons in which annualized sales are relatively constant, say, summer, spring and fall, and winter. Then, the EOQ model is applied separately to each period. During the transitions between seasons, inventories would be either run down or else built up with special seasonal orders.

EOQ RANGE

Thus far, we have interpreted the EOQ and the resulting inventory values as single point estimates. It can be easily demonstrated that small deviations from the EOQ do not appreciably affect total inventory costs, and, consequently, that the optimal ordering quantity should be viewed more as a range than as a single value.[12]

---

[12]This is somewhat analogous to the optimal capital structure in that small changes in capital structure around the optimum do not have much effect on the firm's weighted average cost of capital.

To illustrate this point, we examine the sensitivity of total inventory costs to ordering quantity for Cotton Tops. Table 22-3 contains the results. We conclude that the ordering quantity could range from 5,000 to 8,000 units without affecting total inventory costs by more than 3.4 percent. Thus, managers can adjust the ordering quantity within a fairly wide range without significantly increasing total inventory costs.

<table>
<tr><td>SELF-TEST</td><td>Why are safety stocks required?</td></tr>
<tr><td>QUESTIONS</td><td>Conceptually, how would you evaluate a quantity discount offer from a supplier?</td></tr>
<tr><td></td><td>What impact does inflation typically have on the EOQ?</td></tr>
<tr><td></td><td>Can the EOQ model be used when a company faces seasonal demand fluctuations?</td></tr>
<tr><td></td><td>What is the effect of minor deviations from the EOQ on total inventory costs?</td></tr>
</table>

THE PAYMENTS PATTERN APPROACH TO MONITORING RECEIVABLES

In Chapter 20, we discussed two methods for monitoring a firm's receivables position: days sales outstanding and aging schedules. These procedures are useful, especially for monitoring an individual customer's account, but neither is totally suitable for monitoring the aggregate payment performance of all credit customers, especially for a firm that experiences fluctuating credit sales. In this section, we present another way to monitor receivables, the *payments pattern approach*.

The primary point in analyzing the aggregate accounts receivable situation is to see if customers, on average, are paying more slowly. If so, accounts receivable will build up, as will the cost of carrying receivables. Further, the payment slowdown may signal a decrease in the quality of the receivables, hence an increase in bad debt losses down the road. The DSO and aging schedules are useful in monitoring credit operations, but both are affected by increases and decreases in the level of sales.

TABLE 22-3	EOQ SENSITIVITY ANALYSIS	
ORDERING QUANTITY	**TOTAL INVENTORY COSTS**	**PERCENTAGE DEVIATION FROM OPTIMAL**
3,000	$10,512	+31.4%
4,000	8,960	+12.0
5,000	8,275	+3.4
6,000	8,023	+0.3
6,500	8,000	0.0
7,000	8,019	+0.2
8,000	8,170	+2.1
9,000	8,423	+5.3
10,000	8,750	+9.4

Thus, changes in sales levels, including normal seasonal or cyclical changes, can change a firm's DSO and aging schedule even though its customers' payment behavior has not changed at all. For this reason, a procedure called the *payments pattern approach* has been developed to measure any changes that might be occurring in customers' payment behavior.[13] To illustrate the payments pattern approach, consider the Hanover Company, a small manufacturer of hand tools which commenced operations in January 1996. Table 22-4 contains Hanover's credit sales and receivables data for 1996. Column 2 shows that Hanover's credit sales are seasonal, with the lowest sales in the fall and winter months and the highest during the summer.

Now assume that 10 percent of Hanover's customers pay in the month the sale is made, that 30 percent pay in the first month following the sale, that 40 percent pay in the second month, and that the remaining 20 percent pay in the third month. Further, assume that Hanover's customers have the same payment behavior throughout the year; that is, they always take the same length of time to pay. Column 3 of Table 22-4 contains Hanover's receivables balance at the end of each month. For example, during January Hanover has $60,000 in sales. Ten percent of the customers paid

HANOVER COMPANY: RECEIVABLES DATA FOR 1996 (THOUSANDS OF DOLLARS)						TABLE 22-4
			BASED ON QUARTERLY DATA		BASED ON YEAR-TO-DATE DATA	
MONTH (1)	CREDIT SALES (2)	RECEIVABLES (3)	ADS[a] (4)	DSO[b] (5)	ADS (6)	DSO (7)
January	$ 60	$ 54				
February	60	90				
March	60	102	$2.00	51 days	$2.00	51 days
April	60	102				
May	90	129				
June	120	174	3.00	58	2.50	70
July	120	198				
August	90	177				
September	60	132	3.00	44	2.67	49
October	60	108				
November	60	102				
December	60	102	2.00	51	2.50	41

[a]ADS = Average daily sales.
[b]DSO = Days sales outstanding.

[13]See Wilbur G. Lewellen and Robert W. Johnson, "A Better Way to Monitor Accounts Receivable," *Harvard Business Review,* May–June 1972, 101–109; and Bernell Stone, "The Payments-Pattern Approach to the Forecasting and Control of Accounts Receivable," *Financial Management,* Autumn 1976, 65–82.

during the month of sale, so the receivables balance at the end of January was $60,000 − 0.1($60,000) = (1.0 − 0.1)($60,000) = 0.9($60,000) = $54,000. By the end of February, 10% + 30% = 40% of the customers had paid for January's sales, and 10 percent had paid for February's sales. Thus, the receivables balance at the end of February was 0.6($60,000) + 0.9($60,000) = $90,000. By the end of March, 80 percent of January's sales had been collected, 40 percent of February's had been collected, and 10 percent of March's sales had been collected, so the receivables balance was 0.2($60,000) + 0.6($60,000) + 0.9($60,000) = $102,000; and so on.

Columns 4 and 5 give Hanover's average daily sales (ADS) and days sales outstanding (DSO), respectively, as these measures would be calculated from quarterly financial statements. For example, in the April–June quarter, ADS = ($60,000 + $90,000 + $120,000)/90 = $3,000, and the end-of-quarter (June 30) DSO = $174,000/$3,000 = 58 days. Columns 6 and 7 also show ADS and DSO, but here they are calculated on the basis of accumulated sales throughout the year. For example, at the end of June ADS = $450,000/180 = $2,500 and DSO = $174,000/$2,500 = 70 days. (For the entire year, sales are $900,000; ADS = $2,500, and DSO at year-end = 41 days. These last two figures are shown at the bottom of the last two columns.)

The data in Table 22-4 illustrate two major points. First, fluctuating sales lead to changes in the DSO, which suggests that customers are paying faster or slower, even though we know that customers' payment patterns are not changing at all. The rising monthly sales trend causes the calculated DSO to rise, whereas falling sales (as in the third quarter) cause the calculated DSO to fall, even though nothing is changing with regard to when customers actually pay. Second, we see that the DSO depends on an averaging procedure, but regardless of whether quarterly, semiannual, or annual data are used, the DSO is still unstable even though payment patterns are *not* changing. Therefore, it is difficult to use the DSO as a monitoring device if the firm's sales exhibit seasonal or cyclical patterns.

Seasonal or cyclical variations also make it difficult to interpret aging schedules. Table 22-5 contains Hanover's aging schedules at the end of each quarter of 1996. At the end of June, Table 22-4 showed that Hanover's receivables balance was $174,000. Eighty percent of April's $60,000 of sales had been collected, 40 percent of May's $90,000 of sales had been collected, and 10 percent of June's $120,000 of sales had

TABLE 22-5	HANOVER COMPANY: QUARTERLY AGING SCHEDULES FOR 1996 (THOUSANDS OF DOLLARS)						
AGE OF ACCOUNTS (DAYS)	VALUE AND PERCENTAGE OF TOTAL VALUE OF ACCOUNTS RECEIVABLE AT THE END OF QUARTER ENDING						
	MARCH 31		JUNE 30		SEPTEMBER 30		DECEMBER 31	
0–30	$ 54	53%	$108	62%	$ 54	41%	$ 54	53%
31–60	36	35	54	31	54	41	36	35
61–90	12	12	12	7	24	18	12	12
	$102	100%	$174	100%	$132	100%	$102	100%

been collected. Thus, the end-of-June receivables balance consisted of 0.2($60,000) = $12,000 of April sales, 0.6($90,000) = $54,000 of May sales, and 0.9($120,000) = $108,000 of June sales. Note again that Hanover's customers had not changed their payment patterns. However, rising sales during the second quarter created the impression of faster payments when judged by the percentage aging schedule, and falling sales after July created the opposite appearance. Thus, neither the DSO nor the aging schedule provides an accurate picture of customers' payment patterns if sales fluctuate during the year or are trending up or down.

With this background, we can now examine another basic tool, the *uncollected balances schedule,* as shown in Table 22-6. At the end of each quarter, the dollar amount of receivables remaining from each of the three month's sales is divided by that month's sales to obtain three receivables-to-sales ratios. For example, at the end of the first quarter $12,000 of the $60,000 January sales, or 20 percent, are still outstanding; 60 percent of February sales are still out; and 90 percent of March sales are uncollected. Exactly the same situation is revealed at the end of each of the next three quarters. Thus, Table 22-6 shows that Hanover's customers' payment behavior has remained constant.

HANOVER COMPANY: QUARTERLY UNCOLLECTED BALANCES SCHEDULES FOR 1996 (THOUSANDS OF DOLLARS)				TABLE 22-6

QUARTER	SALES	REMAINING RECEIVABLES	RECEIVABLES/SALES
Quarter 1:			
January	$ 60	$ 12	20%
February	60	36	60
March	60	54	90
		$102	170%
Quarter 2:			
April	$ 60	$ 12	20%
May	90	54	60
June	120	108	90
		$174	170%
Quarter 3:			
July	$120	$ 24	20%
August	90	54	60
September	60	54	90
		$132	170%
Quarter 4:			
October	$ 60	$ 12	20%
November	60	36	60
December	60	54	90
		$102	170%

Recall that at the beginning of the example we assumed the existence of a constant payments pattern. In a normal situation, the firm's customers' payments pattern would probably vary somewhat over time. Such variations would be shown in the last column of the uncollected balances schedule. For example, suppose customers began to pay their accounts slower in the second quarter. That might cause the second quarter uncollected balances schedule to look like this (in thousands of dollars):

QUARTER 2, 1997	SALES	REMAINING RECEIVABLES	RECEIVABLES/SALES
April	$ 60	$ 16	27%
May	90	70	78
June	120	110	92
		$196	197%

We see that the receivables-to-sales ratios are now higher than in the corresponding months of the first quarter. This causes the total uncollected balances percentage to rise from 170 to 197 percent, which, in turn, should alert Hanover's managers that customers are paying slower than they did earlier in the year.

The uncollected balances schedule permits a firm to monitor its receivables better, and it can also be used to forecast future receivables balances. When Hanover's pro forma 1997 quarterly balance sheets are constructed, management can use the receivables-to-sales ratios, coupled with 1997 sales estimates, to project each quarter's receivables balance. For example, with projected sales as given below, and using the same payments pattern as in 1996, Hanover's projected end-of-June 1997 receivables balance would be as follows:

QUARTER 2, 1997	PROJECTED SALES	RECEIVABLES/SALES	PROJECTED RECEIVABLES
April	$ 70,000	20%	$ 14,000
May	100,000	60	60,000
June	140,000	90	126,000
		Total projected receivables =	$200,000

The payments pattern approach permits us to remove the effects of seasonal and/or cyclical sales variation and to construct an accurate measure of customers' payments patterns. Thus, it provides financial managers with better aggregate information than the days sales outstanding or the aging schedule. Managers should use the payments pattern approach to monitor collection performance as well as to project future receivables requirements.

Except possibly in the inventory and cash management areas, nowhere in the typical firm have computers had more of an impact than in accounts receivable management. A well-run business will use a computer system to record sales, to send out bills, to keep track of when payments are made, to alert the credit manager when an account becomes past due, and to take action automatically to collect past-due accounts (for example, to prepare form letters requesting payment). Additionally, the payment history of each customer can be summarized and used to help establish credit limits for customers and classes of customers, and the data on each account can be aggregated and used for the firm's accounts receivable monitoring system. Finally, historical data can be stored in the firm's database and used to develop inputs for studies related to credit policy changes, as we discuss in the next section.

Define days sales outstanding (DSO). What can be learned from it? Does it have any deficiencies when used to monitor collections over time?

What is an aging schedule? What can be learned from it? Does it have any deficiencies when used to monitor collections over time?

What is the uncollected balances schedule? What advantages does it have over the DSO and the aging schedule for monitoring receivables? How can it be used to forecast a firm's receivables balance?

ANALYZING PROPOSED CHANGES IN CREDIT POLICY

In Chapter 20, we discussed credit policy, including setting the credit period, credit standards, collection policy, and discount percentage, as well as factors that influence credit policy. A firm's credit policy is reviewed periodically, and policy changes may be proposed. However, before a new policy is adopted, it should be analyzed to determine if it is indeed preferable to the existing policy. In this section, we discuss procedures for analyzing proposed changes in credit policy.

If a firm's credit policy is *eased* by such actions as lengthening the credit period, relaxing credit standards, following a less tough collection policy, or offering cash discounts, then sales should increase: *Easing the credit policy stimulates sales.* Of course, if credit policy is eased and sales rise, then costs will also rise because more labor, materials, and so on, will be required to produce the additional goods. Additionally, receivables outstanding will also increase, which will increase carrying costs. Moreover, bad debts and/or discount expenses may also rise. Thus, the key question when deciding on a proposed credit policy change is this: Will sales revenues increase more than costs, including credit-related costs, causing cash flow to increase, or will the increase in sales revenues be more than offset by higher costs?

Table 22-7 illustrates the general idea behind the analysis of credit policy changes. Column 1 shows the projected 1997 income statement for Monroe Manufacturing under the assumption that the firm's current credit policy is maintained throughout the year. Column 2 shows the expected effects of easing the credit policy by extending the credit period, offering larger discounts, relaxing credit standards, and easing collection efforts. Specifically, Monroe is analyzing the effects of changing its credit terms from 1/10, net 30, to 2/10, net 40, relaxing its credit standards, and putting less pressure on slow-paying customers. Column 3 shows the projected 1997 income statement incorporating the expected effects of an easing in credit policy. The generally looser policy is expected to increase sales and lower collection costs, but discounts and several other types of costs would rise. The overall, bottom-line effect is a $7 million increase in projected net income. In the following paragraphs, we explain how the numbers in the table were calculated.

TABLE 22-7	MONROE MANUFACTURING COMPANY: ANALYSIS OF CHANGING CREDIT POLICY (MILLIONS OF DOLLARS)

	PROJECTED 1997 NET INCOME UNDER CURRENT CREDIT POLICY (1)	EFFECT OF CREDIT POLICY CHANGE (2)	PROJECTED 1997 NET INCOME UNDER NEW CREDIT POLICY (3)
Gross sales	$400	+$130	$530
Less discounts	2	+ 4	6
Net sales	$398	+$126	$524
Production costs, including overhead	280	+ 91	371
Profit before credit costs and taxes	$118	+$ 35	$153
Credit-related costs:			
Cost of carrying receivables	3	+ 2	5
Credit analysis and collection expenses	5	− 3	2
Bad debt losses	10	+ 22	32
Profit before taxes	$100	+$ 14	$114
State-plus-federal taxes (50%)	50	+ 7	57
Net income	$ 50	+$ 7	$ 57

NOTE: The above statements include only those cash flows incremental to the credit policy decision.

Monroe's annual sales are $400 million. Under its current credit policy, 50 percent of those customers who pay do so on Day 10 and take the discount, 40 percent pay on Day 30, and 10 percent pay late, on Day 40. Thus, Monroe's days sales outstanding is $(0.5)(10) + (0.4)(30) + (0.1)(40) = 21$ days, and discounts total $(0.01)(\$400,000,000)(0.5) = \$2,000,000$.

The cost of carrying receivables is equal to the average receivables balance times the variable cost percentage times the cost of money used to carry receivables. The firm's variable cost ratio is 70 percent, and its pre-tax cost of capital invested in receivables is 20 percent. Thus, its cost of carrying receivables is $3 million:

$$(DSO)\begin{pmatrix} \text{Sales} \\ \text{per} \\ \text{day} \end{pmatrix}\begin{pmatrix} \text{Variable} \\ \text{cost} \\ \text{ratio} \end{pmatrix}\begin{pmatrix} \text{Cost} \\ \text{of} \\ \text{funds} \end{pmatrix} = \text{Cost of carrying receivables}$$

$$(21)(\$400,000,000/360)(0.70)(0.20) = \$3,266,667 \approx \$3 \text{ million.}$$

Only variable costs enter this calculation because this is the only cost element in receivables that must be financed. We are seeking the cost of carrying receivables, and variable costs represent the firm's investment in the cost of goods sold.

Even though Monroe spends $5 million annually to analyze accounts and to collect bad debts, 2.5 percent of sales will never be collected. Bad debt losses therefore amount to $(0.025)(\$400,000,000) = \$10,000,000$.

Monroe's new credit policy would be 2/10, net 40 versus the old policy of 1/10, net 30, so it would call for a larger discount and a longer payment period, as well as a relaxed collection effort and lower credit standards. The company believes that these changes will lead to a $130 million increase in sales, to $530 million per year. Under the new terms, management believes that 60 percent of the customers who pay will take the 2 percent discount, so discounts will increase to $(0.02)(\$530,000,000)(0.60) = \$6,360,000 \approx \$6$ million. Half of the nondiscount customers will pay on Day 40, and the remainder on Day 50. The new DSO is thus estimated to be 24 days:

$$(0.6)(10) + (0.2)(40) + (0.2)(50) = 24 \text{ days.}$$

Also, the cost of carrying receivables will increase to $5 million:

$$(24)(\$530,000,000/360)(0.70)(0.20) = \$4,946,667 \approx \$5 \text{ million.}^{14}$$

The company plans to reduce its annual credit analysis and collection expenditures to $2 million. The reduced credit standards and the relaxed collection effort are expected to raise bad debt losses to about 6 percent of sales, or to $(0.06)(\$530,000,000) = \$31,800,000 \approx \$32,000,000$, which is an increase of $22 million from the previous level.

The combined effect of all the changes in credit policy is a projected $7 million annual increase in net income. There would, of course, be corresponding changes on the projected balance sheet — the higher sales would necessitate somewhat larger cash balances, inventories, and, depending on the capacity situation, perhaps more fixed assets. Accounts receivable would, of course, also increase. Since these asset increases would have to be financed, certain liabilities and/or equity would have to be increased.

The $7 million expected increase in net income is, of course, an estimate, and the actual effects of the change could be quite different. In the first place, there is uncertainty — perhaps quite a lot — about the projected $130 million increase in sales. Indeed, if the firm's competitors matched its changes, sales might not rise at all. Similar uncertainties must be attached to the number of customers who would take discounts, to production costs at higher or lower sales levels, to the costs of carrying additional receivables, and to bad debt losses. In the final analysis, the decision will be based on judgment, especially concerning the risks involved, but the type of quantitative analysis set forth above is essential to the process.

---

[14]Since the credit policy change will result in a longer DSO, the firm will have to wait longer to receive its profit on the goods it sells. Therefore, the firm will incur an opportunity cost due to not having the cash from these profits available for investment. The dollar amount of this opportunity cost is equal to the old sales per day times the change in DSO times the contribution margin (1 − Variable cost ratio) times the firm's cost of carrying receivables, or

$$\text{Opportunity cost} = (\text{Old sales}/360)(\Delta \text{DSO})(1 - v)(k)$$

$$= (\$400/360)(3)(0.3)(0.20)$$

$$= \$0.2 = \$200,000.$$

For simplicity, we have ignored this opportunity cost in our analysis. For a more complete discussion of credit policy change analysis, see Eugene F. Brigham and Louis C. Gapenski, *Intermediate Financial Management*, 5th ed. (Fort Worth, Tex.: Dryden Press, 1996), Chapter 23.

Describe the procedure for evaluating a change in credit policy using the income statement approach.

Do you think that credit policy decisions are made more on the basis of numerical analyses or on judgmental factors?

ACCOUNTS RECEIVABLE AND INVENTORY FINANCING

In Chapter 21, we introduced the use of collateral — mainly accounts receivable and inventory — to secure short-term loans. In this section, we provide a more thorough discussion of the use of security in short-term financing.

In the past, state laws varied greatly with regard to the use of security in financing. Today, however, all states except Louisiana operate under the *Uniform Commercial Code (UCC),* which standardized and simplified the procedures for establishing loan security. The heart of the Uniform Commercial Code is the *Security Agreement,* which spells out the rights of the lender and the borrower in the event of a default, and the UCC-1, which lists the specific pledged assets. The assets can be items of equipment, accounts receivable, or inventories. Both the Security Agreement and the UCC-1 are filed with the secretary of the state in which the property resides. This enables potential new lenders to check to see if property is free and clear before making a loan secured by the property. Procedures under the Uniform Commercial Code for using accounts receivable and inventories as security for short-term credit are described in the following sections.

ACCOUNTS RECEIVABLE FINANCING

Accounts receivable financing involves either pledging receivables or selling them outright (called factoring). The *pledging of accounts receivable* is characterized by the fact that the lender not only has a claim against the receivables but also has *recourse* to the borrower, so if the person or firm that bought the goods does not pay, the selling firm must take the loss. Therefore, the risk of default on the pledged receivables remains with the borrower. The buyer of the goods is not ordinarily notified about the pledging of the receivables, and the lender is generally either a commercial bank or one of the large industrial finance companies.

Factoring, or *selling accounts receivable,* involves the purchase of receivables by the lender, generally without recourse to the borrower, which means that if the purchaser of the goods does not pay for them, the lender rather than the seller of the goods takes the loss. Under factoring, the buyer of the goods is typically notified of the transfer and is asked to make payment directly to the financial institution. Since the factoring firm assumes the risk of default on bad accounts, the factor must make the credit check. Accordingly, factors provide not only money but also a credit department for the borrower. Incidentally, the same financial institutions that make loans against pledged receivables also serve as factors. Thus, depending on the circumstances and the wishes of the borrower, a financial institution will provide either form of receivables financing.

INVENTORY FINANCING

A substantial amount of credit is secured by inventories. If a firm is a relatively good credit risk, the mere existence of the inventory may be a sufficient basis for an unsecured loan. However, if the firm is a relatively poor risk, the lending institution may insist upon collateral, which can take the form of a blanket lien against all inventory or either trust receipts or warehouse receipts against specific inventory items.

A *blanket inventory lien* gives the lending institution a lien against all the borrower's inventories. However, the borrower is free to sell inventories, so the value of the collateral can be reduced below the level that existed when the loan was granted. Because of the inherent weakness of the blanket lien, another procedure for inventory financing was developed — the *security instrument* (also called a *trust receipt*), which is an instrument acknowledging that goods are held in trust for the lender. When trust receipts are used, the borrowing firm, upon receiving funds from the lender, delivers a trust receipt for the goods. The goods can be stored in a public warehouse or held on the premises of the borrower. The trust receipt acknowledges that the goods are held in trust for the lender and that any proceeds from the sale of trust goods must be transmitted to the lender at the end of each day. Automobile dealer financing is one of the best examples of trust receipt financing.

Like trust receipts, *warehouse receipt* financing uses inventory as security. A *public warehouse* is an independent third-party operation engaged in the business of storing goods. Items which must age, such as tobacco and liquor, are often financed and stored in public warehouses. The borrower cannot remove the goods until the lender has been repaid, so the warehouse operation protects the lender. However, at times a public warehouse is not practical because of the bulkiness of goods and the expense of transporting them to and from the borrower's premises. In such cases, a *field warehouse* may be established at the borrower's place of business. To provide inventory supervision, the lending institution employs a third party, a field warehouse company, which acts as an agent for the lending institution.

What is the difference between pledging receivables and factoring receivables?
Explain the differences among blanket liens, trust receipts, and warehouse receipts.

SELF-TEST QUESTIONS

SUMMARY

■ The *cash conversion cycle* is the length of time between paying for raw materials and receiving cash from the sale of finished goods:

$$
\begin{array}{cccc}
\text{Cash} & \text{Inventory} & \text{Receivables} & \text{Payables} \\
\text{conversion} = \text{conversion} + & \text{collection} & - & \text{deferral} \; . \\
\text{cycle} & \text{period} & \text{period} & \text{period}
\end{array}
$$

■ The *Baumol model* provides insights into the optimal cash balance. The model balances the opportunity cost of holding cash against the transactions costs associated with obtaining cash either by selling marketable securities or by borrowing.

$$\text{Optimal cash infusion} = \sqrt{\frac{2(F)(T)}{k}}.$$

■ Firms generally set their target cash balances at the level which holds the risk of running out of cash to some acceptable level. *Monte Carlo simulation* can be helpful in setting the target cash balance.

■ Inventory can be grouped into three categories: (1) *raw materials,* (2) *work-in-process,* and (3) *finished goods.*

■ *Inventory costs* also can be divided into three parts: carrying costs, ordering costs, and stock-out costs. In general, *carrying costs* increase as the level of inventory rises, but *ordering costs* and *stock-out costs* decline with larger inventory holdings.

■ *Total carrying cost (TCC)* is equal to the percentage cost of carrying inventory (C) times the purchase price per unit of inventory (P) times the average number of units held (A): TCC = (C)(P)(A).

■ *Total ordering cost (TOC)* is equal to the fixed cost of placing an order (F) times the number of orders placed per year (N): TOC = (F)(N).

■ *Total inventory costs (TIC)* equal total carrying cost (TCC) plus total ordering cost (TOC): TIC = TCC + TOC.

■ The *economic ordering quantity (EOQ)* model is a formula for determining the order quantity that will minimize total inventory costs:

$$\text{EOQ} = \sqrt{\frac{2(F)(S)}{(C)(P)}}.$$

Here F is the fixed cost per order, S is annual sales in units, C is the percentage cost of carrying inventory, and P is the purchase price per unit.

■ The *reorder point* is the inventory level at which new items must be ordered.

■ *Safety stocks* are held to avoid shortages (1) if sales increase more than was expected or (2) if shipping delays are encountered on inventory ordered. The cost of carrying a safety stock, which is separate from that based on the EOQ model, is equal to the percentage cost of carrying inventory times the purchase price per unit times the number of units held as the safety stock.

■ Firms can use *days sales outstanding (DSO)* and *aging schedules* to help monitor their receivables position, but the best way to monitor aggregate receivables is the *payments pattern approach.* The primary tool in this approach is the *uncollected balances schedule.*

■ If a firm *eases its credit policy* by lengthening the credit period, relaxing its credit standards and collection policy, and offering (or raising) its cash discount, its sales should increase. However, its costs will also increase. A firm should ease its credit policy only if the costs of doing so will be offset by higher expected revenues. In general, credit policy changes should be evaluated on the basis of incremental profits.

■ Accounts receivable financing involves either pledging or factoring receivables. Under a *pledging* arrangement, the lender not only has a claim against the borrower's receivables but also has recourse against the borrower. *Factoring* involves the purchase of accounts receivable by the lender, generally without recourse to the borrower.

■ There are three primary methods of inventory financing: (1) An *inventory blanket lien* gives the lender a lien against all of the borrower's inventories. (2) A *trust receipt* is an instrument that acknowledges that goods are held in trust for the lender. (3) *Warehouse receipt financing* is an arrangement under which the lender employs a third party to take control of the borrower's inventory and to act as an agent for the lender.

This chapter concludes our discussion of working capital management and financing. In Part VII, we discuss several special topics, beginning with derivatives and risk management in Chapter 23.

QUESTIONS

Define each of the following terms:
a. Cash conversion cycle; inventory conversion period; receivables collection period; payables deferral period
b. Baumol model
c. Total carrying cost; total ordering cost; total inventory costs
d. Economic ordering quantity (EOQ); EOQ model; EOQ range
e. Reorder point; safety stock
f. Aging schedule; days sales outstanding (DSO)
g. Payments pattern approach; uncollected balances schedule
h. Pledging receivables; factoring
i. Recourse
j. Inventory blanket lien; trust receipt; warehouse receipt financing; field warehouse

Indicate by a +, −, or 0 whether each of the following events would probably cause average annual inventory holdings to rise, fall, or be affected in an indeterminate manner:
a. Our suppliers change from delivering by train to air freight. _____
b. We change from producing just-in-time to meet seasonal demand to steady, year-round production. _____
c. Competition in the markets in which we sell increases. _____
d. The general rate of inflation rises. _____
e. Interest rates rise; other things are constant. _____

SELF-TEST PROBLEMS

(SOLUTIONS APPEAR IN APPENDIX C)

ST-1 **CREDIT POLICY CHANGES** The McCue Company expects to have sales of $10 million this year under its current operating policies. Its variable costs as a percentage of sales are 80 percent, and its cost of capital is 16 percent. Currently the firm's credit policy is net 25 (no discount for early payment). However, its DSO is 30 days, and its bad debt loss percentage is 2 percent. McCue spends $50,000 per year to collect bad debts, and its federal-plus-state-plus-local tax rate is 50 percent.

The credit manager is considering two alternative proposals, given below, for changing the firm's credit policy. Find the expected change in net income, taking into consideration anticipated changes in carrying costs for accounts receivable, the probable bad debt losses, and the discounts likely to be taken, for each proposal. Should a change in credit policy be made?

Proposal 1: Lengthen the credit period by going from net 25 to net 30. The bad debt collection expenditures will remain constant. Under this proposal, sales are expected to increase by $1 million annually, and the bad debt loss percentage on *new* sales is expected to rise to 4 percent (the loss percentage on old sales should not change). In addition, the DSO is expected to increase from 30 to 45 days on all sales.

Proposal 2: Shorten the credit period by going from net 25 to net 20. Again, collection expenses will remain constant. The anticipated effects of this change are (1) a decrease in sales of $1 million per year, (2) a decline in the DSO from 30 to 22 days, and (3) a decline in the bad debt loss percentage to 1 percent on all sales.

ST-2 **EOQ MODEL** The Bertin Breads Company buys and then sells (as bread) 2.6 million bushels of wheat annually. The wheat must be purchased in multiples of 2,000 bushels. Ordering costs, which include grain elevator removal charges of $3,500, are $5,000 per order. Annual carrying costs are 2 percent of the purchase price per bushel of $5. The company maintains a safety stock of 200,000 bushels. The delivery time is 6 weeks.
  a. What is the EOQ?
  b. At what inventory level should a reorder be placed to prevent having to draw on the safety stock?
  c. What are the total inventory costs?
  d. The wheat processor agrees to pay the elevator removal charges if Bertin Breads will purchase wheat in quantities of 650,000 bushels. Would it be to the firm's advantage to order under this alternative?

PROBLEMS

22-1 **CASH CONVERSION CYCLE** The Boudreaux Corporation has an inventory conversion period of 75 days, a receivables collection period of 38 days, and a payables deferral period of 30 days.
  a. What is the length of the firm's cash conversion cycle?

b. If Boudreaux's annual sales are $3,375,000 and all sales are on credit, what is the firm's investment in accounts receivable?

c. How many times per year does Boudreaux turn over its inventory?

RELAXING COLLECTION EFFORTS The Boyd Corporation has annual credit sales of $1.6 million. Current expenses for the collection department are $35,000, bad debt losses are 1.5 percent, and the days sales outstanding is 30 days. The firm is considering easing its collection efforts such that collection expenses will be reduced to $22,000 per year. The change is expected to increase bad debt losses to 2.5 percent and to increase the days sales outstanding to 45 days. In addition, sales are expected to increase to $1,625,000 per year.

Should the firm relax collection efforts if the opportunity cost of funds is 16 percent, the variable cost ratio is 75 percent, and taxes are 40 percent?

ECONOMIC ORDERING QUANTITY The Gentry Garden Center sells 90,000 bags of lawn fertilizer annually. The optimal safety stock (which is on hand initially) is 1,000 bags. Each bag costs the firm $1.50, inventory carrying costs are 20 percent, and the cost of placing an order with its supplier is $15.

a. What is the economic ordering quantity?

b. What is the maximum inventory of fertilizer?

c. What will be the firm's average inventory?

d. How often must the company order?

TIGHTENING CREDIT TERMS Kim Mitchell, the new credit manager of the Vinson Corporation, was alarmed to find that Vinson sells on credit terms of net 90 days while industrywide credit terms have recently been lowered to net 30 days. On annual credit sales of $2.5 million, Vinson currently averages 95 days of sales in accounts receivable. Mitchell estimates that tightening the credit terms to 30 days would reduce annual sales to $2,375,000, but accounts receivable would drop to 35 days of sales and the savings on investment in them should more than overcome any loss in profit.

Vinson's variable cost ratio is 85 percent, and taxes are 40 percent. If the interest rate on funds invested in receivables is 18 percent, should the change in credit terms be made?

MONITORING OF RECEIVABLES The Russ Fogler Company, a small manufacturer of cordless telephones, began operations on January 1, 1996. Its credit sales for the first 6 months of operations were as follows:

MONTH	CREDIT SALES
January	$ 50,000
February	100,000
March	120,000
April	105,000
May	140,000
June	160,000

Throughout this entire period, the firm's credit customers maintained a constant payments pattern: 20 percent paid in the month of sale, 30 percent paid in the month following the sale, and 50 percent paid in the second month following the sale.

a. What was Fogler's receivables balance at the end of March and at the end of June?

b. Assume 90 days per calendar quarter. What were the average daily sales (ADS) and days sales outstanding (DSO) for the first quarter and for the second quarter? What were the cumulative ADS and DSO for the first half-year?

c. Construct an aging schedule as of June 30. Use 0-30, 31-60, and 61-90 day account ages.

d. Construct the uncollected balances schedule for the second quarter as of June 30.

22-6 **RECEIVABLES FINANCING** Finnerty's Funtime Company manufactures plastic toys. It buys raw materials, manufactures the toys in the spring and summer, and ships them to department stores and toy stores by late summer or early fall. Funtime factors its receivables; if it did not, its October 1996 balance sheet would appear as follows (thousands of dollars):

Cash	$ 40	Accounts payable	$1,200
Receivables	1,200	Notes payable	800
Inventories	800	Accruals	80
Current assets	$2,040	Current liabilities	$2,080
Fixed assets	800	Mortgages	200
		Common stock	400
		Retained earnings	160
Total assets	$2,840	Total liabilities and equity	$2,840

Funtime provides extended credit to its customers, so its receivables are not due for payment until January 31, 1997. Also, Funtime would have been overdue on some $800,000 of its accounts payable if the preceding situation had actually existed.

Funtime has an agreement with a finance company to factor the receivables for the period October 31 through January 31 of each selling season. The factoring company charges a flat commission of 2 percent of the invoice price, plus 6 percent per year interest on the outstanding balance; it deducts a reserve of 8 percent for returned and damaged materials. Interest and commissions are paid in advance. Note, however, that interest is not recognized as an expense until the end of the 90-day period. No interest is charged on the reserved funds or on the commission.

a. Show Funtime's balance sheet on October 31, 1996, including the purchase of all the receivables by the factoring company and the use of the funds to pay accounts payable. Ignore tax effects, and assume all proceeds from receivables factored are applied to accounts payable.

b. If the $1.2 million is the average level of outstanding receivables, and if they turn over four times a year (hence the commission is paid four times a year), what are the total dollar costs of receivables financing (factoring) and the effective annual interest rate?

22-7 **OPTIMAL CASH TRANSFER** Barenbaum Industries projects that cash outlays of $4.5 million will occur uniformly throughout the year. Barenbaum plans to meet its cash requirements by periodically selling marketable securities from its portfolio. The firm's marketable securities are invested to earn 12 percent, and the cost per transaction of converting securities to cash is $27.

a. Use the Baumol model to determine the optimal transaction size for transfers from marketable securities to cash.

b. What will be Barenbaum's average cash balance?

c. How many transfers per year will be required?

d. What will be Barenbaum's total annual cost of maintaining cash balances? What would the total cost be if the company maintained an average cash balance of $50,000 or of $0 (it deposits funds daily to meet cash requirements)?

SPREADSHEET PROBLEM 1

Altman Auto Parts is considering changing its credit terms from 2/15, net 30, to 3/10, net 30, in order to speed collections. At present, 60 percent of the firm's customers take the 2 percent discount. Under the new terms, discount customers are expected to rise to 70 percent. Regardless of the credit terms, half of the customers who do not take the discount are expected to pay on time, while the remainder will pay 10 days late. The change does not involve a relaxation of credit standards; therefore, bad debt losses are not expected to rise above their present 2 percent level. However, the more generous cash discount terms are expected to increase sales from $1 million to $1.2 million per year. The firm's variable cost ratio is 75 percent, the interest rate on funds invested in accounts receivable is 12 percent, and its tax rate is 40 percent.

a. What is the days sales outstanding before and after the change?

b. Calculate the discount costs before and after the change.

c. Calculate the dollar cost of carrying receivables before and after the change.

d. Calculate the bad debt losses before and after the change.

e. What is the incremental profit from the change in credit terms? Should the firm change its credit terms?

f. (1) Suppose the sales forecast is lowered to $1,100,000. Should the firm change its credit policy? What if the sales forecast dropped to $1,036,310?

   (2) Suppose the payment pattern of customers remains unchanged with the new credit plan; that is, 60 percent still take the discount, 20 percent pay on time, and 20 percent pay late. Also, the variable cost ratio rises to 78 percent. How does all this affect the decision, assuming the sales forecast remains at $1,200,000?

SPREADSHEET PROBLEM 2

The following inventory data have been established for the Adler Corporation:

   (1) Orders must be placed in multiples of 100 units.

   (2) Annual sales are 338,000 units.

   (3) The purchase price per unit is $3.

   (4) Carrying cost is 20 percent of the purchase price of goods.

   (5) Cost per order placed is $24.

   (6) Desired safety stock is 14,000 units; this amount is on hand initially.

   (7) Two weeks are required for delivery.

a. What is the EOQ?

b. How many orders should the firm place each year?

c. At what inventory level should a reorder be made? [Hint: Reorder point = Safety stock + (Weeks to deliver × Weekly usage) – Goods in transit.]

d. Calculate the total costs of ordering and carrying inventories if the order quantity is (1) 4,000 units, (2) 4,800 units, or (3) 6,000 units. What are the total costs if the order quantity is the EOQ?

e. What are the EOQ and total inventory costs if

   (1) Sales increase to 500,000 units?

   (2) Fixed order costs increase to $30? Sales remain at 338,000 units.

   (3) Purchase price increases to $4? Leave sales and fixed costs at original values.

MINI CASE

SECTION I: RECEIVABLES MANAGEMENT   Rich Jackson, a recent finance graduate, is planning to go into the wholesale building supply business with his brother, Jim, who majored in building construction. The firm would sell primarily to general contractors, and it would start operating next January. Sales would be slow during the cold months, rise during the spring, and then fall off again in the summer, when new construction in the area slows. Sales estimates for the first 6 months are as follows (in thousands of dollars):

January	$100	March	$300	May	$200
February	200	April	300	June	100

The terms of sale are net 30, but because of special incentives, the brothers expect 30 percent of the customers (by dollar value) to pay on the 10th day following the sale, 50 percent to pay on the 40th day, and the remaining 20 percent to pay on the 70th day. No bad debt losses are expected, because Jim, the building construction expert, knows which contractors are having financial problems.

a. Assume that, on average, the brothers expect annual sales of 18,000 items at an average price of $100 per item. (Use a 360-day year.)
   (1) What is the firm's expected days sales outstanding (DSO)?
   (2) What is its expected average daily sales (ADS)?
   (3) What is its expected average accounts receivable level?
   (4) Assume that the firm's profit margin is 25 percent. How much of the receivables balance must be financed? What would the firm's balance sheet figures for accounts receivable, notes payable, and retained earnings be at the end of one year if notes payable are used to finance the investment in receivables? Assume that the cost of carrying receivables had been deducted when the 25 percent profit margin was calculated.
   (5) If bank loans have a cost of 12 percent, what is the annual dollar cost of carrying the receivables?

b. What are some factors which influence (1) a firm's receivables level and (2) the dollar cost of carrying receivables?

c. Assuming that the monthly sales forecasts given previously are accurate, and that customers pay exactly as was predicted, what would the receivables level be at the end of each month? *To reduce calculations, assume that 30 percent of the firm's customers pay in the month of sale, 50 percent pay in the month following the sale, and the remaining 20 percent pay in the second month following the sale. Note that this is a different assumption than was made earlier.* Use the following format to answer Parts c and d:

MONTH	SALES	END-OF-MONTH RECEIVABLES	QUARTERLY SALES	ADS	DSO = (A/R)(ADS)
Jan	$100	$ 70			
Feb	200	160			
Mar	300	250	$600	$6.67	37.5
Apr	$300				
May	200				
Jun	100				

d. What is the firm's forecasted average daily sales for the first 3 months? For the entire half-year? The days sales outstanding is commonly used to measure receivables performance. What DSO is expected at the end of March? At the end of June? What does the DSO indicate about customers' payments? Is DSO a good management tool in this situation? If not, why not?

e. Construct aging schedules for the end of March and the end of June (use the format given below). Do these schedules properly measure customers' payment patterns? If not, why not?

AGE OF ACCOUNT (DAYS)	MARCH A/R	%	JUNE A/R	%
0–30	$210	84%		
31–60	40	16		
61–90	0	0	___	___
	$250	100%		

f. Construct the uncollected balances schedules for the end of March and the end of June. Use the format given below. Do these schedules properly measure customers' payment patterns?

MONTH	MARCH SALES	CONTRIBUTION TO A/R	A/R-TO-SALES RATIO	MONTH	JUNE SALES	CONTRIBUTION TO A/R	A/R-TO-SALES RATIO
Jan	$100	$ 0	0%	Apr			
Feb	200	40	20	May			
Mar	300	210	70	Jun		___	___

g. Assume that it is now July of Year 1, and the brothers are developing pro forma financial statements for the following year. Further, assume that sales and collections in the first half-year matched the predicted levels. Using the Year 2 sales forecasts as shown next, what are next year's pro forma receivables levels for the end of March and for the end of June?

MONTH	PREDICTED SALES	PREDICTED A/R-TO-SALES RATIO	PREDICTED CONTRIBUTION TO RECEIVABLES
Jan	$150	0%	$ 0
Feb	300	20	60
Mar	500	70	350
	Projected March 31 A/R balance =		$410
Apr	$400		
May	300		
Jun	200		
	Projected June 30 A/R balance =		

h. Assume now that it is several years later. The brothers are concerned about the firm's current credit terms, which are now net 30, which means that contractors buying building products from the firm are not offered a discount, and they are supposed to pay the full amount in 30 days. Gross sales are now running $1,000,000 a year, and 80 percent (by dollar volume) of the firm's *paying* customers generally pay the full amount on Day 30, while the other 20 percent pay, on average, on Day 40. Two percent of the firm's gross sales end up as bad debt losses.

The brothers are now considering a change in the firm's credit policy. The change would entail (1) changing the credit terms to 2/10, net 20, (2) employing stricter credit standards before granting credit, and (3) enforcing collections with greater vigor than in the past. Thus, cash customers and those paying within 10 days would receive a 2 percent discount, but all others would have to pay the full amount after only 20 days. The brothers believe that the discount would both attract additional customers and encourage some existing customers to purchase more from the firm — after all, the discount amounts to a price reduction. Of course, these customers would take the discount and, hence, would pay in only 10 days. The net expected result is for sales to increase to $1,100,000; for 60 percent of the paying customers to take the discount and pay on the 10th day; for 30 percent to pay the full amount on Day 20; for 10 percent to pay late on Day 30; and for bad debt losses to fall from 2 percent to 1 percent of gross sales. The firm's operating cost ratio will remain unchanged at 75 percent, and its cost of carrying receivables will remain unchanged at 12 percent.

To begin the analysis, describe the four variables which make up a firm's credit policy, and explain how each of them affects sales and collections. Then use the information given in Part h to answer Parts i through n.

i. Under the current credit policy, what is the firm's days sales outstanding (DSO)? What would the expected DSO be if the credit policy change were made?

j. What is the dollar amount of the firm's current bad debt losses? What losses would be expected under the new policy?

k. What would be the firm's expected dollar cost of granting discounts under the new policy?

l. What is the firm's current dollar cost of carrying receivables? What would it be after the proposed change?

m. What is the incremental after-tax profit associated with the change in credit terms? Should the company make the change? (Assume a tax rate of 40 percent.)

	NEW	OLD	DIFFERENCE
Gross sales		$1,000,000	
Less discounts	___	0	___
Net sales		$1,000,000	
Production costs	___	750,000	___
Profit before credit costs and taxes		$ 250,000	
Credit-related costs:			
Carrying costs		8,000	
Bad debt losses		20,000	
Profit before taxes		$ 222,000	
Taxes (40%)	___	88,800	___
Net income	___	$ 133,200	___

n. Suppose the firm makes the change, but its competitors react by making similar changes to their own credit terms, with the net result being that gross sales remain at the current $1,000,000 level. What would the impact be on the firm's post-tax profitability?

SECTION II: INVENTORY MANAGEMENT Andria Mullins, financial manager of Webster Electronics, has been asked by the firm's CEO, Fred Weygandt, to evaluate the company's inventory control techniques and to lead a discussion of the subject with the senior executives. Andria plans to use as an example one of Webster's "big ticket" items, a customized computer microchip which the firm uses in its laptop computer. Each chip costs Webster $200, and in addition it must pay its supplier a $1,000 setup fee on each order. Further, the minimum order size is 250 units; Webster's annual usage forecast is 5,000 units; and the annual carrying cost of this item is estimated to be 20 percent of the average inventory value.

Andria plans to begin her session with the senior executives by reviewing some basic inventory concepts, after which she will apply the EOQ model to Webster's microchip inventory. As her assistant, you have been asked to help her by answering the following questions:

a. Why is inventory management vital to the financial health of most firms?

b. What assumptions underlie the EOQ model?

c. Write out the formula for the total costs of carrying and ordering inventory, and then use the formula to derive the EOQ model.

d. What is the EOQ for custom microchips? What are total inventory costs if the EOQ is ordered?

e. What is Webster's added cost if it orders 400 units at a time rather than the EOQ quantity? What if it orders 600 per order?

f. Suppose it takes 2 weeks for Webster's supplier to set up production, make and test the chips, and deliver them to Webster's plant. Assuming certainty in delivery times and usage, at what inventory level should Webster reorder? (Assume a 52-week year, and assume that Webster orders the EOQ amount.)

g. Of course, there is uncertainty in Webster's usage rate as well as in delivery times, so the company must carry a safety stock to avoid running out of chips and having to halt production. If a 200-unit safety stock is carried, what effect would this have on total inventory costs? What is the new reorder point? What protection does the safety stock provide if usage increases, or if delivery is delayed?

h. Now suppose Webster's supplier offers a discount of 1 percent on orders of 1,000 or more. Should Webster take the discount? Why or why not?

i. For many firms, inventory usage is not uniform throughout the year, but, rather, follows some seasonal pattern. Can the EOQ model be used in this situation? If so, how?

j. How would these factors affect an EOQ analysis?
   (1) The use of just-in-time procedures.
   (2) The use of air freight for deliveries.
   (3) The use of a computerized inventory control system, wherein as units were removed from stock, an electronic system automatically reduced the inventory account and, when the order point was hit, automatically sent an electronic message to the supplier placing an order. The electronic system ensures that inventory records are accurate, and that orders are placed promptly.
   (4) The manufacturing plant is redesigned and automated. Computerized process equipment and state-of-the-art robotics are installed, making the plant highly flexible in the sense that the company can switch from the production of one item to another at a minimum cost and quite quickly. This makes short production runs more feasible than under the old plant setup.

SELECTED ADDITIONAL REFERENCES AND CASES

Key references on cash balance models include the following:

Daellenbach, Hans G., "Are Cash Management Optimization Models Worthwhile?" *Journal of Financial and Quantitative Analysis,* September 1974, 607–626.

Miller, Merton H., and Daniel Orr, "The Demand for Money by Firms: Extension of Analytic Results," *Journal of Finance,* December 1968, 735–759.

Mullins, David Wiley, Jr., and Richard B. Homonoff, "Applications of Inventory Cash Management Models," in *Modern Developments in Financial Management,* Stewart C. Myers, ed. (New York: Praeger, 1976).

Stone, Bernell K., "The Use of Forecasts for Smoothing in Control-Limit Models for Cash Management," *Financial Management,* Spring 1972, 72–84.

The following cases from the Cases in Financial Management: Dryden Request *series focus on the credit policy decision:*

Case 33, "Upscale Toddlers, Inc.," and Case 50, "Mitchell Lumber Co.," which deal with credit policy changes.

Case 34, "Texas Rose Company," and Case 34A, "Bridgewater Pool Company," which focus on receivables management.

PART VII

SPECIAL TOPICS

CHAPTER 23

DERIVATIVES AND RISK MANAGEMENT

*C*orporate financial managers are generally thought of as models of caution, paid to manage a company's finances prudently and conservatively. But recent events at Procter & Gamble, Gibson Greetings, and Metallgesellschaft, a German company, have shaken that image. Each of these companies incurred huge losses on derivatives transactions which were supposedly undertaken to reduce risk.

A look at how P&G got into trouble with risky derivatives shows how tempting it can be for a company to try to magnify its returns, but how difficult it is to predict the risks involved. P&G profited handsomely with derivatives in the early 1990s. Sensing more opportunity for gain, the P&G treasury staff asked Bankers Trust in late 1993 to create a derivative whose returns would depend on both U.S. and German interest rates. Bankers Trust, perhaps the most aggressive dealer in exotic securities, gave P&G three choices. P&G chose the most aggressive, the derivative that promised the greatest reward but entailed the greatest risk.

The transaction involved two complex swaps. P&G was allowed to issue floating rate debt at below-market rates, but, in return, the company had to give Bankers Trust a series of "put options" that gave the bank the right to sell to P&G U.S. Treasury bonds (in one swap deal) and German government bonds (in the other deal) at a fixed price. If interest rates in both countries were constant or fell, there would be no problem for P&G—the bonds would be worth more on the open market than the fixed price, so Bankers Trust would not require P&G to buy them. But if rates rose, P&G would have to buy bonds at above-market prices.

Rates climbed rapidly after the deal was struck, causing bond prices to plunge, so P&G was saddled with a rising liability to buy bonds at above-market prices. Bankers Trust said that it advised P&G to cut its losses and get

*out of the swaps, but P&G wouldn't budge. When the first losses hit, P&G prob-
ably said, "Oh-oh, we have a problem. But let's wait and see what interest rates
do." By the time P&G bit the bullet and closed out the position, they had a pre-
tax loss of $157 million.*

*P&G contended that it was victimized by Bankers Trust, and it sued, contend-
ing that the bank did not disclose all the risks involved in the transactions. Said
a P&G spokesperson, "These transactions were intended to be hedges. We use
swaps to manage and reduce our borrowing costs, not to make money. The swaps
turned out to be speculative transactions that were highly leveraged and clearly
did not fit our policy." On the other hand, Bankers Trust claimed that P&G is a
sophisticated company and that it knew the rules of the game. The lawsuit was
finally settled after more than two years of haggling, with Bankers Trust agreeing
to cover about 80 percent of P&G's losses. Yet, the topic of derivative use and
abuse has continued to be one of the hottest topics in the financial press.*

*In this chapter, we will discuss risk management, a topic of increasing impor-
tance to financial managers. We begin with a discussion of derivative securities — primarily options — because such securities form the backbone of most
financial risk management strategies.*

The term *risk management* can mean many things, but in business it involves identifying events that could have adverse financial consequences and then taking
actions to prevent and/or minimize the damage caused by these events. Years ago,
corporate risk managers dealt primarily with insurance — they made sure the firm
was adequately insured against fire, theft, and other casualties and that it had adequate liability coverage. More recently, the scope of risk management has been
broadened to include such things as controlling the costs of key inputs such as
petroleum by purchasing oil futures, or protecting against changes in interest rates
or exchange rates through dealings in the interest rate or foreign exchange markets.
In addition, risk managers try to ensure that actions designed to hedge against risk —
as P&G claimed its derivatives transactions were supposed to be — are not actually
increasing risks.

Since perhaps the most important aspect of risk management involves derivative
securities, we begin the chapter with a discussion of derivatives. *Direct claim securities,* such as stocks and bonds, are pieces of paper that represent claims against
real assets such as land, plant, and equipment, and even whole businesses. *Indirect
claim securities,* or *derivatives,* are securities whose values are determined by the
market price (or interest rate) of some other security. Derivatives include options,
whose values depend on the price of some underlying stock; interest rate and
exchange rate futures and swaps, whose values depend on interest rate and exchange
rate levels; and commodity futures, whose values depend on commodity prices.

BACKGROUND ON DERIVATIVES

An historical perspective is useful when studying derivatives. One of the first formal
markets for derivatives was the futures market for wheat. Farmers were concerned
about the price they would receive for their wheat when they sold it in the fall, and

millers were concerned about the price they would have to pay. The risks faced by both parties could be reduced if they could establish a price earlier in the year. Accordingly, mill agents would go out to the wheat belt and buy contracts from farmers which called for the farmers to deliver grain at a predetermined price. Both parties benefited from the transaction in the sense that their risks were reduced. The farmers could concentrate on growing their crop without worrying about the price of grain, and the millers could concentrate on their milling operations. Thus, *hedging with futures* lowered aggregate risk in the economy.

The earliest futures dealings were between two parties who arranged transactions between themselves. Soon, though, middlemen came into the picture, and *trading* in futures was established. The Chicago Board of Trade was an early marketplace for this dealing, and *futures dealers* helped make a market in futures contracts. Thus, farmers could sell futures on the exchange, and millers could buy them there. This improved the efficiency and lowered the cost of hedging operations.

Quickly, a third group — *speculators* — entered the scene. As we will see in the next section, most derivatives, including futures, are highly leveraged, meaning that a small change in the value of the underlying asset will produce a large change in the price of the derivative. This leverage appealed to speculators. At first blush, one might think that the appearance of speculators would increase risk, but this is not necessarily true. Indeed, speculators add capital and players to the market, and this probably stabilizes the market somewhat. Of course, derivatives markets are inherently volatile due to the leverage involved, hence risk to the speculators themselves is high, but their bearing of that risk probably makes the derivatives markets more stable for the hedgers.

Natural hedges, defined as situations in which aggregate risk can be reduced by derivatives transactions between two parties (called *counterparties*), exist for many commodities, for foreign currencies, for interest rates on securities with different maturities, and even for common stocks where portfolio managers want to "hedge their bets." Think about cotton farmers and cotton mills, copper mines and copper fabricators, importers and foreign manufacturers for currency exchange rates, electric utilities and coal miners, oil producers and oil users, bankers making long-term loans but obtaining funds as short-term deposits, and the like. In all such situations, hedging can reduce aggregate risks and thus benefit the economy.

Hedging can also be done in situations where no natural hedge exists. Here one party wants to reduce some type of risk, and another party agrees to sell a contract which protects the first party from a specific event or situation. Insurance is an obvious example of this type of hedge. Note, though, that with nonsymmetric hedges risks are generally transferred rather than eliminated, although insurance companies may be able to eliminate certain types of risk through diversification.

The derivatives markets have grown more rapidly than any other major market in recent years, for a number of reasons. First, analytical techniques such as the Black-Scholes Option Pricing Model, which is discussed in the next section, have been developed to help establish "fair" prices, which make the counterparties more comfortable with deals. Second, computers and electronic communications make it much easier for counterparties to deal with one another. Third, globalization has greatly increased the importance of currency markets and the need for reducing the exchange rate risks brought on by global trade. Recent trends and developments are sure to continue if not accelerate, so the use of derivatives for risk management purposes is sure to grow.

Note, though, that derivatives do have a potential downside. These instruments are highly leveraged, so small miscalculations can lead to huge losses. Also, they are complicated, hence not well understood by many people. This makes mistakes more likely than with less complex instruments, and it makes it harder for a firm's top management to exercise proper control over derivatives transactions. One 28-year-old, relatively low-level employee, operating in the Far East, entered into transactions that led to the bankruptcy of the oldest British bank (Barings Bank), the institution that held the accounts of the Queen of England. Orange County, California, went bankrupt due to its treasurer's speculation in derivatives. Hundreds of other horror stories can be told.

The P&G, Orange County, and Barings Bank affairs make the headlines, causing some people to argue that derivatives should be regulated out of existence to "protect the public." However, derivatives are used far more often to hedge risks than in harmful speculations, but these beneficial transactions never make the newspapers or television. So, while the horror stories do point out the need for top managers to exercise control over the personnel who deal with derivatives, they certainly do not justify the elimination of derivatives.

In the balance of this chapter, we discuss how firms can manage risks, and the use of derivatives in risk management.

SELF-TEST QUESTION | What is a "natural hedge"? Give some examples of natural hedges.

OPTIONS

An *option* is a contract which gives its holder the right to buy (or sell) an asset at some predetermined price within a specified period of time. *Pure options* are instruments that (1) are created by outsiders (generally exchanges which specialize in options) rather than the firm; (2) are bought and sold primarily by investors, speculators, and corporate risk managers; and (3) are of importance to both individual investors and financial managers. Moreover, financial managers should understand option theory because such an understanding will help them structure warrant and convertible financings, and also because option theory provides useful insights into other facets of corporate finance.

OPTION TYPES AND MARKETS

There are many types of options and option markets.[1] To illustrate how options work, suppose you owned 100 shares of General Computer Corporation (GCC), which, on March 22, 1996, sold for $53.50 per share. You could give (or sell) someone else the right to buy your 100 shares at any time during the next four

---

[1]For an in-depth treatment of options, see Don M. Chance, *An Introduction to Derivatives* (Ft. Worth, Tex.: Dryden, 1995).

months at a price of, say, $55 per share. The $55 is called the *strike,* or *exercise, price.* Such options exist, and they are traded on a number of exchanges, with the Chicago Board Options Exchange (CBOE) being the oldest and the largest. This type of option is defined as a *call option,* because the purchaser has a "call" on 100 shares of stock. The seller of an option is called the option *writer.* An investor who "writes" call options against stock held in his or her portfolio is said to be selling *covered options.* Options sold without the stock to back them up are called *naked options.* When the exercise price exceeds the current stock price, a call option is said to be *out-of-the-money.* When the exercise price is below the current price of the stock, the option is *in-the-money.*

You can also buy an option which gives you the right to *sell* a stock at a specified price within some future period — this is called a *put option.* For example, suppose you think GCC's stock price is likely to decline from its current level of $53.50 sometime during the next four months. For $218.75 you could buy a four-month put option giving you the right to sell 100 shares (which you would not necessarily own) at a price of $50 per share ($50 is the strike price). If you bought a 100-share contract for $218.75 and then GCC's stock actually fell to $45, your put option would be worth ($50 − $45)(100) = $500. After subtracting the $218.75 you paid for the option, your profit (before taxes and commissions) would be $281.25.

Table 23-1 contains an extract from the March 22, 1996, Listed Options Quotations Table as it would appear in a daily newspaper. This extract, which focuses on GCC, U.S. Medical, and Sport World's options, reflects the trading which occurred on the previous day. On March 21, Sport World's April (1-month), $55 call option sold for $0.50. Thus, for $0.50(100) = $50 you could buy options that would give you the right to purchase 100 shares of Sport World's stock at a price of $55 per share at any time during the next month.[2] If the stock price stayed below $55 during that period,

| | | MARCH 22, 1996, LISTED OPTIONS QUOTATIONS | | | | | | TABLE 23-1 |

		CALLS — LAST QUOTE			PUTS — LAST QUOTE		
CLOSING PRICE	**STRIKE PRICE**	**APRIL**	**MAY**	**JULY**	**APRIL**	**MAY**	**JULY**
GENERAL COMPUTER CORPORATION (GCC)							
53 ½	50	4¼	4¾	5 ½	⅝	1⅜	2³⁄₁₆
53 ½	55	1⁵⁄₁₆	2¹⁄₁₆	3 ⅛	2⅝	r	4½
53 ½	60	⁵⁄₁₆	¹¹⁄₁₆	1 ½	6⅝	r	8
U.S. MEDICAL							
56 ⅝	55	4¼	5⅛	7	2¼	3¾	r
SPORT WORLD							
53 ⅛	55	½	1⅛	r	2⅛	r	r

NOTE: r means not traded on March 21.

---

[2]Actually, the *expiration date,* which is the last date that the option can be exercised, is the Friday before the third Saturday of the exercise month. Thus, the April options actually have a term one day less than four weeks. Also, note that option contracts are generally written in 100-share multiples.

you would lose your $50, but if it rose to $65, then your $50 investment would have grown to ($65 − $55)(100) = $1,000 in less than 30 days. That translates into a very healthy annualized rate of return. Incidentally, if the stock price did go up, you would probably not actually exercise your options and buy the stock—rather, you would sell the options, which would then have a value of $1,000 versus the $50 you paid, to another option buyer.

Option trading is one of the hottest financial activities in the United States. In addition to options on individual stocks, options are also available on several stock indexes such as the NYSE Index and the S&P 100 Index, permitting one to bet on a rise or fall in the general market as well as on individual stocks. The leverage involved makes it possible for speculators with just a few dollars to make a fortune almost overnight. Also, investors with sizable portfolios can sell options against their stocks and earn the value of the option (less brokerage commissions), even if the stock's price remains constant. Further, options can be used to create hedges which protect the value of an individual stock or portfolio. We will discuss hedging strategies in more detail later in the chapter.[3]

Conventional options are generally written for six months or less, but a new type of option called a *Long-term Equity AnticiPation Security (LEAPS)* recently made its debut. Like conventional options, LEAPS are listed on exchanges and are tied both to individual stocks and to stock indexes. The major difference is that LEAPS are long-term options, having maturities of up to 2½ years. One-year LEAPS cost about twice as much as the matching three-month option, but because of their much longer time to expiration, LEAPS provide buyers with more potential for gains.

Corporations such as GCC, on whose stocks options are written, have nothing to do with the option market. The corporations do not raise money in the option market, nor do they have any direct transactions in it, and option holders do not vote for corporate directors or receive dividends. There have been studies by the SEC and others as to whether option trading stabilizes or destabilizes the stock market, and whether this activity helps or hinders corporations seeking to raise new capital. The studies have not been conclusive, but option trading is here to stay, and many regard it as the most exciting game in town.

FACTORS THAT AFFECT THE VALUE OF A CALL OPTION

An analysis of Table 23-1 provides some insights into call option valuation. First, we can see that there are at least three factors which affect a call option's value: (1) For a given striking price, the higher the stock's market price in relation to the strike price, the higher will be the call option price. Thus, Sport World's $55 April call option sells for $0.50, whereas U.S. Medical's $55 April option sells for $4.25. This difference arises because U.S. Medical's current stock price is $56⅝ versus only $53⅛

---

[3]It should be noted that insiders who trade illegally generally buy options rather than stock because options increase the profit potential. Note, though, that it is illegal to use insider information for personal gain, and an insider would be taking advantage of the option seller. Insider trading, in addition to being unfair and essentially equivalent to stealing, hurts the economy: Investors lose confidence in the capital markets and raise their required returns because of an increased element of risk, which raises the cost of capital and thus reduces the level of investment.

for Sport World. (2) For a given stock price, the higher the strike price, the lower will be the call option price. Thus, all of GCC's call options, regardless of exercise month, decline as the strike price increases. (3) The longer the option period, the higher will be the option price, because the longer the time before expiration, the greater the chance that the stock price will climb substantially above the exercise price. Thus, for all striking prices, option prices increase as the expiration date is lengthened. Other factors that affect option values, especially the volatility of the underlying stock, are discussed in later sections.

FORMULA VALUE VERSUS OPTION PRICE

How is the actual price of a call option determined in the market? We shall, shortly, present a widely used model (the Black-Scholes model) for pricing call options, but first it is useful to establish some basic concepts. To begin, we define a call option's *formula value* as follows:

$$\text{Formula value} = \frac{\text{Current price}}{\text{of the stock}} - \text{Strike price.}$$

For example, if a stock sells for $50, and its option has a strike price of $20, then the formula value is $30. The formula value can be thought of as the value of the option if it expired today. Note that the calculated formula value of a call option could be negative, but realistically the minimum formula value of an option is zero. Note also that an option's formula value can be thought of as its first approximation value, because it provides a starting point for finding the actual value of the option.

Now consider Figure 23-1, which presents some data on Space Technology Inc. (STI), a company which recently went public and whose stock price has fluctuated widely during its short history. The third column in the tabular data shows the formula values for STI's call option when the stock was selling at different prices; the fourth column gives the actual market prices for the option; and the fifth column shows the premium of the actual option price over its formula value. At any stock price below $20, the formula value is zero; above $20, each $1 increase in the price of the stock brings with it a $1 increase in the option's formula value. Note, however, that the actual market price of the option lies above the formula value at each price of the common stock, but the premium declines as the price of the common stock increases. For example, when the common stock sold for $20 and the option had a zero formula value, its actual price, and the premium, was $9. Then, as the price of the stock rose, the *formula value's increase* matched the stock's increase dollar for dollar, but the *market price* of the option climbed less rapidly, causing the premium to decline. The premium was $9 when the stock sold for $20 a share, but it had declined to $1 by the time the stock price had risen to $73 a share. Beyond this point, the premium virtually disappeared.

FIGURE 23-1	SPACE TECHNOLOGY INC.: OPTION PRICE AND FORMULA VALUE

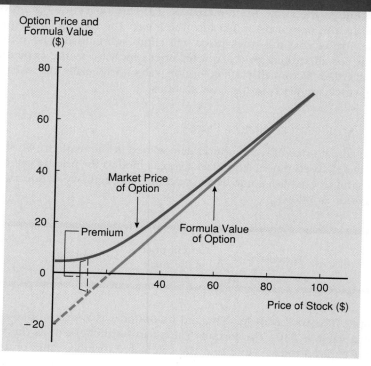

PRICE OF STOCK (1)	STRIKE PRICE (2)	FORMULA VALUE OF OPTION (1) − (2) = (3)	MARKET PRICE OF OPTION (4)	PREMIUM (4) − (3) = (5)
$20.00	$20.00	$ 0.00	$ 9.00	$9.00
21.00	20.00	1.00	9.75	8.75
22.00	20.00	2.00	10.50	8.50
35.00	20.00	15.00	21.00	6.00
42.00	20.00	22.00	26.00	4.00
50.00	20.00	30.00	32.00	2.00
73.00	20.00	53.00	54.00	1.00
98.00	20.00	78.00	78.50	0.50

Why does this pattern exist? Why should a call option ever sell for more than its formula value, and why does the premium decline as the price of the stock increases? The answer lies in part on the speculative appeal of options — they enable someone to gain a high degree of personal leverage when buying securities. To illustrate, suppose STI's option sold for exactly its formula value. Now suppose you were thinking of investing in the company's common stock at a time when it was selling for $21 a share. If you bought a share and the price rose to $42, you would have made a 100 percent capital gain. However, had you bought the option at its formula value ($1 when the stock was selling for $21), your capital gain would have been $22 − $1 = $21 on a $1 investment, or 2,100 percent! At the same time, your total loss potential with the option would be only $1 versus a potential loss of $21 if you purchased the stock. The huge capital gains potential, combined with the loss limitation, is clearly worth something—the exact amount it is worth to investors is the amount of the premium. Note, however, that buying the option is riskier than buying STI's stock, because there is a higher probability of losing money on the option. If STI's stock price remains at $21, you would break even if you bought the stock (ignoring transaction costs), but you would lose your entire $1 option investment.

Why does the premium decline as the price of the stock rises? Part of the answer is that both the leverage effect and the loss protection feature decline at high stock prices. For example, if you were thinking of buying STI stock when its price was $73 a share, the formula value of the option would be $53. If the stock price doubled to $146, the formula value of the option would go from $53 to $126. The percentage capital gain on the stock would still be 100 percent, but the percentage gain on the option would now be only 138 percent versus 2,100 percent in the earlier case. Notice also that the potential loss per dollar of potential gain on the option is much greater when the option is selling at high prices. These two factors, the declining leverage impact and the increasing danger of larger losses, help explain why the premium diminishes as the price of the common stock rises.

In addition to the stock price and the exercise price, the price of an option depends on three other factors: (1) the option's term to maturity, (2) the variability of the stock price, and (3) the risk-free rate. We will explain precisely how these factors affect call option prices later, but for now, note these points:

1. The longer an option has to run, the greater its value and the larger its premium. If an option expires at 4 P.M. today, there is not much chance that the stock price will go way up, so the option must sell at close to its formula value, and its premium must be small. On the other hand, if the expiration date is a year away, the stock price could rise sharply, pulling the option's value up with it.

2. An option on an extremely volatile stock is worth more than one on a very stable stock. If the stock price rarely moves, then there is only a small chance of a large gain. However, if the stock price is highly volatile, the option could easily become very valuable. At the same time, losses on options are limited, so large declines in a stock's price do not have a corresponding bad effect on option holders. Therefore, the more volatile a stock, the higher the value of its options.

3. The payoff on an option will occur in the future, so the value of the option is, in a sense, the present value of an expected future payoff. The higher the discount rate used to find the PV, the lower the value of the option.

Because of Points 1 and 2, in a graph such as Figure 23-1, if everything else were constant, then the longer an option's life, the higher its market price line would be above the formula value line. Similarly, the more volatile the price of the underlying stock, the higher is the market price line. We will see precisely how these factors, and also the risk-free rate, affect option values when we discuss the option pricing model.

SELF-TEST
QUESTIONS

What is an option? A call option? A put option?

Define a call option's formula value. Why is the actual market price of a call option usually above its formula value?

What are some factors which affect a call option's value?

INTRODUCTION TO OPTION PRICING

In the next section, we will discuss a well-known option pricing model, but it is useful first to go through a simple example. Assume that one-year call options are available on Butler Company, a Midwestern firm which produces cellular telephones. Each option has an exercise price of $35, and Butler's stock is now selling for $40 a share. Assume further that when the options expire one year hence, Butler's shares will be selling at one of only two possible prices, $30 or $50. Under these simple conditions, what is the value of a call option on Butler's stock?

To answer this question, we proceed as follows:

1. **Examine the payoffs at maturity.** At expiration, the stock price will be either $30 or $50, and the value of the option at expiration will depend on Butler's stock price. Thus, we have the following situation at expiration:

	STOCK PRICE	STRIKE PRICE	OPTION VALUE	
Low	$30	$35	$ 0	(option is worthless)
High	50	35	15	(expiration value)
Range	$20		$15	

2. **Equalize the range of payoffs.** Note that the range of payoffs as shown in Step 1 is $20 on the stock (from a low of $30 to a high of $50) and $15 on the option (from $0 to $15). The payoff ranges would be identical on the two investments if you could buy 0.75 shares of Butler's stock (or 75 shares of the stock and 100 options). In this situation, the payoff matrix would look like this:

	STOCK PRICE	VALUE OF 0.75 SHARES	OPTION VALUE
Low	$30	$22.50	$ 0
High	50	37.50	15
Range	$20	$15.00	$15

3. **Create a riskless hedge.** You can now make a riskless investment by buying 0.75 shares of Butler's stock and selling 1 call option. The sale of the call option will not affect the final value of your investment if the price of the stock declines, but it will lower your value by $50 − $35 = $15 if the price rises. Here is the resulting payoff matrix:

	STOCK PRICE	VALUE OF 0.75 SHARES	+	EFFECT OF THE CALL ON INVESTMENT'S VALUE	=	VALUE OF INVESTMENT
Low	$30	$22.50	+	$ 0	=	$22.50
High	50	37.50	+	(15)	=	22.50

If the stock price at expiration is $30, the stock investment is worth $22.50, but the call will not be exercised, hence it will not affect your portfolio's value. On the other hand, if the stock price is $50 at expiration, the value of the stock investment would rise from $22.50 to $37.50, but the holder of the call would exercise his or her option. Thus, you must provide one share at the exercise price, $35, which you must purchase at the market price of $50, hence you would incur a $15 loss. Therefore, regardless of what happens to the price of the stock, your portfolio's value is $22.50 — you have created a riskless portfolio by buying the stock and writing (selling) a call option on that stock.

4. **Valuing the call option.** To this point, we have not specified what price you would charge for the call. However, we have seen that your riskless portfolio will provide a sure $22.50 at option expiration in one year. If the risk-free rate is 8 percent, the value of the portfolio today is $22.50/1.08 = $20.83. Since Butler's stock is currently selling at $40 a share, creating the riskless portfolio would require a stock investment of 0.75($40) = $30. Since your total investment outlay to create the riskless portfolio must be equal to or less than $20.83, the present value of the portfolio, you must be able to sell the call option for at least $30 − $20.83 = $9.17 in order to break even. Assuming that competition exists in the options market, $9.17 will be the equilibrium price of the option.

Clearly, this example is unrealistic—Butler's stock price could be almost anything after one year, and you could not purchase 0.75 shares of stock (but you could do so in effect by buying 75 shares and selling 100 options). Still, the example does illustrate that investors can, in principle, create riskless portfolios by buying stocks and selling call options against those stocks, and the return on such portfolios should be the risk-free rate. If call options are not priced to reflect this condition, arbitrageurs will actively trade stocks and options until option prices reflect equilibrium conditions. In the next section, we discuss the Black-Scholes Option Pricing Model, which is based on the general premise we developed here—the creation of a riskless portfolio—but which is applicable to "real-world" option pricing because it allows for a complete range of ending stock prices.

SELF-TEST QUESTIONS : Describe how a risk-free portfolio can be created using stocks and options. How can such a portfolio be used to help estimate a call option's value?

THE BLACK-SCHOLES OPTION PRICING MODEL (OPM)

The *Black-Scholes Option Pricing Model (OPM)* was developed in 1973, and it helped give rise to the rapid growth in options trading.[4] This model, which has been programmed into the permanent memories of some hand-held calculators, is widely used by option traders.

In deriving their option pricing model, which estimates the value of a call option, Black and Scholes made the following assumptions:

1. The stock underlying the call option provides no dividends or other distributions during the life of the option.

2. There are no transaction costs for buying or selling either the stock or the option.

3. The short-term, risk-free interest rate is known and is constant during the life of the option.

4. Any purchaser of a security may borrow any fraction of the purchase price at the short-term, risk-free interest rate.

5. Short selling is permitted, and the short seller will receive immediately the full cash proceeds of today's price for a security sold short.[5]

6. The call option can be exercised only on its expiration date.

7. Trading in all securities takes place in continuous time, and the stock price moves randomly in continuous time.

The derivation of the Black-Scholes Option Pricing Model rests on the concept of a riskless hedge such as the one we set up in the last section. By buying shares of a stock and simultaneously selling call options on that stock, an investor can create a risk-free investment position, where gains on the stock will exactly offset losses on the option, and vice versa. This riskless hedged position must earn a rate of return equal to the risk-free rate; otherwise, an arbitrage opportunity would exist, and people trying to take advantage of this opportunity would drive the price of the option to the equilibrium level as specified by the Black-Scholes model.

---

[4]See Fischer Black and Myron Scholes, "The Pricing of Options and Corporate Liabilities," *Journal of Political Economy,* May/June 1973, 637–659.

[5]Suppose an investor (or speculator) does not now own any IBM stock. If the investor anticipates a rise in the stock price and consequently buys IBM stock, he or she is said to have *gone long* in IBM. On the other hand, if the investor thinks IBM's stock is likely to fall, he or she could *go short,* or *sell IBM short.* Since the short seller has no IBM stock, he or she would have to borrow the shares sold short from a broker. If the stock price falls, the short seller could, later on, buy shares on the open market and pay back the ones borrowed from the broker. The short seller's profit, before commissions and taxes, would be the difference between the price received from the short sale and the price paid later to purchase the replacement stock.

The Black-Scholes model consists of the following three equations:

$$V = P[N(d_1)] - Xe^{-k_{RF}t}[N(d_2)]. \qquad \text{23-1}$$

$$d_1 = \frac{\ln(P/X) + [k_{RF} + (\sigma^2/2)]t}{\sigma\sqrt{t}}. \qquad \text{23-2}$$

$$d_2 = d_1 - \sigma\sqrt{t}. \qquad \text{23-3}$$

Here

V = current value of a call option with time t until expiration.

P = current price of the underlying stock.

$N(d_i)$ = probability that a deviation less than d_i will occur in a standard normal distribution. Thus, $N(d_1)$ and $N(d_2)$ represent areas under a standard normal distribution function.

X = exercise, or strike, price of the option.

$e \approx 2.7183$.

k_{RF} = risk-free interest rate.

t = time until the option expires (the option period).

$\ln(P/X)$ = natural logarithm of P/X.

σ^2 = variance of the rate of return on the stock.

Note that the value of the option is a function of the variables we discussed earlier: (1) P, the stock's price; (2) t, the option's time to expiration; (3) X, the strike price; (4) σ^2, the variance of the underlying stock; and (5) k_{RF}, the risk-free rate. We do not derive the Black-Scholes model — the derivation involves some extremely complicated mathematics that go far beyond the scope of this text. However, it is not difficult to use the model, and, under the assumptions set forth previously, if the option price is different from the one found by Equation 23-1, this would provide the opportunity for arbitrage profits, which would, in turn, force the option price back to the value indicated by the model.[6] As we noted earlier, the Black-Scholes model is widely used by traders, so actual option prices conform reasonably well to values derived from the model.

In essence, the first term of Equation 23-1, $P[N(d_1)]$, can be thought of as the expected present value of the terminal stock price, while the second term, $Xe^{-k_{RF}t}[N(d_2)]$, can be thought of as the present value of the exercise price. However, rather than try to figure out exactly what the equations mean, it is more productive to work out some values and to see how changes in the inputs affect the value of a call option.

---

[6]*Programmed trading,* in which stocks are bought and options are sold, or vice versa, is an example of arbitrage between stocks and options.

OPM ILLUSTRATION

The current stock price, P, the exercise price, X, and the time to maturity, t, of the option can be obtained from a newspaper such as *The Wall Street Journal*. The risk-free rate, k_{RF}, used in the OPM is the yield on Treasury bills with a maturity date equal to the option expiration date. The stock price variance, σ^2, can be estimated by calculating the variance of the percentage change in daily stock prices for the past year, that is, the variance of $(P_t - P_{t-1})/P_t$ on a daily basis.

Assume that the following information has been obtained:

P = $20.

X = $20.

t = 3 months or 0.25 years.

k_{RF} = 12% = 0.12.

σ^2 = 0.16. Note that σ = 0.4%, so this stock fluctuates about 0.4 percent per day, which is about right for an average stock.

Given this information, we can now use the OPM by solving Equations 23-1, 23-2, and 23-3. Since d_1 and d_2 are required inputs for Equation 23-1, we solve Equations 23-2 and 23-3 first:

$$d_1 = \frac{\ln(\$20/\$20) + [0.12 + (0.16/2)](0.25)}{0.40(0.50)}$$

$$= \frac{0 + 0.05}{0.20} = 0.25.$$

$$d_2 = d_1 - 0.20 = 0.05.$$

Note that $N(d_1) = N(0.25)$ and $N(d_2) = N(0.05)$ represent areas under a standard normal distribution function. From Table A-5 in Appendix A at the end of the book, we see that the value $d_1 = 0.25$ implies a probability of $0.0987 + 0.5000 = 0.5987$, so $N(d_1) = 0.5987$. Similarly, $N(d_2) = 0.5199$. We can use those values to solve Equation 22-1:

$$V = \$20[N(d_1)] - \$20e^{-(0.12)(0.25)}[N(d_2)]$$

$$= \$20[N(0.25)] - \$20(0.9704)[N(0.05)]$$

$$= \$20(0.5987) - \$19.41(0.5199)$$

$$= \$11.97 - \$10.09 = \$1.88.$$

Thus, the value of the option, under the assumed conditions, is $1.88. Suppose the actual option price were $2.25. Arbitrageurs could simultaneously sell the option and buy the underlying stock, and earn a riskless profit. Such trading would occur until the price of the option was driven to $1.88. The reverse would occur if the option sold for less than $1.88. Thus, investors would be unwilling to pay more than $1.88 for the option, and they could not buy it for less, so $1.88 is the *equilibrium value* of the option.

To see how the five OPM factors affect the value of the option, V, consider Table 23-2. Here the top row shows the base case input values we used above to illustrate the OPM and the resulting option value, V = $1.88. In each of the subsequent rows, the boldfaced factor is increased, while the other four are held constant at their base

EFFECTS OF OPM FACTORS ON THE VALUE OF A CALL OPTION						**TABLE 23-2**

	INPUT FACTORS					
CASE	P	X	t	k_{RF}	σ^2	V
Base case	$20	$20	0.25	12%	0.16	$1.88
Increase P by $5	**25**	20	0.25	12	0.16	5.81
Increase X by $5	20	**25**	0.25	12	0.16	0.39
Increase t to 6 months	20	20	**0.50**	12	0.16	2.81
Increase k_{RF} to 16%	20	20	0.25	**16**	0.16	1.99
Increase σ^2 to 0.25	20	20	0.25	12	**0.25**	2.27

case levels. The resulting value of the call option is given in the last column. Now let's consider the effects of changes in each factor:

1. **Current stock price.** If the current stock price, P, increases from $20 to $25, the option value increases from $1.88 to $5.81. Thus, the value of the option increases as the stock price increases, but by less than the stock price increase, $3.93 versus $5.00. Note, though, that the percentage increase in the option value, ($5.81 − $1.88)/$1.88 = 209%, far exceeds the percentage increase in the stock price, ($25 − $20)/$20 = 25%.

2. **Exercise price.** If the exercise price, X, increases from $20 to $25, the value of the option declines. Again, the decrease in the option value is less than the exercise price increase, but the percentage change in the option value, ($0.39 − $1.88)/$1.88 = −79%, exceeds the percentage change in the exercise price, ($25 − $20)/$20 = 25%.

3. **Option period.** As time to expiration increases from t = 3 months (or 0.25 years) to t = 6 months (or 0.50 years), the value of the option increases from $1.88 to $2.81. This occurs because the value of the option depends on the chances for an increase in the price of the underlying stock, and the longer the option has to go, the higher the stock price may climb. Thus, other factors held constant, a six-month option is worth more than a 3-month option.

4. **Risk-free rate.** As the risk-free rate increases from 12 to 16 percent, the value of the option increases slightly, from $1.88 to $1.99. Equations 23-1, 23-2, and 23-3 suggest that the principal effect of an increase in k_{RF} is to reduce the present value of the exercise price, $Xe^{-k_{RF}t}$, hence to increase the current value of the option.[7] The risk-free rate also plays a role in determining the values of the normal distribution functions $N(d_1)$ and $N(d_2)$, but this effect is of secondary

---

[7]At this point, you may be wondering why the first term in Equation 23-1, $P[N(d_1)]$, is not discounted. In fact, it has been, because the current stock price, P, already represents the present value of the expected stock price at expiration. In other words, P is a discounted value, and the discount rate used in the market to determine today's stock price includes the risk-free rate. Thus, Equation 23-1 can be thought of as the present value of the end-of-option-period spread between the stock price and the strike price, adjusted for the probability that the stock price will be higher than the strike price.

importance. Indeed, option prices in general are not very sensitive to interest rate changes, at least not to changes within the ranges normally encountered.

5. **Variance.** As the variance increases from the base case 0.16 to 0.25, the value of the option increases from $1.88 to $2.27. Therefore, if all other factors are held constant, the riskier the underlying security, the more valuable the option. This result is logical. First, if you bought an option to buy a stock that sells at its exercise price, and if $\sigma^2 = 0$, then there would be a zero probability of the stock going up, hence a zero probability of making money on the option. On the other hand, if you bought an option on a high-variance stock, there would be a fairly high probability that the stock would go way up, hence that you would make a large profit on the option. Of course, a high-variance stock could go way down, but as an option holder, your losses would be limited to the price paid for the option — only the right-hand side of the stock's probability distribution counts. Put another way, an increase in the price of the stock helps options holders more than a decrease hurts them, so the greater the variance, the greater is the value of the option. This makes options on risky stocks more valuable than those on safer, low-variance stocks.

This concludes our discussion of options and option pricing theory. The next section discusses some other types of derivative securities.

SELF-TEST
QUESTIONS What is the purpose of the Black-Scholes Option Pricing Model?

Explain what a "riskless hedge" is and how the riskless hedge concept is used in the Black-Scholes OPM.

Describe the impact that an increase in each of the following factors would have on the value of a call option:

(1) Stock price

(2) Exercise price

(3) Option period

(4) Risk-free rate

(5) Stock price variance

OTHER TYPES OF DERIVATIVES

Put and call options represent an important class of derivative securities, but there are other types of derivatives, including futures, swaps, structured notes, inverse floaters, and a host of other "exotic" contracts.

FORWARD CONTRACTS AND FUTURES

The first type of future contract was actually called a *forward contract*, under which one party agreed to buy a commodity at a specific price at a specific future date and the other party agreed to make the sale. Goods are actually delivered under forward contracts. Unless both parties are financially strong, there is a danger that one party will default on the contract, especially if the price of the commodity changes markedly after the agreement is reached.

A *futures contract* is similar to a forward contract, but with three key differences: (1) Futures contracts are "marked to market" on a daily basis, meaning that gains and losses are noted and funds must be put up to cover losses. This greatly reduces the default risk of futures vis-á-vis forward contracts. (2) With futures, physical delivery of the underlying asset is virtually never taken—the two parties simply settle up with cash for the difference between the contracted strike price and the actual price on the expiration date. (3) Futures contracts are generally standardized instruments that are traded on exchanges, whereas forward contracts are generally tailor-made, are negotiated between two parties, and are not traded after they have been signed.

Futures and forward contracts were originally used for commodities such as wheat, where farmers would sell futures contracts to millers, enabling both parties to lock in prices and thus reduce their risk exposure. Commodities futures are still important, but today more trading is done in foreign exchange and interest rate futures. To illustrate how foreign exchange futures are used, suppose GE arranges to buy electric motors from a German manufacturer on terms that call for payment of 1 million marks in 180 days. GE would not want to give up the free trade credit, but it might be afraid the mark would appreciate against the dollar during the next six months, in which case the dollar cost of the million marks would rise. GE could buy a forward contract under which it agreed to buy the million marks in 180 days at a fixed price and thus lock in the dollar cost of the motors. The transaction might be conducted through a money center bank, which would try to find a German company (a "counterparty") that needed dollars in six months, or GE could buy a futures contract on an exchange.

Interest rate futures represent another huge and growing market. For example, suppose Simonset Corporation decides to build a new plant at a cost of $20 million, and it plans to finance the project with 20-year bonds which would carry a 10 percent interest rate if they were issued today. However, the company will not need the money for about six months. Simonset could go ahead and sell 20-year bonds now, locking in the 10 percent rate, but it would have the money before it was needed, so it would have to invest in short-term securities which yield only 5 percent. However, if Simonset waits six months to sell the bond issue, interest rates might be higher than they are today, in which case the value of the plant would be reduced, perhaps to the point of making the investment unprofitable.

One solution to Simonset's dilemma involves interest rate futures, which are based on a hypothetical 20-year Treasury bond with an 8 percent semiannual coupon. If interest rates in the economy go up, the value of the hypothetical T-bond will go down, and vice versa. In our example, Simonset is worried about an increase in interest rates. Should rates rise, the hypothetical Treasury bond's value would decline. Therefore, Simonset could sell T-bond futures for delivery in six months to hedge its position. If interest rates rise, Simonset will have to pay more when it issues its own bonds, but it will make a profit on its futures position because it will have sold the bonds at a higher price than it will have to pay to cover (repurchase) them. Of course, if interest rates decline, Simonset will lose on its futures position, but it will get to pay a lower interest rate when it issues its bonds.

Interest rate and exchange rate futures can, of course, be used for speculative as well as hedging purposes. One can buy a T-bond contract on $100,000 of bonds with only $5,000 down, in which case a small change in interest rates will result in a very large gain or loss. We will discuss exchange rate and interest rate futures in more detail in a later section.

SWAPS

A *swap* is just what the name implies — two parties agree to swap something, generally obligations to make specified payment streams. Most swaps today involve either interest payments or currencies. To illustrate an interest rate swap, suppose Company A has a 20-year, $100 million floating rate bond issue outstanding, while Company F has $100 million of 20-year, fixed rate debt. Thus, each company has an obligation to make a stream of interest payments, but one payment stream is fixed while the other will vary, depending on the future course of interest rates.

Now suppose Company A has stable cash flows and wants to lock in its cost of debt, while Company F has cash flows that fluctuate with the economy. Recognizing that interest rates also move with the economy, Company F has concluded that it would prefer variable rate debt. If the companies swapped their payment obligations, an *interest rate swap* would occur. Of course, the swap might involve a side payment; for example, if interest rates had fallen sharply since Company F issued its bonds, then its payment obligations would be relatively high, and it would have to make a side payment to effect the swap. Similarly, if the credit risk of one company was higher than that of the other, the less risky company would be concerned about the ability of its "counterparty" to make the required payments. This too would lead to the need for a side payment.

Currency swaps are similar to interest rate swaps. To illustrate, suppose Company A, an American firm, had issued $100 million of dollar-denominated bonds to fund an investment in Germany. Meanwhile, Company G, a German firm, had issued $100 million of mark-denominated bonds to make an investment in the United States. Company A will earn marks but be required to make payments in dollars, and Company G will be in a reverse situation. Thus, both companies will be exposed to exchange rate risk. However, this risk would be eliminated if the companies swapped payment obligations. As with interest rate swaps, differences in credit risks could lead to the need for side payments.

Originally, swaps were arranged between companies by money center banks, which would match up counterparties. Such matching still occurs, but today most swaps are between companies and banks, with the banks then taking steps to ensure that their own risks are hedged. For example, Citibank might arrange a swap with Company A, which would agree to make specified payments in marks to the bank, and the bank would in turn make the dollar payments Company A would otherwise owe. The bank would charge a fee for setting up the swap, and these charges would reflect the creditworthiness of Company A. To protect itself against exchange rate movements, the bank would hedge its position, either by lining up a German company which needed to make dollar payments or else by using currency futures.

STRUCTURED NOTES

The term *structured note* often means a debt obligation which is derived from some other debt obligation. For example, in the early 1980s, investment bankers began buying large blocks of long-term, noncallable Treasury bonds and then *stripping* them to create a series of zero coupon bonds. The zero with the shortest maturity was backed by the first interest payment on the T-bond issue, the second shortest zero was backed by the next interest payment, and so forth, on out to a 30-year zero backed by the last interest payment plus the maturity value of the T-bond. Zeroes formed by stripping T-bonds were one of the first types of structured notes.

Another important type of structured note is backed by the interest and principal payments on mortgages. In the 1970s, mortgages backed by federal agencies were purchased by Wall Street firms, assembled into pools, and placed with a trustee. Then bonds called *Collateralized Mortgage Obligations (CMOs),* which were backed by the mortgage pool held in trust, were sold to pension funds, individuals for their IRA accounts, and other investors who were willing to invest in CMOs but who would not have purchased individual mortgages. This *securitization* of mortgages made billions of dollars of new capital available to home buyers.

CMOs are more difficult to evaluate than straight bonds for two reasons. First, the underlying mortgages can be prepaid at any time, and the prepayment proceeds are used to retire part of the CMO debt itself. Therefore, the holder of CMO is never sure when his or her bond will be called. Second, a variety of structured notes can be created, ranging from notes whose cash flows can be predicted with virtual certainty to other notes whose payment streams are highly uncertain. For example, investment bankers can (and do) create notes called *IOs,* (for *Interest Only*), which provide cash flows from the interest component of the mortgage amortization payments, and *POs* (for *Principal Only*), which are paid from the principal repayment stream. In each case, the value of the note is found as the PV of an expected payment stream, but the length and size of the stream are uncertain. Suppose, for example, that you are offered an IO which you expect to provide payments of $100 for 10 years (you expect the mortgages to be refinanced after 10 years, at which time your payments will cease). Suppose further that you discount the payment stream at a rate of 10 percent and get a PV of $614.46. You have $614.46 to invest, so you buy the IO, expecting to earn 10 percent on your money.

Now suppose interest rates increase. The discount rate would increase, which implies that the value of the IO should decline. Conversely, if rates fall, the discount rate would drop, and that would imply an increase in the IO's value. However, if rates decline sharply, this might lead to a rash of mortgage refinancings, in which case your payments, which would come from interest only, would cease (or be greatly reduced), and the value of your IO would fall sharply. Similarly, a sharp increase in interest rates would reduce refinancing, lengthen your expected payment stream, and perhaps increase the value of your IO.

Investment bankers can slice and dice a pool of mortgages into a bewildering array of structured notes, ranging from "plain vanilla" ones with highly predictable cash flows and little risk to "exotic" ones (sometimes called "toxic waste") whose risks are almost incalculable but surely large.

Securitizing mortgages through CMOs serves a useful economic function — it provides an investment outlet for pension funds and others with money to invest, and it makes more money available to homeowners at a reasonable cost. Also, some investors want relatively safe investments, while others are willing to buy more speculative securities for the higher expected returns they provide. Structured notes permit a partitioning of risks to give investors what they want.

Inverse Floaters

A floating rate note has an interest rate that rises and falls with some interest rate index. For example, the interest rate on a $100,000 note at prime plus 1 percent would be 9 percent when the prime rate is 8 percent, and the note's rate would move up and down with the prime rate. Since the cash flows associated with the note would rise and fall as the discount rate used to value it rises and falls, the market value of the note would be relatively stable.

With an *inverse floater*, the rate paid on the note moves counter to market rates. Thus, if interest rates in the economy rose, the interest rate paid on an inverse floater would fall, lowering its cash interest payments. At the same time, the discount rate used to value the inverse floater's cash flows would rise along with other rates. The combined effect of lower cash flows and a higher discount rate would lead to a very large decline in the value of the inverse floater. Thus, inverse floaters are exceptionally vulnerable to increases in interest rates. Of course, if interest rates fall, the value of an inverse floater will soar.

Self-Test Question

Briefly describe the following types of derivative securities:
  (1) Futures
  (2) Swaps
  (3) Structured notes
  (4) Inverse floaters

Risk Management

As businesses become increasingly complex, it is becoming more difficult for CEOs and directors to know what problems might lie in wait. Therefore, they need someone to systematically look for potential problems and to design safeguards to minimize potential damage.

Most larger firms have risk managers who report to the chief financial officer, while the CFOs of smaller firms personally assume risk management responsibilities. In any event, risk management is becoming increasingly important, and is something finance students should understand. Therefore, in the remainder of this chapter we discuss the basics of risk management, along with some commonly used risk management tools.

Fundamentals of Risk Management

It is useful to begin our discussion of risk management by defining some commonly used terms that describe various kinds of risks. Some of these risks can be mitigated, or managed, and that is what risk management is all about.

1. *Speculative risks* are situations that offer the chance of a gain but might result in a loss. Thus, investments in new projects and marketable securities involve speculative risks.

2. *Pure risks* are risks that offer only the prospect of a loss. Examples include the risk that a plant will be destroyed by fire or that a product liability suit will result in a large judgment against the firm.

3. *Demand risks* are associated with the demand for a firm's products or services. Because sales are essential to all businesses, demand risk is one of the most significant risks that firms face.

4. *Input risks* are risks associated with input costs, including both labor and materials. Thus, a company that uses copper as a raw material in its manufacturing process faces the risk that the cost of copper will increase and that it will not be able to pass this increase on to its customers by raising its prices.

5. *Financial risks* are risks that result from financial transactions. For example, if a firm plans to issue new bonds, it faces the risk that interest rates will rise before the bonds can be brought to market. Similarly, if the firm enters into contracts with foreign customers or suppliers, it faces the risk that fluctuations in exchange rates will result in unanticipated losses.

6. *Property risks* are associated with destruction of a firm's productive assets. Thus, the threat of fire, floods, and riots imposes property risks on a firm.

7. *Personnel risks* are risks that result from employees' actions. Examples include the risks associated with employee fraud, embezzlement, or suits based on charges of age or sex discrimination.

8. *Environmental risks* include risks associated with polluting the environment. Public awareness in recent years, coupled with the huge cost of environmental cleanup, has increased the importance of environmental risks.

9. *Liability risks* are associated with product, service, or employee liability. Examples include the very large judgments assessed against asbestos manufacturers and some health care providers, as well as costs incurred as a result of improper actions of employees, such as driving corporate vehicles in a reckless manner.

10. *Insurable risks* are risks that typically can be covered by insurance. In general, property, personnel, environmental, and liability risks can be transferred to insurance companies. Note, though, that the ability to insure a risk does not necessarily mean that the risk *should be* insured. Indeed, a major function of risk management involves evaluating all alternatives for managing a particular risk and then choosing the optimal alternative.

Note that the risk classifications just mentioned are somewhat arbitrary, and different classifications are commonly used in different industries. However, the list does provide an idea of the wide variety of risks to which a firm can be exposed.

AN APPROACH TO RISK MANAGEMENT

Firms often use the following three-step approach to risk management.

1. **Identify the risks faced by the firm.** First, the risk manager must identify the potential risks faced by his or her firm.

2. **Measure the potential impact of each risk.** Some risks are so small as to be immaterial, whereas others have the potential to doom the company. It is useful to segregate risks by potential impact and then to focus on the most serious threats.

3. **Decide how each relevant risk should be handled.** In most situations, risk exposure can be reduced by utilizing one or more of the following techniques:

   a. **Transfer the risk to an insurance company.** Often, it is advantageous to insure against, hence transfer, a risk. However, insurability does not necessarily mean that a risk should be covered by insurance. In many instances, it might be better for the company to *self-insure,* which means bearing the risk directly rather than paying another party to bear the risk.

   b. **Transfer the function that produces the risk to a third party.** In some situations, risks can be reduced most easily by passing them on to some other company that is not an insurance company. For example, suppose a furniture manufacturer is concerned about potential liabilities arising from its ownership of a fleet of trucks used to transfer products from its manufacturing plant to various distribution points across the country. One way to eliminate this risk would be to contract with a trucking company to do the shipping, which, in effect, passes the risks involved with transportation to a third party.

   c. **Reduce the probability of occurrence of an adverse event.** The expected loss arising from any risk is a function of both the probability of occurrence and the dollar loss if the adverse event occurs. In some instances, it is possible to reduce the probability that an adverse event will occur. For example, the probability that a fire will occur can be reduced by instituting a fire prevention training program, replacing old electrical wiring, and using fire-resistant materials in areas that have the greatest fire potential.

   d. **Reduce the magnitude of the loss associated with an adverse event.** Continuing with the fire risk example, the dollar cost associated with a fire can be reduced by such actions as installing sprinkler systems, designing facilities with self-contained fire zones that can be isolated if a fire occurs, and locating facilities in proximity to a fire station.

   e. **Totally avoid the activity that gives rise to the risk.** For example, a company might discontinue a product or service line because the risks outweigh the rewards, as with the recent decision by Dow-Corning to discontinue its manufacture of silicon breast implants.

Note that risk management decisions, like all corporate decisions, should include a rigorous cost/benefit analysis for each feasible alternative. For example, suppose it would cost $50,000 per year to conduct a comprehensive fire safety training program for all personnel in a high-risk plant. Presumably, this program would reduce the expected value of future fire losses. An alternative to the training program would be to place $50,000 annually in a reserve fund set aside to cover future fire losses. Both alternatives involve expected cash flows, and from an economic standpoint the choice should be made on the basis of the lowest present value of future costs. Thus, the same financial management techniques applied to other corporate decisions can also be applied to risk management decisions. Note, though, that if a fire occurs and a life is lost, the trade-off between fire prevention and expected losses may not sit well with a jury. The same thing holds true for product liability, as Ford, GM, and others have learned.

Define the following terms:
   (1) Speculative risks
   (2) Pure risks
   (3) Demand risks
   (4) Input risks
   (5) Financial risks
   (6) Property risks
   (7) Personnel risks
   (8) Environmental risks
   (9) Liability risks
  (10) Insurable risks
  (11) Self-insurance
Should a firm insure itself against all of the insurable risks it faces? Explain.

SELF-TEST QUESTIONS

RISK IDENTIFICATION AND MEASUREMENT

The first step in a corporate risk management program is to identify all potential losses, and the second step is to assess their likelihoods of occurrence and loss potentials. In this section, we discuss risk identification and measurement.

Risk identification is the process by which a business systematically and continuously identifies those current and potential risks that might adversely affect it. Most corporate risk managers use a checklist to identify risks, and smaller firms without risk managers usually rely on the risk management services of insurance companies or else hire risk management consultants to identify and measure the risks that they face. The checklists, which are published by insurance companies, the American Management Association, and the Risk and Insurance Management Society, are many pages long, so we will not present one here.[8] For small firms, it may be possible for a single individual to apply the checklist to his or her firm to identify the risks, but larger, multidivisional firms must involve a number of people in the risk identification process.

After risks have been identified, it is necessary to measure the firm's degree of exposure to each risk. This involves estimating (1) *loss frequency* (or loss probability) and (2) *loss severity* (dollar value of each loss). In general, loss exposure is more a function of the severity of losses than of their frequency. A potential catastrophic loss, even though its frequency is rare, is far more serious than frequent small losses.

---

[8]For one example, see C. Arthur Williams, Jr., Michael L. Smith, and Peter C. Young, *Risk Management and Insurance* (New York: McGraw-Hill, 1995), Chapter 3.

For example, suppose a company uses trucks to deliver its products. In any year, the probability of an accident that damages one of its trucks is relatively high, whereas the probability of a death or injury liability claim is relatively low. However, the potential severity of the liability loss is so much greater than potential damage losses that virtually all firms consider their liability risk exposure to be greater than their collision risk exposure.

There are several approaches to measuring loss severity. Two of the most common are (1) the maximum loss approach, and (2) the average loss approach. The *maximum loss* is the dollar loss associated with the worst case scenario, while the *average loss* is the average dollar loss associated with a particular peril, such as a plant fire, considering that a wide range of possible losses can occur.

To illustrate, Table 23-3 contains a risk manager's estimates for the probabilities and dollar losses associated with a fire at a given plant. There is a 99 percent probability that no fire will occur and a 1 percent probability that there will be a fire. The expected loss is only $5,650, but if a fire does occur, the damage could range from $100,000 to $2,000,000. The company could easily afford the $5,650 annual expected loss, but a large fire loss would put it out of business, and it would lose all of its value as a going concern.

A fire insurance policy which fully protects against fire would cost $5,650 plus administrative costs and insurance company profit. In this case, all risk of fire would be transferred to the insurance company. However, the risk manager might decide that the company could withstand losses of up to $1 million, hence that only the risk of losses of $1 million or more should be transferred to an insurer. The probability of a loss of $1 million or more during a given year is 0.10% + 0.05% = 0.15%, and the expected loss to an insurance company which assumed that risk would be $2,000. Therefore, the firm could buy a policy with a $1 million deductible at a relatively low premium cost.[9]

TABLE 23-3	PROBABILITIES AND DOLLAR LOSSES FROM A FIRE

PROBABILITY OF OCCURRENCE	DOLLAR LOSS
99.00%	$ 0
0.15	100,000
0.20	250,000
0.30	500,000
0.20	750,000
0.10	1,000,000
0.05	2,000,000
100.00%	Expected loss = $ 5,650

[9]Although we have been dealing with discrete distributions here, loss probabilities could be specified by continuous distributions, hence Monte Carlo simulation could be a useful tool in the risk measurement process.

How do most companies identify the risks they face?

What two factors are combined to measure the degree of risk exposure?

What is the goal of risk identification and measurement?

PROPERTY LOSS EXPOSURES

One of the first risks that comes to mind when discussing corporate risk management is the risk of property losses. In general, property is divided into two classes: (1) *real property,* which consists of land and buildings, and (2) *personal property,* which is all property other than real property. In a business setting, real property is the company's land and buildings such as corporate headquarters, plants, stores, and warehouses, while personal property includes the company's manufacturing equipment, vehicles, furniture and fixtures, and inventories.

The perils most commonly associated with property losses are (1) *physical perils,* which include such natural events as fires, floods, explosions, and windstorms; (2) *social perils,* which are associated with the behavior of people and include theft, strikes, vandalism, and embezzlement; and (3) *economic perils,* which stem from external economic events, such as a competitor's introduction of a new product that significantly reduces the value of inventory.

Property losses are classified as direct or indirect. *Direct losses* occur when the property itself is destroyed, damaged, or lost. Thus, the loss of a manufacturing plant and its contents by fire is a direct loss. *Indirect losses* stem from direct loss; the loss of profits during the time when fire damage is being repaired is an example.

To measure a firm's potential exposure to property losses, the risk manager must attach a value to the firm's property. Property appraisers have developed several standards of measurement for assigning property values. Here are the six most common appraisal measurements.

1. **Original cost.** The original cost of property is merely the dollar cost at the time of acquisition. In general, original cost is not a very good measure of an asset's true value, primarily because it does not consider the impact of factors that affect value over time.

2. **Book value.** Book value is the original cost of the property less the accumulated amount of accounting depreciation. Book value does consider the wear and tear on an asset, at least as measured by accountants, but it does not consider the impact of inflation, competition, or technological change.

3. **Market value.** The market value of an asset is the current value of the asset as set by supply and demand conditions in the marketplace. Some assets, such as vehicles, have an easily determined market value, but for assets such as a manufacturing plant it may be virtually impossible to determine a market value.

4. **Tax appraisal value.** Many types of property are appraised for tax purposes, so this value is known for many corporate assets. However, tax appraisals may not be current, and they are often set at less than true market value to reduce valuation appeals.

5. **Economic value.** The economic value of an asset is the present value of the cash flows it is expected to produce. For some assets, such as securities, the

economic value should be the same as the market value. For other assets, such as a manufacturing plant, the economic and market values may differ depending on who operates the plant, because different owners may be able to create different cash flow streams due to varying management skills and synergies. Also, some assets, such as office equipment, do not directly produce cash flow streams, and for them the economic value method is obviously inappropriate.

6. **Replacement value.** Replacement value is the cost to replace the property. Because of inflation, the replacement values for many assets are considerably higher than their book values, but in some cases technological or other developments make it possible to replace an asset at less than its book value.

In general, property loss exposures are managed either by retaining the risk or by passing it to an insurer. Basic insurance can usually be purchased to cover losses associated with fire, smoke, lightning, windstorm and hail, explosion, riot, and aircraft and vehicle accidents. Because of the adverse selection problem associated with flood insurance, this type of coverage can generally be obtained only through subsidized government programs.[10]

In addition to basic coverage, additional coverage can usually be obtained to protect against losses due to burglary and vandalism. Finally, coverage can be purchased that offers protection against income loss and employee dishonesty. Needless to say, the more risk that is passed on to the insurer, the higher the cost of the policy. One of the biggest issues in risk management is to determine what risks should be retained by the firm rather than passed on to insurers.

SELF-TEST QUESTIONS

What is the difference between real property and personal property?
Define the following terms:
(1) Physical perils
(2) Social perils
(3) Economic perils
(4) Direct losses
(5) Indirect losses
List six procedures used to value property.

LIABILITY LOSS EXPOSURES

In addition to property loss exposure, businesses also face exposure to liability losses. For our purposes, the term *liability* involves the concept of a cost that can be imposed when a responsibility is not met. Companies risk liability losses through five categories of exposure: (1) bailee exposure, (2) ownership exposure, (3) business operation exposure, (4) employee action exposure, and (5) professional exposure.

In many business activities, a business takes possession of personal property owned by a person or another business and performs some service pertaining to the

---

[10]Only those businesses that face high risk of floods would buy flood insurance. Further, because floods typically cause widespread damage, the premiums charged by commercial insurers for flood insurance would be exorbitantly high.

property, such as repair or storage, and then returns the property to the owner. In legal language, such transactions are called *bailments,* and the business having temporary possession of the property is called the *bailee.* Although the legal complexities associated with bailment are too extensive to discuss here, it is obviously important for companies that act as bailees to fully understand the liability exposure that such arrangements create.

Ownership of real and personal property brings with it significant liability exposures. In essence, injuries that occur on a business's real property and/or as a result of its personal property can give rise to liability losses. Again, the legal specifics go beyond the scope of this chapter, but risk managers must be familiar with the nature of the potential liability that results from property ownership.

The liability exposure that arises from business operations is often the most critical exposure that firms face. First, businesses may be sued for creating a *nuisance,* which is an activity that harms third parties. Much of what is now controlled by environmental regulation was formerly considered as a nuisance. Thus, water and air pollution, as well as noise pollution, may subject a firm to civil suits as well as to the penalties specified in our environmental protection laws.

Another potential liability exposure is *patent and copyright infringement.* Here, firms violate invention or creative work protection laws, hence wrongfully use the works of others. Suits of this nature, if won, tend to have very large settlements, so they can constitute large risks for some firms. For example, Apple Computer sued Microsoft Corporation for $5.5 billion for copyright infringement. Apple argued that Microsoft's Windows software illegally duplicated the "look and feel" inherent in the screen images (icons) that helped make Apple's Macintosh computer successful. "I'll move to Canada if Apple wins," said Steve Ballmer, one of Microsoft's vice-presidents. However, the move was not necessary, because the court dismissed Apple's claim, ruling that the general appearance of a program is not protected by copyright law. On the day following the ruling, Microsoft's shares surged $11\frac{7}{8}$ to $128\frac{7}{8}$, a sign that the potential liability was clearly worrying investors.

A firm that uses *unfair trade practices* also creates the potential for large liability exposures. In fact, treble damages can be assessed in such suits, which can present a serious financial threat to just about any firm.

Firms also face potential liability problems from defects in the goods and services they provide. Such risk exposure is called *product liability.* Auto manufacturers have lost millions of dollars in suits related to faulty design and construction. For example, Audi faced hundreds of lawsuits related to "sudden acceleration" problems, and other automakers lost millions of dollars on lawsuits connected with faulty gas tanks. Similarly, four firms associated with producing breast implants were forced to establish a $4.5 billion fund to settle class action lawsuits related to implant injuries. Of course, the exposure to such liability varies a great deal depending on the type of product or service sold. Because of inflation and the generous temperament of many juries, product liability exposures have become increasingly important in recent years. Thus, every risk manager has to constantly monitor his or her firm's product liability exposure, for it can have negative effects both through damage judgments and through sales lost due to bad publicity.

To illustrate the difficulties encountered in identifying potential risks, consider the situation faced by Keene Corporation, once a NYSE company and a leading manufacturer of heat-absorbing composite materials used in a variety of aerospace, defense, and commercial applications. In 1968, Keene acquired for $8 million a small manufacturer of insulation products which, to conform to customers' specifications at the time, contained asbestos. Keene stopped production of these products in 1972 and closed the company down in 1976 — losing its entire investment. Unfortunately for Keene, this did not mark the end of the saga. Laws passed *after the insulation business was closed, and enforced retroactively,* forced Keene and its insurers to spend over $500 million on asbestos litigation, and these charges eventually forced the company into bankruptcy. In total, Keene lost more than a half-billion dollars and ended up bankrupt because it made the mistake of acquiring a company — which it bought 20 years earlier for $8 million — with a product liability exposure.

Another type of liability involves *improper actions by employees,* such as sexual harassment. For example, in 1994 the world's largest law firm, Baker & McKenzie, was hit with $6.9 million in punitive damages in a sexual harassment suit brought by a former secretary in the firm. Punitive damages, which generally are not covered by insurance, are meant to deter and punish wrongdoing. In this instance, the firm was punished for not doing enough to prevent sexual harassment by a senior partner who brought in a lot of revenue and also for not taking appropriate action after the sexual harassment had been reported. The jury's award was nearly twice the $3.7 million in punitive damages sought by the secretary's lawyers. If the decision is not reversed, it will amount to about 10 percent of the law firm's net worth.

The final type of liability exposure applies to professionals such as doctors, lawyers, accountants, and architects. In general, businesses that provide services requiring advance training and licensing are exposed to *professional liability.* There has been a dramatic increase in the number of malpractice lawsuits in recent years and in the dollar amounts of the judgments. Professional liability losses can be especially damaging because they affect both the firm's cash and its reputation. As with property loss exposures, the usual approach for handling liability exposures is either to self-insure or to pass the risk to an insurer. Liability insurance, including professional liability, can be purchased, but it is often difficult for insurers to adequately pool the risks involved. For example, liability losses among some physicians in southern Florida became so great in the late 1980s that malpractice premiums, which are based on location, rose above $100,000 a year. Many physicians were unable to afford such premiums, so they either retired or left to practice elsewhere. Hospitals face a similar problem, and to deal with it, many states require hospitals to join insurance pools for malpractice protection.

For all types of liability coverage, deductibles are common, whereby the business has to pay some part of the award, say, $100,000, with the insurer covering the remainder.

SELF-TEST QUESTIONS

Within the context of this chapter, what is meant by the term "liability"?

Define the following terms:

    (1) Bailment

    (2) Bailee

    (3) Nuisance

    (4) Patent and copyright infringement

    (5) Product liability

    (6) Professional liability

FINANCIAL LOSS EXPOSURES

Firms are subject to numerous risk exposures due to interest rate, stock price, and exchange rate fluctuations in the financial markets. For an investor, one of the most obvious ways to reduce financial risks is to hold a broadly diversified portfolio of stocks and debt securities, including international securities and debt of varying maturities. There are also other ways to limit risks associated with financial transactions, and we discuss some of the more common methods in this section.[11] In particular, we discuss derivatives markets and their use in reducing the risks associated with financial and commodity markets.

INTEREST RATE AND REINVESTMENT RATE RISK EXPOSURE

In our discussion of bond valuation in Chapter 7, we discussed interest rate and reinvestment rate risk. *Interest rate (price) risk* is the risk that the price of a debt security will fall as a result of increases in interest rates, and *reinvestment rate risk* is the risk of earning a return less than expected when debt principal or interest payments are reinvested at rates less than the original yield to maturity.

To illustrate how to reduce interest rate and reinvestment rate risks, we will consider a firm which is obligated to pay a worker a lump sum retirement benefit of $10,000 at the end of 10 years.[12] Assume that the yield curve is horizontal, the current interest rate on all Treasury securities is 9 percent, and the type of security used to fund the retirement benefit is Treasury bonds. The present value of $10,000, discounted back 10 years at 9 percent, is $10,000(0.4224) = $4,224. Therefore, the firm could invest $4,224 in Treasury bonds and expect to be able to meet its obligation 10 years hence.

Suppose, however, interest rates change from the current 9 percent rate immediately after the firm has bought the Treasury bonds. How would this affect the situation? The answer is, "It all depends." If rates fall, then the value of the bonds in the portfolio will rise, but this benefit will be offset to a greater or lesser degree by a decline in the rate at which the coupon payment of 0.09($4,224) = $380.16 can be reinvested. The reverse would hold if interest rates rise above 9 percent. Here are some examples (for simplicity, we assume annual coupons):

1. **The firm buys $4,224 of 9 percent, 10-year maturity bonds; rates fall to 7 percent immediately after the purchase and remain at that level:**

$$\text{Portfolio value at the end of 10 years} = \frac{\text{Future value of 10 interest payments of \$380.16 each compounded at 7\%}}{} + \text{Maturity value}$$

$$= \$5,252 + \$4,224 = \$9,476.$$

---

[11]In Chapter 26, which covers multinational finance, we discuss the risks involved with holding foreign currencies and procedures for reducing such risks.

[12]For more information on pension plan management, see Chapter 27.

Therefore, the firm cannot meet its $10,000 obligation, and it must contribute additional funds.

2. **The firm buys $4,224 of 9 percent, 40-year bonds; rates fall to 7 percent immediately after the purchase and remain at that level:**

$$\begin{array}{l} \text{Portfolio value at} \\ \text{the end of 10 years} \end{array} = \$5{,}252 + \begin{array}{c} \text{Value of 30-year, 9\% bonds} \\ \text{when } k_d = 7\% \end{array}$$

$$= \$5{,}252 + \$5{,}272 = \$10{,}524.$$

In this situation, the firm has excess capital at the end of the 10-year period.

3. **The firm buys $4,224 of 9 percent, 10-year bonds; rates rise to 12 percent immediately after the purchase and remain at that level:**

$$\begin{array}{l} \text{Portfolio value at} \\ \text{the end of 10 years} \end{array} = \begin{array}{c} \text{Future value of} \\ \text{10 interest payments} \\ \text{of \$380.16 each} \\ \text{compounded at 12\%} \end{array} + \begin{array}{c} \text{Maturity} \\ \text{value} \end{array}$$

$$= \$6{,}671 + \$4{,}224 = \$10{,}895.$$

This situation also produces a funding surplus.

4. **The firm buys $4,224 of 9 percent, 40-year bonds; rates rise to 12 percent immediately after the purchase and remain at that level:**

$$\begin{array}{l} \text{Portfolio value at} \\ \text{the end of 10 years} \end{array} = \$6{,}671 + \begin{array}{c} \text{Value of 30-year, 9\% bonds} \\ \text{when } k_d = 12\% \end{array}$$

$$= \$6{,}671 + \$3{,}203 = \$9{,}874.$$

This time, a shortfall occurs.

Here are some generalizations drawn from the examples:

1. If interest rates *fall,* and the portfolio is invested in relatively short-term bonds, then the reinvestment rate penalty exceeds the capital gains, so a net shortfall occurs. However, if the portfolio had been invested in relatively long-term bonds, a drop in rates would produce capital gains which would more than offset the shortfall caused by low reinvestment rates.

2. If interest rates *rise,* and the portfolio is invested in relatively short-term bonds, then gains from high reinvestment rates will more than offset capital losses, and the final portfolio value will exceed the required amount. However, if the portfolio had been invested in long-term bonds, then capital losses would more than offset reinvestment gains, and a net shortfall would result.

If a company has many cash obligations expected in the future, the complexity of estimating the effects of interest rate changes is obviously expanded. Still, methods have been devised to help deal with the risks associated with changing interest rates. Several methods are discussed in the following sections.

ZERO COUPON BONDS AND STRIPPED TREASURIES   We discussed zero coupon bonds in Chapter 17, where we indicated that they were devised to eliminate reinvestment rate risk. In our example of a firm needing $10,000 in 10 years, the purchase of a 10-year zero coupon bond would eliminate all risks associated with changes in interest rates. The firm would, in our example, simply purchase a zero coupon bond which promised to pay $10,000 in 10 years.

IMMUNIZATION   Bond portfolios can be *immunized* against interest rate and reinvestment rate risk, much as people can be immunized against flu. In brief, immunization involves selecting bonds with coupons and maturities such that the benefits or losses from changes in reinvestment rates are exactly offset by gains or losses in the prices of the bonds. In other words, if a bond's reinvestment rate risk exactly matches its interest rate price risk, then the bond is immunized against the adverse effects of changes in interest rates.

To see what's involved, refer back to our example of a firm which buys $4,224 of 9 percent Treasury bonds to meet a $10,000 obligation 10 years hence. In the example, we see that if the firm buys bonds with a 10-year maturity and interest rates remain constant, then the obligation can be met exactly. However, if interest rates fall from 9 percent to 7 percent, a shortfall will occur because the coupons received will be reinvested at a rate of 7 percent rather than the 9 percent reinvestment rate required to reach the $10,000 target. But, suppose the firm had bought 40-year rather than 10-year bonds. A decline in interest rates would still have the same effect on the compounded coupon payments, but now the firm would hold 9 percent coupon, 30-year bonds in a 7 percent market 10 years hence, so the bonds would have a value greater than par. In this case, the bonds would have risen by more than enough to offset the shortfall in compounded interest. Bonds with a maturity somewhere between 10 and 40 years would result in a breakeven situation in which the reinvestment shortfall was exactly offset by capital gains.

DURATION   The key to immunizing a portfolio is to buy bonds which have a *duration* equal to the years until the funds will be needed. Duration cannot be defined in simple terms like maturity, but it can be thought of as the weighted average maturity of all the cash flows (coupon payments plus maturity value) provided by a bond, and it is exceptionally useful to help manage the risk inherent in a bond portfolio. The duration formula and an example of the calculation are provided below, but first we present some additional points about duration:

1. Duration is to a bond what payback is to a capital budgeting project, because the longer the duration, the longer funds are tied up in the bond.

2. To immunize a bond portfolio, buy bonds which have a duration equal to the number of years until the funds will be needed. In our example, the firm should buy bonds with a duration of 10 years.

3. A corporate treasurer (or any other investor) who is terribly concerned about declines in the market value of his or her portfolio should buy bonds with low durations. (This is important even if the investor buys a bond mutual fund.) The percentage change in the value of a bond (or bond portfolio) will be approximately equal to the bond's duration times the percentage point change in interest rates. Therefore, a 2 percentage point increase in interest rates will lower the value of a bond with a 10-year duration by about 20 percent, but the value of a five-year duration bond will fall by only 10 percent. So, twice the duration, twice the volatility.

4. The duration of a zero coupon bond is equal to its maturity, but the duration of any coupon bond is less than its maturity. (Remember, the duration is a weighted average maturity of the cash flows, the only cash flow from a zero occurs at maturity, and coupon bonds have cash flows prior to maturity.) Further, the higher the coupon rate, the shorter the duration, other things held constant, because a high coupon bond provides significant early cash flows even if it has a long maturity.

Duration is calculated using this formula:

$$\text{Duration} = \sum_{t=1}^{n} \frac{t(\text{PVCF}_t)}{\sum_{t=1}^{n} \text{PVCF}_t} = \sum_{t=1}^{n} \frac{t(\text{PVCF}_t)}{\text{Value}}.$$

Here n is the bond's years to maturity, t is the year each cash flow occurs, and PVCF_t is the present value of the cash flow at Year t discounted at the current rate of interest. Note that the denominator of the equation is the PV of the cash flows, which is the current market value of the bond.

To illustrate the duration calculation, consider a 20-year, 9 percent annual coupon bond bought at its par value of $1,000. It provides cash flows of $90 per year for 19 years, and $1,090 in the 20th year. To calculate duration, we used a spreadsheet set up as follows:

t (1)	CF (2)	PVCF (9%) (3)	PVCF/VALUE = PVCF/$1,000 (4)	t(PVCF/VALUE) (5)
1	$ 90	$ 82.57	0.08257	0.08257
2	90	75.75	0.07575	0.15150
•	•	•	•	•
•	•	•	•	•
•	•	•	•	•
19	90	17.50	0.01750	0.33258
20	1,090	194.49	0.19449	3.88979
		Value = $1,000.00		Duration = 9.95011

Column 1 gives the year each cash flow occurs, Column 2 gives the cash flows, Column 3 shows the PV of each cash flow, Column 4 shows the percentage of each PV cash flow to the total PV of cash flows, and Column 5 multiplies each year by its percentage of the PV of total cash flows. The sum of the weighted percentages is the bond's duration.

Since a 20-year bond's 9.95 duration is close to that of our illustrative firm's 10-year liability, if the firm bought a portfolio of 20-year bonds and then reinvested the coupons as they came in, the accumulated interest payments, plus the value of the bond after 10 years, would be close to $10,000 irrespective of whether interest rates rose, fell, or remained constant at 9 percent.

Unfortunately, other complications arise. Our simple example looked at a single interest rate change which occurred immediately after funding. In reality, interest rates change every day, which causes bonds' durations to change, and this, in turn, requires that bond portfolios be *rebalanced* periodically to remain immunized. Still, this can be done, and computer programs are available to assist in the rebalancing process.

HEDGING WITH FUTURES

One of the most useful tools for reducing interest rate, exchange rate, and commodity price exposure is to hedge in the futures markets. Most financial and real asset transactions occur in what is known as the *spot, or cash, market,* where the asset is delivered immediately (or within a few days). *Futures, or futures contracts,* on the other hand, call for the purchase or sale of a financial or real asset at some future date, but at a price which is fixed today.

In 1996, futures contracts were available on more than 30 real and financial assets traded on 14 U.S. exchanges, the largest of which are the Chicago Board of Trade (CBOT) and the Chicago Mercantile Exchange (CME). Futures contracts are divided into two classes, *commodity futures* and *financial futures.* Commodity futures, which cover oil, various grains, oilseeds, livestock, meats, fibers, metals, and wood, were first traded in the United States in the mid-1800s. Financial futures, which were first traded in 1975, include Treasury bills, Treasury notes and bonds, certificates of deposit, Eurodollar deposits, foreign currencies, and stock indexes.

To illustrate how futures contracts work, consider the CBOT's contract on Treasury bonds. The basic contract is for $100,000 of a hypothetical 8 percent coupon, semiannual payment Treasury bond with 20 years to maturity. Table 23-4 shows an extract from the Treasury bond futures prices which appeared in a past issue of *The Wall Street Journal.*

The first column gives the delivery month; the next three columns give the opening, high, and low prices on that contract for that day. The opening price for the June future, 100-20, means 100 plus 20/32, or 100.625 percent of par. Column 5

FUTURES PRICES   **TABLE 23-4**

TREASURY BONDS (CBOT) — $100,000; PTS. 32NDS OF 100%

						LIFETIME		
DELIVERY MONTH (1)	OPEN (2)	HIGH (3)	LOW (4)	SETTLE (5)	CHANGE (6)	HIGH (7)	LOW (8)	OPEN INTEREST (9)
June	100-20	101-11	100-07	100-16	−13	104-03	98-16	188,460
Sept	99-25	100-18	99-16	99-24	−11	102-05	99-10	42,622
Dec	99-00	99-24	98-24	98-30	−10	101-11	98-06	5,207

SOURCE: *The Wall Street Journal.*

gives the settlement price, which is typically the price at the close of trading. Column 6 reports the change in the settlement price from the preceding day — the June contract dropped by 13/32. Columns 7 and 8 give the life-of-contract highs and lows. Finally, Column 9 shows the "open interest," which is the number of contracts outstanding.

To illustrate, we focus on the Treasury bonds for December delivery. The settlement price was 98-30, or 98 plus 30/32 percent of the $100,000 contract value. Thus, the price at which one could buy $100,000 face value of 8 percent, 20-year Treasury bonds to be delivered in December was 98.9375 percent of par, or 0.989375($100,000) = $98,937.50. The contract price declined by 10/32 of 1 percent of $100,000, or by $312.50, from the previous day, so if you had bought the contract yesterday, you would have lost $312.50. Over its life, the contract's price has ranged from 98.1675 to 101.3438, and there were 5,207 contracts outstanding on the December futures, representing a total value of about $520 million.

Note that the contract declined by 11/32 of a percent on this particular day. Why would the value of the bond futures contract decline? Since bond prices decline when interest rates rise, we know that interest rates rose on that day. Moreover, we can calculate the implied rates inherent in the futures contracts. (*The Wall Street Journal* formerly provided the implied yields, but now one must calculate them.) Recall that the contract relates to a hypothetical 20-year, semiannual payment, 8 percent coupon bond. The closing price (settlement price) was 98 and 30/32, or 98.9375 percent of par. Using a financial calculator, we can solve for k_d in the following equation:

$$\$989.375 = \sum_{t=1}^{40} \frac{\$40}{(1 + k_d/2)^t} + \frac{\$1,000}{(1 + k_d/2)^{40}}.$$

The solution value for the six-month rate is 4.054, which is equivalent to a nominal rate of 8.108 percent. Since the price of the bond (contract) fell by 10/32 that day, we could find the previous day's closing (settlement) price and its implied interest rate, which is 8.073 percent. Therefore, interest rates rose by 3.5 basis points, which was enough to lower the value of the contract by $312.50. Thus, the futures contract for December delivery (seven-month futures) of this hypothetical bond sold for $98,937.50 for 100 bonds with a par value of $100,000, which translates to a yield to maturity of about 8.1 percent. This yield reflects investors' beliefs about the interest rate level which will prevail in December. The spot yield on T-bonds was about 7.9 percent at the time, so the marginal trader in the futures market was predicting a 20-basis-point increase in yields over the next seven months.

Now suppose that three months later interest rates in the futures market had fallen from the earlier levels, say, from 8.1 to 7.5 percent. Falling interest rates mean rising bond prices, so the December contract would then be worth about $105,138. Thus, the contract's value would have increased by $105,138 − $98,938 = $6,200.

When futures contracts are purchased, the purchaser does not have to put up the full amount of the purchase price; rather, the purchaser is required to post an initial *margin,* which for CBT Treasury bond contracts is $3,000 per $100,000 contract. However, investors are required to maintain a certain value in the margin account, called a *maintenance margin.* If the value of the contract declines, then the owner may be required to add additional funds to the margin account, and the more the contract value falls, the more money must be added. The value of the contract is checked at the end of every working day, and margin account adjustments are made at that time. This is called "marking to market." If an investor purchased our illustrative contract and then sold it later for $105,138, he or she would have made a profit of $6,200 on a $3,000 investment, or a return of over 200 percent in only three months. It is clear, therefore, that futures contracts offer a considerable amount of leverage. Of course, if interest rates had risen, then the value of the contract would have declined, and the investor could easily have lost his or her $3,000, or more. Futures contracts are never settled by delivery of the securities involved. Rather, the transaction is completed by reversing the trade, which amounts to selling the contract back to the original seller.[13] The actual gains and losses on the contract are realized when the futures contract is closed.

Futures contracts and options are similar to one another — so similar that people often confuse the two. Therefore, it is useful to compare the two instruments. A *futures contract* is a definite agreement on the part of one party to buy something on a specific date and at a specific price, and the other party agrees to sell on the same terms. No matter how low or how high the price goes, the two parties must settle the contract at the agreed-upon price. An *option,* on the other hand, merely gives someone the right to buy (call) or sell (put) an asset, but the holder of the option does not have to complete the transaction. Note also that options exist for individual stocks and for "bundles" of stocks such as those in the S&P and Value Line indexes, whereas futures are used for commodities, debt securities, and stock indexes. The two types of instruments can be used for the same purposes. One is not necessarily better or worse than another—they are simply different.

SECURITY PRICE EXPOSURE

Firms are obviously exposed to losses due to changes in security prices when securities are held in investment portfolios, and they are also exposed during times when securities are being issued. In addition, firms are exposed to risk if they use floating rate debt to finance an investment that produces a more or less fixed income stream. Often, these risks can be mitigated by using *derivatives.* As we discussed earlier in this chapter, derivatives are securities whose value stems, or is derived, from the values of other assets. Thus, options and futures contracts are derivatives, because their values depend on the prices of some underlying asset such as stocks, bonds, or commodities. Now we will explore the use of two types of derivatives, futures and swaps, to help manage certain types of risk.

FUTURES Futures are used for both speculation and hedging. *Speculation* involves betting on future price movements, and futures are used because the inherent leverage in the contract enhances expected returns. *Hedging,* on the other hand, is done

---

[13]The buyers and sellers of most financial futures contracts do not actually trade with one another, even though a contract cannot be bought without a seller, and vice versa. Each trader's contractual obligation is generally with the futures exchange. This feature helps to guarantee the fiscal integrity of the trade. Incidentally, commodities futures traded on the exchanges are settled in the same way as financial futures, but in the case of commodities much of the contracting is done off the exchange, between farmers and processors, as *forward contracts,* and in these cases actual deliveries occur.

by a firm or individual for protection against a price change that would otherwise negatively affect profits. For example, rising interest rates and commodity (raw material) prices can hurt profits, as can adverse currency fluctuations. If two parties have mirror-image risks, then they can enter into a transaction that eliminates, as opposed to transfers, risks. Of course, one party to a futures contract could be a speculator, the other a hedger. Thus, to the extent that speculators broaden the market and make hedging possible, they help decrease risks to those who seek to bear less risk.

There are two basic types of hedges: (1) *long hedges,* in which futures contracts are bought in anticipation of (or to guard against) price increases, and (2) *short hedges,* where a firm or individual sells futures contracts to guard against price declines. Recall that rising interest rates lower bond prices and thus decrease the value of bond futures contracts. Therefore, if a firm or individual needs to guard against an *increase* in interest rates, a futures contract that makes money if rates rise should be used. That means selling, or going short, on a futures contract. To illustrate, assume that in May Carson Foods is considering a plan to issue $10,000,000 of 20-year bonds in September to support a capital expenditure program. The interest rate would be 10 percent if the bonds were issued today, and at that rate the project would have a positive NPV. However, Carson's financial manager fears that interest rates may rise over the next four months, and that when the issue is actually sold, the interest rate would be substantially above 10 percent, which would make the project a bad investment. Carson can protect itself against a rise in rates by hedging in the futures market.

In this situation, Carson would be hurt by an increase in interest rates, so it would use a short hedge. It would choose a futures contract on that security most similar to the one it plans to issue, long-term bonds. In this case, Carson would probably hedge with Treasury bond futures. Since it plans to issue $10,000,000 of bonds, it would sell $10,000,000/$100,000 = 100 Treasury bond contracts for delivery in September. Carson would have to put up 100($3,000) = $300,000 in margin money and also pay brokerage commissions. We can see from Table 23-4 that each September contract has a value of 99 plus 24/32 percent, so the total value of the 100 contracts is 0.9975($100,000)(100) = $9,975,000. Now suppose renewed fears of inflation push the interest rate on Carson's debt up by 100 basis points, to 11 percent, over the next four months. If Carson issued 10 percent coupon bonds, they would bring only $920 per bond, because investors now require an 11 percent return. Thus, Carson would lose $80 per bond times 10,000 bonds, or $800,000, as a result of delaying the financing. However, the increase in interest rates would also bring about a change in the value of Carson's short position in the futures market. Since interest rates have increased, the value of the futures contract would fall, and if the interest rate on the futures contract also increased by the same full percentage point, from 8.025 to 9.025 percent, the contract value would fall to $9,059,000. Carson would then close its position in the futures market by repurchasing for $9,059,000 the contracts which it earlier sold short for $9,975,000, giving it a profit of $916,000, less commissions.

Thus, Carson would, if we ignore commissions and the opportunity cost of the margin money, offset the loss on the bond issue. In fact, in our example Carson more than offset the loss, pocketing an additional $116,000. Of course, if interest rates had fallen, Carson would have lost on its futures position, but this loss would have been offset by the fact that Carson could now sell its bonds with a lower coupon.

If futures contracts existed on Carson's own debt, then the firm could construct a *perfect hedge,* in which gains on the futures contract would exactly offset losses on the bonds. In reality, it is virtually impossible to construct perfect hedges, because in most cases the underlying asset is not identical to the futures asset.

Note too that if Carson had been planning an equity offering, and if its stock tended to move fairly closely with one of the stock indexes, the company could have hedged against falling stock prices by selling short the index future. Even better, if options on Carson's stock were traded in the option market, then it could use options rather than futures to hedge against falling stock prices.

The futures and option markets permit flexibility in the timing of financial transactions, because the firm can be protected, at least partially, against changes that occur between the time a decision is reached and the time when the transaction will be completed. There is, however, a cost for this protection — commissions plus the opportunity cost of the margin money. Whether or not the protection is worth the cost is a matter of judgment, and it depends on management's risk aversion as well as the company's strength and ability to assume the risk in question. In theory, the reduction in risk resulting from a hedge transaction should have a value exactly equal to the cost of the hedge. Thus, a firm should be indifferent to hedging. However, many firms believe that hedging is worthwhile. Trammell Crow, a large Texas real estate developer, recently used T-bill futures to lock in interest costs on floating rate construction loans, while Dart & Kraft used Eurodollar futures to protect its marketable securities portfolio. Merrill Lynch, Salomon Brothers, and the other investment banking houses hedge in the futures and options markets to protect themselves when they are engaged in major underwritings.

SWAPS A *swap* is another method for reducing financial risks. As we noted earlier, a swap is an exchange.[14] In finance, it is an exchange of cash payment obligations, in which each party to the swap, often called a "counterparty," prefers the payment type or pattern of the other party. In other words, swaps occur because the parties involved prefer the terms of someone else's debt contract, and the swap enables each party to obtain a preferred payment obligation. Generally, one party has a fixed rate obligation and the other a floating rate obligation, or one has an obligation denominated in one currency and the other in another currency.

Major changes have occurred over time in the swaps market. First, standardized contracts have been developed for the most common types of swaps, and this has had two effects: (1) Standardized contracts lower the time and effort involved in arranging swaps, and thus lower transactions costs. (2) The development of standardized contracts has led to a secondary market for swaps, which has increased the liquidity and efficiency of the swaps market. Thus, swaps are becoming a commodity-type item, and a number of international banks now make markets in swaps and

---

[14]For more information on swaps, see Clifford W. Smith, Jr., Charles W. Smithson, and Lee Macdonald Wakeman, "The Evolving Market for Swaps," *Midland Corporate Finance Journal,* Winter 1986, 20–32; and Mary E. Ruth and Steve R. Vinson, "Managing Interest Rate Uncertainty amidst Change," *Public Utilities Fortnightly,* December 22, 1988, 28–31.

offer quotes on several standard types. Also, as noted above, the intermediaries now take counterparty positions in swaps, so it is not necessary to find another firm with mirror-image needs before a swap transaction can be completed. The intermediary would generally find a final counterparty for the swap at a later date, so intermediary positioning helps make the swap market more operationally efficient.[15]

To further illustrate a swap transaction, consider the following situation. An electric utility currently has outstanding a five-year floating rate note tied to the prime rate. The prime rate could rise significantly over the period, so the note carries a high degree of interest rate risk. The utility could, however, enter into a swap with a counterparty, say, Citibank, wherein the utility would pay Citibank a fixed series of interest payments over the five-year period, and Citibank would make the company's required floating rate payments. As a result, the utility would have converted a floating rate loan to a fixed rate loan, and the risk of rising interest rates would have been passed from the utility to Citibank. Such a transaction can lower both parties' risks — because a bank's revenues rise as interest rates rise, Citibank's risk is actually lower if it has floating rate obligations.

Longer-term swaps can also be made. Recently, Citibank entered into a 17-year swap in an electricity cogeneration project financing deal. The project's sponsors were unable to obtain fixed rate financing on reasonable terms, and they were afraid that interest rates would increase and make the project unprofitable. The project's sponsors were, however, able to borrow from local banks on a floating rate basis and to arrange a simultaneous swap with Citibank for a fixed rate obligation.

COMMODITY PRICE EXPOSURE

In the last section, we discussed the use of financial futures to hedge against various types of risk. Actually, futures markets were established for many commodities long before they began to be used for financial instruments. We can use Porter Electronics, which uses large quantities of copper as well as several precious metals, to illustrate inventory hedging. Suppose that in May 1996, Porter foresaw a need for 100,000 pounds of copper in March 1997 for use in fulfilling a fixed price contract to supply solar power cells to the U.S. government. Porter's managers are concerned that a strike by Chilean copper miners will occur, which could raise the price of copper in world markets and possibly turn the expected profit on the solar cell contract into a loss.

Porter could, of course, go ahead and buy the copper that it will need to fulfill the contract, but if it does it will incur substantial carrying costs. As an alternative, the company could hedge against increasing copper prices in the futures market. The New York Commodity Exchange trades standard copper futures contracts of 25,000 pounds each. Thus, Porter could buy four contracts (go long) for delivery in March

---

[15]The role of banks in the global swap market is worrisome to the Federal Reserve and other central banks. When banks take positions in swaps, they are themselves exposed to various risks, and if the counterparties cannot meet their obligations, a bank could suddenly become liable for making two sets of payments. Further, swaps are "off balance sheet" transactions, so it is currently impossible to tell just how large the swap market is or who has what obligation. The fear is that if one large multinational bank gets into trouble, the entire worldwide swap market could collapse like a house of cards. See "Swap Fever: Big Money, Big Risks," *Fortune,* June 1, 1992.

1997. Assume that these contracts were trading in May for about $1.00 per pound, and that the spot price at that date was about $1.02 per pound. If copper prices do rise appreciably over the next 10 months, the value of Porter's long position in copper futures would increase, thus offsetting some of the price increase in the commodity itself. Of course, if copper prices fall, Porter would lose money on its futures contract, but the company would be buying the copper on the spot market at a cheaper price, so it would make a higher-than-anticipated profit on its sale of solar cells. Thus, hedging in the copper futures market locks in the cost of raw materials and removes some uncertainties, or risks, to which the firm would otherwise be exposed.

Eastman Kodak uses silver futures to hedge against short-term increases in the price of silver, which is the primary ingredient in black-and-white film. Many other manufacturers, such as Alcoa with aluminum and Archer Daniels Midland with grains, routinely use the futures markets to reduce the risks associated with input price volatility.

THE USE AND MISUSE OF DERIVATIVES

Most of the news stories about derivatives are related to financial disasters. Much less is heard about the benefits of derivatives, but because of these benefits, more than 90 percent of the largest U.S. companies use derivatives on a regular basis. Moreover, according to McKinsey & Company, by the year 2000 it will be necessary for all CFOs to understand derivatives to do their job well. Even now, sophisticated investors and analysts are demanding that firms use derivatives to hedge certain risks. For example, Compaq Computer was recently sued by a shareholder group for failing to properly hedge its foreign exchange exposure. The shareholders lost the suit, but Compaq got the message and now uses currency futures to hedge its international operations. In another example, Prudential Securities reduced its earnings estimate for Cone Mills, a North Carolina textile company, because Cone did not sufficiently hedge its exposure to changing cotton prices. These examples lead to one conclusion: if a company can safely and inexpensively hedge its risks, it should do so.

There can, however, be a downside to the use of derivatives. Hedging is invariably cited by authorities as a "good" use of derivatives, whereas speculating with derivatives is often cited as a "bad" use. Some people and organizations can afford to bear the risks involved in speculating with derivatives, but others are either not sufficiently knowledgeable about the risks they are taking or else should not be taking those risks in the first place. Most would agree that the typical corporation should use derivatives only to hedge risks, not to speculate in an effort to increase profits. Hedging allows managers to concentrate on running their core businesses without having to worry about interest rate and currency fluctuations, and commodity price variability. However, problems can arise quickly when hedges are improperly constructed or when a corporate treasurer, eager to report relatively high returns, uses derivatives for speculative purposes.

One interesting example of a derivatives debacle involved Kashima Oil, a Japanese firm that imports oil. It pays with U.S. dollars but then sells oil in the Japanese market for yen. Kashima began by using currency futures to hedge, but then it started to speculate on dollar-yen price movements, hoping to increase profits. When the currency markets moved against Kashima's speculative position, lax accounting rules permitted it to avoid reporting the losses by simply rolling over the contract. By the time Kashima bit the bullet and closed its position, it had lost $1.5 billion. Other companies have experienced similar problems.

Our position is that derivatives can and should be used to hedge against certain risks, but that the leverage inherent in some derivatives contracts makes them extremely hazardous instruments. Also, CFOs, CEOs, and board members should be reasonably knowledgeable about the derivatives their firms use, should establish policies regarding when they can and cannot be used, and should establish audit systems to ensure that the policies are carried out. Moreover, a firm's derivatives position should be reported to stockholders, because stockholders have a right to know when situations such as that involving P&G or Kashima might arise. Our guess is that the more information corporations are required to provide about their use of derivatives, the less their use as speculative investments will occur.

SELF-TEST QUESTIONS

What is duration, and how can it be applied to reduce interest rate and reinvestment rate risks?

What is a futures contract?

Explain how a company can use the futures market to hedge against rising interest rates.

What is a swap? Describe the mechanics of a fixed rate to floating rate swap.

Explain how a company can use the futures market to hedge against rising raw materials prices.

How should derivatives be used in risk management? What problems can occur?

SUMMARY

This chapter provided an introduction to derivative securities and corporate risk management. The key concepts covered are listed below:

- A *hedge* is a transaction which lowers risk. A *natural hedge* is a transaction between two *counterparties* where both parties' risks are reduced.

- *Pure options* are financial instruments that (1) are created by exchanges rather than firms, (2) are bought and sold primarily by investors, and (3) are of importance to both investors and financial managers. Moreover, an understanding of options will help financial managers understand warrants and convertibles, which are option-type securities issued by firms.

- The two primary types of options are (1) *call options,* which give the holder the right to purchase a specified asset at a given price (the *exercise* or *strike price*) for a given period of time, and (2) *put options,* which give the holder the right to sell an asset at a given price for a given period of time.

■ The *Black-Scholes Option Pricing Model (OPM)* can be used to estimate the value of a call option.

■ In general, risk management involves the management of unpredictable events that have adverse consequences for the firm. Here the term *management* implies reducing such consequences to the point where there is no significant impact on the financial well-being of the firm.

■ The three steps in risk management are as follows: (1) identify the risks faced by the company, (2) measure the potential impacts of these risks, and (3) decide how each relevant risk should be minimized.

■ In most situations, risk exposure can be minimized by one or more of the following techniques: (1) transfer the risk to an insurance company, (2) transfer the function that produces the risk to a third party, (3) reduce the probability of occurrence of an adverse event, (4) reduce the magnitude of the loss associated with an adverse event, and (5) totally avoid the activity that gives rise to the risk.

■ The *degree of exposure* associated with each risk is defined by (1) *loss frequency* (or loss probability), and (2) *loss severity* (dollar value of each loss).

■ The perils most commonly associated with property losses are typically placed into three categories: (1) *physical perils,* which include such natural events as fires, floods, explosions, and windstorms; (2) *social perils,* which are those associated with the behavior of people and include theft and embezzlement; and (3) *economic perils,* which are those that stem from external economic events, such as a competitor's introduction of a new product that significantly reduces the value of inventory on hand.

■ *Liability* involves the concept of a penalty that can be imposed when a responsibility is not met. Companies risk liability losses through five categories of exposure: (1) bailee exposure, (2) ownership exposure, (3) business operation exposure, (4) employee actions exposure, and (5) professional exposure.

■ *Financial futures* markets permit firms to create *hedge* positions to protect themselves against the damage done by fluctuating interest rates, stock prices, and exchange rates.

■ Bond portfolios can be *immunized* against interest rate and reinvestment rate risks by matching the investment horizon with the *duration* of the portfolio.

■ A *swap* is an exchange of cash payment obligations. Swaps occur because the parties involved prefer someone else's payment stream.

■ *Commodity futures* can be used to hedge against price increases for input materials.

In Chapter 24, we discuss what happens when firms mismanage their risks—bankruptcy, reorganization, and liquidation.

QUESTIONS

23-1   Define each of the following terms:
   a. Derivative
   b. Option; call option; put option
   c. Formula value
   d. Black-Scholes option pricing model
   e. Corporate risk management
   f. Speculative risks; pure risks; demand risks; input risks; financial risks; property risks; personnel risks; environmental risks; liability risks; insurable risks
   g. Real property; personal property
   h. Physical perils; social perils; economic perils
   i. Direct losses; indirect losses
   j. Bailment; bailee
   k. Nuisance
   l. Patent and copyright infringement
   m. Product liability; professional liability
   n. Financial futures
   o. Hedging; natural hedge
   p. Duration
   q. Immunization
   r. Swap
   s. Commodity futures

23-2   Why do options typically sell at prices higher than their formula values?

23-3   Describe how a firm might make the decision whether to self-insure or pass a risk on to an insurance company.

23-4   Suppose you were a corporate risk manager. How might you go about identifying the risks faced by your company?

23-5   Discuss some of the techniques available to reduce risk exposures.

23-6   Discuss some property loss exposures and how companies can deal with those risks.

23-7   Discuss some liability loss exposures and how companies can deal with those risks.

23-8   Explain the concept of duration. How can this concept be used to help reduce interest rate and reinvestment rate risks?

23-9   Explain how the futures markets can be used to reduce interest rate and input price risk.

23-10   How can swaps be used to reduce the risks associated with debt contracts?

PROBLEMS

DURATION Consider the duration of the following bonds:

a. What is the duration of a 3-year, 10 percent, annual coupon bond if its required rate of return, k_d, is 10 percent?

b. What is the duration of a similar risk and maturity bond with a 5 percent coupon? A 15 percent coupon?

HEDGING The Zinn Company plans to issue $10,000,000 of 10-year bonds in December to help finance a new research and development laboratory. It is now May, and the current cost of debt to the high-risk biotech company is 11 percent. However, the firm's financial manager is concerned that interest rates will climb even higher in coming months.

a. Use data in Table 23-4 to create a hedge against rising interest rates.

b. Assume that interest rates in general increase by 200 basis points. How well did your hedge perform?

c. What is a perfect hedge? Are most real-world hedges perfect? Explain.

SPREADSHEET APPLICATIONS

SPREADSHEET PROBLEM

Considine Software Corporation (CSC) options are actively traded on one of the regional exchanges. CSC's current stock price is $10, with a 0.16 instantaneous variance of returns. The current 6-month risk-free rate is 12 percent.

a. What is the value of CSC's 6-month option with an exercise price of $10 according to the Black-Scholes model?

b. What would be the effect on the option price if CSC redeployed its assets and thereby reduced its variance of returns to 0.09?

c. Assume that CSC returns to its initial asset structure; that is, its stock return variance is 0.16. Now assume that CSC's current stock price is $15. What effect does the stock price increase have on the option value?

d. Return to base case (Part a) values. Now assume that the strike price is $15. What is the new option value?

MINI CASE

Assume that you have just been hired as a financial analyst by Tropical Sweets Inc., a mid-sized California company that specializes in creating exotic candies from tropical fruits such as mangoes, papayas, and dates. The firm's CEO, George Yamaguchi, recently returned from an industry corporate executive conference in San Francisco, and one of the sessions he attended was on the pressing need for smaller companies to institute corporate risk management programs. Since no one at Tropical Sweets is familiar with the basics of derivatives and corporate risk management, Yamaguchi has asked you to prepare a brief report that the firm's executives could use to gain at least a cursory understanding of the topics.

To begin, you gathered some outside materials on derivatives and corporate risk management and used these materials to draft a list of pertinent questions that need to be answered. In fact, one possible approach to the paper is to use a question-and-answer format. Now that the questions have been drafted, you have to develop the answers.

a. What is an option? What is the single most important characteristic of an option?
b. Options have a unique set of terminology. Define the following terms:
    (1) Call option
    (2) Put option
    (3) Exercise price
    (4) Striking, or strike, price
    (5) Option price
    (6) Expiration date
    (7) Formula value
    (8) European option
    (9) American option
    (10) Covered option
    (11) Naked option
    (12) In-the-money call
    (13) Out-of-the-money call
    (14) LEAP
c. Consider Tropical Sweets's call option with a $25 strike price. The following table contains historical values for this option at different stock prices:

STOCK PRICE	CALL OPTION PRICE
$25	$ 3.00
30	7.50
35	12.00
40	16.50
45	21.00
50	25.50

    (1) Create a table which shows (a) stock price, (b) strike price, (c) formula value, (d) option price, and (e) the premium of option price over formula value.
    (2) What happens to the premium of option price over formula value as the stock price rises? Why?

d. In 1973, Fischer Black and Myron Scholes developed the Black-Scholes Option Pricing Model (OPM).
   (1) What assumptions underlie the OPM?
   (2) Write out the three equations that constitute the model.
   (3) What is the value of the following call option according to the OPM?

   Stock price = $27.00

   Exercise price = $25.00

   Time to expiration = 6 months.

   Risk-free rate = 6.0%

   Stock return variance = 0.11.

e. What impact does each of the following call option parameters have on the value of a call option?
   (1) Current stock price
   (2) Exercise price
   (3) Option period
   (4) Risk-free rate
   (5) Stock return variance
f. What is corporate risk management? Why is it important to all firms?
g. Risks that firms face can be categorized in many ways. Define the following types of risk:
   (1) Speculative risks
   (2) Pure risks
   (3) Demand risks
   (4) Input risks
   (5) Financial risks
   (6) Property risks
   (7) Personnel risks
   (8) Environmental risks
   (9) Liability risks
   (10) Insurable risks
h. What are the three steps of corporate risk management?
i. What are some actions that companies can take to minimize or reduce risk exposures?
j. How are risk exposures identified and measured?
k. Two of the most widespread risks facing companies are property loss and liability loss exposures. Describe these exposures and the actions that companies can take to reduce them.
l. How can a strategy of diversification reduce risk?
m. What is financial risk exposure? Describe the following concepts and techniques that can be used to reduce financial risks:
   (1) Duration
   (2) Immunization
   (3) Derivatives
   (4) Futures markets
   (5) Hedging
   (6) Swaps
n. Describe how commodity futures markets can be used to reduce input price risk.

SELECTED ADDITIONAL REFERENCES

For additional insights into the use of financial futures for hedging, see the following publications:

Bacon, Peter W., and Richard Williams, "Interest Rate Futures Trading: A New Tool for the Financial Manager," *Financial Management,* Spring 1976, 32–38.

Blake, Marshall, and Nelda Mahady, "How Mid-Sized Companies Manage Risk," *Journal of Applied Corporate Finance,* Spring 1991, 59–65.

Block, Stanley B., and Timothy J. Gallagher, "The Use of Interest Rate Futures and Options by Corporate Managers," *Financial Management,* Autumn 1986, 73–78.

Castelino, Mark G., Jack C. Francis, and Avner Wolf, "Cross-Hedging: Basis Risk and Choice of the Optimal Hedging Vehicle," *Financial Review,* May 1991, 179–210.

Kolb, Robert W., *Understanding Futures Markets* (Glenview, Ill.: Scott, Foresman, 1985).

McCabe, George M., and Charles T. Franckle, "The Effectiveness of Rolling the Hedge Forward in the Treasury Bill Futures Market," *Financial Management,* Summer 1983, 21–29.

Siegel, Daniel R., and Diane F. Siegel, *Futures Markets* (Hinsdale, Ill.: Dryden Press, 1990).

For information on hedging, see

Dolde, Walter, "The Trajectory of Corporate Financial Risk Management," *Journal of Applied Corporate Finance,* Fall 1993, 33–41.

———, "Hedging, Leverage, and Primitive Risk," *Journal of Financial Engineering,* Vol. 4, No. 2.

Marshall, John F., Vipul K. Bansal, Anthony F. Herbst, and Alan L. Tucker, "Hedging Business Cycle Risk with Macro Swaps and Options," *Journal of Applied Corporate Finance,* Winter 1992, 103–108.

For more information on swaps, see

Brown, Keith C., and Donald J. Smith, "Default Risk and Innovations in the Design of Interest Rate Swaps," *Financial Management,* Summer 1993, 94–105.

Einzig, Robert, and Bruce Lange, "Swaps at Transamerica: Applications and Analysis," *Journal of Applied Corporate Finance,* Winter 1990, 48–58.

Goodman, Laurie S., "The Uses of Interest Rate Swaps in Managing Corporate Liabilities," *Journal of Applied Corporate Finance,* Winter 1990, 35–47.

The original Black-Scholes article tested the OPM to see how well predicted prices conformed to market values. For additional empirical tests, see

Galai, Dan, "Tests of Market Efficiency of the Chicago Board Options Exchange," *Journal of Business,* April 1977, 167–197.

Gultekin, N. Bulent, Richard J. Rogalski, and Seha M. Tinic, "Option Pricing Model Estimates: Some Empirical Results," *Financial Management,* Spring 1982, 58–69.

MacBeth, James D., and Larry J. Merville, "An Empirical Examination of the Black-Scholes Call Option Pricing Model," *Journal of Finance,* December 1979, 1173–1186.

Much of the Fall 1993 issue of the Journal of Applied Corporate Finance *is devoted to risk management issues.*

For more information on the derivatives markets, see

Chance, Don M., *An Introduction to Derivatives* (Ft. Worth, Tex.: Dryden, 1995).

Chapman, Alger B. "Duke," "Future of the Derivatives Markets: Products, Technology, and Participants," *Financial Practice and Education*, Fall/Winter 1994, 124–128.

CHAPTER 24

BANKRUPTCY, REORGANIZATION, AND LIQUIDATION

*I*n June 1993, Continental Airlines performed, for the second time, a feat that few companies do even once — emerge from bankruptcy. (TWA managed to duplicate Continental's feat, while Braniff Airlines went into bankruptcy twice but only came out once.) When Continental Airlines Holdings Inc., along with 53 subsidiaries, filed for bankruptcy court protection in December 1990, it owed $3.96 billion. When it emerged from bankruptcy in 1993, the firm was leaner, with only four subsidiaries, it had shaved its debt to $1.8 billion, and it had $635 million in cash. However, with equity of roughly $600 million, the company still had a hefty 3:1 debt-to-equity ratio.

While under court protection—which means that the Bankruptcy Court prevented Continental's creditors from seizing its assets or even collecting interest—the company was able to take many actions that its nonbankrupt competitor airlines could not. In particular, it was able to abrogate and renegotiate its labor contracts. The ability to take this action, along with not having to pay interest on its debt, permitted it to offer very low fares by industry standards and still pare its losses. In 1991, Continental lost more than $300 million, but in 1992, the loss was only $125 million. More important, the lower operating and financing costs made Continental better able to deal with the cutthroat competition which prevailed in the airline industry.

However, the operating and financing advantages brought on by bankruptcy were costly to some parties. The company's reorganization plan, which provided the road map out of bankruptcy, called for paying creditors only a fraction of what they were owed. For example, unsecured creditors received about 5 cents to 40 cents per dollar of claims, depending on the exact type of debt. Creditors also *received some equity in the "new" Continental. In addition, 55 percent of the equity went to Air Canada and Air Partners, a Fort Worth investor group, which poured $450 million dollars of new cash into the airline. In the end, all of the equity went to creditors and new investors—the firm's original stockholders were wiped out.*

After you read this chapter, you will have a good understanding of the basics of bankruptcy. As you go through the material, think about the decisions that Continental's managers had to make regarding bankruptcy and reorganization, and the effects the firm's bankruptcy has had on all of its stakeholders as well as on competing airlines.

Thus far, we have dealt with issues faced by growing, successful enterprises. However, many firms encounter financial difficulties, and some, including such big names as Pan American Airlines and Texaco, are forced into bankruptcy. When a firm gets into trouble, its financial manager must know how to ward off the firm's total collapse and thereby reduce its losses. The ability of a firm to hang on during rough times often means the difference between forced liquidation versus rehabilitation and eventual success. An understanding of bankruptcy is also critical to the executives of healthy firms, because they must know the best way to handle things when their customers or suppliers face the threat of bankruptcy.

FINANCIAL DISTRESS AND ITS CONSEQUENCES

We begin with some background information on financial distress and its consequences.[1] Specifically, we discuss (1) types of financial distress, (2) causes of business failure, and (3) the business failure and bankruptcy record.

TYPES OF FINANCIAL DISTRESS

Financial distress runs the gamut from a vague uneasiness about future profitability to complete disintegration of the firm. Some ways in which financial distress is commonly defined include the following:

1. **Economic failure.** Failure in an economic sense signifies that a firm's revenues do not cover its total costs, including its cost of capital. Businesses that are *economic failures* can continue operating as long as creditors are willing to provide capital and their owners are willing to accept below-market rates of return. Eventually, though, no new capital will be provided when assets wear out and must be replaced, so such firms either close or contract to the point where their smaller level of output provides a "normal" return, at which point they become economically viable.

---

[1]Much of the current academic work in the area of financial distress and bankruptcy is based on writings by Edward I. Altman. For a summary of his work and that of others, see Edward I. Altman, *Bankruptcy and Distressed Restructuring* (Homewood, Ill.: Irwin, 1992).

2. **Business failure.** The term *business failure* is used by Dun & Bradstreet, which is the major compiler of failure statistics, to define any business that has terminated operations *with a resultant loss to creditors.*

3. **Technical insolvency.** A firm is *technically insolvent* if it cannot meet its current obligations as they fall due. Technical insolvency may denote a temporary lack of liquidity, where, given time, the firm may be able to pay off its obligations and survive. On the other hand, if technical insolvency is an early symptom of economic failure, it may be the first stop on the road to financial disaster.

4. **Insolvency in bankruptcy.** A firm is *insolvent in bankruptcy* if the book value of its liabilities exceeds the true market value of its assets. This is a more serious condition than technical insolvency because, generally, it is a sign of economic failure, and it often leads to liquidation of the business. Note that a firm that is insolvent in bankruptcy is not necessarily involved in legal bankruptcy proceedings.

5. **Legal bankruptcy.** Although many people use the term *bankruptcy* to refer to any firm that has "failed," a firm is not *legally bankrupt* unless it has filed for bankruptcy under the federal bankruptcy laws.

CAUSES OF BUSINESS FAILURE

A recent Dun & Bradstreet compilation assigned percentage values to business failure causes, as shown in Table 24-1. Economic factors include industry weakness and poor location, and financial factors include too much debt and insufficient capital. The importance of the different factors varies over time, depending on such things as the state of the economy and the level of interest rates. Also, most business failures occur because a number of factors combine to make the business unsustainable. Further, case studies show that financial difficulties are usually the result of a series of errors, misjudgments, and interrelated weaknesses that can be attributed directly or indirectly to management, and signs of potential financial distress are generally evident in a ratio analysis before the firm actually fails.

CAUSES OF BUSINESS FAILURE	TABLE 24-1

CAUSE OF FAILURE	PERCENTAGE OF TOTAL
Economic factors	37.1%
Financial factors	47.3
Neglect, disaster, and fraud	14.0
Other factors	1.6
	100.0%

SOURCE: Dun & Bradstreet, Inc., *Business Failure Record* (New York, updated annually).

THE BUSINESS FAILURE RECORD

How widespread is business failure in the United States? In Table 24-2, we see that a fairly large number of businesses fail each year, although the failures in any one year are not a large percentage of the total business population. It is interesting to note that whereas the failure rate per 10,000 businesses fluctuates with the state of the economy, the average liability per failure has tended to increase over time, at least into the early 1990s. This is due primarily to inflation, but it also reflects the fact that some very large firms have failed in recent years.

Although bankruptcy is more frequent among smaller firms, it is clear from Table 24-3 that large firms are not immune. However, some firms are thought to be too big or "too important" to fail, and mergers or governmental intervention are often used as an alternative to outright failure and liquidation. The decision to give federal aid to Chrysler in the early 1980s is an excellent illustration. Also, in recent years fed-

TABLE 24-2	HISTORICAL FAILURE RATE OF U.S. BUSINESSES		
YEARS	AVERAGE NUMBER OF FAILURES PER YEAR	AVERAGE FAILURE RATE PER 10,000 BUSINESSES	AVERAGE LIABILITY PER FAILURE
1950–1959	11,119	42	$ 41,082
1960–1969	13,110	52	92,271
1970–1979	9,311	36	296,497
1980	11,742	42	394,744
1981	17,041	61	414,147
1982	24,908	89	626,738
1983	31,334	110	512,953
1984	52,078	107	562,016
1985	57,253	115	645,160
1986	61,616	120	725,850
1987	61,111	102	568,209
1988	57,097	98	693,084
1989	50,361	65	840,507
1990	60,747	74	923,996
1991	88,140	107	1,098,539
1992	97,069	110	971,653
1993	86,133	109	554,438
1994	71,558	86	404,955
1995	71,194	90	525,833

NOTE: Due to statistical revision, data prior to 1984 are not directly comparable to data in 1984 and thereafter.
SOURCE: Dun & Bradstreet, Inc., *Business Failure Record* (New York, 1995).

TWELVE LARGEST NONBANK BANKRUPTCIES (BILLIONS OF DOLLARS)		TABLE 24-3
COMPANY	**LIABILITIES**	**DATE**
Texaco	$21.6	April 1987
Olympia & York	19.8	May 1992
Executive Life Insurance	14.6	April 1991
Mutual Benefit Life	13.5	July 1991
Campeau (Allied and Federated)	9.9	January 1990
First Capital Holdings	9.3	May 1991
Baldwin United	9.0	September 1983
Continental Airlines	6.2	December 1990
Lomas Financial	6.1	September 1989
Macy's	5.3	January 1992
Columbia Gas	5.0	July 1991
LTV	4.7	July 1986

NOTE: There are motivations for filing for bankruptcy other than immediate financial distress. For example, Texaco's bankruptcy was the result of a lawsuit, and Continental Airlines's first filing in 1983 was motivated by a desire to abrogate union contracts.
SOURCE: Data supplied by Edward I. Altman.

eral regulators have arranged the absorption of many large "problem" savings and loan associations and commercial banks by financially sound institutions. In addition, several U.S. government agencies, principally the Defense Department, were able to bail out Lockheed when it otherwise would have failed, and the "shotgun marriage" of Douglas Aircraft and McDonnell was designed to prevent Douglas's failure. Another example of intervention is that of Merrill Lynch taking over Goodbody & Company, which would otherwise have gone bankrupt and would have frozen the accounts of its 225,000 customers while a bankruptcy settlement was being worked out. Goodbody's failure would have panicked investors across the country, so New York Stock Exchange member firms put up $30 million as an inducement to get Merrill Lynch to keep Goodbody from folding. Similar instances in other industries could also be cited.

Why do government and industry seek to avoid failure among larger firms? There are many reasons. In the case of banks, the main reason is to prevent an erosion of confidence and a consequent run on the banks. With Lockheed and Douglas, the Defense Department wanted not only to maintain viable suppliers but also to avoid disrupting local communities. With Chrysler, the government wanted to preserve jobs as well as a competitor in the U.S. auto industry. Even when the public interest is not at stake, the fact that bankruptcy is a very expensive process gives private industry strong incentives to avoid outright bankruptcy. The costs and complexities of formal bankruptcy are discussed in subsequent sections of this chapter, but first some less formal and less expensive remedies and legal actions are examined.

**SELF-TEST
QUESTIONS**
Define the following types of financial distress:
   (1) Economic failure
   (2) Business failure
   (3) Technical insolvency
   (4) Insolvency in bankruptcy
   (5) Legal bankruptcy
What are the major causes of business failure?
Do business failures occur evenly over time?
Which size of firm, large or small, is most prone to business failure? Why?

ISSUES FACING A FIRM IN FINANCIAL DISTRESS

Financial distress begins when a firm is unable to meet scheduled payments or when cash flow projections indicate that it will soon be unable to do so. As the situation develops, these central issues arise:

1. Is the firm's inability to meet scheduled debt payments a temporary cash flow problem (technical insolvency), or is it a permanent problem caused by asset values having fallen below debt obligations (insolvency in bankruptcy)?

2. If the problem is a temporary one, then an agreement with creditors that gives the firm time to recover and to satisfy everyone may be worked out. However, if basic long-run asset values have truly declined, then economic losses have occurred. In this event, who should bear the losses?

3. Is the company "worth more dead than alive"? That is, would the business be more valuable if it were maintained and continued in operation or if it were liquidated and sold off in pieces?

4. Should the firm file for protection under Chapter 11 of the Bankruptcy Act, or should it try to use informal procedures? (Both reorganization and liquidation can be accomplished either informally or under the direction of a bankruptcy court.)

5. Who should control the firm while it is being liquidated or rehabilitated? Should the existing management be left in charge, or should a trustee be placed in charge of operations?

The answers to these questions effectively chart the course of a company in financial distress. In the remainder of the chapter, we discuss the issues surrounding these questions, beginning with informal solutions to financial distress.

**SELF-TEST
QUESTION**
What five major issues must be addressed when a firm is in financial distress?

SETTLEMENTS WITHOUT GOING THROUGH FORMAL BANKRUPTCY

When a firm experiences financial distress, its managers must first decide whether the problem is temporary, and the firm is really financially viable, or whether a permanent problem exists that endangers the firm's life. Then, the firm's managers must decide whether to try to solve the problem informally or under the direction of a bankruptcy court. Because of costs associated with formal bankruptcy, including the disruptions that occur when a firm's customers, suppliers, and employees learn that it has filed under the Bankruptcy Act, it is desirable if possible to reorganize (or liquidate) a firm outside of formal bankruptcy. In this section, we discuss informal settlements.

INFORMAL REORGANIZATION

In the case of an economically sound company whose financial difficulties appear to be temporary, creditors are generally willing to work with the company to help it to recover and reestablish itself on a sound financial basis. Such voluntary plans, commonly called *workouts,* usually require a *restructuring* of the firm's debt, because current cash flows are insufficient to service the existing debt. Restructuring typically involves extension and/or composition. In an *extension,* creditors postpone the dates of required interest or principal payments, or both. In a *composition,* creditors voluntarily reduce their fixed claims on the debtor by accepting a lower principal amount, by reducing the interest rate on the debt, by accepting equity in place of debt, or by accepting some combination of these changes.

A debt restructuring begins with a meeting between the failing firm's managers and creditors. The creditors appoint a committee consisting of four or five of the largest creditors, plus one or two of the smaller ones. This meeting is often arranged and conducted by an *adjustment bureau* associated with and run by a local credit managers' association.[2] Once the decision has been reached that the problems can be worked out, the bureau assigns investigators to make an exhaustive report. Then, the bureau and the creditors' committee use the report to formulate a preliminary reorganization plan. Another meeting between the debtor and the creditors is then held in an attempt to craft a plan that can be agreed upon by all parties. At least three conditions are usually necessary to make an informal debt restructuring feasible: (1) The debtor must be a good moral risk, (2) the debtor must present a reasonable plan to solve its problems, and (3) general business conditions must be favorable to recovery. Many meetings and a great deal of negotiation may be required to reach a final agreement.

In developing the reorganization plan, creditors prefer an extension because it promises eventual payment in full. In some cases, creditors may agree not only to postpone the date of payment but also to subordinate existing claims to vendors

---

[2]There is a nationwide group called the National Association of Credit Management, which consists of bankers and industrial companies' credit managers. This group sponsors research on credit policy and problems, conducts seminars on credit management, and operates local chapters in cities throughout the nation. These local chapters frequently operate adjustment bureaus.

who are willing to extend new credit during the workout period. Similarly, creditors may agree to accept a lower interest rate on loans during the extension, perhaps in exchange for a pledge of collateral. Because of the sacrifices involved, the creditors must have faith that the debtor firm will be able to solve its problems.

In a composition, creditors agree to reduce their claims. Typically, creditors receive cash and/or new securities that have a combined market value that is less than the amounts owed them. The cash and securities, which might have a value of only 10 percent of the original claim, are taken as full settlement of the original debt. Bargaining will take place between the debtor and the creditors over the savings that result from avoiding the costs of legal bankruptcy: administrative costs, legal fees, investigative costs, and so on. In addition to escaping such costs, the debtor gains in that the stigma of bankruptcy may be avoided; as a result, the debtor may be induced to part with most of the savings from avoiding formal bankruptcy.

Often, the bargaining process will result in a restructuring which involves both extension and composition. For example, the settlement may provide for a cash payment of 25 percent of the debt immediately, plus a new note promising six future installments of 10 percent each, for a total payment of 85 percent. In some plans, creditors may end up with senior claims after the reorganization, which could motivate them to agree to the plan even though the amount of the claim had been reduced.

Voluntary settlements are both informal and simple, and also relatively inexpensive because legal and administrative expenses are held to a minimum. Thus, voluntary procedures often result in the largest return to creditors. Although creditors do not obtain immediate payment and may even have to accept less than is owed them, they often recover more money, and sooner, than if the firm were to file for bankruptcy.

In recent years, one factor that has motivated some creditors, especially banks and insurance companies, to agree to voluntary restructurings is the fact that restructurings can sometimes help creditors avoid showing a loss. Thus, a bank that is "in trouble" with its regulators over weak capital ratios may agree to extend further loans which are used to pay the interest on earlier loans in order to keep the bank from having to write down the value of its earlier loans. This particular type of restructuring depends on (1) the willingness of the regulators to go along with the process, and (2) whether the bank is likely to recover more in the end by restructuring the debt or by forcing the borrower into bankruptcy immediately.

We should point out that informal voluntary settlements are not reserved for small firms. International Harvester (now Navistar International) avoided formal bankruptcy proceedings by getting its creditors to agree to restructure more than $3.5 billion of debt. Likewise, Chrysler's creditors accepted both an extension and a composition to help it through its bad years. The biggest problem in informal reorganizations is in getting all the parties to agree to the voluntary plan. This problem, called the *holdout problem,* is discussed in a later section.

INFORMAL LIQUIDATION

When it is obvious that a firm is more valuable dead than alive, informal procedures can also be used to *liquidate* the firm. *Assignment* is an informal procedure for liquidating a firm, and it usually yields creditors a larger amount than they would receive in a formal bankruptcy liquidation. However, assignments are feasible only if the firm is small and its affairs are not too complex. An assignment calls for title to the debtor's assets to be transferred to a third party, known as an *assignee* or *trustee*. The assignee is instructed to liquidate the assets through a private sale or a public auction and then to distribute the proceeds among the creditors on a pro rata basis. The assignment does not automatically discharge the debtor's obligations. However, the debtor may have the assignee write on the check to each creditor the requisite legal language to make endorsement of the check acknowledgment of full settlement of the claim.

Assignment has some advantages over liquidation in federal bankruptcy courts in terms of time, legal formality, and expense. The assignee has more flexibility in disposing of property than does a federal bankruptcy trustee, so action can be taken sooner, before the inventory becomes obsolete or the machinery rusts. Also, since the assignee is often familiar with the channels of trade in the debtor's business, better results may be achieved. However, an assignment does not automatically result in a full and legal discharge of all the debtor's liabilities, nor does it protect the creditors against fraud. Both of these problems can be reduced by formal liquidation in bankruptcy, which we discuss in a later section.

Define the following terms:
(1) Restructuring
(2) Extension
(3) Composition
(4) Assignment
(5) Assignee (trustee)
What three conditions are usually necessary to make an informal debt restructuring feasible?
What are the advantages of liquidation by assignment versus a formal bankruptcy liquidation?

FEDERAL BANKRUPTCY LAW

U.S. bankruptcy laws were first enacted in 1898. They were modified substantially in 1938, then they were changed substantially again in 1978, and some fine-tuning was done in 1986. The primary purpose of the bankruptcy law is to avoid having firms that are worth more as ongoing concerns be put out of business by individual creditors who could force liquidation without regard to the effects on other parties.

The Bankruptcy Reform Act of 1978 was a major revision designed to streamline and expedite proceedings. Currently, our bankruptcy law consists of eight odd-numbered chapters, plus one even-numbered chapter. Chapters 1, 3, and 5 contain general provisions applicable to the other chapters. Chapter 11, which deals with business reorganization, is the most important section from a financial management viewpoint. Chapter 7 details the procedures to be followed when liquidating a firm; generally, Chapter 7 liquidation is not used unless it has been determined that reorganization under Chapter 11 is not feasible. Chapter 9 deals with financially distressed municipalities; Chapter 12 covers special procedures for family-owned farms; Chapter 13 covers the adjustment of debts for "individuals with regular income"; and Chapter 15 sets up a system of trustees who help administer proceedings under the act.

A firm is officially bankrupt when it files for bankruptcy with a federal court. When you read that a company such as Southland (the owner of the 7-Eleven convenience store chain) has "filed for court protection under Chapter 11," this means that the company is attempting to work out a reorganization under the supervision of a bankruptcy court. Formal bankruptcy proceedings are designed to protect both the firm and its creditors. On the one hand, if the problem is technical insolvency, then the firm may use bankruptcy proceedings to gain time to solve its cash flow problems without foreclosure by its creditors. On the other hand, if the firm is bankrupt in the sense that liabilities exceed assets, the creditors can use bankruptcy procedures to stop the firm's managers from depleting assets which should go to creditors.

Bankruptcy law is flexible in that it provides scope for negotiations between a company and its creditors and stockholders. A case is opened by filing a petition with one of the 291 bankruptcy courts serving 90 judicial districts. The petition may be either *voluntary* or *involuntary;* that is, it may be filed either by the firm's management or by its creditors. A committee of *unsecured* creditors is then appointed by the court to negotiate with management for a reorganization, which may include the restructuring of debt. A *trustee* will be appointed by the court if current management is deemed incompetent or if fraud is suspected; otherwise, the existing management will retain control. If no fair and feasible reorganization can be worked out, the firm will be liquidated under the procedures spelled out in Chapter 7.

SELF-TEST QUESTIONS

Define the following terms:
(1) Bankruptcy law
(2) Chapter 11
(3) Chapter 7
(4) Trustee
(5) Voluntary bankruptcy
(6) Involuntary bankruptcy

How does a firm formally declare bankruptcy?

REORGANIZATION IN BANKRUPTCY

It might appear that most reorganizations should be handled informally, because they can be accomplished more quickly and at less cost than through formal bankruptcy. However, two problems — the common pool problem and the holdout problem—often arise to stymie informal reorganizations and thus force debtors into Chapter 11 bankruptcy.[3]

---

[3]The issues discussed in this section are covered in more detail in Thomas H. Jackson, *The Logic and Limits of Bankruptcy Law* (Cambridge, Mass.: Harvard University Press, 1986).

To illustrate the two problems, consider a firm that is having financial difficulties. The firm is worth $9 million as an ongoing concern (this is the present value of its expected future operating cash flows) but only $7 million if it is liquidated. The firm's debt totals $10 million face value—ten creditors with equal priority each have a $1 million claim. Now suppose the firm's liquidity deteriorates to the point where it defaults on one of its loans. The holder of the loan in default has the contractual right to *accelerate* the claim, which means the creditor can *foreclose* on the loan and demand payment of the entire balance. Further, since most debt agreements have *cross-default provisions,* defaulting on one loan effectively places all loans in default.

The firm's market value is less than the $10 million face value of debt, regardless of whether the firm remains in business or liquidates, so all of the creditors cannot be paid in full. However, the creditors in total clearly would be better off if the firm is not shut down, because they can recover $9 million if the firm is to remain in business but only $7 million if the firm is liquidated. The problem here, which is called the *common pool problem,* is that, in the absence of protection under the Bankruptcy Act, individual creditors would have an incentive to foreclose on the firm even though the firm is worth more collectively as an ongoing concern.

An individual creditor would have the incentive to foreclose because it could then force the firm to liquidate a portion of its assets to pay off the creditor's $1 million claim in full. The foreclosure by a single creditor would reduce the value of the assets, hence operating cash flow, so the value of the remaining creditors' claims would be reduced by the foreclosure. Of course, all the creditors recognize the gains to be had from this strategy, so they would storm the debtor with foreclosure notices. Even those creditors who understand the merits of keeping the firm alive would be forced to foreclose, because the foreclosures of the other creditors would reduce the payoff to those who do not. In our hypothetical example, if seven creditors foreclosed and forced liquidation, they would be paid in full, and the remaining three creditors would receive nothing.

With many creditors, as soon as a firm defaults on one loan, there is the potential for a disruptive flood of foreclosures that would make the creditors collectively worse off. In our example, the creditors would lose $2 million in value if a flood of foreclosures were to force the firm to liquidate. If the firm had only one creditor, say, a single bank loan, the common pool problem would not exist—if a single bank had loaned the company $10 million, it would not force liquidation to get $7 million when it could keep the firm alive and eventually realize $9 million.

Chapter 11 of the Bankrupcy Act provides a solution to the common pool problem because of its *automatic stay* provision. *An automatic stay, which is forced on all creditors in a bankruptcy, limits the ability of creditors to foreclose to collect their individual claims.* However, the creditors can collectively foreclose on the debtor and force liquidation.

While bankruptcy gives the firm a chance to work out its problems without the threat of creditor foreclosure, it does not give the debtor free reign over the firm's assets. First, bankruptcy law requires the debtor firm to request permission from the court to take many actions, and the law also gives creditors the right to petition the bankruptcy court to block almost any action the firm might take while in bankruptcy. Second, *fraudulent conveyance* statutes, which are part of debtor-creditor law in most states, protect creditors from unjustified transfers of property by a firm in financial distress.

To illustrate fraudulent conveyance, suppose a holding company is contemplating bankruptcy protection for one of its subsidiaries. The holding company might be tempted to sell some or all of the subsidiary's assets to itself (the parent company) for less than the true market value. This transaction would reduce the value of the subsidiary by the difference between the true market value of its assets and the amount paid, and the loss would be borne primarily by the subsidiary's creditors. Such a transaction would likely be voided by the courts as a fraudulent conveyance. Note also that transactions that favor one creditor at the expense of another can be voided under the same law. For example, a transaction in which an asset is sold and the proceeds are used to pay one creditor in full at the expense of other creditors could be voided. Thus, fraudulent conveyance laws also protect creditors from each other.[4]

The second problem that bankruptcy law mitigates is the *holdout problem.* To illustrate this problem, consider again our example with ten creditors owed $1 million each but only $9 million worth of assets. The goal of the firm is to avoid liquidation by *remedying* the default. In an informal workout, this would require a reorganization plan that is agreed to by each of the ten creditors. Suppose the firm offers each creditor new debt with a face value of $850,000 in exchange for the old $1,000,000 face value debt. If each of the creditors accepted the offer, the firm could be successfully reorganized. The reorganization would leave the equity holders with some value—the market value of the equity would be $9,000,000 − 10($850,000) = $500,000. Further, the creditors would have claims worth $8.5 million, much more than the $7 million value of their claims in liquidation.

Although such an exchange offer seems to benefit all parties, it is unlikely to be accepted by the creditors. Here's why: Suppose seven of the ten creditors tender their bonds; thus, seven creditors each now have claims with a face value of $850,000 each, or $5,950,000 in total, while the three creditors that did not tender their bonds each have a claim with a face value of $1 million. The total face value of the debt at this point is $8,950,000, which is less than the $9 million value of the firm. In this situation, the three holdout creditors would receive the full face value of their debt. However, this would not happen, because (1) all of the creditors would be sophisticated enough to realize this would happen, and (2) each creditor would want to be one of the three holdouts that gets paid in full. Thus, it is likely that none of the creditors would accept the offer, so the holdout problem makes it very difficult to reorganize the firm's debts. Again, if the firm had a single creditor, there would be no holdout problem.

The holdout problem is mitigated in bankruptcy proceedings because the bankruptcy court will lump the creditors into classes. Each class is considered to have

---

[4]Note that federal bankruptcy law contains *voidable preference* provisions that are similar to state fraudulent conveyance laws. The bankruptcy code requires that all transactions undertaken by the firm in the six months prior to bankruptcy filing be reviewed by the court for fraudulent conveyance.

accepted a reorganization plan if a majority of the creditors in the class (holding at least two-thirds of the amount of debt) vote for the plan, and the plan will be approved by the court if it is deemed to be "fair and equitable" to the dissenting parties. This procedure, in which the court mandates a reorganization plan in spite of dissent, is called a *cramdown,* because the court crams the plan down the throats of the dissenters. The ability of the court to force acceptance of a reorganization plan greatly reduces the incentive for creditors to hold out. Thus, in our example, if the reorganization plan offered each creditor a new claim worth $850,000 in face value, along with information that each creditor would probably receive only $700,000 under the liquidation alternative, it would have a good chance of success.

It is easier for a firm with few creditors to informally reorganize than it is for a firm with many creditors. A recent study examined 169 publicly traded firms that experienced severe financial distress from 1978 to 1987.[5] About half of the firms reorganized without filing for bankruptcy, while the other half were forced to reorganize in bankruptcy. The firms that reorganized without filing for bankruptcy owed most of their debt to banks, and they had fewer creditors. Generally, bank debt can be reorganized outside of bankruptcy, while a publicly traded bond issue held by thousands of individual bondholders makes reorganization difficult.

Filing for bankruptcy under Chapter 11 has several features in addition to the automatic stay and cramdown provisions:

1. Interest and principal payments, including interest on delayed payments, may be delayed without penalty until a reorganization plan is approved (the plan may call for even further delays). This permits cash generated from operations to be used to sustain operations rather than paid to creditors.

2. The firm is permitted to issue *debtor in possession (DIP) financing.* DIP financing enhances the ability of the firm to borrow funds for short-term liquidity purposes, because such loans are, under the law, senior to all other unsecured debt.

3. The debtor firm's managers are given the exclusive right for 120 days after filing to submit a reorganization plan, plus another 60 days to obtain agreement on the plan from the affected parties. The court may also extend these dates. After management's first right to submit a plan has expired, any party to the proceedings may propose an alternative reorganization plan.

Under the prior bankruptcy laws, most formal reorganization plans were guided by the *absolute priority doctrine.* This doctrine holds that creditors should be compensated for their claims in a rigid hierarchical order, and that senior claims must be paid in full before junior claims can receive even a dime. However, an alternative

---

[5]See Stuart Gilson, Kose John, and Larry Lang, "Troubled Debt Restructurings: An Empirical Study of Private Reorganization of Firms in Default," *Journal of Financial Economics,* October 1990, 315–354.

position, the *relative priority doctrine,* holds that more flexibility should be allowed in a reorganization, and that a balanced consideration should be given to all claimants. The current law represented a movement away from absolute priority and toward relative priority.

The primary role of the bankruptcy court in a reorganization is to determine the *fairness* and the *feasibility* of the proposed plan of reorganization. The basic doctrine of fairness states that claims must be recognized in the order of their legal and contractual priority. Feasibility means that there is a reasonable chance that the reorganized company will be viable. Carrying out the concepts of fairness and feasibility in a reorganization involves the following steps:

1. Future sales must be estimated.

2. Operating conditions must be analyzed so that future earnings and cash flows can be predicted.

3. The capitalization rate applied to these cash flows must be determined.

4. This capitalization rate must then be applied to the estimated cash flows to obtain an estimate of the company's value.

5. The company's capital structure after it emerges from Chapter 11 must be determined.

6. The reorganized firm's securities must be allocated to the various claimants in a fair and equitable manner.

The primary test of feasibility in a reorganization is whether the fixed charges after reorganization will be adequately covered by earnings. Adequate coverage generally requires an improvement in earnings or a reduction of fixed charges, or both. Among the actions that must generally be taken are the following:

1. Debt maturities are usually lengthened, and some debt is usually converted into equity.

2. When the quality of management has been substandard, a new team must be given control of the company.

3. If inventories have become obsolete or depleted, they must be replaced.

4. Sometimes the plant and equipment must be modernized before the firm can operate and compete successfully.

5. Reorganization may also require an improvement in production, marketing, advertising, and other functions.

6. It is sometimes necessary to develop new products or markets to enable the firm to move from areas where economic trends are poor into areas with more potential for growth.

ILLUSTRATION OF A REORGANIZATION

Reorganization procedures may be illustrated with an example involving the Columbia Software Company, a regional firm that specializes in selling, installing, and ser-

COLUMBIA SOFTWARE COMPANY: BALANCE SHEET AS OF MARCH 31, 1996 (MILLIONS OF DOLLARS)		TABLE 24-4
ASSETS		
Current assets	$ 3.50	
Net fixed assets	12.50	
Other assets	0.70	
Total assets	$16.70	
LIABILITIES AND EQUITY		
Accounts payable	$ 1.00	
Accrued taxes	0.25	
Notes payable	0.25	
Other current liabilities	1.75	
$7\frac{1}{2}$% first mortgage bonds, due 2004	6.00	
9% subordinated debentures, due 1999[a]	7.00	
Common stock ($1 par)	1.00	
Paid-in capital	3.45	
Retained earnings	(4.00)	
Total liabilities and equity	$16.70	

[a]The debentures are subordinated to the notes payable.

vicing accounting software for small businesses.[6] Table 24-4 gives Columbia's balance sheet as of March 31, 1996. The company had been suffering losses running to $2.5 million a year, and, as will be made clear in the following discussion, the asset values in the balance sheet are overstated. Because the firm was insolvent, it filed a petition with a federal court for reorganization under Chapter 11. Management filed a plan of reorganization with the court on June 13, 1996. The plan was subsequently submitted for review by the SEC.[7]

The plan concluded that the company could not be internally reorganized and that the only feasible solution would be to combine Columbia with a larger, nationwide software company. Accordingly, the court solicited the interest of a number of software companies. Late in July 1996, Moreland Software showed an interest in Columbia. On August 3, 1996, Moreland made a formal proposal to take over

---

[6]This example is based on an actual reorganization, although the company name has been changed and the numbers have been changed slightly to simplify the analysis.

[7]Reorganization plans must be submitted to the Securities and Exchange Commission (SEC) if (1) the securities of the debtor are publicly held, and (2) total indebtedness exceeds $3 million. However, in recent years the only bankruptcy cases that the SEC has become involved in are those that are either precedent setting or that involve issues of national interest.

Columbia's $6 million of $7\frac{1}{2}$ percent first-mortgage bonds, to pay the $250,000 in taxes owed by Columbia, and to provide 40,000 shares of Moreland common stock to satisfy the remaining creditor claims. Since the Moreland stock had a market price of $75 per share, the value of the stock was $3 million. Thus, Moreland was offering $3 million of stock plus assuming $6 million of loans and $250,000 of taxes — a total of $9.25 million for assets that had a book value of $16.7 million.

Moreland's plan is shown in Table 24-5. As in most Chapter 11 plans, the secured creditors' claims are paid in full (in this case, the mortgage bonds are taken over by Moreland Software). However, the total remaining claims of the unsecured creditors equal $10 million against only $3 million of available funds. Thus, each unsecured creditor would be entitled to receive 30 percent before the adjustment for subordination. Before this adjustment, holders of notes payable would receive 30 percent of their $250,000 claim, or $75,000. However, the debentures are subordinated to the notes payable, so an additional $175,000 must be allocated to notes payable from the subordinated debentures. In Column 5, the dollar claims of each class of debt are restated in terms of the number of shares of Moreland common stock received by each class of unsecured creditors. Finally, Column 6 shows the percentage of the original claim each group received. Of course, both the taxes and the secured creditors were paid off in full, while the stockholders received nothing.[8]

TABLE 24-5	COLUMBIA SOFTWARE COMPANY: REORGANIZATION PLAN (MILLIONS OF DOLLARS)

SENIOR CLAIMS

Taxes	$ 250,000	Paid off by Moreland
Mortgage bonds	$6,000,000	Assumed by Moreland

The reorganization plan for the remaining $10 million of liabilities, based on 40,000 shares at a price of $75 for a total market value of $3 million, or 30 percent of the remaining liabilities, is as follows:

JUNIOR CLAIMS (1)	ORIGINAL AMOUNT (2)	30% OF CLAIM AMOUNT (3)	CLAIM AFTER SUBORDINATION (4)	NUMBER OF SHARES OF COMMON STOCK (5)	PERCENTAGE OF ORIGINAL CLAIM RECEIVED (6)
Notes payable	$ 250,000	$ 75,000	$ 250,000[a]	3,333	100%
Unsecured creditors	2,750,000	825,000	825,000	11,000	30
Subordinated debentures	7,000,000	2,100,000	1,925,000[a]	25,667	28
	$10,000,000	$3,000,000	$3,000,000	40,000	30%

[a]Because the debentures are subordinated to the notes payable, $250,000 − $75,000 = $175,000 must be redistributed from the debentures to the notes payable.

---

[8]We do not show it, but $365,000 of fees for Columbia's attorneys and $123,000 of fees for the creditors' committee lawyers were also deducted. The current assets shown in Table 24-4 were net of these fees. Creditors joke (often bitterly) about the "lawyers first" rule in payouts in bankruptcy cases. It is often said, with much truth, that the only winners in bankruptcy cases are the attorneys.

The bankruptcy court first evaluated the proposal from the standpoint of fairness. The court began by considering the value of Columbia Software as estimated by the unsecured creditors' committee and by a subgroup of debenture holders. After discussions with various experts, one group had arrived at estimated sales of $25 million per year. It further estimated that the profit margin on sales would equal 6 percent, thus producing estimated future annual earnings of $1.5 million.

This subgroup analyzed price/earnings ratios for comparable companies and arrived at 8 times future earnings for a capitalization factor. Multiplying 8 by $1.5 million gave an indicated total value of the company of $12 million. Since the mortgage bonds assumed and taxes paid by Moreland Software totalled $6,250,000, a net value of $5,750,000 was left for the other claims. This value was almost double that of the 40,000 shares of Moreland stock offered for the remainder of the company. Thus, the subgroup concluded that the plan for reorganization did not meet the test of fairness. Note that under both Moreland's plan and the subgroup's plan, the holders of common stock were to receive nothing, which is one of the risks of ownership, while the holders of the first-mortgage bonds were to be assumed by Moreland, which amounts to being paid in full.

The bankruptcy judge examined management's plan for feasibility, observing that in the reorganization Moreland Software would take over Columbia's properties. The committee judged that the direction and aid of Moreland would remedy the deficiencies that had troubled Columbia. Whereas the debt/assets ratio of Columbia Software had become unbalanced, Moreland has only a moderate amount of debt. After consolidation, Moreland would still have a relatively low 27 percent debt ratio.

Moreland's net income before interest and taxes had been running at a level of approximately $15 million. The interest on its long-term debt after the merger would be $1.5 million and, taking short-term borrowings into account, would total a maximum of $2 million per year. The $15 million in earnings before interest and taxes would therefore provide an interest charge coverage of 7.5 times, exceeding the norm of 5 times for the industry.

Notice that the question of feasibility would have been irrelevant had Moreland offered $3 million in cash rather than in stock, and had it offered to pay off the bonds rather than take them over. It is the court's responsibility to protect the interests of Columbia's unsecured creditors. Since the creditors are being forced to take common stock or bonds guaranteed by another firm, the creditors' committee felt the need to look into the feasibility of the transaction. If Moreland had made a cash offer, however, the feasibility of its own operation after the transaction was completed would not have been a concern.

Moreland Software was told of the subgroup's analysis and concern over the fairness of the plan. Further, Moreland was asked to increase the number of shares it offered. Moreland refused, and no other company offered to acquire Columbia. Because no better offer could be obtained, and the only alternative to the plan was liquidation (with an even lower realized value), Moreland's proposal was ultimately accepted by the creditors despite some disagreement with the valuation.

PREPACKAGED BANKRUPTCIES

In recent years, a new type of reorganization that combines the advantages of both the informal workout and formal Chapter 11 reorganization has become popular. This new hybrid is called a *prepackaged bankruptcy,* or *pre-pack.*[9]

In an informal workout, a debtor negotiates a restructuring with its creditors. Even though complex workouts typically involve corporate officers, lenders, lawyers, and investment bankers, workouts are still less expensive and less damaging to reputations than are Chapter 11 reorganizations. In a prepackaged bankruptcy, the debtor firm gets all, or most of, the creditors to agree to the reorganization plan *prior* to filing for bankruptcy. Then, a reorganization plan is filed along with, or shortly after, the bankruptcy petition. If enough creditors have signed on before the filing, a cramdown can be used to bring reluctant creditors along.

A logical question arises: Why would a firm that can arrange an informal reorganization want to file for bankruptcy? The three primary advantages of a prepackaged bankruptcy are (1) reduction of the holdout problem, (2) preserving creditors' claims, and (3) taxes. Perhaps the biggest benefit of a prepackaged bankruptcy is the reduction of the holdout problem — a bankruptcy filing permits a cramdown that would otherwise be impossible. By eliminating holdouts, bankruptcy forces all creditors in each class to participate on a pro rata basis, which preserves the relative value of all claimants. Also, filing for formal bankruptcy can at times have positive tax implications. First, in an informal reorganization in which the debtholders trade debt for equity, if the original equity holders end up with less than 50 percent ownership, the company loses its accumulated tax losses. In formal bankruptcy, the firm gets to keep its loss carryforwards. Second, in a workout, when debt (worth, say, $1,000) is exchanged for debt (worth, say, $500), the reduction in debt of $500 is considered to be taxable income. However, if this same situation occurs in a Chapter 11 reorganization, the difference is not treated as taxable income.[10]

All in all, prepackaged bankruptcies make sense in many situations. If sufficient agreement can be reached among creditors through informal negotiations, a subsequent filing can solve the holdout problem and result in favorable tax treatment. For these reasons, the number of prepackaged bankruptcies has grown dramatically in recent years.

REORGANIZATION TIME AND EXPENSE

The time, expense, and headaches involved in a reorganization are almost beyond comprehension. Even in $2 to $3 million bankruptcies, many people and groups are involved: lawyers representing the company, the U.S. Bankruptcy Trustee, each

---

[9]For more information on prepackaged bankruptcies, see John J. McConnell and Henri Servaes, "The Economics of Pre-Packaged Bankruptcy," *Journal of Applied Corporate Finance,* Summer 1991, 93–97.

[10]Note that in both tax situations — loss carryforwards and debt value reductions — favorable tax treatment can be available in workouts if the firm is deemed to be legally insolvent, that is, if the market value of its assets is demonstrated to be less than the face value of its liabilities.

class of secured creditor, the general creditors as a group, tax authorities, and the stockholders if they are upset with management. There are time limits within which things are supposed to be done, but the process generally takes at least a year and probably much longer. The company must be given time to file its plan, and creditor groups must be given time to study and seek clarifications to it and then file counterplans to which the company must respond. Also, different creditor classes often disagree among themselves as to how much each class should receive, and hearings must be held to resolve such conflicts.

Management will want to remain in business, while some well-secured creditors may want the company liquidated as quickly as possible. Often, some party's plan will involve selling the business to another concern, as was the case with Columbia Software in our earlier example. Obviously, it can take months to seek out and negotiate with potential merger candidates.

The typical bankruptcy case takes about two years from the time the company files for protection under Chapter 11 until the final reorganization plan is approved or rejected. While all of this is going on, the company's business suffers. Sales certainly won't be helped, key employees may leave, and the remaining employees will be worrying about their jobs rather than concentrating on their work. Further, management will be spending most of its time on the bankruptcy rather than running the business, and it won't be able to take any significant action without court approval, which requires filing a formal petition with the court and giving all parties involved a chance to respond.

Even if its operations do not suffer, the company's assets will surely be reduced by its own legal fees and the required court and trustee costs. Good bankruptcy lawyers charge from $150 to $250 per hour, depending on the location, so those costs are not trivial. The creditors will also be incurring legal costs. Indeed, the sound of all of those meters ticking at $200 an hour in a slow-moving hearing can be deafening.

Note that creditors also lose the time value of their money. A creditor with a $100,000 claim and a 10 percent opportunity cost who ends up getting $50,000 after two years would have been better off settling for $41,500 initially. When legal fees, executive time, and general aggravation are taken into account, it might even make sense to settle for $20,000 or $25,000.

Both the company in trouble and its creditors know the drawbacks of formal bankruptcy, or their lawyers will inform them. Armed with a knowledge of how bankruptcy works, management may be in a strong position to persuade creditors to accept a workout which appears to be unfair and unreasonable on the surface. Or, if a Chapter 11 case has already begun, creditors may at some point agree to settle just to stop the bleeding.

SELF-TEST QUESTIONS

Define the following terms:
- (1) Common pool problem
- (2) Holdout problem
- (3) Automatic stay
- (4) Cramdown
- (5) Fraudulent conveyance

    (6) Absolute priority doctrine
    (7) Relative priority doctrine
    (8) Fairness
    (9) Feasibility
    (10) Debtor in possession financing
    (11) Prepackaged bankruptcy

What are the advantages of a formal reorganization under Chapter 11?

What has been the recent trend regarding absolute versus relative priority doctrines?

How do courts assess the fairness of proposed reorganization plans?

How do courts assess the feasibility of proposed reorganization plans?

Why have prepackaged bankruptcies become so popular in recent years?

LIQUIDATION IN BANKRUPTCY

If a company is "too far gone" to be reorganized, then it must be liquidated. Liquidation should occur when the business is worth more dead than alive, or when the possibility of restoring it to financial health is so remote that the creditors run a high risk of greater loss if operations are continued. Earlier we discussed *assignment,* which is an informal liquidation procedure. Now we consider *liquidation in bankruptcy,* which is carried out under the jurisdiction of a federal bankruptcy court.

Chapter 7 of the Federal Bankruptcy Reform Act deals with liquidation: (1) It provides safeguards against fraud by the debtor, (2) it provides for an equitable distribution of the debtor's assets among the creditors, and (3) it allows insolvent debtors to discharge all their obligations and thus be able to start new businesses unhampered by the burden of prior debt. However, formal liquidation is time consuming, it can be costly, and it results in the extinction of the business.

The distribution of assets in a liquidation under Chapter 7 of the Bankruptcy Act is governed by the following priority of claims:

1. **Secured creditors, who are entitled to the proceeds of the sale of specific property pledged for a lien or a mortgage.** If the proceeds from the sale of pledged property do not fully satisfy a secured creditor's claim, the remaining balance is treated as a general creditor claim (see Item 9 below).[11]

---

[11]When a firm or individual who goes bankrupt has a bank loan, the bank will attach any deposit balances. The loan agreement may stipulate that the bank has a first-priority claim on any deposits. If this is the case, the deposits are used to offset all or part of the bank loan; this is called, in legal terms, "the right of offset." In this case, the bank will not have to share the deposits with other creditors. Loan contracts often designate compensating balances as security against a loan. Even if the bank has no explicit claim against deposits, the bank will attach the deposits and hold them for the general body of creditors, including the bank itself. Without an explicit statement in the loan agreement, the bank does not receive preferential treatment with regard to attached deposits.

2. **Legal fees and other expenses to administer and operate the bankrupt firm.** These costs include legal fees incurred in trying to reorganize.

3. **Expenses incurred after an involuntary case has begun but before a trustee is appointed.**

4. **Wages due workers if earned within three months prior to the filing of the petition in bankruptcy.** The amount of wages is limited to $2,000 per employee.

5. **Claims for unpaid contributions to employee pension plans that should have been paid within six months prior to filing.** These claims, plus wages in Item 4, may not exceed the $2,000-per-wage-earner limit.

6. **Unsecured claims for customer deposits.** These claims are not to exceed a maximum of $900 per individual.

7. **Taxes due to federal, state, county, and other government agencies.**

8. **Unfunded pension plan liabilities.** These liabilities have a claim above that of the general creditors for an amount up to 30 percent of the common and preferred equity, and any remaining unfunded pension claims rank with the general creditors.[12]

9. **General, or unsecured, creditors.** Holders of trade credit, unsecured loans, the unsatisfied portion of secured loans, and debenture bonds are classified as *general creditors*. Holders of subordinated debt also fall into this category, but they must turn over required amounts to the senior debt.

10. **Preferred stockholders.** These stockholders can receive an amount up to the par value of their stock.

11. **Common stockholders.** These stockholders receive any remaining funds.[13]

To illustrate how this priority system works, consider the balance sheet of Whitman Inc., shown in Table 24-6 Assets have a book value of $90 million. The claims

---

[12]Pension plan liabilities have a significant bearing on bankruptcy settlements. As we discuss in Chapter 27, pension plans may be funded or unfunded. Under a funded plan, the firm makes cash payments to an insurance company or to a trustee (generally a bank), which then uses these funds (and interest earned on them) to pay retirees' pensions. Under an unfunded plan, the firm is obligated to make payments to retirees, but it does not provide cash in advance. Many plans are actually partially funded—some money has been paid in advance, but not enough to provide full pension benefits to all employees.

If a firm goes bankrupt, the funded part of the pension plan remains intact and is available for retirees. Prior to 1974, employees had no explicit claims for unfunded pension liabilities, but under the Employees' Retirement Income Security Act of 1974 (ERISA), an amount up to 30 percent of the equity (common and preferred) is earmarked for employees' pension plans and has a priority over the general creditors, with any remaining pension claims having status equal to that of the general creditors. This means, in effect, that the funded portion of a bankrupt firm's pension plan is completely secured, but that the unfunded portion ranks somewhat above the general creditors. Obviously, unfunded pension fund liabilities should be of great concern to a firm's unsecured creditors.

[13]Note that if different classes of common stock have been issued, differential priorities may exist in stockholder claims.

TABLE 24-6	WHITMAN INC.: BALANCE SHEET AT LIQUIDATION (MILLIONS OF DOLLARS)		
Current assets	$80.0	Accounts payable	$20.0
Net fixed assets	10.0	Notes payable (to banks)	10.0
		Accrued wages (1,400 @ $500)	0.7
		Federal taxes	1.0
		State and local taxes	0.3
		Current liabilities	$32.0
		First mortgage	$ 6.0
		Second mortgage	1.0
		Subordinated debentures[a]	8.0
		Total long-term debt	$15.0
		Preferred stock	$ 2.0
		Common stock	26.0
		Paid-in capital	4.0
		Retained earnings	11.0
		Total equity	$43.0
Total assets	$90.0	Total liabilities and equity	$90.0

[a]The debentures are subordinated to the notes payable.

are indicated on the right-hand side of the balance sheet. Note that the debentures are subordinated to the notes payable to banks. Whitman has filed for bankruptcy under Chapter 11, and since no fair and feasible reorganization could be arranged, the trustee is liquidating the firm under Chapter 7.

The assets as reported in the balance sheet are greatly overstated; they are, in fact, worth less than half the $90 million at which they are carried. The following amounts are realized on liquidation:

From sale of current assets	$28,000,000
From sale of fixed assets	5,000,000
Total receipts	$33,000,000

The distribution of proceeds from the liquidation is shown in Table 24-7. The first-mortgage holders receive the $5 million in net proceeds from the sale of fixed property, leaving $28 million available to the remaining creditors, including a $1 million unsatisfied claim of the first-mortgage holders. Next are the fees and expenses of administering the bankruptcy, which are typically about 20 percent of gross proceeds (including the bankrupt firm's own legal fees); in this example, they are assumed to be $6 million. Next in priority are wages due workers, which total $700,000, and taxes due, which amount to $1.3 million. Thus far, the total amount of claims paid from the $33 million received from the asset sale is $13 million, leav-

WHITMAN INC.: DISTRIBUTION OF LIQUIDATION PROCEEDS (MILLIONS OF DOLLARS)	TABLE 24-7

DISTRIBUTION TO PRIORITY CLAIMANTS

Proceeds from the sale of assets	$33.0
Less:	
1. First mortgage (paid from the sale of fixed assets)	5.0
2. Fees and expenses of bankruptcy	6.0
3. Wages due to workers within three months of bankruptcy	0.7
4. Taxes due to federal, state, and local governments	1.3
Funds available for distribution to general creditors	$20.0

DISTRIBUTION TO GENERAL CREDITORS

GENERAL CREDITORS' CLAIMS (1)	AMOUNT OF CLAIM[a] (2)	PRO RATA DISTRIBUTION[b] (3)	DISTRIBUTION AFTER SUBORDINATION ADJUSTMENT[c] (4)	PERCENTAGE OF ORIGINAL CLAIM RECEIVED[d] (5)
Unsatisfied portion of first mortgage	$ 1.0	$ 0.5	$ 0.5	92%
Second mortgage	1.0	0.5	0.5	50
Notes payable (to banks)	10.0	5.0	9.0	90
Accounts payable	20.0	10.0	10.0	50
Subordinated debentures	8.0	4.0	0.0	
Total	$40.0	$20.0	$20.0	

[a]Column 2 is the claim of each class of general creditor. Total claims equal $40.0 million.
[b]From the top section of the table, we see that $20 million is available for distribution to general creditors. Since there are $40 million of general creditor claims, the pro rata distribution will be $20/$40 = 0.50, or 50 cents on the dollar.
[c]The debentures are subordinate to the notes payable, so up to $5 million could be reallocated from debentures to notes payable. However, only $4 million is available to the debentures, so this entire amount is reallocated.
[d]Column 5 shows the results of dividing the Column 4 final allocation by the original claim shown in Column 2, except for the first mortgage, where the $5 million received from the sale of fixed assets is included in the calculation.

ing $20 million for the general creditors. In this example, we assume that there are no claims for unpaid benefit plans or unfunded pension liabilities.

The claims of the general creditors total $40 million. Since $20 million is available, claimants will initially be allocated 50 percent of their claims, as shown in Column 3, before the subordination adjustment. This adjustment requires that the subordinated debentures turn over to the notes payable all amounts received until the notes are satisfied. In this situation, the claim of the notes payable is $10 million, but only $5 million is available; the deficiency is therefore $5 million. After transfer of $4 million from the subordinated debentures, there remains a deficiency of $1 million on the notes; this amount will remain unsatisfied.

Note that 90 percent of the bank claim is satisfied, whereas a maximum of 50 percent of other unsecured claims will be satisfied. These figures illustrate the usefulness of the subordination provision to the security to which the subordination is made.

Since no other funds remain, the claims of the holders of preferred and common stocks are completely wiped out. Studies of the proceeds in bankruptcy liquidations reveal that unsecured creditors receive, on the average, about 15 cents on the dollar, while common stockholders generally receive nothing.

SELF-TEST QUESTIONS

Describe briefly the priority of claims in a formal liquidation.

What is the impact of subordination on the final allocation of proceeds from liquidation?

In general, how much do unsecured creditors receive from a liquidation? How much do stockholders receive?

RECENT BUSINESS FAILURES

This section sketches two of the more prominent recent business failures. They provide additional insights into the bankruptcy process.

EASTERN AIRLINES

During the 1980s, Eastern Airlines was plagued by seemingly unending woes, from incessant labor strife to occasionally poor service, which caused the airline to lose hundreds of millions of dollars.[14] Finally, under its chairman, Frank Lorenzo, the company filed for Chapter 11 bankruptcy in March 1989 after a showdown with its unions. Lorenzo, who was determined to break the unions' strike, insisted that he could restore Eastern to profitability if given enough time. Every few months, the company would submit projections to the bankruptcy court showing that the airline was about to turn the corner, while creditors complained that the forecasts were wildly optimistic.

The bankruptcy judge stated early on that keeping Eastern flying was in the "public interest" and that this goal outweighed the "parochial" concerns of the creditors. Thus, the court allowed Lorenzo to sell off assets and use the proceeds to cover operating losses. In early 1990, the unsecured creditors demanded that a trustee be appointed to run Eastern, and Martin Shugrue was appointed by the court in April. By then, however, $1.2 billion in assets that could have gone to creditors had been sold, and the funds had evaporated. Although analysts gave Eastern almost no chance of surviving, Shugrue launched an expensive program to restore the carrier to health. About $35 million was spent on national TV ads featuring the trustee as the leader of a new Eastern, and millions more were poured into new leather seats and increased flight attendants for first-class passengers to try to steal full-fare passengers from rival carriers which had better reputations for service, such as Delta.

When the Persian Gulf war slowed air travel and sent fuel prices upward, it became obvious to all, even the court, that Eastern would never make it, so the court

---

[14]For more information on the Eastern bankruptcy, see "Eastern: The Wings of Greed," which was published in the November 11, 1991, issue of *Business Week*.

finally agreed to shut it down for good on January 18, 1991. By that time, however, Eastern had wasted another $530 million in its attempt to stay afloat. In May 1996, as we write this, the process drones on. Martin Shugrue has moved on to greener pastures—he is trying to resurrect Pan American—and a new Eastern trustee is supervising the work of 40 people sifting through 7,000 boxes of documents. So far, about $95 million has been paid to lawyers and other bankruptcy officials, but the news is not all bad. About 70,000 unsecured creditors—each with claims under $100,000—were paid about $200 million, or 11 cents on the dollar. About 80 large unsecured creditors remain, and the hope is that they will get 13 cents on the dollar. Still, the unsecured creditors are getting only a small fraction of what they would have received if Eastern had been liquidated in a timely manner.

REVCO

On December 29, 1986, Revco Drug Stores went private in a leveraged buyout.[15] At the time, Revco was one of the nation's largest retail drug chains, operating over 2,000 stores in 30 states. The buyout increased management's ownership in the company from 3 percent to 31 percent, but it also raised the company's indebtedness from $309 million to $1.3 billion, including $700 million in subordinated notes (junk bonds). Immediately after the buyout, the company only had $35 million in common equity out of $1.7 billion in capital, for an equity ratio of only 2 percent. Given the heavy debt burden, several analysts stated that a hiccup would throw the company into bankruptcy.

Indeed, on April 15, 1988, Revco announced that it could not make a $46 million interest payment on its subordinated notes. In a press release issued that day, the company said: "Revco believes that its business is strong and its operations solid; however, our current capitalization is not the appropriate one for the company. After evaluation, Revco's board has determined that a financial restructuring is appropriate." The company and its creditors wanted to avoid the costs of a Chapter 11 bankruptcy, so they made several attempts at a workout. For example, in mid-May Revco's management proposed that bondholders exchange their subordinated notes for a new class of common stock that would leave then-current stockholders with only 5 percent ownership. Such a restructuring was consistent with the argument that the LBO team paid too much for the company and that any equity value remaining after the overpayment was destroyed by poor operating performance. However, this proposal failed because the company's stockholders would not agree to go along with it.

As Revco's fortunes fell, Magten Asset Management, a firm that specializes in investing in distressed companies, began buying Revco's senior subordinated notes at about 50 cents on the dollar. By late June, Magten had accumulated more than 25 percent of that particular security, which gave it veto power over any reorganization plan, whether private or under court supervision. Such power gave Magten the right to hold out for higher returns before consenting to any reorganization plan. On July 7, 1988, bondholders agreed to a one-month "standstill," whereby creditors

---

[15]For more detail on the Revco buyout and subsequent failure, see Karen H. Wruck, "What Really Went Wrong at Revco," *Journal of Applied Corporate Finance,* Summer 1991, 79–92.

agreed not to take action against Revco for missing its June interest payments. However, the company's cash flow was not improving, and on July 22 Magten demanded full and immediate payment of all principal and interest due. This action triggered cross-default provisions, which put Revco in default on all its borrowings. On July 28, 1988, Revco filed for protection under Chapter 11 of the Bankruptcy Act.

Following the formal bankruptcy filing, numerous reorganization plans were proposed, but most failed because of disagreements among the various claimants. In September 1991, creditors filed a plan in which they would get 100 percent ownership of the company in return for agreeing to lighten Revco's current debt load of $1.5 billion. In addition, the plan called for Salomon Brothers, an investment bank which had collected almost $40 million in fees on the original over-leveraged LBO deal, to pay $9.5 million to the creditors in return for an agreement to drop several proposed suits against Salomon. In the plan, banks that had lent Revco $306 million would receive $205 million of new 12 percent notes due December 31, 1998, a small amount of cash, and some new convertible preferred stock. The value of this package of securities was estimated at about 60 cents on the dollar. Holders of Revco's subordinated notes did not fare even that well. They would get common stock in the post-bankruptcy Revco, but no cash or notes. These notes had been trading at about 18 cents on the dollar, reflecting investors' beliefs that the final reorganization plan would leave little for bondholders. Revco's stockholders would receive nothing—stockholders are almost always wiped out when creditors are forced to accept less than their original claims.

Finally, in June 1992 the plan was accepted, and Revco emerged from bankruptcy. With several former creditors now on the board, the first order of business was to fire the chairman, Boake Sells. Then, the board created a committee of five executives to lead the company. In spite of its years of problems, many analysts predicted a bright future for Revco once it shed its onerous debt burden. In fact, the company did well, becoming an industry leader in the use of technology and in 1994 doubled in size by acquiring Hook-Super X. Then, in 1995, Revco was almost acquired by Rite Aid, but the acquisition was blocked on antitrust grounds.

SELF-TEST QUESTION

What are the most important points to be learned from the bankruptcy situations of Eastern Airlines and Revco Drug Stores?

OTHER MOTIVATIONS FOR BANKRUPTCY

Normally, bankruptcy proceedings do not commence until a company has become so financially weak that it cannot meet its current obligations. However, bankruptcy law also permits a company to file for bankruptcy if its financial *forecasts* indicate that a continuation of current conditions would lead to insolvency. This provision was used by Continental Airlines in 1983 to break its union contract and hence to lower labor costs. Continental demonstrated to a bankruptcy court that operations under the then-current union contract would lead to insolvency in a matter of months. The company then filed a reorganization plan that included major changes in all its contracts, including its union contract. The court sided with Continental and allowed the company to abrogate its contract. Continental then reorganized as a nonunion carrier, and that reorganization turned the company from a money loser into a money maker.[16] Congress changed the law after the Continental affair to make it more difficult for companies to use bankruptcy to break union contracts, but this case did set the precedent for using bankruptcy to help head off financial problems as well as to help solve existing ones.

Bankruptcy law has also been used to hasten settlements in major product liability suits. The Manville asbestos and A. H. Robins dalkon shield cases are examples. In both situations, the companies were being bombarded by thousands of lawsuits, and the very existence of such huge contingent liabilities made normal operations impossible. Further, in both cases it was relatively easy to prove (1) that if the plaintiffs won, the companies would be unable to pay the full amount of the claims, (2) that a larger amount of funds would be available to the claimants if the companies continued to operate rather than liquidate, (3) that continued operations were possible only if the suits were brought to a conclusion, and (4) that a timely resolution of all the suits was impossible because of their vast number and variety. The bankruptcy statutes were used to consolidate all the suits and to reach settlements under which the plaintiffs obtained more money than they otherwise would have received, and the companies were able to stay in business. The stockholders did poorly under these plans, because most of the companies' future cash flows were assigned to the plaintiffs, but, even so, the stockholders probably fared better than they would have if the suits had been concluded through the jury system.

What are some situations other than immediate financial distress that lead firms to file for bankruptcy?

SELF-TEST QUESTION

SOME CRITICISMS OF BANKRUPTCY LAWS

Although bankruptcy laws, for the most part, exist to protect creditors, many critics claim that current laws are not doing what they were intended to do. Before 1978, most bankruptcies ended quickly in liquidation. Then Congress rewrote the laws, giving companies more opportunity to stay alive, believing that this was best for managers, employees, creditors, and stockholders. Before the reform, 90 percent of Chapter 11 filers were liquidated, but now that percentage is less than 80 percent, and the average time between filing and liquidation has almost doubled. Indeed, large public corporations with the ability to hire high-priced legal help have a very good chance of avoiding, or at least delaying, liquidation, often at the expense of creditors and shareholders.

Critics believe that bankruptcy is great for business these days — great for consultants, lawyers, and investment bankers, who reap hefty fees during bankruptcy proceedings, and for managers, who continue to collect their salaries and bonuses as

---

[16]As we discussed in the opening section, Continental's fortunes declined again in 1990 when it was unable to successfully integrate several acquisitions, including Eastern, and the company filed for bankruptcy a second time.

long as the business is kept alive. The problem, according to critics, is that bankruptcy courts allow cases to drag on too long, depleting assets that could be sold to pay off creditors and shareholders. Too often, quick resolution is impossible because bankruptcy judges are required to deal with issues such as labor disputes, pension plan funding, and environmental liability — social questions that should be solved by legislative action rather than by bankruptcy courts.

For example, LTV Corporation was in bankruptcy from 1986 to 1993, mainly because of pension disputes between the company, its workers, retirees, and the federal government. During this time, the Dallas-based conglomerate spent $162 million in legal and consulting fees, but, under the final reorganization plan, creditors got only 4 to 53 cents on the dollar, and stockholders got nothing.

Critics contend that bankruptcy judges ought to realize that some sick companies should be allowed to die — and quickly. Maintaining companies on life support does not serve the interests of the parties the bankruptcy laws were meant to protect. One proposal for overhauling the system calls for limiting the time that companies have to file a reorganization plan. A debtor is supposed to have only 120 days, but the deadline is almost never enforced. It might make more sense to set a deadline of six months or a year and then stick to it. "Bankruptcy is like open-heart surgery — the longer you stay under the knife, the lower the chance of success," says James E. Spiotto, a creditor's lawyer with Chapman & Cutler in Chicago. "We should be seeking a quick, efficient way to give companies a fresh start."

Other critics think the entire bankruptcy system of judicial protection and supervision needs to be scrapped. Some even have proposed a kind of auction procedure, where shareholders and creditors would have the opportunity to gain control of a bankrupt company by raising the cash needed to pay the bills. The rationale here is that the market is a better judge than a bankruptcy court as to whether a company is worth more dead or alive.

Finally, note that companies operating under the protection of Chapter 11 can damage and perhaps even bankrupt their otherwise healthy competitors. To illustrate, Eastern Airlines' cash costs were low during its bankruptcy because it did not have to service its debt, and it was also generating cash by selling off assets. Eastern used its cash to advertise heavily and to cut fares, both of which siphoned off traffic from other airlines. Obviously, this hurt the other airlines and indeed led to other airline bankruptcies. Had Eastern been put down in a timely fashion, the airline industry would be a lot healthier today.

SELF-TEST QUESTION According to critics, what are some problems with the bankruptcy system?

USING MULTIPLE DISCRIMINANT ANALYSIS TO PREDICT BANKRUPTCY

As we have seen, bankruptcy, or even the possibility of bankruptcy, can cause significant trauma for a firm's managers, investors, suppliers, customers, and community. Thus, it would be beneficial to be able to predict the likelihood of bankruptcy so that steps could be taken to avoid it or at least to reduce its impact. One approach to bankruptcy prediction is *Multiple Discriminant Analysis (MDA)*, a statistical technique similar to regression analysis. In this section, we discuss MDA in detail, and we illustrate its application to bankruptcy prediction.[17]

THE BASICS OF MULTIPLE DISCRIMINANT ANALYSIS

Suppose a bank loan officer wants to segregate corporate loan applications into those likely to default and those not likely to default. Assume that data for some past period are available on a group of firms which includes both companies that went bankrupt and companies that did not. For simplicity, we assume that only the current ratio and the debt/assets ratio are analyzed. These ratios for our sample of firms are given in Columns 2 and 3 at the bottom of Figure 24-1. The Xs in the graph represent firms that went bankrupt, while the dots represent firms that remained solvent. For example, Point A in the upper left section is the point for Firm 2, which had a current ratio of 3.0 and a debt ratio of 20 percent, and a dot indicates that the firm did not go bankrupt. Point B, in the lower right section, represents Firm 19, which had a current ratio of 1.0 and a debt ratio of 60 percent, and the X indicates that it did go bankrupt.

The objective of discriminant analysis is to construct a boundary line through the graph such that if the firm is to the left of the line, it is not likely to become insolvent, whereas it is likely to go bankrupt if it falls to the right. This boundary line is called the *discriminant function,* and in our example it takes this form:

$$Z = a + b_1(\text{Current ratio}) + b_2(\text{Debt ratio}).$$

Here Z is called the *Z score,* a is a constant term, and b_1 and b_2 indicate the effects of the current ratio and the debt ratio on the probability of a firm going bankrupt.

Although a full discussion of discriminant analysis would go well beyond the scope of this book, some useful insights may be gained by observing these points:

1. The discriminant function is fitted (that is, the values of a, b_1, and b_2 are obtained) using historical data for a sample of firms that either went bankrupt or did not during some past period. When the data in the lower part of Figure 24-1 were fed into a "canned" discriminant analysis program (the computing centers of most universities and large corporations have such programs), the following discriminant function was obtained:

$$Z = -0.3877 - 1.0736(\text{Current ratio}) + 0.0579(\text{Debt ratio}).$$

---

[17]This section is based largely on the work of Edward I. Altman, especially these three papers: (1) "Financial Ratios, Discriminant Analysis, and the Prediction of Corporate Bankruptcy," *Journal of Finance,* September 1968, 589–609; (2) with Robert G. Haldeman and P. Narayanan, "Zeta Analysis: A New Model to Identify Bankruptcy Risk of Corporations," *Journal of Banking and Finance,* June 1977, 29–54; and (3) Salomon Brothers, with John Hartzell and Matthew Peck, "Emerging Market Corporate Bonds, A Scoring System," May 15, 1995. The last article reviews and updates Altman's earlier work and applies it internationally.

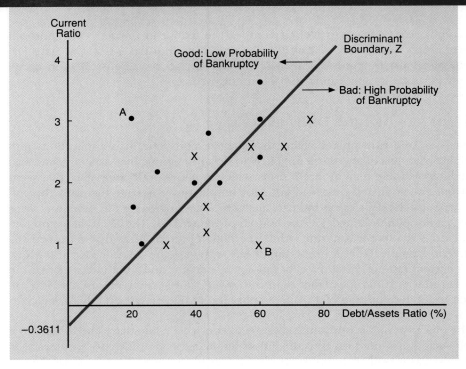

FIGURE 24-1 DISCRIMINANT BOUNDARY BETWEEN BANKRUPT AND SOLVENT FIRMS

FIRM NUMBER (1)	CURRENT RATIO (2)	DEBT/ASSETS RATIO (3)	DID FIRM GO BANKRUPT? (4)	Z SCORE (5)	PROBABILITY OF BANKRUPTCY (6)
1	3.6	60%	No	−0.780	17.2%
2(A)	3.0	20	No	−2.451	0.8
3	3.0	60	No	−0.135	42.0
4	3.0	76	Yes	0.791	81.2
5	2.8	44	No	−0.847	15.5
6	2.6	56	Yes	0.062	51.5
7	2.6	68	Yes	0.757	80.2
8	2.4	40	Yes[a]	−0.649	21.1
9	2.4	60	No[a]	0.509	71.5
10	2.2	28	No	−1.129	9.6
11	2.0	40	No	−0.220	38.1
12	2.0	48	No[a]	0.244	60.1
13	1.8	60	Yes	1.153	89.7
14	1.6	20	No	−0.948	13.1
15	1.6	44	Yes	0.441	68.8
16	1.2	44	Yes	0.871	83.5
17	1.0	24	No	−0.072	45.0
18	1.0	32	Yes	0.391	66.7
19(B)	1.0	60	Yes	2.012	97.9

2. This equation was plotted on Figure 24-1 as the locus of points for which Z = 0. All combinations of current ratios and debt ratios shown on the line result in Z = 0.[18] Companies that lie to the left of the line (and also have Z values less than zero) are not likely to go bankrupt, while those to the right (and have Z greater than zero) are likely to go bankrupt. It can be seen from the graph that one X, indicating a failing company, lies to the left of the line, while two dots, indicating nonbankrupt companies, lie to the right of the line. Thus, the discriminant analysis failed to properly classify three companies.

3. Once we have determined the parameters of the discriminant function, we can calculate the Z scores for other companies, say, loan applicants at a bank. The Z scores for our hypothetical companies, along with their probabilities for going bankrupt, are given in Columns 5 and 6 of Figure 24-1. The higher the Z score, the worse the company looks from the standpoint of bankruptcy. Here is an interpretation:

Z = 0: 50-50 probability of future bankruptcy (say, within two years). The company lies exactly on the boundary line.

Z < 0: If Z is negative, there is a less than 50 percent probability of bankruptcy. The smaller (more negative) the Z score, the lower the prob-

---

[18]To plot the boundary line, let D/A = 0% and 80%, and then find the current ratio that forces Z = 0 at those two values. For example, at D/A = 0,

$$Z = -0.3877 - 1.0736(\text{Current ratio}) + 0.0579(0) = 0$$

$$0.3877 = -1.0736(\text{Current ratio})$$

$$\text{Current ratio} = 0.3877/(-1.0736) = -0.3611.$$

Thus, −0.3611 is the vertical axis intercept. Similarly, the current ratio at D/A = 80% is found to be 3.9533. Plotting these two points on Figure 24-1, and then connecting them, provides the discriminant boundary line, which is the line that best partitions the companies into bankrupt and nonbankrupt. It should be noted that nonlinear discriminant functions may be used, and we could also use more dependent variables.

Figure 24-1 footnote

[a]If the "Z score" in Column 5 is negative, the firm should not go bankrupt, but a positive Z score predicts bankruptcy. There were three misclassifications. Firm 8 had Z = −0.649, so MDA predicted no bankruptcy, but it did go bankrupt. Similarly, MDA predicted bankruptcy for Firms 9 and 12, but they did not go bankrupt. The following tabulation shows bankruptcy and solvency predictions versus actual results:

	Z POSITIVE: MDA PREDICTS BANKRUPTCY	Z NEGATIVE: MDA PREDICTS SOLVENCY
Did subsequently go bankrupt	8	1
Remained solvent	2	8

The model did not perform perfectly, as two predicted bankruptcies remained solvent and one firm that was expected to remain solvent went bankrupt. Thus, the model misclassified 3 out of 19 firms, or 16 percent of the sample. Its success rate was 84 percent.

ability of bankruptcy. The computer output from MDA programs gives this probability, and it is shown in Column 6 of Figure 24-1.

Z > 0: If Z is positive, the probability of bankruptcy is greater than 50 percent, and the larger Z, the greater the probability of bankruptcy.

4. The mean Z score of the companies that did not go bankrupt is -0.583, while that for the bankrupt firms is +0.648. These means, along with approximations of the Z score probability distributions of the two groups, are shown in Figure 24-2. We may interpret this graph as indicating that if Z is less than about -0.3, there is a very small probability that the firm will go bankrupt, whereas if Z is greater than +0.3, there is only a small probability that it will remain solvent. If Z is in the range ±0.3, called the *zone of ignorance,* we are uncertain about how the firm should be classified.

5. The signs of the coefficients of the discriminant function are logical. A high current ratio is good, and since its coefficient is negative, the higher the current ratio, the lower the probability of failure. Similarly, high debt ratios produce high Z scores, and this is consistent with a higher probability of bankruptcy.

6. Our illustrative discriminant function has only two variables, but other characteristics could be introduced. For example, we could add such variables as the rate of return on assets, the times-interest-earned ratio, the days sales outstanding, the quick ratio, and so forth.[19] Had the rate of return on assets been introduced, it might have turned out that Firm 8 (which failed) had a low ROA, while Firm 9 (which did not fail) had a high ROA. A new discriminant function would be calculated:

$$Z = a + b_1(\text{Current ratio}) + b_2(\text{D/A}) + b_3(\text{ROA}).$$

Firm 8 might now have a positive Z, while Firm 9's Z might become negative. Thus, it is likely that by adding more characteristics we would improve the accuracy of our bankruptcy forecasts. In terms of Figure 24-2, this would cause each probability distribution to become tighter, narrow the zone of ignorance, and lead to fewer misclassifications.

ALTMAN'S MODEL

In a classic paper, Edward Altman applied MDA to a sample of corporations, and he developed a discriminant function that has seen wide use in actual practice. Altman's function was fitted as follows:

$$Z = 0.012X_1 + 0.014X_2 + 0.033X_3 + 0.006X_4 + 0.999X_5. \qquad \text{24-1}$$

Here

---

[19]With more than two variables, it is difficult to graph the function, but this presents no problem in actual usage because graphs are only used to explain MDA.

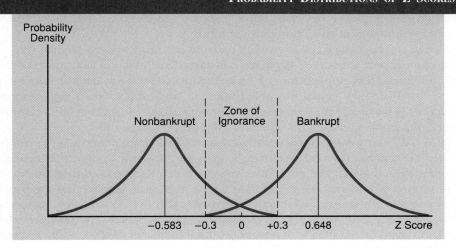

PROBABILITY DISTRIBUTIONS OF Z SCORES FIGURE 24-2

X_1 = net working capital/total assets.

X_2 = retained earnings/total assets.[20]

X_3 = EBIT/total assets.

X_4 = market value of common and preferred stock/book value of debt.[21]

X_5 = sales/total assets.

The first four variables in Equation 24-1 are expressed as percentages rather than as decimals. (For example, if X_3 = 13.3%, then 13.3, *not* 0.133, is used as its value.) Also, Altman's 50-50 point was 2.675, and not 0.0 as in our hypothetical example; his zone of ignorance was from Z = 1.81 to Z = 2.99; and in his model the *larger* the Z score, the less the probability of bankruptcy.[22]

Altman's function can be used to calculate a Z score for MicroDrive Corporation based on the data presented previously in Chapter 2, Tables 2-1 and 2-2. Here is the calculation, ignoring the small amount of preferred stock, for 1996:

X_1 = \$400/\$2,000 = 0.200 = 20.0%   20.0 × 0.012 = 0.240

X_2 = \$660/\$2,000 = 0.330 = 33.0%   33.0 × 0.014 = 0.462

X_3 = \$266/\$2,000 = 0.133 = 13.3%   13.3 × 0.033 = 0.439

X_4 = [50(\$28.50) + 1(\$102)]/(\$300 + \$800) = 1.388 = 138.8%   138.8 × 0.006 = 0.833

X_5 = \$3,000/\$2,000 = 1.5   1.5 × 0.999 = 1.499

Z = 3.473

[20]Retained earnings is the balance sheet figure, not the addition to retained earnings for the year.

[21][(Shares of common outstanding)(Price per share) + (Shares of preferred)(Price per share of preferred)]/Balance sheet value of total debt, including all short-term liabilities.

[22]These differences reflect the software package Altman used to generate the discriminant function. Altman's program did not specify a constant term, and his program simply reversed the sign of Z from ours.

Since MicroDrive's Z score of 3.473 is above the 2.99 upper limit of Altman's zone of ignorance, the data indicate that there is virtually no chance that MicroDrive will go bankrupt within the next two years. (Altman's model predicts bankruptcy reasonably well for about two years into the future.)

Altman and his colleagues' later work updated and improved his original study. In their more recent work, they explicitly considered such factors as capitalized lease obligations, and they applied smoothing techniques to level out random fluctuations in the data. The new model was able to predict bankruptcy with a high degree of accuracy for two years into the future, and with a slightly lower but still reasonable degree of accuracy (70 percent) for about five years.

MDA has been used with success by credit analysts to establish default probabilities for both consumer and corporate loan applicants, and by portfolio managers considering both stock and bond investments. It can also be used to evaluate a set of pro forma ratios as developed in Chapter 12, or to gain insights into the feasibility of a reorganization plan filed under the Bankruptcy Act. Altman's model has also been used by Salomon Brothers, Morgan Stanley, and other investment banking houses to appraise the quality of junk bonds used to finance takeovers and leveraged buyouts. The technique is described in detail in many statistics texts, while several articles cited at the end of this chapter discuss financial applications of MDA. The interested reader is urged to study this literature, for MDA has many potentially valuable applications in finance.

When using MDA in practice it is best to create your own discriminant data using a recent sample from the industry in question. It is not reasonable to assume that the financial ratios of a steel company facing imminent bankruptcy are the same as for a retail grocery chain in equally dire straits. If both firms were analyzed using Z scores calculated with the same equation, it might turn out that the grocery chain had a relatively high score, signifying (incorrectly) a low probability of bankruptcy, while the steel company had a relatively low score, indicating (correctly) a high probability of bankruptcy. The misclassification of the grocery company could result from the fact that it has very high sales for the amount of its book assets, hence its X_5, which has the largest coefficient, is much higher than for an average firm in an average industry facing potential bankruptcy. To remove any such industry bias, the MDA analysis should be based on a sample with characteristics similar to those of the firm being analyzed. Unfortunately, though, it is often not possible to find enough firms that have recently gone bankrupt to conduct an industry MDA.

SUMMARY

This chapter discussed the main issues involved in bankruptcy and financial distress in general. The key concepts are listed below:

■ There are several definitions of financial distress: (1) *economic failure,* (2) *business failure,* (3) *technical insolvency,* (4) *insolvency in bankruptcy,* and (5) *legal bankruptcy.*

■ The proportion of businesses that fail fluctuates with the economy, but the average liability per failure has tended to increase over time due to inflation and to an increase in the number of billion-dollar bankruptcies in recent years.

■ The fundamental issue that must be addressed when a company encounters financial distress is whether the company is "worth more dead than alive"; that is, would the business be more valuable if it continued in operation or if it were liquidated and sold off in pieces?

■ In the case of a fundamentally sound company whose financial difficulties appear to be temporary, creditors will frequently work directly with the company, helping it to recover and reestablish itself on a sound financial basis. Such voluntary reorganization plans are called *workouts.*

■ Reorganization plans usually require some type of *restructuring* of the firm's debts, involving either an *extension,* which postpones the date of required payment of past-due obligations, or a *composition,* by which the creditors voluntarily reduce their claims on the debtor or the interest rate on their claims.

■ When it is obvious that a firm is worth more dead than alive, informal procedures can sometimes be used to *liquidate* the firm. *Assignment* is an informal procedure for liquidating a firm, and it usually yields creditors a larger amount than they would receive in a formal bankruptcy liquidation. However, assignments are feasible only if the firm is small and its affairs are not too complex.

■ Current *bankruptcy law* consists of nine chapters, designated by Arabic numbers. For businesses, the most important chapters are *Chapter 7,* which details the procedures to be followed when liquidating a firm, and *Chapter 11,* which contains procedures for formal reorganizations.

■ Since the first bankruptcy laws, most formal reorganization plans have been guided by the *absolute priority doctrine.* This doctrine holds that creditors should be compensated for their claims in a rigid hierarchical order, and that senior claims must be paid in full before junior claims can receive even a dime.

■ Another position, the *relative priority doctrine,* holds that more flexibility should be allowed in a reorganization and that a balanced consideration should be given to all claimants. In recent years, there has been a shift away from absolute priority toward relative priority. The primary effect of this shift has been to delay liquidations so as to give managements more time to rehabilitate companies in an effort to provide value to junior claimants.

■ The primary role of the bankruptcy court in a reorganization is to determine the *fairness* and the *feasibility* of proposed plans of reorganization.

■ Even if some creditors or stockholders dissent and do not accept a reorganization plan, the plan may still be approved by the court if the plan is deemed to be "fair and equitable" to all parties. This procedure, in which the court mandates a reorganization plan in spite of dissent, is called a *cramdown.*

■ In the last few years, a new type of reorganization that combines the advantages of both the informal workout and formal Chapter 11 reorganization has become popular. This new hybrid is called a *prepackaged bankruptcy.*

■ The distribution of assets in a *liquidation* under Chapter 7 of the Bankruptcy Act is governed by a specific priority of claims.

■ *Multiple Discriminant Analysis (MDA)* is one technique for predicting business failure. MDA uses a set of economic variables, such as the current ratio and debt ratio, to establish the probability of failure.

QUESTIONS

24-1   Define each of the following terms:
a. Failure; insolvency; legal bankruptcy
b. Informal restructuring; reorganization in bankruptcy
c. Assignment; liquidation in bankruptcy
d. Fairness; feasibility
e. Absolute priority doctrine; relative priority doctrine
f. Bankruptcy Reform Act of 1978; Chapter 11; Chapter 7
g. Priority of claims in liquidation
h. Extension; composition
i. Workout; cramdown
j. Prepackaged bankruptcy
k. Holdout
l. Multiple discrimination analysis; Z score

24-2   "A certain number of business failures is a healthy sign. If there are no failures, this is an indication (a) that entrepreneurs are overly cautious, and hence not as inventive and as willing to take risks as a healthy, growing economy requires; (b) that competition is not functioning to weed out inefficient producers; or (c) that both situations exist." Discuss this statement.

24-3   How could financial analysis be used to forecast the probability of a given firm's failure? Assuming that such analysis is properly applied, could it always predict failure?

24-4   Why do creditors usually accept a plan for financial rehabilitation rather than demand liquidation of the business?

24-5   Would it be possible to form a profitable company by merging two companies, both of which are business failures? Explain.

24-6   Would it be a sound rule to liquidate whenever the liquidation value is above the value of the corporation as a going concern? Discuss.

24-7   Why do liquidations usually result in losses for the creditors or the owners, or both? Would partial liquidation or liquidation over a period limit their losses? Explain.

24-8   Are liquidations likely to be more common for public utility, railroad, or industrial corporations? Why?

REORGANIZATION The Verbrugge Publishing Company's 1996 balance sheet and income statement are as follows (in million of dollars). Verbrugge and its creditors have agreed upon a voluntary reorganization plan. In this plan, each share of the $6 preferred will be exchanged for one share of $2.40 preferred with a par value of $37.50 plus one 8 percent subordinated income debenture with a par value of $75. The $10.50 preferred issue will be retired with cash.

BALANCE SHEET

Current assets	$168	Current liabilities	$ 42
Net fixed assets	153	Advance payments	78
Goodwill	15	Reserves	6
		$6 preferred stock, $112.50 par value (1,200,000 shares)	135
		$10.50 preferred stock, no par, callable at $150 (60,000 shares)	9
		Common stock, $1.50 par value (6,000,000 shares)	9
		Retained earnings	57
Total assets	$336	Total claims	$336

INCOME STATEMENT

Net sales	$540.0
Operating expense	516.0
Net operating income	$ 24.0
Other income	3.0
EBT	$ 27.0
Taxes (50%)	13.5
Net income	$ 13.5
Dividends on $6 preferred	7.2
Dividends on $10.50 preferred	0.6
Income available to common stockholders	$ 5.7

a. Construct the pro forma balance sheet assuming that reorganization takes place. Show the new preferred at is par value.

b. Construct the pro forma income statement. How much does the proposed recapitalization increase income available to common shareholders?

c. *Required earnings* is defined as the amount that is just enough to meet fixed charges (debenture interest and/or preferred dividends). What are the required pre-tax earnings before and after the recapitalization?

d. How is the debt ratio affected by the reorganization? If you were a holder of Verbrugge's common stock, would you vote in favor of the reorganization?

LIQUIDATION At the time it defaulted on its interest payments and filed for bankruptcy, the McDaniel Mining Company had the following balance sheet (in thousands of dollars). The court, after trying unsuccessfully to reorganize the firm, decided that the only recourse was liquidation under Chapter 7. Sale of the fixed assets, which were pledged as collateral to the mortgage bondholders, brought in $400,000, while the current assets were sold for another $200,000. Thus, the total proceeds from the liquidation sale were $600,000. Trustee's costs amounted to $50,000; no single worker was due more than $2,000 in wages; and there were no unfunded pension plan liabilities.

Current assets	$ 400	Accounts payable	$ 50
Net fixed assets	600	Accrued taxes	40
		Accrued wages	30
		Notes payable	180
		Total current liabilities	$ 300
		First mortgage bonds[a]	300
		Second mortgage bonds[a]	200
		Debentures	200
		Subordinated debentures[b]	100
		Common stock	50
		Retained earnings	(150)
Total assets	$1,000	Total claims	$1,000

[a]All fixed assets are pledged as collateral to the mortgage bonds.
[b]Subordinated to notes payable only.

a. How much will McDaniel's shareholders receive from the liquidation?
b. How much will the mortgage bondholders receive?
c. Who are the other priority claimants in addition to the mortgage bondholders? How much will they receive from the liquidation?
d. Who are the remaining general creditors? How much will each receive from the distribution before subordination adjustment? What is the effect of adjusting for subordination?

24-3   **BANKRUPTCY PREDICTION** The balance sheet of the McDaniel Mining Company at the time it filed for bankruptcy is given in Problem 24-2. McDaniel's EBIT was $80,000 based on sales of $1,200,000, and its common stock market value was $200,000. Use the Altman multiple discriminant bankruptcy prediction model in answering the following questions.
a. What does the Altman model predict about the bankruptcy potential of McDaniel Mining?
b. Is the Altman model more sensitive to some variables than to others?

24-4   **LIQUIDATION** The following balance sheet represents Boles Electronics Corporation's position at the time it filed for bankruptcy (in thousands of dollars):

Cash	$ 10	Accounts payable	$ 1,600
Receivables	100	Notes payable	500
Inventories	890	Wages payable	150
		Taxes payable	50
Total current assets	$ 1,000	Total current liabilities	$ 2,300
Net plant	4,000	Mortgage bonds	2,000
Net equipment	5,000	Subordinated debentures	2,500
		Preferred stock	1,500
		Common stock	1,700
Total assets	$10,000	Total claims	$10,000

The mortgage bonds are secured by the plant, but not by the equipment. The subordinated debentures are subordinated to notes payable. The firm was unable to reorganize under Chapter 11; therefore, it was liquidated under Chapter 7. The trustee, whose legal and administrative fees amounted to $200,000, sold off the assets and received the following proceeds (in thousands of dollars):

ASSET	PROCEEDS
Plant	$1,600
Equipment	1,300
Receivables	50
Inventories	240
Total	$3,190

In addition, the firm had $10,000 in cash available for distribution. No single wage earner had over $2,000 in claims, and there were no unfunded pension plan liabilities.

a. What is the total amount available for distribution to all claimants? What is the total of creditor and trustee claims? Will the preferred and common stockholders receive any distributions?

b. Determine the dollar distribution to each creditor and to the trustee. What percentage of each claim is satisfied?

MINI CASE

Kimberly MacKenzie, president of Kim's Clothes Inc., a medium-sized manufacturer of women's casual clothing, is worried. Her firm has been selling clothes to Russ Brothers Department Store for more than ten years, and she has never experienced any problems in collecting payment for the merchandise sold. Currently, Russ Brothers owes Kim's clothes $65,000 for spring sportswear that was delivered to the store just two weeks ago. Kim's concern was brought about by an article that appeared in yesterday's *Wall Street Journal* that indicated that Russ Brothers was having serious financial problems. Further, the article stated that Russ Brothers' management was considering filing for reorganization, or even liquidation, with a federal bankruptcy court.

Kim's immediate concern was whether or not her firm would collect its receivables if Russ Brothers went bankrupt. In pondering the situation, Kim also realized that she knew nothing about the process that firms go through when they encounter severe financial distress. To learn more about bankruptcy, reorganization, and liquidation, Kim asked Ron Mitchell, the firm's chief financial officer, to prepare a briefing on the subject for the entire board of directors. In turn, Ron asked you, a newly hired financial analyst, to do the groundwork for the briefing by answering the following questions.

a. What are the various levels, or degrees, of financial distress?

b. (1) What are the major causes of business failure?
   (2) Do business failures occur evenly over time?
   (3) Which size of firm, large or small, is more prone to business failure? Why?

c. What key issues must managers face in the financial distress process?
d. What informal remedies are available to firms in financial distress? In answering this question, define the following terms:
   (1) Workout
   (2) Restructuring
   (3) Extension
   (4) Composition
   (5) Assignment
   (6) Assignee (trustee)
e. Briefly describe U.S. bankruptcy law, including the following terms:
   (1) Chapter 11
   (2) Chapter 7
   (3) Trustee
   (4) Voluntary bankruptcy
   (5) Involuntary bankruptcy
f. What are the major differences between an informal reorganization and reorganization in bankruptcy? In answering this question, be sure to discuss the following items:
   (1) Common pool problem
   (2) Holdout problem
   (3) Automatic stay
   (4) Cramdown
   (5) Fraudulent conveyance
g. What is a prepackaged bankruptcy? Why have prepackaged bankruptcies become more popular in recent years?
h. Briefly describe the priority of claims in a Chapter 7 liquidation.
i. Assume that Russ Brothers did indeed fail, and that it had the following balance sheet when it was liquidated (in millions of dollars):

Current assets	$40.0	Accounts payable	$10.0
Net fixed assets	5.0	Notes payable (to banks)	5.0
		Accrued wages	0.3
		Federal taxes	0.5
		State and local taxes	0.2
		Current liabilities	$16.0
		First mortgage	$ 3.0
		Second mortgage	0.5
		Subordinated debentures[a]	4.0
		Total long-term debt	$ 7.5
		Preferred stock	$ 1.0
		Common stock	13.0
		Paid-in capital	2.0
		Retained earnings	5.5
		Total equity	$21.5
Total assets	$45.0	Total claims	$45.0

[a]The debentures are subordinated to the notes payable.

The liquidation sale resulted in the following proceeds:

From sale of current assets	$14,000,000
From sale of fixed assets	2,500,000
Total receipts	$16,500,000

For simplicity, assume that there were no trustee's fees or any other claims against the liquidation proceeds. Also, assume that the mortgage bonds are secured by the entire amount of fixed assets. What would each claimant receive from the liquidation distribution?

SELECTED ADDITIONAL REFERENCES AND CASES

For a better understanding of multiple discriminant analysis and its use to predict corporate bankruptcy, see

Collins, Robert A., "An Empirical Comparison of Bankruptcy Prediction Models," *Financial Management,* Summer 1980, 52–57.

Eisenbeis, Robert A., "Pitfalls in the Application of Discriminant Analysis," *Journal of Finance,* June 1977, 875–900.

Joy, O. Maurice, and John O. Tollefson, "On the Financial Application of Discriminant Analysis," *Journal of Financial and Quantitative Analysis,* December 1975, 723–739.

For more information on bankruptcy costs, see

Altman, Edward I., "A Further Empirical Investigation of the Bankruptcy Cost Question," *Journal of Finance,* September 1984, 1067–1089.

Guffey, Daryl M., and William T. Moore, "Direct Bankruptcy Costs: Evidence from the Trucking Industry," *Financial Review,* May 1991, 223–235.

Warner, Jerold B., "Bankruptcy Costs: Some Evidence," *Journal of Finance,* May 1977, 337–347.

In addition to those articles cited in the chapter, the Summer 1991 issue of the Journal of Applied Corporate Finance *contains the following relevant works:*

Fitts, Peter, et al., "Bankruptcies, Workouts, and Turnarounds: A Roundtable Discussion," 34–61.

Gilson, Stuart C., "Managing Default: Some Evidence on How Firms Choose between Workouts and Chapter 11," 62–70.

Weiss, Lawrence A., "The Bankruptcy Code and Violations of Absolute Priority," 71–78.

The following articles and publications provide insights into various aspects of bankruptcy:

Brown, David T., "Claimholder Incentive Conflicts in Reorganization: The Role of Bankruptcy Law," *Review of Financial Studies,* 1989, 109–123.

Business Failure Record (New York: Dun & Bradstreet, Inc., updated annually).

Eberhart, Allan C., William T. Moore, and Rodney Roenfeldt, "Security Pricing and Deviations from the Absolute Priority Rule in Bankruptcy Proceedings," *Journal of Finance,* December 1990, 1457–1469.

Franks, Julian R., and Walter N. Torous, "An Empirical Investigation of U.S. Firms in Reorganization," *Journal of Finance*, July 1989, 747–769.

Harris, Richard, "The Consequences of Costly Default," *Economic Inquiry*, October 1978, 477–496.

McConnell, John J., Ronald C. Lease, and Elizabeth Tashjian, "Prepacks as a Mechanism for Resolving Financial Distress," *Journal of Applied Corporate Finance*, Winter 1996, 99–106.

The following bankruptcy case can be found in the Cases in Financial Management: Dryden Request *series:*

Case 39, "Mark X Company (B)," which examines both liquidation and restructuring alternatives for a firm in financial distress.

CHAPTER 25

MERGERS, LBOS, DIVESTITURES, AND HOLDING COMPANIES

On July 31, 1995, the mouse roared — Mickey Mouse that is — for that's when Disney's chairman, Michael Eisner, announced that Disney planned to acquire broadcast powerhouse Capital Cities/ABC for almost $19 billion in stock and cash. The acquisition, one of the largest ever, created an unrivaled global entertainment production and distribution giant, with revenues of about $20 billion.

The deal called for Disney to pay $65 plus one share of Disney stock for each share of Cap Cities/ABC, for a total price of about $124 per share. Thomas Murphy, chairman of Cap Cities/ABC, said that the two sides were able to come to an agreement only because Disney was willing to include Disney stock in the price, which gave Cap Cities/ABC shareholders a stake in the upside potential of the new company. When the deal took place, Cap Cities/ABC shareholders could ask for all stock or all cash rather than accept the primary cash-plus-stock offer. However, they were not guaranteed their choice, because Disney would only issue about 155 million new shares, the same number as Cap Cities/ABC had outstanding.

Disney, which had about $3 billion in debt, borrowed another $10 billion to help finance the cash portion of the deal. Although $13 billion is a great deal of debt, it still represents only about 20 percent of the market value of the new company, and the new company will generate an annual cash flow of $4.6 billion, far more than enough to service the debt. Interestingly, the deal was struck without the help (and cost) of investment bankers. Cap Cities/ABC was counseled by Warren Buffett, the firm's largest stockholder, while Disney sought the advice of a longtime Disney investor, Texas billionaire Sid Bass. Investment *bankers were only brought in at the end of the negotiations, mostly to provide fairness opinions.*

Mr. Eisner said that he believes huge synergies will result from the acquisition. Examples include getting more Disney-produced shows on the ABC television network, the use of Disney's syndication muscle to sell programs produced by ABC, and the joint packaging of the Disney Channel and Cap Cities' ESPN. According to Mr. Eisner, the new company will be a "fantastic combination" which has the capability of becoming the "strongest creative company in the world." Warren Buffett, no stranger to mergers and acquisitions, said, "This deal makes more sense than any deal I've ever seen with the possible exception of Cap Cities' acquisition of ABC a decade ago." He added, "It's a wonderful marriage of the number one content company [Disney] and the number one distribution company [Cap Cities/ABC]."

Only more time will tell whether the acquisition will fulfill the high expectations of the participants, but there is no doubt that mergers and acquisitions are an important part of the financial landscape. As you read this chapter, think about the motivations behind Disney's acquisition, and what specific actions had to be taken to establish a price for Cap Cities/ABC and to bring the deal to completion.

Most corporate growth occurs by *internal expansion,* which takes place when a firm's existing divisions grow through normal capital budgeting activities. However, the most dramatic examples of growth, and often the largest increases in firms' stock prices, result from *mergers,* the first topic covered in this chapter. *Leveraged buyouts,* or *LBOs,* occur when a firm's stock is acquired by a small group of investors rather than by another operating company. Since LBOs are similar to mergers in many respects, they are also covered in this chapter. Conditions change over time, and, as a result, firms often find it desirable to sell off, or *divest,* major divisions to other firms that can better utilize the divested assets. Divestitures are also discussed in the chapter. Finally, we discuss the *holding company* form of organization, wherein one corporation owns the stock of one or more other companies.

RATIONALE FOR MERGERS

Many reasons have been proposed by financial managers and theorists to account for the high level of merger activity in the United States. Some of the motives behind corporate mergers are presented in this section.[1]

SYNERGY

The primary motivation for most mergers is to increase the value of the combined enterprise. If Companies A and B merge to form Company C, and if C's value

---

[1]As we use the term, *merger* means any combination that forms one economic unit from two or more previous ones. For legal purposes, there are distinctions among the various ways these combinations can occur, but our focus is on the fundamental economic and financial aspects of mergers.

exceeds that of A and B taken separately, then *synergy* is said to exist. Such a merger should be beneficial to both A's and B's stockholders.[2] Synergistic effects can arise from four sources: (1) *operating economies,* which result from economies of scale in management, marketing, production, or distribution; (2) *financial economies,* including lower transactions costs and better coverage by security analysts; (3) *differential efficiency,* which implies that the management of one firm is more efficient and that the firm's assets will be more productive after the merger; and (4) *increased market power* due to reduced competition. Operating and financial economies are socially desirable, as are mergers that increase managerial efficiency, but mergers that reduce competition are both undesirable and illegal.[3]

In 1995, Lotus Development Corporation was acquired by IBM. Lotus had an outstanding group of software developers, and it owned the Notes system for communicating between PC users. However, its marketing was relatively weak, and it had a shortage of capital. IBM, on the other hand, had an outstanding marketing organization and a huge pool of capital, so it should be able to increase the market value of Lotus's assets. This merger clearly was based on potential synergies.

TAX CONSIDERATIONS

Tax considerations have stimulated a number of mergers. For example, a profitable firm in the highest tax bracket could acquire a firm with large accumulated tax losses. These losses could then be turned into immediate tax savings rather than carried forward and used in the future.[4] Also, mergers can serve as a way of minimizing taxes when disposing of excess cash. If a firm has a shortage of internal investment opportunities compared with its cash flow, it could (1) pay an extra dividend, (2) invest in marketable securities, (3) repurchase its own stock, or (4) purchase another firm. If the firm pays an extra dividend, its stockholders would have to pay immediate taxes on the distribution. Marketable securities often provide a good temporary parking place for money, but generally the rate of return on such securities is less than that required by stockholders. A stock repurchase would result in a capital gain for the remaining stockholders. Also, a repurchase might push up the firm's stock price to a level which is temporarily above the equilibrium price, so the company would have to pay too much for the repurchased shares, which would be disadvantageous to remaining stockholders. Finally, a repurchase designed solely to avoid dividend payments might be challenged by the IRS.

---

[2]If synergy exists, then the whole is greater than the sum of the parts. Synergy is also called the "2 plus 2 equals 5 effect." The distribution of the synergistic gain between A's and B's stockholders is determined by negotiation. This point is discussed later in the chapter.

[3]In the 1880s and 1890s, many mergers occurred in the United States, and some of them were obviously directed toward gaining market power rather than increasing efficiency. As a result, Congress passed a series of acts designed to ensure that mergers are not used as a method of reducing competition. The principal acts include the Sherman Act (1890), the Clayton Act (1914), and the Celler Act (1950). These acts make it illegal for firms to combine if the combination tends to lessen competition. The acts are enforced by the antitrust division of the Justice Department and by the Federal Trade Commission.

[4]Mergers undertaken only to use accumulated tax losses would probably be challenged by the IRS. However, because many factors are present in any given merger, it is hard to prove that a merger was motivated only, or even primarily, by tax considerations.

However, using surplus cash to acquire another firm has no immediate tax consequences to the acquiring firm or its stockholders, and this fact has motivated a number of mergers.

Purchase of Assets below Their Replacement Cost

Sometimes a firm will be touted as an acquisition candidate because the cost of replacing its assets is considerably higher than its market value. For example, in the early 1980s oil companies could acquire reserves cheaper by buying other oil companies than by doing exploratory drilling. Thus, Chevron Corporation acquired Gulf Oil to augment its reserves. Similarly, in the 1980s several steel company executives stated that it was cheaper to buy an existing steel company than to construct a new mill, and LTV (the fourth largest steel company) acquired Republic Steel (the sixth largest) for $700 million in a merger that created the second largest firm in the industry.

Of course, the true value of any firm is a function of its future earnings power, not the cost of replacing its assets. Thus, acquisitions should be based on the economic value of the acquired assets, not on their replacement cost.

Diversification

Managers often give diversification into other lines of business as a reason for mergers. They contend that diversification helps stabilize a firm's earnings stream and thus benefits its owners. Stabilization of earnings is certainly beneficial to employees, suppliers, and customers, but its value is less certain from the standpoint of stockholders. If a stockholder is worried about the variability of a firm's earnings, he or she could diversify more easily than could the firm. Why should Firm A acquire Firm B to stabilize earnings when a stockholder in Firm A could sell some of his or her stock in A and use the proceeds to purchase stock in Firm B? Stockholders can create diversification more easily than can the firm.

Of course, if you were the owner-manager of a closely held firm, it might be nearly impossible for you to sell part of your stock to diversify, because this would dilute your ownership and perhaps also generate a large capital gains tax liability. In this case, a diversification merger might well be the best way to achieve personal diversification.

Some academicians have used option pricing theory in an effort to gain some insights into the ways stockholders and debtholders are affected by mergers. If one views stock ownership as a call option, then the value of the stock is increased by an increase in earnings variability, but lowered by a decrease in variability. Assume that two firms have the same variability of earnings. If these two firms merge, and their earnings are not perfectly positively correlated, then the earnings of the combined firm will have less variability than the premerger earnings of the separate firms. This decrease in earnings variability would, according to option theory, lower the value of the combined firm's equity. Conversely, the value of the debt would increase, because the probability of default would lessen. Therefore, according to this view of option theory, using mergers for diversification results in a transfer of wealth from stockholders to debtholders, leaving the total value of the combined firm equal to the sum of the premerger values, assuming no synergistic effects.

However, it is possible for the stockholders to avoid these theoretical losses by financing the merger with debt, or to recoup them by issuing additional debt based on the increased debt capacity of the combined firm, and then using the proceeds to repurchase equity. Also, note that the option theory results assume that no synergies exist and that operating income stability has no beneficial effects for shareholders. These assumptions are correct for individual stocks, upon which option theory is based, but they are questionable for whole firms. And, of course, if the assumptions are not correct, then corporate diversification could benefit stockholders.

MANAGERS' PERSONAL INCENTIVES

Financial economists like to think that business decisions are based only on economic considerations, especially maximization of firms' values. However, some business decisions are based more on managers' personal motivations than on economic analyses. Many people, business leaders included, like power, and more power is attached to running a larger corporation than a smaller one. Obviously, no executive would admit that his or her ego was the primary reason behind a merger, but egos do seem to play a prominent role in many mergers.

It has also been observed that executive salaries are highly correlated with company size — the bigger the company, the higher the salaries of its top officers. This too could play a role in corporate acquisition programs.

After many hostile takeovers, the managers of the target companies lose their jobs, or at least their autonomy. Therefore, managers who own less than 51 percent of their firms' stock look to devices that will lessen the chances of their firms' being taken over. Mergers can serve as such a device. For example, when Enron was under attack, it arranged to buy Houston Natural Gas, paying for Houston primarily with debt. That merger made Enron much larger, hence harder for any potential acquirer to "digest," and the much higher debt level resulting from the merger made it harder for any acquiring company to use debt to buy Enron. Such *defensive mergers* are hard to defend on economic grounds. The managers involved invariably argue that synergy, not a desire to protect their own jobs, motivated the acquisition, but observers suspect that many mergers today are designed more to benefit managers than stockholders.

Managers' personal incentives as a basis for mergers represent another example of the agency problem. Of course, there is nothing wrong with executives feeling good about increasing the size of their firms, or getting paid a higher salary as a result of growth through mergers — provided the mergers make economic sense from the stockholders' viewpoint. There have been quite a few stockholder suits against managers who resisted hostile takeovers where the acquiring company offered a high premium. Perhaps there should also be some suits against managers who paid too high a price for target companies, hence diluted the wealth of their own shareholders.

BREAKUP VALUE

Firms can be valued by book value, economic value, or replacement value. Recently, analysts and takeover specialists have begun to recognize *breakup value* as another basis for valuation. Analysts estimate a company's breakup value, and if this value is higher than the firm's current market value, then a takeover specialist could acquire the firm at or even above its current market value, sell it off in pieces, and earn a substantial profit.

SELF-TEST
QUESTIONS
Define synergy. Is synergy a valid rationale for mergers? Describe several situations that might produce synergistic gains.

Give two examples of how tax considerations can motivate mergers.

Suppose your firm could purchase another firm for only half of its replacement value. Would this be sufficient justification for the acquisition?

Discuss the merits of diversification as a rationale for mergers.

Can managers' personal incentives motivate mergers? Explain.

What is breakup value?

TYPES OF MERGERS

Economists classify mergers into four groups: (1) horizontal, (2) vertical, (3) congeneric, and (4) conglomerate. A *horizontal merger* occurs when one firm combines with another in its same line of business — for example, when one computer manufacturer acquires another, or when two retail food chains merge. The merger of Burroughs and Sperry to form Unisys was a horizontal merger, because both firms manufactured computers and electronics products. An example of a *vertical merger* would be a steel producer's acquisition of one of its own suppliers, such as an iron or coal mining firm, or an oil producer's acquisition of a petrochemical firm which uses oil as a raw material. *Congeneric* means "allied in nature or action," hence a *congeneric merger* involves related enterprises but not producers of the same product (horizontal) or firms in a producer-supplier relationship (vertical). IBM's acquisition of Lotus is an example of a congeneric merger. A *conglomerate merger* occurs when unrelated enterprises combine, as illustrated by Mobil Oil's acquisition of Montgomery Ward.

Operating economies (and also anticompetitive effects) are at least partially dependent on the type of merger involved. Vertical and horizontal mergers generally provide the greatest synergistic operating benefits, but they are also the ones most likely to be attacked by the U.S. Department of Justice as anticompetitive. In any event, it is useful to think of these economic classifications when analyzing prospective mergers.

SELF-TEST
QUESTION
What are the four economic types of mergers?

LEVEL OF MERGER ACTIVITY

Four major "merger waves" have occurred in the United States. The first was in the late 1800s, when consolidations occurred in the oil, steel, tobacco, and other basic industries. The second was in the 1920s, when the stock market boom helped financial promoters consolidate firms in a number of industries, including utilities, communications, and autos. The third was in the 1960s, when conglomerate mergers were the rage. The fourth began in the 1980s and is still in progress.

The "merger mania" that began in the 1980s was motivated by a number of factors: (1) the relatively depressed condition of the stock market at the beginning of the decade (for example, the Dow Jones Industrial Index in early 1982 was below its 1968 level); (2) the unprecedented amount of inflation that occurred during the 1970s and early 1980s, which increased the replacement value of firms' assets even while a weak stock market reduced their market values; (3) the Reagan administration's stated view that "bigness is not necessarily badness," which reflected a more tolerant attitude toward large mergers; (4) the general belief among the major natural resource companies that it was cheaper to "buy reserves on Wall Street" through mergers than to explore and find them in the field; (5) the development of an active junk bond market, which helped raiders obtain the capital needed to make tender offers for target firms; (6) attempts to ward off raiders by use of defensive mergers; (7) the decline of the dollar, which made U.S. firms relatively cheap for foreign firms to acquire, combined with huge U.S. trade deficits, which gave foreign firms large pools of funds to invest in the United States; and (8) technological developments which led to "strategic mergers" such as the AT&T-McCaw and IBM-Lotus combinations.

As can be seen from Table 25-1, some huge mergers have occurred in recent years.[5] However, mergers in the 1990s have been significantly different from those of the 1980s. Most 1980s mergers were financial transactions in which buyers sought to buy companies that were selling at less than their true values as a result of incompetent or sluggish management. If a target company could be managed better, if redundant assets could be sold, and if operating and administrative costs could be cut, profits would rise, and the result would be a rapid increase in market value. In the 1990s, on the other hand, most of the mergers have been strategic in nature — companies are merging with other companies to enable the consolidated company to better position itself to compete in the world economy. Indeed, many recent mergers have involved companies in the defense, media, computer, and health care industries, all of which are experiencing rapid structural changes and intense competition.

Other differences between the 1980s and the 1990s are the way the mergers were financed and how the target firms' stockholders were compensated. In the 1980s, cash was the preferred method of payment, because large cash payments could convince even the most reluctant shareholder to approve the deal. Moreover, the cash was generally obtained by borrowing, which left the consolidated company with a heavy debt burden, which in many cases led to difficulties. In the 1990s, stock has replaced borrowed cash as the merger currency of choice for two reasons: (1) Many of the 1980s mergers were financed with junk bonds which later went into default. These defaults, along with the demise of Drexel Burnham, the leading junk bond dealer, made it difficult to arrange debt-financed mergers. Without the availability of debt financing, companies that might have used borrowed

---

[5]For detailed reviews of the 1980s merger wave, see Andrei Shleifer and Robert W. Vishny, "The Takeover Wave of the 1980s," *Journal of Applied Corporate Finance,* Fall 1991, 49–56; Edmund Faltermayer, "The Deal Decade: Verdict on the '80s," *Fortune,* August 26, 1991, 58–70; and "The Best and Worst Deals of the '80s: What We Learned from All Those Mergers, Acquisitions, and Takeovers," *Business Week,* January 15, 1990, 52–57.

TABLE 25-1	THE FIVE BIGGEST MERGERS (BILLIONS OF DOLLARS)			
COMPANY		YEAR	VALUE	TYPE OF TRANSACTION
AT&T-McCaw Cellular		1994	$18.9	Acquisition for common stock
Disney-Capital Cities/ABC		1996	18.8	Acquisition for cash and common stock
Time-Warner Communications		1990	14.1	Acquisition for cash
Chevron-Gulf		1984	13.3	Acquisition for cash
Philip Morris-Kraft		1988	12.9	Acquisition for cash

cash have been forced to offer stock. (2) During the 1990s, most mergers have been strategic — as between AT&T and McCaw, IBM and Lotus, and Disney and Cap Cities/ABC—where both companies' managers realized that they needed one another. Most of these mergers have been friendly, and stock swaps are easier to arrange in friendly mergers than in hostile ones. Also, both sets of managers have been concerned about the postmerger financial strength of the consolidated company, and the surviving company will obviously be stronger if the deal is financed with stock rather than debt.

Although the larger 1990s mergers have generally been stock-for-stock, many of the smaller mergers have been for cash. Even here, though, things have been different. In the 1980s, companies typically borrowed to get the money to finance cash acquisitions. In the 1990s, corporate cash flows have been very high, so companies have been able to pay for their smaller acquisitions out of cash flow.

Yet another factor in the 1990s has been an increase in the acquisition of U.S. companies by foreign buyers. The dollar has been weak, especially relative to the mark and the yen, and the falling dollar has lowered the cost of U.S. companies to German and Japanese acquirers.

SELF-TEST
QUESTIONS

What are the four major "merger waves" that have occurred in the United States? What are some reasons for the current wave?

HOSTILE VERSUS FRIENDLY TAKEOVERS

In the vast majority of merger situations, one firm (generally the larger of the two) simply decides to buy another company, negotiates a price with the management of the target firm, and then acquires the target company. Occasionally, the acquired firm will initiate the action, but it is much more common for a firm to seek acquisitions than to seek to be acquired.[6] Following convention, we call a company that

---

[6]However, if a firm is in financial difficulty, if its managers are elderly and do not think that suitable replacements are on hand, or if it needs the support (often the capital) of a larger company, then it may seek to be acquired. Thus, when a number of Texas, Ohio, and Maryland financial institutions were in trouble in the 1980s, they lobbied to get their state legislatures to pass laws that would make it easier for them to be acquired. Out-of-state banks then moved in to help salvage the situation and minimize depositor losses.

seeks to acquire another the *acquiring company* and the one which it seeks to acquire the *target company.*

Once an acquiring company has identified a possible target, it must (1) establish a suitable price, or range of prices, and (2) tentatively set the terms of payment—will it offer cash, its own common stock, bonds, or some mix of these items? Next, the acquiring firm's managers must decide how to approach the target company's managers. If the acquiring firm has reason to believe that the target's management will approve the merger, then it will simply propose a merger and try to work out some suitable terms. If an agreement is reached, then the two management groups will issue statements to their stockholders indicating that they approve the merger, and the target firm's management will recommend to its stockholders that they agree to the merger. Generally, the stockholders are asked to *tender* (or send in) their shares to a designated financial institution, along with a signed power of attorney which transfers ownership of the shares to the acquiring firm. The target firm's stockholders then receive the specified payment, either common stock of the acquiring company (in which case the target company's stockholders become stockholders of the acquiring company), cash, bonds, or some mix of cash and securities. This is a *friendly merger,* or a *friendly tender offer.*

The 1995 acquisition of Scott Paper by Kimberly-Clark typifies a friendly merger. After negotiations between the two boards, Kimberly-Clark announced that the managements of the two firms had agreed to the deal. Each Scott shareholder would receive 0.78 share of Kimberly-Clark for each share owned, a deal worth about $6.8 million. The acquisition combined the Kleenex brand name of Kimberly-Clark with Scott's brands, giving Kimberly-Clark coverage of both the high-end and low-end markets for tissues and other paper products. Furthermore, Scott Paper's strong presence in Europe gave Kimberly-Clark a much better position from which to expand its overseas sales. The merger was approved by the shareholders of both firms, and no antitrust issues were raised. Therefore, the merger was completed just a few months after the announcement.

Often, however, the target company's management resists the merger. Perhaps the managers feel that the price offered is too low, or perhaps they simply want to keep their jobs. In either case, the acquiring firm's offer is said to be *hostile* rather than friendly, and the acquiring firm must make a direct appeal to the target firm's stockholders. In a hostile merger, the acquiring company will again make a tender offer, and again it will ask the stockholders of the target firm to tender their shares in exchange for the offered price. This time, though, the target firm's managers will urge stockholders not to tender their shares, generally stating that the price offered (cash, bonds, or stocks in the acquiring firm) is too low.

The battle between Shamrock Holdings and Polaroid illustrates a failed hostile merger attempt. It began in the summer of 1988, when Polaroid's stock was trading in the low $30s. At the time, many analysts had declared that Polaroid was a likely takeover candidate because of its sluggish performance but strong brand name. Also, Polaroid was expected to receive a substantial settlement from its successful suit against Eastman Kodak, which had been found guilty of violating Polaroid's instant camera patents.

Then, Shamrock Holdings, the investment vehicle of the Roy E. Disney family, proposed a friendly takeover, was rebuffed, and made a $45-per-share hostile tender offer. Polaroid responded to the unwanted offer (1) by selling a block of its stock to a newly established employee stock ownership plan (ESOP), (2) by selling another block to a friendly investor (a *white squire*), and (3) by buying back 22 percent of its outstanding shares at $50 a share. To finance all of this, Polaroid added $536 million in bank debt. Additionally, Polaroid restructured its operations by cutting its work force by 15 percent through a voluntary early retirement program. Shamrock responded to these actions (1) by initiating a proxy fight to elect a new slate of officers at Polaroid, and (2) by filing a court suit challenging the legitimacy of Polaroid's defensive maneuvers.

After nine months of heated exchanges between the companies, an accord was reached in March 1989. Polaroid agreed to pay Shamrock $20 million in compensation for expenses incurred in the battle, and Shamrock signed an agreement promising not to seek control of Polaroid for 10 years. Also, Polaroid agreed to spend $5 million in advertising on Shamrock's radio and television stations, and to distribute to shareholders much of its pending award from Kodak. In addition, Shamrock agreed to drop all litigation, as well as its proxy fight. Although defeated, Shamrock ended up making about $35 million before taxes, considering both the cash settlement and the price increase on the Polaroid shares it owned. Stanley P. Gold, Shamrock's president, said that the decision to settle was sealed by Delaware court decisions upholding Polaroid's defenses. "It isn't that I went away quietly; I tried as hard as I could," he said. Polaroid ended up with more debt, although it still had a strong balance sheet, and a $36-per-share stock price. Polaroid's president and CEO said, "The fundamental changes and initiatives put in place during this period made us stronger, despite the pressure." (Note: In May 1996, Polaroid's stock was selling for $43, $2 below the $45 offered in 1988. Meanwhile, the market as measured by the Dow Jones industrials had risen more than 70 percent. Were Polaroid's shareholders well served by its managers' resistance to the Shamrock takeover?)

The 1995 battle of Ingersoll-Rand and Clark Equipment illustrates a hostile takeover that succeeded. The battle began in March, when Ingersoll-Rand, an industrial machinery maker, approached Clark, a construction equipment manufacturer, with a proposal to negotiate a friendly acquisition. After Clark's management rebuffed the proposal, Ingersoll-Rand announced a hostile, all-cash tender offer of $77 per share for Clark's stock. The shares, which were selling for just over $50 prior to the offer, immediately jumped to $83 in anticipation of a competing bidder or the prospect of a higher price. Clark's board rejected the offer, but in view of the high price set on the bid, the board came under intense pressure to negotiate a deal. Adding to the pressure was the fact that Clark, unlike most companies, elected all of its directors each year, so the entire seven-member board ran the risk of being ousted at the next shareholder meeting — only a month away. With the pressure mounting, Clark's board agreed to a sweetened $86-per-share deal only one week after the hostile tender offer was launched.

The Clark acquisition illustrates three points. First, an all-cash offer that is high enough will generally overcome any resistance by the target firm's management. Second, and this appears to be a trend in the 1990s wave, strategic buyers often begin the hostile bidding process with a "preemptive" or "blowout" bid. The idea here is to offer such a high premium over the preannouncement price that (1) no other bidders will be willing to jump into the fray, and (2) it will be impossible for the target company's board to turn down the bid. Third, if a hostile bid is eventually accepted by the target's board, the deal ends up as "friendly," regardless of the length or acrimony during the hostile phase.

In another takeover, IBM is reported to have negotiated with Lotus for almost two years before launching its hostile tender offer on June 5, 1995. The week before the offer was announced, Lotus's stock sold for $30 per share. IBM offered $60 per share, a 100 percent premium. IBM is reported to have decided to make a preemptive bid, one that would make Lotus's stockholders likely to tender their stock and one that was too high for some "white knight" to match or exceed. IBM had a cash hoard in excess of $10 billion, so it was unlikely that its bid could be stopped. Indeed, on June 11, Lotus's board agreed to the takeover at a price of $64 per share, so again, a hostile offer ended up as a friendly merger.

What is the difference between a hostile and a friendly merger?   **SELF-TEST**
Describe the mechanics of a typical friendly takeover and of a typical hostile takeover.   **QUESTIONS**

MERGER REGULATION

Prior to the mid-1960s, friendly acquisitions generally took place as simple exchange-of-stock mergers, and a proxy fight was the primary weapon used in a hostile control battle. However, in the mid-1960s corporate raiders began to operate differently. First, they noted that it took a long time to mount a proxy fight — they had to first request a list of the target company's stockholders, be refused, and then get a court order forcing management to turn over the list. During that time, the target's management could think through and then implement a strategy to fend off the raider. As a result, management won most proxy fights.

Then raiders began saying to themselves, "If we could take an action that would bring the decision to a head quickly, before management can take countermeasures, that would greatly increase the probability of a successful takeover." That led the raiders to turn from proxy fights to tender offers, which had a much shorter response time. For example, the stockholders of a company whose stock was selling for $20 might be offered $27 per share and be given two weeks to accept. The raider, meanwhile, would have accumulated a substantial block of the shares in open market purchases, and additional shares might have been purchased by institutional friends of the raider, who promised to tender their shares in exchange for the tip that a raid was to occur.

Faced with a well-planned raid, managements were generally overwhelmed. The stock might actually still be worth more than the offered price to other potential bidders, but management simply did not have time to get this message across to stockholders, or to find a friendly competing bidder (white knight), or anything else. This situation was thought to be unfair, and as a result, Congress passed the Williams Act in 1968. This law had two main objectives: (1) to regulate the way acquiring firms can structure takeover offers and (2) to force acquiring firms to disclose more information about their offers. Basically, Congress wanted to put target managements in a better position to defend against hostile offers. Additionally, Congress believed that shareholders needed easier access to information about tender offers — including information on any securities that might be offered in lieu of cash — in order to make rational tender-versus-don't-tender decisions.

The Williams Act placed the following three major restrictions on acquiring firms: (1) Acquirers must disclose their current holdings and future intentions within 10 days of amassing at least 5 percent of a company's stock, and they must disclose the source of the funds to be used in the acquisition. (2) The target firm's shareholders must be allowed at least 20 days to tender their shares; that is, the offer must be "open" for at least 20 days. (3) If the acquiring firm increases the offer price during the 20-day open period, all shareholders who tendered prior to the new offer must receive the higher price. In total, these restrictions were intended to reduce the ability of the acquiring firm to surprise management and to stampede target shareholders into accepting an inadequate offer. Prior to the Williams Act, offers were generally made on a first-come, first-served basis, and they were often accompanied by an implicit threat to lower the bid price after 50 percent of the shares were in hand. The legislation also gave target managements more time to mount a defense, and it gave rival bidders and white knights a chance to enter the fray and thus help a target's stockholders obtain a better price.

Many states have also passed laws designed to protect firms in their states from hostile takeovers. At first, these laws focused on disclosure requirements, but by the late 1970s several states had enacted takeover statutes so restrictive that they virtually precluded hostile takeovers. In 1979, when MITE Corporation, a Delaware firm, made a hostile tender offer for Chicago Rivet and Machine Co., a publicly held Illinois corporation, Chicago Rivet sought protection under the Illinois Business Takeover Act. The constitutionality of the Illinois act was contested, and the U.S. Supreme Court found the law unconstitutional. The court ruled that the Illinois law put undue burdens on interstate commerce. The opinion also stated that the market for securities is a national market, and even though the issuing firm was incorporated in Illinois, the state of Illinois could not regulate interstate securities transactions.

The Illinois decision effectively eliminated the first generation of state merger regulations. However, the states kept trying to protect their state-headquartered companies, and in 1987 the U.S. Supreme Court upheld an Indiana law which radically changed the rules of the takeover game. Specifically, the Indiana law first defined "control shares" as enough shares to give an investor 20 percent of the vote, and it went on to state that when an investor buys control shares, those shares can be voted only after approval by a majority of "disinterested shareholders," defined as those who are neither officers nor inside directors of the company, nor associates of the raider. The law also gives the buyer of control shares the right to insist that a shareholders' meeting be called within 50 days to decide whether the shares may be voted. The Indiana law dealt a major blow to raiders, mainly because it slows down the action. Delaware (the state in which most large companies are incorporated) later passed a similar bill, and so did New York and a number of other important states.

The new state laws also have some features which protect target stockholders from their own managers. Included are limits on the use of golden parachutes, onerous debt-financing plans, and some types of poison pills. Since these laws do not regulate tender offers per se, but rather govern the practices of firms in the state, they have, at least up to this point, withstood all legal challenges. But when companies such as IBM offer 100 percent premiums for companies such as Lotus, it is hard for any defense to hold them off.

Is there a need to regulate mergers? Explain.

Do the states play a role in merger regulation, or is it all done at the national level?

ANALYSIS OF A POTENTIAL MERGER

In theory, merger analysis is quite simple. The acquiring firm simply performs an analysis to value the target company and then determines whether the target can be bought at that value or, preferably, for less than the assessed value. The target company, on the other hand, should accept the offer if the price exceeds the value of the target firm, assuming it continued to operate independently. Theory aside, however, some difficult issues are involved. In this section, we first discuss valuing the target firm, the initial step in a merger analysis. Then, we discuss two other important considerations: setting the bid price and postmerger control. In the next section, we will discuss structuring the takeover bid.

Several methodologies are used to value target firms, but we will confine our discussion to the two most commonly used methods: discounted cash flow analysis and market multiple analysis. However, regardless of the valuation methodology, it is crucial to recognize two facts. First, the business being valued typically will not continue to operate as a separate entity, but rather will become part of the acquiring firm's portfolio of assets. Thus, any changes in operations occurring as a result of the proposed merger that will affect the value of the business must be considered in the analysis. Second, the goal of merger valuation is to value the target business's equity, or ownership position, because a business is acquired from its owners, not from its creditors. Thus, although we use the phrase "valuing the firm," we are focusing on the value of the firm's equity stake rather than on its total value.

DISCOUNTED CASH FLOW ANALYSIS

The *discounted cash flow (DCF)* approach to valuing a business involves the application of capital budgeting procedures to an entire firm rather than to a single project. To apply this method, two key items are needed: (1) a set of pro forma statements that develop the incremental cash flows expected to result from the merger and (2) a discount rate, or cost of capital, to apply to these projected cash flows.

PRO FORMA CASH FLOW STATEMENTS Obtaining accurate postmerger cash flow forecasts is by far the most important step in a merger analysis. In a pure *financial merger,* in which no synergies are expected, the incremental postmerger cash flows are simply the expected cash flows of the target firm if it continued to operate independently. In an *operating merger,* where the two firms' operations are to be integrated and the acquiring firm plans to change the target firm's operations to get better results, forecasting future cash flows is more difficult.

Table 25-2 shows the projected cash flow statements for Apex Corporation, which is being considered as a target by Hightech, a large conglomerate. The projected data are for the postmerger period, and all synergistic effects have been included. Apex currently uses 30 percent debt, but if it were acquired, Hightech would increase Apex's debt ratio to 50 percent. Both Hightech and Apex have a 40 percent marginal federal-plus-state tax rate.

TABLE 25-2	HIGHTECH CORPORATION: PROJECTED POSTMERGER CASH FLOW STATEMENTS FOR THE APEX SUBSIDIARY AS OF DECEMBER 31 (MILLIONS OF DOLLARS)				
	1997	1998	1999	2000	2001
1. Net sales	$105.0	$126.0	$151.0	$174.0	$191.0
2. Cost of goods sold	80.0	94.0	111.0	127.0	137.0
3. Selling and administrative expenses	10.0	12.0	13.0	15.0	16.0
4. Depreciation	8.0	8.0	9.0	9.0	10.0
5. EBIT	$ 7.0	$ 12.0	$ 18.0	$ 23.0	$ 28.0
6. Interest[a]	3.0	4.0	5.0	6.0	6.0
7. EBT	$ 4.0	$ 8.0	$ 13.0	$ 17.0	$ 22.0
8. Taxes (40%)[b]	1.6	3.2	5.2	6.8	8.8
9. Net income	$ 2.4	$ 4.8	$ 7.8	$ 10.2	$ 13.2
10. Plus depreciation	8.0	8.0	9.0	9.0	10.0
11. Cash flow	$ 10.4	$ 12.8	$ 16.8	$ 19.2	$ 23.2
12. Less retentions[c]	4.0	4.0	7.0	9.0	12.0
13. Plus terminal value[d]					150.2
14. Net cash flow to Hightech[e]	$ 6.4	$ 8.8	$ 9.8	$ 10.2	$161.4

[a]Interest payments are estimates based on Apex's existing debt, plus additional debt required to increase the debt ratio to 50 percent, plus additional debt required after the merger to finance growth while maintaining the 50 percent target capital structure.

[b]Hightech will file a consolidated tax return after the merger. Thus, the taxes shown here are the full corporate taxes attributable to Apex's operations: there will be no additional taxes on any cash flows passed from Apex to Hightech.

[c]Some of the cash flows generated by the Apex subsidiary after the merger must be retained to finance Apex's asset replacements and growth, while some will be transferred to Hightech to pay dividends on its stock or for redeployment within the corporation.

[d]Apex's available cash flows are expected to grow at a constant 10 percent rate after 2001. The value of all post-2001 cash flows as of December 31, 2001, is estimated by use of the constant growth model to be $150.2 million:

$$V_{2001} = \frac{(\$23.2 - \$12.0)(1.10)}{0.182 - 0.10} = \$150.2 \text{ million.}$$

In the next section, we discuss the estimation of the 18.2 percent cost of equity. The $150.2 million is the PV at the end of 2001 of the stream of cash flows for year 2001 and thereafter.

[e]These are the net cash flows projected to be available to Hightech by virtue of the acquisition of Apex. These cash flows could be used for dividend payments to Hightech's stockholders, to finance asset expansion in Hightech's other divisions and subsidiaries, and so on.

Lines 1 through 4 of the table show the operating and depreciation cash flows that Hightech expects for the Apex subsidiary if the merger takes place, and Line 5 contains the earnings before interest and taxes (EBIT) for each year. Unlike a typical capital budgeting analysis, a merger analysis usually incorporates interest expense into the cash flow forecast, which is shown on Line 6. This is done for three reasons: (1) acquiring firms often assume the debt of the target firm, so old debt having different coupon rates is often part of the deal; (2) the acquisition is often financed partially by debt; and (3) if the subsidiary is to grow in the future, new debt will have to be issued over time to support the expansion. Thus, debt associated with a merger is typically more complex than the single issue of new debt associated with a normal capital project, and the easiest way to properly account for the complexities of merger debt is to specifically include each year's expected interest expense in the cash flow forecast. Therefore, we are using what could be called the *equity residual method* to value the target firm, because the estimated net cash flows are a residual which belongs solely to the acquiring firm's shareholders.

Line 7 contains the earnings before taxes (EBT), and Line 8 gives taxes based on Hightech's 40 percent marginal rate. Line 9 lists each year's net income, and depreciation is added back on Line 10 to obtain each year's cash flow, which is shown on Line 11. Since some of Apex's assets are expected to wear out or become obsolete, and since Hightech plans to expand the Apex subsidiary should the acquisition occur, some equity funds must be retained and reinvested in the subsidiary. These retentions, which are not available for transfer from Apex to the parent, are shown on Line 12. Finally, we have projected only five years of cash flows, but Hightech would likely operate the Apex subsidiary for many years—in theory, forever. We applied the constant growth model to the 2001 cash flow to estimate the value of all cash flows beyond 2001. (See Note d to Table 25-2.) This "terminal value" of the Apex subsidiary, which represents its projected value at the end of 2001, is shown on Line 13.

The net cash flows shown on Line 14 are the flows that would be available to Hightech's stockholders, and these are the basis of the valuation.[7] Of course, the postmerger cash flows attributable to the target firm are extremely difficult to estimate, and in a complete merger valuation, just as in a complete capital budgeting analysis, the component cash flow probability distributions should be specified, and sensitivity, scenario, and simulation analyses should be conducted. Indeed, in a friendly merger the acquiring firm would send a team consisting of literally dozens of accountants, engineers, and so forth, to the target firm's headquarters to go over its books, to estimate required maintenance expenditures, to set values on assets such as real estate and petroleum reserves, and the like.

ESTIMATING THE DISCOUNT RATE   The bottom-line net cash flows shown on Line 14 belong to Hightech's stockholders, so they should be discounted at the cost of equity rather than at the company's overall cost of capital. Further, the cost of equity

---

[7] We purposely kept the cash flows relatively simple to help focus on the key issues of the valuation process. In an actual merger valuation, the cash flows would be much more complex, normally including such items as additional capital furnished by the acquiring firm, tax loss carry-forwards, tax effects of plant and equipment valuation adjustments, and cash flows from the sale of some of the subsidiary's assets.

used should reflect the riskiness of the cash flows in the table, hence the appropriate discount rate is Apex's cost of equity, not that of either Hightech or the consolidated postmerger firm.

Although we will not illustrate it here, Hightech could perform a risk analysis on the Table 25-2 cash flows just as it does on any set of capital budgeting flows. Scenario analysis and Monte Carlo simulation could be used to give Hightech's management a feel for the risks involved with the acquisition. Apex is a publicly traded company, so we can assess directly its market risk. Apex's market-determined premerger beta was 1.28. However, this reflects its premerger 30 percent debt ratio, while its postmerger debt ratio will increase to 50 percent. The Hamada equations, which were developed in Chapter 14, can be used to approximate the effects of the leverage change on beta. First, we obtain the unlevered beta of Apex's assets:

$$b_U = \frac{b_L}{1 + (1 - T)(D/E)} = \frac{1.28}{1 + (1 - 0.40)(0.30/0.70)} = \frac{1.28}{1.26} = 1.02.$$

Next, we relever Apex's asset beta to reflect its new 50 percent debt ratio:

$$b_L = b_U[1 + (1 - T)(D/E)]$$
$$= 1.02[1 + (1 - 0.40)(0.50/0.50)] = 1.02(1.6) = 1.63.$$

Finally, we use the Security Market Line to estimate Apex's postmerger cost of equity. If the risk-free rate is 10 percent and the market risk premium is 5 percent, then Apex's cost of equity, k_s, after the merger with Hightech, would be about 18.2 percent:[8]

$$k_s = k_{RF} + (RP_M)b = 10\% + (5\%)1.63 = 18.15\% \approx 18.2\%.$$

VALUING THE CASH FLOWS   The current value of Apex to Hightech is the present value of the cash flows expected to accrue to Hightech, discounted at 18.2 percent (in millions of dollars):

$$V_{1996} = \frac{\$6.4}{(1.182)^1} + \frac{\$8.8}{(1.182)^2} + \frac{\$9.8}{(1.182)^3} + \frac{\$10.2}{(1.182)^4} + \frac{\$161.4}{(1.182)^5} \approx \$92.8.$$

Thus, the value of Apex to Hightech is $92.8 million.

MARKET MULTIPLE ANALYSIS

Another method of valuing a target company is *market multiple analysis,* which applies a market-determined multiple to net income, earnings per share, sales, book value, or, for businesses such as cable TV or cellular telephone operators, the num-

---

[8]In this example, we used the Capital Asset Pricing Model to estimate Apex's cost of equity, and thus we assumed that investors require a premium for market risk only. We could have also conducted a corporate risk analysis, in which the relevant risk would be the contribution of Apex's cash flows to the total risk of the postmerger firm.

In actual merger situations among large firms, companies almost always hire an investment banker to help develop valuation estimates. For example, when General Electric acquired Utah International, GE hired Morgan Stanley to determine Utah's value. We discussed the valuation process with the Morgan Stanley analyst in charge of the appraisal, and he confirmed that they applied all of the standard procedures discussed in this chapter. Note, though, that merger analysis, like the analysis of any other complex issue, requires judgment, and people's judgments differ as to how much weight to give to different methods in any given situation.

ber of subscribers. The DCF method applies valuation concepts in a precise manner, focusing on expected cash flows, while market multiple analysis is more ad hoc. To illustrate the concept, note that the forecasted net income of Apex is $2.4 million in 1997, rising to $13.2 million in 2001, for an average of $7.7 million over the five-year forecast period. Furthermore, assume that the average ratio of stock price to net income (earnings) per share of publicly traded companies similar to Apex is found to be 12. That is, the average earnings per share is $1.50, and the average stock price is $18, giving similar firms a *market multiple* of $18/$1.50 = 12.

To estimate Apex's value using the market P/E multiple approach, simply multiply its $7.7 million net income by the market multiple of 12 to obtain the value of $7.7(12) = $92.4 million. Since equity multiples are typically used in such analyses, the resulting value is the equity, or ownership, value of the firm. Note that we used the average net income over the coming five years to value Apex. The market P/E multiple of 12 is based on the current year's income of comparable companies, but Apex's current income does not reflect synergistic effects or managerial changes that will be made. By averaging future net income, we are attempting to capture the value added by Hightech to Apex's operations.

Note that earnings (or cash flow) measures other than net income can be used in the market multiple approach. For example, another commonly used measure is *earnings before interest, taxes, depreciation, and amortization (EBITDA)*. The procedure would be identical to that just described, except that the market multiple would be based on EBITDA rather than net income.

As noted above, in some businesses such as cable TV and cellular telephone, an important element in the valuation process is the number of customers a company has. The acquirer has an idea of the cost required to obtain a new customer and the average profit per customer. For example, telephone companies have been paying about $2,000 per customer for cellular operators. Medical companies such as HMOs have applied similar logic in acquisitions, basing their valuations on the number of people insured. Of course, the cash flows produced by acquired businesses are the really fundamental factor, but if the acquiring firm can generate more cash flow per customer than the target, then customers will be a key determinant of the price to be paid, so the valuation will be based, in part, on some multiple times the number of customers.

SETTING THE BID PRICE

Using the DCF valuation results, $92.8 million is the most Hightech could pay for Apex — if it pays more, then Hightech's own value will be diluted. On the other hand, if Hightech can get Apex for less than $92.8 million, Hightech's stockholders will gain value. Therefore, Hightech will bid something less than $92.8 million when it makes an offer for Apex.

Figure 25-1 graphs the merger situation. The $92.8 million is shown as a point on the horizontal axis, and it is the maximum price that Hightech can afford to pay. If Hightech pays less, say, $82.8 million, then its stockholders will gain $10 million from the merger, while if it pays more, its stockholders will lose. What we have, then, is a 45-degree line which cuts the X axis at $92.8 million, and that line shows how much Hightech's stockholders can expect to gain or lose at different acquisition prices.

FIGURE 25-1	A VIEW OF MERGER ANALYSIS (MILLIONS OF DOLLARS)

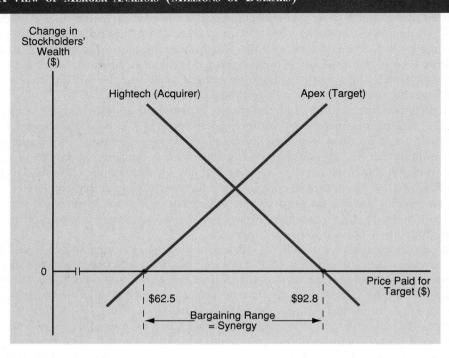

Now consider the target company, Apex. It has 10 million shares of stock which sell for $6.25, so its value as an independent operating company is presumably $62.5 million. [In making this statement, we assume (1) that the company is being operated as well as possible by its present management, and (2) that the $6.25 market price per share does not include some "speculative merger premium" in addition to the PV of operating cash flows.] If Apex is acquired at a price greater than $62.5 million, its stockholders will gain value, while they will lose value at any lower price. Thus, we can draw another 45-degree line, this one with an upward slope, that shows the effect of the merger price on Apex's stockholders.

The difference between $62.5 and $92.8 million, or $30.3 million, represents synergistic benefits the merger is expected to produce. Here are some points to note:

1. If there were no synergistic benefits, the maximum bid would be equal to the current value of the target company. The greater the synergistic gains, the greater the gap between the target's current price and the maximum the acquiring company could pay.

2. The greater the synergistic gains, the more likely a merger is to be consummated.

3. The issue of how to divide the synergistic benefits is critically important in any merger analysis. Obviously, both parties will want to get as much as possible. In our example, if Apex's management knew the maximum price that Hightech could pay, it would argue for a price close to $92.8 million. Hightech, on the other hand, would try to get Apex at a price as close to $62.5 million as possible.

4. Where, within the $62.5 to $92.8 million range, will the actual price be set? The answer depends on a number of factors, including whether Hightech offers to pay with cash or securities, the negotiating skills of the two management teams, and, most importantly, the bargaining positions of the two parties as determined by fundamental economic conditions. To illustrate the latter point, suppose first that there are many companies similar to Apex that Hightech could acquire, but no company other than Hightech that could gain synergies by acquiring Apex. In this case, Hightech would probably make a relatively low, take-it-or-leave-it offer, and Apex would probably take it because some gain is better than none. On the other hand, if Apex has some unique technology or other asset that many companies want, then once Hightech announces its offer, others will probably make competing bids, and the final price will probably be close to or even above $92.8 million. A price above $92.8 million would presumably be paid by some other company which had a better synergistic fit or, perhaps, whose management was more optimistic about Apex's cash flow potential. In Figure 25-1, this situation would be represented by a line parallel to that for Hightech but shifted to the right of the Hightech line.

5. Hightech would, of course, want to keep its maximum bid secret, and it would plan its bidding strategy carefully and consistently with the situation. If it thought that other bidders would emerge, or that Apex's management might resist in order to preserve their jobs, it might make a high "preemptive" bid in hopes of scaring off competing bids and/or management resistance. On the other hand, it might make a low-ball bid in hopes of "stealing" the company.

We will have more to say about these points in the sections that follow, and you should keep Figure 25-1 in mind as a reference point as you go through the rest of the chapter.

POSTMERGER CONTROL

The employment/control situation is often of vital interest in a merger analysis. First, consider the situation in which a small, owner-managed firm sells out to a larger concern. The owner-manager may be anxious to retain a high-status position, and he or she may also have developed a camaraderie with the employees and thus be concerned about keeping operating control of the organization after the merger. If so, these points would be stressed during the merger negotiations.[9] When a publicly owned firm not controlled by its managers is merged into another company, the acquired firm's management is also worried about its postmerger position. If the acquiring firm agrees to retain the old management, then management may be willing to support the merger and to recommend its acceptance to the stockholders. If the old management is to be removed, then it will probably resist the merger.[10]

SELF-TEST QUESTIONS

What is the difference between an operating merger and a financial merger?

Describe the way postmerger cash flows are estimated in a DCF analysis.

What is the basis for the discount rate in a DCF analysis? Describe how this rate might be estimated.

Describe the market multiple approach.

What are some factors that acquiring firms consider when they set the bid price?

What impact does postmerger control have on a merger analysis?

STRUCTURING THE TAKEOVER BID

The acquiring firm's offer to the target's shareholders can be in the form of cash, stock of the acquiring firm, debt of the acquiring firm, or a combination of the three. The structure of the bid is extremely important since it affects (1) the capital structure of the postmerger firm, (2) the tax treatment of the acquiring firm and the target's stockholders, (3) the ability of the target firm's stockholders to benefit from future merger-related gains, and (4) the types of federal and state regulations to which the acquiring firm will be subjected. In this section, we focus on how taxes and regulation influence the way in which acquiring firms structure their offers.

---

[9]The acquiring firm may also be concerned about this point, especially if the target firm's management is quite good. Indeed, a condition of the merger may be that the management team agree to stay on for a period such as five years after the merger. In this case, the price paid may be contingent on the acquired firm's performance subsequent to the merger. For example, when International Holdings acquired Walker Products, the price paid was an immediate 100,000 shares of International Holdings stock worth $63 per share plus an additional 30,000 shares each year for the next three years, provided Walker Products earned at least $1 million during each of these years. Since Walker's managers owned the stock and would receive the bonus, they had a strong incentive to stay on and help the firm meet its targets.

Finally, if the managers of the target company are highly competent but do not wish to remain on after the merger, the acquiring firm may build into the merger contract a noncompetitive agreement with the old management. Typically, the acquired firm's principal officers must agree not to affiliate with a new business which is competitive with the one they sold for a specified period, say, five years. Such agreements are especially important with service-oriented businesses.

[10]Managements of firms that are thought to be attractive merger candidates often arrange *golden parachutes* for themselves. Golden parachutes are extremely lucrative retirement plans which take effect if a merger is consummated. Thus, when Bendix was acquired by Allied, Bill Agee, Bendix's chairman, "pulled the ripcord of his golden parachute" and walked away with $4 million. If a golden parachute is large enough, it can also function as a poison pill — for example, where the president of a firm worth $10 million would have to be paid $8 million if the firm is acquired, this will prevent a takeover. Congress has recently reduced the value of golden parachutes by increasing the tax consequences to the firm, but they still exist.

The form of payment offered to the target's shareholders determines the personal tax treatment of these stockholders. Target shareholders do not have to pay taxes on the transaction if they maintain a substantial equity position in the combined firm, defined by the IRS to mean that at least 50 percent of the payment to target shareholders is in the form of shares (either common or preferred) of the acquiring firm. In such *nontaxable offers,* target shareholders do not realize any capital gains or losses until they sell the equity securities they received. However, capital gains must be taken and treated as income in the transaction year if an offer consists of more than 50 percent cash and/or debt securities.

All other things being equal, stockholders prefer nontaxable offers, since they may then postpone the realization of capital gains and the payment of taxes. Furthermore, if the target firm's stockholders receive stock of the acquiring firm, they will benefit from any newly realized value after the merger takes place. Most target shareholders are thus willing to sell their stock for a lower price in a nontaxable offer than in a taxable offer. As a result, one might expect nontaxable bids to dominate. However, this is not the case—roughly half of all mergers have been taxable, and, as noted in Table 25-1, three of the top five mergers have been all-cash deals.

Prior to 1986, if a firm paid more than book value for a target firm's assets in a taxable merger, it could write up those assets, depreciate the marked-up value for tax purposes, and thus lower the postmerger firm's taxes vis-à-vis the taxes of the two firms operating separately. At the same time, the target firm did not have to pay any taxes on the write-up at the time of the merger. Under current law, if the acquiring company writes up the target company's assets for tax purposes, then the target company must pay capital gains taxes in the year the merger occurs. (These taxes can be avoided if the acquiring company elects not to write up acquired assets and depreciates them on their old basis.)

Note also that in 1986 the maximum capital gains tax rate on personal income rose from 20 percent to 28 percent, a 40 percent increase. This, of course, means that target companies' stockholders now net less from a merger than they would have under the old law. When one considers the combined effects of the corporate and personal tax changes, it is clear that the tax treatment of mergers is significantly less favorable today than it was prior to 1987. This means that a lot less money ends up in the pockets of selling stockholders, so they require larger premiums to sell.

Securities laws also have an effect on the construction of the offer. As we discussed in Chapter 16, the SEC has oversight over the issuance of new securities, including stock or debt issued in connection with a merger. Therefore, whenever a corporation bids for control of another firm through the exchange of equity or debt, the entire process must take place under the scrutiny of the Securities and Exchange Commission. The time required for such reviews allows target managements to implement defensive tactics and other firms to make competing offers, and as a result, nearly all hostile tender offers are for cash rather than securities.

What are some alternative ways of structuring takeover bids?
How do taxes influence the payment structure?
How do securities laws affect the payment structure?

SELF-TEST QUESTIONS

THE ROLE OF INVESTMENT BANKERS

Investment banks are involved with mergers in a number of ways: (1) they help arrange mergers, (2) they help target companies develop and implement defensive tactics, (3) they help value target companies, (4) they help finance mergers, and (5) they speculate in the stocks of potential merger candidates. These merger-related activities have been quite profitable. For example, the investment bankers and lawyers who arranged the Campeau-Federated merger earned fees of about $83 million — First Boston and Wasserstein Perella split $29 million from Campeau, and Goldman Sachs, Hellman & Friedman, and Shearson Lehman Hutton divided up $54 million for representing Federated. No wonder investment banking houses are able to make top offers to finance graduates!

ARRANGING MERGERS

The major investment banking firms have merger and acquisition groups which operate within their corporate finance departments. (Corporate finance departments offer advice, as opposed to underwriting or brokerage services, to business firms.) Members of these groups strive to identify firms with excess cash that might want to buy other firms, companies that might be willing to be bought, and firms that might, for a number of reasons, be attractive to others. Also, if an oil company, for instance, decided to expand into coal mining, then it might enlist the aid of an investment banker to help it locate and then negotiate with a target coal company. Similarly, dissident stockholders of firms with poor track records might work with investment bankers to oust management by helping to arrange a merger. Investment bankers are reported to have offered packages of financing to corporate raiders, where the package includes both designing the securities to be used in the tender offer, plus lining up people and firms who will buy the target firm's stock now and then tender it once the final offer is made. The financing role is discussed in more detail in a later section.

Investment bankers have occasionally taken illegal actions in the merger arena. For one thing, they are reported to have *parked stock* — purchasing it for a raider under a guaranteed buy-back agreement — to help the raider de facto accumulate more than 5 percent of the target's stock without disclosing the position.

DEVELOPING DEFENSIVE TACTICS

Target firms that do not want to be acquired generally enlist the help of an investment banking firm, along with a law firm that specializes in helping to block mergers. Defenses include such tactics as (1) changing the bylaws so that only one-third of the directors are elected each year and/or so that a 75 percent approval (a *supermajority*) versus a simple majority is required to approve a merger; (2) trying to convince the target firm's stockholders that the price being offered is too low; (3) raising antitrust issues in the hope that the Justice Department will intervene; (4) repurchasing stock in the open market in an effort to push the price above that being offered by the potential acquirer; (5) getting a white knight who is acceptable to the target firm's management to compete with the potential acquirer; (6) getting a "white squire" who is friendly to current management to buy enough of the target firm's shares to block the merger; and (7) taking a poison pill, as described next.

Poison pills — which occasionally really do amount to committing economic suicide to avoid a takeover — are such tactics as borrowing on terms that require immediate repayment of all loans if the firm is acquired, selling off at bargain prices the assets that originally made the firm a desirable target, granting such lucrative golden parachutes to their executives that the cash drain from these payments would render the merger infeasible, and planning defensive mergers which would leave the firm with new assets of questionable value and a huge debt load. Currently, the most popular poison pill is for a company to give its stockholders *stock purchase rights* which allow them to buy at half-price the stock of an acquiring firm, should the firm be acquired. The blatant use of poison pills is constrained by directors' awareness that excessive use could trigger personal suits by stockholders against directors who voted for them, and, perhaps in the near future, by laws that would further limit management's use of pills. Still, investment bankers and antitakeover lawyers are busy thinking up new poison pill formulas, and others are just as busy trying to come up with antidotes.[11]

To illustrate a typical poison pill, consider Chrysler's poison pill share rights purchase plan. Chrysler's stockholders received one full right in the poison pill plan for each share of common stock held. Each right entitles the holder to buy one-hundredth of a share of Chrysler junior participating cumulative preferred stock for $120. However, the primary purpose of the rights is to act as a poison pill. Certain events, as described next, will cause the rights either to "kick in" and hence entitle holders to buy Chrysler common stock at half its market value, or to "flip over" and hence entitle holders to buy common stock in an acquiring entity at half its market value.

A "kick in" will occur if a shareholder acquires 20 percent or more of the firm's common stock. Further, Chrysler's board could trigger the "kick in" if an owner of 10 percent or more of the firm's stock has "adverse" intentions, where "adverse" intentions are defined as any intentions to take actions that are detrimental to the long-term interests of Chrysler and its shareholders. A "kick over" will occur if a hostile takeover occurs, which is any takeover that is not supported by Chrysler's board of directors.

Another takeover defense that is being used is the employee stock ownership plan (ESOP). ESOPs are designed to give lower-level employees an ownership stake in the firm, and current tax laws provide generous incentives for companies to establish such plans and fund them with the firm's common stock. As we discussed earlier, Polaroid used an ESOP to help fend off Shamrock Holdings's hostile takeover attempt. Also, Procter & Gamble recently set up an ESOP that, along with an existing profit-sharing plan, eventually will give employees a 20 percent ownership stake in the company. Since the trustees of ESOPs generally support current management

---

[11]It has become extremely difficult and expensive for companies to buy "directors' insurance" which protects the board from such contingencies as stockholders' suits, and even when insurance is available it often does not pay for losses if the directors have not exercised due caution and judgment. This exposure is making directors extremely leery of actions that might trigger stockholder suits.

in any takeover attempt, and since up to 85 percent of the votes is often required to complete a merger, an ESOP can provide an effective defense against a hostile tender offer. Procter & Gamble stated that its ESOP was designed primarily to lower its costs by utilizing the plan's tax advantages and to improve employees' retirement security. However, the company also noted that the ESOP would strengthen its defenses against a takeover.

ESTABLISHING A FAIR VALUE

If a friendly merger is being worked out between two firms' managements, it is important to document that the agreed-upon price is a fair one; otherwise, the stockholders of either company may sue to block the merger. Therefore, in most large mergers each side will hire an investment banking firm to evaluate the target company and to help establish the fair price. For example, General Electric employed Morgan Stanley to determine a fair price for Utah International, as did Royal Dutch to help establish the price it paid for Shell Oil. Even if the merger is not friendly, investment bankers may still be asked to help establish a price. If a surprise tender offer is to be made, the acquiring firm will want to know the lowest price at which it might be able to acquire the stock, while the target firm may seek help in "proving" that the price being offered is too low.[12]

FINANCING MERGERS

Many mergers are financed with the acquiring company's excess cash. However, if the acquiring company has no excess cash, it will require a source of funds. Perhaps the single most important factor behind the 1980s merger wave was the development of the junk bond market and its role in financing acquisitions.

As noted in Chapter 17, Drexel Burnham Lambert was the primary developer of junk bonds, defined as bonds rated below investment grade (BBB/Baa). Prior to Drexel's entry on the scene, it was almost impossible to sell low-grade bonds to raise new capital. Drexel then pioneered a procedure under which a target firm's situation would be appraised very closely, and a cash flow projection similar to that in Table 25-2 (but much more detailed) would be developed. Part of the cash flow projection would generally include cash flows from major asset sales.

With the cash flows having been forecasted, Drexel's analysts would figure out a debt structure — amount of debt, maturity structure, and interest rate — that could be serviced by the cash flows. With this information, Drexel's junk bond people, operating out of Beverly Hills, would approach financial institutions (savings and loans, insurance companies, pension funds, and mutual funds) and wealthy individu-

---

[12]Such investigations must obviously be done in secret, for if someone knew that Company A was thinking of offering, say, $50 per share for Company T, which was currently selling at $35 per share, then huge profits could be made. One of the biggest scandals to hit Wall Street recently was the disclosure that Ivan Boesky was buying information from Dennis Levine, a senior member of the investment banking house of Drexel Burnham Lambert, about target companies that Drexel was analyzing for others. Purchases based on such insider information would, of course, raise the prices of the stocks and thus force Drexel's clients to pay more than they otherwise would have had to pay. Levine and Boesky, among others, went to jail for their improper use of inside information.

als with a financing plan and offer a rate of return several percentage points above the rate on more conservative investments. Drexel's early deals worked out well, and the institutions that bought the bonds were quite pleased. These results enabled Drexel to expand its network of investors and thus increased its ability to finance larger and larger mergers (and LBOs). T. Boone Pickens, who went after Phillips, Texaco, and several other oil giants, was an early Drexel customer, as was Ted Turner.

To be a successful investment banker today in the mergers and acquisitions (M&A) business, a banker must be able to offer a financing package to clients, whether they are acquirers such as Ted Turner who need capital to take over companies such as MGM or else target companies such as Union Carbide trying to finance stock repurchase plans or other defenses against takeovers. Drexel was the leading player in the merger financing game, but since Drexel's bankruptcy in early 1990, the role of chief takeover financier remains unfilled. However, Merrill Lynch, Morgan Stanley, Salomon Brothers, and others are all eager for the title.

Arbitrage Operations

Arbitrage generally means simultaneously buying and selling the same commodity or security in two different markets at different prices, and pocketing a risk-free return. However, the major brokerage houses, as well as some wealthy private investors, are engaged in a different type of arbitrage called *risk arbitrage*. The *arbitrageurs,* or "arbs" as they are called, speculate in the stocks of companies that are likely takeover targets. Vast amounts of capital are required to speculate in a large number of securities and thus reduce risk, and also to make money on narrow spreads, but the large investment bankers have the wherewithal to play the game. To be successful, arbs need to be able to sniff out likely targets, assess the probability of offers reaching fruition, and move in and out of the market quickly and with low transactions costs.

The risk arbitrage business has been rocked by insider trading scandals. Indeed, the most famous arb of all, Ivan Boesky, was caught buying inside information from executives of some leading investment banking houses to help make his millions. The Boesky affair slowed down risk arbitrage activity, but with deals such as IBM's offer of $60 per share for Lotus's $30 stock, risk arbitrage is not about to go away.

What are some defensive tactics that firms can use to resist hostile takeovers?

What is the difference between pure arbitrage and risk arbitrage?

What role did junk bonds play in the merger wave of the 1980s?

Self-Test Questions

Who Wins: The Empirical Evidence

All the recent merger activity has raised two questions: (1) Do corporate acquisitions create value, and, (2) if so, how is the value shared between the parties?

Financial researchers include corporate acquisitions as part of "the market for corporate control." Under this concept, management teams are viewed as facing constant competition from other management teams. If the team that currently controls a firm is not maximizing the value of its assets, then an acquisition will likely occur and increase the firm's value by replacing its poor managers with good managers. Further, under this theory intense competition will cause managers to combine or divest assets whenever such steps would increase the value of the firm.

Most researchers agree that takeovers increase the wealth of the shareholders of target firms, for otherwise they would not agree to the offer. However, there is a debate as to whether mergers benefit the acquiring firm's shareholders. In particular, managements of acquiring firms may be motivated by factors other than shareholder wealth maximization. For example, they may want to merge merely to increase the size of the corporations they manage, because increased size usually brings larger salaries plus job security, perquisites, power, and prestige.

The validity of the competing views on who gains from corporate acquisitions can be tested by examining the stock price changes that occur around the time of a merger or takeover announcement. Changes in the stock prices of the acquiring and target firms represent market participants' beliefs about the value created by the merger, and about how that value will be divided between the target and acquiring firms' shareholders. As long as the market participants are neither systematically wrong nor biased in their perceptions about the effects of mergers, examining a large sample of stock price movements will shed light on the issue of who gains from mergers.

One cannot simply examine stock prices around merger announcement dates, because other factors influence stock prices. For example, if a merger was announced on a day when the entire market advanced, the fact that the firm in question's price rose would not necessarily signify that the merger created value. Hence, studies examine *abnormal returns* associated with merger announcements, where abnormal returns are defined as that part of a stock price change caused by factors other than changes in the general stock market.

Many studies have examined both acquiring and target firms' stock price responses to mergers and tender offers.[13] Jointly, these studies have covered nearly every acquisition involving publicly traded firms from the early 1960s to the present, and they are remarkably consistent in their results: on average, the stock prices of target firms increase by about 30 percent in hostile tender offers, while in friendly mergers the average increase is about 20 percent. However, for both hostile and friendly deals, the stock prices of acquiring firms, on average, remain constant. Thus, the evidence strongly indicates (1) that acquisitions do create value, but (2) that shareholders of target firms reap virtually all of the benefits.

In hindsight, these results are not too surprising. First, target firms' shareholders can always say no, so they are in the driver's seat. Second, takeovers are a competitive game, so if one potential acquiring firm does not offer full value for a potential target, then another firm will generally jump in with a higher bid. Finally, managements of acquiring firms might well be willing to give up all the value created by the merger, because the merger would enhance the acquiring managers' personal positions with no explicit cost to their shareholders.

---

[13]For an excellent summary of the effects of mergers on value, see Michael C. Jensen and Richard S. Ruback, "The Market for Corporate Control: The Scientific Evidence," *Journal of Financial Economics,* April 1983, 5–50.

It has also been argued that acquisitions may increase shareholder wealth at the expense of bondholders — in particular, concern has been expressed that leveraged buyouts dilute the claims of bondholders. Specific instances can be cited in which bonds were downgraded and bondholders did suffer losses, sometimes quite large, as a direct result of an acquisition. However, most studies find no evidence to support the contention that bondholders on average lose in corporate acquisitions.

Explain how researchers can study the effects of mergers on shareholder wealth. Do mergers create value? If so, who profits from this value? Do the research results discussed in this section seem logical? Explain.	**Self-Test Questions**

CORPORATE ALLIANCES

Mergers are one way for two companies to join forces, but many companies are striking cooperative deals, called *corporate,* or *strategic, alliances,* which fall far short of merging. Whereas mergers combine all of the assets of the firms involved, as well as their managerial and technical expertise, alliances allow firms to create combinations that focus on specific business lines that offer the most potential synergies. These alliances take many forms, from simple marketing agreements to joint ownership of worldwide operations.

One form of corporate alliance is the *joint venture,* in which parts of companies are joined to achieve specific, limited objectives.[14] A joint venture is controlled by a management team consisting of representatives of the two (or more) parent companies. Joint ventures have been used often by U.S., Japanese, and European firms to share technology and/or marketing expertise. For example, General Electric recently announced a joint venture with Britain's unrelated General Electric Company to manufacture appliances, medical equipment, and electrical products. In the same month, Whirlpool announced a joint venture with the Dutch electronics giant Philips to produce appliances under Philips's brand names in five European countries. By joining with their foreign counterparts, U.S. firms were attempting to gain a strong foothold in Europe. Although alliances are new to some firms, they are established practices to others. For example, Corning Glass now obtains over half of its profits from 23 joint ventures, two-thirds of them with foreign companies representing almost all of Europe, as well as Japan, China, South Korea, and Australia.

What is the difference between a merger and a corporate alliance? What is a joint venture? Give some reasons why joint ventures may be advantageous to the parties involved.	**Self-Test Questions**

---

[14]Cross-licensing, consortia, joint bidding, and franchising are still other ways for firms to combine resources. For more information on joint ventures, see Sanford V. Berg, Jerome Duncan, and Phillip Friedman, *Joint Venture Strategies and Corporate Innovation* (Cambridge, Mass.: Oelgeschlager, Gunn and Hain, 1982).

LEVERAGED BUYOUTS

The pros and cons of *leveraged buyouts (LBOs)* were discussed in detail in Chapter 16. In an LBO a small group of equity investors, usually including current management, acquires a firm in a transaction financed largely by debt. The debt is serviced with funds generated by the acquired company's operations and, often, by the sale of some of its assets. Generally, the acquiring group plans to run the acquired company for a number of years, boost its sales and profits, and then take it public again as a stronger company. Naturally, the acquiring group expects to make a substantial profit from the LBO, but the inherent risks are great due to the heavy use of financial leverage. To illustrate the profit potential, Kohlberg Kravis Roberts & Company (KKR), a leading LBO specialist firm, averaged a spectacular 50 percent annual return on its LBO investments during the 1980s. However, the weak economy and strong stock prices have dampened the returns on LBO investments, so recent activity has been slower than in its heyday of the 1980s.

A good example of an LBO was KKR's buyout of RJR Nabisco. RJR, a leading producer of tobacco and food products with brands such as Winston, Camel, Planters, Ritz, Oreo, and Del Monte, was trading at about $55 a share in October 1988. Then, F. Ross Johnson, the company's chairman and CEO, announced a $75-a-share, or $17.6 billion, offer to outside stockholders in a plan to take the firm private. This deal, if completed, would have been the largest business transaction up to that time. After the announcement, RJR's stock price soared to $77.25, which indicated that investors thought the final price would be even higher than Johnson's opening bid. A few days later KKR offered $90 per share, or $20.6 billion, for RJR. The battle between the two bidders raged until late November, when RJR's board accepted KKR's revised bid of cash and securities worth about $106 a share, for a total value of about $25 billion. Of course, the investment bankers' fees reflected the record size of the deal — the bankers received almost $400 million, with Drexel Burnham Lambert alone getting over $200 million. Johnson lost his job, but he walked away with a multimillion-dollar golden parachute.

KKR wasted no time in restructuring the newly private RJR. In June 1989, RJR sold its five European businesses to France's BSN for $2.5 million. Then, in September RJR sold the tropical fruit portion of its Del Monte foods unit to Polly Peck, a London-based food company, for $875 million. In the same month, RJR sold the Del Monte canned foods business to an LBO group led by Citicorp Venture Capital for $1.48 billion. Next, in October 1990 RJR sold its Baby Ruth, Butterfinger, and Pearson candy businesses to Nestlé, a Swiss company, for $370 million. In total, RJR sold off more than $5 billion worth of businesses in 1990 to help pay down the tremendous debt taken on in the LBO. In addition to asset sales, in 1991 RJR went public again by issuing more than $1 billion in new common stock at $56.25 per share (adjusted for a 1:5 reverse split in 1995), which placed about 25 percent of the firm's common stock in public hands. Also, as the firm's credit rating improved due to retirement of some of its debt, RJR issued about $1 billion of new debt at significantly lower rates and used the proceeds to retire even more of its high-cost debt.

The RJR Nabisco story is the classic LBO tale — a company is taken private in a highly leveraged deal, the private firm's high-cost junk debt is reduced through asset sales, and finally the company again goes public, which gives the original LBO deal-makers the opportunity to "cash out." This story, however, did not have a fairytale ending. When KKR finally sold its last shares of RJR Nabisco in early 1995, the investment fund that provided the capital ended up making about $60 million on a $3.1 billion investment, hardly a stellar return. The best a KKR spokesman could say about the deal was that "it preserved investors' equity." The fund was largely financed by outside investors, with KKR putting up only $126 million of the original investment. Even though the return on their fund investment was the same as that received by outside investors, KKR earned an additional $500 million in transactions, advisor, management, and directors' fees.

Regardless of the outcome of the RJR Nabisco deal, there have been some spectacularly successful LBOs. For example, in one deal that fueled the LBO wave, William Simon and Raymond Chambers bought Gibson Greeting Cards in 1982 for $1 million in equity and $79 million in debt. Less than 18 months later, Simon's personal investment of $330,000 was worth $66 million in cash and stock. However, there have also been some spectacular failures. For example, in 1988 Revco became the first large LBO to file for Chapter 11 bankruptcy. It turned out that sales were nearly $1 billion short of the $3.4 billion forecasted at the time of the drugstore chain's buyout.[15]

What is an LBO?	**SELF-TEST**
Have LBOs been profitable in recent years?	**QUESTIONS**
What actions do companies typically take to meet the large debt burdens resulting from LBOs?	
How do LBOs typically affect bondholders?	

DIVESTITURES

Although corporations do more buying than selling of productive facilities, a good bit of selling does occur. In this section, we briefly discuss the major types of divestitures, after which we present some recent examples and rationales for divestitures.

TYPES OF DIVESTITURES

There are three primary types of divestitures: (1) sale of an operating unit to another firm, (2) setting up the business to be divested as a separate corporation and then giving (or "spinning off") its stock on a pro rata basis to the divesting firm's stockholders, and (3) outright liquidation of assets.

---

[15]For a more detailed discussion of the impact of the RJR LBO on the firm's different classes of investors, see Nancy Mohan and Carl R. Chen, "A Review of the RJR-Nabisco Buyout," *Journal of Applied Corporate Finance,* Summer 1990, 102–108. For interesting discussions of highly leveraged takeovers, see Martin S. Fridson, "What Went Wrong with the Highly Leveraged Deals? (Or, All Variety of Agency Costs)," *Journal of Applied Corporate Finance,* Fall 1991, 57–67; and "The Economic Consequences of High Leverage and Stock Market Pressures on Corporate Management: A Round Table Discussion," *Journal of Applied Corporate Finance,* Summer 1990, 6–57.

Sale to another firm generally involves the sale of an entire division or unit, usually for cash but sometimes for stock of the acquiring firm. In a *spin-off,* the firm's existing stockholders are given new stock representing separate ownership rights in the division which was divested. The division establishes its own board of directors and officers, and it becomes a separate company. The stockholders end up owning shares of two firms instead of one, but no cash has been transferred. Finally, in a *liquidation* the assets of a division are sold off piecemeal, rather than as an operating entity. To illustrate the different types of divestitures, we present some recent examples in the next section.

DIVESTITURE ILLUSTRATIONS

1. In 1987, United Airlines sold its Hilton International Hotels subsidiary to Ladbroke Group PLC of Britain for $1.1 billion. Later, United divested its Hertz rental car unit and Westin hotel group. The sales culminated a disastrous strategic move by United to build a full-service travel empire. The failed strategy resulted in the firing of Richard J. Ferris, the company's chairman. The move by the airline into nonairline travel-related businesses had been viewed by many analysts as a mistake, because there were few synergies to be gained. Further, analysts feared that United's managers, preoccupied by running hotels and rental car companies, would not maintain the company's posture in the highly competitive airline industry. The funds raised by the divestitures were subsequently paid out to United's shareholders as a special dividend.

2. IU International, a multimillion-dollar conglomerate that was listed on the NYSE, spun off three major subsidiaries — Gotaas-Larson, an ocean shipping company involved in petroleum transportation; Canadian Utilities, an electric utility; and Echo Bay Mines, a gold mining company. IU kept its distribution and manufacturing operations. IU's management originally acquired and combined several highly cyclical businesses such as ocean shipping and gold mining with stable ones such as utilities in order to gain overall corporate stability through diversification. The strategy worked reasonably well from an operating standpoint, but it failed in the financial markets. IU's diversity kept it from being classified in any particular industrial group, so security analysts did not follow it, hence did not understand it or recommend it to investors. (Analysts tend to concentrate on an industry, and they do not like to recommend — and investors do not like to invest in — a company they do not understand.) As a result, IU had a low P/E ratio and a low market price. After the spin-offs, the package of securities rose in value from $10 to $75, which greatly exceeded general stock market gains.

3. AT&T was broken up in 1984 to settle a Justice Department antitrust suit filed in the 1970s.[16] For almost 100 years AT&T had operated as a holding company which owned Western Electric (its manufacturing subsidiary), Bell Labs

---

[16]Another forced divestiture involved Du Pont and General Motors. In 1921, GM was in serious financial trouble, and Du Pont supplied capital in exchange for 23 percent of the stock. In the 1950s, the Justice Department won an antitrust suit which required Du Pont to spin off (to Du Pont's stockholders) its GM stock.

(its research arm), a huge long-distance network which was operated as a division of the parent company, and 22 Bell operating companies, such as Pacific Telephone, New York Telephone, Southern Bell, and Southwestern Bell. AT&T was reorganized into eight separate companies—a slimmed-down AT&T which kept Western Electric, Bell Labs, and the long-distance operations, plus seven new regional telephone holding companies that were created from the 22 old operating telephone companies. The stock of the seven new telephone companies was then spun off to the old AT&T's stockholders. A person who held 100 shares of old AT&T stock owned, after the divestiture, 100 shares of the "new" AT&T plus 10 shares of each of the seven new operating companies. These 170 shares were backed by the same assets that had previously backed 100 shares of old AT&T common.

The AT&T divestiture resulted from a suit by the Justice Department, which wanted to divide the Bell System into a regulated monopoly segment (the seven regional telephone companies) and a manufacturing/long-distance segment which would be exposed to competition. The breakup was expected to strengthen competition and thus speed up technological change in those parts of the telecommunications industry that are not natural monopolies.

4. After its forced breakup, AT&T lost little time in building itself up. In 1991 it acquired computer maker NCR, while in 1994 it bought McCaw Cellular Communications, a cellular phone operator. Then, in 1995, AT&T made a surprise announcement. With no signs that the massive combination of technology assets would pay off, and with AT&T's stock in the doldrums, the company announced that it would split itself into three parts. The surviving AT&T will include the core $53 billion long-distance and cellular phone businesses. The division which makes the switching equipment used by local and long-distance companies will be spun off under the name Lucent Technologies. AT&T will also spin off its loss-plagued computer business (the former NCR). AT&T shares took off on the announcement, adding more than $6 to the share price. This added nearly $11 billion to AT&T's stock value—more than enough to make up for the purchase of NCR and the ensuing losses. One reason for the breakup was the fact that AT&T and the local telephone companies are entering one another's markets, and the locals were reluctant to buy equipment from a competitor (AT&T). Therefore, Lucent was losing business to other manufacturers. Also, the breakup permitted the managers in each of the three entities to focus exclusively on the problems and opportunities unique to that line of business. Now they can concentrate their time in those areas in which they have the greatest expertise, and not be distracted by events in other business lines.

5. Some years ago, Woolworth liquidated every one of its 336 Woolco discount stores. This made the company, which had had sales of $7.2 billion before the liquidation, 30 percent smaller. Woolco had posted operating losses of $19 million the year before the liquidation, and its losses in the six months preceding it had climbed to an alarming $21 million. Woolworth's CEO, Edward F. Gibbons, was quoted as saying: "How many losses can you take?" Woolco's demise necessitated an after-tax write-off of $325 million, but management

believed that it was better to go ahead and "bite the bullet" than to let the losing stores bleed the company to death.

6. As a result of some imprudent loans to oil companies and to developing nations, Continental Illinois, one of the largest U.S. bank holding companies, was threatened with bankruptcy. Continental then sold off several profitable divisions, such as its leasing and credit card operations, to raise funds to cover bad-loan losses. In effect, Continental sold assets in order to stay alive. Ultimately, Continental was bailed out by the Federal Deposit Insurance Corporation and the Federal Reserve, which (1) arranged a $7.5 billion rescue package and (2) provided a blanket guarantee for all of Continental's $40 billion of deposits, which kept deposits in excess of $100,000 from fleeing the bank because of their uninsured status.

As the preceding examples illustrate, the reasons for divestitures vary widely. Sometimes the market feels more comfortable when firms "stick to their knitting"; the United Airlines divestiture is an example. Similarly, IU International demonstrates that there are cases in which a company becomes so complex and diverse that analysts and investors just do not understand it and consequently ignore it. Other companies need cash either to finance expansion in their primary business lines or to reduce a large debt burden, and divestitures can be used to raise this cash; Continental Bank illustrates this point. The actions listed also show that running a business is a dynamic process — conditions change, corporate strategies change in response, and as a result firms alter their asset portfolios by acquisitions and/or divestitures. Some divestitures, such as Woolworth's liquidation of its Woolco stores, occur in order to unload losing assets that would otherwise drag the company down, while the first AT&T example is one of the many instances in which a divestiture is the result of an antitrust settlement, and the second AT&T spin-off illustrates a situation where the parts of the business can operate more efficiently alone than together.

SELF-TEST QUESTIONS

What are some reasons that companies divest assets?

What are the three primary types of divestitures?

HOLDING COMPANIES

Holding companies date from 1889, when New Jersey became the first state to pass a law permitting corporations to be formed for the sole purpose of owning the stocks of other companies. Many of the advantages and disadvantages of holding companies are identical to those of large-scale operations already discussed in connection with mergers and consolidations. Whether a company is organized on a divisional basis or with subsidiaries kept as separate companies does not affect the basic reasons for conducting a large-scale, multiproduct, multiplant operation. However, as we show next, the use of holding companies to control large-scale operations has some distinct advantages and disadvantages.

ADVANTAGES OF HOLDING COMPANIES

1. **Control with fractional ownership.** Through a holding company operation, a firm may buy 5, 10, or 50 percent of the stock of another corporation. Such fractional ownership may be sufficient to give the acquiring company effective working control over the operations of the company in which it has acquired stock ownership. Working control is often considered to entail more than 25 percent of the common stock, but it can be as low as 10 percent if the stock is widely distributed. One financier says that the attitude of management is more important than the number of shares owned: "If management thinks you can control the company, then you do." In addition, control on a very slim margin can be held through relationships with large stockholders outside the holding company group.

2. **Isolation of risks.** Because the various operating companies in a holding company system are separate legal entities, the obligations of any one unit are separate from those of the other units. Therefore, catastrophic losses incurred by one unit of the holding company system are not translatable into claims on the assets of the other units. However, we should note that while this is a customary generalization, it is not always valid. First, the parent company may feel obligated to make good on the subsidiary's debts, even though it is not legally bound to do so, in order to keep its good name and to retain customers. Examples of this include American Express's payment of more than $100 million in connection with a swindle that was the responsibility of one of its subsidiaries, and United California Bank's coverage of its Swiss affiliate's multimillion-dollar fraud loss. Second, a parent company may feel obligated to supply capital to an affiliate in order to protect its initial investment; General Public Utilities' continued support of its subsidiaries' Three Mile Island nuclear plant is an example. And, third, when lending to one of the units of a holding company system, an astute loan officer may require a guarantee by the parent holding company. To some degree, therefore, the assets in the various elements of a holding company are not really separate. Still, a catastrophic loss, as could occur if a drug company's subsidiary distributed a batch of toxic medicine, may be avoided.[17]

DISADVANTAGES OF HOLDING COMPANIES

1. **Partial multiple taxation.** Provided the holding company owns at least 80 percent of a subsidiary's voting stock, the IRS permits the filing of consolidated returns, in which case dividends received by the parent are not taxed. However, if less than 80 percent of the stock is owned, then tax returns cannot be consolidated. Firms that own more than 20 percent but less than 80 percent of another corporation can deduct 80 percent of the dividends

---

[17]Note, though, that the parent company would still be held accountable for such losses if it were deemed to exercise operating control over the subsidiary. Thus, Union Carbide was held responsible for its subsidiary's Bhopal, India, disaster, and Dow Chemical may be held liable for Dow-Corning's multibillion dollar silicone breast implant product liability judgment.

received, while firms that own less than 20 percent may deduct only 70 percent of the dividends received. This partial double taxation somewhat offsets the benefits of holding company control with limited ownership, but whether the tax penalty is sufficient to offset other possible advantages is a matter that must be decided in individual situations.

2. **Ease of enforced dissolution.** It is relatively easy for the U.S. Department of Justice to require dissolution by disposal of stock ownership of a holding company operation it finds unacceptable. For instance, in the 1950s Du Pont was required to dispose of its 23 percent stock interest in General Motors Corporation, acquired in the early 1920s. Because there was no fusion between the corporations, there were no difficulties from an operating standpoint in requiring the separation of the two companies. However, if complete amalgamation had taken place, it would have been much more difficult to break up the company after so many years, and the likelihood of forced divestiture would have been reduced.

HOLDING COMPANIES AS A LEVERAGING DEVICE

The holding company vehicle has been used to obtain huge degrees of financial leverage. In the 1920s, several tiers of holding companies were established in the electric utility and other industries. In those days, an operating company at the bottom of the pyramid might have $100 million of assets, financed by $50 million of debt and $50 million of equity. Then, a first-tier holding company might own the stock of the operating firm as its only asset and be financed with $25 million of debt and $25 million of equity. A second-tier holding company, which owned the stock of the first-tier company, might be financed with $12.5 million of debt and $12.5 million of equity. Such systems were extended to five or six levels. With six holding companies, $100 million of operating assets could be controlled at the top by $0.78 million of equity, and the operating assets would have to provide enough cash income to support $99.22 million of debt. *Such a holding company system is highly leveraged — its consolidated debt ratio is 99.22 percent, even though each of the individual components has only a 50 percent debt/assets ratio.* Because of this consolidated leverage, even a small decline in profits at the operating company level could bring the whole system down like a house of cards. This situation existed in the electric utility industry in the 1920s, and the Depression of the 1930s wreaked havoc with the holding companies and led to federal legislation which constrained holding companies in that industry.

SELF-TEST QUESTIONS

What is a holding company?

What are some of the advantages of holding companies? What are some of the disadvantages?

Summary

This chapter included discussions of mergers, divestitures, holding companies, and LBOs. The key concepts covered are listed below:

■ A *merger* occurs when two firms combine to form a single company. The primary motives for mergers are (1) synergy, (2) tax considerations, (3) purchase of assets below their replacement costs, (4) diversification, and (5) gaining control over a larger enterprise.

■ Mergers can provide economic benefits through *economies of scale* or through *concentration of assets* in the hands of more efficient managers. However, mergers also have the potential for reducing competition, and for this reason they are carefully regulated by governmental agencies.

■ In most mergers, one company (the *acquiring firm*) initiates action to take over another (the *target firm*).

■ A *horizontal merger* occurs when two firms in the same line of business combine.

■ A *vertical merger* combines a firm with one of its customers or suppliers.

■ A *congeneric merger* involves firms in related industries, but for which no customer-supplier relationship exists.

■ A *conglomerate merger* occurs when firms in totally different industries combine.

■ In a *friendly merger,* the managements of both firms approve the merger, whereas in a *hostile merger,* the target firm's management opposes the merger.

■ An *operating merger* is one in which the operations of the two firms are combined. A *financial merger* is one in which the firms continue to operate separately, hence no operating economies are expected.

■ In a *merger analysis,* the key issues to be resolved are (1) the price to be paid for the target firm and (2) the employment/control situation.

■ Two methods are commonly used to determine the *value of the target firm:* (1) the *discounted cash flow (DCF)* method and (2) the *market multiple* method.

■ A *joint venture* is a *corporate alliance* in which two or more companies combine some of their resources to achieve a specific, limited objective.

■ A *divestiture* is the sale of some of a company's operating assets. A divestiture may involve (1) selling an operating unit to another firm, (2) *spinning off* a unit as a separate company, or (3) the outright *liquidation* of a unit's assets.

■ The *reasons for divestiture* include to settle antitrust suits, to clarify what a company actually does, to enable management to concentrate on a particular type of activity, and to raise capital needed to strengthen the corporation's core business.

■ A *holding company* is a corporation which owns sufficient stock in another firm to achieve working control of it. The holding company is also known as the *parent company,* and the companies which it controls are called *subsidiaries,* or *operating companies.*

■ Advantages to holding company operations include the following: (1) control can often be obtained for a smaller cash outlay, (2) risks may be segregated, and (3) regulated companies can separate regulated from unregulated assets.

■ Disadvantages to holding company operations include (1) tax penalties and (2) the fact that incomplete ownership, if it exists, can lead to control problems.

■ A *leveraged buyout (LBO)* is a transaction in which a firm's publicly owned stock is acquired in a mostly debt-financed tender offer, and a privately owned, highly leveraged firm results.   Often, the firm's own management initiates the LBO.

QUESTIONS

25-1   Define each of the following terms:
   a. Synergy
   b. Horizontal merger; vertical merger; congeneric merger; conglomerate merger
   c. Friendly merger; hostile merger; defensive merger
   d. Operating merger; financial merger
   e. White knight; white squire; poison pill; golden parachute
   f. Leveraged buyout
   g. Joint venture
   h. Divestiture; spin-off
   i. Holding company; operating company; parent company

25-2   The four economic classifications of mergers are (1) horizontal, (2) vertical, (3) congeneric, and (4) conglomerate. Discuss how each type of merger differs in (a) the likelihood of governmental intervention and (b) the possibilities for operating synergy.

25-3   Firm A wants to acquire Firm B. Firm B's management agrees that the merger is a good idea. Might a tender offer be used?

25-4   Distinguish between operating mergers and financial mergers.

25-5   Suppose a holding company has subsidiaries which have issued preferred stock and bonds to public investors (all of the subsidiaries' common stock is owned by the holding company). The holding company's major asset is its stock in its subsidiaries, but the parent company does own in its own right certain operating assets. The holding company also issues its own bonds and preferred stock.

   Given this information, discuss the relative riskiness of investments in the common, preferred, and bonds both of the holding company itself (the parent) and of the operating subsidiaries. Assume that all the operating assets are equally risky.

Two large, publicly owned firms are contemplating a merger. No operating synergy is expected. However, since returns on the two firms are not perfectly positively correlated, the standard deviation of earnings would be reduced for the combined corporation. One group of consultants argues that this risk reduction is sufficient grounds for the merger. Another group thinks this type of risk reduction is irrelevant because stockholders could themselves hold the stock of both companies and thus gain the risk reduction benefits without all the hassles and expenses of the merger. Whose position is correct?

PROBLEMS

SIMPLE MERGER ANALYSIS Mary's House of Beauty wishes to acquire Jane's Nail Emporium for $300,000. Mary expects the merger to provide incremental cash flows of about $55,000 a year for 10 years. She has also calculated her marginal cost of capital for this investment to be 12 percent. Conduct a capital budgeting analysis for Mary to determine whether she should purchase Jane's store.

MERGER ANALYSIS Mehran Electric Corporation is considering a merger with the Rodriguez Lamp Company. Rodriguez is a publicly traded company, and its current beta is 1.40. Rodriguez has barely been profitable, so it has paid only 20 percent in taxes over the last several years. Additionally, Rodriguez uses little debt, having a market value debt ratio of just 25 percent.

If the acquisition is made, Mehran plans to operate Rodriguez as a separate, wholly owned subsidiary. Mehran would pay taxes on a consolidated basis, and thus the federal-plus-state tax rate would increase to 40 percent. Additionally, Mehran would increase the debt capitalization in the Rodriguez subsidiary to a market value of 40 percent of assets. Mehran's acquisition department estimates that Rodriguez, if acquired, would produce the following net cash flows to Mehran's shareholders (in millions of dollars):

YEAR	NET CASH FLOW
1	$1.20
2	1.40
3	1.65
4	1.80
5 and beyond	Constant growth at 5%

These cash flows include all acquisition effects. Mehran's cost of equity is 16 percent, its beta is 1.0, and its cost of debt is 12 percent. The risk-free rate is 10 percent.

a. What discount rate should be used to discount the given cash flows?
b. What is the dollar value of Rodriguez to Mehran?
c. Rodriguez has 1.2 million common shares outstanding. What is the maximum price per share that Mehran should offer for Rodriguez? If the tender offer is accepted at this price, what would happen to Mehran's stock price?

SPREADSHEET APPLICATIONS

SPREADSHEET PROBLEM

T. S. Hawkey Inc., a large building materials manufacturer, is evaluating the possible acquisition of the Marvin Laurence Company, a small aluminum siding manufacturer. Hawkey's analysts project the following postmerger cash flows for Laurence (in thousands of dollars):

	1997	1998	1999	2000
Net sales	$250	$288	$312	$338
Selling and administrative expenses	25	31	38	40
Interest	12	15	16	18

Cost of goods sold as a percentage of sales (including depreciation): 65%
Terminal growth rate of cash flows available to Hawkey: 8%

If the acquisition is made, it will occur on January 1, 1997. All cash flows are assumed to occur at year end. Laurence's current market-determined beta is 1.50, but its investment bankers think that its beta would rise to 1.68 if the merger takes place. Depreciation-generated funds would be used to replace worn-out equipment, so they would not be available to Hawkey's shareholders. The risk-free rate is 8 percent, and the market risk premium is 6 percent. The postmerger tax rate would be 40 percent.

a. What is the appropriate discount rate for valuing the acquisition?
b. What is Laurence's terminal value? What is the value of the Laurence Company to Hawkey?
c. If sales in each year were $100,000 higher than the base case amounts, and if the cost of goods sold/sales ratio were 60 percent, what would Laurence be worth to Hawkey?
d. With sales and the cost of goods sold ratio at the Part c levels, what would Laurence's value be if its beta were 1.8, k_{RF} rose to 10 percent, and RP_M rose to 7 percent?
e. Leaving all values at the Part d levels, what would the value of the acquisition be if the terminal growth rate rose to 20 percent or dropped to 3 percent?

MINI CASE

The CompuMax Company, a regional computer retailer, is cash rich due to several consecutive good years. One of the possible uses for the excess funds is an acquisition. Pam Olson, a recent B-school graduate, has been asked to place a value on Pacific Computer Products Inc., a small mail order hardware and software company that sells nationwide.

Listed next are the estimates of Pacific's earnings potential which Pam developed (in millions of dollars):

	1997	1998	1999	2000
Net sales	$10.0	$20.0	$25.0	$30.0
Cost of goods sold	6.0	12.0	15.0	18.0
Selling/administrative expenses	1.0	1.5	2.0	2.0
Depreciation	2.0	4.0	5.0	6.0
Interest expense	0.5	1.0	1.2	1.5
Cash flow plow-back	1.0	2.5	3.0	4.0

The interest expense listed is the sum of interest (1) on Pacific's existing debt, (2) on new debt that CompuMax would issue to help finance the acquisition, and (3) on new debt expected to be issued over time to help finance expansion within the Pacific division. The cash flow plow-back represents depreciation and retained earnings which would be reinvested within the Pacific division to help finance its growth.

Pacific currently uses 20 percent debt financing and pays taxes at a 30 percent rate. The beta coefficients of the large mail order houses average 1.5. If the acquisition takes place, CompuMax would increase Pacific's debt ratio to 50 percent. Further, since CompuMax is highly profitable, taxes on the consolidated firm would be 40 percent.

Pam estimates the risk-free rate to be 10 percent, the market risk premium to be 5 percent, and the cash flow stream would grow at a constant 7 percent rate after 2000. CompuMax's management is new to the mergers game, so Pam asked you, her assistant, to answer some basic questions about mergers and perform the merger analysis. To structure the task, Pam developed the following questions:

a. Several reasons have been proposed to justify mergers. Among the more prominent are (1) tax considerations, (2) diversification, (3) control, (4) purchase of assets at below replacement cost, (5) breakup value, and (6) synergy. In general, which of the reasons are economically justifiable? Which are not? Explain.

b. Briefly describe the differences between a hostile merger and a friendly merger.

c. Use the data developed previously to construct Pacific's cash flow statements for 1997 through 2000. Why is interest expense deducted in merger cash flow statements whereas it is not normally deducted in capital budgeting cash flow analysis? Why are retentions deducted in the cash flow statement?

d. Conceptually, what is the appropriate discount rate to apply to the cash flows developed in Part c? What is the numerical estimate? How much faith can be placed on this estimate?

e. What is the estimated terminal value of the acquisition; that is, what is the estimated value of the Pacific Division's cash flows beyond 2000? What is the value of Pacific to CompuMax? Suppose another firm were evaluating Pacific as an acquisition candidate. Would they obtain the same value? Explain.

f. Assume that Pacific currently has 10 million shares outstanding. These shares are traded relatively infrequently, but the last trade, made several weeks ago, was at a price of $1.00 per share. Should CompuMax make an offer for Pacific? If so, how much should they offer per share?

g. Assume that publicly traded companies in Pacific's line of business have stock prices in the range of 4 to 5 times earnings before interest, taxes, depreciation, and amortization (EBITDA). Use the market multiple approach to value the target company.

h. There has been considerable research conducted to determine whether mergers really create value, and, if so, how this value is shared between the parties involved. What are the results of this research?

i. What merger-related activities are undertaken by investment bankers?

SELECTED ADDITIONAL REFERENCES AND CASES

Considerable empirical investigation has been conducted to determine whether stockholders of acquiring or acquired companies benefit most from corporate mergers. One of the classic works in this field is

Mandelker, Gershon, "Risk and Return: The Case of Merging Firms," *Journal of Financial Economics,* December 1974, 303–335.

Two of the more recent works are

Black, Bernard S., and Joseph A. Grundfest, "Shareholder Gains from Takeovers and Restructurings between 1981 and 1986: $162 Billion Is a Lot of Money," *Journal of Applied Corporate Finance,* Spring 1988, 5–15.

Jarrell, Greg A., and Annette B. Poulsen, "The Returns to Acquiring Firms in Tender Offers: Evidence from Three Decades," *Financial Management,* Autumn 1989, 12–19.

For some additional insights into merger returns, see

Elgers, Pieter T., and John J. Clark, "Merger Types and Shareholder Returns: Additional Evidence," *Financial Management,* Summer 1980, 66–72.

Mueller, Dennis C., "The Effects of Conglomerate Mergers," *Journal of Banking and Finance,* December 1977, 315–347.

Wansley, James W., William R. Lane, and Ho C. Yang, "Abnormal Returns to Acquired Firms by Type of Acquisition and Method of Payment," *Financial Management,* Autumn 1983, 16–22.

For an interesting test of the existence of synergy in mergers, see

Haugen, Robert A., and Terence C. Langetieg, "An Empirical Test for Synergism in Merger," *Journal of Finance,* September 1975, 1003–1014.

For more insights into the likelihood of acceptance of a cash tender offer, see

Hoffmeister, J. Ronald, and Edward A. Dyl, "Predicting Outcomes of Cash Tender Offers," *Financial Management,* Winter 1981, 50–58.

Some additional works on tender offers include

Dodd, Peter, and Richard Ruback, "Tender Offers and Stockholder Returns," *Journal of Financial Economics,* November 1977, 351–373.

Kummer, Donald R., and J. Ronald Hoffmeister, "Valuation Consequences of Cash Tender Offers," *Journal of Finance,* May 1978, 505–516.

The following article examines the effect of merger accounting on stock price:

Hong, Hai, Gershon Mandelker, and R. S. Kaplan, "Pooling versus Purchase: The Effects of Accounting for Mergers on Stock Prices," *Accounting Review,* January 1978, 31–47.

For a selection of articles on LBOs, see the Spring 1989 issue of the Journal of Applied Corporate Finance *and the Spring 1992 issue of* Financial Management.

The Summer 1989 issue of the Journal of Applied Corporate Finance *also focuses on mergers and acquisitions.*

For a selection of articles on LBOs, see the Spring 1989 issue of the Journal of Applied Corporate Finance.

For a very interesting discussion of many of the important merger issues, see

"A Discussion of Mergers and Acquisitions," *Midland Corporate Finance Journal,* Summer 1983, 21–47.

Other recent articles that pertain to this chapter include the following:

Baker, George P., "Beatrice: A Study in the Creation and Destruction of Value," *Journal of Finance,* July 1992, 1081–1119.

Baker, George P., and Karen H. Wruck, "Lessons from a Middle Market LBO: The Case of O. M. Scott," *Journal of Applied Corporate Finance,* Spring 1991, 46–58.

Eckbo, B. Espen, "Mergers and the Value of Antitrust Deterrence," *Journal of Finance,* July 1992, 1005–1029.

Ezzell, John R., H. Christine Hsu, and James A. Miles, "An Analysis of Regulated Rates of Return for Wholly Owned Subsidiaries," *Journal of Financial Research,* Summer 1991, 167–180.

Kaplan, Steven, and Michael S. Weisbach, "The Success of Acquisitions: Evidence from Divestitures," *Journal of Finance,* March 1992, 107–138.

Mitchell, Mark L., and Kenneth Lehn, "Do Bad Bidders Become Good Targets?" *Journal of Applied Corporate Finance,* Summer 1990, 60–69.

Mohan, Nancy, M. Fall Ainina, Daniel Kaufman, and Bernard J. Winger, "Acquisition/Divestiture Valuation Practices in Major U.S. Firms," *Financial Practice and Education,* Spring 1991, 73–81.

Morck, Randall, Andrei Shleifer, and Robert W. Vishny, "Do Managerial Objectives Drive Bad Acquisitions?" *Journal of Finance,* March 1990, 31–48.

Romano, Roberta, "Rethinking Takeover Regulations," *Journal of Applied Corporate Finance,* Fall 1992, 47–57.

Weaver, Samuel C., Robert S. Harris, Daniel W. Bielinski, and Kenneth F. MacKenzie, "Merger and Acquisition Valuation," *Financial Management,* Summer 1991, 85–96.

Wruck, Karen H., "What Really Went Wrong at Revco?" *Journal of Applied Corporate Finance,* Summer 1991, 79–92.

The following cases in the Cases in Financial Management: Dryden Request *series illustrate merger analysis:*

Case 40, "Nina's Fashions, Inc.," Case 40A, "Nero's Pasta, Inc.," and Case 40B, "Computer Concepts/CompuTech," which focus on merger valuation.

MULTINATIONAL FINANCIAL MANAGEMENT

From the end of World War II until the 1970s, the United States dominated the world economy, but that situation no longer exists. Raw materials, finished goods, services, and money flow freely across most national boundaries, as do innovative ideas and new technologies. World-class U.S. companies are making breakthroughs in foreign labs, obtaining capital from foreign investors, and putting foreign employees on the fast track to the top. Dozens of top U.S. manufacturers, including Dow Chemical, Colgate-Palmolive, Gillette, Hewlett-Packard, and Xerox, sell more of their products outside the United States than they do at home. Service firms are not far behind, as Citicorp, Disney, McDonald's, and Time Warner all receive more than 20 percent of their revenues from foreign sales.

The trend is even more pronounced in profits. In recent years, Coca-Cola and many other companies have made more money in the Pacific Rim and western Europe than in the United States. As U.S. companies begin to reap half or more of their sales and profits from abroad, they are finding it useful to blend into the foreign landscape in order to win product acceptance and avoid political problems.

At the same time, foreign-based multinationals are arriving on American shores in ever greater numbers. Sweden's ABB, the Netherlands's Philips, France's Thomson, and Japan's Fujitsu and Honda are all waging campaigns to be identified as American companies that employ Americans, transfer technology to America, and help the U.S. trade balance and overall economic health. Few Americans know or care that Thomson owns the RCA and General Electric names in consumer electronics or that Philips owns Magnavox.

This chapter was coauthored by Professor Roy Crum of the University of Florida.

The emergence of "world companies" raises a host of questions for governments seeking to shape their nations' economic destinies. For example, should domestic firms be favored, or does it make no difference what a company's nationality is as long as it provides domestic jobs? Should a company make an effort to keep jobs in its home country, or should it produce where total production costs are lowest? What nation controls the technology developed by a multinational corporation, particularly if the technology can be used in defense applications? What obligations does a multinational company headquartered in a given country have to adhere to rules imposed by its home country with respect to its operations outside the home country? And if a U.S. firm such as Xerox produces copiers in Japan and then ships them to the United States, should they be reflected in the trade deficit in the same way as Toyotas imported from Japan? Keep these questions in mind as you read this chapter. At the end, you should have a better appreciation of both the problems facing governments and the unique difficulties encountered by financial managers of multinational companies.

Managers of multinational companies face a wide range of issues that are not present when a company operates in a single country. In this chapter, we highlight the key differences between multinational and domestic corporations, and we discuss the impact these differences have on the financial management of multinational businesses.

MULTINATIONAL, OR GLOBAL, CORPORATIONS

The term *multinational,* or *global, corporation* is used to describe a firm that operates in an integrated fashion in two or more countries. During the period since World War II, a new and fundamentally different form of international commercial activity has developed, and this has greatly increased worldwide economic and political interdependence. Rather than merely buying resources from foreign concerns, multinational firms now make direct investments in fully integrated operations, from extraction of raw materials, through the manufacturing process, to distribution to consumers throughout the world. Today, multinational corporate networks control a large and growing share of the world's technological, marketing, and productive resources.

Companies, both U.S. and foreign, go "international" for six primary reasons.

1. **To seek new markets.** After a company has saturated its home market, growth opportunities are often better in foreign markets. Thus, such home-grown firms as Coca-Cola and McDonald's have aggressively expanded into overseas markets, and foreign firms such as Sony and Toshiba now dominate the U.S. consumer electronics market.

2. **To seek raw materials.** It is not surprising that U.S. oil companies such as Exxon have major subsidiaries around the world to ensure access to the basic resources needed to sustain the company's primary business line.

3. **To seek new technology.** No single nation holds a commanding advantage in all technologies, so companies are scouring the globe for leading scientific and design ideas. For example, Xerox has introduced more than 80 different office copiers in the United States that were engineered and built by its Japanese joint venture, Fuji Xerox. Similarly, versions of the superconcentrated detergent that Procter & Gamble first formulated in Japan in response to a rival's product are now being marketed under the Ariel name in Europe and under the Cheer and Tide labels in the United States.

4. **To seek production efficiency.** Companies in high-production-cost countries are shifting production to low-cost countries. For example, GE has production and assembly plants in Mexico, South Korea, and Singapore, and Japanese manufacturers are shifting some of their production to lower-cost countries in the Pacific Rim. Even BMW and Mercedes-Benz, in response to high production costs in Germany, have built assembly plants in the United States. The ability to shift production from country to country has important implications for labor costs in all countries. For example, when Xerox threatened to move its copier rebuilding work to Mexico, its union in Rochester, New York, agreed to work rule and productivity improvements that kept the operation in the United States. Some multinational companies make decisions almost daily on where to shift production. When Dow Chemical saw European demand for a certain solvent declining, the company scaled back production at a German plant and shifted it to another chemical which had previously been imported from the United States. Relying on complex computer models for making such decisions, Dow runs its plants at high capacity and thus keeps capital costs down.

5. **To avoid political and regulatory hurdles.** The primary motivation for Japanese auto companies to produce in the United States was to get around U.S. import quotas. Now Honda, Nissan, Toyota, Mazda, and Mitsubishi are all assembling automobiles or trucks in the United States. One of the factors that prompted U.S. pharmaceutical maker SmithKline and Britain's Beecham to merge was that they wanted to avoid licensing and regulatory delays in their largest markets, western Europe and the United States. Now SmithKline Beecham can identify itself as an inside player in both Europe and the United States. Finally, when Germany's BASF launched biotechnology research at home, it confronted legal and political challenges from the environmentally conscious Green movement. In response, BASF shifted its cancer and immune system research to two laboratories in Boston suburbs. This location is attractive not only because of its large number of engineers and scientists but also because the Boston area has better resolved controversies involving safety, animal rights, and the environment. "We decided it would be better to have the laboratories located where we have fewer insecurities about what will happen in the future," said Rolf-Dieter Acker, BASF's director of biotechnology research.

6. **To diversify.** By establishing worldwide production facilities and markets, firms can cushion the impact of adverse economic trends in any single country.

For example, General Motors softened the blow of poor sales in the United States during the 1990–1991 recession with strong sales by its European subsidiaries. In general, geographic diversification works because the economic ups and downs of different countries are not perfectly positively correlated.

The past decade has seen an increasing amount of investment in the United States by foreign corporations. This "reverse" investment, which is of concern to U.S. government officials, has actually been growing at a higher rate in the past few years than has U.S. investment abroad. These trends are important because of their implications for eroding the traditional doctrine of independence and self-reliance that has always been a hallmark of U.S. policy. Just as U.S. corporations with extensive overseas operations are said to use their economic power to exert substantial economic and political influence over host governments in many parts of the world, it is feared that foreign corporations are gaining similar sway over U.S. policy. These developments suggest an increasing degree of mutual influence and interdependence among business enterprises and nations, to which the United States is not immune.

The world economy is quite fluid. Here are a few of the recent events which have dramatically changed the international financial environment:

1. The disintegration of the former Soviet Union and the movement toward market economies in the newly formed countries have created a vast new market for international commerce.

2. The reunification of Germany, coupled with the collapse of communism in eastern Europe, has created significant new opportunities for foreign investment.

3. The European Community and the European Free Trade Association have created a "borderless" region where people, capital, goods, and services move freely among the 19 nations without the burden of tariffs. Negotiations are also under way to create a single "Eurocurrency," which would greatly simplify economic exchange among the participating countries.

4. The North American Free Trade Agreement (NAFTA) has moved the economies of the United States, Canada, and Mexico much closer together, and made them more interdependent.

5. In recent years, U.S. bank regulations have been loosened dramatically. One key deregulatory feature was the removal of interest rate ceilings, thus allowing banks to attract foreign deposits by raising rates. Another key feature was the removal of barriers to entry by foreign banks, which resulted in more cross-border banking transactions. Still, U.S. commercial and investment banks do not have as much freedom as foreign banks, which has led many U.S. banks to establish subsidiaries in Europe that can offer a wider range of services, hence increase global competition in the financial services industry.

SELF-TEST QUESTIONS | What is a multinational corporation?
Why do companies "go international"?

MULTINATIONAL VERSUS DOMESTIC FINANCIAL MANAGEMENT

In theory, the concepts and procedures discussed in the first 25 chapters of the text are valid for both domestic and multinational operations. However, six major factors distinguish financial management in firms operating entirely within a single country from that in firms that operate in several different countries:

1. **Different currency denominations.** Cash flows in various parts of a multinational corporate system will be denominated in different currencies. Hence, an analysis of exchange rates, and the effects of fluctuating currency values, must be included in all financial analyses.

2. **Economic and legal ramifications.** Each country in which the firm operates will have its own unique economic and legal systems, and these differences can cause significant problems when the corporation tries to coordinate and control the worldwide operations of its subsidiaries. For example, differences in tax laws among countries can cause a given economic transaction to have strikingly dissimilar after-tax consequences, depending on where the transaction occurred. Similarly, differences in legal systems of host nations, such as the Common Law of Great Britain versus the French Civil Law, complicate many matters, from the simple recording of a business transaction to the role played by the judiciary in resolving conflicts. Such differences can restrict multinational corporations' flexibility to deploy resources as they wish, and can even make procedures that are required in one part of the company illegal in another part. These differences also make it difficult for executives trained in one country to operate effectively in another.

3. **Language differences.** The ability to communicate is critical in all business transactions, and here U.S. citizens are often at a disadvantage because we are generally fluent only in English, while European and Japanese businesspeople are usually fluent in several languages, including English. Thus, they can invade our markets more easily than we can penetrate theirs. This factor cannot be stressed too strongly.

4. **Cultural differences.** Even within geographic regions that are considered relatively homogeneous, different countries have unique cultural heritages that shape values and influence the conduct of business. Multinational corporations find that matters such as defining the appropriate goals of the firm, attitudes toward risk taking, dealings with employees, the ability to curtail unprofitable operations, and so on, can vary dramatically from one country to the next.

5. **Role of governments.** Most decision models in finance assume the existence of a competitive marketplace in which the terms of trade are determined by the participants. The government, through its power to establish basic ground rules, is involved in this process, but its participation is minimal. Thus, the market provides both the primary barometer of success and the indicator of the actions that must be taken to remain competitive. This view of the process is reasonably correct for the United States and Western Europe, but it does not accurately describe the situation in most of the world.

Frequently, the terms under which companies compete, the actions that must be taken or avoided, and the terms of trade on various transactions are determined not in the marketplace but by direct negotiation between the host government and the multinational corporation. This is essentially a political process, and it must be treated as such. Thus, our traditional financial models have to be recast to include political and other noneconomic facets of the decision.

6. **Political risk.** A nation is free to place constraints on the transfer of corporate resources and even to expropriate without compensation the assets of a firm. This is *political risk,* and it tends to be largely a given rather than a variable that can be changed by negotiation. Political risk varies from country to country, and it must be addressed explicitly in any financial analysis. Another aspect of political risk is terrorism against U.S. firms or executives abroad. For example, U.S. executives have been kidnapped and held for ransom in several South American countries.

These six factors complicate financial management within multinational firms, and they increase the risks faced by the firms involved. However, prospects for high profits, diversification opportunities, and other factors often make it worthwhile for firms to accept these risks and learn how to manage them.

SELF-TEST   Identify and briefly explain six major factors that complicate financial management
QUESTION   in multinational firms.

EXCHANGE RATES

An *exchange rate* specifies the number of units of a given currency that can be purchased for one unit of another currency. Exchange rates appear in the financial sections of newspapers each day. Selected rates from a recent issue of *The Wall Street Journal* are given in Table 26-1. The values shown in Column 1 are the number of U.S. dollars required to purchase one unit of foreign currency; this is called a *direct quotation.* Thus, the direct U.S. dollar quotation for the German mark is $0.7110, because one German mark could be bought for 71.10 cents. The exchange rates given in Column 2 represent the number of units of foreign currency that can be purchased for one U.S. dollar; these are called *indirect quotations.* The indirect quotation for the German mark is M1.4065. (The "M" stands for *Mark;* it is equivalent to the symbol "$.") Normal practice in the United States is to use indirect quotations (Column 2) for all currencies other than British pounds, for which direct quotations are given. Thus, we speak of the pound as "selling at $1.59" but of the mark as "being at 1.40."

It is also a universal convention on the world's foreign currency exchanges to state all exchange rates except British pounds on a "dollar basis" — that is, as the foreign currency price of one U.S. dollar as reported in Table 26-1, Column 2. Thus, in all currency trading centers, whether in New York, Frankfurt, London, Tokyo, or anywhere else, the exchange rate for the German mark would be displayed as M1.4065.

	DIRECT QUOTATION: U.S. DOLLARS REQUIRED TO BUY ONE UNIT OF FOREIGN CURRENCY (1)	INDIRECT QUOTATION: NUMBER OF UNITS OF FOREIGN CURRENCY PER U.S. DOLLAR (2)
British pound	$1.5910	0.6285
Canadian dollar	0.7069	1.4147
Dutch guilder	0.6338	1.5778
French franc	0.19996	5.0010
German mark	0.7110	1.4065
Italian lira	0.0005944	1,682.50
Japanese yen	0.011007	90.85
Spanish peseta	0.007731	129.35
Swiss franc	0.8523	1.1734

ILLUSTRATIVE EXCHANGE RATES — **TABLE 26-1**

NOTE: Column 2 equals 1.0 divided by Column 1. However, rounding differences do occur.
SOURCE: *The Wall Street Journal*, March 14, 1995.

This convention eliminates confusion when comparing quotations from one trading center with those from another.

We can use the data in Table 26-1 to show how one works with exchange rates. Suppose a U.S. tourist on holiday flies from New York to London, then to Paris, then on to Munich, and finally back to New York. When she arrives at London's Heathrow Airport, she goes to the bank to check the foreign exchange listing. The rate she observes for U.S. dollars is $1.5910; this means that £1 will cost her $1.5910. Assume that she exchanges $2,000 for $2,000/$1.5910 = £1,257.07 and enjoys a week's vacation in London, spending £757.07 while there.

At the end of the week she travels to Dover to catch the Hovercraft to Calais on the coast of France and realizes that she needs to exchange her 500 remaining British pounds for French francs. However, what she sees on the board is the direct quotation between pounds and dollars ($1.5910) and the indirect quotation between francs and dollars (FF5.0010). (For our purposes, we assume that the exchange rates in effect at the start of the trip remain in effect throughout our example. This is unrealistic for reasons explained later in this chapter.) The exchange rate between pounds and francs is called a *cross rate,* and it is computed as follows:

$$\text{Cross rate} = \frac{\text{Dollars}}{\text{Pound}} \times \frac{\text{Francs}}{\text{Dollar}} = \frac{\text{Francs}}{\text{Pound}}$$

$$= 1.5910 \text{ dollars per pound} \times 5.0010 \text{ francs per dollar}$$

$$= 7.9566 \text{ francs per pound.}$$

Therefore, for every British pound she would receive 7.9566 French francs, so she would receive 7.9566 × 500 = 3,978.30 ≈ 3,978 francs.

When she finishes touring in France and arrives in Germany, the American tourist again needs to determine a cross rate, this time between French francs and German marks. The dollar-basis quotes she sees, as shown in Table 26-1, are FF5.0010 per dollar and M1.4065 per dollar. To find the cross rate, she must divide the two dollar-basis rates:

$$\text{Cross rate} = \frac{\dfrac{\text{Marks}}{\text{Dollar}}}{\dfrac{\text{Francs}}{\text{Dollar}}} = \frac{\text{Marks}}{\text{Franc}}$$

$$= \frac{\text{M1.4065 per \$}}{\text{FF5.0010 per \$}} = \text{M0.2812 marks per franc.}$$

Then, if she had FF3,000 remaining, she could exchange them for 0.2812 × 3,000 = M843.60, or about 844 marks.

Finally, when her vacation ends and she returns to New York, the quotation she sees is M1.4065, which tells her that she can buy 1.4065 marks for a dollar. She now holds 50 marks, so she wants to know how many U.S. dollars she will receive for her marks. First, she must find the reciprocal of the quoted indirect rate,

$$\frac{1}{\text{M1.4065}} = \$0.7110,$$

which is the direct quote shown in Table 26-1, Column 1. Then she will end up with

$$\$0.7110 \times 50 = \$35.55.$$

In this example, we made three very strong and generally incorrect assumptions. First, we assumed that our traveler had to calculate the appropriate cross rates. For retail transactions, it is customary to display the cross rates directly instead of a series of dollar rates. Second, we assumed that exchange rates remain constant over time. Actually, exchange rates vary every day, often dramatically. We will have more to say about exchange rate fluctuations in the next section. Finally, we assumed that there were no transactions costs involved in exchanging currencies. In reality, small retail exchange transactions such as those in our example usually involve fixed and/or sliding scale fees that can easily consume five or more percent of the transaction amount.

SELF-TEST QUESTIONS

What is an exchange rate?

Explain the difference between direct and indirect quotations.

What is a cross rate?

THE INTERNATIONAL MONETARY SYSTEM

From the end of World War II until August 1971, the world was on a *fixed exchange rate system* administered by the International Monetary Fund (IMF). Under this system, the U.S. dollar was linked to gold ($35 per ounce), and other currencies were then tied to the dollar. Exchange rates between other currencies and the dollar were controlled within narrow limits but then adjusted periodically. For example, in 1964 the British pound was adjusted to $2.80 for £1, with a 1 percent permissible fluctuation about this rate.

Fluctuations in exchange rates occur because of changes in the supply of and demand for dollars, pounds, and other currencies. These supply and demand changes have two primary sources. First, changes in the demand for currencies depend on changes in imports and exports of goods and services. For example, U.S. importers must buy British pounds to pay for British goods, whereas British importers must buy U.S. dollars to pay for U.S. goods. If U.S. imports from Great Britain exceeded U.S. exports to Great Britain, there would be a greater demand for pounds than for dollars, and this would drive up the price of the pound relative to that of the dollar. In terms of Table 26-1, the dollar cost of a pound might rise from $1.5910 to $2.0000. The U.S. dollar would be said to be *depreciating,* because a dollar would now be worth fewer pounds, whereas the pound would be *appreciating.* In this example, the root cause of the change would be the U.S. *trade deficit* with Great Britain. Of course, if U.S. exports to Great Britain were greater than U.S. imports from Great Britain, Great Britain would have a trade deficit with the United States.[1]

Changes in the demand for a currency, hence exchange rate fluctuations, also depend on capital movements. For example, suppose interest rates in Great Britain were higher than those in the United States. To take advantage of the high British interest rates, U.S. banks, corporations, and even sophisticated individuals would buy pounds with dollars and then use those pounds to purchase high-yielding British securities. These purchases would tend to drive up the price of pounds.[2]

Before August 1971, exchange rate fluctuations were kept within the narrow 1 percent limit by regular intervention of the British government in the market. When

---

[1]If the dollar value of the pound moved up from $1.59 to $2.00, this increase in the value of the pound would mean that British goods would now be more expensive in the United States. For example, a box of candy costing £1 in England would rise in price in the United States from about $1.59 to $2.00. Conversely, U.S. goods would become cheaper in England. For example, the British could now buy goods worth $2.00 for £1, whereas before the exchange rate change £1 would buy merchandise worth only $1.59. These price changes would, of course, tend to *reduce* British exports and *increase* imports, and this, in turn, would lower the exchange rate, because people in the United States and other nations would be buying fewer pounds to pay for English goods. Before 1971, the 1 percent limit severely constrained the market's ability to reach an equilibrium between trade balances and exchange rates.

[2]Such capital inflows would also tend to drive down British interest rates. If rates were high in the first place because of efforts by the British monetary authorities to curb inflation, the international currency flows would tend to thwart that effort. This is one of the reasons domestic and international economies are so closely linked.

A good example of this occurred during the summer of 1981. In an effort to curb inflation, the Federal Reserve Board helped push U.S. interest rates to record levels. This, in turn, caused a flow of capital from European nations to the United States. The Europeans were suffering from a severe recession and wanted to keep interest rates down in order to stimulate investment, but U.S. policy made this difficult because of international capital flows. Just the opposite occurred in 1992, when the Fed drove short-term rates down to record lows in the United States to promote growth, while Germany and most other European countries pushed their rates higher to combat the inflationary pressures of reunification. Thus, investment in the United States was dampened as investors moved their money overseas to capture higher interest rates.

the value of the pound was falling, the Bank of England would step in and buy pounds to push up their price, offering gold or foreign currencies in exchange. Conversely, when the pound rate was too high, the Bank of England would sell pounds. The central banks of other countries operated similarly.

Of course, a central bank's ability to control its exchange rate was limited by its supply of gold and foreign currencies. With the approval of the IMF, a country could *devalue* its currency—which means to officially lower its value relative to other currencies—if it experienced persistent difficulty over a long period in preventing its exchange rate from falling below the lower limit, and if its central bank was running out of the gold and other currencies that could be used to buy its own currency and thus prop up its price. For just these reasons the British pound was devalued from $2.80 per pound to $2.50 per pound in 1967. This lowered the price of British goods in the United States and elsewhere and raised the prices of foreign goods in Britain, thus reducing the British trade deficit that had been putting pressure on the pound in the first place. Conversely, a nation with an export surplus and a strong currency might *revalue* its currency upward, as West Germany did on several occasions.

Devaluations and revaluations occurred only rarely before 1971. They were usually accompanied by severe international financial repercussions, partly because nations tended to postpone needed measures until economic pressures had built up to explosive proportions. For this and other reasons, the old international monetary system came to a dramatic end in the early 1970s, when the U.S. dollar, the foundation upon which all other currencies were anchored, was cut loose from the gold standard and, in effect, allowed to "float."

The United States and other major trading nations currently operate under a system of *floating exchange rates,* whereby currency prices are allowed to seek their own levels without much governmental intervention. The central bank of each country does intervene to some extent, buying and selling its currency to smooth out exchange rate fluctuations, and there have been agreements by groups of countries to keep the relative values of their currencies within a predetermined range.

Each central bank also tries to keep its average exchange rate at a level deemed desirable by its government's economic policy. This is important, because exchange rates have a profound effect on the levels of imports and exports, which in turn influence the level of domestic employment. For example, if a country is having a problem with unemployment, its central bank might encourage a *decline* in the value of its currency. This would cause its goods to be cheaper in world markets and thus stimulate exports, production, and domestic employment. Conversely, the central bank of a country that is operating at full capacity and experiencing inflation might try to raise the value of its currency to reduce exports and increase imports. Under the current floating rate system, however, such intervention can affect the situation only temporarily, because market forces will prevail in the long run.

Exchange rate fluctuations can have a profound impact on international monetary transactions. For example, in 1985 it cost Honda Motors 2,380,000 yen to build a particular model in Japan and ship it to the United States. The model carried a U.S. sticker price of $12,000. Since the $12,000 sales price was the equivalent of (238 yen per dollar)($12,000) = 2,856,000 yen, the automaker had built a 20 percent markup into the U.S. sales price. However, three years later the dollar had depreciated to 128 yen. Now if the model still sold for $12,000, the yen return to Honda would be only (128 yen per dollar)($12,000) = 1,536,000 yen, and the automaker would be losing about 35 percent on each auto sold. Even though U.S. prices held firm, the 46 percent depreciation of the dollar against the yen turned a healthy profit into a loss. In fact, for Honda to maintain its 20 percent markup, the model would have to sell in the United States for 2,856,000 yen/128 yen per dollar = $22,312.50. This situation, which had grown even worse by 1996, led Honda to build its most popular model, the Accord, in Marysville, Ohio.

The inherent volatility of exchange rates under a floating system increases the uncertainty of the cash flows for a multinational corporation. Because these cash flows are generated in many parts of the world, they are denominated in many different currencies. Since exchange rates can change, the dollar-equivalent value of a company's consolidated cash flows can also fluctuate. For example, Toyota estimates that each one-yen drop in the dollar reduces its annual net income by about 10 billion yen. This is known as *exchange rate risk,* and it is a major factor differentiating the multinational corporation from a purely domestic one. However, there are numerous ways for a multinational corporation to manage and limit its exchange rate risk, and several of them are discussed in the next section.

Before closing our discussion of the international monetary system, we should note that not all currencies are *convertible.* A currency is convertible when the nation which issued the currency allows it to be traded in the currency markets and is willing to redeem it at market rates. This means that, except for limited central bank influence, the issuing government loses control over the value of its currency. Lack of convertibility creates major problems for international trade. For example, consider the situation faced by Pepsico when it wanted to open a chain of Pizza Hut restaurants in the Soviet Union. The Russian ruble is not convertible, so Pepsico could not take the profits from its restaurants out of the Soviet Union in the form of dollars. There was no mechanism to exchange the rubles it earned in Russia for dollars, so the investment in the Soviet Union was essentially worthless to the U.S. parent. However, Pepsico arranged to use the ruble profit from the restaurants to buy Russian vodka, which it then shipped to the United States and sold for dollars. Pepsico managed to work things out, but lack of convertibility significantly inhibits the ability of a country to attract foreign investment.

What is the difference between a fixed exchange rate system and a floating rate system? Which system is better? Explain.

What does it mean to say that the dollar is depreciating with respect to the British pound? For a U.S. consumer of British goods, would this be good or bad? How could changes in consumption arrest the decline of the dollar?

What is a convertible currency?

SELF-TEST QUESTIONS

TRADING IN FOREIGN EXCHANGE

Importers, exporters, and tourists, as well as governments, buy and sell currencies in the foreign exchange market. For example, when a U.S. trader imports automobiles from Germany, payment will probably be made in German marks. The importer buys marks (through its bank) in the foreign exchange market, much as one buys common stocks on the New York Stock Exchange or pork bellies on the Chicago Mercantile Exchange. However, whereas stock and commodity exchanges have organized trading floors, the foreign exchange market consists of a network of brokers and banks based in New York, London, Tokyo, and other financial centers. Most buy and sell orders are conducted by computer and telephone.[3]

Spot Rates and Forward Rates

The exchange rates shown earlier in Table 26-1 are known as *spot rates,* which means the rate paid for delivery of the currency "on the spot" or, in reality, no more than two days after the day of the trade. For most of the world's major currencies, it is also possible to buy (or sell) currencies for delivery at some agreed-upon future date, usually 30, 90, or 180 days from the day the transaction is negotiated. This rate is known as the *forward exchange rate.* For example, if a U.S. firm must make payment to a Japanese firm in 30 days, the U.S. firm's treasurer can buy Japanese yen today for delivery in 30 days, paying the 30-day forward rate of $0.0110 per Japanese yen (which equals 90.53 yen per dollar). Forward rates are analogous to futures prices on commodity exchanges, where contracts are drawn up for wheat or corn to be delivered at agreed-upon prices at some future date. The contract is signed today, and the future dollar cost of the Japanese yen is then known with certainty. Purchase of a forward contract is one technique for eliminating the volatility of future cash flows caused by fluctuations in exchange rates. This technique, which is called "hedging," will be discussed in more detail shortly.

Recent forward rates for 30-, 90-, and 180-day delivery, along with the current spot rates for some commonly traded currencies, are given in Table 26-2. If one can obtain *more* of the foreign currency for a dollar in the forward than in the spot market, the forward currency is less valuable than the spot currency, and the forward currency is said to be selling at a *discount.* Thus, because 1 dollar could buy 0.6285 British pounds in the spot market but 0.6306 pounds in the 180-day forward market, forward pounds sell at a discount as compared with spot pounds. Conversely, if a dollar would buy *fewer* units of a currency in the forward than in the spot market, the forward currency is worth more dollars than the spot currency, and the forward currency is said to be selling at a *premium.* We see in Table 26-2 that Japanese yen and German marks were selling at a premium.

Hedging in the Foreign Exchange Markets

Individuals and corporations can buy or sell forward currencies as a means of *hedging exchange rate exposure.* For example, suppose that on March 13, 1995, a U.S. firm buys televisions from a Japanese manufacturer for 100 million Japanese yen. Payment is to be made in Japanese yen 90 days after the goods are shipped, or on

---

[3]For a more detailed explanation of exchange rate determination and operations of the foreign exchange market, see Mark Eaker, Frank Fabozzi, and Dwight Grant, *International Corporate Finance* (Ft. Worth, Tex.: Dryden Press, 1996).

		FORWARD RATES			
SELECTED SPOT AND FORWARD EXCHANGE RATES, MARCH 13, 1995 (NUMBER OF UNITS OF FOREIGN CURRENCY PER U.S. DOLLAR) TABLE 26-2					
	SPOT RATE	30 DAYS	90 DAYS	180 DAYS	FORWARD RATE AT A PREMIUM OR DISCOUNT
British pound	0.6285	0.6287	0.6291	0.6306	Discount
Japanese yen	90.85	90.53	89.92	88.89	Premium
German mark	1.4065	1.4049	1.4022	1.3980	Premium

NOTES:
a. These are representative quotes as provided by a sample of New York banks. Forward rates for other currencies and for other lengths of time can often be negotiated.
b. When it takes more units of a foreign currency to buy one dollar in the future, the value of the foreign currency is less in the forward market than in the spot market, hence the forward rate is at a *discount* to the spot rate.
SOURCE: *The Wall Street Journal,* March 14, 1995.

June 12, so the Japanese firm is extending trade credit for 90 days. The Japanese yen has been strong recently, and the U.S. company is apprehensive that the dollar will weaken even more because of large trade deficits. If the Japanese yen appreciates rapidly, more dollars will be required to buy the 100 million yen, and the profits on the television sets will be lost. Still, the U.S. firm does not want to forgo 90 days of free trade credit by paying cash. It can take the trade credit and protect itself by purchasing 100 million Japanese yen for delivery in 90 days. The 90-day rate is 89.92 yen, so the dollar cost is 100,000,000/89.92 = $1,112,100. When payment comes due, regardless of the spot rate on that day, the U.S. firm can obtain the needed Japanese yen at the agreed-upon price of $1,112,100. The U.S. firm is said to have *covered* its trade payables with a *forward market hedge.*

Note that it would cost the firm only 100,000,000/90.85 = $1,100,715 to buy the yen on the spot market, but it would effectively lose its trade credit, so it must decide which course of action has the greatest net benefit, including all costs involved. For example, there are commissions that must be paid to exchange the currencies on the spot market or to purchase the forward contract. Also, if the yen weakens against the dollar over the next 90 days, the firm would have been better off had it waited and bought the yen in the spot market when the payment would become due.

The forward market permits multinational firms to transfer exchange rate risk to professional risk takers, for a price. Forward contracts can be written in any amount, for any length of time, and between any two currencies as long as the two parties to the contract are in agreement. Some forward contracts are entered into directly by individuals or firms without going through an intermediary. Usually, however, forward contracts are negotiated between banks and their clients and are tailored to the specific needs of the client.

As an alternative to forward contracts, which tend to be specialized as opposed to standardized, the Chicago Mercantile Exchange opened its International Monetary Market (IMM) currency futures market in 1972. The IMM currently offers contracts on the British pound, Canadian dollar, German mark, Japanese yen, Swiss franc, and Australian dollar. Because an organized market exists for futures contracts, they can be executed more rapidly and less expensively than forward contracts can be negotiated. However, futures contracts are limited to a few currencies, and only a limited number of fixed maturity dates are available.

Firms engaged in international trade can hedge with futures or with forward contracts. When hedging with futures contracts, losses on trade transactions are offset by gains on the futures position. When hedging with forward contracts, the currency is normally delivered for use in the trade transaction. Currently, dollar volume in the forward market exceeds volume in the futures market, because most large contracts take place in the forward market. However, more and more small firms that do not have transactions large enough for the forward market are now using the currency futures market to reduce exchange rate risk.

SELF-TEST QUESTIONS

Differentiate between spot and forward exchange rates.

Briefly explain what it means for a forward currency to sell at a discount, and at a premium.

What does "hedging exchange rate exposure" mean? Explain why a firm might wish to do this and how it might be done.

INFLATION, INTEREST RATES, AND EXCHANGE RATES

Relative inflation rates, or the rates of inflation in foreign countries compared with that in the home country, have many implications for multinational financial decisions. Obviously, relative inflation rates will greatly influence future production costs at home and abroad. Equally important, they have a dominant influence on relative interest rates and exchange rates. Both of these factors influence the methods chosen by multinational corporations for financing their foreign investments, and both have a notable effect on the profitability of foreign investments.

The currencies of countries with higher inflation rates than that of the United States tend, by definition, to depreciate over time against the dollar. Some countries for which this has been the case include France, Italy, Mexico, and all the South American nations. On the other hand, the currencies of Germany, Switzerland, and Japan, which in general have had less inflation than the United States, have appreciated relative to the dollar. *In fact, a foreign currency will, on average, depreciate (or appreciate) at a percentage rate approximately equal to the amount by which its inflation rate exceeds (or is less than) our own.*

Relative inflation rates also affect interest rates. The interest rate in any country is largely determined by its inflation rate, hence countries currently experiencing higher rates of inflation than the United States also tend to have higher interest rates. The reverse is true for countries with lower inflation rates.

It is tempting for a multinational corporation to borrow in countries with the lowest interest rates. However, this is not always the best strategy. Suppose, for example, that interest rates in Germany are lower than those in the United States because of Germany's lower inflation rate. A U.S. multinational firm could therefore save interest by borrowing in Germany. However, because of relative inflation rates, the mark can be expected to appreciate in the future, causing the dollar cost of annual interest and principal payments on German debt to rise over time. Thus, *the lower interest rate could be more than offset by losses from currency appreciation.* Similarly, one should not expect multinational corporations to avoid borrowing in a country such as Brazil, where interest rates have been very high, because future depreciation of the Brazilian cruzeiro could make such borrowing end up being relatively inexpensive.

What effects do relative inflation rates have on relative interest rates?

What happens over time to the currencies of countries with higher inflation rates than that of the United States? To those with lower inflation rates?

Why might a multinational corporation decide to borrow in a country such as Brazil, where interest rates are high, rather than in a country like Germany, where interest rates are low?

SELF-TEST QUESTIONS

INTERNATIONAL MONEY AND CAPITAL MARKETS

Owning the stock of U.S. multinational corporations that invest directly in foreign countries is one way for U.S. citizens to invest in world markets. Another way is to purchase stocks, bonds, or various money market instruments issued in foreign countries. U.S. citizens actually do invest substantial amounts in the stocks and bonds of large corporations headquartered in Europe, and to a lesser extent in firms headquartered in the Far East and South America. They also buy securities issued by foreign governments. Such security investments are known as *portfolio investments,* and they are distinguished from *direct investments* in physical assets by U.S. corporations.

From World War II through the 1960s, the U.S. capital markets dominated world markets, so individuals could confine their investments solely to U.S. securities and still have the opportunity to own most of the world's securities. Today, however, the value of U.S. securities outstanding represents less than one-fourth the value of all securities. Clearly, it is important for both managers and investors to have an understanding of international markets, because these markets may offer opportunities for raising or investing capital that are better than those available domestically.

EURODOLLAR MARKET

A *Eurodollar* is a U.S. dollar deposited in a bank outside the United States. (Although they are called Eurodollars because they originated in Europe, Eurodollars are really any dollars deposited in any part of the world other than the United States.) The bank in which the deposit is made may be a non-U.S. bank, such as Barclay's Bank in London; the foreign branch of a U.S. bank, such as Citibank's Paris branch; or even a foreign branch of a third-country bank, such as Barclay's Munich branch. Most Eurodollar deposits are for $500,000 or more, and they have maturities ranging from overnight to about one year.

The major difference between Eurodollar deposits and regular U.S. time deposits is their geographic locations. The two types of deposits do not involve different currencies — in both cases, dollars are on deposit. However, Eurodollars are outside the direct control of the U.S. monetary authorities, so U.S. banking regulations, such as fractional reserves and FDIC insurance premiums, do not apply. The absence of these costs means that the interest rate paid on Eurodollar deposits tends to be higher than domestic U.S. rates on equivalent instruments.

Although the dollar is the leading international currency, German marks, Swiss francs, Japanese yen, and other currencies are also deposited outside their home countries; these *Eurocurrencies* are handled in exactly the same way as Eurodollars.

Eurodollars are borrowed by U.S. and foreign corporations and governments for various purposes, but especially to pay for goods exported from the United States and to invest in U.S. security markets. Also, U.S. dollars are used as an international currency, or international medium of exchange, and many Eurodollars are used for this purpose. It is interesting to note that Eurodollars were actually "invented" by the Soviets in 1946. International merchants did not trust the Soviets or their rubles, so the Soviets bought some dollars (for gold), deposited them in a Paris bank, and then used these dollars to buy goods in the world markets. Others found it convenient to use dollars this same way, and soon the Eurodollar market was in full swing.

Eurodollars are usually held in interest-bearing accounts. The interest rate paid on these deposits depends (1) on the bank's lending rate, as the interest a bank earns on loans determines its willingness and ability to pay interest on deposits, and (2) on rates of return available on U.S. money market instruments. If rates in the United States were above Eurodollar deposit rates, these funds would be sent back and invested in the United States, whereas if Eurodollar deposit rates were significantly above U.S. rates, which is more often the case, more dollars would be sent out of the United States to become Eurodollars. Given the existence of the Eurodollar market, and the easy flow of dollars to and from the United States, it is easy to see why interest rates in the United States cannot be insulated from those in other parts of the world.

Interest rates on Eurodollar deposits (and loans) are tied to a standard rate known by the acronym *LIBOR,* which stands for *London InterBank Offer Rate.* LIBOR is the rate of interest offered by the largest and strongest London banks on dollar deposits of significant size. In May 1996, LIBOR rates were over half a percentage point above domestic U.S. bank rates on time deposits of the same maturity — 4.82 percent for three-month U.S. CDs versus 5.55 percent for LIBOR CDs. The Eurodollar market is essentially a short-term market; most loans and deposits are for less than one year.

INTERNATIONAL BOND MARKETS

Any bond sold outside the country of the borrower is called an international bond. However, there are two important types of international bonds: foreign bonds and Eurobonds. *Foreign bonds* are bonds sold by a foreign borrower but denominated in the currency of the country in which the issue is sold. For instance, Northern Telcom (a Canadian company) may need U.S. dollars to finance the operations of its subsidiaries in the United States. If it decides to raise the needed capital in the domestic U.S. bond market, the bond will be underwritten by a syndicate of U.S. investment bankers, denominated in U.S. dollars, and sold to U.S. investors in accordance with SEC and applicable state regulations. Except for the foreign origin of the borrower, this bond will be indistinguishable from those issued by equivalent U.S. corporations. Since Northern Telcom is a foreign corporation, however, the bond will be called a foreign bond.

The term *Eurobond* is used to designate any bond sold in some country *other than* the one in whose currency the bond is denominated. Examples include a British firm's issue of pound bonds sold in France, a Ford Motor Company issue denominated in dollars and sold in Germany, and a German firm's sale of mark-denominated bonds in Switzerland. The institutional arrangements by which Eurobonds are marketed are different than those for most other bond issues, with the most important distinction being a far lower level of required disclosure than is usually found for bonds issued in domestic markets, particularly in the United States. Governments tend to be less strict when regulating securities denominated in foreign currencies than they are on home-currency securities because the bonds' purchasers are generally more "sophisticated." The lower disclosure requirements result in lower total transaction costs for Eurobonds.

Eurobonds appeal to investors for several reasons. Generally, they are issued in bearer form rather than as registered bonds, so the names and nationalities of investors are not recorded. Individuals who desire anonymity, whether for privacy reasons or for tax avoidance, like Eurobonds. Similarly, most governments do not withhold taxes on interest payments associated with Eurobonds. If the investor requires an effective yield of 10 percent, a Eurobond that is exempt from tax withholding would need a coupon rate of 10 percent. Another type of bond—for instance, a domestic issue subject to a 30 percent withholding tax on interest paid to foreigners—would need a coupon rate of 14.3 percent to yield an after-withholding rate of 10 percent. Investors who desire secrecy would not want to file for a refund of the tax, so they would prefer to hold the Eurobond.

More than half of all Eurobonds are denominated in dollars. Bonds in Japanese yen, German marks, and Dutch guilders account for most of the rest. Although centered in Europe, Eurobonds are truly international. Their underwriting syndicates include investment bankers from all parts of the world, and the bonds are sold to investors not only in Europe but also in such faraway places as Bahrain and Singapore. Up to a few years ago, Eurobonds were issued solely by multinational firms, by international financial institutions, or by national governments. Today, however, the Eurobond market is also being tapped by purely domestic U.S. firms, because they often find that by borrowing overseas they can lower their debt costs.

In closing, we should note that more and more European financial transactions are being made, not in the currency of one country, but rather in *European currency units (ECUs)*. The ECU, which is simply a unit of account, is made up of the currencies of the 12 countries that belong to the European monetary system. For example, at one point in time the ECU might consist of 1.332 French francs, 0.6242 German marks, 0.2198 Dutch guilders, 6.885 Spanish pesetas, and so on, where the weights represent the relative sizes of each country's economy. The ECU is recognized as a means of payment among European governments and private businesses. It is also used in international money and capital markets and as a foreign currency reserve by Europe's central banks. Although no ECU paper bills or coins exist, it is treated as any other currency — companies can make ECU deposits at banks, obtain ECU loans, and engage in ECU foreign exchange spot and forward transactions. Depending on exchange rate fluctuations of the individual currencies, which, at least in theory, are kept within narrow limits by governmental actions, one ECU might translate into, say, 10 German marks, or 33 French francs, or 12 Dutch guilders. Thus, companies can deposit an amount in a single currency, have it converted into ECUs as the unit of account, earn interest in ECUs at some stated rate, and then, at maturity, receive the ECU proceeds in some currency that may or may not be the currency originally deposited. The purpose of the ECU is to create a "currency" that is less volatile than its component currencies and that will also facilitate trade within Europe.

INTERNATIONAL STOCK MARKETS

New issues of stock are sold in international markets for a variety of reasons. For example, a non-U.S. firm might sell an entire issue in the United States because it can tap a much larger source of capital than in its home country. Also, a U.S. firm may tap a foreign market because it wants to create an equity market presence to accompany its operations in that country. Large multinational companies also occasionally issue new stock simultaneously in multiple countries. For example, Alcan Aluminum, a Canadian company, recently issued new stock in Canada, Europe, and the United States simultaneously, using different underwriting syndicates in each market.

In addition to new issues, outstanding stocks of large multinational companies are increasingly being listed on multiple international exchanges. For example, Coca-Cola's stock is traded on six stock exchanges in the United States, including the NYSE, four stock exchanges in Switzerland, and the Frankfurt stock exchange in Germany. Some foreign stocks are listed in the United States — an example here is Royal Dutch Petroleum, which is listed on the NYSE. In addition to direct listing, U.S. investors can invest in foreign companies through *American Depository Receipts (ADRs),* which are certificates representing ownership of foreign stock held in trust. About 1,300 ADRs are now available in the United States, with most of them traded on the over-the-counter (OTC) market. However, more and more ADRs are being listed on the New York Stock Exchange, including Germany's Daimler-Benz, England's British Airways, Japan's Honda Motors, and Italy's Fiat Group.

INTERNATIONAL PORTFOLIO DIVERSIFICATION

One reason for investing in foreign securities is to obtain global diversification. To see what is involved, consider Figure 26-1, which shows the Capital Market Line (CML) as we developed it back in Chapter 5. The brown shaded area represents the feasible set of portfolios of domestic risky assets; the gray shaded area represents the addition to the feasible set when international assets are included; R_F represents the rate of return on domestic riskless assets; M_D is the domestic market port-

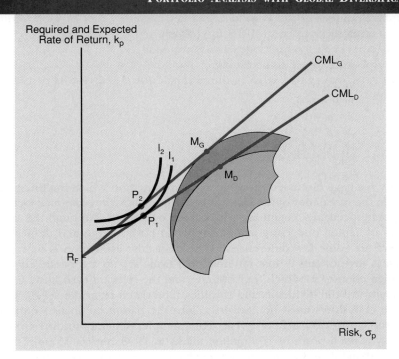

PORTFOLIO ANALYSIS WITH GLOBAL DIVERSIFICATION | **FIGURE 26-1**

folio; and M_G is the *global market portfolio,* which contains foreign as well as domestic risky securities. Note that there are no riskless foreign assets — even foreign Treasury bills are risky because of exchange risk. Since returns on foreign securities are not perfectly correlated with those on domestic securities, the inclusion of foreign assets in the portfolio shifts the boundary (or feasible) set of portfolios upward and to the left. This has the effect of rotating the CML upward, from CML_D to CML_G. This, in turn, permits an investor to move from portfolio P_1, on indifference curve I_1, to portfolio P_2, on the higher indifference curve I_2. P_2 contains a combination of domestic and foreign stocks, plus riskless U.S. government securities, and it is better than P_1 in that it provides a higher expected return for a lower level of risk.

The theoretical results depicted in Figure 26-1 have been borne out by historical risk/return performance. During a recent 10-year period, a portfolio consisting exclusively of U.S. stocks produced a return of 14.7 percent with a standard deviation of 15.4 percent. By holding 10 percent of the portfolio in foreign equities, the historical return was increased to 15.2 percent, and the standard deviation fell to 15.0. At 30 percent foreign stock holdings, the portfolio return climbed to 16.1 percent, while the standard deviation stood at 15.2 percent. We see, then, that the addition of foreign equities to an all-U.S. portfolio can increase the portfolio's return and, at the same time, lower its risk.

MULTINATIONAL CAPITAL BUDGETING

Up to now, we have discussed the general environment in which multinational firms operate. In the remainder of the chapter, we will see how international factors affect key corporate decisions, beginning with capital budgeting. Although the same basic principles of capital budgeting analysis apply to both foreign and domestic operations, there are some key differences. First, cash flow estimation is more complex for overseas investments. Most multinational firms set up a separate subsidiary in each foreign country in which they operate, and the relevant cash flows for the parent company are the dividends and royalties repatriated from the subsidiaries. Second, these cash flows must be converted into the parent company's currency and thus are subject to exchange rate risk. For example, General Motors's German subsidiary may make a profit of 100 million marks in 1998, but the value of this profit to GM will depend on the dollar/mark exchange rate. How many *dollars* will 100 million marks buy?

Also, dividends and royalties are normally taxed by both foreign and home-country governments. Furthermore, a foreign government may restrict the amount of the cash flows that may be *repatriated* to the parent company. For example, some governments place a ceiling, stated as a percentage of the company's net worth, on the amount of cash dividends that a subsidiary may pay to its parent. Such restrictions are normally intended to force multinational firms to reinvest earnings in the foreign country, although restrictions are sometimes imposed to prevent large currency outflows, which might affect the exchange rate.

Whatever the host country's motivation for blocking repatriation of profits, the result is that the parent corporation cannot use cash flows blocked in the foreign country to pay current dividends to its shareholders, nor does it have the flexibility to reinvest these cash flows elsewhere in the world, where expected returns may be higher. Hence, from the perspective of the parent organization, *the cash flows relevant for the analysis of a foreign investment are the cash flows that the subsidiary is actually expected to send back to the parent.* The present value of these cash flows is found by applying an appropriate discount rate, and this present value is then compared with the parent's required investment in the project to determine the project's NPV.

In addition to the complexities of the cash flow analysis, *the cost of capital may be different for a foreign project than for an equivalent domestic project because foreign projects may be more or less risky.* A higher risk could arise from two primary sources — (1) exchange rate risk and (2) political risk — while a lower risk might result from international diversification.

Exchange rate risk relates to what the basic cash flows will be worth in the parent company's home currency. The foreign currency cash flows to be turned over to the parent must be converted into U.S. dollars by translating them at expected future exchange rates. An analysis should be conducted to ascertain the effects of exchange rate variations, and, on the basis of this analysis, an exchange rate risk premium should be added to the domestic cost of capital to reflect the *exchange rate risk* inherent in the investment. As we have seen, it is sometimes possible to hedge against exchange rate fluctuations, but it may not be possible to hedge completely, especially on long-term projects. Even if hedging is possible, the costs of doing so must be subtracted from the project's cash flows.

Political risk refers to potential actions by a host government which would reduce the value of a company's investment. It includes at one extreme the expropriation without compensation of the subsidiary's assets, but it also includes less drastic actions that reduce the value of the parent firm's investment in the foreign subsidiary such as higher taxes, tighter repatriation or currency controls, and restrictions on prices charged. The risk of expropriation is small in traditionally friendly and stable countries such as Great Britain or Switzerland. However, in Latin America, Africa, the Far East, and eastern Europe, the risk may be substantial. Past expropriations include those of ITT and Anaconda Copper in Chile, Gulf Oil in Bolivia, Occidental Petroleum in Libya, Enron Corporation in Peru, and the assets of many companies in Iraq, Iran, and Cuba.

Several organizations rate the political risk of countries. For example, International Business Communications, a London company, publishes the *International Country Risk Guide,* which contains individual ratings for political, financial, and economic risk, along with a composite rating for each country. Table 26-3 contains

		SELECTED COUNTRIES RANKED BY COMPOSITE RISK			TABLE 26-3
RANK	COUNTRY	POLITICAL RISK	FINANCIAL RISK	ECONOMIC RISK	COMPOSITE RISK
1	Switzerland	93.0	50.0	39.5	91.5
9	United States	78.0	49.0	39.5	83.5
10	Canada	81.0	48.0	37.0	83.0
25	Venezuela	75.0	40.0	36.0	75.5
50	Israel	58.0	33.0	34.5	63.0
75	Panama	47.0	24.0	38.0	54.5
100	Peru	45.0	28.0	21.5	47.5
125	Burma	27.0	9.0	22.5	28.5
129	Liberia	10.0	8.0	12.0	15.0

NOTE: A total of 129 countries are ranked, but only 9 are shown here.
SOURCE: *International Country Risk Guide.*

selected portions of a recent report. The political variable — which makes up 50 percent of the composite rating — includes factors such as government corruption and the gap between economic expectations and reality. The financial rating looks at such things as the likelihood of losses from exchange controls and loan defaults. The economic rating takes into account such factors as inflation and debt-service costs.

The maximum, or least risky, score is 100 for the political factors and 50 each for the financial and economic factors. The United States is ranked ninth, below Switzerland, Luxembourg, Norway, Austria, Germany, Netherlands, Brunei, and Japan. Liberia, as shown in Table 26-3, is ranked last.

If a company's management has a serious concern that a given country might expropriate foreign assets, it will probably not make significant investments in that country. However, companies can take steps to reduce the potential loss from expropriation in three major ways: (1) by financing the subsidiary with local capital, (2) by structuring operations so that the subsidiary has value only as a part of the integrated corporate system, and (3) by obtaining insurance against economic losses from expropriation from a source such as the Overseas Private Investment Corporation (OPIC). In the latter case, insurance premiums would have to be added to the project's cost.

Capital budgeting in a multinational setting can be illustrated with data from International Electronics Corporation (IEC), which is analyzing a proposal to build a plant in Caribia to assemble electronic equipment for sale worldwide through the company's marketing and distribution facility in Curaçao. If the project is accepted, a new subsidiary, IEC Caribia, will be incorporated in Caribia. It will be financed solely with common stock, all of which will be owned by the parent firm.

While the corporate income tax in Caribia is a low 20 percent compared with the 50 percent federal-plus-state rate that IEC pays in the United States, the government of Caribia places several restrictions on multinational corporations that will have an impact on the analysis. To preserve investment capital in Caribia, the government prohibits the removal of contributed equity until the investment is sold or otherwise liquidated. Thus, depreciation cash flows cannot be repatriated until the end of the project's life. Dividends are not subjected to a tax, but they must come only from net income, and they are restricted to a maximum of 20 percent of the original equity in any year. At the end of the project's life, any reinvested earnings can be repatriated to the parent. The investment, to be made in January 1997, consists almost entirely of plant and equipment, and the cost will be $10 million or 50 million Caribian pesos (P50 million). Because of the nature of technological change in the electronics industry, IEC bases its analysis on a time horizon of five years. At the end of the five years (in December 2001), the company estimates that the book value of the facility, 25 million Caribian pesos, is the best estimate of its market value.

The Caribian government recognizes that IEC has developed and patented much of the technology employed in the operations, and it is willing to compensate the company for its use. IEC and the Minister of Commerce have reached an agreement that establishes a royalty rate of 10 percent of gross revenues to be paid directly to the parent. IEC also wanted to receive management fees, but they are prohibited by law in Caribia. Table 26-4 summarizes the projected income statements for the Caribian subsidiary.

PROJECTED END-OF-YEAR NET CASH FLOWS TO THE U.S. PARENT (MILLIONS OF CARIBIAN PESOS)					TABLE 26-4
	1997	1998	1999	2000	2001
Revenues	50.00	55.00	60.00	65.00	70.00
Operating costs	30.00	30.00	35.00	35.00	40.00
Depreciation	5.00	5.00	5.00	5.00	5.00
Royalties (10% of revenue)	5.00	5.50	6.00	6.50	7.00
Income before tax	10.00	14.50	14.00	18.50	18.00
Caribian tax (20%)	2.00	2.90	2.80	3.70	3.60
Net income	8.00	11.60	11.20	14.80	14.40
Dividend repatriated (10.0 maximum)	8.00	10.00	10.00	10.00	10.00
U.S. tax on dividend	3.00	3.75	3.75	3.75	3.75
After-tax dividend	5.00	6.25	6.25	6.25	6.25
Royalty (10% of gross revenues)	5.00	5.50	6.00	6.50	7.00
U.S. tax on royalty (50%)	2.50	2.75	3.00	3.25	3.50
After-tax royalty	2.50	2.75	3.00	3.25	3.50
Net cash flow	7.50	9.00	9.25	9.50	9.75

The data in Table 26-4 are straightforward down to "Dividend repatriated." In the 1997 column, we see that net income, 8 million pesos, is less than 20 percent of the 50 million pesos of original equity (0.2 × 50 million = 10 million pesos, which is the maximum dividend in any year). Therefore, the entire 8 million pesos in 1997 can be returned to the parent as a dividend. Dividends in subsequent years are limited to 10 million pesos.

IEC reports its worldwide net income to the U.S. Internal Revenue Service, but it receives *tax credits* for taxes paid overseas, including a credit for taxes paid by its subsidiary to the Caribian tax authorities. The amount of the credit depends on the dividend payout ratio of the subsidiary. With a 100 percent payout, the parent would pay the difference between the assumed U.S. tax rate of 50 percent and the Caribian tax rate of 20 percent. For example, in 1997, when the payout was 100 percent, the subsidiary earned 10 million pesos before Caribian tax and paid 2 million in tax (20 percent) to the Caribian government. Therefore, an additional 30 percent tax, or 3 million pesos, must be paid to the U.S. government. The total tax on the dividend is limited to 5 million pesos, or 50 percent of taxable income; this is the same rate as would be paid if the subsidiary had been located in the United States, in which case it would have paid an assumed 50 percent tax on 10 million pesos of net income.[4]

---

[4]If the foreign tax rate had been higher than the U.S. tax rate, the tax credit would be greater than the taxes owed to the U.S. government on equivalent before-tax earnings by a U.S. firm. This deficit could be used to offset U.S. taxes on income from other foreign subsidiaries in any part of the world. Note that in this example we assume a 50 percent U.S. tax rate.

In 1998 through 2001, net income exceeds 10 million pesos, the maximum dividend payment allowed under Caribian law, so dividends are set at 10 million. To see what is involved, consider 1998. Theoretically, the United States could tax the 14.5 million peso pre-tax income, getting 14.5(0.5) = 7.25 million pesos, less a credit of 2.9 million pesos, for a net tax bill of 4.35 million pesos, but this is not done. Alternatively, the United States could treat as taxable income only the dividends repatriated, which would produce a net tax bill of 10(0.5) − 2.9 = 2.1 million pesos, but this is not done either. Under U.S. law, taxes are collected on the portion of income that is actually repatriated. In the years 1998 to 2001, we proceed as follows: (1) We "gross up" the dividend payment to determine the before-tax net income required to produce the actual dividend payment. This is equal to the dividend repatriated divided by (1.0 − Caribian tax rate), or 10/0.8 = 12.5 million pesos. Had IEC Caribia had 12.5 million pesos of income, it would have paid 20 percent, or 2.5 million pesos, in taxes and had 10 million left for the dividend which it actually paid. (2) We now multiply this 12.5 million before-tax equivalent amount by the difference between the tax rate in the United States and the Caribian rate, or 30 percent, getting 0.30(12.5) = 3.75 million pesos. This is the U.S. tax on the income repatriated in 1998.[5]

However, 3.75 million pesos is not the total U.S. tax liability. An additional source of taxable income to the parent is the royalties paid by IEC Caribia. Royalties are an operating expense to the subsidiary, so they are not subject to Caribian tax. To the parent, however, they are income, and the royalties are taxed at the full 50 percent tax rate. Total operating cash flow to the U.S. parent, then, is the sum of the after-tax dividend and the after-tax royalty. This is shown in the last line of Table 26-4.

Since cash flows from depreciation cannot be repatriated until the company is liquidated at the end of 2001, they must be reinvested locally. Assume that there are no other attractive real asset investments available, so the depreciation cash flows will be invested in Caribian government bonds which earn 8 percent annual interest, with interest not subject to tax until it is repatriated. The accumulated and interest-compounded depreciation cash flow at the termination of the project is shown in Table 26-5 to be 27.166 million pesos after adjusting for Caribian and U.S. taxes.

Operating profits that exceed the dividend repatriation restrictions are also assumed to be invested in 8 percent Caribian government bonds. As shown in Table 26-6, the U.S. tax adjustment is more complex than it was for the depreciation cash flows because Caribian tax is only due on the interest income, but U.S. tax is due on both interest and "grossed up" operating profits. The total after-tax cash flow from blocked operating profits, approximately 8 million pesos, will be added to the 2001 end-of-project cash flow.

The next steps in the analysis are (1) to convert the annual cash flows as developed in Tables 26-4, 26-5, and 26-6, plus the terminal value (assumed to be equal to the ending book value) from pesos to dollars, and (2) to find the net present value of the project. We assume that a 12 percent cost of capital is appropriate for this

---

[5]Notice that the foreign subsidiary's payout ratio has a major effect on total corporate taxes paid—if no dividends are repatriated, no U.S. taxes are paid. This works as an incentive for multinational corporations to reinvest earnings overseas. It also explains why U.S. oil companies and other multinationals often have very low U.S. taxes in relation to their reported income.

DEPRECIATION CASH FLOWS REPATRIATED (MILLIONS OF CARIBIAN PESOS)				TABLE 26-5
YEAR OF DEPRECIATION	**AMOUNT OF DEPRECIATION**		**COMPOUNDING FACTOR AT 8 PERCENT**	**TERMINAL VALUE IN 2001**
1997	5.0	×	$(1.08)^4$ =	6.802
1998	5.0	×	$(1.08)^3$ =	6.299
1999	5.0	×	$(1.08)^2$ =	5.832
2000	5.0	×	$(1.08)^1$ =	5.400
2001	5.0	×	$(1.08)^0$ =	5.000
	25.0		Total	29.333
			Less depreciation	25.000
			Taxable income	4.333
			Caribian tax (20%)	0.867
			After Caribian tax	28.466
			U.S. tax (30%)	1.300
			After U.S. tax	27.166

BLOCKED OPERATING PROFITS (MILLIONS OF CARIBIAN PESOS)				TABLE 26-6
YEAR EARNED	**AMOUNT OF BLOCKED PROFITS**		**COMPOUNDING FACTOR AT 8 PERCENT**	**TERMINAL VALUE IN 2001**
1997	0.0	×	$(1.08)^4$ =	0.000
1998	1.6	×	$(1.08)^3$ =	2.015
1999	1.2	×	$(1.08)^2$ =	1.399
2000	4.8	×	$(1.08)^1$ =	5.184
2001	4.4	×	$(1.08)^0$ =	4.400
	12.0		Total	12.998
			Less investment	12.000
			Taxable income	0.998
			Caribian tax (20%)	0.200
			After Caribian tax	12.798
			U.S. tax[a]	4.799
			After U.S. tax	7.999

[a]Caribian taxes have already been paid on the blocked profits. The pre-tax income that gave rise to the 12.0 million pesos of blocked profits was 12.0/0.8 = 15.0. U.S. taxes at a rate of 30 percent must be paid on this income: 15.0(0.3) = 4.50. In addition, a 30 percent U.S. tax must be paid on the 0.998 million pesos of interest income: 0.998(0.3) = 0.299. Therefore, the total U.S. tax payable upon repatriation of the interest-accumulated blocked profits is 4.50 + 0.299 = 4.799 million pesos.

TABLE 26-7	PROJECT CASH FLOWS (IN MILLIONS)					
		1996	1997	1998	1999	2000	2001

	1996	1997	1998	1999	2000	2001
1. Initial investment (pesos)	(50.000)					
2. Cash flow from operations (pesos)		7.500	9.000	9.250	9.500	9.750
3. Depreciation cash flow (pesos)						27.166
4. Blocked profits (pesos)						7.999
5. Terminal value (pesos)						25.000
6. Net cash flow (pesos)	(50.000)	7.500	9.000	9.250	9.500	69.915
7. Forecasted exchange rate	5.00	5.00	5.25	5.51	5.79	6.08
8. Dollar cash flow	($10.000)	$1.500	$1.714	$1.679	$1.641	$11.499
9. NPV at 12% = $1.468						

investment.[6] These steps are shown in Table 26-7. Row 6 gives the annual net cash flows in pesos; the component parts of these cash flows are shown in Rows 1 through 5. The estimated exchange rates are shown in Row 7. The current rate, 5 pesos to the dollar, is expected to hold during 1997, but the peso is expected to depreciate thereafter at a rate of 5 percent per year.

Dividing the peso cash flows in Row 6 by the exchange rates in Row 7 gives the expected net cash flows in dollars shown in Row 8. Finally, the NPV of the dollar cash flows, $1.468 million, is shown in Row 9. Since its NPV is positive, the project should be accepted.

SELF-TEST QUESTIONS

List some key differences in capital budgeting as applied to foreign versus domestic operations.

What are the relevant cash flows for an international investment?

Why might the cost of capital for a foreign project differ from that of an equivalent domestic project? Could it be lower?

What adjustments might be made to the domestic cost of capital for a foreign investment due to exchange rate risk and political risk?

INTERNATIONAL CAPITAL STRUCTURES

Significant differences have been observed in the capital structures of U.S. corporations in comparison with their German and Japanese counterparts. For example, the Organization for Economic Cooperation and Development (OECD) recently reported that, on average, Japanese firms use 85 percent debt to total assets (in

---

[6]This hurdle rate is based on the cost of capital employed in the project, adjusted as appropriate for risks associated with the foreign environment and any diversification or other benefits that are applicable.

book value terms), German firms use 64 percent, and U.S. firms use 55 percent. Of course, different countries use somewhat different accounting conventions with regard to (1) reporting assets on a historical versus a replacement cost basis, (2) the treatment of leased assets, (3) pension plan funding, and (4) capitalizing versus expensing R&D costs, and these differences make comparisons difficult. Still, even after adjusting for accounting differences, researchers find that Japanese and German firms use considerably more financial leverage than U.S. companies.

Why do international differences in financial leverage exist? Since finance theory regards taxes as a major reason for using debt, the effects of differential tax structures in the three countries have been examined. The interest on corporate debt is deductible in each country, and individuals must pay taxes on dividends and interest received. However, capital gains are not taxed in either Germany or Japan. The conclusions from this analysis are as follows: (1) From a tax standpoint, corporations should be equally inclined to use debt in all three countries. (2) Since capital gains are not taxed in Germany or Japan, but are taxed in the United States, and since capital gains are associated more with stocks than with bonds, investors in Germany and Japan should show a preference for stocks as compared with U.S. investors. (3) Investor preferences should lead to relatively low equity capital costs in Germany and Japan, and this, in turn, should cause German and Japanese firms to use more equity capital than their U.S. counterparts. Of course, this is exactly the opposite of the actual capital structures, so differential tax laws cannot explain the observed capital structure differences.

If tax rates cannot explain the different capital structures, what else might explain the observed differences? Another possibility relates to bankruptcy and agency costs. Actual bankruptcy, and even the threat of potential bankruptcy, imposes a costly burden on firms with large amounts of debt. Note, though, that the threat of bankruptcy is dependent on the *probability* of bankruptcy. In the United States, the costs of monitoring equity investments are comparatively low — corporations produce quarterly reports, pay quarterly dividends, and must comply with relatively stringent audit and SEC requirements. These conditions are less prevalent in the other countries. Conversely, debt-monitoring costs are probably lower in Germany and Japan than in the United States. In Germany and Japan, the bulk of corporate debt consists of bank loans as opposed to publicly issued bonds, but, more important, the banks are closely linked to the corporations which borrow from them. German and Japanese banks often (1) hold major equity positions in their debtor corporations, (2) vote the shares of individual shareholders for whom banks hold shares in trust, and (3) have bank officers on the boards of debtor corporations. Given these close relationships, the banks are more directly involved with firms' affairs, and as a result they are also more accommodating in the event of financial distress than U.S. bondholders would be. This, in turn, suggests that a given amount of debt gives rise to a lower threat of bankruptcy for a German or a Japanese firm than for a U.S. firm with the same business risk. Thus, an analysis of bankruptcy costs and equity-monitoring costs leads to the conclusion that U.S. firms ought to have more equity and less debt than firms in Japan and Germany.

We cannot state that one financial system is better than another in the sense of making the firms in one country more efficient than those in another. However, as U.S. firms become increasingly involved in worldwide operations, they must become increasingly aware of worldwide conditions, and they must be prepared to adapt to conditions in the various countries in which they do business.

SELF-TEST QUESTION   Why do international differences in financial leverage exist?

MULTINATIONAL WORKING CAPITAL MANAGEMENT

CASH MANAGEMENT

The objectives of cash management in a multinational corporation are similar to those in a purely domestic corporation: (1) to speed up collections and to slow down disbursements as much as is feasible, and thus to maximize net float; (2) to shift cash as rapidly as possible from those parts of the business where it is not needed to those parts where it is needed; and (3) to obtain the highest possible risk-adjusted, after-tax rate of return on temporary cash balances. Multinational companies use the same general procedures for achieving these goals as domestic firms, but because of longer distances and more serious mail delays, lockbox systems, electronic funds transfers, and other techniques are especially important.

Although multinational and domestic corporations have the same objectives and use similar procedures, the multinational corporation faces a far more complex task. As noted earlier in our discussion of political risk, foreign governments often place restrictions on transfers of funds out of the country, so although IBM can transfer money from its Salt Lake City office to its New York concentration bank just by pressing a few buttons, a similar transfer from its Buenos Aires office is far more complex. Buenos Aires funds are denominated in australs (Argentina's equivalent of the dollar), so the australs must be converted to dollars before the transfer. If there is a shortage of dollars in Argentina, or if the Argentinean government wants to conserve dollars to purchase strategic materials, then conversion, hence the transfer, may be blocked. Even if no dollar shortage exists in Argentina, the government may still restrict funds outflows if those funds represent profits or depreciation rather than payments for purchased materials or equipment, because many countries, especially those that are less developed, want profits reinvested in the country in order to stimulate economic growth.

Once it has been determined what funds can be transferred out of the various nations in which a multinational corporation operates, it is important to get those funds to locations where they will earn the highest returns. Whereas domestic corporations tend to think in terms of domestic securities, multinationals are more likely to be aware of investment opportunities all around the world. Most multinational corporations use one or more global concentration banks, located in money centers such as London, New York, Tokyo, Zurich, or Singapore, and their staffs in those cities, working with international bankers, know of and are able to take advantage of the best rates available anywhere in the world.

CREDIT MANAGEMENT

Like most other aspects of finance, credit management in the multinational corporation is similar to but more complex than that in a purely domestic business. First, granting credit is more risky in an international context because, in addition to the normal risks of default, the multinational corporation must also worry about exchange rate fluctuations between the time a sale is made and the time a receivable is collected. For example, if IBM sold a computer to a Japanese customer for 90 million yen when the exchange rate was 90 yen to the dollar, IBM would obtain 90,000,000 = $1,000,000 for the computer. However, if it sold the computer on terms of net/6 months, and if the yen fell against the dollar so that one dollar would now buy 112.5 yen, IBM would end up realizing only 90,000,000/112.5 = $800,000 when it collected the receivable. As we discussed earlier, hedging can reduce this risk, but at a cost.

Credit policy is generally more important for a multinational corporation than for a purely domestic firm for two reasons. First, much U.S. trade is with poorer, less developed nations, and in such situations granting credit is generally a necessary condition for doing business. Second, and in large part as a result of the first point, developed nations whose economic health depends upon exports often help their manufacturing firms compete internationally by granting credit to foreign countries. In Japan, for example, the major manufacturing firms have direct ownership ties with large "trading companies" engaged in international trade, as well as with giant commercial banks. In addition, a government agency, the Ministry of International Trade and Industry (MITI), helps Japanese firms identify potential export markets and also helps potential customers arrange credit for purchases from Japanese firms. In effect, the huge Japanese trade surpluses are used to finance Japanese exports, thus helping to perpetuate their favorable trade balance. The United States has attempted to counter with the Export-Import Bank, which is funded by Congress, but the fact that the United States has a large balance of payments deficit is clear evidence that we have been less successful than others in world markets in recent years.

The huge debt which countries such as Brazil, Mexico, and Argentina owe the international banks, including many U.S. banks, is well known, and this situation illustrates how credit policy (by banks in this case) can go astray. The banks face a particularly sticky problem with these loans, because if a sovereign nation defaults, the banks cannot lay claim to the assets of the country as they could if a corporate customer defaulted. Note too that although the banks' loans to foreign governments are getting most of the headlines, many U.S. multinational corporations are also in trouble as a result of granting credit to business customers in the same countries where bank loans are on shaky ground.

By pointing out the risks in granting credit internationally, we are not suggesting that such credit is bad. Quite the contrary, for the potential gains from international operations far outweigh the risks, at least for companies (and banks) that have the necessary expertise.

INVENTORY MANAGEMENT

As with most other aspects of finance, inventory management in a multinational setting is similar to but more complex than that in a purely domestic one. First, there is the matter of the physical location of inventories. For example, where should Exxon keep its stockpiles of crude oil and refined products? It has refineries and marketing centers located worldwide, and one alternative is to keep items concentrated in a few strategic spots, from which they can then be shipped to various locations as needs arise. Such a strategy might minimize the total amount of inventories needed to operate the global business and thus might minimize the firm's total investment in inventories. Note, though, that consideration will have to be given to potential delays in getting goods from central storage locations to user locations all around the world. Both working stocks and safety stocks would have to be maintained at each user location, as well as at the strategic storage centers. Problems like the Iraqi occupation of Kuwait and the subsequent trade embargo, which brought with it the potential for a shutdown of production of about 25 percent of the world's oil supply, complicate matters even more.

Exchange rates also influence inventory policy. If a local currency, say, the Danish krone, were expected to rise in value against the dollar, a U.S. company operating in Denmark would want to increase stocks of local products before the rise in the krone, and vice versa if the krone were expected to fall.

Another factor that must be considered is the possibility of import or export quotas or tariffs. For example, Apple Computer Company recently obtained certain memory chips from Japanese suppliers at bargain. Then U.S. chipmakers charged the Japanese with dumping chips in the U.S. market at prices below cost, so they sought to force the Japanese to raise prices. That led Apple to decide to increase its chip inventory.[7] Then, computer sales slacked off, and Apple ended up with an oversupply of expensive computer chips. As a result, Apple's profits were hurt, and its stock price fell, demonstrating once more the importance of careful inventory management.

As mentioned earlier, another danger in certain countries is the threat of expropriation. If that threat is large, inventory holdings will be minimized, and goods will be brought in only as needed. Similarly, if the operation involves extraction of raw material such as oil or bauxite, processing plants may be moved offshore rather than located close to the production site.

Taxes must also be considered, and they have two effects on multinational inventory management. First, countries often impose property taxes on assets, including inventories, and when this is done, the tax is based on holdings as of a specific date, say, January 1 or March 1. Such rules make it advantageous for a multinational firm (1) to schedule production so that inventories are low on the assessment date, and (2) if assessment dates vary among countries in a region, to hold safety stocks in different countries at different times during the year.

---

[7]The term "dumping" warrants explanation, because the practice is so potentially important in international markets. Suppose Japanese chipmakers have excess capacity. A particular chip has a variable cost of $25, and its "fully allocated cost," which is the $25 plus total fixed cost per unit of output, is $40. Now suppose a Japanese firm can sell chips in the United States at $35 per unit, but if it charges $40 it will not make any sales because U.S. chipmakers sell for $35.50. If the Japanese firm sells at $35, it will cover variable cost plus make a contribution to fixed overhead, so selling at $35 makes sense. Continuing, if the Japanese firm can sell in Japan at $40, but U.S. firms are excluded from Japanese markets by import duties or other barriers, the Japanese will have a huge advantage over U.S. manufacturers. This practice of selling goods at lower prices in foreign markets than at home is called "dumping." U.S. firms are required by antitrust laws to offer the same price to all customers and, therefore, cannot engage in dumping.

Finally, multinational firms may consider the possibility of at-sea storage. Oil, chemical, grain, and other companies that deal in a bulk commodity that must be stored in some type of tank can often buy tankers at a cost not much greater—or perhaps even less, considering land cost—than land-based facilities. Loaded tankers can then be kept at sea or at anchor in some strategic location. This eliminates the danger of expropriation, minimizes the property tax problem, and maximizes flexibility with regard to shipping to areas where needs are greatest or prices highest.

This discussion has only scratched the surface of inventory management in the multinational corporation—the task is much more complex than for a purely domestic firm. However, the greater the degree of complexity, the greater the rewards from superior performance, so if you want challenge along with potentially high rewards, look to the international arena.

What are some factors that make cash management especially complicated in a multinational corporation?

Why is granting credit especially risky in an international context?

Why is credit policy especially important for a multinational firm?

SELF-TEST QUESTIONS

SUMMARY

This chapter discussed the most important differences between multinational and domestic financial management. Some of the key concepts are listed below:

- *International operations* are becoming increasingly important to individual firms and to the national economy. A *multinational corporation* is a firm that operates in two or more nations.

- Companies go "international" for six primary reasons: (1) *to expand their markets*, (2) *to obtain raw materials*, (3) *to seek new technology*, (4) *to lower production costs*, (5) *to avoid trade barriers*, and (6) *to diversify*.

- Six major factors distinguish financial management as practiced by domestic firms from that practiced by multinational corporations: (1) *different currency denominations*, (2) *different economic and legal structures*, (3) *languages*, (4) *cultural differences*, (5) *role of governments*, and (6) *political risk*.

- The number of U.S. dollars required to purchase one unit of foreign currency is called a *direct quotation*, while the number of units of foreign currency that can be purchased for one U.S. dollar is an *indirect quotation*.

- Financial forecasting is more difficult for multinational firms, because *exchange rate fluctuations* make it difficult to estimate the dollars that overseas operations will produce.

■ Prior to August 1971, the world was on a *fixed exchange rate system* whereby the U.S. dollar was linked to gold and other currencies were then tied to the dollar. After August 1971, the world monetary system changed to a *floating system* under which major world currency rates float with market forces, largely unrestricted by any internationally agreed-upon limits. The central bank of each country does intervene in the foreign exchange market, buying and selling its currency to smooth out exchange rate fluctuations, but only to a limited extent.

■ *Spot rates* are the rates paid for delivery of currency "on the spot," while the *forward exchange rate* is the rate paid for delivery of currency at some agreed-upon future date, usually 30, 90, or 180 days from the day the transaction is negotiated. The forward rate can be at either a *premium* or a *discount* to the spot rate.

■ Granting credit is more risky in an international context because, in addition to the normal risks of default, the multinational firm must worry about *exchange rate changes* between the time a sale is made and the time a receivable is collected.

■ Credit policy is especially important for a multinational firm for two reasons: (1) Much trade is with less-developed nations, and in such situations granting credit is a necessary condition for doing business. (2) The governments of nations such as Japan whose economic health depends upon exports often help their firms compete by granting credit to foreign customers.

■ Foreign investments are similar to domestic investments, but political risk and exchange rate risk must be considered. *Political risk* is the risk that the foreign government will take some action which will decrease the value of the investment, while *exchange rate risk* is the risk of losses due to fluctuations in the value of the dollar relative to the values of foreign currencies.

■ Investments in *international capital projects* expose the investing firm to exchange rate risk and political risk. The relevant cash flows in international capital budgeting are the dollar cash flows which can be turned over to the parent company.

■ *Eurodollars* are U.S. dollars deposited in banks outside the United States. Interest rates on Eurodollars are tied to *LIBOR*, the London interbank offer rate.

■ U.S. firms often find that they can raise long-term capital at a lower cost outside the United States by selling bonds in the *international capital markets*. International bonds may be either *foreign bonds*, which are exactly like regular domestic bonds except that the issuer is a foreign company, or *Eurobonds*, which are bonds sold in a foreign country but denominated in the currency of the issuing company's home country.

Define each of the following terms:
a. Multinational corporation
b. Exchange rate
c. Fixed exchange rate system; floating exchange rates
d. Deficit trade balance
e. Devaluation; revaluation
f. Exchange rate risk; convertible currency
g. Spot rate; forward exchange rate
h. Discount on forward rate; premium on forward rate
i. Hedging exchange rate exposure
j. Repatriation of earnings; political risk
k. Eurodollar; Eurobond; international bond; foreign bond

Under the fixed exchange rate system, what was the currency against which all other currency values were defined?

Exchange rates fluctuate under both the fixed exchange rate and floating exchange rate systems. What, then, is the difference between the two systems?

If the French franc depreciates against the U.S. dollar, can a dollar buy more or fewer French francs as a result?

If the United States imports more goods from abroad than it exports, foreigners will tend to have a surplus of U.S. dollars. What will this do to the value of the dollar with respect to foreign currencies? What is the corresponding effect on foreign investments in the United States?

Why do U.S. corporations build manufacturing plants abroad when they could build them at home?

Should firms require higher rates of return on foreign projects than on identical projects located at home? Explain.

What is a Eurodollar? If a French citizen deposits $10,000 in Chase Manhattan Bank in New York, have Eurodollars been created? What if the deposit is made in Barclay's Bank in London? Chase Manhattan's Paris branch? Does the existence of the Eurodollar market make the Federal Reserve's job of controlling U.S. interest rates easier or more difficult? Explain.

EXCHANGE RATES If British pounds sell for $1.79 (U.S.) per pound, what should dollars sell for in pounds per dollar?

CURRENCY APPRECIATION Suppose that 1 French franc could be purchased in the foreign exchange market for 15 U.S. cents today. If the franc appreciated 10 percent tomorrow against the dollar, how many francs would a dollar buy tomorrow?

26-3   **CROSS EXCHANGE RATES** Recently the exchange rate between U.S. dollars and the French franc was FF5.6 = $1, and the exchange rate between the dollar and the British pound was £1 = $1.79. What was the exchange rate between francs and pounds?

26-4   **CROSS EXCHANGE RATES** Look up the three currencies in Problem 26-3 in the foreign exchange section of a current issue of *The Wall Street Journal.* What is the current exchange rate between francs and pounds?

26-5   **EXCHANGE RATES** Table 26-1 lists foreign exchange rates for March 13, 1995. On that day how many dollars would be required to purchase 1,000 units of each of the following: Italian lira, Japanese yen, and Swiss francs?

26-6   **EXCHANGE RATES** Look up the three currencies in Problem 26-5 in the foreign exchange section of a current issue of *The Wall Street Journal.*
a. What is the current exchange rate for changing dollars into 1,000 units of lira, yen, and Swiss francs?
b. What is the percentage gain or loss between the March 13, 1995, exchange rate and the current exchange rate for each of the currencies in Part a?

26-7   **RESULTS OF EXCHANGE RATE CHANGES** Early in September 1983, it took 245 Japanese yen to equal $1. Almost 10 years later, in June 1993, that exchange rate had fallen to 106 yen to $1. Assume the price of a Japanese-manufactured automobile was $8,000 in September 1983 and that any price change resulted solely from exchange rate fluctuations.
a. Has the price, in dollars, of the automobile increased or decreased during the 10-year period because of changes in the exchange rate?
b. What would the dollar price of the automobile be in June 1993, again assuming that the car's price was affected only by exchange rates?

26-8   **HEDGING** Celec French Imports has agreed to purchase 15,000 cases of French wine for 16 million francs at today's spot rate. The firm's financial manager, Dennis O'Connor, has noted the following current spot and forward rates:

	U.S. DOLLAR/FRANC	FRANC/U.S. DOLLAR
Spot	0.17748	5.6344
30-day forward	0.17699	5.6499
90-day forward	0.17612	5.6781
180-day forward	0.17487	5.7186

On the same day, Mr. O'Connor agrees to purchase 15,000 more cases of wine in 3 months at the same price of 16 million francs.
a. What is the price of the wine, in U.S. dollars, if it is purchased at today's spot rate?
b. What is the cost, in dollars, of the second 15,000 cases if payment is made in 90 days and the spot rate at that time equals today's 90-day forward rate?
c. If Mr. O'Connor is concerned about the dollar losing value relative to the franc in the next 90 days, what can he do to reduce his exposure to exchange rate risk?
d. If he does not hedge his exposure to exchange rate risk, and the exchange rate for the French franc is 5.00 to $1 in 90 days, how much will he have to pay for the wine (in dollars)?

26-9   **FOREIGN INVESTMENT ANALYSIS** After all foreign and U.S. taxes, a U.S. corporation expects to receive 3 pounds of dividends per share from a British subsidiary this year. The exchange rate at the end of the year is expected to be $1.76 per pound, and the pound is expected to depreciate 5 percent against the dollar each year for an indefinite period. The dividend (in pounds) is expected to grow at 10 percent a year indefinitely. The parent U.S. corporation owns 10 million shares of the subsidiary. What is the present value of its equity ownership of the subsidiary? Assume a cost of equity capital of 14 percent for the subsidiary.

EXCHANGE GAINS AND LOSSES You are the vice-president of International InfoXchange, headquartered in Chicago, Illinois. All shareholders of the firm live in the United States. Earlier this month you obtained a loan of 5 million Canadian dollars from a bank in Toronto to finance the construction of a new plant in Montreal. At the time the loan was received, the exchange rate was 87 U.S. cents to the Canadian dollar. By the end of the month it has unexpectedly dropped to 80 cents. Has your company made a gain or loss as a result, and by how much?

CAPITAL BUDGETING ANALYSIS The Smith-Capone Corporation of Chicago manufactures typewriters for the world market. In early 1997, the company's board of directors requests the international planning department of the company to evaluate a proposal for setting up a wholly owned subsidiary in Paralivia, a country of 50 million people in South America. The subsidiary will make typewriters for the Paralivian market. Paralivia is a rapidly developing country which has effectively invested its rich oil revenues to support a growing industrial economy. Currently, it imports all of its typewriters from abroad, and Smith-Capone is expected to capture a large portion of this market.

Political sentiment in Paralivia regarding foreign investments has been somewhat lukewarm because such investments have overtones of foreign economic control. Not long ago, the government passed a law requiring all foreign investments to pass to local ownership after 6 years or less. Paralivia recently adopted a parliamentary system of government after 20 years of military dictatorship under General Francisco, but the transition of power was peaceful. Gordon Lidder, chairman of the board of Smith-Capone, has expressed concern about the stability of the new government, but "usually reliable" sources indicate that the government has popular support and is unlikely to be toppled for at least 5 to 10 years.

The following financial information on the proposed project is available:

Paralivian currency: Because the inflation rate in Paralivia is about 5 percent higher than that in the United States, the Paralivian ringo is expected to depreciate relative to the dollar by about 5 percent a year. When the investment will be made, the exchange rate is expected to be 2 ringos per dollar.

Investment: The estimated investment is $30 million in 1998 for inventory, plant, and equipment. The parent corporation, Smith-Capone, will provide all the capital in the form of equity in the subsidiary. The project will begin to generate earnings in 1999. At the end of 6 years, in 2004, all plant and equipment will be sold to the Paralivian government for 20 million ringos. This amount of money, plus all accumulated cash, will be repatriated as a liquidating dividend.

Repatriation: Only dividends may be repatriated by the subsidiary to the parent company. Cash flows from depreciation may not be repatriated except as part of the liquidating dividend in 2004. However, these cash flows can, in the meantime, be invested in local money market instruments to yield a 15 percent tax-free return.

Taxes: The Paralivian corporate income tax rate is 25 percent. There is also a 10 percent withholding tax on dividends. The U.S. federal-plus-state tax rate is 50 percent on the gross earnings of the foreign subsidiary. However, the parent company gets a tax credit for taxes already paid to foreign governments. In the case of the liquidating dividend, the tax treatment is quite different. The Paralivian government will not tax this dividend. Smith-Capone has obtained a ruling from the U.S. Internal Revenue Service that the liquidating dividend also will not be taxed by the U.S. government.

Cost of capital: Based on the sovereign and exchange risk characteristics of Paralivia, Smith-Capone gives Paralivia a BB rating and requires a rate of return of 20 percent on equity.

Projected demand, costs, and exchange rates:

YEAR	DEMAND FOR TYPEWRITERS (THOUSANDS)	PRICE (RINGOS)	UNIT VARIABLE OPERATING COST (RINGOS)	EXCHANGE RATE (RINGOS PER DOLLAR)
1999	50	1,000	400	2.1
2000	55	1,000	420	2.2
2001	60	1,100	440	2.3
2002	70	1,100	460	2.4
2003	80	1,200	490	2.5
2004	90	1,200	540	2.6

Fixed cost: Depreciation expense is 10 million ringos per year. Consider this to be the only fixed cost of the project.

Use the information above to answer the following questions.

a. Excluding the liquidating dividend, estimate the after-tax dividend received by the parent company each year.

b. Estimate the liquidating dividend, remembering that blocked depreciation flows are reinvested at 15 percent.

c. What is your recommendation for the project? (Consider its NPV, and specify any other relevant considerations.)

MINI CASE

Citrus Products Inc. is a medium-sized producer of citrus juice drinks with groves in Indian River County, Florida. Until now, the company has confined its operations and sales to the United States, but its CEO, George Gaynor, wants to expand into Europe. The first step would be to set up sales subsidiaries in Spain and Portugal, then set up a production plant in Spain, and, finally, distribute the product throughout the European Common Market. The firm's financial manager, Ruth Schmidt, is enthusiastic about the plan, but she is worried about the implications of the foreign expansion on the firm's financial management process. She has asked you, the firm's most recently hired financial analyst, to develop a 1-hour tutorial package that explains the basics of multinational financial management. The tutorial will be presented at the next board of directors' meeting. To get you started, Ms. Schmidt has supplied you with the following list of questions.

a. What is a multinational corporation? Why do firms expand into other countries?

b. What are the six major factors which distinguish multinational financial management from financial management as practiced by a purely domestic firm?

c. Consider the following illustrative exchange rates.

	U.S. DOLLARS REQUIRED TO BUY ONE UNIT OF FOREIGN CURRENCY
Spanish peseta	0.0093
Portuguese escudo	0.0067

(1) Are these currency prices direct quotations or indirect quotations?

(2) Calculate the indirect quotations for pesetas and escudos.

(3) What is a cross rate? Calculate the two cross rates between pesetas and escudos.

(4) Assume Citrus Products can produce a liter of orange juice and ship it to Spain for $1.75. If the firm wants a 50 percent markup on the product, what should the orange juice sell for in Spain?

(5) Now assume Citrus Products begins producing the same liter of orange juice in Spain. The product costs 200 pesetas to produce and ship to Portugal, where it can be sold for 400 escudos. What is the dollar profit on the sale?

(6) What is exchange rate risk?

d. Briefly describe the current international monetary system. How does the current system differ from the system that was in place prior to August 1971?

e. What is a convertible currency? What problems arise when a multinational company operates in a country whose currency is not convertible?

f. What is the difference between spot rates and forward rates? When is the forward rate at a premium to the spot rate? At a discount? How can a firm use the forward markets to hedge a future currency transaction?

g. What impact does relative inflation have on interest rates and exchange rates?

h. Briefly discuss the international money and capital markets.

i. What is the impact of multinational operations on each of the following financial management topics?

(1) Cash management

(2) Capital budgeting decisions

(3) Credit management

(4) Inventory management

SELECTED ADDITIONAL REFERENCES AND CASES

Perhaps the best way to obtain more information on multinational financial management is to consult one of the many excellent textbooks on the subject. For example, see

Eaker, Mark R, Frank J. Fabozzi, and Dwight Grant, *International Corporate Finance* (Fort Worth, Tex.: Dryden Press, 1996).

Levi, Maurice, *International Finance* (New York: McGraw-Hill, 1996).

Madura, Jeff, *International Financial Management* (St. Paul: West, 1995).

Shapiro, Alan C., *Multinational Financial Management* (Boston: Allyn and Bacon, 1992).

For some recent articles on multinational financial management, see

Black, Fischer, "Equilibrium Exchange Rate Hedging," *Journal of Finance,* July 1990, 899–907.

Carre, Herve, and Karen H. Johnson, "Progress Toward a European Monetary Union," *Federal Reserve Bulletin,* October 1991, 769–783.

Choi, Jongmoo Jay, and Anita Mehra Prasad, "Exchange Risk Sensitivity and Its Determinants: A Firm and Industry Analysis of U.S. Multinationals," *Financial Management,* Autumn 1995, 77–88.

Frankel, Jeffrey A., "The Japanese Cost of Finance," *Financial Management*, Spring 1991, 95–127.

Hammer, Jerry A., "Hedging Performance and Hedging Objectives: Tests of New Performance Measures in the Foreign Currency Market," *Journal of Financial Research*, Winter 1990, 307–323.

Hunter, William C., and Stephen G. Timme, "A Stochastic Dominance Approach to Evaluating Foreign Exchange Hedging Strategies," *Financial Management*, Autumn 1992, 104–112.

Kester, George W., Rosita P. Chang, and Kai-Chong Tsui, "Corporate Financial Policy in the Pacific Basin: Hong Kong and Singapore," *Financial Practice and Education*, Spring/Summer 1994, 117–127.

Lee, Insup, and Steve B. Wyatt, "The Effects of International Joint Ventures on Shareholder Wealth," *Financial Review*, November 1990.

Mahajan, Arvind, "Pricing Expropriation Risk," *Financial Management*, Winter 1990, 77–86.

Pauls, B. Dianne, "U.S. Exchange Rate Policy: Bretton Woods to Present," *Federal Reserve Bulletin*, November 1990, 891–908.

Two finance journals recently devoted entire issues to multinational financial management. See Financial Management, Winter 1991, and Journal of Applied Corporate Finance, Winter 1991 and Winter 1994.

The following case from the Cases in Financial Management: Dryden Request *series focuses on multinational capital budgeting:*

Case 18, "Alaska Oil Corporation."

CHAPTER 27

PENSION PLAN MANAGEMENT

*I*n 1995, GTE Corporation initiated a strategy that, if adopted by other firms, would have a significant effect on how companies manage their pension plan assets. The $12 billion pension fund organized a contest among some of the biggest money management names on Wall Street. Goldman Sachs, Morgan Stanley, J. P. Morgan, and the Boston firm of Grantham, Mayo, Van Otterloo & Company are each getting close to $1 billion to invest worldwide as they see fit. At the end of the exercise, which will last three to five years, the best performers likely will win a larger share of GTE's pension business.

The four managers' results will be measured against a benchmark index with 45 percent U.S. stocks, 25 percent foreign stocks, 20 percent U.S. bonds, 5 percent foreign bonds, and 5 percent money market funds. Further, the managers will be rewarded for good performance beyond mere bragging rights: Those who do well can earn as much as twice the standard fee, while those who perform poorly can lose up to two-thirds of the standard fee.

The GTE contest is unusual because most pension funds make their own broad asset allocation choices and then pick one or more individual managers within each category to invest solely within that category. The new approach, which turns over a chunk of the fund to a few broad-based managers with global reach, will reduce much of the time spent by GTE's pension fund staff in choosing and monitoring a large number of individual managers, whose results often wind up canceling one another out anyway. In addition, it leaves the asset allocation

---

This chapter was coauthored by Professor Jim Bicksler of Rutgers University. Professor Russ Fogler of the University of Florida also provided important contributions.

decision, which is by far the biggest factor in determining investment performance, to the outside managers.

GTE admits that the new approach is untried. According to GTE's pension fund chief, John Carroll, "If you want to stay ahead of your peers, you've got to do something different, which may or may not be the right thing." But he added, "If these four money managers can't beat the fixed allocation, then I don't think anybody can."

GTE was once known in the pension community for having an unusually large number of money managers — 60 for U.S. stocks alone in 1984. Since he was hired in 1985, Carroll has whittled the number down and shifted more of the actual stock and bond picking functions to GTE's internal managers. He also began negotiating performance fees for GTE's outside equity managers in 1986. Since his arrival, GTE's results have been excellent, with an average annual return of more than 14 percent for the past decade.

Pension plan management is important both to the employees, who depend on the plan for retirement income, and to the company itself, whose very existence could be threatened by poor pension plan management. Although this chapter cannot make you an expert in pension plans and their management, it can inform you about the key issues that managers and employees must face.

Pension plans are an important component of the U.S. financial system: (1) In 1996, pension funds had an aggregate market value of more than $5 trillion, and they owned more than 25 percent of all U.S. stocks and more than 40 percent of all corporate bonds. (2) Pension plans provide workers with the majority of their retirement income. (3) Contributions to pension plans are an important component of most compensation plans, and they affect both labor productivity and economic stability. (4) The rate of return on pension plan assets can have a major effect on corporate earnings, employees' retirement incomes, or both. (5) Because pension plans are large and concentrated owners of corporate stocks, their managers play an important role in corporate governance.

In this chapter, we discuss the different types of pension plans, their management and regulation, and their effects on both individuals and firms.

THE ROLE AND SCOPE OF PENSION PLAN MANAGEMENT

Most companies—and practically all government units — have some type of employee pension plan. Typically, the chief financial officer (CFO) administers the plan, and he or she has these three specific responsibilities: (1) deciding on the general nature of the plan, (2) determining the required annual payments into the plan, and (3) managing the plan's assets. Obviously, the company does not have total control over these decisions — employees, often through their unions, have a major say about the plan's structure, and the federal government imposes strict rules on certain aspects of all plans. Still, companies have considerable latitude regarding several key decisions, and these decisions can materially affect the firm's profitability and its employees' welfare.

Although a few firms have provided pensions since the turn of the century, the real start of large-scale pension plans dates from 1949, when the United Steelworkers negotiated a comprehensive retirement plan in their contract with the steel companies. Other industries followed, and the plans grew rapidly thereafter. Under a typical pension plan, the company (or governmental unit) agrees to provide retirement payments to employees. These promised payments constitute a liability, and the employer is required to establish a *pension fund* and place money in it each year in order to have sufficient assets to meet pension payments as they come due.

Pension plan assets represent a large fraction of total assets for many firms. If the pension fund is managed well and produces relatively high returns, the firm's required contributions can be minimized. However, if the fund does not perform well, then the firm will have to increase contributions to the fund, which will have a negative effect on earnings.

Pension fund management is an important but complex job. Indeed, pension fund administration requires so much specialized technical knowledge that companies typically hire specialists as consultants to help design, modify, and administer their plans. Still, because the plans are under the general supervision of the financial staff, and because the plans have such significant implications for the firm as a whole, it is important that financial managers understand the basics of pension plan management.

SELF-TEST QUESTIONS

What are the three primary responsibilities of the CFO regarding pension fund management?

Why is pension fund management important to most firms?

KEY CONCEPTS

Certain concepts are used frequently in pension plan management, and it is useful to discuss them at the outset. We will have more to say about many of these items in later sections.

DEFINED CONTRIBUTION PLAN

Under all pension plans, the employer agrees to pay something to employees when they retire. Rather than specifying exactly how much each retiree will receive, companies can agree to make specific payments into a retirement fund and then have retirees receive benefits that vary depending on the plan's investment success. This type of plan is called a *defined contribution plan.* For example, a trucking firm might agree to make payments equal to 15 percent of all union members' wages each year into a pension fund administered by the Teamsters' Union, and the fund would then dispense benefits to retirees. Such plans do not have to be administered by unions—they could be administered by a bank's trust department, or the monthly payments applicable to each employee could simply be paid into a mutual fund of the employee's choice and credited to the employee's account.

A defined contribution plan is, in effect, a savings plan that is funded by employers, although many plans also permit additional contributions by employees. The firm is obligated, in bad times as well as in good, to make specified contributions on behalf of participating employees. There are a number of different defined contribution plans, such as money purchase pension plans, thrift plans, 401(k) plans, and Employee Stock Ownership Plans (ESOPs).[1] Defined contribution plans are not subject to the rules of the Employee Retirement Income Security Act of 1974 (discussed later). Additionally, such plans are portable (also discussed later) in that the assets belong to the employee whenever he or she terminates employment. Since the sponsoring firm does not guarantee any specific dollar payments to participants upon retirement, participants in a defined contribution plan bear all of the investment risk associated with poor portfolio performance. However, most defined contribution plans allow participants to choose among several investment alternatives, so each individual can match his or her own risk preference.

To illustrate a defined contribution plan, consider the one offered by Merck. Employees can contribute up to 15 percent of their pre-tax salaries into the plan, which is deductible from the employees' taxable income. Further, the company will match an employee's contribution by 50 cents on each dollar up to 5 percent of salary. For example, if an employee making $50,000 per year contributes the maximum 0.15($50,000) = $7,500, Merck will chip in an additional $2,500 for a total contribution of $10,000. Since all contributions are made from pre-tax income, employees must pay income taxes on all retirement benefits received. In other words, since contributions to the plan are deducted from taxable income, benefits received from the plan are fully taxed.

DEFINED BENEFIT PLAN

Under a *defined benefit plan,* the employer agrees to give retirees a specifically defined benefit, such as $500 per month, 50 percent of his or her average salary over the five years preceding retirement, or 2.5 percent of his or her highest annual salary for each year of employment. The payments could be fixed as of the retirement date, or they could be indexed to increase as the cost of living increases. The key, though, is that payments to retirees, not the cost to the company, are specified (defined).

Defined benefit plans differ in several important respects from defined contribution plans. Most important, the sponsoring firm, not the participants, bears the risk of poor portfolio performance. The company has a firm obligation to its retirees that must be met regardless of how well or poorly the pension plan assets perform. While defined benefit participants expect to receive a particular amount based on salary and years of service, most still bear purchasing-power risk — that is, the risk that inflation will eat away at the purchasing power of a fixed pension payment.[2]

---

[1]An ESOP uses a stock bonus plan and/or a money purchase plan to invest in the firm's common stock. In a KASOP, which is a variation of the ESOP, the firm's contribution consists of shares of its common stock, but employee contributions can be invested in other alternatives.

[2]The plight of many retirees in the former Soviet Union provides a vivid example of purchasing-power risk. One Russian retiree, who was at least able to live on her monthly government pension prior to the breakup, found herself with a pension worth only $8 per month after the breakup and subsequent inflation. If U.S. inflation gets bad, U.S. pensioners could find themselves in the same boat.

To illustrate a defined benefit plan, consider the plan offered by Eastman Kodak. Assuming an employee had 30 years of service and a final annual income of $50,000, Kodak's plan promises to pay $19,700 per year at age 65. This is 1.31 percent of the final salary for each year of service. Thus, an employee who started with Kodak at age 21 could quit work at age 51 and begin to collect his or her pension at age 65. Alternatively, full benefits could be collected when the employee's years of service plus age equals 85, so an employee could begin with Kodak at age 25, work to age 55, and collect full benefits. If a vested employee does not meet one of these guidelines for full benefits, he or she can still receive retirement benefits, but at less than the full amount.

PROFIT SHARING PLAN

A third type of plan calls for the employer to make payments into the retirement fund, but with the payments varying with the level of corporate profits; this is a *profit sharing plan.* For example, a computer manufacturer might agree to pay 10 percent of its pre-tax profits into a fund which would then invest the proceeds and pay benefits to employees upon their retirement. These plans are operated like defined contribution plans in the sense that each employee's funds are maintained in a separate account, and benefits depend on the plan's performance. Profit sharing plans can be operated separately or used in conjunction with defined benefit or defined contribution plans. For example, a drug company might have a defined benefit plan which pays employees 1.0 percent of their final average salary for each year of employment and, in addition, have a profit sharing plan which calls for putting 5 percent of the firm's pre-tax profits into an account for retired employees. As noted above, under most profit sharing plans, a separate account is maintained for each employee, and each employee gets a share of the contribution each year based upon his or her salary. The employee's account builds up over time just as if the employee were putting money into a mutual fund, which may in fact be the case.

VESTING

If employees have a right to receive pension benefits even if they leave the company prior to retirement, then their pension rights are said to be *vested.* If the employee loses his or her pension rights by leaving the company prior to retirement, the rights are said to be *nonvested.* Most defined benefit plans today have *deferred vesting,* which means that pension rights are nonvested for the first few years, but become fully vested if the employee remains with the company for a prescribed period, say, five years. The costs to the company are clearly lower for plans with deferred vesting, because such plans do not cover employees who leave prior to vesting. Moreover, deferred vesting tends to reduce turnover, which, in turn, lowers training costs. However, it is much easier to recruit employees if the plan offers early vesting. Also, many argue that vesting is socially desirable, and as a result there has been a tendency over time for Congress to require vesting for more and more employees and within a shorter and shorter period of time.

Currently, companies with defined benefit plans are required to vest participants at least as fast as either the five-year rule or the three-to-seven-year rule:

1. **Five-year rule.** Under this rule, participants must be fully vested after five years of service. This is called *cliff vesting*—the participant is either vested or not vested, with no partial vesting.

2. **Three-to-seven-year rule.** Under this rule, participants are partially vested according to the number of years of service:

YEARS OF SERVICE	PERCENT VESTED
3	20%
4	40
5	60
6	80
7	100

Of course, employers may offer plans that vest pension rights more quickly than mandated by these two vesting rules.

PORTABILITY

Portable means "capable of being carried," and a *portable pension plan* is one that an employee can carry from one employer to another. Portability is extremely important in occupations such as construction, where workers move from one employer to another fairly frequently. A defined contribution plan is always portable, because the plan's assets are held in the employees' names. However, for a defined benefit plan to be portable, both the old employer and the new employer must be part of the same plan—it would simply not be feasible for an IBM employee to leave IBM and go to work for Delta Airlines and take along a share of the IBM plan. (Note, however, that if the employee's rights under the IBM plan were vested, then he or she could receive payments from both Delta's and IBM's plans upon retirement.) Where job changes are frequent—as in trucking, construction, and coal mining—union-administered plans are used to make portability possible.

FUNDING

Under either a defined contribution plan or a profit sharing plan, the company must make required annual contributions to the plan. However, under a defined benefit plan the company promises to give employees pensions for some unknown number of future years, so its true costs are uncertain. However, pension fund actuaries can determine the present value of the expected future benefits under a defined benefit plan, and this present value constitutes a liability of the plan. This liability may be measured (1) by the present value of *all projected* benefits accrued by present workers, or (2) by the present value of *vested* benefits earned to date. The vested amount is obviously smaller, and it represents the expected present value of the benefits that would be paid to workers if the firm went out of business today or if all workers resigned today. The value of the fund's assets can easily be determined: it is the current market value of the fund's assets. If the present value of expected retirement benefits is equal to assets on hand, then the plan is said to be *fully funded.* If assets exceed the present value of benefits, the plan is *overfunded.* If the present value of benefits exceeds assets, the plan is *underfunded,* and an *unfunded pension liability* exists.

ACTUARIAL RATE OF RETURN

The discount rate used to determine the present value of future benefits under a defined benefit plan, and the rate of return at which the fund's assets are assumed to be invested, is called the *actuarial rate of return.*

The actuarial rate of return is a critical element in pension plan management because it has a significant impact on the employer's required annual contributions. A higher assumed actuarial rate leads to lower current contribution requirements for two reasons: (1) the present value of benefits will be lower, and (2) the plan's assets will be assumed to earn more, hence to grow at a faster rate. Since the actuarial rate is a forecast of the expected future rate of return on the plan's assets, there is a great deal of room for judgment. Some firms base their actuarial rate on recent plan performance, while others base the rate on long-term historical returns on different asset classes and then apply these historical returns to the plan's current asset mix to get a weighted average. If the estimates are unbiased, errors in actuarial rate assumptions should balance out over time. However, if a firm purposely sets its actuarial rate too high in order to hold down its contributions, its pension plan will build up a large unfunded deficiency.

ERISA

The *Employee Retirement Income Security Act of 1974 (ERISA)* is the basic federal law governing the structure and administration of corporate pension plans. ERISA requires that companies fully fund their defined benefit pension plans, although it gives them up to 30 years to make up for underfunding of past service benefits. For example, if a company agreed in 1995 to double payments to all employees who retire in the future, it would immediately have a large unfunded liability. If the company had to come up with the money to fully fund its plan, it would not be able to offer the improved benefits. The prolonged adjustment period is obviously important in such a situation.

In addition, ERISA has several other provisions which affect the management of defined benefit plans. First, ERISA mandates that pension funds be managed according to the "prudent man" rule, which focuses on diversification as the cornerstone of portfolio management. This has resulted in pension funds diversifying into such investments as real estate, international stocks and bonds, LBOs, and venture capital. Second, ERISA sets the mandatory vesting requirements discussed earlier to prevent situations whereby long-term employees are fired or laid off just before their benefits are vested. Finally, ERISA established the Pension Benefit Guarantee Corporation (PBGC), which we discuss next.

PBGC

The *Pension Benefit Guarantee Corporation (PBGC)* was established by ERISA to insure corporate defined benefit pension funds. The PBGC, which is an agency within the U.S. Department of Labor, steps in and takes over payments to retirees of bankrupt companies with underfunded pension plans. Currently, the PBGC is paying benefits to some 350,000 retirees from about 1,800 companies, including Pan American Airlines, Eastern Airlines, Allis-Chalmers, Republic Steel, and LTV Corporation.

Funds for the PBGC come from premiums paid by sponsors of defined benefit plans. Currently, the premium is $19 per participant per year, plus an additional fee of $9 per $1,000 of unfunded liabilities, not to exceed a total of $72. However, the ultimate backers of the PBGC are the taxpayers, and some critics have voiced concern over its financial soundness. The bankruptcy of Pan Am alone brought $840 million of unfunded pension liabilities to the PBGC. The current deficit is about $3 billion, and about 16,000 of the 66,000 plans that are covered by the PBGC are underfunded, with a total potential deficiency of about $30 billion. Furthermore, projections indicate that the guarantee fund will be in the red by a much greater amount by the end of the decade. To help control costs, the PBGC does not cover company-promised health insurance for retirees. Further, PBGC payments to retirees are capped at about $28,000 per year per plan, which for some highly paid workers is much less than their plan originally promised. Finally, the PBGC does not guarantee pensions that are paid by annuities purchased by plans from insurance companies. This feature is important, because in the 1980s, many companies terminated overfunded defined benefit plans, used a portion of the plan's assets to purchase insurance contracts to cover promised benefit payments, and then recovered the excess assets for the company.

CONTRIBUTIONS TO THE PLAN

Actuaries calculate each year how much a company must pay into a defined benefit fund in order to keep it fully funded (or to move it toward full funding). These contributions are a tax-deductible expense, just as are wages. Obviously, if a company agrees to an increase in benefits, this increases its required contribution and consequently lowers its reported profits and cash flow to stockholders. Also, if pension benefits are tied to wages, then any wage increase will also require an increase in payments to the pension plan. Payments also depend on the investment performance of the pension fund — if the fund's managers do a good job of investing its assets, then required annual contributions will be reduced, and vice versa if the fund's investment performance is poor.

FASB

The *Financial Accounting Standards Board (FASB),* together with the SEC, establishes the rules under which a firm reports its financial condition to stockholders. FASB Statement 87, "Employers' Accounting for Pension Plans," and Statement 35,

"Accounting and Reporting by Defined Benefit Plans," provide guidance for reporting pension costs, assets, and liabilities. The reporting of defined contribution plans is relatively straightforward — the annual contribution is shown on the income statement, and a note to the financial statements explains the entry. However, reporting for defined benefit plans is much more complex. Basically, a firm with a defined benefit plan must report the following information in its annual report:[3]

1. The plan's overall funding status must be shown directly on the firm's balance sheet if the plan is underfunded; overfunding, however, is not reported directly on the balance sheet.

2. The annual pension expense must be shown on the firm's income statement, and the difference between the actual contribution and the pension expense is accumulated and shown on the balance sheet.

3. A full description of the pension plan, including the employee groups covered, type of benefit formula, funding policy, and types of assets held, must be included in the notes section.

4. The breakdown of the annual pension expense—including (a) the required contribution to cover new obligations, (b) the interest cost to cover the passage of time, and (c) the actual return on plan assets for the period—must be included in the notes section.

5. A schedule which reconciles the plan's status as shown on the balance sheet must be included in the notes section.

6. The actuarial discount rate used, and any justified difference between this rate and the rates used to project the benefit obligation or to project the return on the plan's assets, must appear in the notes section.

7. The amounts and types of securities issued by the employer and/or related parties that are held by the plan must be reported in the notes section.

SELF-TEST QUESTION

Define the following terms:
(1) Defined benefit plan; defined contribution plan; profit sharing plan
(2) Vested; nonvested; deferred vesting
(3) Portability
(4) Fully funded; overfunded; underfunded
(5) Actuarial rate of return
(6) ERISA
(7) PBGC
(8) Plan contributions
(9) FASB reporting

---

[3]FASB Statement 87 is very complex, hence we cannot discuss its provisions in detail in this text.

PENSION FUND MATHEMATICS

It is clear from the preceding definitions that the calculation of the present value of expected future benefits is of primary importance in defined benefit pension plans. This calculation determines both the required contribution to the fund for the year and the reported unfunded liability or surplus. Thus, it is essential that financial managers understand the basic mathematics which underlies the benefits calculation.

To illustrate the process, let us begin with the following assumptions:

1. A firm has only one employee, age 40, who will retire 25 years from now, at age 65, will die at age 80, and hence will live for 15 years after retirement. There is no uncertainty about these facts.

2. The firm has promised a benefit of $10,000 at the end of each year following retirement until death. For accounting purposes, 1/25 of this $10,000 payment will be vested each year the employee works for the company.

3. No uncertainty regarding the contribution stream exists; that is, the company will definitely make the required payments, in equal annual installments over the next 25 years, in order to build up the fund to the level needed to make the payments of $10,000 per year during the employee's 15-year retirement life.

4. The pension fund will earn 8 percent on its assets; this rate is also known with certainty.

The problem is to find (1) the present value of the future benefits and (2) the company's required annual contributions. We find these values as follows:

Step 1. Find the present value (at retirement) of a 15-year regular annuity of $10,000 per year:

$$\text{PV of an annuity of \$10,000 per year for 15 years at 8\%} = \$10,000(\text{PVIFA}_{8\%,15}) = \$85,594.79.$$

(Using a financial calculator, enter PMT = 10000 [or − 10000], n = 15, and i = 8; then solve for PV = $85,594.79.)

Step 2. Find the set of equal annual cash contributions required to accumulate $85,594.79 over 25 years:

$$\text{Annual cash contribution to establish a fund of \$85,594.79 over a 25-year period at 8\%} = \frac{\$85,594.79}{\text{FVIFA}_{8\%,25}} = \$1,170.83.$$

(Using a financial calculator, enter FV = 85594.79 [or −85594.79], n = 25, and i = 8; then solve for PMT = $1,170.83.) Thus, the company must contribute $1,170.83 per year to satisfy its pension requirements. If it makes these payments each year, it will be able to report a fully funded position.

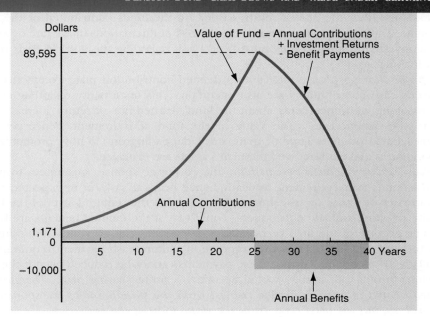

PENSION FUND CASH FLOWS AND VALUE UNDER CERTAINTY | **FIGURE 27-1**

A graphical representation of the contribution and benefit cash flows and fund value is presented in Figure 27-1. The "Value of Fund" line is drawn continuously, although in reality it would be a step function. Note also that setting up a pension plan for this worker requires analysis over a 40-year horizon.

The rate of return assumed makes a substantial difference in the annual contribution. If we had assumed a return of 9 percent rather than 8 percent, the annual contributions would have dropped from $1,170.83 to $951.67. Thus, annual contributions would have fallen by 18.7 percent from only a one percentage point change in the assumed investment rate. Conversely, if we had assumed a 7 percent return, the annual contributions would have increased to $1,440.01, a 23 percent increase. Assumptions about how long the worker will live, years before retirement, and, if the payment is based on salary, annual raises will have similarly large effects on the required annual contribution.

Draw a sketch which summarizes the mathematics of pension funding.
How can discounted cash flow (DCF) concepts be used to estimate the annual funding requirement?

SELF-TEST QUESTIONS

RISKS INHERENT IN PENSION PLANS

Different types of plans differ with regard to the certainty of cash contributions, investment earnings, and promised benefits at retirement. In a *defined contribution plan,* the corporation, or *plan sponsor,* contributes a guaranteed amount which will be invested for eventual payments to the beneficiaries. No guarantee, however, is made about either the rate of return earned on the funds contributed or the final payments. Thus, the beneficiaries assume the risk of fluctuations in the rate of return on the invested money, so they must bear a risk regarding the level of their retirement incomes.

A *profit sharing plan* is similar to a defined contribution plan, except that the sponsor's cash contributions are also uncertain. This uncertainty regarding contributions, along with uncertainty about the fund's earned rate of return, increases the risk to the beneficiaries. The value of the fund at retirement, hence retirees' incomes, could be quite large or quite small, depending on (1) how profitable the corporation is and (2) how well the plan's assets are managed.

Finally, under a *defined benefit plan,* the corporate sponsor guarantees to pay a stated amount from retirement to death, hence bears all risks of unexpected variations in rates of return on investment. Note too that the required level of the fund, and the resulting annual contributions, could vary if the defined benefits are based on some average of the final years' salaries, for salaries can grow at a rate different from the assumed level. Thus, the corporation's future cash payment requirements are relatively uncertain. Further, these payments cannot be reduced even if the corporation's profits fall, as they would be under a profit sharing plan. *Therefore, a defined benefit plan is by far the riskiest from the standpoint of the sponsoring corporation, but the least risky from the standpoint of the employees.*

Large corporations generally use defined benefit plans, while smaller ones typically use profit sharing and/or defined contribution plans. As a result, approximately 75 percent of current pension plans are defined contribution or profit sharing plans, but they include only 35 percent of the total number of employees participating in pension plans. The reason for this situation lies in the relative ability to bear risk — large firms such as GM, GE, and IBM can assume the risks inherent in defined benefit plans better than their employees, but many small firms simply do not have the stability required to assume such long-term risks, and consequently both they and their employees are better off under a defined contribution and/or a profit sharing plan. However, the high and volatile inflation of the 1970s and early 1980s has motivated even some larger companies to terminate their defined benefit plans in favor of defined contribution plans. So, there is a strong trend away from defined benefit plans.

RISKS TO THE CORPORATION

The allocation of risks inherent in pension plan operations depends on how the plans are structured. Under a defined benefit plan, the risks fall primarily on the corporation. If the plan calls for defined contributions, then risks are shared. Under a profit sharing plan, almost all the risk falls on the beneficiaries. Risk to the corporation under a defined benefit plan can be further subdivided into (1) uncertainty about the annual cash contribution and (2) uncertainty about the firm's obligations in the event it goes bankrupt.

RISKS OF ANNUAL CASH CONTRIBUTIONS   The *minimum annual cash contribution* is the sum of (1) the amount needed to fund projected future benefit payments that were accrued during the current period, (2) the amount (which could be zero) that must be contributed to make up for not having funded all benefits for service that occurred prior to the current period, and (3) an additional amount (which could be zero or negative) required to offset unexpected deviations from the plan's actuarial assumptions, especially deviations in the earned rate of return and in employee turnover and wage rates. This minimum cash contribution can be expressed by the following equation:

$$\text{Minimum cash contribution} = NC + PS + AG,$$

where

NC = normal contribution, which is a figure based on funding the present value of benefits earned for service during the current period, discounted at the actuarial rate. NC can vary widely depending on the assumptions made about the return on pension plan assets, future employee turnover, and future salary increases.

PS = past service, which is the make-up contribution for unfunded past service. The minimum PS make-up under ERISA is the amount required to amortize the unfunded liability on a straight line basis over 30 years. The company can, if it has the cash and chooses to do so, set PS equal to the full unfunded liability and hence immediately bring the plan up to full funding. However, for tax purposes the IRS will allow as a deduction only amounts based on amortization over a 10-year or longer period.

AG = actuarial gains and losses from the assumed actuarial forecast, amortized over 15 years at the plan's assumed rate of interest. These actuarial gains or losses could occur because of deviations in employee turnover, final salaries, life expectancy, and so on, and also because of deviations between actual and expected investment performance for the fund's assets.

In our Figure 27-1 illustration of pension fund mathematics, the annual cash contributions were known with certainty. In actual plans, there are three key types of actuarial assumptions which reflect real-world risks: (1) *decrement assumptions*, which allow the actuary to adjust annually for the probability that any employee will leave the company (that is, terminate employment, become disabled, retire, or die); (2) *future salary assumptions*, which take into account expected future average wage increases, which will, of course, affect the final salary and hence defined benefit payments based on the final salary; and (3) *discount rate assumptions*, which explicitly forecast the portfolio's expected future rate of return, which is used both to compound the fund's growth from investment and to discount and thus find the present value of future benefits.

At the end of each year, the assumptions are examined and modified if necessary, and actuaries determine the present value of expected future benefits. Then the deviation between this value and the actual value of the fund's assets is calculated, and it becomes part of an account called "total cumulative actuarial gains and losses." Then the annual cash contribution is adjusted by an amount sufficient to amortize this cumulative amount over a 15-year period. For example, suppose a fund were set up on January 1, 1996, and money were deposited based on a set of actuarial assumptions. Then, at the end of the year, the actual actuarial conditions were examined and compared with the assumed conditions, and the actual value of the fund was compared with the money that would be needed for full funding under the revised actuarial assumptions. Any difference between the actual and required fund balance would be added to the cumulative gains and losses account, and the required annual contribution would be increased or decreased by an amount sufficient to amortize this account's balance over a 15-year period. The same method would be used at the end of 1997; the cumulative gains and losses account would be adjusted, and a new 15-year amortization payment for actuarial gains and losses would be determined. To illustrate, suppose the cumulative amount in the actuarial gains and losses account at the end of 1996 were a $15 million shortfall, and the actuarial earnings rate were 8 percent. Under these conditions, in 1997 the value of AG would be $1.75 million, because this level of AG would eliminate the deficiency over 15 years. If everything else remained constant, then AG would remain at $1.75 million for 15 years. However, in future years new deviations are bound to occur, and the cumulative amount of actuarial gains and losses will rise or fall, requiring new calculations and new values for AG. All of this is designed to build the fund up to its required level but, at the same time, to smooth out the required annual cash contribution and thus smooth out the firm's reported profits and cash flows.

BANKRUPTCY LIENS   Prior to ERISA, employees had no claim against a corporation's assets in the event of bankruptcy. Of course, if a defined benefit plan were fully funded, bankruptcy would present no problem for employees, but bankruptcies did impose serious hardships on members of plans that were not fully funded. Congress elevated the priority of unfunded vested pension liabilities in the event of bankruptcy, and today unfunded vested liabilities have a lien with the same priority as federal taxes on up to 30 percent of the stockholders' equity. Thus, the pension fund ranks above the unsecured creditors for up to 30 percent of common and preferred equity, and any unsatisfied pension claims rank on a par with those of the general creditors.[4]

If one of the subsidiaries of a holding company had been operating at a loss, and consequently had a low net worth, and if the subsidiary also had an unfunded pension liability which was greater than its net worth, then the parent company would probably be better off without the subsidiary than with it. This situation has undoubtedly led some companies to spin off or otherwise dispose of subsidiaries. Such spin-offs have a detrimental effect on the PBGC, which in fact sued International Harvester (IH) for selling its Wisconsin Steel subsidiary three years before the subsidiary went bankrupt and turned its underfunded pension plan over to the PBGC. The PBGC claimed that the purpose of the divestiture was to rid IH of its subsidiary's pension liability. Several recent leveraged buyouts of divisions of corporations may also have been motivated in part by pension plan considerations.

---

[4]Note that if a company has been suffering losses prior to bankruptcy, which is generally the case, its equity will be low, and 30 percent of a low number is lower yet. Nevertheless, PBGC must still make full payments as specified in the company's plan to all vested pension holders, subject to the limits noted previously.

EFFECTS OF PENSION PLANS ON STOCK PRICES   The value of a firm's stock is obviously affected by its pension plan, but because of the uncertainties inherent in pension plan calculations, devising reasonable accounting procedures for reporting both the annual pension expense and the corporation's pension liabilities has proved to be quite difficult. FASB Statement 87 was designed both to increase the disclosure of information about a pension fund's condition and to mandate more uniformity in choosing the actuarial rate of return used to calculate the present value of benefits. However, because of the vast variety of funding techniques and the great difficulty involved in forecasting future pension liabilities, reported pension plan data must still be viewed with a certain amount of skepticism.[5]

Can investors make sense of pension fund accounting data? To help answer this question, researchers have examined the relationship between corporations' market values and their pension fund liabilities, and they concluded that investors recognize the existence of unfunded pension liabilities and lower the firm's value accordingly.[6] This and other evidence indicates that investors are well aware of the condition of companies' pension funds, and that unfunded pension liabilities do reduce corporate value.

RISKS TO BENEFICIARIES

Although the preceding section might suggest that most of the risks inherent in a defined benefit pension plan are borne by the PBGC or the corporate sponsor, this is not entirely true. For example, suppose that in 1996 a corporation went bankrupt and its employees were laid off. It is true that the PBGC will provide the promised retirement payments when the employees actually retire. But suppose an employee is 50 years old now, his or her benefits are $10,000 per year, and retirement, as defined by the plan, is 15 years away. If the firm is in an industry where employment is declining, such as steel or textiles, the worker will have a hard time finding a new job offering comparable wages. Moreover, even if the worker could get another job that provides the same salary and an equivalent pension plan, his or her benefits will still be adversely affected. The benefits under the bankrupt company's plan will be frozen — the past benefits from the now-bankrupt firm will not be increased as a result of pay increases over the worker's remaining employment life, as they probably would have been had the original employer not gone bankrupt. The worker's benefits under his or her new plan, assuming he or she does get a new job, would rise with inflation, but the worker's retirement income will be the sum of payments under the old frozen plan and the new one, and these benefits will almost certainly be lower than they would have been had no bankruptcy occurred. To illustrate, if his or her plan were terminated, a 50-year-old manager with a $100,000 annual salary typically would rate a yearly pension of $36,000 when he or she reaches age 65. However, if the manager had been able to continue working at the company, and salaries had increased by 5 percent annually, then the pension benefit would have

---

[5]FASB Statement 87 was passed by a 4–3 vote, which reflects the lack of consensus regarding the proper accounting treatment for pension plans.

[6]For example, see Martin Feldstein and Randall Morck, "Pension Funds and the Value of Equities," *Financial Analysts Journal,* September–October 1983, 29–39.

come to about $75,000 a year. Thus, bankruptcy still imposes hardships on workers, and a realization of this fact has been a major factor in unions' acceptance of reduced wages and benefits in situations where bankruptcy and resulting layoffs would otherwise have occurred.

It should also be recognized (1) that prior to the 1930s most people had to depend on personal savings (and their children) to support them in their old age, (2) that Social Security was put into effect in 1933 to provide a formalized retirement system for workers, (3) that corporate pension plans did not really "take off" until after World War II, and (4) that even today many workers, especially those employed by smaller firms, have no formal retirement plan other than Social Security. Also, when the Social Security Act was passed in 1933, it was supposed to be based on insurance principles in the sense that each person would pay into the system and then receive benefits which, actuarially, were equivalent to what he or she had paid in. Thus, Social Security was designed to help workers provide for their own future. Today, Social Security has become an income transfer mechanism in that workers with high salaries get less out of the system than they pay in, while low-salaried workers get more out than they pay in. In a sense, the Social Security system, including Medicare, has become a "safety net" for all older Americans, irrespective of their payments into the system. Even so, few people want to be totally dependent on the income provided by Social Security, so private pension plans are still a vital part of the American economic scene.

SELF-TEST QUESTION   Consider the three types of pension plans: (1) defined benefit, (2) defined contribution, and (3) profit sharing. Describe how each plan type affects the risks to the corporation and the risks to beneficiaries.

ILLUSTRATION OF A DEFINED BENEFIT VERSUS A DEFINED CONTRIBUTION PLAN

Many corporations and governmental units give their employees a choice between a defined benefit plan and a defined contribution plan. The implications of these plans ought to be understood both by employees and by the agencies responsible for paying the prescribed benefits. Although pension plan status would rarely be the primary factor when choosing a job, it still should be given at least some consideration. Our example does not correspond (to our knowledge) exactly with the plan of any university, but the University of Florida and UCLA do have plans that are similar to our hypothetical University DB (for defined benefit), while the University of Wisconsin and many private colleges have plans similar to our hypothetical University DC (for defined contribution).

Here are the assumptions used in the illustration:

1. It is now 1997.

2. The employee is 30 years old, earns $30,000 per year, and plans to retire in 35 years, at age 65.

3. Both universities provide for immediate vesting. (This is not always the case.)

4. The rate of inflation is expected to be 6 percent per year. Salaries will also increase at this same rate.

5. Pension fund assets are expected to earn a return of 10 percent.

6. The employee is expected to live for 15 years past retirement at age 65, or to age 80.

UNIVERSITY DB: DEFINED BENEFIT

This school has a defined benefit plan which offers 2 percent of the average salary paid during the last year the employee works for the university for each year of service at the university. Thus, if the employee worked for one year and then resigned, we would have the following situation:

1. The annual benefit at age 65 would be 0.02($30,000) = $600.

2. The amount needed to establish an annuity of $600 per year for 15 years (assuming payment at the end of each year) would be

$$\text{PV of the annuity} = \sum_{t=1}^{15} \frac{\$600}{(1.10)^t} = \$4,564.$$

3. The university will have to put up $162 today to provide the required annuity 35 years from now.[7]

$$\text{PV of the PV of the annuity} = \$4,564/(1.10)^{35} = \$162.$$

Thus the cost to the university is $162. (The cost to the university would have been $4,564 had the employee been 64 years old instead of 30; this helps explain why older workers sometimes have a hard time landing jobs.)

4. Given an inflation rate of 6 percent, the real (1997) value of the income for the employee from this pension would be $78 in the first year of retirement:

$$\text{Real income} = \$600/(1.06)^{35} = \$78.$$

If the person remained at University DB until retirement, and if his or her salary increased with inflation, then the final salary would be $30,000(1.06)^{35} = $230,583 per year, and his or her retirement income would be 0.02(35)($230,583) = $161,408, or 70 percent of the $230,583 final salary. The real (1997 dollar) retirement income would be $21,000, or 70 percent of the 1997 employment income, $30,000.

UNIVERSITY DC: DEFINED CONTRIBUTION

This school has a defined contribution plan under which an amount equal to 6 percent of each employee's salary is put into a pension fund account. The fund

---

[7]We have assumed that inflation in wages is not built into the funding requirement. If a 6 percent wage inflation were built in, then the cost would rise from $162 to $1,245 (as determined by a simple spreadsheet model).

keeps track of the dollar amount of the contribution attributable to each employee, just as if the university had put the money into a bank time deposit or mutual fund for the employee. (Indeed, the money may actually go into a mutual fund.) Here is the situation if the employee worked for one year and then resigned:

1. The university would contribute 0.06($30,000) = $1,800 to the employee's account in the pension fund. This is the university's cost, and it would be the same irrespective of the employee's age.

2. The fund's assets would earn 10 percent per year, so when the employee retired, the value of his or her share of the fund would be

$$\text{Value in fund} = \$1,800(1.10)^{35} = \$50,584.$$

3. At a 10 percent rate of return, this $50,584 would provide an annuity of $6,650 per year for 15 years. To get this result, enter N = 15, I = 10, PV = $50,584, and FV = 0, and press PMT to obtain $6,650.

4. The real (1997) retirement income for this person would be

$$\text{Real income} = \$6,650/(1.06)^{35} = \$865.$$

If the person remained at University DC, his or her retirement fund would accumulate to $1,024,444 over the 35-year employment period (we used a spreadsheet model to obtain this amount). This would provide a retirement income of $134,688, or 58 percent of the $230,583 final salary. The real (1997 dollar) retirement income would be $17,524, or 58 percent of the 1997 employment income.

CONCLUSIONS

1. A young employee who has a high probability of moving would be better off under a defined contribution plan such as the one offered by University DC.

2. A worker who planned to spend his or her entire career at one school would be better off at University DB, with its defined benefit plan.

3. The economic consequences of changing jobs are much worse under the defined benefit plan because benefits are frozen rather than increased with inflation. Therefore, defined benefit plans contribute to lower employee turnover, other factors held constant.

4. It is much more costly to a university (or to a company) to hire older workers if it operates under a defined benefit plan than if it operates under a defined contribution plan. In our example, the 1997 cost to provide pension benefits to a 30-year-old employee under the defined benefit plan would be $162 versus $4,564 for a 64-year-old employee earning the same salary. The average cost per employee to the university would depend on the age distribution of employees. However, the cost would be $1,800 per employee, irrespective of age, under the defined contribution plan. Thus, defined benefit plans carry

with them an economic incentive to discriminate against older workers in hiring, while defined contribution plans are neutral in this regard. Of course, it is illegal to discriminate on the basis of age, but other reasons could be stated for favoring younger workers.

5. If one were to vary the assumptions, it would be easy to show that employees are generally exposed to more risks under the defined contribution plan, while employers face more risks under the defined benefit plan. In particular, the pension benefits under the defined contribution plan are highly sensitive to changes in the rate of return earned on the pension fund's investments. Likewise, the costs to University DB would vary greatly depending on investment performance, but University DC's costs would not vary with respect to changes in investment performance.

6. We could have changed the facts of the example to deal with an "average man" with a life expectancy of 70.6 years and an "average woman" with a 78.2-year life expectancy. Obviously, an average woman would receive benefits over a longer period and thus would need a larger accumulated sum in the plan upon retirement, hence would have a higher actuarial annual required cost to the university than an average man under the defined benefit plan. Thus, other factors held constant, there is an economic incentive for employers to discriminate against women in their hiring practices if they use defined benefit plans. Defined contribution plans are again neutral in this regard.

SELF-TEST QUESTIONS

Would a young worker with a high probability of changing jobs be better off under a defined contribution or a defined benefit pension plan? Explain.

Would a company with a defined benefit plan or a company with a defined contribution plan have more economic incentive to hire younger workers? Explain.

Would a company with a defined benefit plan or a company with a defined contribution plan have more economic incentive to hire men? Explain.

DEFINED BENEFIT VERSUS DEFINED CONTRIBUTION PLANS: THE EMPLOYEE CHOICE

Since many large employers offer both defined benefit and defined contribution plans, many employees have to choose between the two types of plans. This is not an easy decision to make, because it depends on both the specifics of the plans and the situation of the individual. Each individual must examine his or her expected cash flows from wages and investments and pick the plan that provides the incremental cash flows (both costs and benefits) that maximize his or her expected utility. Clearly, an employee must consider a vast array of economic variables such as expected work life, potential job changes, vesting provisions, risk of inadequate funding, and inflation. These factors can vary so much among individuals and employers that meaningful generalizations are impossible.

To illustrate the complexity of the decision, consider only one of the relevant factors, inflation. Participants in a defined benefit plan face substantial inflation risk.

For example, assume an individual retires at age 65 and receives a fixed pension each year. (Most defined benefit plans promise fixed *nominal* payments, so there is no adjustment for inflation once the worker retires.) If the annual inflation rate is 5 percent, each dollar would buy 78 cents worth of goods and services after 5 years, and only 61 cents after 10 years. If the inflation rate is 10 percent, purchasing power would fall to 62 cents after 5 years and to only 39 cents after 10 years. For individuals who retire before age 65 and hence face 20 or more years of retirement, inflation can easily erode the purchasing power of their pensions to only a small fraction of the original dollar amount.

The inflation factor also increases the complexity of decisions under a defined contribution plan because the participant must choose among a number of investment alternatives, including money market funds, fixed income funds, balanced funds, company stock, and stock funds. Then, the ability of the fund to withstand the ravages of inflation depends on the performance of the investments chosen for the portfolio. Many studies have looked at the ability of various portfolio combinations to maintain a fixed real return under inflation.[8] Although it is common "wisdom" that stocks are a good hedge against inflation, studies show that stock returns and inflation are often negatively correlated—when inflation heats up and the plan portfolio needs to perform best, stocks do poorly. Some studies have suggested that a portfolio consisting of T-bills and commodity futures can be a good hedge against inflation, but very few defined contribution plan participants would be willing to place their assets in such a portfolio. In recent years, a few financial institutions have offered, as a more realistic alternative, certificates of deposit with returns that are tied to the consumer price index. Better yet, the U.S. Treasury announced in 1996 plans to issue a T-bond whose interest rate is indexed to offset inflation. This security can be used by investors in defined contribution plans to provide a constant real-dollar pension.

SELF-TEST QUESTIONS

What are some factors that should be considered by an employee when choosing between a defined benefit and a defined contribution plan?

Explain how inflation affects payments from a defined benefit plan and from a defined contribution plan.

DEVELOPING A PLAN STRATEGY

When an employer establishes a pension plan, the plan type may be influenced by competitive conditions in the labor market. For example, unions generally seek defined benefit plans in order to cushion beneficiaries from the investment risks that would exist under a defined contribution or profit sharing plan. Even if a firm has the economic power to resist a defined benefit plan, it may still agree to one on the

---

[8]For example, see Zvi Bodie, "An Innovation for Stable Real Retirement Income," *Journal of Portfolio Management,* Fall 1980, 5–13.

grounds that such a plan would, for the reasons set forth earlier, reduce its turnover rate. Still, there is no universal answer as to whether a defined benefit or a defined contribution plan is better for a particular company.

A defined benefit plan provides tax-planning flexibility, because firms can vary the fund contribution from year to year. Thus, in highly profitable years firms can make large contributions, which decrease taxable income and hence reduce taxes. Defined contribution plans do not afford such flexibility, because the specified contributions must be made each year regardless of the firm's profitability. However, defined contribution plans do not require firms to increase fund contributions if the fund's investment performance is poor.[9] In addition, defined benefit plans have higher administrative costs as well as the burden to make promised pension payments regardless of pension fund performance. Although firms' circumstances vary widely, in recent years there has been a tendency for small firms to adopt defined contribution or profit sharing plans, while larger, and presumably more stable, firms tend to adopt defined benefit plans. Note, however, that high administrative costs and the regulatory burden of ERISA have driven a large number of firms to replace defined benefit plans with defined contribution plans.

Assuming a firm has decided on a defined benefit plan, proper strategic planning requires integrating the plan's funding and investment policies into the company's general corporate plan. The *funding strategy* involves two decisions: (1) How fast should any unfunded liability be reduced, and (2) what rate of return should be assumed in the actuarial calculations? The *investment strategy* must answer this question: Given the assumed actuarial rate of return, how should a portfolio that minimizes the risk of not achieving that return be structured?

Pension fund managers use *asset allocation models* to help plan funding and investment strategies. These models use computer simulation to examine the risk/return relationships of portfolios with various mixes of assets, including stocks, bonds, T-bills, real estate, international assets, and so on, under different economic scenarios. Several conclusions emerge from the model runs. First, the very nature of pension funds suggests that safety of principal is a paramount consideration, so pension fund managers ought not to "reach" for the highest possible returns. Second, as we discussed in Chapter 4, for a given level of return, the inclusion of more types of assets generally reduces the portfolio's risk, because returns on different asset types are not perfectly correlated. And third, choices among the possible portfolios are limited by the introduction of managerial constraints, such as (1) that the portfolio value should not drop more than 30 percent if a 1930s level depression occurs and (2) that the portfolio should earn at least 10 percent if a 1970s level of inflation rate occurs.

Pension fund managers must also consider the effects of portfolio selection and actuarial assumptions on required contributions. First, note that the most commonly

---

[9]The distinction between a pension *plan* and a pension *fund* should be noted. A pension plan is a contract between the participants and the firm which spells out the rights and obligations of each party. A pension fund is the investment portfolio that provides the collateral which secures the contractual pension benefits.

used measure of a pension plan's cost is the ratio of pension contributions to payroll. Now suppose salary inflation heats up to 15 percent, causing the company's projected benefit payments under a final pay plan to grow by 15 percent per year for active participants. Such a situation might not affect the percentage of pension costs to payroll costs, because payroll costs inflate rapidly during such times. However, if a company has a large number of retirees relative to actives, and if the payments to retirees are fixed while the reinvestment rate rises on assets held for retirees (because inflation pushes up interest rates), then pension costs as a percentage of payroll might even decline. On the other hand, in a 1930s-style depression a company with a lot of retirees on defined benefits might be in substantial trouble. For example, suppose production cutbacks caused employees to be laid off, and many of them elected to take early retirement. This would reduce payroll expenses but increase retirement expenses. At the same time, the pension fund, if it were heavily invested in stocks, would decline substantially in value, which, in turn, would lead to higher required contributions to the fund. For such a company, pension expenses could become an intolerably high percentage of the reduced payroll and operating income.

These examples illustrate the interdependence of business policies, economic conditions, and pension fund planning. Pension fund consultants have developed "asset-liability simulators" which produce (1) probability distributions for a plan under different portfolio mixes and (2) probability distributions for plan contributions over time, assuming different investment strategies.[10] These models are helpful, but it is difficult to develop realistic assumptions about asset and liability interrelationships under different economic scenarios.

Asset allocation models generally indicate that portfolios consisting of 25 to 50 percent bonds and 50 to 75 percent stocks provide adequate diversification for safety along with a satisfactory expected return. Additionally, it is now recognized that further benefits can be gained by investing in assets other than stocks and bonds. Indeed, many pension funds make minimum commitments to at least four asset categories, and some fund managers are now committing a percentage of their funds to international securities and to such "hard assets" as timberland, oil and gas reserves, and precious metals, mainly as inflation hedges.

To illustrate one company's approach to asset allocation, consider Table 27-1, which contains the recent asset allocation of General Electric's pension fund. GE's pension fund is diversified along three lines. First, the fund contains numerous types of securities, including stocks, bonds, real estate, options, and venture capital. Second, the portfolio contains both domestic and international securities. Finally, although it is not apparent from Table 27-1, the fund is diversified across maturities so that securities more or less continuously mature, and the proceeds can be either paid out to beneficiaries or reinvested in other securities.

---

[10]An excellent description of several such simulation models is found in the May 1982 *Journal of Finance.* Included are articles by Louis Kingsland, Howard E. Winklevoss, and Alice B. Goldstein and Barbara G. Markowitz, plus excellent discussions of these articles by William F. Sharpe and Irwin Tepper.

GENERAL ELECTRIC COMPANY: PENSION FUND ASSETS (MILLIONS OF DOLLARS)		TABLE 27-1

ASSET CATEGORY	VALUE	PERCENT OF PORTFOLIO
Cash/short-term equivalents	$ 1,703	5.9%
Common stock:		
GE	$ 184	0.6%
Actively managed domestic portfolios	5,704	19.8
Passive (indexed) domestic portfolios	5,337	18.5
Actively managed international portfolios	1,647	5.7
Passive (indexed) international portfolios	201	0.7
Total equities	$13,073	45.3%
Fixed income:		
Domestic bonds	$ 8,448	29.3%
International bonds	90	0.3
Total fixed Income	$ 8,538	29.6%
Real estate:		
Ownership	$ 1,782	6.2%
Mortgages	412	1.4
Total real estate	$ 2,194	7.6%
Specialized investments:		
Guaranteed investment contracts	$ 1,619	5.6%
Options	66	0.2
Venture capital	254	0.9
Private placement	1,387	4.8
Total specialized investments	$ 3,326	11.5%
Total assets	$28,834	100.0%

SOURCE: *Nelson's Directory of Plan Sponsors and Tax Exempt Funds*, updated annually.

What is a plan's funding strategy? What is a plan's investment strategy? What are asset allocation models? What types of assets are held in pension funds? Why?

SELF-TEST QUESTIONS

PENSION FUND INVESTMENT TACTICS

Three factors have a major influence on pension funds' investment tactics: (1) the dollar amount of assets, (2) the mix of the funds' liabilities between those attributable to active workers and those attributable to retired beneficiaries, and (3) the tax situation facing the corporate sponsor. To show how these characteristics affect funds' investment tactics, we next discuss three topics: (1) active workers versus retirees, (2) performance measurement, and (3) procedures for controlling management fees and transactions costs.

ACTIVE WORKERS VIS-À-VIS RETIREES

Many pension fund managers view pension fund liabilities as consisting of (1) benefits due now to plan participants who are already retired, and (2) benefits due in the future to current employees. With this view in mind, note that a common investment tactic involves segregating pension fund assets into two parts: a "retiree portfolio" that provides income to current retirees and a "worker portfolio" that builds value for current workers. Then, as current workers retire, the assets of the fund are shifted from the worker portfolio to the retiree portfolio.

The retiree portfolio is usually invested in fixed-income securities chosen to produce a cash payment stream that matches the required retiree pension payments. In managing the retiree portfolio, fund managers often use *immunization* techniques such as *duration* to eliminate, or at least significantly reduce, the risk associated with changing interest rates.[11] Simply put, matching the duration of the portfolio to the duration of the required payments ensures that any loss of market value due to rising interest rates is offset by additional interest income, and vice versa. Matching asset and liability durations balances interest rate and reinvestment rate risks in such a way that the realized return on the portfolio is very close to the targeted actuarial rate of return, regardless of how interest rates vary.

The active worker portfolio usually includes some relatively risky assets such as stocks and real estate. To reduce the risk inherent in such a portfolio, pension fund managers often use a hedging technique called *portfolio insurance,* which does not appreciably affect upside potential but limits the downside risk. There are many approaches to portfolio insurance, but most involve buying or selling options or futures contracts that would gain about the same amount of value that the portfolio would lose if the market were to take a sudden fall.

PERFORMANCE MEASUREMENT

Pension fund sponsors generally evaluate the performance of their portfolio managers on a regular basis and then use this information as a basis for allocating the fund's assets among portfolio managers. Suppose a fund's common stock portfolio provided a total return of 16 percent during a recent year—is this good, bad, or average performance? To answer this question, the portfolio's market risk (beta) should be estimated, and then the portfolio's return should be compared with the Security Market Line (SML). Suppose, for example, that the "market" portfolio, say, the S&P 500, returned 15 percent, that 20-year Treasury bonds returned 9 percent, and that our fund's equity portfolio had a beta of 0.9 (that is, it was invested in stocks that had below-average market risk). An SML analysis would lead to the visual compari-

---

[11]Duration is the weighted average time to receipt of cash flows from a bond. For a zero coupon bond, duration equals term to maturity. A coupon bond has a duration that is less than its term to maturity, and the higher the coupon for any given maturity, the shorter its duration. See Chapter 23 for an expanded discussion of duration.

ALPHA ANALYSIS   FIGURE 27-2

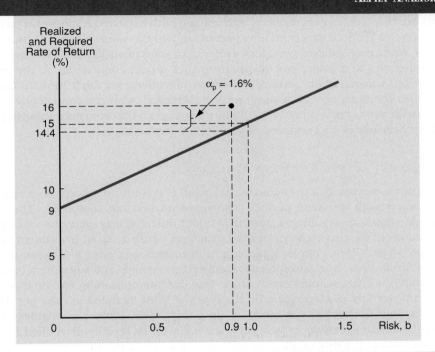

son shown in Figure 27-2, which indicates that the portfolio did better than expected—it is said to have an *alpha* (α) of 1.6 percentage points. Alpha measures the vertical distance of a portfolio's return above or below the Security Market Line. Looked at another way, alpha is the portfolio's extra return (positive or negative) after adjusting for the portfolio's market risk.[12]

Alpha analysis adds substantially to a pension manager's knowledge about his or her equity portfolio's results, but several shortcomings must be recognized. First, alpha analysis relies on the CAPM, which, as we discussed in Chapter 4, is an ex ante equilibrium concept which in theory requires that all risky assets be included in the market portfolio (for example, human capital and residential real estate), so market proxies such as the Standard & Poor's 500 Index result in some degree of measurement

---

[12]The Jensen alpha, so called because this performance measure was first suggested by Professor Michael Jensen, is very popular because of its ease of calculation. Theoretically, its purpose was to measure the performance of a single portfolio versus the market portfolio, after adjusting for the portfolio's beta. However, this measure is not useful in evaluating the performance of portfolios which include real estate and other assets which are not actively traded. This fact has led to the development of a number of other portfolio performance measures. For a discussion of these measures, see Jack L. Treynor and Fischer Black, "How to Use Security Analysis to Improve Portfolio Selection," *Journal of Business,* January 1973, 66–86.

error.[13] Second, the statistical significance of alpha is often too low to make strong statements about the portfolio's relative performance. And third, all of the measurements are based on ex post results which contain both expected returns plus unanticipated returns that resulted from unexpected random economic events. Thus, a large positive alpha may indicate good luck rather than good management, and vice versa.

Another way to measure portfolio performance is peer comparison. At the end of each year, managers with similar investment objectives, say, high growth, can be ranked on the basis of total realized return. Managers who are consistently in the top quartile have done a better job than their peers. Unfortunately, though, good past performance is no guarantee of good future performance.

MANAGEMENT OF PENSION FUND MANAGERS

In Chapter 4, we saw that the standard deviation of returns on a portfolio is reduced when assets with less than perfect positive correlation are combined. The same principle applies to combining portfolios under different managements. Further, it is common practice to classify portfolio managers by their stated investment objectives, or "styles." For example, some equity managers specialize in emerging high-growth firms, others specialize in energy-related companies, and still others invest in well-established, large-capitalization firms. One pension consulting firm divides managers into five groups, depending on the types of firms included in their portfolios: Group A: high-quality growth firms; Group B: high-yield, low-price volatility firms; Group C: small, aggressive growth companies; Group D: broadly diversified companies; and Group E: a mix of all types of firms. Since the groups' returns are not perfectly correlated, a pension fund manager could, by diversifying among portfolio managers with different styles, control the pension fund's expected risk/return relationship. If a pension fund manager targets on equaling a specific index, such as the S&P 500, then the weights assigned to each group would be chosen to correspond to the weightings of these groups in the index. If a pension fund manager wants to try to "beat the market," then he or she should attempt to forecast which groups will perform best and then "tilt" the allocation to favor those particular groups.

Fund administrators can manage their funds' assets with company employees (in-house management) or with external managers (out-of-house management). Insurance companies and bank trust departments are often used as external managers, but "boutique" managers, who have more flexibility than the major institutions, have had strikingly better performance and are capturing an ever-increasing share of the money management market. Regardless of whether a fund is using internal or external managers, if different managers specialize in different types of stocks, then it will be necessary to diversify among managers.

There are a number of professional money management firms that specialize in managing pension fund assets, as well as numerous firms that assist pension sponsors in picking money managers and provide consulting services on transactions

---

[13]Although managerial performance statistics exhibit about 80 to 90 percent correlation regardless of the index used, Richard Roll presents some interesting examples which show how easily rankings can be changed by measurement procedures. See Richard Roll, "Ambiguity When Performance Is Measured by the Securities Market Line," *Journal of Finance,* September 1978, 1051–1069.

costs, interest rate forecasts, and domestic and foreign investment climates. The use of multiple managers can help a fund achieve better diversification and earn higher returns by drawing on different managers' specialized knowledge of particular segments of the market. In general, the fund's assets are invested on either an *active* or a *passive* basis. Active managers select stocks with the idea of "beating the market," while passive management is based on the idea of achieving average returns while minimizing transactions costs and management fees.

The simplest type of passive management is to utilize an *index fund,* which is a portfolio whose securities are selected and rebalanced periodically to achieve a rate of return that will be nearly the same as that of an index such as the S&P 500. The goal is to minimize transactions costs and management fees while achieving average returns. This approach is based on the assumption of market efficiency, for *if the market is efficient, then all costs and fees associated with active management merely reduce the fund's return.* In practice, index funds often concentrate their purchases on a subset of the securities in the broad index. Recall from our discussion of working capital that an increase in "order size" produces a corresponding reduction in transactions costs. This principle also applies in portfolio management, and it leads to "S&P-like portfolios" which actually have fewer stocks than the S&P 500. Selection of securities for the proxy portfolio is usually done by matching the industrial sector percentages of the portfolio to the mix of the target index.[14]

Some fund administrators have employed what is called the *active-passive* concept in an attempt to earn more than an index such as the S&P 500. The fund would be set up as follows. First, the plan administrator selects a series of managers with expertise in different segments of the market, and each manager is required to confine his or her purchases to the type of stocks in which they specialize. Second, each manager is allocated a percentage of the pension fund's assets equal to the percentage of the particular group to the index. For example, if a particular manager specializes in energy stocks, and if energy stocks represent 20 percent of the capitalization of the S&P 500 Index, then this manager would be given 20 percent of the pension fund's equity assets to invest. Each manager's allocation would be based on this same principle, and any remaining assets would be invested on a pro rata basis in stocks that are not on any manager's list. These residual assets would thus be invested in a passive fund that merely buys and holds the required stocks. Thus, every stock in the index (say, the S&P 500) would either be available for purchase by one of the active managers or else held in the passive fund. If the active managers are indeed superior stock-pickers in their specialized areas, then the overall portfolio's excess risk-adjusted return (or "alpha") will be positive.[15]

How have portfolio managers generally performed in the past? One recent study indicates that money managers having an active investment style have underper-

---

[14]For an excellent discussion of constructing passive portfolios, see Andrew Rudd, "Optimal Selection of Passive Portfolios," *Financial Management,* Spring 1980, 57–66.

[15]Robert Monks, former director of the PBGC, has argued that it is impossible for pension funds to "beat the market" because they are, in effect, the market. He goes on to assert that pension plan sponsors should replace the active management of securities with active involvement in the long-term operations of the companies that they own. He argues that, instead of trying to add value by juggling stocks, sponsors should add value through active, informed ownership. See the September 2, 1985, issue of *Fortune,* 97–99.

formed the S&P 500 Index by one to two percentage points per year over the long term.[16] On the other hand, the study found that money managers are very good at selling their services to firms and convincing them not to adopt a passive investment style. Thus, the money management industry offers an array of differentiated products all sold as a way to beat the market, and it provides individuals who are good at establishing working relationships with in-house pension fund managers and at providing "hand-holding" services.

To illustrate one company's approach to managing its pension fund, consider Table 27-2, which shows how Amoco recently allocated its $4.8 billion defined ben-

TABLE 27-2	AMOCO DEFINED BENEFIT PENSION FUND (MILLIONS OF DOLLARS)

ASSET CATEGORY	VALUE	PERCENT OF PORTFOLIO
Cash/short-term equivalents	$ 485	10.1%
Common stock	3,200	66.6
Fixed-income securities	650	13.5
Real estate	300	6.2
Financial futures	125	2.6
Venture capital	50	1.0
Total assets	$4,810	100.0%

MANAGEMENT FIRM	PORTFOLIO TYPE
Acadian Assets Management	International stocks
Boston International Advisors	International stocks
Chase Investors Management	Domestic stocks
Corporate Property Investors	Real estate
Equitable Real Estate Management	Real estate
Fayez Sarofim & Company	Domestic stocks
Fidelity Management and Research	Domestic stocks
Fischer, Francis, Trees & Watts	Fixed income
Forstmann Leff Associates	Domestic stocks
Franklin Portfolio Associates	Domestic stocks
Pacific Investment Management	Fixed income
Security Capital Management	Fixed income
State Street Bank & Trust	International stocks

SOURCE: *Nelson's Directory of Plan Sponsors and Tax Exempt Funds,* updated annually.

---

[16]See Josef Lakonishok, Andrei Shleifer, and Robert W. Vishny, "The Structure and Performance of the Money Management Industry," *Brookings Papers on Economic Activity,* 1992.

efit fund between asset classes, along with a list of the firm's outside managers. Note that more than 66 percent of the portfolio is invested in stocks, while fixed-income investments account for more than 13 percent. Five of the outside managers focus on domestic stocks, three specialize in international stocks, three focus on fixed-income investments (bonds), and two focus on real estate.

How is Jensen's alpha used to judge the performance of common stock fund managers? Can you think of any other ways?

What is the difference between active and passive portfolio management?

"TAPPING" PENSION FUND ASSETS

Corporate sponsors administer defined benefit plans with assets running into the hundreds of billions of dollars. To what extent should a corporation be able to invest its fund's assets to the corporation's own advantage? Or, if the plan is overfunded — perhaps because investment results were better than the actuaries had assumed — should the company be able to take assets out of the plan? (Obviously, we are talking about defined benefit plans only; companies are not permitted to touch the assets of defined contribution or profit sharing plans.) Here are some examples of recent actions which have been called into question:

1. When Occidental Petroleum acquired Cities Service, their combined pension plans had assets of $700 million, but the vested funding requirement was only $300 million. Occidental terminated the old defined benefit plans, replaced them with a new defined contribution plan, and took $400 million out of the fund's assets. Similarly, FMC Corporation recently restructured its plan to recoup about $325 million from it. FMC's pension investments had earned an average return of about 16 percent over the past 10 years, placing it near the top in performance ratings. FMC used outside advisors and investment funds for its plan, and the vast bulk of the plan's assets were invested in stocks. Recent estimates suggest that, in total, corporate pension funds are overfunded by about $300 billion, so there is a lot of scope for actions such as those of Occidental and FMC.[17]

2. Some cash-short companies have been making required payments to their funds by using their own stock, bonds, and real property rather than cash. This is legal under ERISA provided that a fund has no more than 10 percent of its sponsor's own securities and assets, and provided that the Department of Labor agrees that the transaction is made at a fair price. Thus, Exxon recently contributed a $5.4 million office complex to its plan; Boise Cascade added timberland worth $16 million to its plan; and U.S. Steel, Alcoa, Armco, Reynolds

---

[17]We should point out that this type of action can be taken only (1) when approved by the plan's beneficiaries, (2) in conjunction with the establishment of a new pension plan, and (3) after approval by the Labor Department, Internal Revenue Service, and the PBGC if the new plan is a defined benefit plan.

Metals, and Republic Steel all contributed their own newly issued securities rather than cash.

3. Grumman Corporation, Bendix Corporation, and others have attempted to use their pension funds to help thwart hostile takeover attempts, or to help the fund's company take over another firm. For example, Grumman's pension fund bought 1.2 million of its shares, paying a 43 percent premium over the pre-bid price, to help fend off a takeover attempt by LTV. The takeover failed, but the fund incurred an immediate $16 million paper loss on these shares.[18] Similarly, Bendix tried (unsuccessfully) to stop its fund's trustee from tendering 4.5 million shares of its stock to Martin Marietta.

These examples raise some interesting issues: (1) Do the excess assets in a defined benefit plan belong to the sponsoring company or to the employees? Legally, they belong to the company, but a number of union leaders have argued that they ought to belong to the workers. (2) Should the PBGC get involved in reversions such as Occidental's? Since Occidental switched from a defined benefit to a defined contribution plan, it left the PBGC's jurisdiction (and also eliminated the $19 annual employee "head tax"), but if it had simply reduced the funding level of a defined benefit plan from overfunded to fully funded, the plan would have been exposed to more risk after assets were removed. (3) Should companies be able to use fund assets to help fight off takeovers? There are no easy answers to these questions. Obviously, actions which would either violate existing laws or jeopardize the safety of the plan should not be permitted, but many actions are not clear-cut. Given the importance of pension plans, it is safe to assume that the debate will continue.

SELF-TEST QUESTIONS
How can companies "tap" excess pension fund assets?
Do pension plan assets belong to the sponsoring company or to the employees?

RETIREE HEALTH BENEFITS

Most companies offer health care benefits as part of their retirement packages, usually until retirees reach age 65 and become eligible for Medicare. The plans typically cover hospitalization, some physicians' fees, and prescription drugs, with employers paying the entire cost of the coverage. Some firms even pay for supplemental coverage after age 65, the so-called Medigap insurance. Until recently, not much attention was paid to such benefits — firms merely paid the benefits each year and, if the cost was material, reported the annual cost as a note to the firm's annual report. Companies were able to overlook retiree health care costs because the number of retirees was small compared with active workers, health care costs were affordable, and many companies didn't even have a feel for the potential liability created by such benefits.

---

[18]Although the Grumman pension fund eventually made a $13.2 million profit on the Grumman stock it purchased, a lawsuit brought against the plan's trustees resulted in a ruling which held that trustees are liable for actions in using the fund to counter takeover attempts. This ruling sends a clear signal that plan assets must be managed, according to ERISA, for the "sole and exclusive benefit" of beneficiaries.

However, with the population aging and health care costs soaring, companies that have estimated their retiree health care liabilities have been shocked — at many companies, the liability of estimated future costs represents 20 to 40 percent of the firm's net worth, and for some smokestack companies, it exceeds net worth. For low-income retirees, health care benefits can cost corporations three times more than pension benefits. To try to stem the flow, many companies are reducing retiree health care benefits. Until now, most of the reductions have been minor, such as mandating second opinions and increasing co-payments. However, corporate planners and consultants say that changes are likely to become more prevalent and more profound. Possibilities range from adding "keep healthy" programs for retirees to cutting back benefits or even eliminating retiree health care altogether.

Perhaps the most important factor forcing companies to consider retiree health care benefits is the Financial Accounting Standards Board (FASB) rule that requires companies to set up a reserve for future medical benefits of retirees. Prior to FASB Statement 106, companies merely deducted retiree medical payments from income in the year that they were paid. Now firms must take current write-offs to account for vested future medical benefits, which impacts both the income statement and the balance sheet. The new rule was implemented in 1993, and companies could either take a one-time charge or amortize the write-off over 20 years. Some strong companies, such as General Electric, took the write-off. Its liability totalled $1.8 billion, but GE had over $20 billion of book equity to absorb the charge. Other companies, however, found it impossible to take the one-time charge option. For example, General Motors had a $24 billion liability but only $28 billion in book equity, so a one-time charge would have just about wiped out its net worth. Thus, GM had to amortize its current liability. The rationale behind Statement 106 is clear: retiree health care costs should be reported just like pension costs—at the time the benefits are earned by workers.

The new accounting rule, coupled with health care costs that have been increasing at about twice the rate of inflation, has resulted in 65 percent of all companies scrapping or cutting back on retiree health benefits. This is particularly true of medium-size and small firms. For example, Capital Holding Company, a Louisville insurance and financial services firm, has already taken its relatively small charge of $80 million. But, to hold down future accounting charges, as well as cash costs, the firm canceled its retiree health benefits package for all workers under age 55. Some firms have decreased or even canceled health benefits for current retirees. For example, Navistar International recently announced it would "restructure" the benefits package of its current retirees. The change, which requires retirees to pick up a larger share of their health care tab, would save the company about $90 million a year. However, such actions have been challenged in the courts. Employee health care costs, including retiree costs, are clearly a significant concern for corporate managers. Indeed, one of the pressing issues of the late 1990s will be getting these costs under control without creating undue hardships for employees.

Do retiree health care benefits pose a significant problem for many corporations? Explain.

What impact has FASB Statement 106 had on the reporting of retiree health benefits?

SELF-TEST QUESTIONS

SUMMARY

This chapter provides an introduction to pension fund management. The key concepts covered are listed below:

- Most companies, and almost all governmental units, have some type of employee pension plan. The management of these plans is important to employees, who use pensions to provide post-retirement income, and to stockholders, who bear the costs of pension plans.

- Pension funds are big business, totalling about $4.4 trillion in assets.

- There are three basic types of pension plans: (1) defined contribution plans, (2) defined benefit plans, and (3) profit sharing plans.

- Under a *defined contribution plan,* companies agree to make specific payments into a retirement fund, perhaps 10 percent of an employee's salary, and then retirees receive benefits based on the total amount contributed and the investment performance of the fund.

- Under a *defined benefit plan,* the employer agrees to give retirees a specifically defined benefit, such as $500 per month or 50 percent of their final year's salary.

- In a *profit sharing plan,* companies make contributions into an employee-owned account, but the size of the payments depends on corporate profits.

- If an employee has the right to receive pension benefits even if he or she leaves the company, the benefits are said to be *vested.* Congress has set maximum limits on the amount of time it takes employees to become vested.

- A *portable pension plan* can be carried from one employer to another. Defined contribution plans are portable because the contributions and fund earnings effectively belong to the employee. Also, unions manage the pension funds in some industries, enabling employees with defined benefit plans to move among firms in that industry without losing benefits.

- Under defined contribution or profit sharing plans, the firm's obligations are satisfied when the required contributions are made. However, under a defined benefit plan companies must cover all promised benefits. If the present value of expected retirement benefits equals the assets in the fund, the plan is said to be *fully funded.* If fund assets exceed the present value of expected benefits, the fund is *overfunded.* If assets are less than the present value of expected benefits, the plan is *underfunded.*

- The discount rate used to determine the present value of future benefits under a defined benefit plan is called the *actuarial rate of return.* This rate is also the expected rate of return on the fund's assets.

- The *Employee Retirement Income Security Act of 1974 (ERISA)* is the basic federal law governing the structure and administration of corporate pension plans.

- The *Pension Benefit Guarantee Corporation (PBGC)* was established by ERISA to insure corporate defined benefit pension funds. Funds used by the PBGC come from fund sponsors, and these funds are used to make payments to retirees whose firms have gone bankrupt with underfunded pension funds. However, taxpayers will have to pay if the PBGC does not have sufficient funds to cover its payments to bankrupt firms' retirees.

- The different types of pension plans have different risks to both firms and employees. In general, a defined benefit plan is the riskiest for the sponsoring organization but the least risky from the standpoint of employees.

- Assuming a company has a defined benefit plan, it must develop the fund's *funding strategy:* (1) How fast should any unfunded liability be reduced, and (2) what actuarial rate of return should be assumed?

- A defined benefit plan's *investment strategy* must answer this question: Given the assumed actuarial rate of return, how should the portfolio be structured so as to minimize the risk of not achieving the target return?

- The performance of pension fund managers can be assessed in two ways: (1) The fund's beta can be estimated, and the return can be plotted on the Security Market Line (SML). (2) The fund's historical performance can be compared with the performance of other funds with similar investment objectives.

- In general, fund assets can be invested either on an *active* basis, in which case the manager attempts to "beat the market," or on a *passive* basis, in which case the manager strives to minimize expenses yet to match the performance of some index such as the S&P 500.

- Pension fund managers use *asset allocation models* to help evaluate funding and investment strategies.

- During the major bull market of recent years, many defined benefit plans have become overfunded. Some corporate sponsors have terminated their overfunded plans, used some of the proceeds to buy annuities to cover the plan's liabilities, and then reclaimed the remainder.

- Retiree health benefits have become a major problem for employers for two reasons: (1) these costs are escalating faster than inflation, and (2) a recent Financial Accounting Standards Board (FASB) ruling forces companies to accrue the retiree health care liability rather than merely expensing the cash flows as they occur.

QUESTIONS

Define each of the following terms:

a. Defined benefit plan
b. Defined contribution plan

    c. Profit sharing plan
    d. Vesting
    e. Portability
    f. Fully funded; overfunded; underfunded
    g. Actuarial rate of return
    h. Employee Retirement Income Security Act (ERISA)
    i. Pension Benefit Guarantee Corporation (PBGC)
    j. FASB reporting requirements
    k. Funding strategy
    l. Investment strategy
    m. Asset allocation models
    n. Jensen alpha
    o. Active portfolio management
    p. Passive portfolio management
    q. "Tapping" fund assets
    r. Retiree health benefits

27-2   Suppose you just started employment at a large firm that offers both a defined benefit plan and a defined contribution plan. What are some of the factors that you should consider in choosing between the two plans?

27-3   Suppose you formed your own company several years ago and now intend to offer your employees a pension plan. What are the advantages and disadvantages to the firm of both a defined benefit plan and a defined contribution plan?

27-4   Examine the annual report of any large U.S. corporation. Where are the pension fund data located? What effect does this information have on the firm's financial condition?

27-5   A firm's pension fund assets are currently invested only in domestic stocks and bonds. The outside manager recommends that "hard assets" such as precious metals and real estate, and foreign financial assets, be added to the fund. What effect would the addition of these assets have on the fund's risk/return trade-off?

27-6   How does the type of pension fund a company uses influence each of the following:

    a. The likelihood of age discrimination in hiring?
    b. The likelihood of sex discrimination in hiring?
    c. Employee training costs?
    d. The likelihood that union leaders will be "flexible" if a company faces a changed economic environment such as those faced by the airline, steel, and auto industries in recent years?

27-7   Should employers be required to pay the same "head tax" to the PBGC irrespective of the financial condition of their plans?

PROBLEMS

27-1   BENEFITS AND CONTRIBUTIONS The Certainty Company (CC) operates in a world of certainty. It has just hired Mr. Jones, age 20, who will retire at age 65, draw retirement benefits for 15 years, and die at age 80. Mr. Jones's salary is $20,000 per year, but wages are expected to increase at the 5 percent annual rate of inflation. CC has a defined benefit plan in which workers receive 1 percent of the final year's wage for each year employed. The retirement benefit, once started, does not have a cost-of-living adjustment. CC earns 10 percent annually on its pension fund assets. Assume that pension contribution and benefit cash flows occur at year-end.

a. How much will Mr. Jones receive in annual retirement benefits?

b. What is CC's required annual contribution to fully fund Mr. Jones's retirement benefits?

c. Assume now that CC hires Mr. Smith at the same $20,000 salary as Mr. Jones. However, Mr. Smith is 45 years old. Repeat the analysis in Parts a and b under the same assumptions used for Mr. Jones. What do the results imply about the costs of hiring older versus younger workers?

d. Now assume that CC hires Ms. Brown, age 20, at the same time that it hires Mr. Smith. Ms. Brown is expected to retire at age 65 and to live to age 90. What is CC's annual pension cost for Ms. Brown? If Mr. Smith and Ms. Brown are doing the same work, are they truly doing it for the same pay? Would it be "reasonable" for CC to lower Ms. Brown's annual retirement benefit to a level that would mean that she received the same present value as Mr. Smith?

PERFORMANCE MEASUREMENT Houston Metals Inc. has a small pension fund which is managed by a professional portfolio manager. All of the fund's assets are invested in corporate equities. Last year, the portfolio manager realized a rate of return of 18 percent. The risk-free rate was 10 percent and the market risk premium was 6 percent. The portfolio's beta was 1.2.

a. Compute the portfolio's alpha.

b. What does the portfolio alpha imply about the manager's performance last year?

c. What can the firm's financial manager conclude about the portfolio manager's performance next year?

PLAN FUNDING Consolidated Industries is planning to operate for 10 more years and then cease operations. At that time (in 10 years), it expects to have the following pension benefit obligations:

YEARS	ANNUAL TOTAL PAYMENT
11–15	$2,500,000
16–20	2,000,000
21–25	1,500,000
26–30	1,000,000
31–35	500,000

The current value of the firm's pension fund is $6 million. Assume that all cash flows occur at year-end.

a. Consolidated's actuarial rate of return is 10 percent. What is the present value of the firm's pension fund benefits?

b. Is the plan underfunded or overfunded?

MINI CASE

Southeast Tile Distributors Inc. is a building tile wholesaler that originated in Atlanta but is now considering expansion throughout the region to take advantage of continued strong population growth. The company has been a "mom and pop" operation supplemented by part-time workers, so it currently has no corporate retirement plan. However, the firm's owner, Andy Johnson, believes that it will be necessary to start a corporate pension plan to attract the quality employees needed to make the expansion succeed. Andy has asked you, a recent business school graduate who has just joined the firm, to learn all that you can about pension funds, and then prepare a briefing paper on the subject. To help you get started, he sketched out the following questions:

a. How important are pension funds to the U.S. economy?
b. Define the following pension fund terms:
   (1) Defined benefit plan
   (2) Defined contribution plan
   (3) Profit sharing plan
   (4) Vesting
   (5) Portability
   (6) Fully funded; overfunded; underfunded
   (7) Actuarial rate of return
   (8) Employee Retirement Income Security Act (ERISA)
   (9) Pension Benefit Guarantee Corporation (PBGC)
c. What two organizations provide guidelines for reporting pension fund activities to stockholders? Describe briefly how pension fund data are reported in a firm's financial statements. (Hint: Consider both defined contribution and defined benefit plans.)
d. Assume that an employee joins the firm at age 25, works for 40 years to age 65, and then retires. The employee lives another 15 years, to age 80, and during retirement draws a pension of $20,000 at the end of each year. How much must the firm contribute annually (at year-end) over the employee's working life to fully fund the plan by retirement age if the plan's actuarial rate of return is 10 percent? Draw a graph which shows the value of the employee's pension fund over time. Why is real-world pension fund management much more complex than indicated in this illustration?
e. Discuss the risks to both the plan sponsor and plan beneficiaries under the three types of pension plans.
f. How does the type of pension plan influence decisions in each of the following areas:
   (1) The possibility of age discrimination in hiring?
   (2) The possibility of sex discrimination in hiring?
   (3) Employee training costs?
   (4) The militancy of unions when a company faces financial adversity?
g. What are the two components of a plan's funding strategy? What is the primary goal of a plan's investment strategy?
h. How can a corporate financial manager judge the performance of pension plan managers? What is the difference between "active" and "passive" management?
i. What is meant by "tapping" pension fund assets? Why is this action so controversial?
j. What has happened to the cost of retiree health benefits over the last decade? How are retiree health benefits reported to shareholders?

SELECTED ADDITIONAL
REFERENCES

For more information on how pension fund management has been affected by the Employee Retirement Income Security Act of 1974 (ERISA), including the establishment of the Pension Benefit Guarantee Corporation (PBGC), see

Treynor, Jack L., W. Priest, and Patrick J. Regan, *The Financial Reality of Pension Funding Under ERISA* (Homewood, Ill.: Dow Jones-Irwin, 1976).

The following articles provide additional insights into the relationship between pension plan funding and capital costs:

Malley, Susan L., "Unfunded Pension Liabilities and the Cost of Equity Capital," *Financial Review,* May 1983, 133–145.

Regan, Patrick J., "Pension Fund Perspective: Credit Ratings and Pension Costs," *Financial Analysts Journal,* September–October 1983, 19–23.

For more information on pension plan terminations, see

Alderson, Michael J., and K. C. Chen, "The Consequences of Terminating the Pension Fund," *Midland Corporate Finance Journal,* Winter 1987, 55–61.

Haw, In-Mu, William Ruland, and Ahmed Hamdallah, "Investor Evaluation of Overfunded Pension Plan Terminations," *Journal of Financial Research,* Spring 1988, 81–88.

Other pertinent works include

Bicksler, James L., and Andrew H. Chen, "The Integration of Insurance and Taxes in Corporate Pension Strategy," *Journal of Finance,* July 1985, 943–957.

Black, Fischer, "The Tax Consequences of Long-Run Pension Policy," *Financial Analysts Journal,* July–August 1980, 25–31.

Bodie, Zvi, "Pension Funds and Financial Innovation," *Financial Management,* Autumn 1990, 11–22.

Bodie, Zvi, and Leslie E. Papke, "Pension Fund Finance," *Pensions and the Economy,* Zvi Bodie and Alicia H. Munnell, eds. (Philadelphia: University of Pennsylvania Press, 1992).

Bodie, Zvi, and J. Shoren, eds., *Financial Aspects of the United States Pension System* (Chicago: University of Chicago Press, 1983).

Bulow, Jeremy I., "What Are Corporate Pension Liabilities?" *Quarterly Journal of Economics,* August 1982, 435–452.

Copeland, Thomas E., "An Economic Approach to Pension Fund Management," *Midland Corporate Finance Journal,* Spring 1984, 26–39.

Logue, Dennis E., *Managing Corporate Pension Plans* (New York: HarperCollins, 1991).

Munnell, Alicia H., "Guaranteeing Private Pension Benefits: A Potentially Expensive Business," *New England Economic Review,* March–April 1982, 24–47.

Oldfield, G. S. "Financial Aspects of the Private Pension System," *Journal of Money, Credit and Banking,* February 1977, 48–54.

Warshawsky, Mark J., "Pension Plans: Funding, Assets, and Regulatory Environment," *Federal Reserve Bulletin,* November 1988, 717–730.

Warshawsky, Mark J., H. Fred Mittelstaedt, and Carrie Cristea, "Recognizing Retiree Health Benefits: The Effect of SFAS 106," *Financial Management,* Summer 1993, 188–199.

For an excellent discussion of the relationship between pension funding policy and the firm's overall financial policy, see

Bodie, Zvi, Jay O. Light, Randall Morck, and Robert A. Taggart, Jr., "Funding and Asset Allocation in Corporate Pension Plans: An Empirical Investigation," National Bureau of Economic Research Working Paper #1315.

The Winter 1994 issue of the Journal of Applied Corporate Finance *contains several articles pertaining to pension plan management.*

APPENDIX A

MATHEMATICAL TABLES

TABLE A-1   PRESENT VALUE OF $1 DUE AT THE END OF n PERIOD:

Equation: Financial Calculator Keys:

$$PVIF_{i,n} = \frac{1}{(1 + i)^n}$$

n [N]   i [I]   [PV]   0 [PMT]   1.0 [FV]

TABLE VALUE

PERIOD	1%	2%	3%	4%	5%	6%	7%	8%	9%	10%
1	.9901	.9804	.9709	.9615	.9524	.9434	.9346	.9259	.9174	.9091
2	.9803	.9612	.9426	.9246	.9070	.8900	.8734	.8573	.8417	.8264
3	.9706	.9423	.9151	.8890	.8638	.8396	.8163	.7938	.7722	.7513
4	.9610	.9238	.8885	.8548	.8227	.7921	.7629	.7350	.7084	.6830
5	.9515	.9057	.8626	.8219	.7835	.7473	.7130	.6806	.6499	.6209
6	.9420	.8880	.8375	.7903	.7462	.7050	.6663	.6302	.5963	.5645
7	.9327	.8706	.8131	.7599	.7107	.6651	.6227	.5835	.5470	.5132
8	.9235	.8535	.7894	.7307	.6768	.6274	.5820	.5403	.5019	.4665
9	.9143	.8368	.7664	.7026	.6446	.5919	.5439	.5002	.4604	.4241
10	.9053	.8203	.7441	.6756	.6139	.5584	.5083	.4632	.4224	.3855
11	.8963	.8043	.7224	.6496	.5847	.5268	.4751	.4289	.3875	.3505
12	.8874	.7885	.7014	.6246	.5568	.4970	.4440	.3971	.3555	.3186
13	.8787	.7730	.6810	.6006	.5303	.4688	.4150	.3677	.3262	.2897
14	.8700	.7579	.6611	.5775	.5051	.4423	.3878	.3405	.2992	.2633
15	.8613	.7430	.6419	.5553	.4810	.4173	.3624	.3152	.2745	.2394
16	.8528	.7284	.6232	.5339	.4581	.3936	.3387	.2919	.2519	.2176
17	.8444	.7142	.6050	.5134	.4363	.3714	.3166	.2703	.2311	.1978
18	.8360	.7002	.5874	.4936	.4155	.3503	.2959	.2502	.2120	.1799
19	.8277	.6864	.5703	.4746	.3957	.3305	.2765	.2317	.1945	.1635
20	.8195	.6730	.5537	.4564	.3769	.3118	.2584	.2145	.1784	.1486
21	.8114	.6598	.5375	.4388	.3589	.2942	.2415	.1987	.1637	.1351
22	.8034	.6468	.5219	.4220	.3418	.2775	.2257	.1839	.1502	.1228
23	.7954	.6342	.5067	.4057	.3256	.2618	.2109	.1703	.1378	.1117
24	.7876	.6217	.4919	.3901	.3101	.2470	.1971	.1577	.1264	.1015
25	.7798	.6095	.4776	.3751	.2953	.2330	.1842	.1460	.1160	.0923
26	.7720	.5976	.4637	.3607	.2812	.2198	.1722	.1352	.1064	.0839
27	.7644	.5859	.4502	.3468	.2678	.2074	.1609	.1252	.0976	.0763
28	.7568	.5744	.4371	.3335	.2551	.1956	.1504	.1159	.0895	.0693
29	.7493	.5631	.4243	.3207	.2429	.1846	.1406	.1073	.0822	.0630
30	.7419	.5521	.4120	.3083	.2314	.1741	.1314	.0994	.0754	.0573
35	.7059	.5000	.3554	.2534	.1813	.1301	.0937	.0676	.0490	.0356
40	.6717	.4529	.3066	.2083	.1420	.0972	.0668	.0460	.0318	.0221
45	.6391	.4102	.2644	.1712	.1113	.0727	.0476	.0313	.0207	.0137
50	.6080	.3715	.2281	.1407	.0872	.0543	.0339	.0213	.0134	.0085
55	.5785	.3365	.1968	.1157	.0683	.0406	.0242	.0145	.0087	.0053

CONTINUED   TABLE A-1

PERIOD	12%	14%	15%	16%	18%	20%	24%	28%	32%	36%
1	.8929	.8772	.8696	.8621	.8475	.8333	.8065	.7813	.7576	.7353
2	.7972	.7695	.7561	.7432	.7182	.6944	.6504	.6104	.5739	5407
3	.7118	.6750	.6575	.6407	.6086	.5787	.5245	.4768	.4348	.3975
4	.6355	.5921	.5718	.5523	.5158	.4823	.4230	.3725	.3294	.2923
5	.5674	.5194	.4972	.4761	.4371	.4019	.3411	.2910	.2495	.2149
6	.5066	.4556	.4323	.4104	.3704	.3349	.2751	.2274	.1890	.1580
7	.4523	.3996	.3759	.3538	.3139	.2791	.2218	.1776	.1432	.1162
8	.4039	.3506	.3269	.3050	.2660	.2326	.1789	.1388	.1085	.0854
9	.3606	.3075	.2843	.2630	.2255	.1938	.1443	.1084	.0822	.0628
10	.3220	.2697	.2472	.2267	.1911	.1615	.1164	.0847	.0623	.0462
11	.2875	.2366	.2149	.1954	.1619	.1346	.0938	.0662	.0472	.0340
12	.2567	.2076	.1869	.1685	.1372	.1122	.0757	.0517	.0357	.0250
13	.2292	.1821	.1625	.1452	.1163	.0935	.0610	.0404	.0271	.0184
14	.2046	.1597	.1413	.1252	.0985	.0779	.0492	.0316	.0205	.0135
15	.1827	.1401	.1229	.1079	.0835	.0649	.0397	.0247	.0155	.0099
16	.1631	.1229	.1069	.0930	.0708	.0541	.0320	.0193	.0118	.0073
17	.1456	.1078	.0929	.0802	.0600	.0451	.0258	.0150	.0089	.0054
18	.1300	.0946	.0808	.0691	.0508	.0376	.0208	.0118	.0068	.0039
19	.1161	.0829	.0703	.0596	.0431	.0313	.0168	.0092	.0051	.0029
20	.1037	.0728	.0611	.0514	.0365	.0261	.0135	.0072	.0039	.0021
21	.0926	.0638	.0531	.0443	.0309	.0217	.0109	.0056	.0029	.0016
22	.0826	.0560	.0462	.0382	.0262	.0181	.0088	.0044	.0022	.0012
23	.0738	.0491	.0402	.0329	.0222	.0151	.0071	.0034	.0017	.0008
24	.0659	.0431	.0349	.0284	.0188	.0126	.0057	.0027	.0013	.0006
25	.0588	.0378	.0304	.0245	.0160	.0105	.0046	.0021	.0010	.0005
26	.0525	.0331	.0264	.0211	.0135	.0087	.0037	.0016	.0007	.0003
27	.0469	.0291	.0230	.0182	.0115	.0073	.0030	.0013	.0006	.0002
28	.0419	.0255	.0200	.0157	.0097	.0061	.0024	.0010	.0004	.0002
29	.0374	.0224	.0174	.0135	.0082	.0051	.0020	.0008	.0003	.0001
30	.0334	.0196	.0151	.0116	.0070	.0042	.0016	.0006	.0002	.0001
35	.0189	.0102	.0075	.0055	.0030	.0017	.0005	.0002	.0001	*
40	.0107	.0053	.0037	.0026	.0013	.0007	.0002	.0001	*	*
45	.0061	.0027	.0019	.0013	.0006	.0003	.0001	*	*	*
50	.0035	.0014	.0009	.0006	.0003	.0001	*	*	*	*
55	.0020	.0007	.0005	.0003	.0001	*	*	*	*	*

*The factor is zero to four decimal places.

TABLE A-2   PRESENT VALUE OF AN ANNUITY OF $1 PER PERIOD FOR n PERIOD:

Equation: Financial Calculator Keys:

$$PVIFA_{i,n} = \sum_{t=1}^{n} \frac{1}{(1+i)^t} = \frac{1 - \dfrac{1}{(1+i)^n}}{i} = \frac{1}{i} - \frac{1}{i(1+i)^n}$$

	n	i		1.0	0
	N	**I**	**PV**	**PMT**	**FV**
			TABLE VALUE		

NUMBER OF PERIODS	1%	2%	3%	4%	5%	6%	7%	8%	9%
1	0.9901	0.9804	0.9709	0.9615	0.9524	0.9434	0.9346	0.9259	0.9174
2	1.9704	1.9416	1.9135	1.8861	1.8594	1.8334	1.8080	1.7833	1.7591
3	2.9410	2.8839	2.8286	2.7751	2.7232	2.6730	2.6243	2.5771	2.5313
4	3.9020	3.8077	3.7171	3.6299	3.5460	3.4651	3.3872	3.3121	3.2397
5	4.8534	4.7135	4.5797	4.4518	4.3295	4.2124	4.1002	3.9927	3.8897
6	5.7955	5.6014	5.4172	5.2421	5.0757	4.9173	4.7665	4.6229	4.4859
7	6.7282	6.4720	6.2303	6.0021	5.7864	5.5824	5.3893	5.2064	5.0330
8	7.6517	7.3255	7.0197	6.7327	6.4632	6.2098	5.9713	5.7466	5.5348
9	8.5660	8.1622	7.7861	7.4353	7.1078	6.8017	6.5152	6.2469	5.9952
10	9.4713	8.9826	8.5302	8.1109	7.7217	7.3601	7.0236	6.7101	6.4177
11	10.3676	9.7868	9.2526	8.7605	8.3064	7.8869	7.4987	7.1390	6.8052
12	11.2551	10.5753	9.9540	9.3851	8.8633	8.3838	7.9427	7.5361	7.1607
13	12.1337	11.3484	10.6350	9.9856	9.3936	8.8527	8.3577	7.9038	7.4869
14	13.0037	12.1062	11.2961	10.5631	9.8986	9.2950	8.7455	8.2442	7.7862
15	13.8651	12.8493	11.9379	11.1184	10.3797	9.7122	9.1079	8.5595	8.0607
16	14.7179	13.5777	12.5611	11.6523	10.8378	10.1059	9.4466	8.8514	8.3126
17	15.5623	14.2919	13.1661	12.1657	11.2741	10.4773	9.7632	9.1216	8.5436
18	16.3983	14.9920	13.7535	12.6593	11.6896	10.8276	10.0591	9.3719	8.7556
19	17.2260	15.6785	14.3238	13.1339	12.0853	11.1581	10.3356	9.6036	8.9501
20	18.0456	16.3514	14.8775	13.5903	12.4622	11.4699	10.5940	9.8181	9.1285
21	18.8570	17.0112	15.4150	14.0292	12.8212	11.7641	10.8355	10.0168	9.2922
22	19.6604	17.6580	15.9369	14.4511	13.1630	12.0416	11.0612	10.2007	9.4424
23	20.4558	18.2922	16.4436	14.8568	13.4886	12.3034	11.2722	10.3711	9.5802
24	21.2434	18.9139	16.9355	15.2470	13.7986	12.5504	11.4693	10.5288	9.7066
25	22.0232	19.5235	17.4131	15.6221	14.0939	12.7834	11.6536	10.6748	9.8226
26	22.7952	20.1210	17.8768	15.9828	14.3752	13.0032	11.8258	10.8100	9.9290
27	23.5596	20.7069	18.3270	16.3296	14.6430	13.2105	11.9867	10.9352	10.0266
28	24.3164	21.2813	18.7641	16.6631	14.8981	13.4062	12.1371	11.0511	10.1161
29	25.0658	21.8444	19.1885	16.9837	15.1411	13.5907	12.2777	11.1584	10.1983
30	25.8077	22.3965	19.6004	17.2920	15.3725	13.7648	12.4090	11.2578	10.2737
35	29.4086	24.9986	21.4872	18.6646	16.3742	14.4982	12.9477	11.6546	10.5668
40	32.8347	27.3555	23.1148	19.7928	17.1591	15.0463	13.3317	11.9246	10.7574
45	36.0945	29.4902	24.5187	20.7200	17.7741	15.4558	13.6055	12.1084	10.8812
50	39.1961	31.4236	25.7298	21.4822	18.2559	15.7619	13.8007	12.2335	10.9617
55	42.1472	33.1748	26.7744	22.1086	18.6335	15.9905	13.9399	12.3186	11.0140

CONTINUED   **TABLE A-2**

NUMBER OF PERIODS	10%	12%	14%	15%	16%	18%	20%	24%	28%	32%
1	0.9091	0.8929	0.8772	0.8696	0.8621	0.8475	0.8333	0.8065	0.7813	0.7576
2	1.7355	1.6901	1.6467	1.6257	1.6052	1.5656	1.5278	1.4568	1.3916	1.3315
3	2.4869	2.4018	2.3216	2.2832	2.2459	2.1743	2.1065	1.9813	1.8684	1.7663
4	3.1699	3.0373	2.9137	2.8550	2.7982	2.6901	2.5887	2.4043	2.2410	2.0957
5	3.7908	3.6048	3.4331	3.3522	3.2743	3.1272	2.9906	2.7454	2.5320	2.3452
6	4.3553	4.1114	3.8887	3.7845	3.6847	3.4976	3.3255	3.0205	2.7594	2.5342
7	4.8684	4.5638	4.2883	4.1604	4.0386	3.8115	3.6046	3.2423	2.9370	2.6775
8	5.3349	4.9676	4.6389	4.4873	4.3436	4.0776	3.8372	3.4212	3.0758	2.7860
9	5.7590	5.3282	4.9464	4.7716	4.6065	4.3030	4.0310	3.5655	3.1842	2.8681
10	6.1446	5.6502	5.2161	5.0188	4.8332	4.4941	4.1925	3.6819	3.2689	2.9304
11	6.4951	5.9377	5.4527	5.2337	5.0286	4.6560	4.3271	3.7757	3.3351	2.9776
12	6.8137	6.1944	5.6603	5.4206	5.1971	4.7932	4.4392	3.8514	3.3868	3.0133
13	7.1034	6.4235	5.8424	5.5831	5.3423	4.9095	4.5327	3.9124	3.4272	3.0404
14	7.3667	6.6282	6.0021	5.7245	5.4675	5.0081	4.6106	3.9616	3.4587	3.0609
15	7.6061	6.8109	6.1422	5.8474	5.5755	5.0916	4.6755	4.0013	3.4834	3.0764
16	7.8237	6.9740	6.2651	5.9542	5.6685	5.1624	4.7296	4.0333	3.5026	3.0882
17	8.0216	7.1196	6.3729	6.0472	5.7487	5.2223	4.7746	4.0591	3.5177	3.0971
18	8.2014	7.2497	6.4674	6.1280	5.8178	5.2732	4.8122	4.0799	3.5294	3.1039
19	8.3649	7.3658	6.5504	6.1982	5.8775	5.3162	4.8435	4.0967	3.5386	3.1090
20	8.5136	7.4694	6.6231	6.2593	5.9288	5.3527	4.8696	4.1103	3.5458	3.1129
21	8.6487	7.5620	6.6870	6.3125	5.9731	5.3837	4.8913	4.1212	3.5514	3.1158
22	8.7715	7.6446	6.7429	6.3587	6.0113	5.4099	4.9094	4.1300	3.5558	3.1180
23	8.8832	7.7184	6.7921	6.3988	6.0442	5.4321	4.9245	4.1371	3.5592	3.1197
24	8.9847	7.7843	6.8351	6.4338	6.0726	5.4509	4.9371	4.1428	3.5619	3.1210
25	9.0770	7.8431	6.8729	6.4641	6.0971	5.4669	4.9476	4.1474	3.5640	3.1220
26	9.1609	7.8957	6.9061	6.4906	6.1182	5.4804	4.9563	4.1511	3.5656	3.1227
27	9.2372	7.9426	6.9352	6.5135	6.1364	5.4919	4.9636	4.1542	3.5669	3.1233
28	9.3066	7.9844	6.9607	6.5335	6.1520	5.5016	4.9697	4.1566	3.5679	3.1237
29	9.3696	8.0218	6.9830	6.5509	6.1656	5.5098	4.9747	4.1585	3.5687	3.1240
30	9.4269	8.0552	7.0027	6.5660	6.1772	5.5168	4.9789	4.1601	3.5693	3.1242
35	9.6442	8.1755	7.0700	6.6166	6.2153	5.5386	4.9915	4.1644	3.5708	3.1248
40	9.7791	8.2438	7.1050	6.6418	6.2335	5.5482	4.9966	4.1659	3.5712	3.1250
45	9.8628	8.2825	7.1232	6.6543	6.2421	5.5523	4.9986	4.1664	3.5714	3.1250
50	9.9148	8.3045	7.1327	6.6605	6.2463	5.5541	4.9995	4.1666	3.5714	3.1250
55	9.9471	8.3170	7.1376	6.6636	6.2482	5.5549	4.9998	4.1666	3.5714	3.1250

TABLE A-3   Future Value of $1 at the End of n Period:

Equation:

$FVIF_{i,n} = (1 + i)^n$

Financial Calculator Keys:

n	i	1.0	0	
N	**I**	**PV**	**PMT**	**FV**
				TABLE VALUE

PERIOD	1%	2%	3%	4%	5%	6%	7%	8%	9%	10%
1	1.0100	1.0200	1.0300	1.0400	1.0500	1.0600	1.0700	1.0800	1.0900	1.1000
2	1.0201	1.0404	1.0609	1.0816	1.1025	1.1236	1.1449	1.1664	1.1881	1.2100
3	1.0303	1.0612	1.0927	1.1249	1.1576	1.1910	1.2250	1.2597	1.2950	1.3310
4	1.0406	1.0824	1.1255	1.1699	1.2155	1.2625	1.3108	1.3605	1.4116	1.4641
5	1.0510	1.1041	1.1593	1.2167	1.2763	1.3382	1.4026	1.4693	1.5386	1.6105
6	1.0615	1.1262	1.1941	1.2653	1.3401	1.4185	1.5007	1.5869	1.6771	1.7716
7	1.0721	1.1487	1.2299	1.3159	1.4071	1.5036	1.6058	1.7138	1.8280	1.9487
8	1.0829	1.1717	1.2668	1.3686	1.4775	1.5938	1.7182	1.8509	1.9926	2.1436
9	1.0937	1.1951	1.3048	1.4233	1.5513	1.6895	1.8385	1.9990	2.1719	2.3579
10	1.1046	1.2190	1.3439	1.4802	1.6289	1.7908	1.9672	2.1589	2.3674	2.5937
11	1.1157	1.2434	1.3842	1.5395	1.7103	1.8983	2.1049	2.3316	2.5804	2.8531
12	1.1268	1.2682	1.4258	1.6010	1.7959	2.0122	2.2522	2.5182	2.8127	3.1384
13	1.1381	1.2936	1.4685	1.6651	1.8856	2.1329	2.4098	2.7196	3.0658	3.4523
14	1.1495	1.3195	1.5126	1.7317	1.9799	2.2609	2.5785	2.9372	3.3417	3.7975
15	1.1610	1.3459	1.5580	1.8009	2.0789	2.3966	2.7590	3.1722	3.6425	4.1772
16	1.1726	1.3728	1.6047	1.8730	2.1829	2.5404	2.9522	3.4259	3.9703	4.5950
17	1.1843	1.4002	1.6528	1.9479	2.2920	2.6928	3.1588	3.7000	4.3276	5.0545
18	1.1961	1.4282	1.7024	2.0258	2.4066	2.8543	3.3799	3.9960	4.7171	5.5599
19	1.2081	1.4568	1.7535	2.1068	2.5270	3.0256	3.6165	4.3157	5.1417	6.1159
20	1.2202	1.4859	1.8061	2.1911	2.6533	3.2071	3.8697	4.6610	5.6044	6.7275
21	1.2324	1.5157	1.8603	2.2788	2.7860	3.3996	4.1406	5.0338	6.1088	7.4002
22	1.2447	1.5460	1.9161	2.3699	2.9253	3.6035	4.4304	5.4365	6.6586	8.1403
23	1.2572	1.5769	1.9736	2.4647	3.0715	3.8197	4.7405	5.8715	7.2579	8.9543
24	1.2697	1.6084	2.0328	2.5633	3.2251	4.0489	5.0724	6.3412	7.9111	9.8497
25	1.2824	1.6406	2.0938	2.6658	3.3864	4.2919	5.4274	6.8485	8.6231	10.835
26	1.2953	1.6734	2.1566	2.7725	3.5557	4.5494	5.8074	7.3964	9.3992	11.918
27	1.3082	1.7069	2.2213	2.8834	3.7335	4.8223	6.2139	7.9881	10.245	13.110
28	1.3213	1.7410	2.2879	2.9987	3.9201	5.1117	6.6488	8.6271	11.167	14.421
29	1.3345	1.7758	2.3566	3.1187	4.1161	5.4184	7.1143	9.3173	12.172	15.863
30	1.3478	1.8114	2.4273	3.2434	4.3219	5.7435	7.6123	10.063	13.268	17.449
40	1.4889	2.2080	3.2620	4.8010	7.0400	10.286	14.974	21.725	31.409	45.259
50	1.6446	2.6916	4.3839	7.1067	11.467	18.420	29.457	46.902	74.358	117.39
60	1.8167	3.2810	5.8916	10.520	18.679	32.988	57.946	101.26	176.03	304.48

CONTINUED   **TABLE A-3**

PERIOD	12%	14%	15%	16%	18%	20%	24%	28%	32%	36%
1	1.1200	1.1400	1.1500	1.1600	1.1800	1.2000	1.2400	1.2800	1.3200	1.3600
2	1.2544	1.2996	1.3225	1.3456	1.3924	1.4400	1.5376	1.6384	1.7424	1.8496
3	1.4049	1.4815	1.5209	1.5609	1.6430	1.7280	1.9066	2.0972	2.3000	2.5155
4	1.5735	1.6890	1.7490	1.8106	1.9388	2.0736	2.3642	2.6844	3.0360	3.4210
5	1.7623	1.9254	2.0114	2.1003	2.2878	2.4883	2.9316	3.4360	4.0075	4.6526
6	1.9738	2.1950	2.3131	2.4364	2.6996	2.9860	3.6352	4.3980	5.2899	6.3275
7	2.2107	2.5023	2.6600	2.8262	3.1855	3.5832	4.5077	5.6295	6.9826	8.6054
8	2.4760	2.8526	3.0590	3.2784	3.7589	4.2998	5.5895	7.2058	9.2170	11.703
9	2.7731	3.2519	3.5179	3.8030	4.4355	5.1598	6.9310	9.2234	12.166	15.917
10	3.1058	3.7072	4.0456	4.4114	5.2338	6.1917	8.5944	11.806	16.060	21.647
11	3.4785	4.2262	4.6524	5.1173	6.1759	7.4301	10.657	15.112	21.199	29.439
12	3.8960	4.8179	5.3503	5.9360	7.2876	8.9161	13.215	19.343	27.983	40.037
13	4.3635	5.4924	6.1528	6.8858	8.5994	10.699	16.386	24.759	36.937	54.451
14	4.8871	6.2613	7.0757	7.9875	10.147	12.839	20.319	31.691	48.757	74.053
15	5.4736	7.1379	8.1371	9.2655	11.974	15.407	25.196	40.565	64.359	100.71
16	6.1304	8.1372	9.3576	10.748	14.129	18.488	31.243	51.923	84.954	136.97
17	6.8660	9.2765	10.761	12.468	16.672	22.186	38.741	66.461	112.14	186.28
18	7.6900	10.575	12.375	14.463	19.673	26.623	48.039	85.071	148.02	253.34
19	8.6128	12.056	14.232	16.777	23.214	31.948	59.568	108.89	195.39	344.54
20	9.6463	13.743	16.367	19.461	27.393	38.338	73.864	139.38	257.92	468.57
21	10.804	15.668	18.822	22.574	32.324	46.005	91.592	178.41	340.45	637.26
22	12.100	17.861	21.645	26.186	38.142	55.206	113.57	228.36	449.39	866.67
23	13.552	20.362	24.891	30.376	45.008	66.247	140.83	292.30	593.20	1178.7
24	15.179	23.212	28.625	35.236	53.109	79.497	174.63	374.14	783.02	1603.0
25	17.000	26.462	32.919	40.874	62.669	95.396	216.54	478.90	1033.6	2180.1
26	19.040	30.167	37.857	47.414	73.949	114.48	268.51	613.00	1364.3	2964.9
27	21.325	34.390	43.535	55.000	87.260	137.37	332.95	784.64	1800.9	4032.3
28	23.884	39.204	50.066	63.800	102.97	164.84	412.86	1004.3	2377.2	5483.9
29	26.750	44.693	57.575	74.009	121.50	197.81	511.95	1285.6	3137.9	7458.1
30	29.960	50.950	66.212	85.850	143.37	237.38	634.82	1645.5	4142.1	10143.
40	93.051	188.88	267.86	378.72	750.38	1469.8	5455.9	19427.	66521.	*
50	289.00	700.23	1083.7	1670.7	3927.4	9100.4	46890.	*	*	*
60	897.60	2595.9	4384.0	7370.2	20555.	56348.	*	*	*	*

*FVIF > 99,999.

TABLE A-4	FUTURE VALUE OF AN ANNUITY OF $1 PER PERIOD FOR n PERIOD:

Equation: *Ordinary annuity*

$$FVIFA_{i,n} = \sum_{t=1}^{n} (1 + i)^{n-t} = \frac{(1 + i)^n - 1}{i}$$

Financial Calculator Keys:

n	i	0	1.0	
N	I	PV	PMT	FV
				TABLE VALUE

NUMBER OF PERIODS	1%	2%	3%	4%	5%	6%	7%	8%	9%	10%
1	1.0000	1.0000	1.0000	1.0000	1.0000	1.0000	1.0000	1.0000	1.0000	1.0000
2	2.0100	2.0200	2.0300	2.0400	2.0500	2.0600	2.0700	2.0800	2.0900	2.1000
3	3.0301	3.0604	3.0909	3.1216	3.1525	3.1836	3.2149	3.2464	3.2781	3.3100
4	4.0604	4.1216	4.1836	4.2465	4.3101	4.3746	4.4399	4.5061	4.5731	4.6410
5	5.1010	5.2040	5.3091	5.4163	5.5256	5.6371	5.7507	5.8666	5.9847	6.1051
6	6.1520	6.3081	6.4684	6.6330	6.8019	6.9753	7.1533	7.3359	7.5233	7.7156
7	7.2135	7.4343	7.6625	7.8983	8.1420	8.3938	8.6540	8.9228	9.2004	9.4872
8	8.2857	8.5830	8.8923	9.2142	9.5491	9.8975	10.260	10.637	11.028	11.436
9	9.3685	9.7546	10.159	10.583	11.027	11.491	11.978	12.488	13.021	13.579
10	10.462	10.950	11.464	12.006	12.578	13.181	13.816	14.487	15.193	15.937
11	11.567	12.169	12.808	13.486	14.207	14.972	15.784	16.645	17.560	18.531
12	12.683	13.412	14.192	15.026	15.917	16.870	17.888	18.977	20.141	21.384
13	13.809	14.680	15.618	16.627	17.713	18.882	20.141	21.495	22.953	24.523
14	14.947	15.974	17.086	18.292	19.599	21.015	22.550	24.215	26.019	27.975
15	16.097	17.293	18.599	20.024	21.579	23.276	25.129	27.152	29.361	31.772
16	17.258	18.639	20.157	21.825	23.657	25.673	27.888	30.324	33.003	35.950
17	18.430	20.012	21.762	23.698	25.840	28.213	30.840	33.750	36.974	40.545
18	19.615	21.412	23.414	25.645	28.132	30.906	33.999	37.450	41.301	45.599
19	20.811	22.841	25.117	27.671	30.539	33.760	37.379	41.446	46.018	51.159
20	22.019	24.297	26.870	29.778	33.066	36.786	40.995	45.762	51.160	57.275
21	23.239	25.783	28.676	31.969	35.719	39.993	44.865	50.423	56.765	64.002
22	24.472	27.299	30.537	34.248	38.505	43.392	49.006	55.457	62.873	71.403
23	25.716	28.845	32.453	36.618	41.430	46.996	53.436	60.893	69.532	79.543
24	26.973	30.422	34.426	39.083	44.502	50.816	58.177	66.765	76.790	88.497
25	28.243	32.030	36.459	41.646	47.727	54.865	63.249	73.106	84.701	98.347
26	29.526	33.671	38.553	44.312	51.113	59.156	68.676	79.954	93.324	109.18
27	30.821	35.344	40.710	47.084	54.669	63.706	74.484	87.351	102.72	121.10
28	32.129	37.051	42.931	49.968	58.403	68.528	80.698	95.339	112.97	134.21
29	33.450	38.792	45.219	52.966	62.323	73.640	87.347	103.97	124.14	148.63
30	34.785	40.568	47.575	56.085	66.439	79.058	94.461	113.28	136.31	164.49
40	48.886	60.402	75.401	95.026	120.80	154.76	199.64	259.06	337.88	442.59
50	64.463	84.579	112.80	152.67	209.35	290.34	406.53	573.77	815.08	1163.9
60	81.670	114.05	163.05	237.99	353.58	533.13	813.52	1253.2	1944.8	3034.8

CONTINUED   **TABLE A-4**

NUMBER OF PERIODS	12%	14%	15%	16%	18%	20%	24%	28%	32%	36%
1	1.0000	1.0000	1.0000	1.0000	1.0000	1.0000	1.0000	1.0000	1.0000	1.0000
2	2.1200	2.1400	2.1500	2.1600	2.1800	2.2000	2.2400	2.2800	2.3200	2.3600
3	3.3744	3.4396	3.4725	3.5056	3.5724	3.6400	3.7776	3.9184	4.0624	4.2096
4	4.7793	4.9211	4.9934	5.0665	5.2154	5.3680	5.6842	6.0156	6.3624	6.7251
5	6.3528	6.6101	6.7424	6.8771	7.1542	7.4416	8.0484	8.6999	9.3983	10.146
6	8.1152	8.5355	8.7537	8.9775	9.4420	9.9299	10.980	12.136	13.406	14.799
7	10.089	10.730	11.067	11.414	12.142	12.916	14.615	16.534	18.696	21.126
8	12.300	13.233	13.727	14.240	15.327	16.499	19.123	22.163	25.678	29.732
9	14.776	16.085	16.786	17.519	19.086	20.799	24.712	29.369	34.895	41.435
10	17.549	19.337	20.304	21.321	23.521	25.959	31.643	38.593	47.062	57.352
11	20.655	23.045	24.349	25.733	28.755	32.150	40.238	50.398	63.122	78.998
12	24.133	27.271	29.002	30.850	34.931	39.581	50.895	65.510	84.320	108.44
13	28.029	32.089	34.352	36.786	42.219	48.497	64.110	84.853	112.30	148.47
14	32.393	37.581	40.505	43.672	50.818	59.196	80.496	109.61	149.24	202.93
15	37.280	43.842	47.580	51.660	60.965	72.035	100.82	141.30	198.00	276.98
16	42.753	50.980	55.717	60.925	72.939	87.442	126.01	181.87	262.36	377.69
17	48.884	59.118	65.075	71.673	87.068	105.93	157.25	233.79	347.31	514.66
18	55.750	68.394	75.836	84.141	103.74	128.12	195.99	300.25	459.45	700.94
19	63.440	78.969	88.212	98.603	123.41	154.74	244.03	385.32	607.47	954.28
20	72.052	91.025	102.44	115.38	146.63	186.69	303.60	494.21	802.86	1298.8
21	81.699	104.77	118.81	134.84	174.02	225.03	377.46	633.59	1060.8	1767.4
22	92.503	120.44	137.63	157.41	206.34	271.03	469.06	812.00	1401.2	2404.7
23	104.60	138.30	159.28	183.60	244.49	326.24	582.63	1040.4	1850.6	3271.3
24	118.16	158.66	184.17	213.98	289.49	392.48	723.46	1332.7	2443.8	4450.0
25	133.33	181.87	212.79	249.21	342.60	471.98	898.09	1706.8	3226.8	6053.0
26	150.33	208.33	245.71	290.09	405.27	567.38	1114.6	2185.7	4260.4	8233.1
27	169.37	238.50	283.57	337.50	479.22	681.85	1383.1	2798.7	5624.8	11198.0
28	190.70	272.89	327.10	392.50	566.48	819.22	1716.1	3583.3	7425.7	15230.3
29	214.58	312.09	377.17	456.30	669.45	984.07	2129.0	4587.7	9802.9	20714.2
30	241.33	356.79	434.75	530.31	790.95	1181.9	2640.9	5873.2	12941.	28172.3
40	767.09	1342.0	1779.1	2360.8	4163.2	7343.9	22729.	69377.	*	*
50	2400.0	4994.5	7217.7	10436.	21813.	45497.	*	*	*	*
60	7471.6	18535.	29220.	46058.	*	*	*	*	*	*

*FVIFA > 99,999.

TABLE A-5		VALUES OF THE AREAS UNDER THE STANDARD NORMAL DISTRIBUTION FUNCTION								
z	0.00	0.01	0.02	0.03	0.04	0.05	0.06	0.07	0.08	0.09
0.0	.0000	.0040	.0080	.0120	.0160	.0199	.0239	.0279	.0319	.0359
0.1	.0398	.0438	.0478	.0517	.0557	.0596	.0636	.0675	.0714	.0753
0.2	.0793	.0832	.0871	.0910	.0948	.0987	.1026	.1064	.1103	.1141
0.3	.1179	.1217	.1255	.1293	.1331	.1368	.1406	.1443	.1480	.1517
0.4	.1554	.1591	.1628	.1664	.1700	.1736	.1772	.1808	.1844	.1879
0.5	.1915	.1950	.1985	.2019	.2054	.2088	.2123	.2157	.2190	.2224
0.6	.2257	.2291	.2324	.2357	.2389	.2422	.2454	.2486	.2517	.2549
0.7	.2580	.2611	.2642	.2673	.2704	.2734	.2764	.2794	.2823	.2852
0.8	.2881	.2910	.2939	.2967	.2995	.3023	.3051	.3078	.3106	.3133
0.9	.3159	.3186	.3212	.3238	.3264	.3289	.3315	.3340	.3365	.3389
1.0	.3413	.3438	.3461	.3485	.3508	.3531	.3554	.3577	.3599	.3621
1.1	.3643	.3665	.3686	.3708	.3729	.3749	.3770	.3790	.3810	.3830
1.2	.3849	.3869	.3888	.3907	.3925	.3944	.3962	.3980	.3997	.4015
1.3	.4032	.4049	.4066	.4082	.4099	.4115	.4131	.4147	.4162	.4177
1.4	.4192	.4207	.4222	.4236	.4251	.4265	.4279	.4292	.4306	.4319
1.5	.4332	.4345	.4357	.4370	.4382	.4394	.4406	.4418	.4429	.4441
1.6	.4452	.4463	.4474	.4484	.4495	.4505	.4515	.4525	.4535	.4545
1.7	.4554	.4564	.4573	.4582	.4591	.4599	.4608	.4616	.4625	.4633
1.8	.4641	.4649	.4656	.4664	.4671	.4678	.4686	.4693	.4699	.4706
1.9	.4713	.4719	.4726	.4732	.4738	.4744	.4750	.4756	.4761	.4767
2.0	.4773	.4778	.4783	.4788	.4793	.4798	.4803	.4808	.4812	.4817
2.1	.4821	.4826	.4830	.4834	.4838	.4842	.4846	.4850	.4854	.4857
2.2	.4861	.4864	.4868	.4871	.4875	.4878	.4881	.4884	.4887	.4890
2.3	.4893	.4896	.4898	.4901	.4904	.4906	.4909	.4911	.4913	.4916
2.4	.4918	.4920	.4922	.4925	.4927	.4929	.4931	.4932	.4934	.4936
2.5	.4938	.4940	.4941	.4943	.4945	.4946	.4948	.4949	.4951	.4952
2.6	.4953	.4955	.4956	.4957	.4959	.4960	.4961	.4962	.4963	.4964
2.7	.4965	.4966	.4967	.4968	.4969	.4970	.4971	.4972	.4973	.4974
2.8	.4974	.4975	.4976	.4977	.4977	.4978	.4979	.4979	.4980	.4981
2.9	.4981	.4982	.4982	.4982	.4984	.4984	.4985	.4985	.4986	.4986
3.0	.4987	.4987	.4987	.4988	.4988	.4989	.4989	.4989	.4990	.4990

APPENDIX B

ANSWERS TO SELECTED END-OF-CHAPTER PROBLEMS

e present here some intermediate steps and final answers to selected end-of-chapter problems. Please note that your answer may differ slightly from ours due to rounding differences. Also, although we hope not, some of the problems may have more than one correct solution, depending upon what assumptions are made in working the problem. Finally, many of the problems involve some verbal discussion as well as numerical calculations; this verbal material is not presented here.

2-1   a.   Current ratio = 1.98 ×; DSO = 75 days; Total assets turnover = 1.7 ×; Debt ratio = 61.9%.

2-2   A/P = $90,000; Inv = $90,000; FA = $138,000.

2-4 $\dfrac{NI}{S}$ = 2%; $\dfrac{D}{A}$ = 40%.

2-5 $262,500; 1.19 ×.

2-6   Sales = $2,592,000; DSO = 36 days.

2-7   TIE = 3.5 ×.

2-8   ROE = 24.5%.

2-9   7.2%.

2-11 a.   +5.54%.
      b(2).   + 3.21%.
         (3).   + 2.50%.

3-1   a. k_1 = 9.20%; k_5 = 7.20%.

3-3   a.   8.20%.
      b.   10.20%.
      c. k_5 = 10.70%.

3-5 Refund_{2000} = $19,950.

3-6   **a.**   Personal tax = $20,144.
     c.   MD yield = 7.59%;
          choose FL bonds.
     d.   18.18%.

3-7   **a.** k_1 in Year 2 = 13%.

3-8 k_1 in Year 2 = 15%; Year 2
     inflation = 11%.

3-9   Tax = $107,855; NI =
     $222,145; Marginal tax rate =
     39%; Average tax rate = 33.8%.

3-10   **a.**   Tax = $61,250.
      b.   Tax = $15,600.
      c.   Tax = $4,680.

3-11   1.5%.

3-12   AT&T bonds = 8.8%.

3-13   6.0%.

4-1   **a.** $0.5 million.

4-2   **a.** k_i = 6% + (5%)b_i.
     b.   15%.
     c.   Indifference rate = 16%.

4-3   **a.** $\bar{k}_A$ = 11.30%.
     c. σ_A = 20.8%; σ_p = 20.1%.

4-4   **a.** b_X = 1.3471; b_Y = 0.6508.
     b. k_X = 12.7355%; k_Y =
      9.254%.
     c. k_p = 12.04%.

4-5   **a.** $\hat{k}_M$ = 13.5%; $\hat{k}_J$ = 11.6%.
     b. σ_M = 3.85%; σ_J = 6.22%.
     c. CV_M = 0.29; CV_J = 0.54.

4-6   **a.** $\hat{k}_Y$ = 14%.
     b. σ_X = 12.20%.

4-7   **a.** b_A = 1.40.
     b. k_A = 15%.

4-8   **a.** k_i = 15.5%.
     b(1). k_M = 15%; k_i = 16.5%.
     c(1). k_i = 18.1%.

4-9 b_N = 1.16.

4-10 b_p = 0.7625; k_p = 12.1%.

4-11 b_N = 1.1250.

4-12   4.5%.

5-1   **b.**   X: 10.6%; 13.1%.
      M: 12.1%; 22.6%.
     c.   8.6%.

6-1   **a.** $530.
     d. $445.

6-2   **a.** $895.40.
     b. $1,552.90.
     c. $279.20.
     d. $500.03; $867.14.

6-3   **a.**   ≈ 10 years.
     c.   ≈ 4 years.

6-4   **a.** $6,374.96.
     d(1). $7,012.46.

6-5   **a.** $2,457.84.
     c. $2,000.
     d(1). $2,703.62.

6-6   **a.**   Stream A: $1,251.21.

6-7   b.   7%.
      c.   9%.
      d.   15%.

6-8   a. $881.15.
      b. $895.40.
      c. $903.05.
      d. $908.35.

6-9   a. $279.20.
      b. $276.85.
      c. $443.70.

6-10 a. $5,272.40.
      b. $5,374.00.

6-11 a.   Universal = 7%;
           Regional = 6.14%.

6-12 a.   PMT = $6,594.94.

6-13 a.   Z = 9%; B = 8%.
      b.   Z = $558.39; $135.98;
           32.2%; B = $1,147.20;
           $147.20; 14.72%.

6-14 a. $61,203.
      b. $11,020.
      c. $6,841.

6-15 $1,000 today is worth more.

6-16 a.   15% (or 14.87%).

6-17 7.18%.

6-18 12%.

6-19 9%.

6-20 a. $33,872.
      b. $26,243.04 and $0.

6-21 ≈ 15 years.

6-22 6 years; $1,106.01.

6-23 $PV_{7\%}$ = $1,428.57;
      $PV_{14\%}$ = $714.29.

6-24 $893.26.

6-25 $984.88 ≈ $985.

6-26 57.18%.

6-27 a.   FV = $1,432.02.
      b.   PMT = $93.07.

6-28 i_{Nom} = 15.19%.

6-29 PMT = $36,948.95 or
      $36,949.61.

7-1   a. $1,251.26.
      b. $898.90.

7-2   a. $1,250.
      b. $833.33.
      d.   At 8%, V = $1,196.31.

7-3   b.   PV = $5.29.
      d. $30.01.

7-4   a.   7%.
      b.   5%.
      c.   12%.

7-5   a(1). $9.50.
       (2). $13.33.
      b(1).   Undefined.

7-7   a.   YTM = 3.4%.
      b.   YTM ≈ 7%.
      c. $878.06.

7-8   a. P_0 = $54.11.

7-9   a.   YTM = 8%; YTC = 6.1%.

7-10 **a.** $P_0 = \$21.43$.
 b. $P_0 = \$26.47$.
 d. $P_0 = \$40.54$.

7-11 **a.** New price = \$31.34.
 b. Beta = 0.49865.

7-12 **a.** V_L at 5 percent = \$1,518.97; V_L at 8 percent = \$1,171.15; V_L at 12 percent = \$863.79.

7-13 **a.** YTM at \$829 $\approx$ 15%.

7-14 **a.** 13.3%.
 b. 10%.
 c. 8%.
 d. 5.7%.

7-15 \$23.75.

7-16 **a.** $k_C = 10.6\%$; $k_D = 7\%$.

7-17 \$25.03.

7-18 Bond = 9.33%.

7-19 YTC = 6.47%.

7-20 $P_0 = \$19.89$.

8-1 **a.** 10.0%.
 b. 8.0%.
 c. 6.0%.

8-2 10.25%.

8-3 **a.** \$15,000,000.
 b. \$3,000,000; \$12,000,000.
 c. $k_s = 12.0\%$; $k_e = 12.4\%$.
 d. \$6,000,000.
 e. (1) 8.4%.
   (2) 8.6%.

8-4 **a.** 4.8%; 12.3%.
 b. 10.05%
 c. \$432,000.
 d. 10.40%.

8-5 CL = \$10,000,000 (11.14%); LTD = \$19,782,600 (22.03%); CE = \$60,000,000 (66.83%).

8-6 **a.** 8.0%.
 b. \$0.864.
 c. 12.0%.
 d. \$6 million.
 e. \$15 million.
 f. 15%; 12.71%.

9-1 $NPV_S = \$814.33$; $NPV_L = \$1,675.34$.
 $IRR_S = 15.24\%$; $IRR_L = 14.67\%$.
 $MIRR_S = 13.77\%$; $MIRR_L = 13.46\%$.
 $PI_S = 1.081$; $PI_L = 1.067$.

9-2 **a.** \$0; – \$10,250,000; \$1,750,000.
 b. 16.07%.

9-3 **a.** $NPV_A = \$18,108,510$; $NPV_B = \$13,946,117$. $IRR_A = 15.03\%$; $IRR_B = 22.26\%$.
 b. $NPV_\Delta = \$4,162,393$; $IRR_\Delta = 11.71\%$.

9-4 **d.** 7.61%; 15.58%.

9-6 **a.** Undefined.
 b. $PV_C = -\$911,067$; $PV_F = -\$838,834$.

10-2 **a.** \$89,000.
 b. \$26,220; \$30,300; \$20,100.
 c. \$24,380.

10-3 **a.** \$88,400.
 b. \$46,770; \$52,890; \$37,590; \$33,510;

$29,940.

c.   − $10,000.

d. $46,051.

10-5   a.   3 years.

b.   No.

10-6   a.   NPV = $106,537.

11-1   Oil plant; PV_{Costs} = $4,645,188.

11-2   a. $117,779.

b. $445,060; 3.78; High.

11-3   a.   16.5%.

11-4   a.   15.3%.

b. $38,589.

11-5 $10 million.

11-6 $42,000.

11-7 $62,000.

12-1   a. $13.44 million.

b.   Notes payable = $31.44 million.

c.   Current ratio = 2.00 ×; ROE = 14.2%.

d(1).   − $14.28 million.

(2).   Total assets = $147 million; Notes payable = $3.72 million.

(3).   Current ratio = 4.25 ×; ROE = 10.84%.

12-2   a.   Total assets = $33,534; AFN = $2,128.

b.   Notes payable = $4,228;

AFN = $70; ΔInterest = $213.

12-3   a.   AFN = $128,783.

b.   Notes payable = $220,392; ΔInterest = $8,371; AFN = $8,028.

c.   3.45%.

12-4   a.   AFN = $667.

b.   Increase in notes payable = $51; Increase in C/S = $368.

12-5   a. $480,000.

b. $18,750.

12-6   AFN = $360.

13-1   a.   ROI = 21.25% > WACC = 15%.

b. $Q_{BE_{Old}}$ = 40; $Q_{BE_{New}}$ = 45.45.

13-2   a. ROE_C = 15%; σ_C = 11%.

13-3   c. $20.28; $17.96.

13-4   a.   V = $3,283,636.

b. $16.42.

c. $1.81.

13-5   a.   14.0%.

c. $38.85.

14-1   a. b_U = 1.13.

b. k_{sU} = 15.65%; 5.65%.

c.   1%; 2.42%; 4.62%.

d.   4.62%.

14-2   a. $V_U = V_L$ = $20 million.

b. k_{sU} = 10%; k_{sL} = 15%.

c. S_L = $10 million.

d. $WACC_U$ = 10%; $WACC_L$ = 10%.

14-3 **a.** $V_U = \$12$ million; $V_L = \$16$ million.
  b. $k_{sU} = 10\%$; $k_{sL} = 15\%$.
  c. $S_L = \$6$ million.
  d. $WACC_U = 10\%$; $WACC_L = 7.5\%$.

14-4 **a.** $V_U = 9.6$ million.
  b. $V_L = \$12.93$ million.
  c. $\$3.33$ million versus $\$4$ million.
  d. $V_L = \$20$ million; $\$0$.
  e. $V_L = \$16$ million; $\$4$ million.
  f. $V_L = \$12.64$ million; $\$4$ million.

14-5 **a.** $V_U = V_L = \$14,545,455$.
  b. At $D = \$6$ million: $k_{sL} = 14.51\%$; $WACC = 11.0\%$.
  c. $V_U = \$8,727,273$; $V_L = \$11,127,273$.
  d. At $D = \$6$ million: $k_{sL} = 14.51\%$; $WACC = 8.63\%$.
  e. $D = V = \$14,545,455$.

14-6 **a.** A: $\$32.5$ million; B: $\$30.0$ million.
  b. Project B.

14-7 **a.** Harris: $\$10.0$ million; Broske: $\$10.0$ million.

15-4 **a.** $\$6.00$.
  b. 60%.
  c. $\$66.67$ versus $\$100.00$.

15-5 No repurchase $= \$36$.
  Repurchase $= \$36.40$.

16-1 **a.** $\$24.75$.
  b. $\$24.00$.

16-2 **a.** $\$700,000$.
  b. $\$3,700,000$.
  c. $-\$2,300,000$.

16-3 964,115.

16-4 **a.** 1996: $\$12,000$; $\$6,000$; $\$90,000$.
  b. Edelman: $g_{EPS} = 8.0\%$; $g_{DPS} = 7.4\%$.
  e. 1996: $\$3.00$; $\$1.50$; $\$22.50$.
  f. Kennedy: 15.00%; Strasburg: 13.64%.
  g. 1996: Kennedy: 50%; Strasburg: 50%.
  h. Kennedy: 43%; Strasburg: 37%.
  i. Kennedy: $8 \times$; Strasburg: $8.67 \times$.

17-1 **a.** $\$2,570,925$.
  b. $\$1,558,201$.
  c. $\$2,774,097$.
  d. $\$1,769,842$.

17-2 PMT $= \$402,115$.

17-3 18.4%.

17-4 **c.** YTM $\approx 39\%$.
  d. $V = \$41.96$; $\$150.00$.

18-1 **a.** Energen: 50%; Hastings: 33%.
  b. D/A $= 50\%$.

18-2 **a.** NAL $= \$44,204$.

19-1 **a.** (1) $-\$5$, or $\$0$.
    (2) $\$0$.
    (3) $\$5$.
    (4) $\$75$.
  d. 10%; $\$100$.

19-3 **a.** 14.1%.
  b. $\$12$ million before-tax.

19-4 **b.** Plan 1: 49%; Plan 2: 53%; Plan 3: 53%.
     c. Plan 1: $0.59; Plan 2: $0.64; Plan 3: $0.88.
     d. Plan 1: 19%; Plan 2: 19%; Plan 3: 50%.

19-5 **b.** 11.65%.

20-1 **a.** $ROE_T = 11.75\%$; $ROE_M = 10.80\%$; $ROE_R = 9.16\%$.

20-2 **a.** $1,600,000.
     c. Bank = $1,200,000; Books = −$5,200,000.

20-3 **b.** $420,000.
     c. $35,000.

20-4 **a.** Feb. surplus = $2,000.

20-5 **a.** Oct. loan = $22,800.

20-6 **a.** 103,350.
     b. $97,500.

20-7 **a.** DSO = 28 days.
     b. $70,000.

21-1 **a.** $100,000.
     c(1). $300,000.
     (2). Nominal cost = 36.73%; Effective cost = 43.86%.

21-3 **a.** $300,000.

21-4 **a.** 11.73%.
     b. 12.09%.
     c. 18%.

21-5 **b.** $384,615.
     c. Cash = $126.90; NP = $434.60.

21-6 **a(1).** $27,500.
     (3). $25,833.

21-7 **b.** 14.69%.
     d. 20.99%.

21-8 **a.** 44.54%.

21-9 **a.** $k_d = 12\%$.
     b. $k_d = 11.25\%$.
     c. $k_d = 11.48\%$.
     d. $k_d = 16\%$. Alternative b has lowest interest rate.

21-10 Nominal cost = 14.69%; Effective cost = 15.66%.

21-11 Bank loan = 13.64%.

21-12 **d.** 8.3723%.

22-2 $\Delta NI = -\$3,450$.

22-3 **a.** 3,000 bags.
     b. 4,000 bags.
     c. 2,500 bags.
     d. Every 12 days.

22-4 $\Delta NI = +\$28,115$.

22-5 **a.** March: $146,000; June: $198,000.
     b. Q1: ADS = $3,000; DSO = 48.7 days; Q2: ADS = $4,500; DSO = 44.0 days; Cumulative: ADS = $3,750; DSO = 52.8 days.
     c. 0–30 days: 65%; 31–60 days: 35%.
     d. Receivables/Sales = 130%.

22-6 **b.** Total dollar cost = $160,800; 15.12%.

23-1 **a.** 2.74 years.

23-2   b.   Net gain: $587,223.

24-1   a.   Total assets: $327 million.
        b.   Income: $7 million.
        c.   Before: $15.6 million.
              After: $13.0 million.
        d.   Before: 35.7%.
              After: 64.2%.

24-2   a. $0.
        b.   First mortgage holders:
              $300,000.
              Second mortgage holders:
              $100,000.
        c.   Trustee's expenses:
              $50,000.
              Wages due: $30,000.
              Taxes due: $40,000.

24-4   a. $3,200,000; $7,000,000;
              No.

25-1   NPV = $10,761.

25-2   a.   19.3%.
        b. $10.37 million.
        c. $8.64; Nothing.

26-1   0.5587 pounds per dollar.

26-2   6.0606 francs per dollar.

26-3   10.0200 francs per pound.

26-5   Lira: $0.59.
        Yen: $11.01.
        Swiss francs: $852.30

26-7   b. $18,490.57.

26-8   a. $2,839,698.99.
        b. $2,817,844.00.
        d. $3,200,000.00

26-9 $58.67/share.

26-10 $350,000 gain.

27-1   a. $80,865.
        b. $856.
        c. $10,613; $1,409.
        d. $1,021.

27-2   a.   0.8%.

27-3   a. $6,772,460.

A P P E N D I X C

SOLUTIONS TO SELF-TEST PROBLEMS

CHAPTER 2

Billingsworth paid $2 in dividends and retained $2 per share. Since total retained earnings rose by $12 million, there must be 6 million shares outstanding. With a book value of $40 per share, total common equity must be $40(6 million) = $240 million. Since Billingsworth has $120 million of debt, its debt ratio must be 33.3 percent:

$$\frac{\text{Debt}}{\text{Assets}} = \frac{\text{Debt}}{\text{Debt} + \text{Equity}} = \frac{\$120 \text{ million}}{\$120 \text{ million} + \$240 \text{ million}}$$
$$= 0.333 = 33.3\%.$$

a. In answering questions such as this, always begin by writing down the relevant definitional equations, then start filling in numbers. Note that the extra zeros indicating millions have been deleted in the calculations below.

(1)
$$\text{DSO} = \frac{\text{Accounts receivable}}{\text{Sales}/360}$$

$$40 = \frac{\text{A/R}}{\$1,000/360}$$

$$\text{A/R} = 40(\$2.778) = \$111.1 \text{ million.}$$

(2)
$$\text{Quick ratio} = \frac{\text{Current assets} - \text{Inventories}}{\text{Current liabilities}} = 2.0$$

$$\frac{\text{Cash and marketable securities} + \text{A/R}}{\text{Current liabilities}} = 2.0$$

$$2.0 = \frac{\$100 + \$111.1}{\text{Current liabilities}}$$

$$\text{Current liabilities} = (\$100 + \$111.1)/2 = \$105.5 \text{ million.}$$

(3)
$$\text{Current ratio} = \frac{\text{Current assets}}{\text{Current liabilities}} = 3.0$$

$$\frac{\text{Current assets}}{\$105.5} = 3.0$$

Current assets = 3.0($105.5) = $316.50 million.

(4)
$$\text{Total assets} = \text{Current assets} + \text{Fixed assets}$$
$$= \$316.5 + \$283.5 = \$600 \text{ million.}$$

(5)
$$\text{ROA} = \text{Profit margin} \times \text{Total assets turnover}$$

$$= \frac{\text{Net income}}{\text{Sales}} \times \frac{\text{Sales}}{\text{Total assets}}$$

$$= \frac{\$50}{\$1,000} \times \frac{\$1,000}{\$600}$$

$$= 0.05 \times 1.667 = 0.0833 = 8.33\%.$$

(6)
$$\text{ROE} = \text{ROA} \times \frac{\text{Assets}}{\text{Equity}}$$

$$12.0\% = 8.33\% \times \frac{\$600}{\text{Equity}}$$

$$\text{Equity} = \frac{(8.33\%)(\$600)}{12.0\%}$$

$$= \$416.50 \text{ million.}$$

(7)
$$\text{Total assets} = \text{Total claims} = \$600$$

$$\text{Current liabilities} + \text{Long-term debt} + \text{Equity} = \$600$$

$$\$105.5 + \text{Long-term debt} + \$416.5 = \$600$$

$$\text{Long-term debt} = \$600 - \$105.5 - \$416.5 = \$78.$$

Note: We could have found equity as follows:

$$\text{ROE} = \frac{\text{Net income}}{\text{Equity}}$$

$$12.0\% = \frac{\$50}{\text{Equity}}$$

$$\text{Equity} = \$50/0.12$$

$$= \$416.67 \text{ million (rounding difference).}$$

Then we could have gone on to find current liabilities and long-term debt.

b. Kaiser's average sales per day were $1,000/360 = $2.8 million. Its DSO was 40, so A/R = 40($2.8) = $111.1 million. Its new DSO of 30 would cause A/R = 30($2.8) = $83.3 million. The reduction in receivables would be $111.1 − $83.3 = $27.8 million, which would equal the amount of cash generated.

(1)
$$\text{New equity} = \text{Old equity} = \text{Stock bought back}$$

$$= \$416.5 - \$27.8$$

$$= \$388.7 \text{ million.}$$

Thus,

$$\text{New ROE} = \frac{\text{Net income}}{\text{New equity}}$$

$$= \frac{\$50}{\$388.7}$$

$$= 12.86\% \text{ (versus old ROE of 12.0\%).}$$

(2)
$$\text{New ROA} = \frac{\text{Net income}}{\text{Total assets} - \text{Reduction in A/R}}$$

$$= \frac{\$50}{\$600 - \$27.8}$$

$$= 8.74\% \text{ (versus old ROA of 8.33\%).}$$

(3) The old debt is the same as the new debt:

$$\text{Debt} = \text{Total claims} - \text{Equity}$$

$$= \$600 - \$416.5 = \$183.5 \text{ million}$$

$$\text{Old total assets} = \$600 \text{ million.}$$

$$\text{New total assets} = \text{Old total assets} - \text{Reduction in A/R}$$

$$= \$600 - \$27.8$$

$$= \$572.2 \text{ million.}$$

Therefore,

$$\frac{\text{Debt}}{\text{Old total assets}} = \frac{\$183.5}{\$600} = 30.6\%,$$

while

$$\frac{\text{New debt}}{\text{New total assets}} = \frac{\$183.5}{\$572.2} = 32.1\%.$$

CHAPTER 3

a. Average = (6% + 7% + 8% + 9%)/4 = 30%/4 = 7.5%.
b. $k_{\text{T-bond}} = k^* + IP = 3.0\% + 7.5\% = 10.5\%$.
c. If the 5-year T-bond rate is 11 percent, the inflation rate is expected to average approximately 11% − 3% = 8% during the next 5 years. Thus, the implied Year 5 inflation rate is 10 percent:

$$8\% = (6\% + 7\% + 8\% + 9\% + I_5)/5$$

$$40\% = 30\% + I_5$$

$$I_5 = 10\%.$$

ST-2

	1997	1998	1999
THOMPSON'S TAXES AS A CORPORATION			
Income before salary and taxes	$60,000	$90,000	$110,000
Less: salary	(40,000)	(40,000)	(40,000)
Taxable income, corporate	$20,000	$50,000	$ 70,000
Total corporate tax	$ 3,000[a]	$ 7,500	$ 12,500
Salary	$40,000	$40,000	$ 40,000
Less exemptions and deductions	(16,250)	(16,250)	(16,250)
Taxable personal income	$23,750	$23,750	$ 23,750
Total personal tax	$ 3,562[b]	$ 3,562	$ 3,562
Combined corporate and personal tax:	$ 6,562	$11,062	$ 16,062
THOMPSON'S TAXES AS A PROPRIETORSHIP			
Total income	$60,000	$90,000	$110,000
Less: exemptions and deductions	($16,250)	(16,250)	(16,250)
Taxable personal income	$43,750	$73,750	$ 93,750
Tax liability of proprietorship	$ 7,180[c]	$15,580	$ 21,180
Advantage to being a corporation:	$ 618	$ 4,518	$ 5,118

[a]Corporate tax in 1997 = (0.15)($20,000) = $3,000.
[b]Personal tax (if Thompson incorporates) in 1997 = (0.15)($23,750) = $3,562.
[c]Proprietorship tax in 1997 = $5,850 + (0.28)($43,750 − $39,000)
$$= \$5,850 + 0.28(\$4,750)$$
$$= \$5,850 + \$1,330 = \$7,180.$$

The corporate form of organization allows Thompson to pay the lowest taxes in each year; therefore, on the basis of taxes during the 3-year period, Thompson should incorporate his business. However, note that to get money out of the corporation so he can spend it, Thompson will have to have the corporation pay dividends, which will be taxed to Thompson, and thus he will, sometime in the future, have to pay additional taxes.

CHAPTER 4

ST-1 a. The average rate of return for each stock is calculated simply by averaging the returns over the 5-year period. The average return for each stock is 18.90 percent, calculated for Stock A as follows:

$$k_{Avg} = (-10.00\% + 18.50\% + 38.67\% + 14.33\% + 33.00\%)/5$$
$$= 18.90\%.$$

The realized rate of return on a portfolio made up of Stock A and Stock B would be calculated by finding the average return in each year as k_A(% of Stock A) + k_B(% of Stock B) and then averaging these yearly returns:

YEAR	PORTFOLIO AB'S RETURN, k_{AB}
1992	(6.50%)
1993	19.90
1994	41.46
1995	9.00
1996	30.65
	k_{Avg} = 18.90%

b. The standard deviation of returns is estimated, using Equation 4-3a, as follows (see Footnote 5):

$$\text{Estimated } \sigma = S = \sqrt{\frac{\sum_{t=1}^{n} (k_t - \bar{k}_{Avg})^2}{n-1}}.$$

For stock A, the estimated σ is 19.0 percent:

$$\sigma_A = \sqrt{\frac{(-10.00 - 18.9)^2 + (18.50 - 18.9)^2 + \ldots + (33.00 - 18.9)^2}{5-1}}$$

$$= \sqrt{\frac{1,445.92}{4}} = 19.0\%.$$

The standard deviation of returns for Stock B and for the portfolio are similarly determined, and they are as follows:

	STOCK A	STOCK B	PORTFOLIO AB
Standard deviation	19.0	19.0	18.6

c. Since the risk reduction from diversification is small (σ_{AB} falls only from 19.0 to 18.6 percent), the most likely value of the correlation coefficient is 0.9. If the correlation coefficient were −0.9, the risk reduction would be much larger. In fact, the correlation coefficient between Stocks A and B is 0.92.

d. If more randomly selected stocks were added to the portfolio, σ_p would decline to somewhere in the vicinity of 18 percent; see Figure 4-8. σ_p would remain constant only if the correlation coefficient were +1.0, which is most unlikely. σ_p would decline to zero only if the correlation coefficient, r, were equal to zero and a large number of stocks were added to the portfolio, or if the correct proportions were held in a two-stock portfolio with r = −1.0.

CHAPTER 5

ST-1 a. For Security A:

P_A	k_A	$P_A k_A$	$(k_A - \hat{k}_A)$	$(k_A - \hat{k}_A)^2$	$P_A (k_A - \hat{k}_A)^2$
0.1	−10%	−1.0%	−25%	625	62.5
0.2	5	1.0	−10	100	20.0
0.4	15	6.0	0	0	0.0
0.2	25	5.0	10	100	20.0
0.1	40	4.0	25	625	62.5

$$\hat{k}_A = 15\%. \qquad\qquad \sigma_A = \sqrt{165} = 12.8\%.$$

b. $$w_A = \frac{\sigma_B (\sigma_B - r_{AB}\sigma_A)}{\sigma_A^2 + \sigma_B^2 - 2r_{AB}\sigma_A\sigma_B}$$

$$= \frac{25.7[25.7 - (-0.5)(12.8)]}{(12.8)^2 + (25.7)^2 - 2(-0.5)(12.8)(25.7)}$$

$$= \frac{824.97}{1,153.29} = 0.7153.$$

or 71.53% invested in A, 28.47% in B.

c. $$\sigma_P = \sqrt{w_A\sigma_A)^2 + (1 - w_A)^2(\sigma_B)^2 + 2w_A(1 - w_A)r_{AB}\sigma_A\sigma_B}$$

$$= \sqrt{(0.75)^2(12.8)^2 + (0.25)^2(25.7)^2 + 2(0.75)(0.25)(-0.5)(12.8)(25.7)}$$

$$= \sqrt{92.16 + 41.28 - 61.68}$$

$$= \sqrt{71.76} = 8.47\%, \text{ when } w_A = 75\%.$$

$$\sigma_P = \sqrt{(0.7153)^2(12.8)^2 + (0.2847)^2(25.7)^2 + 2(0.7153)(0.2847)(-0.5)(12.8)(25.7)}$$

$$= 8.38\%, \text{ when } w_A = 71.53\%. \text{ This is the minimum } \sigma_P.$$

$$\sigma_P = \sqrt{(0.5)^2(12.8)^2 + (0.5)^2(25.7)^2 + 2(0.5)(0.5)(-0.5)(12.8)(25.7)}$$

$$= 11.13\%, \text{ when } w_A = 50\%.$$

$$\sigma_P = \sqrt{(0.25)^2(12.8)^2 + (0.75)^2(25.7)^2 + 2(0.25)(0.75)(-0.5)(12.8)(25.7)}$$

$$= 17.89\%, \text{ when } w_A = 25\%.$$

% IN A	% IN B	$\hat{k}_P$	σ_P
100%	0%	15.00%	12.8%
75	25	16.25	8.5
71.53	28.47	16.42	8.4
50	50	17.50	11.1
25	75	18.75	17.9
0	100	20.00	25.7

Calculations for preceding table:

$\hat{k}_p = w_A(\hat{k}_A) + (1 - w_A)(\hat{k}_B)$

$= 0.75(15) + 0.25(20)$ $= 16.25\%$ when $w_A = 75\%$.

$= 0.7153(15) + 0.2847(20)$ $= 16.42\%$ when $w_A = 71.53\%$.

$= 0.5(15) + 0.5(20)$ $= 17.50\%$ when $w_A = 50\%$.

$= 0.25(15) + 0.75(20)$ $= 18.75\%$ when $w_A = 25\%$.

d.

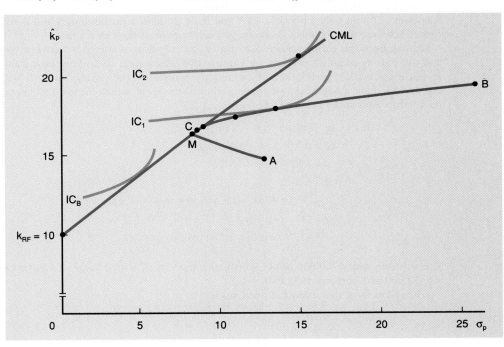

e. See indifference curve IC_1 above. At the point where $\hat{k}_p = 18\%$, $\sigma_p = 13.5\%$.

$$\hat{k}_p = w_A(\hat{k}_A) + (1 - w_A)\,(\hat{k}_B)$$
$$18 = w_A(15) + (1 - w_A)\,(20)$$
$$= 15w_A + 20 - 20w_A$$
$$5w_A = 2$$
$$w_A = 0.4 \text{ or } 40\%.$$

Therefore, to an approximation, your optimal portfolio would have 40 percent in A, 60 percent in B, with $\hat{k}_p = 18\%$ and $\sigma_p = 13.5\%$. (We could get an exact σ_p by using x = 0.4 in the equation for σ_p.)

f. The existence of the riskless asset would enable you to go to the CAPM. We would draw in the CML as shown on the graph in part d. Now you would hold a portfolio of stocks, borrowing on margin to hold more stocks than your net worth, and move to a higher indifference curve, IC_2.

You can put all of your money into the riskless asset, all in A, all in B, or some in each security. The most logical choices are (1) hold a portfolio of A and B plus some of the riskless asset, (2) hold only a portfolio of A and B, or (3) hold a portfolio of A and B and borrow to leverage the portfolio, assuming you can borrow at the riskless rate.

Reading from the graph, we see that your $\hat{k}_p$ at the point of tangency between your IC_2 and the CML is about 22 percent. We can use this information to find out how much you invest in the market portfolio and how much you invest in the riskless asset. (It will turn out that you have a *negative* investment in the riskless asset, which means that you borrow rather than lend at the risk-free rate.

$$\hat{k}_p = \alpha(k_{RF}) + (1 - \alpha)\,(\hat{k}_M)$$
$$22 = \alpha(10) + (1 - \alpha)\,(16.8)$$
$$= 10\alpha + 16.8 - 16.8\,\alpha$$
$$-6.8\,\alpha = 5.2$$
$$\alpha = -0.76 \text{ or } -76\%, \text{ which means that you borrow.}$$
$$1 - \alpha = 1.0 - (-0.76)$$
$$= +1.76 \text{ or } 176\% \text{ in the market portfolio.}$$

This investor, with $200,000 of net worth, thus buys stock with a value of $200,000(1.76) = $352,000 and borrows $152,000.

The riskiness of this leveraged portfolio is

$$\sigma_p = \sqrt{(-0.76)^2(0)^2 + (1.76)^2(8.5)^2 + 2(-0.76)\,(1.76)\,(0)\,(8.5)\,(0)}$$
$$= \sqrt{(1.76^2(8.5)^2}$$
$$= (1.76)\,(8.5) = 15\%.$$

Your indifference curve suggests that you are not very risk averse. A risk-averse investor would have a steep indifference curve (visualize a set of steep curves that were tangent to CML to the left of Point C). This investor would hold some of A and B, combined to form portfolio M, and some of the riskless asset.

g. Given your assumed indifference curve, you would, when the riskless asset becomes available, change your portfolio from the one found in Part e (with $\hat{k}_p = 18\%$, $\sigma_p = 13.5\%$) to one with $\hat{k}_p \approx 22.0\%$ and $\sigma_p \approx 15.0\%$.

h.
$$k_A = k_{RF} + (k_M - k_{RF})\, b_A$$
$$15 = 10 + (16.8 - 10)\, b_A$$
$$= 10 + (6.8)\, b_A.$$
$$b_A = 0.74.$$
$$20 = 10 + (6.8)\, b_B$$
$$b_B = 1.47.$$

Note that the 16.8 percent value for k_M was approximated from the graph. Also, note that this solution *assumes* that you can borrow at $k_{RF} = 10\%$. This is a basic — but questionable — CAPM assumption. If the borrowing rate is *above* k_{RF}, then CML would turn down to the right of Point M.

Chapter 6

a.

1/1/97   8%   1/1/98   1/1/99   1/1/00   1/1/01
                −1,000   FV = ?

$1,000 is being compounded for 3 years, so your balance on January 1, 2001, is $1,259.71:

$$FV_n = PV(1 + i)^n = \$1,000(1 + 0.08)^3 = \$1,259.71.$$

Alternatively, using a financial calculator input N = 3, I = 8, PV = −1000, PMT = 0, and solve for FV = $1,259.71.

b.

1/1/97   1/1/98   1/1/99   1/1/00   1/1/01
   2%
            −1,000   FV = ?

The effective annual rate for 8 percent, compounded quarterly, is

$$\begin{aligned} \text{Effective annual rate} &= \left(1 + \frac{0.08}{4}\right)^4 - 1.0 \\ &= (1.02)^4 - 1.0 = 0.0824 = 8.24\%. \end{aligned}$$

Therefore, FV = $1,000(1.0824)^3 = \$1,000(1.2681) = \$1,268.10$. Alternatively, use FVIF for 2%, $3 \times 4 = 12$ periods:

$$FV_{12} = \$1,000(FVIF_{2\%,12}) = \$1,000(1.2682) = \$1,268.20.$$

Alternatively, using a financial calculator, input N = 12, I = 2, PV = −1000, PMT = 0, and solve for FV = $1,268.24.

Note that since the interest factors are carried to only four decimal places, rounding differences occur. Rounding differences also occur between calculator and tabular solutions.

c.
```
   1/1/97   8%   1/1/98      1/1/99      1/1/00      1/1/01
   ├──────────────┼────────────┼────────────┼────────────┤
                 -250         -250         -250         -250
                                                       FV = ?
```

As you work this problem, keep in mind that the tables assume that payments are made at the end of each period. Therefore, you may solve this problem by finding the future value of an annuity of $250 for 4 years at 8 percent:

$$\text{FVA}_4 = \text{PMT}(\text{FVIFA}_{i,n}) = \$250(4.5061) = \$1,126.53$$

Alternatively, using a financial calculator, input N = 4, I = 8, PV = 0, PMT = −250, and solve for FV = $1,126.53.

d.
```
   1/1/97   8%   1/1/98      1/1/99      1/1/00      1/1/01
   ├──────────────┼────────────┼────────────┼────────────┤
                   ?            ?            ?            ?
                                                   FV = 1,259.71
```

N = 4; I = 8; PV = 0; FV = 1259.71; solve for PMT = $279.56.

$$\text{PMT}(\text{FVIFA}_{8\%,4}) = \text{FVA}_4$$
$$\text{PMT}(4.5061) = \$1,259.71$$
$$\text{PMT} = \$1,259.71/4.5061 = \$279.56.$$

Therefore, you would have to make 4 payments of $279.56 each to have a balance of $1,259.71 on January 1, 2001.

ST-2 a. Set up a time line like the one in the preceding problem:

```
   1/1/97   8%   1/1/98      1/1/99      1/1/00      1/1/01
   ├──────────────┼────────────┼────────────┼────────────┤
           PV = ?                                      1,000
```

Note that your deposit will grow for 3 years at 8 percent. The fact that is now January 1, 1997, is irrelevant. The deposit on January 1, 1998, is the PV, and the FV is $1,000. Here is the solution:

N = 3; I = 8; PMT = 0; FV = 1000; solve for PV = $793.83.

$$\text{FV}_3(\text{PVIF}_{8\%,3}) = \text{PV}$$
$$\text{PV} = \$1,000(0.7938) = \$793.80 = \text{Initial deposit to accumulate } \$1,000.$$

(Difference due to rounding.)

b.
```
   1/1/97   8%   1/1/98      1/1/99      1/1/00      1/1/01
   ├──────────────┼────────────┼────────────┼────────────┤
                   ?            ?            ?            ?
                                                   FV = 1,000
```

Here we are dealing with a 4-year annuity whose first payment occurs one year from today, on 1/1/98, and whose future value must equal $1,000. You should modify the time line to help visualize the situation. Here is the solution:

N = 4; I = 8; PV = 0; FV = 1000; solve for PMT = \$221.92.

$$PMT(FVIFA_{8\%,4}) = FVA_4$$

$$PMT = \frac{FVA_4}{(FVIFA_{8\%,4})}$$

$$= \frac{\$1,000}{4.5061} = \$221.92 = \begin{array}{l}\text{Payment necessary}\\\text{to accumulate \$1,000.}\end{array}$$

c. This problem can be approached in several ways. Perhaps the simplest is to ask this question: "If I received \$750 on 1/1/98 and deposited it to earn 8 percent, would I have the required \$1,000 on 1/1/01?" The answer is no:

1/1/97	8%	1/1/98	1/1/99	1/1/00	1/1/01
		−750			FV = ?

$$FV_3 = \$750(1.08)(1.08)(1.08) = \$944.78.$$

This indicates that you should let your father make the payments rather than accept the lump sum of \$750.

You could also compare the \$750 with the PV of the payments:

1/1/97	8%	1/1/98	1/1/99	1/1/00	1/1/01
		−221.92	−221.92	−221.92	−221.92
		PV = ?			

N = 4; I = 8; PMT = −221.92; FV = 0; solve for PV = \$735.03.

$$PMT(PVIFA_{8\%,4}) = PVA,$$

$$\$221.92(3.3121) = \$735.02 = \text{Present value of the required payments.}$$

(Difference due to rounding.)

This is less than the \$750 lump sum offer, so your initial reaction might be to accept the lump sum of \$750. However, this would be a mistake. The problem is that when you found the \$735.02 PV of the annuity, you were finding the value of the annuity *today*, on January 1, 1997. You were comparing \$735.02 today with the lump sum of \$750 one year from now. This is, of course, invalid. What you should have done was take the \$735.02, recognize that this is the PV of an annuity as of January 1, 1997, multiply \$735.02 by 1.08 to get \$793.82, and compare \$793.82 with the lump sum of \$750. You would then take your father's offer to make the payments rather than take the lump sum on January 1, 1998.

d.

1/1/97	i = ?	1/1/98	1/1/99	1/1/00	1/1/01
		−750			1,000

N = 3; PV = −750; PMT = 0; FV = 1000; solve for I = 10.0642%.

$$PV(FVIF_{i,3}) = FV$$

$$FVIF_{i,3} = \frac{FV}{PV}$$

$$= \frac{\$1,000}{\$750} = 1.3333.$$

Use the Future Value of $1 table (Table A-3 in Appendix A) for 3 periods to find the interest rate corresponding to an FVIF of 1.3333. Look across the Period 3 row of the table until you come to 1.3333. The closest value is 1.3310, in the 10 percent column. Therefore, you would require an interest rate of approximately 10 percent to achieve your $1,000 goal. The exact rate required, found with a financial calculator, is 10.0642 percent.

e.

1/1/97	$i = ?$	1/1/98	1/1/99	1/1/00	1/1/01
		−186.29	−186.29	−186.29	−186.29
					FV = 1,000

$N = 4$; $PV = 0$; $PMT = -186.29$; $FV = 1000$; solve for $I = 19.9997\%$.

$$PMT(FVIFA_{i,4}) = FVA_4$$

$$\$186.29(FVIFA_{i,4}) = \$1,000$$

$$FVIFA_{i,4} = \frac{\$1,000}{\$186.29} = 5.3680.$$

Using Table A-4 at the end of the book, we find that 5.3680 corresponds to a 20 percent interest rate. You might be able to find a borrower willing to offer you a 20 percent interest rate, but there would be some risk involved—he or she might not actually pay you your $1,000!

f.

1/1/97	4%	1/1/98		1/1/99		1/1/00		1/1/01
		−400	?	?	?	?	?	?
								FV = 1,000

Find the future value of the original $400 deposit:

$$FV_6 = PV(FVIF_{4\%,6}) = \$400(1.2653) = \$506.12.$$

This means that on January 1, 2001, you need an additional sum of $493.88:

$$\$1,000.00 - \$506.12 = \$493.88.$$

This will be accumulated by making 6 equal payments which earn 8 percent compounded semiannually, or 4 percent each 6 months:

$N = 6$; $I = 4$; $PV = 0$; $FV = 493.88$; solve for $PMT = \$74.46$.

$$PMT(FVIFA_{4\%,6}) = FVA_6$$

$$PMT = \frac{FVA_6}{(FVIFA_{4\%,6})}$$

$$= \frac{\$493.88}{6.6330} = \$74.46.$$

g.

$$\text{Effective annual rate} = \left(1 + \frac{i_{Nom}}{m}\right)^m - 1.0$$

$$= \left(1 + \frac{0.08}{2}\right)^2 - 1 = (1.04)^2 - 1$$

$$= 1.0816 - 1 = 0.0816 = 8.16\%.$$

h. There is a reinvestment rate risk here because we assumed that funds will earn an 8 percent return in the bank. In fact, if interest rates in the economy fall, the bank will lower its deposit rate because it will be earning less when it lends out the funds you deposited with it. If you buy certificates of deposit (CDs) that mature on the date you need the money (1/1/01), you will avoid the reinvestment risk, but that would work only if you were making the deposit today. Other ways of reducing reinvestment rate risk will be discussed later in the text.

Bank A's effective annual rate is 8.24 percent:

$$\text{Effective annual rate} = \left(1 + \frac{0.08}{4}\right)^4 - 1.0$$
$$= (1.02)^4 - 1 = 1.0824 - 1$$
$$= 0.0824 = 8.24\%.$$

Now Bank B must have the same effective annual rate:

$$\left(1 + \frac{i}{12}\right)^{12} - 1.0 = 0.0824$$

$$\left(1 + \frac{i}{12}\right)^{12} = 1.0824$$

$$1 + \frac{i}{12} = (1.0824)^{1/12}$$

$$1 + \frac{i}{12} = 1.00662$$

$$\frac{i}{12} = 0.00662$$

$$i = 0.07944 = 7.94\%.$$

Thus, the two banks have different quoted rates — Bank A's quoted rate is 8 percent, while Bank B's quoted rate is 7.94 percent; however, both banks have the same effective annual rate of 8.24 percent. The difference in their quoted rates is due to the difference in compounding frequency.

CHAPTER 7

a. This is not necessarily true. Because G plows back two-thirds of its earnings, its growth rate should exceed that of D, but D pays higher dividends ($6 versus $2). We cannot say which stock should have the higher price.

b. Again, we just do not know which price would be higher.

c. This is false. The changes in k_d and k_s would have a greater effect on G — its price would decline more.

d. The total expected return for D is $\hat{k}_D = D_1/P_0 + g = 15\% + 0\% = 15\%$. The total expected return for G will have D_1/P_0 less than 15 percent and g greater than 0 percent, but $\hat{k}_G$ should be neither greater nor smaller than D's total expected return, 15 percent, because the two stocks are stated to be equally risky.

e. We have eliminated a, b, c, and d, so e should be correct. On the basis of the available information, D and G should sell at about the same price, $40; thus, $\hat{k}_s$ = 15% for both D and G. G's current dividend yield is $2/$40 = 5%. Therefore, g = 15% − 5% = 10%. Note that to reach this conclusion we assumed that Stock G's price is $40.

ST-2 **a.** Pennington's bonds were sold at par; therefore, the original YTM equaled the coupon rate of 12%.

b.
$$V_B = \sum_{t=1}^{50} \frac{\$120/2}{\left(1 + \frac{0.10}{2}\right)^t} + \frac{\$1,000}{\left(1 + \frac{0.10}{2}\right)^{50}}$$

$$= \$60(\text{PVIFA}_{5\%,50}) + \$1,000(\text{PVIF}_{5\%,50})$$

$$= \$60(18.2559) + \$1,000(0.0872)$$

$$= \$1,095.35 + \$87.20 = \$1,182.55.$$

Alternatively, with a financial calculator, input the following: N = 50, I = 5, PMT = 60, FV = 1000, and solve for PV = $1,182.56.

c.
$$\text{Current yield} = \text{Annual coupon payment/Price}$$

$$= \$120/\$1,182.55$$

$$= 0.1015 = 10.15\%.$$

$$\text{Capital gains yield} = \text{Total yield} - \text{Current yield}$$

$$= 10\% - 10.15\% = -0.15\%.$$

d.
$$\$916.42 = \sum_{t=1}^{13} \frac{\$60}{(1 + k_d/2)^t} + \frac{\$1,000}{(1 + k_d/2)^{13}}.$$

Try $k_d = 14\%$:

$$V_B = \text{INT}(\text{PVIFA}_{7\%,13}) + M(\text{PVIF}_{7\%,13})$$
$$\$916.42 = \$60(8.3577) + \$1,000(0.4150)$$
$$= \$501.46 + \$415.00 = \$916.46.$$

Therefore, the YTM on July 1, 1994, was 14 percent.

Alternatively, with a financial calculator, input the following: N = 13, PV = −916.42, or PMT = 60, FV = 1000, and $k_d/2$ = I = ? Calculator solution = $k_d/2$ = 7.00%; therefore, k_d = 14.00%.

e.
$$\text{Current yield} = \$120/\$916.42 = 13.09\%.$$
$$\text{Capital gains yield} = 14\% - 13.09\% = 0.91\%.$$

f. The following time line illustrates the years to maturity of the bond:

```
    1/1/94      7/1/94      1/1/95      7/1/95      1/1/96    12/31/00
    ├──────┼──────┼──────────┼──────────┼──────────┼ · · · ──┤
        3/1/94
```

Thus, on March 1, 1994, there were 13⅔ periods left before the bond matures. Bond traders actually use the following procedure to determine the price of the bond:
(1) Find the price of the bond on the next coupon date, July 1, 1994.

$$V_{B\ 7/1/94} = \$60(\text{PVIFA}_{7.75\%,13}) + \$1,000(\text{PVIF}_{7.75\%,13})$$
$$= \$60(8.0136) + \$1,000(0.3789)$$
$$= \$859.72.$$

Note that we could use a calculator to solve for $V_{B\ 7/1/94}$ or we could substitute i = 7.75% and n = 13 periods into the equations for PVIFA and PVIF:

$$PVIFA = \frac{1 - \dfrac{1}{(1+i)^n}}{i} = \frac{1 - \dfrac{1}{(1+0.0775)^{13}}}{0.0775} = 8.0136.$$

$$PVIF = \frac{1}{(1+k)^n} = \frac{1}{(1+0.0775)^{13}} = 0.3789.$$

(2) Add the coupon, $60, to the bond price to get the total value, TV, of the bond on the next interest payment date: TV = $859.72 + $60.00 = $919.72.

(3) Discount this total value back to the purchase date:

$$\text{Value at purchase date (March 1, 1994)} = \$919.72(PVIF_{7.75\%,4/6})$$

$$= \$919.72(0.9515)$$

$$= \$875.11.$$

Here

$$PVIF_{7.75\%,2/3} = \frac{1}{(1+0.0775)^{2/3}} = \frac{1}{1.0510} = 0.9515.$$

(4) Therefore, you would have written a check for $875.11 to complete the transaction. Of this amount, $20 = ($\frac{1}{3}$)($60) would represent accrued interest and $855.11 would represent the bond's basic value. This breakdown would affect both your taxes and those of the seller.

(5) This problem could be solved *very* easily using a financial calculator with a bond valuation function, such as the HP-12C or the HP-17B. This is explained in the calculator manual under the heading, "Bond Calculations."

The first step is to solve for g, the unknown variable, in the constant growth equation. Since D_1 is unknown but D_0 is known, substitute $D_0(1 + g)$ as follows:

$$\hat{P}_0 = P_0 = \frac{D_1}{k_s - g} = \frac{D_0(1 + g)}{k_s - g}$$

$$\$36 = \frac{\$2.40(1 + g)}{0.12 - g}.$$

Solving for g, we find the growth rate to be 5 percent:

$$\$4.32 - \$36g = \$2.40 + \$2.40g$$

$$\$38.4g = \$1.92$$

$$g = 0.05 = 5\%.$$

The next step is to use the growth rate to project the stock price 5 years hence:

$$\hat{P}_5 = \frac{D_0(1 + g)^6}{k_s - g}$$

$$= \frac{\$2.40(1.05)^6}{0.12 - 0.05}$$

$$= \$45.95.$$

[Alternatively, $\hat{P}_5 = \$36(1.05)^5 = \$45.95.$]

Therefore, Ewald Company's expected stock price 5 years from now, $\hat{P}_5$, is $45.95.

ST-4   **a.** (1) Calculate the PV of the dividends paid during the supernormal growth period:

$$D_1 = \$1.1500(1.15) = \$1.3225.$$
$$D_2 = \$1.3225(1.15) = \$1.5209.$$
$$D_3 = \$1.5209(1.13) = \$1.7186.$$
$$PV\ D = \$1.3225(0.8929) + \$1.5209(0.7972) + \$1.7186(0.7118)$$
$$= \$1.1809 + \$1.2125 + \$1.2233$$
$$= \$3.6167 \approx \$3.62.$$

(2) Find the PV of Snyder's stock price at the end of Year 3:

$$\hat{P}_3 = \frac{D_4}{k_s - g} = \frac{D_3(1 + g)}{k_s - g}$$
$$= \frac{\$1.7186(1.06)}{0.12 - 0.06}$$
$$= \$30.36.$$
$$PV\ \hat{P}_3 = \$30.36(0.7118) = \$21.61.$$

(3) Sum the two components to find the value of the stock today:

$$\hat{P}_0 = \$3.62 + \$21.61 = \$25.23.$$

Alternatively, the cash flows can be placed on a time line as follows:

Enter the cash flows into the cash flow register, I = 12, and press the NPV key to obtain $P_0 = \$25.23$.

b. $\hat{P}_1 = \$1.5209(0.8929) + \$1.7186(0.7972) + \$30.36(0.7972)$
$$= \$1.3580 + \$1.3701 + \$24.2030$$
$$= \$26.9311 \approx \$26.93.$$
(Calculator solution: $26.93.)

$\hat{P}_2 = \$1.7186(0.8929) + \$30.36(0.8929)$
$$= \$1.5345 + \$27.1084$$
$$= \$28.6429 \approx \$28.64.$$
(Calculator solution: $28.64.)

c.

YEAR	DIVIDEND YIELD	+	CAPITAL GAINS YIELD	=	TOTAL RETURN
1	$\dfrac{\$1.3225}{\$25.23} \approx 5.24\%$		$\dfrac{\$26.93 - \$25.23}{\$25.23} \approx 6.74\%$		$\approx 12\%$
2	$\dfrac{\$1.5209}{\$26.93} \approx 5.65\%$		$\dfrac{\$28.64 - \$26.93}{\$26.93} \approx 6.35\%$		$\approx 12\%$
3	$\dfrac{\$1.7186}{\$28.64} \approx 6.00\%$		$\dfrac{\$30.36 - \$28.64}{\$28.64} \approx 6.00\%$		$\approx 12\%$

Chapter 8

a. *After-tax cost of debt:*

$$k_d(1 - T) = 12\%(1 - 0.40) = 12\%(0.60) = 7.20\%.$$

Cost of preferred stock:

$$k_{ps} = \frac{D_{ps}}{P_n} = \frac{\$11}{\$100 - \$5} = \frac{\$11}{\$95} \approx 11.6\%.$$

Cost of retained earnings (using DCF method):

$$k_s = \hat{k}_s = \frac{D_1}{P_0} + g = \frac{D_0(1 + g)}{P_0} + g$$

$$= \frac{\$3.60(1.09)}{\$60} + 9\% \approx 15.5\%.$$

Cost of retained earnings (using CAPM method):

$$k_s = k_{RF} + (k_M - k_{RF})b_i$$
$$= 11\% + (14\% - 11\%)1.51 \approx 15.5\%.$$

Cost of new common stock:

$$k_e = \frac{D_1}{P_0(1.0 - F)} + g = \frac{\$3.924}{\$60(0.9)} + 9\% \approx 16.3\%.$$

Since we are using the DCF k_s estimate as our final estimate for k_s, we can use the DCF k_e estimate as our final estimate for k_e. If this condition did not hold, we would apply the 16.3% − 15.5% = 0.8% flotation cost adjustment to the final k_s estimate.

b. LCI's forecasted retained earnings are $17,142.86(1 − 0.30) = $12,000. Thus, the retained earnings break point, BP_{RE}, is $20,000:

$$BP_{RE} = \frac{RE}{\text{Equity fraction}} = \frac{\$12,000}{0.60} = \$20,000.$$

c. *WACC using retained earnings:*

$$WACC_1 = w_d k_d(1 - T) + w_{ps}k_{ps} + w_{ce}k_s$$
$$= 0.25(7.20\%) + 0.15(11.6\%) + 0.60(15.5\%) \approx 12.9\%.$$

WACC using new common stock:

$$WACC_2 = 1.80\% + 1.74\% + 0.60(16.3\%) \approx 13.3\%.$$

d. See the graph below..

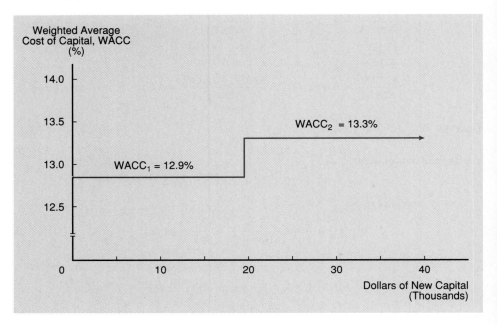

e. Depreciation-generated cash flow pushes the retained earnings break point to the right by the amount of depreciation expense. Thus, the break point would shift to $20,000 + $10,000 = $30,000.

CHAPTER 9

ST-1 **a.** *Payback:*

To determine the payback, construct the cumulative cash flows for each project:

	CUMULATIVE CASH FLOW	
YEAR	**PROJECT X**	**PROJECT Y**
0	($10,000)	($10,000)
1	(3,500)	(6,500)
2	(500)	(3,000)
3	2,500	500
4	3,500	4,000

$$\text{Payback}_X = 2 + \frac{\$500}{\$3,000} = 2.17 \text{ years.}$$

$$\text{Payback}_Y = 2 + \frac{\$3,000}{\$3,500} = 2.86 \text{ years.}$$

Net Present Value (NPV):

$$NPV_X = -\$10,000 + \frac{\$6,500}{(1.12)^1} + \frac{\$3,000}{(1.12)^2} + \frac{\$3,000}{(1.12)^3} + \frac{\$1,000}{(1.12)^4}$$

$$= \$966.01.$$

With a financial calculator, input the following: $CF_0 = -10000$, $CF_1 = 6500$, $CF_2 = 3000$, $CF_3 = 3000$, $CF_4 = 1000$, $I = 12$, and solve for $NPV_X = \$966.01$.

$$NPV_Y = -\$10,000 + \frac{\$3,500}{(1.12)^1} + \frac{\$3,500}{(1.12)^2} + \frac{\$3,500}{(1.12)^3} + \frac{\$3,500}{(1.12)^4}$$

$$= \$630.72.$$

With a financial calculator, input the following: $CF_0 = -10000$, $CF_1 = 3500$, $CF_2 = 3500$, $CF_3 = 3500$, $CF_4 = 3500$, $I = 12$, and solve for $NPV_Y = \$630.72$.

Internal Rate of Return (IRR):
To solve for each project's IRR, find the discount rates which equate each NPV to zero:

$$IRR_X = 18.0\%.$$
$$IRR_Y = 15.0\%.$$

With a financial calculator, input the cash flows and interest rate as done in the NPV calculation, but, rather than using the NPV key, press the IRR key to arrive at the IRR.

Modified Internal Rate of Return (MIRR):
To obtain each project's MIRR, begin by finding each project's terminal value (TV) of cash inflows:

$$TV_X = \$6,500(1.12)^3 + \$3,000(1.12)^2$$
$$+ 3,000(1.12)^1 + \$1,000 = \$17,255.23.$$
$$TV_Y = \$3,500(1.12)^3 + \$3,500(1.12)^2$$
$$+ \$3,500(1.12)^1 + \$3,500 = \$16,727.65.$$

Now, each project's MIRR is that discount rate which equates the PV of the TV to each project's cost, $10,000:

$$MIRR_X = 14.6\%.$$
$$MIRR_Y = 13.7\%.$$

With a financial calculator, input the following: $N = 4$, $PV = -10000$, $PMT = 0$, $FV = 17255.23$, and solve for $I = MIRR_X = 14.6\%$. For Project Y input the following: $N = 4$, $PV = -10000$, $PMT = 0$, $FV = 16727.65$, and solve for $I = MIRR_Y = 13.7\%$.

Profitability Index (PI):

$$PI_X = \frac{PV \text{ benefits}}{PV \text{ costs}} = \frac{\$10,966.01}{\$10,000} = 1.10.$$

$$PI_Y = \frac{\$10,630.72}{\$10,000} = 1.06.$$

b. The following table summarizes the project rankings by each method:

	PROJECT THAT RANKS HIGHER
Payback	X
NPV	X
IRR	X
MIRR	X
PI	X

Note that all methods rank Project X over Project Y. Additionally, both projects are acceptable under the NPV, IRR, MIRR, and PI criteria. Thus, both projects should be accepted if they are independent.

c. Choose the project with the higher NPV at k = 12%, or Project X. Note that both projects have 4-year lives—if Project X and Project Y had different lives and were repeatable, a different procedure would be required. This point is discussed in Chapter 10.

d. To determine the effects of changing the cost of capital, plot the NPV profiles of each project.

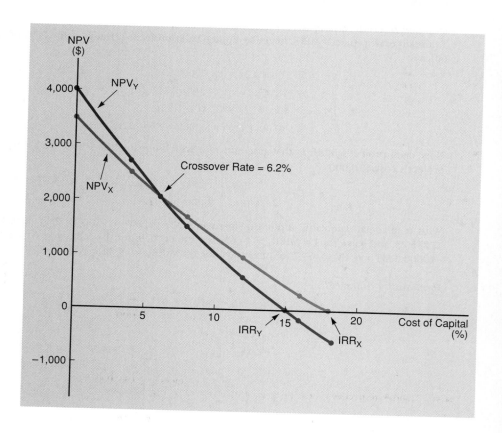

DISCOUNT RATE	NPV_X	NPV_Y
0%	$3,500	$4,000
4	2,545	2,705
8	1,707	1,592
12	966	631
16	307	(206)

The crossover rate occurs at about 6 to 7 percent. To find this rate exactly, create a Project Δ, which is the difference in cash flows between Projects X and Y:

YEAR	PROJECT X − PROJECT Y = PROJECT Δ NET CASH FLOW
0	$ 0
1	3,000
2	(500)
3	(500)
4	(2,500)

Then find the IRR of Project Δ:

$$IRR_\Delta = \text{Crossover rate} = 6.2\%.$$

Thus, if the firm's cost of capital is less than 6.2 percent, a conflict exists since $NPV_Y >$ NPV_X, but $IRR_X > IRR_Y$. Note, however, that when k = 5.0%, $MIRR_X = 10.64\%$ and $MIRR_Y = 10.83\%$, hence the modified IRR ranks the projects correctly, even to the left of the crossover point.

e. The basic cause of the conflict is differing reinvestment rate assumptions between NPV and IRR. The conflict occurs in this situation because the projects differ in their cash flow timing.

CHAPTER 10

-1 a. *Estimated investment requirements:*

Price	($50,000)
Modification	(10,000)
Change in net working capital	(2,000)
Total investment	($62,000)

b. *Operating cash flows:*

		YEAR 1	YEAR 2	YEAR 3
1.	After-tax cost savings	$12,000	$12,000	$12,000
2.	Depreciation*	19,800	27,000	9,000
3.	Depreciation tax savings**	7,920	10,800	3,600
	Net cash flow (1 + 3)	$19,920	$22,800	$15,600

*Depreciable basis = $60,000; the MACRS percentage allowances are 0.33, 0.45, and 0.15 in Years 1, 2, and 3, respectively; hence depreciation in Year 1 = 0.33($60,000) = $19,800, and so on.

**Depreciation tax savings = T(Depreciation) = 0.4($19,800) = $7,920 in Year 1, and so on.

c. *End-of-project cash flows:*

Salvage value	$20,000
Tax on salvage value*	(6,320)
Net working capital recovery	2,000
	$15,680

*Sale price	$20,000
Less book value	4,200
Taxable income	$15,800
Tax at 40%	$ 6,320

Note that Book value = Depreciable basis − Accumulated depreciation
= $60,000 − $55,800 = $4,200.

d. *Project NPV:*

$$\text{NPV} = -\$62,000 + \frac{\$19,920}{(1.10)^1} + \frac{\$22,800}{(1.10)^2} + \frac{\$31,280}{(1.10)^3}$$

$$= -\$1,547.$$

Using a financial calculator, input $CF_0 = -62000$, $CF_1 = 19920$, $CF_2 = 22800$, $CF_3 = 31280$, and $I = 10$; then solve for NPV = −$1,546.81.

Since the earth mover has a negative NPV, it should not be purchased.

ST-2   First determine the net cash flow at $t = 0$:

Purchase price	($8,000)
Sale of old machine	3,000
Tax on sale of old machine	(160)*
Change in net working capital	(1,500)**
Total investment	($6,660)

*The market value is $3,000 − $2,600 = $400 above the book value. Thus, there is a $400 recapture of depreciation, and the firm would have to pay 0.40($400) = $160 in taxes.
**The change in net working capital is a $2,000 increase in current assets less a $500 increase in current liabilities, which totals a $1,500 increase in net working capital.

Now, examine the operating cash inflows:

Sales increase	$1,000
Cost decrease	1,500
Pre-tax operating revenue increase	$2,500

After-tax operating revenue increase:

$2,500(1 − T) = $2,500(0.60) = $1,500.

Depreciation:

YEAR	1	2	3	4	5	6
New*	$1,600	$2,560	$1,520	$960	$880	$480
Old	350	350	350	350	350	350
Change	$1,250	$2,210	$1,170	$610	$530	$130
Depreciation tax savings**	$ 500	$ 884	$ 468	$244	$212	$ 52

*Depreciable basis = $8,000. Depreciation expense in each year equals depreciable basis times the MACRS percentage allowance of 0.20, 0.32, 0.19, 0.12, 0.11, and 0.06 in Years 1-6, respectively.
**Depreciation tax savings = T(Δ Depreciation) = 0.4(Δ Depreciation).

Now recognize that at the end of Year 6 the firm would recover its net working capital investment of $1,500, and it would also receive $800 from the sale of the replacement machine. However, since the machine is fully depreciated, the firm must pay 0.40($800) = $320 in taxes on the sale. Note also that by undertaking the replacement now, the firm foregoes the right to sell the old machine for $500 in Year 6; thus, this $500 in Year 6 must be considered as an opportunity cost in that year. There is no tax effect here since the $500 salvage value would equal the old machine's Year 6 book value.

	0	1	2	3	4	5	6
Net investment	($6,660)						
After-tax revenue increase		$1,500	$1,500	$1,500	$1,500	$1,500	$1,500
Depreciation tax savings		500	884	468	244	212	52
Working capital recovery							1,500
Salvage value on new machine							800
Tax on salvage value							(320)
Opportunity cost of old machine							(500)
Net cash flow	($6,660)	$2,000	$2,384	$1,968	$1,744	$1,712	$3,032

With a financial calculator, input the following: CF_0 = −6660, CF_1 = 2000, CF_2 = 2384, CF_3 = 1968, CF_4 = 1744, CF_5 = 1712, CF_6 = 3032, and I = 15 to solve for NPV = $1,334.89.

The net present value of this incremental cash flow stream, when discounted at 15 percent, is $1,335. Thus, the replacement should be made.

CHAPTER 11

11-1 a. First, find the expected cash flows:

YEAR	EXPECTED CASH FLOW			
0	0.2(−$100,000) + 0.6(−$100,000) + 0.2(−$100,000) = ($100,000)			
1	0.2($20,000)	+ 0.6($30,000)	+ 0.2($40,000)	= 30,000
2				30,000
3				30,000
4				30,000
5				30,000
5*	0.2($0)	+ 0.6($20,000)	+ 0.2($30,000)	= 18,000

Next, determine the NPV based on the expected cash flows:

$$NPV = -\$100,000 + \frac{\$30,000}{(1.10)^1} + \frac{\$30,000}{(1.10)^2} + \frac{\$30,000}{(1.10)^3} + \frac{\$30,000}{(1.10)^4}$$
$$+ \frac{\$30,000 + \$18,000}{(1.10)^5} = \$24,900.$$

Using a financial calculator, input the following: $CF_0 = -100000$, $CF_1 = 30000$, $N_j = 4$, $CF_5 = 48000$, and $I = 10$ to solve for NPV = $\$24,900.19 \approx \$24,900$.

b. For the worst case, the cash flow values from the left-most cash flow column are used to calculate NPV:

$$NPV = -\$100,000 + \frac{\$20,000}{(1.10)^1} + \frac{\$20,000}{(1.10)^2} + \frac{\$20,000}{(1.10)^3} + \frac{\$20,000}{(1.10)^4} + \frac{\$20,000 + \$0}{(1.10)^5}$$
$$= -\$24,184.$$

Using a financial calculator, input the following: $CF_0 = -100000$, $CF_1 = 20000$, $N_j = 5$, and $I = 10$ to solve for NPV = $-\$24,184.26 \approx -\$24,184$.

Similarly, for the best case, use the values from the right-most column. Here the NPV is $70,259.

If the cash flows are perfectly dependent, then the low cash flow in the first year would mean a low cash flow in every year. Thus, the probability of the worst case occurring is the probability of getting the $20,000 net cash flow in Year 1, or 20 percent. If the cash flows are independent, then the cash flow in each year could be low, high, or average, and the probability of getting all low cash flows would be $0.2(0.2)(0.2)(0.2)(0.2) = 0.2^5 = 0.00032$.

c. Under these conditions, the NPV distribution is

P	NPV
0.2	($24,184)
0.6	26,142
0.2	70,259

Thus, the expected NPV is $0.2(-\$24,184) + 0.6(\$26,142) + 0.2(\$70,259) = \$24,900$. Note that, as is generally the case, the expected NPV is the same as the base case NPV found in Part a. The standard deviation is $29,904:

$$\sigma^2_{NPV} = 0.2(-\$24,184 - \$24,900)^2 + 0.6(\$26,142 - \$24,900)^2$$
$$+ 0.2(\$70,259 - \$24,900)^2$$
$$= 894,261,126.$$
$$\sigma_{NPV} = \sqrt{894,261,126} = \$29,904.$$

The coefficient of variation, CV, is $\$29,904/\$24,900 = 1.20$.

d. Since the project's coefficient of variation is 1.20, the project is riskier than average, hence the project's risk-adjusted cost of capital is 10% + 2% = 12%. Now the project should be evaluated by finding the NPV of the base case as in Part a, but using a 12 percent discount rate. The differential risk-adjusted NPV is $18,357, and thus the project should be accepted.

a. *Cost using retained earnings:*

$$k_s = \hat{k}_s = \frac{D_1}{P_0} + g = \frac{(\$1.85)(1.08)}{(\$50)} + 0.08 = 12.0\%.$$
$$WACC_2 = 0.3(8\%)(0.6) + 0.7(12.0\%) = 9.84\%.$$

2 *Cost using new common stock:*

$$k_e = \hat{k}_e = \frac{D_1}{P_0(1 - F)} + g = \frac{(\$1.85)(1.08)}{(\$50)(0.85)} + 0.08 = 12.7\%.$$

$$WACC_2 = 0.3(8\%)(0.6) + 0.7(12.7\%) = 10.33\%.$$

Break point:

$$\text{Break point} = \frac{\$56,000(0.5)}{0.7} + \$35,000$$

$$= \$40,000 + \$35,000 = \$75,000.$$

b. The MCC and IOS schedules are shown next:

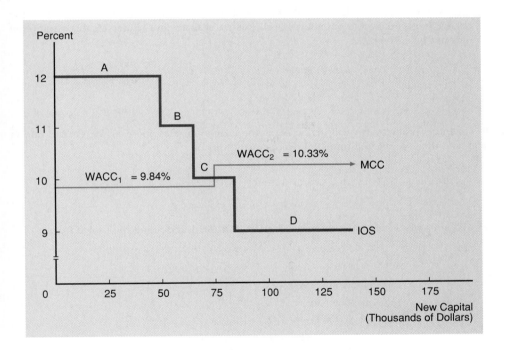

c. From this graph, we conclude that the firm should definitely undertake Projects A and B, assuming that these projects have about "average risk" in relation to the rest of the firm. Now, to evaluate Project C, recognize that one-half of its capital would cost 9.84 percent, while the other half would cost 10.33 percent. Thus, the cost of the capital required for Project C is 10.09 percent:

$$0.5(9.84\%) + 0.5(10.33\%) = 10.09\%.$$

Since the cost is greater than Project C's return of 10 percent, the firm should not accept Project C.

d. The solution implicitly assumes (1) that all of the projects are equally risky and (2) that these projects are as risky as the firm's existing assets. If the accepted projects (A and B) were of above-average risk, this could raise the company's overall risk, and hence its cost of capital. Taking on these projects could result in a decline in the company's value.

e. If the payout ratio were lowered to zero, this would shift the break point to the right, from $75,000 to $115,000:

$$\text{Break point} = \frac{\$56,000(1.0)}{0.7} + \$35,000$$
$$= \$80,000 + \$35,000 = \$115,000.$$

As the problem is set up, this would make Project C acceptable. If the payout were changed to 100 percent, the break point would shift to the left, from $75,000 to $35,000:

$$\text{Break point} = \frac{\$56,000(0.0)}{0.7} + \$35,000$$
$$= \$0 + \$35,000 = \$35,000.$$

The optimal capital budget would still consist of Projects A and B. This assumes that the change in payout would not affect k_s or k_d; as we shall see in Chapter 15, this assumption may not be correct.

CHAPTER 12

ST-1   To solve this problem, we will define ΔS as the change in sales and g as the growth rate in sales, and then we use the three following equations:

$$\Delta S = S_0 g.$$
$$S_1 = S_0(1 + g).$$
$$AFN = (A^*/S)(\Delta S) - (L^*/S)(\Delta S) - MS_1(1 - d).$$

Set AFN = 0, substitute in known values for A^*/S, L^*/S, M, d, and S, and then solve for g:

$$0 = 1.6(\$100g) - 0.4(\$100g) - 0.10[\$100(1 + g)](0.55)$$
$$= \$160g - \$40g - 0.055(\$100 + \$100g)$$
$$= \$160g - \$40g - \$5.5 - \$5.5g$$
$$\$114.5g = \$5.5$$
$$g = \$5.5/\$114.5 = 0.048 = 4.8\%$$
$$= \text{Maximum growth rate without external financing.}$$

ST-2   Assets consist of cash, marketable securities, receivables, inventories, and fixed assets. Therefore, we can break the A^*/S ratio into its components—cash/sales, inventories/sales, and so forth. Then,

$$\frac{A^*}{S} = \frac{A^* - \text{Inventories}}{S} + \frac{\text{Inventories}}{S} = 1.6.$$

We know that the inventory turnover ratio is sales/ inventories = 3 times, so inventories/ sales = 1/3 = 0.3333. Further, if the inventory turnover ratio can be increased to 4 times, then the inventory/sales ratio will fall to 1/4 = 0.25, a difference of 0.3333 − 0.2500 = 0.0833. This, in turn, causes the A^*/S ratio to fall from A^*/S = 1.6 to A^*/S = 1.6 − 0.0833 = 1.5167.

This change has two effects: First, it changes the AFN equation, and second, it means that Weatherford currently has excessive inventories. Because it is costly to hold excess inventories, Weatherford will want to reduce its inventory holdings by not replacing inventories until the excess amounts have been used. We can account for this by setting up the revised AFN equation (using the new A*/S ratio), estimating the funds that will be needed next year if no excess inventories are current on hand, and then subtracting out the excess inventories which are currently on hand:

Present conditions:

$$\frac{\text{Sales}}{\text{Inventories}} = \frac{\$100}{\text{Inventories}} = 3,$$

so

$$\text{Inventories} = \$100/3 = \$33.3 \text{ million at present.}$$

New conditions:

$$\frac{\text{Sales}}{\text{Inventories}} = \frac{\$100}{\text{Inventories}} = 4,$$

so

$$\text{New level of inventories} = \$100/4 = \$25 \text{ million.}$$

Therefore,

$$\text{Excess inventories} = \$33.3 - \$25 = \$8.3 \text{ million.}$$

Forecast of funds needed, first year;

$$\Delta S \text{ in first year} = 0.2(\$100 \text{ million}) = \$20 \text{ million.}$$
$$\text{AFN} = 1.5167(\$20) - 0.4(\$20) - 0.1(0.55)(\$120) - \$8.3$$
$$= \$30.3 - \$8 - \$6.6 - \$8.3$$
$$= \$7.4 \text{ million.}$$

Forecast of funds needed, second year:

$$\Delta S \text{ in second year} = gS_1 = 0.2(\$120 \text{ million}) = \$24 \text{ million.}$$
$$\text{AFN} = 1.5167(\$24) - 0.4(\$24) - 0.1(0.55)(\$144)$$
$$= \$36.4 - \$9.6 - \$7.9$$
$$= \$18.9 \text{ million.}$$

3 a.

$$\text{Full capacity sales} = \frac{\text{Current sales}}{\text{Percentage of capacity at which FA were operated}} = \frac{\$36,000}{0.75} = \$48,000.$$

$$\text{Percentage increase} = \frac{\text{New sales} - \text{Old sales}}{\text{Old sales}} = \frac{\$48,000 - \$36,000}{\$36,000} = 0.33$$
$$= 33\%.$$

Therefore, sales could expand by 33 percent before Van Auken Lumber would need to add fixed assets.

b.

VAN AUKEN LUMBER: PRO FORMA INCOME STATEMENT FOR DECEMBER 31, 1997 (THOUSANDS OF DOLLARS)

	1996	(1 + g)	PRO FORMA 1997
Sales	$36,000	(1.25)	$45,000
Operating costs	30,783	(1.25)	38,479
EBIT	$ 5,217		$ 6,521
Interest	1,017		1,017
EBT	$ 4,200		$ 5,504
Taxes (40%)	1,680		2,202
Net income	$ 2,520		$ 3,302
Dividends (60%)	$ 1,512		$ 1,981
Addition to RE	$ 1,008		$ 1,321

VAN AUKEN LUMBER: PRO FORMA BALANCE SHEET FOR DECEMBER 31, 1997 (THOUSANDS OF DOLLARS)

	1996	(1 + g)	ADDITIONS	1997	AFN	1997 AFTER AFN
Cash	$ 1,800	(1.25)		$ 2,250		$ 2,250
Receivables	10,800	(1.25)		13,500		13,500
Inventories	12,600	(1.25)		15,750		15,750
Total current assets	$25,200			$31,500		$31,500
Net fixed assets	21,600			21,600*		21,600
Total assets	$46,800			$53,100		$53,100
Accounts payable	$ 7,200	(1.25)		$ 9,000		$ 9,000
Notes payable	3,472			3,472	+2,549	6,021
Accruals	2,520	(1.25)		3,150		3,150
Total current liabilities	$13,192			$15,622		$18,171
Mortgage bonds	5,000			5,000		5,000
Common stock	2,000			2,000		2,000
Retained earnings	26,608		1,321**	27,929		27,929
Total liabilities and equity	$46,800			$50,551		$53,100
AFN =				$ 2,549		

*From Part a we know that sales can increase by 33% before additions to fixed assets are needed.
**See income statement.

c.

VAN AUKEN LUMBER: PRO FORMA INCOME STATEMENT FOR DECEMBER 31, 1997 (THOUSANDS OF DOLLARS)

	1ST PASS 1997	FINANCING FEEDBACK	2ND PASS 1997
Sales	$45,000		$45,000
Operating costs	38,479		38,479
EBIT	$ 6,521		$ 6,521
Interest	1,017	+306*	1,323
EBT	$ 5,504		$ 5,198
Taxes (40%)	2,202		2,079
Net income	$ 3,302		$ 3,119
Dividends (60%)	$ 1,981		$ 1,871
Addition to RE	$ 1,321		$ 1,248

*Δ in interest = $2,549 × (0.12) = $306.

VAN AUKEN LUMBER: PRO FORMA BALANCE SHEET FOR DECEMBER 31, 1997 (THOUSANDS OF DOLLARS)

	1ST PASS 1997	FINANCING FEEDBACK	2ND PASS 1997
Total assets	$53,100		$53,100
Accounts payable	$ 9,000		$ 9,000
Notes payable	6,021		6,021
Accruals	3,150		3,150
Total current liabilities	$18,171		$18,171
Mortgage bonds	5,000		5,000
Common stock	2,000		2,000
Retained earnings	27,929	−73*	27,856
Total liabilities and equity	$53,100		$53,027
AFN =			73

*Δ in RE addition = $1,248 − $1,321 = −$73.
NOTE: The cumulative AFN for the first 2 passes = $2,549 + $73 = $2,622.

d. The rate of return projected for 1997 under the conditions in Part c is (calculations in thousands):

$$\text{ROE} = \frac{\$3,119}{\$29,856} = 10.45\%.$$

If Van Auken Lumber attained the industry average DSO and inventory turnover ratio, this would mean a reduction in financial requirements of:

$$\text{Receivables:} \frac{\text{New A/R}}{\$45,000/360} = 90$$

$$\text{New A/R} = \$11,250.$$

$$\Delta \text{ in A/R} = \$13,500 - \$11,250 = \$2,250.$$

$$\text{Inventory:} \frac{\$45,000}{I} = 3.33; I = \$13,500.$$

$$\Delta \text{ in Inventory} = \$15,750 - \$13,500 = \$2,250.$$

$$\text{Total } \Delta = \$2,250 + \$2,250 = \$4,500.$$

If this freed capital was used to reduce equity, the new figures for common equity would be $29,856 − $4,500 = $25,356. Assuming no change in net income, the new ROE would be:

$$\text{ROE} = \frac{\$3,119}{\$25,356} = 12.3\%.$$

One would, in a real analysis, want to consider both the feasibility of maintaining sales if receivables and inventories were reduced and also other possible effects on the profit margin. Also, note that the current ratio was $25,200/$13,192 = 1.91 in 1996. It is projected to decline in Part c to $31,500/$18,244 = 1.73, and the latest change would cause a further reduction to ($31,500 − $4,500)/$18,244 = 1.48. Creditors might not tolerate such a reduction in liquidity and might insist that at least some of the freed capital be used to reduce notes payable. Still, this would reduce interest charges, which would increase the profit margin, which would in turn raise the ROE. Management should always consider the possibility of changing ratios as part of financial projections.

CHAPTER 13

ST-1   a.

$$S = \frac{(\text{EBIT} - k_dD)(1 - T)}{k_s}$$

$$= \frac{[\$4,000,000 - 0.10(\$2,000,000)](0.65)}{0.15} = \$16,466,667.$$

$$P_0 = S/n = \frac{\$16,466,667}{600,000} = \$27.44.$$

$$V = D + S = \$2,000,000 + \$16,466,667 = \$18,466,667.$$

b.

$$\text{WACC} = (D/V)(k_d)(1 - T) + (S/V)(k_s)$$

$$= \left(\frac{\$2,000,000}{\$18,466,667}\right)(10\%)(0.65) + \left(\frac{\$16,466,667}{\$18,466,667}\right)(15\%)$$

$$= 14.08\%.$$

c. Under the new capital structure,

$$S = \frac{[\$4,000,000 - 0.12(\$10,000,000)](0.65)}{0.17} = \$10,705,882.$$

$$V = \$10,000,000 + \$10,705,882 = \$20,705,882.$$

The new value of the firm will thus be $20,705,882. This value belongs to the *present* stockholders and bondholders, so we may calculate the new equilibrium price of the stock, P_1:

$$P_1 = \frac{V_1 - D_0}{n_0} = \frac{\$20,705,882 - \$2,000,000}{600,000} = \$31.18.$$

$$\text{Check: Shares repurchased} = \frac{\text{New debt}}{P_1} = \frac{\$8,000,000}{\$31.18} = 256,575.$$

$$P_1 = \frac{S_1}{n_1} = \frac{\$10,705,882}{600,000 - 256,575} \approx \$31.18.$$

$$\text{WACC} = \left(\frac{\$10,000,000}{\$20,705,882}\right)(12\%)(0.65) + \left(\frac{\$10,705,882}{\$20,705,882}\right)(17\%) = 12.56\%.$$

Thus, the proposed capital structure change would increase the value of the firm and the price of its stock (from $27.44 to $31.18), and lower its cost of capital. Therefore, the firm should increase its use of financial leverage. Of course, it is possible that some amount of debt other than $10 million would result in an even higher value, but we do not have enough information to make this determination.

CHAPTER 14

1 a. Value of unleveraged firm, $V_U = \text{EBIT}(1 - T)/k_{sU}$:

$$\$12 = \$2(1 - 0.4)/k_{sU}$$
$$\$12 = \$1.2/k_{sU}$$
$$k_{sU} = \$1.2/\$12 = 10.0\%.$$

Therefore, $k_{sU} = \text{WACC} = 10.0\%$.

b. Value of leveraged firm according to MM model with taxes:

$$V_L = V_U + TD.$$

As shown in the following table, value increases continuously with debt, and the optimal capital structure consists of 100 percent debt. Note: The table is not necessary to answer this question, but the data (in millions of dollars) are necessary for Part c of this problem.

DEBT, D	V_U	TD	$V_L = V_U + TD$
$ 0	$12.0	$ 0	$12.0
2.5	12.0	1.0	13.0
5.0	12.0	2.0	14.0
7.5	12.0	3.0	15.0
10.0	12.0	4.0	16.0
12.5	12.0	5.0	17.0
15.0	12.0	6.0	18.0
20.0	12.0	8.0	20.0

c. With financial distress costs included in the analysis, the value of the leveraged firm now is

$$V_L = V_U + TD - PC,$$

where

$V_U + TD$ = value according to MM after-tax model.

P = probability of financial distress.

C = present value of distress costs.

D	$V_U + TD$	P	PC = (P)\$8	$V_L = V_U + TD - PC$
$ 0	$12.0	0	$ 0	$12.0
2.5	13.0	0	0	13.0
5.0	14.0	0.0125	0.10	13.9
7.5	15.0	0.0250	0.20	14.8
10.0	16.0	0.0625	0.50	15.5
12.5	17.0	0.1250	1.00	16.0
15.0	18.0	0.3125	2.50	15.5
20.0	20.0	0.7500	6.00	14.0

NOTE: All dollar amounts in table are in millions.

Optimal debt level: D = $12.5 million.

Maximum value of firm: V = $16.0 million.

Optimal debt/value ratio: D/V = $12.5/$16 = 78%.

d. The value of the firm versus debt value with and without financial distress costs is plotted next (millions of dollars):

V_L = Value without financial distress costs.

V_B = Value with financial distress costs.

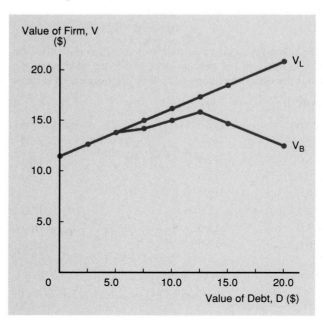

CHAPTER 17

a. $100,000,000/10 = $10,000,000 per year, or $5 million each 6 months. Since the $5 million placed into the sinking fund will be used to retire bonds immediately, no interest will be earned on it.

b. The debt service requirements will decline as follows (in millions of dollars):

SEMIANNUAL PAYMENT PERIOD (1)	SINKING FUND PAYMENT (2)	OUTSTANDING BONDS ON WHICH INTEREST IS PAID (3)	INTEREST PAYMENT[a] (4)	TOTAL BOND SERVICE (2) + (4) = (5)
1	$5	$100	$6.0	$11.0
2	5	95	5.7	10.7
3	5	90	5.4	10.4
.	.	.	.	.
.	.	.	.	.
.	.	.	.	.
20	5	5	0.3	5.3

[a]Interest is calculated as (0.5)(0.12)(Column 3); for example: interest in Period 2 = (0.5)(0.12)($95) = $5.7.

The company's total annual cash bond service requirement will be $21.7 million for the first year (semiannual payments 1 and 2). The requirement will decline by 0.12($10,000,000) = $1,200,000 per year for the remaining years.

c. Here we have a 10-year, 9 percent annuity whose future value is $100 million, and we are seeking the annual payment, PMT, in this equation:

$$\$100,000,000 = \sum_{t=1}^{10} PMT(1 + k)^t$$

$$= PMT(FVIFA_{9\%,10})$$

$$= PMT(15.193)$$

$$PMT = \$6,581,979 = \text{Sinking fund payment.}$$

The solution could also be obtained with a financial calculator: Input N = 10, I = 9, PV = 0, and FV = 100000000, and press the PMT key to obtain $6,582,009. The difference is due to rounding.

d. Annual debt service costs will be $100,000,000(0.12) + $6,582,009 = $18,582,009.

e. If interest rates rose, causing the bonds' price to fall, the company would use open market purchases. This would reduce its debt service requirements.

CHAPTER 18

a. *Cost of leasing:*

	YEAR 0	YEAR 1	YEAR 2	YEAR 3	YEAR 4
Lease payment	($10,000)	($10,000)	($10,000)	($10,000)	$0
Payment tax savings	4,000	4,000	4,000	4,000	0
Net cash flow	($ 6,000)	($ 6,000)	($ 6,000)	($ 6,000)	$0

PV cost of leasing @ 6% = ($22,038)

b. *Cost of owning:*

c. In our solution, we will consider the $40,000 cost as a Year 0 outflow rather than including all the financing cash flows. The net effect is the same since the PV of the financing flows, when discounted at the after-tax cost of debt, is the cost of the asset.

	YEAR 0	YEAR 1	YEAR 2	YEAR 3	YEAR 4
Net purchase price	($40,000)				
Maintenance cost		($1,000)	($1,000)	($1,000)	($1,000)
Maintenance tax savings		400	400	400	400
Depreciation tax savings		5,280	7,200	2,400	1,120
Residual value					10,000
Residual value tax					(4,000)
Net cash flow	($40,000)	$4,680	$6,600	$1,800	$6,520

PV cost of owning @ 6% = ($23,035)

Since the present value of the cost of leasing is less than the present value of the cost of owning, the truck should be leased. Specifically, the NAL is $23,035 − $22,038 = $997.

Use the cost of debt because most cash flows are fixed by contract and consequently are relatively certain; thus lease cash flows have about the same risk as the firm's debt. Also, leasing is considered as a substitute for debt. Use an after-tax cost rate to account for interest tax deductibility.

d. The firm could increase the discount rate on the residual value cash flow. Note that since the firm plans to replace the truck after 4 years, the residual value is treated as an inflow in the cost of owning analysis. This makes it reasonable to raise the discount rate for analysis purposes. However, had the firm planned to continue using the truck, then we would have had to place the estimated residual value as an additional Year 4 outflow in the leasing section, but without a tax adjustment. Then, higher risk would have been reflected in a *lower* discount rate. This is all very ad hoc, which is why analysts often prefer to use one discount rate throughout the analysis.

Chapter 20

The Calgary Company: Alternative Balance Sheets

	RESTRICTED (40%)	MODERATE (50%)	RELAXED (60%)
Current assets	$1,200,000	$1,500,000	$1,800,000
Fixed assets	600,000	600,000	600,000
Total assets	$1,800,000	$2,100,000	$2,400,000
Debt	$ 900,000	$1,050,000	$1,200,000
Equity	900,000	1,050,000	1,200,000
Total liabilities and equity	$1,800,000	$2,100,000	$2,400,000

THE CALGARY COMPANY: ALTERNATIVE INCOME STATEMENTS

	RESTRICTED	MODERATE	RELAXED
Sales	$3,000,000	$3,000,000	$3,000,000
EBIT	450,000	450,000	450,000
Interest (10%)	90,000	105,000	120,000
Earnings before taxes	$ 360,000	$ 345,000	$ 330,000
Taxes (40%)	144,000	138,000	132,000
Net income	$ 216,000	$ 207,000	$ 198,000
ROE	24.0%	19.7%	16.5%

a. First, determine the balance on the firm's checkbook and the bank's records as follows:

	FIRM'S CHECKBOOK	BANK'S RECORDS
Day 1: Deposit $500,000; write check for $1,000,000	($500,000)	$500,000
Day 2: Write check for $1,000,000	($1,500,000)	$500,000
Day 3: Write check for $1,000,000	($2,500,000)	$500,000
Day 4: Write check for $1,000,000; deposit $1,000,000	($2,500,000)	$500,000

After Upton has reached a steady state, it must deposit $1,000,000 each day to cover the checks written 3 days earlier.

b. The firm has 3 days of float; not until Day 4 does the firm have to make any additional deposits.

c. As shown above, Upton should try to maintain a balance on the bank's records of $500,000. On its own books it will have a balance of *minus* $2,500,000.

CHAPTER 21

a. and b.

INCOME STATEMENTS FOR YEAR ENDED DECEMBER 31, 1996 (THOUSANDS OF DOLLARS)

	VANDERHEIDEN PRESS		HERRENHOUSE PUBLISHING	
	A	B	A	B
EBIT	$ 30,000	$30,0000	$ 30,000	$ 30,000
Interest	12,400	14,400	10,600	18,600
Taxable income	$ 17,600	$ 15,600	$ 19,400	$ 11,400
Taxes (40%)	7,040	6,240	7,760	4,560
Net income	$ 10,560	$ 9,360	$ 11,640	$ 6,840
Equity	$100,000	$100,000	$100,000	$100,000
Return on equity	10.56%	9.36%	11.64%	6.84%

The Vanderheiden Press has a higher ROE when short-term interest rates are high, whereas Herrenhouse Publishing does better when rates are lower.

c. Herrenhouse's position is riskier. First, its profits and return on equity are much more volatile than Vanderheiden's. Second, Herrenhouse must renew its large short-term loan every year, and if the renewal comes up at a time when money is very tight, when its business is depressed, or both, then Herrenhouse could be denied credit, which could put it out of business.

CHAPTER 22

ST-1 Under the current credit policy, the firm has no discounts, collection expenses of $50,000, bad debt losses of $(0.02)(\$10,000,000) = \$200,000$, and average accounts receivable of (DSO)(Average sales per day) = $(30)(\$10,000,000/360) = \$833,333$. The firm's cost of carrying these receivables is (Variable cost ratio)(A/R)(Cost of capital) = $(0.80)(\$833,333)(0.16) = \$106,667$. It is necessary to multiply by the variable cost ratio because the actual *investment* in receivables is less than the dollar amount of the receivables.

Proposal 1: Lengthen the credit period such that
1. Sales increase by $1 million.

2. Discounts = $0.

3. Bad debt losses = $(0.02)(\$10,000,000) + (0.04)(\$1,000,000)$

$$= \$200,000 + \$40,000$$

$$= \$240,000.$$

4. DSO = 45 days on all sales.

5. New average receivables = $(45)(\$11,000,000/360)$

$$= \$1,375,000.$$

6. Cost of carrying receivables = (v)(k)(Average accounts receivable)

$$= (0.80)(0.16)(\$1,375,000)$$

$$= \$176,000.$$

7. Change in cost of carrying receivables = $\$176,000 - \$106,667$

$$= \$69,333.$$

8. Collection expenses = $50,000.

Analysis of proposed change:

	INCOME STATEMENT UNDER CURRENT POLICY	EFFECT OF CHANGE	INCOME STATEMENT UNDER NEW POLICY
Gross sales	$10,000,000	+$1,000,000	$11,000,000
Less discounts	0	+ 0	0
Net sales	$10,000,000	+$1,000,000	$11,000,000
Variable costs (80%)	8,000,000	+ 800,000	8,800,000
Profit before credit costs and taxes	$ 2,000,000	+$ 200,000	$ 2,200,000
Credit-related costs:			
Cost of carrying receivables	106,667	+ 69,333	176,000
Collection expenses	50,000	+ 0	50,000
Bad debt losses	200,000	+ 40,000	240,000
Profit before taxes	$ 1,643,333	+$ 90,667	$ 1,734,000
Taxes (50%)	821,666	+ 45,333	867,000
Net income	$ 821,667	+ 45,334	$ 867,000

The proposed change appears to be a good one, assuming the assumptions are correct.

Proposal 2: Shorten the credit period to net 20 such that
1. Sales decrease by $1 million.

2. Discount = $0.

3. Bad debt losses = (0.01)($9,000,000)

$$= \$90,000.$$

4. DSO = 22 days.

5. New average receivables = (22)($9,000,000/360)

$$= \$550,000.$$

6. Cost of carrying receivables = (v)(k)(Average accounts receivable)

$$= (0.80)(0.16)(\$550,000)$$

$$= \$70,400.$$

7. Collection expenses = $50,000.

Analysis of proposed change:

	INCOME STATEMENT UNDER CURRENT POLICY	EFFECT OF CHANGE	INCOME STATEMENT UNDER NEW POLICY
Gross sales	$10,000,000	−$1,000,000	$9,000,000
Less discounts	0	0	0
Net sales	$10,000,000	−$1,000,000	$9,000,000
Variable costs (80%)	8,000,000	− 800,000	7,200,000
Profit before credit costs and taxes	$ 2,000,000	−$ 200,000	$1,800,000
Credit-related costs:			
Cost of carrying receivables	106,667	− 36,267	70,400
Collection expenses	50,000	0	50,000
Bad debt losses	200,000	− 110,000	90,000
Profit before taxes	$ 1,643,333	−$ 53,733	$1,589,600
Taxes (50%)	821,666	− 26,866	794,800
Net income	$ 821,667	−$ 26,867	$ 794,800

This change reduces net income, so it should be rejected. The firm will increase profits by accepting Proposal 1 to lengthen the credit period from 25 days to 30 days, assuming all assumptions are correct. This may or may not be the *optimal,* or profit-maximizing, credit policy, but it does appear to be a movement in the right direction. However, before a final decision is made, the riskiness of the change must be considered.

ST-2   a.

$$EOQ = \sqrt{\frac{2(F)(S)}{(C)(P)}}$$

$$= \sqrt{\frac{(2)(\$5,000)(2,600,000)}{(0.02)(\$5.00)}}$$

$$= 509,902 \text{ bushels.}$$

Since the firm must order in multiples of 2,000 bushels, it should order in quantities of 510,000 bushels.

b.   Average weekly sales = 2,600,000/52

$$= 50,000 \text{ bushels.}$$

Reorder point = 6 weeks' sales + Safety stock

$$= 6(50,000) + 200,000$$

$$= 300,000 + 200,000$$

$$= 500,000 \text{ bushels.}$$

c. Total inventory costs:

$$TIC = CP\left(\frac{Q}{2}\right) + F\left(\frac{S}{Q}\right) + CP(\text{Safety stock})$$

$$= (0.02)(\$5)\left(\frac{510,000}{2}\right) + (\$5,000)\left(\frac{2,600,000}{510,000}\right) + (0.02)(\$5)(200,000)$$

$$= \$25,500 + \$25,490.20 + \$20,000$$

$$= \$70,990.20.$$

d. By ordering 650,000 bushels at a time, ordering costs would be reduced to $1,500, so total inventory costs would be:

$$\text{TIC} = (0.02)(\$5)\left(\frac{650,000}{2}\right) + (\$1,500)\left(\frac{2,600,000)}{650,000}\right) + (0.02)(\$5)(200,000)$$

$$= \$32,500 + \$6,000 + \$20,000$$

$$= \$58,500.$$

Since the firm can reduce its total inventory costs by ordering 650,000 bushels at a time, it should accept the offer and place larger orders. (Incidentally, this same type of analysis is used to consider any quantity discount offer.)

APPENDIX D

SELECTED EQUATIONS

CHAPTER 2

$$\text{Current ratio} = \frac{\text{Current assets}}{\text{Current liabilities}}.$$

$$\text{Quick, or acid test, ratio} = \frac{\text{Current assets} - \text{Inventories}}{\text{Current liabilities}}.$$

$$\text{Inventory turnover ratio} = \frac{\text{Sales}}{\text{Inventories}}.$$

$$\text{DSO} = \begin{array}{c} \text{Days} \\ \text{sales} \\ \text{outstanding} \end{array} = \frac{\text{Receivables}}{\text{Average sales per day}} = \frac{\text{Receivables}}{\text{Annual sales}/360}.$$

$$\text{Fixed assets turnover ratio} = \frac{\text{Sales}}{\text{Net fixed assets}}.$$

$$\text{Total assets turnover ratio} = \frac{\text{Sales}}{\text{Total assets}}.$$

$$\text{Debt ratio} = \frac{\text{Total debt}}{\text{Total assets}}.$$

$$\text{D/E} = \frac{\text{D/A}}{1 - \text{D/A}}, \text{ and D/A} = \frac{\text{D/E}}{1 + \text{D/E}}.$$

$$\text{Times-interest-earned (TIE) ratio} = \frac{\text{EBIT}}{\text{Interest charges}}.$$

$$\begin{array}{c} \text{Fixed charge} \\ \text{coverage ratio} \end{array} = \frac{\text{EBIT} + \text{Lease payments}}{\text{Interest charges} + \text{Lease payments} + \dfrac{\text{Sinking fund payments}}{(1 - \text{Tax rate})}}.$$

$$\text{Profit margin on sales} = \frac{\begin{array}{c}\text{Net income available to} \\ \text{common stockholders}\end{array}}{\text{Sales}}.$$

$$\text{Basic earning power ratio} = \frac{\text{EBIT}}{\text{Total assets}}.$$

$$\text{Return on total assets (ROA)} = \frac{\text{Net income available to common stockholders}}{\text{Total assets}}.$$

$$\text{ROA} = \left(\frac{\text{Profit}}{\text{margin}}\right)(\text{Total assets turnover}).$$

$$\text{Return on common equity (ROE)} = \frac{\text{Net income available to common stockholders}}{\text{Common equity}}.$$

$$\text{Price/earnings (P/E) ratio} = \frac{\text{Price per share}}{\text{Earnings per share}}.$$

$$\text{Book value per share} = \frac{\text{Common equity}}{\text{Shares outstanding}}.$$

$$\text{Market/book (M/B) ratio} = \frac{\text{Market price per share}}{\text{Book value per share}}.$$

$$\text{ROE} = \left(\frac{\text{Profit}}{\text{margin}}\right)\left(\frac{\text{Total assets}}{\text{turnover}}\right)\left(\frac{\text{Equity}}{\text{multiplier}}\right)$$

$$= \left(\frac{\text{Net income}}{\text{Sales}}\right)\left(\frac{\text{Sales}}{\text{Total assets}}\right)\left(\frac{\text{Total assets}}{\text{Common equity}}\right)$$

$$= \frac{\text{Net income}}{\text{Common equity}}.$$

$$\text{Rate of return on investors' capital} = \frac{\text{Net income} + \text{Interest}}{\text{Debt} + \text{Equity}}.$$

CHAPTER 3

$$k = k^* + IP + DRP + LP + MRP.$$

$$k_{RF} = k^* + IP.$$

$$IP_n = \frac{I_1 + I_2 + \ldots I_n}{n}.$$

$$\begin{array}{l}\text{Equivalent pre-tax yield} \\ \text{on taxable bond}\end{array} = \frac{\text{Muni yield}}{1 - T}.$$

CHAPTER 4

$$\hat{k} = \sum_{i=1}^{n} k_i P_i.$$

$$\sigma^2 = \sum_{i=1}^{n} (k_i - \hat{k})^2 P_i.$$

$$\sigma = \sqrt{\sigma^2} = \sqrt{\sum_{i=1}^{n} (k_i - \hat{k})^2 P_i}.$$

$$\text{Semivariance} = SV = \sum_{i=1}^{m} (k_i - \hat{k})^2 P_i.$$

$$CV = \frac{\sigma}{\hat{k}}.$$

$$\hat{k}_p = \sum_{i=1}^{n} x_i \hat{k}_i.$$

CHAPTER 5

$$\sigma_p = \sqrt{\sum_{i=1}^{n} (k_{P_i} - \hat{k}_P)^2 P_i}.$$

$$Cov(AB) = \sum_{i=1}^{n} (k_{Ai} - \hat{k}_A)(k_{Bi} - \hat{k}_B)P_i.$$

$$r_{AB} = \frac{Cov(AB)}{\sigma_A \sigma_B}.$$

$$\sigma_p = \sqrt{x^2 \sigma_A^2 + (1-x)^2 \sigma_B^2 + 2x(1-x)r_{AB}\sigma_A \sigma_B}.$$

Minimum risk portfolio: $x = \dfrac{\sigma_B(\sigma_B - r_{AB}\sigma_A)}{\sigma_A^2 + \sigma_B^2 - 2r_{AB}\sigma_A\sigma_B}.$

Capital Market Line (CML): $\hat{k}_p = k_{RF} + \left(\dfrac{\hat{k}_M - k_{RF}}{\sigma_M} \right)\sigma_p.$

Security Market Line (SML): $k_i = k_{RF} + (k_M - k_{RF})b_i.$

$$b_p = \sum_{i=1}^{n} x_i b_i.$$

$$b_i = \frac{Cov(\bar{k}_i, \bar{k}_M)}{\sigma_M^2} = \frac{r_{iM}\sigma_i \sigma_M}{\sigma_M^2} = r_{iM}\left(\frac{\sigma_i}{\sigma_M} \right).$$

$$\sigma_i^2 = b_i^2 \sigma_M^2 + \sigma_{e_i}^2.$$

$$k_i = k_{RF} + (\lambda_1 - k_{RF})b_{i1} + \cdots + (\lambda_j - k_{RF})b_{ij}.$$

CHAPTER 6

$$FV_n = PV(1 + i)^n = PV(FVIF_{i,n}).$$

$$PV = FV_n\left(\frac{1}{1+i} \right)^n = FV_n(1+i)^{-n} = FV_n(PVIF_{i,n}).$$

$$PVIF_{i,n} = \frac{1}{FVIF_{i,n}}.$$

$$FVIFA_{i,n} = [(1+i)^n - 1]/i.$$

$$PVIFA_{i,n} = [1 - (1/(1+i)^n)]/i.$$

$$FVA_n = PMT \sum_{t=1}^{n} (1+i)^{n-t} = PMT(FVIFA_{i,n}).$$

$$FVA_n \text{ (Annuity due)} = PMT(FVIFA_{i,n})(1+i).$$

$$PVA_n = PMT \sum_{t=1}^{n} \left(\frac{1}{1+i}\right)^t = PMT(PVIFA_{i,n}).$$

$$PVA_n \text{ (Annuity due)} = PMT(PVIFA_{i,n})(1+i).$$

$$PV \text{ (Perpetuity)} = \frac{\text{Payment}}{\text{Interest rate}} = \frac{PMT}{i}$$

$$PV_{\text{Uneven stream}} = \sum_{t=1}^{n} CF_t \left(\frac{1}{1+i}\right)^t = \sum_{t=1}^{n} CF_t(PVIF_{i,t}).$$

$$FV_{\text{Uneven stream}} = \sum_{t=1}^{n} CF_t(1+i)^{n-t} = \sum_{t=1}^{n} CF_t(FVIF_{i,n-t}).$$

$$FV_n = PV\left(1 + \frac{i_{\text{Nom}}}{m}\right)^{mn}.$$

$$\text{Effective annual rate} = \left(\frac{1 + i_{\text{Nom}}}{m}\right)^m - 1.0.$$

$$\text{Periodic rate} = i_{\text{Nom}}/m.$$

$$i_{\text{Nom}} = APR = (\text{Periodic rate})(m).$$

$$FV_n = PVe^{in}.$$

$$PV = FV_n e^{-in}.$$

CHAPTER 7

$$V = \sum_{t=1}^{N} \frac{CF_t}{(1+k_t)^t}.$$

$$V_B = \sum_{t=1}^{N} \frac{INT}{(1+k_d)^t} + \frac{M}{(1+k_d)^N} = INT(PVIFA_{k_d,N}) + M(PVIF_{k_d,N}).$$

$$V_B = \sum_{t=1}^{2N} \frac{INT/2}{(1+k_d/2)^t} + \frac{M}{(1+k_d/2)^{2N}} = \frac{INT}{2}(PVIFA_{k_d/2,2N}) + M(PVIF_{k_d/2,2N}).$$

$$\text{Value of callable bond} = \sum_{t=1}^{N} \frac{INT}{(1+k_d)^t} + \frac{\text{Call price}}{(1+k_d)^N}.$$

$$V_{ps} = \frac{D_{ps}}{k_{ps}}.$$

$$\hat{P}_0 = \text{PV of expected future dividends} = \sum_{t=1}^{\infty} \frac{D_t}{(1+k_s)^t}.$$

$$\hat{P}_0 = \frac{D_0(1+g)}{k_s - g} = \frac{D_1}{k_s - g}.$$

$$\hat{k}_s = \frac{D_1}{P_0} + g.$$

Chapter 8

Component cost of debt $= k_d(1 - T)$.

$\dfrac{\text{Component cost}}{\text{of preferred stock}} = k_{ps} = \dfrac{D_{ps}}{P_n}$.

$\hat{k}_M = \dfrac{D_1}{P_0} + g = k_{RF} + RP_M = k_M$.

k_s = Company's own bond yield + Risk premium.

$\hat{k}_e = \dfrac{D_1}{P_0(1 - F)} + g$.

$g = b(r)$.

$WACC = w_d k_d(1 - T) + w_{ps}k_{ps} + w_{ce}(k_s \text{ or } k_e)$.

$BP = \dfrac{\text{Total amount of lower cost of capital of a given type}}{\text{Fraction of this type of capital in the capital structure}}$.

Chapter 9

$NPV = \displaystyle\sum_{t=0}^{n} \dfrac{CF_t}{(1 + k)^t}$.

$IRR: \displaystyle\sum_{t=0}^{n} \dfrac{CF_t}{(1 + IRR)^t} = 0$.

$PI = \dfrac{\displaystyle\sum_{t=0}^{n} \dfrac{CIF_t}{(1 + k)^t}}{\displaystyle\sum_{t=0}^{n} \dfrac{COF_t}{(1 + k)^t}}$.

$MIRR: \displaystyle\sum_{t=0}^{n} \dfrac{COF_t}{(1 + k)^t} = \dfrac{\displaystyle\sum_{t=0}^{n} CIF_t(1 + k)^{n-t}}{(1 + MIRR)^n}$.

CHAPTER 10

$$\text{Project CF}_t = \frac{\text{CF}_t \text{ for corporation}}{\text{with project}} - \frac{\text{CF}_t \text{ for corporation}}{\text{without project}} .$$

OWNERSHIP YEAR	CLASS OF INVESTMENT			
	3-YEAR	5-YEAR	7-YEAR	10-YEAR
1	33%	20%	14%	10%
2	45	32	25	18
3	15	19	17	14
4	7	12	13	12
5		11	9	9
6		6	9	7
7			9	7
8			4	7
9				7
10				6
11				3
	100%	100%	100%	100%

$$\text{NPV(no inflation)} = \sum_{t=0}^{N} \frac{\text{RCF}_t}{(1+k_r)^t} = \sum_{t=0}^{N} \frac{\text{NCF}_t}{(1+k_n)^t}.$$

$$\text{NPV(with inflation)} = \sum_{t=0}^{N} \frac{\text{NCF}_t}{(1+k_n)^t} = \sum_{t=0}^{N} \frac{\text{RCF}_t(1+i)^t}{(1+k_r)^t(1+i)^t}.$$

CHAPTER 12

$$\text{AFN} = (A^*/S)\Delta S - (L^*/S)\Delta S - MS_1(1-d).$$

$$\text{Full capacity sales} = \frac{\text{Actual sales}}{\begin{array}{c}\text{Percentage of capacity at}\\\text{which fixed assets were operated}\end{array}}.$$

$$\text{Target FA/Sales ratio} = \frac{\text{Actual fixed assets}}{\text{Full capacity sales}}.$$

Required level of FA = Target FA/Sales ratio (Projected sales).

CHAPTER 13

$$\text{EBIT} = PQ - VQ - F.$$

$$Q_{BE} = \frac{F}{P - V}.$$

Total risk = σ_{ROE}.

Business risk = $\sigma_{ROE(U)}$.

Financial risk = $\sigma_{ROE} - \sigma_{ROE(U)}$.

$$S = \frac{(EBIT - k_dD)(1 - T)}{k_s}.$$

$$V = D + S.$$

$$V = \frac{EBIT(1 - T)}{WACC}.$$

$$V = \frac{(EBIT - k_dD)(1 - T)}{k_s}.$$

$$WACC = \left(\frac{D}{V}\right)k_d(1 - T) + \left(\frac{S}{V}\right)k_s.$$

$$EPS = \frac{(EBIT - k_dD)(1 - T)}{Original\ shares - Debt/Price}.$$

CHAPTER 14

$$V_L = V_U = \frac{EBIT}{WACC} = \frac{EBIT}{k_{sU}}.$$

$$k_{sL} = k_{sU} + (k_{sU} - k_d)(D/S).$$

$$V_L = V_U + TD.$$

$$V_U = \frac{EBIT(1 - T)}{k_{sU}}.$$

$$k_{sL} = k_{sU} + (k_{sU} - k_d)(1 - T)(D/S).$$

$$V_L = V_U + TD - \left(\begin{array}{c} PV\ of \\ expected \\ financial\ distress \\ costs \end{array}\right) - \left(\begin{array}{c} PV\ of \\ agency \\ costs \end{array}\right).$$

$$CF_L = (EBIT - I)(1 - T_c)(1 - T_s) + I(1 - T_d).$$

$$V_L = V_U + \left[1 - \frac{(1 - T_c)(1 - T_s)}{(1 - T_d)}\right]D.$$

$$V_U = \frac{EBIT(1 - T_c)(1 - T_s)}{k_{sU}}.$$

$$k_{sL} = k_{RF} + (k_M - k_{RF})b_U + (k_M - k_{RF})b_U(1 - T)(D/S).$$

$$b = b_U[1 + (1 - T)(D/S)].$$

$$b = b_U + b_U(P/S) + b_U(1 - T)(D/S).$$

CHAPTER 15

$$k_i = k_{RF} + (k_M - k_{RF})b_i + (D_i - D_M)\lambda_i.$$

CHAPTER 17

Accrued value at end of Year n = Issue price $\times (1 + k_d)^n$.

Interest in Year n = Accrued value$_n$ - Accrued value$_{n-1}$.

Tax savings = (Interest deduction)(T).

CHAPTER 18

NAL = PV cost of owning − PV cost of leasing.

CHAPTER 19

$$\text{Price paid for bond with warrants} = \text{Straight-debt value of bonds} + \text{Value of warrants}.$$

$$\text{Conversion price} = P_c = \frac{\text{Par value of bond given up}}{\text{Shares received}}$$

$$= \frac{\text{Par value of bond given up}}{\text{CR}}.$$

$$\text{Conversion ratio} = CR = \frac{\text{Par value of bond given up}}{P_c}.$$

CHAPTER 20

$$\text{Accounts Receivable} = \frac{\text{Credit Sales}}{\text{per day}} \times \text{Length of collection period}.$$

$$\text{ADS} = \frac{\text{Annual sales}}{360}.$$

Receivables = ADS × DSO.

CHAPTER 21

$$\text{Approximate trade credit percentage cost} = \frac{\text{Discount percent}}{100 - \text{Discount percent}} \times \frac{360}{\text{Days credit is outstanding} - \text{Discount period}}.$$

$$\text{Face value}_{\text{Discount}} = \frac{\text{Funds received}}{1.0 - \text{Nominal rate (fraction)}}.$$

$$\text{Face value}_{\text{Simple/CB}} = \frac{\text{Funds required}}{1.0 - \text{CB (fraction)}}.$$

$$\text{Face value}_{\text{Discount/CB}} = \frac{\text{Funds required}}{1.0 - \text{Nominal rate(fraction)} - \text{CB(fraction)}}.$$

$$\text{Approximate rate}_{\text{Add-on}} = \frac{\text{Interest}}{\text{Amount received}/2}.$$

CHAPTER 22

$$\text{Inventory conversion period} = \frac{\text{Inventory}}{\text{Sales}/360}.$$

$$\text{Receivables collection period} = \text{DSO} = \frac{\text{Receivables}}{\text{Sales}/360}.$$

Payables deferral period = Payables/Credit purchases per day.

$$\begin{array}{c} \text{Inventory} \\ \text{conversion} \\ \text{period} \end{array} + \begin{array}{c} \text{Receivables} \\ \text{collection} \\ \text{period} \end{array} - \begin{array}{c} \text{Payables} \\ \text{deferral} \\ \text{period} \end{array} = \begin{array}{c} \text{Cash} \\ \text{conversion} \\ \text{cycle} \end{array}.$$

Total costs = Holding costs + Transactions costs

$$= \frac{C}{2}(k) + \frac{T}{C}(F).$$

$$C^* = \sqrt{\frac{2(F)(T)}{k}}.$$

$$\text{Cost of carrying receivables} = (DSO)\left(\begin{array}{c} \text{Sales} \\ \text{per} \\ \text{day} \end{array}\right)\left(\begin{array}{c} \text{Variable} \\ \text{cost} \\ \text{ratio} \end{array}\right)\left(\begin{array}{c} \text{Cost} \\ \text{of} \\ \text{funds} \end{array}\right).$$

$$\text{Opportunity cost} = \left(\frac{\text{Old sales}}{360}\right)(\Delta DSO)(1-v)(k).$$

$$A = \frac{\text{Units per order}}{2} = \frac{S/N}{2}.$$

$$TCC = (C)(P)(A).$$

$$TOC = (F)(N) = F(S/2A).$$

$$TIC = TCC + TOC$$

$$= (C)(P)(A) + F(S/2A)$$

$$= (C)(P)(Q/2) + (F)(S/Q).$$

$$EOQ = \sqrt{\frac{2(F)(S)}{(C)(P)}}.$$

CHAPTER 23

$$\text{Formula value} = \begin{array}{c} \text{Current price} \\ \text{of stock} \end{array} - \text{Striking price}.$$

$$V = P[N(d_1)] - Xe^{-k_{RF}t}[N(d_2)].$$

$$d_1 = \frac{1n(P/X) + [k_{RF} + (\sigma^2/2)]t}{\sigma\sqrt{t}}.$$

$$d_2 = d_1 - \sigma\sqrt{t}.$$

$$\begin{array}{c} \text{Price paid for} \\ \text{bond with warrants} \end{array} = \begin{array}{c} \text{Straight-debt} \\ \text{value of bond} \end{array} + \begin{array}{c} \text{Value of} \\ \text{warrants} \end{array}.$$

$$\text{Conversion price} = P_c = \frac{\text{Par value of bond given up}}{\text{Shares received}}.$$

$$\text{Conversion ratio} = CR = \frac{\$1,000}{P_c}.$$

$$\text{Duration} = \sum_{t=1}^{n} \frac{t(PVCF_t)}{\sum\limits_{t=1}^{n} PVCF_t} = \sum_{t=1}^{n} \frac{t(PVCF_t)}{\text{Value}}.$$